History of the Borough of Preston and its Environs, in the County of Lancaster

Preston from the South.

[illegible] Quay, Preston.

HISTORY

OF THE

BOROUGH OF PRESTON

AND ITS

ENVIRONS,

IN THE

COUNTY OF LANCASTER;

BY

CHARLES HARDWICK,

MEMBER OF, AND CONTRIBUTOR TO, THE LANCASHIRE AND CHESHIRE HISTORIC SOCIETY; AUTHOR OF "FRIENDLY SOCIETIES, THEIR HISTORY, FINANCIAL PROSPECTS," ETC.

"Nothing extenuate, nor set down aught in malice."—*Shakespere.*
"The first object of History is Truth."—*Lamartine.*

PRESTON:

WORTHINGTON & Co., TOWN HALL CORNER.
LONDON: SIMPKIN, MARSHALL, & Co.

MDCCCLVII.

WORTHINGTON AND CO.,
PRINTERS,
NO. 1, CHURCH-STREET, TOWN HALL CORNER,
PRESTON.

TO

HIS WORSHIP THE MAYOR,

THE

ALDERMEN,

AND

COMMON COUNCILLORS,

OF THE

BOROUGH OF PRESTON,

THIS WORK

IS RESPECTFULLY DEDICATED, BY

THE AUTHOR.

ADVERTISEMENT.

EARLY in 1855, Messrs. John Worthington and Co. announced their intention of publishing by subscription, a History and Topographical description of the Borough of Preston and its Environs, before the close of that year. Independently of the fact that a considerable portion of the then projected work was unwritten at the time, other circumstances afterwards transpired, which induced the publishers to considerably enlarge their original design Amongst these may be mentioned the discovery, by the author, of a Roman station at Walton-le-dale, which necessitated a complete revision of the then presumed Roman topography of Lancashire, the excavations of the Castle Hill, Penwortham, by the Lancashire and Cheshire Historic Society, where unique and most interesting remains were discovered; and the probable connection, first suggested by the author, of the Cuerdale treasure with the great battle of Brunanburh. These and other important additions have necessarily delayed the publication. The work was originally announced to consist of upwards of four hundred pages, with sixty illustrations on steel. It is now presented to the subscribers at the price first fixed, although the letter-press has been extended to upwards of seven hundred pages, and the pictorial illustrations augmented about fifty per cent. From these facts, it will be evident that the publishers have no alternative, but to slightly increase the price of the work to non-subscribers, in order to avoid pecuniary loss. They trust, however, that the arduous exertions of the author and themselves in the production of the work in its present more complete form, will induce their fellow-townsmen especially, to liberally accord their patronage to the undertaking, and thus compensate them by a more extended circulation, for the additional labour and capital expended in the production of the work.

Town Hall Corner,
Sep., 1857.

PREFACE.

A correct appreciation of the Present is impossible without considerable knowledge of the Past. Many of the most striking manifestations in the existing generation, owe much of their peculiarities to influences long since passed away, and which, except to the antiquary and the scholar, are practically expunged from the memory of mankind. Hence much of the flimsy Utopism, superficial criticism, and self-sufficiency, of a large section of the self-styled "practical men" of every age. No great step in human progress has instantaneously resulted from the inspiration of intuitive genius, however brilliant. Civilization is a process, which, year by year, age by age, and century by century, is gradually unfolding itself. The very recorded retrogressions are but the partial ebbings of the still onward tide of human advancement. A knowledge of how great principles and results originated and became gradually developed, is essential in order that man may proceed with wisdom and dignity towards the ever-retreating goal of future excellence.

Much has been done for history during the past half century. It has become gradually more and more emancipated from the thraldom of temporary party feeling and existing political power. Its legitimate objects and honours are no longer confined to the production of agreeable narratives, or semi-romances, compounded from shreds of historic truth and the playful vagaries of untrammelled fancy; nor to eloquent dissertations on past events, elaborated in the spirit of the forensic advocate, for the demonstration of some foregone conclusion. Each of these may be valuable in its particular sphere, but the true historic structure is still incomplete It must not hang pendent from the ornament of Art, however gorgeous, however captivating, such ornament may be; its foundations must rest upon the rock of Science. Before a judge sums up a case, and leaves the verdict in the hands of a jury, it is not only necessary that he should hear the arguments of advocates, but that he should carefully examine and balance the evidence advanced. So with history: the procuration and methodical digestion of facts form the base of the gorgeous superstructure. The recent establishment of several local archæological and historic associations has already done good service to the cause of truth Each has furnished valuable contributions to the rapidly increasing stock of material available for the construction of what has long been pronounced a desideratum,—a more complete and truthful history of Britain.

All men naturally feel more interest in the historical associations of their own race than they do in those of any other portion of mankind. The study of that which immediately pertains to them and theirs is more interesting, and therefore more pursued. If this be true in a national sense, it may be expected to operate even more powerfully within limits still more contracted. The soil daily trodden by the foot of any reflecting being, the locality, with whose present struggles, progress, or decay, he is practically acquainted; whose traditions and "folk lore" were fixed in his memory and his heart, long before more exact knowledge or cultivated judgment enabled him to test their accuracy or correctly weigh their value, must possess historic reminiscences, not only capable of commanding his attention, by exciting in the imaginative faculty agreeable and healthy sensations, but of teaching him valuable lessons in profound practical wisdom The dullest familiar scene is encircled with a sacred halo, when associated with some mighty deed of a by-gone age. Its physical impress may, perhaps, be superficially erased, but its spiritual influence still permeates, with a subtlety cognizant only to cultivated intelligence, the sentiment and aspiration of the mass of mankind.

Preston and its environs are rich in historic incident. When conjoined to the fact that all works professing in any way to be a history of the locality, were "out of print" at the booksellers', this will, I conceive, be a sufficient justification of the present undertaking. In the compilation of the work, I have endeavoured to practically carry out the views above enunciated. A local contributor is called upon, especially, to labour diligently in what may be termed the production of the raw material of history. With its more profound philosophy he has relatively little to do; with romantic effect, artistic grouping, and brilliant word-painting, still less. Whenever I have felt disposed to indulge in either the one or the other, I have endeavoured carefully to keep it distinct from the main body of known and acknowledged truths. How far I may have succeeded, either in this or any other particular, is not for me to decide. That I have done something towards the collection and arrangement of materials for a history of my native town, will, doubtless, be acknowledged. I am, however, fully sensible that such a work is, from its very nature, imperfect even under the most favourable circumstances. The character of the labour to be performed, itself necessitated the communication of the author's intention to the public; and, consequently, a very natural desire has been several times expressed that the publication should take place at as early a period as possible. From a desire to respond to this feeling, I fear I may have been somewhat hurried and overtasked during the time the work has been passing through the press I mention this not with the view to forestall legitimate criticism, but rather for the purpose of respectfully soliciting such additional information, as well as reference to materials, documentary or otherwise, as may be calculated to throw further light upon any portion of my subject I shall carefully, from time to time, revise my own private copy, and append such further information as may appear desirable, with the view that it may be available for future publication.

I may as well here call attention to the fact, that much additional matter relative to the Roman topography of Lancashire and the probable site of the battle of Brunanburh, will be found in the appendix.

Nothing now remains but the pleasing duty of expressing my best thanks to the many kind friends who have facilitated my investigations, and otherwise aided me in the practical execution of the work. Without the least invidious distinction, I especially beg to acknowledge my obligations to Mr. Alderman Brown, the Rev. W. Thornber, Mr William Dobson, Mr. Charles J. Ashfield, and Mr. Dearden. To the following gentlemen I am likewise deeply indebted for much courteous attention and most valuable information:—Jno Robson, esq., M. D, Warrington, the Rev. A. Hume, D.C L, etc., Liverpool; Charles Roach Smith, esq., F.S.A., etc, etc., Strood, Kent, A. W. Franks, esq, M.A, of the British

Museum; Trenham Reeks, esq., of the Museum of Practical Geology, London; and John Hodgson Hinde, esq., Felton, Northumberland. The various authors consulted, and other sources of information, will be found sufficiently indicated in the course of the work.

CHARLES HARDWICK.

Preston, August 9th, 1857.

CONTENTS.

PART I.—HISTORICAL.

PAGE

CHAPTER I.—BRITISH AND ROMAN PERIODS.

CHAPTER II.—SAXON AND DANISH PERIODS.

CHAPTER III —FROM THE NORMAN CONQUEST TO THE ACCESSION OF JAMES I.

CHAPTER IV.—FROM JAMES I. TO THE "RESTORATION"

CHAPTER V.—FROM THE "RESTORATION" TO VICTORIA.

CHAPTER VI.—MUNICIPAL GOVERNMENT, GUILD MERCHANT, ETC

PART II.—TOPOGRAPHY, ETC.

PART III.—THE ENVIRONS.

CHAPTER I.—THE VALLEY OF THE RIBBLE.

A RAMBLE FROM LYTHAM TO RIBCHESTER.

CHAPTER II.—THE HUNDRED OF AMOUNDERNESS.

CHAPTER III.—THE HUNDRED OF BLACKBURN.

CHAPTER IV.—THE HUNDRED OF LEYLAND.

APPENDIX.

BIOGRAPHY.

CHRONOLOGICAL TABLE.

INDEX.

LIST OF PLATES.

ERRATA AND ADDENDA.

In chapter 1, for *Ptolomy*, read *Ptolemy*.

At line 1, page 18, for *is supposed to have been* read *was*

At lines 10, and 16, page 41, for *earthern* read *earthen*.

At lines 10, 11, and 12, page 46, for *Beyond Bamber-bridge, its line is indicated by a road marked "Cinder Path," in Cuerden Hall Park*, read *It appears to have been continued in a straight line to near the Parker's Arms Inn, where the Roman road and the present highway become nearly identical*

In note k, at page 62, for *In the year* 601 —*Ethelwerd's Chron*, read *In the year* 596 — *Saxon Chron* According to Ethelwerd, Pope Gregory in 601, "sent to Augustine the pall of apostleship."

At line 31, page 81, for *on this spot* read *near this place*

At the end of the first paragraph on page 111, add see page 591.

At page 146, line 7, for 1616 read 1611.

At line 6, page 150, for 1663, read 1633.

At the fifth line from the bottom of page 152, for see page 4, read see page 41.

At line 20, page 156, for 1752, read 1572

At page 172, fourth line from the bottom, for *Cheetham* read Chetham. At the last line of page 177, ditto. At page 202, ditto.

At page 197, third line from bottom, for *Mossap* read *Mossop*

At page 208, lines 4, and 43, for *Herald's College* read Heralds' College

At page 210, sixth line from the bottom, for *Woodcock* read Kellet.

At line 20, page 236, after the words *Mathematician* insert *and—M'Intosh*. In the same line for *names* read *heads*, as suggested in the note.

At line 15, page 269, for 1565, read 1566

At line 10, page 306, for *Edward III* read Edward I

At page 316, second line from the bottom, fill the blank with *James*, in the fourth line with *Richard*, in the sixth line with *John*, and in the eight line with *Jonathan*

At page 334, third line from the bottom, for 1834, read 1804.

At line 34, page 336, for 1837, read 1857

After line 11, page 350, add 1762, Nicholas Fazakerley, Edmund Starkie.

At page 353, fifth line from the bottom for *c* read *d*

At line 29, page 369, for *Gardens* read *Garden*

At line 22, page 373, for *Dr Cartwright was not, however*, read *It has been asserted that Dr. Cartwright*, etc. The date of Kinlock's first loom is eight years posterior to the doctor's earliest patent, as shown in the preceding paragraph.

At page 394, line 11, move the first letter, p, to the commencement of the line above.

At page 432, ninth line from the bottom, for Jno Able Smith read Jno. Abel Smith

At line 438, page 22, for 1734, read 1732.

At page 473, remove one of the marks of quotation, after the word *vain*, in the twenty-first line, and place the double apostrophe (") after the word mistaken, in the following line.

At line 4, page 478, for *Saint's* read *Saints'*.

At line 14, page 510, for *funish* read *furnish*.

At page 511, second line of note, for *Reliquœ* read *Reliquiœ*.

At line 10, page 516, for *is* read *are*.

At line 14, page 559, insert the word *who married a* before the word *cousin*

At page 568, line 36, strike out *and a Unitarian chapel*. The building has been converted into cottages

At page 575, line 13, for *alter* read *altar*.

At line 11, page 597, for *Edward VII* read *Edward VI*.

At line 30, page 602, for *fayry* read *fayr*.

At page 636, fifth line from the bottom, for *nearer the latter town* read *nearer to that town*.

At line 28, page [illegible], for [illegible], read page [illegible]

'STON AND ITS ENVIRONS.

ART I.—HISTORICAL.

...D ROMAN PERIODS.

" dwellers by the
...f the ancient
...ation of
...be,

...of
...f a
...an

...ns
...of
...is,
...and,

...osition,
...ions of
...north-
...d that
...at or
...f the

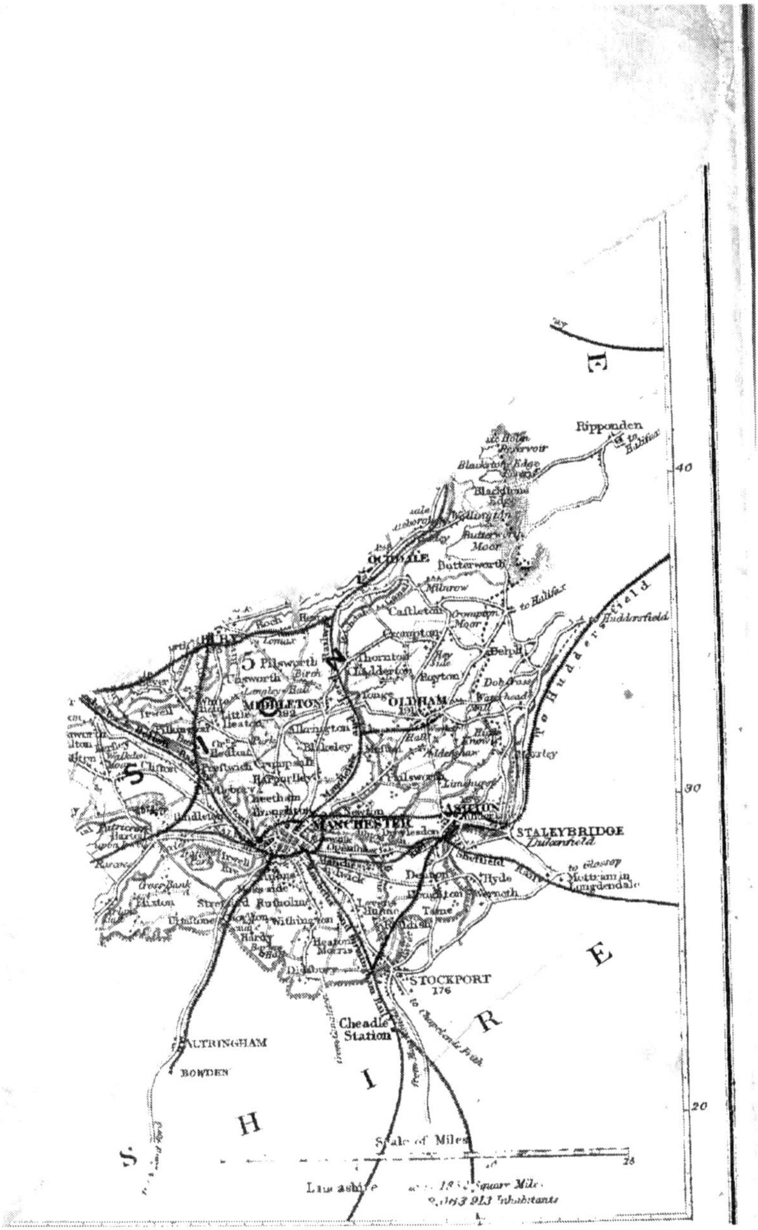

Ripponden
MIDDLETON
OLDHAM
MANCHESTER
STALEYBRIDGE
STOCKPORT
176
Cheadle Station
ALTRINGHAM
BOWDEN
Castleton
Butterworth
Milnrow
Crompton
Royton
Pilsworth
Hyde
Denton
Prestwich
Blakeley
Cheetham
Withington
Didsbury
Flixton
Urmstone
Stretford
Rusholme
E
S
H
I
R
E
40
30
20
Scale of Miles

PRESTON AND ITS ENVIRONS.

PART I.—HISTORICAL.

CHAPTER I.—BRITISH AND ROMAN PERIODS.

The Aborigines—Celtæ, Belgæ, etc.—The Brigantes—The Setantii, or "dwellers by the waters"—Conquest by the Romans—Agricola's march—Remains of the ancient inhabitants, etc.—Britain under the Romans—Remains of the Roman occupation of Lancashire—The Seteia, the Belisama, the Portus Setantiorum and the Moricambe, of Ptolomy identified with the Dee, the Ribble, the Wyre, and Morecambe Bay—Ribchester the Rigodunum of Ptolomy, and Walton-le-dale the Coccium of Antoninus—The route of the tenth iter of the latter authority—Discovery of a Roman station at Walton—Ribchester not a seaport at the time of the Roman occupation.

The early history of any locality presents but inconsiderable modifications of the more prominent characteristics pertaining to the community of which it forms a part. A history of Preston and its neighbourhood is, therefore, of necessity, to some extent, a history of Lancashire; and, though in a still more limited sense, of the British Empire.

The testimony of ancient historians, as well as its geographical position, indicates that Britain was originally peopled by successive migrations of the Celtæ or Keltæ, the Cimbri or Kimbri, and the Belgæ, from the north-western portion of the continent of Europe. Many writers contend that the island was likewise peopled by Teutonic, or German tribes, at or previous to our earliest historic period.[a] Cæsar, indeed, speaks of the

---

a Dr. Robson, in Lancashire and Cheshire Historic Society's Proceedings and Papers, vol. 5, p. 208.—Mr. Thomas Wright, do., vol. 8, p. 141.

Belgæ as of German origin, somewhat intermixed with the Celtæ, of Gaul. The Belgæ are believed by others to have been a mixed race of Kimmerians and Germans. The locality occupied by the Cimbri, after their settlement in the north-west of Europe, still remains a matter of conjecture. Strabo places them on the north of the river Elbe, and includes them amongst the German tribes.[b] The advent of the Angles, the Saxons, and the Jutes, after the departure of the Romans, does not therefore necessarily constitute, as is often supposed, the first infusion of Teutonic blood into the inhabitants of Britain.[c] Some commercial intercourse existed between the Phœnicians, the Greek and Roman merchants, and the aborigines, anterior to the age of Julius Cæsar, especially upon the southern and eastern coasts; where agricultural pursuits and more settled habits had enhanced the wealth of the community, and developed, relatively, a higher degree of civilization. Certain localities are described by Herodotus as the "Tin Islands," (Cassiterides) whence the merchants of Carthage and Massalia (Marseilles) procured large quantities of that metal. These are supposed to have been the Scilly Islands, and the south-western promontory of Britain, or Cornwall.[d] The natives, generally, and especially those inhabiting the midland and northern portions of Britain, were described by the early traders as a most ferocious people, who disfigured themselves by a species of tattooing. An infusion or the juice of a sea-weed called *woad* was employed to discolour the skin with bluish streaks, for the purpose of rendering their aspect terrible to their enemies.[e] They were partially clothed with the skins of wild animals, and dwelt chiefly in hovels amongst morasses and dense forests. Like most other uncivilized tribes, they were

b "It is probable the Cimbri who invaded Italy were composed of mixed tribes, both Teutonic and Celtic, for in their war with Marius, the description of their arms and the name of their chief, Bojorix, appears to designate them as Celtæ.—Knight Pen. Cyclop. Art. Cimbri.

c Mr. J. Hodgson Hinde (Lan. and Ches. His. Soc. Trans. vol. viii, p. 2) inclines, however, to the opinion that the Belgæ, on their migration to Britain, included but little of the Teutonic element. He says, "Even in Cæsar's time the Germans were but recent colonists in their adopted country, and it is more probable that the Belgæ were the last remnant of the original Celtic population of Germany, and were driven across the Rhine by the invading Germans, than that they were themselves a portion of the invading host."

d "Till the Belgæ came over into Britain, either no commerce at all was pursued by the islanders, or the commerce was confined to a few promontories on the south-west and a few vessels from Phœnicia. The Belgæ were strongly actuated by a commercial spirit, and pursued its directions so vigorously, that, within a century from their first entrance into the island, the most westerly tribes certainly carried on a considerable commerce with the Phœnicians, and all of them afterwards a much more considerable one with the Romans of Narbonne and the Greeks of Marseilles. In consequence of the latter, the native commodities of the island in the time of Augustus were regularly exported into Gaul, and conveyed by barges upon the rivers, or by horses upon the roads, across the Gallic continent to both. * * *

"The Belgæ settled in Britain about three hundred and fifty years B. C."—Rev. John Whitaker's History of Manchester.

e Mr. Thornber says a species of woad yet grows upon the coast of Morecambe Bay.

semi-nomadic in their habits, and existed principally on the produce of the chase, pasturage, and plunder.

The ancient Britons were not only a warlike, but, relatively, a free and liberty-loving people. Though divided into many small tribes or petty states, governed by transient military despotisms or more regularly constituted authority, the people do not appear to have been subjected to servile degradation in an equal degree with their relatives and neighbours, the continental Gauls. Yet they were not the less superstitious idolaters. Notwithstanding their military courage and physical prowess, they quailed with infantile terror beneath the anathemas of Druidical priests, who shed the blood of their fellow-men as a sacrifice to their savage deities,—personifications of the worst passions of a ruffian humanity.

The "Country of the Brigantes" is the name by which that portion of the island was distinguished, which included the Lancashire of the present day. The Brigantes occupied the territory which lies between the Scottish border on the north, and the Mersey and Humber on the south. Tacitus says the tribe of the Brigantes was the most numerous in the whole province of Britain. In a further sub-division, the inhabitants of the western coast between the Cumbrian and Welch mountains, were called the Volantii and the Setantii, Sistuntii, or Segantii, "the dwellers in the country of the waters." The Setantii were, therefore, the principal ancient inhabitants of Lancashire. The Rev. John Whitaker is of opinion that about the commencement of the Christian era the Setantii and Volantii acknowledged the supremacy of the Brigantine chiefs.

Dr. T. Dunham Whitaker, speaking of the Setantii, says,—"Thus situated, on an elevated level, along the sources of numerous brooks and of some considerable rivers, their name may be referred to the great characteristic feature of their country, *Se cond uii*,—the *Head* of the Waters."

The Volantii most probably occupied the hilly portion of the country to the north and east, and the Setantii the more level and marshy country near the coast. [f]

Little is known of this people, distinctive from the general aboriginal character, previously to the conquest of the country by the Romans. The polished southern warriors eventually introduced amongst the rude savages the arts and luxuries of civilized life, as some compensation for the loss of national liberty. The Britons, though often defeated in bloody battles, were, however, not easily subdued. They contrived to harass and

---

f The Rev. John Whitaker says the name is expressive of a maritime situation. "It is compounded of SE, TAN, TIU; or, S, IS, TAN, TIU, signifying either simply THE COUNTRY OF W. .ER, or discriminately THE INFERIOUR AND SOUTHERLY COUNTRY OF WATER, and expresses the particular position of Lancashire with respect to the Volantii and the sea."—His. Man. vol. I, p. 7.

disquiet the enemy to such an extent that the acquisition of any portion of Britain remained more a nominal than a tangible achievement till about a century after the arrival of Julius Cæsar. This renowned commander first landed on the British coast in the fifty-fifth year before Christ. In the year 43, during the reign of Claudius, the Romans, under Plautius, again invaded Britain. He was followed by Ostorius Scapula and Suetonius Paulinus. The former defeated Caractacus, and sent him in chains to Rome. The latter, after many sanguinary conflicts, finally routed the army of Boadicea, Queen of the Iceni, who, rather than grace the triumph of the conqueror, committed suicide. The combined efforts of these generals completely subdued the southern Britons. The Druids were put to the sword, or burnt upon their own altars. The sacred groves were destroyed, and the performance of their religious rites prohibited under severe penalties. Such extreme violence towards the faith of a conquered people was never indulged in by the Romans in any other instance; and was evidently an act of stern political necessity, arising from the abject deference paid by the inhabitants to the dictum of the Druidical priesthood, rather than one of simple religious intolerance.

The Brigantes are first mentioned by the Roman historians as in active collision with the imperial troops during the reign of the Emperor Claudius. They espoused the cause of the Iceni, and were defeated by Ostorius.[g] After the death of Galba, an insurrection broke out amongst them. Venutius, one of their most distinguished chieftains, had married the Queen Cartismandua, who had basely betrayed the brave Caractacus. The lady proved equally false to her husband; but Fortune refused to smile upon her second perfidy. She escaped with difficulty to her Roman allies, and Venutius not only remained master of the Brigantine territory, but for a considerable period successfully resisted the progress of the imperial arms. In the reign of Vespasian, the prætor Petilius Cerealis defeated the Brigantes, after a sanguinary struggle, and added the greater portion of their territory to the Roman province.

The Roman domination was not, however, fully established in the north-west of England till the reign of Domitian, when the civil and military government was entrusted to Julius Agricola. Under his commanding genius the whole country was systematically reduced to submission. Agricola entered the territory of the Setantii, according to his son-in-law, Tacitus, in the year 79. The previous ill success of the Brigantine arms dispirited the Setantii, and Lancashire became an easy acquisition. Tacitus says,—

---

g The Iceni inhabited the modern counties of Suffolk, Norfolk, Cambridge, and Huntingdonshire.

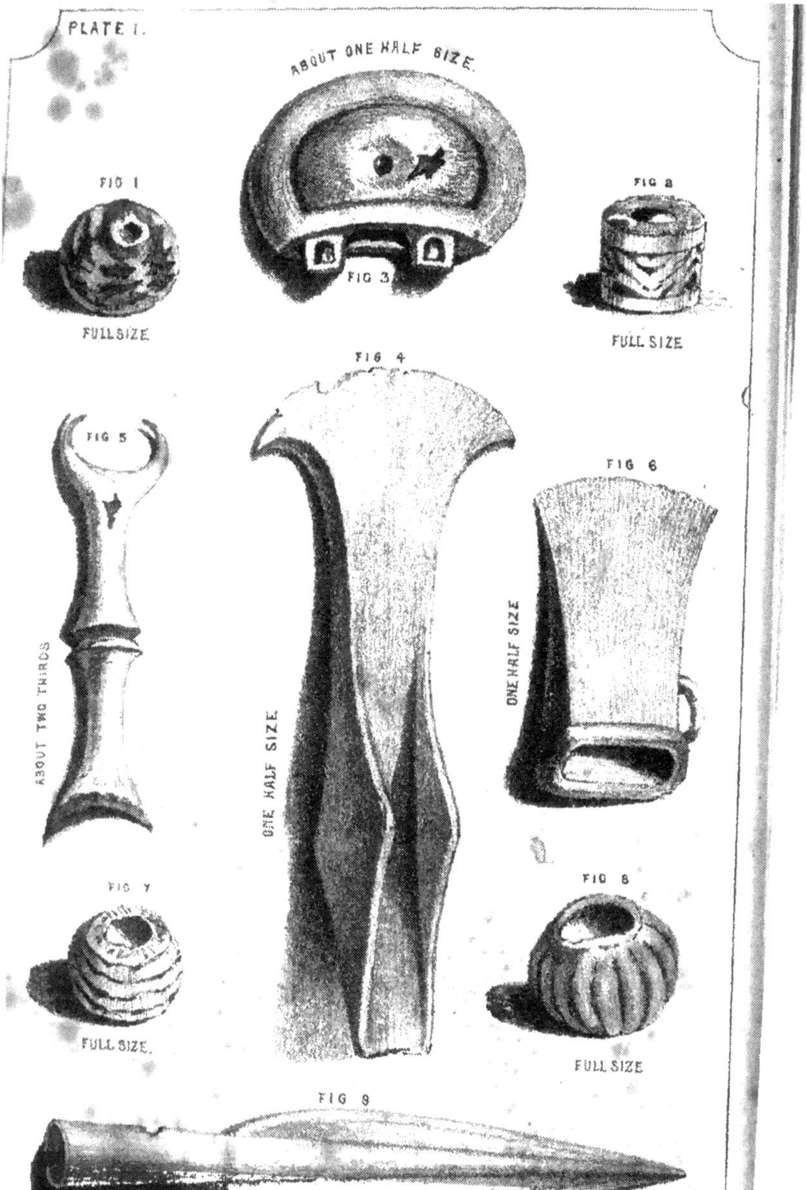
PLATE I.
ABOUT ONE HALF SIZE.
FIG 1
FULLSIZE
FIG 3
FIG 2
FULL SIZE
FIG 4
FIG 5
ABOUT TWO THIRDS
ONE HALF SIZE
FIG 6
ONE HALF SIZE
FIG 7
FULL SIZE.
FIG 8
FULL SIZE
FIG 9

"In the early part of the summer, Agricola personally inspected his soldiers, praised the forward, stirred up the slothful, and marked out the stations himself He explored the estuaries and woods, and kept the enemy in continual alarm by sudden incursions. When he had completely over-awed the people, he stayed his operations in order to exhibit to them the blessings of peace. By these means many cities, which till then had been free, submitted and gave hostages, and were surrounded by posts and fortified places. These were selected with so much skill and judgment that no newly-explored part of Britain was ever before so peaceable. The following winter was spent in the execution of the wisest designs. To pacify men rejoicing in warfare, and to incline them by idleness to pleasure, he exhorted them privately, and assisted them publicly, to erect temples, courts of justice, and habitations By praising the forward and chastising the slothful, he diffused a spirit of emulation which operated like a sense of duty. He instructed the sons of their chiefs in the liberal arts; and professed to prefer the genius of the Britons to the attainments of the Gauls. Thus, those who lately disdained the Roman language began to cultivate its beauties. Our dress became the fashion, and the toga was frequently seen. By degrees they yielded to the charms of vice, the porch, baths, and elegant banquets; and that was called humanity by the simple-minded natives which in truth was but a link in the chain of slavery."

Within four years, Agricola extended his conquests northward to the Firth of the Tay. He afterwards instituted a line of garrisons extending from the Clyde to the Forth, so as effectually to protect the Roman province from the forays of the fierce barbarians who preferred the barren hills and liberty to "inglorious ease" purchased by submission. Although Agricola's civil administration was of so prudent and conciliatory a character that he established, on a permanent foundation, the authority his military genius had achieved, his brilliant services, unfortunately for himself, were more valuable than even princely munificence could adequately recompense. The jealousy of the Emperor Domitian, therefore, repaid him with regal ingratitude.

Many remains of the ancient inhabitants have been discovered in the neighbourhood of Preston. About fifteen years ago, a very superior bronze celt or axe, and a spear head of similar metal, were found at Cuerdale, by Mr. Richardson, the late tenant of the estate, while making a deep drain in what he termed the "cars *or red water* land." This celt was forwarded to London for the inspection of some archæological society, and a common one of the form of fig. 6, plate I, returned in its stead. It is probably of British manufacture. The Rev. W. Thornber and others have discovered several remains of the aborogines in the "Fylde country," consisting of bronze celts, paalstabs, or battle and other axes; spear and arrow heads, a bronze knife, amulets, "Druids' eggs" or "adder stones," skin canoes, "Beltain" or "Teanla cairns" formed of "fire-broken stones;" bone needles, rude urns, etc. Several of Mr. Thornber's celts are large and of superior workmanship. Fig. 4, plate I, is an excellent specimen of this species of implement. It was found near the Roman agger in the Fylde. Mr. Thornber mentions, likewise, some remains of supposed British hovels near Pilling, and a singular pathway, buried above six feet deep in Rawcliffe moss, which is generally regarded to be either of British or Romano-British construction, but more probably the latter. It is fashioned of rude oaken planks, laid upon sleepers of the same material. "Sometimes," says Mr. Thornber, "it is composed of one huge tree, at others of two or three, and its width varies from 20 inches to something more. It has been traced by Mr. Banister and myself for a mile and a half in the interior of the moss; but to pass over the sullen desolation, it will have to run about the same distance farther." This singular road is named "Kate's" or "Danes' pad;" but all ancient remains are invariably attributed to the Danes in this part of the county. Some writers are of opinion that this road was constructed by the Romanized Britons and Roman legionaries in the reign of Severus. The following extract from Herodian's description of this emperor's expedition to subdue the revolted barbarians in the north, demonstrates that this conjecture is by no means improbable. He says,—

"He more especially endeavoured to render the *marshy places stable by means of causeways*, that his soldiers, treading with safety, might pass them, and having firm footing, fight to advantage. For many parts of the British country being constantly flooded by the tides of the ocean, become marshy. In these the natives are accustomed to swim and traverse about, being immersed as high as their waists: for, going naked as to the greater part of their bodies, they contemn the mud. * * * Of a breastplate or a helmet they know not the use, esteeming them as impediments to their progress through the marshes; from the vapours and exhalations of which the atmosphere in that country always appears dense. * * * His army having passed beyond the rivers and fortresses which defended the Roman territory, there were frequent attacks and skirmishes, and retreats on the side of the barbarians. To these, indeed, flight was an easy matter, and they lay hidden in the thickets and marshes through their local knowledge; all which things being adverse to the Romans, served to protract the war."

Those who are acquainted with the Fylde country, and especially the neighbourhood of Pilling and Rawcliffe, will readily perceive that a truer picture of the locality could not have been painted had the author specially alluded to this swampy district. Mr. Thornber describes the course of this singular road as "across the mosses of Rawcliffe, Stalmine, and Pilling, to the ancient sea beach of Scronka." The same authority mentions a singularly formed iron or steel fibula, a wooden drinking bowl, "hooped with two brass bands, and having two handles," found in Stalmine moss, together with a pewter "colon" or wine strainer, which he considers to have been used by the "Romanised Britons." "But," he adds, "the greatest treasure disclosed here was taken out of a ditch by Richard Fairclough. It consists of an anvil, scissors or shears, and many thin plates of brass. And the greatest curiosity is a brass stirrup of good workmanship." The stirrup is of singular form, and quite unique. It is difficult to decide by what people it was manufactured. Mr. Thornber asks, "Is it Roman?" On the line of the Roman agger from Kirkham to Poulton, called likewise "Danes' pad," Mr. Thornber has collected many remains, including iron galloway shoes, fragments of peculiarly formed panniers, and a curious vehicle (a kind of sledge), preserved in the dry gravel or the surrounding peat, which he attributes to the "Romanised Britons." Querns or hand corn mills have likewise been found near the line of the Roman agger. A Celtic stone hammer was found some years ago at Longridge. It is at present deposited in the museum of the Institution, Avenham. A somewhat similar hammer was found in the neighbourhood of Garstang, and near Winmarley, in the same parish, a "rude oaken box, fastened together by pins of the same material, containing a fine collection of celts and other instruments." Dr. Whitaker, in reference to these articles, says,—

"It is not improbable that they are partly Roman and partly British, as there are spears' heads exactly resembling those of the lower empire, while the celts decidedly belong to the original inhabitants of the country, but it may be difficult to fix the antiquity, or to decide the use of the tubes which appear amongst them. These instruments, with the remains of the box in which they were contained, still continue in the possession of the farmer's servant by whom they were discovered." [h]

It is much to be regretted that relics of this description are not immediately, on their being discovered, deposited in some public museum, not simply to ensure their preservation, but for their intrinsic value with reference to archæological and historical investigation. Bronze celts, etc., have at various times been taken from the Ribble, and indications of British location have been found at Walton-le-dale and other places. The ordinary celt, fig. 6, plate I, was found at Walton, together with the bronze articles, figs. 3, 5, and 9. They were deposited in the museum of the Literary and Philosophical Institution, Preston, by Mr. Adam Lambster, and are described as Roman. They belong to that class of articles to which it is difficult to assign a precise date. They are generally described, in consequence, as "Romano-British." Dr. Robson and others are of opinion that the bronze celts are not "British battle axes," but Roman chisels and carpenters' implements. The chief of these are most probably of Roman manufacture. Some antiquaries regard the term "Greaves town" in the township of Ashton, as indicative of the presence of the Druidical priesthood.[i] This conclusion is, however, not very satisfactory. In 1854, two curious glass beads were found near the house of Mr. Henry Threlfall, at Hollowforth, near Broughton. The workmen were digging for "subsoil," in which the beads were deposited. One is nearly spherical, but irregular in form, owing to some imperfection in the workmanship. The other is cylindrical, with the perforation scarcely in the centre, from a similar

h His. Richmondshire, vol. 2, p. 457.

i Whittle's His. of Preston, vol. 1, p. 10.

cause. The colours are yet very brilliant. The spherical one has yellow zigzag marks upon the dull green ground of the glass, and the other is still more elaborated. The circular edges are ornamented with a band of brilliant yellow, and the intermediate space is filled with white, green, and red waved lines. Plate I, figs 1 and 2.

Mr. Edward Benn, in a paper read before the Lancashire and Cheshire Historic Society, in January, 1855, after exhibiting several curious beads of this description, which had been found in Ireland, expresses a doubt whether any of a similar character had been "discovered in the ground elsewhere," and concludes that "till such shall prove the fact they must be classed as Irish." He expresses a hope that "those who are in possession of facts confirming what is stated or otherwise, will make this information known, as it is only by such co-operation that the truth can be reached." From this it would appear that specimens of these aboriginal ornaments are very rare in this country. Mr. Benn further adds, "These articles are found under such circumstances as would lead one to infer that they belonged to an age so distant as to seem quite incredible,—in those localities, indeed, in which are discovered those great fossil teeth, said to have been of an extinct horse. * * I do not mean to assert that the teeth have been found in absolute connection with the beads, but both have been discovered at the same depth in the subsoil and in the alluvial soil, as I have taken pains to ascertain."

There is considerable difficulty in determining the precise date of any ancient beads. They appear to have been used from the earliest known period. Some may have been manufactured in the countries where they are found, but the greater probability is that the bulk were made by the Romans and more civilised people of the continent, and exported to Britain and the provinces. Venice has been, from time immemorial, celebrated for the manufacture of such articles. At the present day, trinkets, beads, and other rude ornaments, as well as tomahawks, and, it is said, wooden idols, are fashioned in England for the barbarian tribes of America and the east. The two beads, figs. 7 and 8, plate I, were found by Mr. Thornber, near the base of the Roman agger in the Fylde. No 8 exactly resembles the centre one figured by Mr. Benn. It is likewise of *terra cotta,* and has been of a beautiful azure colour. Beads of this character are often found in connection with Roman interments. Fig. 7 is made apparently from a piece of "spar," the parallel bands are merely the veins in the original stone. In the tombs of the pagan Saxons, beads of a somewhat similar character are often found. Several are preserved in the British museum, and in the Faussett collection.

The Rev John Whitaker says, "The large branching horns of the segh" (wild deer) "have been found oftener in this than in any other county in the kingdom."[k] Dr. Leigh mentions one dug up towards the end of the 17th century, at Larbrick, near Preston, having the entire head of the stag, and even the vertebræ of the neck, adhering to it; and another, still larger, found a few years before "in the moss at Meales." J. Whitaker alludes to a third, fished out of the sea, in 1727, near Cartmel.

Horns of the segh and other extinct animals have since been dredged from the bed of the river Many similar relics were discovered amongst the alluvial detritus accumulated in the valley of the Ribble, when digging for the foundations of the North Union and East Lancashire railway bridges. Amongst others are remains of the gigantic ox *(Bos primigenius)*, skulls and horns of the long-faced ox *(Bos longifrons)*, skulls of the wild boar *(Sus scrofa)*, skulls of the wild bear *(Ursus arctos)*, etc. Several specimens are preserved in the museum of the Literary and Philosophical Institution, at the Institution for the Diffusion of Knowledge, Avenham, and at the Ribble Navigation Company's office.

Dr. Leigh figures the skull of a rhinoceros belonging to the "antidiluvian period," found "under a moss in Lancashire," which is copied by Buckland, in his "*Reliquiæ Diluvianæ*." Leigh likewise mentions that, during the drainage of Martin Mere, by "that Ingenious Gentleman and Generous Undertaker, *Thomas Fleetwood*, of Bank, Esq.," no less than eight canoes were found, cut from the solid tree, one of which he figures.[l] He likewise engraves a bronze celt and a "stone not unlike a whetstone," found in a "*morass*, in *Sawick*, about nine miles distant from the Meer."

Leigh further adds: "I have likewise seen a Brass Kettle, which was given me by Major *George Westby*, and a small Mill-stone, found in those places, as likewise Beads of Amber. 'Tis plain these could not be brought there by Noah's Deluge, since in those early days the Refining of Metals was not known, and 'tis very probable such kind of Mill-stones were not made use of."[m]

Several of the articles recently discovered on the site of the "Saxon castle," at Penwortham, mentioned in the Domesday survey, will be found fully described in the third chapter of the present work. Fig. 1, plate VI, represents what has been pretty generally pronounced to be a portion of an ancient British canoe paddle.

The names of the principal rivers, hills, and valleys in the county, as well as some other local appellations, still exhibit distinct evidence of

k History of Manchester, vol. 1, p. 352.

l Nat. His. of Lan., Ches., etc., pages 18 and 181.

m Ibid, p. 59. Leigh's work was published in the year 1700.

British origin. The Rev. J. Davies, in an interesting dissertation on the "Races of Lancashire," gives, amongst others, the following, as derived from the ancient Celtic language, represented by the Welsh, the Irish, and the Gaelic of the present day:—

"The Douglas, flowing into the estuary of the Ribble. Welsh du, black, and glas, a greenish blue, or sea green, so called from the colour of the stream.—The Ribble. The name of this well-known river has much perplexed antiquarian philologists. I can only venture to suggest that it may be compounded of rhe (active, fleet), and bala (a shooting out, a discharge, the outlet of a lake), and may refer to its rapid course as an estuary.—The Calder, a tributary of the Ribble: Mr. Baxter describes the first part of this word from calai, muddy. In Welch llai (pr. somewhat like the English clay) signifies "mud," and also "gloom," but this is not, I think, the origin of "cal" in Calder. More probably from Welch call, what goes or turns about. n The latter part is doubtless from the Welch dyr, a stream.—The Darwen, another tributary of the Ribble: Welch dyr, and gwen, white, beautiful.—The Lune, on which the town of Lancaster stands. This word is probably the same as Alun in Wales, from Welch al, chief, and aun, un, a contraction of afon, a river. This contraction of "afon" is not uncommon; it is found in Cornbrook, near Manchester (Cor aun, narrow stream).—The Wyre, a river that flows into Morecambe Bay. Welch gwyr, pure, fresh, lively.—Loud, Welch llwth, glib, slippery.—Bay of Morecambe, Welch mawr, Gaelic mor, great, and cam, crooked, winding, and Winander, or Winder Mere, Welch gwn, fair, beautiful, and dyr, water, stream.—Crag Valley, a long irregular valley near Blackstone Edge. Welch craig, a rock. This valley is also called the Vale of Turvin: Welch terfyn (pr. turvin), a boundary, terræ finis. This valley was probably in old time the boundary in this part between the Sistuntii of Lancashire and the Brigantes of Yorkshire.—Pendle Hill. Welch pen, head or summit, a common name in Wales for a lofty summit, as Penmaenmawr, Penrhyn, &c.; Gael, ben, binnear, hill. This word is written in our old records "Penhull," and is an instance of three parts of a single name, all having the same meaning, and marking three successive changes of language. Welch pen; Anglo-Saxon hull; English hill.—Coniston Old Man, a corruption, as Dr. Whitaker has pointed out, of alt maen, lofty hill.—Rivington Pike: Welch pic or pig, a pointed end, a beak, Armorican picq; French pic, as in the Pic du Midi.—Mellor, near Blackburn. Welch maelawr, a mart or market.—Catterall, near Garstang. Welch cad or cat, war, and rhail, a fence. There was doubtless a British encampment here.—Peel, on the Roman road from Manchester to Blackrod: Welch pill, a small fortress, a stronghold. This word is common in the county as a local name. There is an ancient British encampment near Stockport (the moat of which is still visible), which the country people call the Peel. The rude towers to which the northern borderers brought their prey, after a foray, are still called by this name.—Rossall, on the moorland, near Fleetwood: Welch rhos, a moor.—Carnforth and Scotforth, in the north of the county: Welch carn, a heap of stones, fordd, a road. The Celtic word "fordd," now appropriated to a road over a stream, means simply "a road" or "passage." The word "Scot" may be a sign of the ancient Irish Scoti, of whose permission to dwell in the country the Welch Triads have given us an account.—Penketh, Pendleton, Penwortham: here the first syllable is the Welch pen, head or summit. There are some other names of places which may probably be referred to a Celtic origin, as Heskin, Hesketh (Welch hesg, sedge, rushes).—The number of Celtic names of places is much less than of the names of natural objects, or of the Celtic words found in the dialect. The Saxons or Danes gave their own names to the town or village of which they took possession, while the river that flowed by, or the hill that rose above it, retained its original Celtic appellation."

Britain, whilst under the Roman dominion, was visited by the Emperors Hadrian and Severus, both of whom, together with Lollius Urbicus, the general in command under Antoninus Pius, recovered several revolted

n Dr W[illegible] pr[illegible] "[illegible]" or narrow as the interpretation.

provinces, and strengthened the northern defences, by the erection of military posts, earthern ramparts, and stone walls, extending from the Irish Sea to the German Ocean.

In the reign of Antoninus Pius, the Brigantes again rebelled, and made an aggressive movement into the neighbouring district of the Gernania, then subject to the Romans. They were, in turn, attacked and defeated by the Roman General. Severus died A.D. 210, or 211, at Eboracum, (York), the capital of the Brigantes. Three large hills yet point out the spot where his funeral obsequies are said to have been celebrated. After the death of Severus, his son Caracalla made peace with the Caledonians, and Britain appears to have enjoyed the blessings of internal tranquillity during the reigns of several succeeding emperors In the joint reign of Diocletian and Maximian, the Roman Admiral, Carausius, successfully assumed the purple in Britain (A.D. 288). On his death the province was re-united to the empire, and was afterwards, on its division, included in the possessions of Constantius Chlorus. The latter died at York, in the year 307, at which city his son, Constantine the Great, was proclaimed emperor. Constantine divided the Roman territories into the Eastern and Western Empires. From this period the power of the Roman people in Britain began sensibly to decline. The northern barbarians infested the interior, and the coasts were ravaged by Saxon pirates. The usurper Maximus first raised the standard of revolt in Britain in the year 381, and passed over to Gaul, carrying with him, according to some authorities, the flower of the British youth. He was defeated by Theodosius. Similar usurpations, including the temporarily successful one by Constantine, followed with similar results.[o] Britain suffered severely in the conflicts which preceded the final departure of the Romans from the island.

In the division of the British territory made by Severus, Lancashire formed part of the province Britannia Superior, of which Eboracum (York) was the principal city. In the reign of Constantine a new division was introduced, when the county was included in the province named Maxima Cæsariensis.

The religion of the Romans during their occupation of Britain was the Pantheistic idolatry. Some writers assert that Christianity was preached in the island as early as the time of the Apostles. A British Christian church, certainly, was founded centuries before the advent of Augustine

---

o The British troops, which followed the usurpers to the continent, were permitted to retain possession of Armorica, in the north-west of Gaul, where they founded the modern Bretagne or Brittany. Their number was further increased by the emigration of British people from Cornwall, and other places in the island, on the success of the Saxon invaders.

and Paulinus. The precise amount of truth there may be in the former statement it is now difficult to determine.[p] However this may be, the little light of Christian revelation which glimmered during the latter portion of the Roman period, was soon absorbed in the huge darkness of the succeeding Saxon idolatry. In a few generations the retrograde movement had annihilated the best portion of the Roman civilization. Internal wars and domestic treason completed the work, and Britain relapsed into barbarism.[q]

Notwithstanding the destructive influence of time, and of agricultural improvement, indubitable remains of several Roman roads and stations can yet be traced in various parts of Britain. As might be anticipated, from the imperfect character of the few ancient records which have descended to us, considerable difference of opinion has been expressed by antiquaries respecting the identity of existing localities with those of the Roman topography.

In this respect Lancashire appears to be rather more unfortunate than many other portions of Great Britain. The venerable Camden expressed a fear that he would "give little satisfaction either to himself or his readers," when he entered upon the consideration of the archæological remains pertaining to this county.[r] Although much has been discovered and written since his time, the subject still remains enveloped in considerable obscurity, the more eminent modern antiquaries and historians by no means agreeing even in the general outline.

What Byron so eloquently says of Rome itself, and the mystery still enshrouding many of its colossal remains, applies with two-fold force to the difficulties which present themselves to the local antiquarian topographer in one of the most remote provinces of the empire:—

"The double night of ages and of her
Night's daughter, Ignorance, hath wrapt and wrap
All round us; we but feel our way to err:
The Ocean has his chart, the stars their map,
And Knowledge spreads them on her ample lap;
But Rome is as the Desert, where we steer
Stumbling o'er recollections; now we clap
Our hands and cry 'Eureka!' it is clear—
When but some false mirage of ruin rises near."[s]

p In the year 1702, while removing the rubbish from the chief tribunal of the Druids in Anglesea, a brass medal of our Saviour was found, on which was inscribed in Hebrew—"This is Jesus the Mediator," from which it is inferred the Christian religion had been preached here in the early part of the first century; and it seems probable that this medal was the property of some of its ministers who had been condemned and sacrificed by the Druids —Burton's Mon. Ebor. b 1, p. 3.

q Mr. Kemble is of opinion that the population of Britain at the termination of the Roman occupation was as numerous as at the latter portion of the seventeenth century.

r Gough's edition, vol. 3, p 127.

s Childe Harold's Pilgrimage, canto 4th

The ancient Geographer, Ptolomy, mentions three estuaries and one "portus," which are, by universal consent, assigned to the coasts of Lancashire and Cheshire; but still, notwithstanding their strongly marked and distinctive characteristics, little approaching to a unity of opinion respecting their precise identity has yet been arrived at by those most conversant with the subject.[ŧ] The "*Seteia Æstuarium*" has pretty generally been assigned to the Dee, and the "Moricambe *Æstuarium*" to Morecambe Bay. But the "*Belisama Æstuarium*" and the "*Setantiorum Portus*" have been shifted from place to place, according to the judgment or caprice of the several antiquarian topographers. The *Belisama* is identified with the Ribble by Camden and Dr. T. D. Whitaker; and with the Mersey by the Rev John Whitaker, Horsley, Mr. Edward Baines, and others. The "*Portus Setantiorum*" is the Ribble, in the opinion of John Whitaker, Horsley, and Baines; while Stukeley and T. D. Whitaker place it on the Lune. Baxter supposed it to be the mouth of the Mersey; and Kuerden quaintly says, "They (the Romans) had likewise their *Limen* or Portus Setantiorum at or near the now Pyle of Foudra upon the river Ken." Camden fancied there was some error in the expression "Limen," and that Windermere lake was alluded to by the ancient geographer. And lastly, Percival, Mr. Thornber, Mr. Just, and others, identify it with the Wyre.

Ptolomy mentions a town or city on the Belisama, named Rigodunum. This has been variously placed upon the Mersey, at Warrington, and at Ribchester, on the Ribble. Dr. Kuerden enters into a long series of arguments to show that Preston occupies the site of this Roman city. John Whitaker regards Rigodunum and the Coccium of Antoninus as one and the same place, and fixes the site at Blackrod. He says "Caer Cocciu imports literally the City of Supremacy," and that "Rigodunum literally signifies the 'Fortress of Royalty.'" Dr. T. D. Whitaker gives a totally different derivation, but still fuses the two names into one, and places the compound at Ribchester. Ancient authorities mention other places besides those referred to in the Itinera of Antoninus which are believed to pertain to Lancashire, namely, Veratinum, which has been placed at Warrington; Colunium, or Calanea, at Colne; the Ad Alaunam of "Richard of Cirencester," and the Longovicus of the "Notitia," at Lancaster; on account of the supposed retention of portions of the Roman names in the modern designations.

According to Ptolomy the latitudes and longitudes of the following places on the coast are,—

ŧ Ptolomy's work was compiled about the year 130.

	Roman east long.	North lat.
Ituna	18° 30′	58° 45′
Moricambe Æstuarium	17 30	58 20
Setantiorum Portus	17 20	57 45
Belisama Æstuarium	17 30	57 20
Seteia Æstuarium	17 —	57 —

He places Rigodunum at 57° 30′ north latitude, and 40 minutes to the east of the "portus." It must be understood, however, that Ptolomy's figures are all much too high; and from his limited means of information, and the imperfect state of geographical and astronomical science at the period in which he lived, the *relative* positions of towns, &c., are often very erroneous. This, of course, materially increases the difficulty of local identification at the present day. The 15th degree of east longitude from Ferro, on the modern maps of the ancient world, crosses Morecambe Bay; Ptolomy is, therefore, two degrees and a half in excess. The mouth of the Ribble is about 53° 40′ north latitude. If the Ribble be the Belisama, the ancient geographer is in excess 3° 40′.

Assuming the Seteia estuary to be the Dee, Ptolomy's figures would place the Belisama at about Longton, on the Ribble; the Portus in the midst of Morecambe Bay; the Moricambe Æstuarium near the centre of the Cumberland and Westmoreland hills! and the Ituna not only a few miles to the *north* of the Solway, but about a degree to the *east* of Carlisle! The "Itinerary of Antoninus" does not mention any of these names.

There is another, although a doubtful authority, in whom, however, the Rev. John Whitaker appears to have placed unbounded confidence, viz., "Richard, of Cirencester," or "Ricardus Corinensis," a monkish writer of the fourteenth century. The history of his famous work is somewhat singular. Mr. Charles Julius Bertram, professor of the English Language at the Royal Marine Academy, Copenhagen, in 1747, sent to Dr. Stukeley a copy of a manuscript which he stated he had discovered at Copenhagen, entitled "*De Situ Britanniæ,*" purporting to be written by Richard. Stukeley published an analysis of the work, with the "Itinerary," in 1755; and the same year Bertram published the original at Copenhagen. Richard professes to have compiled his "itinera" from certain fragments written by a Roman general, and from Ptolomy and other authors. Antonine only gives fourteen routes, and one hundred and thirteen stations, in his Itinerary; while Richard has eighteen journeys, and one hundred and seventy-six stations. Some parties regard the manuscript as a forgery, and Bertram himself as the compiler of it. Dr. T D. Whitaker considers Richard to be entitled to no more respect as an authority than a modern historiographer. He says: —

"He may be proved to have had no ancient materials which we have not, and he wanted some that we possess. The *Fragmenta quædam a Duce quodam Romano consignata* appear to have been the Itinerary of Antonine; the basis of his map was that of Ptolomy, whom he expressly mentions; and his general divisions of Roman Britain were taken from the *Notitia*. To have adjusted all these, and to have formed an account of Roman Britain from the result, would have required a judicious and faithful hand. This last the Monk had not: on the contrary, he was possessed with the general spirit of his profession in the middle ages—something between bold conjecture and inventive fraud. He laid out new itinera; he imagined colonies, towns invested with *Jus Latii*, and others merely stipendiary, long after these distinctions were abolished; he inserted some names which, though real, were posterior to the Roman empire in Britain, and some which may safely be affirmed to have been fabricated by himself." [u]

Richard asserts Coccium to have been one of the cities that enjoyed the privilege alluded to, which implies that the native inhabitants were not governed by a *Roman* præfect and quæstor, but by officers elected from amongst themselves.

The Itinerá of Antoninus make no mention of the Portus Setantiorum, or of the town of Rigodunum; [v] but Richard has the following iter commencing at the former place, and passing across the country to York:—

Iter VII. Richard.

A Portu Sistuntiorum Eboracum usque sic.

Rerigonio	m. p.[w]	23.
Ad Alpes Peninos	"	8
Alicana	"	10.
Isurio [x]	"	18.
Eboraco	"	16.

It is by some believed that Richard (or Bertram), either by accident or design, substituted Rerigonium for the Rigodunum of Ptolomy.[y] The Rerigonius Sinus he has correctly placed near the mouth of the Clyde, which circumstance undoubtedly tends to confirm the opinion that its introduction into the Lancashire iter is an error. The elder Whitaker, however, accepted the alteration, and placed Rerigonium at Ribchester, and the "Portus Setantiorum" at the "Neb of the Naze," near Freckleton, on the Ribble.

u History of Whalley, p. 13.

v The "work of Antoninus is merely what its name imports, an itinerary or road book; but it extends over the whole Roman empire in its widest sense. * * The name of Antoninus, under which it now passes, has been retained, perhaps, more from the convenience of having some conventional author to refer it to, than from any good reason for believing that such was really the author's name. In the different MSS. of the work it is variously ascribed to Julius Cæsar, Antonius Augustus, Antoninus Augustalis, and Antoninus Augustus." The entire work has been assigned to Æthicus, "a geographical writer of uncertain date, but not later than the fourth century." The Itinerary must, from its nature, have received many additions subsequent to its original compilation. Some of the routes in Britain could not have been inserted prior to the erection of the wall of Severus, as that rampart is mentioned therein.—See Pen. Cyclop.—Art. Antoninus.

w M. P. signifies Millia Passuum, or miles intervening.

x Dr. Stukeley's copy says,—Isurio—19.

y Dr. Robson,—Lan. and Cheshire Historic Society's Transactions.

The existence of a Roman road from Ribchester to Kirkham, and the near agreement of the distance between the "Neb of the Naze" and the former place, with the figures in Richard's iter, appeared very conclusive, and consequently the Ribble for a long period remained in comparatively undisputed possession of the distinction of being the Roman "*portus*." The *Belisama* was removed to the Mersey, and Ptolomy himself made answerable for errors in the distances which could not be overlooked. But in the early part of the present century, another champion appeared, who impugned the authority of Richard. Dr. T. Dunham Whitaker fancied the *portus* at the *Lune*. Others, and especially the Rev. W. Thornber, having discovered that no traces whatever existed of a Roman highway from Kirkham to the "Neb of the Naze," while an agger, evidently of Roman construction, continued the road from Kirkham to near Poulton, consequently claimed the portus for the Wyre.

Dr. Whitaker exposes the error of the Historian of Manchester, with respect to the distance between the Dee and the Mersey, and replaces the Belisama at the Ribble. The elder Whitaker certainly "strained a point" *to suit his theory,* when he said, "*from the Seteia,* advancing twenty miles *to the north, Ptolomy goes thirty to the east to the Æstuary Belisama. This is plainly the Mersey, because Belisama* is at the distance of the Mersey"! The fact is, as has been previously stated, Ptolomy's distance accords with the Ribble as nearly as possible.[1] His successor, however, commits himself in a similar manner, at the opposite end of the line, or what becomes of the thirty-five geographical miles from the portus to Moricambe, if the former be on the Lune? Indeed, the Lune and the Wyre both discharge themselves into the bay of Morecambe; the latter certainly at its extreme southern point. Some, however, are of opinion that a channel of the Wyre formerly entered the Irish sea between Rossall College and "Cleveleys." But for the embankments artificially constructed, the high spring tides would at the present time force a passage in this direction. The truth of this was practically demonstrated during the heavy gale a few years ago.

Ptolomy makes the portus twenty-five minutes north of the Belisama, and ten minutes to the west. These figures exceed the distance of both Wyre and Lune, and indicate the port to be at Dr. Kuerden's locality, near the "Pyle of Foudra." But, if such be the case, where is the Moricambe Æstuarium? By this arrangement we have the portus on the northern shore

---

1 At so high a latitude, a minute of longitude is but about one half a geographical mile. John Whitaker appears not to notice this fact He continually speaks of Ptolomy's minutes as miles, whether of latitude or longitude.

of Morecambe Bay, and can scarcely be expected to travel thirty-five miles *further* in that direction, with the hope of finding the Moricambe Æstuarium!

The elder Whitaker's argument that so considerable an object as the Mersey *could not* be overlooked, is valueless, from the simple fact that, under any arrangement, a "considerable object" *has* been overlooked by the geographer; and why not the Mersey as well as any other? It is probable, for more than one reason. The present *embouchure* of that river is, from the sea, a much less "considerable object" than Morecambe Bay, the mouth of the Ribble, or that of the Dee. No Roman remains of any description have ever been found at or near Liverpool; and none of their roads tend towards that port. Again, it is the opinion of some that the rivers Mersey and Dee once united, the promontory of the Wirral being a large island in the estuary common to both.[a] However this may be, it does not require any very great stretch of the imagination, on looking at a map at the present time, to regard the bay included between Formby Point and the Point of Ayr as the "Setcia Æstuarium," into which debouche both the Mersey and the Dee. It must not be forgotten that Ptolomy speaks, not of *rivers*, but *estuaries*, under which term he includes the large *bay* of Morecambe. The latter receives the Lune, the Wyre, the Kent, and the Leven. The Ribble estuary conducts into the Irish Sea, not only the waters of the stream of that name, but likewise those of the Douglas. The "Portus Setantiorum" implies not necessarily either estuary or river,—of any importance at least,—but simply a commercial harbour.

According to the Historian of Whalley, the word Belisama signifies "Head of the Waters;" and "Rhiu-bel, from which the present name is obviously formed, has exactly the same meaning, namely, the Head River." The elder Whitaker calls Belisama, the "Head Stream, or King of the Currents," and "Rhi-bel, King River." Leigh says "*Bellisama*, in the *Phœnician* language, signifies *the Moon*, or the *Goddess of Heaven*," and that "*Ribel*, now the name of the same river, in the Armenian Tongue, signifies *Heaven*."[b] He contends that the Brigantes were a mixed people, composed of Britons, Phœnicians, and Armenians Mr. Thornber says that Belisama means "Queen of Heaven," and that the Romans paid divine honours to the Ribble under the title of "Minerva Belisama." The

a See Ormerod's History of Cheshire, vol. 2. A large tract of country, extending from the confluence of the Mersey and the Weaver to Helsby and Frodsham, is still occasionally subjected to inundation If this theory be correct, the mouth of the Mersey must have been originally very shallow, as well as narrow, from the weaker action of the fresh water current. In Grose's map the embouchure is partially blocked by a small island.

b Natural History of Lan. and Ches., and Peak of Derbyshire, p. 76., book 3

temple at Ribchester is supposed to have been dedicated to this goddess. The deification of rivers was common to the Roman people; the Wharfe, in Yorkshire, whose source is almost identical with that of the Ribble, was endowed with celestial attributes under the name "Verbeia." Camden says, "After the Mersey this is the next river that falls into the ocean, the old name whereof is not entirely lost, for Ptolomy calls the estuary here Belisama, and we the Ribell, perhaps by joining to it the Saxon word Rhe, which signifies a river." [c]

If there be much weight in etymological evidence, the identity of the Ribble with the Belisama estuary would seem clearly demonstrated. The inconsistency of the elder Whitaker, in his interpretation of the terms Rhibel and Belisama, and his investment of the Mersey with the Roman title, is self-evident But this semi-romance writer had a pet theory to substantiate He was determined upon fixing the *portus* at Ribble; consequently every other fact or argument is tortured into subserviency to this purpose.

An eminent modern archæologist [d] would, however, extract from the name Ribble a character directly opposite to that of "Head River" or "King River" After demonstrating that Don or Tan is often applied to a superior stream, and Dee or Tee to a relatively inferior one in its vicinity, he applies the Belisama to the Mersey, for the purpose of furnishing the necessary complement to the river Dee! But, independently of the important fact that Bel is neither Tan nor Don, the reasoning is unsatisfactory, inasmuch as a "disparaging diminutive" in the modern word Ribble, might, equally with Dee, indicate the presence of a superior stream in *its* neighbourhood. This, therefore, is but shifting the difficulty from one river to the other. But supposing the term "ripple" does not, like "Dee," imply a comparative quality, the fact that the term Ri-bel, or Rhi-bel, is continually used by the older writers speaks infinitely louder for its *origin* than the Norman-Latin "Ripa" of the Domesday surveyors. Again, Ribble is precisely such a river as would demand the superior appellation, inasmuch as it is the chief current into which four lesser, but not, relatively, insignificant streams, discharge themselves, viz:—the Hodder, the Calder, the Darwen, and the Douglas The ancient name of the Mersey seems to be lost Might it not, if found, furnish the necessary

c Mr. Davis's opinion has been previously given. It is by no means either decisive, or even satisfactory to himself. He says, "I can only venture to suggest that it may be compounded of rhe (active fleet,) and bala (a shooting out, a discharge, the outlet of a lake,) and may refer to its rapid course as an estuary" The Ribble, however, can by no means be called a rapid stream; many of its tributaries exceed it in this particular.

d W. Bell, Phil. Dr and Secretary to the British Archæological Society for Foreign correspondence P[illegible] Lanc and Ches. Hist Soc.—Session 3, 1851

complement to the Dee in the presence of the word Don, or Tan, or some of their variations, without troubling the Belisama at all? Baxter calls it Tinna, which has been identified with Tyne. The present name of the Mersey from its source to Stockport is "Tame." Dr. Bell himself makes Tyne a variation of Tan. If "Tame" will not answer the purpose, it is, at least, much nearer the mark than Belisama. But the strongest evidence against Dr. Bell's position is furnished by the fact that the Dee and the Mersey, as the slightest glance at a map will show, are so nearly of *equal* magnitude, that the terms Don and Dee, as interpreted by him, cannot with propriety be applied to them. In Knight's Pen. Cyclop, both rivers are stated to be fifty-five miles in length![e]

It is necessary to bear in mind that the Mersey is but a *modern* seaport, and depends much upon artificial adjuncts for its safety as a harbour. When Humphrey Brereton undertook the dangerous task of carrying despatches from Lord Stanley and Elizabeth of York to the Earl of Richmond, in the reign of Richard III., he embarked at Liverpool, "a port," says Agnes Strickland, "then little known to the rest of England;" and, for which reason, together with the circumstance that "the shipping and all matters there were at the command of the house of Stanley,"[f] doubtless it was selected. Its character was so low as late as the end of the seventeenth century, that William III. preferred Hoylake, on the coast of Cheshire, for the embarkation of the troops with which he defeated James II. in Ireland.

"Mere" is a term generally applied to lakes in Lancashire and Cheshire, as Windermere, Marton Mere, Martin Mere, Rosthorn mere, Mere-mere, etc., etc. May not the term Mersey be derived from mere and sea, or sea-lake, from the peculiar form of its estuary and narrow *embouchure*? This, of course, is merely a conjecture, and may possibly justify a polite intimation that, in this interpretation of the difficulty, the suggester is a long way "at sea" himself. Etymological evidence is, unquestionably, of the greatest value to the antiquarian topographer, but, like many other precious articles, it is, on account of its very importance, more subjected to the risk of being counterfeited than gross or vulgar material[g]

e Article,—"Cheshire." The same work, article, "Dee," states "The whole course of this river, from Bala pool to the beginning of the æstuary, may be about seventy miles," thus making the Dee the larger instead of the lesser river. The Severn being a much more important stream than the Dee, would better answer Dr. Bell's purpose. One of its chief affluents is named the Teme.

f Lives of the Queens of England, vol. 4, p. 15.

g Since the above was written, the author noticed for the first time, the term "Sea-lake" applied to the estuary of the Mersey, on a "plan of Liverpool and the pool, as they appeared about the year 1650," re-published opposite page 82 of the 6th session of the Transactions of the Lan. and Ches. His. Society. South of Manchester, at this day, the river is not known by many of the peasantry as the Mersey. It is called by them the "Cheshire waters" The modern name appears to have been derived from the estuary, and not from the fresh water stream.

There could scarcely be a doubt as to the identity of the Moricambe Æstuarium with the present Morecambe Bay, if it were known with certainty that such was its designation anterior to the time of Camden. Some parties, however, entertain an opinion that this learned antiquary may have been the first to apply the name to what was previously termed Lancaster Bay, from a conviction of its identity with Ptolomy's Æstuary, because an etymological rendering of the term Moricambe ("great bend") described its peculiar form and character. The universality of its present appellation by the most illiterate of the peasantry of the neighbourhood is, however, decidedly against this supposition. Lancaster Bay is a smaller inlet on the southern shore of the larger indentation. A map of Lancashire, dated 1598, numbered 6159, HL. MSS, and re-published in 1821, in "Gregson's Fragments," gives the name "Morcalm Bay." Lancaster Bay is not mentioned

Dr. Whitaker's affection for the Lune as the *portus* appears to have mainly resulted from a desire to reconcile, as nearly as possible, its latitude, as given by Ptolomy, with that of York, according to the same geographer. Yet he confesses that Ptolomy "is known to have taken his accounts of our British coasts from the observations of mariners." Consequently, relying upon various imperfect authorities, he may rationally be supposed *much more likely to err* in the relative positions of two localities, the one situated near the eastern and the other on the western coast, than he would respecting the distances of four "considerable objects" within a few miles of each other. Besides, the high latitude of Moricambe *must* be an error of Ptolomy, if the estuaries described belong to *the coasts of Lancashire and Cheshire*, which is not denied. This can be demonstrated from his own figures and a reference to the local facts. He makes the entire distance from the "*Seteia*" to "*Moricambe*" 1° 20′, or eighty geographical miles; while the real distance, including both extremities, is little if any more than fifty! Ptolomy's distances, being derived from early mariners, and being generally in excess, might, perhaps, with some probability, be regarded as sailing routes rather than geographical measurements. With a very slight allowance on this score, if the Dee and the Mersey be considered as one, or the latter overlooked, the relative positions of the *Seteia*, the *Belisama*, and the *Portus* will accord with the Dee, the Ribble, and the Wyre. *Moricambe*, however, will still show a considerable excess, unless the deep indentation of the coast line be assumed as a compensation. But this does not satisfactorily meet the difficulty. Ptolomy, or some of his transcribers, has evidently recorded a blunder in the latitude of Moricambe, for he makes it but twenty-five miles south of the *Ituna*, which is acknowledged to be the Solway. The entire latitude distance from *Seteia* to *Ituna* agrees with that of the Dee and Solway, quite as near as can be expected from the imperfect character of Ptolomy's information.[h] The Wyre, likewise, accords with the distance (one degree) of the *portus* from *Ituna*. The chief confusion arises from the latitude assigned to Moricambe. If this were corrected so as to agree with Ituna, there would be no difficulty, the breadth of the bay being still sufficient to give to its centre a considerably higher latitude than the Wyre, and thus preserve the *sequence* of Ptolomy, which would not be done if the *portus* were placed at the "Pyle of Foudra," or scarcely so if at the Lune. This arrangement implies an error of half a degree in the latitude of *Moricambe*. The relative longitudes of all the places, on this supposition (with the exception of the *Ituna*, where there is an evident blunder of one degree,) coincide, considering the circumstances, remarkably well. Under any other theory, the two corrections suggested are necessary, while the remaining figures do not present anything like so near an approximation.

Dr. Whitaker, not wishing his own arrangement to be disturbed, affects to *ridicule* the claims of Wyre. There is, however, little grace and less logic exhibited in the effort. He says,—

> "About three miles south of the town of Poulton, the agger of a Roman road was distinctly visible till within the last ten or twelve years, since which time immense quantities of gravel have been conveyed away for repairs of the roads and garden walks. Its direction was such as to show that it had been a branch from the road now visible on Fulwood Moor, which led from Ribchester to the neb of the Naze, tending to the estuary of Wyre. It does indeed prove, beyond a doubt, that the Romans had a settlement, as it was antecedently probable, that they would have, on that estuary, as well as on those of the Lune or Ribble;[i] but it neither proves nor renders probable, that the mouth of the Wyre was the Setantiorum Portus."[k]

The circumstance would, doubtless, have possessed considerably more value in the estimation of the learned doctor, if it had assisted in the demonstration, and not tended to the overthrow, of his favourite hypothesis. The single fact that the best constructed Roman road in Lancashire passed through the Fylde country to Ribchester and York, is of more value as evidence relative to the site of the *portus* than the whole presented by any other existing remains. Why should the Romans construct such a work? It could not be for the purpose of simply occupying the then swampy district. Or, if so, how does it happen that the precisely similar tract of

---

h The excess is not more than eight or ten miles.

i "I agree with Mr. Whitaker that there has been a Roman port about Freckleton, towards which the Watling-street, as it is called, first described by Dr. Leigh upon Fulwood Moor, evidently tends"—His. Whalley, p. 13.

The road in question was described before Leigh's time by Dr. Kuerden, and pronounced Roman by Dugdale.

k Richmondshire, vol. 2, p. 443.

country between the Ribble and Mersey has hitherto yielded no such evidence of permanent occupation by the Romans? The inference is obvious. It was not the bogs and morasses of the Fylde, but the estuary of the Wyre that gave value to the district in the estimation of the Roman people.

There is yet another important fact in favour of the Wyre. Ptolomy places Rigodunum at fifteen minutes south of the portus, and forty minutes to the east. Dr. Whitaker, himself, identifies Rigodunum with Ribchester. Although these figures are slightly in excess (as is usual with Ptolomy,) for the mouth of the Wyre, the alternative of any other Lancashire harbour, except Peel,—and that has previously been disposed of,—but increases the discrepancy, especially with respect to longitude.

Again, Wyre is not an "*insignificant river*," as is sneeringly asserted by Dr. Whitaker; at least, its *harbour* is not, and that is the question at issue It possesses one quality not likely to be overlooked by a people who could never entirely overcome their dread of tidal seas: "*As safe as Wyre*" has been a proverb from time immemorial amongst the denizens of the Fylde country Wyre is, at present even, unquestionably the best natural harbour on the coast of Lancashire, and is large and deep enough to accommodate vessels of much greater burthen than any chartered by the Greek or Phœnician merchants, or built by the Roman people for either naval or commercial purposes. The Roman ships of war were merely galleys propelled by oars. The fleets were composed of large numbers of vessels, but the individual ships were small in comparison with the craft of the present day. The vessels with which Julius Cæsar invaded Britain were so small, that he was enabled to have the whole dragged upon shore in a few days. The great bulk of the Danish vessels, which scoured the seas centuries after the departure of the Romans, were probably not above thirty tons burthen. Snorre says the largest of them did not carry more than from twenty to forty men and a couple of horses [1] Camden speaks of "eight hundred vessels larger than barks" being annually laden by the Romans with grain at the British ports," for the supply of their garrisons upon the frontiers of Germany The "Portus Setantiorum," doubtless, was frequented by vessels of this class.

Dr. Whitaker's attempt to invalidate the term *Berge-rode* is equally unsatisfactory, and, by its weakness, rather tends to strengthen the position of his opponents than otherwise. In reply, the Rev. W. Thornber pertinently observes:—

---

1 Heimskringla vol 1, p 317

"I cannot but remark here that Dr. Whitaker seems to write with some asperity, when he refers to this subject. The manner in which, by substituting W for B, he reads Werge-rode for Berge-rode, thus discarding the antient name given to the coast along the Wyre by Harrison, our oldest topographer, and by Saxton, our first national surveyor; and affirming that the former of these inscribed the title of Berge-rode,[m] in small characters *as if in doubt*, and that the latter servilely followed, is really unworthy of that most erudite antiquarian." [n]

Several Roman remains have been discovered in the Fylde, near the line of the road and the banks of the Wyre, as well as at Kirkham. Amongst others, two copper coins of Hadrian were found near the church at Poulton, and a large medal of Germanicus in a garden behind the Market-place. A coin of Domitian has likewise been discovered at the "Breck," which is nearer the "Skippool," or estuary of the "Skippon" brook, at its junction with the Wyre. From the direction of the road, and the natural advantages of the locality, it is probable the Roman vessels were "beached" not far from the "Skippool"

Other important remains likewise attest the Roman occupation of the country at the mouth of the Wyre. Some parties conjecture, and not without reason, that they may have had a landmark, or even a *pharos*, at Fenny. If the port were on the Wyre, something of the kind would be necessitated. The country people to this day pronounce Fenny as if spelt "Phaney." [o] In 1840, some brickmakers discovered about four hundred silver denarii between Rossall Point and Fenny. This treasure consisted of coins of Trajan, Hadrian, Vespasian, Titus, Domitian, Antoninus, Severus, Caracalla, Sabina, Faustina, etc., about forty of which are in the possession of the Rev. W. Thornber. [p] This gentleman, likewise, mentions several other interesting relics of the Romans or Romanised Britons, found in the neighbourhood of the Wyre estuary. A curious road, previously mentioned, called Kate's or Danes' Pad, considerable remains of which have been found by Mr. Thornber, Mr. Banister, and others, several feet below Rawcliffe moss, appears to have traversed the swamps in the direction of the Wyre from Lancaster. As the Danes were not road makers, this path is generally regarded as of Roman or ancient British construction Tradition has so strongly preserved the memory of Danish ravage in the Fylde country, that the native inhabitants instinctively refer all matters ancient or mysterious, to the Scandinavian marauders.[q]

---

m "The Romans termed castles and towns 'Bergi,' and rode signifies a station for ships"

n His. Blackpool, p. 15.

o Mr. Thornber, however, thinks the name "Fenny" originated from the swampy nature of the district.

p The remaining portion of these coins was purchased at the sale of the effects of Sir Hesketh Fleetwood, Bart., at Rossall Hall, by Mr. Alderman Brown, of Preston, of whose collection they at present form the chief feature.

q See Lan. and Ches. His. Soc. Proceedings, Session 3rd, 1851, and page 6, of the present work.

The identity of the stations mentioned in the tenth iter of Antoninus has equally provoked much learned disquisition, some of which has tended to envelope the question in still deeper obscurity, rather than to shed additional light upon it.

The Tenth Iter reads as follows :—

A Glanoventa Mediolanum, m. p. C L.

Galava	m. p	XVIII.[r]
Alone	„	XII.
Galacum	„	XIX.
Bremetonacis	„	XXVII.
Coccio	„	XX.
Mancunio	„	XVII
Condate	„	XVIII.
Mediolano	„	XVIII.

Some authorities consider this iter to commence at Lanchester, in the county of Durham; others somewhere upon the Solway, and that it traverses the "Lakes District." All agree that it proceeds southwards through Lancashire and Cheshire.

Richard of Cirencester gives a somewhat similar route, but the discrepancy is such as to admit of no reconciliation with the northern portion of the iter of Antonine. He says,—

Luguballia	
Brocavonacis	XXII.
Ad Alaunam	——
Coccio	——[s]
Mancunio	XVIII.
Condate	XXIII.
Mediolano	XVIII.

---

r The Roman mile consisted of eight stadia, measuring about 1,618 yards. It was consequently less than an English mile by nearly one-twelfth —Penny Cyclop.

From a careful measurement between existing columns on the Appian Way in the neighbourhood of Rome by Bianchini, and from other sources, M. Danville estimates the Roman mile at 755 toises, or 1,593 yards, English measure.—Hist. de l'Academie, t. 88, p. 661.

s The elder Whitaker says Dr. Stukeley's copy fills up the blank after Coccio with sixty-six miles ! Mr. Edward Baines (His. Lan , vol 1, p. 15) gives a portion of Richard's iter as follows :—

Brocavonacis		
Ad Alaunam	m. p.	XXXXVII.
Coccio	„	XXXVI.
Mancunio	„	XVIII.
Condate	„	XXIII.

This, though not so indicated, is, however, evidently "corrected" to suit the elder Whitaker's theory, [illegible]

Referring to these itinera, and other inland stations supposed to pertain to Lancashire, the elder Whitaker observes.—

"The Sistuntii had the towns of Coccui, Bremetonac, Rerigon, Veratin, and our own Mancenion · all acknowledging the first to be, what the name Coccui, or supreme, undeniably imports it to have been, the British metropolis of Lancashire. Such was the principality of the Sistuntian Britons, subject to its own capital, and governed by its own regulus."

He then proceeds to assign to each of these "towns" a precise locality; and, with a daring dogmatism, utterly repugnant to the true spirit of antiquarian research, asserts that such and such places "MUST" be the localities stated by him, though often upon the flimsiest of evidence, and sometimes even from the merest conjecture. Blackrod was both Coccui and Rigodunum; Overborough, Bremetonac; Ribchester, Rerigon; Warrington, Veratin; and Mancenion, Manchester.

Mr. Edward Baines adopts this arrangement, as he had previously done the dictum of the same authority respecting the portus and estuaries; that is, so far as he appears to follow any given system. By a singular inconsistency, he makes, on the same page, Coccium to be both at Blackrod and Ribchester.[t]

Watson and Percival fixed Coccium at Blackrod.[u] Camden placed Rigodunum at Ribchester, and Coccium at Cockey. Kuerden thought Preston occupied the site of Rigodunum. Horsley gave Coccium to Ribchester, and Rigodunum to Warrington. The Rev. T. Sibson assigned Coccium to Wigan, and Dr. Robson placed it a little to the north of Preston. John Whitaker calls Colne, by etymological inference, the Roman Colunium or Calanca. From a similar mode of reasoning, he makes the Ad Alaunam of Richard, which some regard as identical with the Longovicus of the Notitia, to be Lancaster.[v]

Dr. Whitaker, after soundly rating Richard for presuming to substitute Rerigonium for Rigodunum, makes the latter and Coccium identical, and gives the twin-named city a "local habitation" at Ribchester. For this he advances the following arguments:—

"Without repeating reasons so lately adduced for restoring the Ribble to its ancient name of Belisama, I shall now assume the point as proved, at least with the degree of evidence which such investigations admit of, and shall merely state, that upon this river Ptolomy places his Rigodunum; and upon this river also the Itinerary of Antonine, *if the line of the tenth Iter* and the two given stations between which it is interposed,

---

t His Lan, vol. 1, p. 15.

u Watson was the first to adopt this arrangement, nearly a century ago. Jno. Whitaker followed, but shifted the station a mile further north to the banks of the Douglas.

v The *Notitia Imperii* was compiled at the very close of the Roman domination in Britain, and gives the titles and countries of the legionaries and their auxiliaries, which held the garrisons and the more important military posts at that period together with the incontrovertible evidence of remains, (I draw *no argument from the numbers* which upon every hypothesis are allowed to be corrupt,) be allowed to interpret, has fixed the station of Coccium. Yet *no concurrence of roads, no discovered remains*, lead to the supposition that *two* stations or towns of eminence in the age of Ptolomy or of Caracalla were planted on the banks of the Ribble. How then is this apparent difficulty to be solved? A little attention to British etymology and to the obvious appearance of the place will remove every doubt. In the first place let the name as it stands in Ptolomy be stripped of the Roman termination *dunum;* and with a British aspirate at the end it becomes Rigoch. In the next place cut off from the itinerary name its Roman generic termination, and we have *Cochiu.* G and C are convertible; some manuscripts of the Itinerary read Goccium, and the radical syllable *Coch* or *Gosh* is the same in both. *Gosh* in the British language, is red—*Rhigoch*, Red River; and *Gochiu* or *Cochiu*, Red Water. And accordingly, the stone, the sand, the soil of Ribchester, are alike distinguished by this very colour, which would naturally arrest the attention of the first inhabitants, and occasion a name peculiarly significant and proper. [w]

It appears, however, from some observations in his History of Richmondshire,[x] published afterwards, that misgivings had arisen in his mind as to the route of the tenth iter of Antonine. He says,—

"That this place (Ribchester) was the Coccium of the Itinerary, is *proved by the distances (?)* and illustrated by the etymology of the name coch ui, or red water, which is the general complexion of the shelving banks of the Ribble, above and beneath the station. That it was one of Agricola's stations is evident, not only from its *coinciding* with his *acknowledged line of march* to subdue the Brigantes, but from coins as early as Vespasian, and other remains of the Higher Empire there discovered. That it was not merely a military post, but a city of great elegance and wealth, is evident, not only from the numbers, but the superior style and workmanship of the remains which have been brought to light. That notwithstanding the opulence of Ribchester, the great line of march northward, from Mancunium to Bremetonacæ, was carried in the Lower Empire through *the low country by Preston and Lancaster, in order to avoid the difficulties of the Bowland Fells*, has been elsewhere proved."

It is almost a pity to disturb a theory so nicely expressed and apparently so clearly demonstrated. But facts and dispassionate investigation are often stern enemies to fanciful speculation. The learned doctor does not inform us *how the distances had contrived to assimilate*, since his anterior expression of indifference to the test which they furnish. He had likewise previously stated that the higher line was a firmer and a better road, but this is emphatically denied by the Rev. Mr. Sibson. By the latter authority, Blackrod is shown, in contradiction to John Whitaker's assumption, to possess no military road near it, but merely a "vicinal way," although Mr. Edward Baines, misquoting the historian of Manchester, who alluded to his own location at Castle-field, discourses of "Roman roads expanding like radii from a centre," still to be seen in the neighbourhood! Dr. Whitaker speaks of the "mile-stone" found a little to the south of Lancaster, inscribed to the emperor Julius Philipus, who reigned between the years 244 and 249, as probable evidence that the road was

w History of Whalley, p. 12.

x Vol. 2, p. 458.

constructed during his life-time.[y] It is equally probable, however, that mile-stones might be placed upon any given route, years after a road was first constructed, and very certain that the ruggedness of the country over Bowland Fells would be quite as objectionable during the higher as during the lower empire. The doctor's namesake, notwithstanding his sturdy determination to make the most of Manchester, which was the true cause of many of his errors, candidly acknowledges that, in his judgment, "Agricola's main body advanced by way of Warrington," and that "*a detachment*" went by Manchester, Ribchester, etc., and afterwards "re-united with the army in the county of Cumberland!" But, supposing the first construction of the road by Julius Philipus be conceded, it may still be the tenth iter of Antonine, the work known by that name having received, as has been previously shown, many additions after his reign. From the face of the country it is evidently the *natural* route. It formed part of a great line of British road from Cornwall to Cumberland, previous to the Roman occupation, similar to the Ermyn-street on the eastern coast, and the Watling-street from London to North Wales. Several authorities contend that the Romans merely adopted and improved many such aboriginal tracks. To crown the whole, considerable remains of a Roman station have lately been discovered on the lower route at Walton-le-dale, near Preston. This important disclosure relieves the antiquarian topographer from the disagreeable necessity of confounding the Coccium of Antoninus with the Rigodunum of Ptolomy, the red rock, earth, etc., characterising the Ribble near Preston, as markedly as at Ribchester. Amongst the remains already discovered are coins of the higher empire,—Titus Vespasian, Domitian, and Antoninus Pius,—the former of which coincide with the date of Agricola's march.

The Rev. Mr. Sibson, of Ashton-in-Mackerfield, made a very minute survey of the Roman road which enters the county at Warrington, and passes through Haydock to Standish and Wigan. He describes its appearance in almost every field on a large portion of the route, and anticipated the recent discovery at Walton. "From Standish," he says,—

"The Roman road then passes through Welsh Whithill, Euxton Burgh, Rose Whit-hill, Bamber Green to Walton, *where it is probable there has been a fortified camp to protect the pass of the Ribble*. The Roman road from Preston to Lancaster appears to have gone over Fulwood Moor, Cadley Causeway,[z] through Broughton, Barton, and Bilsborough, along Fleet-street in Claughton, and through Borough, near Lancaster. * * * * The road runs through a level country, on hard and dry ground; this road is *much broader and better constructed* than that through Ribchester, and it has

y Mr. Baines mentions another Roman Milliarium, found at Burrough, a few miles south of Lancaster.—His. Lan., vol. 4, p. 544.

z This is an error. Cadley causeway formed a part of the Watling-street, which crossed the road from the south to the north, on Fulwood moor, nearly at right angles.

been shown that this road passes through a continual line of small fortresses from Manchester to Lancaster." [a]

A Roman highway from Manchester unites with this road near Wigan, and here Mr. Sibson placed Coccium.

Dr. Robson, in a paper read at a meeting of the members of the Lancashire and Cheshire Historic Society, held at Warrington, after a visit of inspection, says, the road at Haydock is formed of a "substructure of rude masses of sand-stone built up together, is *six or seven yards wide*, and covered with a thick bed of gravel, while, in some places, the sod has been previously removed, and a layer of sand spread below. The depth of the road in the centre is between two and three feet, the stone foundation being about one-half." The late Rev. Mr. Just, of Bury, surveyed the road from Manchester by Ribchester to Overborough, which he considered to be the tenth iter of Antoninus. Roman roads possess distinctive characteristics, and are not easily confounded with modern highways. Their formation and peculiarities are thus described by Mr. Just:—

"The Romans constructed three kinds of ways or roads, the first kind during conquest was the 'via militaris' properly so called, or the elevated highway from military station to station. The second was the 'via publica,' or public road, made subsequently for intercourse from one place to another, and to facilitate the arts of peace, and communication with the Roman capital. The third were the private roads, or 'viæ privatæ,' called also 'viæ vicinales,' because, according to Ulpian, 'ad agros et vicos ducunt.' He further adds that the military ways were elevated three feet and upwards above the surface of the ground They were paved on their summits throughout their whole length, and were hence also called 'viæ stratæ,' whence we derive our word *street*. From their elevation likewise we term them highways. Their direction was generally in perfectly straight lines, from one high point of ground to another. This arose from their being lines of defence to the troops, as well as of passage. * * The average width of such roads was about twenty-one feet or a little more; and the line chosen out for them, was on the highest ground that their direction would permit. The public ways, except in the vicinity of Rome, or the head quarters of their provinces, were not paved, nor elevated above the surface of the ground They were not laid out on the high grounds, between place and place, but on lower grounds, and were not necessarily straight. They were covered with 'glareæ' or gravel, and were fourteen feet wide, sufficient to allow two carriages or vehicles to pass one another. The private or vicinal ways were less broad, seldom exceeding seven feet in width. They had here and there broader places to allow vehicles to pass, in case two should meet, travelling in opposite directions. They had also cross roads or 'diverticula,' leading to less frequented places than the ordinary roads. Many of our high roads, public roads, and bye and cross roads, were on the lines laid out by the Romans" [b]

Amongst such a mass of uncertain evidence, daring conjecture, and conflicting opinion, it is difficult to arrive at a very satisfactory conclusion. The great errors of the elder antiquaries appear to have resulted

a "Mr. Sibson says Ex-tun-burh is Saxon for Water town fort, Bamberg is War-town; and Walton, Val-tun, or fortified town. The Rev. J Whitaker says *Gual* is the British word for rampart, and is formed into *Wall*, *Val*, *Bal*, and *Ual* or *al*."—See Mr. Sibson's communication, published in Baines's Lan, vol. 3—Ashton-in-Mackerfield.

b Lan. and Ches. His. Soc, vol. 1, p. 69.

from a determination to map out distinctly the entire neighbourhood, notwithstanding the paucity and imperfect character of their materials. All topography which depends primarily on the discovery of antiquarian remains, must, of necessity, for a long period, be imperfect and progressive. The discovery of unquestionable relics in a few localities does not invalidate the possibility, or even probability, that similar evidence of Roman occupation may hereafter be brought to light in other places. Could the roots of the trees that now penetrate the *then* crust of the soil communicate the secrets of their dark homes to mankind, we might possibly learn that the Roman remains hidden from human ken considerably exceed in importance those already discovered.

The documentary evidence relating to this period is likewise very scanty and imperfect, and the best of it acknowledged to be, to some extent, corrupted. For a lengthened period yet to come, the most rational conclusions can but be regarded in the light of probabilities, which may, in turn, be required to give way before facts presented by future discovery.

Many historians regard the Itinera of Antoninus as purely *military* routes, although the fact is by no means certain. After the first conquest of a country, the social necessities of the people and the government administration would demand some system of internal communication, altogether independent of military matters. Modern authors, as well as the promiscuous public, are too much in the habit of associating the clang of arms and the murderous battle struggle with everything pertaining to the "world's conquerors." To contemplate the Roman people quietly governing a subjugated territory, and encouraging the arts of peace, in any corner of the earth, would be, in the estimation of many parties, simply to UN-Romanise the imagination! Yet the fact is undeniable, nevertheless. The military routes would doubtless be used for public transit as well as the *viæ publicolæ*, when long peace had rendered them unnecessary for their original purpose. The massive ramparts which surround old cities, such as Chester, York, Calais, etc., have been converted into public promenades under similar circumstances. The military roads in Russia are *post* routes, and are maintained by the government. It is highly probable the stations in the Itinerary were of a somewhat similar character; and although many would be located near the camps or garrisons, others would be simply stations for convenience on the road. Such is the case under the present railway system. Preston is a large and flourishing town; but "Lea Road" is equally a station, notwithstanding its relative insignificance. Dr. Robson contends strongly against the assumption that the Itinera of Antoninus were merely "routes of the Roman legions on march," and supports his position by reference to classic writers of undoubted authority. He says,—

"I would suggest that the Itinerarium of Antoninus is nothing more or less than the book of the Imperial posts, a curious subject, and well worth more attention than I can now bestow upon it. Suetonius tells us that the Emperor Augustus first placed young men at short intervals on the military roads, and afterwards carriages, that he might have the more speedy intelligence of what was doing in every province. It would seem that these couriers were at first merely bearers of despatches which were transferred from one to another on the route, but were afterwards themselves conveyed in carriages so as to give the Emperor an opportunity of examining them personally, if he wished to do so. * * * Continual allusions are made to these posts in the classic authors, especially in such works as the epistles of Pliny and Symmachus But we have in the Theodosian code, which dates about 430, most minute directions and instructions issued by various Emperors, with reference to the service of the Cursus Publicus, which I will venture to translate the 'Imperial Post.' About a century later, we have the following remarkable account from the Anecdota of Procopius.—'The Roman Emperors of former times devised a plan by which whatever was doing amongst their enemies,—any sedition in states, anything connected with the governors, or whatever else might happen, should be told them, and come to their knowldge as soon as possible. The conveyance of the annual tribute was also safely and rapidly managed by the same means, which was a *public course* They appointed stations—eight,—never less than five,—as a day's journey, for a well girt man. In each station or stable were forty horses, and stable men in proportion, and thus the couriers, having a constant change of trained horses, at times go ten day's journey in a single day.' * * * The great object of these posts was to convey regular and sure intelligence to the seat of government; and officers called *Agentes in rebus* and *Curiosi*, who seem to have combined the functions of high police, post masters, and imperial messengers, had the superintendence of them. They included horses, mules, asses, and oxen, with the farriers, smiths, and hostlers requisite for such an establishment; carriages of various sorts, both light and heavy, the weight allowed for each being fixed by the Imperial Rescript. Certain officers (in the fourth century,) the Prætorian Prefect, and the master of the Palace, were, besides the Emperor, the only persons who could grant warrants for the use of the Imperial Posts, and then merely to the highest officers. Any attempt to abuse this privilege was severely punished. Thus, stations or stages were fixed only upon certain roads, very few indeed compared with the number of military ways we have in the kingdom, and seeming to bear the same relation to them, as the later mail coach routes to the highways." c

The Itinerary of Antoninus contains two of these routes, which are universally admitted to have passed through Lancashire. One (the second iter) crosses the country from York, by Manchester to Chester, and the other traverses the county from north to south. The latter is the tenth iter, concerning which antiquaries are so much divided in opinion. Jno. Whitaker "*must*," of course, take it through Manchester, which he seemed determined *should* be the great centre. To effect this, he had to pursue an extremely irregular route, and disregard materially the distances. The figures in the itinera are acknowledged to be, to some extent, corrupt, as they vary in the different MSS. So each antiquarian topographer accepts or rejects them as best suits his convenience! Nevertheless, in the absence of better information than mere conjecture, the distances, in

c "Cod. Theod., Tom 2, Art. Cursus Publicus.—See Lan. and Ches. His. Soc Trans., Session 3, p 75, and [illegible], p. 201.

the main, must be regarded as the best available evidence for the demonstration of the identity of any route.

The second iter of Antoninus, commencing at Deva (Chester,) and proceeding east, gives the next station at Condate, and the one following at Mamucium, or as it is written in some MSS., Manutium. The tenth iter, travelling northward, begins with Mediolanum, and proceeds to Condate, Mancunium (or as it is sometimes written, Mancocunium,) Coccium, Bremetonacis, etc. Jno Whitaker assumed that Mamucium and Mancocunium were one and the same place, and made the itinera become identical from Mamucium to Condate, notwithstanding the glaring improbability of such a circumstance. The tenth iter, by this interpretation, traverses a portion of the line of the second. To effect this thoroughly inexplicable feat, it is required to depart nearly at right angles from its direct course. In this singularly ingenious theory he was supported by his namesake and successor, the Historian of Whalley. Every other consideration is, by these writers, rendered subservient to this assumption. Since their time, however, important discoveries have been made in South Lancashire and Cheshire, which refute some of the elder Whitaker's daring assertions and conjectures, and have given birth to another and a more probable theory on this subject.

Dr. Robson contends that the tenth iter refers to the road which enters the county at Warrington, and proceeds by Standish and Preston to Lancaster; that the crossing with the second is at Condate, and that Mamucium and Mancocunium are two distinct places [d] This interpretation makes the iter traverse the two counties in a very direct line, and avoids the twist necessitated by the single road for both routes between Condate and Mamucium, on the Whitaker theory. After repudiating the authority of Richard of Cirencester, Dr. Robson thus demonstrates his position :—

"I have already alluded to the evidence, and the necessity of adhering strictly to it till some new proof is exhibited. All that we have at present is the Itinera of Antoninus, and if, without altering in any way that evidence, we find it accordant with existing remains, we do all that can be done towards identifying a route so described. The second iter of Antoninus, in describing the road from York to Chester, has the last station but one, Mamucium, or Manutium, as written in some MSS. No one has ever doubted that this place was Castlefield, near Manchester; and between this place and Chester, at eighteen miles from the former, and twenty miles from the latter, is Condate, which agrees with great precision with the position of Stockton Heath [near Warrington.] If, again, we take the tenth iter, and reverse it, beginning at Middlewich, and considering it

---

d The name of the modern town of Manchester was written Mamchester till near the end of the fifteenth century. In the Saxon Chronicle it is Mameceaster. The name or termination, "caster," or "chester," is indicative of the presence of a Roman castrum or camp, at the period when the Saxon nomenclature was introduced. Sarn, street, stone and stane, with Strat and Stan—when compounded as in Stratford, Standish, etc ,—generally indicate the course of a Roman or ancient British road.

as Mediolanum, we have seventeen miles to the north, on the line of a great Roman road, Condate at Stockton Heath—proceeding along the same road direct north, in eighteen miles we arrive at Mancunium, or, as read in other MSS., Mancocunium, which would take us to Standish, seventeen miles further north brings us to the Lancashire Watling-street,"[e] (on Fulwood Moor, near Preston,) "and where we should naturally expect to find a post of some sort. this would be Coccium; and at twenty miles beyond this is Lancaster, or the station of Bremetonaк, or Bremetonacæ. Now, in this statement I have changed neither names nor figures. The existence of the road no one doubts, and I feel confident that proofs of Roman occupation will be found at Standish, and at the intersection of the roads to the north of Preston, if carefully looked for. And when we know that such proofs have been found only lately in Middlewich and Stockton Heath, we may confidently expect that a proper search will be followed by successful results, not merely at the two spots already named, but at other places on the line of road."[f]

The elder antiquaries appear to have fancied that the towns mentioned by Ptolomy *must* have formed stations in the itinera. But this is evidently untenable, as the Itinerary mentions only a portion of the Roman roads in Britain. The very fact that Ptolomy *mentions* Rigodunum and that Antoninus *does not*, is better evidence than any other extant that the tenth iter of the latter did not pass by that place. The Itinerary did not necessarily, out of mere compliment, include "all places of importance." As the work was compiled chiefly for government purposes, the direct line, other facts being equal, must logically command the preference; and especially so in this instance, where diversion not only falsifies the distances and increases the difficulty of transit, but carries the line through a country less likely to have been populous. The better condition of the remains of the higher Roman road, at the present time, may be attributed to the circumstance that, being off the great line of more modern traffic and agricultural improvement, it has suffered less from the depredations of road makers and road repairers, as well as enterprising farmers, who are generally very active in clearing away all such impediments to the progress of the plough

Although the evidences of Roman occupation have been discovered at Walton, instead of at Fulwood, as was anticipated by Mr. Robson, still the general distances of the stations present a much nearer approximation to the figures in the iter than those on any other route. Had the remains been found about a mile to the north instead of to the south of Preston, all the figures would have satisfactorily coincided. Roman coins have been

e The Rev. John Whitaker makes Guetheling derived from "the Guetheli, or Gatheli, of Ireland." He considers the name of the road to be derived from the place or people to which it led, and that it was used by the British, previous to the Roman era. He says "the Guethling, or Watling-street, must have been originally denominated by the Britons, Sarn Guethelin, or the road of the Irish. * * * From the joint testimony of Richard's Itinerary, and Bede's History, it appears that the Roman road, which reaches from Sandwich to Caernarvon, was distinguished among the Romans by the British name of Guetheling, or Watling-street." This solution, however, is by no means considered satisfactory. The question still continues to puzzle the learned. The Lancashire Watling street does, certainly, cross the county from York to the coast opposite to Dublin.

f His[illegible] and Ches. Proceedings; Session 3, 1850-1, p. 76.

found at Standish, and it is just possible the distance of the crossing of the roads on Fulwood moor, from Bremetonicis, may have been marked instead of the station opposite the ford below; or, it may simply be one of the many acknowledged errors in the work itself.[g]

Camden placed Coccium at Cockey, simply on account of the similitude of the names Some little enquiry by the author, as to the existence of local terms which may have been corrupted from words indicative of the presence of the Roman people at Walton, has, he fears, not been very successful. This, at the best, is dangerous ground to tread upon. The following observations may, however, perhaps suggest something more to the purpose.

It has previously been intimated that Mr. Sibson thought it probable there had been a "fortified camp," at Walton, "to protect the pass of the Ribble" He adds, that Walton is Val-tun, or fortified town. The Rev. Jno Whitaker says Gual is the British word for rampart, and is formed into *Wall*, *Val*, *Bal*, and *Ual* or *Al*. Dr. Kuerden, in his description of Preston, near two centuries ago, says: "There is, likewise, below the Churchgate barrs, another public foot-way, southward, leading towards the bridge over Rible into London road; and this passage, at its entrance, out of town, *was* called Cocker-hole." Many elderly inhabitants remember the term "Cocker-hole-lane" being the common name applied to the present Water-street. If by this we are to understand that the road led to a "Cocker Hall," or to a hollow place named "Cocker-hole," it would exactly identify the neighbourhood of Walton with the word. This is by no means improbable, as will appear from the following presentment at the Court Leet, at Preston, in the year 1657:—

"We find that a comon footpath & highway to Ribble bridge, down by Albon Steepe, up a baulke lying between the lands late of John Sudell, fellmaker, & a field called waterwillows & the said Albon Steepes to Cockerhole.—
Ordered to maintain a style."

On a map of the township, of the date of 1774, in the possession of Mr. Philip Park, some fields, between Albyn bank and Church-street, are described as "Waterwillows" A wood behind the Roman station is

g Mr. Robson has since concluded it probable that Wigan, in the neighbourhood of Standish, may be the site of the Roman Mancocunium. Mr Sibson had previously selected this site for Coccium, regarding Mancocunium as Manchester. There is a good Roman way from Manchester to Wigan, and several remains have been found near the church. Standish, from its elevated position, may have been a "*specula*," or out-post of observation, in connection with the station. Dr. Leigh describes minutely the contents of a "copper urceolus," found near Standish. He likewise mentions "an Idol," found near Up-holland, in the neighbourhood, concerning which, he says, "this I take to be Victory, the *Genius* of that Place." The "urceolus" contained "Two Hundred *Roman* Coins, and two Gold Rings, of the *Equites Aurati*, or *Roman* Knights," together with a "signet," the figure upon which he describes as "Mars leaning with his Left Hand upon a Spear, holding in his Right Hand a *Victoriola*, or small Victory, with a Target at his Right Foot."

named, on the ordnance map, Cockshot's wood, though this is doubtless modern. A station on the East Lancashire Railway, not very far from Walton, on the road towards Ormskirk, is called Cocker-bar. Dr. Kuerden's footpath evidently traversed the Roman way to the ford at Ribble It was joined, at the ford over the Swilbrook, by another track of a similar character, which he thus describes·—"Another *remarkable* foot passage toward Rible Bridge is through the church yard southward, by the publiq schoole and antient place called Chappel of Avenam, over the Swilbrook southward, by west field to the aforesaid Bridge of Rible; and this passage is called the *Stoneygate,* being the greatest foot tract to the Burrough of Preston." Walton-le-dale is the present title of the village, the valley being named Cuerdale. This, too, has but a limited signification, the more comprehensive title being Ribblesdale. The Roman station is only about a mile distant from the spot where the immense Saxon and Danish treasure was found a few years ago. May not Cuerdale be a corruption of Caer dale, the dale of the camp, or fortified town? Walton is written in the Domesday survey *Waletune.* The neighbouring townships are not named, the great portion of Blackburn hundred being waste or forest. In the sixteenth century map, re-published in "Gregson's Fragments," Cuerdale is written Coverdale (pronounced Coucrdale), while Cuerden, in the immediate neighbourhood, is styled Kerdon.

The discovery of a second station on the Ribble, completes a double line of forts, to guard the passes over the principal rivers in Lancashire. One is at the head of the tidal estuaries of the Mersey, the Ribble, and the Lune, which, Tacitus observes, Agricola himself "surveyed and fixed the stations;" namely, Condate at Stockton-heath, near Warrington; Coccium at Walton, near Preston, and Bremetonacis at Lancaster, on the Lune. The higher, or inland line, on the same rivers, is formed by Mamutium, at Manchester; Rigodunum at Ribchester, and Ad Alaunum at Overborough, near Kirkby Lonsdale. For precisely a similar reason to that advanced in favour of Lancaster, by Jno Whitaker and others, Ad Alaunum may be placed at Overborough. If this assumption be granted, there will remain no difficulty in the reconciliation of this portion of the tenth iter of Richard with that of Antoninus The first may have proceeded through the eastern portion of Westmoreland, and the latter by the coast of Cumberland; the routes only becoming identical at Lancaster, where, according to Perceval and others, a third joins them from Carlisle, Penrith, and Kendal. Presuming Antonine's iter to have passed through the centre of the "Lakes district," the Roman camp, alluded to by West, the Historian of Furness, near the head of Windermere

Lake, will accord with the distance of the station mentioned after Bremetonacis, namely—Galacum, twenty-seven Roman miles. The direct line would still be nearly preserved by way of Keswick, and Old Carlisle, to the Solway, opposite Annan. On this supposition, however, the distance between Bowness, at the western extremity of the Picts' Wall and Old Carlisle, would not agree with the figures in the iter.

It is much more probable that Agricola would first secure the estuaries along the coast of Cumberland, as well as Lancashire, before he operated in the interior of the country; and that Antonine's route commenced at Maryport, and proceeded by Egremont, Muncaster, and Dalton, to Lancaster. The distances, by this route, very nearly accord. The Roman road through Dalton, and along the coast, is well known,[h] and Maryport abounds with remains. This is the easiest route for transit, and was most probably an ancient British trackway. Dr. Giles, in his commentary on Richard of Cirencester's itinerary, says: "A road appears to have skirted the western coast, as the Ermyn Street did the eastern. Besides these, there is reason to conjecture, from several detached pieces, that another road followed the shores round the island." Referring to the former, he states that portions of it were "never adopted by the Romans."[i] Its course is thus described:—

"It appears to have commenced on the coast of Devon, perhaps not far from the mouth of the Ex, and to have gone by Exeter, Taunton, Bridgewater, Bristol, Gloucester, Kidderminster, Claverly, Weston, High Offley, Betley, Middlewich, Northwich, Warrington, Preston, Lancaster. Here probably dividing into two branches, one ran by Kendal, Penrith, and Carlisle, to the extreme parts of the island, while the other passed by Kirkby Lonsdale, and Orton, to Kirkby Thure, from whence it continued under the name of the MAIDEN WAY, by the Wall and Bewcastle, into the interior parts of Scotland. On this street were *Isca*, Exeter, *Uxella*, possibly near Bridgewater, *Glevum*, Gloucester, *Branogenium*, Worcester, *Salinæ*, Droitwich, *Coccium*, Blackrode,[j] and *Lugaballium*, Carlisle."[k]

Richard's tenth iter proceeds through Scotland, to Luguballium, (Carlisle) Brocavonacis, Ad Alaunum, and Coccium. From this point, southward, the route is identical with that of Antoninus. The figures in Richard's iter, under every theory, are very unsatisfactory. It is probable that the ancient British road, through Lancashire towards Carlisle, was not converted into a regular Roman highway till the reign of Julius

---

h See West's History of Furness; and "A Day in Low Furness," by James Stonehouse, in Lan. and Ches. His. Soc. Trans., vol. viii., p. 228.

i Doubtless the Romans used these roads. By non-adoption must be understood that they were not re-constructed on the Roman military system.

j Now corrected to Walton, near Preston. Evidence of British occupation beneath the Roman remains, at the confluence of the Ribble and Darwen, strengthens the claim of Walton to the site of Coccium.

k Bohn's edition, p. 479.

Philippus, and apparently not then further than Lancaster; although unquestionable remains near Kendal, Penrith, etc., attest to their occupation of the country. The Setantian Britons apparently submitted to Agricola without a serious struggle, in consequence of the previous subjugation of the superior Brigantine tribes. Under these circumstances, the existing British track, with slight improvements, may have served the purpose of the Roman general. With reference to the difficulties in this portion of the tenth iter of Richard, Dr. Giles says:—

"As we have none of the intermediate stations between Carlisle and the Wall" (of Antoninus Pius, between the Firths of Forth and Clyde), "every commentator may choose what route he pleases, although none will coincide with the distances of the Itinerary From Carlisle, if we place any reliance on the numbers, the next station, *Brocavonacis*, can only be fixed at Brougham. Thence the road to the banks of the Lune, as well as the station on it, is uncertain; for, whether we choose Overborough or Lancaster, we know of no road" (of Roman construction) "to direct us; and the only reason for preferring the latter is the supposed site of the next station, *Coccium*, at Blackrode, and the course of the road through Lancaster, tending more immediately to that point than the road through Overborough."[1]

This, in conjunction with the known remains of a road of Roman construction, in Furness, tends to confirm the opinion that the *main* line of communication followed the coast to Maryport, and hence its obtaining a record in the Itinerary of Antoninus Several remains have been found in Furness Amongst others, a silver coin of the reign of Otho, which would lead to the presumption that the district was occupied by the troops of Agricola. The invasion by that general did not take place until about ten years after the death of Otho, who only reigned ninety-five days. Hence the great scarcity of coins minted by him

Roman remains have been found at Kirkham, and other places in Lancashire, and probably many remain yet undiscovered, of which the names of the locations even, are not recorded in any of the extant writings of the Roman historians or topographers

Till better evidence be produced to support the claims of other places, the following may be regarded as the most probable interpretation of the Roman topography of this part of Britain .—

Setcia Æstuarium ... .Estuary of the Dee.
Belisama Æstuarium...... ...Estuary of the Ribble.
Portus Setantiorum ....Wyre Harbour.
Moricambe Æstuarium....... .Morecambe Bay.
Bremetonacis....................Lancaster.
Coccium...... ....Walton, near Preston.
Mancocunium, or Mancunium, Wigan
Condato .. ..Stockton-heath, near Warrington.
Mediolanum ....Middlewich

[1] Bohn's Edit on, p. 498.

Mamucium....................Manchester.
Rigodunum ....Ribchester.
"Ad Alaunam" ....Overborough.
Calunium, or Calanea ......Colne.
Veratinum ....supposed Warrington (very doubtful).
Longovicus ....the "Ad Alaunam" of Richard, or unknown.
"Ad Alpes Peninos" of Richard, near Pendle Hill

THE TENTH ITER OF ANTONINUS.

A GLANOVENTA MEDIOLANUM. M. P. CL.

Glanoventa		Maryport.
Galava ....M. P.	XVIII.,	near Egremont.
Alone	XII.	Muncaster.
Galacum	XIX.	Dalton.
Bremetonacis	XXVII.	Lancaster.
Coccio	XX.,	Walton, near Preston.
Mancunio..................	XVII.,[m]	Wigan.
Condate....................	XVIII.,	Stockton-heath, near Warrington.
Mediolano	XVIII.,	Middlewich.

The elder Whitaker regarded Coccium as the capital of the Setantian territory. He asserts that Caer Coccui imports literally the "City of Supremacy."! This is, however, rather a different interpretation to the "red-water" of the erudite gentleman's successor, the equally learned Historian of Whalley. Truly, the "city of supremacy" of a tribe of ancient Britons, would present but a very poor figure, in comparison with a third-rate modern village. If there be any truth in John Whitaker's interpretation of the term Coccium, it can only apply to the location of the Aborigines, and not to that of the Roman people. Chester appears to have been their most important military station in this district, and Ribchester perhaps the next. Camden says, in his quaint and careful manner,—"The British towns, before the invasion of the Romans, were only woods, fortified with a ditch and rampire, according to Cæsar and Strabo, whose evidence is unexceptionable."[n] The low mound, at Walton, situated near the confluence of the rivers Ribble and Darwen, is a locality very likely to have been selected for a stronghold by the Aborigines, and its central position amongst the Setantian people is in favour of John Whita-

m Richard gives XVIII. This is probably correct Antonine's total, CL., being one mile in excess of his details.

n "Their towns or villages were a confused parcel of huts, placed at a distance from each other, generally in the middle of a wood, of which the avenues were defended with slight ramparts of earth, or with the trees cut down to clear the ground."—Aspin's Complete Chronology.

ker's supposition. When the surrounding country was clothed with primæval forest, it must have presented the very model of a fastness to the eyes of a people who dwelt for security amongst morasses and dense woods. The broad stream of the Ribble forms a natural fosse on the north and east, while the lesser, though not insignificant, Darwen, encloses the site on the west, and partially on the south. The lower lands, in the immediate vicinity of the streams, would, doubtless, at the period referred to, be sufficiently swampy to accord with the most fastidious ancient Briton's taste, with respect to fortification. A glance at Robert Porter's map, (plate II) published in 1738, will show that the locality must formerly have presented even more attractions of this character than at present. The Darwen, in its course from the site of Walton Hall, towards its junction with the Ribble, made an elliptical curve eastward, something like that of the latter river at "Red Scar," only of smaller dimensions. This formed an additional double moat, which protected the mound on the south. The present straight course of the Darwen, to its *embouchure*, is artificial. The remains of the old channel may yet be distinctly seen. The centre of the curve reaches nearly to the weaving shed, lately erected by Mr. Calvert. The site likewise commands the natural ford, or "pass of the Ribble," a circumstance of the highest importance in a military point of view. A foundation wall, about eight yards long, eighteen inches in breadth, and nearly a foot in depth, was discovered below the level of the Roman remains, during the recent excavation, at the southwestern corner of the mound. The wall was formed of irregularly shaped, but perfectly adjusted, fragments of the red sandstone rock, of the neighbourhood, which had become partially disintegrated. The Romans first taught the British people the use of mortar. As no mortar or other cement had been employed in the construction of this foundation, the presumption is, that it was the work of the original inhabitants. Axes, spear heads, and other bronze articles, supposed to be British, or "Romano-British," had previously been found at Walton. Some remains of this class are preserved in the museum of the Literary and Philosophical Society. See plate I, figs. 3, 5, 6, and 9. Figs. 3 and 5 appear to have been used in connection with harness. The latter is probably a portion of a "bit." There are no specimens in the British Museum *precisely* similar, but many somewhat resembling them in general character. The Romans often selected the sites of the native towns or encampments, for their stations. Similar remains of the Aborigines have been found at Castlefield, Manchester, and other places. The probability, therefore is, that Agricola, in this instance, merely retained possession of a fortress previously occupied by the discomfited native inhabitants.

PLATE 2

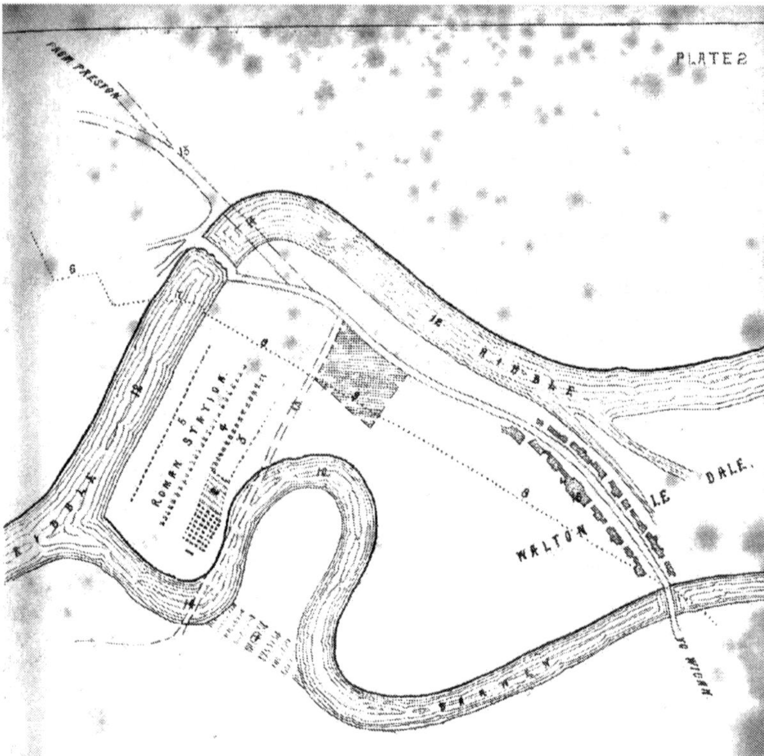

REFERENCE.

No. 1. THE "PLUMP" IN WHICH THE ROMAN REMAINS WERE FOUND.
2 MR. MAITLAND'S GARDEN, IN WHICH REMAINS WERE FOUND.
3.4.5. THE THREE TERRACES.
6 THE ZIG-ZAG INDENTATION
7 LARGE GRAVEL BED AND FORD
8 SUPPOSED ROMAN ROAD
9 MR. CALVERT'S WEAVING SHED, IN WHICH THE WORKMEN FOUND REMAINS OF ROAD
10 OLD COURSE OF THE DARWEN, ACCORDING TO ROBERT PORTER'S MAP, PUBLISD. IN 1738
11 PRESENT COURSE OF THE DARWEN.
12 THE RIBBLE
13 NEW ROADS
14 NEW BRIDGES
15 OLD VILLAGE OF WALTON-LE-DALE
16 STRONG EARTHEN RAMPART

——— THE SOLID LINES ARE FROM ROBERT PORTER'S MAP.
- - - - THE BROKEN LINES INDICATE SUCH MODERN ADDITIONS AS ARE NECESSARY

These interesting relics of past ages were brought to light, like many others, by purely fortuitous circumstances. The author of this work being aware of the existence of a tradition which identified a mound, planted with trees, and known by the name of "The Plump," on "Walton Flats," with the burial place of the "Scotch warriors," slain in Cromwell's celebrated victory over the Duke of Hamilton, in 1648, visited the spot several times in June, 1855, for the purpose of examining its structure, and ascertaining whether or not existing remains countenanced the tradition. Some workmen, employed by the highway surveyor, had commenced digging for stones and gravel. This, fortunately, afforded an excellent opportunity for a minute inspection. The labourers, being resident in the neighbourhood, were aware of the tradition, and fully expected to meet with some memorials of the "great battle."

During the temporary absence of the excavators, the author picked up a curious piece of metal, which, from its configuration, had evidently formed part of some manufactured article. It seemed too thin to be either a fragment of a skull-cap, or a piece of plate armour. It, however, distinctly bore the impression of a blow from a pointed instrument, and some stains upon it appeared like clotted blood. The metal itself, likewise, was peculiar,—apparently a mixture of tin and lead. It served to stimulate further investigation.[o]

Three brass coins were next found by the workmen, one of which was illegible from corrosion. The second merely exhibited the general form of the head of the potentate in whose reign it had been coined; but, on the reverse of the third, the letters S. C. were distinctly visible, which at once demonstrated its Roman origin.[p] The labourers thought it a Scotch penny, from the imperfect figure on the reverse bearing some resemblance to a kilted highlander. Thus, whilst searching for relics of the Commonwealth period, proofs of Roman occupation were disclosed. Instead of the *debris* of a sanguinary struggle, which a lapse of two centuries has invested with traditionary interest and historic dignity, the earth disgorged food for the archæologist, which must have been entombed in her capacious and ever-hungry maw, upwards of fourteen hundred years.[q]

Remembering Mr. Robson's injunction, the author immediately instituted a stricter search. Specimens of Roman pottery were found in abun-

---

o This fragment proved to be a portion of a Roman pewter vessel. It had probably been used for cooking purposes.

p The S. C. signifies Senatus Consultum, which imports that the coin was issued by decree of the senate.

q The Roman dominion in Britain was entirely extinguished before the middle of the fifth century.

dance, after the attention of the labourers had been directed to its peculiar character and importance. During this exploration, an area of nearly one hundred superficial yards was excavated, to the depth of about three feet. Above the original vegetable soil, resting upon a yellow loamy clay, or "sea sludge," as the labourers termed it, on which lay the British foundation wall, previously alluded to,—was spread a mass of boulders, mixed with *glareæ*, or gravel. In and upon the surface of this stratum, the Roman remains were discovered. The stones and gravel only extending to a certain distance, the excavators relinquished their task, and filled up the cavity, or, doubtless, many other interesting relics would have been procured. The workmen, who were accustomed to dig for road materials, from the first pronounced the stone and gravel layer to be of artificial construction. The discovery of the red-rock foundation wall, below this stratum, confirmed their opinion. The mound extends considerably further to the east, north, and west of the excavation. Two, or even three, separate terraces may still be distinctly perceived, descending towards the Ribble, notwithstanding the garden cultivation to which the greater portion has been subjected for some years past. This peculiar, and evidently artificial, formation of the ground, Dr. Robson remarked, bore great resemblance to the site of the Roman station at Caer-rhun, near Conway, the Conovium of Antoninus.[r] On digging a small hole, on the extreme west side of the mound, it was ascertained that the Roman remains extended fifteen yards further in that direction. Mr Martland, of the Bridge Inn, Walton, the tenant of the adjoining garden land, had previously exposed a large quantity of bright red clay, fragments of pottery, etc., considerably to the east of the "Plump;" but not being aware of their archæological importance, the prettier portions of the "red lustrous ware" were given to his children, and the remainder re-consigned to the earth. Many fragments of Roman earthenware have since been picked up at the eastern extremity of this garden. Beneath the trees in the "Plump," the vegetable soil and alluvial deposits had accumulated to the depth of about two feet above the Roman remains. In the adjoining garden, the stratum of boulders and gravel is nearer the surface. Much of it has been removed during the last few years. This portion, being the most elevated land in the immediate neighbourhood, has been rarely covered by even the highest floods, and consequently but little river *debris* is found upon the third or upper terrace. Such is not the case, however, with the lower ones. Here the periodical deposits have formed a consider-

r On the author communicating the discovery to Dr. Robson, that gentleman immediately visited Walton, [illegible] the remains, and neighbourhood of the site, and courteously communi[illegible] most [illegible] subject.

able depth of soil. On stepping across these terraces, from south to north, the highest and middle *plateaux*, are found to be each about thirty yards in breadth, and the lower one from fifty to sixty,—in all about one hundred and twenty yards. (Plate II, figs. 3, 4, and 5) This does not include the inner ditch and rampart, on the bank of the Ribble. The terraces are elevated from two to three feet above each other. From the western extremity of the mound to what appears to have been the earthern vallum, skirting the main highway, from the south to the ford over the Ribble, the distance is about three hundred yards.

Opposite to the centre of the station, on the north, the earthern rampart rises about twenty feet above the ordinary level of the Ribble, and is nearly forty yards in breadth! (Plate II, fig. 16.) A large edifice, called "Flatts House," and several outbuildings have been erected upon it. A portion of this mound, on the eastern side of the house, has lately been removed. A deep ditch, between it and the lower terrace of the station, may yet be seen, as well as some remains of a strong earthern embankment, considerably within the modern "cop," constructed to exclude the flood waters of the Darwen. As it is scarcely conceivable that so large a quantity of earth would be removed, simply for the erection of modern buildings, the presumption is, that the mound formed a portion of the original defence of the station. From this plateau, the Roman garrison could effectually protect the ford, or "pass of the Ribble" Till about the end of the last century, as elderly inhabitants yet remember, a warehouse stood upon this mound. It was used to store alum, from the mines in Samlesbury, near Hoghton Tower, previous to its being floated down the river in barges, when the height of the tide permitted. At low water, remains of a strong wall facing this mound, may yet be seen in the Ribble. Barges have, till within a comparatively recent period, occasionally discharged coals, in the Darwen, for Sir Henry Hoghton, Bart. Notwithstanding the obstruction to the navigation of the river, between Walton and the quay at Preston, Roman vessels would, at high springs and floods, be enabled to reach the station. Doubtless, modern Walton occupies the site of the neighbouring British village, town, or "city," as the fancy of the antiquarian topographer may be pleased to designate it It is, likewise, not improbable that the residence of the governor of the station may have preceded Walton Hall, a mansion of the Hoghton family, pulled down upwards of twenty years ago.

Amongst the remains discovered, are five coins. One, a "second brass," is totally illegible. Another, a "first brass," from the general configuration of the head, on the obverse, is most probably a Titus Vespasian. The third is a "first brass," of Domitian, much corroded. The fourth is a "second brass," of Domitian, with the name of the Emperor perfectly legible. The fifth, which is in tolerable preservation, distinctly presents the effigy of Antoninus Pius, with, apparently, the Antonine column on the reverse.[s]

The other metallic substances include fragments of two pewter dishes, several large and smaller iron nails, a very small piece of copper, two or three pieces of thin sheet lead, "crumpled up," and another specimen, the form of which, indicates previous fusion, like a brazier's lump of solder. The nails, from the oxidising of the iron, are thickly encrusted with sand and gravel, and the lead is covered with a white coating, from a similar cause. Fig. 5, plate III, shows the form of one of these nails, when stripped of the sand and gravel. A bronze fibula, or toga button, (as the fastening is in the centre,) was likewise found. It bears marks of elegant and elaborate chasing, and some remains of purple enamel. (Plate III, figs. 2 and 4.) Another fibula, of a different form and character, was picked up by Mr. Martland's son, together with a small rod or bar, of iron, plated with silver. The rod is about three inches and a half long, and one tenth of an inch in diameter. It is believed to have formed part of a stylus, or, more probably, a lady's hair pin. The fibula is of fine brass. A small circle in the centre, is ornamented with brilliant red enamel, resembling, in appearance, the stone setting of a modern finger ring. (Plate III, figs. 6 and 7.)

Amongst the stone articles, are a large portion of the "ass," or lower stone of a quern, or hand corn-mill, formed of millstone grit, (plate III, fig. 8); several large fragments of "riders," or upper millstones, cut from lava, (plate I, fig. 1); and one small wheel, or "spindle head," about an inch and a half in diameter, fashioned from a very fine bluish stone. It is perforated in the centre, and bears on one side, marks of friction, produced by rapid revolution. (Plate III, fig. 3.)

Mr. Robson expressed an opinion, that some of the "blue lava" stones, discovered at Walton, were fragments of potter's wheels.

A precisely similar upper "quern stone," to the one figured on plate III, was found at Ribchester, in Mr. Patchet's garden, and deposited by the late Dr. Moore, in the museum of the Literary and Philosophical Institution, Preston.[t]

---

s Other brass coins have since been found by the workmen. Some years ago, a silver coin, of the higher empire, was discovered. The mound had evidently been previously disturbed in several places, but by parties incapable of appreciating, or even recognizing the archæological treasures it contained.

t Mr. Joseph Clarke, F.S.A., in a valuable contribution to vol. 7, of the Lan. and Ches. Historic Soc. Pro[illegible] the following observations upon the hand corn-mills of the Roman people, and the mat[illegible] they were formed:- "The querns or millstones discovered there (Colches-

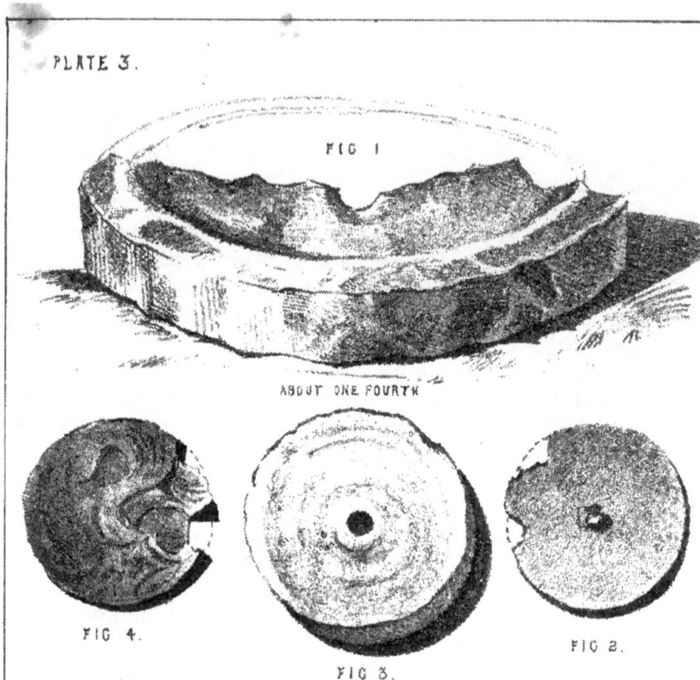

REMAINS FOUND AT WALTON-LE-DALE

PLATE 4.

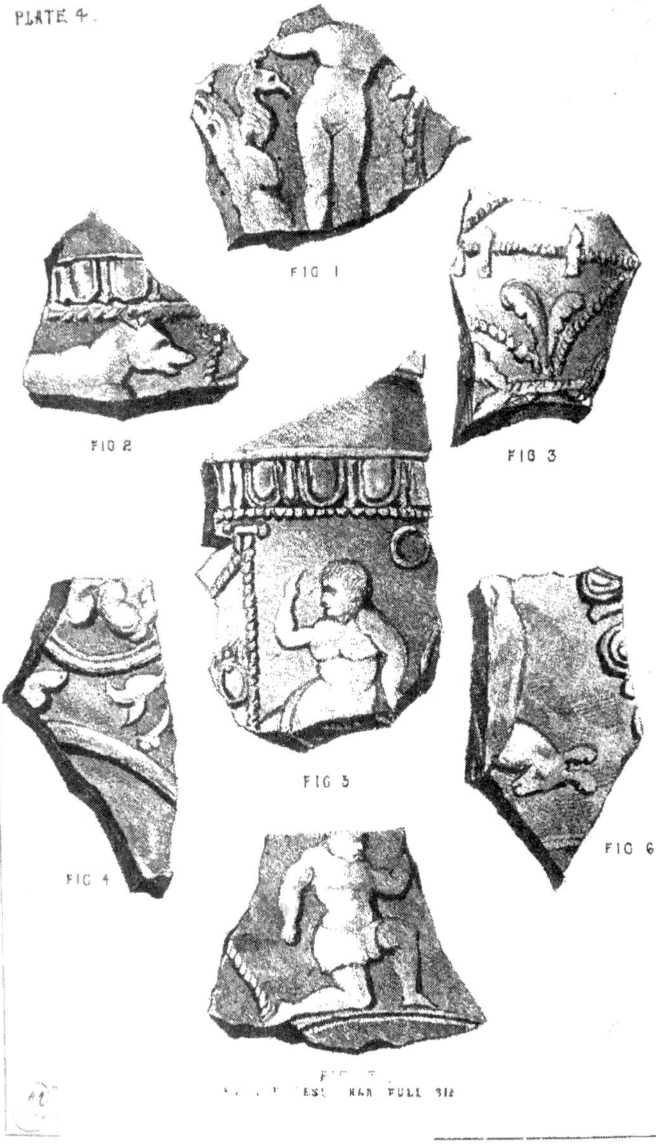

... LESS THAN FULL SIZE

ROMAN POTTERY FOUND AT WALTON-LE-DALE

The specimens of earthenware discovered, are exceedingly numerous, and appear to have been formed from five or six distinct clays, or composition pastes. Some pieces of "Roman red lustrous ware," exhibit elegant and well executed figures in relief, a few of which are represented on plate IV. Many of the ornamental "patterns" on these fragments, are identical with those on some specimens, figured in the catalogue of the "Museum of Practical Geology," especially the bowls, numbered 28, 38, 39, and 80. The first three were found at Roman stations in Britain, and the fourth near Cologne. One fragment, discovered at Walton, likewise exhibits, in relievo, a portion of the figure of the Medicean Venus, precisely similar to those depicted on one of the bowls referred to. (No. 28.) Fig. 1, plate IV, resembles the figure, commonly known to artists as the antique "young Apollo;" fig. 2, the Roman wolf; fig. 5, a Jupiter, or some emperor; fig. 6, a deer; and fig. 7, a fighting gladiator. Other specimens exhibit the forms of lions, birds, etc., common to Roman "lustrous ware." A single fragment presents a good example of a peculiar species of Roman earthenware, often discovered in Germany and Britain, on which, lines of dots and figures in relief, are added, after the vase has been formed and turned in the lathe. This specimen is unglazed. (Plate V, fig. 1). There are numerous fragments of *amphoræ*, *mortaria*, and lesser vessels of great variety of form. A large *amphora* handle exhibits the potter's mark. From superficial decay, all the letters are not very legible; but it appears to resemble P V C R M, F V C B M, or E V C R. M.[u] (plate V, fig. 3). The fragments of mortaria present the

ter), as elsewhere in deserted Roman habitations, are found to be a deposit of lava, from a quarry, near Andernach, on the Rhine. The uppermost stone of a Roman quern very much reduced by abrasion, the aperture for the stick used in turning it being worn through to the under surface, rendering it useless, was lately (1855) found at Maidstone, and is now in the possession of Mr. C. Roach Smith. It is pronounced by Mr. Brayley to be trachitic lava, containing pyroxene crystals of augite; none of which substance is found in England, and but a very small portion in the north west of Ireland; though it is abundant at Andernach, and other places on the Rhine."

Querns, or hand corn mills, have been used by primitive people from the earliest known periods. They are yet to be found in India, Persia, Turkey, and Siberia; in parts of Spain, Italy, Africa, and Ireland. Dr. Johnson remarks, in his Tour in the Hebrides, that the housewives who were too far distant from the water-mills, in Skye and Rassa, grind their oats in a quern or hand mill.

In the Hebrew language, the lower stone was called an ass, and the upper one a rider. "Thus," says Dr. Hume, "when we are told in Judges, c. ix, v. 53, and 2nd. Sam., c. xi, v. 21, that 'a certain woman cast a piece of a *millstone* upon Abimelech's head, and all to break his skull,' it is, in reality, cast a piece of *rider*, or a fragment from an upper millstone. Again, when it is related in Matthew, c. xviii, v. 6, 'that it were better that a millstone were hanged about his neck, and that he were cast into the sea,' it is the *ass* millstone, in the original, that is the lower one. How natural and forcible does the illustration thus become. The stone is of a suitable size to be brought, to be sustained, and to cause drowning; without being absurdly large as a modern millstone would be."

u Mr. Roach Smith considers the last interpretation to be the most probable. It may be translated as from the hand *(manus)* or manufactory of Eucranus. Another amphora handle, and a portion of a Samian bowl, bear the potter's name, but they are too much injured to admit of satisfactory interpretation.

peculiarities observable in this class of Roman earthenware. Grains of quartz have been imbedded in the paste of the interior, apparently after the bowl has been turned, for the purpose of producing a rubbing or grinding surface. Two necks of vases, with single handles, (plate V, figs. 2 and 4) formed of rude clay, and unglazed, resemble those found at Stockton-heath, and figured opposite to page 33, volume 2, of the "Transactions of the Lancashire and Cheshire Historic Society." Fragments of a dark blue or black ware are very numerous. The clay is of a coarse kind; the form of the vessels generally broad and shallow, with a plain, or but slightly ornamented rim (fig. 5, plate V). They appear to have been used for cooking purposes. Large pieces of fine red clay, kneaded into a paste, were likewise continually met with, as well as a few fragments of Roman tiles and bricks. Some lumps of mixed clays, including brown, white, and red, were picked up, apparently the refuse of a potter's workshop. One of these lumps seems to have been cut with a knife, and is curiously tinged with a pale pinkish or purple colour, as if the result of fire or chemical action. A fragment of vitreous material was likewise found, resembling stone china, or very rude glass. It is, therefore, probable that a brick-kiln, and an establishment for the manufacture of the coarser kinds of pottery existed at Walton.[v]

Amongst other miscellaneous articles, taken from the surface of the Roman gravel, are two fragments of the jaw of some large herbaceous animal. One consisted of the entire half of the lower maxillary bone, but it was in such a decomposed condition that it broke into fragments on removal. The teeth, however, are quite perfect. A few fragments of other bones were met with, and a horn of the extinct ox, the ***Bos Lon-***

---

v "The Romans appear to have had a brick-kilne at every stationary town. Their clay is generall found to be finely tempered, compactly kneaded, beautifully red, and completely burnt. And their bricks were constantly about sixteen English inches and three quarters in length, and eleven and a quarter in breadth. But the Romans of the first century never raised any structures of these materials. * * Bricks, as well as stones, however, must have been used in the foundation of the structures, and in the funnels of the chimneys.'—Rev. J. Whitaker.

The buildings, like those of the primitive Britons, were formed of wood. The greater part of the edifices of Rome itself, were constructed of timber, at the time of Nero. Hence the terrific character of the conflagration which occurred during his reign.

"Roman red ware was not uncommonly known by antiquarians as Samian, from Samos having been famous for its manufacture of a red pottery. The Samian potters were famous about B.C. 900; but it may be doubted if any vessels, there manufactured, have ever been found at the Roman stations in England. * * It is not improbable that a considerable portion, at least, of this ware, was derived from southern Germany. * * The manufacture and character of this bowl," (No. 80) "closely agrees with the specimens of similar pottery found in England, where there is little evidence of any of it having been made."—Catalogue of Museum of Practical Geology, London, 1855.

"Pottery can only be found, in any quantity, where there has been a regular settlement, and it may be considered as a proof of a long established and quiet homestead."—Dr. Robson: Lan. and Ches. His. Soc. Papers, vol. 5, p. 204.

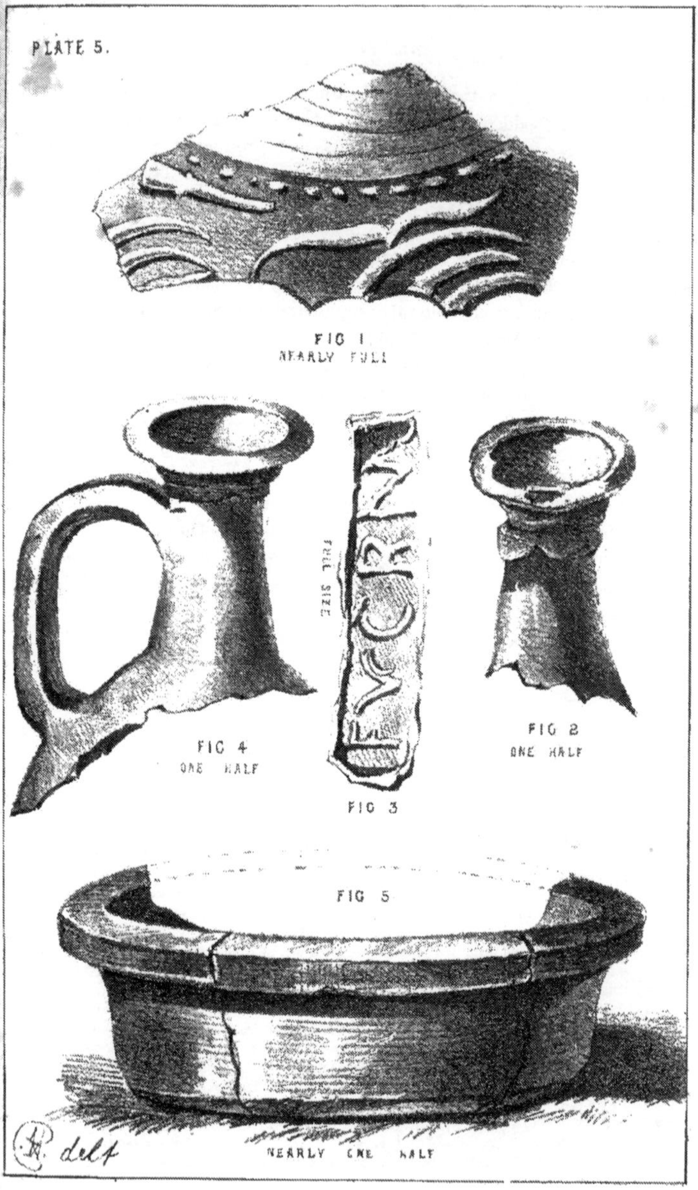

ROMAN POTTERY FOUND AT WALTON-LE-DALE

gifrons. The jaw, most probably, belonged to this animal. A precisely similar horn, taken from the bed of the river, is deposited in the museum of the Literary and Philosophical Society. The Rev. W. Thornber has in his possession, a skull of the *Bos Longifrons,* found in the Roman station at Kirkham. Another specimen, discovered at the same place, was rather broader across the forehead (probably the *Bos Latifrons*). Near these skulls was found an iron axe (a *securis,* or *dolabra,*) likewise in Mr. Thornber's possession.[w]

The wood employed in the construction of the buildings on the station, appears to have perished. A small piece, fossilised, bearing the marks of a sharp instrument, was, however, picked from the heap of stones and gravel, in August last, and deposited with the remains previously discovered. The trees, which formed the "Plump," were cut down during the winter following the discovery of the station, and its picturesque aspect destroyed. The mound has likewise been slightly reduced by the removal of the road materials, and a wider distribution of the soil. Further investigation will, doubtless, bring to light many other relics of the Roman occupation, as a considerable portion of the ground yet remains unexplored.[x]

Notwithstanding the accumulation of alluvial deposit, a broad ridge is still traceable, from the immense natural gravel bank or ford, at the Ribble, towards the present bridge over the Darwen. The workmen employed in the erection of Mr. Calvert's weaving shed, which crosses its line, came, at some distance below the surface, upon a compact mass of road material, so hard that a pick-axe could scarcely enter it. The agger is probably the remains of the original earth work, which protected the

---

w The principal remains found at Walton, were exhibited in May, 1856, before the archæological section of the Lan. and Ches. His. Soc., by the author of this work, who read a paper on their discovery, and afterwards deposited a portion in the museum of the society. It is intended to place the remainder in some public institution in Preston. In the paper alluded to, the jaw is described as that of a horse. An examination of some specimens of the *Bos Longifrons,* in the British Museum, has since induced the conclusion that the horn and teeth belong to the same animal. The British Museum contains, likewise, a Roman altar, described as "for libations," on which are sculptured two skulls of this extinct ox. From this circumstance, it would appear probable that Mr. Thornber's axe is a *securis,* or instrument of sacrifice.

x Some curious stories are related respecting the mound at Walton. Mr. Martland informed the author, that about thirteen or fourteen years ago, a deep hole, near the site of the present cabin, was dug by some unknown persons, in one night. The hole was nine or ten feet long, by about six in width. The materials excavated were principally stones and gravel. Three days elapsed before he and his assistants completed the filling up of this trench. A silver coin, (supposed to be Roman) was found at this time. Mr. Martland likewise remembers hearing of a large hole having been dug under somewhat similarly mysterious circumstances, near the same spot, about sixty years ago. The place was watched every evening for a fortnight, before the hole was filled up, with a view to ascertain whether the midnight excavators would resume their labours. Nothing, however, was discovered which either identified the parties, or explained their object.

station on the east. The road to the ford appears to have run parallel to it on the eastern side. During the last summer, 1856, when the workmen had removed the superior soil, previous to the formation of a new road to the "Flatt's House," crossing the Roman line at right angles, the author perceived, within a breadth of about six yards, some remains of gravel, and many small fragments of ashlers, formed of Whittle gritstone, partially disintegrated The road materials in this place had evidently been removed, these fragments alone remaining. Near Brownedge chapel, a little further south, a portion of the Roman road appears to still exist. It is marked on the ordnance map as the "Mainway-gate." Beyond Bamber-bridge, its line is indicated by a road marked "Cinder Path," in Cuerden Hall Park. On the north bank of the Ribble, opposite the ford, a zigzag indentation in the face of the steep ascent may still be seen. This hollow would appear, from the verdict quoted from the Preston Court Leet record, at page thirty-three, to have been anciently termed "Cocker-hole". From this place, the road passed in a straight line, by the Swilbrook, and Albyn bank, to Church street, in Preston, which it intersected near the site of the Blue Bell Inn. Here it made a slight angle, passing to the east of "Patten House," which probably occupied the site of Ergham's "Manor House," alluded to by Nichols[y] On a map of Preston, dated 1774, a part of which will be found in the topographical portion of the present volume, its course is indicated by the names, "Gt. Pathway Field," "Causeway Meadow," and "Pathway Meadow," to the Moor Brook, which it crossed at Charnock Fold. This carries it in a straight line to the remains described by Mr. Clay and Mr. Cartwright, on Preston Moor. On the first cultivation of the moor, its course was distinctly visible It crossed the line of the present path from the principal carriage-way to the lodge, near the artificial lake, making, with it, a figure somewhat in the form of the letter X. During the construction of the sewerage of the "Freehold Park" estate, in Fulwood, remains were discovered on the section allotted to Mr. Brewer. A small portion of the Roman agger may yet be seen on Preston Moor, where the land slopes towards the brook, opposite to Mr. Brewer's plot. This road intersected the one from the *Portus Setantiorum*, to Ribchester, and York, (the sixth iter of Richard) on the line of the present "Watling-street," about midway between the "Withy Trees Inn," and Fulwood Barracks.

y "The house that Ergham, Mayor of Preston, (in 1328) occupied, was entirely built out of the remains of Ribble-cestre, and a princely mansion it was, erected at the end of Finkle-street, and termed the '*Manor House of Priest-town*' (Nicoll's Researches)"—Whittle's His. of Preston, vol. 2, p. 17 —When the above was written, the existence of a Roman station in the immediate neighbourhood, was unknown. Hence the supposition that the materials alluded to, were procured from Ribchester.

It is highly probable, that an outwork existed near the angle in the road at Church-street Perhaps the Parish Church may have been erected upon the site of some such post, or more probably, Ergham's Manor House replaced the ruined outpost.

The Rev. John Clay, in one of his interesting lectures upon the Ribble, in 1845, gives some particulars respecting the destruction of these roads, which are the more valuable and the more worthy of preservation, as the progress of modern improvement has nearly obliterated all traces of them in the immediate neighbourhood of the town. Mr Clay says:—

"In the course of our enquiries about these roads, we were fortunate in meeting a fine old man, upwards of ninety years of age, named Richard Dewhurst, living on Cadley Moor, in a cottage in which he and his father before him were born. His memory respecting this road seemed very clear. He recollected 'hacking up' and carting away —seventy years ago—the gravel of which it was formed, beginning from the Withy Trees, crossing Cadley Moor, and continuing past Mrs Grimshaw's house, in the direction of Cottam Mill. There can be no doubt that this was a portion of the Watling-street; for the old man's memory brings it to Tanterton Hall, where its traces re-appear.—Mr. Cartwright and I found faint evidences of it yet remaining near Plungington, and also near the lodge of water belonging to Cadley Mill Our informant also well remembered that another road, constructed of similar materials, crossed Preston Moor, and entered the Watling street. On this road, his fellow-workmen, employed in removing the gravel, found some Roman coins.—The tradition which had come down to our venerable informant was, that these roads stretched across the whole country. The 'one reaching from east sea to west sea, the other from the north sea to the south sea.' And as to the maker of the roads, tradition further declared that they were all made in one night by the author of evil."

Another old man, named Thomas Dewhurst, who died in 1855, upwards of ninety years of age, frequently stated that, in his youth, he assisted to cart away the gravel from off Watling-street.

Dr. Leigh visited Ribchester in 1699. He speaks of the Roman way from thence to Preston, as well as one to Lancaster, and another to Manchester. He does not appear to have made any particular survey. Nichols, in 1793, carefully traced the road from Wigan to Lancaster It had, not long previously, been the only highway from Preston to the south. Before the first coach left Preston, in 1771, the traffic was performed by means of "strings of pack horses, thirty and forty in a gang;" and the causeway had become so dilapidated in many places, as to be scarcely passable. Hence numerous divergements from the direct line took place, which may perhaps account for the otherwise apparently unaccountable meanderings of some portions of the modern highway following its track.

Kuerden describes these roads as they appeared nearly two hundred years ago. It has been previously observed he laboured hard to prove that Preston occupied the site of the Rigodunum of Ptolomy. He makes Ribchester the Coccium of Antoninus, and Lancaster the Longovicus of the Notitia. Speaking of the road from the coast to Ribchester, he says.—

"This highway by the country people at this day cald the Watling Street, & was wel vewed by the learned and incomparable antiquary, William Dugdell, Norroy King of Armes in his last visitation of the Gentry within the county of Lancaster, An Do 1664, where by him and many other diligent observers there finding a rampire cast up with gravel, & the largeness of the bulk thereof, was judged to be a Roman strata.—Besides it was observed that from this Ribodunum [Preston] to the other Roman garrison, the Longovicum or Caerwerid of the Britons, their Green Citty, there was another lesser strata leading betwixt them, as diuers signes of a like Rampire ouer Preston and Ful. wood more, towards Garstang, by Broughton, are yet conspicuous to the inquisitive observations of many learned men as well as vulgar people."

Dr. Kuerden likewise mentions, that, not many years previously to his recording the circumstance, "a Roman Vrne, in which was found great store of ancient coynes," was dug up in Myerscough Park, near to the line of the Roman road. The doctor states that he had himself seen most of these coins, which were originally in the possession of "that ingenious gentleman, Edward Towneley, Esq., the proprietor & owner of the park of ground where this vrne was found." Kuerden conjectured the locality "to have been some Taberna, or bathing place for the Roman soldiers" on march.

Some of the elder Lancashire antiquaries were of opinion that the Roman road, from the south to the north, crossed the Ribble by the ford at Penwortham, and passed between Tulketh and the Maudlands. This was first conjectured by Percival The notion was, however, immediately ridiculed by J. Whitaker. Yet, with characteristic daring, he afterwards mentions the circumstance as probable, when it did not affect his favourite theory.[z] The notion has been followed by E Baines, and others. The recent discoveries at Walton, however, point out the upper ford to have been the locality where the *great* Roman road passed the Ribble. The pretensions of the "square area" on the Maudlands to Roman construction have been fully exploded[a]

The lower ford may, however, have been used by the Romans, and vicinal ways may have led to it, as to many other places not upon the line of the principal highway.[b] The Domesday record testifies to a Saxon Castle at Penwortham, and the site is termed "Castle Hill" to this day. From its position and scarped form, it is very probable this peaked hill was used by the Romans as a "*specula*," or out-post of observation, in connection with the station at Walton. A similar mound on the nose of the opposite promontory at Ashton, lately destroyed, may likewise have been used for this purpose. From "Castle Hill" both the Kirkham and Walton stations might be seen, while the Ashton mound commanded the

z History of Manchester, vol. 1, ps 117, and 108.

a See account of the Magdalen Hospital, in Chapter III of the present volume.

b Mr. Edward Baines mentions the discovery of a portion of a road of this character.

entire view of the estuary of the Ribble. The latter must not be confounded with the site of the temporary monastery. The ordnance map marks this much nearer to Tulketh Hall.[c]

John Whitaker says:—

"The Roman British chiefs had previously inhabited castles for their mansions, and the Saxons followed their example They equally possessed their fortresses on settling in the provinces, which were also the houses of their lords, and the capitals of their seignories. In Lancashire, particularly, they inhabited many, and some of them were probably erected by themselves, but most by the Britons before them. They had in all probability no less than twelve considerable ones to the south of the Ribble, Whall-ey, Wal-ton, Child-wall, Win-wick, Black-bourne, Seph-ton, Stand-ish, and Penwortham, Wigan, Rochdale, Middleton, and Bury. * * * They became the origin of villages and the groundwork of towns."

In August, 1856, a vase, containing a hundred Roman denarii, was discovered at the foot of the old "Wery Wall," Lancaster. They were of the higher empire, the latest being of the time of Trajan. Roman tiles, pottery, etc., have been frequently found at Lancaster.

In February, 1856, a large earthenware jar, of Roman manufacture, was discovered in the neighbourhood of Hooley Wood, near Heywood, on the property of Mr Jno. Fenton The vase contained about a thousand small brass coins, chiefly of the lower empire A somewhat similar treasure was found in 1837, on removing the rock above the tunnel formed for the canal at Whittle, near Chorley. Other proofs exist of the presence of the Roman people on the line of the great road from Warrington to Lancaster. An oaken box was found in Leyland moss, in 1820, containing about twenty-eight coins, chiefly of the higher empire, five of which are in the collection of Miss Farington. This lady, likewise, possesses a massive gold ring, bearing the letters S. P Q. R, found at Leyland, and a large portion of a hoard of about one hundred and twenty-six Roman coins, discovered at Worden, in 1850. Roman coins are likewise said to have been found at Woodplumpton, and at Longton, on the Ribble.[d]

c Particulars of the recent excavations at Castle Hill, and the objects discovered, are given in Chapter III. The term "castle" must not be understood in a modern sense. The remains of strong stone fortresses in this country are nearly all Norman A fortified residence is all that is implied, without any reference to its relative strength.

d "In the month of July, 1820, a coin of the Emperor Vespasian was found of copper zinc," [probably Roman brass] "near Woodplumpton Church, having the following inscription — 'Imp CÆSAR VESPASIANUS AUG PRU. TRP COS III.' The head is good relief, and on the reverse side a figure with the letters S C.

"On the eighth day of May, 1819, seventeen Roman coins, of copper zinc, and eleven of silver; they had been contained in a wooden box, several of them were legible, and are coins of Nerva Trajan, Hadrian, Antonine, and Faustina, the daughter of Antonine, and wife of Marcus Aurelius. These coins may be seen at Mr. Westmore's, in the Friargate."—Whittle's His. of Preston, vol. 1, p. 14. 1821.

The last named are doubtless,—those now in the possession of Miss Farington. They were exhibited in the temporary museum formed at the Institution, Avenham, in June, 1856, on the occasion of the visit of the Members of the Lan. and Ches. His Soc., and described as found on Leyland Moss, in 1820.

These hoards have most probably been buried by their owners in the troubled period which preceded and followed the departure of the Roman legions from the country. The localities may have been out-posts of the neighbouring garrisons or stations, or more probably the residences of governors, or other functionaries, or even wealthy natives or colonists.[e] The discovery of the hoard of Roman coins at Whittle, and the circumstance, that part of the quern found in the station at Walton, is made of Whittle stone, render it probable that the quarries were worked during the Roman occupation. It is by no means improbable that either one or the other of the now celebrated alkaline and chalybeate springs of Whittle, were likewise known to them. Remains of a Roman way can be traced in the neighbourhood In 1836, the work-men employed in boring for coal, and through whose operations the alkaline spring was discovered, found a silver denarius of the Emperor Valerian, and a medal in silver of Philip the Elder, which bears the motto, "Salus Augusti." "On the obverse is Hygeia, the Goddess of Health, standing with her usual attributes, the serpent, etc."[f]

According to the Notitia, the mere stations which had been erected by the Romans in the interior of Britain, to secure their conquests, were generally abandoned about the time of the second Theodosius, or during the first half of the fifth century The decay of Coccium may therefore be presumed to have commenced about this period. The larger towns pro-bably flourished for some time after the departure of the Roman military governors. They were eventually either destroyed or occupied by the victorious Saxons

Dr. Whitaker says :—

"Ribchester underwent a sudden and violent demolition about the close of the Roman empire in Britain. In consequence of this, it must have been wholly abandoned, so that the ancient name was lost, and when at some uncertain period in the Saxon era, a few settlers began to gather about the spot, attracted, perhaps, by the remains of Roman buildings, they could only describe it in general terms as the Chester or Roman fortress on the Ribble" [g]

A tradition still remains that Roman Ribchester was destroyed by an earthquake, and another that it was reduced to ashes, in the early part of the fourteenth century, during the great inroad of the Scots under Bruce

e "A. 418. In the ninth year, also, after the sacking of Rome by the Goths, those of Roman race who were left in Britain, not bearing the manifold insults of the people, bury their treasures in pits, thinking that hereafter they might have better fortune, which never was the case, and taking a portion, assemble on the coasts, spread their canvass to the winds, and seek an exile on the shores of Gaul "—Ethelwerd's Chronicle.

"A 418. This year the Romans collected all the treasures that were in Britain, and some they hid in the earth, so that no one has since been able to find them, and some they carried with them into Gaul "—Saxon Chronicle.

f See "Brief Account of Whittle-le-Woods Alkaline Springs,"—Galt, Manchester, 1856.

g Richmondshire, vol. 2, p 458

Both are highly improbable. Had *Roman* Ribchester remained a place of any importance till the period referred to, it could scarcely have failed to have attracted the notice of some of the elder chroniclers or topographers. True, the *Saxon village* may have shared the fate of Preston, in the celebrated foray of our northern neighbours, and hence the tradition! An earthquake in England, of sufficient magnitude to bury a Roman "city," (to use the elder Whitaker's emphatic style,) "*must*" have found some one to record it. Other facts, however, demonstrate that this tradition can have no better foundation than the vague conjecture of ignorant peasants; who, on first discovering remains of ancient buildings beneath the soil, naturally attributed their subterranean location to the action of some earthquake, in that mysterious period usually denominated the "olden time."

Camden attributed the origin of Preston to the decay of Ribchester. He says:—

"Then the *Rhibel* turning Westward, gives its name to a village called at this day *Rhibel Chester*, where so many signs of *Roman* Antiquity, Statues, coins, Pillars, pedestals of Pillars, Chapiters, Altars, Marbles, and inscriptions, are commonly dug up, that this hobbling Rhyme of the Inhabitants does not altogether seem groundless.—

'It is written upon a Wall in Rome,
Ribchester was as Rich as any Town in Christendome.'

"But when the Grandeur of the City, having come to its full period, was at last destroyed by either Wars or Earthquakes (for so it is commonly supposed,) somewhat lower, where the tide flows up the Rhibell, and is called by Ptolomy *Belli-sama æstuarium*; from the ruins of Ribelchester sprang *Preston*, a large Town, handsome for these parts, and populous, so call'd from the Religious, for the name in our language signifies *Priests' Town*."

Rigodunum may have been, relatively, an important and flourishing place, during the latter portion of the Roman occupation of Britain; yet it is highly probable the traditionary tales of its magnificence and extent, owe more to the speculations of enthusiastic antiquaries, than to the sober fact. The stupendous remains, which attest the massive grandeur of the "Eternal City," have become, as it were, daguerreotyped upon the public imagination, and have invested with a mystic and shadowy splendour, almost everything which bears the name of Rome. It is very evident, however, from the absence of remains, that a large portion of Rigodunum must have been, like Rome itself, at the time of Nero, built of wood. Even its most important public building could not, successfully, compete with many an ordinary village church. With reference to the remains of the temple supposed to have been dedicated to Minerva, Dr. Whitaker, himself, confesses that "every appearance about this work, indicated, at once, provincial barbarism, and a declining age of art. For the column was ill wrought, and the different diameters so varied from each other, as to show that it had never been struck from a centre"! The columns taken from the river may still be seen at Ribchester. They form the porch to the principal inn of the village.[h] They are not only very diminutive in stature, but very contemptible in point of workmanship. It is to be hoped, for the reputation of the defunct "city," that these paltry pillars did *not* form a portion of the vaunted "Temple of Minerva."

The discovery at Walton throws considerable light upon the much canvassed probability of Ribchester having been a "sea-port, during the Roman occupation of Britain. The affirmative rested chiefly on a vague tradition, and a conjecture of the ever daring elder Whitaker, endorsed by the Historian of Whalley. The latter learned antiquary, however, afterwards discovered that his position was not tenable, and honourably acknowledged it. He observes:—

"All the nautical remains discovered about Anchor Hill prove nothing more than the existence of a ferry, which the Romans must have had, and which our English ancestors enjoyed, as late as Edward III.; and with respect to the disclosure of an anchor, I know of nothing to negative the opinion, that as the Calder rises in a valley abounding with iron, the ore might be transported to Ribchester, and manufactured there for the use of their port below.[i]

Both Dr Leigh and Mr Oddy, of Blackburn, had, in 1699, decided against the importance of the anchor, rings, etc. Mr. Oddy, in a letter to the Dr., says:—

"When we were at *Ribchester* together, and had carefully viewed the Place, you may remember I gave you my Opinion and Reasons why *Ribchester* had never been Navigable so high, and that Doubt raised about the place called *Anchor-Hill*, may easily be solved, that that Bank was a Rampire of the Fortress is very visible, under which there is yet a broad and deep Foss leading towards the River, serving, as I conceive, for a double use, viz, as a Trench to Fortifie the Place, and a Canal (like to that up to *Holbourn-bridge*, London,) for Boats for the Garrison upon all Occasions, to pass over and re-pass the River, which is not fordable thereabouts but in dry Weather; and we may reasonably suppose there was a great Number of Boats of all sorts, belonging to so large a Fort and City, the *Anchor-Hill*, so called, being as it were a little Dock or Hithe, for the Building or Repairing them, and that the Anchors, Rings, and Nails there found, were only for their use, and not for Ships, they being *far too little* either for Ships of Burden or War."[j]

Mr. Edward Baines, however, in 1836, published the following singular paragraph on this subject, from which we might infer that *he* thought Ribchester had been a sea-port in the time of the Romans:—

"It must be allowed Preston was *not* a Roman station, but that when, by the gradual recession of the waters, or by that mighty convulsion of nature which threw up the huge mass of Pendle, and deranged the whole system of plants and minerals in the vale of the Ribble to a great extent, Ribchester sunk into decay, Preston rose upon its ruins, and became the principal port of Lancashire."[k]

---

h The occupier of the inn informed the author, that one of these pillars is of modern construction, fashioned in imitation of the other three, in order to complete the porch.

i His. of Richmondshire, vol 2, p. 458.

j Nat His. Lan. and Ches, etc, b 3, p 2.

k His. Lan. vol 4, p. 293.

He further adds in a note,—"No Roman remains have been found here," (Preston) "while at York, Lancaster, Ribchester, and Manchester, they abound."

Some antiquaries appear to expect that all remains ought to "come into court," at their bidding, or thenceforth "hold their peace." Such a condition would, unquestionably, free them from the occasionally somewhat disagreeable necessity of reconciling their theoretical elaborations, with after discovered facts. It would, however, have been very remarkable, indeed, if any such remains could have survived the mighty convulsion alluded to! In comparison with the elevation of the "huge mass of Pendle," the Roman occupation of England is but a thing of yesterday, as the veriest tyro in geology can, at the present time, easily understand. But Mr. Baines appears to have afterwards discovered himself, that his "mighty convulsion" was a huge blunder, for the Rev. J. Clay, in 1845, quotes him as an authority on the opposite side of the question He then says, "There is geological demonstration that Ribchester was not a port in the time of the Romans, derived from the fact that the Ribble passes not only over the sand, but over the solid rocks, in its course between Ribchester and Preston, in several places." Mr Clay ridicules this idea, and gives a very elaborate essay on the geological structure of the valley of the Ribble, and contends that the upper portion *may have risen* some twenty feet, while the lower portion, about Lytham, "which had felt less of the earthquake, would retain its usual elevation above the sea." [l]

Mr Clay, however, fell into an error, precisely similar, though less in degree, to that of the Historian of Lancashire, with respect to the *time* when these events took place. The very existence of the Roman ford, at Walton, ought to have thrown grave doubt upon the assumption, and have suggested that these great changes alluded to, must have been effected *anterior* to the Roman occupation. Truly, with a view to sustain this theory, it might be argued that the river was only crossed at low water, as is still the case at Hesketh bank, a few miles lower down the stream, and yet permit sufficient tidal influx to float the Roman vessels past, towards Ribchester.[m] The discovery of the remains, in the centre of the alluvial deposit, between the Ribble and the Darwen, opposite to the natural ford over the former, and the horizontal position of the strata, furnish better evidence, as to the condition of the valley, with respect to tidal action, during the Roman occupation, than a thousand speculations, however

l Lecture on the Ribble, at the Preston Literary and Philosophical Institution.

m It is but simple justice to Mr. Clay, to state here, that further consideration had induced him to abandon this position, previously to the discovery at Walton. The theory is, however, yet maintained by many others ingenious. Geological periods, and the dates of written chronicles, are two widely distinct matters. All historical time is relatively included in the last hour of geological existence. Evidence, as to *when* such events, as those alluded to, *occurred*, must be produced, or the conclusion arrived at remains unsatisfactory. The circumstance, that the red rock "crops out," as it is technically expressed, at an angle, while the immense depth of river *debris*, in the valley, is stratified horizontally, is satisfactory proof that the latter has been deposited *since* the elevation of the former, at whatever period that event occurred. The discovery at Walton may be fairly said to set this question at rest; for, if the tide had, at the time referred to, risen six feet higher, or, what would amount to precisely the same thing, had the level of the valley been depressed but six feet, the station could not have existed. Indeed, it must have required *then* as *now*, to be well embanked, to ensure protection from the ravages of the winter floods, providing the river current and tidal flow were no greater than at the present time. In all human probability, the valley of the Ribble presents, at the present hour, nearly the same *general* features as when the Roman legions left the country. Its superficial aspect may have changed; the alluvial deposits may have increased; the river channel may have become "sanded up" or diverted; marshy swamps may have been converted into solid earth; the dense oak forests, which once crowned its banks, may have fallen beneath the axe of civilization; but no *proof* has yet been advanced that its *great* outlines have changed since the day when the painted Setantian warriors succumbed to Roman discipline and Roman valour, and resigned their stronghold, in the midst of the swamps of Walton, to the soldiers of the victorious Agricola.

PART I.—HISTORICAL.

CHAPTER II.—SAXON AND DANISH PERIODS.

Departure of the Roman legions—Struggles of the Britanni with the native population—The Picts and Scots—The Anglo-Saxon invasion—The Battles of King Arthur—The Saxon Heptarchy—The kingdom of Northumbria—Introduction of Christianity—Battle at Whalley—Battle at Winwick, and death of King Oswald—Danish Invasions—King Alfred—Grant of lands in "Haemundernes"—Rise of Preston—Danish Ravages—Athelstan's grant of lands on the Ribble—The Cuerdale hoard—Battle of Brunanburh—Struggles with the Danes—Canute—Harold—William the Conqueror—Condition of the people—The population of Lancashire composed of varied elements

When the Roman empire began to be seriously threatened in its very heart, by the fierce hoards from the north and east of Europe, the frontier provinces were either conquered by the invaders, or deserted from necessity by the imperial armies The Romans finally evacuated Britain, after nearly four centuries of domination. Some authorities state their departure took place in the year 410; others say nearer the middle of the fifth century. The Saxon historians have almost unanimously asserted, that the native inhabitants, accustomed to repose under the protection of the invincible Roman legions, had lost all warlike spirit or training, and that their newly-acquired liberty was, to them, a misfortune rather than a blessing. They are described as unable to defend themselves from the incursions of the Picts and Scots, who broke through the Roman lines of defence, and plundered the northern portions of the country. A single legion, or less than ten thousand men, granted by the generosity of their former masters, is stated to have been sufficient to chastise the invaders; yet, British courage was at that time insufficient for the protection of its native soil, against so paltry an enemy! When the legions retired, the savage foe again raised his vanquished head. Rome was once more appealed to for succour, and generously she granted it. The fierce Pict was again discomfited, and the effeminate Briton re-presented with the liberty he was still incompetent to preserve. In the meantime Alaric, one of the most redoubtable of the barbarian chieftains, commenced his devastating career. Rome had now occupation sufficient from her own foes, and could no longer afford to fight the battles of others The Britons, left to their fate, are said to have cowardly fled into the mountains, leaving the best parts of the country an undisputed prey to the predatory enemy. This, if true, would indeed present the saddest, the most humiliating page in our national history.

Modern historians, however, have endeavoured to erase some portion of this stain from the conventional character of the aboriginal Britons. The Rev. J Whitaker denounces the whole story as devoid of truth, and asserts that the native Britons fought valiantly, and themselves defeated the Picts and Scots, in the first instance, without Roman assistance. He says: "This false representation was begun by Gildas, and copied afterwards by Bede; and has been faithfully transcribed by every historian since." The Britons *applied*, he confesses, to the consul Ætius for aid, but he asserts, that the Roman functionary was unable or indisposed to spare the requisite troops.

According to Zosimus, who lived in the first half of the fifth century, the Britons themselves revolted against the Roman authority and expelled them from the island. He says,—

"The Barbarians beyond the Rhine, ravaging everything at their pleasure, compelled both the inhabitants of the Britannic islands as well as some of the Celtic nation, to revolt from the empire of the Romans, and to live independent of them, no longer obeying their laws. The people, therefore, of Britain taking up arms and braving every danger, freed their cities from the invading barbarians, and the whole Armoric, and other provinces of Gaul, imitating the Britains, liberated themselves in like manner—expelling the Roman prefects, and setting up a civil polity according to their own inclination This defection of Britain, and of the Celtic nations, took place during the time of Constantine's usurpation, 407—411 ' the barbarians rising up in consequence of the neglect of the government " [a]

Sharon Turner, in his History of the Anglo Saxons, sums up the conflicting evidence in the following terms:—

"Thus the authentic history from 407, is, that the barbarians, excited by Gerontius, assailed both Gaul and Britain, that Constantine" (the rival Emperor) "could give no help, because his troops were in Spain; that Honorius could send none because Alaric was overpouring Italy; that the Britons thus abandoned, armed themselves, declared their country independent, and drove the barbaric invaders from their cities; that Honorius sent letters to the British States, exhorting them to protect themselves, and that the Romans never again recovered possession of the island."

From about the year 410, Britain ceased to acknowledge the Roman domination. Hengist and Horsa did not land in England till 449. The country in the meantime was divided into a series of petty states, and the national strength consequently weakened by disunion and intestine strife. In this semi-defenceless condition the Picts and Scots successfully plundered the northern provinces, while Saxon, Irish and other pirates occasionally ravaged the coasts. Doubtless the narrative of Gildas has reference, if correct, to this period and Rome may have been applied to for the aid she was incapable of rendering The previous repulses of the Picts and

a Mon. Hist, 778

Scots by a single Roman legion, alluded to by the same writer, may have had reference to the victories of Theodosius over the combined forces of the Saxon pirates and the northern hoards, in the preceding century.

Many writers are of opinion that by the term Picti or Picts, the painted men or semi-savage natives are described, and that the Britanni consisted of the Roman colonists and the "Romanised Britons," who endeavoured to retain their authority in the island for some time after the departure of the imperial troops. The revolted natives, joined by the northern barbarians, appear to have triumphed over the Britanni. The Teutonic element of the population, aided by the adventurous Angles, Saxons, and Jutes, however, eventually acquired the supreme authority, and Britain was again subjected to foreign domination. This seems the most consistent interpretation of this somewhat obscure chapter in the national history. Mr. Thomas Wright, indeed, contends that:—

"The Britons, who struggled against the invasions of the Picts and Scots, and Saxons, were a mixture of races foreign to the island, and lived congregated in towns, and that when the Anglo-Saxons at last obtained the ascendency, the remains of this population continued to exist among them, and became part of the Saxon states, while the peasantry probably continued to exist in the same servile condition as before. In fact, that the popular story that the people who resisted the Saxons was the ancient Celtic population of the island, and that it retired before the conquerors, until it found a last refuge in Wales, is a mere fiction." [b]

According to Gildas, the succour denied at Rome was granted by the Anglo-Saxons, and the northern plunderers were speedily ejected. This, however, has been disputed by some modern historians. Hengist and Horsa brought with them but three ships, calculated to convey only a very few troops. Sharon Turner says.—

"As their numbers were too few for conquest, their visit must have been either a matter of accident, or for the purpose of transient depredation. Nennius says they were exiles. Many authorities mention that the Saxons were invited, and many that they came accidentally. It is most likely that the first arrival off the island was casual, but that their landing and subsequent increase were the result of invitation"

Another author says:—

"Hengist and Horsa are poetical names (both in the Anglo-Saxon denoting a horse); and their exploits are, if not entirely fabulous, of so doubtful a character as to deserve little credit. * * * Hengist died, leaving a reputation out of all proportion to the real extent of his achievements. The ravages of others seem to have been ascribed to him, and his pre-eminence has probably resulted from his priority in point of time, rather than from the wider extent or greater destructiveness of his devastations. Even their priority in point of time is questionable; for it has been supposed that during the decline of the Roman power, the east coast, or the Saxon shore, had been to a considerable extent colonized by Saxons. Hengist's dominion never extended beyond Kent, and it may be questioned if he ever took the title of king." [c]

Be that as it may, the British chiefs soon discovered they had entered into an alliance with their future most implacable enemy. The Saxons,

b Lan and Ches His Soc. Transactions, vol. 8, p 147.
c Pen. Cyclop, Art. Kent.

having fulfilled the letter of their contract, speedily ignored both its spirit and purpose. A fertile, and, for the period, a well cultivated country, was virtually in their possession. Might and right are synonymous in the lexicon of barbarian military adventurers. The slightest excuse, real or imaginary, sufficed to induce a complication and a quarrel with the people, whose interests they affected to defend. For nearly a century and a half, the country became the theatre of a series of fierce and sanguinary combats. Some of the more resolute of the native inhabitants yielded their liberty but with their lives. The ultimate subjugation of the Britons cost the best blood of their ferocious invaders Northumberland and part of the Lowlands of Scotland, were subdued by a body of Angles, under their chief Ida, who founded the kingdom of Bernicia. On his death, one of his subordinate chieftains, named Ella, entered the British territory called Deifyr, in 559, and established the Saxon kingdom of Deira. When Adelfrid, king of Bernicia, married Acca, daughter of Ælla, the Deïrian monarch, he banished his infant brother-in-law, Edwin, and formed, by the union of all the counties lying between the then Scottish border and the Mersey and the Humber, the kingdom of Northumbria, which thus became one of the most powerful of the heptarchy Dr. Whitaker, the historian of Whalley, however, advances what he considers satisfactory proof, that the southern portion of the county belonged to the neighbouring kingdom of Mercia; or, in other words, that the Ribble, and not the Mersey, formed the southern boundary of the Northumbrian territory near the west coast. Mr. Baines, however, rejects the learned doctor's inference. He says.—

"This argument he" (Dr Whitaker) "rests principally on the authority the *Status de Blackburnshire*, from which it appears that the parish of Whalley was, from the earliest times, a portion of the diocese of Litchfield, which diocese, as he contends, never passed the Mercian kingdom. It is further urged that the peculiar dialect of the Northumbrian kingdom ceases on the confines of the parish of Whalley, where the Mercian dialect commences. On the first of these points, (the historical argument as it is called,) it is well known that in the early ecclesiastical division of Britain there was great eccentricity, and that it is extremely difficult to fix the limits of the respective dioceses at this distant period: and on the second, it would be unsafe to draw a conclusion of this nature from the variety of dialects in the different parts of Northumbria, seeing that there is a still more marked difference between the dialects of the West Riding of Yorkshire, than exists between those to the north and to the south of the Ribble. To these theories are opposed the generally received opinion, that the kingdom of Mercia was terminated on its north western boundary by the river Mersey; and the positive fact that in the Saxon chronicle, the highest existing authority perhaps upon this subject, Manchester is said to be in Northumbria. The passage is conclusive upon this point — 'This year went king Edward with an army, late in the harvest, to Thelwall; and ordered the borough to be repaired, and inhabited and manned. And he ordered another army also from the population of Mercia, the while he sat there, to go to Manchester, *in Northumbria*, to repair and to man it.'

"To contend, in opposition to this evidence that the Saxon Chroniclers did not know the limits of their own kingdom within nearly a degree of latitude, and to compare their records with the vague notions of certain of the uninformed inhabitants of the south of

England, who call all persons born north of the Trent, Yorkshiremen, is to push a favourite theory to the confines of absurdity. A line in Nennius would seem to favour a conclusion of quite an opposite nature, by representing Mercia as included in Northumbria: 'Pendor primus separavit regnum Merciorum a regno Nordorum.' But it would be as unjust to appropriate Mercia to the Deiri on this unsupported evidence, as to appropriate the most important part of the county of Lancaster to Mercia, on the authority of a vague ecclesiastical division, which might or might not be co-extensive with the civil jurisdiction of that kingdom. [d]

The boundary of the Mercian and the Northumbrian kingdoms may have varied at different periods. The Domesday survey incorporates the northern part of Lancashire with Yorkshire, and describes that portion south of the Ribble, as though it formed an *apanage* to Cheshire Lancashire is not described by its present name. The Ribble, according to Palgrave's map, formed the southern boundary of the Cumbrian principality, at the time of Edmund I., who conferred it upon Malcolm, king of Scotland, and united the land between the Ribble and Mersey to the Northumbrian territory. Sharon Turner says:—

"This kingdom of Mercia made the eighth which these bold adventurers succeeded in founding. It was formed the latest of all The first enterprises of the Angles against the district in which it was raised, were those of inferior chieftains, whose names have not survived their day; and it seems to have been at first considered *as a part of Deira*, or an appendage to it, Its foundation is dated in 586. But although Crida is named as its first sovereign, yet it was his grandson, Penda, who is represented as having first separated it from the dominion of the northern Angles."

The country which eventually formed the Saxon heptarchy, was but gradually wrenched, in fragmentary portions, from the dominion of the native inhabitants In the west, and in the north especially, the Saxons were oftimes defeated by Ambrosius and his brother Uter, in the country of the Deiri. [e]

Both at Manchester and York their leaders submitted, and, with chains in their hands, and ashes upon their heads, ignominiously sued for mercy from the previously despised Britons. But the most redoubtable British warrior of this period, was the renowned king Arthur, the son of Uter and the Lady Igren, Duchess of Cornwall. The exploits of this chieftain have furnished themes for so many bards, romance writers, and retailers of legendary lore and supernatural adventures, that sober history has, to some extent, become inextricably blended with the fictions engrafted upon it. It is said that he was victorious in every battle. The Rev. J Whitaker contends that four of these celebrated conflicts were fought upon the banks of the Douglas, a small river which rises amongst the mosses in

d His. Lan., vol. 1, p. 51.

e Bernicia comprised the lowland country of Scotland, lying between the Forth and the Tweed and the county of Northumberland. The boundaries of the Kingdom of the Deiri about coincide with those of the country of the Brigantes, and include the counties of Lancashire, Yorkshire, and Westmoreland, Cumberland, and Durham.' The Kingdom of Northumbria was formed by the union of Bernicia and the country of the Deiri.

the neighbourhood of Blackrod, and empties itself into the estuary of the Ribble, opposite to the Naze Point. According to Nennius, the second, third, fourth, and fifth battles of Arthur were fought upon a "river, by the Britons called Duglas, in the region Linnuius." The Rev. J. A. Giles, D.C.L., in his annotations to Nennius, gives a variation in the name of the river, namely, Dubglas. He considers it to refer to the "little river, Dunglas," which formed the southern boundary of Lothian. He, however, records Whitaker's opinion in favour of the Lancashire stream Nennius says the tenth battle was fought on the banks of the river Trat Treuroit Dr. Giles gives "Ribroit" as a varied reading of this name, and refers it to the "Brue, in Somersetshire, or the Ribble, in Lancashire."

Jno. Whitaker advances, amongst much conjectural matter, as to the Douglas battles, the following interesting historical and antiquarian details:—

"The name of the river concurs with the tradition, and three battles prove the notice true. On the traditionary scene of this engagement, remained till the year 1770, a considerable British barrow, popularly denominated Hasty Knoll. It was originally a vast collection of small stones taken from the bed of the Douglas; and great quantities had been successively carried away by the neighbouring inhabitants Many fragments of iron had been also occasionally discovered in it, together with the remains of those military weapons which the Britons interred with their heroes at death. On finally levelling the barrow, there was found a cavity in the hungry gravel, immediately under the stones, about seven feet in length, the evident grave of the British officer, and all filled with the loose and blackish earth of his perished remains At another place, near Wigan, was discovered, about the year 1741, a large collection of horse and human bones, and an amazing quantity of horse shoes, scattered over a large extent of ground —an evidence of some important battle upon the spot. The very appellation of Wigan is a standing memorial of more than one battle at that place, *Wig* signifying, in Saxon, a fight, and *Wig-en* being its plural.[f] According to tradition, the first battle fought near Blackrode, was uncommonly bloody, and the Douglas was crimsoned with blood to Wigan. Tradition and remains concur to evince the fact, that a second battle was fought near Wigan Lane, many ages before the rencontre in the civil wars. * * * The defeated Saxons appear to have crossed the hill of Wigan, where another engagement or engagements ensued, and in forming the canal there about the year 1735, the workmen discovered evident indications of a considerable battle on the ground. All along the course of the channel, from the termination of the dock to the point of Poolbridge, from forty to fifty roods in length, and seven or eight yards in breadth, they found the ground everywhere containing the remains of men and horses. In making the excavations, a large old spur, carrying a stem four or five inches in length, and a rowel as large as a half-crown, was dug up; and five or six hundred weight of horse shoes were collected The point of land on the south side of the Douglas, which lies immediately fronting the scene of the last engagement, is now denominated the Parson's meadow, and tradition very loudly reports a battle to have been fought in it. * * *

---

f It is somewhat singular, that Lancashire people, especially in the middle and southern portions of the county, use the term "*Wigen*," or "Wigan," at the present time, as nearly synonymous with "a sound thrashing," or at the least "a tremendous onslaught." A Lancashire seaman in the Black Sea fleet, previously to the late siege of Sebastopol, writing to his uncle in the Fylde country, promised that his venerable relative's advice "to give the Russians Wiggen and no mistake," should be carried out to the letter The Rev T. Sibson, however, gives a very different interpretation to the term. He says, "Wigan, or Wæg-on, is Saxon for Way-on, a town on the Roman way."

"These four battles were fought upon the river Douglas, and in the region Linuis. In this district was the whole course of the current from its source to the conclusion, and the words 'super flumen quod vocatur Duglas, quod est in Linuis,' shew the stream to have been less known than the region. This was therefore considerable; one of the cantreds or great divisions of the Sistuntian Kingdom, and comprised, perhaps, the western half of South Lancashire. From its appellation of Linuis, or the Lake, it seems to have assumed the denomination from the Mere of Marton,[f] which was once the most considerable object within it, and was traversed by the Romans in canoes of a single tree."[g]

Geoffrey of Monmouth speaks only of one battle on the banks of the Douglas. He says.—

"The Saxons, under the command of Colgrin, were attempting to exterminate the whole British race. They had also entirely subdued all that part of the Island which extends from the Humber to the sea of Caithness. * * * Hereupon assembling the youth under his command, he" (Arthur) "marched to" (towards) "York, of which, when Colgrin had intelligence, he met him with a very great army, composed of Saxons, Scots and Picts, by the river Duglas; where a battle happened with the loss of the greater part of both armies Notwithstanding, the victory fell to Arthur, who pursued Colgrin to York, and there besieged him."[h]

But the prowess of king Arthur, and his famous "Knights of the Round Table," aided by the magical lore of "the great and skilful Merlin," could oppose no more than a temporary barrier to the progress of the Saxon arms. After the death of Arthur, the country, exhausted even by his successful efforts, gradually succumbed to the authority of the indomitable and implacable foe.[i]

Notwithstanding the sanguinary ferocity, and the grovelling and remorseless character of their heathen superstitions, the Saxon heart enshrined an instinctive love of personal liberty. A modern writer pertinently remarks, that, "The system of government established by our Saxon ancestors, had in it the germ of freedom, if it did not always exhibit the fruits."[j] The truth of this is attested, not only by the wise laws and constitutional government of the Great Alfred, but by the generous and patriotic sentiment, expressed in the will of this enlightened ruler, namely, "It is but just, the English people should remain as free as their own thoughts." Hume says, respecting the religion of the Saxons:—

"They believed that if they obtained the favour of this divinity," (Woden, their God of War, and chief idol) "by their valour," (for they made less account of the other virtues) "they should be admitted after their death into his hall, and, reposing on couches,

g Martin Mere is evidently here alluded to. Marton Mere is situated on the northern bank of the Ribble, a little to the eastward of Blackpool Both of these shallow lakes have latterly been subjected to extensive draining operations, and considerable quantities of valuable land rescued from the waves, and brought into profitable cultivation

h His. Britain, book 9, c. 1.

i Neither Bede nor Gildas make any mention of Arthur. Some writers regard him as a purely fictitious or poetical personage, embodying the national characteristics of valour and superstition. Some of the genuine exploits attributed to him, may have been performed by others, as in the case of Hengist and Horsa.

j Baines's His. of Lan.

should satiate themselves with ale from the skulls of their enemies whom they had slain in battle. * * * We know little of the other theological tenets of the Saxons; we only learn that they were polytheists; that they worshipped the sun and moon; that they adored the god of thunder, under the name of Thor; that they had images in their temples; that they practised sacrifices, believed firmly in spells and enchantments, and admitted a general system of doctrines which they held as sacred, but which, like all other superstitions, must carry the air of the wildest extravagance, if propounded to those who are not familiarized to it from their earliest infancy."

The time, however, approached when the Saxons became converts to Christianity. Ethelbert, king of Kent, had married the French princess, Bertha, only daughter of Caribert, king of Paris. This lady, being a Christian, stipulated for the free exercise of her religion She brought with her a French bishop, and by her own exemplary conduct, her piety, and womanly tact, she impressed upon her husband and immediate attendants, a favourable sense of the power and influence of the Christian doctrines.

Gregory the Great soon afterwards was induced to send missionaries to England, for the conversion of the Saxons.[k] He had seen exposed for sale, in the Roman market place, some beautiful children, the offspring of mercenary parents, in the kingdom of Northumberland. These children were Angles, from the district of the Deiri [l]

Augustine, a Roman monk, with about forty associates, arrived in Kent in the year 596. The king was converted, and the men of Kent followed his example. Augustine was made archbishop of Canterbury.

Edwin, after defeating his treacherous brother-in-law, Adelfrid, ascended the Northumbrian throne. This talented and popular prince espoused Ethelburga, the daughter of the Christian queen of Kent. This pious lady successfully imitated the example set by her mother. Through the instrumentality of Paulinus, a zealous and intelligent ecclesiastic, not only her warlike and prudent husband, but the high priest of the Saxon paganism, the nobles, and the bulk of the people of his kingdom, were converted to the Christian faith Paulinus was made bishop of Northumbria in the year 627 Paulinus is believed to have visited Whalley, though upon very doubtful evidence. The "*Status de Blackburneshire*" mentions a tradition, that Augustine preached there, and that one of the crosses, in the church-yard, was erected to commemorate the event. Dr. Whitaker thinks Augustine to be a mistake for Paulinus. The conversion of the people of Lancashire is generally attributed to the preaching and example of this prelate *Ethelwerd* and the *Saxon Chronicle* record, however, that in 565, Columba "came from Scotia (Ireland) to preach to the

k In the year 601 Ethelwerd's Chron

l The settlers in Kent, and the Isle of Wight, were principally Jutes The remainder of the southern counties, excepting Cornwall, were peopled by Saxons; Mercia and Northumbria were inhabited by Angles

Picts." Bede attributes the conversion of the "Southern Picts" to the ministration of Nimas, from North Wales, at even an earlier period. Mr. Thornber is of opinion that the locality near Lytham, called *Kilgrimol*, is the site of a Culdee cell or cemetery, and that it was founded by the disciples of Columba. We are informed by Bede, that the lands at Ripon were first "given to those that followed the doctrine of the Scots, to build a monastery upon." From the same authority, we learn that in 635, *Aidan* was sent, at the request of king Oswald, from Iona, "to administer the word of faith to him and his nation" According to Bishop Turner, the "lands in Amounderness, on the Ribble," were first granted to Eata, a Culdee abbot, of Mailros, on the erection of the monastery at Ripon. If such were the case, it is highly probable that the doctrines of Columba were taught in this neighbourhood.[m] The lands are said to have been afterwards transferred to Wilfred, an opponent of the Culdee apostle. According to Dr. Giles, "the ancient name of Iona was I, or Hi, or Aoi, which was Latinized into Hyona, or Iona. The common name of it now is, I-colum-kill, the Island of Colum of the Cells." The term Kilgrimol is certainly suggestive of the location of a "Culdee cell, or cemetery." It is regarded in this light by Ormerod, the historian of Cheshire Mr. Thornber says, the place retains the name of "Church and Cross Slack to this day," and that the foundation deed of Richard Fitz Roger, who afterwards erected a "cell" on the site of the present church, states, that "over the ditch of the previous cell, or cemetery, there was thrown by him a cross." Mr. Thornber is inclined to think a wooden church existed at the time of the Domesday survey. He says:—

"We have the name of Reginald of Durham for recording that the grandfather of the founder of the Norman priory at Lytham, at the end of the reign of Richard the Lion, had pulled down the ancient church, which had been constructed of shingles, and had built another of stone. This, then, is an undoubted fact, though the Domboc mentions no church, because there was no endowment land to be taxed; and it does not deteriorate from the wooden one having been of Culdee origin, when we read in Bede, that "after *the manner of the Scots* Finan built Lindisfarne, not of stone, but of hewn oak, and covered it with reeds.[n]

This, however, is not absolutely conclusive. The Domesday book mentions none of the places of worship in Amounderness, in connection with the land It merely intimates that the latter belonged to Preston, *together with three churches upon it*. These there is no difficulty in identifying

m "Churches were built in several places; the people joyfully flocked together to hear the word; money and land were given of the King's bounty to build monasteries, the English, great and small, were, by their Scottish masters, instructed in the rules and observance of regular discipline, for most of them that came to preach were monks. Bishop Aidan was himself a monk of the Island called Hii"—Bede's Eccles. His.

n Lecture delivered at Preston, on "The Lands and People on the Ribble before the Conquest," Feb., 1856.

with Preston, Kirkham, and St. Michael's Church Town. Is it not more probable, that the "cell, or cemetery," of the disciples of Eata, at Kilgrimol, gradually fell into decay, after the transfer of the "lands on the Ribble," to the rival sect, headed by Wilfred, or, may it not have been destroyed in one of the many incursions of the heathen Danes? There is no evidence to show that the "ancient church, constructed of shingles," was not erected after the Norman invasion. Richard I. died in 1199, one hundred and nineteen years after the commencement of the compilation of the Domesday survey.

A farm, in Fulwood, bears the name of Killingsough. Gossips say that it acquired this title from the circumstance that a large number of human bones were exhumed, during some draining operations. As the act for enclosing Fulwood Moor, of which it forms a part, was not obtained till 1811, this is highly improbable. The term is evidently of much older date. The spot is not very far distant from another deep ravine, from one side of which, numerous small cannon balls have been taken The latter are undoubtedly relics of Cromwell's victory over Langdale, in 1648. Killingsough may be the burial place of the slain, though it is scarcely probable the bodies would be removed so far from the dingle where the struggle took place May not Killingsough, like Kilgrimol, indicate the site of a Culdee cell, or cemetery, or indeed of the earliest place of Christian worship, after the grant to Eata, abbot of Mailros? The church at Stalmine, is dedicated to St. Oswald, and that at Poulton to St Chad, another disciple of the Culdee apostle.

On the death of Edwin, who fell whilst fighting against the army led by Penda, the pagan king of Mercia, and the Welsh monarch, Cadwallon, the Northumbrians relapsed into heathenism.

Paulinus retired with the queen dowager to Kent. Eanfrid, son of Ethelfrith, succeeded to the throne of Bernicia, and Osric, grandson of Ella, to that of Deira. Osric fell in battle with Cadwallon, and Eanfrid was cruelly butchered by the same "hero," while treating for peace, and defended by only twelve soldiers [o] Oswald, the brother of Earnfrid succeeded, and amply avenged this treachery. After a fierce struggle on the banks of the Denise, Cadwallon, and the flower of his army were destroyed. Bede says, that owing to the talents of Oswald, the provinces of the Deiri and the Bernicians, which, till then, had been at variance, were peacefully united, and moulded into one people. Oswald re-established Christianity in his dominions He was regarded as a person of great sanctity Oswald eventually perished in a battle against Penda, the heathen Mercian.

o Bede.

ruler. He was slain, according to the Saxon Chronicle, "on the nones of August, 642, at Maserfield" Camden, Capgrave, etc, place Maserfield near Oswestry, in Shropshire; but Archbishop Usher, Alban, Butler, Powell, Dr. Cowper, and others, are of opinion the engagement took place near Winwick, in the county of Lancashire. The name is still retained in the title of the neighbouring district, Mackerfield. The church at Winwick is dedicated to St. Oswald, and an inscription, on the outside of the south wall, supports the tradition. On the death of Oswald, his brother Oswy ascended the Northumbrian throne. He placed Oswin, son of Osric, over the Deiri; but afterwards repenting of the act, caused him to be murdered. Oswy defeated Penda, and introduced Christianity into the Mercian territory. The bishopric of Litchfield was shortly afterwards established The scene of Penda's defeat is supposed to have been that of his previous victory over Oswald. A local historian says:—

"Penda and upwards of thirty of his principal officers were drowned in their flight, having been driven into the river Winweyde, the waters of which were at that time much swollen by heavy rains There is no stream in England which is more liable to be suddenly flooded than the stream which joins the Mersey below Winweck, and there both the resemblance of the names, and the probability of the fact, induce me to think that Penda met with his death within two or three miles of the place at which Oswald had fallen." p

Camden, Dr. Giles, and others, however, place this battle at Winwidfield, near Leeds. It is not certainly known at what period the direct government of the western portion of the kingdom of Deira first passed from the native British princes to the Northumbrian monarchs Mr Hodgson Hinde says:—

"The reign of Osric extended from the year 642 to 684, during which period, whatever might be his success against the Picts and Scots, we have no record of any attempt to bring the British population of his own dominions under his more immediate control. This work seems to have been reserved for his son and successor, Ecgfrith, to whose reign may be ascribed, with tolerable certainty, the complete subjugation of the Britons of Lancashire, Cumberland, and Galloway, the entire remnant of the native population within his limits, with the single exception of Strathclyde."q

There are some errors in this paragraph Osric I succeeded Edwin in 634. On the death of Oswald in 642, "*Oswy*, his brother, succeeded to the kingdom of the Northumbrians, and he reigned two less (than) thirty years." The same authority says: "670. This year Oswy, king of the Northumbrians, died, and Egfrid, his son, reigned after him. 685. * * And the same year, on the third of June, Egfrid was slain, near the North sea, and a great army with him." r Bede says, Egfrid was slain

p Historical Notes on the Valley of the Mersey, by Thomas Baines.—Lan. and Ches. His. Soc. Pro., Session 5.

q Paper on "State of the Western Portion of the Ancient Kingdom of Northumberland, down to the period of the Norman Conquest."—Trans. Lan and Ches. His. Soc, vol 8.

r Saxon Chronicle.

on the 20th of May," and adds, "from that time the hopes and strength of the English" (Northumbrian) "crown began to 'waver and retrograde'; for the Picts recovered their own lands which had been held by the English and the Scots that were in Britain, and some of the Britons their liberty, which they have now enjoyed for about forty-six years."

The Saxon Chronicle says that in the year 798, "there was a great fight at Hwelleage (Whalley), in the land of the Northumbrians, during Lent, on the fourth of the nones of April, and there Alric, the son of Heardbearht, was slain, with many others with him." From the same authority, it appears that four years earlier, "Ethelred, king of the Northumbrians, was slain by his own people." This revolt had been preceded by a year of the most deplorable famine. "Forewarnings came over the land of the Northumbrians, and miserably terrified the people; there were excessive whirlwinds and lightnings; and fiery dragons were seen in the air." Eardulph, the successor of Ethelred, was king at the period of the Whalley battle. Simeon, of Durham, says that the great leader of the faction was a Saxon nobleman, named Wada, and that he was defeated by the king, at a place called Billangahoh, near Whalley.[s] Billinge Hill and the township of Billington still retain something of the Saxon name; while Langho, a very small village, not far from the river, has preserved almost entirely the latter portion of it. Waddow, near Clitheroe, is interpreted to mean, the hill of Wada; and Waddington, the town or village over which the rebellious chieftain ruled. Not far from Langho, on the south bank of the Ribble, just below its confluence with the Calder, may be seen the remains of a large mound, supposed by Dr. Whitaker, as the probable sepulchre of Alric. The spot is marked on the ordnance map as the "site of a tumulus." On the north bank of the Ribble, opposite the "foot of Calder," two other *tumuli* rise distinctly from the level valley. One is nearly thirty feet high; the other somewhat less. They are between two and three hundred yards asunder, and are described on the ordnance map as "lowes," or hills. They are evidently of artificial construction, and may cover the remains of some warriors slain in this conflict.[t]

---

s Simeon of Durham's words are:—

"A.D. 798. Conjuratione facta ab interfectoribus Ethelredi regis Wada Dux in illa Conjuratione cum illis bellum inivit contra Eardwlphum regem in loco qui appellatur ab Anglis Billangahoh juxta Walalega et ex utraque parte plurimis interfectis Wada Dux cum suis in fugam versus est."—Leland, Col.: vol. 1, p. 350.

"A.D. 798. A conspiracy having been organized by the murderers of Ethelred, the King, Wada, the chief of that conspiracy, commenced a war against Eardulph, and fought a battle at a place called by the English, Billangahoh, near Walalega, and, after many had fallen on both sides, Wada and his army were totally routed."

t "To these sepulchral mounds our Anglo-Saxon forefathers gave the name of low *(hlæw)* and barrow *(beorh, bearw)*."—"The Celt, the Roman, and the Saxon," by Thomas Wright, M.A., F.S.A. etc.

After a long series of factious rebellions, domestic treasons, and intestine wars, the country became thoroughly demoralised, and is said to have eventually passed, along with the remaining kingdoms of the heptarchy, under the domination of Egbert, king of Wessex. The Northumbrians, however, like the Mercians and the people of East Anglia, still retained the privilege of choosing a nominal sovereign, though he possessed little more power than a feudal chief, and paid tribute to Egbert.

Thus, after the expiration of nearly four hundred years from the departure of the Romans, the country was again, to some extent, united under one government. From this date the "Kingdom of England" is generally supposed to commence. Under the Romans, it was merely a province of their extensive empire; under the ancient Britons and early Saxons, an aggregate of petty kingdoms and semi-nomadic tribes.

This popular view of the question, however, scarcely exhibits Egbert's true position. Sharon Turner says:—

"He had made all the Anglo-Saxon Kingdoms subordinate to his own, but the tale, that he assembled the Anglo-Saxon states, and abolishing the distinction between Saxons and Angles, and all provincial appellations, commanded the island to be called England, and procured himself to be crowned and denominated King of England, seems not to be entitled to our belief."

Egbert does not appear to have been absolutely monarch of all England, but he possessed sufficient power to dictate terms to his rivals, who still retained the form of authority. Alfred the Great, even, can only be regarded as the first "king" of all the *Anglo-Saxon* people. It was not until the reign of Athelstan, that the Danes in Northumbria submitted to the direct government of a Saxon prince

The country was first divided into counties, hundreds, and tithings, during the dominion of our Saxon forefathers Mr Baines says:—

"These divisions, as they now stand, according to Mr. Justice Blackstone, owe their origin to Alfred,[u] who, to prevent the rapines and disorders which formerly prevailed in the realm, instituted *Tithings*, so called from the Saxon, because ten freeholders with

[u] J. Whitaker, and others, maintain that these divisions took place at a much earlier period. He says:—"The tything, hundred, and county, constituted part of that original polity which the Saxons brought with them from Germany The tything and shire are both mentioned in the laws of the West Saxons, before the close of the seventh century, and during the reign of Ina. And the tything, the shire, and the hundred, are noticed in the capitularies of the Franks, before the year 630, and the reign of Dagobert. All the three institutions would commence originally among the kindred nations of the Franks and Saxons." After some elaborate argument on the subject, he continues: "The tything of our Saxon ancestors was nothing more than the manour of the present day. The ten families that were incorporated into the deanery, became the ten lordships of a manour. And the eleventh that was appointed to preside over the rest, was thereby made the capital of a manour. * * * The seignior of a tything became what a lord of a manour continues to this day, the one regent and justiciary of the district; and his court was made, as it remains at present, the one tribunal of the manour. And accordingly that manorial judicature, which is particularly calculated to preserve the peace of the whole, is actually denominated the View of Frank Pledge and the Tything-court to this moment"

their families composed one. These all dwelt together, and were sureties or pledges to the king for the good behaviour of each other. Tithings, towns, or vills, are of the same signification in law, and had each of them originally a church and celebration of divine service. As ten families of freeholders made a town, so ten tithings composed a superior division called a *hundred*, consisting of ten times ten families The hundred is governed by a high constable or bailiff, and formerly there was regularly held in it a court for the trial of causes, which is now fallen into disuse. An indefinite number of these hundreds make a *county* or shire, the government of which is confined to the shire-reeve or sheriff, upon whom its civil administration devolves. South Lancashire was first parcelled into three hundreds, Blackburn, Derby, and Salford,[v] which had afterwards taken from them Newton, Warrington, and Leyland hundreds, the two former of which have since merged into the hundred of West Derby. To these are to be added the hundreds of Lonsdale and Amounderness in the north, making in the whole six. These hundreds all took their names from the towns or villages which constitute the heads of their respective centuries, and the custom which still continues, of making the hundreds responsible for the excesses of a lawless mob, is an appendage to the Saxon system of tithings."

Alfred's exertions were incessant in the purification of the grossly tyrannical judicial practices, which then prevailed to an enormous extent. The Anglo Saxon parliament, called the Wittenagemot, or "Assembly of Wise Men," composed of earls, prelates, and landowners, sanctioned these salutary innovations. Alfred's execution of forty-five justices, as murderers, because they had condemned to death unjustly, persons upon whose causes they had adjudicated, may be quoted as an example of his inflexible integrity. Speaking of the hundred or wapentake courts of this period, Hume observes —

"Their method of decision deserves to be noted as being the origin of juries; an institution admirable in itself and the best calculated for the preservation of liberty, and the administration of justice that ever was devised by the wit of man. * * The people in imitation of their ancestors, the ancient Germans, assembled there in arms; whence a hundred was sometimes called a wapentake, and its court served both for the support of military discipline, and the administration of civil justice."

Alfred was likewise the first to embody a regular militia for the defence of the country, as well as to establish a permanent naval force for the protection of the coasts He was a great patron of learning and the mechanical arts, which, previously to his reign, had become almost universally neglected. He, himself, observes,—"When I took the kingdom, there were few on the south side of the Humber, the most improved part of England, who could understand their daily prayers in English, or translate a letter from the Latin. I think there were not many beyond the Humber There were so few that I cannot indeed recollect one single instance, on the south of the Thames."

Sharon Turner, and other writers, are of opinion that the "Guilda Mercatoria," or "Guilds Merchant," originated about this period. They are by others, however, believed to be of much older date. They exhibit

---

[v] Salford, the only hundred that has not been dismembered, has within its limits, a hundred townships.

considerable affinity to the protective legislation necessitated by the lawless character of the early period in the history of any people [w]

During the long wars between the ancient inhabitants and their Saxon conquerors, many of the Roman cities and strongholds were either wholly or partially destroyed, and, from their ruins, towns and castles were subsequently erected. Preston, the chief town in the hundred of Amounderness, is, essentially, of Saxon origin, and dates, at the earliest, in the opinion of several authorities, from about the year 705, when Archbishop Wilfrid, primate of the Northumbrian kingdom, "re-edified" the monastery and church at Ripon, in Yorkshire. The ceremony of consecration appears to have been performed with much pomp, and was witnessed by many Saxon princes and nobles. It has previously been noticed, that Bishop Tanner states, "Alchfrid, King of the Northumbers, gave this place" (Ripon) "first to abbot Eata, to build a monastery, but before it was finished he was sent away, and St Wilfrid was made abbot here, before A.D. 661." The statement of Bede would seem to confirm this. Other historians say, the monastery was founded by Wilfrid, and omit all notice of Eata Dugdale observes,—

"In the life of Wilfrid, quoted by Leland, the *earliest* endowment of Ripon appears to have consisted of certain lands bordering upon the river Ribble; in Hacmunderness, in Gedene, in the territory called Dunutinge, or Duninge, and in Aetlevum. Peter of Blois, in another life of St Wilfrid, states that upon the first construction of the building, certain persons who were present at its consecration and dedication to St. Peter, gave other lands, viz. Ribble and Hasmundesham, and Marchese, and land in the parts of Duninge; and that Wilfrid gave a copy of the Gospels, as also a library, and many other books of the Old and New Testament; together with certain tablets skilfully wrought with gold and precious stones." [x]

Mr. Baines is of opinion that about the period of the grant, "the parish church of Preston was erected, and on the canonization of archbishop Wilfrid, the new edifice was dedicated to that saint." This conjecture is, however, substantiated by no positive evidence.

The name "Preston" is a contraction of "Priest's town," and corroborates the assumption of its ecclesiastical origin. There are upwards of forty places in England which possess a similar patronymic; from which, and other local appellations derived from the same source, it would appear the clergy, during the Saxon period, frequently settled upon the lands granted to them as religious endowments, by the warlike chiefs and princes, and thus formed the original *nuclei* of many towns and villages. Camden attributed the rise of Preston to the decay of Ribchester. He was, of course, not aware of the existence of the Roman station at Walton. It is not improbable that the location of the priests may have been originally

w See Municipal History.

x Monasticon Anglicanum; edition, 1846.

called "Hasmundesham," or Haemundesham" It would appear to be so named by Peter of Blois, at the period of the grant. As stated by Mr. Baines, the name of the hundred is nearly always derived from the chief town or village

Little, however, appears to be known relative to Preston, for upwards of two hundred years after the time of Wilfrid. In 930, the hundred of Amounderness was granted to the cathedral church at York, by Athelstan, son of Edward the Elder. The reason why the monks of Ripon transferred their property, does not precisely appear. Perhaps the insecure nature of the tenure, owing to the depredations of the piratical Northmen, rendered the "lands near the Ribble, in *Hasmundernesse*," scarcely worth the charges and risk attending their defence. It is, however, recorded that Athelstan *purchased* the whole of Amounderness. In this case, the pecuniary consideration may have alone induced the monks to relinquish their possessions. It is more probable, however, the lands were seized by some successful Danish invaders

The incursions of the Scandinavian rovers, including Danes, Norwegians, and Swedes, which commenced previously to the partial union of the Saxon kingdoms under Egbert, again involved the country in a series of sanguinary contests. Victory sometimes smiled for a time upon the prowess of the invaders, and then transferred her favour to the indomitable Saxon.

The renowned "sea-king," Ragnar Lodbrog, was defeated by the Northumbrian Prince Ella, and subjected to a torturing death. An expedition was fitted out by the Northmen, to avenge the piratical old warrior. It was commanded by his three sons, Halfden, Ingwar, and Hubba. Northumbria was suffering at the time all the evils of civil commotion. For a series of years, domestic treason and fierce internal strife had desolated the country and weakened its power Sharon Turner says:—

"Of all the Anglo-Saxon governments, the kingdom of Northumberland had been always the most perturbed Usurper murdering usurper is the prevailing incident. A crowd of ghastly monarchs pass swiftly along the page of history as we gaze; and scarcely was the sword of the assassin sheathed before it was drawn against its master, and he was carried to the sepulchre which he had just closed upon another. In this manner, during the last century and a half, no fewer than seventeen sceptred chiefs hurled each other from their joyless thrones, and the deaths of the greatest number were accompanied by hetacombs of their friends"

The princes in various parts of England were disunited. The successor of Egbert had ceased to exercise the predominant influence amongst the kings of the Saxon heptarchy. Each petty monarch regarded the Scandinavian "vikingr" more in the character of allies, while their forces only threatened their neighbours. There existed no truly national spirit or compact; hence the success which attended these brave but cruel and lawless warriors. Contrary to the expectation of the Anglo-Saxon monarchs, the Northmen first landed in East Anglia, where they wintered without molestation. The weak king even complied with their demand, and furnished horses for their troops. In the following spring, they entered Yorkshire. Ella was defeated at York, and put to death with the most frightful tortures. Ingwar assumed the sceptre, and ruled from the Humber to the Tyne. In 870, the fourth year of their arrival, the invaders ravaged the eastern portion of the country, burnt the monasteries, butchered the clergy at the altars, and committed the most appalling atrocities. Edmund, king of East Anglia, was barbarously murdered, and another of the Saxon kingdoms compelled to succumb to the prowess of the barbarian invaders.

At length Alfred the Great appeared upon the scene. After numerous vicissitudes of fortune, he totally defeated the Danish monarch at Eddington. The remnant of the defeated army was afterwards besieged in their fortified camps, and compelled to surrender at discretion The generosity, or more probably the necessities, of Alfred, however, induced him to divide the kingdom with his late enemies. He granted them lands in Northumbria and East Anglia, where the greater portion of the Scandinavian warriors and adventurers had settled, and become to some extent incorporated amongst the resident English people.[y] The Danish monarch, and nearly the whole of his army, accepted Christian baptism as a pledge of future amity. Alfred acted as sponsor for Godrun, and gave him the name of Athelstan. In his civil government, this wise and upright monarch made no distinction between his Saxon and Danish subjects. He placed them, with respect to the administration of the laws, upon a basis of perfect equality This for some time preserved the tranquillity of the country. The Danish pagan chieftains governed in Northumbria till near the conclusion of the reign of Alfred, when Anarawd sought the friendship of Alfred, and adopted the Christian faith. But eventually, notwithstanding Alfred's clemency, fresh discontents arose between the rival nationalities. On the death of the Danish princes, Guthrum and Guthred, their followers revolted against the Saxon authority. This happened at the time when large bodies of piratical Danes, under Hastings, were laying waste the county of Kent, and thus increased the difficulties of the king. The greater portion of the country was again subjected to pillage and desolation.

Alfred's genius, however, proved equal to every emergency. After a series of desperate conflicts, the military power of the national enemy, if not absolutely destroyed, was for a time, thoroughly prostrated. Twenty of their vessels were taken at sea, and the crews hanged as pirates. The

---

y According to the Saxon Chronicle, Halfden, the Danish chieftain, in the year 876, "apportioned the lands of Northumbria, and they thenceforth continued flourishing and tilling them."

valiant Hastings was at length forced to yield to the superior genius of his distinguished rival. This renowned Danish chieftain fortified the city of Chester, during his struggle with Alfred. In his retreat before the Saxon monarch, he passed with his army through Northumbria into East Anglia, for the purpose of avoiding the forces of his enemy in Mercia. The Danes of East Anglia and Northumbria, on the approach of the victorious monarch hastened to make humble submission. The Britons inhabiting the glens and valleys of Wales acknowledged his authority. Hume says:—

"This great prince, had now, by prudence and justice and valour, established his sovereignty over all the southern parts of the island from the English channel to the frontiers of Scotland; when he died in the vigour of his age and the full strength of his faculties, after a glorious reign of twenty nine years and a half, in which he deservedly attained the appellation of Alfred the Great, and the title of Founder of the English monarchy."

This title must, however, be received with some considerable limitation, as the Danes in the north and eastern portions of the country fairly divided the sovereignty.

On the death of Alfred, his son Edward, surnamed the Elder, ascended the throne. His title was, however, disputed by his cousin Ethelwald, who prevailed upon the Danish population in East Anglia and Northumbria to espouse his cause Another fierce struggle ensued, but the military prowess of Edward eventually triumphed. Ethelwald was slain in a sanguinary encounter at Bury St Edmonds. The remainder of this prince's reign was chiefly occupied in warlike operations against both the foreign and domesticated Danish people, in which he met with almost uninterrupted success. Edward (A. D 921) likewise reduced the Cumbrian Britons to subjection. Notwithstanding the occasional conquests of preceding Northumbrian princes, this territory, which at one period extended south as far as the Ribble, appears to have continually re-asserted its independence of both the Anglo Saxon and Danish authority. Edward likewise reduced the East Anglians to submission, and compelled both Sidroc and Reginald, pretenders to the Northumbrian crown, to yield to his military superiority, and depart from the territory

Mr. Thomas Baines observes, in his paper on the Valley of the Mersey:—

In the year 911 the Northumbrians themselves began the war, for they despised the peace which King Edward and his 'witan' offered them, and overran the land of Mercia. After collecting *great booty* they were overtaken *on their march home*, by the forces of the West Saxons and the Mercians, who put them to flight and slew many thousands of them Two Danish kings and five earls were slain in this battle [z] Amongst the earls slain was *Agmund, the governor*, from whom the hundred of Agmunderness, was probably named"

Ethelwerd states this battle, which was fought at "Wodnesfield," in Gloucestershire, took place in 909, and the Saxon Chronicle in 911. Sharon

z The Saxon Chron says two Kings, Ecwils and Halfdene. Ethelwerd adds a third, Hingwar

Turner prefers 910 Ethelwerd says that the provinces of Northumberland and Mercia were, at the time of this outbreak, "ruled," under the king, by earl Ethered. The same authority records, that, in 913, "a fleet entered the mouth of the river Severn, but no severe battle was fought there that year. Lastly the greater part of that army" (the Danish) "go to Ireland, formerly called Bretannis by the great Julius Cæsar."

This opinion relative to the derivation of the name "Amounderness" was promulgated by the elder Whitaker, and followed by Mr Edward Baines, as well as his son, as above quoted It cannot however be reconciled with the testimony of *Ethelwerd* and the Saxon Chronicle. These authorities expressly declare that the "first arrival" of Danish vessels on the coast did not take place till about the year 787. As the hundred is described in the Ripon grant, in 705, by the name Hacmunderness, a Danish origin for the term must be rejected. The Messrs. Gibson, in their "Etymological Geography," say, "Anderness (for Ackmunderness)," signifies "a headland, a promontory, sheltered by *Oaks*, (*ac*, oak; and *mund* protection)." At page 93, of the same work, however, they say "Munden or Munder" means "Mouth, (*mund*, German, *muth*, Saxon)—the part where a river empties itself, its *Mouth* or *Mouths*" As the hundred of Amounderness lies between the broad estuary of the Ribble and the still more important Morecambe Bay, and includes within its boundaries the estuary of the Wyre, it is probable the middle portion of the name may have been derived from this circumstance. On this supposition, it may be thus interpreted: "The promontory of the estuaries, clothed with oaks;" or the "Ack" may have been derived from the place of meeting of the hundred, or wapentake; as "Appletree hundred," in Derbyshire.

Edward the elder repaired the fortress of Manchester, and garrisoned it with Mercian soldiers, with the view to overawe and keep in check the refractory Northumbrians. His sister Ethelfleda aided him in his enterprises with judgment and heroism, worthy of the daughter of the great Alfred.

Athelstan, his successor, anxious to secure the attachment of the Northumbrian people marched into the country at the head of his army, and conferred the title of king upon the Danish chieftain, Sigtryg, grandson of Ragnar Lodbrog. Further to secure his interest and friendship, he gave him his sister Editha in marriage. Sigtryg embraced Christianity, but shortly afterwards relapsed into his old idolatry, and discarded his wife Athelstan promptly resolved to avenge this insult, but Sigtryg's death prevented its consummation Anlaf and Godefrid, his sons by a previous marriage, presuming upon their father's title, assumed the sovereign power without consulting Athelstan They were, however, speedily defeated and forced to quit the territory. Anlaf fled to Ireland, and Godefrid to Scotland Athelstan pursued the latter, and demanded the fugitive from the Scottish king, who complied and entered into a treaty with the powerful English monarch.[a]

Ten years afterwards, Anlaf resolved upon another attempt to win the Northumbrian crown. Though assisted by the Anglo-Danes in Northumbria, Welsh malcontent princes, Scandinavian pirates, and Constantine, king of the Scots, the brave, enterprising, and able Danish chieftain was totally routed by Athelstan, in a sanguinary engagement, near Brunanburh. The victory was decisive. The grandson of Alfred the Great, not only reigned undisputed monarch of all England, but he exercised something more than a nominal sway over Scotland and Wales

The records of the Saxon and Danish periods of our history are meagre, and sometimes contradictory. Probably few were ever written. Some may have been lost or destroyed by their Norman successors, for it is seldom the policy of conquerors to preserve the national memorials of a subjugated people. That the county of Lancaster was often the scene of their struggles for supremacy, is attested both by tradition and discovered remains. In May, 1840, an immense treasure, belonging to this period, was accidentally disclosed at Cuerdale, near Preston. The winter floods had disturbed the alluvial soil on the south bank of the Ribble, near to Cuerdale Hall, and some workmen were employed in repairing the damage. The spade of one struck upon a decayed wooden box, which immediately, to their surprise, disgorged a large quantity of silver coins, and other valuable articles. A lining of lead had partially protected the contents from the action of air and water. The coins had been placed in the box in regular order, and those in the centre were nearly as bright and perfect as when first minted. The treasure was eventually claimed for the queen, as Duchess of Lancaster, and specimens sent to the British and various local museums. Many of the coins unquestionably found their way surreptitiously into the hands of collectors, consequently, there is some difficulty in determining the precise number discovered. It is pretty generally

---

a The copy of the Saxon Chronicle, preferred by Dr Giles, gives the date 926. "This year fiery lights appeared in the north part of the heavens, and Sihtric perished, and king Athelstan, obtained the kingdom of the Northumbrians, and he ruled all the kings who were in the island; first Howel, king of the West-Welsh, and Constantine, king of the Scots; and Owen, king of the Monmouth people; and Aldred, son of Ealdult, of Bambrough, and they confirmed the peace by pledge, and by oaths, at the place which is called Eamot, on the 4th before the Ides of July, and they renounced all idolatry, and after that submitted to him in peace" One MS. of the Saxon Chronicle further adds that in 933, "king Athelstan went into Scotland, as well with a land army as with a fleet, and ravaged a great part of it."

believed, however, that the chest originally contained about 10,000 coins. Many of the silver rings and smaller bars were likewise "appropriated," before any record of the "find" was made

Mr. Jno Lindsay[b] states "the whole treasure, exclusive of a considerable number of coins which it is supposed were dispersed before they could be taken possession of, was reported as follows:—

About 6800 coins, weighing about	304	ounces Troy.
Sixteen ingots of silver, about 8¼oz. each	132	do.
Small bars of silver.	725½	do.
Manufactured articles of rude workmanship, consisting of rings, armlets, chains, etc.,	103½	do.
	1265	do."

Mr. Hawkins, the vice-president of the Numismatic Society, gives the following summary of the then known contents of the chest found at Cuerdale[c]:—

"The hoard consisted of about 975 ounces of silver in ingots, ornaments, etc., besides about 7000 coins of various descriptions, viz:—

	ENGLISH.	A.D.		A.D.
2	Æthelred, East Anglia .. about	860		
23	Ethelstan	870	to	890
2	Ciolwlf, Mercia	874		
867	Alfred	872		901
45	Eadward	901		925
1770	St. Eadmund	—		—
1	Archbishop Ceolnoth	830		870
59	Phlegmund	891		923
2	Sitric	—		—
	FRENCH.	**A.D.**		**A.D.**
34	Louis	814	to	928
727	Carolus	840		923
7	Carloman	879		884
197	Eudes, or Odo	888		898
11	Lambert	894		898
13	Berengarius	883		924

UNCERTAIN.[d]

304	Sigfred
486	Ebraice, or Evreux
23	Quentovici, or Quanage
1860	Cunnetti
1	Avaldus
315	Various

ORIENTAL .. 27

b View of the Coinage of the Heptarchy, 1842, p. 124.

c Numis. Chron. April, 1842.

d Mr. Hawkins considered these to be French.

The following description of these numismatic and historic treasures is from the pen of the distinguished Danish scholar and antiquary, J. J. A. Worsaae,[e]—

"Amongst the coins, besides a single Byzantine piece, were found several Arabic or Kufic, some of north Italy, about a thousand French, and two thousand eight hundred Anglo-Saxon pieces, of which only eight hundred were of Alfred the Great. But the chief mass, namely, three thousand pieces, consisted of peculiar coins, with the inscriptions 'Siefredus Rex,' 'Sievert Rex,' 'Cnut Rex,' 'Alfden Rex,' and 'Sitric Comes' (jarl); and which therefore, merely from their preponderating number, may be supposed to be the most common coins at that time, and in that part of north England where the treasure had been concealed. Cnut's coins were the most numerous, as they amounted to about two thousand pieces, of different dies, which proves a considerable and long continued coining.

"Not only are the names of Sitric (Sigtryg), Alfden (Halvdan), Cnut (Knud), Sievert (Sivard), and Siefred (Sigfred), visibly of Scandinavian origin, but they also appear in ancient chronicles as the names of mighty Scandinavian chiefs, who in the ninth and tenth centuries ravaged the western lands. Sitric Comes is certainly that Sitric Jarl, who fell in a battle in England about the year 900. Alfden is undoubtedly the same king 'Halfden,' who at the close of the ninth century so often harried South England,—where he even besieged London, till he fell in the battle of Wednesfield in 910. Cnut, whose name is found inscribed on the coins in such a manner that one letter stands on each of the four arms of a cross, while the inscription R. E X, (Rex) is inclosed between them, is probably he whom the Danes called 'Knud Dancast' (or the Dane's Joy), a son of the first Danish monarch Gorm the Old; as it is truly related of him that he perished in Vesterviking (or the Western lands). Sigfred must either have been the celebrated viking, for whose adventurous expedition, France, and its capital, Paris, in particular, had to pay dearly, or that Sigefert, or Sigfred, who, in the year 897, ravaged the English coasts with an army of Danes from Northumberland.

"The steady connection which the vikings in England maintained with France, affords a natural explanation why their coins were imitations both of contemporary English, or Anglo-Saxon, and of French coins. Thus on the reverse of Cnut's coins just mentioned, we sometimes find the inscription 'Elfred Rex,' which is purely Anglo-Saxon; and sometimes the particular mark for Carolus, or Charles (Karl), which otherwise is only found on the French Carlovingian coins.

"A very frequent inscription on the Scandinavian coins here alluded to, is 'Ebraice Civita,' or 'The city of York,' whose ancient name 'Eabhroig,' and in the barbarous Latin of the time 'Eboracum,' was converted into 'Ebraice.' On other contemporary coins struck at York, namely, on some of what is called St Peter's money, York is also called 'Ebraice' and 'Ebraicit.' For the Cuerdale coins, in order to express the name 'Ebraice,' coins of French Kings of the city of 'Ebroicas,' or Evreux, in Normandy, seem to have been particularly chosen as patterns; for, by a slight change of a few letters this Ebroicas could be converted in Ebraice, which was the easier process at a time when the art of stamping coins was not much practised. An additional proof that these coins were really minted by Scandinavian kings in Northumberland, and in the city of York, is, that none such have been found in any other part of England; whilst, on the contrary, one of Canute's coins, which have been so frequently mentioned, was dug up, together with English and French coins of the same kind as those found at Cuerdale, at Harkirke, near Crosby, also in Lancashire, and consequently at places whose names ending in *kirke* (church), and *by* (town), bear witness no less than that of Cuerdale (from *dal*, a valley), to the dominion of the Northmen in those parts.

"Should any doubt still exist that, so early as the ninth century, Danish-Norwegian kings and jarls minted a considerable number of coins in York, in imitation of contemporary Anglo-Saxon and French coins, it is at all events certain that the Northumbrian kings, Regnald, Anlaf or Olaf, and Erik, who resided in York during the first half of the tenth century, caused coins of their own to be minted there, and which agree exactly

e "Danes and Norwegians in England, etc." 1852, p. 49.

with the historical accounts. Regnald, who reigned from about 912 to 944, was a son of king Sigtryg, and brother to the Olaf before mentioned, who fought at the battle of Brunanborg, Erik († 951) is either king Erik Blodoxe, of Norway, or a son of king Harald Blaatand, of Denmark, who is said to have ruled in Northumberland about the same time.

"In the main points these coins are also imitations of the Anglo-Saxon, but are distinguished from them by various and very striking peculiarities which show them to have been coined both by Danes and Norwegians, and by conquerors"

The Rev. J. Clay, in one of his lectures on the Ribble, gives a calculation, by which he arrives at the opinion that the "hoard was worth within thirteen (Saxon) pounds, the whole yearly rental of South Lancashire, when William the Conqueror bestowed it upon Roger of Poictou"

It is difficult to determine when and by whom this immense treasure was deposited. It has been conjectured to have been the property of some Saxon or Danish monarch; the hidden wealth of some religious establishment, or powerful local chieftain; plunder taken in war, and even "the stock in trade of a Saxon silversmith." From the dates of the coins, which include many previously scarce specimens of Alfred's reign, and others totally new to collectors, Mr. Hawkins concluded that the treasure was deposited about the year 910, soon after the battle of Wodensfield, previously alluded to The Rev. J. Clay inclined to this opinion. He says:—

"That some of the contests involved in these campaigns, took place in Lancashire, may be inferred from what I have already mentioned—the erection, in 912, of a fort at Manchester, to curb the predatory propensities of the Northumbrian Danes. In old maps, the scenes of ancient battles are noted by a pair of crossed swords; and this mark appears on the map given by Whitaker, in his History of Whalley, on the site of the discovery at Cuerdale. It is a curious fact, also, that a tradition has existed—no one can tell how long—of a certain treasure being hidden, or lost, somewhere in Cuerdale; and my friend, Mr. B. F. Allen, has heard the old inhabitants of Walton declare, that a field, which he can yet point out, and within three quarters of a mile of the actual 'find,' was carefully turned over in the hope of making a discovery." [f]

The great and decisive victory, which placed the sceptre of all England in the hands of Athelstan, was gained at Brunanburh, in the year 934—7. Historians and topographers have hitherto failed to satisfactorily point out the true locality indicated by the Saxon word Brunanburh Mr. Thomas Baines, in his "Historical Notes on the Valley of the Mersey," has the following observations on this subject:—

"Sharon Turner, in his History of the Anglo-Saxons, states that great doubt exists as to the place where the battle was fought, but mentions Bromborough, in Cheshire, on the south bank of the Mersey, as a probable site. It is certainly much more likely than any other of the places which have been mentioned, namely Bamboro', in the present county of Northumberland; Bourne, in Lincolnshire, and Banbury, in Oxfordshire The expedition was fitted out at Dublin, was commanded by the Danish chief of that city; and the wreck of the army fled there after the fight which took place on the sea shore. These circumstances are all mentioned in the splendid poem in honour of this victory, which is preserved in the Saxon Chronicle, and which is probably the finest specimen of Anglo-Saxon poetry now in existence."

---

f Lecture on the Ribble

g This place is called Bromborough.

Sharon Turner's observations are as follows:—

"It is singular that the position of this famous battle is not ascertained. The Saxon song says it was at Brunanburh; Ethelwerd, a contemporary, names the place Brunandune; Simeon of Durham, Weondune or Ethrunnanwerch, or Brunnan byrge; Malmsbury, Brunsford; Ingulf says Brunford, in Northumbria. These, of course, imply the same place: but where was it? Camden thought it was at Ford, near Bromeridge, in Northumberland. Gibson mentions that in Cheshire there is a place called Brunburh. [g] I observe that the Villare mentions a Brunton in Northumberland."

It is termed "Bellum Brune," or the Battle of the Brune, in the *Brut y Tywysogion*, or the "Chronicle of the Princes of Wales," and in the *Annales Cambriæ*. Henry, of Huntingdon, calls the locality Brunesburh; and the name is variously written by Geffrei Gaimar, as Brunewerche, Brunswerce, and Brunewest. Dr. Giles, in his annotation of Ethelwerd's Chronicle, fixes Brunanburh at Brumby, in Lincolnshire, but assigns no reason for his preference of this site. The following is a translation of the song referred to:—

"A.D. 937.
Here Athelstan, king
Of earls, the Lord
Of heroes, the bracelet-giver,
And his brother eke,
Edmund etheling,
Life-long glory
In battle won,
With edges of swords,
Near Brunanburh.
The board-walls they clove,
They hewed the war-lindens,
Hamora lafan'
Offspring of Edward.
Such was their noble nature
From their ancestors,
That they in battle oft,
'Gainst every foe,
The land defended,
Hoards and homes.
The foe they crushed;
The Scottish people
And the shipmen
Fated fell.
The field 'dæniede'
With warriors' blood,
Since the sun, up
At morning tide,
Mighty planet,
Glided o'er grounds,
God's candle bright,
The eternal Lord's,
Till the noble creature
Sank to her settle.
There lay many a warrior,
By javelins strewed;—
Northern-man
Over shield shot;
So the Scots eke,
Weary war-sad.
West Saxons onwards
Throughout the day,
In numerous bands
Pursued the footsteps
Of the loathed nations.
They hewed the fugitives,
Behind, amain,
With swords mill-sharp.
Mercians refused not
The hard-hand play
To any heroes,
Who with Anlaf,
Over the ocean,
In the ship's bosom,
This land sought—
Fated to the fight.
Five kings lay
On the battle-stead.
Youthful kings
By swords in slumber laid.
So seven eke
Of Anlaf's earls.
Of the army countless:—
Shipmen and Scots.
There was made flee
The North-men's chieftain,
By need constrained,
To the ship's prow
With a little band.
The bark drove afloat—
The king departed—
On the fallow flood

[g] This place is called Bromborough.

His life he preserved.
So there eke the sage
Came by flight,
To his country, north,
Constantine—hoary warrior.
He had no cause to exult
In the communion of swords.
Here was his kindred band
Of friends o'erthrown—
On the folk-stead
In battle slain;
And his son he left
On the slaughter-place,
Mangled with wounds.
Young in the fight,
He had no cause to boast.
Hero grizzly-haired,
Of the bill-clashing,
The old deceiver;
Nor Anlaff, the moor,
With the remnant of their armies,
They had no cause to laugh,
That they in war's works
The better men were;
In the battle-stead,
At the conflict of banners—
Meeting of spears—
Concourse of men—
Traffic of weapons—
That they on the slaughter-field
With Edward's offspring played.
The Northmen departed
In their nailed barks;
Bloody relic of darts,
On roaring ocean,
O'er the deep water
DUBLIN *to seek* —
Again IRELAND,
Shamed in mind.
So too the brothers,
Both together,
King and etheling,
Their country sought—
West Saxon's land,
In the war exulting.
They left behind them
The corse to devour,
She sallowy kite—
And the swarthy raven
With horned nib—
And the dusky pada,
Erne white-tailed,
The corse to enjoy;
The greedy war-hawk—
And the grey beast,
Wolf of the wood.
Carnage greater has not been
In this island, ever yet,
Of people slain before this,
By edges of swords;
As books us say and old writers,
Since from the east hither
Angles and Saxons
Came to land, and
O'er the broad seas
Britain sought;
Mighty war-smiths
The Welsh o'ercame—
Earls most bold
This land obtained." [h]

Ethelwerd's Chronicle describes this celebrated struggle in the following terms:—

"A fierce battle was fought against the barbarians at Brunandune, wherefore that fight is called great even to the present day, then the barbarian tribes are defeated and domineer no longer; they are driven beyond the ocean, the Scots and Picts also bow the neck, the lands of Britain are consolidated together; on all sides is peace, and plenty of all things, nor ever did a fleet again come to land except in friendship with the English." [i]

If Mr. Baines's view be correct, (and in the conflicting and imperfect character of the evidence on the subject, it may at least be pronounced equally plausible with any other,) the deposit of the "Cuerdale coins" may have taken place about this time. It is true Anlaf was ruling chief in Dublin, and that one of the wings of his army "was very numerous, and consisted of the disorderly Irish." [j] The coast of Lancashire being a

---

h Saxon Chronicle.

i The last date in Ethelwerd's Chronicle is 959

j Egil's Saga. These troops are likewise styled "irregular Irish, who always flew from point to point, nowhere steady, yet often injuring the unguarded."—See Sharon Turner's description of the battle.

part of the Danish province of Northumbria, was in every respect best adapted for the landing of this portion of the invading army. Yet the elder historians expressly state that Anlaf commenced the warfare by "entering the HUMBER with a fleet of 615 ships." It is possible, however, this may refer to the landing of the "*fleets of the warriors from Norway and the Baltic*," who joined in the expedition. The great battle did not take place *immediately* on the arrival of these piratical adventurers, for we are told, the governors whom Athelstan had left in Northumbria, were soon overpowered. "Gudrekir fell, and Alfgeirr fled to his sovereign with the tidings" [k] The Irish troops may therefore have landed on the coast of Lancashire, and afterwards joined their victorious *friends* from Scotland, Denmark, and Wales, before Athelstan appeared to check their progress. The English monarch appears to have negociated, at first, for the purpose of gaining time to collect sufficient force to attack the invaders.[l] Anlaf is said to have imitated the expedient of Alfred the Great, and entered the Saxon camp, in the disguise of a humble harper. Athelstan, being informed, after his departure, of the true character of the minstrel, removed his tent to another portion of the ground. In the evening the camp was surprised, and the Bishop of Sherborne, who had taken up the position vacated by the king, was killed in the onslaught.[m] A terrible struggle ensued, but the Saxons eventually triumphed [n] The next day,[o] Athelstan prepared for a general engagement. After a night's rest, a sanguinary struggle took place, the confederated invaders were utterly routed; Anlaf fled to his ships, and sailed for Dublin.

The small "find" of 35 coins of a *similar character* to those discovered at Cuerdale, made in 1611, at Hardkirke, on the property of Mr. Blundell, of Crosby, strengthens Mr Baines's position that the great battle may have been fought upon the west and not upon the east coast, or, at least, that Anlaf most probably embarked at some port in Lancashire, on his flight to Dublin, in 926

Amidst so much contradiction and uncertainty, an attempt to determine which of the many suggested places should be preferred, is a task both difficult and unsatisfactory. Another suggestion for the solution of this great topographical enigma may, therefore, be offered without much presumption. Mr Clay has shown that the site of the Cuerdale "find" is marked on the old map, as the *locality of a battle*. It is well known the Danish and Saxon warriors used the Roman roads in their military operations;

k Egil's Saga
l Egil's Saga
m William of Malmsbury, and Ingulf
n Egil
o Some writers say two days elapsed

and many of their conflicts occurred in their immediate vicinity It is probable enough, the Wyre being the best natural harbour on the coast of Lancashire, that Anlaf's Irish troops and a portion of the Danish rovers landed there, and committed some of the ravages, the memory of which tradition has perpetuated A struggle may have taken place at the "pass of the Ribble," at Walton. The site of the "find" is about a mile from the spot. The direct Roman road into Mercia, passes by Walton and Warrington into Cheshire. From these facts an important question naturally arises Are there any places on this line of road which answer to the Saxon Brunanburh? Yes: at least quite as nearly as any of the localities whose pretensions have hitherto been advanced. The Rev. T. Sibson, in his survey of the Roman road, says, Bamber Green (now called Bamber Bridge) is a corruption from Bam-berg, which signifies "War Town." The neighbouring village is called Brownedge. It is situated on a rising ground, and will represent Brunedune quite as well as Bromeridge! There is as great a probability that Bam-berg is a modernised rendering of Brunanburh as either Bamboro' or Bambury! Bromborough certainly retains the letter R in the first syllable, and may, perhaps, therefore, present the nearest approximation But Bromborough, being on the south side of the Mersey, *is not in Northumbria!* Banbury, in Oxfordshire, as well as Bourne and Brumby, in Lincolnshire, are disqualified for a similar reason. The place must be found somewhere north of the Humber and Mersey. Brownedge is not much more than a mile from Cuerdale. This may be the spot indicated by the crossed swords on the old map engraved in Dr. Whitaker's History of Whalley. Both Bamber Bridge and Brownedge are situated between Cuerden and Cuerdale. The two latter names are evidently Danish, and the two former Saxon.[p] The original burgh or fort, from which the Saxon name is taken, would most probably be situated upon the rising ground of Brownedge. Its commanding site is at present occupied by a Catholic chapel. The great Roman way passes immediately by it. Some outwork on this spot would be absolutely necessary to protect the Roman station, at Walton, from surprise on the south. Hence the probability of the Saxons naming the place Brunanburh, from which Bamberg and Brownedge may have been derived. The syllable an or en is often written in the old Saxon names of towns, though dropped in the modern orthography. Thus Axanminster, Bedanford, and Oxenford, are reduced to Axminster, Bedford, and Oxford.[q] Brunan in the Teutonic signifies "springs"

p Brownedge may possibly be a Norman corruption of Brunedge, the word *brun*, in the French, signifying *brown*

q See Dr Giles's annotations to Ethelwerd's Chronicle.

There are, however, rival localities even in Lancashire. On the Wyre, near the commencement of the Roman agger, or "*Danes Pad,*" in the immediate neighbourhood of the old "Portus Setantiorum," is a place named Bourne or Burn, written in the Domesday survey "Brune." This is the nearest etymological coincidence, and the locality answers well to the description of Brunanburh. Bourne Hall is situated upon a "dune" or hill, which commands a now artificially blocked up channel of the Wyre. Therefore Brunandune or Brunford would strictly apply to it. Edward Baines has, in his Domesday map of Lancashire, placed Brune upon the Ribble, as though it represented the Bryning of the present day. This is evidently a mistake. In the text it is named in order between *Rushale,* (Rossall) and *Torentun,* (Thornton) which identifies it with Bourne.[r]

Bourne is in the neighbourhood of Poulton, "near which town, according to tradition, a great number of bones were ploughed up in an adjoining field, about sixty years ago." [s] It is likewise said, that, being pronounced human, they were buried in the church yard, at Poulton.

Burnley, in Lancashire, is situated on the Brun or Burn. Anglo Saxon remains have been discovered at a place in the neighbourhood, called Saxifield, where tradition says a battle was fought at the time of the heptarchy, and a distinguished chieftain slain.[t] Large quantities of bones and some other confirmatory relics have been found on the spot. The situation of Burnley, in the interior of the country, is, however, detrimental to its claims to the site of the decisive battle of Brunanburh. Many expressions in the poem seem to imply that the final struggle took place near the sea shore.[u]

Not far from Rochdale, is a spot named "Kil-danes," near Bamford. This site is not much over two miles from a place called "Burnedge," or "Brunnidge." Kil-Danes may be a burial place of Scandinavian soldiers slain in battle. A sword belonging to a Danish warrior and other remains have been found here. The great Roman road, from York to Manchester, passes near the place, and a Saxon castle stood not far from the spot. The objection to Burnley, however, applies equally to Rochdale, both places being at some distance from the sea.

r Bryning-with-Kellamergh, near *Warton,* in the parish of Kirkham, is, however, described in a charter of the reign of John, as Brichscrach *Brunn* and Kelgmers*berg*. In the time of Henry III., it is described as Briniage.—See Baines's Lan. : vol. 4, p. 397.

s Thornber's History of Blackpool, 1844. t See Whitaker's Whalley, p. 322.

u Since the above was written Mr. T. T. Wilkinson, F.R.S.A., of Burnley, in a very able and elaborate paper, read before the Lancashire and Cheshire Historic Society, in December last, supports the claims of Saxifield, and brings forward a large number of local facts, which clearly demonstrate that the neighbourhood has been often fortified, and that some great battle has been fought upon the spot; perhaps the one in which Gudrekir fell. The term Saxifield, afterwards given to the place by the Danish settlers in Northumbria, would imply a Saxon location, probably the burial ground of Gudrekir and his followers. The objection mentioned in the text, however, still militates against the claim of Burnley, to the decisive struggle.

The treasure may have been deposited at Cuerdale, on the defeat of one of Athelstan's governors; and Anlaf's troops, unable to maintain their position, may have eventually succumbed to the army of the king, on the banks of the Wyre, or Ribble. It is evident more than one battle was fought during the short campaign. The similarity of the names of the places, and their near neighbourhood, may have caused the confusion of terms exhibited by the Saxon and other chroniclers. The song states that the Mercians "*throughout the day*," of the great fight, "in numerous bands, *pursued the footsteps* of the loathed nations," the rout was continued to the coast, for Anlaf himself is said to have been "made flee, *by need constrained, to the ship's prow*, with a little band. The bark drove afloat—the king departed—on the fallow flood his life he preserved." Athelstan's governor, who retreated on the landing of the invaders, and carried the news to the king, was named Alfgeirr. He fought at the battle of Brunanburh, and was defeated in Anlaf's midnight attack. According to Sharon Turner, he "fled from the field and eventually the country." There is nothing improbable in the conjecture that this governor may have lived at Cuerdale, and have buried the treasure on the landing of the Irish forces under Anlaf. His flight from the country will explain why the hoard was not recovered, the after difficulty of discovering the precise locality of its deposit, and the popular tradition on the subject. The present is, by no means, the first house erected on the site of Cuerdale Hall, as abundant remains of old foundations in the gardens testify. The song especially records that the Saxon warriors defended their "*hoards*" and their homes. Athelstan's presence in the neighbourhood of Preston, at the head of his army, is attested by stronger evidence than mere tradition. In the early part of the seventeenth century, lived one William Elston, who placed upon record the following interesting particulars relative to this monarch The township of Elston, in the parish of Preston, formerly written Ethelestan, is situated on the north bank of the Ribble a little above Cuerdale:—

"It was once told me by Mr Alexander Elston, who was uncle to my father and sonne to Raph Elston, my great grand-father, that the said Raph Elston had a deede or a coppie of a deede in the Saxon tongue, wherein it did appeare that *King Ethelstan lyinge in camp in this county upon occacon of warres*, gave the land of Etheleston vnto one to whom himself was Belsyre." [v]

None of the localities, whose pretensions have hitherto been advanced, exhibit so many concurrent incidents. The Cuerdale "find" included many foreign coins, a fact which strengthens the probability that it may have been deposited in the reign of Athelstan, on account of that monarch's friendly intercourse with the principal European powers. He was not

[v] Mundana Mutabilia, or Ethelestophylax. Harl. MS. 1827, folio 336.

only assisted at the battle of Brunanburh, by Rollo, the Scandinavian conqueror of Normandy, but by the roving vikingr, Thorolf and Egil, who were drawn to his standard by promises of high reward. Whatever site may eventually be preferred for the decisive battle of Brunanburh, there can be little doubt the Cuerdale treasure was deposited during some of the struggles between Athelstan and the sons of Sigtryg. As it contained no coins of Athelstan, the hoard may have belonged to some Scandinavian chieftain, probably Anlaf himself. The large proportion of Danish and foreign coins, included in the treasure is in favour of this supposition. Had Anlaf or any of his jarls buried the chest on their expulsion, in 926, it is highly probable some attempt to recover it would be made, during the invasion which succeeded The treasure, however, if Danish, was more probably deposited at Cuerdale, by the Scandinavian invaders, during the campaign which closed so disastrously for their cause at Brunanburh.

The opinion of a distinguished modern authority is conclusive against the deposit at Cuerdale taking place immediately after the battle of Wodensfield, in 910[w] Worsaae, the celebrated Danish antiquary, speaking of this "find" says: "To judge from the coins, which, with a few exceptions, were minted between the years 815 and 930, the treasure must have been buried in the first half of the tenth century, or almost a hundred years before the time of Canute the Great"

In the year 930, Athelstan granted the whole of Amounderness to the cathedral church at York, and the battle of Brunanburh was fought in 934[x] Thus, the date of the fight, and the previous authority of Athelstan in this part of Northumbria, exactly accord with Worsaae's interpretation of the dates of the coinage. Athelstan had "purchased" Amounderness; a fact which strengthens the probability of one his deputies residing in the neighbourhood.[y] The subject must, however, still be regarded as enveloped in doubt The most probable interpretations yet offered rest principally upon conjecture That some important events transpired in this part of Northumbria, during the Danish struggles, is, however,

---

w Sharon Turner gives the date of the battle 910, Ethelwerd's Chronicle says 909, the Anglo-Saxon Chronicle 911

x Sharon Turner Worsaae (page 34, Danes and Norwegians in England, etc) makes the date of this battle 937 Ethelwerd's Chronicle says 939. Turner mentions the circumstance that one version of the Saxon Chronicle (the MS, book 1) gives the date 937. Still he prefers the year 934.

y During the past year, (1856) a labourer, whilst making drains in the peat at Scotby, near Carlisle, turned up a large number of Saxon coins and several bars of silver They were principally of Edward the Elder and Athelstan. On some of the latter the monarch is styled "King of Britain." A Saxon weapon, like a "bill," was likewise found buried at a depth of six feet. The similarity of the "find," and the name, a Danish expression for the location of the Scotch, render it not improbable that the northern auxiliaries of Anlaf may have buried this treasure about the same period clearly attested by the loud voice of popular tradition. Besides which, numerous proofs exist of the occupation and ravages of the Northmen in the western portion of the kingdom of the Deiri. The Rev. W. Thornber says, "the name of 'Dane's pad,' given to the Roman agger which traverses the Fylde country, is, and ever will be, an everlasting memorial of their ravages and atrocities in this quarter."[z]

About one thousand coins of Canute or *Knut*, were found in 1811, near Lancaster It is generally believed that Canute the Great adopted severe measures in this county. The Fylde traditions may have reference to his acts. Dr. Whitaker states that in the interval between Athelstan's grant and the compilation of the Domesday survey, the church at York had relinquished all claim to the "lands in Amounderness," "owing, it is supposed, to the devastations of the Danes" having rendered them unprofitable. The property therefore escheated to the crown. Again, he says: "This" (Preston) "appears from very early times to have been a very considerable town, and seems to have flourished when Lancaster lay buried in the ashes of Danish ravage."

The Rev. J. Davies likewise testifies, from evidence furnished by the local nomenclature, to the occupation of Lancashire, and especially the valley of the Ribble and the Fylde country, by the Scandinavian people. He says:—

"The track of the Northmen, as permanent landholders in the county, is in the north-east, near the point where the great highroad from Yorkshire leads to Colne, and thence across the county and along the whole of the west. In the north-east we find Balderstone, Osbaldestone, Elstone; and Ulverstone, in the west. Stone is used, I think, as the German stein in the middle ages, and denotes a house of stone or a castle. It is connected chiefly with Danish names, and implies that the Danes, like the later Normans, were obliged to protect themselves by building strongholds[a] Laund, which is the same as Lund, near Sephton, and is often found in the wild hilly country in the north-east part of the county, suggests dark pictures of the barbarous and cruel rites by which the Teutonic deities were propitiated It is the Dan lund, Old Norse lundr a grove, properly a consecrated grove, such as the Teutonic races, like the idolaters of the East, used to set apart as the scene of their "dark idolatry." The well-known Danish termination "by," is found along the whole of the west part of the county, from Kirkby to Nateby (not far from this place is Lund Hill), and thence to Hornby. Other instances are Roby, Westby, West Derby, (which has given its name to one of the hundreds,) Sowerby, Formby, Crosby, and Ribby.¶ Speke also, near Liverpool, is Scandinavian. It signifies a place where mast was obtained for fattening swine, and answers to the Saxon Bearo, and the Old German Parr; Old Norse spika (to feed, to fatten), spik (lard, bacon),

---

z History of Blackpool. In a paper read before the Lancashire and Cheshire Historic Society, on the "Evidences of Roman occupation in the Fylde district," the Rev W Thornber says "These pirates, no doubt from Wyre, made their inroads along its path," (the Roman agger) "and their cruelty and sojourn is so well remembered by tradition in the Fylde, that every remain of antiquity is pronounced Danish."

a Balderstone, Osbaldestone, Elstone, Alstone, are on the Ribble, above Cuerdale In the Fylde country there are local names of a similar character, such as Staining, Stana, etc., as well as other words of Scandinavian origin.

German speck. Another Norse word brecka (a gentle acclivity), is found in Norbreck, Warbreck, Swarbrick, Towbrick, and Kellbricks, all in or near the Fylde country. The appearance of so many names with the same ending, in one particular part, would suggest the idea of related colonists from some place or territory in Scandinavia, but I have not been able to find any place with a similar ending in any country of the north. The word does not now exist, I believe in Danish. [b] Other Scandinavian names are Ormesgill, near Furness, Ormskirk, Tarnsyke (Icelandic tiörn, a pool or lake), and Bearnshew, near Cliviger. The records of Domesday Book confirm the evidence of the local names We learn from them that in the north-east of the county, Ketel had four manors and eighteen carucates of land. In Hoogon (Lower Furness) Earl Tosti had four carucates. In Aldringham, Ernulf, and in Vlarestun, Turulf, had each six carucates. These are all Scandinavian names." [c]

After the decisive victory at Brunanburh, where the son of Constantine, together with several Danish and Welsh princes were slain, Athelstan reigned without opposition and devoted his attention to the arts of peace. This prince, as has been previously observed, granted the whole of Amounderness to the cathedral church of York. For the purpose of fostering industrious habits amongst his people, and encouraging commercial and maritime enterprise, Athelstan decreed that any merchant who should make three long sea voyages with his own manufactures, should be elevated to the rank of thane. He likewise conferred the title of thane upon any ceorl, who possessed five hides of land, a church, a kitchen, a bell-house, and a separate office in the king's hall.

From the time of Athelstan, Preston appears to have risen into a most important provincial town, although little is known respecting its actual condition during the succeeding one hundred and fifty years. It is, described however, in the Domesday survey, (about 1080), as the chief town of the hundred, with six carucates of taxable land. The same document further adds, that all the villages in Amounderness, together with three churches, belonged to Preston.

The lawless Northumbrian Danes again raised the standard of revolt on the accession of Edmund (941). They "invited Anlaf from Ireland," and elected him king. Sharon Turner says, on the authority of the Saxon Chronicle, that "he sailed to York and thence marched towards Mercia, to wrench the crown from the head of Edmund." There is something exceedingly mysterious and unsatisfactory in these voyages of Anlaf, from Dublin to Northumbria. Why he should sail round one half of the island of Britain, when the friendly coast was opposite to him, is utterly incomprehensible. The Danes were remarkable for the rapidity of their movements. Such a voyage would merely lose time, increase the danger, and

b The slope near the Poulton Railway Station, immediately commanding the old harbour at the mouth of the Skippon, at "Skippool," near the termination of the Roman agger, or "Danes Pad," is called The "Breck."

c Races of Lancashire.

forewarn the Saxon monarch. There is sufficient evidence, too, that the Lancashire coast was not only frequently devastated, but colonized by the northern adventurers. In this enterprise Anlaf was successful. Edmund agreed to divide the kingdom, and that "portion north of Watling-street" was assigned to the Danish chieftain, with the condition that the survivor should succeed his rival, and rule over all England. Anlaf, however, died in the following year. Edmund, afterwards, successfully curbed the Danish population, and terminated the "dangerous independence" of five cities, which were previously held by the Danes, on the northern frontiers of Mercia and East Anglia The Northmen were expelled, and a Saxon population placed in possession of these important strongholds. Edmund likewise conquered the Cumberland fastnesses, and conferred the territory upon Malcolm, King of Scotland The latter stipulated to do homage for it to the English monarch, and protect the north from the incursions of the Danes.

It required all the energies of Edred, the successor to Edmund, to keep in check the discontented Northumbrians. They submitted on his appearance with a large military force, but again revolted on the withdrawal of the army. On their re-conquest, the king appointed an English military government to watch their conduct, and enforce obedience He likewise fortified several important garrisons with Saxon troops. During these wars, the counties of York and Lancaster must have suffered severely, from the devastations of both armies.

The three succeeding reigns are chiefly remarkable from the efforts of Dunstan, abbot of Glastonbury, who introduced the Benedictine rule into nearly fifty monasteries to the south of the river Trent. The austerity of the new discipline, it would appear, however, did not meet with much sympathy from the secular clergy of the north. According to "Sim Dunelm," previous to the Norman invasion, there was not a single monk in all the Northumbrian territory.

With the view to check the incursion of the foreign Danes, Edgar established a powerful navy, which, by cruising in three distinct squadrons off different portions of the coast, for a long period overawed their piratical enemies. In the reign of Ethelred, surnamed the *Unready*, however, the Danish rovers renewed their ravages with considerable success. Internal dissention, domestic treason, and the vacillating policy of the king, alternating between a despicable cowardice, and a still more brutal ferocity, frustrated the efforts made for the defence of the country, and encouraged the relentless and implacable foe. The treason of Alfric, Duke of Mercia, saved the Danish fleet from capture or destruction. The pusillanimous monarch, and his degenerate nobility, sacrificed the honour and independence of the country, at the instigation of Siricius, archbishop of Canterbury. They purchased the forbearance of the pirates for the sum of ten thousand pounds! This conduct only served to induce fresh aggressions In 993, Sweyn, king of Denmark, and Olave, king of Norway, sailed up the Humber, compelled the Danish Northumbrians to join their standard, and laid waste the country on all sides. The English army sent to oppose the invaders was defeated, owing to the defection of their generals, three of whom were of Danish descent. *Peace* was again ignominiously purchased for the sum of sixteen thousand pounds! In a few years, the pirates re-appeared, and again triumphed The price of their forbearance had now risen to twenty-four thousand pounds! The Danish army, nevertheless, continued to move from place to place, plundering the inhabitants. The Anglo-Saxon Chronicle states, that all the expeditions fitted out to oppose them, "both by sea and land, effected nothing, except the people's distress and waste of money, and the emboldening of the foes." The country appears to have become thoroughly demoralized. The same authority states, that in the year 1000, "the king went into Cumberland, and ravaged it well nigh all And his ships went out about Chester, and should have come to meet him, but they were not able; then ravaged they Anglesea. And the hostile fleet" (the Danish) "went this summer to Richard's dominions" (Normandy) But they returned the following year, took several towns, plundered the country, and received from the king and his witan, "food, and twenty-four thousand pounds, on condition that they should cease from their evil doings"!! Ethelred afterwards married Emma, sister to Richard II., Duke of Normandy, a descendant from Rolla, the Danish adventurer, who despoiled the French monarch of this portion of his dominions. By this act of policy, he hoped to cement a firm alliance between the two nationalities, which had already amalgamated to some extent in various parts of the country And yet, with a cruelty and baseness worthy of such a poltroon, he, the following year, sought to increase his own security, by issuing orders for the secret assassination of all the Danes in his dominions on a given day. Hume says:—

"It is needless to repeat the accounts transmitted concerning the barbarity of this massacre; the rage of the populace, excited by so many injuries, sanctified by authority, and stimulated by example, distinguished not between innocence and guilt, spared neither sex nor age, and was not satiated without the torture, as well as death, of the unhappy victims."

From the number of Danish people located in Northumbria, the slaughter must have been immense. The now fertile fields of Lancashire, doubtless absorbed a fair proportion of the blood shed during the perpetration of this huge atrocity. The Saxon Chronicle attempts to justify the act, as necessary to the self preservation of the Saxon monarch It coolly says:—

"The King ordered all the Danish-men who were in England to be slain. This was done on St. Brice's mass-day; because it was made known to the king that they would treacherously bereave him of his life, and after that have his kingdom without any gain-saying."

Speedy vengeance followed. Sweyn, king of Denmark, again appeared off the coasts. For four years the country was pillaged. The commanders of the Saxon armies, being of Norman blood, or notorious traitors, played into the hands of the enemy. Thirty thousand pounds again purchased a hollow peace.

Considerable efforts were now made to place the country in a position of defence, and a fleet of about eight hundred ships covered the waters. Treason and internal discord, however, soon effected that which ought to have been the work of an enemy. A terrible period followed. "We hear," says Hume, "of nothing but the sacking and burning of towns, the devastation of the open country; the appearance of the enemy in every quarter of the kingdom" A new peace was ignominiously bought for forty thousand pounds! The tax, named the Danegeld, raised for the purpose of defending the country, was thus employed in her degradation. The Danes speedily renewed their incursions, and levied contributions in Kent. Ethelred fled with his wife to Normandy Sweyn, king of Denmark, died, however, shortly afterwards, but left, in his son Canute, a still more formidable enemy to the Saxon monarch. On the death of Ethelred, his son, Edmund Ironside, weakened by the desertion of his brother-in-law, Edric, and the general devastation of the country, was compelled to enter into a compromise with the Danish king, and divide the territory. Canute reigned in Northumbria, Mercia, and East Anglia. The southern portion of the country alone remained in the possession of the heir of Athelstan. In about a month afterwards, Edmund was murdered at the instigation of his brother-in-law, Edric, when the Danish monarch assumed the sovereignty of England.

The will of Wulfric Spott, Earl of Mercia, executed in 1004, contains the earliest known mention of the rivers Ribble and Mersey by their present names The land between these streams is bequeathed to his heir, subject to a small payment to the monastery at Burton-upon-Trent. Wulfric perished in a battle with the Danes, near Ipswich. On the final triumph of Canute, the earls of Mercia, the most powerful subjects in the country, were deprived of their estates. On the restoration of the Saxon line, a portion was returned, but the southern part of Lancashire was retained by the crown.

Though the commencement of Canute's reign was disgraced by many atrocities, the latter portion of his administration was marked by great judgment and moderation Canute marched through Lancashire into Cumberland, and placed Duncan, grandson of Malcolm, king of Scotland, in possession of the province, subject to the throne of England. Canute married Emma, daughter of the duke of Normandy, widow of Ethelred, and mother of Edward, called the Confessor, who ascended the throne on the demise of his half-brother, Hardicanute, in the year 1043, and thus restored the Saxon dynasty, to the great joy of the people. Edward married Editha, daughter of Earl Godwin, a powerful nobleman, who exercised a kind of vice-royalty over many of the southern provinces. Edward introduced many Normans to his court, and conferred the highest ecclesiastical offices upon these foreigners. This exasperated the powerful English earl, and led to much civil commotion. After the death of Godwin, his son Harold succeeded to the governments of Wessex, Sussex, Kent, and Essex, and to the office of steward of the royal household. The king having no issue, Harold began early to intrigue for the succession. On the death of Siward, duke of Northumberland, he caused his brother Tosti to be invested with the dukedom. Earl Tosti ruled in so brutal and tyrannical a manner, that the people, accustomed to the government of the laws, rose in rebellion against him Morcar, son of Leofric, was elected duke. In conjunction with his brother Edwin, he raised an army from the shires north of the Humber and Mersey. Harold was sent to reduce them to submission; but when he heard of the conduct of his relative, he applauded their resistance, and obtained not only from the king a pardon for past offences, but the confirmation of Morcar in the government of Northumbria. He afterwards married the sister of that nobleman, and by his interest procured the government of Mercia for her brother Edwin. The king regarded his nephew Edward, the son of his elder brother, as heir to the English throne; but this prince dying shortly after his arrival in London, and leaving only a very young and imbecile son, the monarch, who feared the power of Harold and hated the family of his wife, which had caused him so much unhappiness, willed his throne to William, duke of Normandy [d]

d "Nothing can be more fallacious than the idea that it" (the conquest) "was nothing more than a change of dynasty, resulting from a mere personal contest between two pretenders to an *hereditary* crown. The kingship of the Anglo-Saxons was *not* hereditary, nor had they any such thing as an hereditary office, municipal or political, legislative, executive, or judicial. * * The successor in the Anglo-Saxon kingship, or executive office of the state, was constantly selected or approved by the national council; and, as lord Lyttleton has candidly acknowledged in his introduction to the life of Henry II, not only did Harold possess the only right to the crown which the English nation then recognized, but the nation itself had clearly made the wisest selection it could, in choosing as the guardian of their independence in that age, the ablest and most generous spirited statesman and warrior that it then possessed"—Penny Cyclopædia · article, 'Boroughs of England.'

Harold, however, by the general wish of the people, mounted the throne His brother, earl Tosti, declared for the Norman, and, from motives of revenge, collected sixty vessels in the Flemish ports, joined Halfagar, king of Norway, who commanded a fleet of three hundred sail. They entered the Humber, landed their forces, and defeated the earls Morcar and Edwin, brothers-in-law to the king.

Harold, however, soon avenged his relatives. The English populace flocked to his standard with eagerness After a bloody engagement at Standford, the Norwegian army was totally routed, and Halfagar and Tosti were slain. The fleet fell into the hands of Harold; but, with a noble magnanimity, that monarch presented to prince Olave, son to the deceased king, twenty vessels, with permission to return to his country.

But the sun of Harold's fortune, though it rose in such splendour, was destined soon to set in blood The echoes which responded to his soldiers' shouts of victory, had scarcely ceased to vibrate on his ear, when news arrived of the landing of the duke of Normandy, at Pevensey, in Sussex Harold instantly set out to meet him; and after receiving some reinforcements, fought the memorable battle of Hastings, with skill, energy, and desperate valour, worthy of his name and race. He relinquished not his kingdom but with his life With Harold terminated the Saxon dynasty in England, after a continuance, with some interruption from the Danish invaders, for about six hundred years

Though the fine arts, and other luxuries and elegancies of life, received but little consideration from the rude Saxon conquerors of Britain, yet, notwithstanding the general turbulence of their manners, their monarchs encouraged manufactures and the mechanical arts, as well as trade and navigation. Mints were established in several parts of the country. Considerable progress appears to have been made in agriculture, and periodical markets and fairs were instituted. Mr. Kemble is of opinion that there was less land in cultivation during the reign of the first Charles, than there was at the time of the heptarchy. Society was divided into four distinct classes: men of birth, men of property, freemen, and serviles. Fraternities were established for commercial and personal protection, called guilds. Some of these had laws and objects closely resembling modern sick clubs or friendly societies. The power of the king was limited. The "Witenagemot," or council of "wise men," may be regarded as the original germ of the present parliamentary system of government. The absolutism of the Norman dynasty triumphed for a time, but the free spirit of the Anglo-Saxon people retained its vitality, and eventually restored the representative principle. Although at the time of the conquest, Christianity universally prevailed in Lancashire, yet the country is not without its relics of Anglo-Saxon, as well as Celtic and Scandinavian idolatry. The neighbourhood of Preston still retains the names of heathen places of worship, and some of the customs of later times have been traced to the sacred rites of the pagan inhabitants.

The Rev J. Davies says:—

"In the middle of the county we have Anglezark. The first part of the word is, without doubt, from the name of this [Angles] tribe, the second is found also in Grimsargh, Kellamargh, Mansargh, and Goosnargh, all names of places not far from Anglezark, and is probably the Old High German harac, Old Norse hörgr, Anglo-Saxon hearb, gen hearges, a heathen temple or altar. The Old Norse horga (aspretum editius) shows that it meant primarily a lofty grove, and thence a temple encircled with groves (according to Bede's description of a heathen temple, "fanum cum omnibus septis suis,") and, lastly, a temple. It answers therefore to the Danish lund (a sacred grove). We know from Tacitus, that all the Germanic races were wont to celebrate the rites of their dark and cruel worship in the gloomy shade of forests or groves, and the word teaches us, as Wednesbough (Wodensfield), Satterthwaite (Sætere) and Lund, that the Angles were worshippers of the old Teutonic deities, when they took possession of Lancashire. The name was probably given by the Angles themselves, and if so, it indicates that the Anglian speech approached, in some words, to the high German form."

Lingering remnants of the ancient superstitions have been found in the Fylde country by the Rev. W. Thornber. He says.—

"The conjoint worship of the sun and moon, the Samen and Sama, husband and wife of nature, has been from these early times so firmly implanted that ages have not uprooted it. Christianity has not banished it. So prevalent was it in the years 960 and 1102, that it was forbidden in the 16th canon, promulgated in the reign of Edgar, and in those of A. Anslem. The Saxons were guilty of it Nay, in my youth, on Halloween, under the name of Teanla fires, I have seen the hills throughout the country illuminated with sacred flames, and I can point out many a cairn of fire-broken stones,—the high places of the votaries of Bel,—where his rites have been performed on the borders of the Ribble age after age. Nor at this day are these mysteries silenced, with a burning wisp of straw at the point of a fork on Sama's festival, at the eve of All-hallows, the farmer in some districts of the Fylde encircles his field to protect the coming crop from noxious weeds, the tare and darnel, the old wife refuses to sit the eggs under her crackling hen after sunset; the ignorant boy sits astride a stile, as he looks at the new moon, the bride walks not widdershins to church on her nuptial morn; and if the aged parent addresses not the young pair in the words of Hanno, the Carthagenian, in the Pœnula of Plautus, "O that the good Bel-Samen may favour them," or, like the Irish peasant, "The blessing of Sama and Bel go with you," still, we have often heard the benediction, "May the sun shine bright upon you," in accordance with the old adage,

Blest the corpse the rain fell on,
Blest the bride on whom th' sun shone."

The term Anglo-Saxon is generally applied to the inhabitants of England at the period of the conquest The population, however, presented a very mixed character, and included many Celtic people, especially in Cornwall and Cumberland The Danes, Norwegians, and other Scandinavian tribes, formed likewise a large portion of the inhabitants of the northern and eastern counties. The "Englishman" of the present day results from the fusion of these original elements. Even the Saxon royal family was, before the conquest, united with the Danish. The mother of Edmund Ironside was of Scandinavian blood. Worsaae contends, and with reason, that to the Danish people and customs, the modern Britons are indebted for some of their most cherished institutions, and amongst the rest for that great bulwark to the liberty of the subject—trial by jury.

Historians are much divided in opinion respecting the relative proportion of the different races composing the present population of Lancashire. It would appear that in many portions of the south-eastern and midland counties, the Saxon conquerors had almost exterminated, or reduced to serfdom, the ancient inhabitants. In the north and west, the mountain fastnesses, and the almost impassable morasses, afforded rude shelter and an inhospitable asylum. The Cumbrian mountains, the hills of Furness, the swamps of western Lancashire, ("the Country of the Waters") as well as Wales and Cornwall, doubtless furnished retreats for the braver Britons, who, though defeated in the open plain, spurned the yoke of the invaders. The remainder of the native inhabitants became slaves to their conquerors. Mr. Thomas Wright states, that the "Brigantes are believed to have been the original inhabitants of the island, who had been driven northward by successive invasions and settlements, and they appear to have been the least civilised tribe of South Britain; their wild independence was encouraged and protected by the nature of the country they inhabited." [e]

Mr. Thornber contends that "Amounderness, for many a century after the Saxon conquest, was included in the petty kingdom of Cumberland." Camden quotes a document in which Egfrid, king of Northumbria, confers upon St. Cuthbert, bishop of Landisfarne, the land of Carthmel, *and all the Britons in it* (et omnes Britanni cum ea)," as late as the two hundred and twenty-eighth year after the arrival of the Saxon conquerors. [f]

It is, indeed, not known with certainty, whether the northern portion, at least, of the county of Lancaster, was completely subjugated by the Saxons, until the reign of Edward the Elder, in 921. Many defections occurred even after his time, and re-conquest became necessary. Several authorities record that the northern part of Lancashire, including Furtherness or Furness, was inhabited by Britons at a late period of the Saxon domination. Palgrave, in his history of the Anglo-Saxons, says, "*from the Ribble*, in Lancashire, or thereabouts, up to the Clyde, there existed a dense population composed of Britons, who preserved their national language and customs, agreeing in all respects with the Welsh of the present day. So that even to the tenth century, the ancient Britons still inhabited the greater part of the western coast of the island, however much they had been compelled to yield to the political superiority of the Saxon invaders."

e The Celt, the Roman, and the Saxon, p 41.

f Britannia, vol. 3, p. 380.

In his map of England, showing the great earldoms in the reign of Edward the Confessor, the Ribble is made the boundary between the Cumbrian province, then held by a Scottish prince, and Leofric's earldom of Coventry. The boundary has been nearly retained to the present time, in the ecclesiastical division of the archdeaconries of Richmond and Chester. It is to this province Shakspere alludes in his Macbeth. Duncan confers the principality on his son Malcolm, which excites the jealousy of the "predestined" monarch:—

"The Prince of Cumberland! That is a step
On which I must fall down or else o'erleap,
For in my way it lies."

A return made to the king by the prior and convent of Carlisle, in the reign of Edward I., says, "That district was called Cumbria which is now included in the bishoprics of Carlisle, Glasgow, and Whitherne, together with the country lying between the bishopric of Carlisle and the river Duddon."

From these diversified facts, it is highly probable the southern boundary of the Cumbrian kingdom has varied at different periods. Mr. Hodgson Hinde says:—

"So long as the native chieftains were allowed to exercise a subordinate authority, the Northumbrian kings had no occasion to interfere with the internal government of the subject provinces. If the tribute was duly rendered they remained unmolested; if it was withheld, payment was enforced by arms; or, in extreme cases, the refractory state (to use a modern phrase) was 'annexed,' as we have seen in the instance of Elmet."

Mr. Thornber[g] states that he had frequently been "told by those who were reputed judges," that the Fylde country "manners, customs, and dialect, partook far more of the Welsh than the Saxon, and that this was more perceptible half a century ago than at present." He adds, "The pronunciation of the words—laughing, toffey, haughendo,[h] etc., the Shibboleth of the Fylde—always remind me of the deep gutturals of the Welsh, and the frequent use of a particular oath is, alas! too common to both people."

On the other hand, Dr Robson contends that there is "no real ground for the common belief that the inhabitants of Lancashire and Cheshire had been at anytime Welsh or Celtic; that in fact the Celtic tribes, at the earliest historic period, were confined to the western parts of the island; that the extent of their dominions may be traced by the Celtic names of places, both in Wales and Cornwall; and that the rest of England was occupied by a Teutonic race, as it is at the present time."[i]

---

g History of Blackpool, p 17.

h From ackendo, the "half-do," an obsolete measure, yet occasionally used for peas.

i Lan. and Ches. His. Soc. Papers, vol. 7, p. 99.

The Rev. J. Davies, after an elaborate exposition of the etymological evidence furnished by the local nomenclature, decides in favour of the still further mixed character of the population, resulting from succeeding invasion and colonization. He observes.—

"Before the Anglo-Saxon invasion, the county was inhabited by a Celtic population of the younger or Cambrian branch of the Celtic stock; and a considerable number of families, belonging to this race, remained on the soil after the Teutonic invaders had taken possession of it. * * * There is scarcely the slightest trace of the Norman baron in the local names of the county, and only a faint evidence of his race in the dialect. I am inclined to think that, upon the whole, no county in England felt the effects of the Norman conquest less than Lancashire The old records of the county give additional evidence of this fact. The names of the families recorded are almost universally pure Anglo-Saxon, with a slight sprinkling of Celtic There is a trace of the Norman in the south, but along the whole of the east and north of the county, the Saxon or Danish landholder seems to have held in peace the ancestral manor-house he had dwelt in before the conquest, and the haughty insolence of the Norman was comparatively unknown. We may infer, therefore, that the race whose genius and energy have swelled the resources of England to so great an extent, is not much indebted to Norman influences. It is chiefly of Anglian blood, with a considerable mixture of Saxon and Scandinavian, and blended, probably in an equal degree, with that of the Cambrian race." k

Mr. Thomas Wright contends strongly that "at the close of what is called the Roman period of the history of Britain, the remains of the original Celtic population were very small, and perhaps consisted chiefly or entirely of the peasantry who cultivated the land as serfs." Mr Wright suggests the probability, that the present Welsh are not chiefly descendants from the original Celtic population of Britain, but of Armorican adventurers, who, at the decline of the Roman power, invaded the western portion of the island, and simultaneously with the Teutonic tribes on the east and midland, acquired the ascendancy over the Britanni or Romanized Britons; whom he clearly demonstrates, by reference to the Notitia and inscriptions, found at various stations in this country, to have been composed of people from different parts of Europe, and even Asia, and Africa. In Lancashire and its neighbourhood, the following various races are mentioned as included in the "Roman" population of the district.—Nervii at Dictis, in Westmoreland, and at Alionis (Muncaster, in Cumberland); soldiers from Spain and Portugal at Magæ, in Yorkshire, etc.; Moors at Aballaba in the North, and another supposed African tribe at Arbeia, in Westmoreland. From inscriptions, it appears that Lingones from Belgium, Gauls, and Dacians occupied different stations in Cumberland There were Germans at Brougham; Thracians at Bowes, in Yorkshire, Sarmatians at Ribchester, and Frisians at Manchester Amongst the names of officers, on sepulchral remains, are, at Old Penrith, one from Asia Minor; at Old Carlisle, one from Africa, and another from Lower Pannonia. The

k Races of Lancashire a paper published in the Philological Journal.

tribune of the twentieth legion at Chester, was a native of Samosata, in Syria, and the tribune of a cohort, at Maryport, acknowledged Mauritania as the place of his birth.[1] Few women would accompany the Roman colonists, soldiers, or the auxiliaries into Britain. Hence it is but rational to conclude, that during the long period of the imperial dominion, numerous intermarriages with the native population would take place; and, consequently, the principal persons of substance and position, at the time of its decline, would represent, in blood, neither the Romans themselves nor the original Celtic population. The Englishman of the present day, is evidently a compound being, formed from multifarious elements. Like unto his language, almost every other country in the world has contributed to the aggregated stock. To this varied origin, perhaps, more than to any single element, however valuable in itself, may be attributed the strength, elasticity, and indomitable energy, which unquestionably characterises the present inhabitants of Britain; and which is locally exhibited in no more marked a degree than in the county of Lancaster.

---

1 Ethnology of South Britain, at the Period of the Extinction of the Roman Government in the Island, by Thos. Wright, Esq., M.A., F.S.A., etc.—His. Soc. Lan. and Ches. Trans. vol. viii. p. 148.

PART I.—HISTORICAL.

CHAPTER III.—FROM THE NORMAN CONQUEST TO THE ACCESSION OF JAMES I.

The County of Lancaster—Domesday Survey—Results of the Norman Conquest—Roger de Poictou, and Warmus and Abardus Bussell—Value of the Land—"Castle Hill," Penwortham. Discovery of Remains—The Earl of Chester and the Earl Ferrers—Theobald Walter—Charters—Henry Fitz Warren—Right of Pasturage on Fulwood moor—Walter de Preston slain by Robert de Hylton—The Grey Friars Franciscan Convent—The Magdalen Hospital—Ancient Military Outwork on the Maudlands—Edmund Crouchback, earl of Lancaster—Edward I. at Preston—Wars with the Scots—Bruce and Wallace—Plea against the king—Thomas, Earl of Lancaster—Preston nearly destroyed by Bruce—Adam de Banastre and Thomas Earl of Lancaster: Battle near Preston. Edward III at Preston—Henry, earl of Lancaster and Derby made Duke of Lancaster—Value of Property in Preston—John O'Gaunt—Bolingbroke's Rebellion—Wars of the Roses—Henry VI taken prisoner at Clitheroe—Lambert Simnel—Sir William Stanley—Henry VII. at Lathom and Knowsley—Henry VIII. Battle of Flodden Field—The Reformation—The "Pilgrimage of Grace"—Decay of Preston and other Lancashire Towns—Leland's visit to Preston—Levy of Troops—Religious Persecutions—The Spanish Armada—Camden's Description of Preston—Feud between Mr Hoghton, of Lea, and Langton, Baron of Newton and Walton—Condition of the People.

"It is remarkable," observes Mr. E. Baines, "that in the whole of the Saxon Chronicles, the term 'Lancashire' never once occurs, though the neighbouring counties in the kingdom of Northumbria are mentioned in those ancient annals several times. * * It is also remarkable that the name of Lancashire is not to be found in the Domesday book of William the Conqueror, though the manors and lands are described in that imperishable record, with the usual accuracy and precision." The northern portion of Lancashire, Westmoreland, and parts of Cumberland, are included in the Yorkshire survey. Those hundreds south of the Ribble, are described in the Cheshire division under the head "*Inter Ripa et Mersham.*" The remainder of the northern counties are omitted. The earliest recorded mention of Lancashire is in the Pipe Roll, in the Exchequer office, the date is about 1140, or the fifth year of the reign of Stephen. Mr. Baines says: "It is abundantly clear, that sheriffs were elected for this county upwards of a century before Henry III. ascended the throne of these realms."

Dr. Kuerden states that king Egbert divided England into counties, and, "from the river Duden to the river Mersey on the south, was styled Lancasterschyre;" but he mentions no Saxon writer as his authority.

Jno. Whitaker, by inductive reasoning, arrives at the conclusion that the "Sistuntian province was formed into the county of Lancaster about the year 680, and soon after the conquest of it by Egfrid." This is, however, unsupported by any positive evidence, and is extremely improbable. The circumstance that the Domesday survey gives the northern portion to Yorkshire, and describes the southern as land "between the Ribble and Mersey," necessitates the conclusion that the present Lancashire had not been consolidated into one county, at the period of the conquest. It would seem rather to have been a kind of "debateable ground," during the Saxon and Danish periods; portions of it being sometimes governed by independent princes, and sometimes by tributary chieftains, under the Northumbrian kings. The northern part was, unquestionably, at one time, included in the principality of Cumberland. The county appears to have been divided between the Northumbrian and Mercian earldoms, at the latter period of the Saxon *regime*. Hence its anomalous position at the time of the conquest.

The ecclesiastics of York, apparently, did not find their possessions "near Ribble, in Hasmundernesse," worth defence during the struggles which desolated the country. According to the Domesday survey, earl Tosti, brother of king Harold, owned the land in the neighbourhood of Preston, on the north of the Ribble, previous to the conquest. From the same document, it appears that the king held the lands in Leyland and Blackburn hundreds, south of the Ribble.

The following is a translation of the Domesday book, so far as it relates to Preston and its environs :—

"AGEMVNDRENESSE" (AMOUNDERNESS) *under* "*Evrvic-scire*" (YORKSHIRE). "In *Prestvne* (Preston) *Earl Tosti* had six carucates to be taxed.[a] These lands belong thereto; Estun (Ashton) two carucates; *Lea* (Lea) one carucate; *Saleuuic* (Salwick) one carucate; *Clistun* (Clifton) two carucates; *Neutune* (Newton) two carucates; *Frecheltun* (Freckleton) four carucates; *Rigby* (Ribby) six carucates.

Chicheham (KIRKHAM) four carucates; *Treueles* (Treales) two carucates; *Westbi* (WESTBY) two carucates; *Pluntun* (PLUMPTON) two carucates; *Widetun* (WEETON) three carucates; *Fres* (PREESE) two carucates; *Wartun* (WARTON) four carucates.

---

[a] A carucate, carve or plough land, was generally about one hundred acres. Eight oxgangs make a carucate. An oxgang or bovata, as much as a pair of oxen can keep in husbandry. An acre was forty perches in length, and four in breadth. A perch was twenty feet. A hyde of land was an uncertain quantity, generally about one hundred acres; but according to Kelham six carucates make a hyde in that part of Lancashire between the Ribble and the Mersey. J. Whitaker regards, on the authority of Bede, the hyde as a well known standard measure throughout the heptarchy, and that, according to Selden, it contained at the first two hundred and forty acres.

Lidun (LYTHAM) two carucates, *Meretun* (MARTON) six carucates; *Latun* (LAYTON) six carucates; *Stainınghe* (STANING) six carucates, *Carlentun* (CARLTON) four carucates, *Biscopham* (BISPHAM) eight carucates.

Rushale (ROSSALL) two carucates; *Brune* (BOURNE or BURN near Poulton) two carucates; *Torentun* (THORNTON) six carucates, *Poltun* (POULTON) two carucates; *Singletun* (SINGLETON) six carucates, *Greneholf* (GREENHALGH) three carucates.

Eglestun (ECCLESTON), four carucates; another *Eglestun* (ECCLESTON) two carucates; *Edelsuuic* (ELSWICK) three carucates, *Inscip* (INSKIP) two carucates; *Sorbi* (SOWERBY) one carucate; *Aschebi* (NATEBY) one carucate.

Michelescherche (St. MICHAELS) one carucate; *Catrehala* (CATTERALL) two carucates; *Clactune* (CLAUGHTON) two carucates, *Neuhuse* (NEWSHAM) one carucate; *Pluntun*; (PLUMPTON) five carucates.

Brocton (BROUGHTON) one carucate; *Witingheham* (WHITINGHAM) two carucates; *Bartun* (BARTON) three carucates, *Gusansarghe* (GOOSNARGH) one carucate; *Halctun* (HAIGHTON) one carucate.

Trelefelt (THRELFIELD) one carucate; *Watelei* (FULWOOD?) b one carucate; *Chipinden* (CHIPPING) three carucates, *Actun* (ALSTON) one carucate; *Fiscuic* (FISHWICK) one carucate; *Grimesarge* (GRIMSARGH) two carucates.

Ribelcastre (RIBCHESTER) two carucates; *Bileuurde* (BILLSBOROUGH) two carucates; *Suenesat* (SWAINSET) one carucate; *Fortune* (FORTON) one carucate; *Crimeles* (CRIMBLES) one carucate, *Cherestanc* (GARSTANG) six carucates, *Rodecliff* (RAWCLIFFE) two carucates, another *Rodeclif* (RAWCLIFFE) two carucates, a third *ditto*, three carucates; *Hameltune* (HAMBLETON) two carucates.

Stalmine (STALMINE) four carucates; *Pressouede* (PREESALL) six carucates; *Midehope* (MITHOPE or MIDHOPE) one carucate.

All these villages and three churches belong to *Prestune* (PRESTON); of these sixteen have few inhabitants, but how many inhabitants there may be it is not known. The rest are waste. *Roger de Poictou* had it." c

"In BLACHEBURNE HUNDRET," INSERTED UNDER "CESTRE-SCIRE" (Chester).
"*King Edward* held *Blacheburne* (BLACKBURN) There are two hides and two carucates of land. the church had two bovates of this land; and the church of St. Mary's had in *Whalley* two carucates of land, free from all custom. In the same manor there is a wood one mile in length and the same in breadth, and there was an aerie of hawks,— To this manor or hundred belonged twenty-eight freemen, holding five hides and a half and forty carucates of land for twenty-eight manors adjoining. There is a wood six miles long and four broad, and there were the above-said customs.

In the same hundred *King Edward* had *Hunnicot* (HUNCOTE) with two carucates of land, *Waletune* (WALTON) with two carucates of land, *Peniltune* (PENDLETON) half a hide. The whole manor, with the hundred, paid to the king for rent thirty-two pounds two shillings.

Roger de Poictou gave all this land to *Roger de Bush* and *Albert Greslet*, and there are as many men who have eleven carucates and a half; they allowed these to be exempt for three years, and therefore they are not rated."

"In LAILAND HUNDRET. *King Edward* held *Leyland*, where he had one hide and two carucates of land, a wood two miles long and one broad, and an aerie of hawks. To this manor belonged twelve carucates of land, which twelve freemen held as twelve manors. in these are six hides and eight carucates · there are woods six miles long, and

---

b Mr. Ed Baines gives Whalley as the modern representative of *Watelei*. This is evidently an error. Whalley is in Blackburn hundred. As Fulwood is not mentioned it is doubtless, relatively a modern name. The Lancashire Watling-Street crosses this township, and may at the time of the survey have given its name to the cleared land in its vicinity.

c The population of England and Wales at the time of the Conquest has been computed at two millions one hundred and fifty thousand.—Sir George Nicholls, History English Poor Law.

three and a quarenten broad. The men of this manor and of *Salford* did not work as customary for the king at the hall, nor did they reap in August; they only made one hedge in the wood: they were subject to fines for wounding and rape, and had all the other customs of the other superior manors. The whole of the manor of *Leyland*, with the hundred, rendered to the king nineteen pounds eighteen shillings and twopence. Of the land in this manor *Girard* holds one hide and a half, *Robert* three carucates, *Radulph* two carucates, *Roger* two carucates, *Walter* one carucate. There are four radmans, a priest, and fourteen villains, and six bordars, and two neatherds: between them they have eight carucates, wood three miles long and two miles broad, and four aeries of hawks. The whole is worth fifty shillings—part is waste land.

King Edward held *Peneverdant* (Penwortham), where there are two carucates of land, which rendered ten pence. There is now a castle there; and there are two carucates in the demesne, six burgesses, three radmans, eight villains, and four neatherds, between all they have four carucates; there is half a fishery, a wood, and aeries of hawks. As in the time of *king Edward*, it is valued at three pounds." [d]

The people of England did not, however, tamely submit to the yoke imposed by the Norman victor. Several fierce struggles took place in various parts of the country, and especially in the shires north of the Humber and Mersey. The city of York was burned to the ground. The conqueror displayed a ferocity almost unparalleled, especially towards the hardy northmen. So much did he dread their valour, and inherent love of freedom, that, in order to secure himself from further insurrections, he ordered large tracts of the country to be laid waste. Houses, cattle, furniture, and implements of husbandry were given to the flames; and the wretched inhabitants forced to fly from the country, or perish in the wilds and morasses. In some districts, it is said, neither spade nor plough was employed on the land for nine years afterwards. Sir James Mackintosh says:—

"It was a slow, not a sudden conquest. The successive contests in which the conqueror was engaged, ought not to be regarded as, on his part, measures to quell rebellion. They were a series of wars levied by a foreign prince against unconquered and unbending portions of the Saxon people. Their resistance was not a flame casually lighted up by the oppression of rulers: it was the defensive warfare of a nation, who took up arms to preserve, not to recover, their independence. There are few examples of a people who have suffered more for national dignity and legitimate freedom."

Gilbert de Lacy, one of William's subordinate chiefs, penetrated the hills between Lancashire and Yorkshire, and seized upon the hundred of Blackburn. To secure his conquest, an old tradition relates that he expelled all the native proprietors from Blackburn, Rochdale, and the neighbourhood, and established his feudal authority. Previously, the tradition asserts, all the proprietors were equal to each other, and free from the domination of a superior chieftain.[e]

The remaining portion of Lancashire was not easily subdued. So great was the reputation of the Lancashire and Cheshire warriors, and the

---

d It has been computed that the Saxon pound equalled, in relative value, one hundred and ten pounds of the money of the present day.

e Dugdale's Monas. Anglic., p. 792.

dangers of the march, amongst the Setantian estuaries and morasses, that many of William's bravest soldiers flatly refused to enter upon the perilous expedition. Some disease, peculiar to the country, which had, in the preceding year, made sad havoc amongst the Norman troops, attacked their more hardy allies from Brittany and other places, and this increased the terror. William, however, hesitated not. He crossed the mountains by passes previously regarded as impracticable for horses, and appeared before Chester This city was the last in England to submit to the conqueror. It may be presumed, after its capture, that Lancashire yielded without a serious struggle.[f]

From the Domesday survey, which was made about ten years subsequently to the perpetration of this barbarity, it would appear that the western portion of the Northumbrian province (Lancashire) was more leniently dealt with than the eastern (Yorkshire). And yet, the concluding paragraph in the survey of Amounderness, would seem to indicate that even the most favoured had suffered considerably. "Sixteen villages have few inhabitants—how many is not known—the rest are waste."! The three churches mentioned were situated at Preston, Kirkham, and St. Michaels.

The conqueror, under one pretence or another, confiscated the lands of the greater portion of the Saxon nobility and gentry, and bestowed large tracts, together with the "beautiful women," and especially the Saxon heiresses, upon his military leaders; who, in their turn, provided for their inferior followers[g] These lands were held upon feudal tenures; a principle, to some extent, adopted by the Saxon rulers, but more completely developed under the Norman domination. William subjected the lands held by the church, and which were supposed to amount to nearly one third of the kingdom, to similar conditions In this division of the conquered territory, the "Honour of Lancaster" fell to the share of Roger de Poictou, son of Roger de Montgomery, earl of Arundel and Shrewsbury. But owing to his defection, the honour was forfeited previously to the Domesday survey. It was, however, restored to him in the following reign. His participation in an insurrectionary movement at Tewkesbury, compromised him once more, when the "Honour of Lancaster" was transferred to Stephen, afterwards king of England.[h] Roger de Poictou

---

f Order. Vital. Hist. ecclesiat. lib. iv, apud script. rer normann., p. 515

g Dugdale, Monast Anglic

h "Honors were hereditable before the Conquest by earls and barons, and for the most part to such as were of the blood royal, hence the honor of Lancaster had been possessed successively by earls Tosti and Morcar. By the Norman law honors became a feudal patrimony of any of the high barons, and generally adjoined to the principal seat of the baron. The great baron of Lancashire, Roger de Poictou, ranked amongst the Capitales Barones, holding immediately from the crown. The barons who held under him were called Barones Comitatus, (barons of the county) and held free courts for

held three hundred and ninety-eight manors under the crown; the whole of which were confiscated.

Amongst the "barones comitatus," mentioned in Kenion's manuscripts, as holding lands under Roger de Poictou, in Lancashire, are "Ilbert Lacy, baron of Clidero," and Warinus Bussell, baron of Penwortham and Weeton. The same authority states that to the barony of Weeton (between the Wyre and Ribble) was, "temp W. Rufus, an appendant to the barony of Penwortham, and bestowed upon Abardus Bussell, brother of Warinus Bussell, and continued in the renowned noble family of Theobaldus Pincerna," (Theobald Walters) "from whom proceeded the duke of Ormond"

The great difference in the value of landed property, at the period of the conquest, and in the present age of commercial and manufacturing activity, is thus forcibly illustrated by Mr. E Baines.—

"The contrast between the nature of landed possessions in this district, in the time when the dane-geld tax was enforced, in 1086, and the time when the property tax existed, is most striking, in the former, all the lands between Mersey and Ribble were valued at £120,—in the latter at £2,569,761 Allowing for the difference in the value of money, at the two periods, the statement will stand thus —

Annual value in 1086, multiplied by 110 . .	.....£ 13,200
Ditto in 1814, ...	. . 2,569,761
Increased value...	. . .. £2,556,561"

Notwithstanding this marvellous increase, so great has been the growth of manufacturing and commercial enterprise, "between the Mersey and the Ribble," during the succeeding forty years, that even the enormous sum of upwards of two and a half millions sterling falls far short of the present value According to the assessment made in 1841, "for the more easy collecting and levying of the county rates," the aggregate value of the hundreds of Salford, West Derby, and Leyland, was £5,525,626. A parliamentary return issued in 1856, shows that the total assessment for the county rate of Lancashire, is £6,909,656, being the highest of all the counties in the kingdom, with the exception of Middlesex, which is £8,427,336

Roger de Poictou, during the period he held chief sway in Lancashire,

---

pleas and complaints, except those belonging to the earl's sword. The ancient barons in their lordships or baronies, took cognizance of litigations and robberies, and employed the privileges which are called sac, soc, tol, theam, infangthef, outfangthef, ferias et marketas. *Soc* was the power of administering justice; *sac* of hearing and determining causes and disputes without the power of levying forfeitures or fines, *tol* an acquittance from payment of duties and tolls in every part of the kingdom; *theam*, a royalty granted over their villain tenants, as well as over their wives, and children, and goods, to dispose of them at pleasure Spelman calls it a right of trying their bondmen and serfs. *Ingfangthef* was the privilege of trying thieves taken within their lordship; *outfangthef*, a royalty granted by the king, with power to try and punish a thief dwelling out of the baron's liberty or fee, for a theft committed out of his jurisdiction, if he be taken within it. The distinction between an honor and a manor consists principally in the much greater extent of the former."—E Baines His Lan.

erected the castles of Lancaster and Liverpool, and other important *points d'appui*, for the more effectual defence of his possessions It appears from the Domesday survey, that there existed a castle likewise at Penwortham. The site still retains the name of "Castle Hill." Kenion's manuscript says: "On that famous estuary of Ribble, at Penwortham, where remained an ancient castle from the time of the Saxons, here was placed the barony given to Warinus Bussell, who had this place bestowed upon him, temp. William the Conqueror, though it had then no baron Leyland and a great part of Amounderness did anciently belong to the Bussells." Dr. Kuerden, nearly two centuries ago, says.—

"Over against the marsh belonging to this Burrough, under the opposit and high banks at Penwortham, a safe harbour from the western storms, over which was placed a small castle or fort, probably there placed to defend the same, or for the greater preservation of the Burrough of Preston, being placed upon the south bank adjacent to the bondary of their franchises. And it is manifest, by William the Conqueror's grand survey, that such a Castle there placed was then in being, though in later time it hath been demolished, and in the place thereof only a Titular Castle-hill remaining"

Mr Jno Taylor, in a note to the above passage, intimates that tradition asserts the locality to have "anciently been the site of a chapel that was sunk by an earthquake." He considers, however, the more probable conjecture to be, "that it was the outward defence of a watch tower, or a dun, or burg; * * * or the site of a Roman military post"[1] Mr. Taylor describes Castle-hill as "a remarkable mound, surrounded by a fosse or moat, thirty-nine yards square, measured in the centre of the moat, and having the sides facing the four cardinal points" This includes the entire hill A channel of the Ribble, formerly navigable, but now blocked up by the operation of artificial "cauls," or "jetties," defended the hill on the east and north. A deep lane now skirts the eastern boundary; and a fosse yet remains, which divides the mound from the neighbouring church-yard, on the south.

Saxon castles must not be confounded with those erected by the Norman kings or barons. The latter were large and massive structures of stone; but the former do not appear to have been capable of much defence, Dugdale says:—

"In those days (in the Saxon time I mean) were very few such defensible places as we now call castles, that being a French name; so that though the English were a bold and warlike people, yet for want of the like strongholds, they were much less able to resist their enemies.[2]

The discovery of the Roman station at Walton giving additional archæological interest to the neighbourhood, the members of the Lancashire and Cheshire Historic Society selected Preston as the *locale* for their annual

---

1 See Taylor's Brief Description of the Burrough and Town of Preston, page 50 Pub. in 1818.

2 History of Warwickshire.

excursion. They accordingly visited the town in June last, (1856). An influential committee undertook to prepare for their reception, and a temporary museum of interesting local antiquities was formed, at the Institution, Avenham. In addition to an inspection of the site at Walton, it was deemed desirable that excavations should be made in the "Castle hill," Penwortham. The necessary permission having been obtained, workmen were employed on the day previous to the visit, in cutting trenches across the crown of the hill, and in opening various portions of the mound. Remains so interesting, and, at the same time, apparently so irreconcileable, were obtained, that the committee continued the excavations during the remainder of the week.

The following description of the locality and illustrations of the objects discovered, are from the author's drawings and memoranda made at the time:—The mound at Penwortham, denominated "Castle Hill" is situated on the "neb" of a promontory of the table land which rises from about fifty to nearly a hundred feet above the flat alluvial soil of the valley of the Ribble. Though, unquestionably, a portion of the natural elevation, yet it exhibits so distinctly on its surface marks of artificial *form*, that many parties regarded the entire bulk as a *tumulus* or mound of moved earth. It may properly be said to consist of three distinct hills, rising one upon the other. On ascending the lower and of course larger one, at the point of the promontory, a level *plateau* of considerable extent is reached. This is from thirty or forty feet above the surface of the valley. At the further end of this level, a second hill, slightly conical in form, rises nearly twenty feet higher. This is again capped by a smaller mound, of a somewhat irregular shape, about twelve or fifteen feet in height. The whole appears to rise about sixty or seventy feet above the valley. On what had originally been the surface of the second hill, the remains were found. Fig. 4, plate 6, exhibits the profile of the two upper mounds. E indicates the level of the first or larger *plateau*. The hill is separated from the church yard by a ditch (F), which appears to be in part, if not entirely, of artificial construction. The upper mound, from external observation, seems to have been formed by earth removed from this ditch and the sides of the second hill, as it is higher than the neighbouring church yard, on the level table land. In this respect it somewhat resembles the "pike," at Rivington, except that the latter is not cut away from the main hill, by either artificial fosse or natural indentation.

The shaded portion of fig. 4, plate VI, represents a profile of the principal excavations. Fig. 5 is a horizontal or ground plan of the same. The lesser cuttings it is unnecessary to describe. At B and C, the remains were about twelve feet from the surface. At A the distance was about

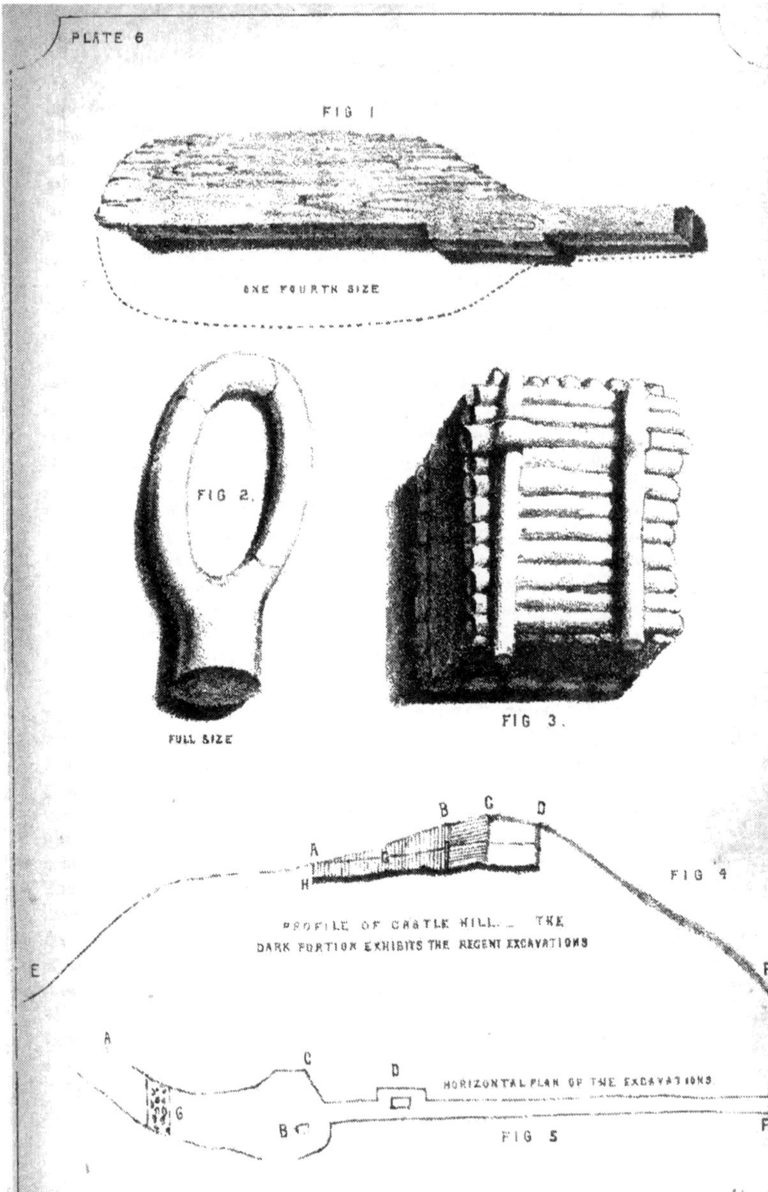

REMAINS FOUND IN THE CASTLE HILL

five feet. The pavement on which they rested continued nearly level from A to B; but from B to C it inclined upwards a little, and was somewhat disturbed and intermixed with clay and the superincumbent *debris*. This portion of the pavement was about a foot higher than that from A to B As a fragment of an upright post was found at B, the more elevated part may have been the flooring of an inner chamber, or perhaps a kind of raised platform or dais A shaft was sunk in the shallow trench at D, to the level of the pavement The result arrived at was, that it would be unnecessary to excavate further in that direction. A beam of timber and other remains were, however, found at the bottom of this cutting. The distance from A to D is about sixteen or seventeen yards The excavation, on the lower level at the widest part, was about four yards in breadth. A transverse section was not made, consequently the extent of the pavement from east to west has not been ascertained. It is probably not more than twenty nor less than sixteen yards. In the thickest portion, including the boulders, the stratum of remains measured two feet six inches in depth (H). It was covered by a layer of quicksand, which was separated from the earth above, by an irregular thin *lamina* of darker matter Over this was a layer of common red sand; then a stratum of clay, covered by a thin black *lamina* of vegetable mould (G.) This was about five feet above the surface of the lower remains. This *lamina* appeared to continue in nearly a horizontal line through the centre of the mound. In the deep cutting it was about seven feet from the surface, but at G not more than two feet. Here the excavators cut through a pavement about two yards in breadth (G). Above the upper "old surface," as it was termed, the soil was composed of sand, clay, and vegetable mould, and was not regularly stratified like that beneath it; though it presented no *positive* indications of having been heaped upon the hill by the action of spade and barrow. This peculiarity in the soil caused much discussion; the position of the remains necessitating that the superincumbent earth, *must* have been placed over them by some process or other. The notion that a cave had been originally scooped out of the hill, and afterwards destroyed by the falling of the upper earth, met with some favour for a short time; but this conjecture is directly opposed to many of the facts. It is infinitely more probable that the mound has been raised at different times, and that the regular stratification is the result of a particular kind of earth having, at each period, been carried up in baskets or panniers. This theory is not, however, without its difficulties as will be presently shown.

The remains, themselves, consist, in the first place, of the relics of a human habitation, covering a superficial area of perhaps not less than two hundred and fifty yards This habitation has been paved with a regular layer of boulders, and afterwards strewed with flags, weeds, and other vegetable matter. Several beams of timber lay upon this mass. The whole was covered with what appeared to have formed a roof, constructed of "wattles and thatch." A section of this mass, which, from being blackened by decomposition, and pressed by the earth above, resembled the contents of a peat-bog, is represented by fig. 3, plate VI. The hazel bark of the "watling" was, in many places, in excellent preservation. The twigs were generally placed parallel to each other, with an under layer at right angles, and a stronger branch occasionally interlacing, to render the mass compact. In some cases the vegetation was well preserved. Stems, leaves, and seeds, of the common dock were interspersed among the mass, as well as many blackened hazel nuts. This vegetable compost contained a large quantity of bones. They were generally broken, and pertained principally to the wild boar, deer, ox, and some smaller animals. Jaw-bones of the boar were rather numerous, and some loose tusks were picked up. They appear to be the refuse of the dinner table, thrown upon the floor, and afterwards covered with successive layers of the vegetable substitute for a carpet This filthy practice remained not uncommon till a much later period of English history than most people imagine.[k]

One large oaken beam is broken at the thinner end, where it shows the remains of a circular perforation A precisely similar beam was discovered *upright*, on the spot marked B, on figs. 4 and 5, plate VI. The thicker

---

k "Domestic cleanliness, in the reign of Queen Mary, was by no means an English characteristic. When a room was out of order, the floor was neither swept nor washed, but received a fresh strewing of green rushes, just like the littering of a farm yard, when it is newly spread with straw, for the accommodation of the cows or pigs, and the old surface remains a festering mass beneath. Thus, layer of rushes accumulated over layer, covering up bones, fragments from the wasteful dining table, and other abominations On occasion of dancing, all this litter was disturbed by a circle being swept in the midst of the hall; the stone floor was thus clear of incumbrances, while the extra littering was heaped up all round. This custom explains an expression used by Shakspere, and the early dramatists and chroniclers, of 'A hall! a hall!' when persons wished to dance. Such was the call by which domestics understood they were to sweep the dancing ring in the hall How noxious the vapours of the newly disturbed compost must have been to persons, warm with dancing, may be supposed * * * The nobles were not a whit cleaner than the country gentry; but as they usually were possessed of several seats, they indulged in the luxury of removing from one to another when the insects, cherished by their dirty customs, became inconvenient. These progresses they elegantly termed 'going to sweeten' "—Agnes Strickland's Queens of England, vol. 5, p. 424.

Erasmus, speaking of the floors of the English houses, says, "they are usually made of clay, covered with rushes that grow in fens, these are so little disturbed, that the lower mass sometimes remains for twenty years together, and in it a collection of filth of every kind. Hence, upon a change of weather, a vapour is exhaled, most pernicious to the human body."—Letter to Dr. Francis.

According to Holinshead, the Spanish ambassadors, who came over with Philip, remarked that the English lived "in houses made of dirt and sticks, but they fared therein as well as their monarch." With such atrociously filthy habits, it ceases to be a matter of surprise that the population of the country was periodically decimated by fevers and plagues.

end was embedded in the earth, amongst the pavement, and was in good preservation. It was about five feet in height The upper portion was much decayed, and had evidently been broken. The first mentioned log is about two and a half yards long, nearly eighteen inches broad, and four inches thick, at the stronger end. It appears to have been riven from the solid tree, and afterwards squared a little with an axe. Remains of other beams of this character were likewise found. A somewhat different beam is "squared" on three sides, but the round surface of the original tree appears on the fourth. Two circular holes perforate this log. They are only about an inch and a half in diameter, and an inch and a quarter deep, and appear to be "peg-holes." This fragment is about four feet long. Others were found resembling it. Another, about eight feet in length, shows the marks of the axe, (which must have been small, and not unlike the form of the bronze celt, in plate I,) used in felling the tree, which still retained the whole of the bark This tree had been used as a stake. Its thickest end was about six inches in diameter. Fig. 1, plate VI, exhibits the form of one half of an oaken canoe paddle, found in a lesser cutting, outside the house, at a depth of six or seven feet, but on a level with the lower pavement. Fig. 2 is a singular wooden loop, formed from a hazel twig. A wooden peg or two, and many other pieces of timber were taken out of the excavation, which presented no additional peculiarities. A portion of the horn of a deer, split up the centre, and bearing marks of a sharp instrument, was likewise found, together with a large fragment of a madrepore, or coralline, said to be sometimes picked up on the coast. A small mussel shell or two were likewise taken from the mass of decaying vegetation.

Several iron articles were found beneath the bones and vegetable matter. These, after exposure to the atmosphere, assumed a beautiful blue colour, not unlike cobalt The old surface soil, in which the boulders were laid, was impregnated with matter of a similar character. This soil, on being first disturbed, was of a pale grey colour, permeated with small white spots. The spots turned to a rich blue after a few hours' exposure to the atmosphere. This stratum, which is only about six inches in thickness, covers the hard solid clay. Mr. Trenham Reeks, of the Museum of Practical Geology, Jermyn-street, London, immediately stated, that the remains had been found amongst bones, and that the blue matter, termed "vivianite," was produced by the contact of phosphate of lime with the surface of the iron. Mr. Franks, of the British museum, informed the author, that iron remains are often well preserved amongst decayed vegetation, and exhibit a blue colour. Both causes may have operated in the present instance.

The metal articles are represented on plate VII There is some difficulty in determining to what period a portion of them belong. Fig. 1 has been pronounced to be a Roman padlock key, similar in character to some found lately at Chester-ford, in Essex, and described by the Hon. R. C. Neville, in a paper inserted in the "Archæological Journal," of March, 1856. It is of iron. Fig. 2 resembles much a similar article found at Settle, in Yorkshire, and figured in Mr. Roach Smith's "*Collectanea Antiqua.*" This is considered to be Roman. Three nails were found, very peculiar in form. Two of them are represented by figs. 4 and 5. Fig. 5 resembles some found in the Roman station at Walton.[l] The only bronze article is fig. 7. Figs. 3 and 6 are lead. The first is evidently a rude bead. A fragment of another larger perforated bead, formed of bone, was likewise picked up. These remains may be reconciled with the Saxon occupation of a Roman out-post. But the presence of the beautiful Norman, or late Saxon spur, fig. 8, is not quite so easily understood.[m] It was certainly thrown from the lowest stratum of remains, and was picked up and partially cleaned in the presence of the author, who immediately sketched it. As it was not observed, however, until thrown to the surface, a *possibility* remained that it might have fallen from the level of the black line G, plate VI, five feet higher, in which the other boulder pavement was found. The presence of the mysterious blue colour upon it, after exposure, however, militates seriously against this conjecture. Several large pieces of leather were likewise taken from the bottom of the excavation. They have formed portions of sandals or some other covering for the feet, as is attested by the forms of several pieces which resemble the sole of the foot. The leather is very thin, and is regularly punctured on the edge with holes, through which the threads have passed by which the "welt" was attached. One of these "welts" still partially adhered when discovered. As the form of the upper portion of these shoes or sandals is not discernible amongst the fragments, it is difficult to decide with certainty to what period they belong.

Many absurd speculations have been advanced, and some ingenious theories propounded, as to the probable history of this mound. None, however, are entirely satisfactory. Some parties contend that, as the Domesday book simply records that a castle existed at the period of the survey, the structure alluded to might have been erected by Roger de Poictou, during the period which elapsed from the conquest to the compilation of the record. The simple fact that the subterranean edifice possessed a "wattle and thatch" *roof*, as well as the form of the hill, and its strati-

l See fig. 5, plate III.

m Mr. Roach Smith and others, describe this spur as Norman. It is of a much more elegant form than any exhibited in the British Museum.

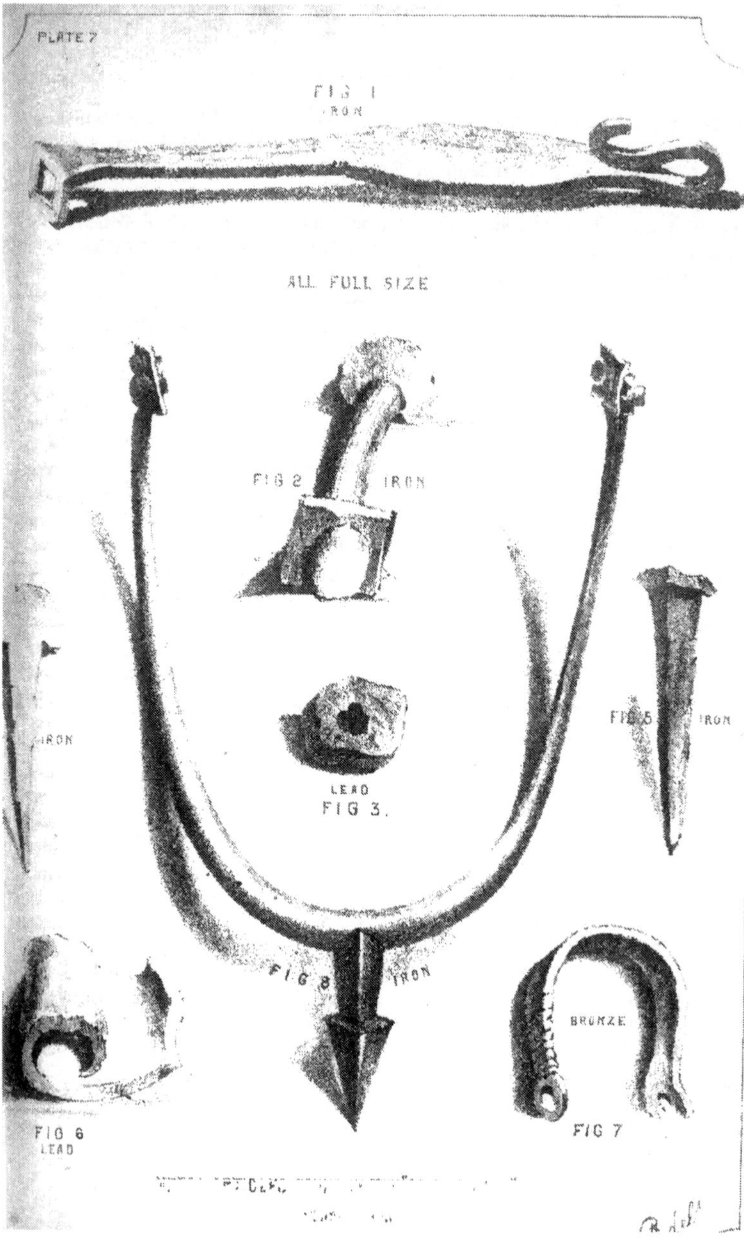
PLATE 7
FIG 1
IRON
ALL FULL SIZE
FIG 2
IRON
LEAD
FIG 3.
FIG 5
IRON
IRON
FIG 8
IRON
BRONZE
FIG 6
LEAD
FIG 7

fication, negatives the notion which was, for a time, rather popular, that the habitation had been scooped out of the hill and entered at its side. The remains likewise do not belong to a people who lived in caves. Mr. Robson, after some consideration, concluded that the building was Saxon, and that "it had been in its turn the royal residence." This, of course, only applies to the petty chief of the neighbourhood. It was the property of the Saxon king of England at the time of Edward the Confessor, and might be occasionally occupied by his representative; or, it may have belonged to some of the independent or tributary chiefs, who ruled the land before the complete annexation of the neighbouring territory by the Northumbrian monarchs. The large level space on the top of the first hill, may have been enclosed by a wooden stockade; hence, perhaps, the term "castle," of the Norman "Dom-boc."

If there ever existed any more important building near Castle-hill, the probability is, as no remains of stone foundations were discovered, that it stood on the site of the present church, and that the mound in question was merely used as a "keep," or out-work. From the Norman spur being found amongst the remains, it is possible that, on the building of the first church, the citadel may have been destroyed, and the mound raised to the level of the dark *lamina*, upon which was found the first or upper pavement. (G.) This may have been used as a beacon or look-out, in some of the early civil wars, and the second addition may have taken place at a later period. Against this assumption, however, there are many objections. The neighbouring tower of the church, if any, would have answered the purpose much better; and hence the difficulty in accounting for the expenditure of so much labour, for so inadequate a purpose. The first church, however, may, perhaps, have been without a tower. The present steeple was most probably, not erected earlier than the reign of Henry VII. The early history of the locality seems less obscure. If, as was previously probable, the Romans had a *specula* on the mound, it is not surprising that some remains of their period should be found amongst those of their successors. In the graves of the Saxon pagan kings, this incident is of frequent occurrence. Mr. Roach Smith says, in his report on the excavations on the site of the Roman castrum at Lymne: "A penny of Eadger, found at the depth of two feet, and also some *iron prick spurs*, suggest that the castrum may have been partially tenanted for some centuries after the Romans had abandoned it." The character of the habitation appears to agree well with the sort of residence occupied by an early Saxon chieftain. Bede, in his relation of the particulars of a miracle performed by a portion of the earth upon which the pious king Oswald died, describes the roof of a Saxon residence as made of "wattles and thatch." This is satisfactory enough. But by whom, and for what purpose, the superincumbent earth has been placed above the remains, is still enveloped in mystery. The subject will doubtless continue for some time an interesting theme for vulgar gossip, as well as antiquarian conjecture.

Perhaps the spur, which creates the greatest difficulty, may, after all, be of *Roman* construction. This is by no means improbable. The opinion of an eminent modern archæologist will countenance the supposition. Mr. Thomas Wright says :—

"Amongst the extensive Roman remains found in the camp at Hod Hill, already alluded to, *were found several spurs of iron*, which *resemble so closely the Norman prick-spurs, that they might be easily mistaken for them.* I suspect that many of the prick-spurs which have been found on or near Roman sites, and hastily judged to be Norman, are, especially when made of bronze, Roman. As far, however, as comparison has yet been made, the Roman and the Saxon spurs are shorter in the *stimulus* than those of the Normans." [n]

The spur found at Penwortham differs in some respects from any of the Norman specimens deposited in the British museum. It is much lighter and more elegant in form. The *stimulus* is not long, for spurs of this class. It is evidently the production of a refined and skilful people. It was unquestionably deposited amongst the soil in which the lower pavement was embedded, as portions still adhered to it at the time of its discovery. Mr. Wright likewise says that the Roman sandals found in England are of leather, of various sizes, and the soles are cut as in our modern right and left shoes." [o] Several of the pieces of leather exhumed at Penwortham are formed precisely in this manner, and they, in other respects, accord with the Roman character. From these facts, in conjunction with the evidence of the remains previously described, it seems probable that the wooden building may have been the structure occupied by the Romano-British soldiers, when the mound was used as a *specula*, or outpost, in connection with the station at Walton. It is infinitely more in accordance with the practice of the Saxon people, to suppose that the higher mound, or "earthen keep," was thrown up by them, when they erected their own stronghold. This appears to have been effected at two distinct periods. The Saxons preferred their keep near or upon the walls of their fortresses. The Normans, on the contrary, generally erected theirs considerably within the external walls. One authority says :—"The Saxons most probably adapted the Roman enclosures to their mode of defence, and it appears that they *often raised a mound on one side of the walls*, on which they erected a keep or citadel. [p] In Grose's Antiquities, a restoration of Dunnington Castle is given, on which is shown a "Saxon mount." Neither the period

n The Celt, the Roman, and the Saxon, p. 348. o Ibid—p. 331.

p Pen. Cyclop.; art, Castle.

when the Norman possessors destroyed the structure existing at the time of the Domesday survey, nor what amount of additional works they erected can now be ascertained. The castle most probably shared the fate of many others during the reign of Henry II. When that prince was duke of Normandy, it was stipulated in a treaty between him and king Stephen, in consequence of the licentious behaviour of some of the garrisons, that all castles built within a certain period should be demolished. Several were accordingly razed; and, on Henry's accession, many others were destroyed. A special license from the king was afterwards necessary to justify the erection of any such stronghold.[q] Had the castle at Penwortham existed much longer than this period, some further record of it must have transpired.

It is by no means improbable that the mound may have been used in Saxon and even Norman times, as a "Mote Hill," where the people assembled periodically, for judicial and other proceedings. The neighbouring promontory, on the west, still retains the name of "Hangsman's Hillock." Castle-hill and its contents bear some resemblance to the "Mote-hill," at Warrington, and the remains found therein. "Constable-hillock," on the banks of the Wyre, in Garstang parish, was used as late as the year 1816, for such purposes. In reference to the friborg, or constablewick, of Garstang, which consisted of eleven neighbouring townships, Mr. E. Baines says:—

"The adjournment of the court to the hillock is obviously the remnant of a custom far more ancient than the institution of the friborg itself. Public courts in the open air may at first have been caused by necessity, and, as Joh. Schildius conceives, continued from motives of religion, under the impression that the proceedings of open courts were immediately subject to the inspection of the Deity. * * * Dr. Hickes preserves the record of the proceedings of a shire mote, in a trial respecting lands, in the reign of Canute, which sat at Ægelnoth's stone, in Herefordshire. The memory of this custom is still retained in the names of several places; the wapentake of Seireke, in the West Riding of Yorkshire, is denominated from the oak under which the courts of that division were held. A German charter, so lately as the year 1248, is dated near the castle Haghen, by the oak commonly called Staleke. Where oaks were absent, other conspicuous natural objects were chosen to mark the place of meeting; the hundred of Appletree, in Derbyshire, took its name from some trees of that kind, the rendezvous of the wapentake; and in the wapentake of Barkstone Ash, in Yorkshire, which was occasioned by the courts held there, * * both stone and tree are obvious. A hillock was the natural substitute for the stone, and Spelman mentions eminences of ground, which, from the use made of them on these occasions, were called Parle Hills. It is not improbable, that the origin of the custom of choosing the constables of the Garstang friborg, by inscribing their names upon pieces of wood, is referable to the holy oak of a remote period."[r]

Mr. Baines mentions an "elevation" in the township of Carnforth, called "Moothaw," on which the "ancient Saxon courts were held."[s]

q Preface to Grose's Antiquities of England and Wales.

r His. Lan., vol. 4, p. 456. s His. Lan., vol. 4, p. 584.

Parlick Fell, near Chipping, is generally supposed to have received its name from the circumstance alluded to by Spelman. Penwortham is written in the Norman Domesday book, Peneverdant. This, most probably, has originated from the green hill, where the manor or other court was held. The formation of the ground is admirably adapted for such a purpose.

King Stephen, having hastily concluded a peace with the Welsh, advanced with his army to Carlisle, to oppose an invasion in favour of the claims of the empress Matilda, to the throne of England. It is, therefore, almost certain, that on this expedition he passed through Preston. In the reign of Stephen, Ranulf, fourth earl of Chester, possessed the lands between the Mersey and the Ribble. In the reign of Henry III., Ranulf de Blundeville, his grandson, received from the king a confirmation of his previous title to these lands, and was appointed, subject to the crown, chief lord of the whole county of Lancaster, with all its "forests, hays, homages, and other appurtenances." As this earl died without issue, his estate was divided amongst his four sisters and co-heiresses. His third sister married William, earl of Ferrers, sixth in descent from Robert de Ferrers, first earl of Derby. This lady's dower, amongst other possessions, consisted of the "manor of West Derby, and all earl Ranulf's lands between the Ribble and the Mersey." The yearly acknowledgment to the king, "as had been usual for lands lying between the rivers Ribble and Mersey," consisted of a "goshawk, or fifty shillings." The earl paid, likewise, fifty pounds for the relief of his wife's inheritance, and one hundred pounds, as a fine, for the misdemeanors of his bailiffs. He was appointed, in the eighth year of this reign, governor of the castle and honor of Lancaster. William, his son and heir, succeeded to the privileges of his father; but his grandson, Robert, earl of Derby, was deprived of his estates and title from his complicity with Simon de Montfort. When Edmund Crouchback, youngest son of Henry III., was created earl of Lancaster, these possessions were united to the honor of Lancaster.

Mr. E. Baines says:—

"The most ancient record after Domesday, is the 'Black Book of the Exchequer,' in which are contained the tenants and fees both 'de veteri feoffamento,' i.e. held in the reign of Henry I., or before; and 'de novo feoffamento,' in that of Henry II., or Stephen. From this document, it appears that Theobald Walter held Amoundernesse by the service of one knight, whence it results that the charter of 5 Richard I, is rather to be considered as a confirmation of a former grant than an original donation. Gilbert Filius Rembr (Gilbert Fitz-Reinfrid), baron of Kendal, in the same record is stated to hold four carucates of land in Preston, and two in Bertune, besides other lands in the hundred but not in the parish of Preston. * * * †

"In 5 Richard I., the king, to reward the services of Theobald Walter, granted to

† His. Lan., vol. 4, p. 297.

him the confirmation of the fee of the lordship of Preston, which, after the defection of Roger Poictou, he had received from the crown. In the sixth year of the same reign, Theobald was made sheriff of the county of Lancaster, and retained that office till the first year of the reign of king John. This baron contributed largely towards the redemption of king Richard I. His son, Theobald, married Maud, sister of Thomas à Becket, the canonized archbishop of Canterbury, and he assumed the official surname, upon receiving the appointment of *Butler* of Ireland, which office was abolished A.D. 1811, on payment of £216,000 to Walter, marquis of Ormonde, out of the public treasury.[u]

"Like many other distinguished men of his time, he" (Theobald Walter) "was a munificent founder of religious houses; and the great abbey of Arklow and Wolheny, and the priory or hospital of St. John the Baptist, at Nenagh, in Ireland, were indebted to him for their primary establishment. He likewise founded the abbey of Cockersand, to which he granted the whole hay of Pylin, in Amounderness, and he was also a liberal benefactor to the abbey of Furness."[v]

Richard I. conferred the earldom and honour of Lancaster upon his brother, the earl of Morton, afterwards king John.

There is some difficulty in determining the date of the ancient document known as the "Custumale of Preston," owing to its present imperfect condition. This deed recites "the liberties of Preston in Amundrenesse," and confers upon the burgesses a "Guild Merchant, with Hanse and other customs belonging to such guild." It appears pretty certain, however, to have been granted either in the reign of Henry I., or that of Henry II.[w]

Another charter was granted by Henry II., which conferred upon the inhabitants similar privileges, liberties, and free customs, as were then enjoyed by the burgesses of Newcastle-upon-Tyne.

King John confirmed these grants, and further accorded the privileges of "the whole toll of the wapentake hundred of Amounderness, and a free fair at Preston, at the Assumption of St. Mary, to last for eight days," together with "the right of pasturage in the forest which is called Fille Wode, and out of the forest itself so much" (wood) "as they shall want, towards building their town."[x]

Henry Fitz-Warren de Lancaster obtained from king John, a confirmation of his right to the "rents of Preston."[y] In the fourth year of this king's reign, letters patent of presentation to the church of Preston, directed to the archidiaconal officials of Richmond, were delivered to master Peter Russiniol.[z] On the death of this ecclesiastic, Henry III. presented the living to Henry, nephew to the bishop of Winchester.[a]

The priory of Lancaster, an appurtenance to the abbey of Sens, in Normandy, possessed the fishery and tithes of Preston. The abbot and Theobald Walter, in the reign of Richard I., disputed each other's pretensions

u His. Lan., vol. 4, p. 301. v His. Lan., vol. 4, p. 289.
w See Municipal History; chap. VI. of the present work.
x Rot. Chart. y Rot. Chart. z Rot. Lit. Pat.
a Testa de Neville, fo. 371, 401.

to the advowson of the churches of Preston and Poulton. The contest terminated by a "quit claim" from the feudal patron of his right in the advowson of Poulton, including the church at Bispham, and all chapels appertaining thereto. The document stipulates that whoever should be presented to the same church by him or his heirs, should pay to the abbot and the prior of Lancaster, every year, ten marks of silver.[b]

The aforesaid Theobald Walter seems to have been more successful in a plaint preferred by him against the free burgesses of Preston, in the reign of king John, "concerning gibbet and goal in Preston;" inasmuch as it appears the burgesses were fined in ten marks and a palfrey, "to have peace" touching the said plaint.[c]

At this period, it was customary for persons of the highest rank to breakfast at five o'clock in the morning, and dine at about half-past ten. Independently of his other evil practices and irregular habits, John excited the contempt of his hardy barons, by slumbering till mid-day.[d] John frequently resided at Lancaster, previously to his accession to the throne; and, according to Dr. Whitaker, appears to have been "a favourite in this part of the country, and a benefactor." There exists no direct evidence to show that John ever visited Preston, but the circumstance is highly probable. Indeed, unless he travelled by sea, he could scarcely avoid passing through the town, on his road from Chester to Lancaster. Henry III. confirmed to the burgesses of Preston, the right of pasturage on Fulwood Moor, which they held under the charter of John. From another charter, granted in the thirty-seventh year of Henry's reign, it would appear the inhabitants of Preston had encroached upon the lands and privileges of the crown, in the forest and enclosure of Fulwood. This charter, however, granted to the burgesses the right, in future, to the lands alluded to, consisting of about three hundred and twenty-four acres, afterwards denominated Preston Moor.

In the fourth year of the reign of Henry III., Walter de Preston, a member of the ancient family of that name, was slain by Robert de Hyltun and Brunus de Salford. The conflict is supposed to have arisen from one of the numerous family feuds, which so strongly characterize the earlier portion of the history of many states. A writ from the king was addressed to the sheriff directing "that if Robert de Hyltun and Brunus de Salford, taken and detained in the prison of Lancaster, shall find him twenty-four good and lawful men of the county, who will engage to have them before the justices itinerant to answer Henry de Preston, Uctred and Robert, brothers

b Registr. S. Mariæ de Lanc., fo. 77.

c Magn. Rot., 3 John.

d Matthew Paris and Hovenden.

of Henry and of Quenilda de Preston, for the 'aforesaid Walter,' brothers of Henry, Uctred, and Robert, and husband of Quenilda, whereof they appeal to them, then he, the sheriff, shall deliver them to the twenty-four, until the arrival of the justices." [e] In reference to this quarrel, Mr. Baines observes that "Robert de Hylton, or Hulton, as the name became subsequently written, was, at this period, steward between the Ribble and Mersey, for William Ferrers, earl of Derby; and, as he was deputy sheriff of the county for the same nobleman, in 1225, it may be presumed that the preceding charge was satisfactorily answered."

An order from king Henry III. was issued, in the seventh year of his reign, commanding Roger Gernet to permit the vassals of the nephew of the bishop of Winchester, "parson of the church of Preston, to have reasonable estovers in the hay of Preston, to repair their houses and enclosures, and to have the other necessaries which the desmene vassals of crown were accustomed to have in the time King John, during the wars between him and his barons." [f]

Preston formerly possessed two institutions of the monastic class. Edmund, earl of Lancaster, son of Henry III., founded a Franciscan convent of Grey Friars, in 1221.[g] It was situated a little to the west of Friargate. Leland, in his quaint manner, thus describes this religious institution in the reign of Henry VIII.:—

"The Grey Freres College in the north west side of the Towne of Preston, in Amundreness, was sett in the soile of a gentleman caullid Prestun, and a Brother or Sunne of his confirmed the first graunt of the site of the House, and one of these two was after a great man of possessions, and Viscount of Gurmaston, as I hard say in Ireland. Diverse of the Prestons were buried yn this House. But the original and great builder of this House was Edmund erle of Lancastre sunne to Henry the thyrde. Sir Robert Holand, that accusid Thomas erle of Lancastre of treason, was a great benefactor of this House, and ther was buried. This Holand, as I hard, was founder of the Priory of Holand, a place of Blake Munkes, by Latham, in Lancastreshire. Ther lay in the Grey Freres at Prestun, divers of the Shirburns and Daltuns, gentilmen."

The site of the "friary" was granted to Thomas Holcroft, on the dissolution of the monasteries, in the reign of Henry VIII.[h] Speaking of the remains of the edifice in 1836, Mr. E. Baines, says:—

"The friary, in its original state, was a small square collegiate building, with a chapel attached to its quadrangular cloisters. By the mutations of time, it became first a residence of the Breres, of Hammerton, in Bowland, of which Oliver Breres, recorder, and one of the council named in the charter of Elizabeth, was a member; and next a house of correction, to which use it continued to be applied till the prison at the bottom of Church-street was erected, in 1790. It is now divided into habitations for cottages; but the shell of the chapel, as well as some remains of three arched windows, pointed, may still be traced. At a short distance from this ruin there was formerly a well, called 'Lady Well,' frequented within living memory by the devout." [i]

e Rot. Lit. Claus. 4 Henry III. f Rot. Lit. Claus. 7 Hen. III. g Notitia Monastica.
h Notitia Mon. i His. Lan., vol. 4, p. 305.

Since 1836, these interesting relics of the past have undergone still further mutation. Friary, house of correction, factory, barrack, and cottages, have all passed away A small portion of the outer wall of the "old friary" alone remains. The whole of the site has been added to the large iron-foundry establishment of Mr Stevenson. The once rural neighbourhood of "Mount Pleasant," and the "Lady Well," has long ago been stripped of its verdant vestment, and covered with buildings; but a small street still perpetuates the name of the locality, and another that of the spring.[j] Mr. Whittle says:—

"During the cutting of the canal in this town, a stone was found adjacent to this convent, with the following figures cut thereon, '1068,' as well as several skulls, and other human bones, together with a leaden conduit, branching from the lady-well to the convent, which supplied the house with water This well stood nearly opposite the house called Mount Pleasant, occupied by Mr Richard Riley. This stone with the above date cannot have belonged to the Grey Friars foundation, because this edifice was built in Henry the third's reign, or the ides of March, A.D. 1221. The datum of 1068, is during the reign of William the Norman" [k]

Mr. Whittle further records that.—

"In July, 1821, a curious silver coin or medal was found near the Franciscan Priory, by a boy of the name of Simpson. It bears the date of 1377 temp. Richard 2nd. Its dimensions was half an inch in diameter, remarkably thin, and in a good state of preservation On one side is the representation of Christ standing on a pedestal, with a small cross in his sinister hand On the pedestal occurred the words 'Jesu Xti,' S.M, meaning Jesus Christ, the Saviour of the World.—The inscription running round the circle is 'Laus tibi soli'—Praise be to thee alone. The figures on the reverse were a bishop kneeling, receiving the standard of authority from the Apostle Peter, the words 'Petrus Cephas,' occur in small letters—and round the margin 'Le lau dux s m. v.'" [l]

"In 1823, the remains of a number of coffins and human bones, were thrown up on digging near the old Friarage, and also a large stone, octagon in shape, which must have been the base of a column belonging to the convent of the Friars minors of this town." [m]

Stephens says "Preston Convent was in the custody of Worcester, which wardenship had nine convents under its care." The mastership was in the gift of the king. An impression of the seal used by the Grey Friars of Preston is preserved in the Augmentation office.[n] Dr. Whitaker, in his History of Richmondshire, gives an engraved fac-simile of a blank form of ecclesiastical absolution, as well as of a grant to Lawrence Horobys, Margery his wife, and their children, by Brother James, warden of the brethren of Preston, "of liberty to choose a confessor, who may absolve each of them once in the year."

The other monastic institution was an ancient hospital dedicated to St. Mary Magdalen. This establishment is mentioned in the Lincoln taxation

j "Mount Pleasant," and Ladywell-street." The "Jolly Tars" public house is said to occupy the site of the spring.

k His of Preston, vol. 1, p 15.

l His. Preston, vol. 2, p 65.

m His Preston, vol. 2, p. 114

n Dugdale's Mon. Anglic.

of 1291. Mr. E. Baines says, the "edifice stood in the Maudlands, *on the eminence now occupied by Tulketh Hall, in Ashton-upon-Ribble,* and was used as a temporary residence for the Cistercian monks, while their magnificent abbey in Furness was building."[o]

The latter portion of the sentence is, doubtless, correct; but there exists considerable confusion in Mr. Baines's statements, with reference to the precise sites of the hospital, and the temporary residence of the Cistercian monks. They must have been not *one,* but *two* distinct establishments, situated about a quarter of a mile from each other. The estate denominated "The Maudlands" is in the township of Preston, and does not include the site of Tulketh Hall. It is separated from the latter by a deep valley, through which flows the "Moor Brook," forming, here, the boundary between the townships of Preston and Ashton-upon-Ribble. After describing a "square area, formed by a ditch, and considerably elevated in the centre, *upon the high ground between Preston and Spaw Brow, and a little to the* EAST *of Tulketh Hall,*" Mr. Baines adds, "In latter times it was the site of a church, dedicated to St. Mary Magdalen, and hence probably called the Maudlands. Seven or eight small pieces of silver were dug up near this mound, some years ago, which appeared to have been suspended and worn, as each of them was perforated."[p]

In the year 1836, five skeletons and several other human bones were dug up by workmen engaged in the formation of new streets on the Maudland estate, on which stood the "perfectly square area" mentioned by Mr. Baines, and which he conjectured to have been originally a Roman out-post. Many other remains of the hospital have likewise been dug up on the Maudlands. A large and handsome Roman Catholic church, dedicated to St. Walburge, now occupies the site of the ancient foundation. During its erection, a stone coffin and some skeletons were exhumed. On the cutting of the Lancaster railway, similar discoveries were made.

Mr. Baines has evidently confounded the picturesque eminence, upon which Tulketh Hall is built, with the neighbouring elevation. The "perfectly square area" has been since removed, and its pretensions to great antiquity dissipated. The whole blunder appears to have arisen from a misapprehension of the following passage, published in 1774, by Thomas West, in his "Antiquities of Furness":—

"The monks placed in this monastery" (Furness Abbey) "were an affiliation from the monastery of Savigny, in Normandy, which had been founded about fifteen years before that of Furness, and fourteen years after the establishment of the Cistercian order. They came into England under the direction of Evanus, or Ewanus, and seated themselves at Tulket, near Preston, in Amounderness, and chose him to be their first abbot. *On a rising ground, at a small distance to the* SOUTH-WEST *of* TULKETH HALL, some ruins,

o His. Lan., vol. 4, p. 304.

p His. Lan., vol. 4, p. 296.

and part of the fosse which surrounded the principal buildings, are still visible. There are, however, good reasons to believe that this fosse or moat is of higher antiquity than either the arrival of Evanus and his monks or the Norman Conquest. Tulket is situated at a small distance from the Roman military way which leads from the mouth of the Ribble over Fulwood to Rib-Chester, and commands a view of the Ribble as far as it is navigable, as also of a great part of the files or fields of Amounderness, and the cultivated part of that side of the county. It is therefore probable that the Romans had there erected some granaries, or other conveniences for the immediate reception of corn, until it could be conveniently transported to their several stations in these parts, and for the better preservation of it from the attempts of the Britons, had defended it with a fosse and vallum. These granaries, together with the strength and pleasant aspect of the place, in all likelihood engaged some man of taste to settle here after the departure of the Romans, and induced him to confer his name upon it, agreeably to the prevailing custom of those times We have not any account of the condition in which the monks found Tulket at the time of their arrival, and some may perhaps imagine from what Leland tells us, that they actually erected a monastery there,[q] but we may with greater probability judge, *from the present ruins*, that during their stay there, they contented themselves with making use of such buildings only as were erected before their coming thither."

The locality alluded to by West, to the *south-west* of Tulketh, in 1855, still presented sufficient evidence to identify it with his description. A mound, situated at the extremity of the elevated headland, overlooked the river just below the "old quay." Considerable remains of a fosse were apparent The workmen employed by Mr Edward Pedder, were laying the land out for villas, and on removing the sod, near the outside of the trench, some remnants of broken brick, etc, might be observed; but no distinctive remains were discovered on cutting through the mound itself; consequently, its Roman pretensions rest merely upon conjecture. It is probable, however, that it may have been used as a *specula*, or look-out, in connection with the station at Walton The clay was being worked into bricks and tiles by the Local Board of Health. Workmen were busily occupied in filling up the trench and levelling the ground. In a short time the locality will present a complete transformation. The fosse was semicircular in form, and detached the "ness" or nose of the promontory from the main land. The view from this point exactly accords with West's description. The prospect, both seaward and up the valley of the Ribble, is very picturesque and extensive.[r]

The "square mound," mentioned by Mr. Baines, on the Maudlands, was removed a few years ago. It was situated between the present St.

q "Stephanus Comes Boloniensis postea Rex Angliæ, dedit Abbati Gaufrido Savaniensi villam, scilicet, Tulket, in provincia quæ vocatur Acmunderness, super ripam fluvii Ribble, ad abbatiam construendam ordinis sui, et ibi fere per tres annos permanserunt —Lelandi Collect tom, 11, p. 357 "

"Stephen, count of Boulogne, afterwards king of England, gave to the abbot Gaufrid, of Savania, a villa, called Tulket, in the province of Amounderness, upon the bank of the river Ribble, to build an abbey of his order; and there they remained for nearly three years."

r See Chap I, page 48. The site of the "Tulketh Monastery" is marked on the ordnance map nearer to Tulketh Hall than this mound.

Walburge's church and the Talbot schools. The iron railing, on the side next to the Wyre railway, passes over the site of its western extremity. The entire work, including the ditch, was about thirty yards in diameter. Its structure and contents proved it to be of comparatively modern formation, and certainly not later than the wars between Charles I. and his parliament. In the ditch were found many staves of wood, which, from appearance, might have formed portions of a palisade or fence. The soil composing the mound, appeared to have been thrown out the ditch. It contained a number of pieces of *tobacco* pipes. A large fragment and one perfect specimen of English mediæval pottery were likewise discovered. The perfect jug is rude in form, and fashioned from a coarse cream coloured clay. It is unglazed, with the exception of an irregular streak near the neck. It perfectly agrees in character with a figure and description of this class of ware given at page 104, of the catalogue of the "Ceramic series," in the Museum of Practical Geology, Jermyn-street, London.[8] As tobacco smoking did not become general in England till the reign of James I., the non-Roman construction of the work is thus satisfactorily attested. In all probability it was erected by Colonel Rosworm, the celebrated German engineer, soon after the capture of Preston by the forces of the parliament under Sir John Seaton, in 1643. Rosworm expressly says, in his appeal to parliament, now published by the "Chetham Society," amongst the "Civil War Tracts," that he personally took part in the siege, and superintended the formation of new defensive works. These were destroyed shortly afterwards by the earl of Derby. The mound, on the Maudlands, appears to have been the remains of an out-work, constructed for the protection of the Friargate entrance to the town. It covered and overlooked the roads from the north and the north-west, or "Fylde country." The Lancaster road, at that period, passed down Water-lane, and turned to the northward, near the present canal aqueduct. In the interior of the *tumulus*, a square brick chamber was discovered, about six feet deep, and of sufficient breadth to admit of the body of a man in an upright position. This was generally regarded as a powder magazine. The situation is well adapted for an out-post of observation, but not in an equal degree to the promontory in Ashton, on the *south-west* of Tulketh, mentioned by West. Its proximity to the town of Preston, however, would render it more eligible for the objects proposed to be attained by Colonel Rosworm.

This mound, though evidently the most modern construction on the Maudlands, previously to the erection of the present edifices, was long

8 These rare relics of the period referred to, are deposited in the Museum of the Literary and Philosophical Society.

regarded by the inhabitants of the neighbourhood with superstitious reverence. Tradition said that the raised ground covered the steeple of a sunken church, and not only children, but adults declared that at midnight on Christmas eve, they had, by placing their ears to the ground, heard subterranean bells ringing a joyful peal in honour of the advent of the Saviour. This superstition was so prevalent, that on the discovery of the brick chamber, previously alluded to, scores of people visited the spot, and retired fully convinced they had seen a portion of the steeple of the sunken edifice, and that its discovery demonstrated the truth of the ancient tradition! This remarkable legend appears to have located itself in other places as well as Preston. A precisely similar story is related in connection with a Roman out-work near Mellor, on the line of ancient road from Ribchester to Manchester.

Mr. Whittle, speaking of the Hospital of St. Mary Magdalen, says:—

"This eleemoysinary institution was standing in the year 1501. temp. Henry 7th, when William Marshall, armiger, was guild Mayor of Preston, being the 16th of Henry 7th. The procession of the confraternities used, as of old, to join procession from St. Mary's hospital, in the Maudlands, and after the said procession, the mass of the Holy Ghost was celebrated with great solemnity, at the mother church of St. Wilfrid. The lands called 'Spittals-moss,' formerly belonged to this magnificent hospice. The Teutonic word spittal (from hospital) signifies, in law, a charitable foundation. * * * Ricardus Blundell, Daniel Pigott, Roger de Preston, and Ricardus de Alston, were trustees to the property in the year 1397, temp. Richard 2nd." t

It is somewhat singular that few traces of the foundations of the ancient hospital have been discovered in modern times; at least, few of much importance. Of the identity of the site, there can, however, be no rational doubt. In a lease, granted during the reign of queen Elizabeth, the estate is described as the "Magdeleynes, and Magdeleyne ridding, within the liberties of the town of Preston." A close of land, containing two acres, is further said to be "neare the capitall messuage called the Magdeleynes, in the said countie."

Dr. T. D. Whitaker, with reference to such institutions as the Friary and Hospital at Preston, says:—

"These small endowed foundations (for they never were permitted to enjoy more than about four acres within their precincts) were always in the immediate neighbourhood of great towns, and that for a very obvious reason, namely, that if they had been placed, like the great monasteries, in distant solitudes, their mendicant inhabitants must often have wanted bread. Their buildings were also adapted to their resources. Most of them resembled colleges, and instead of magnificent churches, had small chapels attached to a mean quadrangle and cloister." u

The brass matrix of the seal of the hospital is preserved in the Fitzwilliam Museum, Cambridge. It is of elliptical form, but with pointed ends, like the Gothic arch. A female figure, apparently the "Magdalen,"

---

t His. Preston, vol. 2, p. 26. u Richmondshire, vol. 2, p. 427.

with a flower-pot in one hand, standing within a Gothic niche, occupies the centre, around which is the following inscription :—

"SIGILLV COMMUNE FRATRUM PRESTONE."

Beneath the feet of the Magdalen, a *fleur de lis* is represented. In her right hand she holds a small reticulated article, apparently an ornamented ointment box.

In the year 1265, Edmund Crouchback, youngest son of Henry III., on the death of Simon de Montford, at the battle of Evesham, was created earl of Leicester. In the following year, he received still further grants from the king, and amongst others the honor, earldom, castle, and town of Lancaster, with the forests of Wiresdale and Lonsdale. This grant, however, was not to affect the interests of Roger de Lancaster. A large share of the forfeited possessions of Simon de Montfort were likewise conferred upon Edmund. These grants were confirmed in the following reign by his brother, Edward I. The house of Lancaster, from this period, exercised great influence in the state. This was still further augmented on the marriage of his son Thomas, his successor, with Alice, sole daughter of Henry de Lacy, earl of Lincoln, by which he became possessed of the lands and fortresses of this distinguished and powerful family.

In the reign of Henry III., the languages spoken in England were more numerous than is generally imagined. The court and nobility used the Provençal and Norman-French; the law of the land was written and administered in the latter; the church services were performed in Latin, and the people generally spoke a corrupted Saxon. A writer of the period[v] says: "Some use strange gibbering, chattering, waffing, and grating; then the Northumbre's tongue (and especially at York) is so sharp, flitting, froyting, and unshape, that we Southron men may not understand that language." It will require another age of railroad influence, yet, before "Southron men" can properly comprehend the discourse of a genuine Lancashire peasant.

Edward I., by his valour and sagacity, having added the principality of Wales to his kingdom, began to turn his thoughts towards Scotland. That country was distracted, at the time, by the pretensions of no less than twelve competitors for the throne. The claimants were, however, eventually reduced to three, John Baliol, Robert Bruce, and John Hastings. Edward, though appointed arbitrator, resolved to secure the crown for himself. As a matter of policy, however, he professed to declare in favour of Baliol; and that prince assumed the reigns of government, as Edward's deputy. Baliol soon perceived the degradation of his position, as a mere

v Trevisa.

vassal of the English crown; and, having procured the pope's absolution from his oath of homage, revolted. The Scots were, however, defeated in several engagements, and Baliol taken prisoner to London.

Sir William Wallace shortly afterwards appeared upon the scene. After many petty successes, the Scots were defeated by Edward, at Falkirk, with immense loss. Wallace was still not disheartened. By his address and self denial, he re-united the jealous Scottish lords. A complete victory was gained over an English army at Roslin, near Edinburgh. Edward, however, shortly afterwards crossed the frontiers, and laid waste the country. Wallace was betrayed into the hands of the English, by the treachery of his friend, Sir John Monteith. Edward, with a ferocity utterly unworthy of his own chivalric valour, hung the Scottish patriot as a rebel, and, after the brutal fashion of the age, further satiated his vengeance on the lifeless body of his valiant foe.

Bruce, at length, escaped from his prison in London, rallied the remnants of the Scottish malcontents, and expelled the English forces from the kingdom. Edward's anger was inflamed to the highest pitch. He summoned his chief nobility and prelates to meet him in arms at Carlisle, and vowed that nothing but the most abject submission should satisfy his resentment. He dispatched a force, under Aymer de Valence, who totally defeated Bruce, in Perthshire. On the king's entry into Scotland, the people offered no resistance. Edward's death, shortly afterwards, however, relieved the Scots from their most terrible foe, and eventually saved the independence of the country. On his way to Scotland, Edward passed through Preston, from which place he issued a proclamation, appointing the archbishop of York and the bishop of Coventry and Litchfield his wardens, during his absence in Scotland. This proclamation is dated "at Preston, the 2nd of July, 1306." Another document was issued by the king, bearing a similar date, and addressed to the pope, complaining of the "malignity of the archbishop of Canterbury." [w]

In the twenty-third year of Edward's reign, the first *recorded* parliamentary representation of the borough took place. The members were William Fitz Paul and Adam Russel, burgesses of Preston.

In the reign of Edward I., a plea of *quo warranto* was moved between the king and the burgesses of Preston. In a writ of *certiorari*, issued to remove the plea into the court of king's bench, the townsmen are "stiled burgesses of Preston in Aundernesse." Adam, son of Ralph, and Robert, son of Roger, bailiffs, and other inhabitants of Preston, appeared and pleaded in the court of king's bench. The question at issue was the right

w Rot. Pat. 34 Ed. I.

of the "bailiffs and community" to have free borough in Preston, market, fair, gallows, infangthef, tumbrel, pillory, and assize of bread and beer, and to be quit of fines, amercements, tolls, and stallage. The charter was produced, by which king John, when earl of Morton, confirmed his father's grant of the liberties cited, and by which he had granted all the tolls of the wapentake of Amoundernesse, a fair at Preston at the Assumption of St. Mary, free, to last eight days; the pasture of the "forest of Fille Wode," and as much of that forest as was necessary to build their town. A charter (I. John) was also produced, confirming the preceding grants. By these charters all the above liberties were claimed, except gallows and infangthef, for which they contended they possessed a prescriptive right, as well as for a market every week, originally held on Wednesday, though latterly on Saturday. The sum of fifteen pounds a year was paid to Edmund, the king's brother, for these privileges. The court adjudicated that the bailiffs and community were in fault as to this matter, and that the liberties should be seized into the king's hands. An extent and valuation was ordered to be made by the Sheriff, but the bailiffs paid ten marks to the king for a respite.[x] The right of Preston to free fishing in the Ribble was disputed. The bailiffs alleged that it was held in common with Henry de Lacy, earl of Lincoln. To this the court assented.[y]

Edward II. was a weak prince, utterly unfitted to carry out the policy of so energetic and enterprising a monarch as his father. He conferred his chief favour upon Piers de Gaviston, or Gavestone, son of a Gascon knight. The influence exercised over the king by this accomplished, but vicious and debauched courtier, roused the indignation of some of the most powerful nobles. Secretly supported by queen Isabel, and headed by the king's cousin, Thomas earl of Lancaster, they rose in arms against the favourite. After a severe struggle with the king, they seized upon Gaviston, at Warwick, and without trial, beheaded him on the spot. The rage of the feeble monarch speedily subsided. He pardoned the earl of Lancaster and the rebellious barons, stipulating merely that they should, on their knees, publicly request his forgiveness.

After a short and hollow truce, Edward marched into Scotland, at the head of a powerful army, with the view of inflicting chastisement upon the Scots. This expedition resulted in the decisive battle of Bannockburn, which seated Bruce firmly upon the throne of Scotland, and wrung from the weak Edward, the fruit of many of his father's most brilliant military achievements.

---

x Plac. coram Rege an. 21, incipiente 22, Ed. I., Rot. 59 a.

y Plac. de Quo War. 20 Ed. I.

The king, after the death of Gaviston, transferred his favour to Hugh de Spencer, and his father; when the nobles again took umbrage. The younger Spencer prevailed upon the king to illegally escheat the barony of Gower, and to confer it upon himself. This exasperated the earls of Hereford and Lancaster. The latter marched to St. Albans, and demanded the banishment of the Spencers, as parties obnoxious to the people, and guilty of gross acts of imposition and oppression. They pillaged the lands of the two favourites, drove off their cattle, and burnt their houses. The lay-barons, in parliament assembled, pronounced the father and son guilty, and sentenced them to banishment and attainder. The following year, the king raised an army, and re-called the Spencers. The earl of Lancaster, feeling the danger of his position, ordered Sir Robert de Holland to reinforce him with five hundred men from Lancashire. Sir Robert owed his entire fortune to the munificence of the earl, who had promoted him from the menial office of butler to the dignity of knighthood. The required force was immediately raised; but, notwithstanding his obligations to the earl of Lancaster, Sir Robert's loyalty overcame his gratitude, and he marched his men to the assistance of the king. The earl, for some time, resisted; but was eventually defeated at Boroughbridge, by Sir Andrew de Harcla, warden of Carlisle and the Marches, and made prisoner. He was treated with much indignity, and even pelted by the mob at Pontefract. When brought before the king, he was refused the privilege of speaking in his own defence. Fresh insults were showered upon him. He was placed upon a wretched horse, and paraded through the streets, with a friar's hood upon his head, to an eminence outside the town, and there beheaded. This Thomas earl of Lancaster was a great favourite with the poorer classes. Miracles were said to have been wrought at his tomb; and it required a special mandate from the king to prevent the populace from worshipping his picture in St. Paul's cathedral. His brother Henry, however, in the following reign, procured an act, repealing the attainder, and took possession of the lordships and lands confiscated by earl Thomas's rebellion.

To add to the king's misfortunes, the Scots made many successful incursions into the northern counties. One of the most destructive of these forays happened in 1323, when, according to Hollinshed, "Robert Bruce entered into England by Carlisle, kept on his way through Cumberland, Westmoreland, and Lancaster, to Preston, which town he burnt, as he had done others in the counties he had passed through, and after three weeks and three days, he returned into Scotland without engaging."

During these conflicts between the king and the powerful barons, great anarchy prevailed in several parts of the country. It appears, from numerous royal proclamations issued at the time, that assault, murder, and rapine, were committed almost with impunity, by armed bands of desperadoes, which included men of rank, as well as lawless soldiery and malefactors of the lowest class. The knights and other dependents of the barons, with the view to obtain pardon for past crimes and excesses, sometimes rose against their feudal chiefs, and espoused the cause of the king. Adam de Banistre, of the house and family of Thomas, earl of Lancaster, wishing to ingratiate himself into the favour of the monarch, declared for the king's full prerogative. Joined with others, he pillaged the earl's castles, and armed about eight hundred of his followers with the weapons intended for the soldiers preparing for the Scottish invasion. About six hundred of the earl's knights and vassals advanced against them. A sanguinary conflict took place on the banks of the Ribble, near Preston. Banistre's whole force charged with impetuosity the advanced division of the earl's little army, and compelled it to fall back; but on the arrival of the remaining portion, his followers were speedily put to the rout. Great numbers were slain in the pursuit, but their leader contrived, for some time, to elude the vigilance of his enemies His place of concealment was at length discovered by the earl's troops, and he was beset on all sides. Still he obstinately refused to surrender, and, with desperate valour, attacked his assailants, killed several, and wounded many others. He was ultimately slain, and his head sent as a trophy to the earl of Lancaster. The followers of the earl, after their victory, entered the hundred of Leyland, on the south of the Ribble, levied contributions to an enormous amount, and committed many other lawless excesses.[z]

Commissioners were appointed by royal authority, in Lancashire, to repress these outrages upon the persons and property of the king's subjects. Amongst others, Edmundus de Botiller, justiciar, Ricardus de Beresford, chancellor, and Magister Walterus de Jeslep, treasurer of Ireland, were entrusted with powers for the maintenance of the public peace, which the combined action of war and famine had seriously disturbed.[a]

A new insurrection against the Spencers, headed by the queen and her celebrated paramour, Mortimer, proved successful. Father and son were executed, and their remains mangled in the most revolting manner. The

z "An old indictment says, 'that the battle took place near Preston, in the valley of the Ribble' This is not the case, for it was fought in Turbary ground, between Leyland and Preston * * * We recollect, about 1820, seeing a reversal of the attainder passed against the Banaster family in consequence of this affray, but of what date we cannot recollect. It was purchased by Lyon, a bookseller, in Preston, and sold for the trifling sum of twenty-one shillings The instrument possessed a large pendant seal of white wax, fastened to a silken bawdry."—Whittle's His. Preston, vol. 2, p 28. Mr Whittle, however, cites no authority against the statement in the "old indictment" referred to.

a Rot. Claus. 8 Ed II.

king was deposed by the parliament, and shortly afterwards murdered at Berkely castle. At the time Mortimer, who had been imprisoned in the tower, for the part he had taken in the previous insurrection of the barons, made his escape from that fortress, while Edward was in Lancashire, from whence he rapidly marched to Wales, with the view of securing the fugitive. Mortimer, however, had embarked for France.

Sir Richard Clayton was rewarded with the "castle, manor, and hundred of Halton, in Cheshire and Lancashire," by Edward III., for services rendered to his mother, queen Isabella.[b] In the reign of Edward II., letters patent were granted for the "paviage of the town of Preston," with powers to collect tolls.[c] A rate on merchandise was granted for a similar purpose, by the "good Duke of Lancaster."

In 1323, the tithes of "Fulwood, Merescough, and Hyde Park," were restored to the rectories of Preston and Lancaster.[d] Edward III. made several irruptions into Scotland. He gained a complete victory at Halidown-hill, in which, it is said, thirty thousand Scots were slain. Edward halted on his way to Scotland at Preston, where he considerably recruited his army. Edward claimed the throne of France, through his mother, daughter to Philip the Fair. He invaded that country, and, aided by his son, the famous Edward, the Black Prince, gained the celebrated victories of Cressy and Poictiers. In the latter, John, king of France, was taken prisoner. While Edward was engaged in the wars with France, the Scots, under David Bruce, invaded England. Lord Percy, who commanded for queen Philippa, gave them battle at Neville's Cross, near Durham, and completely routed the whole army. The king of Scotland and many of his nobles were taken prisoners to London.

About this period, a pestilence of the most fatal character ravaged the country. As many as fifty thousand persons were interred in one burial-ground in London.

To reward the brilliant services, rendered in the French wars, by Henry, earl of Lancaster and Derby, Edward conferred upon him the title of Duke of Lancaster. The county was likewise made a palatinate, under the "thrice noble" John of Gaunt, who married the daughter of Henry, and succeeded to the dukedom. John of Gaunt[e] was fourth son of Edward III. "Law was to be administered by the officers and ministers of the duke, and under his seal, and anciently all offences were said to be against his peace, his sword and dignity," and not, as at present, against the "queen, her crown and dignity." The offices of law, in connection

b Rot. Pat. 1 Ed. III.
c Rot. Lit. Pat.
d Reg. S. Mar, de L. MS.
e So called because he was born at Ghent, in Flanders.

with the palatinate, are still held at Preston. Mr. Baines says: "The house of Lancaster, so renowned in British history, held this place" (Preston) "in high estimation, and nothing but the local situation of their baronial castle on the banks of the Lune, prevented them from establishing the capital of the county where it ought to have been fixed—on the banks of the Ribble." The central position of Preston certainly points it out as the most convenient and desirable locality for the transaction of business pertaining to the whole county.

The first recorded Guild Merchant was celebrated in the reign of Edward III. This king likewise confirmed the grants of his predecessors, and conceded the additional privilege of holding a fair of five days duration, commencing with the vigil of the apostles St. Simon and St. Jude. Additional letters patent were likewise granted for the improvement of the town.

The church and lordship of Preston were held in *capite* by John of Gaunt, duke of Lancaster, in the thirty-fifth year of the reign of Edward III. It is stated that "the high altar, with its appurtenances, was computed to be worth five hundred marks at that time." The lordship appears to have been previously held by Sir Robert de Preston, of Gormanstown, in Ireland, who was knighted by the duke of Clarence, and afterwards became keeper of the seals, and lord high chancellor of Ireland. His descendant, Sir Robert de Preston, was deputy for the duke of York in the government of Ireland. He was created viscount Gormanstown in the reign of Edward IV.

A curious anecdote is related by Ormerod, in his history of Cheshire, which exhibits, strongly, the rude licence of the period. Sir William de Clifton, exasperated at the abbot of Vale Royal, Cheshire, in consequence of some dispute respecting the church at Preston, avenged himself by flogging the secretary of the obnoxious ecclesiastic through the streets of the town.

In 1343, in the reign of Edward III, an inquest of the value of moveable property was made in all the boroughs of the kingdom. From the returns, it appears that Preston was, at the time, the wealthiest of all the royal boroughs in Lancashire; that is, if the term wealth can be appropriately applied to what, at the present day, appears so very humble a condition. The document[f] states, that the "ninth part of the goods of the men dwelling in the borough of Preston," was six pounds, seventeen shillings, and fourpence! This sum is, however, considered to be equivalent to about one hundred pounds of the present coinage. Still this would

---

f Nonarum Inquitiones—Lancashire.

leave the total value of the moveable goods of the Prestonians, in the middle of the fourteenth century, little more than nine hundred pounds!! The ninth part for Wigan, was five pounds, nine shillings, and fourpence, equal to a little over eighty pounds, for Lancaster, six pounds, thirteen shillings, and sixpence; for Liverpool, six pounds, sixteen shillings, and sevenpence These were the only "Royal burghs" in Lancashire Manchester, at this period, did not possess sufficient trade to render it liable to the tax on merchandise and moveable property.

Henry, surnamed Bolingbroke, earl of Derby and Hereford, son of John of Gaunt, in the reign of Richard II, accused the duke of Norfolk, in parliament, of seditious conversation After the rude fashion of the time, the complainant and defendant agreed to decide their quarrel by an appeal to arms. The king, from mere caprice, stopped the combatants, and banished Norfolk for life. Hereford received a somewhat milder sentence. He was required to leave the country for ten years, but this term was afterwards commuted to six. The king promised, by letters patent, that Hereford should, on his return, succeed to any inheritance which might descend to him in the interim. The duke of Lancaster died shortly afterwards. The cupidity of the king overcame his sense of honour. He revoked his letters patent, and seized the possessions of the banished earl.

This conduct exasperated Bolingbroke. He landed in Yorkshire, raised the standard of rebellion, and was joined by the earl of Northumberland, his son Percy, surnamed Hotspur, and other noblemen. The king was detained in Ireland by contrary winds; and when he landed at Milford Haven, the best portion of his army gradually withdrew from him. The weak king submitted without conditions. He was paraded in triumph through Chester and other towns, and afterwards imprisoned in the Tower. Little effort was necessary to induce him to sign a renunciation of his crown, and a declaration of his own unfitness to govern. Bolingbroke was elected king, and ascended the throne by the title of Henry IV. Thus originated the celebrated "Wars of the Roses," which, for a series of years, deluged England with the blood of the bravest of her sons.

The privileges enjoyed by the burgesses of Preston were confirmed by Richard and Henry In the latter reign, letters patent were granted for the "pontage of the river Ribble, juxta Preston," and afterwards for the "paviage of the said bridge." A bridge had existed at Walton, over the Ribble, long previously to the date of this grant. A verdict given in the ninth year of the reign of Henry III, quotes an old boundary deed, in which the bridge is mentioned [g] It is difficult to say by whom this

g His Man., vol 1, p 189.

structure was erected. The Romans forded the stream at the gravel bank, a few yards below. It was probably of Saxon or early Norman construction.

In the reign of Richard II., the earliest recorded enactments, relative to salmon fisheries, were passed, and had special reference to the Ribble, the Wyre, the Lune, and the Mersey. The times during which the rivers might be fished are specified, and justices of the peace appointed conservators of the fisheries. In the reign of Elizabeth, it was enacted that "the meshes of the nets, used in taking salmon, should be two inches and a half broad, and that the fish should not be taken by any other means."

Henry IV.'s reign was disturbed by much civil commotion. The Welsh and Scots rose in arms against him, and his old friend, the earl of Northumberland, by whose aid he ascended the throne, raised the standard of revolt. Henry's courage and discretion, however, proved equal to the crisis. Northumberland's retainers and the malcontents were defeated at Shrewsbury, and his son, the daring Hotspur, slain.

Henry V. increased the military renown of the English, by a successful invasion of France. This prince confirmed the Preston charters, and granted powers for the recovery of such privileges, as might be supposed to have lapsed through neglect, or "non-user," as it is styled in legal phraseology.

The history of Lancashire, during the "Wars of the Roses," is singularly devoid of incident. This appears the more remarkable, as the name of the county furnished the war-cry of one of the contending houses. Mr. Baines says:—

"Although few periods in English history afford so many materials for the pen of the general and local historian, as that comprehended in the reigns of Henry VI., Edward IV., and Richard III., during which time the wars between the houses of York and Lancaster raged with so much fury; and that of the reign of Henry VII., when these intestine broils were happily composed by the union of the rival houses in the persons of Henry VII. and his queen; yet there is no time, from the reign of king Stephen, so destitute of authentic records The savage and murderous contests between the court and the people, appear so to have disorganized society, that the usual communications between the authorities in the provinces and the government were neglected; or, if proclamations and edicts were issued in the several counties, they perished with many of those to whom they were addressed, the usual depositories being found almost entirely destitute of these documents. This paucity of official information is the more extraordinary, seeing that the art of printing, that great engine of multiplication, was introduced into England by William Caxton, in 1471, during the wars of the roses." h

The reign of Henry VI. was singularly unfortunate, both to the monarch and the national glory. The conquests of his father, in France, were lost, and the province of Bayonne, which had been an *apanage* to the English crown for three centuries, was ceded to the French king. The contest

h His. Lan., vol. 1, p. 402.

between the houses of York and Lancaster for the supreme power, continued with varying results for thirty years, during which time, thirteen pitched battles were fought, and many of the most distinguished families in the country nearly annihilated. The county of Lancaster, however, escaped the horrors of direct warfare, though it was not the less subjected to all the evils inevitably resulting from social and political anarchy In the three first engagements, at St Albans, Bloreheath, and Northampton, Fortune favoured the house of York. But the fickle goddess frowned at Wakefield, where the duke of York was slain, after performing prodigies of valour, and his youngest son was cruelly murdered. Edward, earl of March, his eldest son, now duke of York, however, continued the family claim, and defeated the Lancastrian army at Mortimer's Cross. He met with a reverse in a second battle at St. Albans, but not of sufficient importance to prevent his entering London in triumph. Margaret, Henry's queen, assembled an army of sixty thousand men, in the county of York. Edward and the earl of Warwick advanced and gave her battle at Towton, near Tadcaster, where, after a most obstinate and bloody engagement, the Lancastrians were utterly routed. The forthcoming parliament decreed that "Henry of Derbie, otherwise duke of Lancaster, and the heirs of his body coming, were utterly disabled from enjoying any inheritance, estate, or profits, within this realm or dominions of the same for ever."

Henry fled to Scotland, but queen Margaret applied to the court of France for assistance She obtained two thousand men, with whom she landed in England At Hexham, she was joined by volunteers from Scotland and the northern counties. A battle ensued, in which the Lancastrians were totally defeated. The duke of Somerset and the lords Hungerford and Ross were taken prisoners, declared guilty of treason, and beheaded. The queen, after suffering many privations, escaped to the continent. The king was concealed for about twelve months, in the northern counties; but he was eventually discovered, and confined a prisoner in the Tower of London.

"The place of his concealment," according to Mr. Baines, "was Waddington Hall, in the parish of Mitton Magna, in the north eastern part of the county" (Lancashire); "and the person by whom he was betrayed was Sir John Talbot, who, as a reward for his perfidy, received a grant of twenty marks a year from Edward IV., confirmed by his successor, Richard III., and made payable out of the revenues of the county palatine of Lancaster."

Waddington is not in Lancashire, but in Yorkshire. Miss Strickland says, Henry was "taken by the servants of Sir John Harrington, as he sat at dinner, at Waddington Hall.[1] This is not, however, exactly the

[1] Lives of the Queens of England vol. 3 p 279.

case. He appears to have been really captured on the opposite side of the Ribble, in the wood of Clitheroe, in the county of Lancaster. The particulars are related in Warksworth's Chronicle:—

"Also, the same yere, kynge Henry was taken bysyde a howse of religione [i.e. Whalley] in Lancashyre, by the mene of a blacke monke of Abyngtone, [Abingdon] in a wode called Cletherwode [the wood of Clitheroe], besyde Bungerly hyppyngstones, by Thomas Talbott, sonne and heyre to sere Edmunde Talbott, of Basshalle, and Jhon Talbott, his cosyne, of Colebry [i.e. Salesbury in Blackburn], withe other moo; which discryvide [him] beynge at his dynere at Wadyngton halle; and [he was] carryed to London on horsebake, and his leges bownde to the styropes."

The interpolations are by Mr. J. G. Nichols, who says:—

"I have substituted the word 'discryvide' for 'disseyvide,' as it is printed in the Camden society's book, where the editor, Mr. Halliwell, understood the passage as meaning that the king was deceived or betrayed. I take the meaning to be that the black monke of Abington had descried or discovered the king as he was eating his dinner at Waddington Hall; whereupon the Talbots and some other parties in the neighbourhood, formed plans for his apprehension, and arrested him on the first convenient opportunity, as he was crossing the ford across the river Ribble, formed by the 'hyppyngstones' at Bungerley. Waddington belonged to Sir John Tempest, of Bracewell, who was the father-in-law of Thomas Talbot. Both Sir John Tempest and Sir James Harrington, of Brierley, near Barnsley, were concerned in the king's capture, and each received one hundred marks reward, but the fact of Sir Thomas Talbot being the chief actor, is shown by his having received the large sum of £100."[j]

It appears, however, that the hundred marks did not constitute Sir James Harrington's sole reward. Large grants of land, forfeited by Richard Tunstell and other "rebels," were bestowed upon him by Edward IV., "for his services in taking prisoner, and withholding as such, in diligence and valour, his enemy, Henry, lately called Henry VI."[k]

Henry's principal place of concealment in the neighbourhood, appears to have been at Bolton Hall, a little higher on the Ribble, the seat of Sir Ralph Pudsey, who married the daughter of Sir Thomas Tunstell, and whose "rebellion" consisted in his attendance upon the unfortunate king, as an "esquire of the body." Dr. Whitaker engraves, in his history of Craven, the fallen monarch's boots, gloves, and a spoon, which are still preserved at Bolton Hall. Salesbury Hall is likewise on the Ribble, opposite to Ribchester. The "old hall" at Waddington, though much altered in appearance, is still in existence, and a field in the neighbourhood yet retains the name of "king Henry's meadow."

The quarrel of the king with the earl of Warwick, renewed the civil struggles. The "king maker" revolted, and, assisted by the duke of Clarence, raised an army of sixty thousand men. Edward approached them with a large force, near Nottingham; but, from some alarms, decamped in the night, and fled into Holland. Henry was once more seated upon a throne which he was destined not long to occupy. The

j Notes and Queries, vol. 2, p. 229.

k Notes and Queries, vol. 2, p. 316.

duke of Burgundy granted Edward two thousand troops, with which he landed at Ravenspur, in Yorkshire At Barnet, Henry's party was defeated, and the earl of Warwick slain. Queen Margaret and her son were taken prisoners after the battle of Tewkesbury, where the prince was barbarously murdered. King Henry died shortly afterwards in the tower, not without strong suspicions that his death had been brought about by his enemies

King Edward IV, granted to Thomas Molyneux, for an annual consideration of one hundred pounds, four hundred acres of moor and heath land in Fulwood, the tract of turbary called Penwortham Moss, together with the herbage and agistment of Croxteth Park. Henry VI. confirmed all the charters previously granted to the burgesses of Preston.

Soon after the death of Edward IV, his two sons are said to have been murdered in the Tower, by order of their uncle, the duke of Gloucester, who usurped the throne This monarch reigned about two years, and indulged, according to the Tudor writers, in many acts of cruelty and brutal tyranny. His short reign was, however, distinguished by efficient administration, and intelligent civil legislation. A manuscript in the Harleian collection, contains the following somewhat ambiguous paragraph relative to this period: "Aprille, 2 Richard III. The maire and burgesses of Preston in Amonderness haue iij[l] duringe iij yeres, and a perdone of xv[l] due from them" Richard was killed at the battle of Bosworth Field, near Leicester, where his army was defeated by the earl of Richmond, through the defection of Lord Stanley and the forces from Lancashire and Cheshire. The earl ascended the throne with the title of Henry the VII. Descended, through his mother, from John of Gaunt, and his father being half brother to king Henry VI, the victory of the earl of Richmond transferred the crown once more to the house of Lancaster. His marriage with the princess Elizabeth, eldest daughter of king Edward IV., united the contending families, and eventually terminated the wars of the roses. The adherents of the house of York, however, for some time continued to dispute Henry's title, and supported the claims of Lambert Simnel, who assumed, at one period, the title of Edward Plantagent, earl of Warwick, son of the duke of Clarence, and afterwards that of Richard, duke of York, second son of Edward IV Simnel's claim was supported by the Duchess of Burgundy, who entertained a most cordial and inveterate hatred towards Henry VII Simnel landed with several followers from Ireland and the continent, at the "Pile of Foudrey," in Morecambe Bay, Lancashire; where he was joined by many of the disaffected Yorkists, including the chivalrous Sir Thomas Broughton, of Furness. His army was defeated at Stake-field, near Newark, and Simnel himself taken prisoner. Singularly enough, considering the savage character of the times, Henry pardoned the pretender, and conferred upon him a menial office in his own household. The estates of Sir Thomas Broughton, who fell in the battle, were confiscated, and conferred upon the king's stepfather, Lord Stanley, as a reward for the services of his son, Lord Strange.

Another and still more formidable pretender appeared. The Yorkists evidently disbelieved the rumour of the murder of the sons of Edward IV. On the appearance, at the court of the duchess of Burgundy, of Perkin Warbeck, who professed to be the duke of York, and whose resemblance to his assumed father was singularly striking, many of the gentry and nobility supported his claim. The king, however, seized upon several of the leaders of the party, who appeared to credit his pretensions, beheaded them, and confiscated their estates. Sir Robert Clifford, who embarked for Flanders especially to ascertain "the identity of the young prince," pronounced him to be unquestionably the duke of York, with whom he averred he was as well acquainted as with his own son. Hearing of Henry's severities, however, on his return, he threw himself upon his knees before the king, and craved the royal clemency. In return for this favour he denounced all the parties he knew to have favoured Warbeck's pretensions, and, amongst others, Sir William Stanley, brother of Lord Stanley, who, for his services at Bosworth, had been advanced by Henry to the earldom of Derby. Sir William was shortly afterwards found guilty of treason, and executed; though it does not appear his offence extended beyond an expression, "that if he were sure Perkin Warbeck was king Edward's son, he would never bear arms against him." This, however, does not harmonise with his previous preference of the claim of the house of Lancaster to the throne, as evidenced by his services to the earl of Richmond. After his execution, his estates and property, which were very valuable, were seized by the king, and appropriated to his own use. Mr. Baines says, "the general opinion is, that Sir William Stanley was quite as much the victim of Henry's cupidity as his own alleged treason." This is, however, scarcely consistent with the inferences legitimately to be drawn from Mr. Baines's after statement. He says:—

"Henry found sufficient leisure in the summer, after the execution of Sir William Stanley, to visit his mother, for whom he always cherished the most affectionate regard, and his step-father, the earl of Derby, at Knowsley and at Lathom, in this county. So far was the earl from expressing any hostility towards the king, on account of the recent execution of his brother, that he gave all possible effect to the royal progress, and entertained his guest with a sumptuous hospitality, such as has seldom been witnessed in these parts. To promote the king's accommodation, the noble lord built a bridge over the river Mersey, at Warrington, for the passage of himself and suite; which bridge has been found of so much public utility, as to afford a perpetual monument of the visit of Henry VII. to Lancashire."[1]

[1] His. Lan., vol. 1, p. 449.

The execution of Sir William Stanley, if it did not alienate the head of the Derby family from the interest of Henry, was anything but satisfactory to some of his dependents. Agnes Strickland, in her life of Elizabeth of York, who accompanied her royal husband to Lathom, relates, on the authority of White Kennett, the following singular anecdote:—

"While a guest at Lathom House, the king ran a risk of his life from an odd circumstance; the earl of Derby was showing him the country from the leads, when the family fool, who had been much attached to Sir William, the brother of his lord, lately put to death by the king, drew near, and pointing to a precipitous part of the leads, undefended by battlements, close to which the royal guest was standing, said to his lord, in the low deep tone of vengeance, 'Tom, remember Will!' These three words struck the conscience of the king, and he hurried down stairs to his mother and his consort with great precipitation."

Perkin Warbeck, having espoused lady Catherine Gordon, daughter of the earl of Huntley, issued a "royal proclamation," and advanced into Northumberland. After his followers had plundered the country, however, he speedily retreated. Another attempt, in the southern portion of the kingdom, equally failed of success. Though the king appears to have despised Perkin's pretensions, he, nevertheless, ordered his execution, at Tyburn. The earl of Warwick, said to be one of his adherents, notwithstanding his imbecility of mind, through long confinement in the Tower, was beheaded. This unfortunate nobleman is described as the "last of the Plantagenets" in the male line.

One of Henry VII.'s favourite methods of raising money, was by the issuing of a writ, entitled "*Quo Warranto*," which called upon the tenantry of the crown to show their titles to their respective privileges; but, finding little profit from the proceeding, he abandoned it. Amongst others, the "Mayor and Burgesses of Preston," the municipal authorities of Liverpool, Wigan, and Salford, together with some ecclesiastics and noblemen and noble ladies, not even excepting his mother and her family, were served with these warrants! [m]

Dr. Kuerden's manuscript, in Heralds' college, mentions a deed executed at Leigh, in 1498, by which Sir Alexander Hoghton appointed William Galter to officiate as chaplain at "the altar of the crucifix, in the chantry ordained in the parish church of Preston, by Richard Whalley, deceased, who gave it to Sir Alexander, his feoffee." This chantry was familiarly designated "The Hoghton Box"

During this reign, John de Preston was appointed abbot of Cockersand, by the election of the canons. Dr. Whitaker says: "The house of Cockersand was anciently a large proprietor of lands in Preston, the number of their tenants in that town and neighbourhood, amounting to one hundred and thirty-nine, comprehended under the head of Agmundernesse."

m Rolls in Lancaster Castle.

In the year 1485, a plague, or pestilent fever, called the "sweating sickness," afflicted the country, and carried off large numbers of the population.

While Henry VIII. was engaged in successful, but unfruitful military enterprises in France, James IV., king of Scotland, invaded England with a numerous army. Levies of men were made in Cheshire, Lancashire, and the northern counties, to resist the aggression. To these were added about five thousand troops from the king's army. The command was entrusted by the queen regent to Thomas Howard, earl of Surrey, who confronted the enemy at Flodden Field, on the ninth of September, 1513, when one of the most obstinately contested engagements on record ensued. The struggle ended in the total defeat and almost entire annihilation of the Scottish army. The king and the chief of his nobles and prelates perished in the combat. Sir Edward Stanley, fifth son of the earl of Derby, commanded the left wing, consisting chiefly of the levies from Lancashire, Cheshire, and Yorkshire. His valour and tactics, aided by the bravery of his troops, contributed largely to the success of the English, and to the brilliancy of the victory. He was thanked by the king in an autograph letter, and created lord Monteagle, (in allusion to the family crest,) as a reward for his services. Sir Edward Norris, of Speke Hall, Sir William Molineux, of Sefton, and Sir Richard Ashton, of Middleton, in Lancashire, likewise distinguished themselves highly in this campaign, and received the personal thanks of the king. The prowess exhibited by the Lancashire heroes in this celebrated engagement, is enthusiastically extolled in an old ballad, preserved in the Harleian collection of manuscripts, in the British Museum, entitled "the Famous Historie or Songe called Flodden Field," as the following extracts will attest:—

"There is Sr Edward Standley stowte
For Marshiall skill cleare wth out make,
Of *Laytham Howse*, by Lyne came out,
Whose blood will never torne their backe.
All Lancashire will live and dy,
W^th^ him, soe chiefly will Cheshire,
For through his father's force quoth hee
This kingdom first came to my Syre. [m]
* * * * * *
All Lancashire for the most p^te^ (part)
The lusty Standley stowte can lead,
A stock of striplings stronge of heart
Brought vp from babes wth beefe and bread,
From Warton vnto Warrington,

m King Henry VIII. is supposed to speak this. The allusion is to the service rendered by lord Stanley to the earl of Richmond, at Bosworth Field.

From Wiggen vnto Wiresdale,
From Weddecon to Waddington,
From Ribchester vnto Rachdale,
From Poulton to Preston wth pikes
They wth ye Standley howte forthe went,
From Pemberton and Pillin Dikes
For Battell Billmen bould were bent
Wth fellowes fearce and freshe for feight
W^{ch} Halton feilds did turne in foores,
Wth lusty ladds liver and light
From Blackborne and Bolton in ye Moores."

The ancient commission of array, for levying troops in the various counties, to repel foreign invasion, and suppress domestic tumults, began to be superseded about this time by a local authority, called the lieutenancy. The earl of Surrey, created duke of Norfolk, who commanded in chief at the battle of Flodden Field, was first lord lieutenant for Lancashire. He was succeeded by the earl of Shrewsbury. Edward, earl of Derby, followed; and the duties of the lord lieutenancy of the county have been performed, almost ever since, by the head of the Stanley family, although the office is by no means a hereditary one.

The most important feature in the reign of Henry VIII. is the great Protestant Reformation, which now began to monopolise the attention not only of England but of the whole of Europe. This important revolution unquestionably resulted from causation, in the composition of which, large and potent political elements entered. The king's cupidity, lust, and insatiable ambition, hastened, if it did not originate the downfall of the papal authority in this realm.

After the breach with Rome, Henry appointed commissioners to visit and report upon the revenues and conditions of all the monastic institutions and ecclesiastical benefices in the kingdom. Dr. Thomas Leigh and Dr. Thomas Layton visited the Lancashire establishments Their report does not, however, mention either the hospital or friary at Preston, though the Benedictine cell, at Lytham, and the priory, at Penwortham, are included. Henry's pecuniary requirements were pressing He had not patience to wait until the whole of the labour had been completed. In the year 1536, parliament sanctioned the king's resolve to suppress all monastic establishments in England, whose clear yearly income did not exceed £200. This stretch of authority augmented the royal revenues by an annual income of about £160,000, of the present value of money, exclusive of large sums realised by the sale of the plate, jewels, and other property of the ecclesiastics. About three hundred and eighty religious establishments were dissolved under this act of parliament.

Discontent and rebellion followed this wholesale spoliation. An outbreak in Lincolnshire was speedily suppressed; but a more formidable insurrection broke out in Yorkshire and the northern counties. This movement, which originated with a Robert Aske, a gentleman of family, in Yorkshire, was denominated the "*Pilgrimage of Grace*," and was supported by many of the gentry and the heads of religious establishments. For some period, the malcontents were so far successful in their efforts, that the king condescended to treat with them. They disbanded upon the royal promise of a full and complete amnesty.

During this insurrection, the earl of Derby was preparing to march to the abbeys of Whalley and Salley, then besieged by the rebels, when he received the king's command, at Preston, to disband his forces, in consequence of the apparent termination of hostilities. On the reappearance of the malcontents, the earl advanced to Whalley, occupied the abbey, and restored tranquility. The earl, in a letter despatched to the king, states that the northern malcontents purposed to march through Lancashire, "if they had not byn affrayd of me and other your true subgetts soo assembled as is aforesaid at Preston."

Much disaffection still smouldered amongst the people. Minor insurrections broke forth, which were speedily suppressed, and the leaders condemned to death. The king, exasperated at these discontents, repented his former lenity, and wreaked his vengeance on those whom he had previously pardoned in the general amnesty. Amongst the numerous executions which followed this breach of faith, is recorded that of John Paslew, D.D., abbot of Whalley. He was tried at Lancaster, for high treason, at the spring assizes, 1537, and was hung upon a gallows, "erected in front of the house of his birth, in Whalley." [o]

The larger monasteries soon experienced the fate of the minor establishments. After the excommunication of the king by the pope, a bill was passed by parliament, which invested in the crown not only all the property pertaining to the monastic institutions already dissolved, but to all which should "hereafter be suppressed, abolished, or surrendered."

The closing of the two religious houses in Preston, would, probably, take place about the year 1533.

The number of monasteries suppressed in England and Wales amounted to six hundred and forty-five, exclusive of ninety-six colleges, two thousand three hundred and seventy-four chantries and free chapels, and one hundred and ten hospitals. The property thus escheated, according to the Liber Regis, yielded £142,914. 12s. 9¼d. per annum. The total value, at twenty years' purchase, is £2,858,290., equal, at the present day, to £28,582,900.

o Baines's His. Lan., vol. 1, p. 485.

The church property, at this period, is said to have included about one-fourth of the whole of the landed estates in the kingdom.

The greater portion of this enormous property was expended by the king with licentious profusion, or squandered in grants to his favourite courtiers. Henry did profess an intention of founding eighteen new bishoprics with the revenue of the monasteries. A portion of this resolve was consummated; six additional bishoprics were established, viz., Westminster, Oxford, Peterborough, Bristol, Gloucester, and Chester The last-mentioned had previously existed, but had been suffered to merge into that of Lichfield. Fourteen priories or abbeys were converted into cathedral, or collegiate churches. Several ecclesiastics attached to the monasteries were likewise pensioned for life from the revenues of the suppressed establishments.

During the unsettled period which succeeded the dissolution of the monasteries, not only the poor, but the community generally, appear to have suffered much privation. The decay of the national prosperity is recorded in four distinct acts of parliament, passed between 1535 and 1544. One states, "that there hath been in times past many beautiful houses in those places which are now falling into ruin." The act of 1544, amongst other towns of this description, expressly names "Lancaster, Preston, Lyrepool, and Wigan, in Lancashire."

Leland, the "Itinerant" and "King's Antiquary," in the course of a tour through the principal portion of England, undertaken at the command of the king, visited Preston, about this period. His description of the town and neighbourhood, though odd and quaint, is very graphic, and, doubtless, faithful for the period :—

"Within a mile of Preston, I came over *Darwent* River, the which at *Penwardine* Paroche, a celle to *Evesham*, goith into Ribel. This *Darwent* devidith *Lelandshire* from *Anderness*,p and a mile above beyond the place wher I passid over *Darwent*, Mr. Langton dwellith, at *Walton-on-Darwent*, and is Baron of Newton in Macrefield. Half a mile beyond *Darwent* I passed over the great stone bridge of *Rybill*, having v. great arches. From *Ribyl* to *Preston* half a mile. *Preston* hath but one Paro Church. The Market place of the Toun is fair. *Ribil* goith round aboute a greate Peace of the Ground aboute Toune, yet it touchith not the Toune self by space of amost half a Mile. Penwardine semid to me more then half a mile from *Preston*, and ther goith *Ribil* stonding in respect of the Toune of the farther side of *Ribil*, the which ther dividith the Diœcese of *Chestre* from the Diœcese of *York* Penwardine is a Paroch Church and Celle to Evesham Abbey, and standith in Chester Diœcese. Preston is in York Diœcese."

p The Ribble, not the Darwen, divides the Hundred of Amounderness from that of Leyland. The Darwen debouches into the Ribble, in the township of Walton, in the parish of Blackburn. At the present day, the popular opinion in the neighbourhood is, that the Darwen divides the townships of Walton and Penwortham, hence the names "Penwortham Lodge" and "Penwortham Factory," both of which are situated in the township of Walton, the legal boundary being the brook which runs from the higher land to the Ribble, on the western side of these misnamed localities. Perhaps, the Darwen, being the most "natural boundary," may, at some remote period, have divided the hundreds of Leyland and Blackburn.

After the short reign of Edward VI., Mary, the eldest daughter of Henry VIII., ascended the throne. The charters previously conferred upon the borough of Preston, were confirmed by the queen and her husband, Philip, of Spain.

Towards the military levy, made in the early part of Mary's reign, (1553), it appears that Amounderness furnished three hundred, Leyland, one hundred and seventy, and, Blackburn four hundred men.[q]

In the reign of Mary, three inhabitants of Lancashire suffered martyrdom for their adherence to Protestant principles; namely, John Roger, John Bradford, and George Marsh. But this species of religious persecution was not confined solely to the Roman Catholics. In the reign of Edward VI. and Elizabeth, imprisonment and the stake were too often employed in the suppression of obnoxious religious opinion.

Elizabeth ascended the throne in 1558. In the following year, a "great muster," or levy of soldiers for the defence of the nation, was made. The proportion raised in Amounderness was, "two hundred and thirteen harnised, and three hundred and sixty-nine unharnised; in Leyland, twenty-four harnised, and twenty-two unharnised; in Blackburn, four hundred and seven harnised, and four hundred and six unharnised." [r]

Another plague desolated Lancashire and the rest of the country, in 1562. Holinsworth describes it as a "sore sicknesse;" and Stowe records that upwards of 17,000 persons died, in London alone, during the year.

In the year 1574, a "muster," or enrolment of the military strength of the whole kingdom, was taken by order of government. These "musters," or rather levies, ordered to be provided in case of emergency, would seem to have been a kind of precursors of the present militia system. From this, it appears that the number of inhabitants in England and Wales, "able" to bear arms, was 158,509. Of these 55,597 were "armed men," and 11,365 "selected men." "Artificers and pyoneers" numbered 13,105; "demi-launces," 429; and the "light horse," 3,037. The proportion for Lancashire was as follows:—"Able men, 6,000; armed men, 3,600; artificers and pyoneers, 600; demi-launces, 12, and light horse, 90." The hundred of Amounderness contributed "1 demi-launce, 5 light horses, 2 corselettes, 17 cotes of Plate or Almaine Ryvettes, 11 pykes, 22 long bowes, 22 sheff (of arrows), 27 steele cappes, 15 calivers, 20 murrions, and 10 billes." The hundred of Leyland's proportion was "1 demylaunce, 11 light horses, 5 corselettes, 14 cotes of plate Brigund[rs] or Almaine Ryvettes, 14 pykes, 70 stronge boes, 70 sheffes of arrowes, 70 steele cappes or scculles, 10 culivers, 10 morians, and 49

q Birch's MS. r Harl. MSS. Cod. 1926.

billes." Blackburn hundred contributed "2 demi-launces, 13 light horses, 14 corslettes, 34 cotes of plate or Almaine Ryvettes, 14 pykes, 112 large boes, 112 sheffe of arr, 109 steele cappes, 26 calivers, 27 morrians, and 90 billes"

During the troubled period, which succeeded the first adoption of protestant principles by Henry VIII. to the time of Elizabeth, many persons preferred the sacrifice of their religious opinions to the honours and pains of martyrdom. In reference to the general conduct of all classes, and, especially the Lancashire people, Mr. Edward Baines makes the following pertinent observations:—

"The zeal of the Earl of Derby, in favour of the reformed faith, so warmly eulogized by the queen, was the zeal of a convert, and, therefore, perhaps the more lively. In the last reign, his lordship embraced the cause of popery, and the committal of the intrepid George Marsh to that dungeon from which he was liberated only to be conducted to the stake, serves to show that sudden changes in religious faith were not confined to priests but that they were extended to nobles, and, to a certain extent, pervaded the whole people. In the county of Lancaster there was more of consistency than in other parts of the kingdom; and this is a principle which excites respect, even though it should be a consistency in errror * * The reformation was rapid in many parts. In the county of Lancaster it was retrograde. The catholics multiplied, priests were harboured, the book of common prayer, and the service of the church established by law, were laid aside; many of the churches were shut up, and the cures were unsupplied, unless by the rejected catholics."[s]

According to Archbishop Lee, the benefices of the inferior clergy, at that time, were not worth more than four guineas per annum, of the money of the period.

Elizabeth's reign was disturbed by several plots, concocted with a view to the restoration of the Roman catholic religion. The most important were, the attempts to place Mary, Queen of Scots, upon the throne, and the threatened invasion of England, by Philip, king of Spain. The execution of Mary, at Fotheringay Castle, relieved Elizabeth from her formidable competitor. It appeared, on her trial, that Cardinal Allen, a native of Rossall, in Lancashire, then resident at Rome, had long been permitted by Mary to treat her as the legitimate queen of England; and, in conjunction with a jesuit, named Parsons, had entered into negociations, with her consent, for the disinheriting of her protestant son, James VI., of Scotland, and the securing of the succession, to the crown of England, for Philip of Spain

On the alarm of the threatened invasion by the "invincible armada," the lieutenants of the various counties received orders from the queen to levy men for the defence of the country. The gentry, magistrates, and freeholders of the county of Lancaster, were summoned, at their "uttermost peril," to meet Lord Strange, at Preston, on the 13th of July, 1588. That

[s] His. Lan, vol. 1, p 511

the armada might attempt to effect a landing in Lancashire, was, at the time, considered very probable; especially as the harbour of "Pille," on the Morecambe bay, opposite to Rossall point, was regarded, according to the Lansdowne MSS., cod. 56, "the very best haven for landinge with great shyppes in all the southwest coast of England called St. George's Channel.[t] The same document further says:—

"What the Spanyerd meanes to do the Lord knows, for all the countrye being knowne to Doctor Allen, who was borne harde by the pyle," (at Rossall Hall,) "and the inhabytentes ther aboutes all ynfected with his Romish poyson, it is not vnlike but his directione will be vsed for some landinge there." And further—"One Thomas Prestone (a papyshe atheiste) is deputye steward, and commaundes the menrede and landes ther, wch were sometyme members appertayning to the Abbeye of Fornes."

The elements, conjoined to the bravery and skill of the English sailors, under Lord Howard of Effingham, however, destroyed or dispersed the apparently overwhelming naval power of Spain, and effectually freed the country from the threatened danger.

The Rev. W. Thornber, in his History of Blackpool, says:—

"Tradition mentions that one of their ships was driven upon the shore not far from Rossall Point. In this dilemma it was attacked by the country people, instigated either by a desire of plunder, or under the guidance of Fleetwood, the proprietor of the estate, to capture it as a prize. The Spaniards, however, making a most desperate resistance, escaped on the flowing of the tide, and, in revenge, saluted Rossall Hall with their guns. In corroboration of this tradition, two cannon balls are produced, which were found on the removal of the old walls of the mansion, and which, it is asserted, are the identical ones fired by this stranded member of the armada. When the news of the total discomfiture of the Spanish fleet arrived, our noble queen was engaged in feasting on a Michaelmas goose, the whole country, for many a year afterwards, following the example of the court, on the anniversary of that day, celebrated it by partaking of the same excellent fare. Our villages still keep the same feast: the Michaelmas goose annually smokes on the board, in remembrance of the signal overthrow of the boast of Spain; and the guests, notwithstanding the ban of tee-totalism, also imitate the queen in digesting their supper with a cup of brandy."

Notwithstanding the anathemas fulminated upon the head of Elizabeth, by the pope, Sextus V., and his absolution of her subjects from their allegiance, the catholics, as a body, remained faithful to the sovereign, and contributed both ships and men for the defence of the kingdom. Yet such was the virulence and rancour of religious antagonism at the time, that this loyal and patriotic conduct, did not afterwards save them from capital punishment, for such trifling offences against the law, as the harbouring of priests, admitting the supremacy of the pope, denying that of the queen, or receiving ordination on the continent. Religious persecution was not, however, directed solely against the Roman catholics. Nonconformists, of every denomination, under the generic title of recusants, were subjected to similar pains and penalties.

t The endorsement to this document slightly contradicts the opinion expressed in the text. It runs thus:—"Touchinge a place called the Pille, in Lancashire, a dangerous place for Landinge."

Camden, the historian, topographer, and antiquary, in the reign of Elizabeth, mentions Preston as "a large, and for these parts, handsome and populous towne, so called from religious persons, as much as to say Priest's-Towne Preston is vulgarly called Preston in Andernesse, for Acmundesse-nesse, for so the Saxons called this part of the country which runs out with a long compass between *Ribill* and *Cocar*, and forms a promontory resembling a nose, and afterwards called Agmonderness."

Elizabeth confirmed the charters granted to the borough of Preston by her predecessors, and accorded several additional privileges to the burgesses.[u]

In the reign of Elizabeth, a family quarrel, with a fatal termination, occurred near Preston. The particulars illustrate, in a powerful manner, the despotic and arbitrary character of the ancient baronial chieftains, and their disregard for law and order, when their pride or interest was in any way compromised It appears, a feud had existed for some years between the families of Mr. Hoghton, of Lea, in the parish of Preston, and Langton, baron of Walton and Newton, in Makerfield. The latter, desirous of avenging some past indignity, made cause with a widow Singleton, whose cattle had been impounded by his rival. The baron assembled about eighty of his tenants and retainers, marched them to the residence of Mr. Hoghton, and challenged that gentleman and his friends to combat. Finding his house surrounded by his enemies, Mr. Hoghton sallied forth at the head of about thirty followers. A regular battle ensued, in which Mr. Hoghton and his retainer, Richard Baldwin, lost their lives. A magisterial investigation of the affair took place at Preston, when the parties were committed for trial, at the following assizes, for wilful murder. Through the influence of the earl of Derby, who solicited the interest of the high-treasurer, Burleigh, a petition from forty-seven of the belligerents, soliciting the queen's pardon, was favourably received Another petition, from the widow of the deceased Mr. Hoghton, concurring in its prayer, was likewise forwarded. Through this joint effort, a pardon was obtained for the combative baron. In order to effect this compromise, however, Langton entered into an engagement, by which he transferred to the heir of his late rival, as some compensation for the loss of his parent, the valuable manor and estate of Walton-le-dale.[v]

u See Municipal History, chap. vi., of the present volume

v Burke in the Peerage and Baronetage, says —"Thomas Hoghton, Esq., who served the office of sheriff of Lancashire in the 6th year of the reign of Queen Elizabeth, fell in a *duel* with Langton, of Newton, commonly called Baron of Walton and Newton, in the 49th year of the same reign "

"A riot not very dissimilar to that which occurred in 1589, took place at the manor house at Lea, in the parish of Preston, in 1633, for which the offenders were prosecuted in the court of star-chamber, where Sir Richard Hoghton was fined £100, and other two of the rioters £50 each." —Edward Baines's History of Lancashire, vol. 2, p. 4

After the introduction of the art of printing, England made great progress in the march of civilization; yet, even up to the time of Elizabeth, many domestic comforts, regarded at the present day as necessities by the humblest, were unknown. According to Erasmus, the people were generally dirty and slovenly in their habits, and to this he attributes the virulence of the numerous plagues with which the country had, from time to time, been infested. He describes the floors of the houses as made of "clay, and strewed with rushes, under which lay, unmolested, an ancient collection of beer, grease, fragments, bones, spittle, excrement of dogs and cats, and everything that is nasty."

Holinshed, who lived in Elizabeth's reign, states that there was scarcely a chimney to any of the houses in large towns; the smoke found its way through the roof, or out at the door or windows. The walls of the houses were nothing but wattling, plastered over with clay. The people slept on straw pallets, with a good round log under their heads for a pillow. Almost all the furniture and utensils were of wood. The streets of large towns, such as Manchester, Liverpool, and Preston, were unpaved.

The castles and houses of the nobility and gentry were very sumptuous, of their kind; and hospitality of the most profuse character was generally practised by the wealthy barons. The apartments were, nevertheless, often in a most filthy condition.[w]

Much improvement in general manners, social comforts, and domestic appliances, however, took place in the reign of Elizabeth. Holinshed notices the superior style of entertainment at the inns in Lancaster, Preston, etc. In his quaint manner, he informs the reader, that they were well furnished with "napierie, bedding, and tapisserie," and that "each commer is sure to lie in cleane sheets wherein no man hath been lodged since they came from the laundress."

John de Brentford, speaking of Lancashire, about this period, says:—

"The manners and customs of the inhabitants of Lancashire are similar to those of the neighbouring counties, except that the people eat with two-pronged forks! The men are masculine, and, in general, well made; they ride and hunt the same as in the most southern parts, but not with that grace, owing to the whip being carried in the left hand. The women are most handsome; their eyes brown, black, hazel, blue, or grey; their noses, if not inclined to aquiline, are mostly of the Grecian form, which gives a most beautiful archness to the countenance; such, indeed, as is not easy to be described. Their fascinating manners have long procured them the name of Lancashire Witches."

Camden, to some extent, corroborates this. He says:—

"The goodly and fresh complexion of the natives does sufficiently evince the goodness of this county; nay and the cattle too, if you will; for in the oxen, which have huge horns, and proportionate bodies, you will find nothing of that perfection wanting that

---

w See page 106.

Mago the Carthagenian, in Columella required." "This Soil, (Amounderness), bears Oats pretty well, but is not so good for barley; it makes excellent pasture especially towards the Sea, where it is partly Champain; whence a great part of it is call'd the *File*, probably for the *Field*. But being in other places Fenny, 'tis reckond less wholesom. In many places along the Coast there are heaps of Sand, upon which they now and then pour water, till it grows saltish, and then with turf boyl it into a white Salt. Here are also some Quicksands so hazardous to Travellers who think to shorten their Journey when the Tide is out, that they are in danger of being *shipwrack'd and sunk in a Land Journey*, (as *Sidonius* expresses it), especially near the mouth of the *Cockar*, where in a field of Quicksands stood *Cockarsand-Abbey*, formerly a small Monastery of the *Cluniacks*, situated between the mouth of the *Cockar*, and the *Lune* or *Lone*, with a large view of the *Irish* Sea."

The introduction of the art of printing, in 1474, effected a remarkable change in the manners, habits, and tastes of the people. Books, instead of being confined to the libraries of the clergy and a few of the wealthy nobles, began to be eagerly sought for by the more intelligent of the middle class. Literature and the arts met with increased patronage. The result was, that the youthful national intellect rapidly matured, and laid the foundation of much of the after prosperity and glory of Great Britain. The age that produced such minds as Shakspere, Bacon, Spencer, Raleigh, Sidney, and a host of other illustrious men, will ever command the gratitude and reverence of Englishmen, and form one of the most brilliantly illuminated pages consecrated to the record of the gradual development of the genius and enterprise inherent in the Anglo-Saxon race.

PART I.—HISTORICAL.

CHAPTER IV.—FROM JAMES I. TO THE "RESTORATION."

Lancashire gentry Knighted—Institution of the hereditary honour and title of Baronet—Plague—Gunpowder Plot—Witchcraft—Dr. Dee and Edward Kelley: Demonology at Walton-le-Dale—James the First's progress through Lancashire: Festivities at Myerscough, Preston, and Hoghton Tower—Alum Mines at Samlesbury—Petition of Lancashire people in favour of Sunday recreation—Book of Sports—Traditions relating to the King's visit to Hoghton—Civil War between Charles I. and his Parliament—Meeting on Preston Moor—Seizure of Military Stores at Preston, Liverpool, and Manchester—Alexander Rigby, M.P., Sir Gilbert Hoghton, Bart., Lord Strange, Sir Thos. Tildesley, etc., at Walton Hall—Threatened outbreak at Preston—*Fracas* at Manchester—Commencement of Hostilities—Siege of Manchester—Battle of Edge Hill—Defeat of the Earl of Derby, near Chowbent—Battles of Hinfield Moor and Ribble Bridge: Defeat of Sir Gilbert Hoghton—Victory of the Earl of Derby's troops, near Wigan—Meeting of Royalists, at Preston—Ruse at Salesbury Hall, near Ribchester—First Siege of Preston: Surrender of the town to Sir John Seaton—Death of Adam Morte—Surrender of Hoghton Tower to Captain Starkie: Disastrous Explosion, and Destruction of the Fortress—Siege of Lancaster—Successful Surprise of Preston, by the Earl of Derby: Destruction of the Fortifications—Wigan taken by Col. Ashton—Capture of Thurland Castle, by Col. Rigby—Sequestration of Estates—Lord Byron's Successes in Cheshire—Defeat of Byron at Nantwich—First Siege of Lathom House: Gallant Defence by the Countess of Derby—Capture of Bolton by Prince Rupert and the Earl of Derby—Surrender of Liverpool—Battle of Marston Moor—Retreat of Rupert into Lancashire—Seizure of the Mayor and Bailiffs of Preston—Shuttleworth's Victory at Ribble Bridge—Defeat of the Royalists at Ormskirk, and re-capture of Liverpool, by Sir John Meldrum—Distress in Lancashire—Battle of Naseby—Second Siege of Lathom House: Capture of the Fortress—Surrender of the King—Great Battle of Preston, in 1648: Defeat of Langdale and the Duke of Hamilton, by Oliver Cromwell—Famine and Plague—Execution of Charles I.—Establishment of the Commonwealth—Passage of Charles II. through Lancashire—Landing of the Earl of Derby, at Wyre—Lilburne's Pursuit of the Royalists to Ribble Bridge—Battle of Wigan Lane: Defeat of the Earl of Derby, and Death of Sir Thomas Tildesley—Battle of Worcester—Charles II. a fugitive—Capture and Execution of the Earl of Derby—Death of Cromwell—The Restoration—Value of Property in the Boroughs of Lancashire.

By the accession of James I., England and Scotland became united under one head. Immediately after the issuing of the proclamation declaring James king of England, the gentry of Lancashire forwarded to the monarch "a loyal and dutiful response." Sir Thomas Holcroft, Sir Edmund Trafford, and Sir Thomas Gerrard, from Lancashire, were amongst the nobility and gentry who met the king at York, and received the honour of knighthood at his hands. This distinction was shortly afterwards conferred upon several other Lancashire gentlemen, viz., Sir Thomas Hesketh, Sir Thomas Walmsley, Sir Alexander Barlow, Sir Edward Stanley, Sir Thomas Langton, Sir William Norris, and Sir Gilbert Hoghton, eldest son of Sir Richard Hoghton, of Hoghton Tower.

In 1616, James instituted the hereditary honour and title of baronet. Amongst the first eighteen knights elevated to this rank, are Sir Richard Hoghton, of Hoghton Tower; Sir Thomas Gerrard, of Bryn, and Sir Richard Molyneux, of Sefton, in the county of Lancaster. The fees paid on the occasion were devoted towards the subjugation of the province of Ulster, in Ireland. The arms of each baronet, in allusion to the origin of the dignity, include the bloody hand in a field *argent*, previously emblazoned as the heraldic device of the invaded province.

Soon after James's accession, a plague broke out in London, which carried away about one-fifth of the then inhabitants. In the following year, it spread into Lancashire, where it raged for some time with great virulence.

The most memorable event in the reign of James is the celebrated "popish plot," for the destruction of the king, and the members of both houses of parliament. Lord Monteagle, the nobleman who, informed by a mysterious and anonymous epistle of the danger, divulged the fact to the authorities, was himself a Roman catholic, a member of the house of Stanley, and the depository of the title and honour earned by the gallant Sir William Stanley, at Flodden. Peter Heywood, Esq., of Heywood, the individual by whom Guy Fawkes was apprehended, was an active magistrate of the county of Lancaster.

During the reign of James, the superstitious belief in witchcraft and demonology reached its climax, and Lancashire shared in the popular delusion to a very great extent. Faith in the powers and fascinations of "Lancashire witches," is, by no means, extinct at the present day; but the character of their spells, as well as the age and personal charms of the insidious professors, has undergone a complete metamorphosis. The change has, doubtless, been productive of a large increase of social and domestic happiness, in more senses than one. So infatuated were the people, generally, respecting this absurd superstition, that the king himself thought it not beneath his dignity to publish a tract upon the subject, which has perpetuated, not only his shallow-pated credulity, but his petty intolerance. He professes his object to have been to "resolve the doubting hearts of many, both that such assaults of Satan are certainly practised, and that the instruments thereof merit most severely to be punished; against the damnable opinions of those who are not ashamed in publicke print to deny that there can be such a thing as witchcraft; and so maintain the old error of the Sadduces in the denying of spirits."

The principal locality patronised by the Lancashire witches of old for their conferences, and the performance of their pretended incantations, was Malkin Tower, in Pendle forest, in the parish of Whalley. At the Lancaster assizes, in 1612, not less than nineteen persons were tried for this supposed crime. Their names and professional aliases were as follow:—Elizabeth Southern, widow, alias Old Demdike; Elizabeth Device, alias Young Demdike, her daughter; James Device, the son of Young Demdike; Alizon Device, the daughter of Young Demdike; Anne Whittle, widow, alias Chattox, alias Chatter-box, Old Demdike's rival; Anne Redferne, daughter of Anne Chattox; Alice Nutter; Katherine Hewcytt, alias Mould-heeles; Jane Bulcock, of the Mosse End; John Bulcock, her son; Isabel Roby; Margaret Peerson, of Padiham; Jennet Bierley, Ellen Bierley, Jane Southworth, John Ramsden, Elizabeth Astley, Alice Grey, Isabel Sidgreaves, and Lawrence Haye.

The twelve first mentioned are described as "Witches of Pendle Forest," and the latter eight as "Witches of Samlesbury," near Preston. Notwithstanding the improbable and frivolous character of the evidence adduced, ten of the Pendle practitioners fell victims to a combination of their own impostures and the credulity of the age. The old witch Demdike died in prison, and thus escaped the fate of her rivals and companions, who were hanged, king James having, in his sapient treatise, expressly pronounced "those detestible slaues of the Diuel, the witches or enchanters," unworthy of the royal clemency.

Respecting the trial of the Samlesbury offenders, Mr. Baines gives the following particulars:—

"Against Jane Bierley, Ellen Bierley, and Jane Southworth, of Samlesbury, charged with having bewitched Grace Sowerbutts, at that place; the only material evidence adduced was that of Grace Sowerbutts herself, a girl of licentious and vagrant habits, who swore that these women, one of them being her grandmother, did draw her by the hair of the head, and lay her upon the top of a hay mow, and did take her senses and memory from her; that they appeared to her sometimes in their own likeness, and sometimes like a black dog. She further deposed that by their arts they prevailed upon her to join their sisterhood; and that they were met from time to time by four black things going upright, and yet not like men in the face; who conveyed them across the Ribble, where they danced with them, and then each retired to hold dalliance with her familiar, conformable, no doubt, to the doctrine of *Incubi* and *Succubi*, as promulgated by the royal demonologist. To consummate their atrocities, the prisoners bewitched and slew a child of Thomas Walshman's by placing a nail in its navel; and after its burial they took up the corpse, when they ate part of the flesh and made 'an unxious ointment,' by boiling the bones. This was more than even the capacious credulity of the judge and jury could digest; the Samlesbury witches were therefore acquitted, and a seminary priest of the name of Thompson, alias Southworth, was suspected by two county magistrates, to whom the affair was afterwards referred, of having instigated Sowerbutts to make the charge, but this imputation was not supported by any satisfactory evidence. John Ramsden, Elizabeth Astley, Alice Grey, Isabel Sidegreaves, and Lawrence Haye, were all discharged without trial."[a]

The "Iter Lancastrense," a Poem, written in 1636, by the Rev. Rd. Jones, B.D, has the following pertinent lines on the subject:—

"Penigent, Pendle hill, Ingleborough,
Three such hills be not all England thorough:
I long to climb up Pendle, Pendle stands,
Round cop, survaying all ye wilde moore lands,
And Malkins Toure,[b] a little cottage where
Reporte makes caitive witches meete to sweare
Their homage to ye divell, and contrive
The deaths of men and beasts. Lett who will dive
Into this banefull search, I wonder much
If judges sentence with belief on such
Doth passe then sure they would not for lewd gaine
Bad clients fauour, or putt good to paine
Of long pursuite; for terror of ye fiend
Or loue of God they would giue causes end
With equall justice Yet I doe confesse,
Needs must strainge phansies poore ould wiues possesse,
Whoe in those desert mystie moores do liue
Hungrie and colde, and scarce see priest to giue
Them ghostlye counsell. Churches farre doe stand
In lay mens hands, and chappells haue no land
To cherish learned Curates, though Sir Jhon
Doe preach for foure pounds vnto Haselingdon.
Such yeerely rent, with right of hegging corne,[c]
Makes Jhon a sharer in my Ladyes horne;
He drinks and prayes, and fortie yeeres this life
Leading, at home keepes children and a wife.
Theis are ye wonders of our carelesse dayes,
Small store serves him whoe for ye people prayes."[d]

The practice of witchcraft was not always associated with decrepid old women, or withered and helpless wrestlers with poverty, even of the sterner sex The celebrated Dr. Dee, warder of the Collegiate Church, Manchester, considered the suspicions, loudly expressed, respecting his own studies and practices, demanded a public refutation. In a petition to the king, the learned doctor says.—"It has been affirmed that your

a His. Lan., vol I. p. 600

b "Baines confounds Malkin Tower with Hoar-stones" (Boundary Stones), "a place rendered famous by the second case of pretended witchcraft in 1633, but at some distance from the first named spot, the residence of Mother Demdike, which lies in the township of Barrowford. The witch's mansion is now alas! no more It stood in a field a little elevated on a brow above the building at present called Malkin Tower. The site of the house or cottage is still distinctly traceable, and fragments of the plaster are yet to be found embedded in the boundary wall of the field. The old road to Gisborne ran almost close to it"—Rev. T. Corser.

c "*Hegging corn*" Probably an error for begging corn. Mr. Ormerod mentions such a custom existed in Cheshire The clerk of Rochdale parish held such a privilege about 1692.—Corser.

d MS Bodleian Library, Oxford Published by the Cheetham Society, Manchester, and edited by the Rev. Thos Corser, M A

majesty's suppliant was the conjurer belonging to the most honourable privy council of your majesty's predecessor, of famous memory, queen Elizabeth; and that he is, or hath been, a caller or invocator of devils, or damned spirits." He further observes, emphatically "These slanders which have tended to his utter undoing, can no longer be endured; and if on his trial he is found guilty of the offence imputed to him, he offers himself willingly to the punishment of death; yea either to be stoned to death, or to be buried quick, or to be burned unmercifully"

Notwithstanding this indignant protest of the erudite astrologer, many of his studies and experiments might, at that day, have been deemed by a jury of his countrymen equally criminal with the supposed sorceries of the Pendle or Samlesbury witches

The doctor occasionally associated with men whose practices were of a very equivocal character. He was intimate with the renowned Edward Kelley, and, perhaps, owes a considerable portion of his reputation for sorcery to this connection. One of Kelley's most famous exploits was performed in the village of Walton. It is difficult to determine the precise nature of the means by which his impostures were perpetrated, but, it is more than probable, ventriloquism formed no unimportant item in the conjurer's list of accomplishments. This performance is recorded with characteristic gravity and moral horror by Weaver, in his work, entitled "Funerall Monuments," printed in 1631. He says:—

"*Kelley* (otherwise called *Talbot*), that famous English alchymist of our times, who flying out of his owne countrey (after he had lost both his eares at Lancaster) was entertained with *Rodolph* the second, and last of that Christian name, Emperour of Germany; for whom Elizabeth, of famous memory, sent (very secretly) Captaine *Peter Gunne*, with some others, to persuade him to returne backe to his owne natiue home; which hee was willing to doe · and thinking to escape away in the night, by stealth, as he was clammering ouer a wall in his owne house in Prague (which beares his name to this day, and which sometime was an old Sanctuary) he fell downe from the battlements, broke his legges, and bruised his body, of which hurts within a while after he departed this world.

"*Sed quorsum hæc*, you will say. then thus, This diabolicall questioning of the dead, for the knowledge of future accidents, was put in practise by the aforesaid *Kelley*, who, vpon a certaine night, in the Parke of Walton in le dale, in the county of Lancaster, with one *Paul Waring* (his fellow companion in such deeds of darknesse) inuocated some of the infernall regiment, to knowe certaine passages in the life, as also what might bee knowne by the deuil's foresight, of the manner and time of the death of a noble young Gentleman, as then in his wardship. The blacke ceremonies of that night being ended, Kelley demanded of one of the Gentlemans seruants, what corse was the last buried in Law church-yard, a Church thereunto adioyning, who told him of a poore man that was buried there but the same day[e] Hee and the said *Waring* intreated this aforesaid seruant, to go with them to the graue of the man so lately interred, which he did; and withall did helpe them to digge up the carcase of the poore caitiffe, whom by their incantations, they made him (or rather some euil spirit through his Organs) to speake, who deliuered strange predictions concerning the said Gentleman. I was told thus much by the said Seruingman, a secondary actor in that dismall abhorrid businesse: and

[e] "Law" church is Walton church. "Law" signifies a hill or mound.—[See p. 66.]

diuers gentlemen, and others, are now liuing in Lancashire to whom he hath related this story. And the Gentleman himselfe (whose memorie I am bound to honour) told me a little before his death, of this coniuration by *Kelley*, as he had it by relation from his said Servant and Tenant; onely some circumstances excepted, which he thought not fitting to come to his master's knowledge"

In 1663, another gang of witches was hunted up in Pendle Forest, sent to Lancaster, and the whole, seventeen in number, condemned to die. The judge, however, granted a respite; and, eventually, Charles I., by royal clemency, conferred upon the wretched people a free pardon.

The exploits of the witches of Lancashire were so notorious at this period, that a comedy on the subject was produced at the Globe theatre, written by Thomas Heywood and Richard Brown Another drama, about eighty years afterwards, written by Shadwell, depicted the exploits of Old Demdike and her companions. The subject has latterly furnished the groundwork for Harrison Ainsworth's popular novel, "The Lancashire Witches." It is not improbable that Dame Demdike and her compeers may have contributed to the "raw material" from which Shakspere fashioned his celebrated "weird sisters," in Macbeth. The date of the tragedy is not known with certainty. It must, however, have been one of his later productions Demdike was tried in 1612, and Shakspere died in 1616.

The severe laws relative to the supposed practice of demonology and witchcraft, enacted by James, were continued in force for upwards of a century. They were not expunged from the statute book till the ninth year of the reign of George II.

In country districts, in the neighbourhood of Preston, as well as elsewhere, this superstitious belief in the powers of witchcraft still lingers, though in a much milder and, comparatively, harmless form This is attested by the common expression, "surely, the thing's bewitched," applied to a child, or an inanimate object even, that, from any cause or other, appears doggedly to resist the will or labour of the locutor The horse-shoe, so often found nailed on or over the door of a rustic building, the charms and fortune-telling practices of wandering gipsies, as well as occasional cases of successful imposture, which have called for magisterial interference, abundantly demonstrate the fact, that superstitions amongst the uneducated survive, for a lengthened period, their consignment, by cultivated intelligence, to the lumber room of the past.

James I., on his return from a visit to his native country, in 1617, passed through Lancashire, and partook of the hospitality of the lord Gerard, at Ashton Hall; of Edward Tildesley, Esq., at Myerscough; of the mayor and corporation of Preston; of Sir Richard Hoghton, Bart., at Hoghton Tower, and of William, earl of Derby, at Lathom House.

While at Hoghton Tower, the king conferred the honour of knighthood upon Sir Arthur Lake, of Middlesex, and Sir Cecil Trafford, of Lancashire. At Lathom, similar marks of royal favour were extended to the following Lancashire gentlemen:—Sir John Talbot, of Preston; Sir Gilbert Clifton, Sir William Massy, Sir Robert Bendloes, Sir Gilbert Ireland, of the Hutt, and Sir Edward Olbaston.

A private journal, kept by Nicholas Assheton, Esq., of Downham, in the parish of Whalley, describes, in quaint but forcible language, the "doings" of the royal party during his majesty's sojourn in the neighbourhood of Preston. It throws some light, too, upon the domestic habits and social enjoyments of the period. The following extracts have reference to the king's visit:—

"June 1. Sunday. Mr. C. P. moved my brother Sherborne[f] from Sir Richard Houghton, to do him such favour, countenance, grace, and curtesie, as to weare his clothe, and attend him at Houghton, at the king's coming in August, as divers other Gentlemen were moved and would. He likewise moved me. I answered I would bee willing, and redie to doe Sir Richard anie service.

"August 11. My brother Sherborne his taylor brought him a suit of apparall and us two others, and a livery cloake from Sir Richard Houghton, that we should attend him at the King's coming, rather for his grace and reputation, shoeing his neibor's love, then any exacting of mean service.

"August 12. Coz Townley came and broke his fast at Dunnoe, and went away. To Mirescough. Sir Richard gone to meet the King; we after him to ——— There the King slipt into the Forest another way,[g] and we after and overtook him, and went past to the yate; then Sir Richard light; and when the King came in his coach, Sir Richard stept to his side, and tould him ther his Majesties Forest began, and went some ten roodes to the left, and then to the Lodge, the King hunted and killed a buck.

"August 13. To Mirescough, the Comt. Cooz, Assheton came with as gentlemanlie servants as any was ther, and himself excellently well appointed. The King killed five bucks. The Kinge's speeche about libertie to pipeing and honest recreation. We that were in Sir Richard's livery had nothing to do but riding upp and downe.[h]

---

f Mr. Sherborne was brother-in-law to Mr. Assheton.

g "The 'Duchy Park lands,' as those embraced within the limits of the forest are called at the Duchy office, are held on lease from the Crown by Messrs. William and John Humber, of Preston merchants, and the former resides at Myerscough Hall, the property of James Greenhalgh, Esq.

"It appears to be probable that the king slipt into the forest, at some part of the extreme southern boundary, a little to the west of the White Horse public house, as the other gentlemen of the royal party, 'went past to the yate,' that is to the point now known as Park-head Gate, being about seven yards from the boundary of the forest, and close to Hankinson House. The forest, from the south, began at the boundary of the present Park-head farm, and there are still the remains of an ancient direct road leading to the Lodge and two venerable yew trees are pointed out, between an avenue of which tradition reports that the road passed."—Rev. F. R. Raines's Annotations, published by the Cheetham Society.

h "Myerscough Lodge had the distinguished honour of receiving and entertaining two royal visitors. The visit mentioned in this journal, when James I. remained with Edward Tyldesley, Esq., three, but, according to another authority, only two nights, (Cole's MSS. Brit. Mus. vol. xlvi. p. 257), and the other on the 13th August, 1651, when Charles II. 'lodged one night at Myerscoe, Sir Thomas Tyldesley's house;' at that time and previously known as 'the Lodge.'

"The deer were in existence within the memory of aged persons now living, but were destroyed about the year 1778. The park was not walled or fenced, but laid open.

"Myerscough House, and not the Lodge, as stated by Mr. Nichols, was formerly the seat of Charles Gibson, Esq. (maternal grandfather of Charles R. Jacson, of Barton Lodge, Esq.), but is now the property of John Cunliffe, Esq. It is not situated within the forest."—Rev. F. R. Raines.

"August 14. Us three to Preston; ther preparation made for Sir Gilbert Houghton and other Knights.[i] Wee were desyred to be merrie, and at nyght were soe. Steeven Hamerton and wyffe, and Mrs. Doll Lyster supped with us att our lodging. All Preston full.

"August 15. King came to Preston. Ther, at the Crosse, Mr. Beares, the lawyer, made a Speeche and the Corporation presented him with a bowle;[j] and then the King went to a banquet in the Town Hall, and so away to Houghton; ther a speeche made. * * The King hunted and killed a stag. We attend on the Lords' table.

"August 16. Houghton. The King hunting; a great companie; killed affore dinner a brace of staggs. Verie hot; soe he went into dinner. Wee attend the Lords' table,[k] and about four o'clock the King went downe to the allome-mynes,[l] and was ther an hower, viewed them preciselie, and then went and shott at a stagg, and missed. Then my Lord Compton had lodged two brace. The King shott again and brake the thigh bone. A dogg long in coming, and my Lord Compton shott again, and killed him. Late in to supper.

"August 17. Houghton. Wee served the Lords with biskett, wyne and jellie. The Bushopp of Chester, Dr. Morton, preached before the King. To dinner. About four

i Sir Gilbert Hoghton, eldest son and successor of Sir Richard, was knighted at Whitehall 21st July, 1604. He "was in high favour with James and had the honour to be his majesty's servant at court. Sir Gilbert was celebrated for his elegant accomplishments, and especially in dancing. He frequently took part in the beautiful masques in this reign, and is even mentioned by name in Ben Johnson's Anti-masque, 'For the Honour of Wales,' presented before the king and his courtiers in 1618-19."—Raines.

j "The records of the corporation of Preston have been searched in vain for an account of this royal visit. The Crosse was taken down a few years ago, and a tinted lithographic sketch of it was published as it appeared in the year 1274,—but from the style of the architecture it may be allowable to infer that such a structure never existed except in the mind of the artist."—Raines.—[See description of the Market-place in the topographical portion of this work.]

k "A relic of old feudal manners, under which every rank served at the tables of their immediate superiors."—Dr. Whitaker.

l "Sir Richard Hoghton set up a very profitable mine of alum nigh unto Hoghton Tower, in the hundred of Blackburn, within these few years, where store of very good alome was made and sold." —*Webster's History of Metals.*

"The alum mines were held on a joint lease from the Duchy by Mr. Ramsay and Lady Sarah Hoghton, a little before the Restoration, and the latter lessee entered into certain articles of agreement with Captain James Benson, in 1658, to work her ladyship's portion of the mines. These terms appear to have been more advantageous for the lady than for the captain, and in the following year the works failed, and the lessee was ruined, his estate being seized by his creditors, and himself imprisoned. He published (in twenty small quarto pages, about the year 1659) '*A relation of James Benson's undertaking the making of allum at the allum-work in Lancashire, truly opening (opened?) and the instrumental causes of his present condition set forth.*' He states that he found some sympathy in his losses from his cousin, Mr. Justice Sharples, of Blackburn, and from Major John Wiggin, but Dr. Fife, Major Ashurst, and Mr. Thomas Wilson, 'who had been great contrivers and assistants to my Lady,' from 'professed friends became secret and sure enemies.' The captain desired that Lady Hoghton should make him some reparation for his losses, according to the agreement; but she declined doing so, which led him to say that he received 'the hardest measure that ever poor man received from any persons professing truly to fear God,' and that he 'would never have any more to do with any business that concerned her ladyship's honour.' His wish to refer the case to the arbitration of any two or four godly divines, Mr. Eaton and Mr. Tildesley being of the number, was disregarded, and his real or imaginary wrongs remained unredressed. This appears to have been the termination of the working of the alum mines."—Raines.—[The alum mines were worked to a much later period. See p. 4.]

Captain Benson was bailiff of the borough of Preston, in 1644. He was seized, together with the mayor, William Cottam, esq., by Prince Rupert, in September, 1644, after the battle of Marston Moor, and imprisoned in Skipton Castle for eleven months, for his leaning towards the principles professed by the Parliamentarians.

o'clock ther was a rush-bearing[m] and pipeing afore them, affore the King in the Middle Court. Then to supp. Then about ten or eleven o'clock a Maske of Noblemen, Knights, Gentlemen, and Courtiers, afore the King in the middle round in the garden. Some speeches; of the rest dancing the Huckler, Tom Bedlo, and the Cowp Justice of Peace.[n]

"August 18. The King went away aboot twelve to Lathome. There was a man almost slayne with fighting. Wee back with Sir Richard. He to seller, and drunk with us kindlie in all manner of frindlie speake. Preston; as merrie as Robin Hood, and all his fellowes.

"August 19. All this morning wee plaid the Bacchanalians." [o]

m "A Lancashire specimen of 'honest recreation,' suited, no doubt, to the taste of James. The whole scene to a feeling or serious mind is disgusting; a strange medley of dancing, drinking, pipeing, 'rush-bearing,' and preaching, heightened by the unfeeling mention of the King's maiming a noble animal for his sport. I cannot conceive that Bishop Morton would find himself quite at ease in the midst of such a scene."—Dr. Whitaker.

n "A Speeche made to Kinge James at his coming to Hoghton Tower by two conceaved to be the Household Gods; the first attyr'd in a purple taffata mantle, in one hand a palm-tree branch, on his head a garland of the same, and in the other hand a dogge:—

This day, great King for government admir'd!
Which these thy subjects have so much desired,
Shall be kept holy in their heart's best treasure
And vow'd to James as is this month to Cæsar.
And now the Landlord of this ancient Tower,
Thrice fortunate to see this happy hower,
Whose trembleinge heart thy presence setts on fire,
Unto this house (the heart of all the shire)
Does bid thee hearty welcome, and would speake it
In higher notes, but extreme joy doth breake it.
Hee makes his Guest most welcome, in whose eyes
Love-teares do sitt, not that he shouts and cryes.
And we the gods and guardians of this place,—
I of this house, he of the fruitfull chace,—
Since the Hoghtons from this hill took name
Who with the stiffe unbridled Saxons came,
And soe have flurish't in this fairer clyme,
Successively from that to this our tyme,
Still offeringe upp to our Immortall Powers
Sweet incense, wyne, and odoriferous flowers;
While sacred Vesta in her virgin tyre
With vows and wishes tends the hallowed fyre.
Now seeing that thy Majestye we see
Greater than country gods, more good than wee;
We render upp to thy more powerfull Guard
This house; this Knight is thine, he is thy Ward,
For by thy helpinge and auspicious hand
He and his home shall ever, ever stand
And flurish in despite of envious fate;
And then live, like Augustus, fortunate.
And longe, longe may'st thou live! to which both men,
Gods, saints and angells say, 'Amen, amen!'

The Second Tutelar God begins:

Thou greatest of mortalls! [*He's nonplust.*]

The Second God begins againe:*

Dread Lord! the splendour and the glorious raye
Of thy high majestye hath strucken dumbe
His weaker god-head; if t' himselfe he come
Unto thy service straight he will commend
These Foresters, and charge them to attend
Thy pleasure in this park, and shew such sport
To the Chief Huntsman, and thy princely court,
As the small circuit of this round affords
And be more ready than he was in's words."—

Nichol's Progress of James I.

* This must be an error. From the context it is evident it should read, "The *First* God begins againe."

o "We are indebted to the French (and it is no small obligation,) for the temperate elegance of modern tables, and particularly for the practice of drinking wine at dinner. At that time they

From a manuscript in the possession of Sir Henry Bold Hoghton, bart., entitled "Notes of the Diet at Hoghton at the King's cominge there," it appears the royal party were most liberally entertained The following excerpt, giving the bill of fare "for the Lords' table at the dinner on Sunday, the 17th August," will serve to illustrate the notions of good cheer entertained by noblemen and gentlemen at that period:—

"First course. Pullets, Boiled Capon, Mutton boiled, Boiled Chickens, Shoulder of Mutton roast, Ducks boiled, Loin of Veal roast, Pullets, Haunch of Venison roast, Burred Capon, Pastry of Venison hot, Roast Turkey, Veal burred, Swan roast, one, and one for to-morrow, Chicken pye hot, Goose roasted, Rabbits, cold Jiggits of Mutton boiled, Snipe pye, Breast of Veal boiled, Capons roast, Pullet, Beef roast, Tongue pye cold, Sprod boiled, Herons roast cold, Curlew pye cold, Mince pye hot, Custards, Pig roast.

"Second course. Hot Pheasant, one, and one for the King; Quails, six for the King, Partridge, Poults, Artichoke pye, Chickens, Curlew roast, Peas buttered, Rabbits, Duck, Plovers, Red Deer pye, Pig burred, Hot Herons roast, three of a dish; Lamb roast, Gammon of bacon, Pigeons roast, made dish, Chicken burred, Pear tart, Pullets and grease, Dryed Tongues, Turkey pye, Pheasant pye, Pheasant tart, Hog's cheek dryed, Turkey chicks cold."

A somewhat similar "bill of fare," both for Sunday evening's supper and Monday morning's breakfast, received ample justice from the guests.

The celebrated Archie Armstrong, the "king's foole," accompanied his royal master. James was, notwithstanding his soubriquet, "The English Solomon," remarkably fond of "fools," and enjoyed much their rough wit and practical jokes. Sir Arthur Weldon, in his "Court of King James," says:—"After the king supped, he would come forth to see pastimes and fooleries, in which Sir Edward Zouch, Sir George Goring, and Sir John Finit, were the chiefe and master fools (and surely the fooling got them more than any other's wisdome), sometimes presenting David Droman, and Archy Armstrong, the "king's foole," on the back of other fools, to tilt one another, till they fell together by the eares; sometimes they performed antick dances. But Sir John Millicent (who was never known before) was commended for notable fooling, and was indeed the *best extemporary foole* of them all."

were almost wholly divorced It is not above sixty years since," (Whitaker's work was published in 1818,) "the Lancashire gentry were in the habit of adjourning after dinner to the cellars of inns, and drinking themselves drunk with wine immediately drawn from the pipe"—Whitaker.

Miss Strickland (Lives of Queens of England, vol. 5, p. 279), referring to the circumstance of Bishop Ridley, on a pastoral visit to the Princess (afterwards Queen) Mary, being taken by Sir Thomas Wharton, the steward, to the cellar or to the buttery-hatch, and presented with a stirrup-cup observes,—"This custom was in vogue in the middle ages, as a trait of old English hospitality; persons of the highest quality were taken into the cellar, to taste draught wine or ale fresh from the cask, as Cavendish says the duke of Buckingham did in Wolsey's cellar."

According to Sir Arthur Weldon, King James himself was very temperate. "He seldom drank at any one time above four spoonfulls, many times not above one or two."—Court and Character of James I., 8vo., 1650.

Mr. Peter Whittle says, but does not give his authority, that:—

"A grand Masque took place, and a rush-bearing was introduced, in which 'a man was enclosed in a dendrological foliage of fronds,' and was the admiration of the company. This spectacle was exhibited in that part of the garden called the 'middle circular.' Speeches were made in dialogue, wittily pleasant, and all kinds of frolics were carried on to the highest pitch, by Robin Goodfellow, Bill Huckler, Tom Bedloe, old Crambo, Jem Tospot, Dolly Wango, and the Cap Justice. These characters were played to the life, and the Justices Crook, Hoghton and Doddridge, who were present, declared to the King that 'the Cap Justice was acted to the very life.' Sir John Finett, knight, and master of the ceremonies to the King, performed the part of Cap Justice."

Mr. Raines, commenting upon this passage, says:—"This 'dendrological man' was not a more ridiculous exhibition than the characters of men in the shape of hogsheads and barrels in one of the royal Masques, or of the schoolmaster of Linlithgow, who spouted verses to King James, in the form of a lion. In this reign every thing was exhibited in hyperbole. It ought to be named for the honour of the Lancashire ladies that these female characters were always sustained by male performers."

Shakspere evidently intended to burlesque this species of dramatic rhodomontade by his incidental play, "Pyramus and Thisbe," in "A Midsummer Night's Dream." It is doubtful, however, whether there existed any *peculiar merit* in the absence of lady performers in the *Lancashire* exhibitions of this class. It was not until after the "Restoration of Charles II." that the female parts in the regular drama were sustained by women. Shakspere himself never witnessed his Ophelia, his Desdemona, his Juliet, or his Imogen personated, except by boys or clean-shaven young men.

Malone says[p] that Sir William Davenant, Shakspere's godson, in imitation of foreign theatres, first introduced females upon the British stage, and that Mrs. Saunderson, afterwards Mrs. Betterton, was the first lady actress in England. Malone, however, is not certain of this, as he conjectures, in another place, that Mrs. Marshall was the first actress who appeared in any regular drama on the public stage. Waldron, the editor of the edition of Downe's "Roscius Anglicanus," published in 1789, says the first recorded female performer of Ophelia (the part mentioned by Malone), is Mrs. Hughes. A scarce book, entitled *A Royal Arbor of Loyal Poesie,*" by Thomas Jordan, published in 1664, contains a curious prologue, written for the purpose of introducing a lady performer in this character. Amongst other matter, it says:—

"Our women are defective, and so siz'd
You'd think they were some of the Guard disguiz'd;
For (to speak truth) men act, that are between
Forty and fifty, Wenches of fifteen;
With bone so large, and nerve so incomplyant,
When you call *Desdemona*, enter Giant."

Old Downes, the prompter, after informing his readers that Mr. Kynaston

p Supplement, vol. 1, p. 29.

played certain female parts, draws the following very ungallant comparison between him and his fair successors :—"He being then very young, made a complete female stage beauty; performing his parts so well, especially *Anthiope* and *Aglaura*, being parts greatly moving compassion and pity; that it has since been disputable among the judicious, whether any woman that succeeded him so sensibly touched the audience as he."[q] Some of the female characters in the masques, written by Ben Johnson, and by others, previously to the time of Shakspere, for representation at court, were, however, frequently sustained by ladies of rank and title. Indeed, they often appear to have been written expressly for representation by the male and female aristocracy. Henry VIII. occasionally indulged in the practice. The early "mysteries," "miracle plays," and "moralities," were originally performed by priests and others connected with the church. There can be no doubt that the great object aimed at by these representations was the instruction of the rude, unlettered people in the fundamental doctrines of Christianity; and that the practice was well calculated to meet the exigencies of the times. Other amusements or sports gradually became intermixed with these scriptural representations, until some scandal was brought upon the church thereby. The author of a tract, published in 1752, thus denounces the excesses then practised:—"He (the priest) again posteth it (the service) over as fast as he can gallop; for either he hath two places to serve, or else there are sume games to be played in the afternoon, as lying for the whetstone, heathenishe dauncing for the ring, a beare or a bull to be bayted, or else jack-an-apes to ride on horseback, or *an enterlude to be played;* and if no place else can be gotten, it must be doone in the church." "Miracle plays," were acted very constantly at Chester, until 1577, at Coventry, until 1591, at York, until late in the sixteenth century, at Newcastle, until 1598, at Lancaster, *Preston*, and, last of all, at Kendal, in the beginning of the reign of James I.[r] The "properties" and appointments, as well as some of the *dramatis personæ* of the "miracle plays," are singularly repugnant to modern notions of costume and propriety, as will be seen by the following extract from a "bill of expences," inserted in a *Dissertation on the Pageants or Dramatic Mysteries anciently performed at Coventry, and other Municipal Entertainments, by Thos. Sharp*:—"Payd for 2 pound of hayre for the devill's head, 3s.; mending his hose, 8d. Black canvas for shirts for the damned, 4s. Red buckram for wings of angels (represented by naked children), 7s. Paid for a cote for God, and a payre of gloves, 3s." It appears the Devil was a character often introduced into these mysteries and moralities.

q Roscius Anglicanum.

r Pen. Cyclop. art. English Drama.

One writer says:—

"He was made as hideous as possible by the mask and dress which he wore; and from various sources we learn that his exterior was shaggy and hairy, so that in one piece he is mistaken by one of the characters for 'a dancing bear.' His 'bottle nose' and 'evil face' are repeatedly mentioned; and that he was not without a tail is evident from the circumstance that in one place Vice asks him for a piece of it to make a fly-flap. His ordinary exclamation on entering was, 'Ho, ho, ho!' and on all occasions he was given to roaring and crying out, especially when, for the amusement of the audience, he was provoked to it by castigation at the hands of Vice, by whom he was generally, though not invariably, accompanied. * * Malone tells us that 'the principal employment of the Vice was to belabour the Devil.' * * In the moral-plays, as in the miracle-plays before them, the comic ingredients were made to predominate more and more over the serious; and the Vice became a standing vehicle of grosser and more thorough buffoonery than the Devil himself. Thus it was that he came to be so completely confounded with the character of the domestic fool, as to be very commonly dressed in the fool's party-coloured habit, wearing his dagger of lath."[8]

Advantage was taken of James's visit to Sir Richard Hoghton, by the inhabitants of the neighbourhood, to petition his majesty for a removal of the edicts of the commissioners appointed in the reign of Elizabeth, who had issued orders against "pipers and minstrels playing, making and frequenting bear-baiting and bull-baiting, on the Sabbath days, or upon any other days in time of divine service; and also against superstitious ringing of bells, wakes, and common feasts, drunkenness, gaming, and other vicious and unprofitable pursuits." The king received the petition with favour, and, in the following May, published a proclamation, in which he states that, "in his progress through Lancashire, he found it necessary to rebuke some puritans and precise people, and took order that the said unlawful carriage should not be used by any of them hereafter, in the prohibiting and unlawfully punishing of his good people, for using their lawful recreations and honest exercises, upon Sundays after service." The proclamation, after insinuating that the puritanical application of the term Sabbath to Sunday, savoured of Judaism, proceeds to inform us that the "English Solomon" had discovered the county of Lancaster was much infested by two sorts of people, papists and puritans, and that—

"They had maliciously traduced and calumniated his just and honourable proceedings; he had therefore thought proper to clear and make his pleasure manifest to all his good people in these parts; and his majesty's pleasure was, that the bishops of the diocese should take strict order with all the puritans and precisians within the county of Lancaster, and either constrain them to conform themselves, or to leave the country, according to the laws of this kingdom, and canons of this church; and for his good people's recreation, his pleasure was, that after the end of divine service, they be not disturbed, letted, or discouraged from any lawful recreation, such as dancing, either men or women; archery for men, leaping, vaulting, or any other such harmless recreation; nor from having of May-games, Whitson-ales, and Morris-dances, and the setting up of May-poles, and other sports therewith used; so as the same be had in due and convenient time, without impediment or neglect of divine service; and that women should have leave to carry rushes to the church, for the decorating of it according to their old custom; but withal his majesty did here account still as prohibited, all unlawful games to be used on Sundays only, as bear and bull-baitings, interludes, and, at all times, in

[8] Pen. Cyclop., art. English Drama.

the meaner sort of people, by law prohibited, bowling. And likewise did bar from this benefit and liberty all such known recusants, either men or women, as did abstain from coming to church or divine service, they being unworthy of any lawful recreation after the said service, that would not first come to the church and serve God; prohibiting, in like sort, the said recreations to any that though conformed in religion, were not present in the church at the service of God, before their going to the said recreations."

This proclamation was followed by the publication, on the 24th May, 1618, of the celebrated "Book of Sports," in which the royal author undertook to expound what were "lawful sports to be used on Sundays and festivals." On the pain of punishment in the High Commission Court, the bishops were called upon to order the permission to be announced in all the parish churches of their respective dioceses. The "Puritans and precise people of Lancashire," against whom this singular publication was especially directed, were, however, not the only parties who regarded it in the light of a royal sanction to the profanation of the Sabbath. Many clergymen of the Church of England indignantly resisted what they held to be an encroachment upon the clerical function, and a profanation of the sanctuary. Abbot, archbishop of Canterbury, notwithstanding the king's order, *prohibited* its publication by the officiating minister at Croydon. So much disaffection was engendered by the promulgation of these dogmas by the literary monarch, that several historians trace in it one of the principal germs, which, when matured in the following reign, plunged the country into the horrors of civil war.

Apologists have, however, been found for the "Book of Sports," in the persons of the elder D'Israeli and Lord John Manners. These literary advocates of the customs of the "good old times" having adopted a kind of theory that antiquity and goodness are nearly synonymous, doubtless felt the denunciations of the clergy and "precise people" in the light of an oblique attack upon their cherished principle, and consequently entered the lists more for the sake of their own general dogma, than from any particular admiration of the "Book of Sports," or its pedantic author.

Mr. Baines says this "fatal publication" was "suggested, if not written, on the banks of the Darwent," and Mr. Whittle further intimates that there exists "no doubt" upon the matter No evidence is produced, however, in support of these views. The petition of the people, presented to the king during his stay at Hoghton, might very probably *suggest* the compilation of the famous "Book of Sports;" but that it was *written* there is highly improbable In the first place, it was not published till the following year; and again, Mr. Asshcton's diary sufficiently accounts for the consumption of the few days spent at Hoghton Tower and in the neighbourhood of Preston. James appears to have occupied his time and thoughts principally with the shooting of bucks, conferring of dignities, and eating of dinners. His literary efforts would appear to have been confined to the making of a "speeche" or two, one of which certainly had for its theme "libertie to pipeing and honest recreation"

Several traditions yet linger in the neighbourhood respecting the visit of James to Hoghton Tower. One is, that his majesty knighted the loin of beef at the table of Sir Richard Hoghton; and that henceforth it received the appellation of sirloin. A similar story is, however, told of Charles II., and is, perhaps more in accordance with the character and conduct of the "Merrie monarch," than with the pedantry and self-complaisancy of his "learned" grandfather

Another tradition relative to king James's visit, states that on his majesty's arrival at Hoghton, sorely fatigued by the heat of the day and the dusty state of the roads, he was observed to gaze from a window with grave curiosity at a large and peculiarly formed boulder-stone. He speedily discovered that the upper surface bore the following inscription, in the good old Lancashire dialect:—

"Torne me o're, an I'll tel thee plaine."

The monarch's curiosity was still further excited by this invitation, and consequently, after much labour, the stone was overturned. The following minute scrap of rustic wisdom was found carved on the opposite side:—

"Hot porritch softens hard butter-cakes,
So torne me o're again."

The sapient ruler was non-plussed; but he had wit enough to order the stone to be placed in its former position, in order that others might exercise their laudable curiosity and physical power to as little purpose as the royal pedant. In "Traditions of Lancashire," vol 2, p. 175, Mr. Roby states that he had been informed the stone "was in existence less than a century ago, though not in the precise situation above alluded to."

Amongst the nobility and gentry who accompanied James to Hoghton, were the following distinguished personages:—George Villiers, earl, and afterwards marquis and duke of Buckingham, K.G., his majesty's cup bearer and master of the horse;[t] Ludovic, earl, afterwards duke of Richmond; William, third earl of Pembroke, K.G., chancellor of the University of Oxford, and chamberlain of the household; Charles, earl of Nottingham, lord high admiral, John, Viscount Brackley, K.B, afterwards created earl of Bridgewater, Edward Lord Zouche, lord president of Wales; Thomas Moreton, D.D., bishop of Chester, his majesty's chaplain, Sir Francis Fane, knight, afterwards earl of Westmoreland, William, Viscount Knollys, afterwards earl of Banbury; Lord John Mordaunt, afterwards earl of Peterborough; Henry Lord Grey, of Groby, great nephew of Henry, duke of Suffolk, father of Lady Jane Grey; John, Lord Stanhope

t Buckingham fell beneath the dagger of Felton, on the 23rd August, 1628.

of Harrington, vice chamberlain; William, second Lord Compton, created in the following year earl of Northampton; Sir John Tupton, bart.; Sir Arthur Capel, knight, Sir Thomas Brudenell, bart, afterwards Baron Brudenell, and earl of Cardigan; Sir Edward Montague, K.B., afterwards Baron Montague, groom of the bedchamber, Sir John Doddridge; Sir John Crooke and Sir Robert Houghton, the three puisne judges of the king's bench, Sir John Finett, knight, master of the ceremonies to the king; Sir Richard St George, knight, norroy king at arms; Sir Edward Mosley, knight, M P. for Preston in 1614, 1620, and 1623; Sir Edmund Trafford, of Trafford Park, sheriff of Lancashire; Richard Towneley, of Towneley; Ralph Assheton, of Whalley; Nicholas Girlington, of Thurnham Castle; Richard Sherborne, of Stoneyhurst; Richard Shuttleworth, of Gawthorpe; William Anderton, of Anderton, "mayor of the ceremonies" at Preston; together with about one hundred of the chief gentlemen of Lancashire

In the reign of James, the following Lancashire gentlemen, in addition to those already named, received an accession of dignity at the hands of the king:—Sir Thomas Tildesley was knighted at Wimbleton, Sir Hugh Parker, son of Lord Monteagle, was created knight of the bath; Sir Gilbert Gerrard, of Harrow, a junior scion of the family of Gerrard, of Bryn, in Lancashire; Sir Richard Boteler, and Sir Ralph Asheton, of Lever, were each elevated to the rank of baronet.

In the great civil commotions, which, in the reign of Charles I., shook the ancient institutions of the country to their foundations, and prostrated, for a period, the monarchical authority in Britain, the inhabitants of Lancashire enacted a prominent part. Preston was several times the scene of important military operations, and was, alternately, held for the king and for the parliament In this great and memorable struggle between despotic authority and popular liberty, both parties unquestionably committed many of those excesses which are ever incident to violent changes and troubled periods; especially when the principal questions at issue are practically solved, for the time being, by the power of the sword. The leading families of Preston and the neighbourhood, as in other parts of the country, were much divided in opinion as to the merits of the monarchical and parliamentary pretensions, though the popular feeling would appear unquestionably to have favoured representative rather than despotic authority

The principal causes of dispute between the king and his earlier parliaments, arose out of the determination of Charles to levy the impost denominated "ship money," for the support of the navy, without the sanction or authority of the representative body of the nation; the despotic and excessive penalties and fines enforced by the high commission court of Star-Chamber,[p] and his general claim to the right of governing and taxing the country by virtue of the royal prerogative, rather than by the free co-operation and control of parliament, which the ultra-royalists, or supporters of "the divine right of kings," appeared to regard as an instrument in the hands of the monarch, rather than a bulwark for the protection of the liberties of the people. The commons, on the other hand, elated by their successful resistance to the royal encroachments, strenuously laboured not only to legally define, but still further to curtail the royal prerogative An element of strong and even fanatical religious sentiment entered into the contest, and though composed of apparently the most heterogeneous elements, powerfully affected both the leaders and the populace, and influenced largely not only the civil legislation, but the military exploits of the period. The indiscretion of Charles, in the re-publication of his father's foolish tract, entitled the "Book of Sports," estranged from him the more truly pious, as well as the puritanical section of his subjects The puritans hated the Roman Catholics most cordially, and felt jealous of the influence of the queen. The adherents to the "ancient religion," though ofttimes greviously persecuted by both the court and episcopal authority, generally adhered to the crown, as the most endurable or the least embittered of their implacable opponents. Mr. Baines says, "another local cause of the civil wars, was the star-chamber, a branch of which existed at that time under the authority of the court of the duchy of Lancaster, and was probably held at Preston." Amidst these struggles, however, notwithstanding the infatuation, and, occasionally, the criminal irregularities of the human instruments engaged, the present highly prized limited monarchy, or "glorious constitution" of the British people, unquestionably germinated. Its gradual expansion to its present proportions and social importance, has but been the result of after measures, based upon the principles of free representative government, enunciated and fought for by the sturdy old commoners, who first drew the sword against the absolutism of the Stuart dynasty, and paved the way for its final expulsion from the throne of Great Britain.

After an interval of eleven years, the king's pecuniary requirements forced him to employ the constitutional authority of parliament for the levying of additional taxes. The representative body assembled in April, 1640. Before proceeding to supply the king's wants, they entered upon

---

p Sir Richard Hoghton was fined £100 by the court of Star-Chamber, in 1633, and two others £50 each, for an alleged riot at Lea Hall, in the parish of Preston.—[See *ante* p. 142]

the consideration of various grievances to which the people had been subjected, and sought to obtain redress The king, indignant at these proceedings, dissolved the parliament, after a sitting of three weeks. Notwithstanding the prerogative was exercised to the utmost, and every effort made to wring money from the people, Charles was necessitated once more, about six months afterwards, to issue writs summoning a new parliament. This body retained its functions during the whole of the civil war, or "great rebellion," as it was called, and acquired from this circumstance the appellation of the "long parliament." It consisted of about five hundred members. The county of Lancaster was represented by the following gentlemen:—*Knights of the shire*—Ralph Ashton, esq., and Roger Kirby, esq. Borough members,—*Lancaster*, John Harrison, knt., and Thomas Fanshaw, esq ; *Preston*, Richard Shuttleworth, esq , and Thomas Standish, esq ; *Newton*, William Ashurst, esq., and Roger Palmer, knt.; *Wigan*, Orlando Bridgman, esq , and Alexander Rigby, esq.; *Clitheroe*, Ralph Ashton, esq., and Richard Shuttleworth, gent ; *Liverpool*, John Moore, esq., and Richard Wynn, knt. and bart.

This parliament proved no more obedient to the wishes of the king than those which had preceded it Resolutions were passed condemnatory of the king's attempt to "govern the people of England by his sole will and pleasure as an absolute monarch, without the assistance of parliament, as he had lately done" The people's representatives declared "he should be compelled to admit the two houses of parliament to a participation of the legislative authority with him, according to the constitution of England, ever since the first institution of the house of commons in the reign of Henry III."

The disaffection of the country appears to have been confined to no particular class of society; petitions were presented from various localities complaining of grievances. One from Lancashire, signed by "knights, squires, merchants, gentlemen, and freeholders of the county," was introduced, contrary to usage, into the house of commons, by a deputation. The petitioners "complained, as they had done twelve months before, of other grievances, and prayed that such persons as were found to have been instrumental in bringing on arbitrary and insolent government might make reparation to their country and from henceforth be excluded from the exercise of that authority" The petitioners likewise complained of illegal interference by Lord Strange, son of the earl of Derby, in the election of knights of the shire for the county.[q]

The parliament, however, nominated Lord Strange lord lieutenant of

q "Lancashire's Valley of Achor," p. 2.

the county of Chester. Lord Wharton was appointed to the similar office for the county of Lancaster; and the following gentlemen deputy lieutenants:—Sir George Booth, Mr John Moore, Sir Thomas Stanley, Mr. Alexander Rigby, of Preston,[r] Mr. Dodding, Mr. Egerton, Mr Ralph Ashton, of Middleton, Mr J. Hales, Sir William Brereton, Mr. Thomas Standish, of Duxbury, Sir Ralph Ashton, of Downham, Mr. Robert Hide, Mr. Thomas Byrch, Mr. Edmund Hockwood, and Mr. James Bradshaw.

The chancellor of the duchy of Lancaster, by order of parliament, discharged the following parties from being further employed as commissioners of the peace within the county, on account of their real or supposed attachment to the party which supported the royal prerogative:—Sir Gilbert Hoghton, knt. and bart., Robert Holt, of Stubley, Alexander Rigby (of Brough), John Greenhalgh, Edmund Asheton, Sir Alexander Radcliffe, William Farington, Orlando Bridgman, Sir Edward Wrightington, and Roger Kirkeby. The following gentlemen, adherents to the parliament, were made commissioners in their stead:—Sir Ralph Ashton, bart, Ralph Ashton, of Middleton, Richard Holland, John Bradshaw, William Radcliffe, Richard Shuttleworth, John Braddell, John Starkey, Sir Thomas Stanley, bart, John Holcrofte, Thomas Standish, George Dodding, Thomas Fell, and Peter Egerton.

Messrs. Ashton (of Middleton), Shuttleworth, Rigby, and Moore, members of the house of commons, were sent by parliament to Lancashire to embody the militia of the county. Ammunition and ordnance were furnished to Manchester and other places for their defence. In compliance with the prayer of a petition, presented by "the well-affected people of that county," a thousand dragoons were ordered to be equipped for their protection against "papists and other malignants, who had associated and raised great forces both horse and foot to oppress and distress the well-affected subjects in the counties of York, Northumberland, Westmoreland, and Cumberland, and in the counties palatine of Durham, Chester, and Lancashire."

Petitions, remonstrances, and royal concessions, all failing to cement the breach between the king and the commons, Charles fled to York, and issued his celebrated "commission of array." Lord Strange, with the king's authority, summoned the men of Lancashire to arm in the cause of their sovereign. Sir John Girlington, by command of the king, convened a meeting at Preston "for the purpose of promulgating a petition from Lancashire and the king's answer, together with his declarations." Large

[r] Mr. Alexander Rigby, M.P. for Wigan, afterwards colonel, and ultimately judge, was of Middleton, in Goosnargh, near Preston.

numbers likewise assembled upon Ormskirk moor and Bury heath, armed with pikes, muskets, and other weapons. The royal and parliamentary authorities differ materially, both as to the number and temper of the people assembled at these gatherings. Seacombe estimates each meeting at "20,000 men at the least." The meeting at Preston moor was attended by Lord Strange, Lord Molyneux, Sir George Middleton, Sir Alexander Radcliffe, Mr Tildesley, of Myerscough, Mr. William Farington, and many other royalists. Mr. Rigby and Mr. Shuttleworth, members of parliament, were likewise present, with many of their friends. The former gentleman, in a letter to the speaker of the house of commons, dated June 24, 1642, states the number of persons present to have been about five thousand. He says that when Sir John Girlington, the high sheriff, "exhibited the commission of array, and exclaimed, 'For the king! For the king!'" that about 400 persons joined in the cry, and the remainder "prayed for the king *and the parliament*." Mr. Rigby and his colleagues "advised them not to suffer themselves to be draune into armes without direction from parliament and soe dismissed the assembly." The writer further observes :—

"Sir George Middleton, and Master Thomas Tildesley, of Mierscough, and Master Thomas Prestwiche, whose wives are Popish recusants, and Master William Farington, a Justice of Peace, were in our judgments, the most busie and active, and they assisted, countenanced, and abetted the Sheriffe in all the aforesaid passages, and therein pressed and urged him forward, who of himself was thereunto sufficiently inclined, and while these things were in acting upon the moor, Will Sumpner, servant to Master William Farington, who during his late Deputy Lieutenancy, had placed in a private house in Preston, about 13 barrels of gunpowder and some quantity of match, did secretly convey about 6 barrels thereof in Packcloaths upon Packhorses, and the next morning about six of the clocke, and before we had notice in whose house that Powder and Match was lodged, the Sheriffe did convey away out of the Towne and Liberties of Preston the residue of the said Powder and Match, which being made knowne to me, I forthwith repayred to the Sheriffe, and shewed him the order of the Lords and Commons, made the 10th of May last, for disposing of the Magazines, and also a deputation from the Lord Wharton, authorising his Deputy Lieutenants, or any 2 or more of them, to dispose of the Magazines of Lancashire, and then desired him to cause that Powder to be returned to Preston, but he answered that he would not returne it, but would keepe it and defend it with the power of the county, and the Sheriffe and Sir George Middleton then said that that order should not be obeyed, and I thought it not meet for so small a quantity of Powder and Match, though indeed a very considerable quantity for the time and place, to endeavour a returne thereof by force, so that it now remaineth unknowne to me where they (who took it) have disposed it, in the last place I make bold to present my opinion that the Malignant party could not, by any passage at the assembling on Preston Moor, distinguish that the affections of any considerable part thereof enclined unto them, and I verily believe that we lost not, but gained by that day's work, for the safety and peace of the King and Kingdome."

Each party eagerly seized upon the magazines prepared for the use of the militia. The royalists secured thirty barrels of powder at Liverpool; but Sir Thomas Stanley, and Mr. Ashton, of Middleton, forestalled them at Manchester.

On the 15th of July, 1642, a memorable political rencontre, in connection with the civil war, occurred at Manchester. Lord Strange was desirous of obtaining possession of the military magazine in that town. The partisans of the parliament refused to give it up While the negociations were in progress, the high sheriff read the "commission of array" at a royalist dinner, to which Lord Strange had been invited. Parliament had denounced this commission, issued by the king on the 10th of July, 1642, as a violation of the laws of the realm, and accused those who acted under its authority of betraying the liberty of the subject. While the guests were at table, Sir Thomas Stanley, bart., Captain Holcroft, and Captain Birch marched into the town at the head of some parliamentary troops. A skirmish took place between them and the armed followers of Lord Strange, in the course of which a linen weaver or "webster," named Richard Percivall, was slain by the royalists, and several other persons wounded. This is generally regarded as the first overt act of warfare committed in Lancashire by either party. Parliament, in consequence of this *fracas*, ordered Lord Strange to be impeached for high treason

Warburton, in his "Memoirs of Prince Rupert and the Cavaliers," says:—"It is a difficult and unprofitable task to discover where the first blood was shed By some it was said to have been in Somersetshire, by Sir John Stowell, by others in Manchester, by Lord Strange, where one Richard Percivall a linen-webster was killed; by others to have been in Yorkshire, by a body of Northumberland Royal Horse."

Two parliamentary documents, one entitled "*Beginning of Civil Wars in England, or terrible news from the North*—Printed by order of Parliament, July 9, 1642," and the other, "*Manchester Resolutions* against Lord Strange," etc., state "there was upon the 4th day of this instant July, a skirmish between Lord Strange and the Inhabitants of Manchester." The former document distinctly states that Lord Strange appeared on the fourth of July before Manchester "with a great number of armed men," and demanded to know whether the partisans of the parliament were willing to a proposition "he had sent two or three days before for restoring the magazines which were in that town to his own custody, threatening them that if they would not, he would send such a Messenger that would make them Yield, and bring them in due Subjection." This being refused for reasons stated, the document proceeds to say that "Lord Strange marched against the said Towne of Manchester, and shott off three or four Muskets against them, but the Inhabitants seeing that he were come, and that he were resolved to take away the Magazine by force, * * they Resolved every Man to fight it out." The two skirmishes which ensued are then detailed, and the following is announced as the result:—"They ended the Battle with the Sun of the Day, the Lord STRANGE withdrawing his force about two miles from Manchester; having lost as is justly supposed, 27 men; of the other side 11. Captain Bland (who was wounded in the thigh) is well recovered again, praised be God."

This document has been pronounced "a base attempt to excite the country against Lord S. by the most untrue and calumnious reports." —(*March. Coll. Ch.* 1, 197) Ormerod, in his annotations to the "Lancashire Civil War Tracts," appears to endorse this opinion. He says:—"If otherwise it would be difficult to suppose that the events would have been overlooked in the preceding 'Diurnall' in the *Valley of Achor*, and in the impeachment of Lord Strange, the two last of which record the affray on the 15th, connected with Lord Strange's passage through Manchester from Bury to the proposed banquet, and very different proceedings, but notice no earlier bloodshed on the 5th, or any thing according with the statements here given." If the document was published on the date stated, July 9, 1642, and is not an after production, it is equally surprising that nothing is known of a direct contradiction to it, on the part of the supposed slandered royalists.

Preston and the neighbourhood narrowly escaped being the scene of the first outbreak, as will be seen by the following extracts from "A True and Perfect Diurnall of all the Chiefe Passages in Lancashire from the 3 July to the 9 Sent to Five Shopkeepers in London from a friend,[r] July 9, 1642. London, printed for T. U. 1642:"—

"I saw the Militia" (at Manchester) "in number 7 or 8000 well furnished with musketts and pykes, and completely trained by the Captains that were there, and there was a great shout for halfe an houre, '*For the King and Parliament, For the King and Parliament.*'

"Master *Rigbie* told me as we went along" (to Manchester) "that they had sent a letter unto him from Manchester upon Saturday in the night, and the messenger came unto him about one o'clock; the contents of the letter was to meet the rest of the Committee at Manchester, upon Munday betimes. So he wrote an answer by the same messenger who (was) stayed at Walton by a watch which was set by Sir *Gilbert Houghton*, before whom they brought him, and he delivered him Master *Rigbie's* letter, and upon Sunday in the morning Sir *Gilbert* sent for M. *Rigbie*, and being come he said he had a Commission from the King to break open all such letters, Master *Rigbie* asked him if he had taken the protestation, and he told him he had. Then he demanded his letter of him in the name of all the Commons of England; and further told him if he broke it open, it might be he might be the first man that should be made an example in Lancashire; and then he delivered him his letter unbroken up, and intreated him to stay and dine with him, which he did, and when they were at dinner one M. Dawton, a great recusant, and M Tylsley, came in as familiar to Sir *Gilbert*, as if they had been Haile fellow, well met. And M. *Rigbie* told *Gilbert* and M. Tilsley, he could like them well if they were not so familiar with Papists.

"A false messenger came this day," (Wednesday, July 6,) "to Sir *Gilbert Houghton* and told him that the Lord Wharton was come to *Manchester* with 20,000 men, whereupon he sent with all speede to all his tenants, and commanded them that they should be readie upon an hower's warning, and set a stronge watch about his house, but I think

[r] From the context the friend appears to have been a Prestonian. This is the "diurnall" alluded to by Ormerod.

there was no brags in our towne for that day. Then they let honest Protestants go through the streets without scoffing at them, and calling them Roundheads, and *Tylsley* posted up and downe in great fear, it was well if he kept all cleane: and how should it be otherwise, seeing they oppose the King's Majestie's Royall Authority, in the High Court of Parliament, the old and good government of England, the libertie of the subject, the peace and welfare of this land, yea and the pure Protestant religion itselfe, of which when their consciences accuse them, they are filled with guilt and feare, and so cannot stand before God and his armie.

"My Lord *Strange* this night," (Thursday, July 7,) "is at *Walton* with Sir *Gilbert Houghton*, and the High Sheriffe, and Tylesley is there, and they have commanded all betwixt 16 and 60 to be at Preston to-morrow, with the best armes they have. My Lord intends to be there himselfe, but what the event will be I cannot yet tell. The Sheriffe hath been with the Lord *Strange* all this weeke; I believe he's the refuge he plyeth unto when he is in danger.

"Friday, July 8. * * M. *Tylsley* yesterday night said unto *Luke Hodgkinson* in Sir *Gilbert's* buttery that he was told M. Major" (the mayor) "of *Preston*, had thought to have cast him in *Prison*, which if he had he would this day have pulled downe the prison, and M. Major's house should have been set on fire, if he would not have released him. Truly it were well if the Parliament would send for this *Tylsley*, for he is a Captaine, one of the Commission of array, and doth more harme than any man I know. Yesternight when the Lord *Strange* was at supper he received a packet of letters from York, what they were I cannot tell. This day in the morning I spoke with the Sergeant, and he hath delivered the order from the Houses to the Lord *Strange*, and he first told him he would return an answer by word of mouth by him, and afterwards he told him he would send an answer himselfe to Parliament. Five men gave one *Roger Haddock* of Chorley very sore strokes and broke his head to the very scull, because he went with the messenger to show him my Lord's house. The soldiers are all marched out of the Towne to the number of 4000, as I thinke, but the poste is in going, and what this day will bring forth I cannot tell, but they say they shout 'for the King, and my Lord Strange,' and the Sheriffe have set foure barrels of beere abroache at the high Crosse to make the soldiers drinke as they returne backe. The Sergeant is here to arrest the Sheriffe, but it is to no purpose till the company be gone If the Lord *Strange*, the Sheriffe, Sir *Geo Middleton* and *Tylsley* were with you, we should all be quiet Here are many Papists; I beleeve a catalogue of the names of the cheefe of them are sent up. *Tylsley's* Lieutenant, and his Sergeants are Papists. I shall write you more of this dayes proceeding the next poste, my Lord is with them over the moore. Read this letter be sure to M. W. my brother W provide for our safety; we are beset with Papists; I dare not go to the Moore, but my ——— was there, and they told him he was a roundhead, and swore they would kill him. So he came from amongst them. I am in haste. Vale.—*Friday the 8th of July*, 1642."

The king, by proclamation, suspended the laws by which "popish recusants" were disarmed. In a document of this character, addressed "to our trusty and well beloved Sir *William Gerrard, Baronet*, Sir *Cecil Trafford, Knight, Thomas Clifton, Charles Towneley, Christopher Anderton*, and *John Causfield*, esquires, and others of our subjects, Recusants in the county of Lancaster," the king regrets that "the arms taken from the Roman Catholics had been transferred into the possession of others who were disaffected, and for the most part fomenters and exciters of these commotions now raised in this kingdome."

The king, in the first instance, had purposed to unfurl the royal standard at Warrington; but subsequent events induced him to change the scene of operations, and Nottingham was selected as a more central locality.

Lord Strange appeared before Manchester a second time, on the 25th

September, with an army variously stated at from two thousand to four thousand five hundred men, and six or seven pieces of cannon. During his operations against the place, his father died, and he succeeded to the earldom of Derby. The town was filled with parliamentary forces, who defended themselves so resolutely, that the earl retired on the first of October. The reason assigned for this failure, was the king's command that the earl should join the main army at Shrewsbury. A similar attempt on the part of his lordship to get possession of the town of Birmingham was equally unsuccessful According to the parliamentary authorities, he lost six hundred men, and as many prisoners, in the effort. The drawn battle of Edge Hill, in Warwickshire, was fought on the 23rd of October. The earl of Essex commanded the parliamentary forces, and was opposed by the king in person About five thousand men perished in the engagement.

The earl of Derby remained faithful to the royal cause, although he had been treated with some ingratitude, both by the king and his courtiers. On his return to Lancashire, he levied fresh troops; but was defeated in a skirmish at Chowbent and Loaton common No better success attended the royal cause in the hundred of Blackburn Sir Gilbert Hoghton, bart., was defeated on Hinfield moor, by the troops under the command of Colonel Starkie and Colonel Shuttleworth.

The following letter, written by one of the victors, is eminently characteristic of the tone of mind and temper of the warriors of the period:—

"The last Sabbath as wee were going towards the church a poste rode through the countrey informing us that the Earl's troopes were coming towards the *Chowbent*, whereupon the countrey presently rose, and before one of the clocke on that day wee were gathered together 3000 horse and foote, encountering them at *Chowbent* aforesaid, and beate them backe to *Leigh*, killing some and wounding many. Where you might wonder to have seen the forwardnesse of the young youthes, farmer's sons, who indeed were too forward, having had little experience of the like times before this. And so wee Over-rode our Foote, being carried with a fervent desire to overtake them, and to doe some notable service upon them, so that wee drove them to *Loaton* Common, where they, knowing our Foote to be far behinde, turned faces about, and began to make head against us Whereupon a sharpe although a short Incounter; but when they perceived our full and settled resolution, they made away as fast as their Horses could carry them, and wee after them, killing, wounding and taking prisoners about two hundred of them; and wee lost never a man, only wee had three of our men wounded, but not mortally, so that I think they will trouble us no more out of that part of the Countrey, but if they doe wee shall be better provided for them than before, for wee are all upon our Guard, and the Naylers of *Chowbent*, instead of making nayles, have busied themselves with making Bills and Battle Axes And also this Weeke the other part of the countrey meet, and intend not only to stand upon their guard, but to disarm all the Papists and Malignants within their precincts, which wee are resolved upon in our precincts, and also by God's assistance to take the greatest Papists and most dangerous Malignants prisoners and to carry them to *Manchester*, to keep house with Sir *Cecil Trafford*, that Arch-Papist, who is there a Prisoner For now the men of *Blackburn*, *Paduam*, *Burneley*, *Clithero*, and *Colne*, with those sturdy churles in the two forests of *Pendle* and *Rossendale*, have raised their spirits, and have resolved to fight it out rather than their

Beefe and salt Bacon should be taken from them. For the last weeke Sir *Gilbert Houghton* set his Beacon on fire, which stood upon the top of *Houghton* Tower, and was the signall to the Countrey for the Papists and Malignants to arise in the Field,[t] and in *Lealand* Hundred; whereupon great multitudes accordingly resorted to him to *Preston* in *Andernesse,* and ran to Blackburne, and soe through the Countrey, disarming all and pillaging some, which Mr. Shuttleworth, a parliament man, and Mr. Starkie hearing off presently had gotten together out of the places formerly mentioned about 8000 men, met with Sir *Gilbert* and his Catholique Malignants at *Hinfield* Moor, put them to flight, and took away many of their armes; and pursued Sir *Gilbert* so hotley, that he quitted his Horse, leaped into a field, and by the comming on of the night escaped through fur-bushes and by-ways to Preston, and there makes great defence by chaining up *Ribble* Bridge, and getting what force he can into the Towne for his securitie; out of which the Countrey swears they will have him, by God's helpe, with all his adherents, either quicke or dead, soe that by the next poste I hope I shall certifie of some good posture that the country will be in. That Parliament had but sent downe their 1000 Dragoniers into the Countrey ! wee would not have left a Mass-monger nor Malignant of note but wee would have provided a lodging for him. It is reported by some about the Earl of Derby, that he is very melancholy and much perplexed about the unadvised course that he hath run; for the last Thursday at *Warrington,* at dinner, he said he was born under an unfortunate planet, and that he thought some evill Constellation reigned at the time of his birth, with many other such wordes of passion and discontent."

The earl of Derby's troops, however, afterwards defeated a portion of the parliamentary army at Hindley, near Wigan, and drove them into Manchester.

On the 10th of December, the royalists of the county assembled at Preston, for the purpose of "recruiting the king's forces and raising the necessary supplies for their support" The earl of Derby, Sir John Girlington (the sheriff), William Farington, Alexander Rigby, (of Brough), Robert Holt, and Roger Kirby, were amongst the parties present. It was resolved that four hundred horse and two thousand foot soldiers should be raised, and the sum of £8,700 levied upon the county for their support and appointments This force was intended for the use and protection of the county, and for the assistance of the president of the meeting, the earl of Derby, who was styled the "lord general of the county of Lancaster" The funds were confided to the direction of a council, consisting of the high sheriff, Adam Morte (mayor of Preston),[u] James Anderton, and Robert Kirby, with power to call in the aid of several other gentlemen.

At the end of the year, the royalists held the towns of Lancaster, Preston, Wigan, Liverpool, and Warrington; and the parliamentary forces Blackburn, Bolton, Rochdale, and Manchester. During the winter, the

t The Fylde, or more level portion of the hundred of Amounderness.

u Though Mr. Morte was *elected* mayor of Preston, the records of the corporation attest that he declined to serve the office, paying in preference a fine of one hundred marks. He is, however, styled *mayor* of Preston in Sir John Fairfax's dispatches, as well as by the Civil War Tract, entitled "*Orders concluded by Lord Strange and his adherents at Preston,*" etc., printed 29th Dec., 1642.—[See Municipal History; chap 6, of present vol.]

earl of Derby was reinforced by the veterans under Lord Molyneux, and Sir John Seaton was sent with a regiment of fresh troops to Manchester.

From a "contemporary newspaper" report, headed "Continuation of certain Speciall and Remarkable Passages, Jan. 12, 1642-3," number 27, p. 4, it appears that Sir John Talbot, of Salesbury Park, near Ribchester,[v] a Roman catholic, but supposed to be neutral, invited some of the chiefs of the parliamentary party at Manchester to visit him in a "friendly manner," and promised them "very kind usage and some further courtesies by way of compliance with them." But the puritans being suspicious, sent a small body of men to reconnoitre, when it was discovered that "the said Sir John had secretly provided in his stables above one hundred horse fitted with all accoutrements, theire riders being neare at hand upon occasion to set upon the Manchester men. But this being discovered, the Manchester forces being too few to deale with them, retreated back to the towne and about three hundred of them went presently to the said Sir John Talbot's (who was then with all his horse upon flight), pursued them and killed divers of them, took about twenty of his horse, drove others into a river, where the riders were drowned, and their horses taken, and have seized upon the said Sir John's house, where they found good pillage."

At the commencement of the campaign of 1643, Sir Thomas Fairfax, the renowned parliamentary general, fixed his head quarters at Manchester. His first operation was directed against Preston. He despatched major-general Sir John Seaton, at the head of a body of forces, which were further reinforced on their march by the garrisons of Bolton and Blackburn. Sir John appeared before Preston with "about 900 or 1000 Firemen, horse and foot, and about 600 Billmen, Halberdiers and Clubmen," on the 9th of February. The town was fortified with "inner and outer walls of brick," and defended by a brave garrison. On the following morning, the order was given to storm the works. The daring valour of Captain Booth surmounted every obstacle. He scaled the wall, and, at the head of his men, dashed forward with irresistible impetuosity, exclaiming, "Follow me, or give me up for ever!" The garrison defended their works with steady and determined valour. When the outer wall was carried by the parliamentary troops, the cavaliers retired to the inner defence, resolutely maintained their ground "with push of pike," and disputed the breach gallantly, sword in hand. In the mean time, Sir John Seaton having stormed the defences on the eastern side, entered the town

[v] The original says Sir John Talbot resided "within two or three miles of Manchester;" but Mr. Ormerod observes this is evidently an error, as Sir John Talbot resided at "Salebury Park, the Ribble being the river intended."

at Church street. After a combat of two hours, the royalists being driven from the steeple of the church, and their other strongholds, the parliamentary troops obtained complete possession of the place. The chivalrous mayor, Adam Morte, fell mortally wounded in a spirited onslaught upon Colonel Holland's company. He killed one of the besiegers at "push of pike," before he fell. His son died gallantly fighting by his side. It is probable that Morte's death saved the place from total destruction, for he had declared in the heat of the engagement that "he would fire the town rather than surrender it into the hands of rebels." Amongst the officers slain were Captain Hoghton, brother to Sir Gilbert, Serjeant-major Purvey, and Doctor Thomas Westby, a physician. Amongst the prisoners were Mr. Anderton, of Clayton, the commander of the garrison, Captains Farington and Preston, George, son of Sir John Talbot, Mr. Richard Fleetwood, Mr Blundell, of Crosby, (who had his thigh broken), Mr. Abbot, Mr. Mausley, Mr. Thomas Hoghton, and Captain Hoghton (nephew to Sir Gilbert), R. Langton, John Waltham, and William Selby, esquires, "all men of quality," together with Lady Hoghton and Lady Girlington, and about two hundred others of "meaner condition" Sir Gilbert Hoghton and Mr. Towneley, of Towneley, were more fortunate, and escaped by flight.

The capture of Preston was regarded by the parliamentary party as of great importance. Its possession by the puritans interrupted the communications between the royalists of Carlisle and Newcastle, with their friends in South Lancashire and the western counties.

The siege of Preston is described by a puritan writer, in a work published at the time, entitled "Lancashire's Valley of Achor," with much of the peculiar admixture of religion, fanaticism, and military zeal, which so strongly characterised the period. He says:—

"The seventh and eighth of February were devoted to God in Fasting and Prayer in Manchester, to succeed our Forces that were upon their march. The first day was spent, and gave strength to our men to march all night, and to set upon *Preston* the next morning; the second day of fasting, when some of our men soon advantaged themselves by taking of Rible Bridge, and with unspeakable courage set upon the Town, well fortified and manned, which God gave them in two hours, as a present return of prayers. Such courage was raised in the Souldiers that they dared to take hold of their enemy's Muskets put thorow the loop holes, as if the miracle of mercy had been again revived. Psal. 91, 19. *Thou shalt tread upon the Lyon and Adder*. And when the Pikes kept them off from the mud walls, yet by breaking thorow an house some twenty entered the Town; which small number drew down a Troop of Horse to take a prey. But *Moses*, *Aaron*, and *Hur*, being on the top of the hill whilest *Joshua* was fighting in the valley, the Captaine of the Horse was killed, and the Troop scattered. Then came up the rest of our men, killed the Major" (the Mayor) "and some others, chased the enemy, and commanded the Towne. Here Divine Providence took a noble Captaine off his feet, before the dangerous discharge of a Bullet, he stood not to fall, but fell to rise. We lost few men in this dangerous assault, took store of prisoners and armes, and came in the nick of time to relieve the well-affected in *Preston* and thereabouts, upon which the Array were prepared to impose an Oath and heavy Taxations. This prey God plucked out of the teeth of the Lyon and paw of the Bear." [g]

The Rev. John Tilsley, the pastor of Dean, who was present at this storming of the town, in a letter to "an eminent Divine in London," amongst other details, has the following observations, highly characteristic of the manners and sentiments of the period :—

"We have not lost above three or four men, (very strange,) falling upon them in their Workes. Of theirs I saw lying in one street end, at least five or six, besides other parts of the Towne severall, and many in the Houses, not calling for quarter: And as if men must have been singled out for slaughter we could scarce have picked out better, the Major" (Mayor), "(that was resolute to desperateness in the cause, that had oftentimes been heard sweare '*He would fire the town ere he gave it up, and beginne with his own house*') was slain, and that very day he had appointed to constrain the well-affected, or to have seiz'd on their estates, *Sir Gilbert Houghton's* brother, a Captain and a desperate papist, *Mr. Westby*, a Physician and a desperate papist, a Sergeant to the freehold, that lately came out of *Ireland*, a most wicked wretch, were of the number of the slain. Severall of our men are shot, but none mortally (its notable), many are shot in two or three or four severall places, and neither to death nor dangerously; we have taken some prisoners of note, * * and many others with many arms, and a large part of things justly, and by plunder (alas that, it is so much lamented but most hard to be prevented) seized on; more prisoners of note we had been possessed of, but that honest flight rescued them. * * * So soon as matters were settled, we sung praises to God in the street (Sir, it was wonderfull to see it), the sun brake forth and shined brightly and hot, in the time of the exercise, as if it had been Midsummer. Truly, Sir, we owe (subordinate to God) a great deal to *Sir John Seaton*; things are artificially and methodically done, past what they were before, he is a man of wonderfull care and unwearied industry, onely rather too harsh for our northern, knotty, riggid dispositions, had he the meek spirit and smooth tongue of *S. M Sparrow*, he were peerlesse and without parallel doubtlesse." [h]

Another letter to a member of the House of Commons, "certified by some gentlemen of repute in the same County," and ordered by parliament to be printed, furnishes the following additional details:—

"We tooke three pieces of ordnance, a murdering piece, a great number of musquiets, and many horses, with two or three colours, and divers were pillaged to a purpose. Few friends have suffered to any value; there were but two barrells of powder found in the town. We had only three or four common souldiers, not an officer slain on our side; we gave the enemy no leisure to annoy us with their guns, and the execution done was most with the sword" [i]

The town was afterwards re-fortified by Colonel Rosworm, the celebrated engineer, a "brave and skilful soldier—tried in the German wars." Rosworm was ordered to take a part in the assault by Major-general Seaton. He attached himself to Colonel Holland's regiment, and by his skill and bravery contributed much to its successful result. [a]

Captain Birch, after the surrender of Preston, proceeded to Lancaster, and took possession of the town, together with twenty-one pieces of brass

---

g Lancashire Civil War Tracts, edited by Ormerod, and published by the Manchester Cheetham Society h Ibid i Ibid.

a Rosworm's Tract [See chap 1, page 48, and chap 3, page 117.] The supposed Roman mound on the Maudlands, was evidently an outwork of Colonel Rosworm's defences.

cannon which had been seized on board a Spanish ship, from Dunkirk, in the river Lune.[b] The castle surrendered on the seventeenth of February

About five days after the fall of Preston, Sir John Seaton dispatched Captain Starkie with three troops, to besiege Hoghton Tower, the residence of Sir Gilbert Hoghton The place speedily surrendered, but while the captors were congratulating themselves upon the valuable acquisition of ordnance, ammunition and small arms, which fell into their hands, the tower suddenly blew up, and hurried into eternity, or seriously wounded, about sixty of the victors, Captain Starkie himself being amongst the killed. The roundheads accused the defeated cavaliers of perfidy and the wilful destruction of the fortress, but this was denied by the royalists, and no evidence was advanced which demonstrated the truth of the assertion. On the contrary, the author of "Lancashire's Valley of Achor" lectures his own party very severely for their remissness on the occasion, and throws the entire blame upon the parliamentary soldiers. He says:—

"Our men going down to take the Tower, and finding it prepared for entrance, possessed themselves of it, till being burthened with the weight of their swearing, drunkenesse, plundering, and wilfull waste at *Preston*, it dispossessed them by the help of Powder, to which their disorders laid a Train fired by their neglected Matches, or by that great Souldier's Idoll—*Tobacco*. However it was, sure it is, that the place so firmly united, chose rather to be torn in pieces than to harbour the possessours. O that this thundering Alarm might ever sound in the eares of our Swearing, Cursing, Drunken, Tobacco-abusing Commanders and Souldiers unto unfeigned Repentance. For do they think that those upon whom the Tower fell and slew them, were sinners above the rest of the Army?"

Success now patronised for a time the previously defeated loyalists. The earl of Derby, after a fruitless attempt upon Bolton, marched his forces by way of Kirkham to Lancaster, where he burned ninety houses, and nearly the same number of barns, or other outbuildings, to the ground. A body of parliamentary forces from Preston, under Major-general Seaton, and Colonel Ashton, attempted to relieve the place, but arrived too late to save the town. The castle, however, remained in the possession of the parliamentary party. The earl of Derby drew off his troops on the approach of Seaton and Ashton, and, taking advantage of the then defenceless state of Preston, suddenly appeared before it, about ten o'clock in the evening of Monday, the twenty-first of March, and summoned the garrison to surrender the town to the king's troops. The mayor, Edmund Werden, Esq., refused to comply, on which the earl gave orders for the immediate storming of the defences. Assaults were made simultaneously on three distinct points, led by Captain Chisnall, Captain Radcliff, and Captain Edward Rosthorne. After an hour's severe

b Puritan Pamphlet. "Lancashire's Valley of Achor."

struggle, the garrison yielded. A royalist account of this siege, published in the *Mercurius Aulicus*, says:—

"In the taking of *Preston* there was killed in the place 80 of the rebels, whereof Captain *Ashworth* and Captain *Will. Shuttleworth* were the chief, and about 3 or 400 prisoners taken, of which Captain *Standish* was one, together with one brass piece of ordnance. That after the said Toune was taken, his Lordship had especial care to preserve the place, and only gave command that the houses of those who had betrayed the Toune before should be responsall to his Majestie for their Masters treason, whose goods his Lordship ordered to be seized and equally divided among the soldiers. The next morning being March 22, the whole Country came in with apparent joy, and made signal affections of their good affections to his Majestie, flinging up their hats and shouting out, *God blesse the King and the Earle of Derby*. And finally to make up the summe, it was advertised also in the same *Expresse*, that the same day Serjeant Major *Brewyer*, who commanded his Lordships regiment of horse, did with a troope of his defeat two troopes of dragooners, being 140 in the totall, under the command of Captaine *Norris*, taking the Captaine himself prisoner, together with 40 of his souldiers, and having killed no lesse than 50 in the very place. So as now the Earle hath abundance of ammunition, the want whereof did hinder his Lordships good proceedings against the Rebells." w

The earl of Derby secured the parliamentary magazine, but, fearing the probability of the place being again transferred by the vicissitude of war to his ever active enemies, he destroyed the defences and military works, and, after compelling Blackburn to surrender, departed for Manchester. On the way, Lord Molyneux and his regiment received an order from the king to join the main army at Oxford. The loss of the veteran troops, led by Molyneux, prevented the earl from attacking Manchester, although he had expressed his determination to reduce the place, if properly supported, or "lay his bones before it."

The tide of success again turned in favour of the parliamentary forces The earl of Derby, after another fruitless attempt upon Bolton-le-moors, fell back upon his entrenchments at Wigan. The strength of these works was so great for the period, that the "piece" was regarded by the royalists as impregnable. Colonel Ashton, assisted by Rosworm, however, surprised the town on the evening of the first of April, and, notwithstanding a gallant defence, the parliamentary "musketeers and club-men" carried the town. The countess of Derby, on hearing of the fall of Wigan, dispatched the following letter to Prince Rupert·—

"My Lord,—I have just received the disastrous news of the loss of Wigan, six miles from this place. It has held out only two hours, having been panic-struck. My husband was twelve miles off, and before he was ready to succour it, it was surrendered. In the name of God, my lord, take pity on us; and if you appear you can conquer it easily, and with much honour to your highness I do not know what I say; but have pity on my husband, my children, and me, who are lost for ever, if God and your highness do not take pity on us.

I am, my lord, your very humble and obedient servant,

"At Ladhom, April 1, 1643. C. DE LA TREMAILLE."

---

w Another authority says that Captain William Shuttleworth was killed at Lancaster, and not at Preston. This accords with the facts stated in the family pedigree, as given by Whitaker, in his History of Whalley, p 339.

Wigan was afterwards abandoned by the parliamentary party, and again re-occupied by the royalists. At Warrington, a few days after the capture of Wigan, the earl was more successful. The royalists gallantly repulsed the Lancashire and Cheshire parliamentary troops, headed by Sir William Brereton.

The earl of Derby advanced from Preston to operate in the hundred of Blackburn. One of the civil war tracts says that "the earl of Derby, the Lord Molineux, Sir Gilbert Hoghton, Colonell Tildesley, with all the other great Papists in this County, issued out of Preston, and on Wednesday now came to Ribchester with eleven Troops of horse, 700 foot, and an infinite number of club men, in all conceived to be 5000." Ashton and Shuttleworth opposed them with some regular troops, and a body of peasantry and militia, hastily levied. A regular engagement, or rather a running fight, took place between Whalley and Salesbury, in which the earl was defeated, and pursued to Ribchester This success appears to have been the precursor of the subsequent declension of the earl of Derby's military power in the county. It was judged of so much importance by the parliamentary party, that a day of thanksgiving was set apart for the victory.

The "colonel-general" Ashton, as he was sometimes called, a few days afterwards (April 22nd), appeared before Wigan, reinforced by the Manchester garrison. Tildesley, who commanded the place, fled to Lathom, and the parliamentary general "demolisht all outworks and fortifications, burnt the new gates and posts that had been set up, and took an oath of the townsmen never to bear arms again against the King and Parliament." [y] The indefatigable Ashton pursued the fugitive royalists to Lathom and Prescot. The earl of Derby retreated back, first upon Lathom, and from thence to Preston, "wether also the *Manchester* forces, giving neither themselves nor their enemies any rest, followed them close, still driving the Earl thence also, and made him fly either to *Hornby Castle* or else to the Queen into the *North*, his forces being driven at least eight miles from *Preston*." He was pursued by Colonel Ashton, whose forces, by reason of his success, were greatly augmented, "many of the earl's soldiers coming in willingly and cheerfully to serve him." The earl of Derby shortly afterwards dispatched a messenger to Colonel Ashton, requesting him not to set fire to his house at Lathom, and promising the sum of three hundred pounds as a compensation, in case the puritan commander should feel disposed to comply; "but," says the chronicler, "the noble Colonel sent him word that he scorned his money or the firing of his house, and desired nothing more of him than to meet with him, and to give him battel; but

y Vicar's Chronicle, March, 1643.

he as I said ran quite away out of the countie and durst not stay to accept that notion."[x]

Tildesley retired to Liverpool, with the determination of holding it for the king; but his ever active opponent, Ashton, laid siege to the place, and succeeded in completely routing the garrison, and capturing the town. The royalists lost eighty killed, three hundred prisoners, and ten guns. New works were constructed by Colonel Rosworm, and the command of the fortress entrusted to Colonel Moore. Warrington surrendered about the same time, and shortly afterwards (about the 20th of June), Ashton completed the discomfiture of the royalists by the capture of the castles of Hornby and Thurland. The scattered partisans of the king fled to the queen at York. Tildesley afterwards distinguished himself by the desperate courage with which he led the cavalry charge over the bridge of thirty-six arches at Burton-on-Trent. He received the honour of knighthood as a reward for his valour and constancy.

The capture of Thurland Castle, the seat of the sheriff, Sir John Girlington, was the result of the energy and skill of Colonel Rigby, of Middleton, near Preston, member of parliament for Wigan. Whitelock says the achievement was the more discoursed of at the time because Rigby was a lawyer, and not a soldier by profession. An attempt was made to relieve the garrison of Thurland. The Lancashire men, amongst the royalists, were led by a namesake of the parliamentary colonel, Mr. Alexander Rigby (of Brough), and Mr. Roger Kirby. To defeat this, Colonel Rigby marched a large detachment of his troops into Furness, fell upon the relieving army, and totally routed it. Two days afterwards, Sir Roger Girlington surrendered the castle, which, according to the prevalent custom, was speedily demolished. The lawyer-colonel, in his official dispatch to the speaker of the house of commons, dated at Preston, October 17th, 1643, says:—

"God so struck the hearts of these our enemies with terrour, that before a blow given their horse began to retreat, our foot gave a great shout, our horse pursued, their's fled; their foot dispersed and fled; they all trusted more to their feet than their hands; they threw away their arms and colours, deserted their magazine drawn with eight oxen, and were totally routed in one quarter of an hour's time; our horse slew some few of them in the pursuit, and drove many of them into the sea; we took their colonel Hudleston, of Millam, two captains, and an ensign, and about foure hundred prisoners, six foot colours, and one horse colour; and their magazin, and some horses, and more arms than men; and all this without the losse of any one man of ours; wee had only one man hurt by the enemy, and only another hurt by himselfe with his own pistoll, but neither mortally; upon the close of the business, all our men with a great shout cried

[x] Vicar's Chronicle. The queen arrived at York on the 8th of March. In one of the Civil War Tracts (Lancashire Massacre), she is said to have pushed her outposts as far as Skipton, *en route* towards Blackburn. According to the earl's own statement, he was desired by the Lancashire gentry to go to the queen and solicit aid from her.

out, 'Glory be to God'; and wee all, except one troop of horse, and one foot company, which I left to quiet the countrey, returned forthwith towards our seige at Thurland"[a]

The parliament being in want of money, passed an act on the first of April, in this year, sequestering the estates of "notorious delinquents." On the other hand, the king instructed Prince Rupert to seize upon the goods and estates of persons in rebellion against him, and apply the property to the support of the royal army. The parliamentary commissioners for this purpose in Lancashire were, Sir Ralph Ashton, and Sir Thomas Stanley, barts.; Ralph Ashton, of Downham; Ralph Ashton, of Middleton, Richard Shuttleworth (member for Preston); Alexander Rigby, John Moore; Richard Holland; Edward Butterworth; John Bradshaw; Wm. Ashurst; Geo. Dodding; Peter Egerton, Nicholas Cunliff, John Starkie; Gilbert Ireland, Thos. Birch; Thos. Fell, Robt. Hyde, Robert Cunliff; Robert Curwin; John Newell, and John Ashurst. Four members of parliament were some time afterwards appointed auditors of the sequestration accounts, namely,—Richard Shuttleworth, Alexander Rigby, John Moore, and Ralph Ashton.

The parliamentary forces in Yorkshire, under Lord Fairfax and his son, being hard pressed by the army of eight thousand men, commanded by the marquis of Newcastle, the Lancashire troops were sent to their assistance. Fairfax, however, was beaten at Adwalton Moor. The Lancashire men were pursued by the marquis to Bradford, from which place he summoned the garrison at Manchester to surrender. This was peremptorily refused, and every preparation made for defence. Col. Rosworm so effectually fortified the heights of Blackstone Edge, that Newcastle was defeated in his attempt to pass the hills.

---

a According to Dugdale, Colonel Alexander Rigby was of "Middleton in Goosnargh," near Preston, and died in 1650. The Rev. T. Corser says.—"He was the *eldest* son and heir of Alexander Rigby, of Wigan and Peel in the county of Lancaster, esq. * * He was the elder brother of George Rigby, of Peel, esq, to whom the estate of Peel appears to have descended, who was Clerk of the Peace for the County of Lancaster, married Beatrice, eldest daughter of William Hulton, of Hulton Park, esq., and re-built the hall at Peel in 1634." The present Lord Kenyon represents this branch of the family. But Dugdale states that "Alexander Rigby, of Preston, was *younger* brother of George Rigby, of Peel, esq, from whom Rigby of that place (now represented by Lord Kenyon), descended"—(Vis. L. 1664, and Noble's Lives of the Regicides)—Colonel Alexander Rigby, "of Preston," as he was generally styled, married Lucy, the daughter of Thomas Leigh, esq, of Adlington, an active royalist. He was member for Wigan in the "long parliament," and, according to Ormerod, was created Baron of the Exchequer in 1649, but afterwards superseded by Cromwell.—Mr. W Beamont, in his observations on "Some Obsolete Peculiarities of English Law," says that when the civil wars were over, Colonel Alexander Rigby "doffed his scarlet coat for a scarlet gown, and going the circuit with Baron Gates, in 1650, they were both fatally struck with gaol fever and died at Croyden"—Alexander Rigby, of Brough, died about 1650. He married Catherine, daughter of Sir Edward Brabazon, of Nether Whitaker, Warwickshire—Dugdale—Alexander Rigby, of Lawton, was sheriff of Lancashire in 1677. He was the "grateful cornet" who erected the monument to Colonel Tildesley, in Wigan Lane.—*Vide* Ormerod's Annotations to "Civil War Tracts," published by the Cheetham Society"

The campaign of 1643 closed with more satisfaction to the royalists in Cheshire, though their success was of but short duration. The marquis of Ormond, at the instigation of the king, made peace with the Irish rebels, and dispatched a force from that country to Chester, consisting of from three thousand to four thousand men. In a very short time afterwards, Lord Byron, who commanded the Cheshire royalists, re-took all the principal strongholds in the county, with the exception of Nantwich, of which place he commenced the siege in December. Byron wrote to the marquis of Newcastle for assistance against the Lancashire parliamentary troops, which threatened to raise the siege; but the marquis, after his victory at Adwalton, having met with some reverses, was in no position to afford succour to the royalists in Cheshire. One portion of his army had been beaten by Fairfax and Cromwell, at Horncastle, in Lincolnshire. The marquis himself had been worsted before Hull, while Colonel Lambert had been successful against the royal troops in the western portion of Yorkshire. Sir Thomas Fairfax, reinforced by Colonels Ashton, Holland, and Booth, and Sir William Brereton, advanced to the relief of Nantwich. A desperate engagement ensued, in which Lord Byron, after a gallant resistance, was totally defeated, and his army almost entirely destroyed. Byron, with difficulty, reached Chester with the remainder of his forces.

Lathom House, the seat of the earl of Derby, was at this period the only place of strength held in the king's name in Lancashire. The earl had left the county, at the request of the queen, in order to personally defend the Isle of Man, against the naval power of the parliament, which had been considerably augmented since the fall of Liverpool. The countess, therefore, commanded the domestic fortress in person, assisted by Major Farmer, and Captains Farington, Charnock, Chisenhall, Rawstorne, Ogle, and Molyneux. On the 28th of February, 1644, Sir Thomas Fairfax arrived before Lathom. In an interview with the countess, he endeavoured to prevail upon her to yield possession of the place to the parliamentary troops, without the shedding of blood; and promised that herself, family, and domestics, should be escorted to Knowsley, where she would be allowed to remain unmolested, in the possession of one-half of her husband's estates. The countess, with the view to gain time, demanded a month, in order that she might receive her husband's instructions relative to the course she ought to take. Fourteen days afterwards, when Fairfax's siege operations were considerably advanced, he again summoned the fortress to surrender. The countess replied, that she "had not forgot her duty to the church of England, to her prince, and to her lord; and that she would defend the trust with her honour and with her life." Fairfax, being called into Yorkshire, Colonel Egerton and Major Morgan continued the siege. In the frequent sallies made by the brave little garrison, the works of the besiegers severely suffered. On one occasion, the royalists captured a large mortar, which had inflicted considerable injury on the place. One shot from this piece of ordnance had fallen into the room occupied by the heroic countess and her family. The parliament, attributing the want of success to the incapacity of the commander, removed Egerton, and entrusted the direction of the siege to Colonel Rigby and Colonel Moore. These officers constructed new works, which were attacked and destroyed in several vigorous sallies. Rigby, however, persevered till June, when, after a four months' investment, he was compelled to raise the siege, on hearing that Prince Rupert's main army of ten thousand men was advancing to the relief of the garrison. The force of the besiegers has been variously estimated at two thousand, three thousand, and four thousand men. Rigby retired to Bolton, and Colonel Moore to Liverpool, and prepared to stand upon the defensive. Thus, the heroic countess triumphed, and the brave parliamentary generals, in this instance, like the French at Saragoza, were

"Foil'd by a woman's hand, before a battered wall."

Prince Rupert having raised the sieges of Newark and Chester, entered Lancashire with an army of nearly ten thousand men, on the 25th of May, 1644, by the "pass" of Stockport, at that period considered "the second key of the county." The prince having effected a junction with the earl of Derby, attacked Bolton on the 28th, in the anticipation of an easy victory, the garrison of the town consisting only of about two thousand soldiers and five hundred club-men. Rigby and his veterans, however, beat him off, with the loss of two hundred men. It was essential to the success of Prince Rupert's mission, the regaining for the king the "lost county of Lancaster," that Bolton should fall. Another assault was, therefore, determined upon This was led by the earl of Derby in person, at the head of his retainers, tenants, and personal friends. It was completely successful, after a fierce and sanguinary struggle. The town was pillaged without mercy. The prince refused quarter, and, consequently, both the inhabitants and the garrison were put to the sword after the place was won. According to Seacombe, the historian of the house of Derby, the greater part of two thousand parliamentary soldiers were killed. Another royalist account makes the number one thousand six hundred slain, and seven hundred prisoners. The puritan author of "An Exact Relation of the Bloody and Barbarous Massacre at Bolton," says, however, and probably with truth:—"Of their and oure side it is conceived there was slain about 1200 or 1500 in all."

Rupert advanced to Liverpool, which, after eighteen days' resistance, fell into his hands. From Liverpool he was summoned by the king to York, then besieged by the parliamentary forces under Cromwell and Fairfax, and threatened by the Scotch puritan army, before which the marquis of Newcastle had fallen back upon the city. On the 2nd of July, the day after the arrival of Prince Rupert, the great and decisive battle of Marston moor was fought. The discretion of the prince by no means equalled his chivalrous courage. Without consulting the marquis, he rashly ordered the royal troops to engage the enemy, and lost on that fatal day, not only the fruits of many a well-fought field, but destroyed the military prestige of the royalists. This defeat so weakened the king's forces, that his chance of success in the conflict with his parliament from that hour gradually declined. In this engagement, the presence of mind, courage, and skill of Oliver Cromwell proved more than a match for the brave but impetuous Rupert. At Marston moor, fifty, and, according to some authorities, eighty thousand British troops were engaged in mutual slaughter. Newcastle, disgusted with the treatment he had received, retired from active life, and afterwards lived abroad. Rupert retreated precipitately with the remnant of his army into Lancashire.

These continual struggles had inflicted much suffering upon the kingdom, and especially upon the county of Lancaster. An ordinance was issued about this period by parliament, that the maimed or wounded officers and soldiers under the command of Rigby and Shuttleworth, together with the widows and orphans of the slain, should be pensioned "out of the several sequestrations of papists and delinquents, within the respective hundreds of Blackburn, Leyland, and Amounderness, or out of assessments provided for that purpose; but that no person should receive by way of maintenance more than four shillings and eightpence per week." [b]

The struggle was renewed in Lancashire on the return of Prince Rupert. On his passage through Preston, he seized upon the persons of William Cottam, the mayor, and William Patten and James Benson, bailiffs of the borough, and immured them in Skipton Castle, doubtless, for their parliamentary predilections. On their liberation, about three months afterwards, they were indemnified by the corporate body for their detention, in the sum of ten pounds to the mayor, and five pounds each to the bailiffs. [c] The mayor, however, presented his share of the grant to his colleagues. Rupert passed through Lancashire, and joined the king at Chester.

In the month of August, Preston was again the scene of a sharp

b Journal of the House of Commons, Aug. 5, 1644.

c Corporation Records.

rencontre between the parliamentary forces and some "malignants," who were endeavouring to effect a junction with the king's forces in Cheshire. The particulars are given in the following dispatch from Colonel Shuttleworth, dated at Whalley.—

"Right Honorable,—upon Thursday last, marching with three of my troops upon Blackburn towards Preston where the Enemie lay, I met 11 of their Colours at Ribble Bridge, within a mile of Preston, whereupon after a sharp fight we took the Lord Ogleby, a Scotch Lord and Col. Ennis, one other Col. slaine, one major wounded, and divers officers and souldiers to the number of 40 in all taken, besides 8 or 9 slain, with the losse of twelve men taken prisoners, which afterwards were released by Sir John Mildrum upon his coming to Preston the night following, from whence the enemie fled.

"Your humble servant,

"NICHOLAS SHUTTLEWORTH."

This spirited action is described more in detail in the "Perfect Diurnal" of the 26th August, 1644.—

"Letters were read directed to the Speaker of the House of Commons, declaring that the Lord *Ogleby* and Col. *Huddleston* marching towards *Latham* House in Lancashire, encountered with Colonell *Doddington* not far from *Preston*, and at first the dispute was very difficult, but Colonell *Shuttleworth* received an alarm upon their engagement (his quarters being neere) delayed not any time to rescue the first undertakers; upon whose approach Colonell *Doddington's* men were put in great courage, and these two valiant Colonells being joined together, charged the enemy with such brave resolution that they were put in disorder, and many of them slain in the place The enemies party consisting of about 400 horse."

The house of commons, on the 8th of August, ordered Fairfax to send a reinforcement of ten thousand horse into Lancashire, to strengthen the parliamentary forces there, and enable them to reduce Liverpool. Major-general Sir John Meldrum defeated the royalists at Ormskirk, on the 20th of August, and captured about thirty gentlemen of position in the county, and upwards of one thousand horsemen. Lords Byron and Molyneux were engaged, but escaped. Meldrum followed the routed army to Liverpool, and immediately proceeded to invest the place by land, while its late governor, Colonel Moore, who was occasionally employed in the naval as well as the military service, blockaded the port. The siege continued until the 14th November. The garrison, harrassed by dejection and famine, seized the officers, and surrendered the town.

The sufferings of the poorer inhabitants of Lancashire, about this period, were most intense In many parts, the people were without food or decent clothing. Their condition was so lamentable, that parliament appointed the 12th of September, 1644, as a day of solemn fast throughout the country, and ordered that *one-half* of the proceeds from collections made in "all the churches within the cities of London and Westminster, and within the lines of communication," should be devoted to the relief of the distressed people of Lancashire.

The public began to tire of the war, and to suspect that the emoluments of office tempted some of the leaders to prolong it. This feeling gave rise to the celebrated "self-denying ordinance," which prohibited members of parliament holding commissions in the army. Fairfax, however, contrived to retain the services of Cromwell, whose great military talents he had early recognised and cultivated.

The royalists, commanded by the king, Prince Rupert, and Sir Marmaduke Langdale, were defeated by the parliamentary forces, under Fairfax and Cromwell, at Naseby, on the 14th of June, 1645, after which the king fell back upon Chester. His army was again defeated on Rowton heath. The parliamentary forces under General Egerton, after a five months' siege, reduced Lathom House, the last stronghold of the king in the county of Lancaster. The countess and family had retired to the Isle of Man; but the fortress, which had been increased in strength by Prince Rupert, was bravely defended by the Lancashire royalists, under the command of Colonel Rawstorne, and others. The fall of Lathom was celebrated with great rejoicing in London and Westminster, as an event of the highest importance to the cause of the parliament. The commons ordered this celebrated stronghold to be dismantled, and all the military works destroyed. Bristol, Chester, and other fortified places speedily submitted. The royalists being utterly discomfited, the king surrendered himself to the Scotch puritan army, which had advanced to Newark, to support the parliamentary generals The struggle now seemed at an end. A royal warrant was issued from Newcastle on the 10th of June, 1646, in which orders were given to "Sir *Thomas Glenham*, Sir *Thomas Tildesley*, Cols. *Washington* and *Blagge*, Governors of Oxford, Lichfield, Worcester, and Wallingford, and all other commanders of any Touns, Castles, and Forts in our Kingdom of England, to quit the same and disband all their forces"

In order to raise funds necessary for so expensive a war, parliament had previously agreed to compound with "delinquents, papists, spies, and intelligencers," for their sequestered estates Large sums of money were now extracted from those persons of property who had supported the cause of the king The Lancashire sequestration committee usually held its sittings at Preston. Several of the royalist gentry, whose descendants still reside in the neighbourhood, compounded for their estates Roman catholics were mulcted, whether they professedly adhered to the king's cause or not.

While the king was a prisoner, some attempts were made by the Scotch and English royalists to turn the scale in his favour. The house of commons appointed a special "Committee of Lancashire," who ordered levies to be made for the defence of the county, and dispatched a body of troops, under Lieutenant-colonel Alexander Rigby, to the assistance of Lambert, who commanded in the north. Meetings of gentry were held at Bolton, Preston, and other places, where it was resolved to raise the whole force of the county, and warrants were issued accordingly. The campaign of 1648 commenced with the defeat of Sir Richard Tempest, on the 4th of July, by Colonel Lilburne. The royalists lost a considerable number of horses and prisoners. The same year, the duke of Hamilton penetrated into England at the head of a numerous army, by the western route Sir Marmaduke Langdale marched from Northumberland on his left flank, with about four thousand English royalists, and effected a junction with the duke near Preston. The king's army was further reinforced by some Irish troops, under General Monroe. The independents and presbyterians having quarrelled on the subject of church discipline, and the Lancashire puritans adhering almost universally to the formula of thelatter, the duke of Hamilton thought it desirable to intimate, on his entrance into the county, that his sole purpose was the "settling of Presbyterian government according to the covenant, and liberating and re-establishing his majesty." Oliver Cromwell received orders from parliament to immediately oppose the progress of the invading forces. He entered Lancashire on the 16th of August, by the Hodder bridge, where he was joined by the local parliamentary troops and the militia, under the brave Colonel Ashton, now advanced to the rank of major-general. A council of war was held on the spot, and prompt action determined upon.

As a rejoinder to the duke of Hamilton's manifesto, the soldiers, both officers and men, of the parliamentary army of Lancashire, published a declaration of their adherence to the solemn league and covenant of the three kingdoms, that "they would support the established government of king, lords, and commons; that as to priests, malignant abettors of former innovations, or other disaffected persons, they detested them from the bottom of their hearts, and would resist them with their lives and fortunes."

By a rapid movement early on the morning of Thursday, the 17th, from Stonyhurst, Cromwell surprised and defeated, after a sharp conflict, the division under Sir Marmaduke Langdale, at Ribbleton moor, before the duke of Hamilton, (whose troops were quartered in the town of Preston, and by the Darwen, at Walton, on the southern bank of the Ribble,) could render him any assistance. The battle was continued in the streets of the town; but the royalists were forced to retreat by the Ribble bridge upon their main body. Here the combat was renewed with gallant determination on both sides, and great slaughter ensued. The Lancashire troops assisted in the storming of the bridge, which was carried at "push of pike," after a severe struggle. At the end of the lane leading from Preston to the bridge at Walton, which was at that period "very narrow and deep," Cromwell himself, by a mere accident, escaped mutilation or death from the huge stones which the royalists hurled at him and his troops from the higher ground.[d] Night put an end to the engagement, and stopped the carnage. Though the Scotch army lay within musket shot of their enemies, they decamped before daylight. Milton, in his sonnet to Cromwell, regarded this victory as of sufficient importance to demand special mention when eulogising the military prowess of his hero,—

"Darwen's stream with blood of Scots imbued;"

with Dunbar and Worcester, are mentioned as his greatest triumphs.

Sir Marmaduke Langdale complained of the apathy or negligence of the duke of Hamilton, and attributed his defeat at Ribbleton moor entirely to the failure of succour from the Scots in his rear. He declared his conviction that had he only received promptly a reinforcement of one thousand foot, that Cromwell would have been defeated. The total royalist forces amounted to about twenty-one thousand men,[e] while Cromwell's army comprised little more than one-third of that number. This decisive victory was unquestionably the result of the superior unanimity and discipline of the parliamentary forces, and of the skill, promptitude, and energy of their commander.[f]

Langdale himself was, for some time, uncertain whether he was merely attacked by the Lancashire troops under General Ashton, or by the van-guard or "forlorn" of the parliamentary army. The irresolute duke of Hamilton was no match for the clear, penetrating intellect and active genius of Cromwell. The former marched with his large army widely scattered, a portion of his horse having been sent forward to Wigan, while his rear-guard, under Monroe, was loitering far behind the main body. Cromwell knew well the game he had to play with such a leader; and, accordingly, by rapid marches, appeared before the enemy when least expected; and, in the words of Thomas Carlyle, "dashed in upon him, cut him in two, drove him north *and* south, into as miserable ruin as his worst enemy could wish." In the evening of this eventful day, Cromwell forwarded from Preston the following dispatch to the "Committee of

---

d Patten's "History of the Rebellion in 1715."

e Another account states that the Scots alone numbered twenty-six thousand men.

f "Hamilton having entered England with a numerous though undisciplined army, durst not unite his forces with those of Langdale; because the English royalists had refused to take the covenant, and the Scottish presbytery, although engaged for the king, refused to join them on any other terms. The two armies marched together, though at some distance; nor could the approach of the parliamentary army under Cromwell oblige the covenanters to consult their own safety, by a close union with the royalists."—Hume.

Lancashire," in which the chief features of the action are sketched with much precision, and apparent candour:—

"*For the Honourable Committee of Lancashire sitting at Manchester. (I desire the "Commander of the Forces there to open this Letter if it come not to their hands.)*"

"'Preston,'[g] 17th August, 1648.

"Gentlemen,—It hath pleased God, this day, to shew His great power by making the Army successful against the common Enemy.

"We lay last night at Mr. Sherburn's, of Stonyhurst, nine miles from Preston, which was within three miles of the Scots quarters.[h] We advanced betimes next morning towards Preston, with a desire to engage the Enemy, and by that time our Forlorn had engaged the enemy, we were about four miles from Preston, and thereupon we advanced with the whole army · and the Enemy being drawn out on a Moor betwixt us and the Town, the Armies on both sides engaged; and after a very sharp dispute, continuing for three or four hours, it pleased God to enable us to give them a defeat, which I hope we shall improve, by God's assistance, to their utter ruin; and in this service your countrymen have not the least share.

"We cannot be particular, having not time to take account of the slain and prisoners; but we can assure you we have many prisoners, and many of those of quality, and many slain; and the Army so dissipated 'as I say.' The principal part whereof, with Duke Hamilton, is on south side Ribble and Darwen Bridge, and we lying with the greatest part of the Army close to them; nothing hindering the ruin of that part of the Enemy's Army but the night. It shall be our care that they shall not pass over any ford beneath the Bridge, to go Northward, or to come betwixt us and Whalley.

"We understand Colonel-General Ashton's are at Whalley; we have seven troops of horse or dragoons that we believe lie at Clitheroe. This night I have sent order to them expressly to march to Whalley, to join to those companies; that so we may endeavour the ruin of this Enemy. You perceive by this letter how things stand. By this means the enemy is broken: and most of their Horse having gone Northwards, and we having sent a considerable party at the very heel of them; and the Enemy having lost almost all his ammunition, and near four-thousand arms, so that the greatest part of the Foot are naked;—therefore, in order to perfecting this work, we desire you to raise your County; and to improve your forces to the total ruin of that Enemy, which way soever they go; and if you shall accordingly do your part, doubt not of their total ruin.

"We thought fit to speed this to you, to the end you may not be troubled if they shall march towards you, but improve your interest as aforesaid, that you may give glory to God for this unspeakable mercy This is all at present from,

"Your very humble servant,

"OLIVER CROMWELL."[i]

g The words in Cromwell's letters within the half quotations have been added to complete the sense, by Thomas Carlyle.

h As may be supposed, the distances are not quite accurate. Stonyhurst is about twelve miles from Preston.

i "The copy of a Letter from Lieutenant-General Cromwell, from Preston, of the 17° *Augusti*, 1648, to the Committee of Lancashire sitting at Manchester, enclosed in a letter from a Member of this House, from Manchester, of 19° *Augusti*, 1648, were this day read. *Ordered*, That it be referred to the Committee at Derby House to send away a copy of Lieutenant-General Cromwell's Letter to the General" (Fairfax), "and to the Lord Admiral," (Warwick).—Journals of House of Commons, Aug. 21, 1648.——The accompanying letter from the member of parliament at Manchester is signed "W. L." Carlyle describes this production as "short and insignificant, about 'dispensations,' 'providences,' etc.;" and conjectures its author to have been "William Langton, the new member for Preston." Both letters are printed in the "Civil War Tracts," published by the Cheetham Society.

On the morning of the 18th, Cromwell pursued the fugitives to Wigan, where both armies remained during the night. The next day, on his retreat to Warrington, the duke defended the "pass at Winwick" resolutely, for some hours; but the ardour of the parliamentary troops was not to be overcome; they forced the pass, and pursued the enemy to Warrington, which immediately capitulated. The remainder of the "malignant" army was cut up in detail by bands of "roundheads," which fell upon the scattered remnants in the various counties over which they were dispersed. The duke of Hamilton was captured at Uttoxeter, in Staffordshire, and Sir Marmaduke Langdale at Nottingham. The following entry in the records of the corporation thus describes this great military achievement:—

"Memorandum.

"Decimo Septimo die Augustie, 1648, 24 Car.

"That Henry Blundell, gent., being mayor of this town of Preston, the daie and yeare aforesaid, Oliver Cromwell, lieutenant-general of the forces of the parliament of England, with an army of about 10,000 at the most, (whereof 1500 were Lancashire men, under the command of Colonel Ralph Assheton, of Middleton), fought a battaill in and about Preston aforesaid, and overthrew Duke Hamilton, general of the Scots, consisting of about 26,000, and of English Sir Marmaduke Langdale and his forces joined with the Scots, about 4000; took all their ammunition, about 3000 prisoners, killed many with very small losse to the parliament army; and in their pursuit towards Lancaster, Wigan, Warrington, and divers other places in Cheshire, Staffordshire, and Nottinghamshire, took the said Duke and Langdale, with many Scottish earls and lords, and about 10,000 prisoners more, all being taken" (or) "slayne, few escaping, and all their treasure and plunder taken. This performed in lesse than one week." ‡

The number of slain, according to the official returns, in this short but decisive campaign, amounted to two thousand five hundred men, with about twelve thousand prisoners, of which the greater portion were captured in the retreat, making a total loss to the royalists of about fifteen thousand men, besides their munitions and implements of war, and a large booty in horses, cattle, and money.

Clarendon says that "Sir Thomas Tildesley was left with a body of English, with which he had besieged the castle of Lancaster and was on the point of reducing it when the Preston news arrived." Sir Thomas therefore fell back upon Monroe's reserves, and a remnant of Sir Marmaduke Langdale's broken forces, which had escaped from the town by the Lancaster road. He advised Monroe to follow Cromwell in the rear, being still equal in numbers to the parliamentary army. Cromwell evidently expected some such attack when he left orders to his detachment resting at Preston "to put their prisoners to the sword if the Scotch should

‡ This extract is printed in Baines's History of Lancashire. No existing corporation record book, however, contains it. One of the date referred to is, however, missing. There exists a memorandum that Dr. Kuerden borrowed some book belonging to the corporation, and did not return it. Mr. Baines therefore has doubtless transcribed it from some of Kuerden's manuscripts. These documents, from decay and the peculiar writing, are extremely difficult to decypher.

presume to advance upon them, because they cannot bring them off with security." Monroe, however, preferred retreating northward, through a "country hostile to him in consequence of his previous plunder." The royalists attempted to reduce the town of Cockermouth, but Major-general Ashton, who followed them from Preston with the Lancashire troops, raised the siege, and afterwards appeared before Appleby, then held by the Scots for the king, which place immediately surrendered. Ashton captured five pieces of cannon, a thousand stand of arms, "twelve hundred horse," and upwards of one hundred officers.

The following dispatch, from the pen of Cromwell, to the speaker of the house of commons, written on the 20th of August, will be read with interest. The details of the several engagements are given with characteristic force and precision:—

"*To the Honourable William Lenthall, Esquire, Speaker of the House of Commons:*
"*These*—

"'Warrington,' 20th August, 1648.

"Sir,—I have sent up this Gentleman to give you an account of the great and good hand of God towards you, in the late victory obtained against the Enemy in these parts.

"After the conjunction of that Party which I brought with me out of Wales with the Northern Forces about Knaresborough and Wetherby,—hearing that the Enemy was advanced with their Army into Lancashire, we marched the next day, being the 13th of this instant August, to Otley (having cast off our Train, and sent it to Knaresborough, because of the difficulty of marching therewith through Craven, and to the end we might with more expedition attend the Enemy's motion) and on the 14th to Skipton, the 15th to Gisburne; the 16th to Hodder Bridge over Ribble,[k] where we held a council of war. At which we had in consideration, Whether we should march to Whalley that night, and so on, to interpose between the Enemy and his further progress into Lancashire and so southward,—which we had some advertisement the Enemy intended, and 'we are' since confirmed that they intended for London itself. Or whether to march immediately over the said Bridge, there being no other betwixt that and Preston, and there engage the Enemy,—who we did believe would stand his ground, because we had information that the Irish Forces under Monro lately come out of Ireland, which consisted of Twelve-hundred horse and Fifteen-hundred foot, were on their march towards Lancashire to join them.

"It was thought that to engage the Enemy to fight was our business; and the reason aforesaid giving us hopes that our marching on the North side of Ribble would effect it, it was resolved we should march over the Bridge, which accordingly we did, and that night quartered the whole Army in the field by Stonyhurst Hall, being Mr. Sherburn's house, a place nine miles distant from Preston. Very early the next morning we marched towards Preston having intelligence that the Enemy was drawing together thereabouts from all his out-quarters, we drew out a Forlorn of about two-hundred horse and four-hundred foot, the horse commanded by Major Smithson, the foot by Major Pownel. Our Forlorn of horse marched, within a mile 'to' where the Enemy was drawn up,—in the

k This is an error. As Cromwell's army advanced by way of Gisburn, he would necessarily pass through Waddington to the "higher bridge," over the *river Hodder*, on his route to Stonyhurst. A considerable portion of this bridge is still in existence, and forms an interesting relic of the important "council of war" which preceded the great battle of Preston.

enclosed grounds by Preston, on that side next us; and there, upon a Moor, about half a mile distant from the Enemy's Army, met with their Scouts and Outguard; and did behave themselves with that valour and courage as made their Guards (which consisted both of horse and foot) to quit their ground; and took divers prisoners; holding this dispute with them until our Forlorn of foot came up for their justification; and by these we had opportunity to bring up our whole Army.

"So soon as our foot and horse were come up, we resolved that night to engage them if we could, and therefore, advancing with our Forlorn, and putting the rest of our Army into as good a posture as the ground would bear (which was totally inconvenient for our horse, being all enclosure and miry ground), we pressed upon them. The regiments of foot were ordered as followeth. There being a Lane, very deep and ill, on to the Enemy's Army, and leading to the Town,[l] we commanded two regiments of horse, the first whereof was Colonel Harrison's and next was my own, to charge up that Lane; and on either side of them advanced the 'Main'-battle,—which were Lieutenant-Colonel Reade's, Colonel Dean's and Colonel Pride's on the right; Colonel Bright's and my Lord General's on the left; and Colonel Ashton with the Lancashire regiments in reserve. We ordered Colonel Thornhaugh's and Colonel Twistleton's regiments of horse on the right, and one regiment in reserve for the Lane; and the remaining horse on the left,—so that, at last, we came to a Hedge-dispute; the greatest of the impression from the Enemy being upon our left wing, and upon the 'Main'-battle on both sides the Lane, and upon our horse in the Lane in all which places the Enemy were forced from their ground, after four hours dispute;—until we came to the Town, into which four troops of my own regiment first entered; and, being well seconded by Colonel Harrison's regiment, charged the Enemy in the Town, and cleared the streets.

"There came no band of your foot to fight that day but did it with incredible valour and resolution; among which Colonel Bright's, my Lord General's, Lieutenant-Colonel Reade's and Colonel Ashton's had the greatest work; they often coming to push of pike and to close firing, and always making the Enemy to recoil. And indeed I must needs say, God was as much seen in the valour of the officers and soldiers of these before-mentioned as in any action that hath been performed; the Enemy making, though he was still worsted, very stiff and sturdy resistance. Colonel Dean's and Colonel Pride's, outwinging the Enemy, could not come to so much share of the action; the Enemy shogging[m] down towards the Bridge, and keeping almost all in reserve, that so he might bring fresh hands often to fight. Which we not knowing, and lest we should be outwinged, 'we' placed those two regiments to enlarge our right wing; this was the cause they had not at that time so great a share in that action.

"At the last the Enemy was put into disorder; many men slain, many prisoners taken: the Duke, with most of the Scots horse and foot, retreated over the Bridge;[n] where,—after a very hot dispute betwixt the Lancashire regiments, part of my Lord General's, and them, being often at push of pike,—they were beaten from the Bridge; and our horse and foot, following them, killed many and took divers prisoners; and we possessed the Bridge over Darwen 'also,' and a few houses there; the Enemy being driven up within musket-shot of us where we lay that night,—we not being able to attempt farther upon the Enemy, the night preventing us. In this posture did the Enemy and we lie

l This "deep lane" was a little to the south of the present road from Longridge. The hollow is now planted with timber.

m "*Shog*, from the same root as *shock*; 'shogging' a word of Oliver's in such cases, signifies moving by pulses, intermittently."—Carlyle.

n This is an error. The Duke, Sir James Turner, and others, swam the ford at Penwortham, on horseback The main body, however, retreated by the lane at the end of Church-street, to the bridge at Walton.

most part of that night. Upon entering the Town, many of the Enemy's horse fled towards Lancaster; in the chase of whom went divers of our horse, who pursued them near ten miles, and had execution of them, and took about five-hundred horse and many prisoners. We possessed in this Fight very much of the Enemy's ammunition, I believe they lost four or five thousand arms. The number of slain we judge to be about a thousand; the prisoners we took were about four thousand.

"In the night the Duke was drawing off his Army towards Wigan; we were so wearied with the dispute that we did not so well attend the Enemy's going off as might have been; by means whereof the Enemy was gotten at least three miles with his rear, before ours got to them. I ordered Colonel Thornhaugh to command two or three regiments of horse to follow the Enemy, if it were possible to make him stand till we could bring up the Army. The Enemy marched away seven or eight thousand foot and about four-thousand horse; we followed him with about three-thousand foot and two-thousand five-hundred horse and dragoons; and, in this prosecution, that worthy Gentleman, Colonel Thornhaugh, pressing too boldly, was slain, being run into the body and thigh and head by the Enemy's lancers. And give me leave to say, he was a man as faithful and gallant in your service as any; and one who often heretofore lost blood in your quarrel, and now his last. He hath left some behind him to inherit a Father's honour; and a sad Widow; —both now the interest of the Commonwealth

"Our horse still prosecuted the Enemy, killing and taking divers all the way. At last the Enemy drew up within three miles of Wigan, and by that time our Army was come up, they drew off again, and recovered Wigan before we could attempt any thing upon them. We lay that night in the field close by the Enemy, being very dirty and weary, and having marched twelve miles of such ground as I never rode in all my life, the day being very wet We had some skirmishing, that night, with the Enemy, near the Town; where we took General Van Druske and a Colonel, and killed some principal Officers, and took about a hundred prisoners; where I also received a letter from Duke Hamilton, for civil usage towards his kinsman Colonel Hamilton, whom he left wounded there. We took also Colonel Hurry and Lieutenant-Colonel Innes, sometimes in your service.[o] The next morning the Enemy marched towards Warrington, and we at the heels of them. The Town of Wigan,[p] a great and poor Town, and very Malignant, were plundered almost to their skins by them.

"We could not engage the Enemy until we came within three miles of Warrington; and there the Enemy made a stand, at a place near Winwick. We held them in some dispute till our Army came up; they maintaining the Pass with great resolution for many hours ours and theirs coming to push of pike and very close charges,—which forced us to give ground; but our men, by the blessing of God, quickly recovered it, and charging very home upon them, beat them from their standing; where we killed about a thousand of them, and took, as we believe, about two-thousand prisoners; and prosecuted them home to Warrington Town, where they possessed the Bridge, which had a strong barricado and a work upon it, fomerly made very defensive. As soon as we came thither, I received a message from General Baillie, desiring some capitulation. To which I yielded. Considering the strength of the Pass, and that I could not go over the River 'Mersey'

o Who 'Van Druske' is, none knows. 'Colonel Hurry' is the ever-changing Sir John Hurry, sometimes called Urry and Hurrey, who whisks like a most rapid actor of all work, ever on a new side, ever charging in the van, through this Civil War Drama The notablest feat he ever did was leading Prince Rupert on that marauding party, from Oxford to High Wycombe, on the return from which Hampden met his death (Clarendon, ii 381). Hurry had been on the Parliament-side before. He was taken, at last, when Montrose was taken, and hanged out of the way. Of Innes ('Ennis') I know nothing at present."—Carlyle.

p This, evidently, is an error. It should read—"The people of Wigan."

within ten miles of Warrington with the Army, I gave him these terms: That he should surrender himself and all his officers and soldiers prisoners of war, with all his arms and ammunition and horses, to me; I giving quarter for life, and promising civil usage. Which accordingly is done: and the Commissioners deputed by me have received, and are receiving, all the arms and ammunition; which will be, as they tell me, about Four-thousand complete arms; and as many prisoners: and thus you have their Infantry totally ruined. What Colonels and Officers are with General Baillie, I have not yet received the list.

"The Duke is marching with his remaining Horse, which are about three-thousand, towards Nantwich; where the Gentlemen of the County have taken about five-hundred of them; of which they sent me word this day. The country will scarce suffer any of my men to pass, except they have my hand-'writing;' telling them, They are Scots. They bring in and kill divers of them, as they light upon them. Most of the Nobility of Scotland are with the Duke. If I had a thousand horse that could but trot thirty miles, I should not doubt but to give a very good account of them: but truly we are so harrassed and haggled out in this business, that we are not able to do more than walk 'at' an easy pace after them.—I have sent post to my Lord Grey, to Sir Henry Cholmely and Sir Edward Rhodes to gather all together, with speed, for their prosecution; as likewise to acquaint the Governor of Stafford therewith.

"I hear Monro is about Cumberland with the horse that ran away, and his 'own' Irish horse and foot, which are a considerable body. I have left Colonel Ashton's three regiments of foot, with seven troops of horse (six of Lancashire and one of Cumberland), at Preston; and ordered Colonel Scroop with five troops of horse and two troops of dragoons, 'and' with two regiments of foot (Colonel Lascelles's and Colonel Wastell's), to embody with them; and have ordered them to put their prisoners to the sword if the Scots shall presume to advance upon them, because they cannot bring them off with security. q

"Thus you have a Narrative of the particulars of the success which God hath given you: which I could hardly at this time have done, considering the multiplicity of business; but truly, when I was once engaged in it, I could hardly tell how to say less, there being so much of God in it; and I am not willing to say more, lest there should seem to be any of man. Only give me leave to add one word, shewing the disparity of forces on both sides; that so you may see, and all the world acknowledge, the great hand of God in this business. The Scots Army could not be less than twelve-thousand effective foot, well-armed, and five-thousand horse; Langdale not less than two-thousand five-hundred foot, and fifteen-hundred horse: in all Twenty-one Thousand;—and truly very few of their foot but were as well armed if not better than yours, and at divers disputes did fight two or three hours before they would quit their ground. Yours were about two-thousand five-hundred horse and dragoons of your old Army; about four thousand foot of your old Army; also about sixteen-hundred Lancashire foot, and about five-hundred Lancashire horse: in all about Eight-thousand Six-hundred You see by computation about two-thousand of the Enemy slain; betwixt eight and nine-thousand prisoners; besides what are lurking in hedges and private places, which the Country daily bring in or destroy. Where Langdale and his broken forces are, I know not; but they are exceedingly shattered.

"Surely, Sir, this is nothing but the hand of God; and wherever anything in this world is exalted, or exalts itself, God will pull it down; for this is the day wherein He alone will be exalted. It is not fit for me to give advice, nor to say a word what use you should

q "It is to be hoped the Scots under Munro will not presume to advance, for the prisoners here in Preston are about four thousand! These are not Baillie's Warrington men 'who surrendered on quarter for life;' these are 'at discretion.'"—Carlyle.

make of this;—more than to pray you, and all that acknowledge God, That they would exalt him,—and not hate His people, who are as the apple of His eye, and for whom even Kings shall be reproved, and that you would take courage to do the work of the Lord, in fulfilling the end of your Magistracy, in seeking the peace and welfare of this Land,—that all that will live peaceably may have countenance from you, and they that are incapable and will not leave troubling the Land may speedily be destroyed out of the Land. And if you take courage in this, God will bless you, and good men will stand by you; and God will have glory, and the Land will have happiness by you in despite of all your enemies. Which shall be the prayer of,

"Your most humble and faithful servant,

"OLIVER CROMWELL.

"*Postscript.* We have not, in all this, lost a considerable Officer but Colonel Thornhaugh; and not many soldiers, considering the service but many are wounded, and our horse much wearied. I humbly crave that some course may be taken to dispose of the Prisoners. The trouble, and extreme charge of the Country where they lie, is more than the danger of their escape. I think they would not go home if they might, without a convoy; they are so fearful of the Country, from whom they have deserved so ill. Ten men will keep a thousand from running away."

According to Captain Hodgson, Colonel Thornhaugh was "run through with a lancier in Chorley, he wanting his arms" (armour). The colonel appears to have been a great favourite, and his death was much lamented He died like Nelson and Wolfe, in the hour of victory. Ludlow says that, "as he lay wounded among his soldiers, he made them open to the right and left, that he might see the enemy run." Mrs. Hutchinson, in the memoir of her husband, pays the following graceful tribute to Col. Thornhaugh's valour and personal integrity:—

"Being at the beginning of the charge on a horse as courageous as became such a master, he made such furious speed to set upon a company of Scotch lancers, that he was singly engaged and mortally wounded, before it was possible for his regiment, though as brave men as ever drew sword, and too affectionate to their colonel to be slack in following him, to come up time enough to break the fury of that body, which shamed not to unite all their force against one man, who yet fell not among them, but being faint and all covered with blood, of his enemies as well as his own, was carried off by some of his own men, while the rest, enraged for the loss of their dear colonel, fought not that day like men of human race; but deaf to the cries of every coward, they killed all, and would not that a captive should live to see their colonel die, but said that the whole Kingdom of Scotland was too mean a sacrifice for that brave man. His soul was hovering to take her flight out of his body, but that an eager desire to know the success of that battle kept it within till the end of the day, when the news being brought him he cleared his dying countenance, and said,—'I now rejoice to die, since God hath let me see the overthrow of this perfidious enemy; I could not lose my life in a better cause, and I have the favour from God to see my blood avenged' So he died, with a large testimony of love to his soldiers, but more to the cause, and was by mercy removed, that the temptations of future times might not prevail to corrupt his pure soul. A man of greater courage and integrity fell not, nor fought not in this glorious cause" [r]

On the 20th of August, Cromwell wrote another characteristic letter from Warrington, in which he laments that himself and army are completely fagged with the labour of beating the enemy:—

r Memoirs of Col. Hutchinson (Bohn's edition), p 320

"*For the Honourable the Committee at York*: *These*—

"Warrington, 20th August, 1648.

"'Gentlemen,'—We have quite tired our horses in pursuit of the Enemy: we have killed, taken and disabled all their Foot; and left them only some Horse, with whom the Duke is fled into Delamere Forest, having neither Foot nor Dragooners. They have taken Five-hundred of them,—I mean the Country Forces 'have,' as they send me word this day.

"They are so tired, and in such confusion, that if my Horse could but trot after them, I could take them all. But we are so weary, we can scarce be able to do more than walk after them. I beseech you therefore, let Sir Henry Cholmely, Sir Edward Rhodes, Colonel Hatcher, and Colonel White, and all the Countries about you, be sent to rise with you and follow them. For they are the miserablest party that ever was: I durst engage myself, with Five-hundred fresh Horse, and Five-hundred nimble Foot, to destroy them all. My Horse are miserably beaten out;—and I have Ten-thousand of them Prisoners.

"We have killed we know not what; but a very great number; having done execution upon them above thirty miles together,—besides what we killed in the Two great Fights, the one at Preston, the other at Warrington 'or Winwick Pass.' The Enemy was Twenty-four thousand horse and foot, whereof Eighteen-thousand horse and Six-thousand foot: and our number about Six-thousand foot and Three-thousand horse at the utmost.

"This is a glorious Day!—God help England to answer His mercies!—I have no more; but beseech you in all your parts to gather into bodies, and pursue. I rest,

"Your most humble servant,

"OLIVER CROMWELL."

"'P.S.'—The greatest part, by far, of the Nobility of Scotland are with Duke Hamilton."[s]

Captain Hodgson, whom Thomas Carlyle describes as an "honest-hearted pudding-headed Yorkshire Puritan," has left a record of his particular doings in this campaign.[t] Amongst other matter, he says:—"The Scots, marched towards Kendal; we towards Ripon, where Oliver met us with horse and foot. We were then between eight and nine thousand; a fine smart Army, fit for action. We marched up to Skipton; the Forlorn of the Enemy's horse" (Langdale's) "was come to Gargrave; having made havoc in the country,—it seems, intending never to come there again."

After the passage of the Hodder, Hodgson says, "we pitched our camp at *Stanyares* Hall" (Stonyhurst,) "a Papist's House, one Sherburne's, and the next morning a Forlorn of horse and foot was drawn out." He then proceeds to inform his readers that at "Langridge Chapel their horse came upon the advanced posts of Sir Marmaduke Langdale, drawn up very formidably. One Major Poundall" (Pownel) "and myself," he continues, "commanded the Forlorn of Foot. And here being drawn up by

s This letter is in the possession of Mr. W. Beamont, of Warrington.

t Captain Hodgson's narrative is printed in "Original Memoirs of the Great Civil War," edited by Sir Walter Scott.

the Moore-side (a mere scantling of us as yet, not half the number we should have been), the General" (Oliver himself) "comes to us and orders us to march. We not having half of our men come up, desired a little patience;" but Cromwell knowing well the value of time at such a juncture, was not inclined to patience, for, "he gives out the word 'March!'" and Captain Hodgson docilely obeys.

When the action is fairly begun, the "honest-hearted pudding-headed" captain appears to want neither courage nor discretion. He says:—

"I met Major-General Lambert,—and coming to him *I told him where his danger lay*, on his left wing chiefly. He ordered me to fetch up *the Lancashire regiment*, and God brought me off both horse and myself. The bullets flew freely: then was the heat of the battle that day.

"I came down to the muir, where I met with Major Jackson, that belonged to Ashton's regiment, and about three hundred men were come up; and I ordered him to march, but he said he would not, till his men were come up. A serjeant belonging to them asked me where they should march. I shewed him the party he was to fight, and he like a true bred Englishman marched and I caused the soldiers to follow him, which presently fell upon the enemy, and losing that wing, the whole army gave ground and fled.

"The Lancashire men were as stout men as were in the world, and as brave firemen. I have often told them they were as good fighters and as great plunderers as ever went to a field."

Sir James Turner, who is described by Thomas Carlyle as "a stout pedant and soldier of fortune, the original *Dugald Dalgetty* of the novels," accompanied the Scotch army, and having "a turn for taking notes," likewise presented the public with a narrative of this disastrous campaign. From this production, a tolerably clear conception of the "Preston Battle" is obtained from an opposite point of view, and several additional details are supplied. After alluding to the dispute amongst the generals and officers respecting the route, he informs his readers that he "was for Yorkshire," simply because he understood "Lancashire was a close country full of ditches and hedges," which would be more favourable to the enemy, whose army was composed of "well-trained soldiers," while the Scots were "raw and indisciplined musketeers." The Yorkshire heaths he thought would furnish more favourable ground, as they might make better use of their horse, and come sooner to "push of pike" with the foot. Hamilton determined for Lancashire, "which," says Sir James, "led us to our ruin." The doughty knight, having satisfactorily made known his own judgment, and the duke's obstinacy, proceeds with his narration as follows:—

"Our march was much retarded by most rainy and tempestuous weather, the elements fighting against us; and by staying for country horses to carry our little ammunition. The vanguard is constantly given to Sir Marmaduke, upon condition that he shall constantly furnish guides; pioneers for clearing the ways, and, which was more than both these, having good and certain intelligence of all the enemy's motions. But whether it was by our fault or his neglect, want of intelligence helped to ruin us. * * *

"Beside Preston, in Lancashire, Cromwell falls upon Sir Marmaduke's flank. The

English imagined it was one Colonel Ashton, a powerful Presbyterian, who had got together 3000 men to oppose us, because we came out of Scotland without the General Assembly's permission. Mark the quarrel. While Sir Marmaduke disputes the matter, Baillie, by the duke's order, marches to Ribble Bridge, and passes it with all the foot except two brigades. This was two miles from Preston.[u] By my lord Duke's command, I had sent some ammunition, and commanded-men to Sir Marmaduke's assistance: but to no purpose, for Cromwell prevailed; so that our English first retired and then fled. It must be remembered that the night before this sad encounter, Earl Calendar and Middleton were gone to Wigan, eight[v] miles from thence, with a considerable part of the cavalry Calendar was come back and was with the Duke, and so was I; but upon the rout of Sir Marmaduke's people, Calendar got away to Ribble, where he arrived safely by a miracle, as I think, for the enemy was between the Bridge and us, and had killed or taken most part of our two brigades of foot.

"The Duke with his guard of horse, Sir Marmaduke with many officers, amongst others myself, got into Preston Town. with intention to pass a ford below it," (at Penwortham,) "though at that time not rideable. At the entry of the Town, the enemy pursued us hard. The Duke faced about, and put two troops of them to a retreat, but so soon as we turned from them, they again turned upon us. The Duke facing the second time, charged them, which succeeded well. Being pursued the third time, my lord Duke cried, *To charge once more for King Charles!* One trooper refusing, he beat him with his sword At that charge we put the enemy so far behind us, that he could not so soon overtake us again. Then Sir Marmaduke and I entreated the Duke to hasten to his army:—and truly here he showed as much personal valour as any man could be capable of. We swam the Ribble River and so got to the place where Lieutenant General Baillie had advantageously lodged the foot, on the top of a hill," (at Walton,) "among very fencible enclosures

"After Calendar came to the infantry, he had sent 600 musqueteers to defend Ribble Bridge. Very unadvisedly, for the way Cromwell had to it was a descent from a hill that commanded all the champaign, which was about an English quarter of a mile in length between the Bridge and that Hill where *our* foot were lodged.[w] So that our musqueteers, having no shelter, were forced to receive all the musket shot of Cromwell's infantry, which was secure within thick hedges, and after the loss of many men, were forced to run back to our foot. Here Claud Hamilton, the Duke's Lieutenant Colonel, had his arm broke with a musket-bullet.

"The Bridge of Ribble being lost, the Duke called all the Colonels together on horseback to advise what was next to be done. We had no choice but one of two. Either stay and maintain our ground till Middleton (who was sent for) came back with his cavalry, Or else march away that night, and find him out. Calendar would need speak first; whereas by the custom of war he should have told his opinion last,—and it was, To march away that night so soon as it was dark. This was seconded by all the rest, except by Lieutenant General Baillie and myself But all the arguments we used,—as the impossibility of a safe retreat, from an enemy so powerful of horse; in so very foul weather, and extremely deep ways; our soldiers exceedingly wet, weary, and hungry; the inevitable loss of all our ammunition,—could not move my lord Duke by his authority to contradict the shameful resolution taken by the major part of his officers.

"After that drumless march was resolved upon, and but few horse appointed to stay in rear of the foot, I inquired What should become of our unfortunate Ammunition, since forward with us we could not get it? It was not thought fit to blow it up that night, lest the enemy should know of our retreat, or rather flight. I was of that opinion too; but for another reason; for we could not have blown it up then, without a visible mischief to ourselves, being so near it. It was ordered it should be done three hours after our departure by a train; but that being neglected Cromwell got it all.

---

u Sir James, as might be expected from the hurried manner in which his observations were made, is very incorrect in his distances. Walton Bridge is but a little more than one mile from the *centre* of Preston. The town and village now nearly meet

v This is probably a clerical error for eighteen Wigan is about seventeen miles from Preston.

w The valley of the Ribble is nearly a mile in breadth The brow at Walton, on the south of the Ribble, is about three quarters of a mile from the bridge.

"Next morning we appeared at Wigan Moor; half our number less than we were;—most of the faint and weary soldiers having lagged behind; whom we never saw again. Lieutenant General Middleton had missed us, for he came by another way to Ribble Bridge.[x] It was to be wished he had stayed with us. He not finding us there, followed our track, but was himself hotly pursued by Cromwell's horse; with whom he skirmished the whole way till he came within a mile of us."

Captain Hodgson furnishes a few additional particulars respecting the capture of the bridge and the baggage of the enemy He says:—

"Colonel Bright's regiment, Col. Pride's, and Colonel Deane's, kept the field; the *Lancashire regiments* and my *Lord General Cromwell's regiment of foot* pursued towards Ribbald Bridge, with most of our horse, where the Scots had six regiments of horse and foot, that had been in no service, besides their great army, with the waggons, near Walton Hall, drawn up in readiness

"There was a long dispute before the *Bridge* was gained, and our horse and foot having routed that party above Walton Hall, they came to their main body, and a matter of six or eight horsemen, commanded by Captain Pockley, kept a gapstead of their whole army, while some of our troopers lighted and turned about Hamilton's waggons, and threw over that wherein was all his plate, as they brought it down the hill; but the Scots having no mind to rescue it, suffered them to carry the prize away in the face of their whole army, though nothing to fright them, but a forlorn hope of horse.—That night our regiment was appointed quarters in Preston."

Cromwell appears to have remained in Lancashire for a few days after the victory at Winwick, and to have afterwards withdrawn the main body of his army into Yorkshire. He was at Wigan on the twenty-third, from which place he dispatched the following letter:—

"'*For the Honourable the Committee at York. These.*'

"Wigan, 23rd August, 1648.

"Gentlemen,—I have intelligence even now come to my hands, That Duke Hamilton with a wearied Body of Horse is drawing towards Pontefract, where probably he may lodge himself, and rest his Horse;—as not daring to continue in those Countries whence we have driven him; the Country-people rising in such numbers, and stopping his passage at every bridge.

"Major-General Lambert, with a very considerable force, pursues him at the heels. I desire you that you would get together what force you can, to put a stop to any further designs they may have; and so be ready to join with Major-General Lambert, if there shall be need. I am marching Northward with the greatest part of the Army; where I shall be glad to hear from you. I rest,

"Your very affectionate friend and servant,

"OLIVER CROMWELL.

"I could wish you would draw out whatever force you have: either to be in his rear or to impede his march. For I am persuaded if he, or the greatest part of those that are with him be taken, it would make an end of the Business of Scotland." [y]

Cromwell, in a letter dated Knaresborough, 1st September, 1648, and addressed to his "worthy Friend, Oliver St. John, Esquire, Solicitor-General," relates a singular circumstance relative to the battle, which has called forth as singular a commentary from the pen of the able but eccentric Carlyle. Cromwell says: "I am informed from good hands,

x There are two roads from Walton to Wigan: one direct, and another through Chorley.

y Newspaper, *Packets of Letters from Scotland and the North*, no. 28 (London, printed by Robert Ibbitson in Smithfield, 29 August, 1648).

that a poor godly man died in Preston, the day before the Fight; and being sick, near the hour of his death, he desired the woman that cooked to him, To fetch him a handful of Grass: She did so; and when he received it, he asked, Whether it would wither or not, now it was cut? The woman said, 'Yea.' He replied, 'So should this Army of the Scots do, and come to nothing, so soon as ours did but appear,' or words to this effect and so immediately died."

Carlyle exclaims, "Does the reader look with any intelligence into that poor old prophetic, symbolic, Deathbed-scene at Preston? Any intelligence of Prophecy and Symbol, in general; of the symbolic Man-child *Mahershalal-hashbaz* at Jerusalem, or the handful of Cut Grass at Preston:—of the opening Portals of Eternity, and what departing gleams there are in the Soul of the pure and the just?—Mahershalal-hashbaz, ('Hasten-to-the-spoil,' so called,) and the bundle of Cut Grass are grown somewhat strange to us! Read; and having sneered duly,—consider."

Many relics of this brilliant victory have been from time to time discovered. On Killingsough Farm, in Fulwood, several iron cannon balls, weighing about seven pounds each, have been picked up at various times. The country people often use them even to this day, as bowls, in their rural games. Gossip lore declares the farm took its name from the circumstance of an immense quantity of human bones being dug up during the construction of a drain or "sough," soon after the enclosure of the moor, in 1813. This, however, is highly improbable. The name is unquestionably of much higher antiquity.[y] Large quantities of leaden bullets, nearly an inch in diameter, have been dug up near the corner of Gamull-lane.[z] Bullets have likewise been found in the garden belonging to Mr. Lawrence Dobson, at Sion Hill, and what is believed by some to be a stone cannon ball, in the grounds at Ribbleton Hall. From its size, this is, however, improbable. The eastern slope of Ribbleton moor towards the brook, exhibits marks of entrenched earth, which may yet perhaps disclose some remains. The present road is modern; the one referred to by Cromwell passed nearer to Mr. Birchall's house. The formation of the land on the farm occupied by Mr. Robert W. Dobson, yet plainly indicates the site of the "deep lane," where the severe struggle took place between Cromwell's horse and the English, under Langdale. On the upper portion of the steep bank overlooking this ravine, several bullets were found in the spring of last year (1856). The "deep lane," near Walton bridge, passed through the strawberry garden to the west of the present road.

---

y See Chap. 2, page 64.

z So named from Sir Francis Gamull, of Cheshire, who formerly owned the neighbouring property. Sir Francis married one of the Hoghtons, of Lea.

Some indications of the quicksand, referred to by Patten, may still be occasionally perceived, notwithstanding the partial filling up of the hollow. A receptacle, for decayed vegetable matter, formed of brick, receives the contents of a drain. In summer time this is generally dry, but in wet weather large quantities of fine sand are discharged with the spring water. When this garden was first cultivated, many coins, bones, and other remains were found. The site of the old Ribble bridge is indicated by a fragment of the centre pier. Two cannon balls, in the possession of Mr. Dearden, weighing between eight and nine pounds each, were found not far from Darwen bridge. The modern structure is near the site of that upon which the advanced guard of Cromwell's army rested on the night of the battle. Bullets have been found upon "Walton Flats," and a sword, the blade of which is much corroded. The latter, together with a small dagger, said to have been picked up in the neighbourhood, is deposited in the museum of the Literary and Philosophical Institution. Several relics of the battle were dug up in Mr. Mansley's garden, some fifty or sixty years ago. An old man informed the author that he remembered, when a boy, hearing of two human skeletons falling from out of the north bank of the Ribble, after a flood, which were pronounced by the people of Walton to be the remains of "Scotch warriors." A short time ago, an iron cannon ball, nearly seven pounds in weight, was found in the clay on the land belonging to Mr. Catterall, behind the "Lane Ends Hotel," at Ashton. The locality is somewhat to the left of the old road to the north, which passed by the old Water-lane and the present Aqueduct-street. This shot was probably fired during the pursuit of the fugitives northward. Or it may have been discharged from the outwork on the Maudlands, at the time of the surprise of the town by the earl of Derby, in 1643. Mr. Peter Whittle, in his History of Preston, publishes the following curious paragraph: "1831, Oct. 22: An ancient iron boot, found at Ingol, near Preston, by Mr. Simpson, sedan carrier, with the initials engraved on it of O. C. 1648, supposed to be the the identical boot of Oliver Cromwell," (!) "or belonging to one of the numerous body of men he commanded when at Preston, during the civil wars."![a] In the spring of 1853, a heavy storm stripped the roof of a thatched cottage at Tenter Hill, Whittingham, and disclosed a previously hidden treasure, consisting of about three hundred silver coins, including half crowns, shillings, and sixpences. Sixty-nine of these coins were presented by the Rev. Mr. Mossap, of Woodplumpton, to the Institution for the Diffusion of Knowledge, at Avenham. They had been minted in the reigns of Philip IV., of Spain, husband of Mary I., of England; Elizabeth; James

a His. Preston, vol. 2, p. 134.

I, and Charles I. Their consignment to the safe keeping of the cottage thatch, most probably took place during the civil war between the king and parliament. Mr. Whittle records the discovery of a similar hoard a little nearer to the scene of Langdale's defeat. He says, "On the 11th day of April, 1812, a gentleman, near Fulwood moor, was making a hole in the floor of his house, when to his surprise he discovered a little below the surface, a quantity of silver coins, of various sizes; they consisted of Edward the 4th, nearly defaced; Charles 1st, James 1st, and Elizabeth, in a fine state of preservation; also a crown piece of Philip the 4th, of Spain." [b]

This short campaign presents one of the most brilliant exhibitions of the military genius of Cromwell. It was fully appreciated both by parliament and the country. The house of commons ordered a general thanksgiving throughout the whole kingdom, for these important victories; and passed a resolution that "the sum of Two-hundred Pounds be bestowed upon Major Berry, and the sum of One-hundred Pounds upon Edward Sexby, who brought the very good news of the very great Success obtained, by the great mercy of God, against the whole Scots Army in Lancashire." [c] Ten thousand copies of the order authorising the day of thanksgiving, were distributed throughout the country. Commissioners were appointed to enquire into the losses of the inhabitants owing to the Scotch invasion, with a view to their compensation. The people suffered severely, not only from war and famine, but from the "plague of pestilence," which had afflicted the country for upwards of three years. A writer of the period says. "There is a very great scarcity and dearth of all provisions, chiefly of all sorts of grain, particularly that by which that country is most sustained (oats), which is full sixfold the price that of late it hath been. All trade by which they have been much supported is utterly decayed. It would melt any good heart to see the numerous swarms of begging poor, and the many families that pine away at home, not having faces to beg. Very many now crave alms at other men's doors, who were used to give others alms at their doors;—to see paleness, nay death appear in the cheeks of the poor, and often to hear of some found dead in their houses or highways for want of bread." To alleviate, to some extent, this misery, parliament ordered collections to be made in all the churches and chapels throughout the whole country. One half of the proceeds was devoted to the relief of the famishing poor, and the other for the support of the wounded soldiers in the county of Lancaster.

The town of Preston suffered severely during a previous visitation of the

b His Preston vol. 1, p. 14

c Journals of the House of Commons

"plague," which, according to entries in the parish church registers, commenced its ravages in November, 1630. The mortality was most excessive during the following months of July and August; the number of interments in the former being 323, and in the latter 199. In 1631, the total number of funerals at the parish church, (at that period the only burial ground in the town) amounted to 951. The population is not supposed to have much exceeded 3000 persons, so that nearly one third were swept away In 1628, the number of burials was 87; in 1629, 66, in 1630, including 20 deaths from the plague, 74; in 1631 (plague year), 951; in 1632, 39; in 1633, 54.

At the conclusion of the war an ordinance was issued for disbanding of the militia of the kingdom, but the Lancashire forces, in the first instance, refused to comply, "but professed for the Covenant, and were encouraged by the clergy." Major-general Lambert was sent to enforce the order, if necessary, by an appeal to arms, when "the Lancashire warriors" submitted to the law, and yielded up Clitheroe castle, which a portion of them occupied, and had threatened to hold until their demands were complied with. Clitheroe, Greenhaugh, and other strongholds, were afterwards "demolished," or rather dismantled by an order of the Council of State.

It occasionally happened, that either from conviction or policy, some of the influential families changed their views and went over to the opposite party during these disastrous civil wars. The son of Major-general Ashton became a warm supporter of Charles II. From a letter addressed to the treasurer of sequestration at the Guildhall, London, and signed by Sir Richard Hoghton, and five other gentlemen, it appears that the son of the cavalier Sir Gilbert, espoused the cause of the parliament The letter says,—

"In regard of the late imminent danger threatened to this countye by that great and potent Armye of the Scottes and Englishe, wee were inforced to raise such a considerable number of Forces for the mutual defence of the Kingdom our selves and neigbor counties that the maytenace thereof hath occasioned the expense of a vast some of monye over and above the profittes arriseinge out of the Sequestrations. The arreres of the Souldiere are soe greate that we are utterly disabled to sattisfie their iust demande in any reasonable measure without some further supply."

Charles I. was executed in January, 1649. "John Bradshaw, serjeant at-law, lord president" at the trial of the king, was a member of an ancient family in Lancashire. He held, likewise, the office of chancellor of the duchy of Lancaster, under the commonwealth.

Promise of favour from parliament, and a considerable mitigation of the fine upon his estates, was offered to the earl of Derby, for the surrender of the Isle of Man. But the earl's spirit was in no humour for yielding to the wishes of the roundheads, although victorious in England He resolutely replied, "I scorn your proffer, I disdain your favour, I abhor your treason, and so far from delivering up this Island to the Parliament, I shall keep it for the King to the utmost of my power; and if you trouble me with any more messages of this nature I will burn the paper and hang the messenger."

The monarchy was abolished by law in England, and the "Commonwealth" established. The Scotch, however, proclaimed the king's son by the title of Charles II. The corporation of Preston imitated the example at the market cross, in July, 1649. The Scotch attached conditions to their proclamation very unpalatable to the king. He was to be of "good behaviour," exhibit a "strict observance of the covenant," and entertain about his person "no other persons but such as were goodly men and faithful to that obligation."

Cromwell, after subduing Ireland in the space of nine months, led his army into Scotland, and at the famous battle of Dunbar routed the Scotch covenanters under Lesley, slew three thousand men, and took nine thousand prisoners. Edinburgh and Leith immediately afterwards fell into his hands.

King Charles II., with the Scotch royalists under Lesley and the new duke of Hamilton, in 1651, advanced into England. Their army amounted to about fourteen thousand men. The king stayed at Ashton Hall, near Lancaster, on the evening of the 12th of August, where, according to one of the civil war tracts, "Hamilton lodged two days before the battail at Preston." [d] The following evening, Charles rested at Myerscough Lodge, the seat of the brave Major-general Sir Thomas Tildesley. After passing the bridge over the Ribble, at Preston, he lodged at Euxton Hall, the residence of the Anderton family; and on the 15th, Sir William Gerard, of Bryn, had the honour to entertain his royal master. The Scottish army passed the Mersey, at Warrington, after a severe skirmish with some cavalry of the commonwealth, under Major-general Lambert. In the mean time, Cromwell, leaving about seven thousand men with General Monk, in Scotland, quickly followed the king into the centre of England.

The earl of Derby, Sir Thomas Tildesley, and a number of officers landed from the Isle of Man, at the mouth of the Wyre, near the site of the present town of Fleetwood, with about sixty horse, and two hundred and fifty foot soldiers. The earl "beat to arms," and was joined, according to Lilburne, not only by "malignant papists and disaffected persons," but likewise by "those who are called presbyterians." Arthur Trevor, on the contrary, in a letter to the marquis of Ormonde, intimates

d The duke of Hamilton, defeated by Cromwell at Preston, in 1648, was executed soon after the king at Westminster. The descendants of the duke of Hamilton retained, until lately, possession of this property.

that the earl's summons to meet him in arms at Preston, was but feebly responded to. His plans were considered to be well laid; but his influence had latterly become much shaken. According to Seacombe, the earl of Derby hastened to Warrington, where, that very night, the Major-general Massey brought in many of the presbyterian party to his lordship, who made *the taking of the Covenant and removal of Papists essential to their joining him.* The earl declined to accede to this proposal, declaring that he "had *men* enough;" but he added, "all the arms are in your possession, without which I shall only lead naked men to slaughter; however, I am determined to do what I can with the handful of Gentlemen now with me for His Majesty's service, if I perish; but if my Master suffer, the blood of another Prince, and all the ensuing miseries of this nation, will lie at your doors." The earl then departed, accompanied only by the gentlemen who came with him from the Isle of Man, and some few Lancashire and Cheshire royalists. He hastened to Preston, where he issued out warrants, and raised about six hundred horse.

Cromwell, with his accustomed sagacity, had previously strengthened the garrisons of Liverpool and Manchester. Colonel Lilburne, who was ordered to watch the movements of the enemy at the head of a body of horse, being reinforced from Liverpool and Chester, attacked, on the 25th of August, the troops led by the earl of Derby, consisting of about one thousand five hundred men, at Wigan lane, where, after a desperate encounter, the royalists were totally routed, the earl himself, slightly wounded, escaping with difficulty The gallant Major-general Sir Thomas Tildesley fell in this engagement. The principal portion of the king's friends, both officers and men, were either slain or taken prisoners at Wigan lane.

From Lilburne's letter to Cromwell, dated "Wiggan 25 Aug. 1651, late in the evening," it appears a skirmish took place near Preston, between the royalists and parliamentary troops, on the day previous to the decisive battle at Wigan lane. He says:—

"The next day I marched after them towards Preston, and lay within two miles of them onely with my own Regiment and about 60 Horse and Dragoons, which is all the Country could assist me with all this while (saving onely one Company from *Manchester* of Foote, and two from *Chester*, which have been with me two days. That night I sent 40 Horse to alarm them (who then wounded Col. Vere) hearing they were to have a Rendezvous at Preston the next day. I did that to give notice to the Town and Countrey I was there to oppose the Earle, and to stay the people from rising with him, who reported it, that none of our Forces were in that Countrey, and made the Countrey beleeve all was their owne, which the people generally tooke for granted, and was coming in apace, as by these inclosed you may perceive

"The next day, in the afternoone, I having not foot with me, a party of the Enemies Horse fell smartly amongst us where our Horses were grasing, and for some space put us pretty hard to it; but at last it pleased the Lord to strengthen us so as that we put them to flight, and pursued them to *Ribble-bridge*, (this was some thing like our business at *Mussleburgh*) and kild and tooke about 30 prisoners, most Officers and Gentlemen, with the loss of two men that dyed next morning; but severall wounded, and divers of our good Horses killed That night came three Companies of Foot, and the next morning hearing of your Excellencies Regiment cumming towards *Manchester*, I onely removed two miles to a more convenient ground, thinking to have staied there till your Regiment could come, which I expected this day, but their weariness frustrated that expectation, and this morning I had intelligence that the Enemy was upon their march, which I thought was a running away from us, being that they began at 11 in the night and marched so fast and privately, but their confidence was much otherwise raised, having increased in their number at Preston."

Sir Thomas Tildesley appears to have been regarded by both parties as a brave and honourable gentleman. He was not unfrequently styled the "*chevalier sans puer et sans reproche.*" Although Sir Thomas resided at Myerscough Lodge, as keeper of the royal forest, his ancestral estates were situated at Tildesley, near Leigh. In the parish church of the latter place his remains were interred. [e]

Cromwell, being joined by the militia of the country, attacked the king at Worcester, on the 3rd of September, and obtained his celebrated "crowning mercy," in the shape of a complete victory The king became a fugitive, disguised himself as a peasant, and was under the necessity of hiding in an oak tree, to save himself from the pursuit of Cromwell's dragoons After a series of narrow escapes, a vessel was at length procured by his friends, by the aid of which he safely landed on the coast of France.

The "Perfect Diurnall," of September 1st, states that all the shipping was "wafted out of the Rivers of *Liverpool*, and set sail with a fair wind for *Wyrewater*, the place where the Frigots rid, that brought the Lord" (Derby) "over with his company, to surprise them and prevent his Lordship from escaping any way by water." It appears that two of the frigates had become wrecks, owing to their running too near in shore for the purpose of landing the horses. These preparations, combined with the activity of the parliamentary generals, were completely successful.

e "There is an unintelligible and very inaccurate passage in *Lloyd's Memoirs*, p. 692, respecting Tyldesley being buried in one grave with Sir Francis Gamul, who certainly survived to 1654, although included by error among the slain in the first account of Wigan fight. The same statement is inaccurate also as to Tyldesley. After his heroic death in the battle-field, and his escape thereby from the scaffold, this last named officer was interred in the north chancel of the church of Leigh, appendant to his ancient mansion of Morleys, where the Earl of Derby seven weeks afterwards, in his way to execution at Bolton, made an unavailing request to visit his grave. Tyldesley is honourably commemorated by Clarendon, and the long series of his exploits proves that he deserved such remembrance. Another memorial (of a more solid but less durable description than Clarendon's praise,) is the PILLAR in Wigan Lane, erected by his grateful cornet Alexander Rigby. Considering the adverse zeal of Tyldesley, the ruling powers may be said to have dealt gently with him He was thrice a prisoner, but always at liberty and in arms again; and no forfeiture is known to have followed his decease, at least so far as related to his estates in Astley and Tyldesley."—Ormerod.—Lancashire Civil War Tracts, published by the Cheetham Society.

Harrison and Lilburne captured, at Middleton, near Lancaster, on their retreat from Worcester, towards Scotland, Generals Lesley and Middleton, and "other eminent officers and commanders, with six hundred private soldiers, horse, and arms."

The earl of Derby was less fortunate than his royal master. He was taken prisoner in Cheshire, on his way to Knowsley, by Major Edge. At a court martial, held on the first of October, at Chester, he was charged with high treason for having corresponded with "Charles Stuart," contrary to the act of parliament, passed on the preceding 12th of August. The earl, in his defence, urged that he had been promised quarter when captured; but this the court overruled. He was sentenced to death, and executed on the 15th of October, at Bolton. This town is said to have been selected for the closing scene of the earl's life, owing to representations that he had been an active instrument in the atrocities practised upon the people when the place was sacked by order of Prince Rupert. It is but simple justice to the earl to state, that he always, even on the scaffold, indignantly denied the truth of this allegation. The belief that he was of a cruel disposition could not have been general; for many of the inhabitants sympathised with his misfortunes, and were "moved to tears" when they witnessed the calm resignation with which he met his fate The earl felt grateful for this unexpected sympathy. Looking upon the people from the scaffold, a few moments before his death, he exclaimed, "There is no man that revileth me; God be thanked." This was the closing scene of the civil war in Lancashire.

In the year 1650, after the execution of Charles I., the parliament entertained a motion for the holding of the assizes at Preston, instead of Lancaster. No resolution, however, was adopted which interfered with the then existing arrangements.

During the troubled period of the civil wars and the commonwealth, Preston, from its central position, was selected as the place of meeting, not only for the "Lancashire committee of sequestration," but likewise for the sittings of the "Lancashire Assembly of Divines." The first meeting of the latter body was held in November, 1646 The episcopal church government was superseded by the presbyterian, and the county divided into classes; the parishes of Preston, Kirkham, Garstang, and Poulton, are described as "VII. classis." Its executive consisted of the following clergymen and lay members. "Ministers—Isaac Ambrose and Robert Yates, Preston; Edward Fleetwood, Kirkham; Thomas Cranage, Gosenargh, Chris. Edmondson, Garstange; and John Sumner. Laymen—Alexander Rigby and William Langton, esquires. Matthew Addison, of Preston, William Sudal, of Preston, and William Cottam, of Preston, aldermen. Edward Downs, of Wesam; Thomas Nickson, of Plompton; Robert Crane, of Leaton; William Latewise, of Catterall, and Richard Whitehead, of Garstange, gentlemen. Edward Veal, of Layton, esquire; Richard Wilkins, of Kirkham, and Edward Turner, of Gosenargh, yeomen."

Cromwell was made "Lord Protector" in 1653, and died in 1658. His administration of the national affairs, both foreign and domestic, was marked by prudence, energy, and promptitude, and notwithstanding the suicidal struggle in which the people of England had been so long engaged, the nation, at no previous period of its history, was more respected for its policy, or feared for its power, than when the chief authority was vested in the person of Oliver Cromwell

His son Richard proved incompetent to discharge the duties of the position held by his father with so much tact and ability. The royalists took heart, and, being eventually seconded by General Monk, who commanded the army of the commonwealth, effected the restoration of Charles II., by a vote of parliament, without the shedding of blood. Charles made a public entry into London, on the 29th of May, 1660, amidst the cheers of the populace. Monk was rewarded for his services by the dukedom of Albemarle, and, amongst other marks of the royal bounty, received a grant of the ancient honour of Clitheroe, which previously appertained to the duchy of Lancaster.

Some notion of the relative wealth of the boroughs of Lancashire may be formed from the amount of their respective assessments for "ship money" in the time of the first Charles. Lancashire was assessed at one ship of 400 tons, and 160 men, or £1,000 in money. The proportion for the borough of Preston was £40, Lancaster, £30; Liverpool, £25; Wigan, £50; Clitheroe, £7 10s.; Newton, £7 10s. The tax continued to be levied with some modification for three years. Mr. Baines says, the arrears owing by Lancashire, at the end of that period, amounted to £172 10s.[f]

[f] His Lan., vol. 2, p. 4.

PART I.—HISTORICAL.

CHAPTER V.—FROM THE RESTORATION TO VICTORIA.

Profligacy of the Court—Test and Corporation Act—Act of Uniformity—Knights of the Royal Oak—Value of Household Goods, etc.—Extinction of Feudalism—Preston in the Seventeenth Century: Dr. Kuerden's description—James II. at Chester—The Revolution—Judge Jeffreys—Disaffection of the Roman Catholics—The Lancashire Plot—Jacobite Rebellion in 1715—Invasion of England by the Scotch Army—Siege of Preston—Surrender of Forster, Derwentwater, and other Stuart Partisans—Sale of Sequestered Estates—Claims of Prestonians for Compensation—Second Jacobite Invasion—Prince Charles Edward Stuart at Preston—Retreat of the Scotch Army—Battle of Culloden—Jacobite Club at Walton-le-Dale—Preston in the Eighteenth Century.

The austerity of the puritan manners, on the accession of Charles, was succeeded by openly expressed contempt for moral principle, and practical indifference to the social and domestic duties. The king, courtiers, and a large portion of the people, wearied with the extreme cant and self glorification of the *soi disant* "saints," rushed to the opposite extreme, and revelled with the zest of escaped prisoners in their newly acquired liberty. Licentiousness and debauchery became fashionable, and, as usual, the multitude servilely bowed before the "respectability" of the reigning idol. The nation, however, recovered from its intoxication more rapidly than its princes. The Stuart dynasty, untaught by misfortune, and incapable of moulding itself into harmony with the progressive spirit of the English people, after a lamentable exhibition of weakness and incapacity, was eventually, within a very few years from the restoration of the profligate Charles, finally expelled from the throne of Great Britain.

The episcopalian party, on the downfall of the "commonwealth," being in the ascendant, exercised all the power conferred by their position to strengthen the authority of the church and the crown. In 1661, the celebrated "Test and Corporation Act" was passed, which required that every mayor, alderman, common councilman, and all other corporate officers, should make specific declaration *against* the "solemn league and covenant,"[a]

a One of the most flagrant of Charles II.'s acts of perfidy, consisted in his persecution of the covenanters, although he himself in his necessity had professed to adopt their peculiar views of church doctrine and government.

and to make oath that he abhorred the traitorous act of taking up arms "by the king's authority against his person," or those commissioned to act on his behalf. With the view to the exclusion from all power of persons who were at heart nonconformists, it was enacted that no corporate officer should be elected, who had not within the preceding twelve months received the Sacrament of the Lord's Supper, according to the formula of the episcopacy or Church of England, as established by law. Next year, the equally memorable "Act of Uniformity" received the sanction of the legislature. By this enactment, every minister holding an ecclesiastical preferment, was compelled to renounce his living if he failed, previously to the feast of St. Bartholomew, to append his signature to a declaration of his "assent and consent" to the contents of the then new book of Common Prayer. To the credit of the ministers of religion at the time, about two thousand preferred poverty and social humiliation to the self reproach attending the barter of conscience for worldly preferment. In the county of Lancaster sixty-seven persons were ejected from their benefices by the rigid enforcement of this act. Amongst these were, the Revs. John Wright, M.A., Billinge; Henry Welch, Chorley; — Lowe, rector of Croston; Jonathan Schofield, Douglas Chapel; Isaac Ambrose, vicar of Garstang; — Bullock, Hambleton; Peter Naylor, Houghton Chapel; Timothy Smith, Longridge Chapel; John Mallinson, vicar of Melling; — White, Melling; Nathaniel Baxter, M.A., vicar of St. Michaels-le-Wyre; and Cuthbert Harrison, Singleton. Other acts were passed prohibiting nonconformist clergymen from teaching in public schools, or dwelling or coming within five miles of any corporate town or other place where he had been minister or had preached unless he took the oath depriving him of the right of private judgment and committing him to the doctrine of passive obedience to the "church and the state" as then established.[b]

Mr. Edward Baines says, on the authority of Goodwin's Lives of the Puritans, in White's Collection, that "the sufferings of the ejected ministers were extreme; it is computed that no fewer than sixty thousand persons suffered on account of their religion in different parts of the kingdom, and that of this number five thousand perished in prison." He further observes, that "in Lancashire, where the catholics were so numerous, a preponderance was given to that party, and the dissenting interest was reduced to the lowest point of depression."

Charles II. with the intention of conferring honourable distinction upon the families of those who had risked life and fortune in the defence of the throne, contemplated the establishment of a special order of knighthood. The members were to be termed "Knights of the Royal Oak," and

b These intolerant enactments were repealed in the reign of George IV.

to be privileged to wear a silver medal, bearing a representation of the king in an oak tree, in allusion to his majesty's hair breadth escape from the dragoons of Cromwell. Charles, however, was proverbially indolent and ungrateful. The project was abandoned, ostensibly lest the distinction should engender ill-feeling between parties whose good will was necessary to the peace and security of the monarchy. The following Lancashire gentlemen were selected for the honour:—Thomas Holt, Thomas Greenhalgh, Colonel Kirby, Robert Holte, Edmund Asheton, Christopher Banester, Francis Anderton, Colonel James Anderton, Roger Nowell, Henry Norris, Thomas Preston, — Farrington, of Worden, — Fleetwood, of Penwortham; John Girlington, William Stanley, Edward Tildesley, Thomas Stanley, Richard Boteler, John Ingleton, and — Walmsley, of Dunkenhalgh.

Preston received two charters from Charles II., confirming and extending the privileges previously enjoyed by the borough [c] The following document, in the possession of the Rev W Thornber, is illustrative of the condition of the middle class in the seventeenth century, as well as of the variation in the monetary value of farming stock and domestic utensils, when compared with that of the present time:—

"A true and perfect inventarye of all the goods and chattels, as well moveable as not moveable, whatsoever, that were of Peter Birkett, late of Borrands within Gressingham, in the County of Lancaster, deceased, taken the sixt day of December, 1661, and prised by Will'm Backhouse of Borrands, Will'm Brathwayte of Gressingham, Allan Harrison of Eskrigg, and James Bell of Gawenhall, and particularly according to their best judgments, as followeth:—Imprimis, his apparel, £1; bedding, 5s.; arkes and chests, 13s. 4d.; old woodden vessell, 5s.; new woodden vessell, cowper timber, and one pair of old bedstockes, 12s.; one brasse pott, three pans, one pewther dubler [dish] and one earthen pott, 10s.; gridiron and branderesth, 3s.; old table, old chaire, wheele and stocke, two old formes, and three old stooles, 3s. 4d.; 2 sackes, 5s . kneading tub and meale, 2s.; one Rakencrooke,[d] paire of tonges, cowper tooles and 3 quishions [cushions], 10s.; hempe and 25 lra [libra, lb] of yarne, 9s , wheeltimber, carle, and carrs, 8s., corne and strawe, £3: one outshoote of hay, £1 6s 8d.; one stacke of hay without dores, 10s.; one scaffold of hay, 10s.; one padd and wooll, 10s., one mare and one colt, £3; 5 geese, 4s ; manure, 5s.; 13 sheepe, £3; ropes, 1s., one cocke and 5 hens, 2s., turfe, 6s. 8d.; loose wood, stees, and forks, 3s.; one poake [bag] and hempseed, 1s.; one calfe, 10s ; 2 heiffers, £3; one ditto, £2; one cow, £2 10s.; another £3 10s. Summa totalis, £29 15s"—Of the four appraisers, only one, James Bell, could write his name, the other three attached their marks.

In 1661, a local token was coined expressly for the Nowells, of Preston, "there being at that time no national copper in England." [e]

The last remains of the feudal system were swept away in the twelfth year of the reign of Charles. The holding of lands in consideration of "Knights' service, chivalry, escuage, petit serjeantry, villanage," etc, was abolished, and "fee-simple, fee-tail, and copyhold" tenures substituted.

---

c See "Municipal History"

d An iron instrument fixed in the chimney, from which kettles, etc., are suspended.

e Whittle's Lecture, in 1849.

Preston, in the reigns of Charles II. and his brother, James II., has been very minutely described by Dr. Kuerden, a native of Cuerden, near Preston, who resided for some time in the town. His historical manuscripts are deposited in the Herald's College, London, and in the library attached to the Cheetham Hospital, Manchester. However valueless at the present day the learned doctor's antiquarian speculations may be considered, his description of the town, as it appeared in his own time, is highly interesting, as will be seen from the following extracts[e]:—

"The antient Burrough is very pleasantly seated upon a high or riseing ground, more especially from the south or west, such a situation as the Britains and Romans in antient time either prefixed or annexed a Dunum or Duno to the names of towns so seated as this Burrough. In those days by Ptolemy it was styled Tibo Dunum, or Tigo Dunum,[f] from the British word Dun, a hill or elevated situation; as may appear in many towns in Gaul and Brittain, that were so seated. as formerly hath been hinted at, as well as on the sight of this Burrough of Preston which southward for many miles, yeilding forth a very fayre and pleasant prospect, as upon London road as far as Chernoc green, distant some 6 or 7 miles, and by the Lirpole road from Ormeschurch more 12 customary miles at least. * * * This Burrough, from the entrance thereunto, upon south, unto the townsend on the north,[g] being a full statute mile in length, though'd be not altogether so much from the eastern part to the west thereof.

"This Burrough is much adorned with its larg square or market place, as likewise with the streets thereof, which are so spacious from one end thereof unto the other, that few of the corporations of England exceed the same, either for streets or market-place. In the midle of the Burrough is placed an ample antient and yet well beautifyed gylde or town hall or toll bothe, to which is annexed, at the end thereof, a counsell chamber for the capitall burgesses or jurors at their court days, to retire for consultation, or secretly to retire themselves from the comon burgesses or the publiq root of people, as occasion shall require. * * * [h]

"Under this hall are ranged two rows of butcher's shopps[i] on either side, and a row at either end, where victualls are exposed dayly for the use of man, excepting Sundays, as also weekly on the public market dayes (etc.,) Wednesday, and Saturday, and Friday

e Kuerden's description of Preston was published in 1818, with notes by Mr. John Taylor. From his preface it would appear that Mr. Taylor was not aware by whom the manuscript was written. He says —"From internal evidence it seems to have been compiled about the year 1682, or perhaps a few years later." "Mr. Taylor conjectures that the manuscript published by him is of the date of 1682, but it is evident that it was written at least four years after that time, seeing that the municipal government described by Dr. Kuerden is that established by the charter of Charles II., granted in 1685"—Edward Baines —The manuscript must have been *originally* compiled previously to the guild of 1682, and additional matter afterwards introduced, for Kuerden speaks of this festival as "now intended, by God's assistance, to be begun, held, and kept, within this borough of Preston, before Roger Sudell, Mayor of this present Gild" Yet he afterwards speaks of the festival of 1662, as the "last gild save one." There is some variation between the manuscript deposited in the Herald's College, as quoted by Mr Baines, and the one possessed by Mr. Taylor, but the purport appears to be generally the same. The above extracts are from Mr. Taylor's copy.

f Kuerden is evidently in error on this subject. [See chap. 1]

g From Church street to Friargate. The latter was at the time the principal road to the north.

h The roof and greater part of the walls of this building fell in 1780. The present edifice was erected shortly afterwards upon the site of the ancient town hall.

i The butchers' shops were not incorporated with the new edifice; but the narrow street leading into the Market place still retains the name of "Old Shambles" The "New Shambles," built in 1715, is speedily to follow the steps of its predecessor. The improvements now in progress by the earl of Derby, in Lancaster road, include the removal of the rude piazza, and the erection of handsome shops upon the site.

being ever a market for fish, butter, and cheese, as likewise in the evening for yarn; Wednesday likewise being a market for fish, butter, and cheese: And upon Saturday, as soon as light appeare, is the market bell for linnen cloth; which ended, yarn appears, bread and fish of all sorts, butter and cheese; as formerly, the fish all in a row upon the fish stones and places adjacent; their butter, cheese, and pullen, and potters about the butter crosse, in the end of Cheapside market; and bread nere unto the fish market.

"The cattell market ordinarily in Church-street, and upon the Saturday only; their horse market in the Fishergate, and begins about the ending of their market for cattell.

"The swyne market over against the church; their sheep early upon the west side of the Market-squarе above the shoomakers' stalls; and the leather cutters' earthern vessell, in Cheepside, and wooden vessell in the west end of the Market-place, below the barley market. The upper corn market beginning at one of clock, upon the corn bell ringing; here standeth for sale rowes of wheat, rye, groats, in their distinct fyles and orders; below them towards the west is the barley and bean market, places in distinct and well ordered rowes, j in which place, before the corn comes into town, was hydes and skinns exposed to sale untill 9 or 10 aclock. Below the fish stones k standeth the stalls of hardwaremen, with all sort of iron instruments; in the midst of the Market-place aside the barley market, are the stalls for brass and pewter, and higher above them ranges of stalls for pedlars and cloth cutters, hosiers and the like · yet notwithstanding all these varyetys of wares and merchandizes thus exposed, most of the burgesses or inhabitants of the Burrough have shops about the Market-place and in other streets, in their houses or nere unto their lodgings, were the several companyes of tradesmen dayly expose wares to sale.

"The streets belonging to this town or burrough are very spacious, good handsome buildings on either side, here and there interwoven with stately fabricks of brickbuilding after the Modish maner, extraordinarily addorning the streets which they belong vnto.

"The first street as you enter upon the south side from the bridge, l is Fenkell-street, unto the barrs; and from the barrs proceeding to the town's hall, is styled the Church-street, all though the other part below the barrs hath been, and is, vulgarly taken for part thereof. m

"From the Church-street, in a straight line proceeding westward, the whole street is called the Fishergate-street.

"And over against the church, proceeding northward to Salter-lane, was esteemed to be Vicars or Vicarage-street, n or alley, by reason that at the end thereof, the ancient vicarage stood before delapidation, and the tithe barn were adjacent.

---

j The grain market was removed to Lune street in 1824, on the erection of the present Corn Exchange.

k The fish stones were removed by order of the corporation, from the Market-place, in 1853, and a fish market established in one of the large rooms of the Corn Exchange, Lune-street. There is, however, no regular fish market at the present time, the removal to the Exchange not conducing to the interest of the trade.

l The old bridge at Walton. The other bridges over the Ribble, near Preston, were not built at the time Kuerden's manuscript was written The bridge is evidently one of the oldest in the northern part of the country, and was long regarded as an important military position. Whitaker, in his history of Manchester, quotes a verdict given in the reign of Henry III., in which an ancient forest boundary record is cited as authority. The forest is described as "beginning at the bridge of the Ribble, going to Steep-clough, betwixt Ribchester and Hadersal—betwixt Chippin and Gosnaig, to the water of Lond or Laund, by the demense of Hornby, to the water of the Lone or Lune, and the current of the Ken or Kent, down the Kent to the sea, along the coast of the sea to the foot of the Wire and the Ribble, and up the Ribble to Ribble Bridge." The old bridge consisted of five arches. A portion of one of the piers in the centre of the river yet marks its site, about fifty yards below the present structure, which was completed at the beginning of the year 1782.

m The entire length from the Town Hall to the House of Correction is now called Church-street. "One of the Church-street bar posts, the Editor well remembers standing close to the house on the scite of which now stands the house and shop occupied by Mr Yates the grocer, at the corner of Cockerhole now Water-street."—Taylor's Notes.

n The present St. John-street and Tithe Barn-street

"From the end of Vicarage-street or lane, a spacious street passed westward, and this is called St. John Street;[o] and from thence a back lane passing beside the town, falling into the Fryergate below the Fryergate barrs.[p]

"And from the west end of St. John's-street," (now called Lord-street) "and the little short street or alley passing southerly into the lower end of Market-place, and this is called the Fryer's Weend.[q]

"And likewise from the midst of St. John's-street," (now Lord-street) "passing by the horsemill southward, into another square with a draw well in the midst thereof, into which square the mayor and counsell did intend to translate their fish stones or fish market, out of the larger market-place.[r]

"And from this lesser square (most of which belongs to that worthy person and purchaser of the town-end, the antient estate formerly belonging to the family of Prestons, but now in possession of Mr. Rigby, Paternoster-row, in London), is another alley lately adorned with new building, passing into the Market-place, at the upper end of the Corne market; and this alley or passage from the aforesaid lesser square hath been antiently called Gin Bow Entry.[s]

"There is likewise below the Churchgate barrs another public footway southward, leading towards the bridge over Ribble into London-road; and this passage at its entrance out of town was called Cockerhole.[t]

"Another remarkable foot passage toward Rible Bridge is through the Churchyard southward, by the publiq schoole and antient place called Chappel of Avenam, over the Swilbrook southward, by West-feld to the aforesaid Bridge of Rible; and this passage is called the Stonygate, being the greatest foot tract to the Burrough of Preston.

"Another passage southward, about the midst of Church Street, more privatly passing either towards the bridge or bote,—and is at present styled the passage through Cockshutt's back side.[u]

"Another foot passage southward, is over against the Shambles or Town Hall, and leadeth by the Minspitt well, and over Avenam to Rible side, passing along the river to the boate or ferry of Penwortham, and this is called Minspitt-lane or Pettycoat-ally, by reason of the frequent carrying of water from this well by woemen, and the milkmaids bringing dayly their milk and butter to the town this way, from beyond the river Rible.[v]

---

o Now named Lord-street. The present St. John-street leading from the church to Tithe-barn-street was till within a few years ago, often called the "Church Weind."

p This street still retains the name Back-lane.

q "Now Anchor-wiend because the house opposite the south end was formerly a public house, known by the sign of the Anchor."—Taylor's Notes.

r Molyneux-square. The Earl of Derby's improvements will erase this little square from the map of Preston. The site will form a part of the new Lancaster-road.

s "Gin Bow Entry" still rejoices in its ancient patronymic, but the "adornment" effected by the "new building" has followed in the wake of all terrestrial beauty, and succumbed to the influence of time.

t Water-street is generally considered to be the ancient "Cocker-hole," although, from a verdict recorded in the "Court Leet Book," and quoted at page 33 of the present work, it would appear that the deep gully by which the Roman way descended to the ford over the Ribble was the true Cocker-hole. Some old people still call Water-street, Cockerhole-lane. More than one passage led to the bridge over Ribble by this hollow. The path described by Kuerden passed most probably over the Roman road, which crossed Church-street near the Blue Bell Inn. Another footpath may have joined this road from near the present Water-street, which appears to be a more modern thoroughfare, opened about the time of the closing of the old footpaths.

u The present Turk's head-court.

v In 1729, a large circular well was sunk by Mr. Robert Abbott and a Mr. Woodcock, upon the site of the "Min Spit Well," and portions of the town supplied with water by means of pipes and a forcing engine. These early "Waterworks" were popularly styled the "Folly," from the supposed Quixotism of the innovation!! A public well, however, remained near the end of the Main-sprit wiend till the Gas Company, having previously purchased the property, erected, in 1850, a large gas holder upon the site. In 1774, the alley was called "Midspit Weint."

"At the west end of the Fishergate, there is one lane or footpath, likewise leading over Avenham, from the Almes-house to the aforesaid boat at Penwortham, and this is called the Almes-house-lane or Passage to the boat.[w]

"From the Church-street or Town Hall westward, in a direct line, continues another spacious street leading towards the river of Rible or Broadgate, as they call it; and this street as far as the buildings extend, is called the Fishergate-street, and the end thereof, at the ford over Rible or the horseway to the boat, when the river is not fordable, is called Broadgate,[x] from whence going southerly they pass over the river, there divided into three streams,[y] a very secure passage if the water be not too deep by fresh or flood; in such cases when they come to the river side at the aforesaid Broadgate, they must follow up the river side eastward, about a quarter of a mile, untill they arrive at the key or wharf over against the boat house, where diverse boats are ready, as occasion may require, for horse or foot to waft them over to the other side, from thence to pass through Leyland-lane to Eccleston; and from thence to passe to Wigan by Standish, or by Maudsley to Ormschurch, and so to Liverpoole; or westward unto Croston, or when over the ford or boat, upon the right hand road, through Penwortham, Longton, Hoole, Ormschurch, and so to Liverpoole.

"Now from the corner end of the Market-street or square, passing by the northwest through a fayre long and spacious street cal'd the Fryergate-street, by reason upon that side of the town was formerly a larg and sumptuous building, formerly belonging to the Fryers Minors or Gray Fryers, but now only reserved for the reforming of vagabonds, sturdy beggars, and petty larcenary thieves, and other people wanting good behaviour; it is now the country prison to entertain such persons with hard work, spare dyet, and whipping, and it is cal'd the House of Correction.[z] And at the upper end of this street without the barrs, is a passage westward, either for horse or foot, by this Fryery or House of Correction, to the upper end of the Marsh, where there is a lower ford to passe over the water to the Church or Hall of Penwortham, although not altogether so safe as the aforesaid Upper Ford; and this passage betwixt the Burrough and the said Pryory is styled the Fryers'-wind.[a]

"When you pass the barrs towards the Townsend Hall now belonging to Mr. Rigby, of Paternoster-rowe, upon the left hand westward lyeth the publiq road by Preston Marsh unto the Fyld Contry, or the plain and westron part of the said Amoundernes

---

w Since called Brewery-lane; now Mount-street. The alms-houses were situated at the north-west corner of this lane.

x The beautiful terrace to the left, when passing from the bottom of Fishergate to Penwortham bridge, is erected upon this Broadgate, which still retains its ancient name

y In the early part of the present century, the "Holm" was a single island, the middle stream having disappeared. The southerly channel which passed beneath Penwortham wood, was sufficiently deep to permit small vessels to discharge their cargoes at the foot of Penwortham brow. Through the influence of an artificial "caul" or weir this southern channel is now totally blocked up The "Holm" has therefore ceased to be an island, and the river now flows in a single stream. The three channels are visible upon a "South Prospect of Preston," drawn and engraved by S. & N. Buck, in 1728. On a plan published in 1738, by Robert Porter, of Goosnargh, two large islands and three smaller ones are distinctly marked The largest is called the "Holme." The present Penwortham bridge was built in the year 1759, on the site of one, which fell shortly after its erection. It is situated midway between the old ford and the ferry The boat house and landing stairs remain to this day. The former which has been somewhat modernised, was a few years ago used as a public house A sculptured stone in the front wall of the building, exhibits the arms of the Fleetwood family, and the date 1626.

z The Friary was converted into cottage dwellings after the erection of the House of Correction, in Church-street, in 1789. Mr. Whittle says the building was used for a time as a cotton factory. Some operations in connection with the staple trade may have been carried on within its precinct. It was certainly, as Miller's map of Preston testifies, for some time used as a barrack. It is now nearly erased. A small part of one of the outer walls alone remains, and forms a portion of a workshop in connection with Mr Stevenson's foundry.—See chap. 2, p. 115.

a Now Bridge-street and Marsh-lane.

hundred, followeing allong the side of the river of Rible towards the market town of Kirkham, and toward that of Poulton.[b]

"But upon the right hand northerly, lyes the great road towards Lancaster by way of Garstang.[c]

"There is likewise when you enter the town upon the south or eastern side, a way to pass by the body of the town, over Preston More and Fulwood by Broughton northward, by Garstang aforesaid, towards the Burrough of Lancaster.[d]

"This burrough is likewise adorned with a spacious wel built or rather re-edified church,[e] for the decent and more commodious solemnization of religious rytes and instruction of the people in sound and healthfull Christian doctrines, and nereunto this church is likewise built a large and hansom schoole house[f] for the better education of their children, and bringing them up in humane learning, making them fitter for trade or other better preferment in the world.[g]

"Adjacent unto which is lately raised a publiq workhouse, to employ the poorer sort of people especially woemen and children in a worsted trade of yarn, thereby better to maintain their family from begging.[h]

"And there are likewise 3 other hospitalls or publiq alms houses erected for the habitation of many old, impotent, decripid, and other of the most needy persons, to preserve them with charity from starveing and extreme necessityes; and these, for many familyes apeece, are placed at the ends of three severall streets for the more commodious assistance.[i]

* * * * * * *

"The bondary confining the franchises and libertyes of this Burrough of Preston, beginneth upon the south side, at the much famed river of Ribell, at a place cal'd the

---

b Near Tulketh hall, three district roads within a very few yards of each other are still visible. The present highway was made by the Wyre Railway Company. The road previously used turns beneath one of the arches of the viaduct. The Old Fylde road went down to the Marsh corner and turned sharply under the brow still nearer Tulketh hall. The remains of this road will soon be erased.

c From Fylde-lane beneath the canal aqueduct. This road is now stopped. Small portions of it, however, yet remain.

d By St. John-street and Park-lane, (formerly Salter-lane) to Gallows-hill, etc.

e "The roof of this church fell in on Wednesday, the 7th of February, 1770. The north and south walls were taken down, and the whole rebuilt in the same and following year. The steeple being in a very dilapidated state, was taken down in the latter end of the year 1811, and the present handsome tower was rebuilt in the year 1816, partly by subscription, and partly out of the regular church leys, through the indefatigable exertions of Mr. John Fallowfield, jun., one of the Church Wardens." —Taylor's notes. The whole of the church, with the exception of the lower portion of the tower, was taken down in 1853. The present handsome structure was completed in 1855.

f The old "Free Grammar School," situated at the bottom of Stonygate, near the old "Shepherd's Library." Rebuilt for shops last year (1856).

g Kuerden's manuscript in the Heralds' College further records that, "for the more eas of the people, there had lately been built on the south side of the church a large spacious and well adorned gallery, for the gentry of the town, who were farmers." The same document likewise adds, "there has been annexed to it" (the school house) "an handsome fabric adjoining to it as a fitting habitation for a schoolmaster, for convenience and ease over the school, a fitting place for the scholars retirement, for making their exercises, as likewise upon occasion, if needful, for a scrivener to make use of with least prejudice to the scholars as to their absence or attendance." The schoolmaster's residence has latterly been converted into an inn or public house, and designated the "Arkwrights' Arms," from the circumstance that the inventor of the spinning jenny set up one of his earliest machines in this building, whilst in the occupation of his patron, Mr. Smalley.

h "This is now occupied as private dwellings, and a large and substantial workhouse has been erected on Preston moor."—Taylor's notes, 1818.

This building was taken down in 1850. The lodge belonging to the factory of Messrs. Jacson and Co., now occupies a large portion of the site. The old workhouse fronted towards Avenham-lane, at the corner of Bolton's court.

i The Heralds' College manuscript gives the following further particulars respecting these

washing stood, j and from thence ascend up, easterly, by a little rill or rivulet called the Swill-brooke, crossing the London road and passing upward to the head thereof, till you come over against the town of Fishwick, k from which the brooke parteth this burrough aforesaid, and from thence the bonds pass to the norward, to the entrance upon Ribbleton more, nere if not close by, the crosse upon the highway a little above Ribchester, l toward the citty of Yorke; and from this crosse, passing by the west side of that more, still norward, through some few closes unto Eavs brook, and thus it is separated from the village of Ribbleton, upon the east from thence, passing down the Eavs brook untill it fallith into the water of Savock, and thus it is parted from the forest of Fullwood and Cadily more, so descending the water Savock to a certain old ditch which is the bondary betwixt Preston and Tulketh, soe following that old ditch southward, by Lancaster-lane, untill you arrive to Preston Marsh, a little west from the water Milne, and so following the milne stream westward, after the north side of the marsh, untill it crosse up southward towards Rible, but following that stream to Rible water; and so following Rible eastward, by the midst of that water, until it come past the boat over against Preston, to the afore mentioned washing steeds, into the Swill-brook."

Referring to Dr. Kuerden's description of the borough of Preston, Mr. Taylor observes that "such, with nearly equal correctness, might have been given as its true description, in the Guild of the year of 1782, a century afterwards. With the exception of the buildings connected with the Waterworks established in 1729, St George's Chapel erected in 1732,[m] and the factory at the lower end of Friargate, in Moor lane, erected by Messrs. Collinson and Watson about the year 1777; it is generally believed that no edifice had been built on a new site in the past century; the population, during this time, remaining nearly stationary at about six thousand inhabitants."

At the period of the revolution, 1688, the population of England and Wales has been computed at "somewhat over five millions and a-half." [n]

The year previous to his expulsion from the throne, James II. visited Chester; on which occasion the corporation of Preston evinced their loyalty by the sending of a deputation from their body to present a dutiful address to the king.

---

hospitals or alms houses —

"1st At the end of the town" (Friargate,) "for eight or ten almspeople.

"2nd. Next near the end of Lemon's Charity.

"3rd. At the end of Fishergate, consisting of eight rooms, erected by the widow of Bartho. Worthington and Eliz Harrison, widow."

j At the foot of Avenham Walks. The mouth of the brook is now converted into a culvert. The entire streamlet, from London-road, will shortly form one of the main sewers of the town.

k The few scattered buildings, between the head of the brook and the Ribble, could scarcely, at the present time, by any stretch of complaisance, be designated a town. That portion of Preston which extends over the brook into the township of Fishwick, has been erected during the present century.

l Ribchester is seven or eight miles east of this boundary. The Heralds' College manuscript, as quoted by Mr. Edward Baines, reads correctly as follows. "nere, if not close by, the crosse upon the highway *leading* to Ribchester." The pedestal of the stone cross still remains.

m An evidently accidental transposition of the figures. St. George's chapel was erected in 1723.

n His. of English Poor Law, by Sir George Nicholls.

At this period, the remedial power of the "king's touch" in cases of "evil," was firmly believed in by others than the vulgar; for it appears the corporation of Preston voted the sum of five shillings each to two poor women afflicted with this disease, towards the expense of travelling to Chester, to avail themselves of the supposed potency inherent in royal digits. This absurd superstition was not entirely discountenanced till the reign of George III.

The corporation of Preston, in 1684, had the very questionable "honour" of entertaining the notorious "Judge Jeffreys," on his return from the assizes at Lancaster. Amongst the papers in the possession of the corporate body, is the following letter from this foul stain upon the judicial ermine of England, dated 29th September, 1684:—

"Sr I recd yours with an accompt of yor communicating my last to yor Brethren & I am shure nothing I sayd therein could be more pleasing to any of you then my being in Condicon to doe you any act of Service or ffriendship is to me and as a Testimony of my Sincerity therein I shall for ye prnt and as long as I live give you ye best assistance I am capable off nor shall yor Corporation be any wayes Injured in any of your priviledges if I can prevent. in my last I hinted to you ye most Pper time for your attendance upon his Sacred Matie & shall hasten ye Confirmation of your Chartr with as much ease both of Charge and Trouble as possible can be. his Matie has again commanded me to take an especiall Care on your behalf and yt you may find ye efferts of his Gratious acceptance of yor unanimous and loyall submission to his Royall pleasure by his bounty in yor next Chartr and so I wish you & all your Brethren all hapiness and remain,

"Sr Your most ffaithful ffriend & oblidged servt:

"London Sept. 29th 84." "Geo: Jeffryes.

"For James Ashton Esq Mayor of Preston att Preston in Lancashire."

During his stay in Preston, Jeffreys ordered the Reverend Thomas Jolly, non-conformist minister, of Wynne House, near Whalley, to find two sureties in two hundred pounds each, for holding conventicles.

Notwithstanding the attachment of the people of England to the principle of hereditary succession, the perverseness and infatuation of the Stuart family, which seemed incapable of adapting itself to the temper and progressive tendencies of the liberty-loving Anglo-Saxon nation, precipitated the revolution, which transferred the crown to the Prince of Orange, and afterwards to the house of Hanover. In this second struggle between the nation and the reigning dynasty, the people of Lancashire appear to have taken no very prominent part. There is some reason to believe, however, that Amounderness narrowly escaped being again the theatre of another sanguinary conflict. One of the places proposed for the secret landing of the king, by his partisans, is said to have been near Blackpool; and "Vauxhall," or "Foxhall," a marine residence belonging to Thomas Tildesley, Esq., the representative of the gallant cavalier who fell at Wigan lane, was prepared for his temporary residence and concealment, should subsequent events have necessitated such an expedient.[o]

After the accession of William III, many schemes were projected by the Roman catholics and the advocates of "legitimacy" and the "divine right of kings," for the restoration of James. Several plots were laid for the assassination or dethronement of William, one of which, named the "Lancashire Plot," caused considerable sensation in the county. Many, however, doubted its reality, and others regarded the affair as a government conspiracy to effect the ruin of certain Lancashire and Cheshire gentlemen, who were known to be well affected towards the Stuarts.

Mr. William Beamont in his commentary upon the "Jacobite Trials at Manchester, in 1694," published by the Cheetham Society, in 1853, from a manuscript copy, boldly says :—

"Had the government believed the plot, or been really in earnest, they might have found evidence to support the charge; and the case would not have been so loosely managed, unless they had purposely designed to let Mr. Lunt escape to serve their purposes elsewhere, or at some other time Possibly they had already discovered that *he might be useful as a spy, and they designed by his means to penetrate the secrets of the disaffected.* He was to be a tame pigeon kept to fly when other flocks were on the wing, in order to allure them into the traps set for them by its owner."

Whatever might be the true character of this "Lancashire Plot," it produced a tragical result in the neighbourhood of Preston. The story runs, that the disaffected in Lancashire, being anxious to receive some promised commissions from King James, dispatched Mr. Edmund Threlfall, of the Ashes, in Goosnargh, to Ireland, to bring them over. At Dublin, Threlfall was introduced to Lunt, the chief agent of the Jacobites. The two landed in the Lune, near Cockerham, early in the morning of the 13th of June, 1689. Singularly enough, Lunt left his saddlebags, containing many of these treasonable commissions, in the boat. These were seized by the custom house officers, who are said to have made "hot pursuit" after the conspirators, but without success. Threlfall and Lunt repaired to Mr. Tildesley's residence, at the Lodge, in Myerscough, where they divided the remaining commissions. The task of delivering those addressed to gentlemen in Yorkshire and Durham was assigned to Threlfall, and Lunt took charge of the Lancashire, Cheshire, and Staffordshire portion. These commissions empowered the parties to whom they were sent to raise "regiments of horse and dragoons." Lunt was indicted but acquitted, and after a series of adventures, disclosed the "plot" on the 16th of June, 1694. The denoument, so far as concerns Threlfall, is thus stated by Kingston :—

"Threlfall, pursuant to the late King's orders, having delivered his share of the commissions and what else he had in charge to the more northern gentlemen, privately returned to his own house at Goosner, in Lancashire, and having notice there that his treasonable practices were discovered by Mr. Kelly and Mr. Dodsworth, and the commissions

o See depositions of Mr. Dodsworth, printed in Kingston's work, p. 271 He there states that it "was reported amongst them that the said King James would land in a month's time."

left in the ship, took all imaginable care to secure himself there till he could find an opportunity to return to the late King in Ireland. But this design encountered a severe disappointment, and he met with the reward of his treachery. For it having been whispered among the party that he was returned, it quickly took air, and a warrant (as I said before) being out against him from the lord lieutenant, he was sought after by a party of the militia, and found by a corporal in a hollow place made for that purpose in a stack of turves. As soon as he was discovered, the corporal attempting to seize him, Threlfall violently snatched the musket out of the corporal's hand and knocked him down with it, but the corporal recovering himself, and finding his own life and the prisoner's escape in such apparent danger, he drew his sword and ran Mr. Threlfall through the body, of which wound he died immediately."

Another account says Mr. Threlfall was "returning through *Cheshire* to Ireland, when he was pursued upon suspicion, and killed as he was endeavouring to defend himself," but this is evidently an error.

Mr. Beamont expresses his surprise at the supineness of government in this matter, from which it would appear that no real fear of the existence of any serious plot was ever entertained. He says, "no reader of either account would suppose that Mr. Threlfall, who had been often seen in the neighbourhood of his own house in this interval, where any ordinary diligence might have taken him, survived the issuing of the warrant against him more than twelve months, and was not killed until about the 20th August, 1690, as appears by the subjoined register of his burial at Goosnargh:—

"'August 1690. Bur, was Edmund Threlfall, of Goosnargh, the 26th day.'"

Mr. Macaulay, in his History of England, eloquently denounces the chief actors in this affair. His masterly exposition of the condition of the rival parties, and the state of society at the period, is especially interesting to the student of Lancashire history. He says:—

"Among the informers who haunted this office was an Irish vagabond, who had borne more than one name, and professed more than one religion. He now called himself Taaffe. He had been a priest of the Roman Catholic church, and secretary to Adda, the papal nuncio, but had since the revolution turned Protestant, had taken a wife, and had distinguished himself by his activity in discovering the concealed property of those Jesuits and Benedictines, who, during the late reign, had been quartered in London. The ministers despised him; but they trusted him. They thought that he had, by his apostacy, and by the part which he had borne in the spoliation of the religious orders, cut himself off from all retreat, and that, having nothing but a halter to expect from King James, he must be true to King William. This man fell in with a jacobite agent named Lunt, who had, since the revolution, been repeatedly employed among the discontented gentry of Cheshire and Lancashire, and who had been privy to those plans of insurrection which had been disconcerted by the battle of the Boyne, in 1690, and by the battle of La Hogue, in 1692. Lunt had once been arrested on suspicion of treason, but had been discharged for want of legal proof of his guilt. He was a mere hireling, and was, without much difficulty, induced by Taaffe to turn approver. The pair went to Trenchard. Lunt told his story, mentioned the names of some Cheshire and Lancashire squires to whom he had, as he affirmed, carried commissions from Saint Germains, and of others, who had, to his knowledge, formed secret hoards of arms and ammunition. His simple oath would not have been sufficient to support a charge of high treason, but he produced another witness whose evidence seemed to make the case complete. The narrative was plausible and coherent; and, indeed, though it may have been embellished by fictions, there can be little doubt that it was true in substance. Messengers and search warrants were sent down to Lancashire. Aaron Smith himself went thither; and Taaffe went with him. The alarm had been given by some of the numerous traitors who eat the bread of William. Some of the accused persons had fled; and others had buried their sabres and muskets and burned their papers. Nevertheless, discoveries were made which confirmed Lunt's depositions. Behind the wainscot of the old mansion of one Roman Catholic family was discovered a commission signed by James Another house of which the master had absconded, was strictly searched, in spite of the solemn asseverations of his wife and servants that no arms were concealed there. While the lady, with her hand on her heart, was protesting on her honour that her husband was falsely accused, the messengers observed that the back of the chimney did not seem to be firmly fixed. It was removed, and a heap of blades, such as were used by horse soldiers, tumbled out. In one of the garrets were found, carefully bricked up, thirty saddles for troopers, as many breastplates, and sixty cavalry swords Trenchard and Aaron Smith thought the case complete; and it was determined that those culprits who had been apprehended should be tried by a special commission. Taaffe now confidently expected to be recompensed for his services, but he found a cold reception at the treasury. He had gone down to Lancashire chiefly in order that he might, under the protection of a search warrant, pilfer trinkets and broad pieces from secret drawers. His sleight-of-hand, however, had not altogether escaped the observation of his companions. They discovered that he had made free with the communion plate of the popish families whose private hoards he had assisted in ransacking. When, therefore, he applied for reward, he was dismissed, not merely with a refusal, but with a stern reprimand He went away mad with greediness and spite. There was yet one way in which he might obtain both money and revenge, and that way he took He made overtures to the friends of the prisoners. He, and he alone, could undo what he had done, could save the accused from the gallows, could cover the accusers with infamy, could drive from office the secretary and the solicitor, who were the dread of all the friends of King James. Loathsome as Taaffe was to the jacobites, his offer was not to be slighted. He received a sum in hand; he was assured that a comfortable annuity for life should be settled on him when the business was done; and he was sent down into the country, and kept in strict seclusion against the day of trial. Meanwhile, unlicensed pamphlets, in which the Lancashire plot was classed with Oates's plot, with Dangerfield's plot, with Fuller's plot, with Young's plot, with Whitney's plot, were circulated all over the kingdom, and especially in the county which was to furnish the jury. Of these pamphlets, the longest, the ablest, and the bitterest, entitled "A letter to Secretary Trenchard," was commonly ascribed to Ferguson. It is not improbable that Ferguson may have furnished some of the materials, and have conveyed the manuscript to the press But many passages are written with an art and vigour which assuredly did not belong to him. Those who judge by internal evidence may perhaps think that, in some parts of this remarkable tract, they can discern the last gleam of the malignant genius of Montgomery. A few weeks after the appearance of the letter, he sank, unhonoured and unlamented, into the grave. There were then no printed newspapers except the *London Gazette*. But since the revolution the newsletter had become a more important political engine than it had previously been. The newsletters of one writer named Dyer were widely circulated in manuscript. He affected to be a tory and a high churchman, and was, consequently, regarded by the fox-hunting lords of manors, all over the kingdom, as an oracle. He had already been twice in prison. but his gains had more than compensated for his sufferings, and he still persisted in seasoning his intelligence to suit the taste of the country gentlemen. He now turned the Lancashire plot into ridicule, declared that the guns which had been found were old fowling-pieces, the saddles were meant only for hunting, and that the swords were rusty relics of Edge Hill and Marston Moor. The effect produced by all this invective and sarcasm on the public mind seems to have been great. Even at the Dutch Embassy, where assuredly there was no leaning towards jacobitism, there was a strong impression that it would be unwise to bring the prisoners to trial. In Lancashire and Cheshire the prevailing sentiments were pity for the accused and hatred of the prosecutors The government, however, persevered. In October four judges went down to Manchester. At present the population of that town is made up of persons born in every part of the British isles, and consequently has no especial sympathy with the landowners, the farmers, and the agricultural labourers of the neighbouring districts. But in the seventeenth century the Manchester man was a Lancashire man. His politics were those of his county. For the old cavalier families of his county he felt a great respect; and he was furious when he thought that some of the best blood of his county was about to be shed by a knot of roundhead pettifoggers from London. Multitudes of people from the neighbouring villages filled the streets of the town, and saw with grief and indignation the array of drawn swords and loaded carbines which surrounded the culprits. Aaron Smith's arrangements do not seem to have been skilful. The chief council for the crown was Sir William Williams, who, though now well stricken in years, and possessed of a great estate, still continued in practice. One fault had thrown a dark shade over the latter part of his life. The recollection of that day on which he had stood up in Westminster Hall, amidst laughter and hooting, to defend the dispensing power and to attack the right of petition, had, ever since the revolution, kept him back from honour. He was an angry and disappointed man, and was by no means disposed to incur unpopularity in the cause of a government to which he owed nothing, and from which he hoped nothing. Of the trial no detailed report has come down to us, but we have both a whig narrative and a jacobite narrative. It seems that the prisoners who were first arraigned did not sever in their challenges, and were consequently tried together. Williams examined, or rather cross-examined, his own witnesses with a severity which confused them. The crowd which filled the court laughed and clamoured. Lunt in particular became completely bewildered, mistook one person for another, and did not recover himself till the judges took him out of the hands of the counsel for the crown. For some of the prisoners an *alibi* was set up. Evidence was also produced to shew, what was undoubtedly quite true, that Lunt was a man of abandoned character. The result, however, seemed doubtful, till, to the dismay of the prosecutors, Taaffe entered the box. He swore with unblushing forehead that the whole story of the plot was a circumstantial lie devised by himself and Lunt. Williams threw down his brief; and, in truth, a more honest advocate might well have done the same. The prisoners who were at the bar were instantly acquitted, those who had not yet been tried were set at liberty; the witnesses for the prosecution were pelted out of Manchester; the clerk of the crown narrowly escaped with life; and the judges took their departure amidst hisses and execrations."

Soon after George I., of the house of Hanover, ascended the throne, the partisans of the Stuarts in Scotland and the north of England, headed by the earls of Mar, Derwentwater, Winton, Nithsdale, and Carnworth, and a Northumberland gentleman, named Forster, raised the standard of revolt, and proclaimed the Chevalier de St. George, son of James II., king, by the title of James III. One division of their forces, under the command of Mr Forster, penetrated into England, notwithstanding the defection of five or six hundred highlanders, who refused to cross the border. The remainder of the rebel forces advanced southward, by Jedburgh, Penrith, etc., to Lancaster, at which place they arrived on Monday, the 7th of November, 1715. During the march from Appleby to Kendal, but three recruits joined the insurgents. This ill success, according to Peter Clarke, caused the Brigadier Mackintosh to put on a "grim countenance," and "Forster and most of the other horsemen were disheartened and full of sorrow." [p] Between Kendal and Lancaster, however, the enthusiasm of highlanders was again excited by the news that large

---

p Clarke had, a month previously to his joining the rebel army, entered into the service of a Mr. Crackenthorpe, a Kendal attorney. Clarke's journal is printed in "Lancashire Memorials," published by the Manchester Cheetham Society, and edited by Dr Hibbert Ware.

numbers of Lancashire people were preparing to join their standard. The news, however, proved deceptive, much to the chagrin of the Scotch protestant Jacobites, who anticipated that the "Tory" or "High Church Party," as one class of the partisans of the Stuart was then called, would be most zealous in their cause. Amongst others who joined them at Lancaster, was Mr. Edward Tildesley, of Myerscough, the representative of the chivalric Sir Thomas Tildesley, who fell at Wigan Lane, in 1651. [q]

A Mr. Patten, protestant minister of Annandale, who accompanied the rebel army in the capacity of chaplain to Mr. Forster, and who, according to his own statement, "saved his life by being an evidence for the king," in a "History of the Rebellion," makes the following severe remarks upon the habits and conduct of this party at the period :—

"A great many Lancashire gentlemen joined us, with their servants and friends. [r] It's true they were most of them Papists, which made the Scotch gentlemen and the highlanders mighty uneasy, very much suspecting the cause; for they expected all the High Church party to have joined them. Indeed that party, who never are right hearty for the cause, 'till they are mellow, as they call it, over a bottle or two, began now to show us their blind side; and that it is their just character, that they do not care for venturing their carcasses any further than the tavern; there indeed with their High Church and their Ormond, they would make men believe, who do not know them, that they would encounter the greatest opposition in the world, but after having consulted their pillows, and the fume a little evaporated, it is observed of them that they generally become mighty tame, and are apt to look before they leap, and, with the snail, if you touch their houses, they hide their heads, shrink back, and pull in their horns. I have heard Mr. Forster say he was blustered into this business by such people as these, but that for the time to come he would never again believe a drunken tory."

Whatever truth there may be in Mr. Patten's graphic description of the convivial habits of the period referred to, the irresolution of the "High Church Party" must unquestionably have resulted from the simple fact, that whilst supporting their views concerning hereditary right, in the person of the Stuart, they were unquestionably aiding in the destruction of what to them was at least of equal importance, the domination of the protestant church of England.

Sir Henry Hoghton, at that time member of parliament for Preston, endeavoured to procure for the king's service, six pieces of cannon, which lay in a vessel at Sunderland, five miles from Lancaster; but being unsuccessful, and hearing of the near advance of the rebel army, he retired with about six hundred militia to Preston. The pavement was taken off the bridge at Lancaster, by the inhabitants, with the view to the obstruction of the passage of the rebel army Colonel Charteris, and another Hanoverian officer, would have blown up the bridge; but discovering that the river was

q "Edward Tyldesley, of the lodge, was descended from an ancient Lancashire family, who flourished in the reign of Henry III His ancestor in 1675 sold the family estate in Tyldesley"—Dr Hibbert Ware· "Lancashire Memorials."

r During the two or three days, the rebel army remained at Lancaster

fordable at low water, they relinquished the project, though not without considerable reluctance.

The conduct of the rebel army appears, on the whole, to have won the esteem of the Lancaster people. William Stout, a quaker gentleman, speaking of their visit, says:—"It was a time of tryall, and in fear that the Scotts and Northern rebells would have plundered us, but they were civill, and to most paid for what they had; but I had five of the Mackintosh officers quartered on me two days, but took nothing of them."

Peter Clarke, in his quaint but pithy journal, informs the lovers of gossip that, on one afternoon, during their sojourn at Lancaster, "the Gentlemen soldiers dressed and trimmed themselves up in their best cloathes, for to drink a dish of tea with the laydys of this towne. The Laydys also here apeared in their best riging, and had their tea tables richly furnished for to entertain their new suitors."

At Lancaster, as elsewhere, the Chevalier de St. George was proclaimed king, and the Reverend Mr. Paul read public prayers for him as the British monarch. The minister of the place was desirous of giving offence to neither party, and made no opposition. The rebel chiefs took possession of the money belonging to the revenue, in the excise office and custom house. They seized the six pieces of cannon, and mounted them upon wheels that belonged to Sir Henry Hoghton's carriages. [s] After releasing one "Tom Syddal, a mob captain," and another prisoner, confined in the castle, according to the Stuart partisans, "for treasonable words," [t] Forster marched his little army southward, with the purpose of seizing Manchester, securing Warrington bridge, and thus isolating Liverpool from the king's forces. The cavalry arrived at Preston on the evening of Wednesday, the 9th of November. The foot soldiers rested at Garstang, and entered Preston on the following day. The whole force amounted to about one thousand six hundred men. Two troops of Stanhope's dragoons occupied the town, but withdrew on the approach of the rebel army. The chevalier was proclaimed king at the Market cross. The Reverend Mr. Paul, who had joined the rebel army at Lancaster, read prayers three times for the heir of the Stuarts, as the lawful monarch of Britain. [u] Patten says, "here they were also joined by a great many gentlemen with their tenants, servants, and

s Patten.

t "Tom Syddal" had not been content with "treasonable words." He had headed a "Sacheverel riot" at Manchester, when a meeting house was destroyed.

u "During the time that the rebels were in Preston, in 1715, the daring zeal of the vicar" (the Rev. Samuel Peploe, B.D.) "for the reigning sovereign, was the subject of general conversation, and he daily read the prayers for the King, on one occasion even in the presence of his Majesty's rival. It is also reported that a rebel soldier forgetful of his allegiance to a higher power, once approached the

attendants, and some of very good figure in the county; but still all Roman catholics. They once resolved to have marched out of Preston, and order was given to get ready on the Friday; but that order was countermanded, and they resolved to continue till the next day, and then to advance." Orders were again issued for the army to march on Saturday morning, when Forster learned that General Wills was advancing from Wigan to give them battle.

Considerable diversity of opinion has been expressed regarding the conduct of Forster during this memorable struggle. From the statements of a "Merse Officer," who served under him, and who, in a journal, noted down the more important passing events at the time, he would appear to have been suddenly afflicted by an unaccountable lethargy, the result, perhaps of a growing conviction that the duties of his position had become infinitely superior to his experience or capacity. Forster had been appointed general in England simply because he was a protestant gentleman, with the view to conciliate the "High Church" party, which, it was thought, would never consent to fight under a Roman catholic commander, however distinguished for military talent. The "Merse Officer" says:—

"Upon Wednesday the 9th of November, the Horse came into Prestoun, and the foot the next day. There we received certain notice of General Wills's being in Wigan, twelve miles distant from us, with two regiments of dragoons, who lay night and day at their horses heads, in order to fly if we should march towards Manchester or Chester. Though we had an opportunity of cutting off the enemy, yet General Forster would not allow us, nor suffer us to march towards Manchester.

"Upon Friday the eleventh, about seven at night, the Earl of Derwentwater received a letter from the Lord M———, informing us that about twelve o'clock, Wills, being joined with seven regiments more, resolved to march towards Preston. When this letter was communicated to General Forster he appeared dispirited, and then, as at all other times, very unfit for such an important command. He had nothing to say, but sent the letter to my Lord Kenmure. His Lordship upon reading it, going with the other persons of note to Mr. Forster's quarters, found him in bed without the least concern. A council being called, it was thought convenient to detach a party of horse towards Wigan, as an advanced guard, and another party of foot to Derrin" (Darwen) "and Ribble bridges, and the whole army had orders to be in readiness to take the field. But to our great surprise, these orders were countermanded by Forster."

The newly-enlisted attorney's clerk, Master Peter Clarke, records a trifling incident that may throw a little light upon the certainly mysterious supineness and lack of military ardour exhibited by the Jacobite chiefs.

Vicar during Divine Service, and drawing his bayonet, threatened Peploe's life if he dared to read the prayer for the elector of Hanover. With an undaunted courage, characteristic of the man, Peploe replied, 'Soldier, do your duty, and I will do mine!' The firmness of his tone, and the dignity of his manner, awed the rebel, who silently retired, and the alarmed congregation proceeded with their devotions. When this anecdote was related to George the First, he was so much affected by the cool heroism of his whig supporter, that he exclaimed in his broken German, with considerable emphasis, 'Peep-low, Peep-low! by ———!' he shall Peep-high—he shall be a Bishop!' a royal determination punctually performed."—Introduction to "Notitia Cestriensis," edited by the Rev. F. R. Raines, M.A. —Peploe was made warden of Manchester in 1718, and succeeded Bishop Gastrell in the see of Chester in 1726.

Peter's propensity to gossip, his professional or his innate gallantry, made him occasionally cast his eyes upon other beings than military warriors, and upon fields of conquest of a somewhat less repulsive character than barricades bristling with pikes, muskets, and cannon. Yes; Peter does not forget to note that:—

"The Ladys in this toune, Preston, are so very beautifull & so richly attired, that the Gentlemen Soldiers from Wednesday to Saturday minded nothing but courting and ffeasting."

Dr. Samuel Hibbert Ware, in his annotations to Clarke's journal, thus speaks of Preston and the apathy of Forster:—

"It would be a charitable supposition to be entertained, that when the important letter actually arrived, the General '*had received some little damage in the course of a convivial entertainment, so as to render it necessary, that instead of studying military despatches, he should retire to bed.*'

"'PROUD PRESTON,' as this aristocratic town was long named, had been selected, and from its central situation, milder climate, and beautiful aspect, deservedly so,—as a winter residence for the leading gentry of the county. The Duke of Marlborough, who was well studied in human nature, while he was aware that the Insurgent force would suffer some detention at Preston, then considered as the district where the Roman Catholics most abounded, must also have calculated upon the allurements incidental to a town long regarded as the metropolis of Lancashire. In directing, therefore, the general operations of the Government forces, the experienced veteran did not overlook the enervating effect liable to result from such gay quarters as THE LANCASHIRE CAPUA was likely to afford. He adverted to PRESTON as the net of the Fowler, in preparation for the wild birds of prey who were to be gathered therein: 'It is here,' said the Duke, with prophetic discrimination, 'that we shall find them!'"

If there be not more of fancy than of logical inference in the conclusion drawn by the learned commentator, the house of Hanover lies under considerable obligation to the fascinations of the Preston *belles* of the period. The fact, as stated by Clarke, certainly admits of no dispute; but that the venerable victor of Blenheim, who, it appears, directed the chief movements of this short campaign, was sufficiently acquainted with the place to predict such a result, is very problematical. The Roman catholics being numerous in the neighbourhood, and the chief supporters of the Stuarts, the insurgents might, with probability, be expected to remain a few days to recruit. The well known military skill of the duke, and the prompt action of Wills and Carpenter, furnish sufficient grounds to predict that the little northern army, led by an inexperienced civilian, would not very easily escape, when the forces of the two subordinate royalist generals began to act in concert. From the previous positions of the armies, the centre of Lancashire appeared, with great probability, likely to become the scene of the conflict.

A dissenting clergyman at Chowbent, well known for combative propensity and his loyalty to the house of Hanover, received an invitation from Sir Henry Hoghton, bart., franked by "George Wills," to bring up his "lusty younge fellows" to the aid of his sovereign. The following copy of Sir Henry's letter to the reverend combatant is preserved in Toulmin's "Life of John Mort:"—

"To the Rev Mr. Woods, in Chowbent, for His Majesty's Service,
" Charles Wills.

"The officers here design to march at break of day for Preston, they have desired me to raise what men I can to meet us at Preston to-morrow, so desire you to raise all the force you can, I mean lusty younge fellows to draw up on Cuerden Green, to be there by 10 o'clock, to bring with them what arms they have fitt for service, and scythes put in streight polls, and such as have not, to bring spades and bill hooks for pioneering with. Pray go immediately all amongst your neighbours and give this notice.

"I am your very faithful servant,

"Wigan 11th Nov. 1715. "H. HOGHTON."

Woods, who entered into the campaign with singular enthusiasm, was assisted by another dissenting minister, named Walker. The former showed so much courage and tact that he was often called, in compliment, "General Woods." There still exists a tradition which asserts that on one occasion his military ardour induced him to draw his sword upon one of his own men, whose conduct betokened fear or cowardice.

A "journal of the proceeding," quoted in Rae's History, says:—"We have it from several good hands, that upon their day's march, Mr. Wood and Mr. Walker, two dissenting ministers in Lancashire, came to General Wills, while he was yet some miles from Preston, and told him they had a considerable party of men well armed for his Majesty's service; and that they were ready to take any post his Excellency pleased to assign to them. As soon as he knew who they were, and had seen their men, he told them, that after he was come to Preston he would assign them a post." Woods and his Chowbent men were employed in guarding the ford at Penwortham, and the bridge at Walton.

Patten strongly censures some of the Jacobite leaders for neglecting to defend the pass at Ribble bridge. He says:—

"The alarm now being given, a body of the rebels marched out of the town as far as Ribble Bridge, posting themselves there, and Mr. Forster with a party of horse, went beyond it to get a certain account of things; when discovering the vanguard of the dragoons, he returned another way, not coming by the bridge. He ordered Mr Patten with all haste to ride back, and give an account of the approach of the King's army, and to give orders to prepare to receive them, whilst he went to view a ford in the river, in order for a passage to come behind them. The foot that were advanced to the bridge were about 100 men; but they were choice, stout, and well armed, and commanded by Lieutenant-Colonel John Farquharson, of Innercall, belonging to Macintosh's battalion: He was a good officer and a very bold man, and would have defended that important pass of the bridge to the last drop, and still the rest had advanced and drawn themselves out of the town, but he was ordered to retreat to Preston. This retreat was another wrong step, and has been condemned on all hands as one of the greatest oversights they could be guilty of; for the river is not fordable but a good way above and below the bridge, which they might have made impassable also, by several methods practised on like occasions. As for the bridge they might have barricaded it so well, that it would have been impracticable to have passed there, or to have dislodged them from it; also they had cannon, which General Wills wanted And here alone indeed it might be said they were in a condition to have made an effectual stand; for here the

King's forces would have been entirely exposed to their fire, having no cover; whereas the rebels could have very much secured themselves against the other's fire, by the bridge and by the rising ground near it. General Wills did indeed expect some difficulty and opposition at this place; * * but understanding by his advanced guard that the rebels had abandoned that post, he was surprised and suspected that then they had some stratagem in hand, and perhaps had lined the hedges, and so made the lane impassable for his men. The lane is indeed very deep, and so narrow that in several places two men cannot ride abreast This is that famous lane at the end of which Oliver Cromwell met with a stout resistance from the King's forces, who from the height rolled down upon him and his men (when they had entered the lane) huge large millstones; and if Oliver himself had not forced his horse to jump into a quicksand, he had luckily ended his days there." v

The Brigadier Mackintosh, when asked, a few days afterwards, at Wigan, by Lord Widdrington, why he had not made a stand at so important a pass as the Ribble bridge, replied, that the post "was not maintainable, because the river was fordable at several places." This is perfectly correct, and doubtless influenced the brigadier in his determination not to fight at the bridge. The number of his forces was insufficient to guard the fords, and successfully defend the pass. Under these circumstances, he expressed his conviction that "the body of the town was the security of the army."

Clarke says:—"Upon Saturday ye 12th November 1715, about 11 a clock in the forenoone, the Earl of Derwentwater ordred 300 Horsemen to go to Rible bridge to oppose Genrall Wills passage over it, but abt an hour after Genrall Wills & his men came into Walton in Le dale, neare unto ye sd Rible Bridge, the sd El Derwentwaters men retired into Preston." Clarke often speaks of the earl of Derwentwater as if he were the commander-in-chief of the rebel forces. This may have arisen from the deference paid to his rank and influence; or it may be explained by the fact that honest Peter himself, being attached to the suite of the earl in some capacity or other, with pardonable egotism, regarded his own immediate superior as the most distinguished and potent individual engaged in the revolt.

The rebels, however, resolutely prepared to defend the town. They erected barricades in the principal streets, and posted men in the houses of the alleys and bye-lanes. Mr Patten, who himself acted as a kind of extraordinary aide-de-camp to the generals, and witnessed the attacks at the three distinct barricades, gives the following description of the defensive works of the besieged:—

v Notwithstanding Mr Patten's political conversion, and his horror of the "licentious freedom" of those who "cry up the old doctrines of passive obedience, and give hints and arguments to prove hereditary right," he appears to have retained all the antipathy of a Stuart partisan to the memory of Oliver Cromwell Yet the loyalty of 1648 became rebellion in 1715, when Mr. Patten's head was in danger Such is the mutation of human dogmatism

"The gentlemen volunteers were drawn up in the Churchyard, under the command of the Earl of Derwentwater, Viscount Kenmure, Earls of Wintoun and Nithsdale. The Earl of Derwentwater signally behaved, having stript into his waistcoat, and encouraged the men by giving them money to cast up trenches, and animating them to a vigorous defence of them. * * * The rebels formed four main barriers, one a little below the church, w commanded by Brigadier Macintosh, the gentlemen in the church yard were to support that barrier in particular, and Lord Charles Murray that which was at the end of a lane leading to the fields. x The third barrier was called the windmill; y this was commanded by Colonel Macintosh: And the fourth was in the street which leads towards Liverpool, z commanded by Major Miller and Mr. Douglass."

Clarke quaintly says.—"And there they made a trensh and made a Baracade ovr agt the church in Church Gate Preston, & there placed two of the ships guns charged with small bullet, and at the out ends of this towne they made trences."

General Wills, with six regiments of "horse and dragoons," and one battalion of foot, commanded by Colonel Preston, advanced, and ordered his forces to pass through a gate, which then led into the fields behind the town, and spread themselves so as to cut off the retreat of the rebels.

A severe struggle took place at the barrier below the church, which Brigadier Mackintosh successfully defended Brigadier Honeywood attacked the point with the following troops:—"Preston's regiment of foot, commanded by Lord Forrester; and a captain and fifty dragoons from each of the five regiments, with a colonel, lieutenant-colonel, and major to command them, to be severally dismounted to sustain Preston's foot, and Brigadier Honeywood's regiment to sustain the whole on horseback." Some of the officers of Preston's regiment being informed that no barrier had been constructed at the end of "the street leading to Wigan," a supported by Honeywood's dragoons, boldly entered, and took possession of "Patten House," the property of Sir Edward Stanley, which overlooked

w In the military map of Preston, published soon after the siege, by A. Boyer, and dedicated to the "immortal fame of Gen Wills," this barrier is placed opposite the court at present named Clark-yard.

x Boyer's map does not clearly indicate this barrier. It was, however, at the end of Tithebarn-street, opposite to which he has depicted a building on fire, as in the other parts of the town upon which the royal troops directed their attacks

y Friargate brow. Boyer exhibits a wooden windmill somewhere about the present entrance to the Fylde road. A more substantial erection of a similar character lately occupied the spot This has since been removed, and the "Ragged School" built upon the site. The barrier is placed about midway between the Market place and the windmill.

z Fishergate. Boyer marks this barrier a little nearer the Town Hall than the present Mount-street.

a Boyer's map indicates a barricade near the then end of Church-street. The site is a little to the westward of the present Water-street, on the spot where the "Church-street barrs" stood Perhaps these "barrs" are alluded to by General Wills. Two inner barricades are marked upon the map, one across Friargate, a little below Anchor-weind, and the other in Church street, on the east side of Mainsprit-weind and the old Shambles These barriers were never attacked A combination of this military plan of Boyer, and the map of the surrounding country, drawn in 1738, by Robert Porter, of Goosnargh, was published in 1847, by Mr Samuel Crane Fisher, Preston It is, however, very defective The town and country are not laid down to the same scale, and some important objects are misplaced.

the entire town, from which place and the opposite house, belonging to a Mr. Eyre, the rebels suffered the greater portion of their loss. Brigadier Mackintosh had originally posted a few troops, under the command of Captain Wogan, in the houses at the end of Church-street; and Captain Innis, with fifty highlanders, held possession of Sir Edward Stanley's mansion. On the advance of Colonel Preston's regiment, the brigadier injudiciously withdrew these troops. Patten says:—

"Preston's men did not come up to the head of the street, but marched into a straight passage behind the houses, and then made a halt till their lieutenant-colonel the Lord Forrester came into the open street with his sword in his hand, and faced Macintosh's barrier, looking up the street and down the street, and viewing how they were posted. There were many shots fired at him, but he returned to his men, and came up again at the head of them into the middle of the street, where he caused some to face the barricade where the brigadier was posted, and ply them with their shot, at the same time commanding another party to march across the street to take possession of those houses. Whilst this was doing, the rebels from the barrier, and from the houses on both sides, made a terrible fire upon them, and a great many of that old and gallant regiment were killed and wounded. The Lord Forrester received several wounds himself. Besides the damage they received on that side, they were sore galled from some windows below them, by Captain Douglas's and Captain Hunter's men. Preston's foot fired smartly upon the rebels, but did little execution, the men being generally covered from the shot, and delivering their own shot securely and with good aim." b

The king's troops, according to Patten, next attacked the barricade defended by Lord Charles Murray. They were received with unflinching courage and forced to retire. The Earl of Derwentwater sent Mr. Patten with a reinforcement, consisting of fifty men. The chaplain, who appears not to have lacked military ardour, passed over this barrier to examine the position and strength of the besiegers. His clergyman's habit saved him from the fire of the enemy. Mr. Patten was not, however, always so fortunate, as on one occasion his horse was shot under him. From the report of the chaplain, Lord Charles Murray prepared for a second conflict, and so well did his men perform their duty, that the king's troops were again repulsed with considerable loss. Patten says, the king's soldiers "were for the most part new listed men, and seemed unwilling to fight; yet the bravery and conduct of experienced officers supply'd very much that defect; * * * nor had they been all old soldiers, could they have beaten Lord Charles from that barrier, which was very strong; the number they had slain from

b General Wills, in his evidence before the House of Lords, stated that, "he came before Preston on the 12th of November last, about one o'clock, and ordered two attacks upon the town; the attack which led to Wigan being commanded by Brigadier Honeywood, *who* beat the rebels from their *first barricade*, and took possession of some houses in the town; the other attack which led to Lancaster, under the command of Brigadier Dormer, who lodged his troops nigh the barricade of the rebels." Patten says, that Lord Widdrington asked Mackintosh, at Wigan, "why he did not make his barrier at the extreme end of the street leading to the town, which would have prevented the king's forces from taking possession of *those houses* below his barrier, which was a great way up the town?" Mackintosh replied, "at the extreme end of the town there were so many lanes and avenues, that to defend them would have required more men than he had."

the barn holes and barrier itself, added very much, so that at last the officers themselves thought fit to give it over."

The Merse officer in his journal, speaks of "Patten House," as Sir H. Hoghton's residence. He describes it as an edifice "whose battlement and battery did command the head of the hollow way that leads from the bridge to the town, and the street in the Mercat-Place, and a great part of the neighbouring fields: This house had a garden at the back of it, with a high brick wall."[c] He further adds that, Forster "ordered Captain M——n" (Maclean) "with his company of gentlemen volunteers to leave this most advantageous post." He then says—

"His Lordship," (Derwentwater) "sent me to the top of the steeple in order to view the enemy's disposition, where I saw a regiment of foot possess themselves of Sir Henry Hortoun's house, and a strong detachment of dragoons on foot, possess another house opposite to Hortouns. I saw them march through Sir Henry's garden, and draw up in battalion at the foot of the Broad Lane. I desired the Earl of Derwentwater to close the right of his men to the range of houses that was from Sir Henry's house to a street northward from the church which was done.[d] I gave, likewise, a signal intimating that the enemy was within the flank of Lord Charles Murray's men, upon which the brave and undaunted Earl of Derwentwater wheeled his gentlemen to the right, covering the head of Back Lane, and received the enemy with a very brisk and successful fire. Lord Charles Murray flanked them with as close a fire, and put them in great confusion and to flight. They sheltered themselves in Sir Henry Hortoun's house. I desired that the said house should be demolished by two pieces of cannon that were ready charged in the front of the church yard, and that the Earl of Derwentwater and Lord Charles Murray should jointly attack the enemy without the town. I went for orders to General Forster, who would by no means allow it, saying, 'that the body of the town was the security of the army.'"[e]

Dr. Hibbert Ware says, the second barrier was "placed on the inside of a hedge which flanked a broad way from Sir Henry Houghton's garden," but he does not mention the authority. Patten House is marked upon the map as situated a little below the present North-road. This confirms the probability that the barrier defended by Lord Charles Murray was situated at the south end of the present Tithe-barn-street. Perhaps General Wills regarded this barricade but as a support to the principal one near the church, and, consequently, spoke of the two conjointly, when he alluded to the "attack which led to Wigan."

---

c The slightest glance at the plan of Preston, dated 1774, and the "South Prospect" of the town and environs, published by S. and N. Buck, in 1728, (copies of which are given in the topographical portion of this work,) will demonstrate that the house alluded to by the Merse officer, is the old residence of the Derby family, called "Patten House," lately destroyed. Its situation and character as described, exactly accord with Buck's drawing. Mr. Eyre's house, on the opposite side of the street, is likewise depicted. Of course, from the prominent part taken by Sir Henry Hoghton during this crisis, it is easily to be understood how a perfect stranger should fall into such an error. The reference to Buck's Prospect describes the house as "Sir Edward Stanley's." The map, of the date 1774, designates the enclosure behind this edifice as "Lord Stanley's Garden." There is no other house, on either the prospect or plan, which, in the slightest degree, resembles the Merse officer's description.

d The present St. John-street.

e Quoting Mackintosh's reason for not defending Ribble-bridge.

Peter Clarke thus describes the attack on the Church-street defences:—"Ab^{t} 2 o'clock this afternoone, 200 of Gen^{r}all Wills men entred the Churchgate street, and the Highland^{r}s firing out of the cell^{r}s and windows, in 10 minutes time kiled 120 of them. The Highland^{r}s also fired the s^{d} 2 ship guns, but the bulletts flew upon the houses, so that no execuc^{i}on was done thereby. A little time after this, a party was sent to burne the houses & barnes where the Highland^{r}s were, at the entrance of the said Church Gate street, and accordingly sev^{r}all houses and barnes were burnt, and so forced the Highland^{r}s to move up furth^{r} into the towne. At this time the wind was North, w^{ch}, if it had been South, the judicious are of opinion that most of the towne wood have been burnt."

Brigadiers Dormer and Munden attacked the barrier on Lancaster-road, with the regiments of Wynn and Dormer, and a squadron of Stanhope's dragoons, dismounted, together with Pitt's and Munden's regiments, and a squadron of Stanhope's horse. This barricade was defended by about three hundred men under Colonel Mackintosh, a relative of the veteran brigadier. Clarke says, "Ab^{t} 4 o'clock, the same day, 300 men were commanded to enter the Back Street, called the Back Ween" (Back Lane), "in Preston, and accordingly they made an attempt, but the Highland^{r}s placing themselves und^{r} garden walles, hedges, and ditches, kiled the Capt and about 140 of his men."

Dormer, who received a shot in the leg, ordered the houses to be set on fire, which was done "with all expedition, burning them up to the barricade" Great diversity of opinion is entertained regarding the loss of the king's troops in this attack. Another account says nine only were slain and about forty wounded. The captain alluded to by Clarke is supposed to have been the son of Lord Ogilvie. He was severely wounded, but ultimately recovered.[f]

[f] Within the last half century several remains of the bodies of the soldiers engaged in this combat have been found in the neighbourhood of Patten-field and Back-lane. About fifty years ago, "nearly a cart load" of bones were dug up in one place. Within a short distance from this sepulchral pit, the skeleton of a gigantic individual was discovered, about eighteen inches below the surface of the ground. As he lay in the earth, he is said to have measured six feet seven inches in length. In the right hand he held the remains of a "basket hilted" sword, and in the left a massive iron key! The latter article excited considerable interest at the time, on account of its colossal proportions. It is said to have been nearly a foot in length. The portion which entered the lock and turned the bolt was between three and four inches square, and the ring at the other extremity large enough to admit the entire hand!* No satisfactory explanation of this singular circumstance has yet been adduced. The "Old Friary" was at the time used as a prison. Scarcely any other building in the town would appear at all likely to require such a massive instrument to open and secure its portal. The nature of its connection with a soldier slain in storming the barricade, however, has not been determined. Patten-field is now built upon. Part of the site is occupied by Patten-street and Trinity church. Other remains were found about twenty years ago, opposite the Wool-pack Inn. In August last, the workmen employed in excavating for the sewerage works in Back-lane, not more than a dozen yards from the Friargate corner, came upon a human skeleton, at a depth of about four feet from the surface. At the time when the hill in Friargate was reduced in height, the road at the Friargate end of Back-lane was raised at this spot about

* The [illegible] witness, still living.

Both parties are accused of setting fire to houses with the view to effect the dislodgement of the enemy, or to cover themselves from observation by the smoke. Clarke says, "Night now approaching, Gen'all Will's men camped round the town, and also burnt sev'all houses at the North end of it." The Merse officer states that, "both armies lay upon their arms, *but General Forster went to bed.* All that night there were constant dropping shots." Honeywood's men fired from Stanley's and Eyre's houses during the night, and killed few of the enemy, amongst whom were Mr. Hume, a cornet, Mr. Scuttery, and a highland gentleman under Lord Nairn. Honeywood's men threw up a "breast-work" or counter barricade, with a view to prevent the escape of the rebels Large numbers decamped, nevertheless, during the night; especially amongst the new recruits, who began to look upon the affair as a desperate adventure. Mackintosh was, on the whole, however, so well satisfied with his success, that he wrote a letter to the Earl of Mar, on the Sunday morning, in which he expressed his confidence that Wills would be defeated.

During the darkness, some confusion arose in consequence of a misunderstanding of an order to put out all lights in the houses, as the illumination exposed persons passing in the streets to the enemy's fire. The inhabitants, instead of extinguishing their candles, lighted up more; which, says Patten, "amused both sides, but did no harm to either." It appears General Wills had ordered the troops occupying the houses of Sir Edward Stanley and Mr. Eyre, to illuminate; and, in error, other parties followed their example.

The Merse officer writes: "By daylight, I espied from the steeple some dragoons on foot, creeping near to our quarters, which party were immediately beat back. About ten o'clock Mr. Carpenter and Mr. Wills joined

two feet six inches. The line of the old pavement was distinctly visible in the excavation Consequently the body had originally been covered with soil to no greater a depth than eighteen inches The back of the skull was pierced in two places. Three or four other skeletons were afterwards found below and around the one first discovered, as well as evidence of the existence of others to the east of the excavation From these circumstances, it is certain the number of slain much exceeded nine Peter Clarke's statement, perhaps, includes the wounded as well as the killed. From his loose manner of expression this is by no means improbable The skeleton of a horse was likewise found in the neighbourhood of the human remains; and a few days afterwards, as the workmen were digging for the purpose of laying a branch drain from the Sun Inn public-house, to the sewer in Back-lane, they discovered, a little below the original level of the street, a hollow shot or grenade, about two inches and three quarters in diameter, and nearly half a pound in weight. It is formed of iron, with the exception of a small portion about the aperture intended for the fusee, which appears to be brass. The original surface is ornamented with two groups of circular lines, crossing each other at right angles. One of these groups resembles in appearance the seam of a cricket ball. As the shell was perfect in form, it most probably belonged to the king's troops, and fell unexploded when the grenadier who endeavoured to project it over the barricade was shot down by the besieged The celebrated Dutch engineer, Coehorn, invented a small mortar for the purpose of throwing light shells, into covered ways, over parapets, and other defensive works From their being portable by a single individual they were named hand grenades, and the soldiers employed in this particular service grenadiers.

their forces." General Carpenter had marched from Newcastle, and expected to have been at Preston on the 12th. On the evening of that day, he received, at Clitheroe, a letter from Sir Henry Hoghton, announcing the commencement of the struggle. Carpenter consequently hastened to the scene of action. He commanded a body of two thousand five hundred horse, composed of Churchill's, Molesworth's, and Cobham's dragoons; and was accompanied by the Earl of Carlisle, Lord Lumley, Colonel Darcey, and other gentlemen. On the junction of the two forces, Carpenter, as superior officer, took the chief command. He complimented Wills, however, upon the courage and skill with which he had so far conducted the operations, observing, "I will not take from you any part of the renown of the victory, or lessen you upon any account. You have begun the affair so well that you ought to have the glory of finishing it." According to the Merse officer, "about eleven of the clock, Mr. Carpenter and Mr. Wills divided their forces and surrounded the town."

Wills has been blamed for not doing this in the first instance. With the force at his command, it is, however, questionable, whether he could have accomplished it, had he made the attempt. He was evidently too weak for what he did undertake. A still further subdivision of his troops would have subjected him to the chance of being cut up piece-meal by vigorous sallies of the enemy. The addition of Carpenter's two thousand five hundred horse to his previous strength, necessarily demanded a new disposition of the besieging forces. For want of troops, Wills had not only been unable to direct an attack upon the Fishergate barricade, but even to prevent large numbers escaping by this outlet. Carpenter, therefore, ordered two squadrons of *horse*, under Colonel Pitt, to cover the ford. Notwithstanding the numbers which escaped, Woods and Walker, the clerical "generals," and their brave Chowbent volunteers, are reported to have acted with so much courage and address, that Wills expressed regret that he had not entrusted a more important post to their care. One authority (Toulmin), says Woods defended the bridge at Walton. He had evidently too much ground to protect for the number of his forces, which would be principally if not entirely composed of footmen.

Carpenter made such disposition of his troops as effectually blockaded the insurgent army, and left them no alternative but to capitulate, or cut their way through the lines of the besiegers.

When the rebels learned from some wounded prisoners that General Carpenter had arrived, their confidence began rapidly to evaporate, although they had been up to the time almost uniformly victorious. The common men had been led to expect that many of the king's troops, when occasion served, would declare for the Stuart, but in this they had been thoroughly deceived, and their enthusiasm had suffered a corresponding depression.

Patten says, one reason why the king's troops failed in their first attack, is to be found in the fact that the rebels were in possession of six pieces of cannon. Yet he acknowledges they did not avail themselves of them, except at the commencement of the contest. In order to account for such apparent neglect, he says, "in short they knew not how to use them, having no engineers among them, and a seaman, who pretended judgment, and upon his own offer took the management of the cannon at the Brigadier's barricado, acted so madly, whether it was that he had too little judgment, or too much ale, or perhaps both, that in levelling one of the pieces to cut off Preston's foot, who advanced to attack us, the ball brought down the top of a chimney. It is true the next he fired did execution, and obliged the regiment to halt; tho' on all occasions they behaved with a great deal of bravery and order."

Several of the rebel chiefs, discovering the true state of affairs, and knowing that their stock of powder would not suffice for a protracted defence, were desirous of trying the effect of negociation. Forster, therefore, by the advice of Lord Widdrington and Colonel Oxburgh, dispatched the latter to treat with the king's generals for the surrender of the town. Oxburgh offered, on behalf of the insurgents, to lay down their arms, on condition that the general would recommend them to the king's mercy. Wills replied that "he would not treat with rebels, for that they had killed several of the king's subjects, and they must expect to undergo the same fate. * * * If they laid down their arms and submitted prisoners at discretion, he would prevent the soldiers from cutting them in pieces, 'till he had further orders, and that he would give them but an hour to consider of it" [g] When Forster was informed of this, he dispatched Mr. Dalziel, brother to the carl of Carnworth, to see if he could get better terms for the Scotch. But the general was inexorable. Patten says:—

"About three in the afternoon, Colonel Cotton, with a dragoon and a drum beating a chamade before them, came up the streets from the king's general the colonel alighted at the sign of the Mitre, where the chief of the rebel officers were got together, and told them he had come to receive their positive answer [h] 'Twas told him there were disputes

g General Wills's evidence before the House of Lords.

h Mr. Whittle identifies this with the present "Mitre Inn," Fishergate This is an error. The "Mitre," of 1715, was situated in the Market-place. The present entry leading to the Strait-shambles was called "Mitre Court," within the memory of many living inhabitants. The buildings on each side of this court belonged to the hotel The small square, opposite the present "Shakspere," formed the court yard The premises to the north of "Mitre Court," were long occupied as the Preston Journal and Preston Chronicle office. A tradition yet remains that Prince Charles Edward occupied apartments in this building in 1745.

between the English and Scots, that would obstruct the yielding, which others were willing to submit to; but if the general would grant them a cessation of arms 'till the next morning at seven, they should be able to settle the matter, and that the gentlemen promised they would then submit. Colonel Cotton sent the drum to beat a chamade before the doors of some houses where the king's men continued firing; to cause them to cease, on account of the cessation which was agreed to, and to order them to withhold till they had notice from the general; but the poor fellow was shot dead upon his horse as he was beating his drum. It is said that this was not done by the king's men, (for they must needs know him to be one of their own drums by his livery and mounting,) but that it was done by some of the rebels, who were averse to all thoughts of surrender. * * * * The common men were one and all against capitulating, and were terribly enraged when they were told of it, declaring that they would die fighting; and that when they could defend their posts no longer, they would force their way out and make a retreat. * * * * Their madness was such that nothing could quiet them for a great while; and it was astonishing to see the confusion the town was in, threatening one another, nay killing one another, but for naming a surrender; one was shot dead and several wounded. In this dilemma, many exclaimed against Mr Forster, and had he appeared in the street, he would certainly have been cut to pieces. * * * * He had actually been killed in his chamber by Mr. Murray, had not I with my hand struck up the pistol with which he fired at him, so that the bullet went through the wainscot into the wall of the room."

Colonel Cotton, on behalf of General Wills, demanded two hostages; and the earl of Derwentwater and Colonel Mackintosh were delivered into his hands.[i] During the conference, according to Oldmixon, six or seven of the insurgents, "people of quality," attempted to leave the town, notwithstanding the promise of the lords that no new works should be thrown up, and that they would to the utmost of their power prevent the people from escaping. Colonel Cotton, to his surprise, found six persons cut to pieces, who had violated this pledge.[j] One of them was Cornet Shuttleworth. The pretender's standard, made of green taffety, with a buff silk fringe, was found in his pocket. On the flag was a representation of a pelican feeding her young, and the following motto:—

"Tantum valet Amor Regis et Patriæ."

Wills is said to have treated the rebel officers with unnecessary rudeness. He told Colonel Mackintosh, in reply to an observation respecting the bravery and hardiness of the Scottish troops, that he might have proved their quality if he had pleased, and it would then have been seen whether the king's troops or a parcel of rebels would have acted the braver part. Even Brigadier Munden acknowledged that Wills received the persons who came to treat with him "with the utmost detestation and contempt." Perhaps the manner in which Mackintosh's troops had received his attack on the barricades had somewhat ruffled his temper.

The Merse officer says:—"Mr. Carpenter and Mr. Wills patched up a

i General Wills's evidence

j "There was a popish priest named Littleton among them * * He contrived a most excellent disguise, for he put on a blue apron, went behind an apothecary's counter, and passed for an assistant or journeyman to the apothecary, and so took an opportunity of getting off."—Patten.

treaty with Mr. Forster, without the knowledge of several worthy noblemen and gentlemen. So soon as the capitulation was reported, the Earl of Wintoun, Captain Philip Lockhart, Major Nairn, and Captain Shafto went to Brigadier Mackintosh, desiring him to allow his foot to flank the hedges on the Lancaster Road, while the Scots gentry, under the command of the Earl of Wintoun and Mr. Charles Radcliffe, forced their way through the enemy The brigadier told them that 'it was too late to make such an attempt, especially after hostages were given on our side.'" The Merse officer further adds:—"I know nothing of the terms of the capitulation, only I heard them, in the general, said to be necessary and honourable, by the Earl of Cranwath, and Lord Widdrington and others."

When Colonel Mackintosh heard of the treaty, he expressed an opinion to Wills that the highlanders would never submit without a struggle. "Go back to your people again," responded the general, "and I will attack the town; and the consequence will be that I will not spare one man of you." Mackintosh accepted the taunting challenge, and returned to his troops; but he found the brigadier, his kinsman, Lord Kenmure, and the other noblemen, had already surrendered.

Lord Forrester received the swords of the officers in the churchyard; but those of the lords were delivered to him at the Mitre Inn. Widdrington requested, as a favour, that his arms might be presented to Lord Kimmergen.

The highlanders laid down their arms in the Market-place, and were, with the common men, imprisoned for about a month in the church; where "they took what care of themselves they could, unripping all the linings from the seats or pews, and making thereof breeches and hose to defend themselves from the extremity of the weather." [k] The prisoners were fed upon bread and water at the cost of the inhabitants. They were ultimately removed to Wigan, Chester, and Lancaster, for trial. Some were executed, others "transported by their own choice," and the remainder were reprieved. The noblemen and gentlemen, who had been secured in the first instance, were placed under guard at the inns called the Mitre, the White Bull, and the Windmill, and in Mr. Wringley's house The chiefs were afterwards removed, by Wigan and Warrington, to London.

The loss on the part of the king's forces was relatively very great. Amongst the wounded officers were Brigadier Honeywood, Major Bland, Lord Forrester, and Major Preston. The latter was made prisoner, and died in the town. The principal loss fell upon Preston's regiment, which sustained the brunt of the battle in Church-street. Captain Ogleby,

k Patten.

Major Lawson, Brigadier Dormer, together with three other captains, two lieutenants, one cornet, and four ensigns, were likewise wounded. There were three captains and one ensign killed. The total loss was upwards of two hundred men in killed and wounded. The rebels were more fortunate, being under cover. Patten estimates their loss in all the actions at seventeen killed, and twenty-five wounded.[1]

The number of prisoners who surrendered, according to some authorities, was fifteen hundred and fifty, of whom ten hundred and eighty-eight were Scotch, and four hundred and sixty-two English. From a list of names, printed at Edinburgh, by "James Moncur, 1715," and corrected by Dr. Ware, from other documents, the number appears to be—Scotch, eleven hundred and three; English, four hundred and sixty-six; total, fifteen hundred and sixty-nine.

According to the government return, the king's troops lost "2 captains, 1 ensign, and 53 private men killed, and two field officers, 4 captains, 2 lieutenants, 4 ensigns, 1 cornet, and 77 private men wounded, and 72 horse killed or lost." Total, "killed 56, wounded 90; in all 146."

Clarke says:—"By the strictest observa'ion of the number of El Derwentwaters men that were killed, were 18 or 19; and of Genrall Carpenters & Wills men two hundred and seaventy."

Dr. Ware says, respecting the government return, that "there is not a single writer on the events of the Rebellion who has treated it as a veracious document." It would doubtless be the policy of the government to conceal as much as possible their loss on the occasion. The morals of the politicians of the day were anything but scrupulous with regard to even more important matters. Patten evidently appears much of the same opinion as Clarke; but he seems to fancy that his new patrons would scarcely relish being told by their proselyte that the official document was framed purposely to mislead.

Peter Clarke flatly accuses the king's troops of burglarious and felonious proceedings after the surrender. It must not be forgotten that Clarke was a lawyer's clerk, in the employment of Mr. Crackenthorpe, the Kendal attorney. He says:—"After the sd two Genralls men had taken whole p'ossion of the sd toune of Preston, they with force and armes broke open doors & locks of chambers and clossetts, and moneys, plate, goods & chatels

1 "I shall take notice of one," says the rebel chaplain, "that was killed, tho' a person of no note, yet he is not to be forgotten, seeing the bravery of mean persons ought not to be buried: He was a lame man and had the care of the gunpowder, which he carried under him on a horse from one post to another. He was told that they wanted powder at Maciatosh's barrier; but if he went they told him he would certainly be shot. He answered, 'I know I cannot avoid that, if I go; but since they want, if I cannot carry it quite up to them, I'll carry it as far as I can;' and so set forward, and both he and his horse were shot dead."

of most of the inhabts of that toun (who were & still are good subjects to his Majesty King Georges Government) contrary to the will of the ownrs of the sd goods ffelonyously did steal, take & carry away contrary to His said Majties peace, crown, and dignity; and also contrary to the laws of this nation in that case made and pvided"

This appears to be but another instance of the acknowledged fact, that, in time of war, the next terror to the peaceable inhabitants, after the enemy, is the troops employed for their protection. It not unfrequently happens that the friendly force is even the more exacting of the two.

James, earl of Derwentwater, William, earl of Nithsdale, Robert, earl of Carnworth, George, earl of Wintoun, William, Lord Widdrington, William, Viscount Kenmure, and William, Lord Nairn, were impeached before the house of lords, and found guilty of treason. Earls Nithsdale and Wintoun escaped from the tower; Lords Widdrington and Nairn, and the earl of Carnworth, were pardoned by the king; but the earl of Derwentwater and Lord Kenmure were beheaded upon Tower Hill.

Nearly fifty others were convicted and executed, with the exception of some who escaped from prison. Amongst the latter were Mr. Forster and the Brigadier Mackintosh, who were confined in Newgate. Lord Charles Murray, son of the duke of Athol, was spared by the clemency of the king, after condemnation by a court martial.

Baines states that the number of prisoners sent to Lancaster was two hundred and fifty; but a journal, written by William Stout, of Lancaster, says that—

"After the Rebellion was suppressed about 400" (of the rebels) "were brought to Lancaster Castell, and a Regiment of Dragoons quartered in the town to guard them. The King allowed them each 4d. a day for maintenance, viz., 2d in bread, 1d. in cheese, and 1d. in small beer And they laid in straw in stables most of them, and in a month's time about 100 of them were conveyed to Liverpool, to be tried, where they were convicted and near 40 of them hanged at Manchester, Liverpool, Wigan, Preston, Garstang, and Lancaster, and about 200 of them continued a year, and about 50 of them died, and the rest were transported to America; except the lords and gentlemen, who were had to London, and there convicted, and their estates forfeited. Whilst they were here I was employed to buy cheese for them, about two or three cwt. a week, of about 12s or 14s a cwt Besides the king's allowance, they had supplies privately from the papists and disaffected, so as to live very plentifully. This year provisions were plentyful and cheap, as also corn and hay, and although a regiment of dragoons was quartered here all the winter, hay was as cheap at the spring as at the fall And although it was hard upon innkeepers, it was a profit to the country, and it was computed that the dragoons and prisoners maintained this year amounted to at least £3,000."

The following is a summary, from an old document, of the executions:—

"Dec. 1715 Major Nairn, Captains Lockhart, Shaftoe and Erskine, shot at Preston 4

"Jan. 28. 1716 Richard Shuttleworth, of Preston Roger Muncaster, of Garstang, attorney; Thomas Cowpe, of Walton-le dale, Will. Butler, and Will. Arkwright, hanged on the gallows hill at Preston m 5

m "On cutting through the Gallows hill, in May, 1817, the workmen discovered two coffins, in which the headless bodies of two of the rebel chiefs executed here, were, no doubt, deposited. According

"Feb. 9 Richard Chorley, esq.; James Drummond,[n] Will. Black, Donald M'Donald, John Howard, Berry Kennedy, and John Rowbottom, hanged at Preston...7

"Feb 10. James Blundell, James Finch, Jno. Macgilliwray, Will. Whalley, and James Bun, hanged at Wigan ... 5

"Feb 11. Tho. Sudell, Will Harris, Stephen Sagar, Jos. Porter, hanged at Wigan, and John Finch, hanged at Manchester ... 5

"Feb. 14 Allan Sanderson, Tho Cartmel, Tho Gorse, and Jos. Wadsworth, hanged at Garstang... 4

"Feb 24. James, earl of Derwentwater, and Lord Visc. Kenmore, beheaded on Tower Hill ... 2

"May 3. Messrs. Collingwood, Burnet, Drummond, and Hunter, hanged at Liverpool ... 4

"May 14. Colonel Oxburgh, hanged at Tyburn ... 1

"July 25. Mr. Gascoigne, hanged at Tyburn ... 1

"July 13. Rev Mr. Paul and Jno Hall, esq, executed at Tyburn[o] ... 2

"Oct. 2. Captain Bruce, Jno Winckley, Thos. Shuttleworth, George Hodson, and — Charnley, hanged at Lancaster"... 5

The document further adds:—"I am certain that four more were executed at Lancaster, of whom I remember the names of two, viz., Mr. Crow, an Aberdeen Scott, and a mathematician, whose *names*[p] were fixed over the castle gates."

The execution, by court martial, of Major Nairn, Captain Lockhart, Mr. Shaftoe, and Mr. Erskine, has been much animadverted upon. In a letter written by a "Gentleman in Prestoun to his friend in the King's camp at Perth," it is stated that,—"When the affair was debated in the Privy Council at London, several of the lords were of opinion that these gentlemen could not be tried as deserters by a Council of War, but by the usual proper civil judicatories." The Lord High Chancellor Cowper appears to have been strongly of this opinion. The writer of the letter, after describing the unavailing efforts of the ministers of Preston to induce them to repent of "that great sin of rebellion," their devotion to the cause they had espoused, and "the most Christian resignation" which they exhibited, further observes:—

"It was not without great difficulty and much intercession, that the first two" (Nairn and Lockhart) "were allowed each a coffin, and a Christian, decent burial; but these, for what reasons I know not, were refused to the other two When they came to the place of execution, Major Nairn, who was to be shot first, desired his face might not be covered, and to have the liberty to give the word of command; but he was refused. After he was shot, Captain Lockhart would not suffer any of the common

---

to tradition, the heads were cut off at the time of execution, and exposed on poles in front of the Town Hall."—Taylor's Notes.—Mr Whittle adds that "near the spot timber was found, which from its appearance had formed the gallows." He further states that, "a hand axe made of brass" was discovered at the same time.

n Charles Chorley, his son, was condemned at Liverpool, but died in prison.

o The composition of Paul and Hall's dying declarations, which were published at this time, is attributed to a celebrated non-juror, Dr. Deacon, then in his youth. Nearly thirty years afterwards, he was actively employed at Manchester, in fomenting the rebellious spirit which again displayed itself in open warfare in 1745

p Query—"heads."

soldiers to touch his friend's body, but, with his own hands, and the help of the two other gentlemen, laid Major Nairn in his coffin, and with the greatest composure of mind, performed the last offices to his dear companion. After which he was shot, and the two others performed the like to his body Then the others were shot, and laid together without a coffin, in a pit digged for that purpose. Which tragical scene being thus finished, Mr. Nairn and Mr. Lockhart were decently buried"

Amongst the others brought to trial, but acquitted or reprieved, were the following Lancashire gentlemen:—Ralph Standish, esq., of Standish; Francis Anderton, esq, of Lostock;[q] John Dalton, esq.; Richard Towneley, esq, of Towneley,[r] (brother-in-law to Lord Widdrington); Edward Tildesley, of the Lodge,[s] Myerscough; Gabriel Hesketh, and his son, Cuthbert Hesketh, and Butler, of Rawcliffe.

A curious document was lately in the possession of William Upcott, esq., formerly of the London institution, relating to the sheriff's disbursements in the trials and execution of the rebels in Lancashire. The following is a portion of it:—

"The charge of Executing 34 rebels.

	£	s.	d.
"Jan. 27, 1715. Erecting gallows, and paid for materialls, hurdle, fire, cart, &c, on executing Shuttleworth and 4 more at Preston, and setting up his head, &c.	12	0	4
"Feb 9. Disbursement on executing old Mr. Chorley,[t] and setting up a head, &c.	5	10	6
"Besides the undersheriffs.			
"Feb. 10. Charge at Wigan on executing Blundell, &c.	7	1	2
"Besides the undersheriffs.			
"Feb. 11. Charge at Manchester on executing Syddall, &c	8	10	0
"Besides the undersheriffs.			
"Feb 16 and 18. Charge at Garstang and Lancaster on executing 4 at either place	22	0	1
"Besides the undersheriffs.			
"Feb. 25. Charge of executing Bennet and 3 more at Leverpoole	10	3	0
"Payd the two executioners	60	0	3
"Payd for horses to carry the executioners to the severall places of execution and their travelling charges.	7	10	0
	£132	15	8

q "Francis Anderton, of Lostock, a papist of Lancashire: He had an estate of £2000 per annum. He was indicted as a baronet; but he pleaded that false, because his eldest brother a popish priest, beyond sea, was alive. He was afterwards found guilty, and received sentence. This gentleman is of pleasant and diverting conversation: He is reported to say, he lost a good estate, for being with the rebels but one day."—Patten.—[Mr. Anderton was pardoned.]

r "Richard Towneley, of Towneley, a papist in Lancashire, he married Lord Widdrington's sister. This gentleman's servants were found guilty of high treason, for being in the rebellion with their master, and some of them afterwards executed in Lancashire; but he was acquitted by the jury at the Marshalsea. After which, endeavouring to go beyond seas, he was retaken into custody, but soon discharged."—Patten.

s "Edward Tildesley, of the lodge, a papist, Lancashire, was acquitted by the jury at the Marshalsea, tho' it was proved he had a troop, and entered Preston at the head of it with his sword drawn. But his sword had a silver handle"—Patten.

t "Richard Chorley, of Chorley, in Lancashire, a papist · A gentleman of singular piety and parts, was ordered for London; but falling sick at Wigan was left behind, and was try'd at Liverpool, found guilty, and executed at Preston, Feb. 1715-16."—Patten.

Woods and Walker, from Chowbent, were rewarded by government for their zealous services, on the representation of General Wills, with an annuity of one hundred pounds per annum each. [u] Woods distributed a portion of his pension amongst his followers, and appropriated a considerable part of the remainder towards the erection of a chapel, at Chowbent. He died in 1759. The exploits of the "parson-general" still furnish matter for conversation and gossip at Chowbent. Tradition asserts that, in addition to the pecuniary reward referred to, Woods was permitted to preach in a gown, and attach a bell to his chapel,—a very remarkable concession at the time. The late Reverend B. R. Davis, who occupied the "general's" pulpit during a period of forty-two years, often stated that Woods's influence procured the liberation from prison of some sturdy dissenter, immured for "conscience sake." He was a stout, venerable looking man, and was regarded as a good practical Christian, and a most useful pastor. He entertained, however, a very humble opinion of his own powers of oratory. It is said, when asked by one of his congregation, if he had secured the services of any talented minister to preach on a certain special occasion, that Woods replied, in the dialect of his district, which it appears he was in the habit of using on all occasions,—"No; but tha may depend on't, I'll get one better than mysel, for I'm sure I cannot find a wurr (worse)." [v]

A curious letter, purporting to be written by one Gabriel Dutton, a quaker, of Liverpool, soon after the defeat of the Jacobites at Preston, to his friend, William Brandine, of Berwick, but strongly suspected to be the composition of "an Independent partisan," shows, in a very clear light, the extent to which religious bigotry and fanatical zeal entered into this contest for the sovereignty of Great Britain:—

---

u Rae's History.

v Many curious anecdotes are related of Woods. Amongst others, he is said to have been an excellent "begger" for public purposes, as he would accept no denial. He was in the habit of soliciting subscriptions from his friends in the following brusque manner:—"Well, Thomas, I've put tha down for so much (naming the sum); and if tha thinks it too little, tha may give as much more as tha will." It is said, that he travelled on horseback as far as Scotland, collecting small sums from dissenters, towards the expenses of erecting his chapel. One day, having met with little success, Woods determined to rest for the evening at *the first mansion* he should meet with. Accordingly, he rode, with perfect *nonchalance*, into the court-yard of a neighbouring hall, ordered a groom to put his horse into the stable, and rapped boldly at the door. He announced himself, and added, "I've come according to *promise!*" The owner of the establishment, somewhat surprised, intimated that he had no knowledge whatever either of his visitor or his business. "May be, may be," rejoined Woods; "but having met wi' little succour to-day, I *promised my horse* wee'd abide o'neet at th' first *hospitable-looking* mansion o'th road." The host was amused at the oddity of the stranger's introduction, and humoured it. The "general's" anecdotes, conversational power, and practical common sense, not only procured a hospitable reception for himself and horse, but a *five-pound note* towards his chapel fund. Woods likewise extracted from Sir Peter Warburton, a "staunch churchman," sufficient timber to form the "first principals" of his dissenting place of worship; no slight feat in those days of intolerance.

"Laverpool, 19 of the 9th Month of the year called 1715.

"Friend William,—I hope thou art now fully convinced that these Backsliders from the Truth, who profanely call themselves the Church of England and the Kirk of Scotland, are nothing but the Worshipers of Baal and Dagon, and thy inward Light will plainly show thee, that if their Tithes be taken from them, these Priests will turn Boars and Wolves to suck out the Heart Blood of the Deluded Flock They have the subtilty of the old Serpent in their Blasphemy and Cursing, which is by them called Preaching, to turn the Brains of their Giddy Hearers, making them believe Lyes that they all may be Damned. If their private interest is in the least touched, immediately the Ecclesiastic Drum is beaten, and Anathema Maranatha is the Word for those who will not go out to Fight the Battles of the LORD against the Mighty. These Sons of Belial are now knocking their heads one against another, but let us, who are the true Enlightened, rejoice.

"Thy Ungodly Kinsman, who sojourneth here, Joseph Fallman, who is a Worshiper of the Scarlet Colloured Whore, is sick almost unto Death, for the Defeat of his Friends at Preston.

"Roger, the High Church Man, laughs yet, and says all will be well, and that the Covenanters will fall before them

"The Pagans who descended from the high Mountains of Scotland, play'd the Devil under the Command of one M'Intosh, who may be compared to Beelzebub, the God of Ekron.

"Fare thee well! all the Congregation of the Faithful wish thee Health. Several of the Sisters long much to be Refreshed with thy presence.

"Notwithstanding of all our care, we hear that one of our Sisters named Hannah, whom we heped would have held forth one of these days, Alas! she has fallen down beneath one of the half Naked Brauny Pagans, tho' its hoped she may rise again, yet she cannot be received into our Bosom, till she be twin'd of the Bloody Offspring of that Anakite

"Keep thy Garments clean, and neither trouble thee whether Rehoboam, or Jereboam, the Son of Nebat, be the Ruler, and learn to be as Indifferent about their Kings and Priests, as thy Friend, "GABRIEL DUTTON.

"To William Brandine, Clothier at Berwick"

Singular stories appear to have been circulated, with the view to affect the more ignorant of the populace, as well as the zealous protestants, with fear and horror of the Jacobites. Had they been successful, the inquisition was to have been immediately introduced into England, and all heretics, men, women, and children, were to be subjected to cruel tortures. In the printshops of London, a representation of a formidable instrument was exhibited, said to have been found amongst the insurgents, and intended to "assist in the purposes of torture, pillage, or murder." Dr. Hibbert Ware gives a small woodcut of this singular engine of cruelty, which is described as "an exact draught of the gagg taken from the rebels at Preston." Dr. Ware likewise gives a copy of a ballad, upon the subject of the "Preston fight," from a "broadside printed in double columns, without any date or place of printing." The original is in the possession of Mr. David Laing, of Edinburgh. It is called "Brigadier Macintosh's Farewell to the Highlands. To an excellent new tune." It is too long, and scarcely of sufficient interest, for insertion at length The following stanzas will serve to give a taste of its quality:—

"My Lord Derwentwater when he found,
that Foster had drawn his left wing round,
Said I wish I were with my dear Wife,
for fear that I will loose my life,
With a fa la la ra da ra da.

M'Intosh he shook his head,
to see his soldiers all ly dead;
It was not for the loss of those,
but I fear we're taken by our foes,
With a fa la, &c.

M'Intosh is a valiant Soldier,
he carried a musket on his shoulder;
Cock your pistols, draw your rapper,
damn you Foster, for you're a traitor.
With a fa la, &c.

My Lord Derwentwater to Foster did say,
thou hast proved our ruin this very Day,
Thou promisedst to stand our friend,
but thou hast proved a rogue in the end.
With a fa la, &c."

On the same day that Preston surrendered to the royal troops, a general action was fought at Sherriff moor, near Dumblane, between the rebel forces under the earl of Mar, and the king's army, led by the duke of Argyle. Both sides claimed the victory; but the result was disastrous to the pretender's cause. The town of Inverness fell into the hands of Simon Fraser, Lord Lovat, who deserted the Jacobite party, and held the town for the reigning monarch. The chevalier himself shortly afterwards appeared in Scotland, but, finding his cause hopeless, re-embarked at Montrose, for the continent.

Dr. Hibbert Ware expresses great indignation at the want of clemency exhibited by the Hanoverians towards the Jacobites in England, during the following year, when Captain Bruce and four other rebels were executed at Lancaster. Very few (about six only) were executed in London, and one or two deserters in Scotland.

Acts of parliament were passed, authorising the indemnification, out of the sequestered estates of the rebels, of such parties as had suffered loss or damage from the military operations consequent upon the rebellion. Commissioners were appointed to "give relief to lawful creditors by determining the claims" The commission was first opened in London, and afterwards adjourned to Preston. The total number of claims registered amounted to 1,696. The inhabitants of Preston alone entered claims to the number of 226, demanding compensation, in accordance with a clause in the act, for injuries and losses sustained, to the amount of £6,462 8s. 10¾d.[w]

The commissioners put up for sale the estate of Richard Chorley, of

w Report of commissioners, dated February 4th, 1718

Chorley, and Walton-cum-Fazakerley, which realised the sum of £5,550, the purchaser being Abraham Crompton. Lord Widdrington's estate, in Lincolnshire, was disposed of at the same time, to Thomas Camplyn, for £32,400. The commissioners' report gives a list of papists who registered their estates and the respective values thereof. The Lancashire estates amounted to four hundred and sixty five in number, of the estimated value of £27,903 7s. 9¼d. The whole of the English forfeited estates were valued at £375,284 15s 3d.; and those in Scotland, £27,771 7s. 7d

Another act of parliament was passed, which ordained that "all Roman catholics, nonjurors and others," who refused to take the oaths of allegiance and supremacy to the Hanoverian family, should furnish to the commissioners appointed, "a register of their estates, setting forth in what parish and township the lands were situated, and by whom they were occupied, the annual value at which they were estimated, and the names, titles, additions, and places of abode of their owners" Returns were furnished under this act, which registered property in England alone of the yearly value of £358,194 5s. 3¾d. The Lancashire estates were valued at £13,158 10s per annum. Amounderness hundred returned seventy-three estates, of the annual value of £2,660 1s. 3d.; Blackburn hundred, twenty-nine estates, annual value £972 10s. 2d.; and Leyland hundred, fifty-four estates, annual value £1,463 13s. 1½d.

It does not appear that the registers were ever used to the detriment of the holders of the property, with the exception of their publication in 1745, "with the view," as it was set forth, "to assist the magistrates and other officers entrusted with the execution of the orders of government, for suppressing the growth and unhappy effects of the insurrection in the north"

On the second of August, 1745, Prince Charles Edward, son to the pretender, landed in the Hebrides, with seven officers, and arms for two thousand men, and caused his father to be proclaimed king of Great Britain, in several of the Scotch towns Having defeated Sir John Cope, at Preston Pans, he took possession of Edinburgh.

On the receipt of this news, the principal of the nobility, gentry, and clergy of Lancashire, met at the Town-hall, Preston, to devise measures for the protection of the country. The earl of Derby addressed the assembly with so much effect that a resolution was passed to raise "five thousand men for the defence of the government."

Prince Charles Edward directed his course southward, and invested the city of Carlisle, which surrendered in three days. The prince and the invading army entered Lancaster on the twenty-fourth of November. His forces amounted to scarcely six thousand men, principally composed of the highland clans, led by their chiefs. On the twenty-seventh, the insurgents arrived at Preston, but did not remain long in the town, the leaders preferring, by forced marches, to get possession of Manchester, where many friends anxiously awaited their coming. They appear, on the whole, to have met with as favourable a reception at Preston, as at any other place in England. Mr. Robert Chambers says.— [y]

"At Preston, for the first time, did a slight gleam of approbation rest on the cause. The bells were rung at their entry, probably by the intervention of the Catholics who abounded in the town. Some huzzas attended the reading of the proclamation, and a few recruits were obtained A Mr Towneley, a Catholic gentleman, here joined the standard, being the first man of distinction who had done so in England. A council of war was held, at which the Prince, ever eager, like his ancestor Bruce, to 'go on,' renewed his assurance of English and French assistance, and thereby prevailed upon the chiefs to continue their southward march. The clansmen had a superstitious dread, in consequence of the misfortunes of their party at Preston, in 1715, that they would never get beyond this town, to dispel the illusion Lord George Murray crossed the Ribble, and quartered a number of men on the other side" y

A contemporary writer states, that on his arrival at Preston, Prince Charles, "who had hitherto marched on foot, mounted on horseback, and surveyed the passes and bridges of the town, taking with him such as had been there in the year 1715." [z]

The forces of the young chevalier generally observed the rules of war in their expedition, and paid for what they required. They, nevertheless, seized upon the public money, and levied contributions upon the towns as they passed Mr. Edward Baines says, "the ladies of Preston were by no means inactive, when the safety of their families or the welfare of the public required their exertion; and it is related of Mrs. Grimshaw, the mother of the worthy mayor of the guild,[a] on the best authority, that while her husband, the under sheriff of the county, was at a distance, providing for the safety of a part of his young family, she raised a sum of several hundred pounds, demanded from the inhabitants, and presented with her

---

y "The cavalry having passed the bridge of Preston, on the 26th, occupied a village near the suburbs," (Walton le dale,) "and our infantry arrived at Preston The Prince held here a council of the chiefs of clans, gave them fresh hopes of being joined by his English partisans on their arrival at Manchester; and persuaded them to continue their march The whole army was allowed to rest itself during the 27th, at Preston On the 28th, our army left Preston, and passed the night at Wigan"—Memoirs of the Rebellion, by the Chevalier De Johnstone

"When the rebels marched from Carlisle to the southward, the people of England in most of the towns through which they passed, shewed the greatest aversion to their cause. Some memoirs written by the rebel officers, mention that Charles ordered his father to be proclaimed king, in all the towns through which they passed, and that no acclamations or ringing of bells were heard, but at Preston and Manchester"—Home's History of the Rebellion in 1745

z His. of the Rebellion in the year 1745 6, reprinted at Ormskirk, in 1808

a Nicholas Grimshaw, Esq., was guild mayor in 1802 and in 1822.

own hands the price of the public safety to the Scottish chiefs, at their head quarters, the White Bull Inn"

Mr. James Ray, of Whitehaven, a volunteer under his royal highness the Duke of Cumberland, in a work entitled "A Compleat History of the Rebellion," rather sarcastically describes the vacillation of the authorities in Preston, under the then perplexing circumstances. He says:—

"In the road to Preston, I picked up another straggler, following his company; and within two miles of that town I met the rebel post, returning with despatches from the army to Scotland, whom I also made prisoner, and took from him 49 letters. I conducted him and the above straggler to Preston, intending to deliver them to the magistrates; but they would neither receive the prisoners nor letters, *for they feared the consequence of so rash an undertaking*, the rebels being but just gone out of the town, and, as I had brought the prisoners into the town, they obliged me to carry them out of it, and told me that among the crowd in the streets, there were several who had worn white cockades, that were for going with the rebels, who would know me again, so that if ever I had the misfortune to be taken prisoner, I might be sure of losing my life, on which a sergeant of militia was hired for one pound five shillings, who with four men to assist him, carried the post and the other straggler to Lancaster."

Mr. Ray, however, acknowledges he received some assistance from the Prestonians. His misfortunes, however, were not yet at an end He continues:—

"After I had secured the prisoners before mentioned, I fled across the country, intending to have gone to Ribchester with the letters, expecting to have been pursued by the rebel hussars, but without my knowledge the gentlemen of Preston had taken care of my safety, by planting a guard upon the bridge, with order to let no person pass, that might give the rebels an account of what had happened, until I was got out of their reach. In the evening I met with a countryman of whom I asked the way, and told him if he met any rebels inquiring after me, to turn them a contrary way which he promised to do; he also told me it was not safe for me to go to Ribchester, but advised me to go to Clitheroe. Before I got into the right road I come to a deep brook,[a] over which there was a long stone laid for foot travellers, and in riding over it one of my horses hinder feet slipped, and we both fell backward into the water, where I was well dipped, but I and my horse happily got out without receiving any other damage. Having no time to lose, I immediately mounted, the water running from my cloaths, but my boots continued full, and my fire arms were likewise wet, so that if I had been pursued, I could have made little resistance. In this plight I was in on a cold frosty night, and knew not the road, till I came to a house where I hired a guide who conducted me over Longridge fell to Clitheroe, where I arrived about ten that night, and had the letters opened by a justice of the peace There was little in them of consequence, but boasting of favours they had never received, saying the people of Lancashire had joined them, so that their army was increased to 24,000 men, and that they were going directly without opposition to London."

At Manchester, Prince Charles was joined by a large number of partisans, who were formed into a regiment, the command of which was given to Francis Towneley, Esq., of Carlisle, nephew to Mr. Towneley, of Towneley, who narrowly escaped in the rebellion of 1715 This corps was denominated the "Lancashire regiment"

a Perhaps the brook which divides the townships of Fulwood and Ribbleton. It crosses the road at the east side of the moor.

The Chevalier de Johnstone, aide-de-camp to Lord George Murray, general of the rebel army, and assistant aide-de-camp to Prince Charles Edward, relates an amusing anecdote relative to the "capture of Manchester," by a sergeant, a woman, and a drummer-boy, from Preston, and the formation of Colonel Towneley's regiment. He says :—

"One of my sergeants, named Dickson, whom I had enlisted from among the prisoners of war at Gladsmuir, a young Scotsman, as brave and intrepid as a lion, and very much attached to my interest, informed me, on the 27th, at Preston, that he had been beating up for recruits all day without getting one, and that he was the more chagrined at this as the other sergeants had had better success. He, therefore, came to ask my permission to get a day's march ahead of the army, by setting out immediately for Manchester, a very considerable town of England, containing 40,000 inhabitants, in order to make sure of some recruits before the arrival of the army. I reproved him sharply for entertaining so wild and extravagant a prospect, which exposed him to the danger of being taken and hanged, and I ordered him back to his company. Having much confidence in him, I had given him a horse, and entrusted him with my portmanteau, that I might always have it with me. On entering my quarters in the evening, my landlady informed me that my servant had called, and taken away my portmanteau and blunderbuss. I immediately bethought me of his extravagant project, and his situation give me much uneasiness. But on our arrival at Manchester, on the evening of the following day, the 29th, Dickson brought me about one hundred and eighty recruits, whom he had enlisted for my company. He had quitted Preston, in the evening, with his mistress and my drummer; and having marched all night he arrived next morning at Manchester, which is about twenty miles distant from Preston,[a] and immediately began to beat up for recruits for the 'yellow-haired laddie.' The populace at first did not interrupt him, conceiving our army to be near the town, but as soon as they knew that it would not arrive till the evening, they surrounded him in a tumultuous manner, with the intention of taking him prisoner, alive or dead. Dickson presented his blunderbuss, which was charged with slugs, threatening to blow out the brains of those who first dared to lay hands on himself or the two who accompanied him, and by turning round continually, facing in all directions, and behaving like a lion, he soon enlarged the circle, which a crowd of people had formed round them. Having continued for some time to manœuvre in this way, those of the inhabitants of Manchester, who were attached to the house of Stuart, took arms and flew to the assistance of Dickson, to rescue him from the fury of the mob, so that he soon had five or six hundred men to aid him, who dispersed the mob in a very short time. Dickson now triumphed in his turn; and putting himself at the head of his followers, he proudly paraded, undisturbed, the whole day with his drummer, enlisting for my company all who offered themselves. On presenting me with a list of one hundred and eighty recruits, I was agreeably surprised to find that the whole amount of his expenses did not exceed three guineas. The adventures of Dickson give rise to many a joke, at the expense of the town of Manchester, from the singular circumstance of its having been taken by a sergeant, a drummer, and a girl. The circumstance may serve to show the enthusiastic courage of our army, and the alarm and terror with which the English were seized. I did not derive any advantage from these recruits, to the great regret of Dickson. Mr Townley, formerly an officer in the service of France, who had joined us some days before, obtained the rank of colonel, with permission to raise a regiment entirely composed of English; and the Prince ordered me to deliver over to him all those whom Dickson had enlisted for me. It was called the Manchester regiment, and never exceeded three hundred men; of whom the recruits furnished by my sergeant formed more than the half These were all the English who ever declared themselves openly in favour of the Prince; and the chiefs of the clans were not far wrong, therefore in distrusting the pretended succours on which the Prince so implicitly relied." [b]

---

a Evidently an error Manchester is about thirty miles from Preston

b Memoirs of the Rebellion in 1745 and 1746, by the Chevalier de Johnstone, edition 1822, p 63.

The bridge at Stockport, having been destroyed by the "Liverpool Blues," the rebel army forded the Mersey near the town, and continued their march through Macclesfield to Derby. Their object it would appear, from one of the Scotch letters detained at Preston by Mr James Ray, was to deceive the king's generals by the rapidity of their movements, and get possession of London by a *coup de main.*[c] Hearing, however, that the duke of Cumberland, brother to George II., was at Lichfield, on his march northwards to meet them, the Jacobites made a feint for Loughborough on the 6th December; and suddenly commenced their famous retrograde movement, by way of Ashbourne, Leek, and Manchester. General Wade was at Wetherby, in Yorkshire, on the 5th, from which place he proceeded to Doncaster. The rebels, therefore, narrowly escaped being hemmed in between two armies, each superior to their own, both in numbers and discipline. They arrived in Preston on the 12th of December, and early on the 13th left for Lancaster, where they opened the jail and released, amongst others, the prisoners taken by Mr. Ray.[d] They entered Scotland on the 20th, and thus completed the retreat in the depth of winter, with scarcely any loss, in about fourteen days, although the distance traversed was nearly two hundred miles. Oglethorp's dragoons, however, more than rivalled them in expedition. They entered Preston soon after the rebels had left it, having marched one hundred miles in three days, over snow and ice.[e] The Duke of Cumberland arrived about one o'clock, on the same day, and issued orders for a vigorous pursuit. The Georgia rangers were dispatched immediately, and Oglethorp with the remainder of the horse continued the chase on the following day; Preston thus narrowly escaped more than a repetition of the horrors of 1715.[f] The

c The following is the pith of the letter referred to —"We have left our baggage at Carlisle castle, and march so light, that neither hedges, ditches, nor devils are able to stop us. We have outstripped Wade, and have nothing to do but to go by Ligonier, and so to London."

d "The insurgent army, about 6000 strong, with Prince Charles Edward at its head, marched through Preston on the 27th of November, on its route to London, to the animating tune of 'The King shall have his own again.' After advancing by Manchester to Derby, the Prince and his followers, to avoid being made prisoners, commenced their retreat to Scotland, and on the 12th of December, at nine in the morning, they again passed through this town, to the less agreeable but equally appropriate sounds of 'Hie thee Charlie home again.'"—E. Baines

e Ray's Compleat History of the Rebellion

f "The Highlanders managed their retreat in such a manner as to unite expedition with perfect coolness, and never to allow the enemy to obtain a single advantage. Though on foot and pursued by cavalry, they kept distinctly ahead of all danger or annoyance for twelve days, two of which they had spent in undisturbed rest at Preston and Lancaster.

"At Wigan, some fanatic, intending to shoot the Prince, fired at O'Sullivan by mistake. Charles would not allow any harm to be done to the assassin. Captain Daniel, who mentions this fact, with bitter comment on what he thought such injudicious clemency, also complains respecting a woman and her sons who were brought before Charles, accused of murdering one of his volunteers at Manchester, and who confessed their crime, but whom he would not allow to be punished."—Robert Chambers· History of the Rebellion.

pretender's forces defeated the king's troops near Falkirk, but they were forced to succumb to the army commanded by the Duke of Cumberland, on the memorable 16th of April, when the heath on Culloden moor drunk the best blood of the Jacobite clans, and decided for ever the fate of the house of Stuart. This was the last battle fought in Britain. Prince Charles Edward was reduced to the greatest privations, and wandered for months amongst the highlands of Scotland to avoid the pursuit of his foes, who were stimulated to increased vigilance by the offer of a reward of £30,000 for his head, or for his apprehension. But the poor highlanders remained faithful to their "prince," and, notwithstanding all the efforts of the triumphant Hanoverians, the "Young Pretender" eventually escaped to France.

The Earl of Kilmarnock and Lord Balmerino, Ratcliffe, the titular Earl of Derwentwater, and Simon Fraser, Lord Lovat, were beheaded; the Earl of Cromartie was convicted but pardoned.

Seventeen of the English partisans, the chief portion of whom belonged to the Lancashire regiment, were tried for high treason, at Southwark, and condemned "to be severally hanged by the neck, not till they were dead, but cut down alive, then their bowels to be taken out and put before their faces, their heads to be severed from their bodies, and their bodies severally divided into four quarters, and there to be at the king's disposal." Eight were executed in the brutal manner prescribed, on Kennington common. The remainder were reprieved. The sufferers were Colonel Francis Towneley,[g] Captain Thomas T. Deacon, James Dawson, John Berwick, George

g "A secret hoard of modern coins found concealed beneath the oak window-sill of a bed-chamber at Gawthorpe Hall, some three years ago, was exhibited," at a meeting of a Manchester antiquarian society, named 'The Brotherhood,' "consisting of ninety-one gold coins, Portuguese and English. Of these, two "broad pieces" of gold, nearly as large as an English crown piece, were Portuguese dobraons, (equivalent to the Spanish doubloon) weighing 436 and 437 grains troy, and dated 1730 and 1732, being then current for £3 12s. Thirty-six Portuguese gold coins, about the size of the English florin, were moidores or Joannes (so named from the king of that name, and familiarly termed "Joes," weighing about 160 grains each, and current for £1 7s. They are of various years from 1693 (in the reign of Peter II.) to 1745 (reign of Joannes or John V.) One piece, rather larger than an English shilling, was half a moidore or Joe, weighing 110 grains, and current for about 13s. 6d. In all there were thirty-nine Portuguese gold coins. Of English guineas, four were of as many different years of the reign of Charles II., three of as many years of James II.; six of three years of William III., nine of four years of Anne, twenty-two of eight years of George I., and eight of five years of George II., the latest date being 1740. In all, fifty-two English guineas and thirty-nine Portuguese gold pieces, weighing 35¾ oz., the Portuguese gold being of twenty-two carats fineness. They were conjectured to have been concealed by the unfortunate Colonel Francis Townley about the period of 1745, the latest date on any coin, while a guest at Gawthorpe, and on his way to join the Pretender. For his share in the rebellion he was executed, and his head placed on Temple Bar. It was mentioned as a tradition, that his next relative offered a neighbouring barber a guinea to procure the skull for him, that this was done, and that on one occasion when one of the Townley family was consulting the late Sir Astley Cooper, and that eminent man wished to elucidate something by reference to a skull, that of the unfortunate Colonel Francis Townley was produced by him. Whether it is still preserved was not known."—*Manchester Guardian*, 1856.

Fletcher, and Andrew Blood; Lieutenant Thomas Chadwick, Adjutant Thomas Syddall, and David Morgan, barrister-at-law, a volunteer in the rebel army. The heads of Colonel Towneley and Captain Fletcher were exposed at Temple-bar, London, those of the others were sent to Manchester and Carlisle. Six others were executed at Brompton and Penrith, nine at Carlisle, and eleven at York. In Scotland, upwards of eighty suffered for treason, and about fifty deserters were executed by military law. The great majority of the rebel chiefs met their fate with remarkable constancy; which circumstance, conjoined to the atrocities committed by the Duke of Cumberland, in the highlands, after the battle of Culloden, created more sympathy for the unfortunate Jacobites than their cause itself was calculated to inspire. The Stuarts had evidently outlived the affections of the English people.

The author of "A Compleat History of the Rebellion" draws a very flattering picture, not only of the beauty of the town of Preston, but of the fairer portion of its inhabitants. He says.—

"Preston or Priest's Town, so called from the religious, who were formerly here in great numbers, as it was first ornamented with the beauty of holiness, to it you may add female beauty, with which it now shines, the ladies being very agreeable, and much gentry live here. This town is situated on a clean delightful eminence, having handsome streets and variety of company, which the agreeableness of the place induces to board here, it being one of the prettiest retirements in England, and may for its beauty and largeness compare with most cities, and for the politeness of the inhabitants none can excel. It is vulgarly called *Proud Preston*, on account of its being a place of the best fashion. 'Tis the residence of the officers belonging to the Chancery of the County Palatine. Here is a handsom church, and a Town-hall where the corporation meet for business, and the gentlemen and ladies for balls and assemblies Here is likewise a spacious Market-place, in the midst of which stands a fine obelisk, [h] the streets are neatly paved, and the houses well built of brick and slates This town being a great thoroughfare, there are many good inns for the reception of travellers, but one in particular, the sign of the Black Bull, kept by Mrs Chorley, I never met with any better, for all kind of eatables, proper attendance, kind usage, and a moderate charge, and where you may have all things done in the most grand and elegant manner if required. [i] This town has a pretty good trade for linen yarn, cloth, cotton, &c" [j]

On his return, the author bestows his commendations on the ladies of Lancashire, *en masse*, with whom he appears to have been upon the very

h This obelisk, or market cross, was taken down and another erected in 1782. The latter was removed in 1852. The site at present remains unoccupied.

i It is somewhat remarkable, that after a lapse of one hundred and twelve years, the "Bull," under the efficient management of Mr Leonard Billington, still receives from travellers precisely similar commendation to that bestowed by our author upon the establishment in good old Mistress Chorley's days. It is generally spoken of by commercial men as one of the very best inns on the road. Neither has it degenerated in grandeur and elegance, "if required," as the patronage of the most aristocratic class of sojourners amply testifies. Fortunately, truth, as well as gallantry, will justify a similar observation with regard to the ladies. The Preston *belles* of the present day reflect no discredit upon either the beauty or the fascinating manners of their renowned great-grandmothers. The "Bull Inn" of the period was situated near the end of the present Avenham-street.

j The "cottons" of 1745, were made of woollen. See chap 8.

best of terms. He says:—"In this county the women are generally very handsome, by which they have acquired the name of 'Lancashire Witches,' which appellation they really deserve, being very agreeable." He speaks however, of certain "Jacobite Witches," whose charms, and their mode of exhibition, he considers "dangerous to the constitution," and "of so attractive a quality, that it's not only in danger of drawing his majesty's good subjects in the civil, but military gentlemen, off their duty."

"John Marchant, gent," in a "History of the present Rebellion," published in 1746, adds his testimony in favour of the beauty of the town during the past century, and the character of its inhabitants. He says:—

"Preston may from its Bigness and Beauty compare with some Cities. * * * * This place from its Situation on a clean delightful Eminence, handsome Streets, and Variety of Company that board here, is reckoned one of the prettiest retirements in *England*. 'Tis a very gay Town, the Residence of the Officers belonging to the Chancery of the County Palatine, and is call'd *Proud Preston*, tho' not near so rich as *Liverpool* or *Manchester*."

Marchant gives the following extract from a letter written by a lady at Preston, to her friend in town, dated December 14th., which furnishes a very piquant specimen of the domestic gossip of the day:—

"Yesterday the Rebel Army re entered our Town, all sufficiently wearied, and out of Humour enough There are with them four Ladies, who seem to be of some distinction, *Lady Ogilvy, Mrs. Murray, Jenny Cameron*, and another, whose name I could not learn, but they say she is the mistress of one *M'Sheridan*, a Popish Priest. The two first were in a Chariot by themselves; the other two in a Coach and Six, with the young Pretender and *M'Sheridan*, who it seems is called *Archbishop of Canterbury* The young Pretender seem'd very faint and sick, and is very assiduously ministered unto by Jenny Cameron. *O'Sullivan*, one of the young Pretender's Councill, a very likely Fellow, made free with our House; from him we learnt some little Anecdotes relating to *Jenny Cameron*. She is, it seems, the Niece of a Person of some Fashion in the Highlands, and was sent by her Uncle to pay his Compliments to the young Pretender, on his March from *Lochabar* to *Perth*. She brought with her a considerable Quantity of Cattle, some Usquebaugh, and other little Presents. When she appear'd before the young Pretender's Tent, who received her very gallantly, she jump'd off her Horse, and she told him with great Frankness, *That she came like the Queen of* Sheba *to partake of the Wisdom of* Solomon· He answered, *And thou shalt my Dear partake of all that* Solomon *is master of.* He took her in his Arms, and retired with her into his Tent, and were there some Time alone, the rest Mr. *Sullivan* says we are to guess. This wild Rabble made no long stay here, nor, I dare say will ever come back again. They look all like hunted Hares, and had rather hear the name of the Devil than the Duke; but don't seem to mind any Body else in particular, except General Oglethorp, whose Vivacity they are no Strangers to; but seem to hope his Forwardness may out run his Judgment, in which, I don't doubt, they will be fatally mistaken. They are march'd or rather gone off, in a very unaccountable manner, galloping, trotting, and running, and, as we say, bidding the Devil take the Hindmost Mr. *Oglethorp* is just now coming into Town; but the post waiting, I can give you no further particulars."

At the meeting of the Lancashire and Cheshire Historic Society, in Dec., 1852, Mr. P. R. Mc. Quie exhibited, amongst other articles of interest, a relic of the "Young Pretender's" army, which is thus described in the minutes of the proceedings —"Sword, captured by Mr. Leatherbarrow's great-grandfather, at Preston, in 1745. The captor was a tailor, and when the rebel rushed up stairs to plunder, he beat him back with his goose!"

There exists a tradition in the Fylde, that Vauxhall, or Foxhall, near Blackpool, one of the seats of the Tildesleys, was fitted up for the reception of Prince Charles Edward, but he did not occupy it. This, however, appears to be but another version of the more probable story, that James II. contemplated a landing on the coast of Lancashire, and that the Tildesleys had prepared Vauxhall for his reception. [k]

In a curious work published at the beginning of the present century, and attributed to Southey, the following singular anecdote is related. At what period the event took place, it would be difficult now to decide, unless the name of the old writer alluded to could be discovered :—

"Preston was our next stage, a large manufacturing town, before we entered it we crossed the River Ribble by a good bridge, and immediately ascended a long hill—it was the only pleasant spot we had seen upon the way. Near this place an officer once met his death in battle by a singular accident. His horse, upon some disgust he took at the guns, as the old writer oddly expresses it, ran off and leapt a ditch; the man's sword fell, and at the same minute he was thrown upon its point, and it ran him through."[l]

The visits of the "Scotch rebels" to Preston have given rise to many other local stories, traditions, etc.; but the promiscuous public are in the habit of strangely confounding three distinct historical events. Cromwell's victory, in 1648, the surrender of Forster, Derwentwater, etc, in 1715, and the visit of the "young Chevalier, Prince Charles Edward," in 1745, are often huddled together "in most admired disorder." This may, perhaps, be excused amongst the rustic population when literary men fall into similar confusion, or from love of "thrilling effect," violate the truth of history.

In a periodical entitled "New Tales of the Borders and the British Isles," of the date of May 8, 1847, a story is published entitled "Preston Peggy," with the following quotation at the head of the chapter.—

"Long Preston Peggy to Proud Preston went,
To see the bold rebels it was her intent:
For in brave deeds of arms she did take much delight,
And therefore she went with the rebels to fight.—*Old Yorkshire Ballad.*"

The scene is laid at Walton and Preston, in 1715. The love story and romantic conduct of the heroine and General Wills may be tolerated or

---

k See page 214.

l Letters from England, No XL, by Don Manuel Alvares Espriella, second edition, 1808.—Mr. Whittle, in his lecture, in 1849, speaks of a tombstone in the parish church-yard, "dated 1642," and inscribed,—"To the memory of Richard Greenfield, who was slain in the lane near Walton bridge, during the civil wars." He describes a rude outline upon it as a representation of a man with a sword run through his body. This may be the party alluded to. The date, however, must be an error. The struggle took place in 1648, when Cromwell's troops attacked the bridge.

excused, but the direct violation of fact in making the earl of Derwentwater carouse at a mock corporation meeting at the village of Walton, the day before the arrival of the rebel army, is reprehensible even in a novelist. The whole is a mass of glaring anachronisms, clashing both with history and tradition, chiefly resulting from a blunder as to the period to which the story refers. Long Preston Peggy was a stalwart heroine in 1745, and not a love-sick maiden in 1715, as will appear from the following extract from a thin quarto "History of Preston," published by Edward Jeffery, London, 1822. Peggy's true future was somewhat less brilliant, likewise, than that pourtrayed in the novel, where the "lowly born maiden" becomes the bride of the nephew of General Wills!"

"It is well known at Long Preston, near Settle, in Yorkshire, that in the year 1745, a buxom, handsome young woman of that place, anxious to see the Pretender and his army, went to Preston, in Lancashire, for that purpose, a distance of about thirty-eight miles, and, after gratifying her curiosity, and staying for some time in or near the rebel camp, returned to her native village. This became so much the subject of general conversation, that it was the occasion of producing a ballad, which obtained as much notoriety in Ribblesdale as the famous historical ballad of Chevy Chase. The gentleman who has furnished this anecdote says, that he has frequently heard her sing the very song, of which she herself was the subject, twenty-five years after the occurrence, and she had then, though advanced in life, the remains of a handsome face and fine person, which had doubtless been impaired by time, and a strong propensity to indulge in spirituous liquors. The strain of—

"Long Preston Peggy to Proud Preston went,
To see the bold rebels it was her intent,"

was seldom carolled from her lips till she had been treated with half a dozen or more glasses of spirits."

Shocking! Peggy surely had, herself, not the least notion that she would ever become the sentimental heroine of a modern romance! Truly,—"Truth is strange; stranger than fiction."

The "mock Corporation at the village of Walton," alluded to by the novelist, continued to exist until within a comparatively recent period. Dr. Whitaker, in his "History of Richmondshire," gives the following interesting particulars respecting this somewhat singular society:—

"At an obscure inn, m in the neighbouring village of Walton, has been held from the beginning of the last century, a meeting of noblemen and gentlemen, styling themselves the mayor and corporation of the ancient borough of Walton. All their proceedings were conducted with ludicrous formality; and they had a register which still

m "The term "obscure inn" can scarcely with propriety be applied to the "Unicorn," at Walton. It is situated at the foot of the bridge which crosses the Darwen, and was unquestionably the principal hostelry within some miles south of Preston, at the time the "mock corporation" held its meetings. Nay, it is more than probable, that it furnished "head quarters" for Cromwell's advanced guard on the evening of the memorable defeat of the duke of Hamilton. Cromwell expressly states that his army occupied the bridge of Darwen, while the enemy lay within musket shot, on the opposite bank of the river. The house at the present day, though somewhat antiquated in its appearance, is one of the most noted and respectable inns in the neighbourhood.

remains, together with a mace or sword of state, and three large staves, covered with silver, on which are inscribed the names of the successive officers of the society from the year 1702. The register does not commence till the year after. The officers of the whimsical fraternity were a mayor, deputy mayor, recorder, two bailiffs, two sergeants, a physician, a jester, a macebearer, a poet laureate, who furnished copies of very bad verses, entered the records, and lastly a town clerk. Under this semblance, however, of sport and jollity, there seems to have been concealed a political purpose. The members who appear till about the year 1740, were the Catholic and Jacobite nobility and gentry, and here seem to have concerted their plans for the restoration of the exiled family.

"In the year 1709, the mayor was the most noble Thomas Duke of Norfolk, Sir Nicholas Sherborne, of Stonyhurst, mayor's boy; Sir Wm. Pennington, bart., town's bailiff, Charles Towneley, of Towneley, deputy mayor.

"In 1711, the mayor was James, the unfortunate earl of Derwentwater.

"In 1715, no meeting was held, for a very obvious reason.

"In the accounts of 1745, is the following entry —'Pd. 2. 6. for fixing the plates upon the staves, which were taken off an account of the *rebels* coming hither'; The word rebels is written on an erasure, and I suspect on the word duke. [n] They were only become rebels after their defeat.

"But about this time I observe a mixture of Whigs, so that as all political confidence must have been destroyed, everything of a political tendency in the society must have ceased.

"The year 1766, is the last in which the meeting continued to be respectable. It has since fallen into the hands of inferior tradesmen, who are still possessed of the ancient insignia of office" (1823), "and who continue to assemble with some of the old formalities, but with neither the danger nor dignity of their predecessors."

The regalia at the present time consists of the following articles:—Two halberds, of a somewhat similar form to those carried before the mayor of Preston. Two very long official staves, painted black and silver mounted One of these was presented by the Earl of Derwentwater, during his mayoralty. It bears the earl's coronet and the following inscription:—"The Right Honourable James Earl of Darwentwater, Viscount Ratcliffe and Langley, and Baron of Tindale, Mayor, 1711. ,On the other is inscribed, "The gift of Banistre Parker, of Extwistle, Esq , for the use of the Huntsman of the Corporation of Walton, 1721." Banistre Parker is an ancestor of the present R. Townley Parker, Esq.

The names of the officers for each year are engraved upon massive silver bands, covering four other long staves of wood. The earliest is dated 1701, and is inscribed: "William Farington, Esq , was Mayor, John Walmsley, Esq., (of Dunkenhalgh), Recorder; Richard Ashton, Robert Parker, (of Extwistle), Esqs , Bailiffs , William Cooten, Chaplain; Thomas Dale, Deputy-mayor." The silver bands for the years 1730, 1735, and 1737, have been lost. If there ever was one for 1715, it has likewise been removed.

The written records, which are in the possession of Mr. Hoghton, son of Sir Henry Bold Hoghton, bart , commence five years later than the inscrip-

---

n Dr Whitaker here alludes to the duke of Cumberland, who followed the "young Chevalier" through Preston, on his retreat to the north

tions upon the staves, and continue until the year 1766; when, according to Dr. Whitaker, the corporation ceased "to be respectable." It was continued for some years afterwards, but merely as a convivial meeting. The subsequent records are of no interest. The last entry is dated 1796. At the period of its first establishment, the parties above named were the only officials; but they afterwards became more numerous. Their various titles appear upon the silver bands attached annually to the staves, viz:—"Swordbearer, Master of the Hounds, Huntsman, House-groper, Slut-kisser, Custard-eater, Physician, Mace-bearer, Town Clerk, Poet Laureate, Jester, Town Serjeant, Mayor's Serjeant, Mayor's Bailiff, Town Bailiff," etc. These offices were held by many of the leading gentry in the county. The names of Towneley, Trafford, Shuttleworth, Farington, Rawstorne, Osbaldeston, Stanley, Holt, Starkie, Parker, Fleetwood, Tildesley, Worthington, Blundell, Chorley, Anderton, Winckley, Sherburne, Ormerod, Tunstall, Nowell, Hesketh, Gillibrand, Rigby, Blackburn, Patten, Assheton, Atherton, Scarisbrick, Bradshaw, and others, frequently occur. The club was unquestionably a Jacobite institution, although we see in the records a few names of Hanoverians; including that of Sir E. Stanley, bart., afterwards Earl of Derby, who was mayor in 1713. In the year 1715 no new appointments took place, there being merely an entry that the officers for the preceding year were continued.

Among the other officers we find the name of Dr. Shepherd, of Preston, as having been the "Physician to the Corporation" on several occasions, and in one instance as the Mayor. In the records are inserted the effusions of some of the laureates, but scarcely any are worthy of transcription. One of these rhymesters tells us, in 1723,—

"I've bought my freedom with a glass of claret,
And am rewarded with the post of laureate;
And if my verses are not on record,
The devil take me if I speak a word."

Another says:—

"First I would praise the worshipful the Mayor,
As fit in all respects to fill the chair:
Next, then, I would his brethren range in order,
And speak the merits of the bright Recorder.
* * * * * *
Many things wrong in these few lines you'll find,
But to his faults let goodness make you blind;
With candour judge him, so his wishes crown,
For if you smile ill-nature dare not frown."

The members of this "corporation" have since ceased to meet, either for political or convivial purposes. The regalia and other property remained for some time in the possession of Sir H. P. Hoghton, bart. These curious relics have been transferred to the custody of Robt. Townley

Parker, esq., recently one of the members for the borough of Preston. They will doubtless be preserved at Cuerden Hall, for many years to come, as interesting memorials of the struggle for supremacy between the house of Hanover and the Stuart dynasty,—of constitutional liberty and arbitrary power

The partisans of the Stuarts did not lose all hope of ultimate success for some time after the retreat of Prince Charles The following curious document, purporting to have been taken from the pocket of a woman on Darwen bridge, in October, 1747, and reprinted as a small handbill in 1815, throws some light upon the local feeling at this period. From the savage tone of the epistle, it is, however, more than probably, the production of a partisan of the house of Hanover, rather than a genuine Jacobite effusion. From the imminent danger attending the slightest indiscretion of speech at that period, it is difficult to conceive for what purpose such unnecessary parade of bloody intention could have been perpetrated. Whoever may have been its author, it exhibits, in a strong light, the rancour and bigotry engendered by religious intolerance and civil strife. From the context, it purports to have been written by some of the Lancashire Jacobites, who joined the pretender's army at Preston, and who were afterwards taken prisoners, and incarcerated in Carlisle Castle:—

"A copy of a letter found the 18th of October, 1747, upon Darwent-Bridge, in Walton, near Preston, in a Woman's Pocket, which contained besides, a Papist Book and two Crosses —

"*To Mr James Ratcliffe, in Whittle-in-le-Woods, near Chorley, in Lancashire*

"*Dear and loving Friends,*—This with my Love to you, and all true friends, and to let you know that we are all in high Spirits, tho' low in diet. Three days before *John* died, the Holy Father of *England*, the Holy Bishop came to us in the Dress of a poor Man, & call'd himself the Father of one of the Prisoners; and gave a Crown to come thro' the Guards to us, and stay'd with us, six days, and lived as we do, laid with us, and pardon'd all our Sins, and made us all into pure Martyrs; and assured us, that we shall not stay half so long in Purgatory as Others, for our Sufferings here, amongst these damnable hereticks, and gave every one of us a Cross, that the Supreme Holy Father the Pope hath sent to preserve our Souls from the Hands of Hereticks The Supreme Holy Father sent 5000 all at once, and this is one that I have sent you, that the Holy Father of *England*, gave *John* upon his dying bed, there is such Virtues belonging to these Crosses, the like was never known in *England* before. And the Supreme King of the World, his Holiness the Pope, hath sent the Holy Father of *England*, (the Bishop) a Letter, to let him know, that the King of *France* hath sworn to his Holiness the Pope, to assist King J—— with 50,000 men, and hath sent 10,000 into *Scotland* already, and will send 20,000 with Prince Charles into Wales, and 10,000 with Prince *Edward* near *London*, on the East side. And his Holiness promised to give 100,000l. out of the Holy Treasury, to maintain the War; and so it is to be done in a very little Time. And sent to the Holy Father of *England*, to order all the Ghostly Fathers, to order all that are able to bear Arms, to be ready on an Hour's warning; and to order the Prisoners to send to where they came from, to those that are loyal, and hath taken the Holy Oath, by the Holy Cross and Blessed Virgin, steadfastly believing that King J—— is the true, right, and lawful Heir of the Crown of *England*, and that G—— is a damned Heretick, a Bastard of *Hanover*, and Usurper to the Crown of

England; and that all Heretics are damned; and to kill, burn and destroy them, or all their Families, or Houses, or Goods, or anything they have; whoever Doth it, shall save his soul from Hell, and merit thereby. So I send you in the behalf of King J—— to go to those that you know are well affected for King J——, and all the Royal Family. The first is *John Abbott*, of the *Hey*, he took the Holy Oath, and sent his Man and 5*l.*; *James Hartley*, sent his Son, and *Arthur Proctor* gave 7*l.* with him, and Fifty Shillings *John Hartley* of *Pipping-street* gave with him; and *Robert Banks*, Shoemaker, took the Holy Oath, and sent his Man and 10*l.*; *Hugh Tootel*, of the *Holt*, took the Holy Oath, and gave 10*l.*, and would have sent *Robert* and a Horse if we had gone forward; and *Hugh Tootel*, of the *Well*, took the Holy Oath, and gave 5*l.*; *James Tootel* of the *Hill Top*, took the Holy Oath, and gave 5*l.*; and *James Tootel* enlisted when I did, and stay'd in *Preston* whilst we did, and walked with us, and swore he would kill some of the Hereticks in a little Time, for he was sure it was no sin; and I am sure he is very loyal to the cause; and my Mistress gave 5*l.* with me, and told me when King J—— was set on the Throne she would marry me; and *Nicholas Madder* 10*l.*, and took the Holy Oath; and *Thomas Burges* 5*l.*, and took the Holy Oath; But as loyal a Man as any that belongs to King J——'s Force is *Benjamin Waddington*, in *Brindle*, he met us at *Manchester*, and took on with us eagerly, and took Listing-Money, and Colonel Townley ordered him to Quarters, and I and other two went with him, and we drank all night, and he put forth very good Healths; the first he drank was King J——'s good Health, and the next Prince *Charles* good Health, and next to Prince *Edward's* Health, and then he drank damnation to the Usurper G——, the *Hanover* Bastard, and all his damnable crew of Bastards; and damnation to *Will*, o and all his undertakings; and hell and damnation light upon their Forces for ever. Then he contrived what death Hereticks should die, and the first he would kill would be *Brown*, that lives at the Watch house in *Brindle*; he said he would tye him neck and Heels, and burn the flesh of his Bones with Red hot Irons; and the Constable *Calvert*, and several other Hereticks in the Town; and the rest of the Hereticks, he would make a great Hole like a Marl pit, and make Fires and burn them by hundreds: It was told to Prince *Charles* that he was a very loyal Man; and a reformed Heretick; Prince *Charles* sent for him, and he had the Honour to kiss his Hand, and gave him two Broad Pieces, and a pair of Pistols; and told him he should have a Captain's Commission of a troop of Dragoons, and an Estate of Five Hundred a Year, when his Father was set on the Throne; and he came with us to *Chorley*, and gave me a good pair of shoes of his feet, for mine was very bad; and I persuaded him to go no further till we came back again, and a great many more that would have gone; and it was very well they did not go, to suffer what we both have suffered, and what we do suffer.

"But we hope to be set at Liberty in a little time, for there's 10,000 *French* landed in *Scotland*, with Lord *Drummond*, and when the *Hanoverian's* Forces are gone to Flanders, Prince *Charles* will land in Wales 20,000 men, and Prince *Edward* with 20,000 in *Ireland*.

"Now let the Hereticks know that we have suffered, Now is their downfall at Hand. Mr. *Skelton* is set at Liberty, for they durst hold him no longer: And the Holy Father of *England* and *He*, has had a letter from the Pope's own Hand, That the King of France has made a Vow to his Holiness the Pope, that he will bring the Hereticks of *England* down, or he will loose both Life and Crown. So dear Friends, be ready, for the Time is at Hand, that the Hereticks must have their Reward, you must go to *Manchester*, and take *Benjamin Waddington* and *James Tootel* with you, and raise what Forces you can, for *Benjamin* sent us word he was there twelve Months ago, and there was above three Hundred Men ready in an Hour's Warning; get them to write a great many Letters for you to drop at the Hereticks' Houses in *Whittle*, *Brindle*, and *Walton*, and in so doing, they cannot know the Hand-writing, and demand great Sums of Money from the damn'd Hereticks; and if they don't obey your Commands, set fire to there Houses in the Night-time, and kill them in their Beds, for all is your own; for the King of *France* has promised an Hundred Thousand Pounds to any one that can take the *Hanover* Cub, (as *Benjamin Waddington* calls him) and be sure to kill *Brown* in *Brindle*,

o The Duke of Cumberland.

and Constable *Calvert*, and those that swore against us; Fire them in their Beds, and if they take you and make you swear, swear freely, for it is no sin to take a false Oath to an Heretick.

"Pray go to *Peter Wearden*, in *Penwortham*, for he has been very Kind to us; and all his Brothers are very loyal, and sent us a great deal of Money; *George Garstang* hath been very Kind.

There is a contrivance in acting to blow up G—— and his Parliament, but the Day is not fixed on yet, but as soon as we hear we will let you know. So no more,

"*From all your Friends*, "WILLIAM HARGREAVES,
"Carlisle, July 11, 1747. and all the rest.

"We have more fresh News which stopp'd in not sending; we hear that *France* will fire *Holland* all before them, and then they will come for *England* in two Months time, and they will fire and burn all the Hereticks, for there is no one to stop them, for the *Hanover* Cub is running and all his Crew, they fly before them like Chaff before the Wind; and we hear there is three Parts out of four of the Kingdom for us; So pray make what haste you can, and go quickly. And pray make much of the Messenger, for she is a very loyal Woman, and hath done great Things for us, she hath gone a Hundred Miles round with letters on his Account; so I pray you, pay her well for coming, and if you have a mind to have any Letters by us to drop, we will write some and send them by her; and if we hear any more News we will send it by her. Pray excuse our bad Writing. *Thomas Wearden* has sent us Word that they are building the Chapel at *Cuerden Green* again, for the damn'd Hereticks dare hold it no longer, for they know their case is bad

"We now must go, but where we do not know, for they dare not hang us; and if they transport us *French* will have us

"Pray think of Rump *Hoghton*, of *Walton*, plague him and fire his house; *Benjamin Waddington* must have Part of his Estate, and *Thomas Wearden & William* his Brother, must have all the rest. Pray now begin to drop Letters and Hostilities upon the Rumps and Hereticks. Now we take our Leave of all. Be not afraid.

"*So we rest*, "WILLIAM HARGREAVES,
"GEORGE HARTLEY,
"(Printed 1747—Reprinted 1815) "GEORGE WARING."

Since the final defeat of the Jacobite party, no event of great national importance has transpired in Preston or its vicinity. The inhabitants appear to have taken the usual average interest in public affairs, and to have duly honoured the coronation festivities and public rejoicings for the great victories which transpired from that period to the present time. The "glorious constitution," and the "prosperity of Britain," were continually pronounced, during the latter portion of the last century, to be on the verge of certain destruction, and as constantly survived the lugubrious prophesy as during the present generation. A somewhat singular specimen of this kind of political vaticination is recorded in an autograph letter, preserved in Dr. Shepherd's library, penned by its learned and worthy founder. It is dated Preston, November 20th, 1757. After duly introducing the business motive of the epistle, the doctor suddenly breaks off, and unfolds to his correspondent his sentiments upon the aspect of the times, in the following despondent terms —

"Our public Affairs interrupt all business and Commerce and our unfortunate conduct has made us so low and despicable amongst the Neighbouring Nations, that I am apprehensive we never shall be able to defend ourselves against our Enemies any longer!"

The learned Prestonian's fears were groundless. In a very short time, the genius and energy of the elder Pitt not only restored the military and naval prestige of Great Britain, but converted the dissatisfaction and despair of the people into boundless confidence and overflowing enthusiasm.

In 1797, a corps, named the "Royal Preston Volunteers," commanded by Lieutenant-colonel Grimshaw, was raised for the defence of the county; and in the following year another corps, commanded by Lieutenant-colonel Watson, was enrolled. A rifle corps was likewise formed, under the command of Captain William Brade, which, in 1808, along with Colonel Grimshaw and his men, voluntarily joined the militia.

These troops were encamped upon ground in the rear of the present barrack, at Fulwood, hence the names of "camp ground," and "camp field," which the locality bears to the present day. Last year, 1856, several bullets were found on the "Freehold Land Estate" in the immediate neighbourhood. They most probably had been deposited during the musket practice of this body of men.

Twice during the latter portion of the last century the celebrated Benjamin Franklin visited the town [p] His only daughter had married a Mr. Richard Bache, of Preston. A musical instrument is still in the possession of the widow of W Taylor, esq., Moss Cottage, which was made by Franklin, during one of his visits, as a toy for the amusement of his niece. It was exhibited at the temporary museum, prepared on the visit of the Lancashire and Cheshire Historic Society, in 1856. It is merely a series of square wooden rods, gradually diminishing in size, so as to form a scale of notes The rods are suspended a few inches apart by common cord. When struck by another rod, a weak but not unpleasing musical sound is produced Mr Edward Baines says, this instrument "is supposed to have been the germ of the harmonicon." Franklin was a friend of General Burgoyne, who represented Preston in several parliaments. Mr W. Dobson says:—"It has been stated that the original house at Cooper Hill, Walton-le-dale, was designed by General Burgoyne, and that a lightning conductor was put to it by Dr. Franklin" [q]

At the period of Prince Charles Stuart's invasion, Preston contained about six thousand inhabitants It at present numbers about eighty thousand. This rapid progress has resulted from the operation of influences more of a domestic or local character, the particulars of which will be fully recorded in succeeding chapters.

---

p In 1771 and 1775

q His Parliamentary Representation of Preston, p 29

PART I.—HISTORICAL.

CHAPTER VI.—MUNICIPAL GOVERNMENT, GUILD MERCHANT, Etc

Origin of Municipalities and Guilds Merchant—Preston Charters—The Custumale—The "Law of the Bretons" and Traditional Customs Probable Roman Origin—Saxon and Norman Boroughs—Charters of Henry II, John, Henry III., and Edward III.—Value of Property in the Lancashire Boroughs · Preston the wealthiest town in the County—Charters of Richard II., Henry IV., Henry V, and Elizabeth—Municipal Hospitality—"Booke of Orders"—By-laws against Foreigners, Public-House Tippling, and Vagabonds—Charitable Bequests—Fees of Inferior Officers—Civil War—Adam Morte's Contumacy—Charities—Imprisonment of Mayor and Bailiffs by Prince Rupert—Cock-fighting—Purchase of the Fee Farm Rent of Preston—Corporate Property in 1650—Grammar Schoolmaster's Salary—Public Wells—Regulations respecting Swine—Corporate Officers fined for neglect of Duty—Regulations respecting the "Corporation Pew" in the Parish Church—Workhouse Regulations—Grants to the Poor—Parliamentary Franchise—Limitation of the number of Freemen—Charters of Charles II—Disputes between the Burgesses and "Foreigners"—Early Guild Festivities—Guilds of 1682, 1762, 1782, 1802, 1822, and 1842—Municipal Reform Act—New Council—Freemen's Rights of Pasturage on Moor and Marsh—Corporation Regalia, etc—Corporate Property—Ribble Navigation—Post-Office—Loyal Addresses—Covered Market—Public Parks—Baths and Washhouses—The Queen at Fleetwood and Preston—Public Health Act—Cemetery—New Town Hall—Value of Corporate Property in 1855—Russian War · Celebration of the Peace—Guild Mayors—Mayors and Bailiffs since the commencement of the last century—Police Commission and Improvement Act—Local Board of Health—Waterworks—Sewerage of the Town—Parochial Affairs

There exists considerable difficulty in determining the precise period when Preston was first elevated to the dignity of a chartered borough or municipality. Mr. Sharon Turner, in his "History of the Anglo-Saxons," satisfactorily shows that "guilds" or social confederations were common anterior to the Norman conquest, yet, from the rules and other documents of several that have survived, it appears that, with a fair allowance for the condition and requirements of the period, they resembled much more, in character and objects, the trades unions and friendly societies of the present century, than corporate bodies, to whom were entrusted the local government of the people, and the protection of privileges enjoyed by chartered localities.

Henry I. is known to have conferred "hanse" privileges upon the curriers and cordwainers of Rouen, in his capacity as duke of Normandy, and to have granted them a charter of incorporation. Hanse and guild are not materially different in general import. The term "guild" is derived simply from the payment of a periodical contribution to a common fund for the benefit of the subscribers, or the prosecution of specific objects. The "Hanse" towns of Germany were incorporated at an early period, and formed a kind of commercial fraternity, with exclusive privileges of trade. The "*custumale*" of Preston, Mr. Edward Baines conjectures to have been granted by Henry II. The pendant seal has been lost, and the document itself is without date The corporation of Preston possesses a certificate, under the hand and seal of Sir Thomas Walmesley, a judge of the Court of Common Pleas, in the reign of James I., stating that he had seen a charter granted by Henry I to the burgesses of Preston, in the first year of that monarch's reign (1100). Mr Baines quotes, (vol. 4, page 303,) a fragment of one of the Kuerden manuscripts, in Heralds' College, from which it appears that in the "28th Henry III, an extent of the town was made by Sir John de Lee and eleven other free and lawful men of the wapentake, who returned that the town of Preston was demesne and made a free borough by the king's grandfather, which sets aside the assertion that Preston was so constituted by a charter of Henry I." Yet, (at page 340, vol. 4) he says:—"Dr. Kuerden asserts the same fact as Sir Thomas Walmesley: 'Preston in Amounderness was constituted a borough by Henry, son of the Empress, as appears ex Bundell Escact. Ao I. H. 3. n. 18.'" The "*custumale*" is, most probably, the document alluded to.

Dr. Whitaker printed the "custumale" apparently, according to Mr. Baines, from an ancient but imperfect copy. The latter authority published a translation by Mr. Cayley, of the Augmentation office, from a manuscript in the possession of the late Nicholas Grimshaw, esq., which, he says, "contains several passages which do not exist in the Latin;" but, "since it faithfully renders the remaining portions of the Custumale, may be considered as accurate with respect to the decayed passages." [a] This curious document, so illustrative of the customs and manners of the inhabitants, as well as of the ancient government of the borough, is as follows:—

"These are the liberties of Preston in Amoundrenesse —1. So that they shall have a Guild Merchant, with Hanse, and other customs, and belonging to such Guild; and so that no one who is not of that Guild shall make any merchandize in the said town, unless

a Kuerden gives a fragment imperfectly An amended translation of this passage, by Mr. Taylor, is as follows —"If any one should wish to be made a burgess let him come into the court, and pay twelve pence to the Prefect, and take his burgage from the pretors, and afterwards give one penny to the pretor's servant, and he shall bear witness that he was made a burgess in court. Also, no one can be a burgess, except he have a burgage twelve feet in front."

with the will of the burgesses —2. If any native [bondman] reside in the same town, and hold my land, and be in the same Guild and Hanse, and pay scoth and loth with the same burgesses for one year and a day, then he shall not be reclaimed by his lord, but shall remain free in the same town.—3 The burgesses of Preston in Amundrenesse shall have soc and sac, tol and them and infangthef, and they shall be quit throughout all my land of toll, lastage, passage, pontage, and stallage, from Lenegeld, [b] and Denegeld, and Gathwite, [c] and all other customs and actions throughout all our land and dominion, as well in England as in other our lands ; and that no sheriff shall intermeddle with the burgesses of Preston in Amundrenesse concerning any plea, or plaint, or dispute, or any other thing pertaining to the aforesaid town, saving [the pleas of] the king's crown —4. If any one wish to be made a burgess, he shall come into court and give to the mayor 12d. and shall take his burgage from the mayor; afterwards he shall give to the mayor's clerk one penny, that he may certify him to have been made a burgess in court —5 Also, when any burgess shall receive his burgage and it shall be a void place, the mayor shall admit him, so that he shall erect his burgage within forty days upon a forfeiture; but if he does not erect it, he shall be in mercy 12d —6. Also, when any burgess shall challenge his burgage against another, and shall prove it to be his right, and the tenant who holds it shall prove that burgage to have been held without challenge many years and days, and name for one year and one day, shall prove himself to have been possessed thereof, and shall prove the same in court by the oath of two of his neighbours to have been so held ; he who shall by them so prove shall hold without contradiction of the claimant whoever that claimant may be, for one day and one year on this side the sea of England —7. Also, if any burgess complain of any matter and another challenge against him, the plaintiff for judgment shall name two witnesses, and shall have one of them at the day and term, and he may have any lawful person for witness and another burgess, but the defendant against a burgess shall be put to his oath at third hand [d] by his peers —7. Also, the amerciament in our court shall not exceed 12d unless for toll evaded, and then the amerciament shall be 12s. —8. Also, a burgess shall be bound to come to no more than three portmotes yearly, unless he shall have plea against him, and unless he shall come to some one great portmote he shall be amerced 12d [e]—9. The mayor shall collect the king's farm at the four terms of the year, and shall go once for the farm, and another time if he pleases, and shall take away [deponet hostium, pull down] the door of the burgage, and the burgess shall not replace his door until he have paid his debt, unless at the will of the mayor —10. Also, if any burgess shall buy any bargain or any merchandize, and give earnest, and he who sold shall repent of his bargain, he shall double the earnest ; but if the buyer shall

b "Dr. Whitaker suggests that this word is formed from the low Latin *lena*, a blanket, but is it not more consistent with the context, to consider it as Langeld, a land-tax ?"—Baines.

c "Dr Whitaker has *Gothewite*, which he takes to be formed from gote, a ditch, or gutter. It is, however, no other than Grithwite, the fine for breach of the peace, a very common term in Saxon and Anglo-Norman laws."—Baines.

d "That is, shall have two witnesses besides himself."—Baines.

e "'A portmote,' says Dr. Whitaker, 'was a court convened for the purpose of hearing and determining causes relating to a harbour It may surely therefore be inferred, that Preston was then a seaport town. There are many reasons for believing that the tides rose much higher up the Ribble than at present' This reasoning, however, is not conclusive, there was a portmote at Manchester, which could not have been at any time a seaport town The word *port* is from the Teutonic, and not from the French or Latin, it signifies any city or walled town as well as a harbour, and it enters into the composition of the names of several inland towns, as Stockport, Aldport, Newport Pagnell, &c."—Baines.—Without the tides rising any higher than at the present time, the Ribble was capable of floating to Preston a large class of the merchant vessels in use at the period referred to. See chap 1, page 52.

have handled the goods, he shall either have the merchandize or 5s. from the seller.—11. Also, if any burgess shall have drink for sale, he shall sell according to the assize made by the burgesses, unless it shall be replaced by the tunnel.—12. Also, a burgess shall not come to the mayor after sunset for any claim, if he is unwilling, unless the claim be made by a stranger.—13. Also, a burgess shall accommodate his lord out of his bargain, and the lord shall pay for it to him within 40 days, but if he doth not, the burgess shall not accommodate him again until he shall pay.—14. Also, no one can be a burgess unless he hold a burgage of 12 feet in front.—15. Also, if a burgess shall sell for more than the assize he shall be in mercy 12d. and he who brought in nothing; so the burgess of the court aforesaid shall have fuel, fire, and water, to make judgment.—16. Also, if any be taken for theft or breach of trust and be condemned, he who sued shall do justice.—17. Also, if a burgess wound another and he shall be willing to agree amicably, he shall give for every bruise the breadth of a thumb 4d. and for every wound 8d.; and whoever is wounded may prove what he has lost by the wound, and the other shall return to him what he has paid to the surgeon for healing the wound: and the arms shall be brought to him, and he shall swear upon his arms that he has been wounded and such things have been done to him, and that, if his friends consent, he will take what is offered to him.—18. Also, if a burgess complain of another burgess that he owes a debt to him, and the other shall acknowledge the debt, the reeve shall command him to avoid the debt, and render the debt within 8 days, upon pain of forfeiture, 8d. for the first week, 12d. for the second, and so for every week until he shall render the debt; but if he shall deny the debt, and the plaintiff hath witnesses, he shall deny by a third hand upon oath, and the plaintiff shall be amerced 12d. And if the defendant shall come with his witnesses, and the plaintiff shall not come, the defendant shall be quit and the plaintiff in mercy; and if the plaintiff shall not be able to come and place any one in his stead before the court, he may take the defendant's oath. And that no plaint or forfeiture shall be set on the burgesses in the court aforesaid exceeding 12d. unless he shall vouched to duel, and duel shall be adjudged to him; but if duel shall be adjudged to him and waged he shall be in mercy 40s.—19. Also, if a burgess marry his daughter or grand-daughter to any one, he may marry her without the license of any one.—20. Also, a burgess may make an oven upon his ground, and take furnage for one load of meal [suma farris, *seam of corn*, Whitaker,] one halfpenny, and he whose meal or corn it shall be, shall find wood to heat the oven.—21. Also, the burgesses shall not go to the oven nor to the kiln unless they please.—22. Also, if any one's kiln shall take fire, and it have one door, he shall give 40d. and if it have two doors half a mark.—23. Also, if the burgesses by the common council of the neighbourhood shall travel for any business of the town, their expenses shall be rendered to them when they return.—24. Also, a stranger may not participate in any merchandize with the burgesses of our town.—25. Also, when a burgess shall be desirous to sell his burgage, his next of kin is to buy that burgage before any other, and when it shall be sold and he hath not another burgage, when the other shall be seized he shall give 4d. from the issue, but if he hath another burgage he shall give nothing.—26. Also, if a burgess shall be in mercy for bread and ale, the first, second, or third time, he shall be in mercy 12d. but the fourth time he shall go the cuck-stool. f—27. Also, if a burgess of the

f "'Ibit at Cuckestolam.' There are several fields adjoining to the corner of the Moor near St. Paul's church, known by the name of the '*Cuck Stool* Pit Field,' to this day. Insolvent burgesses were submitted to the chastisement of the correctional chair, and it is probable that a species of domestic delinquents underwent the same cooling operation. How this matter may be, we have not now the power to determine, but a passage in the history of Liverpool and Ormskirk may shed some light on this curious subject. Not more than forty-five years ago, a Cuck-stool complete stood over a pit, near Longton, on the way from Preston to Liverpool, adjoining the turnpike-road."—Baines.

town die a sudden death his wife and his heirs shall quietly have all his chattels and lands, so that neither his lord nor the justices may lay hands on the houses or chattels of the deceased, unless he shall have been publicly excommunicated, in which case by the council of the priest and of the neighbours they are to be expended in alms.—28. Also, the wife of the deceased may marry whomsoever she please —29. Also, if any one shall demand a debt of another before the reeve, if he be unwilling to pay, the mayor shall render to the plaintiff his debt from the king's purse, and shall distrain the other by his chattels that he pay the debt, or he shall seize the house into his hands —30. Also, the burgesses shall not receive claim from the reeve on a market day unless the claim be made by a stranger.—31 Also, a burgess gives no transit —32. Also, a burgess hath common pasture every where, except in corn-fields, meadows, and hayes.—33. Also, if a burgess shall strike the mayor or reeve of the borough in court, and shall be convicted, he shall henceforth be in mercy for the offence —34 Also, if the reeve shall strike any one out of court, he shall be in mercy for his offence.—35. Also, if a burgess shall strike the reeve out of court, he shall be in mercy 40s.—36 Also, if a burgess shall overcome another, if he confess it, he shall forfeit 12d.; if he deny it, he shall clear himself by oath.—37. Also, if any one bearing false money shall be taken, the reeve shall render to the king the false monies as many as there are, and shall account in the rent of his farm for the goods, and deliver his body to our lord the king for judgment to be done.—38. Also, it shall not be lawful for regrators to buy anything which shall be sold on a market day to a regrator until the bells be rung in the evening, nor in any day in the week, until that which he bought shall be in the town for one night.—39. Also, the aforesaid burgesses shall not go in any expedition unless with the lord himself, unless they may be able to return on the same day.—40. If any one shall be summonod when the justice of the town shall be in the expedition and shall not go, and shall acknowledge himself to have heard, he shall forfeit 12d ; if he denies to have heard the edict, shall clear himself by his own oath, but if he shall have essoin, to wit, either by his wife's lying in childbed of a son, or other reasonable essoin, he shall not pay. If he is going with the person of our lord the king, he shall not have essoin.—41. Also, it is the custom of the borough that no burgess ought to be taken for an accusation by the lord or by the reeve if he have sufficient pledges so of claim made in the borough by any knight, if duel be adjudged between the burgess and knight, the knight may not find a substitute unless it be found that he ought not to fight —42. If the reeve command any burgess by another than his own servant and he shall not come, he shall forfeit nothing —43. Also, no justice shall lay hands on the house or chattels of any deceased.—44. Also, if any one call a married woman a whore, and complaint be made thereof, and witnesses be absent, she may clear herself by her own oath; and he by whom it was said shall do this justice, that he shall take himself by the nose and say he hath spoken a lie, and shall be pardoned · there is the same judgment as to a widow.

"This is the law of Preston in Amoundrenesse which they have from the law of the Bretons."

Considerable difference of opinion obtains as to the precise meaning to be attached to the expression, "which they have from the law of the Bretons." Some conjecture the passage alludes to certain privileges enjoyed by the natives of Brittany or Armorica, others to prescriptive customs descended through the Saxon and Danish periods from the ancient inhabitants, or from the Brittani or "Romanised Britons." Holinshed, in his description of England, says :—

"Martia surnamed Proba, or the Just, was the widow of Gutiline, king of the Britons, and was left protectoress of the realm during the minority of her son. Perceiving much in the conduct of her subjects which needed reformation, she devised sundry wholesome laws which the Britons, after her death, named the Martian statutes. Alfred caused the laws of this excellently learned princess, whom all commended for her knowledge of the Greek tongue, to be established in the realm."

These laws received many additions and improvements up to the time of the Confessor, under whose name they are continually referred to, as the code of the English people. The great effort of the commonalty, Anglo-Norman, as well as Saxon, for some time after the conquest, was directed to procure the re-enactment of these cherished laws The sovereigns of the new dynasty, and especially Henry II., frequently propitiated their subjects by concessions in this direction. It is most probable, therefore, that previously enjoyed municipal laws and privileges of Preston are implied by the "law of the Bretons."

With reference to the opinion that the Roman municipal form of government, including the "Guilds Merchant" and other customs, was adopted or imitated by the Saxon conquerors, one writer says:—

"It is a point of curious inquiry, not yet, so far as we know, fully discussed, to ascertain how far the Saxons, on their invasion of the island, moulded or adapted their political institutions to those which they must have found existing in Roman Britain. The Saxons, we know, ultimately possessed themselves of all the Roman walled cities, of which they formed their boroughs; and it is hardly conceivable that a comparatively small body of invaders would completely overturn all those municipal institutions, which, though less free than their own, would present them, so far as administration was concerned, with useful means for securing and consolidating their acquisitions." g

Mr. Thomas Wright, contends that, as the constitution of the Roman towns, with their *curiales*, or senators, and their municipal officers, were all preserved after the Teutonic conquests, in the cities in Gaul and the other Roman provinces on the continent, they were no doubt also preserved in Britain. He says:—

"We have unfortunately few documents which throw any light on the condition of the towns in England during the Saxon period of our history; but we cannot help recognising in the Roman *curia* the origin of the elective body in our medieval towns, the *probi homines* of the older records, the burgesses, who, like the *curiales* or senators, obtained their rank by birth or election. The *duumviri* answered to the two *ballivi* or bailiffs, or, as the Saxons called them *præfecti* or *reeves*, who were the chief magistrates in our medieval boroughs. The *principales* were the *scabini (echevins)* of the continental towns in England, generally known by the Saxon name of aldermen." h

Mr. Wright, in support of this view, instances several rights and privileges retained in the Saxon period by the Roman municipal towns, and especially Worcester, Exeter, and London. The latter he clearly shows, not only preserved its relative independence, through the stormy period

g Pen Cyclop, art. Britannia

h Celt, Roman, and Saxon, p. 437.

when the Danish and Saxon chieftains contended for mastery, but that the invaders were often beaten back from the walls of London by the free citizens when the monarch was discomfited in the open field. The Norman William was compelled to make conditions with them before they would acknowledge his sovereignty. Mr. Wright says :—"In a dispute with the abbot of Bury, in the twelfth century, the citizens of London, so far from admitting (as Brady supposed), that their privileges were newly acquired from their Norman sovereigns, professed to have enjoyed them from the first foundation of their city, which they carried as far back as the foundation of Rome." [i]

It appears pretty clear that a considerable portion, at least, of the Roman walled towns in Britain, inhabited chiefly by the remains of the Romano-British population, compounded with the Saxon conquerors for the retention of their ancient privileges, and that the Teutonic chiefs, especially on the north-western portion of England, imitated, to a considerable extent, the form and character of the Roman administration. Palgrave, alluding particularly to the Cumbrian Britons, whose territory at one time extended to the Ribble, affirms that "as soon as the royal authority became developed on Roman ground, all their kings took upon themselves, as far as they could, to govern according to the spirit of the Roman policy, and agreeably to the maxims prevailing at the decline of the empire." Mr. Hodgson Hinde says :—

> "At the very period to which on other grounds we have assigned the extermination of the native dynasties in Lancashire" (the reign of Egfrid or Ecgfrith, who ruled from 670 to 685), "we find for the first time in the Northumbrian annals, the appointment of a new class of officers, who are variously styled by Beda—'tribuni,' 'duces,' and 'præfecti,'—whose administration appears to have extended not only to the Britons, but to the subject Picts, and even to the Irish, who were partially subdued by Ecgfrith. After his reign, and the *contraction of the territory of his successors*, the authority of these officers was necessarily confined to the Britons."[j]

The Saxons were originally strongly attached to pastoral or agricultural pursuits, and often declined from a superstitious feeling, to occupy houses built by a people they had conquered Many of the smaller and imperfectly fortified Roman towns were unquestionably destroyed in the sanguinary contests between the Britanni and the "Picts and Scots," and likewise during the gradual conquest by the Teutonic races. Hence Preston most probably rose from the ruins of Roman Coccium, or the victorious Saxon chieftain may have preferred the erection of a new home-

i "Et dicebant cives Lundonienses fuisse de theloneo in omni foro, et semper et ubique, per totam Angliam, a tempore quo Roma primo fundata fuit, civitatem Lundoniæ eodem tempore fundatam. Joscelline de Brakelonde, p 56."—Celt, Roman, and Saxon, p 444.

j Lan and Ches His. Soc. Trans., vol. 8, p. 19 —See chap 2, p 65, of the present work.

stead or "tun," on the northern bank of the river, either from the superstitious feeling referred to, or from a natural preference of the site as a *residence*, if not as a *fortress*. To some extent the Roman forms of municipal government may have been transferred to the new location. This is quite consistent with Mr. Wright's theory. He says:—

"Although the municipal privileges were all derived directly from the Romans, it does not of course follow that such privileges were enjoyed only by towns which had been founded in Roman times. As the Saxons became established throughout the island, they adopted, to a certain degree, the manners of their Roman predecessors, they founded other towns, and they naturally imitated the forms, presented to their view in the Roman models already existing. Most of these were, as the Roman towns had become, *royal towns*, that *is they had no superior lord but the king*. But others, after the conversion of the Saxons to Christianity, gradually sprung up about, and *under the protection of episcopal sees and abbeys, and these eventually received their rights and privileges at the hands of their ecclesiastical protectors*. * * The judicial entries on the fly leaves of the Exeter manuscript, written before and after the Conquest, show us that the municipal forms and conditions of that city underwent no change upon the transfer of the English crown to a Norman line of sovereigns; *and such was probably the case in all other cities and towns then in existence*. But, although their privileges and constitution were in principle untouched, in practice they were frequently trespassed upon. A new race of feudal lords had entered upon the land, who were ignorant of the customs of the people over whom they had intruded themselves, and who had little respect for any customs which stood as obstacles to the gratification of their views of aggrandisement. This must have led to continual riots and disturbances in the old Saxon towns, and to the infringement of their privileges where they had little power to obtain permanent redress. After undergoing all these vexations during a few years, they saw the advantages—or we may perhaps better say the necessity—of *purchasing from the king written charters confirming their old rights*, which became an effective protection in a court of law. Thus originated municipal charters, which are rather to be considered as a *proof of the antiquity, than of the novelty*, of the privileges they grant. They were given most abundantly under Henry II. and his sons, when it became the policy of the English monarchs to seek the support of the independent burghers against a turbulent feudal aristocracy." k

If Walton-le-dale be the Coccium of Antoninus, and ever possessed anything resembling the privileges mentioned by Richard of Cirencester, it is by no means improbable that many of its forms of civil administration, its privileges, and immunities, may have descended through the Saxon municipality of Preston, to the period of the Norman conquest. The phrase, "This is the law of Preston, in Amoundrenesse, which they have from the law of the Bretons," may thus be satisfactorily interpretated. Dr. Kuerden appears to have entertained a firm conviction of the Roman origin of the more antiquated municipal formulæ of the borough of Preston. He says:—

"In antient time of the early Saxons it" (Preston), "was ruled by a Portgrave formerly, and then in Latin call'd Prefectus or Prepositus, being the king's immediate officer in that burrough, which had the liberty of keeping 3 port-motes per annu. Two of them, as I conceive, in success of time being changed into the nature of 2 Leet dayes, after King Alfred's time, and the other grand port-mote to this day" (about 1686) "being styled Magna Curia Lete, being a Court for election of new Magistrates within

k Celt, Roman, and Saxon, p. 449.

the burrough. They had likewise two other officers of note within the burrough then styled Pretores, a title or office no doubt derived from the Roman time, and that there have been such officers within the burrough is manifest from an antient roll or charter of liberties kept amongst their antient records." [l]

A municipal custom, somewhat peculiar, is yet observed in Preston, which may possibly have descended from the Roman period. The mayor and members of the corporation are preceded, on state occasions, by two officers in livery, each bearing a halberd. These weapons are placed outside of the door of the residence of the mayor for the time being, as insignia of his office. There is some difficulty in tracing this practice to any other source than the one suggested, notwithstanding its great antiquity. The right to carry a mace is conceded by the charter of Elizabeth, but no mention is made of halberds. The "Custumale" gives to the mayor, within the borough, the authority of sheriff in all matters "saving the" (pleas of the) "king's crown." Are the halberds carried before the chief magistrate by virtue of this privilege? The sheriff of the county, in the execution of his duty, is escorted by a troop of javelin men. If such be the case, it is not improbable both customs may have originated from the practice of the Romans, whose superior magistrates were escorted by twelve lictors, while those invested with more limited authority were preceded by two. Dr. Leigh, alluding to the improvements effected by the Emperor Trajan, says, "he constituted in *Britain the Municipal Laws;* at Sessions and Assizes ordered the Rods and Axes to be presented to the Backs and Necks of the common people." [m]

The Preston halberds are by no means indifferent modern representatives of the Roman *fasces* and *secures,* or the bundle of rods with an axe stuck in the centre. The shaft is much decorated, and the brass head exhibits an axe as well as a spear. A similar custom is observed at Lancaster, and by many of the "mock corporations," (some of which are of old standing), in the neighbourhood of Preston. The newly incorporated municipality of Blackburn has adopted the halberds; but the practice is not common in other parts of England. Notwithstanding their Roman origin, many practices, peculiar to the Saxon people, were engrafted upon the elder municipal institutions, and some of these contain the germs of the most cherished portions of the present "constitution" of the country. The peculiarity and extent of this modification is thus forcibly described by a modern writer:—

"The municipal organization of the Anglo-Saxons was not confined to their towns; it pervaded the whole territory; the modern distinction between personal and political

---

l The "Custumale" is perhaps the document referred to

m His Lan, Ches, etc., p 73.

freedom was unknown; the right to a weapon for his personal defence, and a vote in the affairs of the town or district, were regarded as inalienably attached to every free man. This leading principle of the Anglo-Saxon polity, directly descended from those continental Germans, whose free spirit Tacitus has so clearly and forcibly exhibited, must be borne in mind to estimate the relative position of the Anglo-Saxon boroughs. They were not like the boroughs of modern times, isolated municipalities in the midst of large tracts of country, subject, in matters of local judicature and taxation, to magistrates directly nominated by the central authority of the state; they were only parts of one great municipal system, extending over the whole territory. The principal boroughs existing at the period of the Norman conquest were the towns still girt by the walls and towers erected under the Roman *regime*. The state of the age, the prevalence of warfare, both on the large and petty scale, the constant liability to foreign incursion, made walls and trenches necessary to the security not only of trading towns, but of isolated mansions; and *byrig*, *burgh*, or borough as it is now written, was still the genuine term for all. But the boroughs by distinction, the boroughs in political estimation, were those towns," (apparently all considerable ones) "which had each, under the name usually of *burgh-reve* or *port reve*, an elective municipal officer, exercising functions analagous to those of the elective *reve* of the shire, or *shire-reve*. [n]

After the conquest, the Norman chieftains for some period abrogated the free municipal liberties of the Saxon people. According to the Domesday survey, guild-halls of municipal towns were included in the grants of the Conqueror. The king's revenue had previously been collected by the elective heads of the shires and municipalities. The Saxon shire *reeve* was displaced and a Norman *viscount* appointed in his stead. A *bailiff*, appointed by the king, superseded the *borough reeve*. It was the practice of the earlier Norman monarchs to farm these bailwicks to the highest bidder, in consequence of which the inhabitants were subjected to the most unprincipled and reckless extortion. With the view to rid themselves of this odious system, beneath which all commercial enterprise or industrial energy must have speedily perished, several of the municipalities were induced to outbid the parties farming their revenues, and thus pay the tax directly to the king. This proved more profitable to the crown, and hence the frequent charters granting the revenue to the *burgesses* in *fee farm*, that is in permanent possession, so long as the stipulated crown "rent" was regularly paid. Under such circumstances the ancient mode of administration would be resumed; but the Norman *mayor* was substituted for *reeve*. This was more agreeable to the Saxon population than the term *bailiff*; mayor signifying a municipal officer in the language of the conquerors. The obnoxious term *bailiff* was, however, retained by many corporate towns. The constitution of all municipal bodies for several centuries after the Conquest, was of a purely democratic character. The Saxon *Folkemote*, or meeting of all the inhabitants, enacted the burgh-laws, or by-laws, levied local taxes, administered justice, sold or leased public lands, appointed the municipal executive, and transacted any other

n Pen. Cyclop., art. Borough.

business affecting the welfare of the general community. The meetings of the urban boroughs were held at the "Mote," "Moot," or Common Hall, which was likewise sometimes denominated, where the Danish nomenclature prevailed, the *hus-tings*, a term now exclusively confined to the arena-set apart for the election of members to serve in parliament. The Norman and Plantagenet princes frequently founded free boroughs in populous manors, to which they granted some of the older municipal privileges. Parties who took land and erected dwellings in these "royal burghs" were exempted from many of the royal and manorial taxes, not only in the town where they resided, but in all the royal boroughs in the kingdom. The land belonging to the king alone conferred these exemptions. All other holders in the borough were subjected to the tax due to the crown. So highly was this privilege valued that large sums were sometimes paid to secure the freedom. An instance is recorded in the borough of Carlisle, where one David *Le-Tinctor*, or David the Dyer, paid a sum equal to ten pounds of the present value of money, to have his own house made into a burgage tenement. The free boroughs, likewise, having the privilege of trying offences committed within their boundaries, escaped the payment of the heavy fees charged in the courts attached to the hundred or county.

The charter of Henry II., which is without date, [o] briefly confers upon the burgesses of Preston the privileges previously granted to "his burgesses of Newcastle-under-Lyne." What these privileges were, can only at the present time be surmised, as the Newcastle charter is lost. The probability is that it differed but very slightly from similar documents of the period, and included immunities from tolls,[p] the privileges of a guild merchant, and judicial authority within the borough.

In the confirmation of this charter by King John, the privileges are described as the "liberties and free customs which the lord H , our father, gave, granted, and by his charter confirmed to the same burgesses, the whole toll of the Wapentake hundred of Amounderness, and a free fair at Preston, at the Assumption of St. Mary, to last eight days." John, in

o "The charter of Henry II. is without date, but in the by-laws of the corporation of Preston, it is said to have been granted in the tenth year of his reign, this, however, appears to be incorrect, for John of Oxford, bishop of Norwich, who is one of the witnesses to the charter, was not made a bishop of Norwich until 1175, about the 21st Henry II. The better opinion, therefore, is that the charter was granted in the 26th year of his reign, 1179 or 1180, in the former of which years he spent his Christmas at Winchester, where the charters appear to have been granted.—See Holinshead, vol. 3, p. 102."—Edward Baines.

p "Thelonium is a payment in towns, markets, and fairs, for goods and cattle bought and sold. According to Bracton (ii 24), it implies a liberty as well to *take*, as to be *free* from toll."—Note to Dr. Lingard's translation of the Preston charters.

addition, granted "the right of pasturage in the forest which is called Fulwood, and out of the forest itself as much (wood) as they shall want towards building their town, on the view of our foresters."

Henry III. confirmed the previously acquired privileges. From the preamble of a second charter, in the year 1252, and the 27th year of his reign, we learn that complaint had been made of encroachment on the part of the burgesses upon the king's forest rights. By this charter, however, Henry confers a legal title to the pasturage, etc., previously disputed. The document says:—

"Whereas it is known to *us* by an inquisition which we caused to be taken by our sheriff of Lancaster, that three hundred and twenty-four acres of land, as well of the old as of the new purpresture,[q] which our burgesses of Preston, in Amounderness, have made under our enclosure of Fulwood, belong to our borough of Preston, and not the said enclosure (which purpresture reaches to the following boundaries, to wit: along the rivulet of Ennisbrock at Ribbleton, as far as where that rivulet falls into the water of Sannocke, and so proceeding along that water of Sannocke, as far as the old dyke, which is the division between Preston and Tulketh), we have granted and by this our charter have confirmed for ourselves and our heirs, that the burgesses and their heirs shall have that purpresture for ever; and that on the moor towards our wood of Fulwood, without the cover of the said wood, and within the said boundaries, they may break up ground, and bring it into cultivation as they shall please, without any impeachment of our foresters or verderors;[r] yet so that they come not within forty perches of the cover of the said wood. Saving also to the burgesses aforesaid, and their heirs aforesaid, their right of turbary and pasturage on the said moor, and of sufficient underwood[s] in the same wood, without waste or impeachment of our foresters or verderors aforesaid."

Edward III., in 1328, after confirming all previous rights and privileges, further grants "to the same burgesses that they and their heirs shall have for ever a weekly market in the aforesaid town of Preston, in the county of Lancaster, and a fair in like manner every year, to last five days, to wit on the vigil and feast of the apostles Simon and Jude, and on the three days next following, provided that market and that fair be not to the prejudice of the adjoining markets and adjoining fairs."

In the reign of Edward III. (1343), an inquiry was made into the value of property of all the boroughs in the kingdom. There were only four "royal burghs" in Lancashire at that period,—Preston, Liverpool, Lancaster, and Wigan. From this document[t] it appears that Preston was the wealthiest of the four:—

"Borough of Preston. The undersigned made inquiry as to the true value of the ninth part of the goods of the men dwelling in the borough of Preston, and found that the true value was £6 17s. 4d. Albert Fitz Robert, John de Wiche, Galfred de Hakenshou, Nicholas de Preston, William Smyth, and Roger de Bluwath."

---

q "Purpresture (from *pour prendre*, to take for one's own use) signifies an encroachment on the right or desemne of the king."—Note to Lingard's Translation.

r "Verderor is one whose office is to look to the preservation of the *vert* in the forest, that is of every thing bearing green leaves, and affording cover for deer."—Ibid.

s "Clausura often means brushwood, to make fences or enclosures."—Ibid.

t Nonarum Inquisitiones,—Lan.

The £6 17s 4d. has been computed to be rather more than equal to £100 of the present value. The whole of the moveable property of Preston at the time would not amount, even with this allowance, to £1000. Liverpool returned £6 16s. 7d., Lancaster £6 13s. 6d., and Wigan £5 9s 4d Manchester had not sufficient trade to be taxed.

Richard II. merely confirmed "to our beloved burgesses now being of the said town of Preston," the privileges granted by his predecessors.

Henry IV., in the second year of his reign (1401), was equally gracious to his "beloved burgesses;" and added powers for the recovery of any of their previously granted privileges which "their predecessors and fore-runners by some chance might not have hitherto fully used"

Henry V's charter (1414), confirms the additional powers granted by his father. Philip and Mary, in 1557, likewise endorsed the acts of their predecessors.

The great charter of Elizabeth, granted in 1565, is, however, a much more important document It more fully sets forth the privileges, duties, and powers of the corporation and burgesses It appears from the preamble, that application had been made to the queen for the gracious extension to the borough of the royal favour, and that in consequence thereof the charter was granted, by which Preston was declared to "be and remain for ever after a free corporate borough in deed fact and name for ever, of one mayor, two bailiffs, and the burgesses of the borough of Preston, in the county of Lancaster; and that the said mayor, bailiffs and burgesses of that borough shall be hereafter one commonalty, and one body corporate and political, in deed fact and name for ever."

Power is then given to the corporate body, to "implead and be impleaded, sue and be sued, defend and be defended, answer and be answered," in all courts within the queen's dominions. The privilege of using a "common seal" is next accorded, with the power to "break, change, or make anew that seal at their pleasure." The document next concedes to the body corporate the right to the acquisition of "demesnes, manors, lands, tenements, rents, revenues, hereditaments, liberties, franchises, rights, jurisdictions, and privileges whatsoever, which are held of us immediately in chief, or otherwise by military service."

The charter next provides for the appointment of "twenty-four of the more discreet and worthy men of the said borough," to be called "principal burgesses," and entrusted with the performance of the functions of a common council, "to make and enact from time to time by themselves, or by the greater part of them, with the mayor of the said borough for the time being, statutes, acts, and ordinances, touching and concerning the public advantage and profit of the same borough, and the inhabitants thereof for the time being." Power is likewise granted to the mayor, bailiffs, and burgesses, "according to their discretion," to "make appoint, and admit other burgesses from among the more worthy inhabitants of that borough to be burgesses of the same borough." The privilege of making by-laws, and the power to punish their infringement, by either corporal punishment or by fine and amercement, is likewise conceded.

The document then proceeds to nominate the first mayor, bailiffs, and other officers, who are to exercise their official functions until the election of their successors, "at the feast of St. Wilfrid, archbishop, next ensuing." The following gentlemen, who are severally styled "our beloved," received the honour of these appointments:—Mayor, Evan Walle; bailiffs, Richard Banester, and William Robson; "twelve principal burgesses," or common councilmen,—Oliver Brerers, William Hodgkynson, Christopher Haidock, Thomas Typpinge, Thomas Walle, William Banester, Thomas Brerers, William Clayton, Henry Blundell, Richard Arram, Richard Banester, and John Hynde. The mayor is appointed clerk to the market, "coroner within the said borough, and the liberties and precincts thereof," and justice of the peace.

"A certain house within the said borough, vulgarly called the Toll-booth, otherwise the Moot-hall," is next ordained to be "the common hall and house of the said mayor, bailiffs, and burgesses and their successors for ever, as well to make therein their assemblies and meetings, as to hold and treat therein all and every their courts, pleas, causes, matters, consultations, and affairs, whatsoever, from time to time."

The charter then provides for the election of the future mayors and other officers, "in the week next before the feast of St. Wilfrid, archbishop." "Two persons[u] of the more discreet and worthy inhabitants of the said borough" are to be chosen, one by the mayor, and the other by the "capital burgessess," who "shall corporally make oath before the mayor that they, with convenient speed, will choose and name twenty-four others of the more discreet burgesses dwelling within the said borough to choose and name, a new mayor, a new bailiff, to be called the town's baylie, and a new sergeant to be called the town's sergeant. * * * And if the twenty-four men aforesaid cannot consent and agree together in their choice, then we will that the choice and will of the major part of the same take effect as was used heretofore."

u Kuerden describes these two officers by the title of "Eleisors." He likewise gives at length the forms of the oaths taken by these officers, and all others acting under the charter of incorporation. From his description it would appear that these elections were followed by much feasting and hospitality, the church bells contributing a "joyful noise" in honour of the newly appointed functionaries.—See "Brief description of Preston," edited by John Taylor.

Provision is then made for the supplying of vacancies, in case of the death of the mayor, bailiff, or town sergeant. The right of election in such cases is vested in the "capital burgesses or the major part of them," who are required to meet for such purpose, within eight days after the death or removal of any of the above-named officials.

Authority is given to the mayor, "whenever it shall so please him to name, choose, and appoint one honest and fit person, being a burgess and inhabitant of the said borough, to be and bear the office of bailiff, called the mayor's baylie, as long as the same mayor shall be or remain in office." The mayor is likewise authorised to appoint a burgess "to be and bear the office of sub-bailiff, called the sergeant-at-mace, * * * for making, performing, and executing proclamations, arrests, processes, executions, and other things pertaining to his office, * * * in like manner and form as the sergeants-at-mace in our city of London do and execute" And likewise "that the same sergeant-at-mace, so named, appointed, and chosen, may and can bear a mace, engraven with our arms, within the limits and bounds of the said borough."

Authority is granted to the corporation to compel the acceptance of any office to which a burgess may have been elected, under the penalties of fine or imprisonment.

In case of the death or removal of a capital burgess, power is given to the mayor and the other capital burgesses still remaining, to elect another to fill the vacancy.

The privilege of holding a Guild Merchant is confirmed in the following terms:—"Moreover, we have granted, and by these, for ourselves, our heirs and successors, we have confirmed to the aforesaid mayor, bailiffs, and burgesses of the said borough of Preston, and their successors, that the said mayor, bailiffs, and burgesses, and their successors, shall have a Gild Merchant in the aforesaid borough, with all the liberties and free customs appertaining to such a gild, as they have heretofore enjoyed." [v]

The charter next invests the corporation with the privilege of "assize and assay [w] of bread, wine, and beer, and other victuals; the ulnage [x] and sealing of all cloths, weights and measures whatsoever, and the amendment and correction thereof, and of all things belonging or appertaining to the office of our clerk of the market."

A court to be held every three weeks, before the mayor, bailiffs, and seneschal,[y] is next granted, with full "power and authority to hear and

v "The members of a gild-merchant, beside other liberties, had that of holding certain pleas of land within their precincts."—Note to Dr Lardner's Translation

w "The power of fixing the price and examining the quality of these articles."—Ibid.

x "Ulnage and sealing imply the office of measurer of the length and breadth of every piece of cloth, and of the searcher, who, by seals, pointed out the faults in each "—Ibid

y The recorder

determine, by plaints in the same, concerning all and every kind of debts, accounts, covenants, and contracts, trespasses by force and arms, or otherwise, done in contempt of us, our heirs and successors," etc. Power is likewise given to receive "all recognizances whatsoever between merchant and merchant, and of doing execution thereupon, according to the statute of merchants lately enacted in the statutes of Acton Burnell." The "view of frank pledge" is next granted, or the power of holding a court, for the reception of pledges or sureties in behalf of all persons above the age of fourteen, as guarantees for their loyalty to the sovereign.

The privilege of holding a weekly market on Saturdays, and two annual fairs, "as heretofore," is next accorded, with a "court of pie-poudre," or "court of record, held at fairs and markets, to do justice between buyers and sellers, and to redress disorders." [z] Upon the body corporate is likewise conferred "the stallage," piccage,[a] fines, amercements, and all other profits, commodities, and emoluments whatsoever appertaining, happening, arising, or belonging to such market, fairs, and court of pie poudre aforesaid."

The ancient limits and boundaries of the borough are confirmed, and the privilege of "perambulating" accorded, "as often as it shall seem to them necessary to be done." This interesting document concludes with a *resume*, or general grant of all the privileges, etc., previously enjoyed.

In the 1st and 2nd Elizabeth, it appears, from the duchy records, that a dispute arose respecting the privileges of the mayor. It was eventually decided that, by grants to the town, they had "omes oid securitates pacis," and that the mayor had continually been in the habit of taking sureties for the peace in Preston

The earliest record of the transactions of the corporation in their possession at the present time, is inscribed:—"This is the Booke of Orders for the Towne of Preston," (in) "Amoundernes in the Countie of Lancaster, Richard Blundell, maior, 1608." From this document it appears that, the maintenance of the character of the town for hospitality and good cheer, originally formed no unimportant item on the roll of municipal duties. On the 26th August, 1612, a resolution was passed, relieving the bailiffs from their then somewhat undue share, in this agreeable but somewhat expensive privilege. The document says:—

"Whereas, heretofore of ancient tyme y[t] hath beene used and accustumed within this towne of Preston, that the Bailives thereof for the time being att the Feast of Easter yearelie, should to their greate and excessive

---

z Note to Dr Lardner's Translation.

a Stallage is the money paid for the liberty of erecting stalls in markets and fairs. Piccage is the money paid for breaking up the ground for similar purposes.—Ibid

charge, provide wine, beare, breade, cheese, ayle, and other bankettinge stuff and provisions, as well for the maior of the said Towne, and his brethren the comon counsell of the same, and all other the burgesses thereof for the time beinge, as alsoe for all other strangers, passengers, and neighbours repairing to the same towne, by reason whereof the concourse and assemblie of people att the same tymes did grow greater, very Turbulent and unrulie, tending" (not only) "to the breache of His Ma[te] peace" (but also) "divers other Inconveniences thereof, very likely to ensue to the greate p.udice of the whole corporation & the peaceable govern[t] thereof, and therein of ancient time used and enjoyed."

The resolution, therefore, provides that the bailiffs should be "eased in some sorte of that greate and unnecessary charge," and that, in lieu thereof, a certain sum should be paid by them for a "more godlie, lawdable, and charitable purpose." The then present, and all future bailiffs, are ordered to pay or cause to be paid to the "Schole maister of the towne of Preston, or to his use, the sume of twentie marks in p[te] of p.ment of his stypende and wages. That is to saie, either of them, six pounds thirteen shillings and four-pence." All defaulters are threatend with the compulsory providing of the "provision, diet, and bankettinge, at the said feast of Easter as hath heretofore been accustomed."

The same resolution orders the bailiffs and common councillors who had not previously made such provision, to procure "decente and comelie gownes of Blacke cloath, or other Blacke stuffe," of the fashion then in use, "to attend upon the maior of this towne for the tyme beinge, for the worshippe of this towne, upon needfull and convemente occasions."

About this period the practice of building, *by licence*, "porches and windowes," and the "fixing of the same into the streetes of this towne, to the greate prejudice of the Anncıente Burgesses," had become so intolerable and occasioned so much litigation, that it was resolved in future no such leave be given, "att the entreatie, mocon" (motion), "or requeste of anie p son or p.sons whatsoever."

An entry in September, 1616, records the gift to the corporation of "one faire silver Bowle, with a cover for the same, Double guilte," by Henry Banester, of Hackney, a native of Preston. In this entry occurs for the first time the name of "alderman" in connection with the corporation minutes. The style previously appears as the "maior, bailiffes, and capital burgesses."

In the following month, several entries of by-laws and orders occur, from which some curious information is derived, relative to the habits and customs of the period, and of the municipal authority. Every householder was compelled to have his or her street doors "shutte in all the tyme of divyne service and sermons upon sabbath daies and other festival days." They were also required to prevent their "children, servantes, or familie, or anie of them beinge above the age of seaven years, to plaie in the open streetes of this town, at anie game or plaie whatsoever, or to sit at the doors or in the streete," under a penalty of four-pence. A councillor not attending the mayor when summoned, was mulcted in the sum of twelve pence, while a freeman for non-attendance to his duty as juryman, was amerced to the extent of six shillings and eightpence. The municipal authorities appear to have entertained a singular horror of all strangers, or "foreigners," as they were termed If any householder of the "town or liberties thereof" admitted any one of this class, who should appear to the council "noe fytt p.son to inhabitte within the same," the party was required to decamp within a month after notice given. The householder was to see to the due execution of this order, or give security that the "foreigner" or any of his family should not become chargeable to the town; or to pay the sum of six and eightpence per week during the time they remained A special licence from the council suspended the operation of the last named condition, but only for the space of three months. All publicans were compelled to sell a full quart of the best beer or ale for a penny The penalty for non-compliance was six shillings and eightpence. A similar fine was enforced upon the courageous individual who presumed to "kepe alehouse or tiplinghouse" without the mayor's licence No person was permitted to tipple or drink in any alehouse for a longer period than one hour at a sitting, nor after the specified hours; nor during divine service, on the sabbath, (except travellers), under a penalty of three shillings and fourpence. The same amount was levied on all who permitted drunken or disorderly persons in their houses, or who neglected to apprehend "rogues, vagabonds, sturdie beggars," or suspicious persons, soliciting alms or offering goods for sale No one was permitted to erect porches or posts on any of the town's wastes, without the mayor's permission, under a penalty of six shillings and eightpence. Any person permitting a "bastard to be born in any of their houses" was called upon to give security that it should not become chargeable to the town

An entry on the 20th of October, exhibits a singular method of relieving the poor at the period. It says, "whereas divers poore people are assigned and app[d] to divers inhabitants houses for their releeffe by meate and drinke" Some party it appears had refused to comply, in consequence of which the council resolved that such person should pay the sum of threepence per day to be demanded weekly by the churchwardens or the collectors for the poor.

In 1632, the first record of several legacies and donations for the benefit of the poor, appears in what is termed "The White Book." Certain benefactions are, however, mentioned in the "Booke of Orders" at an earlier period, and which the council declare shall be applied to the "setting forth and binding of the poorer sorte of children, being free burgesses sonnes or daughters and borne in this towne, to apprentices of Traide and Handie crafte." Some of the earlier leaves of the "White Book" are missing. The matter in the following pages has reference to a legacy of £20, or rather thirty shillings yearly, to the poor, by a William Martin, and a similar bequest by William Dykes, of 50s. per year. No further reference to these charities appears, either in the books of the corporation, or in the report of the charity commissioners. The document then proceeds, however, to record the well-known legacy of George Rogerson, of the sum of £9 per annum. It afterwards states, that all the bequests enumerated have reference to similar objects, and that the proceeds should be applied to the apprenticing of poor children, and to the relief of impotent and aged persons.

The following fees were agreed upon, "to be due & payable att the openinge of the comon box everie faire" by the corporate body, on the 4th of November, 1639:—

"Imprimis, to the steward..................	2s.
Item to the Towne's S^r^iant (Sergeant) for his fee 2^s^ and for aile 2^s^, in toto	4s.
Item to Maior's S^r^iant (sergeant).........	2s.
Item to the vewers 12d. a-peece..........	2s.
Item to the Aile founders, 12^d^ a-piece...	2s."

The scavenger is to have allowed "hym for his wages yearlie for cleaninge the street, *videlt*, all the middle pte of the streete over against Mr Morte, his door, and so all about the Butter cross, the whole Markett-place and all along the Church wall side the some of .. .. 4s.

Item, for dressing the fish-boards yearlie 4s."

The struggle between King Charles I. and the parliament, seriously interfered with the duties and responsibilities of the municipal officers. The general feeling appears to have inclined towards the parliament, but this was balanced by the zealous advocacy of the king's prerogative by several influential parties in the town and neighbourhood. Adam Morte, the brave royalist, who fell, together with his son, in the streets of Preston, when the town was stormed by the parliamentary troops under Major General Seaton, on the 9th of February, 1643, had, during the previous year, been elected to the office of mayor He, however, refused to take the oaths. The council "having maturely considered of the Indignity and Disgrace putt upon them," "to the end that such an unparall'd and unpresidented example may not passe unpunished, lest others in the like kynd may become refractory and disobedient," order that the "said Adam Morte shall be fyned and amerced in the sum of one hundred marks," "for such his greate contempte, disobedience and refusall." But Mr. Morte's contumacy was proof even against this sweeping resolution, to the great confusion of the municipal body In despair they sought the aid of "counsell learned," to determine the correct mode of procedure, under such peculiarly irritating circumstances. It was then decreed that the mayor of the preceding year, Edward Werden, should "continue to act until Adam Morte doe come in and take his oath," or until a new election shall have furnished him with a legally appointed successor. It would appear that Master Edmund by no means relished the responsibility attached to the office of mayor, with the country on the eve of a sanguinary civil war. The council, likewise, thought his misgivings anything but chimerical; for, "in regard many dangers may arise unto him in theis troublesome tymes," they considerately promised to "secure, save harmlesse, losselesse, and indempnified, him the said Edmund Werden, from all losses, charges, and damages, which shall or may happen, or accrue unto him for or concerning the execution of the said office."

There appears to have been some vacillation amongst the members of the municipal body, after the resolution quoted was entered on the book; for it is not attested by the usual signatures. Four days afterwards, a somewhat similar resolution is inserted, in which, however, there is no allusion to the "troublesome tymes." Master Werden is indemnified "from all charges, suits and troubles," but is especially reminded that he must not do "any thinge of greate weighte which may concerne the whole body of this Incorporation but with the advise of the comon counsell of this Towne or the greater parte of them "

Amid the distraction of the civil war, the corporation did not altogether neglect their more pleasing duties as charitable trustees. The record says:—

"Where as several somes of money (and particularly the somes hereafter mencond) have been bequeathed, given, or bestowed upon the towne with intente to relieve the indigente and poore burgesses, and for the puttinge forth of poore children to bee apprentices to some trades for their better educacon & mayntenance."

It unfortunately happens, however, that, by some accident or other, the "sums hereafter mencond" are not mentioned at all! to the great annoyance of the impartial historian, and, perhaps, the greater loss to the "poore children." Whatever may have been the nature of the bequests alluded to, the council resolved that, "at the Michaelmas Leet Court yearlie," two of their body should be appointed, as treasurers or overseers for the poor. The duties of these officers extended to the collection "of all somes of money as are *hereafter menconed*" (!) "or which in tyme to come may bee bestowed or given in any grosse some for the use of the poore people," and to see to their proper disbursement. They were further required to present correct "accounts of their doeings," and "pay over the remayninge somes in their hands to the next succeeding Treasurers"

The unsettled state of the country did not prevent the holding of the guild. Adam Morte's contumacy accidentally conferred the honour of guild mayor upon his predecessor and substitute, Edmund Werden.

The corporation of Preston appears, on the whole, to have had parliamentary predilections; for the royalist general, Prince Rupert, on his passage through Lancashire, in 1644, deemed it prudent to incarcerate in Skipton Castle the worthy mayor, William Cottam, and his bailiffs. On the return of the parliamentary authority, the council passed the following resolution on the subject:—

"Whereas William Cottam, gent., now maior of this Towne and William Patten and James Benson, now Baylives of the same, have by reason of their office (as we conceyve) susteyned imprisonment for the space of twelve weeks in [b] Skipton by command from Prince Rupert when he came to this Towne in an hostile manner In regard to whose imprisonment they have been put to extraordinary charges and expenses, And because wee are bound in conscience to see them eased in this particular we conceyve it fitt, and hereby wee whose names are subscribed doe order that the some of Twenty Pounds shall be paid by this Towne unto them for and in lieue of such their charge, vizt. Tenne pounds to ye said William Cottam, Maior, and fyve pounds a piece to ye said Baylives."

The mayor, however, knowing the "some of five pounds a piece soe allowed unto ye said Baylives" to be "much lesse than their charges and expences were, for and by reason of their said Imprisonm^{t}," generously ordered his own lion's share of the grant to be divided between his subordinate officials. The poverty of the corporation, however, was such, and the method of raising funds by means of "laye" (levy or ley) so unpopular at the time, that out of this paltry sum, a balance of £5. 1s. 6d. remained unpaid until the 5th of October, 1646, two years after the date of the grant.

Mr. Edward Baines quotes a resolution from the corporation records relative to Cromwell's celebrated victory over the duke of Hamilton, in 1648; but this cannot be found either in the "White Book" or any other document at present in the possession of the corporation. It is probable the historian of Lancashire transcribed the resolution or minute from Dr. Kuerden's manuscript There is evidently one book of this date missing. The learned doctor appears, according to a resolution yet extant, to have borrowed some such volume, and neglected to return it

In 1650, the members of the corporation, as patrons of the then national pastime of cock-fighting, were put to some little trouble on account of the rickety condition of the town's cockpit, and the obstreperous conduct of the party occupying the same. It was resolved that the said public edifice,

---

b In the original, the words "in the Castle of" have been erased

which is described as "goods belonging to this Towne," or rather the "cover" thereof, as it is termed, should "be removed in regard it would fall downe & so bee a great charge to repaire being in great Ruyne & decay for want of reparacons" The bailiffs were ordered to remove it to "such convenient place as they shall think fitt nere unto the Towne hall to be employed for the publique use of this Towne."

It would be difficult to determine with certainty where either of these edifices stood. An old building in Back lane is, however, yet pointed out as the site of a cockpit, and may be the spot selected by the bailiffs of the year 1650. A field behind the Adelphi Hotel, at the end of Friargate, (formerly called the "Fighting Cocks,") is described as "cockpit" field, in George Lang's map, dated 1774.

This year, the corporation agreed to purchase the "Fee farme Rent of fifteen pound p[r] ann. lately payable to the crowne of England." [e] In order to raise the necessary funds, the tenants of the corporate estate were "desyred" to "Send to the vse of this Towne fyve yeares Rent. * * * to be returned to London and disposed of for ye purpose aforesaid."

It is not certain that all the tenants complied with this request; but, as there is no mention of any who were contumacious, it is highly probable that such was the case. The following schedule of the corporation property, and its value at this period, will be read with interest:—

"A particular Expresse of ye names of such P.sons, Tenants belonginge to this Towne who have paid in their Rents for fyve years (yet to come) to bee employed for & towards ye purchase of y[e] Fee Farme Rent of XV[l] [£15] payable by this Towne & receyved by Mr. Wm. Sudell, appointed by an order of the Sixth day of May, 1650.

		£.	s.	d.
Of Mr Wm. Farington, of Worden, Esq, his rent, being £6 for the fishinge and Holme		30	0	0
Of Mary Archer, wid. of Thomas Archer for her several rents, for the shopp	5s.	3	10	5
for the house	4s.			
for encrochts	5s. 1d.			
Of Mr Worden for a Burgage	10s.	5	15	0
the Intack	2s. 6d.			
another Intack	2s. 6d			
shopp	8s.			
for a standinge at the Moote hall	20d.	0	8	4
Of Mr. William Sudell for a Barne	14d.	2	6	4
Intacks	2s 6d.			
for a Cottage and Intacks	4s. 8d.			
for porches	1s.			

e "A fee farm rent of £15., reserved by Henry II., and payable at the feast of St. Michæl, and the annunciation was purchased by the corporation under an act of the commonwealth for £127., and conveyed 23rd July, 1650; and again purchased for £247 10s. after the restoration. The conveyance dated 6th June, 1676, states that the 'said premises were parcel of the landes and possessions of the late Duchy of Lancaster, and were by letters patent of the late King Henry II. granted to the burrough and their successors for ever.' The corporation, encouraged by the flatteries of Judge Jefferies, it is said paid dearly for his majesty's favours in this instance."—Edward Baines See page 214.

		£	s.	d.
Of Mr. Willim. Shawe for Intacks	5s.			
Carguawts [d] (?)	3s. 4d	2	16	8
Long Syke	3s.			
Of Rich Bostocke for a butcher's shopp	8s	2	0	0
Of John Mitton for a butcher's shopp	8s.	2	0	0
Of Hugh Blackleach—2 buth. shopps	15s.	3	15	0
2 Standings	4s.	1	0	0
Of George Tasker for a parcell of land att the end of Aram Sykes	4d.	0	1	8
Of Thomas Bickerstaffe new meadows	6s. 8d.	1	13	4
Of John Wall, for midingstead	6d.	0	2	6
Of Mr. Preston for Aram Sykes and Aram bank	7s. 6d	4	1	3
more for the Intacks	8s. 9d			
Of Mr. Blundell for a Smithy	2s	0	10	0
Of Mr. George Addison for a Shopp	3s.	0	15	0
Of John Singletons 2 daughters for a barne	1 s	0	5	0
Of Roger Sudell for 2 butchers shopps	13s. 4d.	3	6	8
for a free rent for ye pitt	4d.	0	7	6
a P.cell of hissell (?) land	1s 2d.			
Of Thos Werden for a Shop and Warehouse	3s	0	15	0
Of Henry Blackhurst for an Intacke D'Holme		0	17	6
Of James Hodgkinson for old Schole house and 2 bayes of buildinge adioyneinge to it, Rent p anm.	vjs. viji	1	13	4
Of Mrs. Williamson for one butcher's shopp	5s. 4d			
for a house at east moreyate	6s 8d.			
for a butcher shopp	6d.			
for a rent of her house in Churchgate	3s. 4d.	4	6	8
for Horridge lands	6d.			
for pte. of Broomefield	12d.			
Rent in toto—17s. 4d.				
Of Mrs. Jennette Morte for one shopp	3s.			
for Intacke	4s			
for free rent out of ye Guildhouse	2s.	2	10	0
for rent of a barne	1s			
Of William Whaley for Intacke	5s.	1	5	0
Of Thomas Walmsley de Holehouse for a croft.	3d.	0	1	3
Of Robte. Bayley for one house @ 3 acres of land	4s. 10d.	1	4	2
Of Thomas Sumpner		6	16	8
Of William Hodgkinson for St Mary Heys	8d.			
for Balshawe house	15d.	2	12	6
for free rent of his hall	3d.			
for free rent of his pte. in Bromefield	1s.			
Of Mr. Edward Hodgkinson for Barkhouse hill	4d.	0	1	8
Of Mr Edward French for Intacks	5s			
and other things, vizt. for herbage in ye lane	2d.	1	10	0
free rent on ye more	4d			
more free rent there	6d.			
Mr. Luke Hodgkinson for the heires of Mr. Henry Assheton,				
for Sackvyle Sykes	vs	5	18	4
new meadows	xvj. viijd.			
4 butcher shopps & lofte over	2s.			
Of Ellen Whalley, widdowe, for a shoppe and warehouse nere the Buttercrosse late belonging to James Whalley, dec. rent 3s.		0	15	0

The corporation was, this year (1650), troubled by the obstreperous conduct of one of the bailiffs. William Curtis, who, utterly oblivious of the exemption from the duty of providing the "banquetinge stuff" and other

d Several words in this document are difficult to decipher

viands for the Easter feast, "not only publiquely refused" to pay the sum of £6. 13s. 4d. to the schoolmaster, but, in the words of the record, "still doeth deny and refuse to pay the same to the great affront of ye corporacon in breaking and contemning their orders and much damage to the schoolema^{r} and the evil encouragement of others for the future." He was ordered to pay, or submit to a levy of ten pounds on his "goods and chattells by distresse & sale."

In 1652, however, a resolution abrogating the previous orders respecting the schoolmaster was passed, and a salary of twenty-two pounds per annum awarded to him. The reason assigned is, that some of the said orders "were dissonant to ye laws of this nacon."

In 1654, the municipal authorities took into consideration the defective supply of water in the town, and ordered that a "drawe well shalbee made in the Bottome of the Markett stidd."

Four years after this step towards sanatory improvement, numerous erratic pigs, which prowled about the town and the neighbouring lanes and enclosures, were subjected to a little judicious municipal regulation. The following extract, from the "White Booke" of the corporation, graphically describes a somewhat singular, but evidently a characteristic scene, not only of Preston, but of other towns and villages, during the latter portion of the seventeenth century. The English evidently had not, at that period, acquired their present character for domestic cleanliness:—

"It is this day ordered by the Maior and Counsell of the Borough aforesaid that all the Inhabitants within this Towne shall keepe up their Swyne in their Backsydes or Swynesties and their safely keepe them until the Swyneheards shall call for them in the morneings and that at ye Swyneheards comeing backe with them from the Moore they shall take up their Swine into their Backsydes or Swynesties and there safely keepe them till the Swynehead shall call for them in the morneinge followinge, and in case any Swyne or piggs shall be taken abroad either in the streets or fields from the tyme that they came from the Moore at Night till morneinge that they be called for by the Swyneheards as aforesaid or from the tyme aforesaid till they come back from the Moore at night, the owners of such Swyne or piggs shall forfeit for every Swyne or pigg soe taken abroad as aforesaid for every tyme four pence, to be immediately levied by distress upon the goods of the offender by such officers as the Maior for the tyme beinge shall appointe, allowinge such officers the Moiety of such forfeiture for his pains to be therein taken."

It appears that the sum of £632. 11s. 11d. accrued from the grants and renewals of freedom at the celebration of the Guild Merchant in 1662, and that, "the expences of the guild and other occasions of this borough" amounted to £230. 13s. 11d., leaving, as the "profits of the Guild," £401. 18s.

It was frequently the custom to fine refractory councillors and aldermen, as well as the mayor, for non-attention to the duties of their respective offices. A Mr. Thomas Martin was fined in the sum of forty pounds for contumacy of this kind, although the record does not say whether he ever paid it or not. Other delinquents were sometimes expelled from the corporate body, for what the council deemed improper conduct.

At the petition of some of the inhabitants, in 1666, a draw well was sunk in Fishergate, at a cost of £21. 0s. 10d. To this and several other wells afterwards sunk, pumps were in course of time attached. These in turn are fast disappearing, in consequence of the superiority of the supply under the new waterworks system.

An entry, of the date of August 4th, 1673, records that as early as 1607, "five pewes or seates within the body of the parish church" were granted to the corporation, by the Lord Archbishop of York. Some little irregularity having been manifested in the attendance of the council at public worship, the following resolution was passed:—

"And Whereas the said maior, aldermen, and comon counsell, (or the major part of them) have ever since that" (the bishop's grant) "in a devout and orderly manner, upon every Lord's day (and other days of Holidays appointed for Divine service and sermon) as well in the aforenoone as afternoone of the same days resorted to and sate in ye said pewes and seates, which use and custom hath been esteemed and is still thought to be very laudable and to manifest very much concord within such an Incorporate community, And whereas some of the said comon counsell have of late foreborn and neglected to come to the said seates, but have sate in other pewes within the said church, by which meanes not only the good design and intent of giving and granting ye said seates as aforesaid hath been frustrated and disappoynted; but also other persons (unconcerned therein) have taken lib.tie to sit in the said seates, which is conceived disorderly and derogatory to ye said bishop's disposition of the seates aforesaid."

The resolution then decrees that all the corporation shall proceed to these sittings, and promulgates the law of precedence to be observed by those privileged to occupy the said "pewes or seates; vizt the maior to the highest seate, the aldermen to the two next adjoining seates, and the rest of the counsell to ye two lowermost, being soe usually sate in and enioyed." A fine of twelve pence for each contravention of this order is put forth, as a terror to the indolent or contumacious. The council, however, considerately granted to Alderman William Sudell the liberty to "sitt in any seate where he thinks conveynent, by reason of his infirmity of hearing."

About this period (1674-5), the mass of the poorer people were so ill employed, and mendicancy so much on the increase, that the corporation, after much consultation, resolved to adopt the advice of a sub-committee of their body, and establish workhouses and storehouses for the purpose of furnishing the more deserving with employment in the woollen manufacture. The following are amongst the resolutions adopted:—

"That ye churchwardens and overseers of ye poore doe deliver unto ye maior and counsell ye names of all ye poore people in ye towne, and that thereout may bee choyse made who of them shall be sett on worke.

"That there be two lusty men appoynted Beadles, to whipp out all vagrants and beggarrs, and that all officers and other P.sons within ye towne bee p.ticularly charged to bee ayding and assisting to ye sd Beadles.

"That the said Beadles for their more Incouragement have ye reward of two shillings for every one they take begging, from ye constable through whose constablery any vagrant or beggar did last passe unpunished.

"That all persons who refuse to worke or refuse to suffer their children to worke bee punished according to law, wherein it is desired yc maior will bee very dilligent.

"That ye Maior and Counsell shall sett ye rates of ye wages of any who are workers and also of all other servants according to yc statutes of this Realme

"That ye wages of such as shall bee imployed in ye workhouse bee weekly paid unto every P.son working or unto theirparents, upon every Friday night at such time as they leave of working.

"That ye Maior and Counsell do appoynt and limitt fitt times when yc workers shall beginn and how long to continue at worke."

On the 24th of February, in the same year, the sum of two hundred pounds was granted for the furtherance of this object.

In 1681, the council were much occupied in the consideration of the elective franchise of the borough. They "resolved and declared *(nemine contradicente),*"—

"That no forreigne Burgesse although he lives within the corporacon hath or ought to have any vote in such elleccon, nor that any p.son entered an Inburgesse (living forth of the sd Burrough att the time of such elleccon) ought to have any vote at such said elleccon, But that the sole right of the elleccon appertaines to the Inburgesses of this corporacon either of the last guild merchant or by coppy of Cort Roll that doe or shall inhabit within the said Burrough att the time of such elleccon. And that the vsage of this corporacon hath, time out of mind, been accordingly; and that to offer or introduce the contrary would bee a great invasion upon the rights of this Burrough."

The corporate body merely granted the limited suffrage referred to in compliance with a decision of the house of commons, the peculiar wording of which was taken advantage of about a century later, and the privilege of voting thrown open to the inhabitants at large.[e]

Previously to the guild of 1682, the municipal authorities, with the view to limit the number of freemen, passed a curious resolution, declaring that no person should be admitted a burgess during the subsequent five years, with the provision, however, that the mayor and council were privileged to bestow the then envied freedom of the borough, "for ye greater reputn, state, & creditt, o' this Incorporacon upon some P.sons of honour, nobility, or or gentry, but upon no or P.sons except it bee upon some rare or speciall occasion that shall or may fall out or happen and now not thought on and yt withall may tend much to ye welfare creditt & benefitt of the towne of Preston."

It appears the total receipts of the guild of 1682 were £569 9s. 3d., and the disbursements £333 19s. 4d., which left a balance, or "remains," as it is termed, of £234 9s. 11d.

The next charter was granted by Charles II. in in 1673.[f] It recapitu-

e See chap. 7. Parliamentary Representation.

f The corporation "Booke of Orders" contains,—"A particular note of all such persons which have lent anie, and what some of money for and towards the renewinge of the Charter of this Towne." A list of eighty-nine names follows, whose total subscription amounted to "four score and nine pounds." The subscriptions range from £3. to 10s. each person.

lates generally the document of Elizabeth, with some slight variations, the most important of which are as follows:—One clause distinctly specifies that the "capital burgesses or the major part of them," have authority to "remove" the mayor, if guilty of "bad behaviour in that office, or for any other reasonable cause." The acquisition of lands and other property is permitted to the corporation, but limited to the annual value of £200. The crown reserves by a special clause the privilege of confirming or rejecting the appointment of any person who may have been elected to the "office or offices of seneschal, recorder, or common clerk."

Charles II. acting it is believed principally under the advice of the notorious Jefferies towards the end of his reign, dispossessed Preston and many other boroughs of all their privileges and chartered rights. A short time before his death, however, either the heart of the monarch relented, or the rapacity of his counsellor had been privately satisfied,[g] for another charter, dated January, 1684-5, which restored all the ancient privileges, was granted to the mayor, bailiffs, and burgesses of Preston. By these "letters patent" some little alteration is made in the form of the executive government. Seven capital burgesses are to be elected, and dignified by the title of aldermen, and, in conjunction with seventeen other capital burgesses, constitute the common council of the borough. The mayor, for the time being, his predecessor in office, the recorder, and the senior alderman are to be justices of the peace within the borough, its liberties, and precincts. The mayor is further invested with the authority of justice of the peace for the county. For these concessions, however, the crown reserved the right to remove from office, at any time, "the mayor, the recorder or seneschal, and his deputy, or any one or more of the bailiffs, aldermen, capital burgesses, and common councilmen, or justices of the said borough." A third annual fair is granted, "for the buying and selling of all and every manner of goods, cattle, wares, and merchandizes," to commence on the 16th March, and continue during three days. The maximum annual value of property to be legally held by the corporation for public purposes, is extended to £500. The charter, which is preserved in the office of the duchy, is accompanied by the following singular memorandum:—

"M[d] that the charter for Preston passed the Greate Seale according to the date, but by reason Mr. James Ashton, who su'd it out, did not pay the fees due to the Chancellor of the Duchy, he refused to put the Duchy or Co. Pal. seale to it, where upon Mr. Ashton tooke it with him to Preston, and there procured the Co. Pal. seale to be put to it, for

g "Jefferies, afterwards Lord Jefferies, Baron of Wem, in Shropshire, was sumptuously entertained by the corporation of Preston, on his return from the assizes at Lancaster, in the autumn of 1684, on the principle probably, that certain of the Indian tribes pay their devotion to the spirit of evil. A letter of the chief justice, in good preservation, is amongst the corporation records, dated 29th of September, 1684."—Edward Baines. See page 214.

which he was turn'd out of his place. This was soe sealed a few days before king Cha. the Second dy'd.

"In Easter Terme following, viz, the beginning of June, the Fees for both Seales were paid, at which time, or two or three days after, the Dutchy Seale was put to the said Charter.

"This memorand was made the 13th day of June, 1685,

"by me

"BEN· AYLOFFE."

After the close of the seventeenth century, the entries in the corporation books are very meagre, and furnish but little matter of historical importance.

The twelfth and last charter was granted by George IV., in 1828.[h] By its provisions every alderman was appointed a justice of the peace within the borough. The mayor's predecessor, and the senior alderman, are invested with the powers and authority of coroners within the same limits. The corporation officers enumerated in this document are the mayor, seven aldermen, seventeen councilmen, recorder, town's bailiff, mayor's bailiff, town's sergeant, mayor's sergeant, town clerk, mace bearer, beadle, bellman, gaoler, market looker, market keeper, and land steward.

The privilege of guild merchant appears to have been held in Preston by prescriptive right anterior to its chartered recognition; yet little information has descended relative to the original *modus operandi* of this ancient institution. It is certain, however, that the necessity for enrolment as a burgess was imperative, at a very early period, upon every person who wished to embark in trade within the jurisdiction of the corporation. The enrolled inhabitants thus secured a complete monopoly of the commerce of the place. One section in the burgesses' oath, preserved by Kuerden, shows that these privileges were jealously guarded even at the end of the seventeenth century. It reads thus:—"You shall know noe foreiner to buy or sell any merchandise, with any other foreiner within this town or the francheses thereof, except at Faire Time, but you shall warn the Mayor or Bailiffs thereof" The following by-law, passed at the guild of 1662, still further illustrates the exclusive privilege of trade enjoyed by the burgesses:—"After the shutting up of the present gyld, no Apprentice for the seven years next ensuing shall be manmitted" (made free) "to trade within this Burrough, nor any other tradesman be admitted as Free, *de novo*, except he bring a new Trade into the town, or great necessity to introduce the same."

h "Attested copies of all the charters ever granted to the borough were procured in the year 1817, when some proceedings at law were pending between the freemen at large and the mayor and council, Translations of these important documents were made by Dr Lingard, and printed with the original Latin under the translator's immediate supervision"—Wilcockson's Authentic Records of the Guild Merchant, p 14.

The burgesses of Preston about this period appear to have been in the habit of strictly enforcing their prohibition against the interference of strangers with the trades monopolised by the privileged companies in the town, as is evidenced by the following entries in the record of the corporation :—

"Whereas ye day abouesaid[1] wee James Coulters of Halifax in the countie of York, Clothier, and Jno. Braithwaite, sone of Nathan Braithwaite of Ovendall, in ye County aforesd, Clothier, each of vs hauing forfeited an end of Cloath to ye Companie of Drap. pt. by sellinge & exposeinge the same to sale Wee are sorrye for ye same and doe p.mise hereby for ye future not to offende in ye Like."

On Jan. 8, 1659, Mr. Peter Ryecroft, of Leeds, consented to forfeit to the drapers' company the sum of twenty pounds should he in the future "sell or expose to sale any woolen Cloath or other Comodity (belonging to ye trades of any of ye foresaid Company) vnto any person within the Corporacon aforesaid, except it bee to ye member or members of ye aforesaid Company or Society."

Orders were granted by the mayor and corporation, and confirmed by the judges of assize, in 1685-6, which authorised the wardens of the company to distrain upon certain persons named "for the sume of fourty shillings A month for one month by past, & soe for the like sume of fourtey shillings for every month hereafter that they shall use the Trades they now follow, contrary to the orders of the said company."

During the past year (1856), a gentleman in Preston, on turning over some old papers, met with the following copy of a letter, addressed to one of the then parliamentary representatives of the borough. It is not signed, but is in the hand-writing of the town clerk at the time, Mr. Henry Smith, and was doubtless his production in a literary as well as a caligraphic sense. It exhibits, in a very marked manner, the exclusive character of the code by which the commercial element of the borough's progress was and had been regulated, and contrasts somewhat oddly with modern notions of free trade and commercial competition :—

"Copy of Lr sent to Mr Fazakerley.
"Preston April 7th 1745

"Sr—The Gentlemen of our Town desire the favour of your Advice and direction in an affair now depending which, in it's Consequence, may very much Affect the interest of the Corporacon— The case is this—

"A Pson who came some years ago to reside in Preston as a Writing Master, Afterwards Marryed in the Town And has since thought fit by degrees to Strike into and Exercise himself in the various trades or Employmts of Printer, Booksellr Stationer, Dealer in China Ware and divers other branches of trade within the Town; and this in an Open Shop and publick Manner, tho' he is not ffree of the Borough nor has serv'd any Apprenticeship to any trade whatsoever —

"Upon this Open Violation of the Customs and priviledges of the Borough, the Mayor and Council were Address'd at their last Meeting with a Petn subscribed by great Numbers of the ffreemen—(A Coppy of Which and of the Order of ye Council made

---

1 Feb. 6th, 1659.

thereon are inclosed)—And as this Attempt is now become the Object of publick attention, it will certainly in it's Consequence, if not controuled, introduce great disorder and very much impair the revenue of the Corporacon heretofore arising from the Admission of ffreemen for liberty of trade in ye Town—Upon which the ffines formerly Sett have varyed according to the Nature of the trades to be exercised: And Sometimes considerable Sums have been pd to make people free, for the priviledge of following some of the branches of business which this Scrivener now insists upon following in a publick defiance of our Customs and by Laws.—And under these Circumstances it is that the gentlmn of the Corporacon have determin'd to resort to Every Legal Means (and Acts of power too) for the checking of this ill Example And desire the favour of you to point out the most proper methods—

"As there is scarce any Precedents of such a Wilful and resolute Attempt heretofore —We have not (that I can find) many footsteps of proceedings on such occasions—only in a late instance of an obstinate Quaker who, after some litigation, was at last brought to submit: But this may be observed that the Custom to Exclude Psons not ffree or that have not serv'd Apprenticeships in the town from ye priviledge of Exercising trades in the Town has been general.—

"Besides the general usage of Excluding fforreigners I have search'd All our Ancient Corp: Books and Find Several Marks and instances of the Custom of debarring Strangers from the Exercise of trades — Which is all that I am (at present) capable of laying before you —

"Whether the by Laws of our Corp: will bind those not of their own body Or whether the penalties thereby inflicted can properly be Levyed by distress, Or what other Method may be most proper and Effectual to be taken to Vindicate the Customs and rights of the Corporacon agst this Invader Your thoughts and directions are required. And if you want further Information in any thing I am Ordered to spare no pains to give you the best I can, Who am Sr."

The name of the offender was William Smith. The corporation books record that the memorial above referred to had been received, and that the council resolved "to make use of their utmost power and of all legal ways and means to restrain the said William Smith from the exercise of so many different trades within the borough, contrary to the ancient custom thereof; and further purpose that the town clerk do forthwith consult the recorder of the corporation how to proceed against the said William Smith in the most legal and effectual manner."

It appears that the subject of "early closing," so much agitated at the present day, is by no means an innovation peculiar to modern notions of the necessity which exists for increased physical recreation and mental culture, amongst the trading portion of the community and their *employes*. In 1662, the merchant companies of Preston entered into a compact with the view to limit the hours of business, as will be seen by the following curious document. What peculiar advantages may have resulted from this effort, it would be difficult now to precisely determine:—

"December the 5th, 1662. Whereas vpon serious consideration of the companie of Mercers, Grocers, Ironmongers, Haberdashers, and Salters, It is thought that the keepinge of Shopps open in the Eveninges vntil nine or Tenn of the clock is imprudent, unprofitable, and discommendable. For reformeinge whereof, Wee, the severall Wardens and Masters Tradesmen of the several Companies aforesaid, doe hereby vollantarily and freely agree, and do hereby covenant, conclude, and bynd our selves, that from henceforth, neither wee ourselves nor anie for vs, shall keepe open our Shopp windowes, or doares, after eight of the clock betwixt the 25th of March and the 29th of September, and after six of the clock betwixt ye 25th of September and the 25th of March. vpon paine of everie one of vs to forfeite for everie such offence five shillings. And that ye wardenes for the tyme being shall destraine the goodes of such offenders vnless the p.tie offending doe presently paie soe much forfeited And that everie p.son that shall offer to opose, rescue, disturbe or sue, anie such warden that shall destraine the said forfeiture and execute this Order, everie such p.son shall forfeite for everie such offence Fower pounds Ten shillings of current money of England for the vse and improvement of the comon stock of the companie abousaid by distresse vpon theire goods or by action in our owne Townes Court in the name of the wardens for the tyme beinge And it is hereby further agreed, that ye Wardens for the tyme beinge shalbe harmelesse Losslesse and indemptnified by the companie aboucsaide for anie thing they shall doe in the execution of this order In witnesse whereof wee doe hereby severally bynde owrselves and have subscribed owr names to this order the daie and yeare first above written."

W. SUDELL, } Wardens."
JOHN SUMPNER. }

(and several others.)

Mr. Edward Baines states, that so late as the year 1772, "the corporation renewed their prosecutions against 'merchant strangers,' who had established themselves in the town without possessing the qualification as freemen of the borough; and in the corporation books of the date of the sixth of April, in that year, the following entry appears:—'Received into stock from the subscribers to Baines's prosecution towards paying Mr. Grimshaw's Bill from Thomas Walshman, £47 7s. 8d.,' and on the credit or opposite side of the ledger,—'Rec^{d} 27th April, 1772, from the Mercers, Grocers, &c., Company, within the borough of Preston, the sum of £45, by the hands of Mr. Walshman and Mr. Derbyshire, the wardens, in full for my cost of the Prosecutions against Mr. Baines to March Assizes last. John Grimshaw!' With the history of this prosecution, one of the last remaining vestiges of feudal policy, we have reason to be familiarly acquainted The effect was to subject Mr. Baines to expences amounting to several hundreds of pounds, and ultimately to oblige him to remove from Preston to Walton-le-dale." [j]

Mr. Wilcockson, in his "Authentic Records of the Guild Merchant," published in 1822, says, this by-law was not "fully and finally abandoned until more enlightened views, combined, perhaps, with political motives, occasioned the corporation to withdraw their countenance from its support, about 30 years ago, since which time all the distinct trading companies have ceased to exist; and persons belonging to separate branches of business, without regard to their being burgesses or not, now arrange themselves into temporary societies a few weeks or months previous to each guild, for the mere purposes of parade."

In 1803, Prince William Frederick, of Gloucester, military commander of the northern district, reviewed the Preston and other volunteer corps

j The historian of Lancashire was second son of the "merchant stranger," against whom the prosecutions were directed.

at Liverpool. He likewise visited Preston, and was met by the municipal authorities at the Bull Hotel, where a loyal address was presented to him.

In the following year, Prince Frederick again visited Preston, accompanied by his father, the duke of Gloucester, brother to his majesty George III. Mr. Whittle says, the prince made an observation to the effect that, "Preston was the handsomest town in England." ! !

The periodical festival of the Guild Merchant originated in the necessity which called together both the resident and non-resident burgesses to renew their freedom, and sanction such laws as, from time to time, might be deemed beneficial to the fraternity. These meetings, in the earlier times, appear to have been held at irregular periods; but, since the year 1562, a Guild Merchant has been regularly celebrated once in each twenty years. The earliest celebration of which any specific record has been preserved, took place in 1329, in the second year of the reign of king Edward III. Five other guilds were held within that time and 1562, namely, in 1397, 1415, 1459, 1501, and 1543. Kuerden says:—

"These are such as doth appeare within the Records and Gild Books that yet remain extant and in being,[k] though some I conceive to be omitted, as one Gild in Henry 6th dayes occasion'd, as I conceive, in those distractions and civil wars betwixt the Houses of Lancaster and York, another Gild Merchant omitted to be kept in K H 8th dayes, occasion'd, as may be thought, by the Revolutions at that time in Church affyres; the next that are wanting may be through the loss of Records in K Ewd. 3rd.[l] dayes, whenas the Scottish army burnt the Burrough of Preston to the very ground."

In Cooke's "Topography of Lancashire," it is stated that, "Preston Guild is, by charter, obliged to be celebrated at the end of every twenty years, in default of which, the elective franchise of the inhabitants in sending members to parliament, and their rights as burgesses would be forfeited." This is, however, an error, no such clause being found in any of the existing charters. The practice of holding a guild at the expiration of every twenty years, originated in a by-law of the corporation, adopted anterior to the granting of the charter of Elizabeth.[m] The latter document, which includes a summary of all known previous grants, is perfectly silent on the matter It is evident, therefore, that the precise periods were dictated by the discretion of the corporation and burgesses themselves, with the view to meet their own wishes and business requirements. The processions, entertainments, and feasting, had no more legal connection with the institution itself, than the anniversary dinners of modern friendly societies have with their provident objects. Business required a periodical *re-union* of parties holding common interests, and the

k Kuerden manuscript was written shortly before the guild of 1682.

l This is an error. Bruce's incursion occurred in the sixteenth year of the reign of Edward II.

m Wilcockson's "Authentic Records"

gathering was seized upon as a favourable occasion for festive enjoyment, and the exhibition of civic hospitality The privilege of the inhabitants to the exercise of the elective franchise in the selection of persons to serve in the national parliament, had no connection with their municipal incorporation. No reference is made to the subject in any of the charters [n]

For a long period previously to the passing of the Corporation Reform Bill, in 1835, the legal business of the guild had ceased to include more than the simple renewal of freedom to those parties who were previously in possession of the privilege, and the admission of others, who, by birthright, purchase, or otherwise, proved their title to a participation of the immunities enjoyed by the free burgesses of the borough. Mr. Wilcockson observes, in his "Authentic Records of the Guild Merchant," that, "since the dissolution of the trading companies, and the extension of the elective franchise to all the inhabitants, the immunities of the burgesses have been much circumscribed. The only rights they at present enjoy (1822), above those possessed by their fellow townsmen, is an exemption from toll, the benefit of turning cattle upon the moor and the marsh, and the exclusive privilege of serving in the corporate offices of the borough."

The festival of the Preston guild has been celebrated from the earliest known periods with great pomp and profuse hospitality Dr. Kuerden has preserved the following record of several of the earlier guilds [o] :—

1329

In 2d of K. Edward 3d, there is mention made of a Grand or Gild Court, holden at Preston, in Amoundernes, before Aubert the Son of Robt *Major*, and William the son of Roger Paulin, and Roger of the Wych, Balives of the same Towne; on Munday after the Feast of the Nativity of St. John Baptist, the yeare raigning of K. Edw 3d after the conquest of the 2d, and at the said Guild divers others confirm'd, that had been made at a procedent Guild.

1397.

Item, A Guild Merchant held here before Will Ergham, then Mayor; and Jeoffry, of the Males, Thomas More, John Haconshawe, Stewards of the sd Gild; Ri: Blundell, Hen: le Counter, Simon of Preston, Johanes Marshall, Ri: of Bretherton, W: de Cane, Jo. Alston, W: de Walton, Mercer, W. Grimbaldeston, and Jo: Lambart, Aldermen; and Clerk of the say'd Gild, on Munday next after the feast of the Ascention of our Lord, in the 20th year of K. Rd. 2d.

1415

Item, Another Gild likewise held here, before H. Johnson, Mayor of that Gild; and W. Clifton, W. Winter, senior, Robt. Males, Stewards of that Gild; W. Ergham, Jo: Blundell, Roger Wich, Jo del Walton, Jo: de Alston, W. de Greenhills, Jo de More, Tho: do Bretherton, Rob Albin, Jo: Lambart, W. Grimbaldeston, Jo: Breton, A. de Marshall, and W. Blundell, Aldermen; and Clerk of the same Gild, upon Munday after Trinity Sunday, in the 3rd yeare of the Raign of K. H. the Fifth.

1459

Item, Another Gild held here before Rob Houghton, Mayor; John Houghton senr. Rob· Preston, Ri Walley, Stewards, Jo Boteler, Rich Blundell, Gilbert Hydson, Rob· Blundell, Rob: Taylor, Ri: Johnson, W. Cook, Jo· Whaley, Rob Coke, Jo·

n See chap. 7.

o These notices are printed from the work published by Mr Wilcockson They are copied from the manuscript printed by Mr. Taylor, previously referred to, with a "few blanks supplied, and one or two corrections made from collating the account with the public documents in the town clerk's office"

Halywell, Aldermen; and W. Walton, Clerk of the same Gild, upon Munday next after the Invention of the Holy Crosse, in the 7 yeare of K. Hen. 6th.

1501.

Item, Another Gild held within this Town of Preston, upon Munday next after the Decolation of St John Baptist, in the 16th yeare of King Hen: 7th, before W Marshall, *Major*; H. Preston, W. Ergham, Law: Houghton, Ri: Aynsworth, Stewards, Adam Skillicome, W. Tipping, Lawr. Whaley, Ri. Tipping, W. Sadler, Ri. Arrowsmith, Tho. Alcock, Tho: Davel, Gilbert Arrowsmith, Will· Bonk, Tho: Wainwright, Aldermen; and William Walton, Clerk of the same Gild

1543.

Item, Another Gild held within this Burrough of Preston, upon Munday next after the Feast of the Ascention of our Lord, in the 34th yeare of the Raign of King Henry 8th, before Tho: Tipping, then Mayor; and Christopher Hadak, Evan Wal, Rad: Dawson, and Oliver Breres, Stewards, Jam Walton, Alex: Clayton, W. Ergham, H. Preston, Jam: Walton, Tho. Camberall, Thos Sadler, and Will. Walton, Clerk of the same Gild.

1562

Item, Another Gild held within this Burrough of Preston, upon Munday after the Decolation of St John Baptist, in the 4th yeare of the Raign of Queen Eliz. before Tho: Wall then Mayor, Evan Wall his Brother, Tho. Tipping, W. Banester, Stewards; Christopher Hadock, Oliver Breres, Rad Dawson, H. Blundel, W. Bostock, W. Preston, Evan Hodgkinson, senr Jo Werden, Jo Banester, Rad. Cumberal, Aldermen; and Lawr: Wal, Clerk of the same Gild.

1582.

Item, Another Gild held within the Burrough of Preston, upon Thursday, being the day after the Decolation of St Jo Baptist, in the 24 Year of the Raign of Queen Eliz: befor George Walton, g then Mayor; W. Hodgkinson, senr Tho Breres, Hen Preston, Stewards, Rog Hodgkinson, Rob· France, Tho· Cooper, senr Ri. Cuerdall, Jams Helm, Jams Dyke, Aldermen; and Roger Gillibrand, Stewards of the said Gild.

1602

Item, Another Gild held within this Burrough of Preston, upon Munday, being the day after the Decolation of St John Baptist, in 44 yeare of the Raign of Queen Elizabeth, before Henry Catterall, Mayor; Wm Hodgkinson, Ri Blundel, and Edmund Lemon, Stewards; Tho Wal, James Hodgkinson, Ri· Cuerdal, Ri: Hodgkinson, Jo: Chorley, Rog Langton, W. Garstang, Jo Hynd, James Weiden, and Nicholas Sudell, Aldermen; and Jo. Breres, Clerk of the said Gild.

1622

Item, Another Gild Merchant, held within this Burrough of Preston, upon Munday next after the Decolation of St. John Baptist, in the 20 yeare of the Raign of King James, before Willm. Preston, g *Major*; Ri Blundall, Rog: Langton, & Hen. Breres, Stewards, Tho: Banister Jo: Crook, Jo; Hynd, W. Walton, Hen: Sudall, Seth Bushel, W. Lemon, Ri Shawe, Geo. Hodgkinson, and W. Wall, gen. Aldermen; and George Hodgkinson Clerke of the said Gild Merchant.

1642.

Item, Another Gild Merchant held within this Burrough of Preston, upon Munday 29th August in the Feast of the Decolation of St John Baptist, in the 18th year of the Raign of King Charles the first, before Edm: Werden, Mayor; Rog: Langton, W. Sudall, Hen· Blundall, g. Stewards; H Sudall, Jams. Wall, George Addison, Jams. Archer, Ad. Mort, W Cottom, Tho. Sumner, Tho Bickerstaffe, Math. Addison, W. Shaw, g Aldermen, and Christopher Banister, Esqr Clerk of the sd Gild.

1662.

Item, Another Gild Merchant held within the Borrough of Preston, 3d day of September, in the 14th yeare of the blessed Raign and happy restoration of our Soveraigne Lord King Charles the 2d before James Hodgkinson, g Mayor; W. Sudal. Tho. Sumner, and Seth Blackhurst, Stewards; W. Baniester, W Turner, Luk: Hodgkinson, Tho: Mertin, Sylvester Jugha, Tho: Walmslev, Lawr Weal, W. Hodgkinson, Tho: Werden, Tho: Rishton, Aldermen of the sd Gild, and Edw Rigby, Esqr clerk of the sd Gild.

1682.

Item, Another Gild Merchant, according to the ancient rights, precedent practice, and laudable custome of this Burrough of Preston upon day of in the 34 yeare of the Raign and happy restoration of our said Soveraign Lord K. Charles 2d now intended, by Gods assistance, to be begun, held, and kept within this Burrough of Preston before Roger Sudall, Mayor of this present Gild. p

p "From the state of the MS here, it is evident that it was originally compiled after the Election of the Guild Mayor in 1681, and before the time of the Guild in 1682. The other officers of this

Kuerden's description of the style in which these municipal carnivals were conducted about two hundred years ago, is not only pertinent to the present section of this history, but instructive as to the habits, manners, and social morals of that period. He says:—

"Upon Munday next after the Decolation of St. John Baptist, about 8 in the morning, all the Companys of Trades, with the Wardens of each Company in their Gowns and long white Rods, each Company ranged into 2 fyles, the flags of each Company displayed, and variety of musick attending each Company, march regularly up and down the streets, wayteing for the Guild Mayor's attendance.

"And the young men within the Town, not being as yet free to Trade of themselves, have a Captain and Leftenant of their own, their ensign bearing the Towns Arms, a Flagg with the Holy Lamb: and they march and attend in the like order, as aforesaid, with their drums and musiq.

"After which marches, a proper man, bearing the great Baner, with the King's Arms: and after that, following in ranks, the Mayor's pensioners or guard before the Baner, with Partezans, and those after with halberts, after which followeth singly the Black Serjeant with his halberd, and then the two Sarjents with their Maces, then the 2 Balives with their white Rods, and the Aldermen in their Robes, and after them the Guild Mayor with his great Staff of Authority, and attended on each side with the Nobility and Gentry of the country, as wel as with the Gentry of the Town.

"The Mayor first proceeding from his own House, with his more private attendance, to the Town Hall, where the 12 Aldermen attend his coming in their brown fur'd Robes, with the rest of his Council in their Gownes appropriat; from whence, with sound of trumpet, they march to the High Crosse in Market-place, where, after proclamation there made that the Guild is now to be opened and solemnized, in the interim the Bells ringing, all the Companys of Trade, souldery, and guards, are ranged in order for their more solemn attendance, (viz.) the Company of Smiths, then that of the Cuttlers and Sadlers Company, having in the midst of their travn, a man on horse back armed Cap-ape, brandishing a naked sword; they marching in order from the Market-crosse towards the Church, their drums beating, music of all sorts playing, they from the Church style divid to the right hand and left, Mr. Mayor, the Nobility and Gentry, passing through them, and so into the Church, where, after prayers performed by the Vicar of the Parish, and a learned Sermon preacht by the Guild Mayor's Chaplin, comonly a man of noted knowledge and eloquence, chosen upon that occasion, where, after Sermon ended, the Mayor with his great attendance is received in the streets by his guards of Souldiers and Companys of Trade, he maks his procession to the Church gate barrs, where he and his attendance are entertained with a speech made by one of the chief Schollars of the School, a Barrel or Hogshead of nappy Ale standing close by the Barrs is broached, and a glass offered to Mr Mayor, who begins a good prosperous health to the King, afterwards to the Queen, the Nobility and Gentry having pledged the same; at each health begun by Mr. Mayor, it is attended with a volley of shot from the musketiers attending; the contry people there present drinking of the remainder, after which the Companys of Trade and others, facing about, march in the same order toward the Fishergate Barrs, where they are entertained with another speech in Latin by a Scholler appointed for the same, where another Hogshead is set a broch with the ceremony of healths and volleys of shott, the people shouting and seizing of the residue left. Then, in the same order, they march in great equipage to the Friergate Barrs, where entertained in the same manner by a 3d speech and another Hogshead of ale as aforesaid, then the Guild Mayor and all his noble retinue, returning back towards the Market place, to the High Crosse, where the Schollmaster himselfe entertains them with a learned speech, and verses concerning the prosperous Government of his Majestie, and his gracious confirmation of their unparaled franchises of a Gild Merchant in such grandeur to be solemnis'd each 20 years; after which a Hogshead of Wine standing at the Crosse, is broached, the King's and Queen's health drunk, with joyfull acclamations of the people and volleys of shot as aforesaid, all the Companys of Trades, Soldiers, Mayor's guards in good order surrounding the High Crosse, Mr. Mayor and his honourable retinue, whilst these things were in

---

Guild were Law. Wall, Thos. Hodgkinson, Geo. Addison, Stewards; James Ashton, John Kellett, Wm Lemon, junr. Thos. Winckley, Christopher Nowell, Rich Taylor, Jno Chorley, Wm. Werden, Joseph Bolton, Ralph Rishton, Aldermen, and Edwd. Rigby, Serjeant at-Law, Clerk of the Gild." —Wilcockson.

performing, afterwards reducing themselves in their methods, march before Mr. Mayor towards the Gild Hall appointed for entertainment, where coming they lodg, and hang out at some of the higher windows, the King's Flag and the Burrough Flag with the Holy Lamb, at which Mr Mayor being present, with great acclamations of the people and a volley of shott, each Company of Tradesmen draw off in order to their respective Halls, appointed for their Societys, their Flag of Trade hung out in like manner before their Halls, and their entertein nobly each their own society, the Forren Burgesses at that solemnity in order marching with their respective fraternityes particepatry in their splendid entertainment, feastings, and what additional treats are sent unto them by the Guild Mayor at that time.

"Here it will be necessary to premise the Checke Roll officers and Servants appointed as necessary for this Grand Solemnity

"Ist The 3 High Stewards of the Guild, one to compare the old Guild Book, what persons are surviving in each family of Burgesses, whether they be inhabitant, remoted, restored, or yet forren Burgesses.

"2d Steward to consider what additional Burgesses since the last Guild are procreated or admitted by Court Roll, since the last Guild.

"3d Steward to be Bonser, and receive the fines at that time to be pay'd; and if any new Compounder or Court Roll Burgess, or Admitted Apprentice, at or before this Guild that is now to compound, or requires confirmation of his Freedome; the 3rd Steward, together with the Benchers, are to appoint a fine for any such, to be payd over to the Stewards, and to be inrolled accordingly, which the Clerk of the Guild is to do in a distinct part of the Guild Book appointed for y[t] purpose.

"Chief Clerke or Senescal is to enroll the same, and the names of the Burgesses, either admitted *de novo*, or claiming antient priviledges within this Burrough

"Controler of the Household is generally chosen out of the 12 Benchers or Aldermen, who is, in the Guild time of entertainment, to survey the inferior officers of the household, walking in his gown, with a white rod in his hand, and giveing directions to other servants, of their dutyes; and to advise with the Clerke of the Kitchen and Master Cook and others, what preparations to be made for each several dayes entertainment in Feasting, and to receive accompts, each morning, of the precedent dayes expences.

"Clerke of the Kitchen, adviseing with the Controler, is to give order to the Master Cook and Butchers, what beef, muttons, and veals to kill; what venison to prepare, what rabets or variety of fowls, as phessants, green geese, ducks, capons, pullets; and the Catterars to provide and to be delivered to the Larderer and Cook, to bee in readynesse with other necessarys of the like nature, and with the Baker what bread and flower for the pastery, and with the Bruer what bear, ale, or malt is in store by the Chief Butler's order, and what wines are in readiness, under the custody of the Yeoman of the Wine Cellar, or what may be wanting, to be provided for, and account given up to the said Clerke of the Kitchen and Controller of the Household. The Clerk of the Kitchens to receive accounts dayly, from his inferior Officers, as relating to their kitchen; and weekly to deliver the same up to the Controller, who at the publiq audit, at the shutting up of the Gild, is to render up his account, and compare them with the accounts of other inferior officers

"The Chief Cook is to give order to his under cooks, for prepairing such victualls, boyld, roast or baked as he, with the Clerke of the Kitchen and Controller, have considered to be needful as occasion of entertainment shall require: and to see each dish furnished and sent up with what art, ornament can possibly be perform'd.

"The Under Cooks to obey their *Masters* with all diligence.

"And the servants in the scullery and turnspitts to be attended upon them, as wel as the servants attending in the slaughter, are to do the like upon occasion.

"Chief Butler to wayt in the buttery, and entertain strangers with all kindness and curtesse, and to take charge of the plates in his custody, to be returned

"The Under Butlers to attend in the cellar, and to draw beer or ale for strangers, either below or in the cellar, for divers suppers or entertainment above staires.

"Yeomen of the Wine Cellar to entertain the gentry with Wine or Sack nobly, in the office or wine cellar, and charg'd with the plates in his custody, to furnish the dining roome or other places of entertainm't above the stares, as he shal receive comand from the Controller or other great Officers of the household.

"Inferior officers of the wine cellar as attendant to the yeoman thereof, and other drawers of wine below.

"Bread Baker and Pantler to provoide and deliver out, upon order, bread, &c. out of the pantry, as occasion shall require, as likewise cheese or butter upon all occasion needfull.

"The Guardian of the Spicery and Sweetmeats, &c. to have Tobacco and Pipes, and to deliver out to Mr. Cook what is necessary for the kitchen, or furnishing of dishes at or aft-r t: - C' ι -

"TABLE WAYTERS, young men appointed decently to carry up meat, and to attend at dinner or supper, to furnish each guest with plates, beer or wine, or other viends, and Gentlemen's Servants to be taken into their number for the like service

"THE 2 GENTLEMEN SEWERS to receive the Dishes of meat from Wayters, and place them decently and in order upon the Tables, the one upon the one side, the other upon the other or opposite part.

"The Tables to be prepar'd and cover'd by the chief or 2d ary Butler furnished with plates, napkins, bread, salt, and beer, ale, and wine, in greater vessells standing in cestrons, close by the side cupboard of plates.

"GENTLEMEN OF THE NAPERY, attending the cupboard of plate and glasses, directs the wayting Men where to be furnished with botles of sack, white or claret, and Renish or Frontiniak, or ale strong, or small beer, and to deliver to them plates, glasses, &c. and see bowls, tankers and the same placed again or redeliver'd after Dinner or Supper.

"The DAPIFER or GENTLEMAN CARVER to attend at the Mayor's Table, and carve as he shall be cald upon.

"The MARSHALL OF THE PROCESSION or MASTER OF THE CEREMONYS, in procession time, to rang in decent order of the Company of Trads, Souldiers and the Mayor's guards or halberts, and when procession is ended, to attend, conduct and see placed, the Gentry according to their due procedency at Table, and after to comit the method thereof to writing for future Guilds remembrance

"USHER OF THE HALL, a proper man in his Gown and black Staf, stil attending below stayrs, and conducting Gentlemen and Strangers up the stayrs. If persons of Honōr they are to be usher'd up by the Master of the Ceremonys, into the great dining Roome to Mr. Mayor or into his retiring Roome.

"GROOM PORTERS in black Gowns, one at the Foregate, another at the Back-gate, to keep of Croud and lett in Gentry and Strangers into the Hall or Butteryes.

"As soon as the Kings Baner and the Flag, with the Holy Lamb, are hung out att the Guild Hall, the Mayor, with his noble Attendants enter the Hall, passing by the Groom Porter, in his black Gown and black Staff, who keeps of pressure of the crowding people. They are conducted up into the dining Roome by the Controuller of the Household and the Usher of the Hall, both in their Gowns and white Staves, where, when arrived, they are kindly and nobly welcomed, and treated with good Sack and Bisket, until Dinner be brought up, which is attended by 6 or 8 able Musitians, with their wind Instruments; and caryeing of the first course, upon the first day of the Guild, is by the Aldermen or 12 Benchers, the senior Aldermen bearing and presenting the first dish unto the attending Gentlemen Sewers, who receiveth that and the other dishes, decently and reverently placing them upon the Table, after which the Mayor with his Master of the Ceremonys moveth the Nobility and Gentry to take their places at the Table, which, when so placed, the Reverend Divine (the Guild Mayors Chaplain for that solemnity) with great reverence, craves a blessing upon the Meat; after which, the carver attending, being cal'd upon, attends in his office as occasion requires, the Attendants at the Table, with reverence being very dutifull in supplying what may be required Att Dinner time, after the 1st Course be served up, the Musick playing upon their stringed Instruments, at a due distance in or near unto the Dyning Roome, as may be most pleasant and audible, to the contentment of the Nobility and Gentry attending at this great Solemnity.

"Against the 2d Course, they goe down towards the Kitchen, attending that service with their wind Instruments to the Dyning Roome After Meat plac'd upon the Table, betake them again to their stringed Instruments as before, their playing melodiously all Diner time, where is all varietye of mirth and good victualls, nothing is wanted that may either give a plenary contentment to the Guests or credit and honour to Mr Mayor, where the King, Queens, and many a noble health, in good liquor, passeth round and round all the Tables; and lastly, after great variety of Fruites and Sweet Meats be sufficiently over, in comes the concluding dish, of all store of Pipes and Spanish Tobacco, drenched well with healths in Spanish Wine; and this last dish served up, after the Chaplain hath given thanks for the plentifull refreshment already made use of

"After the Table is diffurnished of Victualls, the memory of Absent Friends is then revived in the best Wine or Sack, as the Cellar will afford.

"Towards 2 or 3 o'Clock notice is given to the Guards and Companys of Trads to attend again in their Equipage, as before is said, they having sufficiently feasted themselves at their severall Halls, with Flags hung out; each Company having, besides their own splendid provisions, a present at Diner sent them from the Guild Hall, each Company a Venison pasty, piping hott, and a great store of Wine and Sack presented from Mr. Mayor.

* * * * * * * * * * * *

"Mean while new preparations are making ready, about midd afternoone, to entertain the Ladyes who are pleas'd to honor Mr. Mayor with their presence, in the great Dining

Roome, where they are treated most nobly with a splendid supper, rich banquet, pleasant musick, Balls and revellings, where their excellent skill in dancing is expressed to the full; Mrs. Mayores (if any) or otherwise a representative appointed to make them welcome. no gates are shutt this night, no persons of gentry or credit debarred from being spectators (if not active themselves), in this Jubile. I have known 200 or more Ladyes and Gent'ewoemen entertain'd at supper, at 3 or 4 sittings down, the great dining room prepaired with diverse ascents for the ladys better prospect, divers Wislers in antiq apparell, with links and torches to keep of the more intruding of spectators, for greater liberty and freedome to the dancers each—them showing their learned skill and mysteryes in the art of dancing—Corantes, Galliards, Serabrands, with their Castinenetts, French and Country Dances, with great delight to the spectators, and glorious reputation to the deserving actors, coming hither from all parts of the County and neighbouring parts upon this occasion and Grand Solemnity. Morning and Wearines having concluded these revelings; after a new treatmt all depart to their severall apartments with their attendance.

"The 2d Day of the Guild Mr Mayor is attended with his train to the Church, to prayers, his Chaplain there wayting for him about 10 of the clock, after the Ceremony of Prayers ended, other nobility and gentry not being present the 1st day of the Gyld, attend Mr. Mayor the 2d 3d or 4th days to the Gyld Hall, where they dine splendidly and are nobly treated, somwhat resembling the 1st Dayes Entertainmt After dinner in the Burrough or Town Hall, they take their Oaths, pay their Fynes, and are enrolled Burgesses in manner as afsd publq attendance to the Company's, upon extraordinary occasion, being call'd to each day in the 1st Week of the Gyld, is attended with feasting of Forren Burgesses that appear then at court, with great solemnity, as hath been said already.

"Upon Sunday following after divine service and Sermon, The Inhabitant Burgesses, the better and greater sort of which that are Wardens of Companys or Housekeepers, Mr Mayor publiqly entertains at diner the young men of an inferior rank are treated occasionally in the Mayors Cellers and Butteryes, when vacant from Forrein Burgesses.

"Each Company of Trads keepe the Flags daily hanging at their Wardens Hall or Lodging, all the time of the Gyld, and when the Wardens are treated abroad in the Burrough, they attend in order, with their Flags displayd; and upon return, lodge them at their Wardens lodging, each Mr of any trade treating his Warden and Brethren, severally, att his own apartment, thus continuing, for most part of the Gyld, which generally continues about 6 weeks.

"The Mayor this last Gyld, after the first week ended, treats openly every other day, vizt—Mundayes, Wednesdayes, and Frydayes; but it any Nobleman, Baronet, or Kts approach, att any other day as often they doe appeare in Companys, the Mayor having notice thereof, entertains splendidly upon their appearances, as if it had been upon more publiq and solemn feasting dayes or in like manner upon the Judges and Sheriffs return from the Assizes, with their retinues of the long Robe and other gentry

"This Treatment is not much unlike that of the first day of the Gyld, setting Publiq Procession from barrs to barrs aside Most of these strangers, as wel as the Judges themselves, if not already Burgesses, have at this time their freedom granted them, and are enrolled forren Burgesses with great solemnity."

The learned doctor likewise describes, in his usual quaint manner, the fashion in which the proceedings, both civic and festive, were brought to a conclusion:—

"The time of shutting up the Gyld being appointed, all the Companyes of Tradesmen attend (as the first day of the Gyld) and all the Burgesses upon Mr. Mayor, to the Town Hall, the adjourn'd Court being call'd, and the attendance of the Burgesses being required, the orders of each Company then sealed, *de novo*, and included within the Gyld Book, after 3 Proclamations, and the Burgesses inhabitant, being cal'd by their names, the Gyld Book of new Orders is held up before them, and the general heads or contents thereof, declared unto them, it is demanded by the Mayor, whether they approve of what is done, which by their precedent Oath of Burgesses, they were engaged to assent to all such orders to be made according to Regal Authority, and the laudable customs of precedent Gylds, which they with loud acclamations do cry consent—God bless the king.

"Then doth the Clerk of the Gyld draw back the Book, and affixes the Holy Lamb, &c, the Burrough Seal unto the same, in presence of them all; and then the Mayor and Steward, holding up the Book, say, "Here is your Lawe." God bless the king

"And the Clerke of the Gyld, by Proclamation made by the Sergeants, says the Court is adjourned for twenty years, untill a new Gyld be proclaimed and held.

"Then great acclammation by all, God save ye king, and echoed with Drums, Trumpets, and a Volley of Shott.

"Mr. Mayor, with attendance, returns from the Gyld Hall, and each Warden with his company of Trades to their severall apartments

"The Mayor, solaceing the Gentlemen and his own attendance, with Bisket, Ale, Beer and Wine; and after is attended to his own lodging, or to some publiq Tavern, where they give him many thanks and great applause for his *Great Care, Labour, Toyle, and Charge, exhibited with such Grandure*, unparalled by other Burroughs, though injoying the liberty of a Gyld Merchant by their Charters Royall, and so each goes to his own appartment."

No detailed records of the proceedings at the following guilds, previously to that which was celebrated in the year 1762, are known to exist From a pamphlet published by J. Moon, it appears that the festivities, processions, etc., were upon this occasion on a very extensive scale. About three hundred ladies walked in procession on the second day of the guild, "all splendidly and elegantly dressed. * * During the procession, the companies of trade were drawn up in lines, on each side, (many gentlemen also attending) to prevent the ladies from being interrupted, or incommoded by the numerous crowd of spectators, who were assembled to view this uncommon and memorable sight. There was on this occasion an amazing concourse of people from many parts of the kingdom, and from all parts of the country. This spectacle was allowed to surpass any thing of the kind ever seen in the country, and exceeded the expectation of every one present, as well in point of the brilliancy and grandeur that attended it, as in respect of the regularity and decorum, with which it was conducted." The pleasures of the festive season were diversified by balls, public breakfasts, concerts, horsemanship, theatrical performances,[r] tumbling, vaulting, dancing on the stiff rope, * * puppet shows, wild beasts, horses of knowledge, etc. "The Guild Hall, an elegent structure, designed by Mr. Carr, an eminent architect, in York," was erected in anticipation of this festivity. The cost of candles for the illumination of the "state room and adjoining Town Hall" in the several entertainments is said to have amounted to two hundred pounds. The rooms were considered "capable of containing near one thousand people, which number it was conjectured by many appeared therein each ball night."[s] Mr Moon's pamphlet further states that "large quantities of ale and beer, and cold provisions of all sorts, were ordered to be distributed amongst the populace each day," and that the guests and inhabitants were much gratified by the exhibition of reciprocal acts of courtesy, and especially with the conduct of Mr. Mayor,

r In addition to the old theatre in Woodcock's-yard, a "commodious temporary theatre was built for the purpose in Church-street, in which plays were performed by his Majesty's comedians from the Theatre-royal, London"

s This appears an extraordinary number, when considered in relation to the then population of the town, which is supposed to have remained nearly stationary, at six thousand persons, since the time when Kuerden wrote his description, nearly a century previously.

(R. Parker, esq.,) "who was singularly studious to please, and to inspire mirth and festivity into every individual." The pamphlet gives the names of six hundred and twenty-nine persons of the nobility and gentry who dined with the mayor during the jubilee. It likewise records that four hundred and fifty-four persons subscribed one guinea each, for the privilege of attending the ladies' assemblies, on the Tuesday and Thursday evenings during the month.

From a notice of the festivities in the "Liverpool Advertiser," of September 19, 1782, it would appear that some advance had been made at the guild of that year, in the style and character of the popular entertainments The writer thus sums up his observations:—"In a word, the plays, oratorios, masquerades, assemblies, and races, formed a diversity of amusements for every description of taste, and greatly contributed to make up a degree of refulgence such as no former period has equalled, nor is it probable that any future one will surpass. There were upwards of three hundred people at the masquerade, on Tuesday se'night, a number of which assumed characters, which were exceedingly well supported." A neighbouring poet celebrated this festival in tolerable verse,[t] in which the beauty and fascinations of the congregated ladies are highly extolled. The poet, however, frankly acknowledges that,

"—— feasting and dancing, and music, and noise,
Are the soul of a Guild, and the chief of its joys."

At the guild of 1802, amongst the vehicles which perambulated the streets of the town, carrying emblematical devices or machinery with operatives actively engaged in their peculiar callings, was exhibited, for the first time, a miniature steam-engine, and other machinery, "at full work, and performing all the various operations of the cotton factory."[u]

An article in the Monthly Magazine describes the festivities on this occasion, from which the following paragraphs are extracted:—

"The gentlemen's procession commenced on Monday morning, immediately after breakfast, it was preceded by the Marshal, armed cap-a-pee, on horse-back, trumpeters on horse-back, &c.; then came twenty-four young, blooming, handsome women, belonging to the different cotton mills, dressed in a uniform of peculiar beauty and simplicity. Their dress consisted wholly of the manufacture of the town. The ground petticoats were of fine white calico; the head dress was a kind of blue feathered wreath, formed very ingeniously of cotton, so as to look like a garland, each girl carried in her hand the branch of an artificial cotton-tree, as the symbol of her profession The gentlemen walked in pairs, preceded by Lord Derby, and the Hon. T Erskine. They amounted to

t The Rev Thomas Wilson, B D, author of the Achæological Dictionary, and formerly master of the Free Grammar school, Clitheroe

u The cotton spinning business had begun to make some figure in the town at this period The Monthly magazine says,—"This very curious and singular piece of mechanism attracted very great attention" The introduction of the cotton business, and the abandonment of the old claims of the companies to the exclusive privileges of trade, had operated so favourably upon the general prosperity of the town that the population had increased from six thousand to twelve thousand, since the preceding guild

about four hundred, consisting of all the principal noblemen, gentlemen, merchants, and manufacturers of this and the neighbouring counties. At the head of the manufacturers were J. Horrocks, esq, M P., and J. Watson, esq, arm in arm, (the two principal and indeed rival manufacturers of the county,) carrying white wands in their hands; upwards of one hundred workmen and mechanics followed, two and two. They paraded through all the principal streets of the town, attended by bands of music, and flags, with various emblematical devices, &c, and then proceeded to the parish church. In the course of the procession, came Nicholas Grimshaw, esq, the mayor, with his maces, the recorder, bailiffs, aldermen, common-council-men, halbert-men, and other corporation officers, town-crier, beadle, &c., as likewise all the different companies or incorporated bodies, headed by their wardens, with staves of office, in their state dresses, and with the usual insignia, also one of the lodges of free-masons, in their appropriate decorations.

"On Tuesday was the ladies' procession. A numerous body of gentlemen, holding white rods in their hands, walked before, and filed off, making a line on each side of the street, through which the ladies were to pass. The girls from the cotton manufactory, led the van as before, afterwards came the ladies, two and two. The Rev Mr Shuttleworth, rector, and Mrs. Grimshaw, the mayoress, and queen of the guild, walked first; after them came the Countess of Derby, and Lady Charlotte Hornby; Lady Stanley, daughter of Lord Derby, and Lady Ann Lindsay; Lady Susan Carpenter, and the Hon. Mrs. Cawthorne; Lady Gerard, and Lady Houghton; Lady Jerningham, and Lady Fitzgerald. Several other baronets' ladies, and the rest of the other ladies, followed, walking in pairs; in all, near four hundred in number, consisting of the most distinguished ladies in this and the neighbouring counties They were all superbly dressed, and adorned with a profusion of the richest jewels. Each of them wore an elegant fashionable plume of feathers, branching from the *coeffoure*. This part of the spectacle (especially the first *coup d'œil*, when the ladies had all got out of the town-hall into the street), comprehending such a brilliant display of beauty, elegance, and fashion, deservedly attracted universal attention and admiration, and produced one of the grandest, most uncommon, and charming sights ever beheld. So splendid an exhibition of female attractions has seldom been witnessed in this part of the country, and indeed every possible variety of taste, elegance, and art, were displayed by both sexes during the whole festival, in costume, ornaments, and decorations. Some of the dresses worn by the ladies, on this occasion, were said to be worth more than £10,000. On Monday, there was a splendid assembly at the town-hall, (the tickets at half-a-guinea each) which was crowded to an uncommon degree, and on Wednesday night the Mayoress gave a ball at the same place, for which more than 400 tickets were issued. The crowd was so great, that dancing was scarcely practicable. The new theatre at Preston, a very elegant and convenient house, was attended by crowded audiences every night, at double prices; a great part of the pit had been laid into boxes; notwithstanding which, hardly a place was to be had on most of the nights. The prodigious concourse of visitors, especially those of the higher ranks, was such as to excite the astonishment of all the townsmen —More than 200 gentlemen's carriages were daily parading the streets of Preston. The races begun on Wednesday, and the concourse of people on Fulwood Moor was greater than ever before remembered."

The guild of 1822, found a faithful historian in Mr. Isaac Wilcockson, from whose "Authentic Records" the following particulars are gathered:—

In ordinary routine, the senior alderman generally succeeded the retiring chief magistrate; but on this occasion the precedent was set aside, and Nicholas Grimshaw, esq, was elected Guild Mayor, for the second time. William Clayton, esq., was appointed the "Town's Bailiff," and Edmund Grimshaw, esq, the mayor's bailiff, by the nomination of his father. In the April previous to the guild, two of Mr Grimshaw's sons were unfortunately drowned in the river, by the upsetting of a pleasure boat. This bereavement prevented Mrs. Grimshaw from taking part in the festivities, as Lady Mayoress The duties of the position were, however, sustained with becoming dignity by her daughter, the lady of Richard Atkinson, esq., of Stodday Lodge, near Lancaster.

The Town and Guild Halls were re-decorated, and a suite of four temporary rooms, tastefully fitted up, erected upon the spot now occupied by the Corn Exchange. The balls and assemblies, and the Lady Mayoress' public breakfast, were held in the latter, the mayor retaining the Guild-hall rooms for his dining parties, etc. "For six months previous, every joiner, painter, and decorator, was in constant employment, and when the Guild was opened there was scarcely a dwelling in the town, from the mansion of the mayor, to the hovel of the cotter, that did not shew itself off in a holiday garb."

The processions passed off with great *eclat*, especially that of the ladies, on the second day, Tuesday, Sep. 3rd. "Every eye," says Mr. Wilcockson, "was instantly turned towards the spot from which the procession was to approach, in order to gain the earliest glance of the delightful spectacle. The sun shone resplendently; the air cooled by the rain which had fallen in the morning, felt most refreshing. The procession was led by Mrs. Atkinson, supported, as before, by the mayor and the mayor's chaplain. The countess of Wilton, and the Hon. Mr. Stanley, followed, and these were succeeded by a train of beauty and elegance which could not be equalled out of the fair circle of 'Lancashire witches'—'Twas a light that ne'er will shine again, until twenty revolving years shall bring the season of another Guild." About one hundred and sixty ladies appeared, in full ball-room costume, in this procession, which included the countess of Derby, the daughter of Lord Stanley, Lady Hoghton, and many members of some of the most distinguished families in the county.

The exhibition of cotton machinery, in full work, was again one of the chief features in the trades' procession. The commercial companies and fraternities, numbered about as follows:—Tanners and curriers, 60; cotton trade, 800; cordwainers, 40; carpenters, 120; butchers, 70; vintners, 90; tailors, 50;[v] smiths, 100; odd-fellows, 250; plasterers, 100; gardeners, 60; printers and bookbinders, 40; free masons, 450.

It was computed that 50,000 persons joined or witnessed the procession on the first day, which number was increased on the following morning by about ten thousand new arrivals.[w]

v The *journeymen* tailors took umbrage at the place assigned to them in the procession, which was the seventh in the list of thirteen. They refused to walk, alleging that their profession boasted the highest antiquity, and was consequently entitled to the first place, "which," said their written protest, "has always been assigned to them from the creation of the world to the present time (the last guild excepted), and they are resolved never to be disgraced by tamely accepting any other!" Their employers, however, were not so squeamish. They cheerfully accepted the place assigned them by the committee.

w The population of Preston had increased to about twenty-four thousand souls; about double the number inhabiting the town at the guild of 1802. This is sufficient to show that the Preston guild festivities enjoyed more than a local reputation. From the list of distinguished visitors, indeed, it would appear that the gentry from almost every part of the kingdom contributed to the splendour and *eclat* of this ancient municipal jubilee.

The entertainments continued for a fortnight, and comprised dress and fancy costume balls, a masquerade, oratorios, concerts, races, banquets, and various other amusements, including the ascent of Mr. Livingstone, in his large balloon. The lady mayoress's public breakfast was attended by about seven hundred persons The masquerade concluded the festival, which passed off with the "greatest order, harmony, and good feeling;" the civil authorities, notwithstanding the immense congregation of people, being fully equivalent to the preservation of the public peace.

This was the last celebration of the Guild Merchant under the *old regime*. The Corporation Reform Bill, passed in 1835, placed Preston, as well as other "chartered boroughs," under its provisions. The exclusive privileges of the "free burgesses" are now things of the past, but the memory of the great jubilee has not yet departed. It will doubtless continue to be celebrated, as a period of festivity, for a long time yet to come, though judiciously contracted in point of duration. Such was the case in 1842, during the mayoralty of Samuel Horrocks, esq., when the proceedings occupied seven days. The festivities of the previous guilds extended over a fortnight; and the guild books continued open for the registration of freemen during twenty-eight days.

Previously to September, 1842, considerable difference of opinion was expressed relative to the propriety of celebrating the guild in the future, as the alteration in the municipal law rendered the legal portion of the ceremony unnecessary. The reformed council, notwithstanding, resolved that the guild books should be opened as usual, and the procession and festivities conducted with all the splendour of their predecessors. Preparations were accordingly made upon the most extensive scale. The suite of rooms at the Guild Hall were tastefully painted and decorated. The area of the Corn Exchange was covered over, and temporarily converted into a magnificent ball-room, one hundred and twenty-six feet in length, by about sixty-three feet in mean breadth The roof in the centre was thirty-one feet six inches in height, and around the sides, about nine feet The large intermediate space was twenty-one feet high This peculiarity gave the saloon something of the character of a cathedral nave, the pillars supporting the roof being festooned, so as to imitate, to some extent, architectural form and embellishment. The general decorations were very gorgeous; the lights in the "clerestory" were formed of coloured transparencies, resembling stained glass, which much enhanced the effect in the day time The entire floor was covered with a deep crimson drugget. The present large assembly room and the galleries were tastefully decorated, and converted into promenades and refreshment rooms.

On Saturday, the 27th of August, the mayor and corporation met at the Guild Hall, and, after drinking the health of the queen, proceeded to the obelisk in the Market-place, and made proclamation of the guild in the usual form. On their return, the "silver punch bowl" and the "loving cup" [x] were replenished, and the members of the council and their friends commenced the festive enjoyments.

On Monday, the guild court was opened at the Town Hall, and afterwards adjourned to the Exchange. The usual ceremonies being gone through, a Latin oration was spoken by Master Humber, a pupil at the grammar school, with such effect as to call forth an eulogium from the recorder, T. B. Addison, esq., who responded, and from the mayor, who, with his own hands, decorated Master Humber with a silver medal of the guild.

Cricket matches, boat races on the Ribble, wrestling matches, formed the staple amusements during the day. In the evening, a magnificent display of fireworks was given in the Market-place, by Mr. Bywater, of Sheffield.

On Tuesday, the grand guild procession took place, when members of the following trades, accompanied by flags, banners, bands of music, and vehicles, containing craftsmen actively employed in their several occupations, attended the mayor and corporation to church, and afterwards paraded the principal streets of the town, the corporate body joining the procession during a portion of the perambulation. Joiners, plasterers, plumbers, glaziers, and painters, smiths, coachmakers, letterpress printers and engravers, glass cutters, butchers, and members of the various lodges of Freemasons likewise joined the procession.

A bazaar, for the benefit of the Abbey Church of St. Bernard, Charnwood Forest, Leicestershire, was opened in the school-room of the Sisters of Charity, near St. Ignatius Church, and remained open during the week. The bazaar was patronised by the principal Roman catholic families in the town and neighbourhood. Amongst the ladies, the Princess Doria Pamphili, and the countess of Shrewsbury, presided at stalls. The earl of Shrewsbury, the Prince Doria Pamphili, and other illustrious members of the family, were present at the opening. They were prevented, however, from honouring the remaining portion of the guild festivities with their presence, in consequence of a previous engagement, which required their attendance at the earl's beautiful seat, Alton Towers, Staffordshire, on the following morning, to receive, as their guest, his royal highness the duke of Sussex.

---

x The silver bowl was presented to the corporation by the earl of Derby, on the 24th of August, 1742. It will contain nearly two gallons. The loving cup is a beautiful silver tankard, of the capacity of about two quarts.

A grand miscellaneous concert was given in the theatre, in the evening. A second day's "Westmoreland and Cumberland Wrestling" was likewise provided, at which the "Champion's Guild Belt" was carried off by Mr. George Donaldson, of Patterdale.

On Wednesday morning, the oratorio of the Messiah was performed at the parish church. A grand procession of upwards of one hundred ladies, in morning concert dress, accompanied the lady mayoress. The members of several friendly or benefit societies, with their emblems, banners, and regalia, joined the procession to the church, and afterwards perambulated the streets of the town. At the conclusion of the oratorio, the members of the twenty-four lodges, forming the Preston district of the Manchester Unity of Oddfellows, formed in two lines, extending from the church to the Town Hall, between which the ladies in procession returned. Nearly four thousand members of friendly societies took part in the day's proceedings. It was generally remarked that the reputation of the ladies of Preston, for personal attractions, had in no respect degenerated.

A grand full dress ball, in the guild saloon at the Corn Exchange, which was attended by upwards of five hundred persons, furnished amusement for the upper classes in the evening.

On Thursday morning, the performance of Rossini's celebrated "Stabat Mater" took place, at St Wilfred's catholic chapel, and the lady mayoress gave her public breakfast in the grand guild saloon, at the Corn Exchange. The children belonging to the schools of the established church, to the number of about two thousand five hundred, marched in procession to the parish church, and were treated, in conjunction with about two thousand others, which the church would not accommodate, with suitable refreshments. The festivities were varied by horse-racing upon the "Holme," and rowing matches upon the river. In the evening, a grand concert, principally of Italian music, was given in the theatre, and a ball took place in the school room attached to St. Augustine's catholic church.

On the Friday, the scholars belonging to the various religious denominations walked in procession. Those appertaining to the establishment were treated with an excursion to Fleetwood, those belonging to the Roman catholic body, to the performances of Mr. Pablo Fanque's equestrian troupe; and others to suitable refreshments in their respective school-rooms.

The weavers likewise, walked in procession, accompanied by a vehicle, containing one of the trade, with a boy assistant, in the act of weaving fancy cloth.

The afternoon was principally devoted to the races. The festivities were brought to a close in the evening by a grand costume ball in the guild saloon. Nearly a thousand persons were present, the chief portion of whom appeared in elegant and costly fancy dresses. This gathering may, unquestionably, lay claim to the distinction of being the most brilliant and gorgeous spectacle ever presented to the inhabitants of Preston.

Amongst the distinguished visitors at the guild were, his highness the duke of Brunswick, the Baron Audlaw, equerry and chamberlain to the duke of Brunswick; the Prince and Princess Doria Pamphili, the earl and countess of Shrewsbury, the earl of Traquair, the Viscount and Viscountess Castlemaine, the honourable Colin Lindsay, the honourable Miss Handcock, the honourable H. Cholmondeley, Sir R. Brooke, bart., Miss Brooke, Major-General Sir Thomas Whitehead, bart., the Misses Whitehead, the Chevalier Datti, the honourable H. Petre, Sir Thomas de Trafford, Sir Thomas H. Hesketh, bart., and the principal gentry of the town and neighbourhood.

The guild of 1842 passed off, on the whole, to the entire satisfaction both of the inhabitants and their visitors. The town was filled with company, notwithstanding the greatly increased accommodation since the holding of the previous guild festival. The gross receipts of the committee of management amounted to £2,500. After the payment of all demands, a surplus of about £200. remained, which was handed over to the public charities.[y]

At the period immediately previous to the passing of the municipal corporation act, Preston contained about three hundred resident, and three thousand non-resident freemen.[z] These were respectively termed in-burgesses and foreign burgesses. Those who were enrolled at a guild merchant were styled guild burgesses; those entered on other occasions were called burgesses by court roll. Freedom was obtained by grant of the corporation and by birth, but it is the general opinion that in the earlier period of the municipal government of the town "almost every respectable housekeeper was a burgess."

At the time of the passing of the municipal reform act, the following gentlemen formed the corporate body:—

"Mayor, Thomas Troughton, Esq. Recorder, T. B. Addison, Esq. Town-Clerk, Richard Palmer, Esq. Steward and Treasurer, Mr. Philip Park. Aldermen—Nicholas Grimshaw, John Troughton, Thomas Miller, James Mounsey, James Dixon, John Addison, and John Woodburn, Esqrs.

"Common council, or capital burgesses.—Messrs. R. Palmer, R. Friend, J. Taylor, J. Pedder, T. Moor, J. Robinson, J. Paley, C. Buck, T. Petty, W. Taylor, W. O. Pilkington, S. Horrocks, junr., T. German, W. Clayton, E. Grimshaw, J. Paley, junr., Greenhow Crane, Esqrs.

"Town's Bailiff, George Noble, Esq. Mayor's do., Thomas Howard, Esq, Town's Sergeant, Thomas Walton; Sergeant at Mace, H. Bowerbank; Market-looker, Thomas Green; Mace-bearer, George Longworth; Town-cryer, James Curle; Beadle and Hall-keeper, William Topping."

The first election of councillors under the new act took place on the 26th of December; and of the aldermen, on the 31st of December, 1835. The

y For further details of the guild of 1842, see pamphlet published by W. Pollard.

z Municipal cor. rep. co. Lan. p. 1687.

mayor was elected on the first of January, in the following year. The following is a list of the gentlemen comprising the first reformed council:—

"Thomas Miller, Esq, mayor. Aldermen —Messrs James Dixon, Charles Swainson, George Gradwell, Peter Haydock, Thomas German, John Horrocks, John Paley, Thomas Monk, John Lawe, William Taylor, John Noble, Thomas Miller

"Councillors.—St. John's Ward —Messrs. Joseph Walker, Thomas Munday, George Jacson, Joseph Livesey, J. Fallowfield, Edward Leece

"Trinity Ward.—Messrs Francis Sleddon, William Garstang, William Holmes, P. Walker, John Knowles, R Segar.

"Fishwick Ward —Messrs. John Swainson, Thomas Barker, John Horn, S. Horrocks, jun, William Shaw, S. Horrocks, senr.

"Christ Church Ward.—Messrs. John Smith, Richard Pilkington, Thomas Leach, Robert W. Hopkins, Thomas Clayton, Robert Brown

"St. George's Ward.—Messrs John Paley, senr., Richard Arkwright, William Humber, J. Bulman, Richard Threlfall, John Park

"St. Peter's Ward.—Messrs. Thomas Swindlehurst, Robert Gardner, Thomas Carter, Joseph Mitchell, Joseph Pomfret, James Park

"Recorder.—Thomas Batty Addison, Esq. Town Clerk and Coroner.—Richard Palmer, Esq. Steward —Mr. Philip Park."

The limited space which can be devoted to the proceedings of the corporate body, in a work of this character, necessitates allusion but to a few of the more important transactions. For further particulars and details the reader is referred to the published minutes of proceedings.

Early after the inauguration of the reformed council, resolutions were passed for the purpose of disposing of the stock of wine in the corporation cellars, the superflous furniture, etc, and for ascertaining the validity of the claim of the old freemen to the exclusive right of pasturage for their cattle on the moor.[a] It was eventually decided that the ownership of the land in question was vested in the mayor, aldermen, and burgesses, in their corporate capacity; and that the freemen had no exclusive right to the pasturage. The report in conclusion says —

"The 92nd section of the act, by the authority of which this council exists, directs any surplus of the borough fund to be applied for the public benefit of the inhabitants and improvement of the borough.

"The disposing of this surplus to a favoured few cannot be complying with this direction.

"Every inhabitant, free or otherwise, has a right to the benefit of this clause, and your committee think that the long enjoyment by the freemen of their exclusive and originally usurped privileges, ought to reconcile them to the tardy justice now partially done to the public."

The "marsh" land not having been "enclosed" by the preceding corporation, remains as a free pasturage for the cattle of freemen only. Like their brethren of the old parliamentary franchise, these exclusives are fast disappearing, the municipal reform act only recognising for the future the rights or privileges of then existing freemen. No new burgesses of this class can be added either by birth or grant The only other privilege at present enjoyed by the freemen is exemption from toll

a The wine realised £226. 3s 7½d.

In 1816, the claim of the freemen to the pasturage on the moor had been decided "not to be well founded," in the case of Hodgkinson *v*. Clowes, at the Lancaster Lent Assizes. Nothwithstanding this, the exclusives were dissatisfied, and in order to try their right, a cow placed upon the moor, was impounded by the municipal authorities. The decision was again adverse to the freemen's claim. A resolution of the corporation on the 1st of January, 1841, authorises the town-clerk, (in consequence of the "proceedings in the action by the freemen to try the right of pasturage on the moor having terminated)," "to discharge John Hodgkinson, the plaintiff, now in goal for the costs of such action, from further custody."

The reformed corporation have preserved the regalia of their predecessors. These articles are rather numerous and possess some historical interest. In addition to the halberds carried before the chief magistrate, and whose probable origin has been previously discussed, the public processions of the municipal authorities are graced by the presence of one large gold (or silver gilt), and two smaller silver maces. The gold mace was presented to the corporation by the duke of Hamilton, in the reign of Queen Anne. It is ornamented by the royal arms, the borough arms, and the heraldic emblazonments of the donor, together with the letters A. R., and the rose and thistle, each surmounted by the royal crown. The following inscription is engraved upon the handle:—

"The Gift of the High and Mighty Prince, James, Duke of Hamilton, Marquess of Clydsdale, Earl of Aran, Lanerk, and Cambridge, Lord Avon, Polemont, Machanshire and Innerdale, and Knight of the most antient and most noble Order of the Thistle, &c., &c., To the Towne of Preston, in Lancashire, in the year 1703, in Token of his Friendship to that Corporation, and of their civilities to him and Elizabeth Gerard, Dutches of Hamilton, his consort, Testified on several occasions during their abode in that Place, and particularly upon the birth of their son James, Marquess of Clydsdale, who was born at Preston, the 3rd day of January, 1701 [2]." [b]

The two silver maces carry no inscription. They are simply ornamented

b He was the fourth duke of the title. His arms, together with those of the earl of Derby, ornament the west end of the Bull Inn assembly room. The dukes of Hamilton were amongst the most distinguished of the occasional residents of the town, ere the aristocratic element yielded before the rapid progress of commercial enterprise. The nobleman, whose costly gift forms the chief feature of the municipal insignia, was slain in a duel, through the treachery of General Macartney, the second of his antagonist and challenger, Lord Mohun, who was himself killed. Macartney although acquitted of the capital offence, was found guilty of manslaughter. Elizabeth Gerard was only daughter and heiress of Digby, Lord Gerard, from whom the dukes of Hamilton inherited the whole of their Lancashire property.

Agnes Strickland says, in her life of Mary Beatrice of Modena, wife of James II. and mother to the Chevalier de St. George: "The duke of Hamilton was at that time the main pillar of her son's cause in Scotland; he was in correspondence with herself; had just been appointed ambassador to the court of France, secretly empowered, it has generally been supposed, by Queen Anne to make arrangements with the court of St. Germains for the adoption of the exiled prince as her successor, on condition of his remaining quiet during her life, little doubt existing of the duke being able, by his great interest in parliament, to obtain the repeal of the act of settlement for the royal succession." —Lives of Queens of England, vol. 10, p. 128.

by the royal crown of the reign of George II., the letters G. R., and the rose, thistle, and fleur-de-lis.

The wand of office carried by the mayor is silver headed, and bears the following inscription:—"Ex Dono Edwardi Rigby arm." (The gift of Edward Rigby, Esq) Another silver headed wand, apparently more ancient, and probably borne by the mayor before the date of Mr. Rigby's gift, is inscribed "Thomas Sompner gen. Maior of Preston, 1644, Henry Werden and Richard Feilden Bailiffs." A representation of the borough arms accompanies this inscription.

Edward, eleventh earl of Derby, great-grandfather of the present peer, was a native of Preston He served the office of mayor of the borough, and was an alderman at the time of his accession to the chief honours of the family. Soon after his elevation to the peerage, he presented to the corporation a magnificent silver punchbowl, as a mark of his esteem. The heraldic bearings of the noble donor and the Preston arms are engraved upon it, together with the following inscription: "Preston in Amounderness, A.D. 1742. The Gift of the Right Hon[ble] Edward, Earl of Derby, 24th August, 1724" The crest of the Stanley family ornaments the silver ladle.

A large and elegantly chased gold, or silver gilt, cup, bears the following inscription:—"Donum gratulatorium Henrici Banester de London armigeri collatum in usu propriu Maioris de Preston in Andernes ac fratrum eius pro tempore existentium in perpetuum. Anno Domini 1615." "A congratulatory gift of Henry Banester, of London, Esq., bestowed for the particular use of the mayor of Preston, in Andernes [Amounderness], and his brethren for the time being for ever. In the year of our Lord, 1615" The arms of the donor and of the borough are likewise engraved upon it.

The "loving cup," or "Queen Anne's cup," as it is sometimes designated, is of richly cut glass, mounted upon a gold stand. It bears the arms of the Fleetwoods and of the borough, together with the following inscription:—"Prosperity to the Queen, the Church of England, and the corporation of Preston." It is doubtless the gift of one of the Fleetwoods, of Penwortham; although no inscription testifies to the fact.

A silver goblet bears the following rude latin inscription: "Ex dono Radi Longworth, Gent., Rico Hynde, Gent., Maiori Burg sive ville de Preston et successoribus suis in perpetuum. A.D. 1671." "The gift of Radus Longworth, Gentleman, to Richard Hynde, the Mayor, and the burgesses of the town of Preston, and their successors for ever."

A silver claret jug, resembling a coffee pot, is, "The gift of Richard Atherton, of Atherton, Esq, to the corporation of Preston, 1722." It bears the arms of the Athertons, impaled with those of the Faringtons, of Worden.[a]

A gilt oar, emblematical of the port, and a handsome state sword, were presented by Mr. John Addison, during his second mayoralty, in 1845. The corporation regalia likewise includes two massive silver snuff boxes, presented by Mr. Palmer, the town clerk, and Mr. Green, the borough treasurer, in 1814.

The corporation of Preston still possesses the matrices of some of the old borough seals. The oldest bears the head of a king, supposed to be Edward III. Beneath the bust a lion couchant is represented, and on each side of the portrait a crescent, bearing, in heraldic nomenclature, an *etoile* or star. The inscription is as follows:—

"S': EDW': REG': ANGL': AD: RECOGN': DEBITOR':"

There is likewise a portion of what appears to have been a duplicate of this seal, which bears the inscription, "Ex dono, 1663." These seals, however, are believed to have belonged to some of the guild companies, and not to the corporate body. The old corporation seal bears a lamb passant, on a shield encircled by a wreath, and is without inscription or date. The seal at present in use exhibits a lamb couchant, with the letters P.P. (Princeps pacis), and the following inscription:—

"SIGILLVM· COMVNE· VILLÆ· DE· PRESTON."

The moor had been enclosed by the old corporation, and the centre portion reserved for a public park. The new body not only proceeded with this work, but took steps for the securing of land on Avenham brows for the extension of the promenade, and the procuring of a survey of the estuary of the Ribble, with a view to improvements in the navigation. Application was likewise made to the "Lords Commissioners of His Majesty's Treasury," for power to sell a portion of the corporate estate, in order to furnish funds for the carrying out these and other public improvements.

In Feb., 1836, Mr. Philip Park, treasurer, presented an elaborate statement relative to the corporate property, in which he showed that the annual income arising therefrom might fairly be set down at upwards of £3,000. The following is a summary of the annual value of the three distinct classes of property into which he divided the corporate estate:—

	£.	s.	d.
"Rents arising from Lands and Buildings exclusive of the Exchange, in Lune-street, but including the Fishery in the River Ribble	2,283	11	4
Receipts at the Exchange, for the year ending Nov. 12, 1835	492	10	3
Rental of Tolls and Stallage, according to the letting of the current year	471	0	0

a Richard Atherton married Elizabeth, daughter of William Farington, Esq., high sheriff of the county in [illegible]. The present Lord Lilford is descended from this union.

The estate of the "old corporation" was, however, indebted to the amount of £6,052.

In June, 1837, it was resolved "that the present and all future mayors of the borough have an allowance of £150, from the corporation funds, by way of salary"

During 1836 and 1837, valuable surveys of and reports on the navigation of the Ribble, by R Stephenson and Son, and Captain Belcher,[a] were procured by the corporation. At a special meeting, held in Dec., 1837, it was resolved that two hundred and fourteen shares should be taken by the municipal body in the company formed to carry out the suggested improvements, etc. The corporation afterwards considerably increased their number of shares in this undertaking.

In July, 1837, the municipal authorities presented an address of condolence to her present Majesty, on the death of her uncle, William IV, and of congratulation on her accession to the throne.

In 1837 and 1838, steps were taken with the view to the erection of a convenient covered market. A committee was appointed to procure plans, estimates, etc.

In 1839, the corporation memorialised the Postmaster-General respecting the situation of the post-office in Church-street, which they proposed to remove to Fishergate, "because," says the memorial, "the persons to whom two-thirds of the letters sent through the post-office to Preston reside in Fishergate" This is principally caused by the law offices being chiefly situated in that neighbourhood. They likewise prayed for an extension of the limit to free delivery of letters, and an earlier despatch of mails.

The corporation, in 1840, presented loyal addresses to the Queen and Prince Albert, on the occasion of the royal nuptials. A petition from the council was presented against, and other steps taken to oppose, so much of a "Bill to amend the Act for the Establishment of County and District Constables," "as proposed to compel Borough Towns to appoint and maintain the same number of Constables in proportion to the population of the rest of the County, and to adopt the rules in force for the government, pay, clothing, accoutrements, necessaries, and qualifications of County and District Constables, without any discretion being vested in the Watch Committees."

In Dec., 1840, a loyal address was presented to the queen, congratulating Her Majesty on the birth of the Princess Royal.

a Captain Belcher was conducting the survey of the estuary and the coast for the lords of the Admiralty He received a special vote of thanks for his valuable assistance to the surveyor appointed by the corporation.

In 1841, the corporation appeared seriously disposed to erect a covered market. Plans were ordered, and, at several meetings, their details discussed. Three distinct sites were proposed; one to the east of the present Market-place, including a portion of the now open square; another to the west, between Friargate, Fishergate, and Lune street; and a third in the "Orchard."

In 1841, an address of congratulation was presented by the mayor and corporation to the Queen and Prince Albert, on the occasion of the birth of the Prince of Wales. Similar expressions of loyalty were tendered on each succeeding addition to the royal family, and others, of "deep concern" on the occasions when traitorous attempts were made upon her Majesty's life.

After much discussion, the proposition respecting the erection of a covered market was rejected in Feb., 1842, by twenty-four votes to nine, in "consideration of the state of the corporation finances." The absorption of the municipal revenue by the Ribble navigation improvements, led to this decision. The lords of the treasury, this year, granted permission to borrow the sum of £12,000., on security of the corporate property, "the same to be applied in discharging the debt incurred by the corporation on account of the improvement of the navigation of the river Ribble, in meeting present and future payments, and in carrying out further projected improvements." This year the celebration of the guild entailing additional expense upon the mayor, his salary was temporarily raised to £500., "being an addition of £350. to the mayor's usual allowance." The peace of the town was disturbed by serious riotings in August.[a]

In 1843, the corporation and other inhabitants, obtained for Preston its recognition as an independent port of the sixth class, with "privileges as extensive as those granted to the port of Lancaster." Fleetwood, then a "supernumerary port," was made a "creek under Preston." The memorial prayed for the "restoration of Preston to its former rank as an independent port." Steps were likewise taken for the erection of bonded warehouses and a custom house. The stalls erected in Church street and Friargate, on market days, were ordered to be removed to the Shambles and Molyneux square.

In 1844, the corporation resolved to purchase the reversionary interest in six acres of land, in the occupation of Mr. Charles Jackson, "for the purpose of preserving for ever uninjured the public walk at Avenham, and of extending it and forming other walks and public gardens, when the existing interests shall expire, or so soon as a satisfactory agreement can be made with the parties having present interests" therein.

The corporation memorialised the postmaster general, "praying for the

---

a See Chap. 8, Trade and Commerce.

establishment of a mail in the middle of the day, between the towns of Preston, Liverpool, and Manchester; for the removal of the post office to a more convenient situation with better accommodation, and for the establishment of receiving houses for letters." The post-office has since been removed to Lancaster-road.

In 1845, the corporation ordered the purchase of other land in the neighbourhood of Avenham-walk, the widening of the south end of the original promenade, and the formation of the lower terraces. In the following year a "committee of taste" was appointed to conduct these extensions, with power to expend the sum of £500. on the same Other sums were afterwards voted for this object, and the improvement of the Moor park. Application was likewise made to the lords of the treasury for £1078., from the funds granted by parliament for such purposes. The commissioners of woods and forests, however, only recommended the sum of £300., which amount the lords of the treasury eventually granted. Several additions and improvements at the New Quay were also effected this year.

In 1846, and the following year, the question of public baths and wash houses began to be agitated in the council, and the condition of the grammar school and Shepherd's library, with a view to the erection of suitable edifices for their respective objects.

On the 21st of September, 1847, her Majesty the Queen, Prince Albert, and the royal children, landed at Fleetwood, *en route* from Scotland to London Great rejoicing took place. The mayor and corporation voted "a dutiful and loyal address, on the occasion of her visiting her county palatine, disembarking within the limits of our port, and honouring our borough with her presence."[a]

The address was presented by the mayor, recorder, and some of the corporation, through Lord Palmerston, at Fleetwood. The Preston station was crowded by parties anxious to catch a glimpse of the royal party, but owing to other arrangements, the train did not stay at Preston. The mayor and corporation were at the station, and shared in the general disappointment.

The municipal authorities, in 1848, resolved, that the market committee be authorised to obtain all surveys, plans, and valuations, and to take all proceedings which may be necessary to obtain an act of parliament "to erect a covered market between Lune street and the Market place, and between Fishergate and Friargate, in the said borough; and for power to borrow a sum not exceeding £40,000 upon the security of such market, and the tolls, stallage, etc., to be received therein." After some agitation,

a Fleetwood has since been made an independent port.

however, this scheme was, like its predecessor, abandoned; the corporation resources being at the time, in the opinion of the majority of the council, sufficiently taxed by the improvements in progress at Avenham walk, and the prospective erection of baths and wash-houses.

This year was one of great political excitement, serious disturbances being threatened by the more violent of the chartist agitators. In May, the municipal authorities addressed her majesty in terms of congratulation, "on the peaceable issue of the late political agitation," and of assurance of the "unabated loyalty of the council and of the inhabitants of the borough of Preston."

In November, 1848, the sanatary committee submitted a report to the council on the general health of the town, from which it appeared that the average mortality, for the preceding seven years, was at the rate of twenty eight deaths to one thousand of the population. The public health act, of 1848, gave power to the general board to direct a superintendent inspector to visit and inquire into the general sanatary condition of any city, town, or borough, where the proportion of deaths to the population had exceeded twenty three to one thousand. The committee, therefore, recommended, and the council passed, a resolution, requesting the general board of health "to send down an inspector, pursuant to Lord Morpeth's Public Health Act."

At the end of the year 1849, some steps were taken to provide a public cemetery for the town, but the project eventually fell to the ground.

The council in 1850, entered into contracts for the erection of baths and wash houses, and introduced the Public Health Act. The members of the corporation form the local board.

In 1851, another attempt was made to proceed with the proposal to erect a covered market between the Market place and Lune street, which ended in—"doing nothing."

Subsequently to the Queen's landing at Fleetwood, in 1847, her Majesty passed through Preston on two different occasions, without staying for refreshment, or for the reception of any address.[a]

In October, 1852, the Queen determined to stay at Preston, on her route from Balmoral to the metropolis. Extensive preparations were made to accord to her Majesty a suitable reception. The station was gaily decorated with flags, mottoes, etc. The first class refreshment room, which was set apart

a On the 30th September, 1848, the royal train did stay a few minutes; when, says the Preston Chronicle, "from the defective arrangements of the railway authorities, the crowd pressed inconveniently upon the carriages," and created some slight annoyance to the royal party. The queen passed through Preston on the 8th of October, 1851, *en route* from Lancaster to Liverpool and Manchester.

for the royal party, was elegantly decorated; several gentlemen of the town and neighbourhood contributing from their collections many first class works of art for this purpose. Other rooms were likewise prepared for the Queen's suite and servants. The principal of the ladies and gentry, as well as a large concourse of the inhabitants of the town and neighbourhood, attended to gratify themselves, and to do honour to her Majesty and her family. The mayor, Thomas Monk, Esq., presented, on the part of the municipal authorities, a suitable address, and the bishop of Manchester performed a similar office for the clergy. Her Majesty's reception was of the heartiest character, and afforded evident gratification to the royal party, although the time of their sojourn did not much exceed thirty-five minutes.

On the death of Mr. Palmer, in 1852, Mr. Robert Ascroft, solicitor, was appointed town clerk.

In 1853, resolutions were passed with the view to the demolition and the re-erection of the corporate property between Fishergate and the Market-place, Cheapside and the Old Shambles

On her return from Balmoral in October, this year, the Queen again honoured Preston with a brief visit. She stayed about fifteen minutes for refreshment, and was presented with an address by the mayor, on behalf of the municipal authorities. The station and waiting rooms were decorated appropriately, and an enthusiastic welcome greeted the royal party. It may, perhaps, be difficult to decide at what particular point overt exhibitions of loyalty degenerate into troublesome routine; but, if all the towns through which her Majesty passes, on her way to her Scottish retreat, were to entertain her with attention similar to that bestowed upon her by the municipal authorities and sight seeing inhabitants of Preston, the "progress" of the popular Queen would be speedily converted into something very different to the notion of pleasant travelling cherished by ordinary people. The mere fact that her Majesty requires refreshment, on her way from London to Balmoral, demands some little stretch of the imagination to invest it with the character of either a state or a private visit to the ancient and loyal borough.

The corporation having determined upon the erection of new Town-hall buildings, offered prizes for suitable designs. A large number of tasteful and elegant architectural drawings were exhibited at the Institution, Avenham, and the public began to anticipate that a truly splendid edifice would shortly adorn the centre of the town. The project included the entire re-construction of the block of buildings between Cheapside and the Old Shambles. The lower story was devoted to shops, the upper and interior portions to a Town-hall, Exchange, and other public offices. The first prize, of one hundred guineas, was awarded to Mr. Hill, of Leeds, and the second, fifty guineas, to Mr. Gingill, of Bristol. The contemplation of the large expense about to be incurred, had, however, somewhat cooled the enthusiasm of some of the council, for at the meeting ordering the payment of the prizes, it was resolved,—

"That the building committee be re-appointed, and that they be directed to inquire into the expediency of proceeding with or postponing the erection of the new Town-hall buildings; and also of the removal or re-letting the present buildings, or some part thereof, and report their proceedings to a special meeting of the council."

The committee duly reported,[a] and the council passed a resolution, postponing "for the present" the erection of the buildings, the "state of the money market and the town" being assigned as the reason for such postponement.

Mr. Philip Park,[b] presented a report and a plan for rendering the present property to some extent available, and materially reducing the cost. A somewhat similar plan, by Mr. Hill, was approved by the council on the 1st Jan., 1855, for the "re-erection of the Town-hall buildings upon the site of the old buildings, at a cost not exceeding £9,500, leaving the (present) Council-room and Town-hall standing.[c] The committee were empowered to enter into the necessary contracts. In May, the demolition of the old Elizabethan structure in the Market-place commenced, and the site was soon cleared; but all further progress was arrested by the following resolution, passed on the 5th of June:—"That inasmuch as the cost of the new Town-hall buildings will so far exceed the estimate stated by the architect, it is not expedient to proceed with their erection."

From a report presented by Mr. Philip Park, it appears that the annual value of the corporate property, in 1855, was estimated at £4,398 15s. 6d., including the Ribble navigation and railway shares.

The public feeling was much excited by the stirring events of the short but severe and costly war with Russia. The news of the several victories were welcomed with great public rejoicing. On the day set apart for the celebration of the return of peace, however, the demonstration, though highly gratifying in itself, did not present that universality of feeling which was to be desired. The principal mill-owners refused to close their establishments. Notwithstanding, a very large and respectable procession of the inhabitants accompanied the mayor and council to the Marsh, where the troops stationed at the barracks, assisted by the militia, fired *feux de joie*, and performed several military evolutions. An immense crowd of people assembled to witness the proceedings. The town was gaily decorated with flags, banners, etc., and the strains of several bands of music added further zest to the proceedings. In the evening,

a February 27th. b August 24th.

c The estimated cost, according to Mr. Hill's previous plans, was £30,000.

several of the principal tradesmen exhibited appropriate transparent pictures, and otherwise illuminated their places of business. The corporation likewise secured the services of Mr. Bywater, of Sheffield, who exhibited a large selection of fire-works, in the Avenham-park. Thousands witnessed the spectacle; the sloping banks below Ribblesdale-place being literally crowded with human beings.

In Feb., 1857, the mayor, Lawrence Spencer, esq., laid the first stone of an edifice to be erected in Lancaster-road, for the joint accommodation of the police authorities and the magisterial bench.

In 1815, an act of parliament was obtained, to "light, watch, pave, cleanse, and improve the streets, highways, and places within the borough of Preston, * * and to provide fire-engines and firemen for the protection of the said borough."

The town had not previously been without some organization for the protection of property from the ravages of fire. A resolution appears in the corporation book of proceedings as early as 1724, from which it appears the mayor intimated that he had received a letter from "y[e] Hon[ble] Daniel Pulteney, Esq[r] one of y[e] Representatives in Parliam[t] for the Burrough, signifying the said Mr. Pulteney's incencons of making a p.sent to y[e] Town of an engine for y[e] extinguishing of fire, of late invencon & which has been tried with success." The corporation resolved that the sum of twenty pounds should be granted from the corporation revenue, towards the purchase of another engine of "such size, make, and invencon as that intended to be given by Mr. Pulteney." It was likewise recommended to "Mr. Mayor to appoint some proper Pson to goe ab[t] in ord[r] to get contrabucons to defray the remaining p[t] of y[e] charge."

The gas company was established in 1815, and the town lighted with gas in the following year.[d]

On the passing of the Corporation Reform Act, the powers of the Commissioners, under the act of 1815, so far as related to the "watching department," were transferred to the municipal authorities; and, on the introduction of the "Health of Towns Act," in 1850, the remaining powers became vested in the council as the "Local Board of Health."

The works belonging to the Preston Water Company were purchased by the municipal authorities, in the year 1853. Very extensive additions are now in progress for the purpose of securing to the town a first-class supply of water from the best available sources. The municipal authorities as the "Local Board of Health," are likewise, at the present time, introducing a most comprehensive system of sewerage, with the view to the thoroughly efficient drainage of the town.[e]

d See Part II. Gas-works. e See Part II. Water-works.

The following list of all the known guild mayors is from the record in the council chamber:—

1329 Aubert son of Robert	1662 James Hodgkinson
1397 William Ergham	1682 Roger Sudall
1415 Henry Johnson	1702 Josias Gregson
1459 Robert Houghton	1722 Edmund Assheton
1501 William Marshall	1742 Henry Farington
1543 Thomas Tipping	1762 Robert Parker
1562 Thomas Wall	1782 Richard Atherton
1582 George Walton	1802 Nicholas Grimshaw
1602 Henry Catterall	1822 Nicholas Grimshaw
1622 William Preston	1842 Samuel Horrocks
1642 Edmund Werden	

The following list of the mayors, bailiffs, and recorders, from the commencement of the last century to the passing of the Municipal Reform Act, with the exception of a few corrections, and the addition of the officers subsequent to the publication of his work, is extracted from Mr. Taylor's notes to Kuerden's manuscript:—

Dates.	*Mayors*	*Bailiffs*
1701	Josias Gregson *(Guild)*	Joseph Curtis, Josias Drinkwater
1702	Geoffrey Rishton	Rob. Chaddock, Adam Cooper
1703	William Lemon	Rich. Ashton, Rich. Casson
1704	John Atherton	Lawrence Wall, John Orme
1705	Thomas Winckley	Edm. Assheton, Will. Coope.
1706	John Chorley	Benjam. Tod, Thomas Garlicke
1707	Roger Sudell	Wm. Prescot, Jas. Drinkwater
1708	John Harrison	Joseph Brearley, John Waller
1709	John Loxham	James Chorley, John Birchall
1710	George Lamplugh	Thomas Rishton, Thomas Myers
1711	William Gradwell	Will. Hebson, Rob. Ashburner
1712	Richard Ashton	Peter Harrison, Jos. Tomlinson
1713	Edmund Assheton	John Thornton, John Clayton
1714	Lawrence Wall	Hen. Atherton, Jacob Parkinson
1715	William Lemon	John Addison, Richard Price
1716	Robert Chadwick	William Wall, Jos. Drinkwater
1717	Joseph Curtis	John Myers, Richard Addison
1718	Richard Casson	Rich. Atkinson, Will. Harrison
1719	George Lamplugh	Richard King, James Riley
1720	William Gradwell	Will. Hardman, Henry Fisher
1721	Edmd. Assheton *(Guild)*	William Patten, Richard White
1722	Lawrence Wall	Edw. Entwistle, Jos. Drinkwater
1723	John Thornton	James Derbyshire, Henry Smith
1724	John Clayton	William Atherton, John Ravald
1725	Thomas Garlicke	Anth. Davis, Robert Walshman
1726	John Myers	Will. Prichard, John Myers, jun.
1727	Richard Addison	Sir Edward Stanley, baronet, (afterwards Earl of Derby) and Banastre Parker
1728	J. Curtis	W. Shackleton, R. Pedder
1729	E. Ashton	E. Knight, J. Walshman
1730	Lawrence Wall	T. Astley, James Naylor
1731	Sir Edward Stanley, bart, (afterwards Earl of Derby)	Thomas Hesketh, Alexander Osbaldeston
1732	William Atherton	Henry Farington, J. Assheton
1733	J. Clayton	J. Hopkinson, J. Bolton

	Mayors.	*Bailiffs*
1734	J. Myers	J. Hopkins, R. Pedder
1735	Richard Addison	John Winckley, John Garlick
1736	Henry Farington	Lawrence Rawstorne, R. Robinson
1737	E. Assheton	R. Assheton, Dr. Escolme
1738	William Atherton	Thomas Garlick, C. Barton
1739	J. Ravald	H. Orme, J. Todhunter
1740	Lawrence Rawstorne	Thomas Starkie, Richard Shepherd, M.B. (founder of the Shepherd's Library in this town)
1741	Henry Farington *(Guild)*	Dr. Parkinson, R. Prescott *(Guild)*
1742	J. Walshman	J. Dixon, Richard Loxham
1743	William Pritchard	J. Hesketh, Gilbert Woosey
1744	W. Harrison	R. Briggs, Thomas Jackson
1745	J. Darbyshire	Edward Pedder, J. Wilkinson, (afterwards town clerk,—discharged about 1765)
1746	Thomas Starkie	Thomas Winckley, S. Prescott
1747	Richard Shepherd, M.B.	Joseph King, J. Wilkinson
1748	Richard Pedder	J. Astley, Joseph Myers
1749	Thomas Astley	Robert Parker, N. Walton
1750	Lawrence Rawstorne	R. Hesketh, Evelyn Charles Franckes
1751	J. Bolton	William Coward, Will. Green
1752	Robert Parker	Dr. Escolme, R. Livesey
1753	William Prichard	Nicholas Starkie, Robert Moss
1754	Thos. Starkie	Thomas Grimshaw, James Cowburn
1755	Richard Shepherd, M. B.	Thomas Aldred, Ralph Watson
1756	Richard Pedder	J. Whittle, J. Darbyshire
1757	Robert Hesketh	Edward Bolton, John Nabb, (afterwards town clerk)
1758	J. Bolton	William Riddihough, Bartholomew Davis
1759	William Prichard	John Watson, Thomas Wilson
1760	Lawrence Rawstorne	Richard Atherton, John Taylor
1761	Robert Parker *(Guild)*	John Jackson, jun., John Grimshaw,
1762	Thomas Jackson	Fleetwood Hesketh, William Prichard
1763	Edward Pedder	Thomas Pedder, John Smalley
1764	Richard Assheton	Casson, Thomas Aldred
1765	William Prichard	William Leake, Alexander Nowell
1766	Joseph Myers	Thomas Cowburn, Will. Briggs
1767	Robert Moss	Nicholas Winckley, Rob. Farrer
1768	Thomas Grimshaw	Edward Pedder, Richard Wilson
1769	Richard Assheton	J. Woods, J. Nuttall
1770	Edward Pedder	Will. Wickstead, James Knowles
1771	James Cowburn	James Cheetham, Thomas Greaves
1772	Ralph Watson	Thomas Walshman, R. Bailey
1773	Richard Atherton	Edward Atherton, Edward Robert Travers,
1774	Bartholomew Davis	O. Farrer, John Greaves
1775	John Grimshaw	Thomas Cowell, James Heald
1776	Edward Pedder	James Pedder, Thomas Bolton
1777	James Cowburn	John Latus, John Fallowfield
1778	Ralph Watson	Henry Watson, Will. Brandreth
1779	Thomas Pedder	Thomas Briggs, Tho. Winckley
1780	Bartholomew Davis	Richard Loxham, William Serjeant, (died in office, succeeded by Thomas Farrer)
1781	Richard Atherton *(Guild)*	Robinson Shuttleworth, Nich. Grimshaw town clerk

	Mayors.	Bailiffs.
1782	John Grimshaw	Henry Walshman, John Green
1783	William Green	James Cowburn, Joseph Seaton Aspden
1784	Ralph Watson	James Blackhurst, John Heald
1785	Bartholomew Davis	James Moore, Daniel Lyon
1786	Richard Atherton	Richard Newsham, Richard Loxham
1787	Thomas Cowburn	William Wilson, George Blelock
1788	John Grimshaw	Seth German, Henry Fisher
1789	William Green	Rich. Riddihough, Robt. Gornall
1790	Edward Pedder	Hugh Waterworth, Sept. Gorst
1791	Thomas Greaves	James Lorimer, James Cowburn
1792	William Prichard	Ralph Assheton, George Bolton
1793	Robinson Shuttleworth	Geo. Dewhurst, Hugh Dewhurst
1794	James Pedder	Thomas Sill, John Horrocks, (afterwards M. P. for Preston)
1795	Henry Walshman	Roger Fleetwood, Peter Blelock
1796	James Moore	John Troughton, Sam. Horrocks (late M. P. for Preston)
1797	John Fallowfield	William Brakell, Thomas Ogle
1798	Edward Robert Travers	John Startifant, John Whitehead
1799	John Grimshaw	Thomas Starkie Shuttleworth, George Fleming
1800	William Prichard	James Heald, Richard Palmer, (town clerk)
1801	Nicholas Grimshaw *(Guild)*	Thomas Wilson, Thos. Norcross
1802	Samuel Horrocks	William Leighton, Thos. Miller
1803	Daniel Lyon	Robert Friend, James Mounsey
1804	George Blelock	John Taylor, George Cotton, (died in office)
1805	Edward Robert Travers	James Pedder, John Daniel Lyon
1806	John Grimshaw	John Knock Grimshaw, Charles Ambler
1807	Richard Newsham	Thomas Tomlinson, Jas. Dixon
1808	Nicholas Grimshaw	Thos. Moore, Jonathan Lodge
1809	Daniel Lyon	Arthur Milsom, William Brade
1810	George Blelock	Joseph Robinson, John Paley
1811	Edward Robert Travers	Wm. Buck, R. R. W. Robinson, MD.
1812	Nicholas Grimshaw	Charles Buck, Thomas Petty
1813	Richard Newsham	Thomas Green, John Woodburn
1814	Daniel Lyon	Thomas German, William Petty
1815	Edward Robert Travers	James Newsham, Wm. Taylor
1816	John Troughton	Thomas Troughton, John Baron,
1817	Nicholas Grimshaw	Jno. Addison, jun., Rich. Addison
1818	Richard Newsham	T. B. Addison, W. O. Pilkington
1819	Hugh Dewhurst	Thomas Dewhurst, Robert Buxton
1820	Thos. Miller	Saml. Horrocks, jun., Geo. Jacson
1821	Nicholas Grimshaw	Wm. Clayton, Edmd. Grimshaw
1822	Dan. Lyon	John Paley, jun., S. G. Crane,
1823	John Troughton	John Startifant, John Troughton, jun.
1824	Richard Newsham	Alex. Moore, M. D., Rd. Newsham, jun.
1825	Nicholas Grimshaw	Jos. Bray. Wm. Nicholson
1826	Thomas Miller	T. S. Shuttleworth, Wm. A. Hulton
1827	Hugh Dewhurst	Bulman, Geo. Todd
1828	John Troughton	Thos. Troughton, jun., John Abraham
1829	James Mounsey	Jos. Walker, Bowman
1830	Nicholas Grimshaw	S.R. Grimshaw, H. P. Fleetwood
1831	James Dixon	Threlfall, Robt. Brown
1832	John Addison, jun.	Thomas Pedder, John Gorst
1833	John Woodburn	Kaye, Wm. Ainsworth
1834	Thos. Troughton	Geo. Noble, Robt. Troughton

RECORDERS.

Edmund Starkie, Esq., Barrister-at-Law, of this Borough.
John Aspinall, Esq., Serjeant-at-Law, of Standen Hall.
Robert Moss, Esq., Barrister-at-Law, of this Borough, and of Sandhills.
Sir James Alan Park, Knt., one of the Justices of his Majesty's Court of Common Pleas.
Thos. Batty Addison, Esq., Barrister-at-Law, Preston.

The following have been mayors of Preston since the passing of the Municipal Reform Act:—

1836, Thomas Miller; 1836-7, P. Haydock; 1837-8, Thomas German; 1838-9, John Paley, sen; 1839-40, William Clayton; 1840-1, George Jacson; 1841-2, Samuel Horrocks; 1842-3, William Taylor; 1843-4, John Addison; 1844-5, John Paley, jun.; 1845-6, Thos. German; 1846-7, John Paley, jun.; 1847-8, Thomas Birchall; 1848-9, Richard Pedder; 1849-50, James German; 1850-1, John Catterall; 1851-2, Thomas Monk; 1852-3, Peter Catterall; 1853-4, Thomas Walmsley; 1854-5, Wm. Humber; 1855-6, Richard Threlfall, jun.; 1856-7, Lawrence Spencer.

PRESTON POOR-LAW UNION.

In the year 1837, the "New Poor-law Amendment Act" was introduced. Much feeling has been manifested by the rate-payers, and several discussions have taken place at the guardian meetings relative to the workhouse question. The poor-law commissioners, and one section of the guardians, (including a large majority of the ex-officio members of the board), have propounded a scheme for the erection of a new and sufficiently large workhouse, to provide accommodation for the whole union. Another, (with a large majority of the elected guardians), has hitherto successfully opposed this movement. The parties are at present, when in the board-room, nearly balanced; but judging from the circumstance that a majority of the entire body have lately been privately induced to append their signatures to a document in favour of the scheme, its eventual adoption may almost be regarded as a certainty. The outlay in the first instance will unquestionably be heavy, but the annual expenses of conducting one well adapted establishment, it is contended, will be much less than under the present divided and imperfect system.

The following tables exhibit the state of the union at the period when the "Amendment Act" was first introduced, and at the time when the last valuation of rateable property and average expenditure in relief were taken:—

TOWNSHIPS COMPRISING PRESTON POOR LAW UNION.

DISTRICTS.	TOWNSHIPS.	Statute Acres.	Population in 1831.	Parochial Assessment or Rateable Value in 1829.	Average Yearly Expenditure in Relief for 1835-6-7.	Population in 1851.	Parochial Assessment or Rateable Value in 1855.	Average Yearly Expenditure in Relief for 1849-50-51.
PRESTON	Preston	1415	33112	£120,156	£5641	68356	£187,826	£8069
	Fishwick	675	759	4878	107	1005	6353	38
ALSTON	Dutton	1665	490	2069	193	446	1605	197
	Ribchester	2093	1889	3700	448	1650	3265	365
	Dilworth	1074	874	1993	119	834	2674	147
	Alston	1785	1030	3145	163	807	3179	144
	Hothersall	963		1194	51	152	1183	67
	Grimsargh-with-Brockholes	1800	310	2895	92	360	3114	60
	Elston	866	64	1070	7	54	965	1
	Ribbleton	717	170	1458	37	189	1683	48
BROUGHTON	Broughton	2303	620	4941	170	685	6425	104
	Barton	2543	422	3357	169	370	4844	87
	Fulwood	2014	500	4259	90	1748	5843	114
	Lea, Ashton, Ingol, & Cottam	3095	687	7868	284	743	8539	163
	Haighton	1041	192	1490	51	193	980	59
	Woodplumpton	4699	1719	4749	178	1575	9038	181
	Whittingham	2797	710	4574	169	678	4163	164
	Goosnargh	7891	1844	9445	485	1454	7982	383
LONGTON	Farington	3190	672	3053	238	1932	7642	118
	Little Hoole	846	189	1000	65	202	2032	46

LONGTON	Much Hoole........	1622	745	2397	181	775	2760	110
	Hutton........................	1859	715	3200	247	500	3015	123
	Howick..........................	495	132	1066	35	116	923	44
	Longton........................	2907	1744	4786	327	1687	5163	275
	Penwortham	2109	1416	1906	576	1487	7097	327
WALTON-LE-DALE......	Walton-le-dale.................	4239	5767	13820	750	6855	20098	870
	Samlesbury	3799	1948	6121	459	1435	5277	338
	Cuerdale..........................	660	118	1170	57	80	785	9
TOTAL...........	....	61252	58836	221760*	£11347	96368	£314465†	£12651

No.	WORKHOUSES, &c.	Capacity of Accommodation in 1837.	No. of persons therein on the 16th Feb. 1837	Capacity of Accommodation in 1856.	No. of persons therein on the 11th Sept. 1856
1	Preston	300	242	480	237
	Ditto House of Recovery..............................	...	...	50	38
2	Walton-le-dale	150	43	124	89
3	Ribchester	130	43	145	118
4	Wood Plumpton	140	31	64	62
5	Penwortham	100	64	70	44
6	Longton	80	31	discontinu'd	...
7	Goosnargh	130	43	do.	...
8	Alston...	80	7	do.	...
9	Hutton	60	25	do.	...
	TOTAL......	1170	529	933	588

* The county assessment, in 1829, gives the total value at £195,930. The total net annual value of rental is given at £228,309.

† The total will not exactly accord with the addition of the several items, as the shillings and pence of the latter are omitted.

The following additional particulars respecting the Preston Union are extracted from the sixteenth annual report of the registrar-general, published 1855:—

PRESTON UNION, IN THE YEAR 1852.

Area in Statue Acres.	Population in 1851.	Marriages.	Births.	Deaths.	Excess of Births over Deaths.
68035.*	96545.*	1015.	3876.	2909.	967.

Births including Illegitimate Children.		Illegitimate Births		Deaths.	
Males.	Females.	Males.	Females.	Males.	Females.
1975.	1901.	205.	187.	1468.	1441.

* From some unexplained cause the total area of the townships composing the union is 6,783 acres less in the union books than in the registrar-general's report. The deficiency is divided over the various districts. The population in the union books is 181 below that of the registrar-general. The deficiency in this respect is almost entirely confined to the Preston district.

PART I.—HISTORICAL.

CHAPTER VII.—PARLIAMENTARY REPRESENTATION.

Elective principle of Anglo-Saxon Government—Norman Despotism—The Great Charter—Charter of Henry I.—Parliaments summoned by Henry I.—Henry II. and Henry III.—The "Reforming Barons"—Edward I.—Earliest Recorded Representation of Preston, and the County of Lancaster—Boroughs—Lords and Commons—Influence of the Crown—Payment of Members—Preston Unrepresented through Poverty—Henry VI.—Forty Shilling Freeholders—Civil Wars—Cromwell's Parliament—Annual, Triennial, and Septennial Parliaments—Property Qualification—Universal Suffrage at Preston—Disputed Rights—Resolutions of the House of Commons—Rivalry of the Corporation and the Derby Family—The "Great Election"—Serious Riots—Rise of the Manufacturing Interest—The Coalition—The Reform Bill—Election Details—List of Representatives.

The Norman conquest, as has been shown in the previous chapters, did not simply transfer the crown from one dynasty to another, but almost annihilated the civil and political laws of the Saxon people, and transferred nearly the whole of the landed property to the military chiefs of the successful adventurer.

The Anglo-Saxon principle of government was unquestionably representative in its generic character; that of the early Norman princes autocratic, or oligarchial. In process of time, the Anglo-Saxon element began to regain some of its lost influence. This has gradually expanded into the present constitution, composed of a limited monarchy, with a joint oligarchial and representative legislation. One writer says:—

"For a clear exposition of the necessarily republican basis of all the public institutions of the Anglo-Saxons, up to their kingship itself,—which, though now becoming generally understood, it is necessary to insist upon again and again, in opposition to the misstatements on the subject, which are even yet being propagated,—we would refer to Mr. Allen's learned and sagacious 'Inquiry into the Rise and Growth of the Royal Prerogative in England,' 8vo, 1830. The indiscriminating use, by our historians, of the words *king* and *kingdom*, as if bearing precisely the same import, after the Norman conquest as before it, has contributed not a little to the confused apprehension of the matter which has generally prevailed. The very etymology of the Saxon compounds *cyn-ing* and *cyne-dom* (according to modern orthography *kin-ing* and *kin-dom*), denotes an elective national head. The *cyne* or *kin* of the Saxons was synonimous with *nation* or *people;* and *cyne-ing* or *kin ing* (by contraction *king*), implied, as Mr. Allen well remarks, that the individual so designated, was, in his public capacity, not, as some modern sovereigns have been willing to be entitled, the *father* of a people, but their offspring. In the introduction and use of the modern word *kingdom*, we trace a still more remarkable perversion. The Anglo-Saxon *cyne-dom* or *kin-dom* denoted the extent of territory occupied and possessed by the *kin* or nation—an import diametrically differing from that of king-dom, which, in the decline of the Norman tongue as the language of the government implanted by the conquest, was substituted for the Norman *royaulme* (in modern English *realm*)—as the word *king* itself, with as little regard to its etymological derivation, was substituted for the Norman *roy*. Thus it is manifest that the difference of meaning between *kin-dom* and *kingdom* is as wide as that between the principle which recognised the nation at large as the original proprietor of the soil, and that which vests such absolute proprietorship exclusively in the crown—a distinction which it is most important to perceive and bear in mind. It is not possible to form any just conception of the political history of the English municipal towns, without first possessing a more correct notion than is to be gathered from the greater part of our modern historians, of the real character of the great revolution effected in England by a foreign conqueror towards the close of the eleventh century. Want of diligence or of candour has betrayed them into giving always a faint and often a false representation of that transaction." [a]

The conquered people were not only stripped of their property, but of all civil or political influence.

"The highest condition of the English in the rural districts was that of the humble farmer and rustic artizan, whom their Norman masters called *villains*; and in the municipal towns, the townsman or resident householders, according to the Normans the *burgess*,—no longer a freeholder, was placed on precisely the same social level as the *villain*—that of men not indeed personally enslaved like the serfs and bondsmen, but wholly excluded from political rights, and therefore subject, according to the feudal maxims of the Normans, beside the rent of their individual holdings, and besides the rigorous payment of the rents and service due by the old English custom, in the nature of contributions to the general exigences of the state, to arbitrary taxation by the crown, in the shape of occasional levies, called by the Normans *taillages* or *tallages*." [b]

The "Great Charter," wrung from the vacillating John, on the field of Runnymede, by the barons, curtailed greatly the absolutism of the early Norman monarchs, and paved the way for the gradual further enfranchisement of the people. The burgesses of the city of London, and other large towns, actively interested themselves in the procuration of this *magna charta*, which expressly declares that all cities, boroughs, and ports shall "have their liberties and free customs" preserved. A sense of common interest had by this period induced, to some extent, a fusion between the Norman proprietors of the soil, and the wealthier portion of the mercantile Anglo-Saxon people. Still the national council represented solely the barons and the extensive landed proprietors. The lesser holders of land, of the second, third, and other inferior classes, (being all tenants or vassals of the upper class of landholders), together with every other interest, commercial or mercantile, were regarded as "too insignificant" to be represented in the great council of the king.

---

a Penny Cyclopædia, art. Boroughs of England and Wales.

b Ibid. In the eleventh year of the reign of Henry III., a tallage was levied, towards which Preston, contributed fifteen marks, equal to about £150. of the present money. Lancaster paid thirteen marks, and Liverpool eleven marks and a half.

The original charter was really granted by Henry I., who, on espousing Matilda, of Scotland, united the Saxon and Norman royal families. He caused one hundred copies of a digest of the laws of Alfred and Edward the Confessor to be distributed amongst the several bishoprics and principal monasteries. Henry did not, however, scruple to violate his engagement to observe these laws, and it is believed he caused the greater quantity of the copies deposited to be destroyed. According to Rapin, only one could be found, when searched for by the confederated barons in the reign of John. Miss Strickland[c] contends that Henry I., by the advice of his queen, assembled parliaments, in the election of which the burgesses of the chartered boroughs were consulted. She says:—

"Our earliest historian who writes in English, Robert of Gloucester, declares,—

'When his daughter was ten years old, to council there he drew,
On a Whitsuntide, a great parliament he name (held)
At Westminster noble enow, that much folk came.'

"Piers of Langtoft, a parallel historian, who wrote in French, with the most minute detail points out the classes of whom Matilda advised Henry to take counsel, viz., barons, lords of towns, and burgesses. Here are the lines:—

'Mald the good queen gave him in counsell
To love all his folks and leave all his turpeile, (disputing)
To bear him with his barons that held of him their fees (feofs)
And to lords of towns and burgesses of cities:
Through council of Dame Mald, a kind woman and true,
Instead of hatred old, there now was love all new;
Now love they full well the barons and the king,
The king does ilk a deal at their bidding.'"

Long after the first signing of the great charter, however, the levying of *tallage* upon the burgesses as upon the *villains*, was still claimed as an inherent right of the Anglo-Norman crown, and was of itself an abundant source of vexatious oppression.

By virtue of this prerogative, Henry II., under pretence of a crusade, in 1087, procured a list of the more wealthy citizens in the boroughs and towns, and summoned them to appear before him. In consideration of the honour of an interview with his majesty, each party was informed by an interpreter of the amount of contributions which the king's emergencies required. "And thus," says a contemporary chronicle,[d] "did the king take from them a tenth of their properties, according to the estimate of good men and true, that knew what income they had, as likewise what goods and chattels. Such as he found refractory he sent forthwith to prison, and kept them there until they had payed the uttermost farthing. In like manner did he to the Jews within his realm, which brought him incalculable sums."

c Lives of the Queens of England, vol. 1, p. 176.

d Roger de Hoveden, Annales.

Henry III. being in want of money for the prosecution of his wars, and deeply embarassed, had recourse to a kind of parliament, which was convened at Oxford, in 1258. It would appear that the arbitrary spoliations previously practised had begun to produce serious discontent in the nation. A contemporary historian[e] says that, "justice itself was banished from the realm; for the wicked devoured the righteous, the courtier the rustic, the oppressor the innocent, the fraudulent the plain man, and yet all these things remained unpunished." This parliament was composed of "the grandees of the realm, major and minor, with horses and arms, together with the clergy." They were convened together to make "provision and reformation, and ordination of the realm." Amongst other acts, this parliament decreed that four knights should be chosen by each county, whose duty should include the investigation of local grievances, with the view to their removal. Parliament was to meet three times in each year. By a writ in chancery, the sheriffs were commanded to pay "reasonable wages" to the knights delegated, for their public services. Other encroachments upon the absolutism of the monarch were introduced, which eventually involved the king, Prince Edward, and the chief courtiers, in a sanguinary war with the "reforming barons," headed by Simon de Montfort, count of Leicester, and Robert de Ferrers, earl of Derby. In the course of events, the king fell into the power of the former, who, in 1264, summoned a parliament to meet at Worcester. This parliament enacted that the sheriff of each county should return, together with two knights of the shire, "two citizens for each city, and two burgesses for each borough" within his jurisdiction. The defeat of Montfort, shortly afterward, frustrated for a time the enfranchisement of the Saxon citizens and burgesses. Edward I. in in the twenty-third year of his reign, however, had the penetration to see that the innovation was necessary to the peace of the country, and the security of his throne. Though, in his writs he declares, "that it was a most equitable rule that that which concerns all should be approved by all," his main object in calling a council of knights, citizens, and burgesses, was to procure supplies with the least possible trouble and show of injustice. But parliament once formed soon acquired a permanent and influential position in the state. The parties who voted the money for the exigences of the government, required conciliating, and sometimes satisfying as to the wisdom or necessity of the expenditure. As early as the twenty-fifth year of the reign of Edward I. (1297), the right of raising taxes by royal prerogative was disclaimed, and the political existence of a house of representatives guaranteed by statute. The knights of the shire, who pre-

e Ann. Burton, p. 421.

viously held separate consultations, afterwards amalgamated with the citizen and burgess representatives, and formed one council or estate of the realm. The title "commons" appears to have been first used in the writs issued by parliament for the proclamation of Edward III. king, on the deposition of his father Edward II. in the year 1327.[f]

The earliest public record of members serving in parliament for Lancashire, does not extend further back than the twenty-third Edward I. (1295) though it is probable, writs were issued, both for knights of the shire and representatives of the borough towns as early as the forty-ninth Henry III. (1264). Mr Edward Baines says:—

"The boroughs for which returns were made were principally 'walled towns,' held of the king in ancient demesne, and the only places in Lancashire entitled to the privilege, if that could be considered a privilege which was felt as a public burthen, were Lancaster, Preston, Liverpool, and Wigan. The inhabitants of the boroughs, under the feudal system, were for the most part, villeins, either in gross, or in relation to the manor in which the town stood, and belonged to some lord.[g] The former held houses called burgage tenures, at the will of the lord, and carried on some trade such as carpenter, smith, butcher, baker, clothier, or tailor; and the election of members was in the inhabitants of the burgage tenures, so far as they were free agents. There were also in these boroughs certain free inhabitants who held burgages, and were in consequence invested with the elective franchise. In incorporated cities and boroughs, the right of election was generally in the corporate body, or freemen, as they were called, subject to such limitations, however, as the charters imposed. When the wages of the members representing the cities or boroughs were paid out of the rates, the election was in the inhabitant householders paying those rates, and the right of election was hence designated 'scot and lot suffrage.'"

The two first recorded members for Preston were William Fitz-Paul, and Adam Russel They were returned in the year 1295

From this period a house of commons became a necessary condition to the power and security of any English monarch. The absurd attempt to rule without, or in defiance of, this governing element, by the Stuarts, cost them an empire. The Plantagenents and Tudors regarded the "*management*" of the house of commons rather than its "*coercion,*" as the safest method for the accomplishment of their wishes. Some historians are of opinion that the "packing" of the house, in defiance of solemn enactments to secure the purity of election, was the true cause of the fall of the house of Lancaster, in the reign of Henry VI, as the sanction of a really popular representation formed the basis of its permanent restoration in the reign of Henry VII.

The writs being directed to the sheriff, in his capacity of king's bailiff, considerable power was exercised by this official, in influencing the

f "In former times both lords and commons sat together in one house in parliament, says Sir Edward Coke, in his 4th Institute, 23, but this is clearly a mistake, as is shown by Sir Robert Cotton and others, and is decidedly proved by 6, Edward III n. 3, parl. rol, where is said—'The bishops by themselves, the lords by themselves, and the commons by themselves, consulted and advised the king touching the war with Scotland' So that in reality, the early parliaments of England consisted, not of one house, but of three houses."—Edward Baines

g Archæologia.

return of individual members, and even to the suppression of the writ, in the case of an intractable borough. In the seventeenth year of the reign of Edward II., the high sheriff of the county of Lancaster, by a singular act of presumption, claimed for himself the right to the selection of members to represent the county. In the following reign, (thirty-sixth Edward III.,) this stretch of arbitrary power was even exceeded by the audacity of the under sheriffs, Edras Lawrence and Mathew Risheton, who elected themselves, and pocketed the expenses amounting to £18. 16s. This being complained of, writs of enquiry were issued by the king. The investigation resulted in the unseating of these worthies, by authority of the crown. The Norman princes, as well as the Stuarts, frequently testified their notion that a parliament was merely a convenience to aid the monarch in carrying out the behests of his individual will. Richard II., in 1398, summoned the sheriffs, and with unparalleled autocratic insolence charged them to permit of the election of no one who would not promise to agree to the measures of the king. This imbecile monarch, had the daring hardihood to ask of the sheriffs what force each county could furnish, as he proposed raising an army to punish such of his subjects who should act in opposition to his wishes. His solemn impeachment and deposition was the first act of the first "free parliament" called by him; a proof that the majority of the nation had, even then, begun to entertain notions concerning the royal prerogative, very different from those cherished by the descendants of the conqueror.

The power of the commons had, however, by the latter portion of the reign of Richard II., become so much increased, that statutes were enacted by which sheriffs were fined, who did not "literally obey the writ," and the citizens and burgesses subjected "to be amerced or otherwise punished," for neglect or non-compliance, without sufficient excuse. The wages of the members were paid by the burgesses, whose voices were, nevertheless, little more than the mere formal echoes of the wishes of the lords of the soil. Several of the smaller towns consequently petitioned for exemption from so questionable a privilege. It appears the borough of Preston after furnishing its due quota to the legislative wisdom of the nation for seven successive parliaments, "declined the honour," in the reign of Edward II. (1326). It was common about this period for the sheriffs to conclude their returns with an intimation that there were "not any other cities or boroughs within the county, from which any citizens or burgesses can or are accustomed to be sent to the said parliament, by reason of their decay or poverty." The daily stipend, fixed by royal writ, for knights of the shire, was four shillings, and that of the borough representatives, two shillings.

The sittings did not generally extend over a month; yet the burgesses of Preston regarded the representative privilege, either as useless, or as too expensive an article for their indulgence. The expenses of the journey would form a serious item, for, according to Prynne, the time for travelling from Lancashire to Westminster, allowed to members of parliament in the reign of Edward III., was from five days to eight, according to the state of the weather! It can be accomplished now in as many hours!! It must not, however, be forgotten that the *practical* value of two shillings in the reign of Edward II., was more than equivolent to that of a sovereign at the present day.[g] It appears that the burgesses of Preston suffered their right to parliamentary representation to remain in abeyance during a period of 221 years. It was resumed in the first year of the reign of Edward the sixth, A.D. 1547.[h] Lancaster Liverpool, and Wigan, at the same time resumed, by royal authority, their dormant privileges. In the first of Elizabeth, the boroughs of the county were increased in number by the addition of Clitheroe and Newton.[i] Manchester, with the exception of two returns during the period of the commonwealth, remained disfranchised till the passing of the reform bill, in 1832.

In the sixth year of the reign of Henry IV., the king commanded the sheriffs not to return any persons "learned in the law," from which circumstance the legislative assembly, which met at Coventry, was nicknamed, in derision, the "lack-learning parliament."

In the seventh Henry VI. the privilege of voting in the election of knights of the shire was confined to "forty shillings freeholders." All the freeholders previously claimed the right, as at present, in the case of election of coroner,[j] which according to the preamble of the act caused "man-

g Mr. Edward Baines says, vol. 4, p. 345, "the burgesses were required to make payments to the members of 2s. 6d. per day." This is an error. The sum is correctly stated at 2s. in the same work, vol. 1, p. 300, and again at page 308 and 309.

h Mr. Baines (History of Lan. vol. 4, p. 345), says, "Preston resumed the electoral privileges in the first Edward IV. In vol. 1, however, p. 310 and 317, and in the list of members, p. 347. vol. 4, the period is correctly stated as the first Edward VI. These errors having been copied elsewhere, necessitates this comment.

i It was customary about this period, as well as with the Stuarts, to create nomination boroughs, as one means of "managing" the parliament, which sometimes became the property of ladies, as in the case of Mistress Packington, who introduced her nominees to the "free" burgesses, in the following candid and constitutional manner:—"Know ye, Me, the said Dorothy Packington, to have chosen, named, and appointed, my trusty and well-beloved Thomas Lichfield and George Burden, esqrs., to be my burgesses of the said town of Aylesbury. And whatsoever the said Thomas and George, burgesses, shall do in the service of the queen's highness in that present parliament, to be assembled at Westminster, the eighth day of May next ensuing the date hereof, I the same Dorothy Packington do ratify and approve to be my own act as fully and wholly as if I were present there!" This modest document is addressed "to all Christian people to whom this present writing shall come!" By this it would appear the English constitution has not always entirely excluded females from exercising the parliamentary franchise.

j The election of coroners, in whatsoever district of the county they, by arrangement, may practice, always take place at Preston, which gives an undue preponderance to the freeholders of

slaughter, riots, batteries, and divisions amongst the gentlemen and other people of the said counties." A forty shilling freehold of that period would be about equivalent to one of twenty pounds at the present time.

The parliament of 1653, in the time of the commonwealth, consisted of only one hundred and twenty-one persons, including the celebrated "Praise God Barebones," member for London. None of the Lancashire boroughs were represented, but the county sent three knights of the shire. Preston never failed to respond to the summons, from the reign of Edward VI. to the present time; for in this instance, the parliament was a "packed" one, and no writs were issued to any of the Lancashire boroughs.

Parliaments were by statute in the reign of Edward III. ordered to be called annually, and oftener, if required. This was confirmed in the reign of Edward VI. In the sixteenth year of the reign of Charles II., the practice of holding parliaments triennially was adopted. The law so remained until the commencement of the reign of George I., when the present septennial act was introduced. The property qualification was first adopted in the ninth year of the reign of Queen Anne, when it was by statute enacted that no person should be qualified to sit in parliament, as the representative of any city or borough, who was not possessed of a freehold or copyhold estate of the annual value of £300., over and above all incumbrances whatever. The only exceptions were in favour of the eldest sons of peers of the realm, or of persons qualified to sit as knights of the shire.

Preston, previously to the passing of the Parliamentary Reform Bill, in 1832, enjoyed a more democratic suffrage than any other borough in the kingdom. The personal right to the "franchise," it would appear, was not either very clearly defined in law, or reduced to anything like a uniform system by the practice of the burgesses of the various cities and boroughs. The report of the Royal Commission on municipal corporations, printed in 1835, says:—

"Without enquiring when corporations in the country assumed their present form, it may be safely asserted that the body, however, named, which was originally intended to share, and which in fact did share, in the rights which the early charters conferred, embraced the great mass of the householders or inhabitants. By degrees, exclusive qualifications were insisted on with increasing strictness, and with new exceptions, as the privileges to which these exclusive bodies laid claim, rose in importance. This importance again was enhanced by the narrowing of the access to the privilege, and the consequent diminution of the number of individuals sharing in its advantages."

Amongst other muncipalities, Plymouth, with a population of 75,000 (including Devonport), had only 437 freemen, 145 of whom were non-resident! In Norwich, the great bulk of the respectable inhabitants were

---

that neighbourhood, and causes much fraudulent voting. It is probable, however, that ere long, if the office of coroner be not altogether abolished, or the duties consolidated with those of some other public functionary, that the mode of their appointment will be thoroughly reformed.

excluded from the corporate body, while paupers, lodgers, and other parties who contributed not to the rates, exercised the privileges of the freemen! Ipswich presented a still more flagrant pervertion. The resident freemen, out of a population of 20,000, only formed a fifty-fifth part, and about one-ninth of these were paupers! More than one-third were not rated, and many amongst those who were, were often excused payment! More than eleven-twelfths of the property assessed belonged to parties excluded from the privileges of freemen! The commissioners found that in sixteen of the largest cities and boroughs, with an aggregate population of 715,702, there were only 34,697 resident and non-resident freemen! The object sought to be gained by this gradually encroaching exclusiveness, did not arise so much from the desire to prevent the inhabitants generally from interference in municipal affairs, as with the view to the monopoly of the political franchise, which, in proportion to the limitation of numbers, conferred additional personal and pecuniary importance upon the "free and independent burgesses." Many municipal institutions had been preserved solely on account of the political privileges conferred by their incorporation, and numerous instances of gross perversion of municipal authority to political ends, were exposed by the commissioners.

The corporation of Preston had gradually assumed to itself the exclusive right to select the parliamentary representatives of the borough, though not without considerable opposition from the resident freemen. In the year 1661, the corporation returned Mr. Rigby and Mr. Fife; but the *Inn-burgesses* proceeded to the poll and elected Mr. Rigby and Dr. Rishton. The disputed claim was adjudicated upon by the whole House of Commons, and not merely by a select committee, as is the practice at the present time. Mr. Rigby and Dr. Rishton were declared duly elected. This decision, eventually produced results utterly unexpected by either of the litigant parties. The resolution not only repudiated the notion of exclusive privilege claimed by the corporation, but likewise the pretensions of the municipal authorities and burgesses conjoined. It literally declared that the right to vote lay with "the inhabitants at large," and thus created, though evidently unintentionally, a suffrage absolutely *universal*. The following is the resolution passed by the House of Commons:—

"Sergeant Charleton made report from the Committee of Privileges and Elections, that upon the petition of Dr. Fife and Dr. Rishton they had proceeded to examine the matter touching their election for the borough of Preston; and the question being whether the mayor and twenty-four burgesses had only voices or the inhabitants at large; the committee is of opinion that *all the inhabitants* have voices in the election; and the majority of such voices is with Dr. Rishton; and that he is duly elected and ought to sit. Resolved, upon the question that this house do agree with the said committee, that *all the inhabitants of the said borough* of Preston have voices in the election; and that the majority of such voices is with Dr. Rishton; and that the said Dr. Rishton is duly elected a burgess for the said borough, and ought to sit in this house." k

It does not appear that the general population became cognizant of the comprehensive nature of the expressions used in the resolution for a considerable period. However, in 1768, upwards of a century afterwards, the non-freemen resident in the borough claimed the franchise, and proceeded to the poll. The non-freemen were usually designated as "*foreigners*," in contradistinction to the *inhabitants*. This explains the nature of the error committed by parliament, and the century of indifference with which the non-burgesses regarded the decision.[l]

The mayor declared that Sir Peter Leicester, bart., and Sir Frank Standish, were legally elected to represent the borough, although General Burgoyne and Sir Henry Hoghton, through the influence of the earl of Derby, had secured a majority of the voices of "the inhabitants at large." Sir Henry Hoghton and the gallant general, together with some of their friends, petitioned the house of commons, and unseated the chosen of the exclusives. The case was heard by the whole house of commons. The council for the corporation argued that the term "all the inhabitants" had reference only to "such in-burgesses of the last guild, or those admitted since by copy of court roll, as were inhabitants of the place." One hundred and thirteen voted for this view of the case, and one hundred and eighty-three against it. This vote interpreted the previous decision of the house of commons, in 1661, to mean that the elective franchise extended to the "inhabitants at large," or in other words that "all the inhabitants had voices in the election of members." In practice, however, this very comprehensive expression was always understood in a more limited sense. The right was confined to all the *male* inhabitants above twenty-one years of age, who had resided six months in the town, and were untainted with pauperism or crime. So much importance was attached to these proceedings, that the struggle acquired the distinguished appellation of "the great election." Of course the exertions of the Derby family in this matter resulted not from any sympathy with "universal suffrage," as a political principle. During the first seven days of the "great election," their own party did not attempt to poll any persons except freemen. Finding themselves in a minority, their ingenuity was taxed to avert defeat. Some cunning lawyer or other, probably remembering the words of the resolution of the house of commons, suggested the

k Journals of the House of Commons.

l The corporation records contain many allusions to the two distinct classes then occupying the town. "*Foreigners*" are forbidden to graze their cattle on the moor to the "prejudice of the *inhabitants*." The closing of places of business on Sundays is strictly enforced upon both "*foreigners* and "*inhabitants*." The term foreigner appears to have descended from the Roman municipal expedient of polling all their friends, freemen and non-freemen. According to a contemporary document, "the Vicar of the Parish" (the Rev. R. Andrews), stood forward upon the hustings to expound the resolution of 1661." He declared his opinion that all were legally entitled to vote, notwithstanding the previous practice. The hint was acted upon, and the Derby party spared defeat. This undignified *ruse de guerre*, however, produced the most alarming consequences. A letter from Preston, dated February 21st, and quoted in the Gentleman's Magazine for March, 1768, says:—

"The contest here is attended with imminent danger. I have just escaped with many friends. The country is now up in arms. As the town is now abandoned by our men, the cry is *Leave not a freeman alive!* God knows where this will end. I think to-night or to-morrow may be fatal to many. This is shocking work in a civilized country."

The same magazine, in the month following, on the authority of a letter from Lancaster, says, "the violence committed on account of the ensuing election at that town and at Preston exceed belief; murdering, maiming, pulling down the houses, destroying places of public worship, and breaking the furniture and burning the effects of each other, are among the acts of the inflamed mob."

Bands of drunken "roughs," designated "bludgeon-men," were hired by the contending parties ostensibly for "protection and defence." These lawless blackguards were incited to acts of violence by inflammatory placards and election squibs. The Roman catholic chapel of St. Mary, on Friargate brow, was, according to an address published soon afterwards, "scandalously and impiously plundered and violated by a band of unprincipled ruffians." Cottam catholic chapel was almost destroyed, and the one at New House, near Hollowforth, narrowly escaped a similar fate. The mayor of the borough was subjected to the inconvenience and indignity of a public drenching at the Fishergate pump, and his friends so maltreated for their remonstrances, that one of them died in consequence of the injuries he received. A judicial investigation followed these outrages, with the following result:—

"Saturday, 6th May, 1769. The Court of King's Bench gave judgment in the case of the riot at the last general election at Preston, when Mr. Justice Yates, after a most nervous and pathetic speech on the turpitude of riots at elections, pronounced sentence: an officer" (Burgoyne) "was fined £1,000.; four other defendants £100. each, and three months' imprisonment; and three rioters on account of their low circumstances, six months' imprisonment." m

The following extract from a document issued by the Derby party, gives the proportion of voters on each qualification as follows:—

---

nomenclature. Dr. Adam says:—"All those who were not citizens were called by the ancient Romans foreigners (Peregrini), wherever they lived, whether in the city or elsewhere."—Roman Antiquities, page 70.

m Gentleman's Magazine.

	H.	B.	L.	S.
"These are the numbers admitted by the Mayor, and upon which he has made his return	230	259	289	276
"Although by a resolution of the House of Commons, and confirmed by act of parliament, the right of election, for the said borough is vested in the inhabitants at large, who, although rejected by the Mayor, voted for	328	330	1	1
"This is insisted upon to be the true state of the poll	558	589	290	277" [n]

Another attempt was made to limit the franchise in 1780, when Sir John Fenton petitioned against the return of one of the members, on the plea that the "universal suffrage" practice was illegal. The previous decision of the house of commons was, however, adhered to. Mr. Fenton's petition was dismissed, and Burgoyne declared duly elected. The following resolution was passed:—

"That it being the opinion of this Committee that the Resolution of the 18th Dec., 1661, by which all the Inhabitants of the Borough of *Preston* are declared to have voices in the Election, is a last Determination within the meaning of the Act 2 Geo. II.; but it being also the opinion of the Committee that such a right of election is too indefinite,—*Resolved*,—That the Chairman be directed to move for leave to bring in a Bill to ascertain the Description of Inhabitants who shall for the future have Voices in the Election, humbly recommending it to the House that the Right be confined to all In-Burgesses resident and to all other Inhabitant Householders paying Scot and Lot."

The report was considered by the house on the 1st of May. The Derby influence was, however, powerful enough to prevent any action being taken thereupon. It was "ordered that the said report be taken into consideration that day three months."

This silenced for a time the obnoxious proposition. Notwithstanding this confirmation, the singular decision of the committee on the original appeal has ever been regarded, by competent authority, as a direct contravention of the law of the land.[o] Its "legality," however, now became established by precedent; another and last attempt to overthrow the practice, in 1784, being equally unsuccessful. This last effort was made by Ralph Clayton and Michael Angelo Taylor, who in vain petitioned against the return of Hoghton and Burgoyne. The corporation incurred considerable expense in prosecuting their petitions for the exclusion of non-freemen, and consequently, after a private subscription fund was exhausted, they trespassed a little on the corporate revenue for the liquidation of a portion of the charges. They voted the "sum of Fifty pounds to be applied to the discharge thereof, and if the said sum of Fifty pounds shall not be found sufficient, then let any further sum not exceeding £20. be paid and applied for the purpose aforesaid." "All the

n See pamphlet on the "Parliamentary Representation of Preston during the last hundred years," by Mr. W. Dobson.

o Sergeant Merewether's History of Boroughs, p. 365.

inhabitants" from this period peaceably enjoyed the exercise of their singularly acquired privilege till the passing of the reform bill.

The Derby family continued to possess the chief influence over the parliamentary elections, owing to the extent of the franchise, till 1796, when the "manufacturing interest," then comparatively in its infancy, backed by the corporation, resolutely attacked the aristocratic monopoly, and nominated John Horrocks, esq., in opposition to Lord Stanley (the late earl of Derby), and Sir Henry Philip Hoghton, bart. Mr. Horrocks was also supported by the then government, the earl of Liverpool, chancellor of the duchy of Lancaster, and by the "Church and King Club," of Manchester. The contest was a most severe one, not a single "tally" being supposed to remain unpolled at the close. The numbers were, for Lord Stanley, 772; Sir H. P. Hoghton, 756; John Horrocks, esq., 742. Ridiculous exhibitions of party spirit were occasionally indulged in by the rival factions during these contests. The author of the pamphlet previously alluded to, thus cleverly hits off some of the "small spite" exhibited by the rival political zealots:—

"Not merely was the feeling of hostility between the rival competitors for political influence carried into the business of the town, but even into its pleasures, and for six years, from 1786 to 1791, races were held under the auspices of each party, the corporation races being held on Preston moor, the earl of Derby's races, as an opposition meeting, on Fulwood moor, a lease of which had been obtained from the duchy of Lancaster. The political differences which divided the town extended even to sedan chairs! The coats of the chairmen had collars of the colour of one or other of the two great parties, and as the ladies were equally warm in their political sympathies as the rougher sex, they showed their predilections not only in the ribbons they wore, but in the choice of their sedans. A lady of the family of Pedder, or Starkie, or Gorst, would have walked home in a thunder storm, before she would have been carried in a Derbyite or Burgoyne chair, while the wives and daughters of the Shawes, the Hornbys, and the Whiteheads, would have missed going to the best ball of the season, rather than have been taken there in a corporation sedan."[p]

"Church street mill," now the property of Messrs. Ainsworth and Co., owes its origin to political causes. It was built with a view to strengthen the interest of the Derby family against the powerful influence of the corporate body of that day. In those days, when cotton mills were few in number, and labour scarce, the proprietor of a factory could, and did, exercise great influence over the voters employed by him, constraining them, under pain of instant dismissal, to vote for his party or nominees; thus converting that which was intended as a political privilege into an engine of wrong and oppression. Happily for society, such an unconstitutional exercise of power is of much rarer occurrence at the present day. The employer, who would presume to interfere with the conscientious discharge by his workman of his duty to the state, is to some extent, held in

p History of Par. Rep. of Preston during the last hundred years.

check by the force of public opinion, the increased intelligence of the mass of the people, and a wholesome dread of a recent act of parliament.

The growing strength of the manufacturing interest, however, soon became so apparent, that a compromise was eventually agreed upon; and, consequently, in 1802, Lord Stanley and John Horrocks, esq., were elected without a contest. This arrangement was effected, according to Mr. Edward Baines, "through the intervention of Thomas Butterworth Bayley, esq., of Manchester, and ratified by the signatures of eleven gentlemen of Preston, the leaders of the parties, to a written agreement prepared for the purpose." This compromise or "coalition," as it was then called, quietly nominated the members for two succeeding parliaments. At the general election in 1807, an effort was made by the "radicals" to break through the "coalition." Joseph Hanson, esq., of Manchester was nominated, and contested the election during a poll of eleven days' duration. The numbers were, Lord Stanley, 1619; Samuel Horrocks, esq.,[q] 1616; Colonel Hanson, 1002. Some rioting occurred during this struggle; indeed, from the peculiar tone in which the circumstance is alluded to by the Preston Journal of the day, it would appear that an "election row" was no great novelty at that period. The editor observes:—"We are concerned to have to state that a man was killed in an electioneering squabble, last night. We trust that the friends of all parties will recommend more peaceable behaviour than has hitherto been observed." This was written after the second day's polling.

In 1812, Lord Stanley represented the county. His cousin and brother-in-law, Edward Hornby, esq., was nominated for Preston, in conjunction with Samuel Horrocks, esq. The "independent" party brought into the field Edward Hanson, esq., brother to the gentleman, who, in 1807, unsuccessfully opposed the "coalition" nominees. On the fourth day of the election some rioting took place, during which two flags belonging to the "coalition party" were destroyed by their opponents, who afterwards proceeded to break the windows of the public houses "attached to the interest of Mr. Horrocks and Mr. Hornby." They demolished the windows, both glass and frame work, of eight or nine of these establishments, together with the frames and windows of Mr. Horrocks's porter's lodge. "They were, however, at length stopped in their lawless career, on Mr. Nabb, a particular friend of Mr. Hanson's going amongst them and requesting, in the name of Mr. Hanson, that they would desist from these violent proceedings; and, from the readiness with which they complied it is to be regretted that the experiment was not earlier tried."[r]

q John Horrocks, esq., died in 1804, and was succeeded in the representation of the borough, by his brother, Samuel Horrocks, esq.

r Preston Chronicle, October 17th, 1812.

No serious personal injury appears to have resulted from this outbreak. It was considered, however, sufficiently alarming to induce the magistrates to call in and retain the aid of the military, notwithstanding the protest of the friends of Mr. Hanson. The polling lasted eight days, when the numbers were, Horrocks, 1379; Hornby, 1368; Hanson, 727. On the first day, Mr. Horrocks and Mr. Hornby each polled twenty votes and Mr. Hanson nineteen. The "independent" electors apparently preferred watching the tide of events to relieving themselves from their onerous duties!

The suicidal policy of the Stanley family brought its own punishment. The popularity of the "universal suffrage" *coup d'etat*, as it may not improperly be termed, naturally for a time conferred upon nominees of the family the parliamentary honours of the borough. The progress of the cotton business, however, introduced a large number of voters, who were, at the time, completely under the influence of their employers. Hence a counter interest sprung up, which threatened to destroy the aristocratic power and *prestige*. This necessitated the first concession, and the "coalition" resulted. The representation of the borough was virtually *nil*, on most important public questions, as the voice and influence of one member counteracted that of the other. But this was not the only humiliation. As a matter of course, from such elements the independent party sprung into existence, and wrestled with the coalitionists. "Universal suffrage," under those circumstances, became transmuted into an extremely intractable animal, with some of the peculiarities of the hydra. Nay the modern monster vastly exceeded in number of "polls". the many headed victim of Hercules, and became infinitely more voracious. The thirteen hundred and odd votes, which secured the triumph of the coalition party at this election, *cost* the enormous sum of £5671. 17s. 6d.

By a fortunate incident the enfranchised of the present day are enabled to ascertain with unquestionable accuracy, what were regarded as "legitimate election expenses" by their immediate progenitors. The author of the pamphlet previously quoted, accidentally obtained possession of the accounts of the treasurer to the coalition candidates.[8] The following particulars from this document, demonstrate to a certainty, that neither the Stanley nor the corporation influence, nor both combined, was all powerful with even a majority of the "free and independent" burgesses, without immense sacrifice at the altar of Mammon, and copious libations at the shrine of Bacchus; the veritable deities who have long presided over election *mysteries*:—

8 "The late Samuel Crane, Esq., was the treasurer. The accounts appear to have been made up with peculiar care, the various items being entered with great minuteness, and they are scarcely less remarkable for their methodical arrangement than for their singularity."

"First of all in the accounts appear the names of 'staffmen, intended to act as special constables, at 20s. each.' These 'special constables,' or more properly bludgeon-men, were 276 in number, and cost (one of them received 40s.) £277. Something beyond their services was no doubt looked for in return for the 20s.; as, out of the whole number, only seven voted against their paymasters, a few were apparently not voters. Then follows "paid sundry others as under," and twenty-four names are appended with sums varying from 3s to 40s., a total of £19. 14s., but for what is not stated. Most of the parties were voters. One non-elector's name occurs, 'Betty Spencer, 5s.,' but there is no record of the nature of Betty's assistance to the cause. Then another batch of 'staffmen' for £54. 6s. The music cost £188 12s.; the messengers, £29. 15s. 4d.; the captains, or superintendents of districts, £7. 8s.; twelve waiters, at 4s. a day, £24.; solicitors and clerks, £367. 7s. 0d.; this included a retaining fee of £10. 10s. to Mr. T. B. Addison, and one of £5. 5s. to Mr. T. S. Shuttleworth for their services at the next election: overseers of townships, £56. 2s. These were from all the neighbouring villages, and would be in attendance to object to persons from the neighbourhood voting as residents, or to any residents in the town who had relief from their rates, as a person having received relief within twelve months was disqualified The sum of £24 was incurred in bringing twelve men of the 2nd Lancashire Militia from Plymouth to vote, but they came too late; £9. 11s. to men attending the horses for 'the riding,' £577 14s. 6d for ribbons; £94. 14s. 6d for printing and stationery; and £3,807. 13s 7d. for public-houses! Fifty-six publicans had bills varying from £10 to £246. 10s. After the election, an expense of £131. 4s. 7d was incurred in prosecuting some parties for rioting, and Mr Baines had £20 for 'keeping list of the inhabitants.'"†

Nothing daunted by previous defeat, the "independent party" again determined to oppose the "coalition," and, at the ensuing election, in 1818, nominated Dr. Crompton, of Liverpool. This gentleman, in his address expressed the satisfaction he should feel in assisting to rescue "the town of Preston from the degraded state into which it had been plunged by the coalition," but stated that, neither directly nor indirectly, would he "endeavour to obtain one suffrage by means inconsistent with the most perfect purity of election" The only local journal existing at that time in the town, (the Preston Chronicle) in commenting upon this portion of Dr. Crompton's address, makes the following pertinent observations, which until the recent contest (1837), applied with equal force and propriety, not only to the electoral constituency of Preston, but to the enfranchised of most other boroughs.—

'If this example should be followed by the opposite parties, we may hope to see established in this borough, a system of appointing representatives to serve us in parliament, which will render us worthy of the high privileges we possess. Free from the influence of gin and beer, the polling may then be conducted in a manner becoming rational beings, called to exercise an important national duty; and each elector having given a conscientious vote, it will betray a persecuting spirit of the very worst description, should any be made to suffer in person or estate for an act which the law of the land requires to be performed with purity under the solemn pledge of an oath."

From the speeches of the parties nominating Dr. Crompton, it appears

† "Since this was in type the writer has been informed that Betty Spencer at that time was a worker at the Moss Factory, of Messrs Horrockses, Whitehead, Miller, & Co, as the firm then was, and as 'she knew everybody,' she was stationed at the Town-hall to object to any unqualified person who should come up to vote for Mr. Hanson. Several women were thus always engaged at the elections, from thirty to fifty years ago Among these female electioneerers was a woman of the name of Alice Abbott, a quakeress, of a respectable family in the town, who, during the whole of the election of 1796, stood beside Lord Stanley and Sir H. P Hoghton, in the Town-hall, to object to disqualified voters, and few men could have equalled the tact and spirit with which she discharged her duty."

that the old members both enjoyed the private esteem of the liberal party, and that Mr. Hornby's political sentiments and ability met with considerable approval; but the "coalition" was still regarded as most offensive to the "*freedom* of election." At the end of the second day's polling, Dr. Crompton headed Mr. Horrocks by one vote, and Mr. Hornby by five. At the conclusion of the third day, Mr. Horrocks and Dr. Crompton were equal; the votes being, Horrocks and Crompton, 468; Mr. Hornby, 464. At the conclusion of the sixth day, Mr. Horrocks led, and Mr. Hornby and Dr. Crompton were equal, the numbers for the latter being 1166 each. On the seventh day, however, Dr. Crompton fell so far behind, that he declined any further contest. The total numbers polled were: for Horrocks, 1694; Hornby, 1598; Crompton, 1245.

During the election, the general conduct of the belligerent parties was such as to call forth the following eulogy from the local journalist:—

"The active supporters of the respective candidates have evinced throughout the struggle a liberal and gentlemanly conduct towards each other; and we feel a proud satisfaction in stating that the greatest regularity and order have been preserved, and not the slightest disposition to break the peace has been manifested on the part of the great body of the electors. Our streets, as compared with the scenes of brutal drunkenness which have prevailed on all former occasions of this kind, have presented a contrast highly creditable to the present improved state of the public feeling."

The election closed on Thursday, and the successful candidates were "*chaired*" in the usual manner; "that is, they *rode* upon gaily decorated horses, amidst a procession of their friends and admirers, accompanied by music, flags, banners, and other gorgeous paraphernalia." Singularly enough, the parties who conducted themselves so laudably during the excitement of the contest, relapsed into the "brutal drunkenness which had prevailed on all former occasions," immediately after the "chairing" of the members. The journal above quoted thus describes this remarkable transaction and its results:—

"It is with deep regret that we are compelled as faithful historians, to make an abatement from the above favourable report of the proceedings at our election. Up to seven o'clock last evening, no one who witnessed the contest will say that our account of it is overcharged. At that time a great portion of the public-houses were opened at the expense of the returned members, and about ten or eleven o'clock, a mob, whose heads were charged with coalition ale, but with hearts true to Crompton, assembled in front of the Bull and Red Lion Inns, assaulting the company with stones and mud, as they came out; and in the course of the evening broke several windows at the Bull Inn." [v]

A very probable and natural result of the system of *purchase* adopted! A peep into the account book of the worthy treasurer will satisfactorily explain away scepticism on the subject:—

"The election of 1818 was a little more expensive. The music cost £233. 12s. 6d.; the messengers, £19 4s.; the attendants on members at "the riding," £8. 1s.; court fees, £55. 4s.; ribbons, £712 11s. 5d.; law agents and clerks, £422. 6s. 6d.; miscellaneous charges, £250. 14s. 4d.; overseers, £106. 2s. 8d.; *public-houses* £4,111. 4s. 7*d.!*

v Preston Chronicle, June 27th, 1818.

and printing and stationery, £98. 1s. One of the entries quaintly enough describes the payment to "twelve men employed the first day of the election by Mr. ——— to assist in resisting any attempt that might be made to create riot, £1. 16s.!"

On the death of George III., in 1820, parliament was dissolved, and the "independent" party determined upon another contest with the "coalitionists." On this occasion John Williams, esq., afterwards Mr. Justice Williams, was nominated, together with Mr. Henry Hunt, the celebrated "radical reformer," and "hero of Peterloo," as he was sometimes designated. The contest was remarkably severe. Mr. Horrocks, however, always kept the lead; and Mr. Hornby retained the second place on the poll, during the whole period, with the exception of the second day, when the numbers for each were as follows:—Horrocks, 143; Hornby, 141; Williams, 141; Hunt, 141. The election lasted thirteen days. The return at the close gave for Horrocks, 1,902; Hornby, 1,649; Williams, 1,525; Hunt, 1,127. The coalition candidates on this, as on the two previous occasions, issued a joint address; and, notwithstanding their conflicting political sentiments, worked side by side at the election, with as much zeal as if their own votes in parliament were to be devoted to the furtherance of the same principles or measures. A considerable amount of "treating" was practised during this election, which led to rioting. The windows of the Town-hall, Guild-hall, Mr. Friend's shop, under the Guild-hall, the Bull Inn, and the Gentlemen's Coffee Room opposite, were smashed, and some flags destroyed. The mayor, assessor, and town-clerk endeavoured to "read the riot act" from a window of the Grey Horse Inn, Church-street, but they were forced to retreat before a shower of stones. They made their exit by the back premises, and after climbing over some pailings, entered the yard of the Bull Hotel. After an ineffectual attempt to read the proclamation against rioting, from the lower windows of the hotel, they succeeded in effecting their object from the upper story, the great height preventing the missiles projected towards them from causing serious interruption. No person was killed in the uproar, though several received contusions more or less severe. About nine o'clock in the evening of Thursday, a party of the 7th dragoons arrived in the town, but the mob had in a great measure dispersed. The assessor having announced to the candidates that the military should not be allowed to interfere with the election, but simply remain within call in case of further disturbance, all parties appeared satisfied, and the voting proceeded without further interruption. Mr. Hunt left town before the conclusion of the election, in order to prepare for his trial at York, where he was found guilty, along with Messrs. Joseph Johnson, John Knight, Joseph Healy, and Samuel Bamford, "of assembling with unlawful banners, at an unlawful meeting, for the purpose of moving and inciting the subjects of our lord the king, to con-

Bellington's Bull Hotel, Preston

tempt and hatred of the government and constitution of the realm as by law established." The trial arose out of the proceedings of the celebrated 16th of August, in the previous year, in St. Peter's Field, Manchester. Mr. Hunt was afterwards sentenced to two years and six months imprisonment in Ilchester gaol, with a further condition that, at the conclusion of his incarceration, he should enter recognizances to keep the peace for five years, himself in £1000. and two sureties in £500. each. In answer to a question from Mr. Hunt, Mr. Justice Bayley informed the court, that "his confinement was to be with as few privations as the due execution of the sentence would allow." Mr. Hunt being a great favourite with the populace, was cheered loudly as he passed from the court of king's bench, Westminster, to the prison, after the passing of the sentence.

At this election, the purchase money for the very questionable honour of representing Preston in parliament, amounted to the enormous sum of £11,559. 12s. 8d. There must have existed some singular infatuation at the period, to induce parties to make such a sacrifice for the mere political negation of the borough. Mr. Dobson informs his readers, on the authority of the accurate and painstaking treasurer, that:—

"The music cost £454. 11s.; attendance of overseers, £207. 8s. 6d.; advocates and attorneys, £753. 0s. 10d.; ribbons, £1,047. 6s. 9d.; district committees, £403. 5s. 6d.; writers and clerks to committees, £117. 12s. 6d.; *public-houses*, £8,203. 19*s* 4*d*.!! and 'O monstrous! but one half-penny worth of bread to this intolerable deal of sack;' printing and stationery, £129. 6s.! Certain charges entered as expenses were £244. 2s. 3d. There is a memorandum in pencil in the book to the effect that Mr. Williams's expenses were £6,000., but upon what authority this statement is made does not appear." w

Such is the instability of political law, that, at the present day, a meeting similar in character to the one at Peterloo, might be held with perfect impunity; while the exposition of such election accounts as those of the successful candidates, would be visited with the concentrated wrath of a parliamentary committee; and that, in 1857, is no trifling matter.

In June, 1826, the next election took place. Mr. Horrocks having signified his intention to retire from the representation of the borough, the corporation wisely resolved to interfere no more, in their collective capacity, with the free choice of the voters. Mr. Hornby, likewise retired, and his nephew, the honourable E. G. Stanley, (the present earl of Derby) offered himself to the electors, on the family interest. The "coalition" thus collapsed without a struggle, after uninterruptedly maintaining its ground for twenty-four years. Doubtless, the gradually increasing demands of the faithful treasurer had considerable influence in hastening this

w This, of course, is the statement of the "enemy," and consequently merely exaggerated conjecture. Those in the secrets of Mr. Williams's committee state his expenses amounted to about £2,700., a sum large enough, in all conscience, for a *defeated* candidate.

catastrophe. Mr. Stanley solicited the suffrages of the electors on what was then called "whig" principles. Mr. John Wood, (the late chairman of the Board of Inland Revenue) was nominated by the "liberals;" Mr. William Cobbett, by the "radicals," and Captain Barrie, R. N., by the "tories." The contest was maintained with much vigour, during fifteen polling days; the full extent of time then allowed by law for the recording of the votes. During this election an immense amount of violent partisan "speech making" was perpetrated. Some of the candidates and their friends at the hustings, often became heated in temper, and occasionally indulged in indecent or irrelevant personalities. The spacious area of the Corn Exchange, being for the first time available, was selected as the scene for the nomination of the candidates and the voting of the electors. The old system of polling in "tallies" was found very inconvenient with so many candidates; for the number was increased to eight, merely as an election "ruse," to prevent "split votes" being given to opponents, and for obtaining freer access to the polling booths. Each candidate adopting the "ruse" stultified its influence.[x] Sir Thomas Beevor was thus nominated by Mr. Cobbett's friends, Mr. Lawe by Mr. Stanley's, Mr. Phillips by Mr. Wood's, and Captain Colquitt by Captain Barrie's. Some rioting took place, in which banners were torn and windows broken. A military force stationed at Kirkham, was twice called upon to preserve the peace of the town. On the latter occasion, several men, armed with bludgeons, were taken into custody. Though some unpleasant knocks were given and received, no lives were lost on the occasion. The Preston Chronicle of that date says, the military were not sent for on account of the election riots, which, *for Preston,* were not considered excessive, but sufficiently within the control of the police force. The introduction of power looms into the factories, about this period, caused serious apprehension of disturbance of another character, which the drunken recklessness of the election was by no means calculated to allay. The contest was, on several days, very severe between Mr. Wood and Captain Barrie. Notwithstanding, the relative positions of the candidates, at the close of each day's poll, remained the same from the first to the last. The polling continued during the then full legal period of fifteen days. The numbers at the close were:—Stanley, 2944; Wood, 1974; Barrie, 1653; Cobbett, 995. The number of persons voting amounted to 4222. A large number of Roman catholics walked in the procession, on the "chairing" of the members, with the view

x Previously to the passing of the Reform Bill, it was the practice at the hustings to permit each candidate to poll no more than ten voters consecutively, providing his opponent called the attention of the clerks to the fact that he had friends wishful to record their votes. Hence the term "tally," which signified a troop of ten voters, marshalled to the electoral arena by an agent named a captain.

to express their satisfaction at the result. The bulk of them did not vote, in consequence of the friends of Captain Barrie insisting upon the administration of the "oath of supremacy." Several distinguished foreigners visited Preston during the contest, attracted by curiosity to witness the exciting scenes presented by an English parliamentary election. Amongst others, were one of the ministers of the king of Bavaria, whose name did not transpire; the Duke de Monte Bello, (son of the celebrated Marshal Lannes); M. Prosper Duvergier, and Signor Panizzi, (at present chief librarian to the British Museum).

No treasurer's accounts of the expences of this election are available for public instruction. The cost, however, to some of the candidates, must have been immense, far exceeding, it is said, that of any previous struggle.

Another contest took place in Aug., 1830, immediately after the accession of William IV. The candidates were the Hon. E. G. Stanley, John Wood, esq., and Henry Hunt, esq. The polling lasted four days. The following was the result:—Stanley, 2,996; Wood, 2,489, Hunt, 1,308. Although the public houses were liberally patronised by the voters, at the expence of the successful candidates, the election passed off in a very orderly manner. A *fracas* did occur at the polling place, in the Exchange area; but the loss of a coat tail, by one of Mr. Stanley's friends, was the most serious part of the damage. Some gentlemen of influence in the "Tory" party, were said by Mr. Stanley to have subscribed towards the fund raised to meet Mr. Hunt's election expences, with the view to the exclusion of the hon. gentleman, from personal motives, and not sympathy with Mr. Hunt's political character. The general courtesy of the candidates and their friends towards their opponents, presented a striking contrast to the ribaldry at the preceding election. This, however, did not prevent the occasional exchange of a little *badinage* by Mr. Stanley and his democratic competitor.

The "Emancipation Bill" having received the royal assent during the preceding year, the Roman catholic population were, for the first time, enabled to register their votes, without doing violence to their religious sentiments.

Another contest occurred in December, 1830, in consequence of the acceptance of the office of chief secretary for Ireland, under the "reform government," by the Hon. E. G. Stanley, the sitting member. Mr. Hunt was again nominated; but he did not arrive in the town until Tuesday, the 14th December, when the poll had been open during five days. On the first day, Mr. Hunt polled 1,204 votes, and Mr. Stanley only 791. Mr. Stanley gained gradually a little upon his opponent, but he remained in a minority at the close of the poll, on the seventh day. The numbers were :—Hunt, 3,730, Stanley, 3,392 ; majority, 338. Many statements and conjectures were made as to the cause of Mr. Stanley's defeat. The majority gained by Mr. Hunt, on the first day's polling, sadly damaged Mr. Stanley's chance. He is understood to have declined treating the electors, according to *ancient usage,* feeling confident of success, from his large majority at the preceding election. The customary practice, however, was adopted after the first day's polling, but without materially altering his position. The "tory" party, too, or at least a section of them, were either antagonistic to the principles of parliamentary reform, professed by Mr. Stanley, or indifferent to his personal success. The voting was unquestionably of a very irregular character; the number of recorded franchises being greater than the supposed male population of the borough entitled to the privilege. Both sides polled men who had previously registered their votes. Many supported Mr. Stanley, during the *latter* part of the contest, in consideration of the electioneering liberality of his friends, who had previously tendered their "sweet voices" for his opponent, on the first day of the polling. Mr. Stanley, at the conclusion, demanded a scrutiny; but, after more mature consideration, abandoned it. With the exception of some disturbance at the polling booths, there does not appear to have been much rioting, notwithstanding the numerous processions which paraded the streets during the contest. Mr. Hunt's partisans perambulated the town in the evenings, carrying lighted tar barrels, and flags and banners. These processions created considerable excitement, and some terror; but no serious breach of the peace occurred. The defeat annoyed much the Derby family, and caused them for a time to withdraw their countenance from the borough, for which they had successfully nominated one or both representatives during a lengthened period. It has been shown that the influence of the family materially assisted, if it did not entirely procure, the retention of the evidently *illegal* decision of the committee of the house of commons, which vested the franchise in "the inhabitants at large." Thus, the means adopted by the corporation and the Derby family, to monopolize the representation of the borough, eventually defeated both their objects. The Right Hon. E. G. Stanley was afterwards elected for Windsor. Mr. Stanley represented Stockbridge previously to his offering himself for Preston. He was not quite "of age" at the election in 1820, or he would have been nominated in the place of Mr. Hornby. The radicals of England were so overjoyed with their victory, that each voter was presented with a silver medal struck expressly for the occasion. The funds were furnished by a national subscription. On the obverse, surrounded by a wreath of laurel, are the following words :—" H. Hunt, Esq.,

M.P. for Preston, Dec. 24, 1830;" and outside the wreath: "The time is come. The triumph of principle." On the reverse: "One of the 3,730 electors of Preston. The grateful tribute of the people of England." A small democratic political periodical was afterwards established in the town, which bore, as its distinguishing title, "The 3,730."

Another general election took place in April, 1831. Several attempts were made to procure a candidate to oppose Mr. Hunt. Colonel (now General Sir) De Lacy Evans, issued an address, and made a partial canvass of the borough; but a request from Mr. Wood's committee, who thought a contest might endanger their friend's election, in conjunction with his having received an invitation from the borough of Rye, which the gallant colonel had previously contested, induced him to to withdraw. Mr. Wood and Mr. Hunt were therefore returned without opposition. Col. Evans was successful at Rye.

The Parliamentary Reform Act, of 1832, confined the franchise to parties occupying houses of the annual value of ten pounds and upwards. Yet, although the "universal suffrage" principle was destroyed, and the improved practice of registering the electors introduced, the Preston constituency still includes a large number of "potwallopers," as the claimants under the phrase "inhabitants at large" are sometimes designated. By a special clause in the act, all parties who were in possession of the right, or, in other words, were twenty-one years of age, and had resided in the town for six months prior to the bill becoming law, still retained their privileges. They continue, however, gradually to decrease; and, in the course of a few years, but a very small number will remain on the register. In addition to those who die off, parties leaving the town, even though they should return after a six months' absence; all persons who become necessitated to apply for parish relief; together with those who neglect for one year to register themselves, are disfranchised. At the present time (1857), the register contains the names of 1023 persons who claim under the old franchise. Of these, however, 208 likewise possess the new qualification. The true number, therefore, is 815.

In Dec., 1832, the first election took place under the reform act.[y] The candidates were Peter Hesketh Fleetwood, esq., supported chiefly by the "tory party;" the hon. H. T. Stanley, brother to the late member, whig; Mr. Hunt; Captain Forbes, radical; and Mr. Charles Crompton (now Mr. Justice Crompton), liberal. The polling was limited by the act of parliament to two days' duration. Notwithstanding, much rioting occurred, aggravated considerably by the employment of "bludgeon-men,"

y By the boundary act, which followed, the franchise was extended so as to include all qualified persons resident in "the old borough of Preston and the township of Fishwick."

or "roughs," armed with staves and decorated with ribbons, whose ostensible occupation was the protection of the flags and banners of their respective parties; but who not unfrequently themselves created the disturbance they professed to oppose. Much of the rioting might have been prevented if the candidates had mutually consented to the abolition of processions during the contest. They served little purpose, except to congregate the most intemperate and lawless of the population in the public streets, and bring them into collision, when liquor, music, and party zeal had excited their worst passions, and blinded the limited rationality or sense of decorum which they previously possessed. Mr. Hunt's friends again paraded the town in the evenings, carrying lighted tar barrels, banners, etc. The votes were taken for the first time at several distinct poll booths, situated in different portions of the town. The polling of all the voters previously took place in the area of the Corn Exchange; and, anterior to its erection, at the Town-hall. At this election the practice of "*chairing*" the successful candidates was discontinued, at the request of the mayor, Jno. Addison, esq. The contest lay entirely between Mr. Fleetwood and Mr. Stanley on the one hand, and Mr. Hunt and Mr. Forbes, on the other. Mr. Crompton retired before the close of the first day's poll. The numbers at the conclusion were:—Fleetwood, 3,372; Stanley, 3,273; Hunt, 2,054; Forbes, 1,926; Crompton, 118.

In Jan., 1835, another contest took place. Although considerable efforts were made to unseat the old members, Messrs. Fleetwood and Stanley triumphed by a large majority. The former gentleman's votes in the house of commons had gained him many supporters amongst the "liberal" section of the electors, while he still retained the confidence of a majority of his conservative friends. The "radicals" nominated Col. (now Gen.) Thompson, editor of the Westminster Review, author of a pamphlet entitled "Catechism of the Corn Laws," etc., and Mr. Thomas Smith, of Liverpool, a friend and admirer of Mr. Cobbett. Previously to the arrival of Colonel Thompson, he was ably represented by his friend, the learned Dr. Bowring (now Sir John Bowring, governor of Hong Kong), who delivered several eloquent speeches during the election, notwithstanding the call upon his time arising from the circumstance that he was contesting the neighbouring borough of Blackburn, on the "liberal" interest. The peace of the town was again disturbed by hired "bludgeon-men." Many windows were broken, and other damage sustained. The votes recorded were:—Fleetwood, 2,165; Stanley, 2,092; Thompson, 1,385; Smith, 789.

In July, 1837, a general election took place, consequent upon the demise of William IV. R. Townley Parker, esq., of Cuerden, was nominated by the "conservative" party, and Jno. Crawfurd, esq., by the "radical" party. The sitting member, P. Hesketh Fleetwood, esq., again solicited the suffrages of the electors; but the Hon. H. T. Stanley did not again offer himself. Mr. Fergus O'Connor was nominated, with the view to afford him an opportunity of addressing the electors; but he did not go to the poll. The proceedings were again disgraced by much drunkenness and rioting, especially between some "bludgeon-men" and a party of Irish labourers. Several persons were seriously injured, and some property destroyed. The mayor was necessitated to call in the aid of the military, to protect the peace of the borough. The following was the final state of the poll:—Fleetwood, 2,726; Parker, 1821; Crawfurd, 1,562. The act of parliament, which confined the voting to one day's duration, first became operative at this election.

In July, 1841, the "liberals" supported Sir P. Hesketh Fleetwood, bart., and Sir George Strickland, bart. The "conservatives" nominated Mr. Townley Parker, and Mr. Chas. Swainson. The great political parties, who joined issue at this election, were "protectionists and free-traders." Lord Melbourne had been defeated on his free-trade measures, as well as on Sir R. Peel's motion, declaring a want of confidence in the ministry, on the part of the house of commons. The nomination was seriously interrupted by combats of hired "bludgeon-men," and conflicts, disgraceful to all parties concerned, occurred in the streets. The windows of the Bull Hotel and other places were broken, and several of the "hirelings" severely bruised. The result of the polling was in favour of the liberal candidates. For Sir P. H. Fleetwood, bart., there were tendered 1,655 votes; for Sir G. Strickland, bart., 1,629; for R. Townley Parker, esq. 1,270; for Charles Swainson, esq., 1,255. Although the free-traders succeeded at Preston, the protectionists were generally successful throughout the country, and shortly afterwards Sir R. Peel displaced Lord Melbourne. This election is said to have cost the four candidates between £13,000. and £15,000.

The next parliamentary election took place in July, 1847. Sir P. H. Fleetwood, bart., retired, and the "liberals" nominated Charles Pascoe Grenfell, esq., in conjunction with Sir George Strickland, bart. The conservatives again supported R. Townley Parker, esq. Considerable disturbance was created, previously to the day of nomination, by hired "navvies" or "bludgeon-men," and the windows of the Bull and Red Lion Hotels were broken. The borough magistrates issued a proclamation, requesting all parties to aid the authorities in the preservation of the peace, and calling upon all persons concerned in the election, to abstain from the practice of perambulating the town in procession, with music, flags, banners, etc. This proclamation, being respected by all parties, produced a most salutary effect, and the remainder of the contest was not disgraced by further important disturbances. The struggle proved one of the closest in the history of the borough representation. The numbers were—Strickland, 1,404; Grenfell, 1,378; Parker, 1361. Some voters considered the election to be a "dry one," notwithstanding the evidently liberal treatment they received, both in a liquid and pecuniary sense.

Another election took place in July, 1852, and was severely contested. The "liberal" party was divided in opinion respecting the conduct of Mr. Grenfell, who had supported the "ecclesiastical titles bill." Mr. Grenfell's votes and attention to his parliamentary duties, otherwise appeared to have given general satisfaction to his party. The Roman catholic electors, however, refused to vote for him, notwithstanding the certainty that his place would, through their course of policy, be filled by a gentleman whose attachment to the church of England and opposition to their claims, was well known. Sir George Strickland, on the other hand, voted against the measure, and consequently received the strenuous support of the Roman catholic body. James German, esq., likewise offered himself on "liberal" principles. This caused a still further division in the party. The conservatives, perceiving this disunion, rallied round their old friend, R. Townley Parker, esq., and eventually placed him at the head of the poll. The numbers were—Parker, 1,335; Strickland, 1,253; Grenfell, 1,127; German, 692. Mr. German retired soon after eleven o'clock. At the request of the mayor, all the candidates agreed to dispense with the usual custom of parading the town with banners and music. Notwithstanding the intensity of the political excitement, no rioting of any consequence took place. There was upon the whole less drunkenness than at some previous contests; but a general impression remained, that the direct appeals to the pocket sympathies of the "free and independent" electors, exceeded those of many a previous struggle.

After this contest, an act of parliament was passed with the view to the more effectual suppression of corrupt practices at parliamentary elections. Some of its provisions are well calculated to render the investment of a few thousand pounds in the procuration of a seat in the legislature, rather a precarious speculation. A public auditor is appointed for the examination of all election expences accounts. Payment of any, without the sanction of this officer, will, on proof being made, unseat the member.

Mr. Cobden's motion with reference to the conduct of Sir John Bowring, at Canton, being supported by a large section of the conservative as well as of the "Peelite" party, placed Lord Palmerston's government in a minority of sixteen. This implied a vote of censure or a want of confidence in the administration. Lord Palmerston dissolved parliament, and appealed to the country. The energy with which he and his colleagues had conducted the Russian war, after the vacillating policy of the earl of Aberdeen's government had caused much discontent, and the failure of the earl of Derby to maintain the office of premier, told favourably for the veteran war minister. Messrs. Cobden, Bright, Milner Gibson, and other leaders of the "Manchester school," and advocates of the doctrines of the "Peace Society," were rejected by their own friends; other liberals occupied their seats. Several of the conservatives and Peelites likewise were defeated or retired, owing to the unpopularity engendered by their votes on the Chinese question. Thus the *coup* was eventually fatal to those who triumphed in its first success.

The election at Preston, was not however, materially affected by the question. Mr. Townley Parker, who voted adversely to the government, had, for some time previously, expressed a desire, owing to the unsatisfactory state of his health, to retire from the representation of the borough. Sir George Strickland, on the other hand, supported the ministers. The conservatives selected as their candidate, Richard Assheton Cross, esq., barrister-at-law, and brother to Major Cross, of Red Scar, near Preston. This gentleman declared he would give an independent support to the government of Lord Palmerston; and Mr. Grenfell, expressed a similar determination. The latter gentleman, notwithstanding his defeat at the previous election, had not ceased his friendly intercourse with Preston. Although his courteous attention to all parties had procured him many friends, and an impression had long prevailed that Sir George Strickland would not again offer his services, yet his election was by no means regarded as certain by many of his most sanguine admirers. Some of the friends of Sir George, and especially those belonging to the Roman catholic body, anxious to secure his re-election and the second defeat of Mr. Grenfell, at any cost, determined to "plump" their champion. This policy proved fatal to the party. The numbers at the close of the poll were:—Grenfell, 1503; Cross, 1433; Strickland. 1094. The plumpers were as follows:—Strickland, 590; Cross, 296; Grenfell, 75. Total number of electors who recorded their votes, 2495. Total number of electors on the register, 2793; being a decrease of 61 as compared with the register in 1851-2, which was used at the previous contest. The number unpolled, including dead and absent persons, was, in 1857, 289; in 1852, 247.

The most remarkable feature of this election was the relatively quiet and orderly manner in which it was conducted. With a single exception, no literary "passage at arms," in the shape of a "squib" contest, disturbed the even tenor of the proceedings. No bands, no banners, no bludgeon-men, no bribery, treating, or intimidation! strange features in a Preston election. True; perhaps, gold, strong beer, and the "screw," might still be slightly operative in sundry dark corners; but the general opinion appeared to be that the recent act of the parliament, and the publication of some of its provisions, by the joint committees of the candidates, produced a marvellous effect. Some of the friends of the defeated candidate, of course, threatened a petition; but, perhaps, from a wholesome fear, that some of their own agents might not have been quite so discreet as their leaders could have wished, combined with the evident state of opinion, as expressed by the numbers, the threat was not carried out. It is expected the total expenses of the three candidates will amount to no more than £1600. or £1800.[z]

As might have been expected, many of the "free and independent electors," who regarded a couple of sovereigns and "oceans of beer," and "rivers of gin," as in no way discordant with their political sentiments, felt, and sometimes expressed, considerable indignation at the altered state of affairs. But, the great body of the voters and inhabitants, regarded the change with much satisfaction. Had there been a tithe of the intoxicating liquor consumed, which many have been taught to regard as the orthodox quantity on such occasions, serious rioting, must unquestionably have ensued; the feeling of some of the disappointed, amongst the uneducated, being strongly exhibited at the close of the proceedings. Handfuls of mud and discordant hooting might, under higher "spiritual" pressure, have found substitutes in paving stones and extemporary bludgeons.

The next step, in the right direction, is to discountenance the practice of house to house canvass. There are many difficulties in the way; but greater have yielded before combined action. As in the case of bribery and intimidation, its suppression has now become the interest of every influential and well disposed individual; some improvement may, therefore, be looked for in the direction indicated, even if the practice be not entirely discontinued. The application of the provisions of the new law to Municipal elections, would likewise be productive of much benefit, and materially assist in the elevation of the moral tone of society at large.

The following is a list of the gentlemen who have represented the borough of Preston in parliament since the time of Edward I. The earlier portion is extracted from Edward Baines's history of Lancashire, and differs considerably from the one published by Whittle. The latter part of the list (from 1700), has been carefully revised and corrected by Mr. W. Dobson, and published in his pamphlet "on the Parliamentary Representation of Preston during the last hundred years:"—

---

z The precise expenses, after being audited, will be published according to the provisions of the act of parliament. When this sheet was put to press they had not appeared. The result will, however, be found in the appendix.

MEMBERS OF PARLIAMENT FOR PRESTON.

1295.—Willielmus fil' Pauli, Adam Russel.
1298.—Adam fil' Radulphi, Adam de Biri.
1300—Wili' fil' Paulini, (The name of the other Burgess is lost.)
1304—Robertus fil' Willielmi de Preston, Henricus fil' Willielmi de Townhende.
1306.—Robertus fil' Rogeri, Ricardus Banastre.
1307.—Henricus del Kykestyle, Ricardus Banastre.
1326.—Laurencius Travers, Willielmus de Graistok.
1547.—Geo. Frevil, esq., John Hales, esq.
1552-3—Anthony Browne, Tho. Fleetwood.
1553.—Will. Gerard, Anth. Browne.
1554.—Tho. Ruthel, esq., Will. Bernere, esq.
1554.—Rich. Sharborne, kt., John Sylyard, esq.
1555.—John Arundel, esq., John Hearle, esq.
1557.—Rich. Sherborne, kt., Rob. Southwell, knt.
1558-9.—John Alford, Rich. Cooke.
1563.—Gilb. Morcton, esq., Roger Askham, esq.
1571.—Edw. Basshe, esq., Reginald Williams, esq.
1572.—James Hodgekinson, esq., Geo. Horsey, esq.
1585.—Edw. Basshe, esq., Reginald Williams, esq.
1586.—John Brograve, esq., Thomas Hesketh, gent.
1588.—John Brograve, esq., Michael Doughtie, gent.
1592.—James Dalton, Tho. Balbeck, gent.
1597.—John Brograve, esq., John Stanhope, knt.
1601.—John Brograve, attorney of the duchy of Lancaster,—Will. Wood, esq.
1603.—Vincent Skinner, kt., Will. Hall, esq.
1614.—Edward Moseley, knt.
1620.—Edw. Moseley, kt., Will. Pooley, kt.
1623.—Edw. Moseley, kt., Will. Harvey, kt. (in place of Will. Pooley, kt., chosen also for Sudbury.)
1625.—Will. Harvey, knt., Hen. Banister, esq.
1625.—Geo. Gerard, esq., Tho. Farnshaw, esq.
1628.—Rob. Carre, kt., Geo. Gerard, kt.
1640.—Rich. Shuttleworth, esq., Tho. Standish, esq.
1640.—Rich. Shuttleworth, esq., Tho. Standish, esq.
.—William Langton, esq.
1653.—(No return for Preston.)
1654.—Rich. Shuttleworth, esq.
1656.—Rich. Shuttleworth, esq.
1658-9.—Col. Rich. Shuttleworth, esq., Col. Rich. Standish, esq.
1660.—Edward Rigby, Jeffrey Rushton.
1661.—Edward Rigby, Jeffrey Rushton.
1678.—Edward Rigby, Sir Robert Carr.
1681.—Sir Jervis Elwys, Sir Robert Carr.
1685.—Sir John Chichley, Richard Fleetwood.
1688.—James Stanley, Thomas Patten.
1690.—Sir Charles Greenfield, Sir Edward Chisnell.
1695.—Sir Thomas Stanley, Thomas Molineux.
1698.—Henry Ashurst, Thomas Molineux.
1700-1—Henry Ashurst, Edward Rigby.
1701.—Henry Ashurst, Thomas Molineux
1702.—Sir Cyril Wyche, knt., Charles Stanley.
1705.—Edward Rigby, Francis Annesley.
1706.—*Death of Edward Rigby*—Arthur Manwaring.
1708.—Henry Fleetwood, Arthur Manwaring.
1710.—Henry Fleetwood, Sir Henry Hoghton, bart.
1714.—Henry Fleetwood, Edward Southwell.

1715.—Henry Fleetwood, Sir Henry Hoghton, bart.
1722.—Thomas Hesketh, Daniel Pulteney.
1726.—*Daniel Pulteney appointed Clerk of the Council in Ireland*—Daniel Pulteney.
1728.—Sir Henry Hoghton, bart., Daniel Pulteney.
1732.—*Death of Daniel Pulteney*—Nicholas Fazackerley.
1735.—Nicholas Fazackerley, Sir Henry Hoghton, bart.
1741.—Nicholas Fazackerley, James Shuttleworth.
1747.—Nicholas Fazackerley, James Shuttleworth.
1754.—Nicholas Fazackerley, Edmund Starkie.
1761.—Nicholas Fazackerley, Edmund Starkie.
1767.—*Death of Nicholas Fazackerley*—Sir Peter Leicester, bart.
1768.—Sir Peter Leicester, bart., Sir Frank Standish, bart., who were unseated on petition, and in their stead the House of Commons seated Col. John Burgoyne, Sir Henry Hoghton, bart.
1774.—Col. John Burgoyne, Sir Henry Hoghton, bart.
1780.—General John Burgoyne, Sir Henry Hoghton, bart.
1784.—General John Burgoyne, Sir Henry Hoghton, bart.
1790.—General John Burgoyne, Sir Henry Hoghton, bart.
1792.—*Death of General Burgoyne*—William Cunliffe Shawe.
1795.—*Death of Sir H. Hoghton*—Sir Henry Philip Hoghton, bart.
1796.—Lord Stanley, Sir Henry Philip Hoghton, bart.
1802.—Lord Stanley, John Horrocks.
1804.—*Death of John Horrocks*—Samuel Horrocks.
1806.—Lord Stanley, Samuel Horrocks.
1807.—Lord Stanley, Samuel Horrocks.
1812.—Edmund Hornby, Samuel Horrocks.
1818.—Edmund Hornby, Samuel Horrocks.
1820.—Edmund Hornby, Samuel Horrocks.
1826.—Hon. E. G. Stanley, John Wood.
1830.—Hon. E. G. Stanley, John Wood.
1830.—*Hon. E. G. Stanley appointed Chief Secretary for Ireland*, Henry Hunt.
1831.—John Wood, Henry Hunt.
1832.—Peter Hesketh Fleetwood, Hon. Henry Thomas Stanley.
1835.—Peter Hesketh Fleetwood, Hon. Henry Thomas Stanley.
1837.—Peter Hesketh Fleetwood, Robert Townley Parker.
1841.—Sir Peter Hesketh Fleetwood, bart., Sir George Strickland, bart.
1847.—Charles Pascoe Grenfell, Sir George Strickland, bart.
1852.—Robert Townley Parker, Sir George Strickland, bart.
1857.—Charles Pascoe Grenfell, Richard Assheton Cross.

PART I.—HISTORICAL.

CHAPTER VIII.—TRADE AND COMMERCE.

Early Trade—Portus Setantiorum—Roman Commerce—Trade of the Saxons—Norman Conquest—Henry III: Preston the Wealthiest Town in Lancashire—Edward III.—The Woollen Trade—The Flemmings—Condition of the People—Henry VIII.—Woollen Cottons—Progress of Manchester—Revocation of the Edict of Nantes—Assize and Assay—Ulnage and Sealing—Vegetable Cotton—Fustians—Calicoes—Linen Trade—Refugees from the Spanish Netherlands—Early Spinning Machines—British Exports—Rapid Progress of the Cotton Trade—Inventions of Wyatt, Arkwright, Kay, Hargreaves, etc—Disputed Claims—Arkwright's Early Difficulties—Opposition to the Introduction of Machinery—Riots—First Cotton Factory in Preston—Further Improvements in Machinery—Arkwright's Success—Infringements of his Patents—Litigation—Arkwright's Claims as an Inventor—Further Improvements in Machinery—Power Looms—Riots—The Steam Engine—Rapid Extension of Preston—Influence of Trade upon the National Character—Internal Communication—Transit of Goods and Passengers—Roads during the Eighteenth Century—Coaches, Canals, etc.—Progress of Trade and Commerce—Effects of War—Steam Vessels and Railways. RIBBLE NAVIGATION.—Early Commerce—State of the River during the Past Century—Original Company—Surveys of Messrs. Stephenson, etc.—New Company Improvements—Preston an Independent Port—Traffic, Tonnage, etc.—Sale of Land. STRIKES AND LOCKOUTS.—Condition of the People—Decline of Serfdom—Legislative Interference with Labour and Capital—Singular Laws—Wages and Prices of Provisions, etc.—Competition—Early Strikes—Great Strikes in 1836 and 1853-4—Additional Statistics with reference to Trade and Commerce.

PREVIOUSLY to the Norman era little is known which peculiarly characterises the trade or commerce of the people inhabiting the district now known as Lancashire. In all probability their internal barter or "home trade" was limited to the interchange of the rude necessaries of a rural and warlike population. Anterior to the Roman occupation, the aborigines of Britain were almost entirely unacquainted with the use of money. Pieces of brass, iron, and other metals, were sometimes used, but they were not impressed with any distinctive device, and were merely valued according to weight. Doubtless the "Portus" of Ptolemy, whether situated on the Ribble, the Wyre, or the Lune, would afford facilities for commercial enterprise; and it is probable the Roman merchants would not neglect so important and well protected a position.

Referring to the Setantian port, J. Whitaker says:—"It was the only commercial harbour along the whole line of the western coast, and had no rival from the Cluyd to the Land's End. And the exports of the neighbouring region, the lead of Derbyshire, and the salt of Cheshire, the corn, the cattle, and the hides of the whole, must have been all shipped at the port of the Ribble.[a] The British dogs in general were a very gainful article of traffic to the Romans." [b]

Nevertheless, the trade, in the estimation of modern civilization, must have exhibited very insignificant results. The Romans, however, in the early period of their domination in Britain, introduced the woollen manufacture, and probably Lancashire, which afterwards became so celebrated for its textile productions, received its earliest impulse in this direction from the world's conquerors. Gildas, the early British historian, states that at the period of the departure of the Romans, Britain was "adorned with her large spreading fields, pleasantly seated hills, ever famed for good husbandry, which ever mastereth the ground, and mountains most convenient for the changeable pasture of cattle," and was "enriched with the mouths of noble floods, by which outlandish commodities have, in times past, been transported into the same." The arts of agriculture must have made considerable progress under the Roman *regime*, for according to Camden the corn fields of Britain furnished large supplies of grain for the sustenance of the Roman armies defending the Rhine frontier of the empire. The Romans derived considerable revenues from the mineral products of the country. During the reigns of Augustus and Trajan, according to Strabo, mines of gold and silver were worked in Britain. The tin mines of Cornwall, and the salt rocks and pits of Cheshire, presented at that period, likewise, considerable sources of mercantile wealth.

At the time of the settlement of the Romans, according to the Rev. J. Whitaker, the imports consisted principally of "earthenware, salt, and brass." The articles exported were chiefly "tin, gold, silver, iron, lead, hides, cattle, corn, slaves, dogs, gems, pearl muscles, polished horse bits of bone, horse collars, amber toys, and glass vessels." According to the same authority, the articles introduced by the Romans after their occupation included the following:—"Sugar, pepper, ginger, writing paper," and others of a similar character. The exports he states to have been "partly the same as before, and partly the additional particulars of gagate or jet, bears for the foreign amphitheatres, baskets, salt, corn, and oysters." The British jet appears to have been highly prized upon the continent, on account of its superior quality.

The advent of the Saxons, a rude and barbarous people, little acquainted with the refinement of Roman civilization, produced a retrograde movement. The fertility and comparative wealth of the country, tempted these

a See chap. 1, page 14. b Gratius, page 96.

roving warriors. Spoliation and plunder followed their track, and the previously fertile domains relapsed into primitive wildness.

At the time even of the Norman conquest, the Anglo-Saxons "were in general, a rude uncultivated people, ignorant of letters, unskilled in the mechanical arts. * * * The Norman historians, notwithstanding the low state of the arts in their own country, speak of them as barbarians, when they mention the invasion made upon them by the duke of Normandy."[c] Still, according to the learned and venerable Bede, London, though but the capital of one of the minor kingdoms of the heptarchy, as early as the beginning of the seventh century, was regarded as a great commercial port, and enjoyed an extensive trade with the merchants of many European nations. The wiser of the Saxon monarchs were not unmindful of the importance of the industrial arts, in the furtherance of peace and civilization. Skilful foreigners were encouraged to settle in the country, and navigation and commerce progressed under their fostering protection. Markets and fairs were pretty generally established in the more populous portions of the kingdom. Macpherson, in his "Annals of Commerce," states that, in the Anglo-Saxon times, merchants from Cologne and other cities of Germany, visited the southern ports of the island, to purchase the wool of the numerous flocks of sheep which grazed upon the downs and pastures of Britain. The trade and commerce of Lancashire at this period, must have been of a very insignificant character. Such as it was, however, Preston appears to have possessed a greater portion of it than any other town in the county. From the taillage assessed by "Master Alexander de Dorsete and Simon de Hal," in the second year of the reign of Henry III., it appears that Preston paid 15 marks; Lancaster, 14 marks; Liverpool, 11 marks, 7s. 8d.; and the "town" of West Derby, 7 marks, 4s. 4d.[d] Manchester and Wigan are not mentioned in this return.

The commercial enterprise of the kingdom made but little progress during the disturbances which characterised the period of the earlier Norman princes. In the reign of Edward I. laws were enacted for the encouragement of trade, by affording to merchants a cheaper and more expeditious method of recovering their debts. It would appear from the seizure by this king of the property of the Jews, and of "all the wool and leather in the kingdom,"[e] and the increased taxes imposed upon the former article, that the woollen trade had begun to assume some importance. Hume observes, that, "in 1296, the famous mercantile society, called the '*Merchant Adventurers*,' had its origin: it was instituted for the improve-

c Hume. Gul. Pict, p. 202.

d Mag. Rot. 11 H. III. Rot. 1. a. Lankastre.

e Hume.

ment of the woollen manufacture, and the vending of cloth abroad, particularly at Antwerp. For the English at this time scarcely thought of any more distant commerce." Another writer states, however, that soon after the Norman conquest, the merchants of Florence and Venice traded largely with England in the raw material for their woollen manufactures.[f] The inhabitants of Lancashire appear to have always preferred the grazing of cattle to sheep. At the present time M'Culloch says, the chief wealth of the Cheshire farmers consists in their 100,000 milch cows, and that the farmers of Lancashire possess nearly double that number. During the reigns of the earlier Plantagenet princes the manufacture of flax was likewise cultivated to some extent. Mention is made of a "fulling mill" on the banks of the river Irk, near Manchester, in the reign of Edward II.[g] After the marriage of Edward III. with Philippa of Hainault, a considerable impetus was given to the woollen manufacture. According to Fuller, the English, previous to this period, "were ignorant of that art, as knowing no more what to do with their wool than the sheep that ware it, as to any artificial curious drapery; their best clothes then being no better than friezes, such was their coarseness for want of skill in making."[h] The king procured large supplies of continental workmen, whom he distributed over various parts of the kingdom. The Flemings were located chiefly in Norfolk, York, Kendal, Halifax, Manchester, the districts of Rossendale and Pendle, and in the west of England; most of which localities still maintain their original reputation for superior skill in the woollen manufacture. Fuller says the skilful, though poorly remunerated Flemish artisans, were prevailed upon to leave their country by the promises of the king's emissaries. Amongst other temptations, the following were held out:—

"They should feed upon fat beef and mutton till nothing but their fulness should stint their stomach; yea that they should feed on the labours of their own hands, enjoying a proportionable profit of their pains to themselves: their beds should be good, and their bed fellows better; seeing the richest yeoman in England would not disdain to marry their daughters unto them. * * * Those yeomen in whose houses they harboured soon preceded gentlemen, gained great estates to themselves, and arms and worship to their estates. Here they found fuller's earth, a precious treasure, whereof England hath better than all Christendom besides. And now was the English wool improved to the highest profit, passing through so many hands, every one having a fleece of the fleece, sorters, combers, carders, spinners, weavers, fullers, dyers, pressers, packers, and these manufactures have been heightened to the highest degree of perfection."[i]

---

f Daru's Venice. g Kuerden.

h Fuller further observes, in his quaint and humourous style, that after the king's marriage he "began to grow sensible of the great wealth the Netherlands gat by our English wool, in memory whereof the Duke of Burgundy, a century after, instituted the order of the Golden Fleece, wherein indeed the fleece was ours, but the gold theirs, so vast was their emolument by the trade of clothing."

i Church History, p. 110.

From an enquiry[j] into the value of property in all the boroughs of England, made during the reign of this monarch (1343), it appears that Preston was the wealthiest town in Lancashire at that period. Manchester was not at the time a manufacturing town, but the centre of an agricultural population. In this respect the parish was amongst the very first in the county, the produce of the soil being worth eighty marks, or nearly, in the money value of the present day, £800. per annum. Manchester had not even sufficient trade to render it liable to pay the tax upon merchandise and moveable property. Most of the other now large towns were in a similar condition. There were but four "royal boroughs" in the county: Preston, Liverpool, Lancaster, and Wigan. The ninth portion of "the goods of the men dwelling in the borough" of Preston was valued at £6. 17s. 4d.; in Liverpool, £6. 16s. 7d.; in Lancaster, £6. 13s. 6d.; and in Wigan, £5. 9s. 4d. The £6. 17s. 4d. has been computed to be equal to about £100. of our present money; which, multiplied by nine, gives less than £1000., as the value of the "goods" of the Prestonians of that period. Thus the whole county could only boast of "merchandise and moveable property," liable to the tax, amounting to about £3,500. At the same time, according to a similar calculation, the town of Nottingham possessed property of the class named to the value of £50,000., and Bristol £30,000.

A singular piece of legislation was attempted in the reign of this monarch, with the expressed object of "restraining the malice of servants," who refused to work for the same amount of wages they had received previously to the outbreak of a great plague, by which the number of artisans had been considerable lessened, and the value of labour consequently increased.[k] It appears the legislators of that period understood not, or refused to recognise, the modern doctrine in political economy, that all mercantile value depends upon the relative proportion between the supply of, and demand for, any given commodity. This act arbitrarily fixed the wages of the labourer at the price paid before the plague diminished the supply. This rate was fifteen pence per week; but corn at the time sold at tenpence per bushel. The labourers, of course, immigrated to localities where their services commanded higher reward. A second act of parliament was consequently passed, which prohibited a servant leaving, in summer, any town or parish where he usually dwelt in winter, if employment were offered him in his own locality, on the terms of the act. Exceptions were granted during the harvest, to labourers residing in Lancashire, Stafford, Derby,

j Nonarum Inquisitiones.

k According to Stowe fifty thousand persons died of the plague in the city of Norwich, and as many were interred in one burial ground within the precincts of the city of London.

and some other places. Delinquents were punished with "the stocks," or three days' imprisonment.

The great mass of the labouring people were, in fact, slaves, in the truest sense of the term, down to a much later period. Sir. F. M. Eden, in his "History of the Labouring Classes,"[1] says:—

"If we except the baronial proprietors of land, and their vassals, the free tenants and socmen, the rest of the nation seems to have been involved in a state of servitude, which, though qualified as to its effects, was uniform in its principle, that none who had been born in or had fallen into bondage, could acquire an asbolute right of property. * * * In both Magna Charta and the charter of Henry the Third, in 1225, a class of men are mentioned who appear to have been considered in the light of moveable property. The prohibition to guardians from wasting the men and cattle on the estates of minors, is a clear proof that villeins, who held by servile tenures, were looked upon in the light of negroes on a rice, a tobacco, or sugar plantation. Long after the year 1225, they were considered as a saleable commodity. In 1283, a slave and his family were sold by the abbot of Dunstable, for 13s. 4d.; in 1333, a lord granted to a charity several messuages, together with the bodies of eight natives (villeins) dwelling there, with all their cattle and offspring; and in 1339, we meet with an instance of a gift of a neif (a female slave), with all her family, and all that she possessed, or might subsequently acquire."

Other acts of parliament, of a similar character to those of Edward III., were continually passed down to the time of George III. The emancipation of the working classes, as the term is now understood, has been a gradual achievement, extending over many centuries.

In the reign of Edward VI., a law was passed which prohibited any person making cloth, unless he had served a seven years' apprenticeship to the trade. In the first year of the reign of Mary, this act was repealed, in consequence of the injury sustained by the woollen manufacture of the kingdom, through its operation. It was, however, again enacted in the reign of Elizabeth, and continued in force until within a very recent period.

Little is known of the progress of the woollen manufacture in Lancashire, till about the period of the Reformation. In the reign of Henry VIII. (1520), Hollinworth, in his "Mancuniensis," says, "there were three famous clothiers living in the north contre, viz., Cuthbert, of Kendal, Hodgkins, of Halifax, and Martin Brian (some say Byrom), of Manchester. Every one of these kept a great number of servants at work, carders, spinners, weavers, fullers, dyers, sheermen," etc. Leland, the antiquary, visited Lancashire about 1538. He speaks of Manchester as the "fairest, best builded, quickhest, and most populous tounne of al Lancastreshire." He further remarks that "Bolton-upon-Moore market stondith most by cottons, divers villages in the moores about Bolton do make cottons." The statute 33 Henry VIII., abolishing the privilege of "sanctuary" at Manchester, mentions the town as a place where the manufacture of cotton and linen cloths was rapidly increasing the wealth and importance of the

1 Vol. 1, pages 7 and 35.

inhabitants. It had already become a kind of depot or market for the sale of the staple manufactures of the county. Parties congregated thither from various parts of England and Ireland, for traffic in wool and linen yarn. "Many persons," says the statute, "were accustomed to resort to this town with *cottons* to be sold." The cloths, then denominated Manchester and Bolton cottons, like the Kendal and Welsh cottons of the present day, were made from a coarse wool. It appears from the statutes of Edward VI. and Elizabeth, regulating their manufacture, that they were heavy, *milled* goods. The former says, "all the *cottons* called Manchester, Lancashire, and Cheshire cottons, full wrought to the sale, shall be in length twenty-two yards, and contain in breadth three-quarters of a yard in the water, and shall weigh *thirty* pounds in the piece at the least." Camden, in 1590, states that Manchester "excels the towns immediately around it in handsomeness, populousness, *woollen* manufacture, market place, church and college; but did much more excel them in the last age, as well by the glory of its *woollen cloths*, which they call Manchester *cottons*," etc. A modern authority says:—

> "The application of the term 'cottons' to a woollen fabric may either have arisen, as some conjecture, from a corruption of the word 'coatings;' or from the manufacturer having imitated the foreign cottons, which were fustians and other heavy goods, and having given the name to their imitations. It is, however, not a little singular, that a manufacture destined afterwards to eclipse not merely the 'glory' of the old 'Manchester cottons,' but that of all other manufactures, should have existed in name long before it existed at all in fact." [m]

The unsettled state of the continent during the latter portion of the sixteenth century, and the revocation of the edict of Nantes, in 1685, caused many skilled artisans from France and Flanders to seek an asylum in England. Lancashire manufactures consequently received a powerful stimulus, and rapidly increased in extent and importance.

The statute of the 8th of Elizabeth states that the aulneger[n] for the county of Lancashire "shall appoint and have his lawful deputy within every of the several towns of Manchester, Rochdale, Bolton, Blackburn, and Bury." From this it might at first sight appear that the chief manufacture was confined to the localities mentioned. The other important towns of Lancashire were, however, chartered boroughs, and enjoyed the special privilege of appointing their own officers for the performance of these duties. The charter of Elizabeth confers upon "the mayor, bailiffs, and burgesses of the borough of Preston," the privilege of "assize and assay of bread, wine and beer and other victuals, the *ulnage and sealing of all cloths*, weights and measures whatsoever, and the amendment and

---

m History of the Cotton Manufacture, by Edward Baines, jun.

n The duties of the aulneger included the measuring of all cloth offered for sale, and stamping the same with the king's seal and the name of the maker, for which he received the prescribed fee. The length, breadth, and weight of each piece of cloth was regulated by act of parliament.

correction thereof." The population of the borough at this period is not supposed to have much exceeded three thousand persons, but it is evident no inconsiderable portion of them were employed in the woollen manufacture, the then staple trade of the county.

The record of the Preston corporation° contains an entry dated 1633, setting forth the names of poor children who had been apprenticed under certain specified charities. One of these children, Margaret Osbaldeston, is bound "prentice" to Thomas Hodgson, of Preston, chapman, "to be instructed in the art or craft of weavinge Boone Lace, and in other arts which the said Thomas Hodgson now uses." Another is bound apprentice to one Thomas Hesketh, glover.

A resolution of the corporation, in January, 1674-5, ordered the establishment of a workhouse and other offices, for the employment of the poor in the woollen manufacture.

From the passing of the act of the 8th of Elizabeth, nearly a century elapsed, during which authentic records are silent respecting the manufactures of the county; but within that period the cotton manufacture of England must have originated. The plant is supposed to be indigenous to Persia and Hindostan. The cultivation and manufacture of cotton had arrived at considerable perfection amongst the eastern nations anterior to the Christian era. The Aztecs, or aborigines of Mexico, appear to have made great progress in this species of textile manufacture, previously to the time of their conquest by the Spaniards. It is not positively known whether the plant is or is not indigenous to America. The excellence of the Georgian cotton is attributed to the fact that the American colonists originally procured their seed from Smyrna. A species of cotton plant is, nevertheless, found growing in a wild state upon the plains of the new world. Cotton is first alluded to, as an article of commerce, by an Egyptian Greek writer, of the first or second century of the Christian era, who states that cottons were brought by Arab traders to the ports of the Red Sea. Calicoes were exported from Barygaza (now Baroche), and Masalia (now Masalipatam); and Bengal muslins were then, as now, the most esteemed.

The records of the middle ages make no allusion to the manufacture of cotton in Europe. It flourished, however, in Spain under the Mahomedan califs, as early as the tenth century, and by the fourteenth had arrived at great perfection. It was not much cultivated, as a branch of European trade, even at this period. "The silken fabrics of Italy and Sicily were well known and esteemed in the twelfth, thirteenth, and fourteenth centuries; the woollen trade was carried to great extent and perfection in Flanders,

° Books of Orders.

Lombardy, and Romagna at that period; while Greece added to these the manufacture of linen goods, which, with more intellectual arts, she had learned from Egypt; still cotton finds no place in the general enumeration of the fruits of industry and science." [p]

In an old poem, entitled the "Progress of English Policy," published in "Hackluyt's Collection of Voyages," in 1430, the Flemings are described as in the habit of exporting fustians to Spain, and importing similar articles from the Easterlings, Prussia, and Germany. Fustians are mentioned by Guicciardini, as an article of commerce between Italy and the Low Countries, in 1560. They were produced, at a still earlier period, at Barcelona, in Spain. In the middle of the thirteenth century, the manufacturers of this city were incorporated. Their chief productions were sail cloth and fustians. The latter name is supposed to be derived from the Spanish word *fuste*, meaning substance.

The use of the spindle and distaff was superseded, in England, about the end of the reign of Henry VIII., by the spinning wheel; yet the manufacture of cotton received little or no impetus in Britain, and for a long period made but slow progress on the continent of Europe. Fuller, writing in 1662, calls fustians a "foreign commodity." Printed calicoes were first imported into England by the East India Company, in 1631. The name is derived from Calicut, in Hindostan. In 1676, they were first printed in London.[q]

Before the close of the seventeenth century, the linen trade would appear to have made so much progress in Preston, as to have become the staple manufacture. In Jan., 1704-5, the mayor, aldermen, capital and other burgesses, and tradesmen, presented a petition to the house of commons, in which they state that "the making of linen cloth hath, for many ages, been the settled trade of their neighbourhood, and is the sole dependence of *thousands* of families." [r] There is evidently some mistake in the word "thousands," as it is highly probable, at this period, that the entire population of the borough did not consist of more than from twelve to fourteen hundred families. But, from the general tenor of the document, the linen trade of Preston must have been, relatively, both extensive and important.

The precise period at which the cotton manufacture was introduced into England is not yet known. It probably began gradually to develope itself about the close of the sixteenth or the commencement of the seventeenth century. The earliest known allusion to it is in 1641. Cotton was, previously to that period, only employed in the manufacture of candlewick and such inferior articles of the trade.

p "Cotton, from the Pod to the Factory."
q Anderton's History of Commerce.
r Journals of the House of Commons.

The refugees from the persecutions of the duke of Alva, in the Spanish Netherlands, are supposed by some authorities to have introduced the cotton manufacture into England. A portion of these settled at Manchester, and received considerable encouragement, especially from the warden and fellows of the college. The first authentic record of the existence of the cotton manufacture in Manchester, or, indeed, in Great Britain, is found in a work published in 1641, entitled "Treasure of Traffic," by Lewis Roberts, in which he says :—

"The town of Manchester, in Lancashire, must be also herein remembered, and worthily for their encouragement commended, who buy the yarn (linen) of the Irish in great quantity, and weaving it, return the same again into Ireland to sell: Neither doth their industry rest here, for they buy *cotton wool* in London, that comes first from Cyprus and Smyrna, and at home worke the same and perfect it into *fustians*, *vermillions*, *dimities*, and other such stuffes, and then return it to London, where the same is vented and sold, and not seldom sent into forrain parts, who have means at far easier terms, to provide themselves of the said first materials."

From this period the manufacture of cotton goods furnished occupation for a large proportion of the population in various towns and villages in Lancashire. The finished articles were chiefly sold in Manchester; but the principal market for the coarser or unfinished goods was at Bolton. Yet, up to the year 1738, observes Mr. Baines :—

"The machines used in the manufacture were nearly as simple as those of India; though the loom was more strongly and perfectly constructed; and the hand cards, for combing the fibres of the cotton straight, had been adopted from the woollen manfacture. The one thread wheel was also used instead of the distaff; but this well known appendage of the houses of English farmers and peasants scarcely admitted of greater dispatch in spinning than the more ancient instrument."

Notwithstanding, the manufacture progressed rapidly, towards the end of the seventeenth century; and the annual value of the general British export trade more than trebled, between 1662 and 1699. In the latter year it amounted to £6,788,166. The manufacture of cotton continued to advance rapidly during the earlier part of the eighteenth century. Still, in relative importance, as a national staple, it ranked considerably below the woollen manufacture. It was not until after the introduction of those mechanical inventions, which have so immensely augmented the productive power, that the cotton trade of England began to exhibit colossal proportions. The quantity of cotton wool annually imported into Great Britain, on an average of five years, ending with 1705, did not exceed 1,170,881 lbs.; and even so late as from 1771 to 1775, the average import was only 4,764,589 lbs. a year. The quantity of cotton spun into yarn in Great Britain, in the year 1832, amounted to no less than 246,935,124 lbs. The annual value of the goods manufactured was estimated at about £36,000,000 sterling. Nearly a million and a half of persons derived their subsistence from this branch of industry; the greater portion of whom were located in Lancashire.[a] In 1856, the quantity of cotton wool imported

a Baines' History of the Cotton Manufacture

into England, is estimated at upwards of one thousand millions of pounds![t]

A combination of many inventions, with subsequent additions and improvements, effected this mighty social revolution. In 1738, Mr. John Kay, of Bury, invented the "fly shuttle." By the use of this instrument, the weaver was enabled to nearly double the amount of his production. The shuttle had previously been thrown by the hand. In the manufacture of wide cloths, this practice necessitated the employment of two men in the weaving of one piece. The fly shuttle was first introduced into the woollen manufacture. It was not until about 1760, that the cotton weavers adopted it, in conjunction with a further improvement, introduced by Mr. Kay's son, named "the *drop-box*," which enabled the weaver to use any one of three shuttles, containing different coloured weft, without removing them from the lathe. Mr. Kay, on the introduction of his improvement, met with considerable opposition from the operatives. He found it necessary for his personal safety or comfort to remove to Paris.

These inventions necessitated further improvements in the spinning department, as the weavers were unable to procure material for their looms, at the required rate. Dr. Aikin, in his "History of Manchester," says, "the weavers, in a scarcity of spinning, have sometimes been paid less for the weft than they paid the spinner, but durst not complain, much less abate the spinner, lest their looms should be unemployed." When a weaver, from any cause, was desirous of completing a piece in a shorter time than usual, "a new ribbon or a gown was necessary to quicken the exertions of the spinner."[u] "The one-thread wheel, though turning from morning to night in thousands of cottages, could not keep pace either with the weaver's shuttle or with the demand of the merchant. Genius stepped in to remove the difficulty, and, as it were, gave wings to a manufacture which had been creeping on the earth. A mechanical contrivance was invented, by which twelve, twenty, fifty, a hundred, or even more threads could be spun at once, by a single pair of hands."[v]

The distinguished honour of this important invention, the precursor of others pregnant with mighty results and lasting influence upon the social condition of Lancashire, and of the civilization of the world, was, for a long time, pretty generally accorded to a humble hair dresser, who daily exercised his skill upon the perukes and chins of the good people of Preston, at a little shop in Lord-street.[w]

---

t Holt's Annual Circular. u Guest's History of the Cotton Manufacture.

v Baines's History of the Cotton Manufacture.

w The house or shop where Arkwright resided, was pulled down a short time ago. It stood on the north side of Lord-street, a little to the west of Wood-street, and faced Molyneux-square. It was afterwards tenanted by Mr. Clare, hosier. Its site is now occupied by one of the handsome shops, lately erected by the earl of Derby. It forms the southern extremity of Stanley-buildings Lancaster-road.

But, although candid investigation has stripped much of the laurel from the brow of Richard Arkwright, sufficient evidence of his energy, enterprise, mechanical ingenuity, and adaptive skill, still remains to justify his pretensions to a high position amongst the public benefactors of his country. Arkwright might not be the great original mechanical genius he was for some time represented; but he possessed marvellous business qualities, great foresight, and indomitable perseverance. His success was commensurate with his efforts. His qualities were such as transformed a ragged barber[x] into a wealthy knight; while the men of genius, from whom he received original ideas, pined in poverty and comparative neglect.

Mr. Baines, in his "History of the Cotton Manufacture," has satisfactorily proved that the method of spinning by rollers was practised more than thirty years before Arkwright took out his patent for a machine of this character. The original invention is due to John Wyatt, of Birmingham, who, in the name of his partner, Lewis Paul, a foreigner, took out a patent for spinning with rollers, in 1738. Another patent was taken out, by the same parties, in 1748, which included some improvements on the previous machine. The former was worked at Birmingham, and the latter at Northampton; but owing to some defects of construction, or perhaps want of capital or business talent, the speculation did not prove profitable to the projectors. Wyatt wrote a work in 1743, which long remained in manuscript, entitled "A Systematical Essay on the Business of Spinning, or the Manufacture of Cotton Wool into Yarn for various uses," etc. From this work we learn that the business failed in consequence of Wyatt leaving the first establishment at Birmingham to reside in London, for the purpose of disposing of the yarn spun at the manufactory. Mr. Baines observes: "If Wyatt could have applied himself as closely to the direction of his machinery, and to the perfecting of the arrangements of his mill, as Arkwright afterwards did—finding some one to make known and dispose of his yarn—the great impetus to the cotton manufacture might have been given thirty years earlier.

Mr. Kennedy states, "that after the breaking up of Wyatt and Paul's establishment at Northampton, it was purchased by a hat manufacturer at Leominster, and by him applied to the carding of wool for hats; and, about 1760, it was introduced into Lancashire, and re-applied to the carding of cotton, by a gentleman of the name of Morris, in the neighbourhood of Wigan." This evidently alludes to the *carding* and not the spinning

x Arkwright's wardrobe, while preparing his first spinning machine, was in such a tattered condition, that some friends subscribed the means necessary to render him presentable at the poll booth on the occasion of the "great election" at Preston, in 1768. Mr. E. Baines, sen., says he voted for Burgoyne and Hoghton. This is an error. His vote was tendered, according to the poll book yet extant, for the corporation candidates, and rejected on the ground of non-residence.

portion of the machinery. Indeed, Mr. Kennedy afterwards explained, in a communication to Mr. Baines, that it was the *cylinder card* which Mr. Morris used at Leominster and Wigan.

Mr. Charles Wyatt, son of the inventor, says, in a letter, published in the "Repertory of Arts, Manufactures, and Agriculture," in January, 1818: "From a strange coincidence of circumstances, there is the highest probability, that the machinery got into the hands of a *person, who with the assistance of others*, knowing how to apply it with skill and judgement, and to supply what might be deficient, raised upon it, by a gradual accession of profit, an immense establishment and a princely fortune." Mr. Charles Wyatt still more pointedly alludes to Arkwright in the same communication. After minutely describing his father's machines, he says: "Such or nearly such being the early history of this invention, I thought the late Sir Richard would be gratified by possessing the very model to which I have alluded; and I accordingly waited on him at Cromford with the offer, but my reception did not correspond with my expectations."

Arkwright confessed, in the "Case," which he drew up for presentation to parliament, that he was aware "about 40 or 50 years ago, one Paul and others, of London, invented an engine for the spinning of cotton, and obtained a patent for such invention; afterwards they removed to Nottingham and other places. They spent many years and much money in the undertaking but without success; and many families who were engaged with them were reduced to poverty and distress." As Arkwright's "water frame" is regarded as identical in principle with that of Wyatt, though differing in minor details and extent of development, the probability is, that the former had seen the machine of the latter, or read the specifications on which the patent was founded.

But Wyatt was not the only original inventor to whom Arkwright is supposed to have been indebted. Thomas Highs, of Leigh, a reed maker by trade, gave evidence on the trial of the validity of Arkwright's patent, in 1758, and claimed a priority in the invention of spinning by rollers. He stated that he had made a similar machine in 1767, two years previously to Arkwright's patent, and that he employed a man named Kay, a clock-maker, to make wheels and rollers for him. Kay stated that he had, during the same, or in the following year, communicated the plan to Arkwright, at Warrington, and furnished him, at his request, with two models. Highs, however, never perfected a machine, or took out a patent, till some years after Arkwright's successful experiments were well known to the public. The fact that Arkwright engaged Kay to accompany him to Preston and Nottingham, and his remaining in his service for four or five years, is however, strong presumptive evidence that Highs possessed some claim to the invention afterwards perfected by his more successful compeer.

Arkwright was thirty-five years of age when he first met with Kay, the clockmaker, at Warrington, in 1767. He employed this ingenious man to assist him in some experiments, which had for their object the discovery of perpetual motion. Arkwright afterwards devoted his energies in a more profitable direction; but, being no practical mechanic, he engaged Kay to assist him in the construction of his spinning machine. Kay being unable to make all the required machinery, Mr. Peter Atherton, afterwards of Liverpool, was applied to for assistance. He lent Arkwright a smith and watch tool maker, to make the heavier part of the engine. Kay undertook to make the clockmaker's part of it, and to instruct the workmen. In this manner, under Arkwright's personal superintendence, his first spinning machine was constructed.

Arkwright's poverty, for some time, prevented him completing his machine. He repaired to Preston, his native town, and was fortunate enough to secure the sympathy and assistance of Mr. John Smalley, "a liquor merchant and painter." This gentleman allowed Arkwright the use of a room in his own house, for the prosecution of his labours. In this room the first complete machine constructed and afterwards patented by Arkwright, was fitted up. The house is situated at the bottom of Stonygate. It was afterwards for a long period the residence of the Rev. Robert Harris, B.D., head master of the grammar school. It has since been converted into a public-house, and is now known by the sign of the "Arkwright's Arms." The parlour in which the first "spinning engine" was fitted up, has been restored as nearly as possible to its original condition, with the view to enhance the historical interest attached to it.

Another invention, by James Hargreaves, a weaver, of Stand-hill, near Blackburn, called the "spinning-jenny," was introduced in 1767, about the time Arkwright became acquainted with Kay, and two years before he obtained a patent for his "water frame." The machine of Hargreaves, being entirely different in principle from that of Wyatt, must be regarded in the light of an original invention. It is said that Hargreaves first conceived the idea of his "jenny," from the accidental overturning of a one-thread wheel. As the wheel and spindle continued to revolve, he conjectured that a frame might be constructed, in which a number of spindles placed upright would spin several threads at one time. His first experiment was with eight rovings and eight spindles. Mr. Baines thus describes Hargreaves's machine:—

"The rovings which extended to the spindles, passed through two horizontal bars of wood, which opened and shut something like a parallel ruler; when pressed together the clasp held the threads fast. A certain portion of roving being extended from the spindles to the wooden clasp, the clasp was drawn to a considerable distance from the spindles which lengthened out the threads; this was done with the spinner's left hand, and his right hand at the same time turned a wheel, which caused the spindles to revolve rapidly and thus the thread was spun into yarn. By returning the clasp to its first situation, the yarn was wound upon the spindles."

Hargreaves did not patent his invention, but endeavoured to confine the knowledge of it to his own family. In this however, he did not long succeed.

Mr. Guest advocated the claim of Highs, of Leigh, to the invention of the "jenny." The evidence adduced is, however, by no means conclusive. Highs was unquestionably a man of remarkable genius, and is entitled to the gratitude of his country for many partially successful efforts for the improvement of spinning machinery. He certainly invented, at a later period, a kind of "double jenny;" and, according to his evidence on Arkwright's trial, he had made what he called a "perpetual carding machine," in 1773. Highs called his machine, according to the evidence of Thomas Leather, a *jenny*, in compliment to his daughter Jane, the produce from whose labour it was intended to augment.

The perfected roller machines of Arkwright were found to produce a "hard firm thread," well adapted for warps, which had been previously made of linen. Hargreaves's jenny made a superior kind of "weft." The two machines, therefore, rather aided than opposed each other in their practical results, and produced, for the first time in England, a fabric made entirely from cotton.

These inventions were regarded, as most other innovations upon ancient usage, with great jealousy, not only by the workmen, but by the middle classes and gentry, and even by the then established manufacturing capitalists. The workmen fancied the new machinery would supersede their labour, and the wealthier inhabitants feared an augmentation of the poor's rate in consequence. Mr. Baines asserts that they "connived at, and even actually joined in, the opposition to machinery, and did all in their power to screen the rioters from punishment." Hargreaves's house was broken into, and his machines destroyed. He fled to Nottingham, took out a patent in 1770, and entered into partnership with one Mr. James; but his affairs did not prosper. His patent was invaded by a "powerful combination of spinners," he was reduced to poverty, and ultimately perished in the Nottingham workhouse;[y] a striking example of the national ingratitude to one of its greatest benefactors. Many riots occurred in the neighbourhood of Blackburn, in 1779. Jennies, carding engines, and all machines turned by horse or water power, were destroyed. Some progress had, however, been made in public enlightenment on this subject; for jennies, containing no more than twenty spindles, were spared,

---

y Baines's "History of the Cotton Manufacture." The author of "Cotton from the Pod to the Factory," however, says, "Hargreaves died at Nottingham, in 1778, having maintained his family in comfort by the fruits of his invention."

as useful and necessary. Arkwright's large mill, at Birkacre, near Chorley, was destroyed by a mob, notwithstanding a large body of police and military were present, who received no order from the magistracy to prevent or suppress the outrage. The grandfather of the late lamented Sir Robert Peel left the county in disgust, and commenced business at Burton-on-Trent, in Staffordshire. He had been subjected to personal insult at Altham, and his machinery thrown into the river. Thus, the very places where the inventions originated, were deprived, for a time, of the many advantages which resulted from their introduction into other parts of the country.

Arkwright obtained his first patent in 1769, and erected a mill at Nottingham, which was worked by horse power. The necessary capital was advanced by Messrs. Wright, bankers, of that town. By these gentlemen he was afterwards introduced to Mr. Need, a stocking manufacturer, of Nottingham, and Mr. Jedediah Strutt, of Derby, the improver and patentee of the stocking frame. The latter gentleman remedied some practical objections to Arkwright's spinning frame. Messrs. Need and Strutt entered into partnership with Arkwright, and doubtless materially aided in his success. In 1771, a second mill was erected at Cromford, on the banks of the Derwent, near Matlock, Derbyshire. The spinning machinery was worked by water power, hence the name "water-frame," by which Arkwright's invention was for a long period known to the public.

The first cotton mill erected in Preston was built in Moor-lane, in 1777, by Messrs. Collinson and Watson, the year previous to Hargreaves's death. The structure is yet standing, and is used as a weaving establishment. The "yard factory," at the east end of Church-street, was built in 1792, by Mr. John Horrocks; whose energy and enterprise, if it did not found the cotton trade in Preston, unquestionably gave the chief impetus, which, in little more than half a century, converted the quiet aristocratic town, of about 6,000 or 7,000 inhabitants, into a busy hive of industry, with a population augmented more than ten-fold. In 1796 and 1797, Mr. Horrocks erected two other mills upon the "Spital's Moss," and the "Frenchwood Cotton-mill," near Lark-hill. The Lord's factory (Messrs. Ainsworth and Co.'s), was built in 1796. About 1799, the "Old Friary" was transformed from a house of correction into a cotton-mill. Messrs. Riley and Paley's establishment was erected in 1802.

After the first impulse had been given to the cotton manufacture, its progress was by no means rapid. Inventive skill was not wanted to perfect the new machinery, but ignorance and cupidity, intent upon *present* aggrandisement, and blind to the future advantages, for some time successfully crippled its operations. Inventors were either proscribed, or ruthlessly robbed of their rights. Even Arkwright, the most enterprising and successful business man amongst them, was seriously opposed and annoyed by the manufacturers of his time. Notwithstanding the acknowledged superiority of his yarns, the Lancashire capitalists entered into a combination to discountenance the productions of his machinery, and refused to purchase his goods. Arkwright complained, in a pamphlet which he issued in 1782,[z] that:—

"It was not till upwards of five years had elapsed after obtaining his first patent, and more than £12,000. had been expended in machinery and buildings, that any profit accrued to himself and partners. * * The most excellent yarn or twist was produced: notwithstanding which the proprietors found great difficulty to introduce it into public use. A very heavy and valuable stock, in consequence of these difficulties, lay upon their hands; inconveniences and disadvantages of no small consideration followed. Whatever were the motives which induced the rejection of it, they were thereby necessarily driven to attempt, by their own strength and ability, the manufacture of the yarn. Their first trial was in weaving it into stockings, which succeeded; and soon established the manufacture of calicoes, which promises to be one of the first manufactures in the kingdom. Another still more formidable difficulty arose; the orders for goods which they received being considerable, were unexpectedly countermanded, the officers of excise refusing to let them pass at the usual duty of 3d. per yard, insisting on the additional duty of 3d. per yard, as being calicoes, though manufactured in England;[a] besides these calicoes when printed were prohibited. By this unforseen obstruction, a very considerable and very valuable stock of calicoes accumulated. An application to the commissioners of excise was attended with no success; the proprietors, therefore, had no resource but to ask relief of the legislature; which after much money expended, and *against a strong opposition of the manufacturers in Lancashire*, they obtained."

It is somewhat difficult to account for the *animus* exhibited by the Lancashire cotton manufacturers against the introduction of a new and profitable branch of their own trade. The legislature of the country proved, however, more enlightened upon the subject. The ridiculous demands of the "Lancashire manufacturers" were rejected, and a law passed, which states that "a *new* manufacture of stuffs, made *entirely of cotton spun in this kingdom*, had lately been introduced, and some doubts were entertained whether it was lawful to use it, it was declared to be not only a *lawful* but a *laudable* manufacture, and was therefore permitted to be used on paying threepence per square yard when printed, painted, or stained with colours."

The silk and woollen manufacturers of England, towards the conclusion of the preceding century, had succeeded in obtaining the "entire prohibition of Indian silks and calicoes, both plain and printed, for home consumption." Notwithstanding this stringent measure, these elegant fabrics found their way into general use in this country, much to the chagrin of the native manufacturers, whose woollen goods they in some

z The "Case" for presentation to parliament.

a Calicoes were first made in imitation of the cotton goods imported from the East Indies. The name is derived from Calicut, the original place of their manufacture.

measure superseded. Their influence was such, however, that an act was passed, in 1721, which prohibited the use of printed calicoes, under a "penalty of five pounds for each offence on the wearer, and twenty pounds on the seller"! With reference to these singular enactments, Mr. Baines judiciously observes, that the laws passed at the instigation of the British woollen spinners, "though injurious to the public, were (for the time at least), beneficial to the home manufacturer; but the prohibition of English made calicoes was so utterly without an object, that its being prayed for by the cotton manufacturers of this country, is one of the most signal instances on record of the blinding influences of commercial jealousy."

Notwithstanding the value and importance of the inventions already recorded, the remaining machinery of a cotton mill was still of a very imperfect character, especially that portion which prepared the cotton for the spinning frames. Lewis Paul, the partner of Wyatt, took out a patent in 1748, "for two different machines for accomplishing the same purpose; the one a flat, the other a cylindrical arrangement of cards." Mr. Baines, after describing minutely the machine of Paul, says:—

"Here, then, are the carding cylinder, the perpetual carding, and the comb for stripping off the carding. It must be admitted that the invention was admirable and beautiful, but not perfect. Its defects were,—that it had no feeder, the wool being put on by hand,—that the cardings were taken off separately by a moveable comb, which of course required the machine to stop,—and that the perpetual carding was produced by joining short lengths with the hands, whereas now it is brought off the machine in a continuous roll, by a comb attached to the cylinder, and constantly worked against it by a crank. This machine, though so great an improvement on the old method, was not known in Lancashire for twelve years, nor generally practised for more than twenty years after the date of the patent."

Successive improvements were made in these machines by John Lees, of Manchester, in 1772; Messrs. Wood and Pilkington, in 1774; James Hargreaves, the inventor of the jenny, in 1773, and Richard Arkwright, previously to 1775; the latter, with his usual tact and judgment, embodying, improving, and adapting, and afterwards patenting, the various discoveries of his contemporaries. With respect to these inventions, Mr. Baines pronounces the following judgment:—"The cylinder must be ascribed to Paul,—the feeder to Lees,—the mode of producing a perpetual carding to Wood and Pilkington,—the crank and comb to Hargreaves,—but the perfect machine to Arkwright."

Arkwright's patent, in 1775, included improved machinery for drawing and roving. He described himself as "the first and sole inventor," and declared "that the same had never been practised by any other person or persons whatsoever, to the best of his knowledge and belief." The sliver, by the former process, is drawn out and afterwards doubled, to be again drawn out and the previous operation repeated. "Every time the drawing and doubling is repeated, the irregularities in the substance or grist of the sliver will be *reduced* in exactly the same ratio as the doublings are multiplied." [z] Thus a greater uniformity in the thickness and strength of the thread is produced.

"The roving frame performs the first process of spinning, by twisting the sliver into a thick loose thread. This is done by a machine on exactly the same principle as the spinning frame. The carding is drawn out of the can into which it was delivered from the drawing frame; it passes through two or more pairs of rollers, which by their different velocities stretch it out; and it is then slightly twisted and wound on the bobbins. Arkwright, however, did not wind the thread on bobbins, but allowed it to fall into an upright can, revolving rapidly on its axis; the revolution of the can gave the roving its twist, no spindle being used; when the can was filled, the roving was wound upon bobbins at the winding frame. He claimed the can as his own invention, but it was proved at the trial to have been in use long before he obtained his patent." [a]

Arkwright now began to reap the reward of his enterprise and ingenuity. Poets sung his praise, and the reputation of his patented machinery rapidly increased.[b] From his "Case" intended for presentation to parliament, we learn that he "sold to numbers of adventurers residing in the different counties of Derby, Leicester, Nottingham, Worcester, Stafford, York, Hertford, and Lancaster, many of his patent machines. Upon a moderate computation, the money expended in consequence of such grants [c] amounted to at least £60,000. Mr. Arkwright and his partners also expended in large buildings in Derbyshire and elsewhere, upwards of £30,000.; and Mr. Arkwright also erected a very large and extensive building in Manchester, at the expense of £4,000." From these data, he contended that in consequence of his patented inventions, "a business was formed which already employed upwards of five thousand persons, and a capital, on the whole, of not less than £200,000."

---

z Baines: Cotton Manufacture. a Baines: Cotton Manufacture.

b Dr. Darwin, in his "Botanic Gardens," thus eloquently describes the marvels of Arkwright's establishment at Cromford :—

"Where Derwent guides his dusky floods
Through vaulted mountains and a night of woods,
The nymph Gossypia treads the velvet sod,
And warms with rosy smiles the wat'ry god;
His pond'rous oars to slender spindles turns,
And pours o'er massy wheels his foaming urns;
With playful charms her hoary lover wins,
And wields his trident while the Monarch spins.
First, with nice eye, emerging Naiads cull
From leathery pods the vegetable wool;
With wiry teeth *revolving cards* release
The tangled knots, and smooth the ravell'd fleece:
Next moves the *iron hand* with fingers fine,
Combs the wide card, and forms th' eternal line:
Slow with soft lips the *whirling can* acquires
The tender skeins, and wraps in rising spires;
With quicken'd pace *successive rollers* move,
And these retain, and those extend the *rove*:
Then fly the spokes, the rapid axles glow,
While slowly circumvolves the labouring wheel below."

c That is anterior to 1782.

Only three years afterwards it was stated by the counsel employed to oppose Arkwright, that thirty thousand people were employed by the capitalists who acted in defiance of his patents, and that the money sunk in the buildings and machinery of these establishments amounted to near £300,000.

The success of Arkwright thus stimulated the enterprise of other capitalists. His patents were infringed, and his claims to the original inventions disputed. In 1781, nine actions were instituted by Arkwright against persons who had set up his machines, without obtaining from him a license for such proceedings. An association of Lancashire spinners defended the only one tried (that against Colonel Mordaunt), and non-suited Arkwright, on the ground of the obscurity or insufficiency of the specifications in his second patent. Arkwright, thus baffled by his competitors, published the pamphlet already alluded to, in which he argued his claims to special legislative protection.[a] He did not, however, proceed in this direction. In 1785, having obtained new evidence, he commenced another action, with a successful result. But the vast and increasing interest of the manufacturing spinners, especially in Lancashire, was again arrayed against him, as the second decision would subject them to penalties for continuing the use of the machines. An association was formed, which employed the best legal advice, and specially retained scientific gentlemen to expose the technical defects, etc., of the patent, and to procure and digest the evidence necessary to its overthrow. A writ of *scire facias* was obtained from the lord chancellor to try the validity of the patent. The case was heard before Judge Buller. Amongst other witnesses examined against Arkwright's claim were Highs and Kay, and the widow and son of Hargreaves. The result was that the jury, without a moment's hesitation, returned a verdict which nullified the patent. The Manchester spinners were in ecstacies, and overt demonstrations of satisfaction were exhibited by the rival manufacturers. In the following term, a new trial was applied for by Arkwright, on the plea that he had procured evidence

a This pamphlet is entitled, "The Case of Mr. Richard Arkwright and Co., in relation to Mr. Arkwright's invention of an engine for spinning cotton, etc., into yarn; stating his reasons for applying to parliament for an act to secure his right in such invention, or for such other relief as to the legislature shall seem meet." Respecting this pamphlet Mr. Baines remarks, "Whatever were the services Arkwright had rendered his country—and they are delusively and greatly over-rated in this 'Case'—he here asked for an enormous reward. His first patent, obtained in 1769, would expire in 1783, the year after the 'Case' was drawn up; and the second patent, obtained in 1775, would not expire till the end of the year 1789. He was therefore asking for the patent right of all the machines to be continued to him for eight years longer, which alone would have secured to him a large fortune."—Whatever doubt there may be respecting Arkwright's mechanical genius, there can be none as to his business capabilities. His immense fortune was not accumulated without the expenditure of much energy, ingenuity, and commercial tact. In common with most other eager speculators, he had ever a sharp eye to his own interest, and but little practical sympathy for the inventive genius of others.

which contradicted that of his opponents. The rule was refused, Judge Buller expressing his conviction, that on the previous trial Arkwright "had not a leg to stand upon." Arkwright, however, still continued at the head of the principal cotton spinning firm in the country, and for a long period his prices for twist furnished the standard to which all other manufacturers conformed. After accumulating a large fortune, he died at Cromford, in 1792.

Much difference of opinion still obtains, in well informed circles, respecting the precise measure of Arkwright's claims as an inventor. Mr. Baines's summary, though somewhat severe, appears to be candid and based upon the evidence adduced. He says:—

"Truth and justice have compelled us to strip Sir Richard Arkwright of borrowed plumes. We have shown that the splendid inventions which even to the present day (1836) are ascribed to him by some of the ablest and best informed persons in the kingdom, belong substantially to other and much less fortunate men. In appropriating those inventions as his own, and claiming them as the fruits of his unaided genius, he acted dishonourably, and left a stain upon his character, which the acknowledged brilliancy of his talents cannot efface. Had he been content to claim the merit which really belonged to him, his reputation would still have been high, and his wealth would not have been diminished. For in improving and perfecting mechanical inventions, in exactly adapting them to the purposes for which they were intended, in arranging a comprehensive system of manufacturing, and in conducting vast and complicated concerns, he displayed a bold and fertile mind and consummate judgment; which, when his want of education, and the influence of an employment so extremely unfavourable to mental expansion as that of his previous life, are considered, must have excited the astonishment of mankind. Such high merit must be accorded to him. But the still more rare and exalted merit of *original invention*—the *creative faculty*, which devised all that admirable mechanism—so entirely new in its principles, and characteristic of the first order of mechanical genius—which has given a new spring to the industry of the world, and within half a century has reared up the most extensive manufacture ever known,—*this* did NOT belong to Arkwright; this laurel must be taken from the brow of the wealthy knight of Cromford, and if it may be awarded to any one individual, it must be given to the modest insolvent of Birmingham."

The author of the article, "Arkwright, Sir Richard," in the Penny Cyclopædia, claims for the ingenious and energetic Prestonian more original inventive power than Mr. Baines accords; but he advances no new evidence to controvert that already adduced. He says:—

"Even without claiming for him the honour of having been an original inventor,—an honour which, upon the best consideration we can give to the conflicting evidence brought forward, *we are still inclined to award him*,—we may certainly ascribe to him the possession of a clear and comprehensive mind, as well as the most unerring judgment. His plans were all laid with skill, and pursued with energy; he displayed the most unwearied perseverance in pursuit of his object under difficulties which would have borne down most men; and he forms one amongst the bright instances afforded by the annals of this country, that talent, when thus allied with patient energy and persevering industry, will not fail to ensure ultimate success to its possessor."

The description by Thomas Carlyle, the celebrated *litterateur*, of Preston's most distinguished son, written with his characteristic eccentricity and almost savage power, will be read with interest:—

"Richard Arkwright, it would seem, was not a beautiful man, no romance hero with haughty eyes, Apollo lip and gesture like the herald Mercury; a plain, almost gross, bag-cheeked, pot-bellied, Lancashire man, with an air of painful reflection, yet also of copious free digestion; a man stationed by the community to shave certain dusty beards in the northern parts of England, at a halfpenny each. To such end, we say, by forethought, oversight, accident, and arrangement, had Richard Arkwright been, by the community of England and his own consent, set apart. Nevertheless, in strapping of razors, in lathering of dusty beards, and the contradictions and confusions attendant thereon, the man had notions in that rough head of his; spindles, shuttles, wheels and contrivances plying ideally within the same;—rather hopeless looking, which, however, he did at last bring to bear. Not without difficulty! His townsfolk rose in mob around him, for threatening to shorten labour, to shorten wages,—so that he had to fly, with broken wash-pots, scattered household, and seek refuge elsewhere. Nay, his wife, too, as I learn, rebelled; burned his wooden model of his spinning wheel, resolute that he should stick to his razors rather,—for which, however, he decisively, as thou wilt rejoice to understand, packed her out of doors. O reader, what a historical phenomenon is that bag-cheeked, pot-bellied, much-enduring, much-inventing barber! French Revolutions were a-brewing; to resist the same in any measure, imperial Kaisers were impotent without the cotton and cloth of England; and it was this man that had to give England the power of cotton."

Between the years 1774 and 1779, Samuel Crompton, a respectable weaver, residing in one of the cottages forming a portion of the ancient edifice denominated "The Hall i'th Wood," near Bolton, was diligently employed in still further improving the newly introduced spinning machinery. His labours resulted in the production of a machine which combined the principles of Hargreaves's jenny and Arkwright's or Wyatt's roller frame. From this circumstance it received the appellation of "the *mule jenny*."

"The distinguishing feature of the mule is, that the spindles instead of being stationary, as in both the other machines, are placed on a moveable carriage, which is wheeled out to the distance of fifty-four or fifty-six inches from the roller-beam, in order to stretch and twist the thread, and wheeled in again to wind it on the spindles. In the jenny, the clasp which held the rovings, was drawn back by the hand from the spindles; in the mule, on the contrary, the spindles recede from the clasp, or from the roller-beam which acts as a clasp. The rollers of the mule draw out the roving much less than those of the water frame; and they act like the clasp of the jenny, by stopping and holding fast the rove, after a certain quantity has been given out; so that the draught on the thread is chiefly made by the receding of the spindles. By this arrangement, comprising the advantages both of the rollers and the spindles, the thread is stretched more gently and equally, and a much finer quality of yarn can therefore be produced." [b]

Other improvements rapidly followed, step by step, till the present wonderfully complex, but coherent factory machinery resulted. Crompton's first mule was only calculated for about twenty or thirty spindles.

These machines were afterwards enlarged and improved in details by Stones, of Horwich, and others, till Mr. Wright, of Manchester, constructed a *double* mule, by which contrivance no less than four hundred spindles were worked by one frame. As many as twelve hundred are, at the present time, frequently placed in one machine. Kelly, of Lanark, introduced the principle of the *self-acting* mule, as early as 1792. He but partially succeeded, however, and soon afterwards abandoned his experiments. Others followed with indifferent success, till Mr. Roberts, of Manchester,

b Baines's History of the Cotton Manufacture.

of the firm of Sharp, Roberts, and Co., overcame the difficulty. His first patent is dated 1825, and a second, for further improvements, in 1830. The self-acting mule does not require the superintendence of a spinner, a "minder," and a "piecer," to re-unite the threads which accidentally break, being alone necessary to its perfect operation. Amongst other important improvements may be mentioned the "throstle," the "fly frame," and the "tube frame." The first is a modification of Arkwright's spinning machine, by which its speed, and, consequently, amount of productive power is much increased.

As "necessity is the mother of invention," improvements in the weaving machinery rapidly succeeded the introduction of the spinning-frames. The first "power-loom" was patented in England, by Dr. Edmund Cartwright, in 1785, although as early as 1678, a weaving machine, moved by water power, had been constructed by M. de Gennes, but does not appear to have succeeded in practice. Dr. Cartwright's weaving establishment, at Doncaster, notwithstanding the introduction of several valuable improvements in his looms, was commercially unsuccessful, and he abandoned it. The merit of his invention was, however, recognized by parliament, in 1809, when the sum of £10,000. was granted to him, in consideration of the advantage derived by the manufactures of the country from his labours and discoveries.

Dr. Cartwright was not, however, the first native of Great Britain who constructed a power-loom. This honour is claimed for Mr. Andrew Kinloch, who, in 1793, with the assistance of an operative joiner and a clockmaker, set up, at Glasgow, what is described as the "first power-loom ever made." The sum of one hundred pounds was subscribed by some friends, to aid Kinloch in his experiments. Power was applied to his machine by a wheel, turned by the hand. The expenditure of the one hundred pounds produced about ninety yards of cloth. He afterwards set up some power-looms for Messrs. Pollock Shaw, and Co., at Paisley. He removed to Staley-bridge, in 1800, and there set up several looms. A portion of these were removed to, and several others made for, West Hoghton, near Wigan. During some riots, in 1813, the operatives destroyed about one hundred and seventy of his looms, together with other property, at West Hoghton, and would, as Kinloch expressed it, have consigned himself likewise to the flames, if he had not promptly decamped. Kinloch, in 1845, when on a visit to Glasgow, was presented with a handsome silver snuff box, containing fifty sovereigns, as a testimony to his ability as an ingenious mechanic, and as a token of respect for his moral worth. Andrew Kinloch died at the residence of his son, in Preston, on the 15th of Jan., 1849, and was buried in St. Peter's churchyard. When a boy, Kinloch, after a hard race of about eight miles, was captured by a press-gang, and served for some time on board the Shannon frigate. He took part in the memorable struggle between that vessel and the American frigate, Chesapeake. Kinloch has been heard to remark that he turned his attention to the construction of a power-loom, owing to the impression made upon his mind by an observation of Sir Richard Arkwright. The roller machines of the latter produced so large a quantity of twist, that the manufacture of it into cloth became, with the then means, a serious difficulty. This being mentioned to Arkwright, as an objection to his invention, the shrewd Prestonian remarked, that an effort ought to be made to weave cloth by machinery likewise, and the mischief complained of would be obviated. Kinloch was born at Port Glasgow, in the year 1760; and was, consequently, in his eighty-ninth year at the time of his death.

The "power-loom" did not successfully compete with hand labour for many years. The continual necessity which existed for stopping the loom, in order to "dress" the warp, as it unrolled from the beam, was at length overcome by the introduction of the "dressing machine" of Messrs. Radcliffe and Ross, of Stockport, by which the warp is prepared previously to its being placed in the loom. This machine was patented in 1803, and again in 1804. The principal inventor was a workman in the employ of Messrs. Radcliffe and Ross, called Johnson, in whose name the patent was taken out.[c] Radcliffe, however, failed to realise a profit by his ingenuity and enterprise.

Mr. H. Horrocks, cotton manufacturer, of Stockport, patented a power-loom in 1803, which he afterwards improved in 1805, and again in 1813. Radcliffe claimed the method of taking up the cloth introduced by Horrocks as the invention of his workman Johnson. This ingenious individual was known amongst his fellow operatives as "the conjuror," on account of his inventive skill. Horrocks's power-loom, with additional improvements, is the one now generally adopted. It is a compact machine, constructed of iron, and occupies little room. The power-loom and dressing machines, however, did not, for a long period, receive much attention from manufacturers. They were employed chiefly in the production of coarse goods, the finer qualities being still woven by hand labour. Horrocks was unfortunate in his commercial speculations, and ended his days in poverty, "the common destiny of inventors;" business habits and commercial acumen being seldom compatible with the dreamy temperament and delicate sensibility, which usually accompanies creative genius.

c The dressing machine itself has now (1836) in some establishments been superseded, and the warp is dressed in a shorter and simpler way by an improved sizing apparatus.—Baines.

The operatives, fearing for their occupation, employed physical force to prevent the introduction of these machines. Although, in 1813, there were not supposed to be more than two thousand four hundred power-looms in use, the hand-loom weavers became alarmed. Riots took place at Middleton, West Hoghton, etc., and the obnoxious machinery was destroyed. In 1808, a large body of weavers met on Preston moor, to devise means to induce their employers to raise their wages. A military force was in attendance to preserve order, though it does not appear that the destruction of the new weaving machinery formed a part of the objects entertained by the workpeople. In 1818, a body of twelve hundred handloom weavers paraded the streets of Preston, with the view to enforce the manufacturers to increase the remuneration of their labour.

In 1826, serious riots occurred in various parts of Lancashire, and a large number of looms were destroyed. Preston, to some extent, was fortunate during this crisis. The "big factory," at Fishwick, (Messrs. Swainson and Birley's), was converted into a kind of fortress, and armed with cannon. Small arms were likewise provided for the workmen, to defend the establisment, and large quantities of paving stones were stowed upon the roof and in the upper stories. These preparations checked the progress of the rioters, who threatened the town from the Chorley and Blackburn roads.

In 1836, the number of these weaving machines or power-looms in Great Britain, was calculated to be nearly seventy thousand, fifty thousand of which were at work in England alone. Notwithstanding the extensive introduction of power-looms, it is supposed that, between 1820 and 1829, the number of hand-looms remained undiminished. In 1835, about 108,632 power-looms, employed in the manufacture of cotton, are said to have been at work in Great Britain. In 1850, the number had increased to 249,627. In 1835, the total number of power-looms running, including those employed in the woollen, worsted, flax, and silk manufactures, was 115,782; in 1850, 298,916.[d] At the present time, hand-loom weaving has become almost extinct, except for certain kinds of fancy goods. According to Mr. Kennedy, in 1815, the spinning machinery, then in use, was calculated to produce, by the labour of one man, about two hundred times the quantity of yarn more than that in use fifty years previously. Mr. Baines says, the production of cotton goods, in 1836, per individual labourer, was "equal to what could have been done by two or three hundred men sixty years previously." This enormous amount of productive power has been still further augmented by improvements in the machines themselves, and by the increased speed to which they are subjected. In 1857, the spinning

d Parliamentary Report.

machinery, with one man to superintend, will do the work of eight hundred individuals. At the present time, the production of cotton goods by machinery is four or five hundred-fold per man employed, to that of the old distaff and hand-loom system.

Extensive improvements in the machinery and the chemical processes used in bleaching, dyeing, and printing cotton goods, followed in the wake of the spinning and weaving inventions. Mr. Whittle says:—

"At Mosney, near Preston, cylinder printing was invented by Mr. Bell, a Scotchman, and was successfully applied in the year 1785, at Mosney, near Walton-le-Dale, by the house of Livesey, Hargreaves, Hall, and Co., so much celebrated for the extent of their vast concern, and the magnitude of their failure in 1788, which gave a severe shock to the industry of the vicinity of Preston, and even to the town itself." [e]

Additional value was given to these discoveries, by the introduction of Watt's improved steam engines. Wyatt's frames at Birmingham, were turned by asses; and Arkwright first employed horses as the motive power. Wyatt, at Nottingham, and Arkwright, at Cromford, availed themselves of the water wheel. The first discovery of the power of steam, seems due to Solomon De Caus, a Frenchman, in 1615. [f] David Ramsey, a groom of the privy chamber, obtained a patent in England from Charles I. The Marquis of Worcester still further developed the principle. Captain Savery's engine, patented in 1698, was the first which proved of much practical value. The pumping of water from coalpits and other mines, appears to have been the chief object aimed at by the original inventors. Thomas Newcombe improved Savery's machine. A joint patent was taken out in 1705. The movements were simplified, in 1717, by Mr. Beighton. No improvement of importance followed, till 1769, when Watt took out his patent for "lessening the consumption of steam and fuel in fire engines." Watt afterwards became connected with Mr. Boulton, a capitalist, of Soho, Birmingham, and took out another patent in 1775, or rather was invested by a special act of parliament with the "sole use and property of certain steam engines (or fire engines), of his invention," for a period of twenty years. He effected still further improvements, which he patented in 1781, 1782, and 1784.

Messrs. Robinson, of Papplewich, in Nottinghamshire, were the first to introduce Boulton and Watt's engines into a cotton mill, in the year 1785. The first erected in Lancashire, for cotton spinning, was for Mr. Drinkwater, of Manchester, in 1789. The new inventions did not receive the patronage of Arkwright till 1790, when one of Boulton and Watt's engines

e His. Pres. vol. 2, p. 62.

f See the letter of Marian De l'Orme, quoted in Sir John Barrow's autobiography. From this document it appears the Marquis of Worcester originally received his knowledge of the applicability of steam power to machinery from a pamphlet by De Caus. The "Century of Inventions," by the Marquis, was published in 1663.

was set up for him at Nottingham. Messrs. Scott and Stevenson introduced the first into Glasgow, for the purposes of cotton manufacture, in 1792. Other improvements have from time to time been effected, from which the several powerful engines at present in use have resulted.

An improvement in the method of spinning flax was introduced by Mr. Kay, of Preston, about 1822-3. The principal feature in Kay's patent consisted in bringing the drawing and retaining rollers within two and a half inches from each other. Considerable improvements were afterwards effected by Marshall, of Leeds, who introduced steam and "troughs," for "macerating" the flax. Others had previously only steeped the slivers in cold water, contained in "cans." Marshall, eventually succeeded, after much litigation, in overthrowing Kay's patent right, on account of the imperfect character of the specification. Kay's flax mill was situated in Kay-street, Marsh-lane, Preston. Mr. Seed, of Preston, patented a "presser," constructed on what he called the "centrifugal principle." This presser, which was attached to the "roving flyers," was for a long time regarded as the best of many patented articles professing to attain similar results. After some litigation with Mr. Lamb, of Manchester, as to the validity of the patent, Mr. Seed united his interest with that gentleman, and their separate inventions are now amalgamated.

It is to the combined influence of the various inventions thus hastily noticed, that the marvellous development of industrial energy and commercial enterprise presented by the Lancashire cotton manufacture is mainly to be attributed. Preston has played no insignificant part in this mighty social revolution. Not only did she give birth to Arkwright, but she produced or fostered men of similar energy and commercial sagacity, whose united action has converted, in about seventy years, the quiet little chartered borough of six thousand people, with its "well-born" but "ill-portioned old maids and widows," and aristocratic feelings and prejudices, into the second manufacturing town of Lancashire, where about eighty thousand persons find pleasurable or profitable occupation, and where capital, combined with intelligent enterprise, yearly extends the productive power, and adds to the wealth of the locality.

The great social value of these wonderful inventions was, however, for a long period, disputed, not only by the operative population, who suffered at the time from the innovation, but by men of high standing, and acknowledged intelligence. Change of any kind is ever terrible to a certain classes of very amiable individuals. So long as their nests are warmly lined, and their larders well supplied with both necessaries and luxuries, they can perceive nought but misery and desolation in the rear of the social and political antagonism ever attendant upon human progress.

Amongst those whose fears and prejudices overpowered their judgments on this subject, one of the most distinguished was intimately connected with this neighbourhood. Dr. T. D. Whitaker, in his History of Richmondshire,[g] makes the following remarkable observations :—

"Thirty years after" (1745), "in the last generous but hopeless effort to restore the exiled family, Preston merely witnessed the orderly and well conducted march of the insurgents on their way to Derby, and their precipitate and undisciplined retreat with the Duke of Cumberland in close pursuit. Had he been two days earlier it is not improbable that Fulwood moor would have been remembered for what Culloden was, and Falkirk should have been. Times are now altered; and Preston instead of witnessing the noble struggles of loyalty or liberty, and the efforts of contending branches of the same family to recover or retain the throne, has since had nothing better to agitate the fears of its inhabitants than the base and brutal efforts of anarchy, stimulated by those hotbeds of insubordination and sedition, the manufactories, which have debased the manners of the lower orders more rapidly than they have increased the population of the place. It is the nature of the dreadful visitation of Providence, which for our sins, has fallen upon this age and country, that it tends at once to ruin the principles and multiply the number of our species: and if not checked by the removal of the evil into other countries, who, grasping like ourselves at immoderate gain, are insensible to its consequences,

——— ——— mox
Progeniem dabit vitiosiorem." [h]

Never was prophet more unfortunate in his vaticination! Whatever evils may be inseparable from overstrained commercial enterprise, surely they are neither irremediable in themselves, nor more degrading than the vicious habits fostered by war. To the most ordinary mind, at the present day, it would be difficult to suggest any worse occupation in which a people could be employed than the slitting of their neighbours' throats and the devastating of their common country, merely for such an inadequate consideration as the pleasure or profit resulting to *"contendiug branches of the same family" endeavouring " to recover or retain the throne."* These "noble struggles of loyalty and liberty" may be all very grand to boast about; but how the morals of the public are improved by the deeds and influences of civil war is somewhat difficult of comprehension. An act of parliament, passed in 1692 (the fourth year after "the revolution,") tells a rather different story. The preamble declares it was passed expressly for "encouraging the apprehension of highwaymen." The highways and roads had become more infested with thieves and robbers than formerly; and "so many murders and robberies had been committed, that it was become dangerous, in many parts, for travellers to pass on their lawful occasions." It was, therefore, enacted that a gratuity of £40. should be given for the apprehension and conviction of every offender; and as a further inducement, the robber's horse, arms, money, and other property taken with him, were ordered to be transferred to the party effecting the capture.

g Vol. 2, p. 433.
h "Will soon produce a still more vicious progney."—Horace.

Nay more; any one turning informer, and discovering and convicting two other robbers, was to receive a pardon for all previous offences. A modern writer truly observes: [i] "The evil must have been great to warrant the application of such remedies, which lowered the dignity and moral purity of justice, by thus allying it with crime." Ay, and every reader of the "Newgate Calendar" or other "wholesome literary food" of the past generation, knows well the evil continued rife until within a comparatively recent period.

From the statute passed in the second George II., in 1746, the year after the last "noble struggle" between the aforesaid "contending branches of the same family," it seem not only does "insubordination and sedition" result from such conflicts, but that the "manners of the lower orders" are seriously "debased" thereby; nay, that depravity of morals permeated every class of society, to such an extent, that "constables, tithing-men, and peace officers," were required to "seize and secure," not only the *canailles*, the "vagabonds," "sturdy beggars," and "incorrigible rogues," then so prevalent, but "gentlemen" (?) guilty of habitual profane cursing and swearing! The said offenders are ordered to be mulcted in the following proportions:—"A day labourer, a soldier, or a sailor, one shilling; if under the degree of gentlemen, two shillings; and if above that degree, five shillings!" This resulted not from the slightest tincture of puritanism in the government, but from the natural recoil after excessive licence. The preamble of the act expressly declares that "the horrid, impious, and execrable vices of profane cursing and swearing, so highly displeasing to Almighty God, and loathsome and offensive to every Christian," were becoming so common as to justly provoke the divine vengeance. There exists, however, one glorious exception to this rule of a life of plunder and debauchery amongst disbanded troops previously engaged in civil war. It is thus eloquently described by Macaulay:—

> "Fifty thousand men, accustomed to the profession of arms, were at once thrown on the world," [at the period of the restoration] "and experience seemed to warrant the belief that this change would produce much misery and crime, that the discharged veterans would be seen begging in every street, or would be driven by hunger to pillage. But no such result followed. In a few months there remained not a trace indicating that the most formidable army in the world had just been absorbed into the mass of the community. The royalists themselves confessed that in every department of honest industry, the discharged warriors prospered beyond other men, that none was charged with any theft or robbery, that none was heard to ask an alms, and that, if a baker, a mason, or a waggoner, attracted notice for his diligence and sobriety, he was in all probability one of Oliver's old soldiers."[j]

This contrasts oddly with the licentious roystering of the Stuart cavaliers, and speaks volumes in honour of those stern old warriors to

i Sir George Nicholls's History of the English Poor Law.

j History of England, vol. 1, page 154.

whom English liberty owes so much, and who, till lately, have been rewarded by those most benefited, with abuse instead of gratitude. With this exception, however, experience has ever proved that riot, violence, debauchery, famine, and crime, both accompany and follow in the track of the heroes of the sword, and in no case with more revolting and unnatural accessories, than when warriors flesh their weapons in the strife termed, with bitter irony, *civil* warfare! Peace may have its vices, and "indolent ease" may be "inglorious;" commercial enterprise may, nay does, give birth to selfish avarice, and sometimes to cold-hearted tyranny; but the worst of these attributes must be added to the other characteristics of the good old fighting period, or the portraiture is neither true nor complete. Some of the vices of our ancestors, too, have vanished before the progress of mechanical aid in the production of the necessaries and comforts of human existence. Dr. Whitaker himself laments the drunken debaucheries of the Stuart partisans and complains bitterly of the filthy habits and brutal sports which did *not spring* from modern commercial sympathies. He says:—[k]

"Many laudable exertions have been lately made, and are making to procure for our parish churches, not only the removal of annoyances to sight and the smell, but some degree of that silence and sequestration which their sanctity demands. Never was the removal of a nuisance of the last species more loudly called for than at this place," (Preston) "where the parish church is visited by the audacious neighbourhood of one of those human pandemonia, a cockpit; so that, on a hot day when the windows were open, the writer of this has distinctly heard the infernal yells, the diabolical oaths and curses, which issued from that place, while standing before the altar of God."

The Preston cockpit was converted into a Temperance Hall, in the days of mechanical skill and commercial enterprise![l] Pugilism, bull-baiting, and cock-fighting were *virtues* in the deeply lamented defunct age of high "principle" and "noble struggle." The present, with all its faults, and truly they are more than the utilitarian spirit of the hour has yet discovered, or at least willingly acknowledges; the despised present patronises free schools and libraries, cheap books and periodicals, baths and wash-houses, public parks, cheap trips, extensive sewerage, and other sanitary improvements; better *legacies*, at least, to posterity, than bloody victories, however glorious! The "good old times," it must not be forgotten, evoked these struggles, and produced, of necessity, rebels and tyrants as well as patriots and heroes. The best possible cure for this hankering after supposed by-gone perfections, would, if it were practicable, be the transportation of the most antiquated section of the present generation into a country inhabited by a people with dwellings, manners, and intelligence, identical with those so grievously lamented. They would, perhaps, find them-

k History of Richmondshire, vol. 2, p. 425.
l It has since been converted into the "Derby Assembly Room."

selves in a somewhat similar mood to the fashionable young lady, who, compelled by the will of a crabbed old uncle either to marry her great-grand-father or resign a princely fortune, complied with the testator's wishes to the letter, but eloped on the afternoon of the same day with a modern spark of eighteen. Truly no man is a hero to his own valet; and there are no "good old times" to those who live in them! The much abused industrial element of the present age needs nothing but a quiet consignment to the tomb of the past, to draw down unavailing regrets from the stagnant souls of the next generation.

Doubtless, on the first introduction of the factory system, the complexion of the new order of things was much more dingy than at present; hence the virtuous indignation of the erudite antiquary and orthodox theologian. Mankind, however, has gained much and lost little by the change. The true remedies for existing evils are to be found in the volume dedicated to the developement of future progress, and not to the deification of the musty records of the past; in which, after all, men read more of wrong and falsehood than truth and right. When the present edifice shall be completed, the ugly scaffolding which, though necessary to its construction, disfigures its beauty, will be removed. It will then cease to be viewed through the spectacles of prejudice and personal selfishness. Its claims to public consideration will be asserted by an *after* present, when time hath robed it with some of the venerable but profitless weeds which adorn the tottering limbs of its mouldering competitor. And the spirit of this same *after* present, now throbbing in the womb of time, true to the eternal law, will, in turn, dispute *its* perfection; and, wrenching from the mysterious and inexhaustible hoard of natural wealth some new truth, supersede its *protege*, to be itself superseded in turn by the genius of a still more remote but equally active and progressive future.

The improvement in the power for production necessitated a corresponding advance in the means of transit. In the early portion of the eighteenth century, the great bulk of the roads in Lancashire were scarcely passable for carriages, except in very fine weather. They were merely "bridle paths" or "horse-tracks." "There was not a proper carriage road from Liverpool to the great northern highway at Warrington, until about the time of the accession of George III." [m]

In 1720, an act was obtained for making and keeping the river Douglas navigable from Wigan to the Ribble. The preamble declares that the carrying out of the project would be beneficial to trade, advantageous to the poor, and convenient for the carriage of coal, cannel, stones, slate, and other goods and merchandise to and from the towns and places adjacent;

m Thos. Baines's History of Liverpool, p. 401.

and would very much tend to the employment and increase of watermen and seamen, and be a means of preserving the highways. The act limited the charge to 2s. 6d. per ton for the conveyance of goods along the river. In the same year, acts were obtained for rendering the river Weaver available for the carriage of goods between the river Mersey and the Cheshire salt works, and for the conversion of the Irwell and Mersey into a means of communication between Liverpool and Manchester. About this period the first Liverpool dock was completed.

The means for personal locomotion, or the transit of goods, in the interior of the country, were nevertheless very limited at the middle of the eighteenth century. Not a single stage coach left Liverpool "for Manchester, London, or any other place," as late as the year 1753.[n] The roads were infested with robbers; and travellers, in consequence, generally proceeded in companies. Every Friday morning, a kind of caravan or "gang of horses," set out from the Swan with Two Necks, Lad-lane, London, and arrived generally at Liverpool on the following Monday evening; taking four days and three nights for the journey.

"This was considered very swift travelling. The old Lancashire and Cheshire stage-waggons, which started from the Axe Inn, Aldermanbury, London, every Monday and Thursday, were ten days on the road in summer, and eleven in winter; goods were forwarded from Liverpool at about the same speed of travelling, by various carriers to Wigan, Blackburn, Preston, Lancaster, Halifax, Leeds, York, Newcastle-upon-Tyne, and Sheffield. The cost of carrying goods to Sheffield was 3s. 6d. per cwt."[o]

Williamson's Liverpool Advertiser, published in 1756, contains an announcement, that a Mr. Benen travelled regularly from Liverpool to Lancaster. This gentleman politely announces that he has "two good double horses," for the accommodation of ladies. This journal, on the ninth of June, in the same year, contains the following announcement:—

"*Warrington Flying Stage Coach!* Sets out from the Red Lyon Inn, in Warrington every Monday and Thursday evening, and arrives at the Bull Inn, in Wood-street, London, every Wednesday and Saturday evening; and sets out from the Bull Inn, Wood-street, London, every Monday and Thursday morning, and arrives at the Red Lyon Inn, in Warrington, every Wednesday and Saturday evening. Each passenger to pay two guineas, one guinea as earnest, and the other guinea on taking coach; and every passenger to be allowed 14 lbs. of luggage; all above 14lbs. to pay after three pence a pound. Outside passengers and children on safety to pay half price. To be performed, if God permit, by Anthony Jackson and Henry Secrit."

Preston passengers had to ride on horseback to Warrington, to meet this "flying coach."

During the second half of the last century, rapid advances were made in the means of internal communication. In the 10th George II., Scroop, duke of Bridgewater, the predecessor of the more celebrated Duke Francis, obtained an act for the rendering navigable the streamlet which runs from his Worsley estates into the Irwell. This was not carried into effect. His successor, Francis, in the year 1758 (32nd Geo. II.), received parliamen-

n Thos. Baines's His. Liverpool, p. 418. o Ibid.

tary sanction to form a canal from the neighbourhood of Manchester to Worsley mill and Middlewood, and from thence to Hollin's-ferry, on the Mersey. Another change was determined upon, and a new act rendered necessary. This was obtained in the 2nd year of the reign of George III. The canal was made from Manchester to Longford Bridge, near Stretford under the act of 1759, and from thence to Runcorn, on the Mersey, by virtue of the powers conferred by the 2nd George III. This gave a great impulse to the efforts for the improvement of the internal communication by means of navigable canals, and opened a wide field for the development of the genius of Brindley. The river Mersey, at Runcorn, was joined to the Trent, near Wilden ferry. The Leeds and Liverpool canal and others speedily followed. The act was granted in 1769.

Arthur Young, in his tour, refers to the state of the road between Preston and Wigan, in 1770, in the following indignant strain :—

"I know not, in the whole range of language, terms sufficiently expressive to describe this *infernal highway*. Let me most seriously caution all travellers who may accidentally propose to travel this *terrible country, to avoid it as they would the devil*, for a thousand to one but they break their necks or their limbs by overthrows or breakings down. They will here meet with ruts which I actually measured four feet deep, and floating with mud only from a wet summer! What must it therefore be in winter?"

Mr. Whittle states that, in 1771,—

"The route to the metropolis of England from Preston, was by way of Warrington. The first stage-coach established in this town was about this time—Sumpter horses were used previous to this in the carriage of parcels and provisions. Strings of pack horses, thirty and forty in a gang, were used for carrying coals and lime. The leading horse of a gang carried a bell to give warning to travellers coming in the opposite direction, by any sharp turn or narrow pass. It very frequently happened that the Roman causeway between Preston and Wigan, scarcely afforded room to pass" (probably from being out of repair), "they were obliged to make way for each other by plunging into the side road (which was soft, and sometimes almost impassable), out of which they found it difficult to get back upon the causeway." [p]

Doubtless the Roman highway, between Preston and Wigan, had done service for several centuries, without any substantial repair. In 1648, it is described by Oliver Cromwell, in his dispatch to parliament, after the great battle of Preston, in no very favourable terms. He says,—"We lay that night in a field close by the Enemy" (near Wigan); "being very dirty and weary, having marched twelve miles of such ground as I never rode in all my life, the day being very wet."

A stage-coach began to run in April, 1774, three times a week, between Manchester, Warrington, and Liverpool. The vehicle started at seven

---

p His. of Preston, vol. 2, p. 61. Mr. Whittle gives no authority for this statement. It is, however, evidently an extract from some previous writer—probably Nichols, who described the Roman way, in 1793.

o'clock in the morning, and proceeded so slowly that the passengers stayed at Warrington to dine.[q]

Coaches, from Liverpool to Preston, commenced running on the fifteenth of June, 1774. They were oddly named, "Liverpool and Preston machines on steel springs."[r] They started at eight o'clock in the morning, waited for the passengers to dine at Ormskirk, and returned the same evening. The inside fare was eight shillings and sixpence. Fourteen pounds of luggage only were allowed free, one penny per pound being charged for all above that weight.

The war with America caused great stagnation in the trade of the country. In Sep., 1775, a writer in a Lancashire journal says:—

"Our once extensive trade to Africa is at a stand; all commerce with America is at an end. Peace, harmony, and mutual confidence must constitute the balm that can again restore to health the body politic. Survey our docks; count there the gallant ships laid there and useless. When will they be again re-fitted? What become of the sailor, the tradesman, the poor labourer, during the approaching winter?"[s]

The Bridgewater canal, from Manchester to Liverpool, was opened in March, 1776. Passengers were carried from the latter place to Wigan, for one penny per mile, in boats "fitted in an elegant manner."[t]

In Feb., 1778, an inquiry was instituted by the house of lords respecting the injury done to the British commerce from the commencement of the war with America. It appeared that the British had lost 559 ships, after deducting the number of those retaken. Their value was estimated at £1,800,000! American and West Indian produce had risen to an enormous price. On the other hand, this state of things was considered satisfactory, because, forsooth, the English had captured 904 American vessels, of the value of £1,808,000! The historian of Liverpool pertinently remarks that our legislators seem to have overlooked or "forgotten that the enormous sums thus taken from the merchants of England were not transferred to the merchants of America; nor those taken from the merchants of America transferred to the merchants of England; but that the whole were taken from commerce and turned into prize money."[u]

Privateering was very rife about this period, especially after the Spaniards and French joined in the struggle. The famous Paul Jones appeared on the coast. Liverpool was placed in a state of defence. "The Liverpool merchants and shipowners fitted out upwards of one hundred

q Williamson's Liverpool Advertiser. r Ibid. s Liverpool General Advertiser.
t Williamson's Liverpool Advertiser. u Thomas Baines, p. 455.

and twenty privateers, and made a great number of rich prizes." [v] Holland was added to the number of the enemies of Britain, and commerce thus received another deadly thrust. The speed of internal transit improved notwithstanding, for the "London and Liverpool flying machine" performed the distance in forty-eight hours. The "Diligence," however, was not quite so reckless in its motion. It arrived in London in the afternoon of the third day, after treating the passengers to ten hours' rest, on the second evening, at Stony Stratford.[w] The journey from Liverpool, through Preston, to Carlisle, occupied a day and a half, in 1781.[x]

The Liverpool Advertiser announced, early in the year 1782, that the inland navigation had been opened to the river Douglas, and that goods were regularly forwarded, by the canal and river, to Preston.

In Jan., 1783, the London Gazette announced the definite treaty of peace, between England, France, Spain, and the United States. The welcome news was received by the whole nation, and especially by the commercial portion of the community, with great rejoicings. A writer, in the Liverpool paper before quoted, says :—

> "The mercantile world is in a hurry and bustle unknown at any former time. The merchants are endeavouring to out-strip each other in the race of traffic. European goods, and particularly the produce of England, being greatly wanted in the ports of America, the destination of many of the vessels now in the river is altered from the West India islands to the American ports, where it is expected the cargoes will sell at an immense profit."

The interval of peace between the American war and the French revolution, was most valuable for the commercial interests of the country. It has been seen that the great inventions in machinery, and improvement in the means of internal transit, had materially facilitated commercial operations, and given a mighty impetus to the industrial energies of the north of England.

The first mail-coach for the conveyance of letters, etc., was dispatched from London to Bristol, in August, 1784. One to Liverpool speedily followed.

In 1778, the traffic in slaves produced an annual profit to the Liverpool merchants, of from two to three hundred thousand pounds.[y] A long and spirited controversy arose, during this year, as to the morality of this traffic. The Rev. Raymond Harris, a Spanish Jesuit, a native of Seville, settled in Liverpool, astonished the Christian world by the publication of a pamphlet, in which he maintained that the practice was not repugnant to the teachings of the scriptures. It required many years' severe struggling, before those Europeans interested could be brought to acknowledge that

v Thos. Baines's His. of Liverpool, p. 456.
w Prestwich's MS. History of Liverpool.
x Williamson's Liverpool Advertiser.
y Baines's His. Liverpool, p. 471.

so great a source of profit was sufficiently criminal to justify its repression by act of parliament.

Notwithstanding the interruptions of the wars of the French revolution, commercial enterprise still struggled onward. Mr. Thos. Baines says:—[2] "The canal fever, of 1792, was not less intense than the railway fever, of 1845; nor were the undertakings projected at the former period less bold than those of the latter, if allowance be made for the inferiority of the national resources at the former time."

Billinge's Liverpool Advertiser, for Nov. 29, 1796, reports that "the engineers are now completing the survey of the canal from Kendal to Burton, the making of which will commence in a short time. It is expected the canal from Burton, by Lancaster, Garstang, etc., to Preston, will be navigable in the course of next summer." The tram-road and wooden bridge, over the Ribble, by means of which a junction was effected between the Lancaster and the Leeds and Liverpool canals, were not constructed till 1802. It was originally proposed to carry an aqueduct across the Ribble valley. The canal was not opened till 1798.

In 1798, subscriptions were entered into for assisting the government to carry on the war with France. The Irish rebellion broke out in the same year. Volunteer corps for the defence of the country were established in Preston, as well as in other towns in the county. The royal Preston volunteers were commanded by Lieut. Col. Nicholas Grimshaw, and Lieut. Col. J. Watson. Mr. Watson, in conjunction with his partner, Mr. Collinson, first introduced the cotton manufacture into Preston.

In the year 1800, the opening of the Grand Junction Canal completed the inland water communication between the Thames, the Severn, the Mersey, and the Humber, with the exception of the Blisworth tunnel, which was not finished till 1805.

The temporary peace at Amiens, concluded in 1801, proved but a hollow truce. The war was resumed with more determination than ever. Bonaparte assembled his army of 200,000 men, and 2,000 gun-boats, at Boulogne, and threatened to invade England. Volunteer corps were formed with spirit and enthusiasm all over the county. Preston lagged not behind in patriotism. In addition to the militia and volunteers, a regular army of reserve, for the general defence of the kingdom, was formed, the Lancashire contingent to which amounted to 2,425 men. Lord Castlereagh announced, in 1803, that the total naval and military force of the empire of Great Britain amounted to upwards of 700,000 men. The navy included more than five hundred vessels of war, of various sizes.

The destruction of the combined fleets of France and Spain, off Cape

2 His Liverpool, p. 1[illegible].

Trafalgar, by Lord Nelson, in 1805, relieved, to some extent, the fears of the commercial world; and although the war continued, the trading interest of the country was still progressive. In 1807, the traffic between Liverpool and Manchester maintained twenty-seven stage-coaches[a] In 1770, a single vehicle sufficed.

The celebrated Berlin decree, issued by Bonaparte, in 1807, by which, under severe penalties, all trade or correspondence with Great Britain was prohibited,—the counter resolution of the English government, declaring all the ports of the French empire in a state of blockade, and the general embargo laid on all ships in the ports of America, threatened the total subversion of commercial prosperity.

The Preston volunteers, under Lieut. Col. Grimshaw, and the rifle corps, under Captain Brade, in 1808, joined the militia.

Still commerce struggled onward, notwithstanding occasional panics. In 1809, the then Liverpool docks were found "insufficient for the accommodation of the business of the port, which, about that time, had received a sudden impulse from the opening of the trade with Spain and Portugal, and with the Spanish and Portuguese colonies in America" [b]

This proved delusive "After some time" (close of 1810), "it began to be seen that there were no returns for these immense shipments, and then a terrible panic took possession of the public mind, prices falling as rapidly as they had risen. The government, in the hope of ameliorating the distresses of the mercantile and manufacturing classes, agreed to make a considerable loan for the relief of trade." [c]

Before the close of the war, the price of food rose so high that the greatest distress prevailed, and public subscriptions were generally entered into for the purpose of purchasing "rice, peas, potatoes, and other substitutes for bread and flour," which were afterwards sold to the starving poor at reduced prices. In Feb., 1811, a public meeting was held at the Town-hall, Preston. The subscriptions amounted to upwards of one thousand pounds. So severe were the privations of the people at this period, that resolutions of the following character were circulated by local committees.—

"That it be strongly recommended to all housekeepers to be economical in the use of bread and potatoes, to abstain altogether from pastry, and not to use any bread until after the expiration of twenty-four hours from the time of its being baked; and that it be also strongly recommended to all persons who keep horses, to be economical in the feeding of them, by diminishing the quantity as much as possible." [d]

---

a Billinge's Liverpool Advertiser. b Baines's His. Liverpool, p. 539. c Ibid.

d Copy of resolution issued by the Liverpool committee —Baines's His. Liverpool, p. 547. The effect of war upon commerce, at this period, is illustrated by the fact that, in 1809, 92,812,282 lbs of cotton were imported into England. In 1810, the quantity increased to 132,488,935, and again decreased, in 1811, to 91,576,535.

The government of England still adhered to their "orders in council," notwithstanding the complaints of the American people, and the mercantile and industrial classes at home. In June, 1812, Lord Castlereagh announced in parliament the intention of their withdrawal. This reasonable concession, however, came too late. In the same month, the exasperated Americans declared war against England. The struggle lasted two years and a half, with immense loss and little gain to either party. Nearly a thousand merchant ships, on each side, were captured, and converted into prize money. Mr. Thos. Baines says:—

"In the latter part of the war, the risk of capture was so great that the freight on cotton, from Savannah to France, rose to 10d. a pound. At the close of the contest, upwards of 200,000 bales of cotton, which was then more than a year's supply, was piled up in the warehouses of America; whilst in this country, that great article of consumption was sold at prices ruinous to trade." [e]

In 1811, Russia, exhausted by the results of the Berlin decree, had, for some time, indirectly encouraged trade with England; and, at length, notwithstanding the threat of Bonaparte, under certain restrictions, openly authorised it. This led to the celebrated Russian campaign, so fatal to the French armies, and to the prestige of the great Napoleon. Wellington's successes in Spain, conjoined to the defeat of Napoleon at Leipsic, hastened the overthrow of the French emperor. Peace was proclaimed at the close of the year 1813, to the infinite joy of the whole nation.

The trade had increased to such an extent, that the old highways leading to Preston were inadequate to its requirements. The present excellent road from Stanley-street to Walton bridge was cut about 1812. The old way passed over the Swillbrook, a little to the right of the new road, and descended towards the bridge by the valley in Mrs. Walmsley's strawberry garden. The steep hill, at the end of Fishergate, was lowered, and the present embankment, leading towards Broadgate, was constructed shortly afterwards. The new road to Lancaster, over Gallows Hill, and the one to Blackburn, by Brockholes, were not cut till a few years later. [f]

About this period, the application of steam power to navigation began to be introduced. Thus, another powerful auxiliary to commercial enterprise was gained. In 1812, the first steam-boat, for commercial purposes, in Great Britain, was introduced by Mr. Henry Bell, on the river Clyde. In the following year, one plyed on the Yare, between Norwich and Yarmouth. About the same time, a steamer was launched at Bristol, and another at Manchester. In 1814, steam-boats were introduced on the Humber and Thames; and in June, the following year, the first vessel

e His. Liverpool, p. 549.

f The Lancaster-road was cut in 1817, and the Blackburn one in 1821.

propelled by steam power appeared on the waters of the Mersey. She was built on the Clyde, and could accommodate in her cabin about one hundred passengers.[g]

Bonaparte's return from Elba renewed the war; but Wellington's victory at Waterloo, in June, 1815, again brought peace to Europe. From this period, commercial progress was rapid. The deficient harvest of the following year, however, caused great distress. It has been described as "one of the worst ever known in England, both for quantity and quality." At a meeting in Preston, the sum of five hundred pounds was subscribed in one hour for the relief of the poor. The total subscription amounted to one thousand four hundred and nineteen pounds.

The opening of the branch from the Leeds and Liverpool canal, at Wigan, to the duke of Bridgewater's canal, at Leigh, took place in 1820. This was one of the last of the canal extensions in Lancashire. A new and still more wonderful stride in the march of progress followed; the locomotive and the railroad superseded, to a great extent, the water transit, and opened out still greater facilities for commercial intercourse.

In twenty years from the commencement of the century, the town of Preston had doubled its population. According to the census of 1821, the number of inhabitants was 24,627. Half a century previous it did not exceed 6,000. This mainly resulted from the extension of the cotton trade.

In September, 1823, "seventy-two coaches ran in and out of Preston, every Wednesday. Fifteen stage-coaches went in and out of the town, in one hour."[h] In the same year the new road by Brockholes to Blackburn was first projected, and the cutting soon afterwards commenced.

In 1825, application was made to parliament for an act to facilitate the construction of a railway between Liverpool and Manchester.[i] The work was commenced on Chat-Moss, in June, 1826. The first journey to and from Manchester was made on the 14th June, 1830. On the 15th of September following, the railway was formally opened. The duke of Wellington, Sir Robert Peel, bart., and other distinguished personages were present. A cloud was thrown over the enthusiasm of the party, by an accident which caused the lamented death of the Right Honourable William Huskisson.

g His: of Liverpool, p. 566. h Whittle's His. Preston, vol. 2, p. 115.

i A paragraph published in August, 1802, in the Leeds Mercury, quotes a pamphlet, by Richard Lovell Edgeworth, on railroads, of which he claimed the invention. Mr. Edgeworth says that "in 1768, he presented models to the Society of Arts for which he received their gold medal." He however, only proposed to use horse power. Mr. Trevethick, of Cornwall, took out the first patent for a locomotive engine in 1802. One was introduced on a colliery railway near Leeds, in 1811, by Mr. Blenkensop; another at Killingworth colliery, by Mr. George Stephenson, in 1814. Stephenson's after improvements are well known.

Mr. Whittle records that, in June, 1830, "eighty-one coaches ran in and out of the good old town of Preston. About twenty years ago, about a dozen coaches were moving in and out of the town, to the great amazement of the inhabitants. This may be called the *March of Coaching.*"[j]

The Grand Junction railway, which connected both Manchester and Liverpool with Birmingham, was opened in July, 1837.[j]

At the close of 1829, a meeting was held to devise a plan for ameliorating the distress amongst the poor of the town. Soup kitchens were established. The use of Patten house, in Church-street, was granted for the purpose by the earl of Derby. Soup, beds, and blankets, were liberally distributed, and much suffering alleviated.

The first steamer that crossed the Atlantic was the Sirius. She left Cork harbour on the morning of the 4th April, 1838, and arrived at New York, eighteen days afterwards. Her return voyage from New York to Falmouth, occupied twenty-two days. The first steamer that ever left England for America, was the "Great Western." She departed from Bristol, on the 8th of April, in the same year, and arrived at New York, twelve hours after the Sirius, on the 22nd, thus making the run in fourteen days. Severe commercial difficulties were experienced in this year.

The Manchester and Bolton railway was opened to the public, in May, 1838. In September, the same year, the London and Birmingham line was completed. Portions of the distance had previously been available for public transit. The North Union railway from Preston to Wigan, completing the junction to Parkside, was opened on the 22nd of October following. This railway was first projected in 1830.

In 1840, three other railways in connection with Preston were opened; the Preston and Longridge on the 1st of May, the Preston and Lancaster on June 25th, and the Preston and Wyre on the 15th July. In 1841, the junction from Bolton to Euxton was finished, completing the railway communication between Preston and Manchester. Branch lines from the Wyre railway were opened to Blackpool and Lytham shortly afterwards.[k]

In 1845-6, trade was much depressed, and considerable suffering experienced, especially in Ireland, owing to the failing of the potatoe crop.

The line from Preston to Blackburn was completed in 1846, that to Liverpool in 1849, and the branch line connecting Preston with Southport in 1855. An act was afterwards obtained for the construction of a railway in continuation of the Longridge line to Whalley, with an extension to the Maudland's station of the Wyre railway. The expensive cutting and tunnelling through the town, in pursuance of the latter object, has been completed,

j Hist. Prest. vol. 2, p. 130.

k The Blackpool branch was opened in April, 1846; and the one to Lytham in February, 1846.

but the remainder of the scheme has been for some time in abeyance. A branch line from the principal station to the quays on the Marsh was completed in 1846.

RIBBLE NAVIGATION.

Many efforts have been made, from time to time, to render the Ribble navigable for vessels of moderate burthen. Its pretensions to the distinction of being the "Setantian Port" of Ptolemy, have already been disposed of.[1] It has doubtless, from an unknown period, been navigated as far as Preston, by the smaller description of vessels. It has long enjoyed the privileges of a port, and is described as such in several resolutions of the house of commons. Its early history is, however, enveloped in much uncertainty. In the time of Charles the I., when Lancashire was assessed at one ship, of forty tons burthen, and one hundred and sixty men, or £1000. in money; the proportion for Preston was £40., against £30. for Lancaster and £25. for Liverpool. But "ship money" was not levied upon maritime places exclusively; consequently, no relative superiority, in mercantile matters connected with the port, can be inferred from this fact. Wigan appears to have been the most wealthy borough in Lancashire at the period, it being assessed at £50. for ship money.

Mr. E. Baines says, "Preston in this reign seems to have been one of the chief *ports* of Lancaster, paying in 2nd Henry III., no less a talliage than 15 marks."[m] This, however, exhibits not, any more than "ship money," the relative importance of the *port* of Preston.

In the reign of Edward I., a mandate was issued by the magistrates of all the ports in England, prohibiting the exportation of coin, bullion, etc., but no port in Lancashire is mentioned. Later in the same reign, when all the ports on the east, as well as on the west coast, were required to send ships and men to Dublin, for the transportation of the earl of Ulster and troops to Scotland, still Lancashire received no precept for this purpose. From the contiguity of the county to the scene of operations, the inference is obvious. Had Lancashire possessed any important maritime trade, it would doubtless have been called upon to furnish its quota of vessels. Dr. Kuerden, however, towards the end of the seventeeenth century, speaks of the river as if it were used as a port, though not to any great extent. He says:—

"Now westward, below this Burrough of Preston, lyeth a marsh, belonging to the same, wither yet, at higher water, a vessell of reasonable burden may arrive from the Western Sea, guided by a knoweing and well skill'd pylot; though the river below at present is much choked up with sand, and by the destruction of the neighbouring marshes is made more shallow than formerly. The river having been no doubt bound in a nar-

1 See chapter 1, page 14.

m Vol. 4, p. 303. Lancaster paid 13 marks, and Liverpool 11 marks, 7 shillings, and 8 pence.

rower compass, which at present is more dangerous to strangers, which in antient time very probably was much better; and over against the marsh belonging to this burrough, under the opposite and high banks at Penwortham, a safe harbour from the western storms, over which was placed a small castle or fort, probably there placed to defend the same, or for the greater preservation of the Burrough of Preston."

Mr. Murdock Mackenzie was employed by the admiralty about the year 1770, in making a survey of the coast. From his instructions, it appears that the Ribble was, at that period, little frequented, and its few vessels were of very limited burthen. He describes the channel as "crooked, without buoys, perches, and distant land-marks," and intimates that "no instructions will be sufficient for a stranger," to enable him to navigate it with safety. Nevertheless, Preston was regarded in the light of a seaport, as will appear from the following resolution, adopted by the house of commons, on the 26th of April, 1776; and, in pursuance of which, a bill was introduced by Sir H. Hoghton, bart., and received the sanction of the legislature:—

"Resolved,—That Corn, Grain, and Flour, imported into the Port of Preston, be allowed to be landed without payment of the duties, under the like restrictions as Corn, Grain, and Flour, are allowed to be landed at the several ports mentioned in an act made on the 13th year of the reign of his present Majesty, intitled, 'An act to regulate the Importation and Exportation of Corn.'"

The act referred to, was passed with a view to the reduction of the then high price of corn, and other articles of food. The duties were merely nominal.

In the year 1806, an act of parliament was obtained by the principal proprietors of the land in the neighbourhood, "incorporating them a company for the improvement of the Navigation of the River Ribble," but with a limited capital. Forty shares of £50. each, were created. The company likewise obtained power to add twenty more shares, and to dispose of them to parties not immediately interested in the neighbouring lands. The money was spent in the erection of cauls, or jetties. A duty of "2s. 6d. per ton, annually" was levied on each vessel. The river was undoubtedly much improved by the operations of this company, but the investment proved unremunerative. The "memorandum for the company on their interview with the committee appointed by the borough of Preston, on the 17th of May, 1837," gives the following as the state of affairs at that period:—

"By order made at a meeting held 31st January, 1825, interest to that day was added to the principal money advanced, and a statement entered in the order book at that meeting, of the interest of each proprietor in the undertaking, making the total of principal and interest £4706. 13s. 11d., since which no interest has been paid.

"1st Feb. 1830, the value of one share was ascertained to be £200. 8s. 4d., n * * *

n The "Memorandum" gives the following as the original cost of each share:—

"The Price of a share by the Act is	£50
"Since advanced as a loan for each share	25
	£75"

It appears that only one of the proposed additional shares was created.

	£	s.	d.
"On the 1st of Feb., 1830, the value of 41 shares, at £200. 8s. 4d., was	8217	1	8
"The debt due to the Bank of Messrs. Pedder, Fleetwood, and Pedder, on 31st Dec., 1836, was	3884	4	0
	£12,101	5	8"

Notwithstanding the operations of this company, the navigation of the river was for a long time almost exclusively confined to "flats," and "lighters." At the spring tides, which flow as high as Cuerdale, vessels of one hundred and fifty tons burthen occasionally reached the quays at Preston, but the craft generally employed did not exceed sixty or seventy tons burthen. Nevertheless, when Captain Belcher surveyed the coast of Lancashire, in 1836, he found the rise of the tide, in the channel opposite to Lytham, in the month of July, to be not less than twenty-five feet seven and a half inches. Captain Belcher thought so well of the Ribble entrance, that he considered it desirable that a harbour of refuge should be established at Lytham.

From the report of Messrs. Robert Stevenson and Sons, civil engineers, Edinburgh, presented in March, 1837, it appears that the Ribble possesses some natural advantages for maritime purposes. The report says:—

"The off-shore part of the great Lancashire bay, according to the best modern charts, also preserves the same depths of soundings that it had in Mackenzie's time, as appears from his testimony. 'The ground,' he says, 'along the coast is clean sand; and the depth, for two or three leagues, not above five or six fathoms. Ships in moderate weather, or when the wind is off shore, may stop a tide anywhere from three to six miles from the land.' In this great bay, it is observeable that the Ribble holds a central position; and that the land, especially on the northern side of the entrance, stands prominently forward, forming on the whole, perhaps, the best point of departure for a ship that is to be found on this part of the coast. The mariner, with the use of well defined sea-marks, may, therefore, make boldly for the Ribble, and still preserve a good offing at those times when it is not found advisable to enter. The favourable nature of this approach, together with the reasons assigned for believing that the general features of the seaward channels are of a permanent description, induces the reporters, with confidence, to recommend the improvement of the interior or higher parts of this navigation."

The report further states that—

"Although the Ribble, seaward of Lytham, possesses a depth of from 10 to 20 feet at low water of ordinary spring tides, and the rise of tide upon this coast is upwards of 30 feet; yet at the quays of Preston, there is not a depth or rise of more than between six and seven feet of tidal water.o * * * * It appears that off or near the Naze Point, there is a depth of about 17 feet at high water of Spring Tides. What the reporters, therefore propose, is to deepen the navigable channel from thence to the quays of Preston, so as to admit ships drawing at least 14 feet, at high water of these tides."

Messrs. Stevenson were of opinion, by the employment of steam dredging machines, and the excavation of the sand stone rock in the bed of the river,

o One of Messrs. Stevenson's reports states that "the tidal waters at the entrance of the Clyde do not rise more than about one-third of those of the Ribble;" and another that the tide of the latter river "rises fully double the height of that on the coast at the entrance of the Firth of the Tay."

near the quay, that "a large and most useful class of vessels, of from 200 to 300 tons burthen," might navigate the Ribble with facility.

Some other projects were propounded about this time, such as the formation of docks at Preston and at Lytham, together with a ship canal to connect the same, but these were ultimately abandoned.

In 1837, a new Joint Stock Company was projected to carry out the improvements suggested by Messrs. Stevenson. It was proposed to raise £50,000. in shares of £50. each, and it was agreed that the shareholders in the original undertaking "should receive four shares in the new comany for one share in the old company," as a compensation for their prepvious investments. The corporation subscribed for 214 shares, and afterwards considerably increased the number. This undertaking, at the onset, was very warmly supported by one section of the commercial population of Preston; and was as coldly regarded by another. Some parties argued in favour of a line of railway to Fleetwood, where the condition of the harbour was such as to induce them to anticipate a successful rivalry with Liverpool. Others contended that the formation of a railway to Liverpool would remove the necessity for the carrying out of either project.

The company became incorporated under the "1 and 2 Vic. I. & p. c. 8," entitled, "An act to repeal an act passed in the 46th year of the reign of his Majesty King George III., for improving the navigation of the river Ribble, and for further improvement of the said river."

Mr. Baines says, "Preston was formerly a port of more importance than at present." [p] This, however, is merely conjecture, and is not borne out by any documentary evidence. Mr. Baines himself records that "previous to the year 1798, the total amount of tonnage is calculated not to have exceeded 6000 tons of merchandise annually. About the year 1802, a more extensive trade, hitherto confined to the coast, was established between Preston and Drogheda, which proved very beneficial to the town." [q] It was, however, previously to the year 1826, an "independent port, extending from a place on the south side of the river Ribble, called the Hundred end, being the division of the ports of Preston and Liverpool, to another place on the north side of the river Wyre, called Broad Fleet, being the divison of the ports of Preston and Lancaster; and the river Wyre, was then a creek within the port of Preston." [r] The principal custom-house was at that time situated at Preston. In 1826, the custom's business was removed to Lancaster, in "consequence of the Ribble and Wyre being incorporated with the port of Lancaster."

p 1835. His. Lan. vol. 4., p. 361. q Ibid. r Corporation Memorial, 1840.

The number of vessels which entered and cleared at the Preston custom-house, in 1825, was as follows:—

	INWARDS.		OUTWARDS.	
	VESSELS.	TONS.	VESSELS.	TONS.
Irish Coasters..............	277	21,876	181	14,530
Other Coasters	246	13,806	96	5,622
TOTAL..........	523	35,682	277	20,152

In the previous year, the total tonnage was: inward, 33,640, in 514 vessels; outward, 20,253, in 296 vessels.

In the year ending the 5th June, 1830, the tonnage was: inwards, 39,595 tons; outwards, 32,420 tons.

In 1839, Preston was separated from the port of Lancaster, and placed under the newly created port of Fleetwood-on-Wyre. This not being in accordance with either the dignity or interest of the inhabitants of Preston, the corporation, in the following year, presented a memorial to the lords of the treasury, praying that Preston might be restored to its original position as an independent port, with the privilege of bonding goods not wanted for immediate use. This was, however, not fully acceded to, until the year 1843, when the lords of the treasury considered the improvements effected by the company in the navigation of the Ribble justified the change.

In the "Corporation Memorial, praying for permission to raise £12,000. at interest," in 1841, it is set forth that the corporate body is "possessed of nearly the whole of the frontage land to the said river Ribble, within the said borough, extending in length 1,950 yards, and about 84 statute acres of land adjoining, a great part of which has hitherto lain waste and been unproductive; and, in consequence of the improvement in the navigation of the river, the trade now requires the erection of quays, sheds, wharfs, warehouses, and other erections, which will, when erected, be a great benefit to the navigation of the said river and the town and trade of this borough, as well as very considerably augment the revenue of the corporation."

The new company commenced their labours with great vigour. In 1839-40, the rock was excavated near the quays, and the channel of the river below much deepened by the dredging operations. In 1839, a steam tug, the "Lily," was placed upon the river. Previous attempts had been made to navigate the Ribble by steamers; one about the year 1829, and another some time afterwards. The first steamer was named the "Ribble," and the second the "Enterprise." Both were, however, unsuccessful, owing to the difficulties of the navigation.

The rock near the quays was excavated four feet deeper than was originally contemplated by the engineers, by which a depth of twenty feet of water was secured. This was not completed till 1841. In addition to the dredging operations, the channel of the river was protected by stone walls, which the company have gradually extended to the Naze Point. It is understood that a similar walling of the channel of the Douglas will shortly be undertaken.

In 1841, a dock was constructed near Lytham, with the view to afford a safe harbour and anchorage for vessels, until the tides permitted their approach to Preston.

In 1842, the company resolved to increase their capital to the amount authorised by act of parliament. This was effected by the issue of new shares, of the value of £16,666, nearly the whole of which were taken by the old proprietors. At the end of this year, the improvements began to tell, in a financial sense; the tonnage for the half year being, according to the report, "double in amount, as compared with the last corresponding half year."

Spacious quays were erected by the corporation, in 1843; and, Preston having been made a free bonded port, arrangements were made for the erection of suitable warehouses. These were completed in 1845.

From the directors' report, in Jan., 1844, it appears that during the previous year, "no fewer than eleven timber vessels arrived in the Ribble, direct from the British possessions abroad, and that the timber met with a ready sale." The amount of customs duties had increased to £19,375., against £6,309. in the year 1841.

In 1844, the company obtained power to raise, by loan, the sum of £22,000., for the purpose of completing the proposed improvements. The amount received for customs this year, was £23,303. 13s. 2d. The report further states that the tonnage had "gradually risen from £500. to near £2,000. a year."

The want of a lighthouse, at the mouth of the Ribble, began to be seriously felt. To meet the expenses attendant upon such an undertaking, together with a branch railway to the quays, and other improvements, the company, in 1845, created one thousand new shares, which were nearly all taken up by the previous proprietors. The branch railway was completed in the following year.

In 1845, the dues for tonnage at Preston, amounted to £1,812. 7s. 10d., and at Lytham dock to £151. 4s. 9½d.;—total, £1,963. 12s. 7½d. The customs for the same year amounted to £66,921. 4s. 9d.

The failure of the potatoe crop in Ireland, and the general stagnation of trade, in 1846, materially affected the revenue of the navigation, "there being," according to the directors' report, "little or no grain or provisions comparatively" imported from Ireland to Preston. The trade was still dull in the early part of 1847. The channel, however, continued to deepen, and the lighthouse, on the "double stanner," at the river's entrance, was completed. The report states, that "the land reclaimed is fast grassing over, and, in 1848, will become productive to the company. The total quantity they eventually expect to reclaim will not be far short of two thousand acres." The directors further state that several large foreign ships had arrived, and that many more were on their way to the port. The exportation of coal, likewise, continued to increase.

In their report, at the end of 1848, the directors express a "regret that their revenue does not increase to that extent they were promised and led to expect, when they had deepened the river and afforded facilities for vessels to come direct to Preston; they trust, however, that a revival of trade, and more prosperous times, will bring a corresponding increase of revenue." They likewise "thought it prudent, under existing financial circumstances, to suspend, at present, any further outlay in the works beyond what was necessary for repairs."

In their July report, 1849, the directors—

"Have again to regret that they cannot report an increase of revenue, although it was confidently assumed that by a reduction of the tolls (which after much deliberation and discussion was finally resolved upon), a great increase in the exports of coal and imports of iron, would probably be the result. The imports for the half year ending the 30th of June last, of 13,325 tons, in the place of 16,605 tons for the corresponding half year of 1848, and the exports (consisting principally of coal,) of 10,659 tons, in the stead of 12,759 tons, for the corresponding half year, shew a considerable decrease."

During the second half of the year, the trade, however, somewhat improved. This was still further apparent in 1850. During this year, the imports were 30,389 tons, and the exports, 28,096 tons. The report states that—

"Notwithstanding the continued competition with the river from various sources, the increase of the tonnage for the year 1850, over that of 1849, amounts, in imports, to 3,352 tons register, and in exports to 3,427 tons. The directors find that the revenue of the company, for the year 1850, has amounted to £1550. 10s. 3d., and that the interest paid on loans, preference shares, and for bank commission, has been £926. 18s. 3d., leaving a balance of £623. 12s., available for the working expenses of the company."

In 1851, the report intimates that the "pilots and mariners frequenting the river, all concur in their testimony of the great improvement which is being effected in the navigation of the river." The directors likewise published the following analysis of the traffic for the first six months in the years 1849, 1850, and 1851 :—

	Tonnage. Half-year ending 30th June, 1849.	Tonnage. Half-year ending 30th June, 1850.	Tonnage. Half-year ending 30th June, 1851.
Irish Traffic	13,285	14,646	14,276
Iron Traffic	1,087	1,480	2,954
Liverpool Traffic	3,030	3,291	3,459
Other Coasting Traffic	5,961	7,407	6,170
Foreign Traffic	1,247	2,065	3,096
Total	24,610	28,889	29,955

In 1852, the "Gem" steamer was placed upon the river, its predecessor, the "Lily" having been previously disposed of. The imports for the year were 39,716 tons, and the exports 24,888 tons.

The engineer (Mr. P. Park), reported that "the bank of gravel, about three quarters of a mile in length, stretching downwards from the chain-caul, had been efficiently and effectually removed by the dredging operations; 104,940 tons of gravel having been dredged from the river's bed, at a cost, including all wages and repairs, of 3¾d. per ton." Mr. Park likewise intimated that the channel had been much obstructed by forest trees, "some of very large dimensions, in one or two instances containing one hundred cubic feet of timber in each tree." Upwards of one hundred of these trees had been taken from the river's bed during the previous six months, containing from two thousand to three thousand cubic feet of timber; a great proportion of which was found at and near to that part of the river "not inappropriately named 'Peg Hill,' opposite to Ashton marsh."

In 1853, the directors obtained another act of parliament, to facilitate the disposal of reclaimed lands, together with other powers. They report,—

"According to the general wish of the parties connected with the trade of the river, powers were taken * * to levy dues as well upon vessels as upon cargoes. * * * The new scale came into operation on the 1st November last, (1853). From a comparison of the tolls received in the months of November, December, and January last,[s] with the corresponding months of November and December, 1852, and January, 1853, the company's revenue has increased in those months by the sum of £221. 7s. 11d., and the tonnage for the year has increased 1,943 tons. * * The total quantity of land laid down in the deposited plan as reclaimed is 913a. 2r. 4p. which will become available to the company in the autumn of this year."

Mr. W. Threlfall, iron merchant, this year placed upon the Ribble, a fine new steamer, named "The Preston," two hundred and sixty-two tons register. The vessel was intended for the Scotch trade. Land on the

[s] The report is dated February 23rd, 1854.

bank of the Ribble, was let to Messrs. Watson and Allsop, for the building of iron vessels. The dredge was actively employed near the "Savick Caul," a locality which hitherto had presented an important obstruction to the navigation.

In 1854, the directors reported an increased revenue from tolls and dues. The total receipts from this source amounted to £1831. 16s. 3d. The directors likewise published the following statement respecting the reclaimed land, on the 21st of February, 1855:—

ON THE NORTH SIDE OF THE RIVER.

	Quantity of Land reclaimed. A. R. P.	To whom sold.	Price per acre.	Purchase money. £ S. D.
In Lea	49 0 12	Sir. H. B. Hoghton	£26	1275 19 0
In Clifton	146 1 0	J. T. Clifton, esq.	£25	3656 5 0
In Freckleton	47 2 28	H. Pedder, esq.	£25	1191 17 6
In Nwton	36 1 10	Messrs. Fisher & Loxham	£25	907 16 3

ON THE SOUTH SIDE OF THE RIVER.

In Hutton	90 2 20	The purchase money for these lots to be fixed by Arbitration.†
In Hesketh	436 2 10	
In Howick	100 3 29	Vested in the company absolutely, and retained by them.

The dredge was principally employed during this year in cutting a permanent channel through the clay bank at the Naze.

In 1855, land was leased to Messrs. Ogle and Robinson, for the purpose of ship building. Mr. Thomas Smith had previously formed a graving dock and ship building establishment, on the bank of the river. Several large vessels (iron and timber), are at the present time in the course of construction by these firms. One on the stocks, in Mr. Smith's yard, is about a thousand tons burthen; and another, nearly the same size, of iron, will be launched this summer, from Messrs. Ogle and Robinson's establishment.

The "Lady Lindsay" steamer, engaged for the Irish trade, was unfortunately lost at sea, in 1855. Messrs. M'Clure and Tamplin, of Liverpool, advertised their intention of placing screw steamers on the station between Liverpool and Preston. This announcement has not, however, been carried into effect. In the early portion of this year, "in consequence of the interruption of steam communication on the river, and other causes," the directors were "unable to report an increase in the traffic." The receipts of dues and tolls, for the six months ending December 31st, 1855, however, "amounted to £1030. 11s. 10d., while for the corresponding six months, ending 31st December, 1854, they amounted to £780. 3s. 9d.

Mr. Robert Parker was this year appointed managing director for the company. Mr. E. Haydock continues to act as secretary.

† The prices awarded were, for Hutton, £1,184 0s. 0d.; Hesketh, £5,108 0s. 0d.; making the total "amount realised from the sales of land," £13,323. 17s, 9d. The directors' report, dated February 21st, 1856, says,—"The entire quantity of land which will ultimately be recoverable from the river, (exclusive of the 913a. 2r. 4p. now reclaimed) will exceed 3,000 acres."

The engineers report—

"That the company's works have been in a great measure suspended during the past half year (1855); the ordinary repairs of the walls have been duly attended to. The navigable channel is in a very good state, and continues to improve by the action of the flood waters upon its bed. The reclamation of the land is progressing favourably, and the vegetation is gradually extending on both sides of the estuary."

The tolls and dues for the six months ending June 30th, 1856, amounted to £802. 15s. 10d. The amount for the corresponding six months in 1855, was £794. 15s. 4d.

The directors, in their report (August), "regret the entire suspension of steam traffic on the river," and urge upon shareholders "the great importance of rendering every assistance and support" to this species of traffic. They further state, that they "have deemed it prudent, in the present state of the money market, to confine the works to mere repairs of the walls, and to delay the commencement of the important works on Hesketh and Longton marshes. They have now determined to proceed with those works, and accordingly have made arrangements with Messrs. Cooper and Tullis, for the supply of stone for the walls to be formed there."

STRIKES AND LOCKOUTS.

Preston has become somewhat celebrated as the principal "battle field," where the capital and labour engaged in the cotton manufacture fight in defence of what each deems its respective rights or privileges. As a manufacturing town, Preston possesses a few advantages, combined with some drawbacks. It is thirty miles from the chief market at Manchester, and some distance north of the great Lancashire coal field. These are disadvantages; but on the other hand, it is situated a little outside the thoroughly manufacturing area, and, therefore, commands the first offer of the services of a continually immigrating surplus agricultural population. Its markets, from the same cause, being better supplied, provisions are consequently cheaper. This is demonstrated by the prevailing practice of many farmers in the neighbourhood, who regularly transfer their produce to Blackburn, Bolton, etc., simply because, by so doing, they obtain better prices. These circumstances, added to the acknowledged fact, that Preston is a more desirable place of residence than most other neighbouring towns, will explain why the manufacturing capitalists require a somewhat lower rate of wages to compete with the general trade; and, likewise, how they continue so to rule it, notwithstanding the severe struggles consequent upon its supposed injustice.

The true history of the labour and wages question is so little understood, even by those most interested, that a cursory glance at the various statutes affecting labour and capital, and the gradual emancipation of both from the thraldom of legislative domination, will be neither uninteresting nor uninstructive.

It is very gratifying, no doubt, to read or listen to eloquent expositions on the liberty-loving propensities of the Anglo-Saxon people. But, in plain modern English, during what is termed the Saxon period, the self-styled "people" formed but a small portion of the entire population; the great majority being, both in name and in fact, slaves. The free population was divided into two classes, "the Eorl and Ceorl, the men of noble and ignoble descent.

"After the royal family, the highest order in the state was that of ealdorman or earls. The districts which they governed were denominated their shires, confined originally to a small tract of country, but gradually enlarged to the extent of our present counties. The 'thanes,' so called from *thegnian*, to serve, were a numerous and distinguished order of men, divided into several classes of different rank, with different privileges. The lowest class of freemen was that of ceorls or husbandmen; of these some possessed bocland, but not in sufficient quantity to raise them to the rank of thanes; others held land of their lords by the payment of rent, or other free but inferior services. * * * These several classes formed but a small part of the population, of which, perhaps, not less than two-thirds existed in a state of slavery." [u]

These slaves were of various classes, but all were alike deprived of the privileges of freemen. Their persons, families, and goods of every description, were the property of their lord. He could dispose of them as he pleased, either by gift or sale. He could annex them to the soil, or remove them from it. He could transfer them with it to a new proprietor, or leave them by will to his heirs. [v]

It has been previously shown that this state of vassalage was not mitigated during the dominion of the early Norman monarchs. Edward III. encouraged the trading of "merchant strangers;" but passed severe enactments against all workmen who presumed to take more for their labour than they had been accustomed to receive "five or six common years next before." Butchers, bakers, poulterers, and other tradesmen were ordered to sell their provisions at a price dictated by parliament; and the wages of all classes of labourers were fixed by the same authority. Labourers and artificers were compelled to remain in their own localities. Those who left service were put in the stocks, and branded on the forehead with the letter F, "in token of falsity." The mayor and bailiffs of any town were subjected to a fine of ten pounds, if they failed to deliver up any such workman who had left service. In fact, the working men, and, to some extent, even their employers, were still slaves. The very food and clothing of each class was regulated by parliamentary enactment. Workmen were restricted to one trade or mystery, and merchants were permitted to deal in one kind of merchandise only, on pain of fine and forfeiture.

In the reign of Richard II. (1381), the rebellion under Wat Tyler

u Lingard's His. Eng. See Palgrave, Sharon Turner, and others. v Ibid.

broke out. The four conditions demanded by them, and, in the first instance, granted by the king, show what was the state of the people, and the real cause of the rising. They were,—

"1st. The total abolition of slavery for themselves and their children for ever.—2nd. The reduction of the rent of good land to 4d. the acre.—3rd. The full liberty of buying and selling, *like other men*, in all fairs and markets.—4th. A general pardon for all past offences."

The 12th of Richard II. (1388), fixes the wages of labourers, and punishes both the giver and receiver, by a fine equivalent to the excess so given or taken; double the amount for a second offence; and for a third, treble. Forty days' imprisonment were awarded in default of payment. A statute of Henry V. (1416), however, repeals the penalty so far as the giver of higher wages is concerned, because, says the statute, they "will in no wise present such excesses to eschew their own punishment." The workmen, however, are still subjected to "the pain contained in the said statute." Another of the same reign empowers justices to "examine all manner of labourers, servants, and their masters, of all things done contrary to the said ordinances and statutes, and to punish them upon their confession, as though they were convict by inquest." The "glorious days" of the hero of Agincourt lose some of their splendour, when viewed through the medium of these "ordinances and statutes."

With such a system of "honourable labour," it is in no way surprising that the country was over-run by "rogues, vagabonds, and valliant beggars," concerning whom severe enactments follow side by side with the laws regulating capital and labour. When a villein or serf contrived to save a little property, without the knowledge of his owner, he generally contrived to escape and conceal himself in some town. If he were successful, for a year and a day, he acquired his freedom for ever.

The statute prices of labour, in 1350, and in 1444, were as follows. The price of wheat, at the latter period, was, according to Sir Frederick Eden, tenpence per bushel. A fat ox was worth 31s. 3d., a lean do., 13s.; a sheep (1449), 2s. 5½d,; a calf, 2s.; a pig, 3s.; a goose, 3d.; three pigeons, 1d.; a quarter of malt, 4s. :—

	In 1350.	In 1444.
"A master carpenter	3d. per day	5d. per day.
A master or free mason	4d. ,,	4d. ,,
Other common labourers about buildings	1d. ,,	3d. ,,
A mower	5d. ,,	6d. ,,
A reaper	3d. ,,	5d. ,,
Women and other labourers	1d. ,,	4d. ,,

The emancipation of the population from serfdom was a gradual achievement. Mr. Macaulay says[w]:—

[w] History of England, vol. 1, p. 22.

"Moral causes noiselessly effaced, first the distinction between Norman and Saxon, and then the distinction between master and slave. None can venture to fix the precise moment when either distinction ceased. Some faint traces of the old Norman feeling might perhaps have been found late in the fourteenth century. Some faint traces of the institution of villeinage were detected by the curious so late as the days of the Stuarts; nor has that institution to this hour, been abolished by statute."

Though the civil wars between the rival houses of York and Lancaster hastened the progress of emancipation, neither the labour of the workman nor the capital of the employer was freed from legislative dictation. Acts of parliament were continually passed of a similar character to those previously quoted. The limited space available for the examination of this question, in the present work, will permit, however, of reference to only a few of the more important.

The dissolution of the religious houses, in the reign of Henry VIII., induced an increase of vagabondage and mendicany. This, and the partial emancipation of the villeins, necessitated the poor-laws of Elizabeth. The master, previously, was compelled, after his fashion, to keep his serfs, as well as his cattle, whether he employed them or not. A new species of slaves were created, however, after the Reformation; for, by the 1st Edward VI., enacted "for the punishment of vagabonds, and for the relief of the poor and impotant persons," it is ordained that, if a man refuse to labour at statute prices, he is to be branded with the letter V, and declared a slave for two years to any one who shall demand him. Should he attempt to escape, an additional letter S is to be burnt upon his cheek, and himself adjudged to be a slave for life. For any further attempt to escape, he is to suffer death as a felon. "Loitering and idle wanderers," male or female, of three days' duration, are to be marked on the breast with the letter V, sent to their place of birth, and compelled to labour in chains as the slaves of the inhabitants, who are to keep them at work under severe penalties. The master had the privilege of placing a ring of iron about the leg, neck, or arm of his slave, "for the more knowledge and surety of keeping him."

In this reign, combinations, both of capitalists and labourers appear to have been formed. "An Act touching Victuallers and Handicraftsmen" (1548), recites that,—

"Sellers of victuals, not contented with reasonable and moderate gain, have conspired and covenanted together to sell their victuals at unreasonable prices; * * and that artificers, handicraftsmen, and labourers, have made confederacies and promises, and have sworn mutual oaths, not only that they should not meddle one with another's work, or perform and finish that another hath begun; but also to appoint how much work they should do in a day, and what hours and times they shall work, to the great hurt and impoverishment of the king's subjects."

Severe penalties are enacted against all such combinations. Parties belonging to them are subjected, for the first offence, to a fine of ten pounds, or twenty days' imprisonment; for a second offence, twenty pounds, or the pillory; and for a third, to a penalty of forty pounds, or the pillory, and loss of ears; and also, "at all times afterwards to be taken as a man infamous, and his depositions or oath not to be credited."

By the 5th Elizabeth (1562-3), the rate of wages, hours of work, times for meals, etc., are ordered to be settled annually by the justices in session assembled; after calling "unto them such discreet and grave persons as they shall think meet, and, after conferring together respecting the plenty or scarcity of the time, and other circumstances necessary to be considered."

These rates are to be approved by the privy council, and afterwards proclaimed by the sheriffs. Any employer giving excessive wages is subjected to a penalty of five pounds, and ten days' imprisonment; any labourer receiving such, to twenty-one days' imprisonment; and all such contracts are to be void and of none effect.

Strype records that, owing to the threatened disturbances in the north, a strict search was made in every part of the kingdom, on the night of Sunday, the 10th July, 1569, for vagrants, beggars, gamesters, rogues, or gipsies. The search commenced at nine o'clock in the evening, and was continued till four o'clock on the following afternoon. It resulted in the apprehension of thirteen thousand "masterless men." The offence charged against these individuals was, that they had no visible mode of living, "except that which was derived from unlawful games, especially of bowling, and maintenance of archery." The offenders were "all passed to their own counties, under the direction of the magistrates." [x]

In Elizabeth's reign, acts were passed directing how leather should be tanned, and hats and caps manufactured. The hatters' statute orders that all persons above the age of six years, except ladies, lords, knights, and gentlemen worth twenty marks per year in land, to wear upon their heads "one cap of wool, made within this realm of England, and dressed and finished by some of the trade or science of cappers." Contumacy was punished by a fine of 3s. 4d. This was protection to the home manufacturer with a vengeance!

Sir George Nicholls gives the following as the average rate of wages, including the allowance for clothing, for the periods referred to.[y] He says: "It will be seen that an increase had taken place, nearly corresponding with the increase in the price of provisions":—

By the Year.	1495. s.	d.	1593. s.	d.	1610. s.	d.
A bailiff in husbandry	31	8	40	0	52	0
A hine, shepherd, or husbandry servant of the best sort	25	0	34	4	50	0
A common servant in husbandry	20	8	30	0	40	0

x Strype's Ann., vol. 1, p. 572. y His. Eng. Poor-law, vol. I, p. 209.

By the Year.	1495. s.	d.	1593. s.	d.		1610. s.	d.
An inferior servant in husbandry			25	0		29	0
A woman servant	14	0	17	4		26	8
A youth under sixteen	9	8	16	0		20	0
By the Day.							
A mower in harvest, without meat and drink	0	6	0	10		0	10
A reaper or carter, do.	0	5	0	5		0	8
All other labourers without meat and drink — in summer	0	4	0	5		0	7
All other labourers without meat and drink — in winter	0	3	0	4		0	6
Artificers without meat and drink — in summer	0	6	0	8	on an average	0	10
Artificers without meat and drink — in winter	0	5	0	7	on an average	0	8

A document, in the possession of R. Townley Parker, esq., gives the rate of wages as fixed by the magistrates, for the hundred of Blackburn, at the sessions held in Preston, in April, 1673. The local legislators premise their tariff with a declaration, that they have been induced to devote their attention to the subject, in "consideration to what exorbitant height, for want of putting ye laws in execucon, servantes are now growne; for reformation thereof; and to ye end that masters and mistresses of families shall not soe frequently tempte a good servante to leave his service by offering more or greater wages than ye Law permitts." The following is the scale agreed upon; any infringement of which subjected the offenders to similar punishments to those previously recited. The removal of a workman to another parish, without authority, is likewise expressly prohibited:—

Servants and Artificers of Husbandry.

1.—A Bayliffe or foreman of Husbandry yt is hyred with a Gent. or a rich yeomon yt doth not labour himselfe but putteth his whole charge to his servt shall not take by the yeare for his wages with meate & drinke above iij*l*. x*s*. (£3. 10s.)

2.—A chiefe servt in Husbandry to a yeomon or Husbandman yt can mow plow or sowe & doe other Husbandry shall not take for his wages with meate & drinke above ij*l*. x*s*.

3.—A miller shall not take by the year above iij*l*.

4.—An ordinary servt in Husbandry yt can mowe and plowe well shall not take by ye yeare with meate and drinke above ij*l*. x*s*. And every other comon servant in Husbandry shall not take by ye yeare above ij*l*.

5.—A young man betweene the age of 12 and 18 yeares shall not take by the yeare with meate & drinke above xxvj*s*. viij*d*.

6.—A woman servante that taketh charge of Brewinge, Bakeinge, & Kitchinge, Milkehouse, or Maltinge, yt is hired with a gent. or rich yeomon whose wife doth not take the paines & charge upon her, shall not take wages by the yeare with meate and drinke above xxx*s*.

7.—A woman servt yt serveth a Husbandman or farmer or any other woman servt shall not take by the yeare with meate and drinke above xxvj*s*. viij*d*.

Harvest worke.

8.—A Mower of grasse shall not take by the day with meate and drinke above six pence, and without meate and drinke above xij*d*.

9.—A man shearer or Bynder of corne shall not take by the day with meate & drinke above fouer pence & without meate and drinke viij*d*.

10.—A man Haymaker iij*d*. a woman ij*d*. a Weeder or Lowker of corne being a man, shall not take by the day with meate and drinke above ij*d*., without meate and drinke vj*d*., and a woman iiij*d*.

11.—Every man labourer for Ditchinge, Pailinge or Raileinge, Hedgeinge, Threshinge, or other comon labourers, from ye Feast of All Sts to the first day of March, shall not take for wages by the day with meat and drink above iijd., without meate & drinke not above six pence; and from ye first day of March untile All Saintes with meate and drinke not above fouer pence, and without meat and drinke not above Eight pence.

12.—Noe man shall for castinge or settinge any ditch, haveing the Quick wood layed besides him, which ditch is more than one yarde, and Quarter broade and a yard deep, above vjd. for a roode, and when the ditch is bigger or lesser according to the Quantity and rate.

13.—Noe man that scowreth a ditch three spade Breadth and two depth shall not take for one Rood scowring above ijd., and for one spade gripp in breadth and depth for making every roode not above a halfepenny.

14.—Noe man shall take for makeing a rough drye stone wall, hauing the stones layed beside him, which wall is one yard and halfe high & halfe a yard thick, above xijd. a roode without meate and drinke.

ARTIFICERS & HANDICRAFTSMEN.

A master Mason that taketh charge of a mans buildinge, hauinge under him or them one two or three men yt. have been two or three yeares at the occupion, shall not take for wages for himself by the day at any time of the yeare, with meat and drinke, above vjd., and without meat and drinke not above xijd., & for every one yt worketh under him hee shall not take by the day, with meate and drinke, from ye feast of St. Michaell the Archangell untill ye 25th day of March, with meate and drinke not above iij., without meate and drinke not above vjd., and from the 25th day of March, until the feast of St. Michaell the Archangell, with meate and drinke, not above iiijd. and without meate and drinke not above viijd.

16.—A Master Carpenter who taketh charge of buildinges that hath one two or three men under him that hath been two or three yeares at the science, shall not take for wages by the day, with meat and drinke, above vjd., and without meat and drinke not above xijd.

17.—A Mason or other Carpenter that hath but one man or none and that are not masters of a charge of a building but of other work, as Hewing, Squaring, Walling, or such like, or Plumer, Glazier, Lymeburner, Cowper, Bricklayer, or Thatcher, Turner, Brickmaker, Slater or Taylor, shall not take by the day for wages, with meat and drinke, not above vjd. from ye Annunciation of the Blessed Virgin Mary untill Michaelmas and without meate & drinke not above xijd. And from the feast of St. Michael ye Archangell untill ye 25th of March, with meate & drinke, not above iijd., and without meate and drinke, not above viijd., except Thatchers, who may take by ye day throughout ye whole yeare vjd.

18.—A master Taylor that shall make a Gent. or Gentlewoman their Apparell shall not take by the day above vjd., his servante iijd.

CLOATH WORKERS AND DYERS.

19.—Noe Journeyman Webster, fuller, cloath workers, shereman, or dyer shall not take for his wages above iiijd. with meate & drinke, and without meate and drinke not above viijd., and if hee be hired by the yeare, if hee bee a very skillfull workeman in those sciences he shall have iijl. per annum, and comon weavers, cloath-workers, sheremen, fullers, & dyers shall not take for their wages yearly above ijl. xs.

COLLIERS.

20.—No Collier or workeman that is skilfull in getteinge of coaels shall take wages by ye day, without meate and drinke, above xd.

21.—Noe filler or drawer of coaels shall take for his wages by ye day, without meate and drink, above vjd.

22.—Noe Bankesman or drawer up of coaels shall take for his wages by ye day, without meate and drinke, above viijd.

The following documents, in the possession of the Rev. W. Thornber, will serve to show the value of household furniture and farming implements and stock, in Lancashire, at the end of the seventeenth century, and illustrate the difference in the value of money at that period and the present time [z]:—

"October 16th, 1669. Then; a Sale Bill made of all such Goods and Chattells as were sold in open Sale, by Thomas Chippindale, of Borrands, wth in Gressingham, as followeth:—

"Impr.	£.	s.	d.
Britt Chippindale, 6 Bands	00	00	04
Tho. Barber, 6 Bands	00	00	03
Barthol. Parker, Harrow Bulls	00	00	04½
Itm. two Tarr Kitts	00	00	03
ffran. Chapman, a pair of Gripes	00	00	03
Itm. a Spade	00	00	06
Rob. Latas, a Spade	00	00	03½
Rob. Heysam, a Spade	00	00	03
Rich. Thompson, a fforke	00	01	06
Rob. Lutus, a sheep Cribbe	00	00	06½
Mr. Rich. Eskrigge, Timber wood	00	09	08
Itm. for a Plough	00	00	11
Itm. an Ox Calfe	01	01	07
Itm. a Heifer	01	10	00
Anth. Thompson, a Heifer	01	16	08
Bry. Birkett, a Heifer	02	14	06
Marg. Barker, a Heifer	02	16	00
Tho. Townson, a Heifer	02	17	00
Josuah Bryer, a Heifer	03	15	06
Rob. Lucas, a Cow	03	17	06
Tho. Townson, two Oxen	08	09	00
Mr. Rich. Eskrigge, two Oxen	09	16	01
Rob. Chorley, a Cow	03	12	00
Tho. Walters, 10 Sheep	02	07	06
Rich. Thompson, 10 Sheep	01	19	02
James Craven a ffilly	04	03	04
In all	51	11	01½

"A true and perfect Inventory of all the Goods, Chattells, and Debts, wch of late did belong to Thomas Chippindale, late of Borrands, wth in Gressingham, in the County of Lancaster, yeoman, deceased. Apprized the 13th Day of November, Anno Dnj., 1699 as followeth:—

"Impr.	£.	s.	d.
His purss and Apparrill	02	00	00
Bedding and Bedcloths	01	10	00
Cupboards and Chests	00	02	04
Tables, Chaires, and Boards	01	02	00
Brass and Pewther	01	00	00
Wooden vessell, Girdle, & Brand Iron	00	18	06
Hemp, Wooll, & other things	01	14	00
Sacks, Poaks, & Hempseed	00	10	00
Meal, Malt, & a fflesh tubbe	00	15	00
Plough & Plough Gear	00	06	00
Cartts, Wheeles, wth Husband Gear	00	12	00
Corn, Hay, & Straw	16	00	00

z See Chapter 5., page 207, for a similar document, of the middle of the seventeenth century, likewise in the possession of Mr. Thornber.

	£	s.	d.
Sheep & one Mare	10	12	00
Two Cows	06	00	00
Money upon Specialtye a	148	05	00
Money wth out Specialtye	015	11	01
Pullen, Turffe, & Dunghill	000	09	00
"In all	207	17	11

"Apprized by us,
THO. BURTON.
THO. DIXON.
RICH. THOMPSON."

In the 18th and 19th Charles II. (1666), an act for the "encouragement of the woollen manufacture in the kingdom," orders that, under a penalty of £5., no person shall be buried "in any shirt, shift, or sheet," other than what is made from woollen only.

How little the legislators of the earlier portion of the last century understood the coming destiny of commercial and manufacturing Britain, may be gathered from the following "act to preserve and encourage the woollen and silk manufactures," (7th George II., 1720). The preamble declares it "most evident that the wearing and using of printed, painted, stained, and dyed calicoes in apparel, household stuff, furniture, and otherwise, does manifestly tend to the great detriment of the woollen and silk manufactures, and to the excessive increase of the poor, and if not prevented, may be the utter ruin and destruction of the said manufactures, and of many thousands whose livelihoods do entirely depend thereupon." The wearing of printed or dyed calico is forbidden by the statute, under a penalty of five pounds! The seller of it, except for exportation, was mulcted in the sum of £20!! By another act passed the same year, it was resolved, under a penalty of £5., "that no buttons or button-holes made of cloth, serge, drugget, frieze, camblet, or any other stuffs, should be made, set, or bound on any clothes or wearing garments whatsoever, by any tailor or other person." This was passed with the object of relieving the "great impoverishment" of the manufacturers of buttons made of silk, mohair, and thread.

In 1720, another act was passed "for regulating journeymen tailors." It declares that "great numbers of journeymen tailors in and about the cities of London and Westminster, and others who have served apprenticeships, or been brought up in the art and mystery of a tailor, have lately departed from their services without just cause, and have entered into combination to advance their wages to unreasonable prices, and lessen their usual hours of work, which is of evil example, and manifestly tends to the prejudice of trade, to the encouragement of idleness, and to the great

a Invested on special security, or by deed under seal.

increase of the poor." The act then proceeds to denounce all such covenants or agreements for the advancement of wages, or for lessening the usual hours of work, as illegal and void; and subjects all persons offending therein, to two months' imprisonment with hard labour! The men are ordered to work from six in the morning till eight at night, with an allowance, by the employer, of "one penny halfpenny a day for breakfast, and one hour for dinner." The wages were not to exceed two shillings a day, between the 26th of March and the 24th of June; for the remainder of the year, one shilling and eightpence must suffice. It likewise declares that if any journeyman tailor quitteth his labour, or if he, "not being retained or employed, shall refuse to enter into work or employment, after request made for that purpose by any master tailor, for the wages and hours limited as aforesaid, unless it be for some reasonable and sufficient cause to be allowed by two justices of the peace," his Utopian notions respecting personal freedom are to be subjected to the discipline of hard labour in the house of correction, for any period not exceeding two months! In what shape harder labour, than he was expected to perform as a *peaceful citizen*, could be administered or endured, it is difficult, in these days of comparative freedom, to conjecture. The employer's liberty of judgment or action was not a whit more respected. A penalty of five pounds was decreed, on any master tailor or other person who should presume to pay greater wages than those prescribed by the act! one half of which was given to the informer, and the other to the poor of the parish.

Five years afterwards, a similar act was passed "to prevent unlawful combinations of workmen employed in the woollen manufactures." This act, however, prohibits, under a penalty of £10., all manufacturers of woollen cloths from paying any portion of the wages of their weavers, or others in their employ, "in goods or by way of truck, or in any other manner than in money." The employers are protected against violence or dictation on the part of the workmen, by the terrors of a seven years' transportation.

The introduction of some such statutes, to regulate the cotton manufacture, during the late "strike" and "lock-out," at Preston, would have somewhat astonished both the operatives and their employers!

This species of legislation must have, in itself, materially aided in the propagation of mendicancy and vagabondism; against which acts were passed, reeking with the vengeful spirit of the lowest of savageism. Dr. Burn,[b] writing in 1764, forcibly observes:—"The *prevention* of poverty, idleness, and a loose and disorderly education, would do more for this kingdom, than all the gibbets and cauterizations, and whipping posts, and

b History of the Poor Laws.

gaols, in the kingdom; and would render these kinds of discipline less necessary and less frequent." Experience has proved the truth of the doctor's observations. The question may be studied yet to further advantage.

The 20th George II. (1747), empowered justices, not only to fix the rate of wages, but to settle all disputes between masters and workmen. Sir George Nicholls, in his History of the English Poor Law, says,:—[c]

"The last occasion on which the power of limiting wages appears to have been exercised, was a little more than twenty years previous to the passing of the present act (20th George II.), when the justices of the county palatine of Lancaster, 'upon conference with discreet men of the said county,' on the 22nd of May, 1725, established the following as a *maximum* scale:—[d]

	Without Meat and Drink.			With Meat and Drink.		
	£	s.	d.	£	s.	d.
A bailiff in husbandry or chief hind, by the year, ...not above				6	0	0
The best millers	0	0	0	5	0	0
A chief servant in husbandry, that can mow or sow, or do other husbandry well				5	0	0
A common servant in husbandry, of 21 and upwards				4	0	0
A man servant from 20 to 24 years of age				3	10	0
A ditto from 16 to 20 ditto				2	10	0
The best woman servant being a cook, or able to take charge of a household ....not above				2	10	0
A chamber maid, dairy maid, and wash maid or other mean servant ....not above				2	0	0
A woman servant, under 16 years of age				1	10	0
LABOURERS BY THE DAY.						
The best husbandry labourer, from the midst of March to the midst of September	0	1	0	0	0	6
An ordinary sort of husbandry labourer ditto	0	0	10	0	0	5
The best husbandry labourer, from the midst of September to the midst of March ....not above	0	0	10	0	0	5
The ordinary sort of ditto ,,	0	0	9	0	0	4
Man haymaker ,,	0	0	10	0	0	6
Woman haymaker ,,	0	0	7	0	0	3
A mower of hay ,,	0	1	3	0	0	9
Man shearer ,,	0	1	0	0	0	6
Woman shearer ,,	0	0	10	0	0	6
Hedgers, ditchers, pailers, and thrashers ,,	0	0	10	0	0	6
Masons, carpenters, joiners, plumbers, tilers, slaters, coopers, and turners, who are not master workman ....not above	0	1	0	0	0	6
The master workman, who has others working under him ,,	0	1	2			
Bricklayers, plasterers, whiteliners ,,	0	1	0	0	0	6
A master bricklayer, who has others working under his direction	0	1	2			
A pair of sawyers, by the day ,,	0	2	0	0	1	0
A master tailor ,,	0	1	0	0	0	6
A journeyman tailor and apprentice ,,	0	0	10	0	0	5
WORK IN GREAT.						
For an acre of oats, seven yards to the rood ,,	0	5	0			

c Vol. 2, p. 17. d See Sir F. Eden's "State of the Poor," vol. 3, p. 106.

WORK IN GREAT.		Without Meat and Drink. £ s. d.	With Meat and Drink. £ s. d.
For an acre of barley ditto	,,	0 6 0	
For an acre of wheat ditto	,,	0 7 0	
Thrashing, winnowing, or farming a quarter of oats	,,	0 1 0	
Ditto barley, beans, and peas	,,	0 1 6	
Ditto wheat and rye	,,	0 2 0	
WHEELWRIGHTS.			
Sawing a rood of boards, 22 feet to the rood	,,	0 8 0	
Hewing a gang of fellies	,,	0 1 0	
Making a plough	,,	0 2 0	
BRICKMAKERS.			
For casting the clay, moulding it according to the statute, making the kiln, and burning it, having straw and other necessaries laid by, for every thousand of six score to the hundred......not above		0 3 0	
HEDGERS AND DITCHERS.			
For a new ditch out of the whole ground, 4 feet wide, 3 feet deep, 18 inches in the bottom, double set with quicks, and setting a hedge upon it, after the rate of 8 yards to the rood, and gathering sets for the same		0 1 0	
For making a rood of ditch of like breadth and depth, without quicks		0 0 10	
For making a rood of a usual hedge, the stuff laid by		0 0 3	
COLLIERS.			
Miners in high delfe (a standing delfe), for 24 baskets, (a tunn)		0 1 0	
Miners in low delfe (a sitting delfe), for 24 baskets		0 1 3	
PAVIOURS.			
For paving every square yard, having the usual foundation made, and the materials laid by		0 0 1	

Referring to this table, Sir George Nicholls observes :—

"The above order shews the minute precision with which the justices exercised the powers conferred upon them for regulating the rates of wages, and the remuneration of labour; and the scale therein prescribed affords a means of comparison with what is usually paid on like occasions in the present day. In 1725, the price of wheat in the Windsor market, according to the Eton tables, was 43s. 1¼d. a quarter, Winchester measure. At the time I now write (1853), the Mark-lane price of wheat is 44s. the quarter, scarcely differing from what it was a century and a quarter ago, whilst wages have at least doubled since then, and the price of clothing has fallen at least one half."[e]

What British workman would wish to restore the slavery and fare of the first quarter of the eighteenth century? What capitalist would rejoice at the resumption of the paternal authority of the state over such details in his commercial arrangements? The workmen, were however, far the worse used; the object of this species of legislation evidently being to *prevent* the law of supply and demand influencing the gains from their labour. The order referred to, expressly declares the labourer shall not

e His. Eng. Poor Law. vol. 2, p. 49.

receive *above* the specified sum, but is silent as to the acceptance of less!! Truly, personal slavery was not extinct in England, either then, or for some time afterwards. Such selfish class legislation, however, harmonized but indifferently with the growing intelligence of the people. Combinations amongst workmen were formed to resist this system of tyranny, but they were as speedily interdicted by legislative enactment. The 22nd George II. cap. 27, prohibits all combination amongst workmen of every trade. The right to dispose of their labour to the best advantage is thoroughly ignored. With reference to this act, Sir George Nicholls makes the following just, practical, common sense observations:—

"Such a prohibition can only be justified, on the ground of its being necessary for the protection of life and property, or for the preservation of the public peace; but no such cause of justification was adduced on the present, or on the previous occasions, and this absolute prohibition of all combinations must, therefore, be held to have been opposed to justice and sound policy."

Resistance, however, was not extinguished; for in 1768, the 8th George III. declares that the frequent combinations of the London tailors led "to the prejudice of trade, to the encouragement of idleness, and to the great increase of the poor." The act determined that the hours of labour should be from six in the morning to seven in the evening, "with an interval of one hour only for refreshment." It likewise decreed the wages should not exceed 2s. 7½d. per day, except at a period of general mourning; when, for the space of a month, 5s. 1½d. might be paid. Any workman receiving, or master paying, more, was subjected to a penalty of two months' imprisonment and hard labour! And this was not all. In order to prevent the said "masters" evading the law by the employment of workmen who did not reside within five miles of the city of London, a penalty of £500. was imposed, "one half to the king, and the other half to the person suing for the same."

In 1795, (35 George III.) some progress was made in the legislative policy respecting migration in search of employment. It was enacted that poor persons should not be removed to their own parish, until they actually became chargeable. This was a great boon at the time, and relieved the persevering operative from the capricious interference of parish authorities. Previously, the *possibility* that a person might obtain a settlement and become chargeable, was a sufficient excuse for ordering his removal.

At the end of the last century, a practice had become very prevalent of eking out labourers' wages from the poor's rate. Parties were sent "on the rounds," as it was termed, by the overseers; that is each householder in turn was compelled to employ the applicant, or pay a portion towards his sustenance, the remainder being provided by the parish authorities.

An attempt was made by the Berkshire justices to regulate the rate of wages, in 1795, according to the price of provisions. It was decreed that:—

"When the gallon loaf of second flour, weighing 8 lb. 11 oz., shall cost 1s., then every poor and industrious man shall have for his own support 3s. weekly, either produced by his own or his family's labour, or an allowance from the poor rates; and for the support of his wife and every other of his family, 1s. 6d.

"When the gallon loaf shall cost 1s. 4d., then every poor and industrious man shall receive 4s. weekly for his own, and 1s. 10d. for the support of every other of his family.

"And so on in proportion, as the price of bread rises or falls (that is to say) 3d. to the man and 1d. to every other of the family, on every penny which the loaf rises above a shilling.

This "Berkshire Bread-scale" was locally known as the "Speenhamland Act of Parliament." According to Sir George Nicholls, it was extensively adopted in other counties.[f]

Such a practice produced the most unfortunate results. No insignificant portion of the wages of the operative population, especially in the agricultural districts, was derived from the parish. This indiscriminate pauperising of industrious labourers was not eradicated until after the introduction of the much abused "Poor Law Amendment Act," in 1834.

The honour of first propounding a sounder principle of legislation respecting labour and wages, appears to be due to Mr. Pitt. In 1796, he opposed a measure, introduced by Mr. Whitbread, for the purpose of regulating wages, and forcibly observed that, "trade, industry, and barter, would always find their own level, and be impeded by regulations which violated their natural operation, and deranged their proper effect." He contended that to give "justices the power to regulate the price of labour, would be endeavouring to establish, by authority, what would be much better accomplished by the unaided operation of principle."

Considerable advance in the price of provisions, etc., took place at the commencement of the present century. Many reasons have been assigned for the change, none, perhaps, individually, very satisfactory. Various causes may have operated to produce the result. The effect on the working population was severe in the extreme, and especially during the period of scarcity which continued for some time after the conclusion of the war with France. Sir George Nicholls says:—

"Whatever may have been the cause of the rise which took place during the period under consideration, in the price of all the articles necessary for sustaining life, the effect must at the time have borne hard upon those who lived by labour, and must have exposed the working classes generally to much privation; for wages neither rise nor fall in immediate nor in exact proportion to the changes of price. Mechanics and operatives in towns, might succeed in obtaining an advance of wages in some degree commensurate with the advance in prices; but such would not be the case with labourers generally, nor with the agricultural labourers in particular—the advance they obtained was too often, if not most commonly, from the poor-rate. In a debate on the presentation, by Mr. Calvert, in 1817, of petitions from two parishes in Dorsetshire,[g] complaining of the burthen of the poor-rates, which in one year amounted to 19s., and in the other to 21s. in

---

[f] English Poor Law, vol. 2, p. 13

[g] See Hansard's Debates for March 7, 1817.

the pound, Lord Castlereagh, whose official position afforded him the means of obtaining the best information, expressed his conviction, 'that in cases where 19s. or 20s. in the pound were paid for poor-rates, 15s. of that would be found to be wages paid in the shape of poor-rates,' for that the farmers had been long in the habit, in many parts of the country, of paying a great proportion of the wages of farm labour out of the poor-rates."

The good harvest of 1818, materially improved the condition of the labourer, which has gradually progressed since, notwithstanding some important interruptions.

It was not until 1814 (54th George III.), that the act of Elizabeth, which restricted the exercise of any "art, mystery, or manual occupation" to parties who "shall have been brought up therein seven years at the least as an apprentice," was repealed. There is a special provision, however, that "the ancient customs, usages, privileges, or franchises of the city of London," are to remain intact!

It would appear, after all, that the operatives have learned most of their notions, crude, erroneous, or otherwise, respecting the regulation of wages and trade, from their superiors in station and intelligence; and that ancient usage and personal prejudice can prevent progress, in this respect, in wealthy corporations, as well as in working men's trades unions.

After the establishment of the "New Poor-law Board," the commissioners, finding an excess of labour in the southern counties, and a corresponding demand in the manufacturing districts,—

"So far interfered as to put the manufacturers of Lancashire into communication with certain of the most burthened rural parishes, which led to the voluntary removal of many families from places where wages were very low, to others where they were comparatively high, and where, moreover, there was full employment for women and children. A large migration from the most pauperised districts took place in consequence; and the commissioners state that all these migrants were employed, 'and earning collectively as families, three times the amount of wages which they had at any time earned in the districts which they had quitted,' whilst the effect upon the parishes was a proportionate reduction of the rates." [h]

Since the emancipation of the operative population from this state of semi-serfdom, two important struggles have taken place in Preston, with reference to the price of labour, and the conditions of its employment,—one in 1836, and the other in 1853-4. During the present century, some minor efforts amongst various trades have transpired, but not of sufficient public importance to demand special notice. The struggles between the employers and the employed, in the staple manufacture, will sufficiently illustrate those of capital and labour generally.

Mr. Whittle mentions that, as early as 1808, "the cotton weavers of the town assembled on the Moor in great numbers, in order to consult and induce their employers to raise wages." He further records the significant fact, that "the military were ready at a moment's notice on this occasion." [i]

h Sir George Nicholls. English Poor-law, vol. 2, p. 321. i History of Preston, vol. 1, p. 311.

Considerable destitution had prevailed in the town, and subscriptions had been raised for the relief of the poor. As no mention is made of any results from the weavers' meeting, it is most probable no change was effected.

A petition from the manufacturers and inhabitants of Preston, containing 9,812 signatures, was presented to the house of commons, in 1817, "against the exportation of cotton twist." This exhibits a somewhat different principle of commercial legislation to that propounded by the free-trade capitalists during the strike of 1853-4.

In 1818, an unsuccessful attempt was made to raise wages by the weavers. Upwards of 1,200 persons paraded the streets on this occasion.

In 1821, a reduction of ten per cent. being made in the operative cotton spinners' wages, they suspended labour for about three weeks. They resumed their employment, however, without obtaining their object.

Disturbances occurred in 1831, and some damage was done to the mill belonging to Messrs. Birley and Turton, the "big factory," at Fishwick. Wages was not the question at issue on this occasion; but the prevention of the introduction of improved machinery. In the following year, the "martello towers" were erected at the House of Correction, with the view to strengthen the place, which had been threatened with an attack by the rioters.

In 1836, the memorable struggle known as the "spinners' strike," took place. The agitation commenced in October. The strike itself lasted three months. The dispute originated in a demand of the operatives for an equalisation of their wages with the prices paid in Bolton. The employers agreed to give an advance of ten per cent., on condition that the operatives seceded from the trades-union; but this was rejected. On the 7th November, the spinners discontinued their attendance, and consequently the mills were closed. Eight thousand five hundred people were thus suddenly thrown out of employment, seven thousand eight hundred and forty of whom were altogether unconnected with the dispute, as will be seen from the following table, extracted from a paper read before the British Association, at Liverpool, and printed in the "Working Man's Companion," for 1838:—

Spinners	660
Piecers, and children employed by spinners	1320
Card-room hands, reelers, and power-loom weavers	6100
Overlookers, packers, engineers, etc.	420
Total	8500 ǂ

ǂ Mr. Whittle says (His. Preston, vol. 2, p. 174), "upwards of 15,000 persons (including women and children)," were thrown out of employment; but this is evidently an exaggerated statement, formed upon conjecture without positive data.

The same paper gives the following details and statistics relative to this, the first grand struggle between capital and labour in Preston :—

"During the first fortnight of the turn-out, no change was apparent in the condition of the work-people; some meetings were held both by masters and men, but nothing resulted from them. At the commencement of the second fortnight, complaints began to be heard from the card-room hands, and from the shopkeepers of the town.

"Early in December, when the mills had been closed for a month, the streets began to be crowded with beggars, and the offices of the overseers were besieged with applicants for relief. The inmates of the workhouse began to increase rapidly, and scenes of the greatest misery and wretchedness were of constant occurrence. At this period the spinners were receiving from the funds of the union five shillings a-week each, and the piecers, some two, and others three shillings a-week; the card-room hands and power-loom weavers [forming, be it observed, nearly three-fourths of the whole number out of employment] were destitute of all means of support, receiving no assistance except such as the masters afforded them, which (except in the cases of eighteen or twenty individuals who had not joined the union) extended to only one meal a-day for each person.

"In December, £100. was granted by the corporation towards relieving the general distress, and a meeting was convened for the purpose of raising a further sum, and of considering the most effectual means of putting an end to the turn-out; but nothing resulted from it. Towards the middle of December, when the turn-out had lasted six weeks, it was evident that the funds of the union were nearly exhausted.

"By the end of December, the distress had become universal and intense, and the masters came to the resolution of opening their mills, in order to give those who wished for it an opportunity of resuming their work. In doing so, they announced their determination to abide by their former offer of an increase of ten per cent. on the rate of wages; but to require from all those who should enter the mills a written declaration to the effect, that they would not, at any future time, whilst in their service, become members of any union or combination of workmen.

"Immediately on the re-opening of the mills, which took place on the 9th of January, all the card-room hands rushed anxiously to their work; but the continued absence of the spinners rendered it impossible to give them employment.

"At the end of the first week after the mills had been opened, forty spinners were at work, of whom eighteen were those who, as before stated, had not joined the union, and the remaining twenty-two had never before been regularly employed in that kind of work.

"In the course of the second week, the number had increased to one hundred, of whom some were entirely new to the work, and three were seceders from the union; and at the end of the third week, there were one hundred and forty spinners at work, some of the additional forty having been procured from neighbouring towns. Besides this, in two of the factories a few self-acting mules, or spinning-machines, were substituted for common mules, thereby dispensing with the services of the spinners. As the number of the spinners increased, of course a corresponding increase took place in the number of persons employed in the other departments.

"Towards the middle of the fourth week, the supplies from the funds of the union suddenly stopped, and those who had depended on this resource had no alternative left but to endeavour to obtain readmission to the factories. On the 5th of February, exactly three months from the day on which the mills were first closed, work was resumed in all the mills to its usual extent; but about two hundred of the spinners who had been most active in the turn-out, were replaced by new hands, and have since either left the town, or remain there without employment. No systematic acts of violence, or violations of the law, took place during the turn-out. Detachments of military were stationed in the town to preserve order, but their services were not required. Some inflammatory hand-bills appeared on the walls, but without creating much sensation.

"While the turn-out lasted, the operatives generally wandered about the streets without any definite object; seventy-five persons were brought before the magistrates, and convicted of drunkenness and disorderly conduct; twelve were imprisoned or held to bail for assaults or intimidation; about twenty young females became prostitutes, of whom more than one-half are still so, and of whom two have since been transported for theft; three persons are believed to have died of starvation; and not less than five thousand must have suffered long and severely from hunger and cold. In almost every family the greater part of the wearing apparel and household furniture was pawned. In nine houses out of ten, considerable arrears of rent were due; and out of the sum of sixteen hundred pounds deposited in the Savings' bank by about sixty spinners or overlookers, nine hundred pounds were withdrawn in the course of the three months; most of those who could obtain credit got into debt with the shopkeepers. The trade of the town suffered severely; many of the small shopkeepers were nearly ruined, and a few completely so.

The following estimate may be made of the direct pecuniary loss to all classes of operatives in consequence of the turn-out:—

	£.	s.	d.
The wages of the 660 spinners for 13 weeks, at 22s. 6d.	9,652	10	0
1,320 piecers for 13 weeks, at 5s. 6d.	4,719	0	0
6,520 weavers, card-room hands, overlookers, engineers, etc., etc., for 13 weeks,			
8,500 averaging 9s.	38,142	0	0
Estimated loss sustained by hand-loom weavers in consequence of the turn-out	9,500	0	0
Estimated loss sustained by clerks, waggoners, carters, mechanics, dressers, sizers, etc., in consequence of the turn out	8,000	0	0
Total	£70,013	10	0
From which must be deducted—			
Estimated amount of wages earned during the partial resumption of work between the 9th Jan. and the 5th Feb.	5,013	0	0
Estimated value of relief given by the masters	1,000	0	0
Other private charity and parish relief	2,500	0	0
Allowance to the spinners and piecers from the funds of the union	4,290	0	0
	£12,803	0	0
Leaving a net pecuniary loss to the whole body of the Preston operatives of	57,210	10	0

(But to the town at large it may be said the loss was that of the whole sum of £70,013. 10s. as the amount of the deductions are mostly of a charitable nature.)

Loss to the Preston operatives	57,210	0	0
The loss to the masters being three months' interest of £800,000, some of which being sunk capital was not only unproductive, but was taking harm from being rendered useless, has been estimated at	45,000	0	0
And the loss sustained by the shopkeepers from loss of business, bad debts, etc., etc.	4,986	0	0
Making the total loss to the town and trade of Preston, in this unavailing struggle	£107,196	0	0

In Aug., 1842, alarming riots took place throughout the manufacturing districts generally. In Lancashire, the flame appears to have been first lighted at Staley-bridge. The principal object sought was evidently a higher rate of wages, although many other elements entered into the composition of this serious "mass movement." Chartism was rife at the period, and general dissatisfaction prevailed. Mobs scoured the county, and forced the willing workmen to leave their employment. On Friday, the 12th August, a meeting was held in the "Orchard," at Preston.

Some of the mill hands turned out, and endeavoured to compel the closing of several other establishments,—sometimes not without success. On the following morning, this conduct was repeated; but by eight o'clock, the authorities of the town, aided by the police and a detachment of military, put a stop to the career of the mob, but not until a volley of musketry had stretched on the earth eight men, five of whom were mortally wounded. On the Wednesday following, serious riots took place at Farrington, Leyland, and Penwortham, chiefly created by "navigators," or "navvies," as they are now called. Rumours arrived that a powerful mob was marching from Chorley, to compel the Preston mills to close, and to avenge the deaths of the men slain on Saturday. Another, although a bloodless battle, took place at Walton, where the rural police, under Captain Woodford, totally routed the mob, without the assistance of a party of rifles, by whom they were accompanied. About twenty-seven of the rioters were taken prisoners, and several of them punished. The manufacturing activity was not seriously affected by this demonstration; yet the town did not quite recover its habitual tranquility for some time afterwards, notwithstanding the intervention of the guild festivities.

The most important struggle between labour and capital commenced in 1853. In the earlier half of the year, the exports of the kingdom had risen to £41,866,557., against £33,549,392., showing an increase of £8,317,165. The prices of provisions were very high, and although this does not materially affect the rate of wages, it unquestionably stimulated the operatives in their demands. Strikes were pretty general throughout the country. The workmen triumphed at Stockport and other places. The flame at length spread to Preston. The operatives contended that they were entitled to "the ten per cent. which was taken off in 1842, and also the ten per cent. taken from them in 1847-8, and if the manufacturers were men of their word they would not scruple to give it according to their promise." [k] Ten per cent. advance, accordingly was the war cry. This was, at first, partially conceded, but some difficulties arose as to its practical adjustment in two or three mills. An attempt was made by the operatives to assimilate the rates of remuneration in the various mills, taking the most favourable, of course, as the standard. This caused a strike in two or three establishments. The dispute eventually caused the locking up of all the mills, and a determination on the part of both employers and employed to contest the question to the uttermost. The latter were wishful to refer their differences to arbitration, but the "masters" declined all interference with their business arrangements.

---

k Cowell's Speech in the Orchard, Aug. 11th, 1853.

Several meetings were held in the "Orchard" during August; and, by the end of the month, the hands in four or five establishments, either entirely or partially agreed to "strike." At the end of September, about a dozen mills were closed by the employers. This policy was soon afterwards adopted by the remainder of the establishments in Preston and the neighbourhood, with a very few exceptions. This constituted the "lock-out." The struggle lasted till nearly the end of May, in the following year. The commercial prosperity, which heralded the strife, had passed away, and the workmen were compelled to resume their employment on the masters' terms. The affairs of the operatives were managed by two distinct committees, one representing the spinners, and the other the power-loom weavers. The greatest distress was felt by the remainder of the hands unemployed; many of whom did not wish to suspend labour, as they were not in a position to claim relief from the funds of any union.

The total number of hands thrown out of employment, has been variously estimated at from 20,000 to 26,000. The most important facts relative to this "labour battle," may be learned from the statements published by the various parties interested. The "thirty-ninth, and final report of the income and expenditure of the funds subscribed for the Preston power-loom weaver's lock-out, from August 29th, 1853, to May 22nd, 1854, both inclusive," gives the following summary of their expenditure :—

GENERAL EXPENDITURE.

				£	s.	d.
11,619	Weavers...	at 6s. 0d. each	... ...	3,485	14	0
2,343	Winders and Warpers	„ 6s. 0d.	„	702	18	0
523	Beamers and Twisters	„ 6s. 0d.	„	156	18	0
7,791	Helpers	„ 3s. 0d.	„	268	13	0
1,989	Weavers	„ 5s. 6d.	„	2,196	19	6
27	Ditto	„ 4s. 6d.	„	6	1	6
843	Winders and Warpers	„ 5s. 6d.	„	232	7	6
39	Ditto	„ 4s. 6d.	„	8	15	6
226	Twisters and Drawers	„ 5s. 6d.	„	62	3	0
73,562	Weavers	„ 5s. 0d.	„	18,390	10	0
6,247	Winders and Warpers	„ 5s. 0d.	„	1,561	15	0
1,685	Beamers and Twisters	„ 5s. 0d.	„	421	5	0
114,770	Weavers	„ 4s. 0d.	„	22,954	0	0
12,779	Winders and Warpers	„ 4s. 0d.	„	2,555	16	0
3,284	Beamers and Twisters	„ 4s. 0d.	„	656	16	0
2,271	Weavers	„ 3s. 0d.	„	340	13	0
546	Winders and Warpers	„ 3s. 0d.	„	81	18	0
140	Beamers and Twisters	„ 3s. 0d.	„	21	0	0
15,446	Helpers and other hands	„ 2s. 6d.	„	1,930	15	0
12,642	Helpers	„ 2s. 0d.	„	1,264	4	0
3,434	Helpers and other hands	„ 1s. 6d.	„	257	11	0
5,372	Helpers and others...	„ 1s. 0d.	„	268	12	0
871	Helpers	„ 0s. 6d.	„	21	15	6
	Cash to Dressers' Committee			446	5	4
	Cash to Children and other Distressed Cases ...			1,363	7	3½
	Cash to Cloth Lookers' Committee			20	0	0
	Cash paid over to other Committees in Town ...			120	17	3½

	£	s.	d.
Cash to Strikes, Lock-outs, Victims, &c., in other Districts	912	9	11½
Cash to Executive Committee, Propagandist Committee, and Assistants, with Railway Fares	1,368	9	0½
Printing, Stationery, &c.	1,625	1	3½
Cash Removing Families, Emigration, &c. ...	207	0	9
Rent of Committee Rooms, Pay Rooms, &c. ...	80	8	3
Committee Expenses	36	13	11½
Salaries of Secretary, Assistant, and Treasurer	66	19	0
Incidental Expenses...	96	15	2½
Balance on hand	38	13	0¼
TOTAL EXPENDITURE	£64,230	0	10¾

TOTAL OF 38 WEEKS.

Number of Hands paid...278,629.

	£.	s.	d.
Amount paid to Hands...	57,847	0	6
Amount paid to Distressed Cases and to Children...	1,363	7	3½
Amount of Working Expenses, including £207. 0s. 9d., for removing Families	3,481	7	6

AVERAGE OF 38 WEEKS.

Number of hands paid Weekly. .7332½.

	£	s.	d.
Amount paid to Hands Weekly	1469	13	2
Amount paid to Distressed Cases and to Children	33	4	11⅛
Weekly Amount of Working Expenses	91	12	3⅝

The largest amounts contributed to this fund were,—Blackburn, £18,645. 1s. 7¼d.; Preston, £7475. 3s. 8¾d.; Stockport, £6916. 7s. 10d.

In addition to the weavers' and spinners' committees, a third was formed called the "Amalgamated," which received subscriptions for the general cause, and afterwards apportioned the fund amongst the various classes locked out.

The following shows the total expenditure of all the operative committees, from the commencement, including expenses of every kind[1]:—

WEEK.	TOTAL AMOUNT. £	s.	d.	WEEK.	TOTAL AMOUNT. £	s.	d.	WEEK.	TOTAL AMOUNT. £	s.	d.
1	80	1	3½	14	3094	12	6½	27	3592	19	7½
2	381	6	6	15	3089	2	5	28	3634	0	2½
3	561	17	5½	16	3169	5	10½	29	3610	11	8½
4	671	3	8½	17	3213	11	1½	30	3480	19	3
5	707	12	6½	18	3253	3	3	31	3619	14	0
6	1153	15	6½	19	4012	1	8½	32	3604	0	5
7	1317	5	9	20	3237	5	11¾	33	3553	4	10
8	1684	8	6	21	3366	12	4¼	34	3337	0	5
9	2521	9	5½	22	3250	15	0½	35	2808	3	11
10	2569	5	7½	23	3426	19	6½	36	1819	8	10
11	2830	18	3	24	3281	9	9	37	946	15	0
12	2832	1	2½	25	3711	9	7	38	995	15	5½
13	2939	2	7	26	3572	12	6				

Further sums were received and distributed amongst the distressed operatives; but no other balance sheets were published.

From the report of the "Master Spinners and Manufacturers' Defence

[1] Preston Guardian, May 20th, 1854.

Fund," the following table of the probable cost of the struggle is extracted:—

Capital sunk in the establishments of the Associated Manufacturers of Preston...		£1,000,000
Estimated trading loss to the Employers	£50,000	
Loss by depreciation, interest, and other contingencies for 36 weeks	67,000	
Unavoidable expenses in wages, fuel, and other items, during the Strike	28,000	
Loss in working machinery without adequate number, and with inferior description of hands ...	20,000	
		165,000
Loss of wages to the Operatives during the strike		250,000
Loss to the contributors to the Strike Fund, whose contributions have become abortive by its failure:—		
Blackburn	£30,000	
Stockport	10,000	
Preston	7,000	
Ashton, Hyde, Glossop, and Stalybridge ...	10,500	
Over-Darwen	4,000	
All other places and Trades	35,500	
		97,000
Estimated loss of profits to Shopkeepers and Innkeepers	11,250	
Estimated loss to Carriers, Railway Companies, Mechanics, Dressers, Sizers, and other ancillary occupations...	10,000	
		21,250
Total loss to the community by the Preston Strike... ...		£533,250

Perhaps the above figures are as correct as the circumstances permitted, but some of the conclusions are by no means so satisfactory. How the £97,000. contributed by other towns, and spent by the operatives principally in Preston, can be included in the loss to the *community* is difficult to understand. Even the largest portion of the operatives' subscriptions from other towns, can scarcely, with justice, be termed individual loss; for, had they refused to enter into the contest, an amount equal or greater would have been deducted from their earnings, as was proved by the result in many cases. They, at the worst, merely contributed what they perceived they could not retain without such contribution. Had the operatives of Preston gained the "ten per cent.," the operatives of Blackburn, etc. would have retained theirs; and, of course, as the result at Preston was unfavourable, they were compelled to submit to a reduction. How the £11,250. loss to innkeepers and shopkeepers can be *added* to the loss of the capitalists and the loss of the operatives' wages is equally mysterious; as the deficiency referred to could not have taken place, had the £250,000. operatives' wages been forthcoming in the local market. However, the sacrifice was, under any calculation, large enough for all practical teaching. The Preston strikes have furnished valuable material for future reflection, but they have not yet evolved a practical principle, calculated to put an end to such struggles. The passage from serfdom to perfect freedom has not yet been accomplished. The victory obtained by the employers merely demonstrated that which every one previously knew, viz., the strongest party in the end would win. But this is not sufficient to set at rest the mighty question, which yearly throbs with increased vitality beneath the surging mass of mercantile contention. No one really wins in these struggles. They are essentially productive of loss to all, except in so far as they inculcate lessons of wisdom. It is, therefore, the duty and interest of all, that the differences which must occur occasionally between the buyers and sellers of labour, as well as of any other commodity, should be settled in a commercial, and not in a military spirit. A talented writer in the Westminster Review, makes the following observations, which are worthy of the serious consideration of every well-wisher to social progress and national prosperity :—

"Of those problems which this age *must solve*, if it would live and prosper—which it can neither pass by on the other side, nor push off upon its successor—the *true and fit relation between employer and employed*—is one of the most pressing, and the most perplexing. To ascertain what it ought to be, and to make it what it should be, is one of the first tasks allotted to our epoch and country."

The select committee appointed to enquire into the expediency of establishing equitable tribunals for the amicable adjustment of differences between masters and workmen, issued their report last year. A majority of the witnesses examined, express themselves in favour of boards of arbitration between masters and workmen, but they differ as to the constitution of the proposed boards, and still more as regards their jurisdiction. The existing law on the subject of arbitration (the act of 5th George IV., cap. 96), is found to be nearly inoperative, as hardly any one resorts to it, and few are aware of its existence. Three causes are assigned for the failure of this measure;—viz., the unwillingness to go before a magistrate; the reluctance to defer to the decision of unknown arbitrators; and the objection of workmen to the magistrates in manufacturing districts, who are generally manufacturers themselves. To obviate these objections, it has been proposed to establish in the various manufacturing districts, "Courts of Conciliation," like the "*Conseils de Prud'hommes*," in France. The committee believe that the formation of such courts in this country, more especially in the large commercial, manufacturing, and mining districts, would be beneficial; and suggest the introduction of such a measure as an amendment to the present "Arbitration Act." In these "Courts of Conciliation" masters and operatives choose referees from their own class or calling, equal in number, who are presided over by a chairman, unconnected with either party, elected by the referees. The tribunal would be appointed to act for a certain period. These boards of arbitration, on being licensed by the secretary of state, would have full power to act and decide on all questions of existing contracts. The committee, however, think it would be highly impolitic to give to these or to any other tribunal power of forcibly regulating the rate of wages.

ADDITIONAL STATISTICS WITH REFERENCE TO TRADE AND COMMERCE.

The following is an estimate of the quantity of cotton wool imported into Great Britain during the years specified:—

In 1801	... ... 56,004,305 lbs.	In 1841	... ...489,900,000 lbs.
1811	... ... 91,576,535 „	1851	... ...760,142,000 „
1821	... ...129,536,620 „	1855	... ...901,138,000 „
1831	... ...280,674,853 „	1856	... ... 1,021,021,000 „ [m]

The relative proportion of the cotton imported into the various ports of the kingdom, in 1851, is as follows:—Liverpool, 1,748,946 bales; London, 65,800; Glasgow, 67,000; Bristol and Hull, 21,800; total, 1,903,546.

In 1855, Liverpool, 2,142,699; London, 101,000; Bristol and Hull, 700; Scotland, 33,700; total imports into Great Britain in 1855, 2,278,099 bales.

In 1856, Liverpool, 2,308,660; London, 92,700; Bristol and Hull, 4,400; Scotland, 62,300; total 2,468,160.

In 1791, only 68,404 bales were imported into Liverpool; and in 1811, 174,132; in 1821, 413,182; in 1831, 791,582; in 1841, 1,164,269.[n]

In 1850, the actual quantity and value of cotton consumed in the whole kingdom was 584,000,000 lbs., of the value of £17,374,000. The value of the goods manufactured therefrom was £48,490,300.

The value of the goods and twist exported in 1850, is as follows:—goods, £21,432,000; twist, £6,820,000; total, £28,252,000.

The value of the home consumption for the same year was £20,227,600.[o]

In 1850, in England, Wales, Scotland, and Ireland, there were 1,932 cotton factories, containing 20,977,017 spindles for spinning yarn, and 249,627 power-looms for weaving cloths.

In Lancashire, the number of cotton mills in 1850, was 1,235; spindles, 13,955,497; power-looms, 176,947.

In Lancashire, in 1850, there were 26 woollen factories, 238,492 spindles and 4,839 power-looms. In the United Kingdom, 1,497 factories, 1,356,691 spindles, and 9,439 power-looms.

The total number of worsted factories in the United Kingdom in 1850, was 501, spindles 875,830, power-looms 32,617.

---

m Holt's Annual Circular. n Ibid.

o Du Fay and Co.'s Annual Circular.

The total number of flax mills in the three kingdoms in 1850, was 393, spindles 965,031, power-looms 3,670. Lancashire contained 9 flax mills, with 117,356 spindles.

The number of silk mills in the United Kingdom, in 1850, was 277, containing 1,225,560 spindles, and 6,092 power-looms. Lancashire had 29 mills, 162,988 spindles, and 1,977 power-looms.[d]

In 1856, the number of factories in the united kingdom amounted to 5,117, against 4,600 in 1850, and 4,217 in 1838. Of these 2,210 are cotton factories; 1,505 wollen; 525 worsted; 417 flax; and 460 silk. The cotton factories have increased 142 per cent, and the silk 66 per cent. The number of spindles in 1856 amounted to 33,503,580; power-looms 369,205. The actual horse power returned was 161,435. The average value of the cotton goods and yarn exported in the three years, 1853, 1854, and 1855 was, in round numbers, £31,000,000, of woollen and worsted goods and yarn £10,000,000. [e]

According to the parliamentary report, the number of persons employed in factories in the United Kingdom, in 1835, 1850, and in 1856, was as follows:—[c]

	1835.	1850.	1856.
Number of male persons between 13 and 18 years of age	47,768	67,864	72,220
Number of females above 13 years of age	167,130	329,577	387,806
Number of males above 18 years of age	82,336	157,866	176,400
Number of boys under 13 years of age	27,715	21,137	46,071
Number of girls under 13 years of age	28,378	19,638	
TOTAL	353,327	596,082	682,497

In 1856, the number of firms engaged in cotton spinning and the manufacture of cotton goods, in Preston, was about 37; in spinning only, 15; in the manufacture only, 23; total 75. Four new mills were likewise in course of erection, or being filled with machinery.

In the flax trade, in 1856, but two firms were engaged; in the worsted, one, and in silk none. A very few mixed goods are woven in the town.

In 1836, according to Mr. Baines, Preston produced chiefly the following description of cotton cloths:—Superfine printing calicoes and muslins, ginghams, jaconets, muslins, and cotton shirtings. At the present time the character of the goods manufactured remains much the same. The greatest increase has, however, taken place, relatively, in the cotton shirting department.

o Parliamntary Returns: Factory Inspectors' Report.
c The factory act began to be effective in 1834 d Parliamentary Returns.

Royal Hotel & Museum, Southport, Lancashire

Lord St. Southport, Lancashire

Messrs Horrocks, Miller & Co. Yard Factory, Preston.

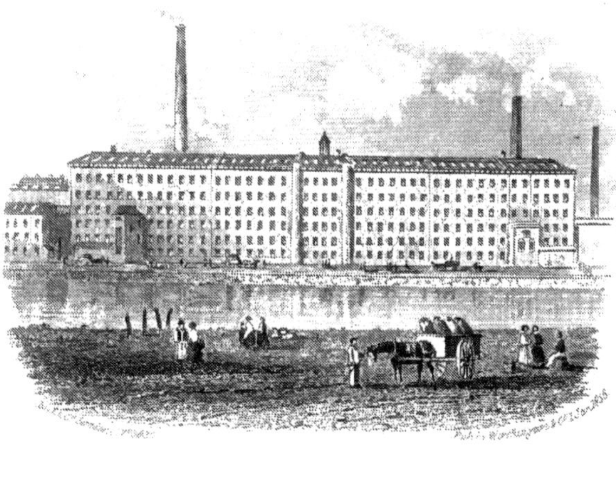

Several of the manufacturing establishments of Preston are very extensive, and the goods produced maintain a first-class reputation in the markets. This is especially the case with "Horrockses' long cloths," a species of stout shirting, manufactured by the firm of Horrockses, Miller, and Co. This firm now possesses ten mills, driven by twelve steam engines, with an aggregate nominal power of 540 horses. Above 3,000 hands are employed, whose labour combined with the action of 154,334 spindles and 2,775 looms, produces weekly about 95,000 lbs. of yarn, and 400,000 yards of cloth weekly. Messrs. Ainsworth and Co. run 54,696 spindles, and 1,100 looms. The large weaving shed belonging to this firm covers 6922 square yards of land, and will contain 2000 thirty-inch power-looms. Messrs. Swainson and Birley's establishment (the "Big Factory," and those of Messrs. Napier and Goodair, as well as some others, are very extensive.

There are likewise in Preston several establishments for the founding of metals and the manufacture of machinery, and some of the cotton manufacturers employ a large number of mechanics, in connection with their mills.

PART II.—TOPOGRAPHY, ETC.

General Aspect of the Town—Preston in the Seventeenth Century—Bucks' Prospect in 1728—Lang's Map in 1774—Shakeshaft's Map in 1809—Miller's Map in 1822—Survey by J. J. Myres, in 1836 and 1846—Further Extensions—PUBLIC SQUARES, PARKS, etc.—Market-place—Winckley-square—Stephenson's Terrace, Deepdale-road—Avenham Walk—Moor Park—The Orchard.—PUBLIC BUILDINGS, INSTITUTIONS, ETC.—The Town Hall—The Corn Exchange—The Court House and Prison—Magistrates' Court and Police Station—Baths and Wash-houses—Fire Brigade Building—Overseers' Buildings—Workhouse—House of Recovery—Dispensary—Gas-works—Water-works—Theatre Royal—Temperance Hall—The Preston Railway Stations.—Dr. Shepherd's Library—Institution for the Diffusion of Knowledge—Literary and Philosophical Institution—The Winckley Club—Law Library.—The Press.—BANKS—Old Bank—Savings Bank—Lawe and Co.—Roskell and Arrowsmith—Lancaster Banking Co.—Preston Banking Co.—BRIDGES—Walton, Penwortham, Tram-road, Brockholes, North Union, East Lancashire.—CHURCHES, CHAPELS, SCHOOLS, CHARITIES, ETC.—Parish Church, St. George's—St. Peter's—St. Paul's—Christ Church—St. Mary's—St. Thomas's—St. James's—All Saint's.—ROMAN CATHOLIC CHAPELS—St. Mary's—St. Wilfrid's—St. Ignatius's—St. Augustine's—St. Walburge's.—CHAPELS OF PROTESTANT DISSENTERS—Unitarian—Friend's—Baptist—Methodist—Independent—Episcopalian—New Jerusalem—Mormon, etc.—The Cemetery.—PUBLIC SCHOOLS—Educational Statistics—Grammar School—Blue Coat School—Commercial—St. John's—Christ Church—St. Peter's—St. Paul's—St. James's—St. Thomas's—St. Mary's—German's—All Saints—Trinity.—ROMAN CATHOLIC SCHOOLS—St. Wilfrid's—St. Augustine's—St. Ignatius's—St. Walburge's.—DISSENTERS' SCHOOLS, ETC.—Wesleyan School—Friends' School—Ragged School—Private Schools.—PUBLIC CHARITIES, PROVIDENT SOCIETIES, ETC.—LAW—Public Offices—County Court, Wapentake Court, etc.

PRESTON is a borough and market town, situated in the township and parish of Preston. It is the principal town in the hundred of Amounderness, and the seat of the legal offices in connection with the duchy and county palatine of Lancaster. Its longitude is 2 deg., 42 min., 30 sec. west from Greenwich; its latitude 53 deg. 45 min. 24 sec., north. The true time at Preston is about 10 min. 50 sec. later than at Greenwich observatory.[a]

Notwithstanding the occasional carpings of a splenetic traveller, who may have passed through the place in foul weather, and visited the sins of the elements upon the streets and buildings, Preston is generally

a These figures are from observations by Mr. Moses Holden, astronomer, Jordan-street, Preston.

and deservedly recognised as one of the cleanest and most pleasantly situated manufacturing towns in England. The cotton factories are erected chiefly to the north and east of the old aristocratic borough, significantly named "Proud Preston," and do not as yet materially interfere with the more "fashionable" or picturesque sections of the district. The generality of manufacturing towns rear their tall chimneys from the lower level and the sloping sides of mountain valleys. They corrupt and almost solidify, with the *debris* of the mills and workshops, the once limpid streamlets; which, converted into open common sewers, crawl like slimy envenomed snakes, through their very hearts, and pollute the surrounding atmosphere; while black heated smoke, belched forth in dense volumes from the sooty nostrils of the forge and the engine furnace, scorches the scanty herbage struggling for existence on the neighbouring sterile slopes. Preston is a striking exception to this rule. Situated upon an elevated bank above the Ribble valley, with a gently undulating surface, it possesses not only the advantage of good natural drainage, but its atmosphere is hourly subjected to the untrammeled action and salutary influence of either the sea or the mountain breeze. That melancholy mixture of smoke and fog, which, during a portion of the winter months, enshrouds many of our modern "hives of industry" in semi-darkness at noon day, is seldom seen at Preston, except in a very diluted condition. The streets and squares are generally clean and well paved, though some exceptions to this rule may yet be found, which are neither creditable to the owners of the properties nor the authorities. Great improvement has, however, latterly been effected in this respect by the operations of the local board of health; and still more and efficient purgation may yet be anticipated on the completion of the extensive public sewerage now in course of construction.

The main thoroughfare of Preston, composed of Fishergate and Church-street, intersects the town nearly in a straight line from east to west. Several good streets from the north enter this line of road nearly at right angles. The principal northern thoroughfare, or what will speedily become such, is not yet completed. It forms nearly a continuous line from the "Gallows Hill" to Church-street. Its southern extremity passes through the "Orchard" and the property of the earl of Derby, in Molyneux-square and the Shambles. From the elegant and substantial buildings erected on this portion of the new street, by the noble proprietor, from designs by the late Mr. Dawson, it is probable that in the course of a few years, Lancaster-road will not only become the handsomest public thoroughfare in Preston, but one that will exhibit artistic excellence rarely surpassed in the street architecture of the largest provincial towns. The Friargate forms still a busy and important thoroughfare, leading from the

Market-place in a north-westerly direction, to the junction of the roads from Lancaster and the Fylde. Fishergate and Church-street divided the old town of Preston nearly into two equal parts. Such, however, is not the case at present. The principal extension of the town, since the introduction of the cotton trade, has been on the north, the north-east, and north-west of this line; the steep bank of the Ribble valley having interfered, to some extent, with its progress southward. The mass of building, exclusive of many suburban erections, extends over an area of about a mile and a half from east to west, by one mile from north to south. The great bulk of the town has been erected during the present century, and, consequently, except in the centre, bears an unmistakably modern aspect.

It is generally thought, previously to the struggle between Charles I. and the parliament, that the town did not contain many more than 3000 inhabitants, and that in point of population it had remained nearly stationary a considerable period. At the end of the seventeenth century it had expanded to about 6000, and did not receive any material addition for nearly one hundred years.[a] In 1801, the impetus imparted by the cotton trade, had raised the number of inhabitants in the township to 11,887.

A large engraving, styled "The South Prospect of Preston, in the county of Lancaster," (a reduced copy of which, in outline, illustrates the present work), was published in 1728, by S. and N. Buck. This view will convey a better notion of the character and extent of the town than any verbal description. The parish church steeple exhibits, at its north western angle, a smaller tower, surmounted by a spire. Church-street, or Fenkel-street, does not appear to have extended very much further than Sir Edward Stanley's house. Avenham walk is quite detached from the town, and "Frenchwood," between it and Walton bridge, presents no more than a couple of trees; a few others skirt the river on the plain below. The old bridge at Walton appears in excellent condition. The river Darwen, though somewhat incorrectly represented in proportion and detail, meanders in its old channel, from Walton-hall to the Ribble. The double "horse shoe form" is an error. The curve next to its junction with the Ribble should be omitted, as there is not sufficient space for the site of the Roman station. The true size and form is given opposite page 38 of this work, from Robert Porter's survey. The hill upon which Walton church stands, is not sufficiently elevated. A similar error is committed on the opposite side of the picture. The site of Penwortham church and the Priory, is much too nearly on a level with the Holme below. The latter appears as two distinct islands. The windmill at the end of Friar-

a Taylor's notes to Kuerden's description.

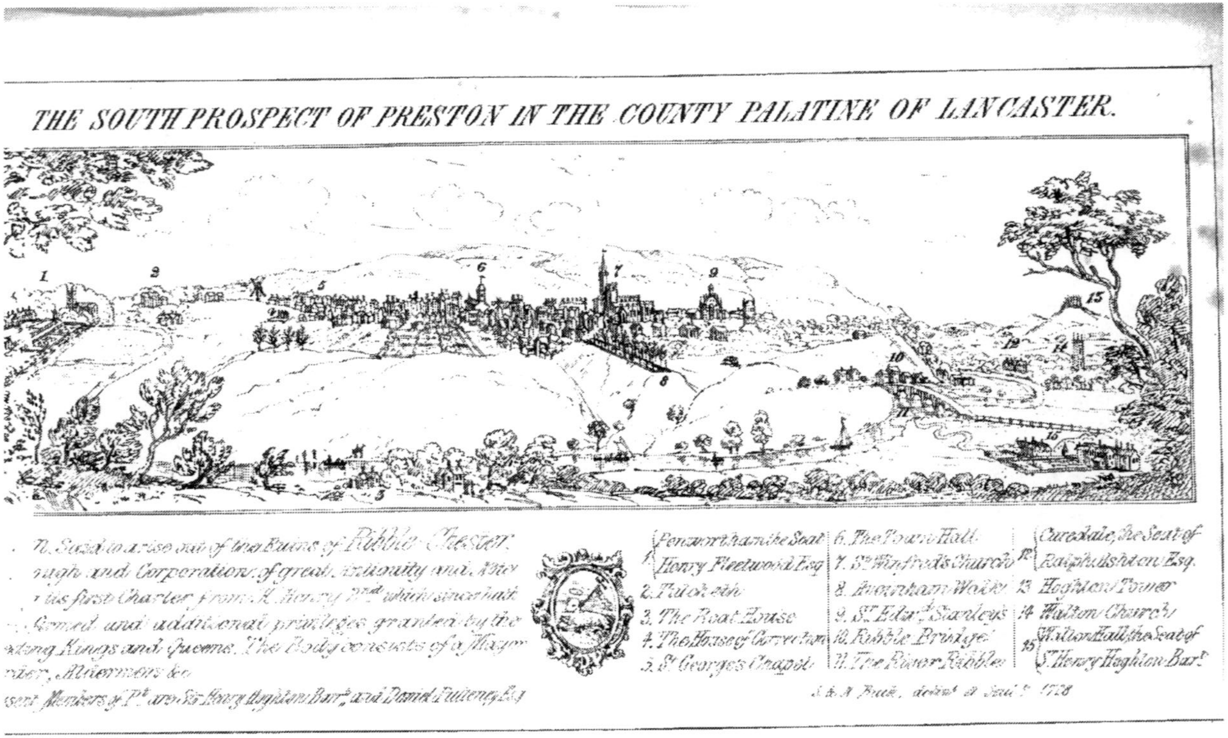
THE SOUTH PROSPECT OF PRESTON IN THE COUNTY PALATINE OF LANCASTER.
1 Penwortham the Seat of Henry Fleetwood Esq
2 Tulketh
3 The Boat House
4 The House of Correction
5 St. George's Chapel
6 The Town Hall
7 St. Winifred's Church
8 Avenham Walk
9 St. Edw.d Stanley's
10 Ribble Bridge
11 The River Ribble
12 Cuerdale, the Seat of Ralph Assheton Esq.
13 Hoghton Tower
14 Walton Church
15 Walton Hall the Seat of S.r Henry Hoghton Bar.t
...n. Said to arise out of the Ruins of Ribble Chester.
...ugh and Corporation of great Antiquity and hav...
... its first Charter from K. Henry 2.nd which since hath ...
... firmed and additional privileges granted by the ...
...ding Kings and Queens. The Body consists of a Mayor ...
...rder, Aldermen &c.
...sent Members of P.t are Sir Henry Hoghton Bar.t and Daniel Pulteney Esq
S. & N. Buck, delin.t et Sculp. 1728

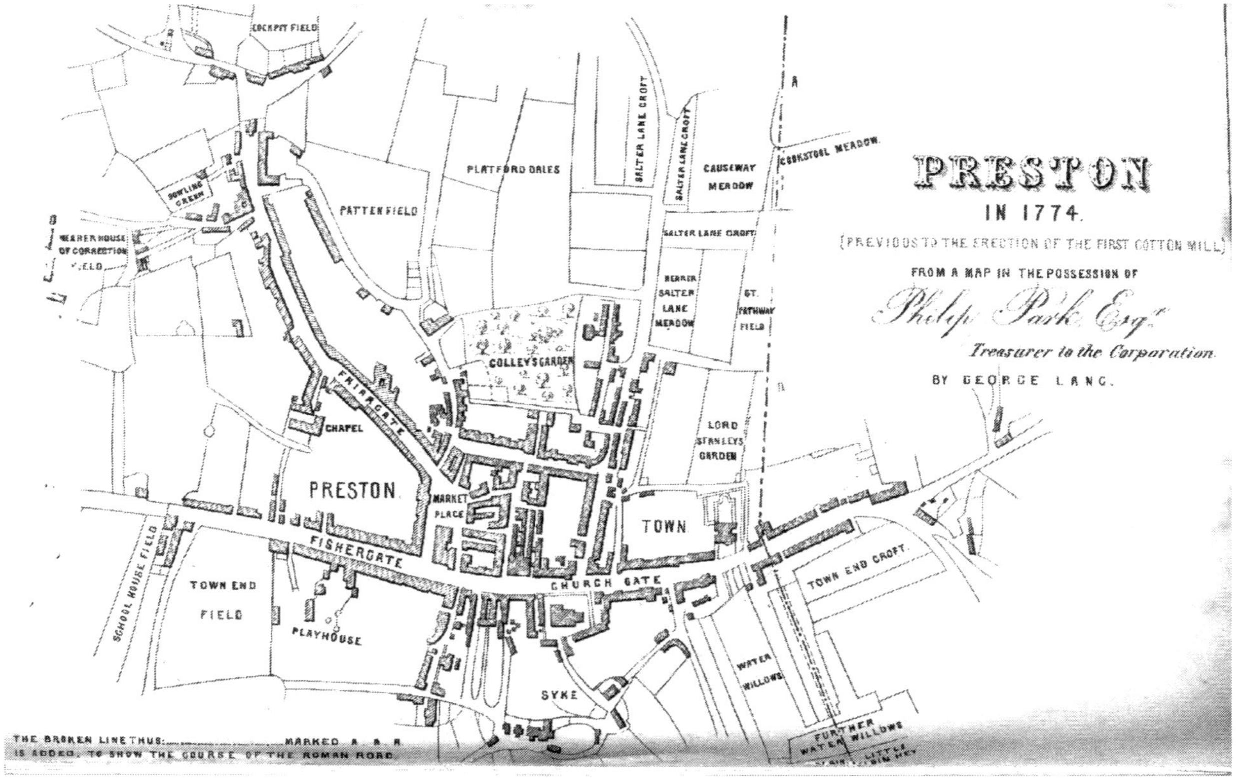
PRESTON
IN 1774.
(PREVIOUS TO THE ERECTION OF THE FIRST COTTON MILL)
FROM A MAP IN THE POSSESSION OF
Philip Park, Esqr.
Treasurer to the Corporation.
BY GEORGE LANG.
COCKPIT FIELD
BOWLING GREEN
WEARER HOUSE OF CORRECTION
PATTEN FIELD
PLATFORD DALES
SALTER LANE CROFT
SALTER LANE CROFT
CAUSEWAY MEADOW
COCKSTOOL MEADOW
SALTER LANE CROFT
NEARER SALTER LANE MEADOW
ST. PATHWAY FIELD
COLLEY'S GARDEN
LORD STANLEY'S GARDEN
FRIARGATE
CHAPEL
PRESTON
MARKET PLACE
TOWN
FISHERGATE
CHURCH GATE
TOWN END CROFT
TOWN END FIELD
SCHOOL HOUSE FIELD
PLAYHOUSE
SYKE
WATER WILLOWS
FURTHER WATER WILLOWS
A
THE BROKEN LINE THUS: MARKED A. A. A.
IS ADDED, TO SHOW THE COURSE OF THE ROMAN ROAD.

gate, from which one of the barricades, erected in 1715, took its name, is outside the town. The "Old Friary," described as the "House of Correction," is likewise detached from the mass of buildings.

A map of the township of Preston was executed by George Lang, a local surveyor of some repute, in 1774. It is at present in the possession of Mr. Philip Park, treasurer to the corporation. It exhibits "Preston Town" at the period immediately preceding the introduction of the cotton manufacture. From this plan it appears that the number of edifices in the borough had increased but very little since the time of Kuerden.[e] The chief mass of building, with a slight exception, on the south of Church-street, is included in a square formed by the present Lord-street, St. John-street, Church-street, and the west side of the Market-place. From its peculiar configuration, this area has evidently constituted the extent of the ancient burg, or walled town, in the time of the Plantagenets. On the north, are a few buildings about the "vicarage" and the present Tithe-barn-street. Chadwick's orchard appears as "Colley's Garden." The enclosure in the rear of "Patten House" is described as "Lord Stanley's Garden." The old "Play-house" is indicated as situated in the midst of an open space up Woodcock's court. Fishergate extends no further than Mount-street. Church-street reaches nearly to the present House of Correction. Friargate appears to be the longest street, although the old "Fighting Cocks Inn," now superseded by the Adelphi, is still a little way in the country. The "Friary" remains the prison described by Kuerden, and is situated at some distance from the town. The site of one of the ancient "cucking stools" is indicated by the name of a field near Meadow-street. Another "cucking stool" stood not far from the present House of Correction. In 1683, the bailiffs were fined 40s. for want of a cuck stool in the town, but the fine was remitted on their supplying the deficiency.[d] The accompanying print is copied from the centre portion of Lang's map.

The town of Preston must, at this period, have presented but a very melancholy aspect. Several of the channels ran down the centre of the streets. Previously to the year 1699, the town was not even lighted by oil lamps. The municipal authorities of that period resolved that, "for the better going in the streets in the winter evenings in the decrease of the moon, or when clouds interpose, it has been thought necessary that some lamps or convex lights should be provided." One was procured at the expense of the corporation, and three others were furnished by private gentlemen. One of these was placed in the Market-square, one near the Parish church, one at the top of Main-sprit-wiend, and another near the Butter-cross. A huge

d Preston in the Olden Time: A lecture by W. Dobson. e See page 208.

lantern, formerly carried by the mayor of the borough is still in the possession of the corporation.[c]

Shakeshaft's map of the town was published in 1809. Though the town had more than doubled its population, scarcely any building is shown on this plan to the west of the "tram road" and the Lancaster canal, with the exception of the "Old Friary" and Butler-street. The greater portion of the land between Friargate, Fishergate, and the canal, is covered with ornamental and kitchen gardens. On the east, Stanley-street exhibits but very few houses. Beyond the new House of Correction, a few cottages and weaving shops, the nucleus of "New Preston," stand at a little distance from the rest of the town. "The Park" yet honestly responds to its cognomen. With the exception of a few houses on the north of Church-street, this now densely populated district, is clothed with verdure and stately trees. Spring Gardens and Everton Gardens are two rows of cottages, with veritable vegetable producing enclosures intervening, the present North-road as yet having no existence. High-street forms the northern boundary in the centre opposite to the "Orchard." Friargate exhibits an unsteady straggling towards the north-west as far as the Moss factory. Singleton-row and Crown-street are detached and surrounded by fields. The entire space south of the Syke-brook or "Avenham Sykes," now the common sewer, is in a rural state from Vauxhall-road to its junction with the Ribble, with the exception of a few houses in Avenham-lane, the "Folly" and Avenham-house. On the south-east, Lark-hill appears a suburban residence, detached from the town, Water-street and a few others of less importance alone creeping towards the "Frenchwood factory."

In 1811, the population of the township had increased to 17,065.

In 1819, the number of inhabited houses was 1,546; uninhabited, including new buildings, 170, and the population 21,958.

In 1821, the township of Preston contained 24,627 persons.

In 1822, Mr. William Miller published a new edition of Shakeshaft's map. The chief distinguishing features between this plan and its predecessor are a slight extension of the extremities of the town, and a greater compactness of building about the centre. North-road and Park-road are both opened, but not much built upon.

In 1831, the township of Preston contained 33,112 inhabitants.

The earl of Derby's house, situated on the north side of Church-street, near the present Derby-street, was pulled down in 1835. This building was named "Patten House." It came into possession of the Derby family after the marriage of Sir Thomas Stanley, in 1688, with Elizabeth, only

c Dobson's Lecture

daughter and heiress of T. Patten, esq., of Preston. It was a large substantial building in the domestic architecture of the period. It stood at some distance from the line of street, the intervening area being enclosed. The Derby family added an iron gateway surmounted by the arms of the family.[d] On the destruction of this residence, some human skeletons were found, which occasioned at the time much idle speculation. From its situation, it is more than probable they were the remains of parties slain in some of the many conflicts which occurred during the civil wars. This was doubtless the house described as belonging to "Sir Henry Horton," by the chroniclers of the seige, in 1715.[e]

In 1836, Mr. J. J. Myres published his map. The population at this time exceeded 36,000. A great change is apparent since 1822. The building in the centre of the town wears a more solid aspect, with the exception of the "Orchard," the land about Derby-street, gardens between Lune-street and the Market-place, and some others to the south of Fishergate. The "Green Bank" and "Maudland" estates are "laid out" for building land, and the Moor-park is enclosed. There are many new streets in the neighbourhood of Fylde-road and "Spital's-moss," and much building land occupied between Fishergate and Bridge-lane, as well as a little to the west of Bow-lane. Avenham-lane has become a principal thoroughfare, and exhibits many branch streets. Between Oxford-street and Alfred street, however, the land is merely "laid out." Such is likewise the condition of the plot between Winckley-square and Avenham-house. On the south-east, London-road has extended over the Swilbrook, and modern Fishwick begins to appear. A large portion of the space between Lark-hill and London-road is, notwithstanding, though marked out on the map, yet unbuilt upon. To the east of Park-road and Park-lane, several branch streets appear. Deepdale-terrace is formed, and Ribbleton-lane shows a few scattered buildings.

The population, according to the census of 1841, was 50,073. In 1846, Mr. Myres published a new edition of his map. The chief peculiarity which it presents, is the increase of buildings upon sites previously laid out. As the town has considerably extended since its publication, Mr. Myres is at the present time engaged in the preparation of another edition.[f]

---

d This gateway at present ornaments the entrance to Howick House, the residence of Thomas Norris, esq. It was purchased, on the demolition of Patten House, by the late W. Rawstorne, esq., and placed in its present position.

e See page 227.

f The Park estate, belonging Saml. Pole Shawe, esq., was opened for building land about the year 1822; Green Bank estate and Ox Heys estate, belonging to the late William Tomlinson and Thomas Tomlinson, esqs., in 1834, to which was added, in 1856, by purchase from John Myers, esq., 100 acres from the Moor Hall estate; Maudlands estate, belonging Edward Pedder, esq., in 1834; Peel Hall

In 1851, the population of the township amounted to 68,356, and it has considerably increased since. After the passing of the Reform Bill, in 1832, the township of Fishwick was incorporated with the borough of Preston. Fishwick had 287 inhabitants in 1801; 295 in 1811; 284 in 1821; 759 in 1831; 756 in 1841; and 1,005 in 1851. The total population of the *borough* of Preston was thus, at the last census, 69,361.

PUBLIC SQUARES, PARKS, Etc.

The Market-place is simply at the present time an opened paved area, nearly square in form. In the reign of Henry VIII., it was described by Leland, the king's antiquary and topograper, as possessing some attraction, though whether from its beauty or its size is rather doubtful, owing to the quaint and curt style of expression used by the erudite gentleman. He merely intimates that "the Market-place of the town is fair."[b] All the buildings which existed in Leland's time have been succeeded by more modern erections, and only a few remains of their immediate successors are now in existence. In 1855, the fine old picturesque pile of "Elizabethan" architecture, which formed so prominent a feature of the Preston Market-place, was razed to the ground. The buildings had become somewhat "rickety," and the corporation proposed to erect a new Town Hall and Exchange upon the site. This intention, however, has not yet been carried out, consequently, at the present time, the only available benefit derived from the demolition of these interesting specimens of the domestic architecture of the seventeenth century, is an increase of market accommodation.

These old houses possess some historical interest. Adam Morte, the mayor, who, together with his son, fell in the seige of Preston, in 1643, occupied one of them.[c] The date of the erection of this edifice (1629), was carved over a doorway, together with the initials I. I. A.[d] The lower house at the eastern corner was an older erection. When the beam over the window was exposed, it exhibited the date 1618, and the initials I . . A.[f]

estate (135 acres), belonging to the trustees of Gen. Fletcher, in 1846; Lancaster-road and Harrison's Hill, in 1835; Freehold Park estate, Fulwood (45 acres), in 1850; Hole House estate, in 1855, (belonging to Lady Shelley,) about 30 acres. In 1851, Swainson, Birley, and Co. opened 7 acres, purchased from Lord Derby; and Edward Stanley, esq., opened, in 1852, several detached fields in the vicinity of Fishergate. The estates at Tulketh and Ashton (100 acres), the property of J. Bray, esq., E. Pedder, esq., and Jno. Able Smith, esq., were opened for building in 1853.

b Leland's Itin., vol. 5, fo. 84, p. 91.

c Morte is described by Prince Rupert, as Major (Mayor), but from the records of the corporation, it appears that, though elected, he refused to serve. See chap. 6, page 235.

d The "frame-work" forming the front of this house was purchased by Mr. Richards, and sent to Longridge, with the view to its re-erection upon the bowling-green belonging to the Railway Hotel.

f The initials I. A. represent James Archer, the name of the original proprietor. The larger building showing the letters I. I. A, (Jenkinson, John and Ann) was built under instructions

The only buildings now remaining in the Market-place, of this period, are the low shops on the western side near Friargate. But the oaken framework has been plastered over, and their true character destroyed. The "Grey Horse Inn," Church-street, is the only good specimen left in Preston of this class of architecture. The environs, however, yet present several excellent examples.

From the earliest incorporation of the borough, a "cross" or ornamental structure of some description, appears to have occupied the centre of the Market-place. Mr. Peter Whittle, a few years ago, published a lithographic print, purporting to be a "perspective view" of the cross, as it appeared in 1273.

The "perspective view" of this "gem of the olden times," as it is styled, however, appears to have been solely indebted for its existence to the ingenious fancy of a modern local architect, assisted by the following description, quoted by Mr. Whittle :—

"The ancient cross in the Market-place, at Preston, in Lancashire, was erected in the year of redemption D,CCCCCCC,LXXIIII—temp. Edward 1st, by Willus Fitzpaul, Armiger, and Burgess in Parliament. This cross consisted of V octagon steps each way from the pavement, and III tiers,—pedestal oblong with blank niches, containing seats for pilgrims—Zig Zag Norman heads terminating at the uppermost step, and slender shafts after the Norman fashion at each angle. Second tier contained within ornamented Norman canopied niches, the statuary, viz.—St. Wilfrid, Archbishop of York, and patron Saint of the church, facing the east. The rest were the B. V. Mary and the Infant Jesus.—St. Joseph, the other was St. John Baptist, patron of the Gild—the Agnus Dei, or the holy Lamb, was placed within a foliated escutcheon, and the motto—"PRINCEPS PACIS," in relievo—the third tier of masonry, had blank niches with Norman heads plain. The whole was XXI feet high exclusive of the steps; on the basement, under the figure of Blessed Wilfrid, was a brass plate bearing the following inscription—'HUMILIATE CAPITA VESTRO DEO;'—rendered 'Bow down your heads to God.'—From Nicholl's Port Folio of 1826."

In the year 1729, the corporation permitted the erection of a "conduit, not to exceed twelve yards by six," on the site of the old cross. But, in

---

contained in the will of John Jenkinson, dated 13th February, 1628, the will says—"Whereas, I hould to mee and my assignes a mesuage with the appurtenances situat lyinge and being in Preston aforesaid in the Markett Place late in the possession of James Breeres, and one barn and croft in St. John's Weend, now or late in the possession of Christopher Banister, Esquire, all being of the yearly rent of twentie six shillings eight pence or thereabouts for" &c., &c.; "*and whereas I had a purpose and intente by the sufferance of the Almightie God to build and erect an house uppon the fronte towards the streete of the said mesuage and have provided divers and sundrie materialls for and towards the said building. It is my mynde and will that the said buildinge and* FRAME *intended to bee erected as afforesaid shall bee accomplished and p,formed in convenient tyme at the direction and discretion of my said loving wyfe or her assignes and that the charge disbursed in the said erecon* and of all things thereunto belonginge shal be taken had and received out of the whole personall estate of me the said John Jenkinson undevyded." The will then bequeaths the building in prospective to his wife Ann, during her life, and afterwards to his two daughters, Grace and Elizabeth.

After passing through various hands, the property was sold to the corporation of Preston, in 1822, by the father of the present Mr. Alderman Walmsley. A detailed account of the owners and occupiers of these premises from the period of their erection, together with other minute information respecting them, was published in the Preston Chronicle, at the time of their demolition, and afterwards reprinted in a pamphlet form.

1738, the mayor and corporation being "wishful to repave and adorn," commanded the external structure to be pulled down, and the basin to be filled up.[a] An obelisk was afterwards erected upon the spot.

In 1782, the authorities entered into a contract with William Roper, stonemason, to "build and compleat a good and sufficient obelisk, upon the base of the old obelisk formerly standing there, but which," says the document, "some years ago, lately fell, or was taken down." The erection was to be "thirty-three feet high, to be computed from the surface of the said old base." This obelisk presented no very peculiar feature, either of beauty or deformity. The shaft was formed of three "clustered" columns, although the rest of the structure partook more of the character of Roman than Gothic architecture. During the latter period of its existence, it admirably served the purpose of a huge lamp post, and thus at least contributed to the comfort and convenience of the inhabitants. It was taken down in 1853, and the Market-place has since remained without either "ornament" or encumbrance. The "fish stones," which formerly stood between the centre of the square and the end of Friargate, were originally erected in 1605,[b] and were removed in 1853.

Several attempts have latterly been made to provide better market accommodation, and some extensive schemes inaugurated, but hitherto all have proved abortive.

Winckley-square, situated to the south of Fishergate, is a large parallelogram, with enclosed gardens in the centre, similar to the "squares" of London. In point of extent and picturesque beauty, this provincial "*rus in urbe*" might successfully compete with many in the metropolis. It is ornamented by some of the handsomest buildings in the town, including the Literary and Philosophical Institution, Mr. Ainsworth's "Italian Villa," Mr. Miller's newly-erected mansion, and the residences of several of the more wealthy and influential of the inhabitants. The statue, erected to the memory of the late Sir Robert Peel, bart., situated within the railing of the garden enclosure, opposite the end of Cross-street, likewise adds to the beauty and interest of the locality. This statue, which is cut from one block of limestone, is considered a very good likeness of the deceased statesman, and certainly possesses considerable pretensions as a local work of art. The general effect, however, is injured by the incongruous character of the drapery of the lower limbs. Mr. Thomas Duckett, the sculptor,[c] in this, his first production of similar

a Conveyance deeds from the Corporation of Preston to Abbatt and Kellett, the founders of the "Folly" Waterworks, now in the possession of the Preston Gas Company.

b Mr. Whittle's Lecture, at Preston, 1849.

c Mr. Duckett is a native of Preston, and has deservedly gained considerable reputation in his profession, especially for bust sculpture, as many excellent and characteristic portraits of several of the gentry of the town and neighbourhood amply testify.

The Prison & Court House, Preston

The Old Market Place, Preston

Stephenson Terrace, Preston.

magnitude, appears to have hesitated whether he should yield to the old fashioned conventionalism, which dogmatically invested all sculpture, portrait or otherwise, with antique drapery, or boldly represent the modern dress in its integrity. The clothing appears to cling to the lower limbs as though it had been soaked in water. Neither one nor the other object has been truly effected; but the vacillation has considerably injured the general effect of the statue. The following inscription is carved upon the pedestal:—

SIR
ROBERT PEEL,
BARONET.

ERECTED
BY PUBLIC SUBSCRIPTION.
1852.

THOMAS MONK, ESQ., MAYOR.

The entire cost of the monument amounted to no more than six hundred and twenty pounds.

STEPHENSON TERRACE, Deepdale-road, or rather the open space in front of it, might be considered a public "square," but for the triangular form of the enclosed and planted area. It is situated upon a portion of what was termed, in the earlier part of the present century, the "Washing Moor," from the number of laundresses, professional and otherwise, who, in the exercise of their vocation, availed themselves of the then public common as a drying ground. This area was judiciously enclosed, and the neat lodge at the southern corner erected by the corporation, in the year 1850. As buildings are rapidly increasing in this direction, the open space thus preserved will, in the course of a few years, be prized as a valuable "lung" to the eastern portion of the town. The handsome stone terrace was erected by Mr. George Mould, contractor, and named after the celebrated engineer.

AVENHAM WALK, though latterly considerably enlarged and improved by the municipal authorities, has long existed as a favourite promenade of the inhabitants. It forms a conspicuous object in the "South Prospect of Preston," published in 1728, by J. and N. Buck. Until 1846, however, the walk extended no further than the present upper terrace. In the previous year, the corporation secured the neighbouring property, including Mr. Jackson's garden, and other lands to the west, lying between the tram-road and the river's edge. The upper walk has been widened at its southern extremity, and two additional terraces added. The latter are chiefly formed of removed earth. The fences in some of the fields below Ribblesdale-place, have been cleared away, with the view of preparing the ground for a public park. The pathways have been much improved, and the railway embankment planted with shrubs; but no further steps have latterly been taken, although it is the intention of the corporation shortly to lay out and plant the whole land in an ornamental manner. The view from the upper terrace invariably receives the warmest commendation from visitors. Few towns, manufacturing or otherwise, of the size of Preston, possess so agreeable a promenade, within five minutes' walk from the business centre of the borough. The beautiful scenery, and the well kept walks, on the banks of the Ribble, form a natural landscape infinitely superior in picturesque aspect, to many artificially formed parks, where the character of the locality has been less favourably adapted to such a purpose.

The Moor Park was enclosed in 1834. Originally horse races were run upon it, under the patronage of the corporation. An opposition meeting was got up by the political supporters of the Derby interest, on Fulwood moor, in 1786.[a] The latter meeting continued until 1833, when the races were abandoned. They were, however, revived during the last guild festivities, when the "Holme," beneath Penwortham church, was converted into a course. They lingered, however, but an odd season or two; and although several efforts, and especially one during the past year, have been made for their revival, the project appears to have entirely failed. The Moor Park already possesses something of an ornamental character. The fine straight avenue, from west to east, called "the ladies' walk," is adorned by plantations, and picturesque entrance lodges. The "Serpentine-road," across the northern side of the moor, is likewise varied by some planting. A small lake and picturesque lodge also add to the variety and beauty of the park. Much, however, is yet required in the shape of landscape gardening before the corporation can be said to have carried out their original purpose. The air is very salubrious, and the situation admirably adapted to meet the growing wants of the town on the north. Even in its present condition, Moor Park is much frequented, and will doubtless, in a short time, become so general a promenade, that further additions to the planting and laying out of the ground may confidently be anticipated.

The Orchard, so well known as an arena for public meetings, is merely a large plot of valuable building land, in the centre of the town. It is highly probable that this area will, in a short period, receive its destined quantity of bricks and mortar. It was formerly a fruit garden, in the occupation of Mr. Chadwick; hence its name,—"Chadwick's Orchard." It is described in Lang's map, in 1774, as "Colley's Garden."

a See chap, 7, p. 333.

Bank Parade & Avenham Walks, Preston.

Bushell Place, Colonade & Avenham Walks, Preston.

The Residence of William Ainsworth Esq.re
Winckley Square, Preston.

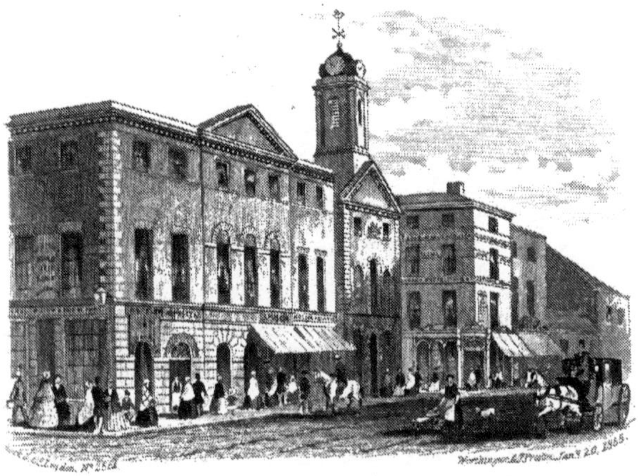

Town Hall, Preston

At Whitsuntide, and other holidays, this plot of land has, for some years, furnished accommodation for the numerous shows, travelling theatres, fly-boats, swing-boxes, whirligigs, etc. On such occasions, the otherwise dingy looking "Orchard" presents a very animated appearance. These shows were, during the festive periods referred to, previously located in the "Lord's field," at the top of Grimshaw-street.

PUBLIC BUILDINGS, INSTITUTIONS, Etc.

The Town Hall.—Preston, doubtless possessed a "Moot," or Town Hall, from the earliest period of its incorporation. No description of such building has been preserved, anterior to the latter portion of the seventeenth century, when Dr. Kuerden records that, "in the midle of the burrough," there "is placed an ample antient and yet well beautifyed gylde or town hall, or toll boothe, to which is annexed, at the end thereof, a counsell chamber for the capitall burgesses at their court days, to retire for consultation." The lower portion of this building, according to the same authority, presented "two rows of butchers' shops on either side, and a row at either end, were victuals" were daily exposed "for the use of man," excepting on Sundays, market days, etc. The roof, and a portion of the walls of this edifice, fell to the ground, on the 3rd of June, 1780. The corporation and burgesses resolved to entirely re-build the structure. They ordered that "the Chimney Piece, with the Town's Arms upon the same," should be "well dressed and fixed up again as the Chimney Piece for the said intended new Town Hall." "The old Cupola, which stood upon the old Town Hall," was likewise "to be well dressed and repaired, and fixed up again upon the new Town Hall." This cupola was removed in 1814, and the present one substituted. The contractors for the erection of the new building were "Robert Bailey, Michael Emmett, and John Emmett, joiners and cabinet makers, of Preston." The amount of the contract is no more than six hundred and fifteen pounds; yet the said Robt. Bailey and Co. covenant that the neighbouring Guild Hall shall be propped up during the work, and left in the same state as it then was, "except as to the paper with which the same was hung." The old music gallery was likewise to be "repaired and cleaned, and fixed up again in the new Town Hall." The contract was signed in 1781, and the building finished in the following year, in time for the guild festivities. No architect's name is mentioned. The present Town Hall, though a substantial structure, is but a mean edifice for so populous and wealthy a borough. Its site encroaches very much upon the busy thoroughfare called the "Old Shambles." The interior of the hall is dark, and not sufficiently spacious for the transaction of the borough magistrates' business. Although this objection will shortly cease to exist, owing to the erection of the new offices and Magistrates' Court in Lancaster-road; still the building is in no way adequate to the growing wants of the town. The guild hall, or council chamber, is certainly a better room, and not ill adapted to its present purpose. Several schemes have been propounded for the erection of a suitable edifice, but none have yet been carried out.[c] In the present Town Hall, the magistrates' bench was formerly situated at the northern end. It has latterly been removed to the niche on the southern side. The hall is decorated with a tablet, on which the names of the guild mayors are inscribed; a bust of the late Thomas German, esq., by Mr. Duckett, and four full length portraits, of the following individuals: George II.; Sir Edward Stanley, bart.; the Hon. Daniel Pulteney; and Nicholas Fazackerley, esq. The portrait of George II. is either a duplicate or a copy of one by Kneller, at Hampton Court. This monarch's picture was presented to the corporation of Preston by Sir Edward Stanley, bart. It was placed in the Town Hall on the king's birthday, October 30th, 1729. Sir Edward Stanley's portrait is supposed to have been painted by the same artist. If the picture of the king be a copy, this is not improbable. Sir Edward Stanley, bart., afterwards earl of Derby, was bailiff of Preston, in 1727, and mayor in 1731. The picture was probably placed in the Town Hall soon after his completion of the duties of the mayoralty. The Hon. Daniel Pulteney was member of parliament for Preston, from 1722 to 1734. Nicholas Fazackerley was member for Preston, from 1734 to his death in 1767. He was likewise recorder of Preston from 1742 to the time of his demise. This picture was painted by a Mr. Davis, brother to Bartholomew Davis, who occupied the civic chair of the borough three different times, namely, in 1774, 1780, and 1785. From the great similarity of manner, it is highly probable Davis painted Pulteney's portrait likewise.

The Corn Exchange is a plain substantial erection, on the west side of Lune-street. It was first opened to the public in 1824. In its original condition, the building, which in form is nearly a parallelogram, contained a large area in the centre, open to the weather. This area, which measures one hundred and thirty-three feet in length, with a mean breadth of sixty-two feet, was covered with a glazed roof in 1853. It forms now not only an excellent corn market, but a spacious hall for general purposes.[d] This building originally provided extensive accommodation for clothiers and others engaged in the woollen trade, as well as for dealers in toys, hardware, trinkets, and fancy goods generally, during the fairs periodically

---

c See chap. 6, p. 311.

d In 1842, the area of the Exchange was temporarily converted into a handsome ball-room, in which were held public assemblies in connection with the guild festivities.

held in the town. The three large rooms in the upper story, fronting Lune-street, were thrown together in 1848, and now form a spacious assembly room, 105 feet long, somewhat in the form of a cross. Its general breadth is about 33 feet, and that of the centre portion, which may be termed the transept, 45 feet. It is upwards of 18 feet in height. In connection with this spacious hall, there is a lengthy promenade, and refreshment and retiring rooms, formed from the upper galleries, which had previously been named the "cloth hall." The rooms below the *salle de bal* are used as a mart for the sale of cheese and butter. The one to the north end was converted into a fish market on the removal of the fish-stones from the central Market-place, in 1853; but the project failed. No regular fish market at present exists. The open area at the front of the Exchange is, on market days, devoted to the sale of eggs, poultry, etc. The pork market is still at the western end of the building. Other shops were formed on the south side in 1853. The external dimensions of the Exchange buildings are, length 193 feet, mean breadth 100 feet.

The House of Correction.—Dr. Kuerden, nearly two centuries ago, described the "old Friary," situated to the south of the present Marsh-lane, as being "only reserved for the reforming of vagabonds, sturdy beggars, and petty larcenary thieves, and other people wanting good behaviour; it is now the country prison to entertain such persons with hard work, spare dyet, and whipping, and it is cal'd the House of Correction."[e] This place remained the common gaol of the neighbourhood until the erection of the modern prison, at the end of Church-street, which was first opened for the reception of criminals in the year 1789. This gaol is said to have been constructed according to the improved plans laid down by the celebrated prison philanthropist, John Howard, who resided for some time in the neighbouring town of Warrington. The site of this edifice was well chosen. A large quantity of land was secured in its immediate vicinity, from which circumstance ample available space has not been wanted for the further extension of the buildings, which the increasing population gradually demanded. At the present time, a large grassed area remains in front of the governor's house, which, with a considerable quantity of land in the rear, and on the south side, still gives a semi-suburban character to the establishment, notwithstanding its comparative proximity to the present centre of the town. Eighteen additional cells were added in 1817. The prison was visited in June, 1819, by the celebrated Mrs. Fry, and her brother, Jno. Gurney, esq., of Norwich. Mrs. Fry again visited the place in Oct., 1820, and expressed herself gratified with the mode of treatment adopted. Mr. Gurney, in his notes, afterwards

e See chap. 3, page 115, and chap. 5, page 211.

published, says,—"About one thousand persons are computed to pass through this House of Correction in the course of the year; and many of them learn in it those habits of industry, and that knowledge of a trade, by which they are enabled to respectably maintain their families when they leave it." The same writer further adds:—"We have indeed in the course of our journey, visited no prison which appeared to us to be so much a house of reformation as the bridewell at Preston. More completely, however, to effect that great object, one thing seems wanting; namely, more religious care and instruction. The prisoners meet for divine worship only once in the week; and there is no school in the prison." Mr. Liddell was governor at this time, he having been appointed in 1817. He was succeeded by Captain Hansbrow, the present governor of Lancaster Castle. A new females' ward was erected in 1842, which contains thirty-three cells, six day rooms, residence for matron and female warders, together with wash-houses, laundry, and other offices. In 1842, the first corridor, or block of sixty cells, under the new regulation for separate confinement, was erected; and, in 1847, a second corridor, or block of ninety-six cells, was added. Previously to these additions, which are on the most approved plans, the prison contained three hundred and ten cells, which, at three persons each, would hold nine hundred and thirty prisoners.[a] In 1832, three "martello towers" were erected upon the walls, with the view to protect the prison from threatened attacks by mobs of machinery breaking operatives. In the previous year, the promptitude and courage of the governor, Captain Hansbrow, frustrated an attempt of this character. The governor's house, which forms the principal front, was re-built in 1834, from designs by Mr. Jno. Dewhurst. It is of undressed stone, in the "castellated style," and although without much pretension to architectural merit, presents a very characteristic and commanding aspect. The chapel has likewise been enlarged and decorated. The benches, communion table, and handsome chairs, railing, reading desk, as well as the decorated roof, emblazoned with golden stars, together with the gilt letters cut from card board, which form the apostles' creed, etc., near the altar, are the productions of prisoners who have been confined in the gaol. A large figure of Christ upon the cross, painted by the chaplain, the Rev. J. Clay, adorns the space above the altar. A large and very superior instrument, which cost eighty guineas, called a "seraphine," has been placed in the chapel, by subscription, collected by the governor, Col. Martin, who contributed twenty-five pounds towards the fund. The chapel, which will contain about five hundred persons, is warmed by gas apparatus. The average

a Governors of gaols are prohibited by statute from lodging *two* criminals in one cell. Each apartment must be occupied by either one or three prisoners,

number of persons confined in the gaol, for the last few years, is about three hundred and fifty. The prisoners are taught in the cells and in classes, on an average about two hours daily. Total separation is practised, except during exercise and working hours, and during divine service in the chapel. At these times, even, the prisoners are always under the eye of an officer, who enforces the strictest silence. The discipline of this gaol has been pronounced by competent authorities, from various continental states, as well as England, to be fully equal, if not superior, to that of any other prison, either in Europe or America. Flogging was discontinued upwards of eleven years ago, except in the cases of criminals under the "Juvenile Act;" but even these are of rare occurrence. There have not been, for some time, any irons or hand-cuffs in the place. Col. Martin appears to prefer, as a portion of his discipline, the principle acted upon in Kuerden's days, when prisoners were "*entertained* with hard work and spare dyet;" one of his maxims being, that if a risoner will not work, he ought not to feed. Parties who have tried the gallant colonel's drill, have often thanked him, on their release, for having taught them how to earn their living by honest industry. Some of the reports of the chaplain of this prison (the Rev. J. Clay), have had a wide circulation, and have attracted considerable attention. The staff of officials consists of the governor, the chaplain, the surgeon, nine male warders, store keeper, taskmaster, two schoolmasters, two porters, four night watchmen (two for each alternate night), one matron, and two female warders.

The Court House is situated to the south of the prison. It is a handsome stone edifice, built about 1829, from designs by Mr. Rickman. In 1849, the dome was removed; and another of rectangular form erected in its place. The latter, which is regarded as a great improvement over the previous plan of lighting the court, was designed by Mr. Geo. Latham. Owing to the weight of business at the sessions, a second smaller court has been fitted up. The principal hall is spacious, and contains a commodious gallery for spectators. A portrait of the late Col. Clayton, of Blackburn, decorates the court. This gentleman had served as a county magistrate fifty years at the time the portrait was placed in its present position. Previously to the erection of this building, the "sessions-house" was attached to the governor's residence.

The Militia Stores.—A large quadrangular building of brick, with square towers at the corners, was erected in 1854, to the south of the Court House, for the purposes of the militia. The clothing, arms, and accoutrements are here deposited. There are likewise apartments for the commanding officer, the adjutant, the staff, and the regimental tradesmen, together with cells, stables, etc.

MAGISTRATES' COURT AND POLICE STATION, LANCASTER-ROAD.—The borough magistrates, at present, hold their court at the Town-hall, and the police-station is in Avenham-street. Spacious premises, from designs by Mr. J. H. Park, are, however, in course of erection, in Lancaster-road, which will afford superior facilities for the transaction of this department of the public business. Previously to the erection of the new police-station, in 1832, the "lock-up" was situated up a dismal alley branching from Turk's-head-court. The Avenham-street establishment is a massive structure, and affords sufficient accommodation for the police requirements; but the site having been purchased by Messrs. Jacson and Co., cotton spinners, with the view to the enlargement of their premises, the erection of new police buildings became necessary. It was therefore determined to erect a suitable court in connection therewith, the Town-hall being ill adapted for the transaction of the magisterial business. The ground floor of the new building will contain a magistrates' clerk's room, superintendent's office, book-keeper's and general police office, store room, washing room, and four cells. The upper story will include a private room for the magistrates, jury or attorney's room, three cells, and a court house, forty feet long by thirty-two feet wide. The principal entrance, in Lancaster-road, will present a front of fifty feet. The depth of the building, with front to Earl-street, will be one hundred and four feet. The estimated cost, including fire-proof floors, internal fittings, etc., is about £3,000. The architectural character of the building may be described as an adaptation of the Italian manner to modern and local requirements.

BATHS AND WASH-HOUSES.—Several projects had been mooted for the establishment of public baths previously to the erection of the present establishment, in Saul-street. In 1836, a prospectus was issued with the object of procuring a capital of £1,000. for the furtherance of this object, in shares of £40. each. The scheme, however, was ultimately abandoned. After considerable discussion, it was eventually agreed, chiefly through the instrumentality of the then mayor, James German, esq., that public baths and wash-houses should be erected by the corporation. In 1851, the Saul-street establishment was opened. It is furnished with every convenience, and fitted up in the most approved manner. The plans of the building are by P. P. Baly, esq., of London, civil engineer. The frontage to Saul-street is upwards of eighty feet in length; and the building extends backward about one hundred and nine feet. There are sixty-three private bath rooms, sixteen first-class for men, eight first-class for women, and thirty-one second-class for men and eight for women. The swimming bath is thirty-four feet by twenty-four feet. This bath is supplied with hot and cold water, and is generally kept tepid. There are likewise vapour and shower baths on the premises. The washing department is fitted up with every convenience for the cleansing and drying of clothes. The old company supplied the water gratuitously, during which time the establishment about paid its working expenses. Since the local board purchased the water company's interest, the usual charge has been made, from which time the expenses have exceeded the receipts. The number both of washers and bathers has slightly decreased during the past year, as will be seen from the following statement:—

NUMBER OF BATHERS AND WASHERS FOR THE PAST FIVE YEARS.

Sep. 1 to Aug. 31.	*Bathers.*	*Washers.*	*Hours Washing.*
1851—2	31,314	6,778	20,164
1852—3	30,296	9,347	24,004
1853—4	27,472	10,775	29,154
1854—5	29,855	10,194	31,279
1855—6	27,294	8,527	26,783

From the capital account of the establishment, it appears that the land, buildings, fittings, etc., cost £11,217. 12s. 7d., which sum was raised by loans on mortgage of the borough rate.

The Fire Brigade Buildings were formerly beneath the "Lock-up," in Avenham-street. In 1852, however, suitable premises were erected in Tithe-barn-street, especially for the accommodation of this branch of the public service. The building is furnished with a tower, in which is placed the alarm bell used in connection with the establishment. The present fire brigade, under the direction of Mr. Superintendent Marriot, is considered to be very efficient. In proportion to the amount of property, destructive fires are very rare in Preston. The first record of the use of a fire-engine in the borough, is found in the corporation minute book, of the year 1724, when Dan. Pulteney, esq., member of parliament for Preston, presented to the corporation "an engine for y[e] extinguishing of fire, of late invencon."[a] The corporation immediately ordered a second engine, of a similar character. The want of adequate protection from fire was so much felt in 1803, that a meeting was held, and a subscription entered into for the purchase of engines. Four were procured soon afterwards. The "Victoria" engine was purchased by the old police commissioners, in 1837. The establishment includes, at the present time, engines of the most approved construction, together with hose-reel and other requisites.

The Overseers' Offices, in Lancaster-road, were erected in 1848. In this building the guardians meet, and the general business of the union is transacted.

The Workhouse, on the Moor, was built in 1788, and has since been enlarged. Considerable discussion relative to the propriety of erecting a

a See chap. 6, p. 313.

suitable edifice for the accommodation of the entire union has been frequently discussed by the guardians; but the project, at present, remains in abeyance.[b]

THE HOUSE OF RECOVERY.—An institution of this character, in connection with the Dispensary, was originally established near the Trinity church, in 1813; but the building on the "Moor" was not erected until 1833. It is at present used more as a fever ward in connection with the Dispensary and the Workhouse.[c]

THE DISPENSARY, in Fishergate, was first established in 1809. It is supported entirely by voluntary contributions and annual donations. The following extracts, from the last report of the house surgeon, for the months of November and December, 1856, and January, February, and March, 1857, show the valuable aid rendered to the poor by this institution:—

"The number of patients admitted during the months of November and December, is 423; of these 34 were accidents; 195 attended personally at the Dispensary; 228 were visited at their own homes. The number for these three months is rather below the average, and can only be accounted for by there having been less illness in the town than is usual at this season. * * * The number of patients admitted during the months of January and February, is 448; of these 26 were accidents: 233 attended at the Dispensary; 255 were visited at their homes. * * * The number of patients admitted last month" (March), "is 219; of these 118 attended at the Dispensary; 100 were seen at home; and 13 were accidents."

Notwithstanding the amount of relief furnished by this institution, it is still very desirable that Preston should ere long possess a large and commodious Infirmary, capable of meeting the requirements of its numerous and increasing population. Perhaps the example of the neighbouring borough of Blackburn may eventually serve to stimulate the benevolence of the wealthy inhabitants of Preston in this direction. From time to time some efforts have been made; but, as yet, without practical results.

GAS WORKS.—Preston has the distinction of being the first provincial town in England into which gas was introduced for public consumption. Its old parish church was the first structure devoted to religious service lighted with gas, not excepting those in the metropolis; and the first government barrack which adopted the improved method of illumination is the one at Fulwood. The gas company in Preston was formed in 1815, chiefly through the instrumentality of the Rev. Joseph Dunn, who had witnessed its successful introduction into the Roman Catholic college, at Stonyhurst. The works were in operation early in 1816. So rapid has been their extension, that the original capital stock of £2000. has, in the short space of forty years, become augmented to £87,000! The old works were erected in Avenham-lane. The company has gradually purchased

b See page 310. c See page 319.

so much of the neighbouring property that the entire space from east to west, between Avenham-street and Glover-street; and from north to south, between Syke-lane and Avenham-lane is now in their possession. Besides which, other extensions have been found necessary, from time to time, to meet the gradually increasing demand. Land in Upper Walker-street, then on the outside of the town, was purchased in 1835, and gas-holders erected on the new station. This was further extended in 1845, and a second establishment commenced for the manufacture as well as for the storing of gas. The property belonging to the old water-works company in Syke-lane was purchased in 1833, and a large gas-holder erected on the site in 1850, when the old "Folly well" was filled up. An additional supply gasholder was afterwards erected at Walton-le-dale. The company first obtained a special act of incorporation in 1839. In 1853, a further act was deemed necessary, and was accordingly procured. The length of the mains from east to west, and from north to south, is about two and a half miles in each direction. The quantity of gas annually manufactured at the present time, is about one hundred and twenty-five millions of cubic feet. The rate of charge has been considerably diminished during the last few years. Meters were gradually introduced between 1835 and 1840. At first the price was fifteen shillings per thousand cubic feet. At present it is four shillings and ninepence, with a discount of ten per cent., if paid within one month from the end of each periodical settlement.

THE WATER WORKS.—Originally Preston was supplied with water from open wells or springs in the town, near which, in process of time, draw-wells were sunk. It is impossible to say when open wells were first constructed. In 1654, the municipal authorities ordered a "drawe well" to be made "in the Bottome of the Markett stidd." Another ancient well was accidentally discovered in 1852, by the workmen employed in excavating for the mains of the new water company in Church-street, a little to the east of Water-street. The well appeared to have been erected over or near the spring which supplied the Syke-brook. It resembled a vault in form, was about two yards deep, four yards long, and three in width. The bottom was flagged, and the upper portion was covered with flags or stone slabs, one of which, though broken, distinctly presented the following inscription:—

"William Turner, MAIOR.
George Addison, } Baylives.
Lawrence Farringdon, }
Anno. 1664."

The vault was full of water at the time of its discovery. It is generally believed to have been an ancient well, used previously to the erection of the town's pumps. The cavity was filled with rubbish by the workmen, but the stone bearing the inscription was removed to the water company's office. Dr. Kuerden, towards the end of the seventeenth century, describes Molyneux-square, now that portion of Lancaster-road immediately south of Lord-street, as having a "drawwell in the midst thereof."[a] The well, sunk at the expense of the corporation, "in the bottom of the Market Stidd," in the year 1654, was most probably near the site of the old fish-stones pump, at the Friargate corner of the square. An open sewer ran down the centre of this thoroughfare to "Brown's channel," which crossed Friargate opposite Lune-street, and which doubtless carried away the overflow from the "Stidd." A drawwell in Fishergate, near the site of the present pump, was constructed in 1666, at the expense of the corporation. A Mr. Kellett, a carpenter, proposed in 1718, to supply the town with water from the Ribble. The project, though encouraged by the corporate body, was not, however, carried into effect. In 1729, Messrs. Abbatt and Kellett received power from the municipal authorities to supply the town with water. Land was leased to them at Avenham, (near the present gas company's office) for the erection of the necessary machinery, and for the procuring of a supply of water. This establishment, from the supposed Quixotic character of the innovation was named the "Folly." The large well occupied the site of an ancient spring, described by Dr. Kuerden as the "Minspitt well," situated at the bottom of "Minspitt-lane or Pettycoat-alley, by reason of the frequent carrying of water from the well by women.[b] The corporation likewise granted Messrs. Kellett and Abbatt power to construct a conduit in the centre of the Market-place, on the site of the old cross, and even furnished materials for the structure, but in 1738, it was ordered to be destroyed.[c] The pipes used by this establishment, were, in the first instance, made of wood, but afterwards lead and iron were substituted. The company gradually assumed more extensive proportions, and added a maltkiln to their business. Owing to the low situation of the spring, power was required to force the water to the higher level of the town. This was effected by the continual perambulation of decrepid old horses around the main shaft of the primitive machinery. The supply from this source, not keeping pace with the extended requirements of the town, another scheme was set on foot in 1825, principally by the late Mr. John Smith, but the commercial panic of 1826 prevented its realization. Soon afterwards Mr. W. Wood erected premises in Ormskirk-road, intended to supply water at least to the tenants of his property in the neighbourhood. As little building has since been placed upon the "Orchard," it may be supposed these "waterworks"

a See page 210. b See page 210. c See page 433.

were never brought into active operation. On the revival of trade, however, Mr. Smith's project was resumed. In 1832, the "Preston Waterworks Company" was incorporated by special act of parliament. The capital was raised in three hundred shares at £50. each, power was granted to borrow a further sum of £10,000. The water was procured and stored in a reservoir at Grimsargh, on the way to Longridge. The concern speedily realised ten per cent. to the shareholders. In 1843, another act of parliament was obtained, authorising an increase of capital, when six hundred new shares, at £50. each were created. Eventually the local board of health purchased the company's interest in these works. By the powers conferred by an act passed in 1853, the sum payable to the shareholders, was assessed by the arbitrator, Sir John Rennie, at £135,225. which, after discharging all liabilities, furnished a dividend of £116. 5s. on each original £50. share. Since the waterworks have become the property of the local board of health, most extensive improvements and additions have been commenced, but most of these are at present in an unfinished state. Recent disagreement, between the local board and Mr. Wrigg, the engineer, which resulted in the resignation of the latter, for a short time put a stop to the works, as well as to the sewerage of the town. Mr. Newton has since been appointed surveyor, and Mr. Hawkesley has reported on the condition, and necessary steps to be taken with respect to the new waterworks. Their speedy completion may, therefore, with some confidence, be anticipated.

The Theatre Royal, in Fishergate, was built in 1802, by a company of shareholders, with a view to provide more efficient accommodation for the festivities incident to the guild of that year. It is a large and commodious building, and is capable of being converted into a first-class provincial house. A smaller theatre previously occupied the site of Messrs. Hunt's maltkiln, in Woodcock's court, Fishergate. See map of Preston in 1774.

The Temperance Hall, in North-road, formerly a maltkiln, was opened on July 5th, 1856. For some years previously, the temperance committee leased from the earl of Derby, the old cockpit, which has since been converted into the "Derby Assembly Room."

Railway Stations.—The great general railway station in Fishergate, has been enlarged from time to time, merely with a view to meet temporary requirements. It consequently presents a singular mixture of styles, from the early dark and clumsy wooden shed, to the light iron and glass roofing, lately so much in fashion. It is intended, however, shortly to remove entirely the present passenger station, and erect premises suitable to the traffic of the locality. A bill was introduced into parliament lately for the carrying out of a magnificent project; but, as the rival companies could not agree as to the relative proportions of the expense, the scheme was dropped. It has been said that more trains pass daily in and out of the Preston station than at any other place. Derby is stated to be the next upon the list. In June, 1853, the return was—London and North Western, 165; East Lancashire, 30; total, 195 trains. In April, 1857, the numbers were as follows:—London and North Western, 255; East Lancashire, 62; total, 317. The goods station of the London and North Western company is situated in Charles-street, and that of the East Lancashire at the lower end of Butler-street. There are likewise branch works in connection with the Crewe establishment, for the repair of locomotive engines, etc. The whole of these buildings, attached to the London and North Western, the East Lancashire, the Lancashire and Yorkshire, the Lancaster and Carlisle, and the Wyre railways, are situated within what is called a "ring fence," and occupy a very considerable space of ground. There is yet standing a small goods-station, in connection with the Wyre line, at the Maudlands. The Longridge railway and the Preston portion of the unfinished Fleetwood and West Riding scheme are now worked together. The station of the former, behind Stephenson-terrace, is to be appropriated in future to the goods department alone, a commodious new passenger station being in course of erection, near the house of recovery, in Deepdale-road. A small station for passengers, has been lately opened on the Maudlands, for the convenience of parties residing at the western side of the town. The Lancaster and Carlisle company are erecting a large and commodious shed on the Maudlands, as an engine depot. Their principal establishment of this character is at Carlisle.

Dr. Shepherd's Library.—A physician of Preston, Richard Shepherd, M.B., who died in November, 1761, bequeathed a valuable library to the mayor and aldermen of the borough, for the public use. Dr. Shepherd likewise devised the proceeds arising from the investment of a sum of £200. as a salary for a librarian; together with the interest accruing from the residue of his personal estate, (about £1000) as a perpetual fund for the further augmentation of the library. The books were deposited for a long period in a suitable building in Shepherd-street; but, owing to the rapid increase of the town, and the change in the character of the locality, the mayor and aldermen determined upon the provision of a more suitable site. A portion of the present grammar school, Cross-street, was originally destined for the reception of Dr. Shepherd's bequest, but the room not proving sufficiently large to meet the probable increase in the number of works, the project was abandoned. Several schemes were entertained for the erection of a suitable edifice on the opposite side of the street, and plans were submitted by Mr. Barry, son of Sir Charles Barry, architect of the new houses of parliament, Westminster, but nothing further resulted. The books have, since May, 1851, been deposited in a large room in the upper portion of the Institution for the Diffusion of Knowledge, at Avenham, where every facility is afforded to readers. The only condition attached to the privilege of free access to this valuable collection of standard works, is a recommendation signed by the mayor or one of the aldermen of the borough. In November, 1836, the library contained 4277 volumes; in January, 1852, 5,700 volumes; and at the present time, about 7,000 volumes.

INSTITUTION FOR THE DIFFUSION OF KNOWLEDGE.—Preston possesses no Mechanics' Institute, at least none which is so styled. There are, however, several libraries and mutual improvement classes, in connection with some of the leading establishments, which might, perhaps, with greater justice, claim the title, than many of the so styled "Mechanics' Institutions." Preston was not, however, backward in the cause of popular education, for as early as October, 1828, the "Institution for the Diffusion of Knowledge" was opened in Cannon-street, avowedly with the same objects as Mechanics' Institutes. From six hundred to eight hundred members joined during the first twelve months of its existence, a large proportion of whom were operatives. At the end of the first year the library contained about 1,500 volumes, and the museum above 800 interesting specimens, chiefly in the departments pertaining to natural history. The institution was, however, too far advanced in its character to meet the then state of the education of the masses, and, like many other Mechanics' Institutes, soon ceased to be much patronised by that class. The number of subscribers, in the course of two or three years, fell to between three and four hundred. Previously to August, 1837, works of fiction, including Shakspeare and dramatic literature generally, were excluded. The committee of the institution originally rented the upper room in a building on the east side of Cannon-street, which served as both library, museum, and lecture room. The lower room was afterwards added, but still the accommodation was very limited. The first effort towards the raising of a fund for the erection of a suitable building was made in 1840, when an exhibition of works of art, scientific apparatus, machinery, etc., was held in the Exchange-rooms. It proved very successful, and realised a profit of £280. This sum was afterwards increased by a legacy of £100., bequeathed by Mr. Hamer Hargreaves, of Manchester, a talented and enthusiastic amateur musician. This gentleman formerly resided in Preston; and was for many years the conductor of the choral society, and chief patron of musical talent in the town. Considerable exertions were afterwards made, and liberal subscriptions resulted. The corporation voted £250. in aid of the building fund. In 1844, it was resolved to erect a suitable edifice in Cross-street. This site was, however, afterwards abandoned. The foundation stone of the present handsome building, at Avenham, was laid in June, 1846, by the then mayor, the late Thomas German, esq. A bazaar was held in the Corn-exchange during the spring of 1849, in aid of the funds. This proved one of the most successful enterprises of the kind ever undertaken in Preston. The total proceeds amounted to about £1,800. In order to raise the necessary funds to complete the building, Thomas Birchall, esq. advanced the sum of £600. This was entirely repaid in the year 1854. The total cost, including fitting, was about £6,000. The building was opened in October, 1849. In architectural character it partakes of the Greek composite order, combined with modern Italian. It was erected from designs by the late Mr. Welch. The portico is, to some extent, imitated from an antique edifice at Athens, known as the "Temple of the Winds." The basement contains several good offices and class rooms. The principal story includes a large library and a reading room of similar dimensions, committe room, ante-rooms, and large lecture hall. The latter including the gallery, will contain about six hundred persons. The platform is spacious, and is tastefully ornamented by an architectural proscenium. A fine oil picture, representing Eve pleading to Adam, decorates the hall. This picture was presented through Thomas Birchall, esq., by the artist, H. O'Neil, Esq. In the sides of the building are other class rooms. The upper story consists of two large exhibition rooms, lighted from the roof, and united by corridors. One of these has been set apart for Dr. Shepherd's library, the trustees of which pay a rent of £40. a year to the council of the institution. From the top of the building, an excellent view is obtained of the town and surrounding country. The approach, or entrance terrace, was not added till 1849. It is in the Italian villa style, and was designed by Mr. George Latham. The cost of this work, about £350, was defrayed by James German, esq., and a few of his friends. The number of members at the present time, about one half of which may be included in the operative class, is nearly six hundred,[a] and the number of volumes in the library upwards of 6,000. Lectures, gratuitous and otherwise, are regularly given in the theatre of the institution; and exhibitions and soirees, are occasionally held in connection with it. The museum has not yet been fitted up within the present building.

[a] The actual numbers on the books in April last, were as follows :—

Out of business, professional, and tradesmen	240
Operatives	264
Females and minors	67
Total	571

Philosophical Institution Preston

[illegible]

Its contents have been greatly neglected, and portions irretrievably injured. The project for the establishment of a free library and museum in Preston has met with some favour. Several meetings have been held, at one of which Lord Stanley and Sir Robert Peel, bart., and at another the Bishop of Manchester, and Sir J. Kay Shuttleworth, bart. advocated the cause with great and much commended eloquence. The subscription list, however, does not exhibit yet, an equal proof of practical zeal in the undertaking. The total amount promised (April, 1857), is £2,274., of which £476. 4s. 6d. is contributed by Preston operatives. Doubtless, the recent praiseworthy example and munificence of William Browne, esq., M.P., will stimulate the local patriotism of the inhabitants of Preston, and, in a short time, the ancient borough will occupy a position in this respect commensurate with its wealth and population. The numerous and attentive audiences, which have frequented the Corn-exchange, during the past season, to listen to a course of lectures, gratuitously provided by the mayor, bears testimony to the increasing desire of the operative population for the acquisition of knowledge.

Literary and Philosophical Institution.—Mr. Whittle mentions a Literary and Philosophical Institution as existing in 1810, and that the late Rev. J. Dunn, and Thos. Batty Addison, esq., were amongst its chief patrons. In September, 1834, a "Society of Arts" was instituted; which, for some time, received the patronage of the principal gentry. Two exhibitions of paintings were held in connection with this institution, one in the society's rooms, Fishergate, and another at the Court-house. In 1838, the committee announced their intention to give a number of prizes, to be competed for by parties residing within twenty miles of Preston. The following is a list of the successful competitors:—Best drawing, in chalk, from the Townley Venus: Chas. Hardwick; second do., William Pilkington. Landscape view of Ribble valley: first prize, G. W. Anthony; second do., W. Pilkington. Best design for a statue of the late John Horrocks: Thomas Duckett. Architecture: George Benson. The society, however, gradually fell into decay; and, eventually, its collection of pictures, etc., was transferred to the new Literary and Philosophical Institution. This society originated in a slight misunderstanding with the committee and some of the members of the Institution in Cannon-street, in 1840. Rooms were fitted up in the Corn Exchange for a library, museum, and lectures. The project so far succeeded as to induce the proprietors and subscribers to determine upon the erection of a suitable building. During the mayoralty of Jno. Addison, esq. (August, 1844), the first stone of the present picturesque edifice was laid. His worship presented a portion of the site. The building was designed by the late

Mr. Welch, and forms, in conjunction with the Winckley Club, and the Grammar School, one of the chief architectural ornaments of the town. The ground floor consists of a committee room and a spacious library and reading room, fifty feet by twenty-four feet. A room over the library, of similar dimensions, is used as a museum. The collection, though somewhat small, is choice and valuable; and includes several interesting local antiquities, and some specimens of the remains of extinct animals, found in the bed of the Ribble. This collection, combined with the specimens deposited at the Institution, Avenham, would form a respectable nucleus for a museum in connection with the projected free library. Above the committee room, vestibule, etc., is the lecture theatre, forty-one feet six inches, by thirty feet, capable of containing upwards of three hundred persons. The roof of the museum is constructed on a similar plan to that of the "guard room," in Lambeth Palace. Mr. Welch attempted, in the first instance, to form the roof of the lecture theatre with stone principals, somewhat in the manner presented in the great hall of Conway Castle, with, however, more of elaborate and elegant detail. During the erection of the edifice, however, this was abandoned, owing to the fears expressed by several parties, that the weight of the stone would be too heavy for the form and strength of the walls. The lecture room and museum, although less in dimensions, bear some resemblance, in general character, to the new library and hall at Lincoln's Inn, London. The Cross-street elevation is one hundred and sixty feet in length. Its architectural ornamentation is of a mixed character. This façade is continued by the building originally intended for Dr. Shepherd's library, and the new Grammar school. The Winckley-square elevation joins the Winckley Club. The two form apparently portions of the same building. The Literary and Philosophical Institution portion consists chiefly of two square towers, surmounted by open octagonal lanterns, the intermediate space being occupied by a large projecting Gothic arch, beneath which is a fine window and gallery, with elaborately enriched parapet. This has been imitated, so far as regards the general outline, from West Stowe Hall, in Suffolk. The Winckley Club portion of this front, consists principally of a square tower, fifty feet in height, and a bold projecting gable, in which is inserted a beautiful oriel window. The Winckley-square front is elaborately decorated with heads, grotesques,and other ornaments, a portion of which were executed by Mr. T. Duckett. The Literary and Philosophical Institution at present numbers nearly two hundred subscribers, including the shareholders. The library contains about four thousand volumes. Additional volumes, for circulation, are procured from a London library, to which the directors subscribe. Lectures are occasionally delivered here, although not so often as at the Institution, Avenham.

The Winckley Club House, in Winckley-square, forms a portion of the same structure or group as the Literary and Philosophical Institution. It consists of a spacious news-room on the ground floor, two billiard rooms above, and offices for servants below. The building is the property of about eighty shareholders. There are likewise between fifty and sixty town, and from fifteen to twenty, country subscribers, chiefly of the upper classes. Previously to the erection of the Winckley Club House, the "Gentlemen's News Room" was at the Guild Hall. The large building at the Church-street corner of the new Lancaster-road, was originally erected for, and was for some time used as, the "Gentlemen's Coffee Room." A "Tradesmen's News Room" was open for many years, over the old Chronicle office, next to the Straight Shambles, Market-place. These establishments are now closed. There are, however, many news rooms, class rooms, and libraries, in connection with some of the important manufacturing and other establishments in the town.

Law Library, Chapel-street.—Mr. Whittle mentions a "Legulean Society," established in 1787, in which the younger members of the legal profession argued points of law. This society has been discontinued; but a library of law books, established many years ago, is still in existence, and receives the patronage of all, or nearly all, the members of the legal profession in the town. This library at present contains nearly a thousand works, composed chiefly of treatises and reports.

The Press.—The history of newspapers is a history of civilization. The development of the press of England has been concurrent with the development of her freedom. In this country, more than in any other, the press is a power in the state. "He who," said Canning, in one of his speeches, at Liverpool, "speculating on the British constitution, should omit from his enumeration the mighty power of public opinion, embodied in a free press, which pervades, and checks, and perhaps, in the last resort, nearly governs the whole, would give but an imperfect view of the government of England." It is not, however, within the province of a local historian to descant upon the national influence of the newspaper, or to trace its gradual development until it has assumed its present gigantic proportions. Those who feel an interest in the history of the general newspaper press, are referred to "The Fourth Estate," an interesting work from the pen of the late Mr. F. K. Hunt. To England belongs the honour of having issued the first printed newspaper. Small pamphlets, containing news, were occasionally published in the reign of James I.,[b] but no continued publication of a newspaper, in the modern sense,

[b] It has been ascertained, beyond a doubt, that the "English Mercurie," a newspaper in the British Museum, purporting to have been issued in the reign of Elizabeth, is a forgery.

took place until the year 1622. The first provincial newspaper, in England, was printed at Norwich, in 1706, at one penny, but "a halfpenny not refused." Warrington has claimed the honour of publishing the first newspaper in Lancashire;[c] but the Warrington Advertiser, appears to have been preceded by the Liverpool Courant, which was issued in 1712, and also by the Manchester Journal, which was sold at a halfpenny per copy, before the newspaper stamp was imposed.[d] It was first published in 1719. The earliest newspaper published in Preston was called "The Preston Journal, with News both Foreign and Domestick." It contained four pages, each measuring about fourteen inches by ten, and was printed by Mr. W. Smith, in Church-street. A few numbers yet preserved have not the publisher's price printed on them. The sheet bore a halfpenny stamp. Its intelligence was of the most meager character; there was rarely any notice of a local occurrence, and seldom even the announcement of a marriage. One of the few original paragraphs, which appeared in the paper, is in the number for February 22nd, 1745. It announces an occurrence, common in Ireland, but seldom known in England, viz., a moving bog; Pilling Moss was actually in motion! This phenomenon caused "much terror and alarm," as well as serious loss. It was occasioned by heavy rains. The cause of such an occurrence is now well understood. The following is the form in which a marriage was announced in the Preston Journal, of Nov., 1744:—"We hear from Lancaster that last week was married there Timothy Stern, of Shipley, Esq., in Yorkshire, to Miss Wigglesworth, daughter and heiress of the late Thomas Wigglesworth, of Woodfields, Esq., a young lady of great beauty and merit, and a fortune of £10,000." Singularly enough, the election of a member of parliament for Clitheroe was inserted amongst the news received from London. The advertisements, too, were few; but some of them give a curious insight into the manners and customs of the period. One announces the sale of "a gang of packhorses and mares, with pack-saddles," belonging to a person at Croston, who was "one of the four monthly Lancashire carriers." In the year 1745, there were two newspapers published in Preston, the second one being called "The True British Courant, or Preston Journal, with News both Foreign and Domestick." Mr. Edward Smith published this paper in the Market-place; but it was printed by Mr. Moon, in Cheapside. Both newspapers were decided partisans of the reigning family, both before and after the

c See "A Morning Ramble in old Warrington," by Dr. Kendrick, printed in the seventh volume of the Lancashire and Cheshire Historic Society's Transactions. The author does not give the date of the first publication of the Warrington paper, but refers to its existence in 1750.

d The earliest imposition of the newspaper stamp took place in 1720. In the first instance, the impost amounted to only one halfpenny each copy.

rebellion, in 1745. From the time of the "young chevalier's" entry into Lancashire, until his return through Preston, homeward, no paper was printed. How long these journals were issued is not known. The next caterer in the news line was the late Mr. Thomas Walker, father of Mr. John Walker, who has lately retired from business as a printer. His newspaper was the Preston Review. It appeared in June, 1791, and was a great step in advance of its predecessors. It contained more frequent allusions to local occurrences, but had few of the characteristics of a modern newspaper. It existed only twelve months. Mr. Thomas Croft next issued a newspaper. It was called the Preston Journal, and was somewhat larger than the Review. Its notices of local events were also more copious, and frequently "leading articles," or comments on political affairs, appeared; although, as was then the case with newspapers generally, they were very meager, and bore little resemblance to the articles published at the present day. Mr. Croft issued the Journal from 1807 to 1812, when he disposed of it to Mr. Isaac Wilcockson, who changed its name to the Preston Chronicle, under which title it continued to be published for many years, by Mr. Wilcockson, and since by his successors, Messrs. Dobson and Son. A copy of this paper, in the earliest period of its existence, contained something less than a fifth of the amount of matter given in the Chronicle and other full-sized papers now published. The Chronicle advocates the political views of the "reformers" or "liberals," and at present enjoys, as a local journal, an extensive circulation. In 1821, Mr. L. Clarke published the Preston Sentinel, which continued in existence twelve months. Mr. Clarke, however, in 1825, issued the first number of the Preston Pilot, which paper is now published by his son, Mr. R. Clarke. The Sentinel was the organ of the "Tory party." The Pilot advocates the politics of the "Conservatives." Its circulation is not extensive. In 1837, the Preston Observer was inaugurated by a company of proprietors. It changed hands several times, and expired in 1840. In the same year, Mr. W. Pollard commenced the publication of the Preston Advertiser, but it had a very short-lived existence. Both these papers advocated "liberal" politics. In 1844, Messrs. Livesey and Son issued the first number of the Preston Guardian. Its politics are "liberal" or "radical." It is now published by Mr. W. Livesey, and commands the largest circulation of any journal in North Lancashire. About the time of the agitation for the repeal of the newspaper stamp duty (1855), several attempts were made to organize in Preston penny newspapers, and penny and even gratuitously circulated advertising sheets. With a single exception, however, these have had but an ephemeral existence. One established by Mr. H. C. Barton, the

Preston Herald, the joint production of a London and a Preston printing-office, is yet published. The Herald professes "conservative" principles. Its circulation is moderate. The Standard, issued by Mr. W. Bailey, continued for some months. The rest were very short-lived. Several other temporary publications, partaking in some degree of the character of local journals, have, from time to time been issued, including "The 3,730," published shortly after Mr. Hunt's first successful contest for the representation of the borough; the "Struggle," issued by Mr. Joseph Livesey, to aid in the procuration of the repeal of the corn-laws; the "Moral Reformer," edited and published by the same gentleman, etc.

BANKS.

THE OLD BANK.—The oldest bank established in Preston is that of Messrs. Pedder and Co., in Church-street. It was first opened for business in 1776. The name of the firm at the commencement was Atherton, Greaves, and Company, the company consisting of Mr. Denison, of London, and the grandfather of the present Mr. Edward Pedder. The establishment was afterwards known as that of Messrs. Pedder, Newsham, Lomax, and Denison. The next change was to Pedder, Newsham, and Co., the late Mr. Paul Fleetwood being a partner. The firm was afterwards changed to Pedder and Fleetwood, and again to Pedder, Fleetwood, and Pedder. Its present title is Pedder and Co. The building in which the business of this establishment is transacted, is an excellent specimen of the style of domestic architecture which prevailed at the earlier portion of the last century, when Preston was the favourite winter residence of the neighbouring nobility and gentry.[e] The noble porch, massive doorway, wainscoted rooms, and broad staircase with its heavy oaken bulustrade, proclaim the original builders and tenants to have moved amongst the classes most favoured by fortune. There are several other houses, since converted into shops, about Church-street and the southern side of the higher end of Fishergate, which yet bear evidence of the class of persons by whom they were originally tenanted. One in Church-street, near to the end of Grimshaw-street, a portion of which, occupied by Mr. Brandreth, though in a dilapidated condition, yet retains a somewhat similar porch to that of the old bank. This building is probably the one described as Mr. Eyre's house, by the parties engaged in the siege of Preston, in 1715.[f]

THE SAVINGS BANK.—Lune-street.—This elegant little edifice was erected in 1842, from a design by Mr. John Latham, at a cost of £1,300. It occupies the site of the premises originally rented by the trustees, and

---

e From an inscription found in the rear of the premises, it appears that the building was erected in 1690.

f See chapter 5, page 227.

Messrs. Pedder & Co. Old Bank Preston

subsequently purchased by them. This bank has now been in operation forty-one years. It was originally opened at the National school, Avenham-lane. Here it remained about two years, when it was removed to more convenient premises, in Chapel-street. In 1830, the trustees leased the premises in Lune-street, when the bank was removed to its present location. In 1830, the number of depositors was 1,234, and the amount deposited, £12,105. 7s. 10d.; in 1836, depositors, 2383, amount deposited, £26,572. 19s. 9d.; in 1846, depositors, 4616, amount deposited, £40,570. 10s. 4d. The following table shows the quantity and character of the business of this valuable institution at the close of the last financial year:—

No. of Depositors.		Total Amount of each Class. £	s.	d.
433	Whose respective Balances on the 20th Nov., 1856, (including Interest did not exceed .... £1 each	168	16	4
1123	.... ditto .... were above £1 and not exceeding .... 5 ,,	2909	15	10
974	.... ditto .... were above 5 and not exceeding .... 10 ,,	6846	19	0
724	.... ditto .... were above 10 and not exceeding .... 15 ,,	8589	4	0
427	.... ditto .... were above 15 and not exceeding .... 20 ,,	7270	11	7
784	.... ditto .... were above 20 and not exceeding .... 30 ,,	18597	9	10
584	.... ditto .... were above 30 and not exceeding .... 40 ,,	19394	0	9
289	.... ditto .... were above 40 and not exceeding .... 50 ,,	12787	12	10
477	.... ditto .... were above 50 and not exceeding .... 75 ,,	28842	3	0
196	.... ditto .... were above 75 and not exceeding ....100 ,,	16868	0	6
147	.... ditto .... were above 100 and not exceeding ....125 ,,	16272	14	3
76	.... ditto .... were above 125 and not exceeding ....150 ,,	10107	3	7
107	.... ditto .... were above 150 and not exceeding ....200 ,,	17624	8	7
1	.... exceeding 200	205	12	11
76	Friendly Societies..............	10399	13	2
33	Charitable Societies..............	1558	8	6
6451 g	Total number of Accounts. Total Balances......	£178,442,	14	1

The bank is open for business every Monday and Saturday, from ten to one o'clock.

Messrs. Lawe, Roskell, Arrowsmith and Co's. Bank, Fishergate, was first opened in July, 1825. In 1833, the partnership was dissolved, after which, the new firm, Messrs. Lawe and Hudson, continued the business in Fishergate. The description of this firm at the present time is Robert Lawe and Co. Messrs. Roskell and Arrowsmith opened, at the time of the dissolution, a new bank, next to the Castle-inn, Market-place, but afterwards removed to the premises at present occupied by them in Fishergate.

The Lancaster Banking Company first opened a branch in Preston, in 1833. This company is about to erect suitable premises for the transaction of their business, a little above their present offices, on the south side of Fishergate. The designs are by Mr. J. H. Park. The new bank will be situated at the western corner of Butler's-court, the covered entrance

g Included in this statement are 152 Depositors in the Branch Bank at Lytham, the amount due to whom is £4301 5s. 0d.

to which will be dispensed with, by which means, this narrow *cul de sac* will be better ventilated, and an angular view of the proposed edifice obtained.

The Preston Banking Company was first established in 1844, on the joint stock principle. Their new offices, on what was once termed the "Terrace," in Fishergate, were opened for business in 1856. It is one of the most elaborately decorated and attractive buildings in the town, and materially improves the general aspect of this portion of Fishergate. It is built of Longridge stone, in the "Italian palazzo style," from designs by Mr. J. H. Park. The first story is in strongly "rusticated work," with arched heads to the doors and windows, carrying carved masks on the key stones. The spandrils of the arches are filled with groups of fruit and flowers, hanging from tiger's mouths, inserted in the "string course." Above this, an elegant Corinthian colonnade forms the *facade* of the second story, each window of which is ornamented by a handsome cornice in the form of a pediment. The whole is surmounted by a massive cornice and carved string course, under which are the third story windows, with moulded architraves. The ground floor is devoted solely to banking purposes. The dimensions of the principal office are fifty-four feet by twenty-six feet. The remainder of the building is occupied as a residence by the manager.

BRIDGES.

Walton.—The Ribble in the immediate vicinity of Preston, is spanned by no fewer than six bridges. The old "bridge of Ribble" was situated a little below the present structure at Walton, immediately contiguous to the great British and Roman ford. It is impossible now to determine, with certainty, when the first bridge was erected over the Ribble. In the reign of Henry III. (1216 to 1272), however, the "bridge of Ribble" is referred to, in a then old boundary deed, as a well known object. In the reign of Henry IV. (1399 to 1413), letters patent were granted for the "pontage of the River Ribble, juxta Preston," and some time afterwards, similar authority was obtained for the "paviage of the said bridge."[h] This structure is described by Leland, in the reign of Henry VIII., as "the great stone bridge of Rybill, having V. great arches." The "South Prospect of Preston," published by S. and N. Buck, in 1728, shews the bridge as it then appeared, with its five pointed arches. Towards the latter end of the last century, however, the old structure exhibited unmistakable symptoms of decay; in consequence of which the present bridge was built. It consists of three large arches, and is considered an

h See chap. 3, p. 128, and chap. 5, p. 209.

Penwortham Bridge near Preston.

View from Avenham Walks Preston.

excellent piece of masonry. Below the western battlement, on the north end of the bridge, is the following inscription:—"Built by Sam[l] & Rob[t] Laws, in 1779, 80, & 81. Under the Inspection of Mr. Rich[d] Threlfall. Cost £4200."

PENWORTHAM BRIDGE is situated a little above the ancient ford described by Kuerden.[1] An act of parliament was obtained in 1750. The preamble declares that a bridge at this place was desirable, inasmuch as the fords were, "by reason of the great freshes and tides, which have, of late years, happened therein, so much worn, and become so deep and *founderous*, that his Majesty's subjects, even at low water, especially in the winter season, cannot pass the same on horseback, or with carts and carriages without imminent danger." It further states that several persons had "lost their lives in endeavouring to pass the said river;" and that, although the place of fording had been "shifted, changed, and removed," still from the "force of the current and the nature of the soil," the new fords had become as difficult and "founderous" as the previous ones; indeed, at the time, it appeared highly probable that the passage of the river at this place would shortly be "entirely lost and rendered impracticable." By the act, power was given to levy tolls for the maintenance of the bridge, to borrow money on the security of such tolls, and to purchase from the owners their right of ferry. The inhabitants of the "villas or townships of Broughton, Barton, Goosenargh, and Whittingham," and "other places in that neighbourhood," who "fetch their coal and cannel from such distant places, that they usually set out in the afternoon or evening of one day, and return home the next," were exempt from toll on their return. Subscriptions to the amount of £2,500. were raised from the principal gentry of the neighbourhood. The corporation of Preston subscribed the sum of five hundred pounds; and the two members for the borough (N. Fazakerley and J. Shuttleworth), a similar sum. The bridge was erected higher up the river than the old ford, to avoid the expense of crossing the then double stream formed by the "Holme." It was completed in 1755; and, in September, 1756, a little more than a year after its being thrown open to the public, owing to some defect in the foundation, one of the piers of the centre arch gave way, and shortly afterwards five other arches fell. The Rev. Randal Andrews, vicar of Preston, passed over the bridge shortly before the accident. Another act was obtained in 1757, which authorised the sum of two thousand pounds to be paid out of the county rate, for the re-construction of the bridge, and conferred power to levy tolls for necessary repairs. The bridge was so much damaged by floods, in 1768, that the toll was enforced. This toll was farmed for two hundred

1 See chap. 5, p. 211.

and seven pounds, and in the following year, for two hundred pounds. From time to time, a bar has been placed on the bridge for similar purposes. During the past year, about three hundred pounds were so raised for the repair of the structure, and the providing of additional accommodation for foot passengers.

Tram-road Bridge.—This wooden structure was erected in 1802. It forms a part of the tram-way formed to connect the Lancaster canal with a branch of that from Liverpool to Leeds, near the "Summit" coal pits. It is now but little used, the line having been leased by the Lancashire and Yorkshire Railway Company. On the brow of the hill, at Avenham, a stationary engine is placed, which, by means of an "endless chain" working round a shaft, erected near the centre of the bridge, raises the waggons, laden with coal, to the level of the high bank of the river. Accidents have frequently occurred, owing to the breaking of the chain, or the accidental detachment of the waggons, when the latter have been violently thrown over the wooden battlement into the "stone delph"[k] below. This bridge has already stood longer than the term originally intended, and is at present in so very dangerous a condition, that the footway over it is stopped during floods.

Brockholes Bridge.—This wooden structure was built when the Blackburn new road was excavated, in 1824. It has several times suffered much damage from the breaking up of the ice, and the winter floods. It is at present in good condition, having sustained little injury during the last few years.

North Union Railway Bridge.—This bridge was opened, together with the line of railway, in October, 1838. It was designed by Mr. Vignoles, civil engineer, and built by Messrs. Mullin and Co. It is one of the finest structures of the kind in England, being light and elegant, and extremely well built. It consists of five elliptical arches, of one hundred and twenty feet span each. From beneath the dry arch, on the north bank of the river, a very singular and powerful echo, repeated many times, is evoked by the utterance of a few words at an ordinary pitch of the voice. The embankment, connecting this viaduct with the southern slope above the valley of the Ribble, is nearly three quarters of a mile long. The construction of the two miles and a half of railway, from the Preston station southward, was let to Messrs. Mullin and Mc. Mahon, of Dublin, at the enormous sum of £80,000.

East Lancashire Railway Bridge.—This structure, first opened for traffic in June, 1846, is situated about half way between the North Union

k This deep hole in the river is so named, because the place was once quarried, and the material used for the erection of a steeple to the Parish church. The red sandstone rock, however, proved very perishable, and the tower was soon afterwards again re-built.

viaduct and the old Tram-road bridge. The river is passed by three arches of iron. On the north side is a dry brick arch over the pathway; and on the south, the railway is carried over the Ribble valley by a long viaduct, formed of brick arches, and an embankment pierced by several others. The amount of Mr. Cornie's contract, for the embankment and viaduct, was about £55,000. Previously to the erection of this bridge, the municipal authorities of Preston, having determined to convert the neighbouring bank of the river into a public park, opposed the East Lancashire Railway Company's bill, when before a committee of the house of commons. A compromise, however, was effected; by which the company not only undertook to provide a public footpath, on the east side of their viaduct over the Ribble, but likewise to plant the slopes of the northern embankment with shrubs and forest trees; and thus promote rather than frustrate, the objects proposed by the corporation.

CHURCHES, CHAPELS, SCHOOLS, PUBLIC CHARITIES, ETC.

THE PARISH CHURCH.—It has been shewn that Preston possessed a parish church during the Saxon period. At what precise time the earliest edifice was erected, is not known. The lands in the neighbourhood were first granted to the monks of Ripon, in 705, on the consecration of their church, after its "re-edification" by Archbishop Wilfrid. As the earliest recorded structure is dedicated to St. Wilfred, its probable erection must be placed some years later. Wilfrid died in the year 709, and was buried at Ripon. Mr. Whittle,[1] however, speaks of the "church of St. Theobald's (St. Wilfrid's afterwards)," being in the year 700, "repaired by Wilfrid, the archbishop of York," but he cites no authority! It is more probable the earliest church dedicated to Wilfrid was built soon after the grant of Amounderness to the ecclesiastics at York, by Athelstan, in 930. Mr. Whittle says, in his first vol., page 72, that the "Parish church of Preston was first dedicated, under God, to his (St. Wilfrid's) memory on the 12th day of October, 957, being the day his remains were deposited on the north side of the high altar, in Canterbury cathedral, by St. Anselm." For this statement, however, he refers to no ancient authority, but speaks of the 12th of October being the "dedication feast for the whole of Preston parish." It is not improbable, however, that a church existed at or near Preston, previously to the time of Athelstan, under the grant to Eata, abbot of Mailros, a disciple of St. Columba, who was afterwards superseded by Wilfrid.[m] The church is mentioned in the Domesday survey, which was compiled between 1080 and 1086.[n] Probably, on its being

1 History of Preston, vol. 2, page 129. m See chapter 2, page 68. n See chapter, 3, page 98.

rebuilt soon after the reformation (about 1581), the Roman saint was discarded, and the Protestant edifice dedicated to St. John, The body of the church having given way, it was again rebuilt, in 1770. In 1814, the tower[o] was taken down and rebuilt, and the chancel in 1817. The choir was renovated in 1823. Dr. Whitaker describes this edifice simply as a "good ordinary parish church." Mr. Edward Baines says, "as a public fabric there is nothing about the parish church of St. John to call for observation. The body of the church consists of two elevations with castellated parapets. The nave is divided from the side aisles by pointed arches deeply hollowed, and resting on octagonal pillars. There are no very ancient monuments; but the copy of one which existed some centuries ago, has been preserved. It is in memory of one of the Travers, of Tulketh, Nateby, Preston," etc.[p] The "old church," as it was termed, certainly well merited the very faint praise of the historians quoted. Its pretensions to architectural beauty or even character were so ambiguous, that it was sometimes quoted in derision as an excellent specimen of "joiners' gothic!" About the middle of the present century, it began to exhibit symptoms of decay, and, as the growing wealth and importance of the town demanded a more creditable structure, a public subscription was entered upon for the purpose of raising funds for the erection of the present edifice. With the exception of the lower portion of the tower, the old building was completely razed in 1853. During its destruction, an old grave stone, which had evidently been buried for many years beneath the then floor of the church, was discovered, bearing the following inscription engraved upon a large plate of brass :—

"HERE LYETH INTERD SEATH BVSHELL WOOLLEN DRAPER BAYLIFE AND A BROTHER OF PRESTON DYING THE XV OF SEPTR 1623 AGED 53 GAVE VNTO HIS KINESFOOLKES AND GOD CHILDREN IN LEGACIES VI· C· L [£600] ALSO XX· L [£20] TO THE POORE OF THIS TOWNE FOR EVER THE VSE [interest] TO BE GIVEN THE SAID POORE BY THE MAIOR OR HIS DEPVTIE AT CHRISTs & EASTER 4 [£4] TO THE POORE OF LEELAND & WALTON AL OVT OF HIS CHARITABLE MINDE."

This plate was sold in a "crumpled" state, with other old brass, to Mr.

---

o This tower is said to have been built of soft red sandstone rock, taken from the bed of the river, at the "stone delph," below Avenham.

p "I Travers by birth a Norman,
To gain victorious conquest,
With William Conqueror in I came
As one chief rol'd among the rest.

His guerdon was a crown,
And ours subjects spoyle,
Some ransom'd tow'r & town,
Some planted English soyle.

Tolketh his castle & herison,
My captives maulger were;
His daughter & his heire Dame Alison
I spoused to my fere.

Thirty winters thus were worn
In spousalls, mirth & glee;
Four begotten I had & borne
Ere crowned was Beauclerk Henerey.

Arnold & Jordan Fitz-Travers, [orders;
The one me succeed, th' other tooke
With Constance & Blanch, my daughters
The one to spousalls, the other vow'd cloysters·

"John Travers, of Tulketh, &c., occurs in the escheats of 36 Edw. III. (p. 2, n. 52.)"

W. Holland, who perceiving some letters upon it, preserved it from the melting pot. Mr. W. Dobson, in a communication to the Lancashire and Cheshire Historic Society, gives the following interesting particulars respecting the discovery of this monumental brass plate:—[q]

"The 'Seath Bushell' whose benevolence is thus recorded, was buried within the Parish Church of Preston, and his interment is recorded in the parish register, next to one dated the 16th of September, 1623, as follows:—Sep. [sepultus, buried] Mr. Seth Bushell, eo: die [the same day.] He was, as stated in the inscription, a "brother of Preston," i.e., a member of the corporation, his signature as 'Seath Bushell' being affixed to some proceedings of that body in the corporation records, in the year 1612. After possessing myself of this plate, which Mr. Holland kindly placed in my hands, with a view to its restoration to the church, I made some enquiries as to the site of Mr. Bushell's grave, and felt anxious to obtain some particulars of one who had shewn such a desire to benefit not only his 'kinesfoolkes,' but the poor of his town and neighbourhood. I learned that when the works in connection with the rebuilding of our Parish Church were in progress (in 1854 and 1855), the workmen were told that if they met with any plates (meaning, no doubt, ordinary coffin plates) they were to bury them. Yet even an ancient coffin plate might have possessed some local, personal, or historical interest. It would have been wiser to have ordered that all should have been submitted to some one in authority, who might have examined them. The workman who met with this plate, which was affixed to a gravestone about two feet below the then level of the church floor, knew that if a brass plate was of so little importance to a churchwarden, it would at least be worth something to a marine store dealer; so he got it removed and sold for old brass. In the progress of the work another workman met with a second brass upon the same gravestone, and this being disclosed in the presence of the parish sexton, some trouble was taken to obtain the former plate also, but of course without success. An inscription, 'Spes altera vitæ' [*sic*], cut in rude old English characters, was above the plates on the gravestone. When I made enquiries (in December last) a few months after the discovery, not a vestige of the stone could be found. It had been destroyed in the course of the work, but fortunately Mr. John Addison, of this town, who saw it soon after its discovery, had taken a rubbing of it, from which this copy has been made.[r] The two brasses are of equal size, nineteen inches by nine; the one discovered last was placed lengthwise on the stone, with the other one crosswise below it. The former bears a rude representation of a person wearing a robe, probably a municipal robe of that era; for our councillors then wore gowns, and rules respecting their attire are in our corporation records.[s] There is also the broad turned down collar seen in portraits of that date. Mr. Bushell, for I deem it to be intended for his effigies, has the close cut hair of the Roundhead of that age, as well as the moustache and 'beard of formal cut' clearly defined."

Nothing is known, with certainty, of the family of this generous Prestonian. He bears the same family name as Dr. William Bushell, the founder of the hospital at Goosnargh. A Seth Bushell, D.D., was vicar of Preston, half a century after the demise of his charitable namesake.[t] He most probably belonged to the same family. His legacy, like some others of a similar character, appears to have been altogether

q Volume 8, page 247.

r "Rubbings" from the brasses and stone accompanied Mr. Dobson's paper.

s See chapter 6, page 273.

t An old pamphlet, bearing the following title, is yet occasionally to be met with:—"The Believer's Groan for Heaven; in a Sermon at the Funeral of the Honorable Sir *Richard Hoghton*, of Hoghton, Baronet, Preached at Preston, in Amounderness, Feb. 14, 1677. By Seth Bushell, D.D. London, Printed for Thos. Sawbridg, at the Three *Flower-de-luces*, in *Little Britain*, and Philip Burton, at *Preston*, in *Lancashire*, 1678."

forgotten. No record of it is found either in the corporation minutes, or in the reports of the "Charity Commissioners." [u] The present footpath in Church-street, to the north of the Parish church, occupies the site of a terrace, which was removed in 1828. The terrace, at the eastern extremity, was ascended by a flight of stone steps. The western end, which was nearly level with the continuing parapet, was ornamented with iron gates. On the removal of this terrace, a small tomb stone, with a double cross sculptured upon it, was discovered. A silver coin of the reign of Charles II., together with a dagger, with a neatly chased handle, and some other relics, were likewise found. The churchyard was formerly planted with trees; but these ornaments to the urban cemetery gradually decayed, after the extension of the town, consequent upon the introduction of the cotton manufacture. The registers of the Parish church have been preserved since 1611. The vestry books contain but few interesting records relating to the church. The following are amongst the most important:—In January, 1644, the sum of fifty pounds was ordered to be disbursed in necessary repairs of the church, a previous grant of thirty pounds for the purpose being found insufficient. A rude plan of the church, dated Sep., 1647, is preserved. The arrangement of the pews, etc., did not differ materially from that which remained in 1853. The chancel was not in existence. A space at the south-east corner of the church is designated as "The aintient burying place of the Lords of Hoghton and Lea." All the pews are alike in size, with the exception of a large square one near the Hoghton sepulchre. In 1668, the record says, "The style att ye lower end of ye churchyard, towards ye east, was built of free stone, which stones were ye gift of Sir Richard Hoghton, Baronett, but ye charge of setting up and making ye said style was by ye town of Preston." In 1674, an order was made to repair the pews and flags, the former being "exceedingly decayed, and undecently kept, and out of order;" and the latter, "exceedingly broken and out of order, so as yey lye in a very undecent and rude manner." Of the date April 5th, 1675, is the following curious entry:—

"At a meeting of ye 24 gent. of ye parish, ordered yt ye pewter flagons belonging to ye church, being 5 in number, and now by use worn out, shall be all exchanged by ye churchwardens for new ones, and yat yere shall also be provided by ye said churchwardens three new plates of ye best pewter for ye service of ye communion, to be decently and well kept for ye future and not lent abroad to any funerals, or emploied in any common services."

The charnel-house appears to have become dilapidated about this period, for, on April 20th, 1675, an order is made "by ye 14 gent. of ye parish of Preston for ye building of a bone and charnel-house." It appears that

u See chap. 6, page 270.

bones had remained scattered about the church and churchyard, which the order declares to be an "indecent and uncomely yinge" [thing]. A penny per funeral is ordered to be paid to the sexton, in consideration that he "do gather up the fragments," place them in the bone-house, and, from time to time, re-commit them to the earth. In April, 1682, a new black hearse cloth is wanted. At the same time, an order is made that "ye church (being foule and uncomly) shall be whitened and beautified." In 1696, a fourth bell is ordered to be procured at a cost of forty pounds. From this entry it appears the Parish church steeple was previously furnished with no more than three bells. From 1689 to 1693, several sums are ordered to be expended in the repair of the bells. In 1694, twenty pounds were expended in the putting up of a new dial in the churchyard, and in repairing the clock. In 1719, a contract was entered into for the purpose of maintaining in good repair the roof and windows of the church. For this service, James Pert, the contractor, is allowed the apparently insignificant sum of £1. 6s. 8d. per annum. It appears that the churchwardens had been in the habit of feasting sumptuously at the parish expense; for, in April, 1731, at a "general meeting of the 24 gentlemen" previously alluded to, it was resolved that the churchwardens should "for the future bear all expenses that may happen, for what is called the churchwardens' dinner, at their coming into office, or any expenses on sacrament day, *except two bottles of wine* to be allowed to any strange clergyman that shall at any time preach." Truly, clerical eloquence at the period was a somewhat droughty affair! In 1752, the "new casting of the peal of eight bells" is ordered, together with "a compleat repair to the clock, and making it a good one." On the 6th November, 1768, the churchwardens are ordered to procure contracts for the taking down and re-building of the church, in consequence of its precarious condition having prevented the celebration of divine service in the usual manner. The "twenty-four gentlemen,"on the 23rd March, 1770, passed the following resolution:—

"Whereas, the nave or body of the Parish Church of Preston hath lately fallen down (but the steeple and vestry room, together with the chancel and north and south walls are yet standing), and the parishioners are thereby prevented from resorting to and attending the services of Almighty God; and whereas it is of absolute necessity that the same shall be forthwith repaired, or totally taken down and re-built, etc."

A rate, amounting to six hundred pounds, towards the necessary expenses, was ordered to be laid. On the 4th of April, following, at a meeting, not of the "four-and-twenty gentlemen," but, (for the first time), of "ye select vestry of ye Parish Church of Preston," Messrs. Woodcock and Roper, masons and carpenters, reported upon the state of the edifice. Amongst other matters they say:—

"We have inspected and examined the present state and condition of ye said Parish Church, and are of opinion that ye tower or steeple thereof, together with ye vestry and porch, are substantial and firm, and will stand, but that the north and south-west walls of ye said church are insufficient and ruinous, and must be taken down and re-built, with ye other part of ye said church that is fallen; that we have now delivered a plan of ye re-building and repairing of ye said parish church, together with an estimate of ye expense thereof, amounting in ye whole to ye sum of £1,400.; having all ye materials of ye old church, except ye lead and timber."

The vestry did not approve of the alterations proposed by the reporters, but ordered that the church should be re-built, "agreeable to the plan upon which the body of the old church was built, and that without any addition, diminution, variation, or any other alteration whatsoever, in the dementions, materials, or workmenship, in the walls, pillars, and roof thereof." A plan, by Mr. John Hird, was eventually approved of. His estimate amounted to £1,006. 10s. In September, 1771, a further rate of £406. 10s. was laid for the purpose of completing the contract. Several parties refused to pay the rate, and were "presented" in the Ecclesiastical court as defaulters. In December, Sir Henry Hoghton, bart., agreed with the vestry for the erection of a gallery "over a certain chappel or aisle, situate at the south eastern corner of the said church, containing, by a late admeasurement thereof, twenty-eight ffeet, or thereabouts, extending westward, from the inside of the east wall to about a ffourth part of the arch next the pulpit." From this it appears that the pulpit was originally placed against the centre pillar on the south of the nave. The vestry meeting, in August, 1790, in consequence of money being wanted for the repair of the church, ordered a rate to be levied in the proportion of one half on the "town district," and "each one quarter" on "the higher and lower districts." This arrangement caused some squabbling and litigation. The case was eventually tried at Lancaster, during the autumn assizes, in 1797. The verdict was in favour of the "ancient custom," by which the three divisions of the parish were rated in equal proportion. The churchwardens reported, in 1799, that they had placed a bench adjoining the vestry, as a baptismal seat, and erected a new font. They had likewise made several other alterations at the west end of the church. The old baptismal seat, on the north side of the middle aisle, by these improvements became unnecessary; it was therefore ordered to be sold, and the proceeds applied to the liquidation of the expenses incurred in the alterations referred to. The burial ground being found too small for the increasing number of inhabitants, in 1801, land was purchased on the south side, from the earl of Derby, for its enlargement. In the same year, the flags belonging to the Royal Preston Volunteers, together with a painting of the royal arms, were deposited in the church. The latter remained at the time of its demolition, but the flags, having fallen into decay, had been previously removed. The churchwardens, it appears, had again contrived to debit the parish with the expenses of a dinner, on the occasion of the "visitation of the officers of the spiritual court." These expenses, however, became so considerable that, in 1808, it was ordered that the churchwardens, in future, should be allowed no more than three shillings and sixpence each, on such occasions, for both dinner and liquor. In 1810, it was discovered that the "turret staircase" of the steeple, and the "cupola," thereupon, were in a dangerous state. It was resolved, by the select vestry, that the steeple should be taken down and re-built. In April, in the same year, the following resolution was placed upon the minute book:—

"It appearing to this meeting that the expense of taking down and rebuilding the steeple in its present form and new casting and replaceing the bells would amount, upon the average of the estimates now produced, to the sum of £1050, it is ordered by the vestry that the sum be raised within this parish for the purposes above mentioned, by £350. in each division thereof, according to the ancient custom within this parish for expenses relating to the church. And it is also ordered that instead of rebuilding the steeple upon the old plan and site, the same be rebuilt upon a new plan, to be approved of by the mayor and aldermen, as vestrymen for the town of Preston, and that the extra expense of the steeple and bells, over and above the said sum of £1050., shall be borne by the town of Preston."

In May, in the following year, however, the town of Preston was relieved from the "extra expense" referred to. Many meetings and discussions took place relative to the subject, but no further progress was made, except in the demolition of the upper portion of the tower. In August, 1812, however, plans were submitted for the rebuilding of the steeple upon the old site, and "preserving the east arch." The estimate amounted to the sum of £1204. 0s. 8d., with an intimation that if it should be thought desirable to carry the tower twenty-seven feet higher, a further expense of £760. would be incurred. This project was carried out. In 1815, the pulpit, reading desk, etc., were removed to their present position near the entrance to the chancel. There is a minute, dated August, 1816, which orders an "engine house" in the church yard to be removed, and the land so occupied to be added to the burial ground. In 1817, Sir Henry Hoghton, bart., communicated to the vestry his intention of taking down and rebuilding the chancel. In the same year funds were raised by subscription for widening "the arch at the entrance of the chancel." In 1820, a new clock was ordered, with four dials. The expense of the extra dials was borne by the "town of Preston." In 1824, the south wall of the churchyard gave way and was shortly afterwards re-erected. In August, 1835, the following resolution was passed:—

"Messrs. Pedder, Birchall, and Smith, having reported to this vestry in favour of procuring the requisite additional free sittings for the poor by erecting a gallery over the present organ gallery, and by bringing forward the organ gallery as far as the east pillar of the first arch,—resolved, that this vestry consents to the erection of the additional gallery, and the extension of the present organ gallery in the mode recommended, and that this vestry also consents to the further extension of the present gallery as pointed out by the Rev. R. Carus Wilson, the vicar, provided that the owners of all seats affected thereby consent thereunto,"

This was carried into effect, and a brass plate on the east wall of the gallery recorded that the "sittings were free and unappropriated for ever, in addition to the 1,500 sittings formerly provided, one hundred of which were free." An upper gallery formerly existed at the west end of the church. On the donation of the organ, in 1802, by John Horrocks, esq., M.P., a minute records that the mayor requested the sanction of the vestry for the taking down of an "upper gallery" in this portion of the edifice. The present structure was completed in 1855, at a cost of about £9,500. This sum was principally raised by subscription. The following six gentlemen guaranteed the payment of the estimated expense: Messrs. T. M. Lowndes, R. Newsham, J. Bairstow, T. Miller, T. Walmsley, and W. Birley. A bazaar, held in April, 1853, in aid of the building fund, realised upwards of £2,000. The new church, which was designed by Mr. Shellard, of Manchester, is regarded as a good specimen of the "flowing decorated style of English architecture." It consists of a nave, two side aisles, chancel, tower and spire, the height of the latter being two hundred and five feet to the top of the vane. The present edifice is built upon the foundations of the old church, with the exception of the entrance porch at the north west, and an addition to the chancel on the south side. The lower portion of the tower of the previous building was not removed. The new structure is calculated to accommodate about 1700 persons. Owing to the liberality of several gentlemen of the town and neighbourhood, the church will shortly be completely glazed with coloured glass. The eastern window is the gift of Sir Henry Bold Hoghton, bart., and was executed by Wailes, of Newcastle, after a design by the donor. It represents the crucifixion, and passages from Christ's passion. The eastern window of the side chancel aisle, was presented by John Bairstow, esq. It represents the four evangelists, with parables from each in rich medallions underneath. The next window, the first on the south, is the gift of John Horrocks, esq., and represents the calling of St. John. The next in order was presented by R. Newsham, esq. The subject represented is Christ blessing the little children. The neighbouring window, the gift of Charles Jacson, esq., represents the Transfiguration. The whole of these were executed by Wailes. The first window from the east, on the north side of the church, is a memorial one, presented by E. C. Lowndes, esq., on which are depicted figures of Faith, Hope, and Charity. It was designed and executed by Lamb, of London. The next window is glazed with the principal portion of the eastern window of the old church. It was presented by the late Thomas German, esq., and was executed by Ballantine, of Edinburgh. The next is a memorial window, erected by John Gorst,

The Parish Church, Preston.
(The Rev Canon Parr, Vicar.)

esq. It contains three figures, St. Stephen, St. Peter, and St. John the Baptist. It was designed and executed by Lamb. The window in the baptistry, by Willimont, of London, is the gift of Thomas Miller, esq. All the nave and clerestory windows have been executed at the expense of Thomas Batty Addison, and John Addison, esqs. They contain medallions representing subjects from scripture, armorial shields of sovereigns who have visited Preston, guild mayors, ecclesiastical functionaries connected with the town and diocese, and several families in the town and neighbourhood. The handsome font in the baptistry was presented by Mrs. W. A. Hulton, Miss Gorst, and Miss Rebecca Gorst. An elegant staircase to the pulpit, of rich open work in polished brass, has recently been added. The church can scarcely yet be said to be in finished state. Several other benefactions have recently been announced. A large brass plate, inserted in the west wall of the north nave, beneath the organ gallery, bears the following inscription:—"This Parish Church of St. John the Evangelist, Preston, was re-built by public subscription in the year of our Lord, M.dccclv, John Owen Parr, M.A., vicar; William Birley, and Miles Myres, Esquires, Churchwardens; Edwin Hugh Shellard, Esquire, Architect." The organ, originally erected in 1802, has since been considerably enlarged. It bears the following inscription:—"The Gift of John Horrocks, esq., M.P., 1802. Repaired and Enlarged by the addition of a Choir organ, at the expense of Samuel Horrocks, Esq., Mayor of the Guild, MD.CCCXLII." It is thus described in the "New History of the Organ," by Edward F. Rimbault, L.L.D :—

"The organ in the Preston Parish Church was originally built by Davis, of London, in 1802, and had a great organ from G.G. to F. in alt, and a swell to fiddle G. No Pedals or pedal pipes—Diagonal bellows.

"In 1822, a set of union pedal pipes (an octave and half), and new bellows, were put in.

"In 1842, a new choir organ was added by Gray and Davison, of London, at the cost of S. Horrocks, Esq., Guild Mayor; but, unfortunately, the great organ, and swell and pedals, received no addition.

"In 1850, the organ was entirely re-built; a new pedal organ added; the swell extended to tenor C.; and several new stops added to it and to the great organ. These additions were made by Jackson, of Liverpool, from funds raised by public subscription.

"In 1854, W. A. Cross, esq., of Red Scar, gave funds for a metal double diapason, and a new great organ sound board; Mr. Greaves, the organist, adding the twentieth at his own expense. Two spare slides were prepared on the great organ sound-board for a wood principal and a wood fifteenth. The organ has now 36 sounding stops, of which the following is a list:—

GREAT, 16 STOPS.

1 Double diapason, bass } in metal	9 Fifteenth, metal
2 Double diapason, treble } in metal	10 Fifteenth, wood
3 Stopped diapason	11 Sesquialtera 3 ranks
4 Open diapason, large scale	12 Mixture, 2 ranks
5 Open diapason	13 Twentieth *
6 Principal, metal	14 Trumpet, bass
7 Principal, wood *	15 Trumpet, treble
8 Twelfth	16 Clarion

CHOIR, 7 STOPS.

17 Stopped diapason	21 Flute
18 Clarabella	22 Fifteenth
19 Dulciana	23 Cromorne
20 Principal	

SWELL, 9 STOPS.

24 Double diapason	29 Fifteenth
25 Stopped diapason	30 Mixture
26 Open diapason	31 Hautboy
27 Keraulophon	32 Cornopean
28 Principal	

PEDAL, 4 STOPS.

33 Open diapason, 16 feet	35 Fifteenth, 4 feet
34 Principal, 8 feet	36 Sesquialtera, 3 ranks

ACCESSORY STOPS, MOVEMENTS, ETC.

1 Couplar, pedals to great	5 Couplar, octave couplar swell
2 Couplar, pedals to choir	6 7 Three composition pedals for great organ stops
3 Couplar, swell to great	
4 Couplar, choir to swell	

COMPASS.

Great and choir organs from from CC to f 3 in alt
Swell from tenor C to f 3 in alt
Pedal CCC to tenor c. [v]

The old church contained but few monuments of interest. Those which existed have been re-built into the present edifice. In the baptistry, beneath the tower, is an altar tomb beneath a Gothic niche, to the memory of Starkie Shuttleworth, esq., of Ashton. The baptistry likewise contains three other mural tablets, one to the memory of Margaret Hornby, of Poulton, 1815; one to William Pritchard, 1803, and another to Thomas and Catherine Greaves, 1811. There are no monuments on the north wall of the body of the church. The south wall, however, presents three small ones, to the memories of Jannet Pedder, 1842; Mary Gertrude Pedder, 1810; and Joseph Atkinson, 1853. On the north wall of the chancel are three monuments, of more pretensions. One, in the Italian manner, is erected to the memory of Dame Mary Hoghton, and dated 1720. The centre one is a neat Gothic structure, bearing the following inscription:—"In Memory of William Hulton, aged XX years, Nicholas Charles Grimshaw, aged XX years, George Henry Grimshaw, aged XVII years, and Joseph Kay, aged XX years, who in a moment of youthful enjoyment were drowned in the River Ribble by the oversetting of a boat, on the 24th day of April, A. D. 1822." The one to the right is inscribed to the memory of Mrs. Ann Broughton, daughter of Sir William Broughton, of Lawford, in Warwickshire, and sister to Lady Hoghton. On the south

v The double diapason, and the stops marked with an asterisk, have not yet been placed in the organ. The latter are intended to be added by the present organist, Mr. Greaves. The donation referred to, by Major Cross, was applied to the general fund for the re-construction of the church.

wall of the chancel are two superior monuments. One is erected to the memory of William St. Clare, M.D. who died in May, 1822. The other is a memorial of the late vicar, the Rev. Roger Carus Wilson, M.A. It is a beautiful work of art executed in Bath stone, by Theakstone, of London. The base exhibits, in relievo, representations of the five churches, erected through Mr. Wilson's instrumentality. There is likewise a small tablet over the arch which divides the chancel from the south aisle. The grave, bearing the oldest date, is situated about the centre of the church yard, on the south. The present stone was placed on the spot a little more than forty years ago, but the following inscription is a literal copy from the original:—"Here lyeth the body of George Rogerson, Salter," (drysalter) "who dyed childles Feb. the 3rd, 1619, aged 68, and gave to the poor of Preston, Nine Pounds yearly out of his lands for ever." Mr. Whittle says:—"In 1806, the stocks were standing in the church-yard, and near to them was a tombstone, dated 1642, 'To the memory of Richard Greenfield, who was slain in the lane near Walton-bridge, during the civil wars.' A rude outline was cut upon it of a man with a sword run through his body.* * * The last person put in the stocks was in 1816, when George Arkwright was placed in the pillory." Mr. Whittle conjectures Richard Greenfield may be the officer alluded to by Southey in his Espriella letters.[w] Another flat stone is inscribed to the memory of Thomas Myers, who was interred on the 12th of January, 1670. There is likewise one dated July 24th, 1690, which covers the remains of Christopher Santer, parish clerk. A large and handsome monument ornaments the churchyard on the south, erected by John Walshman, to the memory of his mother, who died July 14th, 1743. The monument was restored and "beautified" in 1818, by John, son of Roger and Grace Blelock, who are interred beneath it. There were several minor tablets in the old church which have not yet been re-erected. Mr. Whittle, amongst some others of this class, mentions two on the north-east wall of the nave, which he says bore the name of Wall's chapel. After the Norman conquest the church of Preston, with the tithes, fisheries, etc., was granted to the priory of St. Mary, at Lancaster, by Roger de Poictou. St. Mary's was "appropriated" to the Norman Abbey of Syon or Sees. The living reverted to the crown before the 4th year of the reign of John. Henry III. presented it to the nephew of the bishop of Winchester. Henry, duke of Lancaster, was patron in 1359, and John of Gaunt in 1371. The abbot and convent of Whalley were anxious to secure the benefice, and presented a petition to the duke of Lancaster, with an intimation to that effect. They were however, unsuccessful. The duke conferred the living upon his new college at Leicester,

w Lecture at Preston, in 1849. See page 219 of the present volume.

on the 17th of June, 1420. [x] The advowson remained with the dean and canons of St. Mary's College, Leicester, till the time of Edward VI. when it again reverted to the crown. In 1607, the living was vested in the Hoghton family, by James I. They retained possession of it until it was purchased a few years ago, by the "Feoffees of William Hulme, of Hulme and Kearsley, esquire." A chantry was founded in the church by Richard Whalley, in 1498, who "vested lands in Sir Alexander Hoghton, to maintain a chaplain at the altar of St. Crux, in the said chantry." St. Mary's chantry, in Preston church, is mentioned in the return of the commissioners of chantries in Lancashire, in 1548. In 1650, Preston is returned by the "Inquisitors" as a vicarage in the patronage of Sir Richard Hoghton, bart., "the Impropriator of the Tithes." The tithes were valued at £176. 12s. 10d. The return further states:—"Mr. Isaac Ambrose, a painfull Min[r], is Vicar of Preston, and receives for his Sallary the profitts of his whole Vicarage, w[ch] about 30 years since was worth ab[t] 100 markes per ann. but in these distracted troublesome times, the same is not so much worth; besides which there is £50. per ann. of an augment[a] from the Com: of Plund. Min[rs], and £50. per ann. forth of y[e] Revenue of the Duchy of Lancaster, to Mr. Ambrose, as one of the foure Itinerant Ministers within the County." [y] Bishop Gastrell, in his "*Notitia Cestriensis*," gives the following additional particulars respecting the church and living at Preston:—[z]

"Preston, certified by the Vicar anno 1705, not above 57[l], (4[l] of w[ch] to be paid to the Curate of Broughton Chapel, viz. one Acre of Land; Great Tyths of one Township about 12l per annum; Small Tyths and Easter dues uncertain; the rest Surplice Fees. Vide *Pap. Reg.*

"By other accounts it appears to be a good 100[l] per annum, part of wh[ch] is precarious; but the Vicar now allows it to be above 80[l] per annum, in such dues as may be legally demanded, anno 1717.[a]

"Given to 'water dry and barren places in Lancashire,' or to 'direct the People to the glory of a Preaching Minister at Preston,' by Mr. Henry Banaster, of Hackney, 10l per annum. The Mayor and Councill of Preston were Trustees for ye money [£200; being part of a legacy of £600,] wch hath been laid out in Land in Brockholes, near Preston, and is now applied to a Curate.

"Anno 1374, a Clerk instituted to the Rectory of Preston, upon the Presentation of the Duke of Lancaster. *Reg. Charlton*, f. 16.

x "Appropriatio Ecclesiæ de Preston Monaster. de Syon: Dat. 17 die Junii, A. D. 1420."—Dr. Ducarel: Chartæ Miscell. in the Augmentation Office.

y Parl. Inq. Lamb. Libr.

z "Notitia Cestriensis, or Historic Notices of the Diocese of Chester, by the Right Rev. Francis Gastrell, D.D., Lord Bishop of Chester, now first printed from the original manuscript, with illustrative and explanatory notes, by the Rev. F. R. Raines, M.A., F.S.A., Rural Dean, Hon. Canon of Manchester, and Incumbent of Milnrow. Printed for the Chetham Society, M.D.CCC.L."

a The annual value of the living in 1834, was estimated at £665.—Raines.

"The church of Preston in Amounderness belonged to ye Dutchy of Lancaster till it was appropriated to ye Collegiate Church of St. Mary of Leicester; and then a vicaridge was ordained. *MS. Ebor.*

"Anno 142, a Presentation to the Vicarage of Preston, by the Dean and College of St. Maryes of Leicester. *Register of Archdeacon Bowet*, f. 11.

"Value 16l Patron, the College of Leicester. *MS. L.*

"Anno 1580, John Bold, of Northmeals, esq., Patron. *Institution Book*, 2, p. 3.

"35 Elizabeth, Henry Bold, Patron. *Ib.*

"Anno 1603, a vicar presented by virtue of a grant from Sr Richard Houghton, of Houghton Tower. *Ib.* p. 37.

"Anno 1630, the King presented upon ye Outlawry of Sr Richard Houghton. Vide *Subscription Book.* Sir Richard Houghton is afterwards stated to have presented Mr. James Starkie, on the 2d December, 1632. *Inst. Bk.*
"Patron, Sir Henry Houghton, Bart.

"A Reader was nominated by the Mayor and Corporation and other Inhabitants. Vide Nomination, 1695."

Mr. Whittle gives, from various sources, a number of early rectors and vicars of Preston. He introduces the list with the following observations:—"Whitaker, in his History of Whalley, p. 78, stated that the register of Preston cannot be traced later than 1607, and the records of Chester have been searched in vain." We will supply this matter in part, therefore Mr. Whitaker is mistaken. The names supplied by Mr. Whittle are as follows:—

1243.—Benedict Osbaldestone, Clerico, son of Eilfi Osbaldestone. [b]
1297.—Dom. Willus Dacre, who held the advowson till 1322. A Cistercian.
1322.—A prior and two monks of the Cistercian order.
1359.—Henrica de Walton, a Cistercian monk.
1360.—Robert de Burton; Patron, Henry, duke of Lancaster.
1371.—Radbert de Ergham, L.B. of Cockersand Abbey. Patron, John, duke of Lancaster.
1416.—Ricardus de Walton, a Benedictine.
1418.—Dom. John White, pbr. a Benedictine.
1421.—Dom. John Lingard, pbr. do.
1452.—Thos. Bolton, from Furness Abbey, Patron King Henry VI.
1561.—Nicholas Banester.[c] Patrons, Ricardus Werden and others.
1562.—Lawrence Wall, brother to Evan Wall, steward of Preston Guild.
1563.—Roger de Chorley; Patrons, Thomas Parker and Thomas Patchett.
1567.—Leonard de Chorley; Patrons, William Patten and John Bold, North Meols.
1568.—Nicholas Bradshaw.[d]

b Osbaldestone pedigree.

c Strype says, "Banester was an unlearned schoolmaster, for he was ordered to remain in the county of Lancaster, (after being deprived of the living of St. Wilfrid's), the town of Preston excepted: He was vicar of Preston in Queen Mary's days, and was sorely persecuted for conscience sake, being known to be a rank Jesuit."

d Mr. Whittle says, "During Bradshaw's ministry we read from '*Blighted Ambition*,' that 'during Elizabeth's reign, when she fell ill in 1563, she was most seriously affected with a belief in witchcraft, and that the recusants of Preston in Lancashire, shut up St. Wilfrid's church by main force, and caused the Romish ritual of mass to be publicly read: the Bishop of Winchester during the same time broke down the gates of Corpus Christi, and a new college, Oxford, that he might purge the place of Popish delinquents who were there, and to expunge many practices which was symbolizing with the ancient faith.'—Vide vol. 3d."

Mr. Baines[e] gives the following list of the vicars of Preston, from the 6th Elizabeth, "collected from the episcopal registers of Chester and other authentic sources."

VICARS OF PRESTON,

IN THE DEANERY OF AMOUNDERNESS, AND ARCHDEACONRY OF RICHMOND.

Date of Institution.	Vicars.	On whose Presentation.	Cause of vacancy.
	Nicholas Bradshaw		
Sep....29, 1567	Roger Chorley	Thomas Patchett	Death of Nich. Bradshaw
Sep.... 4, 14 Eliz	Nicholas Danyell	John Bold, of North Meols	Resign. of Roger Chorley
Aug...27, 1580	Thomas Wall	The King	Resign. of Nich. Danyell
Dec...21, 35 Eliz	William Sawrey [f]	Henry Bold	Death of Thos. Wall
Feb....12, 1603	John Paler	Robert Parker, yeoman	
May...28, 1621	James Martin	Sir Richard Houghton	Death of John Paler
July...21, 1623	Alexander Bradley	King James, patron by lapse of time	
May...19, 1625	John Inskip	The King	
Nov...18, 1626	Augustine Wildbore	Sir Richard Houghton, Kt. and bart.	
Dec.... 2, 1630	James Starkie	The same [g]	Resignation of Augustine Wildbore
[h]	Seth Bushell	[i]	
Oct....12, 1692	Thomas Birch	Sir Charles Houghton	Resign. of Seth Bushell
May...29, 1700	Samuel Peploe	The same	Death of Thomas Birch
July... 4, 1727	Samuel Peploe, jun.	King George	Promotion of Samuel Peploe to the bishopric of Chester [j]
April 30, 1743	Randal Andrews	William Shaw, for this turn only	Resign. of Samuel Peploe
Oct....30, 1782	Humphrey Shuttleworth	Sir Henry Houghton	Death of Randal Andrews
Sep....26, 1809	James Penny	Sir John Philip Houghton	Resign. of Hum. Shuttleworth
Mar... 1, 1817	Roger Carus Wilson	Wm. Wilson Carus Wilson	Death of James Penny

Roger Carus Wilson died December 15th, 1839. The living was shortly afterwards presented by the trustees of the "Hulme Exhibitions" to the present vicar, the Rev. J. Owen Parr, M.A., and honorary canon of Manchester.

St. George's Chapel.—Preston appears to have possessed only one place of public worship, in connection with the established church, till the year 1723, when a plain brick edifice was erected on the south side of Fishergate, as a chapel of ease to the parish church. This unassuming structure

e History of Lancashire, vol. 4, p. 334.

f Mr. Whittle prints this name Lawrie. There are some other descrepancies between the two lists.

g This is evidently an error. According to the Notitia Cestriensis, the king presented in 1630, owing to "ye outlawry of Sir Rich. Houghton."

h According to the Inquisitors' return previously quoted, Isaac Ambrose was vicar of Preston, in 1650. Mr. Whittle says, "Ambrose remained minister of the church of Preston from 1646 till 1660, and died in 1663, aged 59 years. Ambrose wrote an excellent work, on the 'first, middle, and last things' (in folio), printed after his death, in 1701. He was curate of Garstang for some time. * * The Rev. Oliver Heywood, B.A., the celebrated nonconformist, had an offer of Preston vicarage about 1655-9, from Sir Richard Hoghton, bart., but declined the acceptance on some account."

i Whittle gives in 1662: Thomas Clark; patron, Sir Richard Hoghton; and on January 4, 1667, Seth Bashell, D.D.; patron Sir R. Hoghton.

j Peploe was made warden of Manchester, in 1717, by the king. The then bishop of Chester (Dr. Gastrell), refused to recognise the appointment, on the plea that Peploe's degree had been obtained from the archbishop, at Lambeth, and not at the university of Oxford. The court of King' Bench, however, decided against the bishop.

St. Augustine's Chapel & Rectory, Preston.

[illegible]

was, in 1843-4, faced with stone and otherwise ornamented, the necessary funds being furnished by the liberality of the late T. M. Lowndes, esq.; to whose memory an excellent mural monument in marble, by Mr. Duckett, has been erected in the church, at the expense of his brother E. C. Lowndes, esq. The deceased gentleman, whose patronymic was Gorst, but who assumed the name of Lowndes on succeeding to a large fortune bequeathed by a relative of that name, was distinguished by unostentatious benevolence and liberality. He bestowed for a number of years a considerable portion of his large income in works of charity. By this gentleman's munificence, a new chancel was erected in 1848, and in the following year the present elegant pulpit and reading pew were constructed. St. George's chapel is furnished with a good organ.

Trinity Church.—The rapid increase of the town, in the early portion of the present century, rendered further accommodation for religious worship necessary. In 1814, the first stone of a new church was laid by Sir Henry Hoghton, bart., on a plot of ground then named "Patten Field." In the following year, the edifice was consecrated and dedicated to the Holy Trinity. This church, though constructed in the "decorated" or middle period of English architecture, has but little pretension to architectural beauty. It is, however, a good substantial edifice, with side and end galleries, and a spacious eastern window filled with stained glass, the work of Mr. W. R. Egginton, of Birmingham. Mr. Whittle says,[k] "the total amount of the building of Trinity Church, cost nine thousand and eighty pounds nine shillings and threepence." He further records that "there are fifty sittings subject to an annual rent of one pound each, as a stipend for the officiating minister; the salary is about £150. per annum, besides what the congregation give gratuitously, aided by what is termed Queen Anne's bounty, for which a certain sum of money was expended to obtain this. On the right and left side are excellent free sittings for the use of the working classes of society." The church was erected partially by subscription, and partially from funds derived from the sale of pews. The right of presentation to the living is vested in the trustees and the vicar of Preston alternately. In the year 1824, an organ was erected in the west gallery. This was superseded in 1842, by the present excellent instrument, constructed by Grey, of London.

St. Peter's Church, Fylde-road.—The foundation stone of this church was laid during the "guild week," in 1822, by Mr. Justice Park, the recorder of the borough. The entire expense of its erection, £6,900, was defrayed by the "commissioners for building new churches." The land for the site of both church and burial ground, was presented by Mr. James

k His. of Preston, vol. 1, p. 68.

Allan Park, son of the recorder. This church was built from plans designed by the distinguished architect, Thomas Rickman, of Birmingham. It is in the style of the latter period of English architecture, called perpendicular or florid gothic, and is much admired for the beauty of its general form and elaborate decoration. The present organ, built by Nicholson, of Rochdale, was presented by S. R. Grimshaw, esq., in 1846. This instrument had previously been erected in the church, but was removed by its proprietor to the Corn Exchange assembly room. By the will of the late Thomas German, esq., the sum of £1,000. was invested in trustees for the purpose of erecting a tower and spire to this building. This was completed in 1852. Mr. Joseph Mitchell, of Sheffield, was the architect. Mr. Edward Baines,[l] referring to this edifice and St. Paul's, says:—

"It was generally wished that a spire might be attached to one of the new churches, and that the additional expense should be raised by subscription, but the plans could not be altered. The manufactories still tower over the churches, the highest building in the town being the chimney of a steam engine; and it is an extraordinary fact that previous to the erection of the new catholic chapel of St. Ignatius, and the addition of a spire to the church at Mellor, in Blackburn parish, there was not a spire between the Lune and the Ribble, with the exception of one at Lancaster, nor is there a single spire within fourteen miles of Preston.'

This was written in 1836. During the last twenty years, however, numerous spires have sprung up in the town and neighbourhood.

St. Paul's Church, Park-road.—It was originally intended, when the sum of £12,500 was granted by the commissioners, to expend it in the erection of one church only.[m] But this determination was afterwards abandoned, from a conviction that the accommodation of the inhabitants would be more efficiently attained by two smaller edifices. The first stone of St. Paul's church was laid by the Rev. R. Carus Wilson, vicar, in October, 1823, upon land presented by Samuel Pole Shawe, esq. The building cost rather more than £6,500. It is a very elegant specimen of the early English style of architecture, and was designed by Messrs. Rickman and Hutchinson. An excellent organ was placed in this church, in 1844. It bears the following inscription:—"The gift of Thomas Miller, and Henry Miller, esqs., MDCCCXLIV." A very small organ had been previously used.

Christ Church, Bow-lane.—This church, one of a series erected chiefly through the instrumentality of the Rev. R. Carus Wilson, M.A., late vicar

l His. Lan. vol. 4, p. 337.

m "It is not generally known that the grant of £12,500. was obtained by the bishop of Chester (Lawe), to defray the expenses of *one* church, St. Peter's, on the representation of Nicholas Grimshaw, esq., and Thomas Troughton, esq., but that on the suggestion of the vicar, the commissioners resolved upon the erection of *two* churches out of the original grant, which was effected, exclusive of the burial ground attached to St. Paul's."—Baines's Lancashire, vol. 4, p. 336.

[illegible]

Incumbent the Rev. W. M. [illegible] M.A.

of Preston, was consecrated on the 11th of October, 1836, by the bishop (Sumner) of Chester, and opened for public service by the vicar on the 19th of March, in the following year. It is in the Norman style of architecture, and was designed by Mr. John Latham. The principal entrance is flanked by two octagonal towers, with curious stunted conical caps. These towers are seventy feet in height. The length of the church is about seventy feet, and the breadth fifty-six feet. The building furnishes accommodation for nearly one thousand and fifty people. Four hundred of the sittings are free. The gallery will accommodate about five hundred persons. This church was enlarged in 1852, when several additional sittings were provided. The organ was erected in 1843.

St. Mary's Church.—The first stone of this edifice was laid in May, 1836. It was opened for service in 1838, and enlarged in 1853. It is eighty-six feet in length, and the height of the spire is about one hundred and four feet. In 1849, an organ, built by Messrs. Kirtland and Jardine, was erected, the necessary funds being realised by public subscription. This church likewise owes its existence principally to the exertions of the late Rev. R. Carus Wilson. M.A. The land was presented by Mr. John Smith, who likewise contributed two hundred pounds towards the funds for the erection of a school in connection with the church. The structure was designed by Mr. John Latham, and is in the Norman style of architecture, with a curious spire of a somewhat doubtful character. The enlargement was effected under the superintendence of Mr. Shellard, of Manchester. By the erection of this transept additional accommodation for about four hundred persons is obtained. The original building was constructed to seat about one thousand and fifty persons.

St. Thomas's Church, Lancaster-road.—This is one of the new churches erected through the instrumentality of the late vicar. The necessary funds formed a portion of a legacy of about fifty thousand pounds, bequeathed for church building purposes by Miss Catherine Elizabeth Hyndman. The first stone was laid in August, 1837. The building, which is in the Norman style of architecture, with a nave, side aisles, and a small chancel, was built after designs by Mr. Jno. Latham. The tower supports a spire, one hundred feet in height. It provides accommodation for about eleven hundred persons. The organ was erected in 1855.

St. James's Church, Avenham-lane.—This building was erected in 1837, as a dissenting chapel, by the friends of the Rev. Mr. Fielding. It was afterwards purchased by the late vicar, the Rev. R. Carus Wilson, and consecrated as a place of worship in connection with the Church of England, on the 9th of June, 1841. This church was originally a plain, spacious building of brick. The walls have since been strengthened by stone buttresses, and its general appearance much improved, both externally and internally. The organ was built by Mr. Jackson, of Liverpool, and was erected in 1855.

ALL SAINT'S CHURCH, Elizabeth-street.—The first stone of this structure was laid in October, 1846. The necessary funds were raised by public subscription; many of the contributors belonging to the operative classes. Hence the edifice is often termed the "Poor Man's Church." The subscription originated in a desire to retain to the town the services of the Rev. W. Walling, M.A., formerly pastor of St. James's, but who had resigned his appointment. This church, which is a large and substantial edifice of brick, with a stone peristyle, in the Ionic order of Grecian architecture, will accommodate from fourteen hundred to sixteen hundred people. The designs were furnished by Mr. John Latham.

ROMAN CATHOLIC CHAPELS.

ST. MARY'S, Friargate.—Mr. Baines says,[n] "it does not appear, that at any period since the reformation, when the Franciscan Convent was dissolved, and the Parish Church passed out of their possession into the hands of the protestants, that they" (the Roman catholics) "had ever more than one place of worship in this town, till the year 1793. The original chapel, called St. Mary's, is situated at the top of Friargate-brow." This is not precisely correct. For some time after the reformation, the Roman catholics were, owing to the rigorous persecution to which they were subjected, compelled to worship privately and in secret. The tone of public feeling, in this respect, however, so far improved, that a small thatched building, in a place called Chapel-yard, in Friargate, below Bridge-street, is said to have been used by them as a place of public worship, as early as 1605. This building, after being converted into cottages, and again transformed into a stable, was pulled down a few years ago, and a joiner's shop erected upon the site. It was dedicated to St. Mary, probably in memory of the ancient hospital on the Maudlands. The Rev. George Oliver, D.D., of Exeter, in an account of the "Preston Mission, communicated to a friend in Preston," however, says:—

"The Jesuits, from the accession of King James II., in 1685, at least had the pastoral charge of the Catholics of Preston. Bishop Leyburn, during his visitation of the northern counties, in 1687, confirmed at Preston and Tulketh 1,153 persons, on Sep. 7th. Divine service was then performed in a barn at Fishwick. * * The first chapel in Preston, I believe, was erected in 1761, by Father Patrick Barnewell, in honour of St. Mary, on part of the site of the Convent of Grey Friars. He died shortly after, in 1762. He was succeeded by Father Jos. Smith, who witnessed the spoliation of his chapel by an infuriated mob, in 1768" (during the great election), "and died May 1, about a month afterwards."

The chapel alluded to by Mr. Baines, was opened in the year 1761. The

n His. Lan., vol. 4, p. 336.

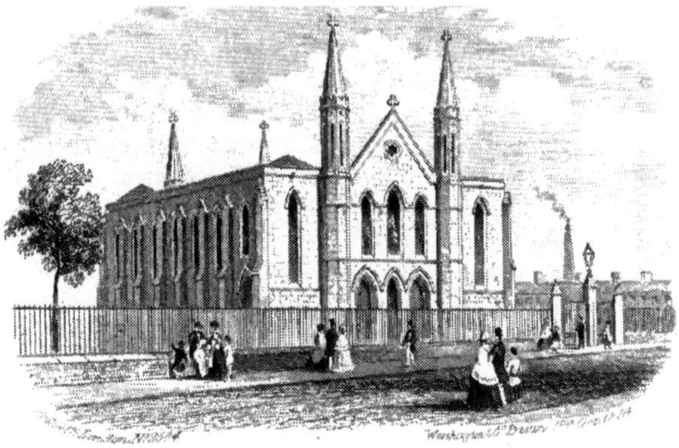

St. Paul's Church, Preston.

Rev. John Miller, M.A. Incumbent.

old building, in Chapel-yard, was closed, and the new one dedicated to St. Mary. It continued to be the only place of worship, in connection with the Roman catholic body, till the erection of St. Wilfrid's, in 1793. It was then in turn closed, and afterwards converted into a cotton warehouse. In 1815, however, the increased population requiring more accommodation, it was re-opened for public worship. During the past year (1856), it was entirely re-built and considerably enlarged. The altar of St. Mary's was embellished by a large oil picture, representing the last supper. The picture painted by Mr. Hill, which formerly decorated the altar at St. Wilfrid's, has been removed to St. Mary's.

St. Wilfrid's, Chapel-street.—This plain but spacious edifice was opened on the 4th of June, 1793. The south end was taken down a few years ago, and the chapel considerably lengthened. Mr. Baines speaks of the old "altar-piece being enriched with several paintings of superior workmanship." The chief subject was the "Ascension." Over the altar was afterwards placed a large and cleverly-executed oil picture, by Mr. Chas. G. Hill, representing the "Taking down from the Cross," copied from an original painting, supposed to be the production of one of the Carracci, which forms a chief feature of the collection at Stonyhurst. This picture has since been removed to St. Mary's, Friargate; St. Wilfrid's chapel has lately been entirely redecorated by Mr. Balfe, of London. The "Crucifixion" forms the subject of the altar-piece. The organ, which was built by Davis, in 1839, was enlarged in 1855. A small and highly decorated building, erected "from a model in Rome," named the "Lady chapel," was added in 1844. The chief of the ornamental decoration was executed by Mr. Taylor Bulmer. The chapel was considerably enlarged and beautified in 1839, at a cost, including the expense of the new organ, of about two thousand pounds. Previously to its enlargement, this edifice was computed to accommodate three thousand persons. A seminary, in connection with the Benedictine Nuns of Ghent, was established contiguous to this chapel, in 1792. The sisterhood removed to Caverswell Castle, in Staffordshire, in 1812.

St. Ignatius's, St. Ignatius-square.—The first stone of this elegant structure was laid on the 27th of May, 1833. It is a cruciform building, in the latter period or perpendicular English style of architecture, and was erected from designs by J. J. Scholes, esq., of London. It is about one hundred and fourteen feet in length, and the breadth of the nave forty-eight feet. There is sitting accommodation for about six hundred persons, and standing room for nearly two hundred others. The building is ornamented with a square tower, surmounted by an ornamental spire, the entire height of which, including the cross, is nearly one hundred and twenty feet. The altar table, which is beautifully carved, and decorated with figures of the apostles, was presented to the church by Jas. Anderton, esq., of Haighton. This church has since been enlarged by an additional sacristy or confessional. Several stained glass windows, by Barnett, of York, and other decorations by Evans, Thompson, and Brown, of Birmingham, have been added at considerable cost. In the immediate neighbourhood is a commodious residence for the clergy, who belong to the Society of Jesuits. The original cost of the building, including the priests' house, exceeded eight thousand pounds. A small tablet says that one thousand and thirty pounds of this sum were raised by small weekly subscriptions of poor catholics in Preston. It contains a very good organ, built by Davis. On the north side of St. Ignatius-square, is a building erected for the accommodation of the "Sisters of Charity."

St. Austin's, St. Austin's-place.—The foundation stone of this edifice was laid in November, 1838. The necessary funds were raised by public subscription. The land was presented by Dr. Briggs, the Roman catholic bishop of the district. It is calculated to seat about one thousand persons. The plan of the building is cruciform, with a sunk stone portico, in the Roman Ionic order, facing Vauxhall-road. It was designed by the late Mr. Tuach. The interior is handsomely decorated, the high altar being adorned by a large oil painting, by Mr. Taylor Bulmer, after a celebrated picture by Paolo Veronese. The excellent organ, by Grey, of London, was erected in 1841.

St. Walburge's, Maudlands.—The first stone of this edifice was laid on Whit-Monday, 1850. It is erected on or near the site of the ancient hospital dedicated to St. Mary Magdalen.[o] It was opened for public worship in August, 1854. It is built in the early decorated period of Gothic architecture, and is one of the largest and handsomest structures in Preston. It is one hundred and sixty-five feet long, by fifty-five feet wide. The western façade, or principal front, is divided into three portions by two lofty buttresses, which rise to a height of sixty-nine feet. This façade is ornamented by a circular or "wheel" window, twenty-two feet in diameter, highly decorated and filled with geometric tracery. Above is a small arcade of five lancet-headed lights. The height from the ground, to the top of the elaborately carved cross, is ninety-one feet. The roof is eighty-three feet from the parapet, and is terminated by highly ornamented ridge tiles. The tower is near the east end, on the south side of the church. It is intended to carry a spire, which will support a cross three hundred feet above the level of the street. The base of this tower is nearly fifty feet square. When complete, the tower itself will be one

o See page 116.

Interior of St. Walburgh's Church, Preston.

The Grammar School, Preston.

hundred and fifteen feet high, and capable of containing a peal of twelve bells. At present it has been built no higher than sixty-one feet. The body of the church is of grey flag, with dressings of white grit; but the tower is of lime stone. The interior is very spacious, and highly ornamented. The east window, which is thirty-five feet high, by twenty-one feet wide, is filled with stained glass. Other windows are likewise decorated in a similar manner. These embellishments are chiefly the gifts of private individuals. Several other decorations are at present in progress. There is a small gallery at the west end of the church capable of holding about one hundred choristers. As there are no other galleries, and as about one-third of the entire area is occupied by the sanctuaries, etc., the building, notwithstanding its large dimensions, is calculated to accommodate no more than one thousand six hundred persons, for which number benches are erected. The present arrangement with regard to the sacristry and confessional, is merely temporary. These are intended to be added to the present edifice, when not only will more internal space be gained, but the exterior outline of the structure will be much improved. There are three altars, highly decorated. The edifice has been erected from designs by Mr. Joseph A. Hansom. The organ was built by Messrs. Hill and Co., in 1855. It contains thirty sounding stops, distributed among two manuals and pedal, in the following manner :—

GREAT, 15 STOPS.

Every Stop throughout.

1	Double open diapason	16 feet	9	Fifteenth	2 feet
2	Open diapason	8 feet	10	Piccolo	2 feet
3	Gamba	8 feet	11	Sesquialtera, 3 ranks	$1\frac{3}{5}$ foot
4	Stopped diapason	8 feet tone	12	Mixture, 3 ranks	
5	Quint	$5\frac{1}{3}$ feet	13	Posaune	8 feet
6	Octave	4 feet	14	Clarion	4 feet
7	Wald Flute	4 feet	15	Cremona	8 feet tone
8	Twelfth	$2\frac{2}{3}$ feet			

SWELL, 12 STOPS.

16	Double open diapason	16 feet	22	Twelfth	$2\frac{2}{3}$ feet
17	Open Diapason	8 feet	23	Fifteenth	2 feet
18	Salicional	8 feet	24	Sesquialtera, 3 ranks	$1\frac{3}{5}$ foot
19	Stopped diapason	8 feet tone	25	Oboe	8 feet
20	Octave	4 feet	26	Cornopean	8 feet
21	Suabe flute	4 feet	27	Clarion	4 feet

PEDAL, 3 STOPS.

28	Open diapason	16 feet	30	Trombone	16 feet
29	Octave	8 feet			

COUPLERS.	COMPASS.
1 Swell to great	Great CC to f 3 in alt.
2 Great to pedal	Swell CC to f 3 in alt.
3 Swell to pedal	Pedal CCC to tenor e.

The Roman Catholics propose to erect a new church and schools under the direction of the secular clergy of St. Austin's, a little to the right of Ribbleton-lane, behind Mr. Seed's cotton mill. Some subscriptions have been collected, and other steps taken in furtherance of this object.

CHAPELS OF PROTESTANT DISSENTERS, Etc.

Mr. Edward Baines[p] considers it "probable that a congregation of protestant dissenters was formed in Preston soon after the passing of the memorable St. Bartholomew's act, 1662." He deduces this opinion chiefly from the fact that the Rev. Isaac Ambrose, one of the most distinguished nonconformist ministers, resided in Preston, during the Commonwealth. No record, however, has been preserved of their occupancy of any special building for public worship.

The Unitarian Chapel, to the north of Church-street, a very small building, with no architectural pretensions, was erected in 1718. It was originally occupied by the Presbyterians.

The Society of Friends originally held their meetings in a building situated between Everton-gardens and Spring-gardens.[q] A more commodious edifice was erected to the north of Friargate, in 1784. This was re-built and considerably enlarged in 1847-8.

The Baptists erected a small chapel in Leeming-street, in 1783. This building was considerably enlarged in 1833. Mr. Baines mentions a "Particular Baptists' place of worship," in Cannon-street, opened 18th December, 1833; and a "Sandemanian, or Scot's Baptist Room," in Church-street, commenced in 1823. The Leeming-street Chapel is at present closed. One portion of the congregation meet at the Institution, Avenham, and the other at Pole-street chapel, the latter building having been purchased by them, in 1855, from the trustees representing Lady Huntingdon's sect. This building, which is calculated to seat nine hundred persons, was erected in 1825.

The Scotch Baptist Chapel, Meadow-street, a very small building, was opened in 1845.

Zoar Chapel, Regent-street, a small building, was erected in 1853, for a party seceding from the Baptist congregation worshiping at Vauxhall chapel.

The Baptists are erecting a new chapel at the corner of Charnley-street, Fishergate. According to the plans prepared by Messrs. Hibbert and Rainford, it is intended to provide sitting for about six hundred and twenty individuals. Beneath the chapel, accommodation will be afforded for schools. The style of the architecture is "Byzantine."

p His. Lan., vol. 4, p. 337. q Baines's His. Lan., vol. 4, p. 337.

The building will be ornamented by a tower, upwards of sixty feet in height, in which it is proposed to place an illuminated clock.

The earliest METHODIST CHAPEL was built in Back-lane, in 1778. The Rev. John Wesley preached in it on two occasions. This building has since been converted into a corn warehouse. In 1817, the large chapel in Lune-street was built. It is capable of seating about two thousand persons. The organ was erected in 1845. A Sunday school was established about the same time. It is attended by about four hundred scholars.

WESLEY CHAPEL, in Park-lane, now North-road, was built in 1838. An organ was erected in 1846. It is a large and commodious building.

THE PRIMITIVE METHODISTS' small chapel, in Lawson-street, was first used for worship about the year 1827. It was lately transferred to the "Mormons, or Latter-day Saints." The Primitive Methodist chapel is at present in Saul-street.

The ORCHARD CHAPEL, for the PROTESTANT WESLEYAN METHODISTS, was built in 1831. It is intended shortly to considerably extend the accommodation afforded by this building. The plan includes the erection of a larger chapel, with school rooms adjoining.

The INDEPENDENT CHAPEL, in Grimshaw-street, was built in 1808. It is at present proposed to take this building down, and erect a larger and more commodious edifice on its site, capable of holding about nine hundred persons.

THE INDEPENDENT CHAPEL, Cannon-street, was originally built in 1825, and very considerably enlarged in 1852. This body had previously a place of worship in Fishergate, at the corner of Chapel-street, erected in 1700. The site has since been converted into shops.

THE VAUXHALL-ROAD CHAPEL, dedicated to St. Paul, which was according to Mr. Baines—

"Originally used, in 1814, by the followers of Mr. Alexander Kilham, a sect of seceders from the Methodists, who contend for a more popular form of church government, was purchased by a congregation of semi-episcopalians, in 1819, and the service according to the ritual of the Church of England was performed here for a short time, by a minister licensed at the quarter sessions, but not ordained by the bishop; it was then purchased by the Wesleyan Methodists, who left it about two years ago" (1834), "and it was occupied for a short time by the General Baptists. It has now" (1836) "reverted to the semi-episcopalians." [r]

It is at present occupied by a Baptist congregation. A Sunday school was erected behind the chapel, in 1849.

EPISCOPALIAN (PRIMITIVE) CHAPEL, Gorst-street, Avenham-lane, was erected in 1837, as a place of worship for the followers of the Rev. Mr. Aitkin. It was then denominated the "New Christian Society's Chapel."

---

r His. Lan., vol. 4, p. 337.

The Countess of Huntingdon's Chapel, Pole-street, was erected in 1825, and dedicated to St. Mark. For two years previously this congregation met in a room in Cannon-street. In 1855, this chapel was purchased by a Baptist congregation. It furnishes accommodation for about nine hundred persons.

The New Jerusalem Church, Avenham-road, was first opened in 1844. It is a small but elegant edifice, in the "mixed Gothic" or middle period of English architecture, erected from drawings by the late Mr. Welch. It will accommodate about two hundred and fifty persons, and was built at the sole cost of Hugh Becconsall, esq. A house for the officiating clergyman, at the rear of the chapel, is included in the general design of the edifice. A small organ was erected in 1856.

The Mormons and some other sects have sometimes used the Cockpit or old Temperance-hall, as a place of worship. This building about two years ago was completely gutted, and converted into the "Derby Assembly Room."

The "Old Institution," Cannon-street, as well as the lecture-hall of the new building at Avenham, have been occasionally used for religious worship.

THE CEMETERY.

On the passing of the "Burials (beyond the Metropolis) Act," 16 and 17 Victoria, steps were taken for the construction of a suburban cemetery. Part of the Farington-hall estate, in Ribbleton, was eventually selected as the site. The required land (about forty-five acres), was purchased from Sir Thomas Hesketh, bart., at the rate of £150. per acre. The grounds were laid out from designs by Messrs. Myres and Veevers, who superintended the general construction of the cemetery, including the fencing, draining, etc. Three very neat and picturesque chapels, in the early English style of architecture, are erected on the ground, from designs by Mr. T. D. Barry, of Liverpool, and Lincoln's-inn Fields, London. The first interment took place on the first of July, 1855. All the burial grounds, within the town, belonging to the Church of England and dissenting congregations were closed at the same time. The burial grounds attached to St. Ignatius and St. Austin's churches, were, however, permitted to be used until the 31st December, 1856. St. Wilfrid's was closed in July, 1855. The three chapels at the cemetery cost about £6000., the land about £6700. The total amount expended, including tenants' compensations, draining, fencing, ornamental planting, commission, etc., was about £25,000. The ground in the cemetery is appropriated as follows:—Church of England portion, 19 acres; Roman Catholic do., 11 acres; Nonconformist do., 7 acres; unappropriated, 8 acres; total 45 acres. The following table, showing the dimensions of the town burial grounds, and the number of interments in each, during the year 1851, is extracted from Mr. Myres's report to the Burial Board :—

	No. of Interments.	Super. sq. yards.
Church of England	1404	25,620
Catholics	733	12,285
Society of Friends	2	635
Unitarian	3	371
Independents	22	518
Baptists	5	575
	2169	40,004

The population of Preston in 1851, being 69,361, the rate of mortality appears to have been about one in thirty-two. The average of the kingdom, according to the Registrar General's returns, was one in 35.35. This apparently high rate of mortality has been explained by a supposition that a large number of non-residents were interred within the borough, although no evidence is produced to show that such actually is the case. Mr. G. T. Clarke, in his report to the General Board of Health, in 1849, gives the annual mortality of Preston, at 2,924. From the opening of the cemetery on the 1st of July, 1855, to the 12th of March, 1857, 1786 persons were buried in the ground belonging to the Church of England; in that appertaining to the Nonconformists, from July, 1855, to February 12th, 1857, 380. The Roman Catholics, in consequence of two of their burial grounds in the town being in use after the opening of the cemetery, had interred, to February 14th, 1857, only 535 persons. Messrs. Myres and Veevers have prepared plans of the cemetery, with reference books, showing the spaces to be used as graves, numbered in consecutive order. From this it appears that the Church of England ground contains room for about 29,200 places of sepulture; that of the Roman Catholics, 15,500; and that appropriated to Nonconformists about 8200. The cemetery has been laid out and planted with great taste. Several ornamented headstones and other monuments have already been erected. In a short time, when the trees and shrubs have advanced in growth, the cemetery will have the appearance of a park or garden, and will doubtless be much frequented as such. The sub-soil is a fine even sand of great depth, in consequence of which, and the excellent superficial drainage, the walks are always dry and clean. The view of the higher lands to the south of the Ribble valley is very picturesque. From the elevated situation of the cemetery, the atmosphere will receive regular and effectual purification. It is proposed shortly to make a second entrance and a new carriage road, a little to the south of Ribbleton-lane. This will give increased facility of approach to parties residing to the north east of the town.

PUBLIC SCHOOLS.

EDUCATIONAL STATISTICS, from the official report of Horace Mann, founded on the census taken in 1851, and published in 1854.[s]

PRESTON (MUNICIPAL BOROUGH), POPULATION 69,542.

SUNDAY SCHOOLS.	No. of Schools	No. of Scholars belonging to Schools. Both Sexes.	Males.	Females.
	35	11,187	5166	6021
Church of England	12	4613	1830	2783
Independents	4	1182	602	580
Baptists	2	329	140	189
Society of Friends	1	104	66	38
Unitarians	1	54	30	24
Wesleyan Methodists	3	1565	679	886
Primitive Methodists	1	217	122	95
Wesleyan Association	1	256	136	120
Lady Huntingdon's connection	1	130	56	74
New Church	1	104	66	38
Undefined Protestant Congregations	1	111	57	54
Roman Catholic	7	2522	1382	1140
DAY SCHOOLS.	88	7677	4243	3434
PUBLIC DAY SCHOOLS	22	5312	3031	2281
PRIVATE DAY SCHOOLS	66	2365	1212	1153
Classification of Public Schools.				
CLASS 1.—Supported by General or Local Taxation	2	189	136	53
CLASS 2.—Supported by Endowments	2	144	144	
CLASS 3.—Supported by Religious Bodies	17	4959	2741	2218
CLASS 4.—Other Public Schools	1	20	10	10
CLASS 1.— Prison School	1	41	39	2
CLASS 1.— Workhouse School	1	148	97	51
CLASS 2.— Grammar School	1	120	120	
CLASS 2.— Other Endowed School	1	24	24	
CLASS 3.— Church of England, *National*	8	2389	1521	1366
CLASS 3.— " *Others*	3	278	163	115
CLASS 3.— Independents .... *British*	1	131	91	40
CLASS 3.— Wesleyan Methodists	2	303	223	80
CLASS 3.— Roman Catholics	3	1358	743	615
CLASS 4.— Other Subscription School of no specific character	1	20	10	10

A comparison with the returns from forty-five of "the principal boroughs and large towns," shows that Preston had above the average

[s] Pages 141 and 182.

number of Sunday scholars in proportion to the population; and below the average number of day scholars.

THE GRAMMAR SCHOOL.—The origin of the grammar school is not known. It was most probably established by the municipal authorities. In the time of Edward VI. a sum of £2. 18s. 2d. per annum was charged upon the lands belonging to the Duchy of Lancaster for a clerk and schoolmaster at Preston. Tanner, in 1705, writing to Dr. Kennett says, "I remember to have met in our old friend Dr. Hutton's collections, with grammar schools at Richmond and Preston, in the fourteenth century, which were under the cognisance of the Archdeacon of Richmond (who you know had Episcopal power), and yet had no relation to any religious houses." In 1612, a resolution was passed by the corporate body, relieving the bailiffs of the borough from the expense of providing "wine, beare, breade, cheese, ayle, and other bankettinge stuffe and provisions" at the "Feast of Easter," on condition that they should in lieu thereof, pay to the "Schole maister of the towne of Preston, or to his use the sume of twentie marks in p^te of p.ment of his stypende and wages. That is to saie, either of them, six pounds thirteen shillings and four pence." In 1650, one William Curtis resisted the payment, but the municipal authorities ordered him to comply or submit to a levy of ten pounds on his "goods and chattels by distresse & sale." In 1652, however, the corporate body themselves pronounced some of the orders respecting the schoolmaster's salary to be "dissonent to ye laws of this nacon." The bailiffs were relieved of the tax, and a salary of £22. per annum voted from the corporate revenues.[t] Land was bequeathed for the support of the school in 1663, by Bartholomew Worthington. At the time of the Charity Commissioners' inquiry, this land produced in ground rents the sum of £46. 3s. per annum. A portion of a close of land in Fishergate, was sold to the Lancaster canal company for £180., the interest arising from which forms a portion of the schoolmaster's salary. The head master, a few years ago, received from the corporation £45. per annum, and the second master £40. Bishop Gastrell speaks of the school and endowment in the early part of the last century, in the following terms:—

> "There is a Free School, taught by a Master and Usher, who are nominated by the Mayor and Councill. The Salary of the Master is 30l per annum, more or lesse, at the discretion of the Mayor and Councill, besides a house and field, worth about 6l per annum, given by Bartholomew Worthington, in 1663. The Usher's Salary is 18l 6s. 8d."[u]

In January, 1855, the municipal authorities published the following particulars relating to the school:—

---

t See chapter 6, pages 272 and 279.

u *Notitia Cestriensis*, vol. 2, part 3, page 464.

The original Endowment of the School now consists of—

	£	s.	d.
The sum of £180. received by the Corporation from the Lancaster Canal Company, for the sale of part of a close of land in Fishergate, which, at £5. per cent., is per year	9	0	0
Ground rents arising from the remainder of the same close	46	3	0
Total	£55	3	0

The following is the present average yearly expense of the Corporation in respect of the Grammar School:—

	£	s.	d.
Payment to the Head Master	100	0	0
„ to the Second Master	45	0	0
„ for Cleaning, Firing, &c	16	0	0
Total	161	0	0
Deduct the amount of the original Endowment, as above	55	3	0
Present yearly expenses out of the Corporation revenue	£105	17	0

Number of Scholars at the School for the half year ending Dec. 1854.	100
Number upon the foundation included in the above	9
Quarterage payable by the Scholars upon the foundation to the Masters	2 guineas ℔ ann.
Quarterage payable by other Scholars to the Masters	8 „

The Scholars in the 1st and 2nd classes pay 2 guineas per year each, and the other Scholars pay 1 guinea per year each, towards the rent of the School Buildings.

The Scholars upon the foundation do not pay anything towards the rent of the School Buildings.

Since the publication of the above, the attendance of pupils has somewhat decreased. The following extract from a communication made by the head master, the Rev. Edwin Smith, M.A., to the municipal authorities, dated January 10th, 1857, exhibits the present condition of the school and the character of the instruction imparted:—

"The number of Scholars who attended at the Grammar School during the half-year ending Christmas, 1856, amounted to 72; five of whom were admitted on the recommendation of the Corporation. The subjects which have engaged the attention of the pupils, have been portions of Euripides, Xenophon, the Holy Scriptures in Greek and English, Tacitus, Virgil, Ovid, Cæsar, Cornelius Nepos, and the elementary books which are usually read in Grammar Schools. The study of the Modern Languages, as well as that of Geography, Chemistry, and of the Histories of Rome and England, has formed a part of the usual routine. The subjects of instruction in Mathematics have been Conic Sections, Trigonometry, Algebra, Euclid, Statics, and Arithmetic. Some of the Mechanical and other drawings produced during the half-year have been very creditable."

At a meeting of the corporation in December, 1856, in accordance with a recommendation from the grammar school committee, a resolution was passed by which ten additional boys, the sons of non-freemen, might be admitted on the same terms as the sons of freemen. The object of this resolution was to afford opportunity for the selection of the more meritorious boys trained in the diocesan, national, and commercial schools in the town, and to place them in a position to complete their education at the grammar school, on the same terms and with the same privileges as the sons of freemen. The mayor usually gives two prizes at the annual examination of the scholars; one for scripture and the other for history. The master's prizes are generally about seven in number. They include Greek, history, mathematics, arithmetic, French, German, writing, etc. Several of the scholars educated at this school have obtained university honours at Cambridge. Amongst these are the following gentlemen:—Messrs. Thomas Humber, Pearson, James T. Brown (double), Walter Clay, and John Eldon Gorst. The latter gentleman was second wrangler of his year, and is, at the present time, a fellow of St. John's. The building referred to by Dr. Kuerden as existing in his day at the bottom of Stonygate, was erected in 1666, upon land belonging to the municipal authorities.[v] The neighbouring house, now converted into the "Arkwright's Arms," was erected in 1728, as a residence for the master, from funds raised by subscription, the corporation contributing the sum of £50. The neighbourhood having altered in character, it was determined to provide more suitable accommodation. The present edifice in Cross-street, was erected in 1841, from designs by Mr. Welch, the necessary funds being furnished by a committee of shareholders. It is a handsome building, in the Tudor style of architecture, and contains on the ground floor, a hall for recreation, sixty feet in length. The principal story consists of a lofty open roofed hall for study, class room, and a transept, forty feet long. On the ground floor of the transept is the school-room, forty feet in length by twenty in width. The windows of the hall bear some resemblance to those of Merton College, Oxford. Adjoining, to the west, is the "Collegiate Library," above which is a school room for the superior classes. The latter, which was originally intended for the reception of the books composing Dr. Shepherd's library, is decorated with some excellent specimens of stained glass by Ballantyne. The principal hall is elaborately ornamented with pictures in distemper, painted by Frank Howard, representing subjects from English history, interspersed with decorative ornaments, mottoes, etc. These embellishments were presented to the school by John Addison, esq., judge of the county court.

Blue Coat School:—Roger Sudell bequeathed, in 1702, some property in Main-sprit-wiend, comprising a "stable and a hayloft," for the purpose of being converted into a school house. Mr. Sudell likewise charged his estate with the sum of £12. per annum for its maintenance; £10. of which was to be devoted to the schoolmaster's salary, and £2. to the purchase of the necessary books for the scholars' use.[w] Other benefactions subsequently augmented the funds to £1000, which, in 1813, was invested in stock. The late vicar afterwards purchased property belonging to the earl of Derby, situated at the top of the wiend, with the money belonging to the trust.

v See page 210. w Report of Charity Commissioners.

At the time of the vicar's death, the trust was indebted to him to the amount of £200. In 1817, the "Blue schools" were amalgamated with the then recently established national schools. The funds afterwards increased, and in 1830, a new school house was erected on the original site in Main-sprit-wiend. The establishment is calculated to afford clothing and education for twenty-five boys and the same number of girls. The number of pupils at the present time is nearly equal to the full amount. Mr. Whittle gives the following as an inscription placed over the doorway of the old school:—"Mr. Roger Sudell, Bachelor, his Catechetical School, A.D. 1701." The *Notitia Cestriensis* contains the following notice of those charities. The bishop, who wrote immediately after the demise of Roger Sudell, makes the original endowment £17. pounds per annum. He says:—

"There is a Charity School for Boyes, endowed with 15l per annum for a master, and 2l per annum for buying Books, Paper, Ink, and Fire; wch endowment wth a School-house, are ye gift of Roger Sudell, [by will dated 26th Jan., 1702.] The Master is nominated by the Vicar and one of Mr. Sudell's executors. [In 1726, his nephew, the Rev. Christopher Sudell, Rector of Holy Trinity, in Chester, (brother of James Sudell, Woollen Draper,) made statutes for the Government of the School.] There, is another Charity School, for Girls, which is maintained by Contributions. 200l was given to both Schools by Wm. Shaw, [in 1720;] 100l by Mr. [Thomas] Loxham, [in 1723;] 10l by Mrs. [Mary] Stanley, [in 1720;] 20 guineas by Mr. Dan. Pultney, [M.P. from 1722 to 1734. His portrait is in the Court House.]"

The additional particulars within brackets are added by Bishop Gartrell's annotator, the Rev. Canon Raines. Pulteney's portrait is in the Town Hall.[x]

CHURCH OF ENGLAND COMMERCIAL SCHOOL, Knowsley-street.—This building was erected in 1844, by Richard Newsham, Esq., as a "testimonial of his gratitude and affection to his honoured parents, for the education of youth of the middle classes in God's word, and other useful learning, according to the principles of the Church of England." The principal subjects taught are such as constitute a sound commercial education, with the addition of vocal music, mapping, elocution, etc. The upper room was formerly devoted to the education of females. It is at present occupied by the junior boys' classes. The girls' school did not prove successful, owing it is supposed to the novelty of such an establishment for the *middle* classes in Preston. Previously to the appointment of the present head master, Mr. H. W. May, a short time ago, the number of male pupils amounted to no more than 19. The number at present instructed is 64. The school is not endowed, therefore the only source of emolument to the teachers is the scholars' fees. The following prizes, amongst others, have been founded in connection with this school:—The Vicar's prize, for general good conduct, by the Rev. Canon Parr; theological prize, for the greatest proficiency in Scripture history, by the Rev. S. Hastings;

x See pages 350 and 438. Mr. Dobson records an election in consequence of Pulteney's death in 1732, Mr. Baines, in 1734. Mr. Dobson's date is correct. See journals of the house of commons.

commercial prize, for writing and book-keeping, by Richard Newsham, esq.; and an arithmetical prize, by the Rev. Canon Parr.

GERMAN'S, Elizabeth-street:—This establishment was built and partially endowed by James German, esq., in 1848. Its superintendence is intrusted to the minister of All Saints' Church. The northern gable bears the following inscription:—"These schools are erected by James German, as an affectionate tribute to the Memory of the late Thomas German, Esq., of this Town, and in grateful Remembrance of his liberal and Christian example." In the boys' lower school about 40 pupils are taught reading, writing, arithmetic, and geography. The upper school is attended by about 80 pupils, who are taught, in addition, English grammar mathematics, and the higher branches of a commercial education. The lower "girls' school" is devoted to infants of both sexes. About 180 children attend this department. In the girls' higher school, about 60 pupils are instructed in the usual branches of education taught in the national establishments. The pupils contribute a portion towards the teachers' salaries.

ST. JOHN'S, Avenham-lane, (boys) formerly called the "National School," was erected by public subscription in 1814. The site, leased from Dr. Bushell's trustees, was presented by the earl of Derby. About 120 pupils at present attend, who are taught "all subjects conducive to a good English and commercial education." The teachers are paid by scholars' fees, subscriptions, and government aid. This was the first national school established in Preston, and was at one time attended by between 600 and 700 children, who were educated free of charge.

ST. JOHN'S, (for girls) Vauxhall-road, was erected in 1828, and enlarged in 1830. The necessary funds were raised by subscription and a bazaar, chiefly through the exertions of the late Rev. R. Carus Wilson. The teachers are remunerated from funds raised by subscription, scholars' fees, and grants from government. About 160 pupils attend. The subjects taught are Scripture, reading, writing, arithmetic, grammar, geography, English history, sewing, knitting, etc.

CHRIST CHURCH, Bow-lane.—This building was erected in 1833. The funds were furnished by local voluntary contributors, with aid from the National Society. About 200 boys and 150 girls daily receive instruction. The subjects taught include reading, writing, arithmetic, grammar, geography, history, drawing, and vocal music. The girls learn knitting, and sewing. The teachers' salaries are paid from children's pence, local voluntary contributions, and aid by the Committee of Council on Education. In these school rooms, upwards of 250 girls, and about 150 boys are taught on Sundays, by 39 voluntary teachers. It is proposed to build, during the present year, an additional school, in connection with Christ church, in Wellfield-road, at a cost of about £2000. There is an infant school in Arthur-street, in connection with Christ church. About 160 pupils are in daily attendance, and receive the rudimentary instruction usually imparted in infant schools. The building was erected in 1838, by voluntary subscriptions and assistance from the National Society. The teachers' salaries are paid from grants by the Committee of Council on Education, voluntary subscriptions, and children's fees.

St. Peter's, Fylde-road, (boys).—Erected by subscription, in 1829. About 240 scholars attend. Salaries paid by voluntary contributions, children's pence, and government grants. Subjects taught, reading, writing, grammar, and geography.

St Peter's, Brook-street, (girls)—Built by subscription, in 1839, for a Sunday and a boys' national school, and enlarged in 1856. Subjects taught: Scripture, geography, grammar, history, writing and arithmetic. Teachers paid by school fees, government grants, and subscriptions. Number of pupils, 278. The infant school in connection is attended by about 260 children.

St Paul's, Carlisle-street and Pole-street.—The first school was built in 1829, in Pole-street, consisting of one story, which is now used as the infant school. The building in Carlisle-street was erected in 1832. This was formerly occupied as a school for boys and girls; it is now entirely devoted to the boys. During the latter half of the past year, another story has been added to the infant school room, and is used for girls. The number of children in daily attendance at these schools is about 650. The subjects taught are the elements of reading, writing, arithmetic, English grammar, English history, geography, and "common things," instruction on the bible and church catechism, with the addition of sewing to the girls; and, if desired, algebra and mensuration to the boys. The salaries of the teachers, the largest staff in the town, consisting of a certificated master, two certificated mistresses, and twenty apprenticed pupil teachers, are derived from the children's pence, voluntary subscriptions, and grants from government. St. Paul's schools have received, in aid of teachers' salaries alone, grants from government, amounting to between £300 and £350. annually. This sum is independent of grants in aid of school apparatus and alterations in the buildings. There is likewise what is termed a "second infant school" in connection with St Paul's, in Fletcher-road, Ribbleton-lane. It was built by subscription, in 1853, and is attended somewhat irregularly, the numbers fluctuating between one and two hundred. The neighbouring plot of land has been secured as the site for a new church, to which it is intended, eventually, to transfer the school.

DEAF AND DUMB SCHOOL, St. Paul's:—About 18 scholars are taught scripture, arithmetic, writing, etc., in the class room of St. Paul's national school. The funds for the payment of the teachers, are raised by subscription.

ST. JAMES'S, Knowsley-street:—About 200 pupils are instructed in the branches of education usually taught in national schools. The building was erected in 1848. The teachers' salaries are paid from funds raised by voluntary contributions, etc. The expence of the erection was defrayed by grants from the Committee of Council of Education, the National Society, and public subscriptions.

ST. THOMAS'S, Lancaster-road and Moor-lane, was erected in 1840, by subscriptions and government grant. The teaching is of a similar character to that of the other national schools. The teachers are likewise remunerated from similar sources. The number of pupils is about 216 boys, 137 girls, and 170 infants. The infant school was erected in 1848.

ST. MARY'S, St. Mary's-street, (two buildings) erected in 1837 and in 1846, by subscription. The schools are attended by about 670 pupils, (including girls and infants.) The teachers are paid by the local national school committee, and from government grants. The subjects taught are reading, writing, arithmetic, geography, history, English grammar, and scripture.

ALL SAINTS' Schools, Isabella-street, were erected by subscription and government grants, in 1853. This establishment is at present used only for girls and infants. The subjects taught are similar to those previously mentioned. About 200 children attend the infant school, and 70 the girls' department. The teachers' salaries are paid from children's pence, funds raised by the local school committee, and government grants.

TRINITY.—There are two schools in connection with this church, one in Trinity-place was erected about the year 1828; the other on Snow-hill some ten or twelve years ago. [y]

---

y The author regrets to state that the present incumbent of Trinity church, with characteristic eccentricity, not only refused to communicate any information respecting these schools; but was likewise so uncourteous as to prohibit others, over whom he possessed influence, from furnishing the necessary data, to enable the writer to complete the educational statistics of the town. The reason assigned by the Rev. F. Langhorne, for this singular conduct, is a fancied slight on the part of the publishers, whose artist, unfortunately, *having only a limited number of illustrations to prepare*, with commendable taste, regarded the Trinity church as a less suitable subject for a pictorial sketch than some other buildings in the town and neighbourhood! These schools, differ little in character from the others connected with the Established Church. It is generally reported that the attendance of pupils is by no means so numerous as formerly. This is more than probable, as the somewhat unamiable, and certainly unclerical, peculiarities of the reverend gentleman have caused a large portion of his flock to decline attendance at the church. It is much to be regretted that so large and commodious a building, situated in a densely populous neighbourhood, should be rendered comparatively useless, owing to unseemly squabbling between the clergyman, the wardens, and other officials.

ROMAN CATHOLIC SCHOOLS.

St Wilfrid's, Fox-street —This building was erected in 1814, by subscriptions raised principally through the exertions of the late Rev. J. Dunn. The schools are supported by voluntary contributions and govern ment grants. The subjects taught are reading, writing, arithmetic, history, geography, English grammar, etc. The number of scholars attending the boys' day schools, is about 160, night school 130, Sunday school, 200. The girls' school is attended by about 160 day, 100 night, and 100 Sunday scholars. This includes the attendance at an infant school, in connection with the establishment.

St Austin's, St Austin's Road —This building was erected by subscription, in 1841 There are about 480 pupils, including boys, girls, and infants. The teachers are paid from funds raised by subscription, and childrens' pence. The subjects taught include reading, writing, English grammar, composition, geography, arithmetic, scripture history, English history, book-keeping. The girls are taught sewing, knitting, and vocal music.

St. Ignatius's, Upper Walker-street —Erected in 1844, by the "Socialists," and called the "Hall of Science." It was converted into a school in 1845 The teachers' salaries are paid from school pence, voluntary contributions, and grants from the Committee of Council on Education. The number of scholars (boys and girls) on the books, is about 464. The ordinary attendance averages about 320. The subjects taught are reading, writing, arithmetic, geometry, algebra, mensuration, English grammar, geography, elements of popular astronomy, history of England, and general history, including that of the bible. The present school, being found inadequate for the accommodation of so large a number of scholars, will shortly be taken down, and a larger and more suitable building erected, to meet the wants of the rapidly increasing Catholic population. The plan has been already approved of by the Committee of Council on Education, and it is expected that the new building will be erected in the course of the present year.

St. Ignatius's, St. Ignatius-square, (for girls) —Erected by subscription, in 1840. The number of pupils in attendance is about as follows:— Day scholars (including infants), 370; night scholars, 300; Sunday scholars, 650. The teachers' salaries are paid by subscriptions. The subjects taught are reading, writing, grammar, arithmetic, needlework, and religion.

St. Walburge's (Talbot schools), Maudlands.—This spacious edifice was built in 1848. The funds were furnished by the munificence of the late W. Talbot, esq, of Preston. The schools are at present supported by voluntary contributions and the pence of the children. The subjects taught are religion, reading, writing, arithmetic, geography, history, elements of natural philosophy, and chemistry. There are about 112 male, and 120 female, day pupils; and 65 male, and 200 female, night scholars. An infant school is established in connection with the Talbot schools, supported by scholars' pence, and voluntary contributions. About 150 pupils are daily in attendance.

Hope-street.—The Roman Catholics have, likewise a school in Hope-street. From the inspector's report, it appears that in April, 1856, seventy-six pupils attended the public examination. The inspector (Mr. Stokes) says :—"This school deserves more suitable premises and a larger teaching force. It belongs to the reformatory class."

DISSENTERS' SCHOOLS, etc.

Wesleyan School, Croft-street.—Erected in 1840. It is attended by about 500 Sunday, and 200 day scholars. The teachers for the latter are paid from the childrens' pence, subscriptions, and government grants. There is likewise a day school in connection with the Wesley chapel, North-road, which is not under government inspection, at which about 160 children receive the ordinary rudimentary education. The teachers are paid by subscriptions and the pupils' pence.

Friends' School, Friargate.—Erected in 1847, by subscription. About fifty scholars are taught a "plain English education." The teachers are paid entirely by the parents of the pupils.

Baptists' School, Pole-street.—In connection with St. Mark's chapel, the Baptist's have a day school at which about fifty boys and forty girls receive education of the usual character.

There are likewise Sunday schools in connection with most of the places of worship.

Ragged Schools.—The experiment of ragged schools was first tried in Preston, in 1848, under the auspices of the Preston Sunday School Union, with the view to meet the requirements of a large class of young persons too vitiated in habits, or wretched in circumstances, to mingle with the ordinary Sunday scholars, and whose moral destitution required most kind consideration and self-denying efforts in order to bring them within the pale of civilised society. The experiment proved so far successful, that it was determined to erect a more suitable building; and accordingly in 1853, the present neat edifice, near the site of the old corn mill, at the bottom of Friargate, was built from designs kindly presented by Mr. J. S. Hardy, of York. It is gratifying to find that increased success continues to reward the philanthropic efforts of the donors and subscribers. At the present time, about 300 young persons avail themselves of the

Sunday and daily evening schools, and are making rapid progress in religious and secular knowledge The large room, formerly Dr Shepherd's library, in Shepherd-street, is now used as a "Ragged Sunday School."

PRIVATE SCHOOLS —In addition to the public schools, the borough of Preston possesses about thirty-six private seminaries of the usual diversified character.

PUBLIC CHARITIES, PROVIDENT SOCIETIES, ETC

The grammar school and blue coat schools have been previously described [z] Mr. Baines gives the following particulars respecting other charitable bequests, on the authority of the Parliamentary Commissioners' report ·—[a]

Bread Money—Up to the year 1812, inclusive, £1. 10s was paid out of the school accounts, and was distributed in bread. After that time, the practice was discontinued; but the vicar determined, in 1828, to revive the charity. In 1710 Mrs. Smith left the interest of £10 for bread

Charities for the Use of the Poor—Richard Houghton, in 1613, left in rent £2. 10s. per annum; Cosney, in 1678, £5. per annum interest, Crook, in 1688, £4 per annum rent, Hodgkinson, in 1697, £2 10s. per annum interest, Dawson, in 1698, £5 per annum interest; William Rishton, in 1729, £5 per annum interest, Parker or Chorley, in 1747, £5. per annum interest. Total per annum £29

George Rogerson's Charity—In 1619, a rent charge of £13., of which £9. was directed to be given to the mayor to assist poor apprentices, and the residue to be laid out in meat and drink for poor prisoners in Lancaster castle.

Banister's Charity—In 1642, a rent of £16., of which £10 is paid to the vicar, and the remaining £6 is applied, together with the produce of Rogerson's charity, in binding out apprentices These funds belong to the corporation.

Thomas Houghton's Charity—In 1649, land for the poor of Preston and Grimsargh, as well as other places. The annual rent is £64, which is divided into four equal parts, of which Preston and Grimsargh receive one. This is subdivided, and two-thirds given to Preston, and one-third to Grimsargh.

Winckley's Charity.—In 1710, the interest of £50 for binding poor apprentices. This and Hodgkinson's charity, in 1697, belong to the corporation, and there is an accumulation of interest amounting to £34. 9s 4d.

Addison's Charity—In 1729, a rent charge of £5 to 20 poor housekeepers.

Henry and Eleanor Rishton's Charity—In 1738, in trust for the poor, £300. Part of the income is applied annually in binding out apprentices, and the remainder is given to poor persons, in sums of 2s. 6d each.

Rigby's Charity—In 1741, the interest of £100 to six poor widows, £5.

Donors Unknown.—Two benefactions, amounting to £70, appear upon paper, written between 1750 and 1760, and are secured upon a close of land in Kirkham, left at the yearly rent of £7. Two-sevenths of the rent are paid to St Michael's parish

Ann Winckley's Charity.—In 1779, the interest of £100 to poor widows. Annual produce £5 2s. 4d

Lost Charities.—Eight benefactions, from the year 1605 to 1631, amounting to £134. Whittingham's in 1690, the interest of £68. Ingham's and Ashton's, in 1609 and 1709, of £7 4s. per annum, probably never received.[b]

Sudell's Charity—£5 10s. per annum, which has not been paid these 60 years [c]

Worthington's Almshouses.—Built in 1663, were taken down about thirty years ago, and the materials sold for £12 12s, which, with other money, was applied to building one almshouse on waste land.

---

z See page 487.

a Report XI, pages 321 and 352.

b See chap 6, page 276

c "Mr. Wm. Sudell, 3l. per annum, Mr James Sudell, of Preston, Woollen Draper, in 1689, for Bibles and Testaments, 1l. per annum, and 30s to the Poor "—*Notitia Cestriensis.*

Corporation Almshouses.—In 1790, six almshouses were built on waste land, and are occupied, rent free, by persons appointed by the corporation. There are also three others at the top of the Clerk-yard, occupied by three persons put in by the mayor. [d]

The Notitia Cestriensis records others not mentioned above, viz: Sir Thomas Hesketh, in 1605, and Seth Bushell, Draper, in 1623, £20. each; [e] Peter Burscough, of Walton, and William Martin, of Preston, in 1631, £40. each; J. Rogertson, Mrs. Sherburn, in 1625, and James Stopford, £10. each; W. Rogertson, £4.; and John Farrington, of Elston, in 1670, 40s. a year. Several poor children have been bound apprentices from the funds bequeathed for this purpose. A committee of the corporate body, at the present time, receives applications, and occasionally grants a sum of £5. each, towards the fees required on apprenticing approved candidates. There are several charitable societies in the borough which distribute relief to the sick and indigent poor. The ladies' charity furnishes medical attendance and necessaries to poor married women of good character, during their confinement owing to childbirth. The Samaritan society relieves the sick poor generally. From the last annual report it appears that the committee during the past year "paid 2,157 visits, and afforded relief in every instance." Upwards of £110. were thus expended.

The Preston District Provident Society was established for the "encouragement of industry, frugality, and forethought, and the suppression of mendicity and imposture." The amount deposited in small sums with the visitors of this society, in 1855, was £484. 19s. 4d.; and in 1856, £611. The depositors receive a premium for their forethough, in the form of very high interest. The money thus granted during the past year amounted to £16. 1s. 9d½.

Friendly Societies.—There are a large number of sick clubs in Preston, instituted by the working classes for the purpose of securing independent provision during sickness and at death. Some of the "burial clubs," are very extensive. One reports its number of members as upwards of 23,000, two others nearly 8000 each, and in a fourth 4500. There are likewise three or four smaller clubs of this character, whose aggregate numbers exceed 4,000. The most extensive affiliated friendly society in the world is the Manchester Unity of Odd-Fellows. Its branches extend to nearly every portion of the British dominions. It numbers at the present time upwards of 262,000 members, who pay a periodical contribution for relief during sickness and a small insurance at death. The Preston district branch consists of twenty lodges, numbering upwards of 2,600 members. The "Ancient Order of Odd-Fellows" have likewise several lodges in the town. The Preston district of the "Independent Order of Mechanics"

d These have been since taken down. e See page 462.

numbers about twenty-five lodges, and nearly 1000 members, a large proportion of which reside within the borough. The "Druids" have about 900 members. The "Foresters" have ten courts, and about 515 members. There are two lodges of "Rechabites," and four of the "Sons of Temperance," numbering together about 500 subscribers. In addition to these are many isolated sick clubs, some of which are held in connection with the Sunday schools. The "Holy Guild of St. Wilfrid," which meets at the Fox-street school room, is instituted for similar objects. It numbers upwards of 200 subscribers. There are likewise branch agencies to some of the "office friendly societies," recently established on the plan of insurance companies. Several of the affiliated societies have additional funds for charitable purposes. One of the most important is a benevolent fund for the relief of widows and orphans. The Manchester Unity branch expends in Preston in this charitable object, nearly £150. annually.

BUILDING CLUBS, ETC.—There are at present ten building clubs in Preston, viz:—the "Odd Fellows," "Second Improved," "Third Improved," "Saving Fund," "Union," "Permanent," "Preston and North Lancashire," "Prince of Wales," "Prince Albert," and the "Victoria." Belonging to these there are about 1570 members, holding about 2680 shares, of £120. each. There is one "Freehold Land Society," with about 196 members, holding 481 shares. This society purchased and laid out the "Freehold Park," in Fulwood; and has since procured another estate in Ribbleton-lane. It was originally established to create voters for the northern division of the county.

LAW.

COUNTY OFFICES.—Although Lancaster is the county town, and still shares with Liverpool the honour of holding the assizes, yet, all the public offices connected with the administration of law in the county and duchy are situated at Preston. This has doubtless resulted from its central position. The shire of Lancaster, being a county palatine, possesses peculiar legal privileges and immunities. The Chancery court exercises powers within the county, similar in character to those of the high court. Its chief officer is entitled the Chancellor of the Duchy, who is generally a nobleman or a distinguished commoner; always connected with the government, and not unfrequently a member of the cabinet. The vice-chancellor presides at the sittings of the courts, which are held periodically at Preston, Liverpool, and Manchester. The other officers are a principal registrar, and several district registrars, and cursitors. The present officers are as follows:—Chancellor of the duchy, the Right Hon. M. Talbot Baines, M.P.; vice-chancellor, Mr. W. M. James, Q. C.; principal registrar, Mr. Peter Catterall; district registrar, Mr. Joseph Catterall, Camden-place;

acting cursitor, Mr. J. B. Dickson, Winckley-street. The keeper of the seal for the duchy is Mr. R. W. Hopkins, Winckley-square; the prothonotary for the court of common pleas of the county palatine, is the Hon. Charles Beaumont Phipps; and the deputy prothonotary, Mr. Edmund R. Harris, Chapel-street; clerk to the crown, Mr. Thomas Starkie Shuttleworth, Fishergate; clerk of the peace, Robert Jno. Harper, esq.; deputy clerks of the peace, Messrs. Gorsts and Birchall, Chapel-street. The present sheriff of the county is Charles Towneley, esq., of Towneley; and the deputy, or under sheriff, Mr. Thomas Birchall, Chapel-street.

The County Magistrates' Court is held every Saturday, at the Town Hall, Preston. Clerks, Messrs. Pilkington and Walker, Chapel-walks. The county magistrates likewise meet in annual session, at the Court House, Preston; where the general business of the county is transacted. Chairman, Mr. T. B. Addison; treasurer, Mr. Christopher Moore Wilson.

The Quarter Sessions for the hundreds of Amounderness, Leyland, and Blackburn, are held at the Court House, Preston. There are, in addition, four intermediate sessions annually, for the greater dispatch of business. A second court is likewise formed, with a similar object. Mr. T. B. Addison is chairman of the principal court.

The County Court, for the recovery of debts under £50., is held every fortnight, at the Court House. Judge, Mr. John Addison. Registrar, Mr. M. Myres, Winckley-street. Mr. Myres is likewise one of the coroners for the county, and, by arrangement, officiates in the Preston district.

The Wapentake Court, of the hundred of Amounderness, has jurisdiction in personal actions where the debt or damages do not amount to forty shillings. Its officers are a steward, who is appointed by the crown in right of the duchy of Lancaster; a deputy steward, who is appointed by the steward; and bailiffs for the execution of processes. The present steward is the duke of Hamilton; the deputy steward Mr. Edmund Robert Harris, Chapel-street. The court is holden every three weeks.

The Borough Court meets every third Friday, at the Town Hall. Its jurisdiction is in personal actions to the amount of £20. Mr. T. B. Addison is judge or assessor; and Mr. Robert Ascroft, Cannon-street, registrar. Mr. Ascroft is likewise town clerk and clerk to the local board of health. Mr. Thomas Dodd, Lune-street, is clerk to the borough magistrates. They sit at the Town-hall, daily, for the purpose of adjudicating in criminal matters.

PART III.—THE ENVIRONS.

CHAPTER I.—THE VALLEY OF THE RIBBLE

A RAMBLE FROM LYTHAM TO RIBCHESTER.

Situation of Preston—The Valley of the Ribble—The Coast of Lancashire—The Horse Bank—Lytham, Southport, etc —St. Cuthbert—Lytham dock—Sub-marine Forest—The "Neb of the Naze"—Drainage of Martin-mere—The Douglas—Freckleton-pool—Portus Setantiorum of Ptolemy—Improvements in the Navigation—Lea, Ashton, Penwortham, Tulketh, etc —Roman outposts—Singular tradition—The Past and the Present—Preston—The River, Bridges, etc.—Avenham walk—Frenchwood—Walton—Historical Revery—Events which have transpired near the Pass of the Ribble—Cuerdale, Hoghton Tower, Red Scar—Ribbleton-moor—Pope-lane—Elston and Alston—Remains of the great Forest of Oaks—Hothersall, Osbaldestone, Balderstone, etc —Historical Events—Ribchester and Salesbury—The Roman road over Longridge Fell—The Country between the Ribble and the Mersey—View from Tootal Height—Concluding Reflections

PRESTON is situated near the junction of what may be termed the Ribble proper, or the fresh water stream, and its tidal estuary The scenery by which it is environed, consequently presents much diversity of character, and furnishes within itself, ample store of the variety necessary to a *continued* enjoyment of even the most charming of individual perfections, natural or artificial. Notwithstanding its present manufacturing importance, and the consequent aggregation of workshops and lean unsentimental looking factory chimneys, yet, thanks to its elevated site, southern aspect, and the mild breezes prevalent from the west, "Proud Preston" still smiles in graceful beauty from the sunny bank, beneath which the ever meandering Ribble flows with seeming reluctance towards its ocean goal Preston does not appear to have yet satisfactorily solved the problem, whether dame Nature intended it for a seaport or an inland town Its western extremity is washed by the tidal wave; its eastern limbs repose amongst green and flowery uplands Like a favoured "child of Beauty," with its right hand it gathereth the rose-lipp'd "shells of ocean," while its left clutches the pale primrose on the mossy bank, or the wild blue hyacinth in the shadowy woodland dell The joyous songs of feathered warblers in the rural grove are mocked by the sea-fowl's mournful cry A neutral ground, where mighty manly Ocean, having spent his fury, and satiated his ambition, rolleth gently to the embrace of the fair Earth, and ratifies their union by gurgling kisses on her peaceful shore.

Few manufacturing towns are so highly favoured by Nature. The pure mountain air and the strong full sea breeze are each within a few minutes' railway ride from the workshop and the counting-house; equally inviting the toil worn operative and the mentally fagged capitalist to partake of their invigorating influence.

The valley of the Ribble is justly celebrated for the rich luxuriance of its general scenery. It has furnished a theme for both poets and prose writers, of more than one age. Drayton, the metrical topographer, makes the Ribble describe its own course, from the Yorkshire hills to the sea, in the following quaint terms:—

"From *Penigent's* proud foot as from my source I slide,
That mountain, my proud sire, in height of all his pride,
Takes pleasure in my course as in his first-born flood,
And *Ingleborrough* too, of that Olympian brood,
With *Pendle*, of the north the highest hills that be,
Do wistly me behold, and are beheld of me.
These mountains make me proud, to gaze on me that stand,
So *Longridge*, once arrived on the Lancastrian strand,
Salutes me, and with smiles me to his soil invites,
So have I many a flood that forward me excites,
As *Hodder* that from Home attends me from my spring.
Then *Calder*, coming down from *Blackstonedge* doth bring
Me easily on my way to Preston, the greatest town
Wherewith my banks are blest, where, at my going down,
Clear *Darwen* on along me to the sea doth drive,
And in my spacious fall no sooner I arrive,
But *Savock* to the north from *Longridge* making way
To this my greatness adds, when in my ample bay,
Swart *Dulas* coming in from Wigan, with her aids,
Short *Taud* and *Dartow* small, two little country maids,
In these low watery lands and moory mosses bred,
Do see me safely laid in mighty Neptune's bed,
And cutting in my course, even through the heart
Of this renowned shire, so equally it part,
As nature should have said, lo! thus I meant to do,
This flood divides this shire, thus equally in two."

Camden describes the "River Ribell" as follows:—

"Running in a swift stream from *Yorkshire* Hills, it passes to the Southward by 3 great mountains. Near its source is *Ingleborough hill*, which to great admiration, shoots out in a vast ridge, rising as it were gradually to the Westward, and towards the end mounts up as if another hill were rais'd upon the back of it. *Penegent*, so called perhaps from its white and snowy head, since *Pengwin* signifies so in the British, is of a great bulk, but not so high as the other: and *Pendlehill*, not far from thence, rises to a great height, and on the top produces a peculiar Plant call'd *Cloudesbury*, as if it were the Offspring of the clouds."

Its historical associations, however, rival in interest the charms of its picturesque aspect. The slumbering echoes of its secluded glens have been often startled into life by the rude clangour of fierce warriors in deadly contention; and more gently awakened by shouts of joyous revelry, attendant upon the peaceful progression of a potent nobility, and a loyal populace, zealous in honour of a princely guest. The aboriginal Briton roamed in freedom amongst its luxuriant primæval woods. The Roman, Saxon, Danish, and Norman—(conquerors by courtesy, though pirates or freebooters, none the less in fact,) alternately dominated over the land; and each has left some well defined footprints behind, to testify to the truth of the "chronicles of old." The pedestrian meets with a new scene of historic interest or natural beauty, at almost every bend of the river's sinuous course.

The coast of Lancashire in general is low and flat, and presents but little variety to the eye of the mariner or tourist. This is especially the case near the mouth of the Ribble. The great breadth of the estuary,[a] and its bell shaped form, prevent the river current and the tidal action from scouring out a deep single channel, like that of the Wyre. A large portion of this space is occupied by the famous "Horse Bank," which, lying between the north and south channels, is suggestive, at low water, of a huge sea monster, slumbering till the returning wave shall arouse him to his duty, as guardian of the river's entrance. The view from this bank presents a kind of compound of Dutch and desert scenery. The broad expanse of firm hard sand, extends in some directions beyond the range of vision. Its dingy yellow monotony is relieved only by indistinct groups, clustered here and there between the middle ground and extreme distance, comprising some three or four hundreds of human beings, busily occupied in shrimping, or the gathering of cockles; the sole produce of this large tract of what may be, not inaptly, termed amphibious territory.[b] On the north horizon, the pretty village of Lytham rises gently from the water's edge. The windmill, the elegant spire of St. John's church, and the bulkier mass of the tower of the elder ecclesiastical structure, on the site of St. Cuthburt's cell, cutting against the sky, agreeably break the long dreary line of sand and sea. These flat village effects, combined with the wooded mass near Lytham Hall, and the few low sand hills stretching towards the modern lighthouse on the extreme western point, beneath the soft light of the moon and a slightly hazy atmosphere, would remind an artistic spectator of a picture by Vanderneer, but for the utterly sterile character of the immediate foreground. The southern prospect, including glimpses of Southport, Churchtown, Crossens, and the North-meols generally, presents a somewhat similar aspect. Almost every considerable object appears to have been subjected to a strange kind of horizontal elongation. Both sea and land seem as if, disliking immediate

a The distance from Lytham point to Southport, is about seven or eight miles.

b There is a tradition that such was not always the case. Dodsworth indeed asserts that, in the reign of James I., the Horse Bank afforded pasturage for cattle. The sea has evidently made considerable encroachment upon the Lancashire coast, even within comparatively modern time.

Clifton Arms Hotel, & Beach, Lytham.

contiguity to human vision, they felt nervously anxious to resolve themselves immediately into middle ground or extreme distance. True, the few far-off buildings, trees, vessels and human figures, when under the influence of mirage, are occasionally converted into spectre-like perpendicular forms of fantastic beauty, which slightly diversify the scene. When, however, the temper of old Boreas has been seriously ruffled in the west, and he rides in sullen anger upon the high tidal "springs," the Horse Bank receives the first brunt of his fury, and the calm expanse of sand and shallow water is converted into a scene of sublime desolation. Then infuriated Ocean leaps and foams, and chafes in reckless ire,

"Like a blind lion wasting all its might!"

His force is not, however, always idly spent in the neighbourhood of this terrible shoal. Too oft the long soughing howl of the dying but still maddened blast, resembles the wild glee of infernal gnomes rejoicing at the addition of another "tall ship" to the many which already "lie buried" in the bosom of the Lancashire "Goodwins." The native seamen occasionally relate strange traditional tales of gallant vessels, laden with fabulous amounts of wealth, said to have been swallowed by this hungry sand bank, in the "olden time;" and they sometimes even speculate upon the probability of a portion of the treasure being recovered! Though the stranded hull and broken mast of a vessel or two may yet be sometimes seen near its western margin, the improvements of the Ribble Navigation Company, including the erection of the lighthouse and the buoying of the channel, have now robbed the once dreaded Horse Bank of nine tenths of its terror.

Situated a little within the mouth of the Lytham estuary, is, to some extent, protected against the north western winds. During the past few years, many elegant villas and handsome shops have been erected. A kind of orderly, quiet gentility, is almost universally regarded as charasteristic of the village and its inhabitants. The general aspect of the place, its cleanliness and neatness, tend to confirm this impression. It is a favourite resort of that class of invalids who find the ruder sea breeze at Blackpool too strong for impaired constitutions. From its smooth, pleasant, and extensive beach, the prospect, though level and monotonous in the immediate vicinity, is, in fine weather, agreeably diversified in the extreme distance. On the horizon, to the south west, the mountains of North Wales are often distinctly visible, reposing in quiet majesty against the calm evening sky. Their apparent contiguity is, however, according to the faith of the "weather-wise" of the locality, much more agreeable to the eye, than gratifying to the judgment. The habitual visitors, as well as the native fishermen, prognosticate, from the atmospheric condition necessary to the realisation of this beautiful accessory to the landscape, that rough weather will shortly intrude its unwelcome presence. The larger buildings of the modern, fashionable bathing place, Southport, and the older spire of the parish church of North Meols, at Churchtown, rise above the mass of level waste, and slightly vary the aspect of the long flat line of coast on the southern bank. As the eye glances towards the east, the land gradually presents more picturesque characteristics, although the immediate vicinity of the river is still low and comparatively uninteresting. The high lands in the neighbourhood of Latham and Standish, are succeeded by the bolder outline of Rivington pike, whose modern stone tower is suggestive of some more ancient military fortress, overlooking and threatening the whole low country bordering on the western coast of Lancashire. Further eastward, the broad form of Winter hill contrasts agreeably with the conical apex of the "pike." Thin clouds of dark vapour, formed by the smoke of Preston, floating lazily towards the upper atmosphere, indicate the locality of the town. The wooded heights of Hoghton and Billinge close in the prospect. The village of Lytham, its pleasant promenade, and its picturesque old windmill, with black sails and crown, and whitewashed walls, occupy the foreground, and shut out much further view to the left.

The distant accessories to the landscape are, however, only distinctly visible during fine weather. The slightest haziness in the atmosphere is sufficient to extinguish the greater portion. In the clear bright days of summer and autumn, however, the prospect is ever agreeably diversified by numerous groups of health and pleasure seekers scattered over the beach. Pony chaises and saddled donkeys, bearing fair visitors and merry laughing children, give life and human sentiment to the scene; doubtless, much to the chagrin of the pious but ungallant St. Cuthbert, whose intense and avowed horror of the "weaker vessel" jostles rather unnaturally against some of the precepts of his divine master. [c]

About a mile above the village, the pedestrian meets with Lytham dock, or Lytham pool. Some small vessels for the fishing or coasting trade are occasionally built here. The two insignificant creeks, however, afford but

c In the reign of Richard I. lands in Lytham were presented to the prior and convent of Durham, for the foundation of a cell of the Benedictine order, dedicated to St. Mary and St. Cuthbert. St. Cuthbert during his lifetime, would not permit a cow to approach his sacred residence at Lindisfarne. He excused himself for this strange freak, by averring that, "*Where there is a cow there must be a woman, and where there is a woman there must be mischief.*" The crabbed old saint carried this unamiable peculiarity with him to the grave. When Edward III. and his queen Philippa rested for a night at the priory at Durham, the saint, say the monks, kicked his heels against his coffin with such violence, that the expulsion of the queen, with but a portion of her clothing, was necessary to propitiate his ire. Nay, so inveterate was his dislike to "lovely woman," that he shook and cracked the walls of a new chapel which one of his successors, Bishop Pudsey, proposed to dedicate to the Virgin Mary!

little room or convenience for shipping. It was low water at the time of our last visit, when about nine or ten sailing vessels and two steamers were laying like hogs in the mud, the ebb of the tide leaving no more water than the scanty supply furnished by a small rippling brook or two. Vessels, however, frequently discharge the whole, or a portion of their cargoes here, into lighters, when the neap tides prevent their getting up to Preston.

About a mile further, the curious observer will distinguish near the tidal line, distinct remains of the celebrated sub-marine forest, which is believed to extend from near the Welsh coast to Morecambe. Where the action of the waves has displaced a portion of the firm "sea sludge" near the river's bank, a thin layer of soft spongy peat is exposed, amongst which fragments of trees lie scattered in curious disorder. Some huge knarled roots appear to occupy still the spot on which they grew; large trunks lay prostrate by their sides, while others crop out of the earth in an oblique direction. Many of these blackened trunks have been lifted from the bed of the river, by the dredging operations of the Ribble navigation company, and are placed, as posts, upon the sea walls, to indicate the depth of the tidal water, and to mark out the channel.

This submarine forest has long attracted the attention of the learned, as well as of the fisherman and rural population along the coast. Various conjectures have been hazarded, as to when and how it became submerged; and there are several traditions still faintly heard in the neighbourhood respecting it. In the Bodlean library, Oxford, is preserved a manuscript poem entitled, "Iter Lancastrense," written in the year 1636, by the Rev. Richard Jones, B.D. This curious work, which has been lately published by the "Chetham Society," Manchester, with annotations by the Rev. Thomas Corser, M.A., contains the following description of the remains of this forest as they appeared upwards of two centuries ago:—

"But greater wonder calls me hence: ye deepe
Lowe spongie mosses yet remembrance keepe
Of Noahs flood: on numbers infinite
Of firre trees swaines doe in their cesses light; [d]
And in summe places, when ye sea doth bate
Downe from ye shoare, tis wonder to relate
How many thowsands of theis trees now stand
Black broken on their rootes, which once dry land
Did cover, whence turfs Neptune yeelds to showe
He did not allways to theis borders flowe."

Ormerod, the historian, [e] says that the coast of Cheshire, though now bare of trees, was once so well timbered, as to give rise to the saying that

d "Cesses," probably excavations filled with water.—*Corser.*

e History of Cheshire, vol. 2, p. 262.

a "man might have gone from tree top to tree top from the Meols-stocks[f] to Birkenhead," and to another proverb to the same purport which says :—

> * "From Blacon Point to Hilbree
> A squirrel might leap from tree to tree."

A considerable portion of the walk further inland towards "Naze Point" is upon "cops" or embankments, erected for the purpose of protecting the reclaimed Marsh lands from the action of floods and spring-tides. From the extreme point of the projecting headland, or the "Neb of the Naze," an extremely beautiful and extensive prospect is obtained. Westward, the green level country, surrounding the broad estuary, owing to the elevation of the point of view, is seen for a considerable distance, gradually resolving itself into yellowish sterile sand-banks, which, in turn, unite gently with the leaden hues of the tidal wave, creeping stealthily from the deep azure of the extreme horizon.

As the eye passes southward and towards the east, the hills which separate the valleys of the Ribble and the Mersey stand forth in bold relief: Rivington, Winter hill, the fells about Darwen, Hoghton, Billinge; and, somewhat obscured by the smoke hovering about Preston, the massive form of old Pendle closes in the scene. The prospect eastward is further diversified on the left by the height of Parlick, and Bleasdale, and Longridge fells. Freckleton pool, the broad extent of flat marsh land and sludgey debris, through which passes the Ribble like a subjugated hero, obedient from necessity and not from will to the dictum of his captors, furnish the foreground. The improvements in the navigation are here very apparent. Large tracts of land are rapidly being reclaimed. The straight parallel lines of the walls may detract somewhat from the river's beauty at this spot; but they, in compensation, have contributed much towards the increased capabilities of the stream for commercial purposes. The middle distance is agreeably diversified by windmills, cottages, clusters of trees, etc., sprinkled upon the higher table land which encloses the low level valley. Preston is seen to advantage from this spot. Its numerous tall chimneys uprear their heads in the midst of a lovely pastoral landscape; which, at this distance, receives but slight blemish from the heavy cloud of coal smoke that crawls leisurely through the morning mist into the clearer upper atmosphere. Beautiful nature and human enterprise, ingenuity, and industry, are here presented in harmonious conjunction. Tradition and historical association likewise contribute to the interest of the scene.

---

f The term "Meol," according to Owen's Welsh Dictionary, means "a heap or pile, a conical hill, its top smooth, or void of rocks and woods." The "star-hills" or "sand-hills" would therefore appear to have given the appellation of "North-Meols" to the district in the neighbourhood of Churchtown and Southport.

A tall chimney, faintly visible against the sky, on the south west horizon, marks the spot where modern mechanical skill [g] has been brought to bear, with so much effect, as to convert the greater portion of a shallow inland lake and immense tracts of surrounding swamp and moss, into some of the best land in the country for agricultural purposes. Martin mere is now nearly extinct. Yet it is supposed that a district in western Lancashire derived its old name "Linius," from the circumstance that it contained within its boundaries a large lake, of which Martin mere is the remnant. The river Douglas, whose present embouchure is opposite the Naze, may have formerly flowed through this lake.[h] The banks of this river have witnessed some struggles which have "shook the nations," both in ancient and more modern times,—from the days of the semi-fabulous King Arthur, and his stalwart knights, to the wars of the Commonwealth, when the chivalrous and gallant Tildesley closed his life of fidelity to the Stuarts, at Wigan-lane. "Freckleton Pool," at the spectator's feet, formed by the junction of the tiny river Dow with the estuary of the Ribble, was long regarded by the learned as the site of the celebrated "Portus Setantiorum" of Ptolemy. The Mersey, the Lune, the Kent, and the Wyre have successively been placed in competition with the Ribble for this distinction, and the superior claims of the last mentioned appear to be pretty generally acknowledged by modern antiquaries. Nevertheless, as Dr. Whitaker confesses, it is more than probable that Roman vessels have floated upon the broad expanse of the "Belisama Estuarium"[i] and discharged their cargoes at Freckleton pool; although it may not have been the chief port of the Setantii mentioned by the learned Egyptian.[j] This is rendered probable by its proximity to the Roman station at Kirkham, the site of which is indicated by the windmill erected on the hill, at the eastern entrance to the town.

The "pool" at Freckleton, though available only for the navigation of small vessels, except during the higher springs, is well sheltered by the promontory of the "Naze" from the westerly winds. There being no dock, however, the various craft are stranded in the mud on the receding of each tide. This circumstance, though it may please the eye of an artist owing to the diversity of picturesque *pose*, incident to vessels in such a predicament, is by no means gratifying to the merchant or shipowner, whose property and business are seriously affected thereby.

g The chimney is connected with the steam pumping machinery erected by Sir Thomas Hesketh, bart.

h Camden, writing in the reign of Elizabeth, says, "near the mouth of the Douglas, is Merton, a large broad lake that empties itself into this river," etc.

i Many of the elder antiquarian topographers indentified the Belisama of Ptolemy with the Ribble. See chapter 1, page 13.

j Ptolemy, the ancient geographer, was a native of Egypt.

The high ground bordering the valley sweeps from the "Naze," in a large curve, by Freckleton and Clifton, to Lea. Considerable tracts of enclosed and marsh land, on the lower "flats," are now covered with verdure, furnishing rich pasturage for large herds of cattle. The valley has, however, yet lost but little of its monotonous level form.

Lea Hall, the scene of the fight between Langton, lord of Newton in Mackerfield, and Mr. Hoghton, the ancestor of the present baronet, stands upon the high bank to the left. Though now converted into a humble homestead for the farmer, it will, nevertheless, arrest for a moment the traveller's attention, and furnish matter for speculation upon the relative degree of security to person and property enjoyed by ourselves in "these degenerate days," and our worthy progenitors in the "good old times."

As we approach Ashton the valley begins to narrow. Suburban villas crown the heights, and the bustle and stir of the town and port arrest the attention. From the promenade on the large embankment, formed by the Navigation Company near the site of the old "chain caul," the appearance of Preston is very imposing, and presents to the eye of the spectator many indications of superior affluence, and commercial and manufacturing enterprise. The high lands at Ashton, belonging to Mr. Pedder and Mr. Bray, are laid out for the erection of villa residences, and several structures have been lately built thereupon. The general site is one of the very finest in the immediate vicinity of Preston. An elegant villa, "Whinfield," recently built by Mr. Henry Newsham Pedder, a little nearer the bank of the river than his brother's mansion, Ashton-park, is most delightfully situated.

From the projecting headland, to the south-west of Tulketh Hall, a fine prospect of the estuary is obtained. The river, although enclosed by walls erected to improve the navigation, here pursues its serpentine course with comparative freedom. The dark form of the "Naze," projects boldly into the watery plain, and shuts out Lytham from the view. The marshes and reclaimed lands of Hutton, Howick, and Longton, stretch away to the left, while the broad expanse of the Irish sea glitters in the sunlight on the extreme horizon.

We are standing upon the site of what was probably one of the Roman *speculæ* referred to in chapter 1.[k] On the opposite promontory of Penwortham, its companion outpost raises its bold conical head towards the sky, as though conscious of its historic dignity, and the traditionary mystery which yet lingers around it. Gossip lore still maintains that a subterranean passage, a kind of ancient "Thames tunnel," once united the priory of Penwortham with the temporary monastery at Tulketh! A germ of

k The recent levelling of the ground has filled up the ditch and reduced the height of the mound nearly ten feet.

Ashton Park, Preston

truth is ever enshrined in any long cherished tradition, however distorted or absurd may be its modern aspect. This notion of a secret passage, in process of time, may have been engrafted upon the mystery which would originally envelope the rude system of telegraphic communication employed by the Roman or Saxon warriors when the promontories were used as outposts or *speculæ*. Their successors, the monks of Evesham, might from policy countenance the tradition, especially in troubled times, on account of the impression of power or security which such a belief would naturally engender amongst the more ignorant of the population.

The dense foliage crowning the heights of Penwortham, conceals from view the mansion built upon the site of the ancient priory; but the grey old tower of the church gently raises its venerable form amidst the rich masses of shadowy verdure, and meekly reflects upon the cold world around, a portion of the golden light breathed upon it, as if in spiritual sympathy, by the declining Day. The immediately surrounding accessories are all, as yet, in excellent keeping with the sentiment of this scene and its historic associations. A very limited draught upon the imagination is alone necessary to realise a vision of the "olden time," when the venerable prior, accompanied by his sumpter horse, issued from its verdant precincts, to convey the tribute rent to the parent establishment at Evesham, including the "good Ribble salmon," of the specified dimensions. Penwortham yet remains clothed in its ancient picturesque costume, gazing, like the representative of twenty generations, with a mixture of contempt and wonder, upon the somewhat unsightly *parvenu* connections of its once respectable *confrere* on the opposite bank of the river. The Old and the New are here in direct collision. It needs "no ghost come from the grave" to tell us which eventually must conquer. The active energy and commercial enterprise of Preston are fast absorbing the suburbs of the town. All around, the face of the country speaks of past, present, and projected change. The woods of Tulketh have bowed to the conqueror, the hill of the Maudlands has yielded its time honoured site to the brickmaker, the railway engineer, and the cotton spinner. The little white cottage, at the foot of the cliff, with its neat garden and "Spa Bath," looks friendless amongst the mass of material activity by which it is surrounded. Nay, the very "Holme" has submitted to the action of a couple of "jetties" or "cauls," resigned its individuality, and become incorporated with the main land. The town appears to be stealthily creeping into the valley. The brick walls of the cottage and the workshop are rapidly approaching the "wooden walls" of commerce. Patches of red and yellow earth, filling up irregularities in the hill side, indicate that, notwithstanding the intervention of the green plot, still named the "Marsh," the town and the river will shortly become closely united.

The Ribble winds with a gentle sweep below the southern portion of the borough, and is, within about the space of a mile, spanned by five bridges, some of no mean pretensions.[l] After passing the quays, the valley becomes gradually more rural and picturesque. The Penwortham bank is occupied by several first class mansions, including the "Oaks," "Hurst Grange," the "Hall," etc. More closely built but still handsome edifices occupy the high land on the Preston side of the stream.

On passing the magnificent dry arch of the North Union Railway bridge, the pedestrian enters the land now partially thrown open as a public park. Though somewhat interfered with by the iron bridge and long line of brick arches forming the viaduct of the East Lancashire railway, this magnificent semi-amphitheatre, in conjunction with the "Avenham-walk," is calculated, with but little assistance from a judicious landscape gardener, to funish one of the most picturesque places of public recreation in England, in the immediate neighbourhood of a manufacturing town.[m]

Passing along from the public walk, over the Swilbrook, the "washing stood," of old Kuerden, but now one of the common sewers of the town, the line of route leads by Frenchwood to Walton. Frenchwood is not yet a misnomer, so far as the vegetable portion of its composition is concerned. How long it may continue so, it would, in the present age of progress, be hazardous to assert.

We are arrived at Walton; and here it is necessary to pause a while. That we may gaze upon the beautiful site to more advantage, and include within our view a larger field of historic interest, let us enter the strawberry garden overlooking the river, and, having climbed its steep side, take our station near the *camera* which crowns its summit. Modern Preston is just behind us, towering with Yankee-like "bounce" over its humbler but older neighbour. For a time we will turn our backs upon the *parvenu;* its numerous steam engines, its power-looms, and its spindles; fit representatives of the substantial, though, perhaps, somewhat soulless Present, and we will gaze upon lowly Walton, and the rich pastoral valley of Cuerdale, while we commune with the visionary Past.

Clouds of ignorance, or, more truly, imperfect knowledge; for conventionalism has invested the term ignorance with contemptuous associations; clouds of uncertainty and imperfectly developed truth rest upon the scene. All is dreary and obscure. Presently a ray of light penetrates the shadowy mass. The eye rests upon one mighty and dense forest of pines.[n] The rhinoceros, the hyena, the tiger, the bear, the wolf, and lesser carni-

l See page 458.
m See page 435.
n The trees forming the submarine forest along the coast, are said to be composed chiefly, if not entirely, of pines.

View from Bushell Place, Avenham Walk, Preston

Valley of the Ribble from the Vicarage, Preston

verous animals, long since extinct in England, hold dominion over it. The voice of man hath not yet "awakened its echoes." [o]

Another wide and dense shadow rests upon the scene. Unrecorded time passeth. Twilight glimmerings succeed, followed by brighter flashes of historic truth. Huge oxen and deer browse beneath umbrageous oaks. The wild bear and grizly boar dispute the empire with savage man, the degenerate son of a previous partial civilization.[p] Yet stagnation with him, as with all other earthly things, is death. Once sunk to the lowest degradation, by the unerring law of eternal motion, he must perish or progress.

Time passeth, and more light penetrates the semi-gloom. Barbarian men have begun to form communities. Society, though rude and imperfect in many of its relations, has germinated. Petty tribes of partially nude and frightfully disfigured human beings have entered into combinations for mutual *defence* against combinations ostensibly formed for a similar purpose! Where the *Dwr-gwen*, the "white and beautiful stream," is wedded to the *Goch-ui*, or the "red-water,"[q] nature hath provided sufficient defence against sudden irruption. Rude huts congregate upon this small peninsula, and the stalwart savage chief increases the strength of his fortification, by barricades formed from the limbs of the then luxuriant forest monarch. Ages pass in desultory but savage warfare. One petty tribe yields to another, until the Setantii, or the "dwellers by the waters," acknowledge a single head. The chief rulers of this tribe assemble at Caer Gochui, or the "fortress of the red water."[r] Its great natural strength, its central position, and the influence of the most distinguished warrior, secure for it the distinction of the "Supreme City." Lesser states in savage neighbourhood are gradually absorbed by greater. The Setantii and their neighbours, the Volantii, become part of the great nation of the Brigantes, which now includes all the country from the western to the eastern coast.

A new era begins to dawn. Britain has attracted the attention of the warriors of all-powerful Rome. After more than a century of gradual conquest, the Brigantine chiefs of the western coast learn that the formidable imperial legions, led by the famed Agricola, are marching to subdue them. The valour and skill of the brave Venutius and his rude charioteers had

o A skull of the rhinoceros was found in Lancashire, and figured by Leigh.—See Buckland's *Reliquæ Diluvianæ*.

p It is held by some, with evident probability, that the earlier settlers in Britain, brought with them some of the knowledge of their eastern forefathers, and that they afterwards degenerated. A few thousand emigrants in Australia, if cut off from all communication with the mother country, would, at the present day, rapidly deteriorate from the European standard.

q The Darwen and the Ribble. r See chapter I, page 37.

prevailed not against the discipline of Rome and the military genius of Suetonius and Cerealis. What was to be hoped for by the lesser tribes when the strength of the nation was broken?

Caer Gochui is crowded with warriors; the cattle of the tribe are driven within the trenches formed by the two rivers The narrow neck of land is strongly fortified. The fords are protected by brave hearts, willing to perish in defence of "hearths and homes," notwithstanding their rudeness The scouts announce the approach of the enemy. The semi-naked Setantii rush to their posts It is in vain! The Roman spears and helmets glisten on the hill. A haze passes over the scene. The fight is over, and Agricola himself is ordering the necessary works to secure the pass of the river and protect his rear. The conqueror presses forward towards the north, and Roman Coccium rises from the ruins of the British fortress Some of the legionaries repose on the banks of the Belisama, or chief river, and teach the natives the arts of peace. Coccium, however, still remains relatively a free town, governed in part by a British prefect,[s] under the *surveillance* of the Roman commander of the fortress or station

Upwards of three centuries more join the irrevocable Past. Luxury and vice have done their work; the power of the once "almighty Rome" is broken! Britain is covered with her roads, fortresses, cities, and colonies. Some slight gleam of Christianity flickers over the land. Civilization has materially advanced amongst the natives, but still they are slaves. The tide of conquest ebbs; the barbarian nations of the north and east devastate the empire, and plunder the "eternal city." The legions in Britain are wanted at home. The subjugated Celtæ and other continental nations revolt and assert their freedom. The Roman governors and the Britanni or "Romano-British" population, can not resist the native onslaught. In vain they solicit imperial succour.

Unused to liberty, the British tribes sink into license, and contend for the superior domination. Emigration has already infused some Teutonic blood into the population of the eastern portion of the country.[t] Their relatives on the continent are invited to aid in the struggle. A period of sanguinary desolation follows. The Teutonic stock triumphs. The Angles settle in the valley of the Rhi-bell, and the little village of Walton springs into existence from the fragmentary remains of Roman Coccium[u]

s Richard of Cirencester

t During the Roman dominion, the south eastern portion of the kingdom must have been inhabited chiefly by German emigrants The commander of the district about Norfolk, Suffolk, Essex, etc, was termed "Comes Littoris Saxonici," or count of the Saxon coast or shore. See chapter 1, page 1, and chapter 2, pages 57 and 93

u See Chapter 1, pages 25, 33 and 37.

Christianity dawns apace. The disciples of Paulinus and St. Columba convert the sanguinary idolaters. The kingdom of Northumbria champions the cause against the pagan Mercians. The pious Oswald marches by the "pass of the Ribble" to his "martyr-grave" at Maserfield.[v] Lands on the Ribble, in "Hacmunderness," are granted to the monks of Ripon, and the "Priest-town" begins to emerge from the darkness of the past.

The next important page of historic record is somewhat mutilated. The Scandinavian vikings ravage the coast, and settle in the valley of the Ribble. Scenes of bloody contention arise. The rovers maintain their footing, and successfully dispute the sovereignty with the Anglian lords. The genius and resolution of Alfred can but save the south and western portions of the island.

The struggle still continues with varied fortune. The "star" of the "right royal" Athelstan, the worthy grandson of the Great Alfred, is now in the ascendant. The Northumbrians and even the Scottish monarch render him homage. With true regal munificence he purchaseth "with his own money, at no little cost," the whole of Amounderness, and bestows it upon the cathedral church of York. The "Priests' town" begins to flourish and becomes the capital of the district.

The Scandinavian population of Northumbria still yearn for a chief of their own blood. The Welsh and Scottish kings seek to humble the growing power of Athelstan. The Danish and Norwegian pirates scouring the seas for plunder, are ever eager for a descent on the British coasts. Anlaf, chief of Dublin, son of the late Scandinavian ruler, Sigtryg, hastens to seize the proffered crown. Northumbria is simultaneously invaded at four points. Gudrekir, one of Athelstan's deputies, is overpowered and slain by the invading hosts from Norway and the Baltic. His colleague Alfgeirr, flies before the "irregular and disorderly Irish" troops under Anlaf; but first buries his coin and other treasure near the "pass of the Ribble," at Cuerdale.[w] The confederate invaders ravage the country. Amounderness, the king's gift to York, is desolated. Athelstan himself shortly afterwards appears upon the scene. A series of murderous struggles ensue. The great grandson of the renowned Ragnar Lodbrog, the terrible Danish pirate king, and the descendant of the honoured Alfred, contend for dominion. The confederated armies are at length routed. The Danish chief, with the remnant of his disorderly Irish followers, escapes with difficulty to his ships in the Wyre and the Ribble. The Scotch and Welsh princes become tributary to Athelstan, the first undisputed possessor of the crown of all England!

v Winwick. See chapter 2, page 64.

w It is not improbable that the treasure may have belonged to the Danish chieftain. See chapter 2, page 83.

The Dane and Saxon alternately triumph; till the decisive battle of Hastings transfers the crown to the "Bastard of Normandy," the most ruthless of the conquerors of Britain.

"Prestune" is now risen into importance. All Amounderness belongs to it, together with three churches. The ford is superseded by the "Bridge of Rible"[x] Several monarchs pass, with retainers or armed force, before the first Edward rests here, on his way to Scotland. In the following reign, Preston expiates, in part, the cruelties of the English in Scotland. The fire-brands of Robert Bruce, consume a large portion of the town, but the "pass of the Ribble" stops the further ravages of the predatory army.

A fierce domestic struggle now disturbs the repose of the valley. Adam de Banistre fruitlessly copes with his relative and superior, Thomas, earl of Lancaster, brother to the king.

The third Edward advances to Scotland. Resting at Preston, he draws many of the youth of the neighbourhood to his standard. The sackage of the town is avenged by the slaughter of thirty thousand Scots, at Halidown-Hill

The house of Lancaster acquires the throne of England. Letters patent provide for the "pontage" of the Ribble, "juxta Preston."[y] A noble structure rises, worthy of the fame of the ecclesiastical builders

The "wars of the roses" disturb not the valley. Their thunder but faintly echoes in the distance.

The Scots, profiting by the absence of Henry VIII., invade England. "Lusty lads, liver and light, from Blackborne and Bolton in ye moores," with other south Lancashire and Cheshire heroes, led by "lusty Stanley, stout" Sir Edward, pass the Ribble. The warriors of Amounderness, including pikemen from Preston and Pilling, "brought up from babes, wth beefe and bread"[z] join them The old song, which celebrates the victory and records the terrible slaughter at Flodden, testifies to the courage and patriotism of the "lads" of Lancashire, exhibited on that fatal field; the record of which furnishes the most mournful page in the annals of Scotland.

A discreet and thoughtful looking man gently draweth his horse's rein, and gazes in silent admiration, upon the "great stone bridge of *Rybill*, having v great arches." It is the learned and accomplished Leland, king Henry VIII's antiquary, on his journey through the country, "in search of England's antiquities."[a] It would be, perhaps, to "consider too curiously," as the gentle Horatio expresses it, if we were to ponder long upon

x See pages 209, and 458. y See page 128.
z Flodden ballad. See page 135. a See page 138

the question whether "deathless fame" is more dependent upon great achievements, or upon the industry, imagination, or prejudice of those by whom they are chronicled! A real living Achilles might possibly cut a sorry figure in a modern drawing room! It is by no means precisely certain whether such a man would, "in these degenerate days," win a peerage, or the championship of the prize ring! On the other hand, there is some truth in the couplet,

> "Full many a flower is born to blush unseen,
> And waste—"

Stay; "The proverb is somewhat musty." If ALL "the secrets of antiquity" were to become suddenly revealed, what a frightful reign of literary terror might ensue! what a revolution in the world's hero-worship! The subject is too painful to contemplate. *Revenons a nos moutons.*

Who is here? Another scholar endeavouring to extract intelligence from the mouldering and imperfect records of the *past?* No. His very opposite! This man wishes to read the *future*! A much more "learned fool" than the most imaginative antiquary; excepting so far, of course, as there may be knavery rather than folly in the composition of the exorcist! Edward Kelly is doubtless well paid for "raising the devil" in Walton park. The promised "secret information," whether derived from such infernal communion, or from a resuscitated corpse in the church-yard, on the top of the hill, was a marketable commodity, very much in demand in the reign of "good Queen Bess." [b]

What have we here? More folly? Shade of the immortal Touchstone! do we gaze upon thy veritable earthly prototype? That "wise fool," Archie Armstrong, accompanied by the august patron and lover of "foolerie," yclept, in eloquent derision, the "English Solomon," with a holiday train of gay gallants, and knightly and noble attendants, furnishes food for "merrie laughter," as the cavalcade passes southward to Hoghton Tower. The courtly Buckingham pays an elegant compliment to the beautiful scenery of the valley, and dreams not of Felton's dagger. "Wise King Jamie" cracks his broadest joke, in still broader Scotch, in happy ignorance that he treads upon the spot, where the cup of Hope will be rudely dashed from the parched lips of his dethroned and imprisoned son! [c]

A widely different "masque" to that performed at Hoghton is now being enacted. The nation's blood, at fever heat, pulsates wildly. Two elements of authority grapple in fierce antagonism. Many conflicting and discordant items enter into the composition of the "Great Rebellion,"

---

b See page 149. c See page 151.

but the true principle at stake is really misunderstood by none. Arbitrary power, or the "Divine Right of Kings," is arrayed against constitutional government, and the progressive spirit of human liberty. The governors and the governed are earnestly endeavouring to solve the grand problem,—which is the master and which is the servant,—by an appeal to that most potent of all human arguments,—physical force. Gay cavaliers, loyal to the Stuart, and cautious legislators, who fear anarchy worse than despotism, measure blades with grim fanatics and stern earnest men, whose patriotism includes "the people" as well as "the crown." Preston and the "pass of the Ribble" is won and lost, and won again; the parliament triumphs; Charles, though still king, is a prisoner.

All is not yet lost The Scotch, who venerate the blood of the Stuart, in conjunction with northern royalists, invade England, and demand the restoration of the captive monarch. The valley of the Ribble is alive with troops. The duke of Hamilton issues his commands from Preston; while Sir Marmaduke Langdale rests on Ribbleton moor. Are we on the eve of a day of vengeance? Is the scaffold to drink the "rebel blood" of the Commonwealth leaders? Not so The master spirit of the time is here, when least expected; one by Nature fitted "to disturb the peace of all the world, and rule it when 'tis wildest." Genius, energy, and military discipline totally annihilate an opponent numerically three-fold the stronger! Oliver Cromwell achieves one of his most brilliant and decisive victories. The exploit is celebrated by the great poetic genius of the age; the crowning wreath is added to the historic interest of the scene:—

> "Cromwell, our chief of men, who through a cloud
> Not of war only, but detractions rude,
> Guided by faith and matchless fortitude,
> To peace and truth thy glorious way has plough'd,
> And on the neck of crowned Fortune proud
> Hast reared God's trophies, and his work pursued,
> WHILE DARWEN STREAM WITH BLOOD OF SCOTS IMBUED,
> And Dunbar field resound thy praises loud,
> And Worcester's laureat wreath. Yet much remains
> To conquer still, Peace hath her victories
> No less renown'd than War; new foes arise
> Threat'ning to bind our souls with secular chains
> Help us to save free conscience from the paw
> Of hireling wolves, whose gospel is their maw." d

The Commons of England behead the king. The Scotch, still true to the Stuart, advance with his son, Charles II., into England. He passes the bridge of Ribble, on his way to Worcester. The faithful, but unskilful and unfortunate earl of Derby, after landing at Wyre, from the Isle of Man, passes the Ribble to the scene of his last defeat at Wigan-lane, where the gallant Tildesley, closes his chivalric career

d Milton's Sonnet "to the Lord General Cromwell."

The Commonwealth passes away with the breath of the man whose genius alone could direct it. Charles II. is restored to the throne of his ancestors, but with a limited prerogative. His brother and successor, James, doubly imbued with the proverbial infatuation of the Stuart race; to whom "necessity" was *not* "the mother of invention," and whose selfish folly experience itself could *not* convert into wisdom, endeavours to follow in the footsteps of his father, and restore absolutism. The liberty-loving spirit of the Anglo-Saxon people is again roused. The last of the Stuart kings in terror flies! By this act he saves his head, but deprives it of its regal ornament.

Time passeth, and the Hanoverian dynasty occupies the throne of the Stuart. The Scotch and the northern "legitimists" are still faithful to the old cause. They invade England and proclaim the son of James king. They are met again at the fatal "pass of the Ribble." Mackintosh prepares to defend the bridge; but withdraws his troops into the town, and erects barricades. The little army under Wells, advances, and Preston is besieged. The Scotch are beaten, and the partizans of the Stuarts shot or hanged as criminals! The "loyalty" of 1648 and 1651, is, by the potency of the magic word "failure," converted into "treason." On the other hand, the spirit of the "great rebellion" had, in the meantime, passed through the alembic of "success," and, in 1688, the "glorious revolution" was the product! Truly, "What's in a name?"

Yet another effort. Prince Charles Edward, or the "young pretender," is received by the Scottish people, and his father is again proclaimed king. England is invaded, and the dreaded "pass of the Ribble" safely reached. Superstition darkly insinuates that a Scottish army can never in triumph proceed beyond it. Some regiments are quartered at Walton, to dissipate the gloomy foreboding. The invaders pass southward to Derby. Will they reach the metropolis? The destinies of the houses of Stuart and Hanover oscillate on the balance! But for a moment, however! The partisans of the "young chevalier" return in a somewhat disorderly plight. Hark! the bugles of the duke of Cumberland echo on the horizon! Is the valley of the Ribble again to witness the destruction of a Scottish army, and the final extinction of hope for the exiled family? No; they make no stand. Like hunted hares they have "doubled," and are hurrying home again, to close the sad drama on Culloden moor.

More than a century passeth. We are arrived at the "ignorant present."(?) The heavy breathing of the steam engine, and the quick whirl of machinery, almost obliterate from the memory the echoes of past struggles. Part of Cromwell's great battle field, upon which we stand, is converted into a fruit and pleasure garden. The deep hollow, where the general's life was in imminent peril, resounds with the merry laughter evoked by holiday enjoyment.[e]

From this spot, a charming *coup d'œil* is yet presented. The village nestles quietly in the valley; while the old church, on the richly wooded height, seems to gaze, with maternal pride, upon the time honoured locality over which it presides. Walton Hall has been razed, and its site usurped by a kitchen garden; but the immediate back ground of the picture yet includes the verdant park and luxuriant foliage. In the middle distance, the angular form of the rocky hill, clothed with its forest mantle, and crowned by the now deserted baronial hall, that once echoed with the mirth and revelry of the princely, noble, and knightly guests of the hospitable Sir Richard Hoghton, bart., gives dignity and variety to the landscape. Beyond, the varied outline of the east Lancashire hills circumscribes the prospect. The river meanders gracefully from the shadowy "deeps," beneath the church, where the nets of fishermen entrap the celebrated Ribble salmon, on their passage to and from the ocean. A little higher, on the bank of the stream, near Cuerdale hall, just hidden by the projecting headlands of Fishwick and Brockholes, stands the sapling planted upon the spot which disgorged the long sought treasure of the days of Athelstan.[f] The broad gravel bank, below the hill on which we stand, yet marks the original ford. In the field on the right, beyond the present Swilbrook lane, the course of the Roman road, is yet indicated by the deep zigzag indentation, on the face of the steep ascent. A large fragment of one of the centre piers, a substantial relic of the past, gradually crumbling beneath the action of time, yet lingers on the site of the ancient viaduct.

To the left, through the dingle in the strawberry garden, passed the "deep narrow lane," on its approach to the bridge, where the victorious Cromwell had nearly met his death. It is not difficult to trace remains of the quicksand into which his horse leaped, when he dexterously avoided the stone hurled upon him, from the high land that commanded the narrow pass.[g] But commercial enterprise has laid its persevering hand upon the locality. Two factory chimneys rise from the bosom of the valley, and more fringe its borders. Yet, but a little time, and Preston and Walton will become united. If not converted into "one flesh," they will at least present one mass of substantial bricks and mortar.

From Cuerdale the Ribble passes through rich pasture lands and well wooded banks, by Brockholes and Samlesbury, towards "Red Scar." Above the modern wooden bridge, slight remnants may yet be seen of the

---

e See pages 184 and 284. f See chapter 2, page 74.

g See chapter 4, page 184, and chapter 5, page 224.

Whitfield, Ashton upon Ribble, Preston.

The Seat of Henry Hawsbaw Podge Esq.re

weir, which was destroyed, after most expensive and exciting litigation, some years ago, on account of its obstruction to the passage of the much prized salmon. Ribbleton moor, the scene of Langdale's defeat, crowns the table land on the left. Samlesbury's rural church reposes quietly in the valley on the opposite bank of the river, no "witches" troubling its pastoral congregation with mystic power, derived from demoniac communion. Lancashire's "angelic" spell workers, have fairly routed their Pandemonian namesakes.[h]

Passing the remains of a fine old Elizabethan hall, now converted into a farm house, the pedestrian, after mounting a steep and rugged path, which occasionally does double duty as a by-road and watercourse, stands upon the plateau overlooking the "Red Scar."

No single picture can do justice to this beautiful and unique scrap of English scenery. The whole is not presentable on canvass, from any one given point of view. It contains rather, within itself, a complete portfolio of sketches. It is a place to *ramble about in*, and not simply to stand *staring at!*

BEAUTIFUL NATURE!

Whene'er I gaze on thy untrained grace
My heart o'erflows once more with Boyhood's gladness;
The guileless smile that lights thy varied face
Re-germinateth Hope and calms my bosom's sadness!

Truly, an Eden spot, fashioned by bounteous nature, to dispel the fierce burning passion and choking heart-ache, engendered by rude collision with the outward world.

The valley of the Ribble is generally about a mile in breadth, and the soil entirely river *debris* or alluvial deposit. The table land rises between one and two hundred feet above this fertile plain. The river, playfully meandering amongst level green meadows and pasture lands studded with cattle, with a divided love, alternately courts the cooling shadows beneath the rugged "scars" and verdant woods which limit its domain on either hand. At the "Red Scar," a semi-circular indentation has been scooped out of the northern bank, by some natural causation. This is so singularly perfect in its form, as to suggest, contrary to the fact, the possibility of Nature having been assisted by Art, in its formation. The river sweeps, from nearly the southern bank, entirely round the foot of this concave precipice, partially forming, in its erratic course, the figure of an ellipse. This is no ordinary or miniature feat of natural geometry, the longest diameter of the "horse shoe," as it is locally termed, being nearly a mile. The high and steep outer bank of the river is superbly robed with rich and

h Several recent occurrences may appear to challenge the truth of this assertion. But the exception only tends to prove the rule.

varied forest foliage. On the western arm of the curve, the bank is so steep, that huge trees are continually being detached from the soil, by the action of frost and rain, and projected, by their own weight, into the stream below. Others, bending over the precipice, like wounded warriors, unable to conquer yet unwilling to yield, cling tenaciously to the crumbling earth. The stream below is full of shallows and rapids. The subject is not quite wild and savage enough for the pencil of Salvator Rosa. It is more suggestive of trout and salmon fishing than of brigands and desperadoes. Our own Tennant would better enter into its sentiment. It would make a glorious picture under his masterly treatment. Owing to the thinness of the plantation at this spot, the best single view of the entire scene is obtained. The water in the opposite reach is still and smooth as a pond. Its transparent bosom reflects darkly the green, brown, and russet of the overhanging woods, with here and there a patch of clear blue sky, and the primrose tinted fringe of a passing sunny cloud. Were Diana a material existence, she would select this retired and sylvan nook as a favourite bath. The "yellow sands" of the inner beach are so smooth, the water so pellucid, and the spot so quiet and secluded, that, at eventide, when the wind's gentle music gives a spirit voice to the forest quire, the poetic faculty may easily realise Shakespere's beautiful vision of the "dainty Ariel" and the loveliest dell in Prospero's enchanted isle!

The river advances towards this seclusion through the open plain, between irregularly broken rows of stately trees, and glitters like molten silver, as it almost imperceptibly glides over the slight terraces of red sandstone rock, which form its bed. In the distance, Pendle Hill, famous in story, as the chief *locale* of the Lancashire witches of old, uplifts his broad shoulders to the sky above the heads of the lesser compeers by whom he is surrounded. Amongst the latter, our old acquaintance, the half rock, half wooded height of Hoghton, with its stern grey embattled mediæval fortress-mansion, like a lingering frown of the dead and mouldering Past upon the fair brow of the living Present, by contrast, heightens the beauty and interest of the scene. The spire of Mellor church crowns the summit of the neighbouring hill; whilst, in immediate contiguity, the ruined tower of a relatively modern windmill indicates, within a trifling distance, the site of a *specula* or outlook, from which the Roman sentinels gazed upon several of the neighbouring stations, and warned their brethren in arms, when the brave though discomfited Celt, indignant beneath the yoke, spurned the conqueror's power, and futilely essayed "one blow more" for their rude but cherished—and all the more cherished, because *lost*—liberty![1]

1 From Ribbleton-moor to the edge of Red Scar, is a perfectly straight road called "Pope-lane," with about three feet of its breadth paved with boulders. A similar pavement is likewise yet in

View from Red Scar, near Preston.

Red Scar, near Preston, the Seat of Wm. Assheton Cross, Esqr.

"Red Scar," the seat of Major Cross, a quaint Elizabethan mansion, with modern additions, is situated on the table land opposite to the centre of the curve. It is no slight privilege to be permitted to ramble through the winding paths, shadowy vistas, and secluded dingles, musical with the voices of singing brooks and birds, embosomed in the depths of these woods, from the lone quietude of which we occasionally catch a glimpse of the bright country beyond. Here are stately halls of Nature's architecture, domed by the azure heaven, and paved in rich mosaic, lustrous with the bloom of the wild blue hyacinth, and flakes of golden sheen by the bright attenuated fingers of stray sunbeams at random flung! Hanging leaves form verdant curtains with quivering fringe, so perfect yet picturesque in form, that sympathetic fancy denies that the rude east wind hath ever breathed upon them, or the eye of living being previously mirrored their beauty!

This little Eden is within about three miles from the manufacturing town of Preston, and yet few of its inhabitants ever visit the spot. Some animals, in dire extremity, are said to feed upon their own limbs. Doth the ravenous appetite for material wealth absorb that portion of the soul which rejoices and expands in the presence of the Beautiful?

After three or four miles ramble by the woods of Elston, Alston-hall is gained. Here the river merrily pursues its picturesque course, and carols away in joyous contentment, while the ruddy and almost perpendicular cliff called "Balderstone scar," on the opposite bank, scowls like a crabbed sentinel, fatigued with lengthened watching. The old mansion at Alston, is now converted into a farmer's homestead; but its fine large hall is yet in excellent preservation.

The chief attraction here, however, is the famous oak, with its "lightning-blasted" limb, huge hollow trunk, and still luxuriant foliage; realising to the view a rare specimen of the forest monarch in his "green old age." Enthusiastic admirers of rural scenery occasionally congregate at this spot, and some six or seven of them have been known simultaneously to enjoy a pic-nic feast within the hollow stomach of the woodland patriarch. This venerable relic of the old forest may almost be truly said to "stand in his pride alone," the last of his noble race.

existence beyond the "scar." It passes through the wood by "Tunbrook." This road is doubtless very ancient. Some regard it as a Roman vicinal way, which led to the mineral springs of Boilton. This is, however, by no means certain. It would be difficult to determine where it communicated with the "Watling-street," as the two roads are rather parallel than otherwise. The term "Pope lane" is a modern designation, derived from a comparatively recent occupant of a farm in the neighbourhood. On Lang's map of Preston, surveyed in 1774, there is a plot of land marked "Causeway field," which strengthens the impression that a vicinal way may have existed, which passed from the great Roman road at Preston over Ribbleton-moor to a villa at or near Red Scar. So beautiful a spot would scarcely be neglected by the refined southern warriors.

Near him, however, a small withered fragment of the old stock, a remnant of a still mightier brother, tottering on the verge of destruction, yet preserves his neighbour from utter solitude.[j]

Rambling along the bank of the Ribble, the pedestrian at length reaches Hothersall Hall. From the table land which overlooks the valley, a beautiful prospect to the west is obtained. The buff coloured buildings of the hall, nestle snugly below. Above, the neat little residence, "the Woodlands," peeps from amidst the foliage which crowns the brow of the hill. The rich verdure of Stubbin's wood and King's wood closes in the landscape on the extreme right, while the luxuriant groves of Alston, Elston, Boilton and Red Scar, vary the perspective line and conduct the eye gradually towards Preston. The shadowy height of Hoghton peeps over the table land of the middle distance, and the chimneys of some of the suburban factories, south of the Ribble, are visible in the horizon. The river from Osbaldestone Hall, on the left or southern bank, flows with a serpentine course, in form of the letter S, to Balderstone scar. Sunderland and Osbaldestone Halls repose securely on the margin of the stream, sheltered by the neighbouring picturesque foliage and the higher lands, from the storm's ruder blasts. The bosom of the valley rejoiceth in rich green pastures and sheets of waving golden grain. The colour and surface of the extensive plain is further varied by numerous flocks of sheep and herds of cattle. Groups of the latter repose upon the cool sands, whilst others stand in listless dreamy enjoyment, mid deep in the clear cool stream, which reproduces somewhat distortedly, within its depths, their somnolent bovine images.

The view eastward is equally picturesque. To the right, the high bank, with its richly wooded knoll and dingle, shelters Osbaldestone Hall, renowned, in the folk-lore of the neighbourhood, for its redoubtable "siege." Let not the reader for a moment fancy that the combatants were mail-clad warriors of the musty days of yore, or their valiant modern representatives, resplendent in scarlet cloth, pipe-clay and stunted cockades! No, the chief of its gallant defenders were "limbs of the law in possession;" gentlemen more famous for deeds on parchment and forensic triumphs, than deeds of

j The trunk of the oak at present flourishing at Alston is nearly ten feet in diameter, at the earth's surface. About three or four feet from the ground, the circumference is upwards of twenty feet. Its companion, which succumbed to the joint action of Time and Boreas, about six and twenty years ago, was a much larger tree. The hollow trunk was so capacious that it was occupied as a shippon, and two "head of cattle" were frequently "sealed" in it! It was likewise often used as a cart-house, the entrance being wide enough, and the internal space sufficiently large, to render it available for this purpose. In its prime, it must have been one of the most magnificent oaks in the kingdom. When this hoary forest monarch fell, a single root still adhered firmly to "mother earth," and retained a portion of the hollow trunk. It yet stands at the end of the garden wall. Although this singular relic puts forth a few leaves and gives other signs of vitality, its robe of ivy but imperfectly conceals the internal decay, which ere long will consign it to the fagot shed.

personal prowess or daring valour. Its assailants consisted chiefly of the peasantry of the neighbourhood, who sympathised with the "distress" of the unfortunate occupier, rather than with the legal instrument commonly so termed, by authority of which his homestead had been successfully invaded.[k]

Near this spot stands what was once a small chapel, now converted into a barn, a fate often attending sacred as well as profane edifices. On the right, Mellor church and mill "come off sharp" against the sky. The old parsonage house and estate is prettily situated on a knoll, in the middle distance, on the north bank of the river. Beyond this peeps the tower of Ribchester church, backed by the high lands of Ramsgrave, Clayton-le-dale, Salesbury, etc. In the extreme distance the broad full profile of huge Pendle closes in the prospect. Near its lower end, the hills in the neighbourhood of the Calder valley, and the moors about Billington, infuse a little rugged variety into this lovely pastoral landscape. There are gossips in the neighbourhood who shake their heads, when they gaze on the old parsonage, and mutter words of disapprobation at the conduct of certain high church dignitaries, whom they (foolishly no doubt) fancy to have appropriated to the uses of others, revenues originally intended to provide for the spiritual wants of the inhabitants of the locality.

Modern Ribchester, though possessing but little attraction to the tourist, is, nevertheless, not the mean and despicable spot it has been described. It is an ordinary well-built country village; without any particularly distinguishing feature. It is chiefly remarkable at the present day, for two grotesque carvings in wood, purporting to represent a black and a white bull. It is not yet decided by connoisseurs, which of the specimens of public house sculpture at Ribchester, or the one which adorns the neighbouring village of Longridge, is the most remarkable for taste or execution. The thing is, however, not of very much consequence, as it is believed the said bulls (evidently Irish) owe their existence to one and the same genius, who studied animal form (?) and wielded his chisel somewhere in the neighbourhood of the "Trough of Bolland."

The parish church stands on the site of the Roman castrum. Part of the artificial fosse is yet visible on the western side of the ancient fortification. Cowley brook bounds the camp on the east, and the Ribble on the south. Though the earth is rich in Roman remains, little of the ancient Rigodunum meets the eye, with the exception of three pillars taken from the river, now forming part of the porch of the principal inn. Other remains are yet preserved by the vicar and Mr. Patchet, but the greater bulk have found their way into the British Museum and public and private

k This sturdy resistance to the constituted authority took place some forty years ago. It required a tolerably significant demonstration on the part of the military, before the law was permitted to take its course.

collections, remote from the locality. Coins are yet often found. In the spring of 1855, the clerk of the church turned up in his garden a silver denarius, of Titus Vespasian, in capital preservation. On the reverse is a female figure, with the inscription "Concordia."

Roman roads in the neighbourhood may yet be traced. Near "Stubbin's nook," about two miles from Ribchester, the pavement of the road from the portus, at the Wyre, may be traced for some distance. On the opposite bank of the river, behind Salesbury Hall, some fragments are visible in the wood to the right of the modern road to Whalley. A little to the west, on the summit of the brow, the remains of what appears to have been a fosse, belonging to an outpost or *specula*, may be seen. It is probable from some such outwork the name "Salesbury" is derived. The road from Manchester, after crossing the ford over the Ribble, passes directly over Longridge fell. Considerable portions of this highway are yet in existence. From "Cherry gate," the modern road, called Stonygate lane, is occasionally identical with it, and sometimes leaves it a little to the left. Remains may easily be detected either in the fence or in the neighbouring fields. After crossing the road from Longridge to Stonyhurst, the ancient way still continues its direct line, leaving the modern zigzag road a little to the right. After passing the summit of the fell, the Roman way turns abruptly to the right, and, crossing the Hodder, enters Yorkshire. Some remains of the agger are yet visible in the fields to the left of the present road.

There are many objects of beauty and historic interest in the environs of Ribchester. Salesbury hall *may have* sheltered Henry VI. when a prisoner to the Talbots, after his capture at "Bungerley hyppyngestones," a little higher up the river.[1] In 1642, the Manchester puritan forces outwitted the then supposed vacillating Talbot, who sought to entrap them by a show of sympathy with their cause. Shortly afterwards, the earl of Derby, being routed by Colonel Shuttleworth, at Whalley, was chased across the Ribble to Ribchester, by the intrepid and indefatigable victor. In the immediate neighbourhood, the venerable "Stydd church," one of the oldest buildings in the county, yet stands a solitary semi-ruin. It is something more than strange, that funds cannot be raised for the restoration of this little monument of past ages. Surely there is antiquarian zeal and enthusiasm sufficient in the county, to make an effort powerful enough to snatch this choice morsel from the devouring maw of Time, ere it be too late. It is mere waste of breath, to expend our eloquence in denouncing the Vandalism which destroys, while we ourselves

1 Henry was captured at Bungerley, near Clitheroe, by Thomas Talbot, of Bashall, near Waddington, Yorkshire, and his cousin John, of Salesbury.—See chapter 3, page 130.

carelessly suffer that which is preserved to us to sink into decay, through practical indifference.

From Longridge fell side, a glorious view of the valley of the Ribble, and the greater portion of south Lancashire, is obtained. The Jesuits' college of Stonyhurst occupies a fine site on its southern slope. The village of Mitton, its ancient church and interesting monuments, lie hid amongst the foliage which luxuriates on the Hodder's banks. At the foot of Pendle, the village of Whalley, with its picturesque abbey ruin, and its long modern railway viaduct, lies cradled in the centre of a lovely amphitheatre of gently sloping hills, rich in varied beauty. A wide expanse of wood and plain, glittering in the sunlight, or reposing in cool transparent shadow, lies at our feet. The whole of our course from Lytham is seen at a glance; the objects which have been familiar to us, during our journey, are spread out like a chart before us. Moderately sized hills, shrunk into puny mounds, have lost their individual importance, but contribute towards the construction of the mighty panorama by which we are environed. Truly the scene is lovely enough to justify the enthusiastic aspiration of the good old poet of 1636, who exclaims :—[m]

I love ye men, ye countrye and ye fare,
And wish heere my poor fortunes settled were,
Far from ye courts ambition, citties strife,
Reposed in silence of a countrye life,
Amongst ye Dingles and ye Appennines,
Whose safetye gaue occasion to ould lines,
Thus riming: 'When all England is alofte
Then happie they whose dwelling's in Christs crofte;'
And where thincke you this crofte of Christe should be
But midst Ribchesters Ribble and Mercy ?"

From the angle of the Roman road on the north, just over the crown of the fell, the valley of the Loud and part of the valley of the Hodder, surrounded by the Bleasdale fells, Parlick pike, the Bowland fells, and the lesser Yorkshire hills, over-capped by the rugged heads of Penigent and Ingleborough, form another landscape of grander proportions and still more powerful features. From "Tootal Height," above the Longridge stone quarries, both valleys may be seen. To the west, from this point, the majestic panorama, like a sea of verdure, stretches from the shores of Morecambe Bay to near the estuary of the Mersey, the glittering sea line sparkling on the horizon. In the centre of this glorious prospect rises "Proud Preston," slightly disfigured, it is true, by the heavy cloud of coal smoke hanging like a sombre pall above its tall thin factory chimneys. Preston has, nevertheless, still good reason to be justly proud of its beautiful site, its historic antecedents, and its present envied position as the second manufacturing town in the county.

m Rev. Richard Jones, B.D. Iter Lancastrense.

An hour's repose on "Tootal Height" is a fitting close to our ramble. Here, while we gaze upon the open honest face of Nature in one of her loveliest moods, and admire the delicate and harmonious blending of the Beautiful with the Grand, we may reflect calmly upon the Past, and, guided by its teachings, we may speculate with profit upon the probable contents of the succeeding pages in the volume of universal and eternal Truth, in which the spirit of all History, present, past, and future, lies enshrined!

PART III.—THE ENVIRONS.

CHAPTER II.—THE HUNDRED OF AMOUNDERNESS.

Origin of the term Amounderness—Boundaries of the Hundred—Norman Proprietors—Harrison's description of Amounderness—Leland's Ditto—The Fylde—Parish of Preston—Fulwood and Myerscough—Parish of Kirkham—Lytham—Bispham, including Blackpool—Poulton, including Fleetwood—St. Michael's—Garstang.

THE origin of the term Amounderness has not yet been satisfactorily explained. It has, however, most probably been derived from *Ac*, oak; *munder*, estuaries, or mouths of rivers; and *ness*, promontory. This interpretation exactly accords with its natural characteristics.[a]

At the period of the Norman conquest, Amounderness included the parishes of Chipping and Ribchester, the Ribble forming the natural boundary between it and "Blackburn-shire." These parishes were, however, afterwards added to the territory of the De Lacies, probably from their contiguity to the stronghold of Clitheroe castle. The original boundaries of Amounderness, as described in the charter of Athelstan, in his grant of the land to the church of St. Peter, at York,[b] appear to have likewise included a considerable portion of the land to the north of the Wyre, at present appertaining to the hundred of Lonsdale. Dr. Whitaker, referring to this document, says:—

"The boundaries on three sides were simple, natural, and strongly defined—the sea, the Ribble, and the Hodder: the limit of the fourth, from the source of the Coker to the point where it falls in with Hodder, is rather obscure, '*ab illo fonte directe in alium fontum qui dicitur Saxonice Duleshope, sic per descensum rivuli in Hodder*.' Dulcshope was, therefore, a fountain which descended into the Hodder, having its source in the great ridge which forms the limit of Bowland to the north. This can be no other than Duneshope, the stream of Whitendale. By this demarcation, the course of Wire, which has long been the boundary between Loynesdale and Amunderness, was wholly neglected, and a right line, defining the two hundreds, carried from the source of Cocker to the top of Whitendale, so that great part of Over Wiresdale would fall within Amunderness."[c]

It has been shown that Lancashire, Westmoreland, etc., were most probably not formed into counties anterior to the Norman conquest. The ecclesiastical divisions of the country are evidently of much more ancient date.[d] In the valor of Pope Nicholas, completed in 1292, in the reign of Edward

---

a See chapter 2, page 73. b See chapter 2, page 70.
c His. Richmondshire, vol. 2, page 420.
d See chapter 2, pages 59 and 93; and chapter 3, page 97.

I., the parishes of Preston, Kirkham, Poulton, Garstang, St. Michael's, Lancaster, and Ribchester, are included in the deanery of Amounderness and the archdeaconry of Richmond When Chester was erected into a distinct bishopric in the 33rd year of the reign of Henry VIII., a new valuation was made, in which the rectory of St Bartholemew, at Chipping, the perpetual curacies of Bispham and Lytham, and the discharged vicarage of Cockerham, are included in the deanery of Amounderness.

The Domesday survey says, that all the villages in Amounderness, including three churches, belonged to Preston. It further adds,—"Of these" (villages) "sixteen have *few* inhabitants—but how many inhabitants there may be is not known." From this it has been supposed that the remainder of the sixty-two villages or townships enumerated therein, were without, or nearly without, inhabitants. It is more probable, however, that forty-six of the villages, possessed an average population, and that the sixteen had partially fallen into decay, in consequence of the ravages of the victorious Norman soldiery. The document further adds that the remaining lands in the hundred were "waste," and that the whole was held by Roger de Poictou [e] It was subsequently conferred upon Theobald Walters, son of Herveus, another follower of the conqueror, whose line according to Dr. Whitaker, still remained unbroken to the present century in the Butlers of Kirkland. [f] Mr Baines says the "name of Walter originally signified an office; and, by Verstigan, in his *Decayed Intelligence*, is derived from the Teutonic 'Wald-huter,' a forester; and, having been assumed by Herveus, Carte is of opinion that he was warden of the forest of Amunderness" On the death of Theobald Walter, Amounderness reverted to the crown, in the possession of which it remained until the 51st year of the reign of Henry III., when, as stated in the pleadings on a *Quo Warranto*, in a subsequent reign, this monarch granted the Wapentake to Edmund Crouchback, earl of Lancaster, with the castle and honour of Lancaster, and the manors of Preston, Rigby, and Singleton. They again merged into the possessions of the crown, on the accession of Henry IV. A portion is still retained by the queen, as duchess of Lancaster.

Harrison, the oldest English topographer, has left the following description of the rivers in Amounderness and the neighbourhood:—

"The Darwent divideth Lalandshire from Andernesse, [g] and it riseth by east, above Darwent Chappell, and soone after uniting itselfe with the Black-burne and Rodlesworth water, it goeth through Howghton parke, by Howghton towre, to Walton hall, and so on to the Ribell As for the Savvocke brooke, it ryseth some what above Longridge chappell, goeth to Browghton towne, Cottam, Lee hall, and so into Ribell; and here is all that I have to say of this river.

"The Wyre riseth eight or ten miles from Garstan, out of a hill in Wyresdale, whence it runneth by Shireshead chappell, and then going by Wadland, Garstang, and Kyrke-

e See chaper 3, page 98. f See chapter 3, page 112.

g This is an error See chapter 3, page 138.

lande hall, it first receyveth the second Calder, that cometh down by Edmersey chappell, then another channel, increasd with sundrie waters, which I will here describe before I begin with the Wire. I suppose that the first water is called Plympton brooke. It riseth south of Gosner, and cometh by Cawforde hall, and ere long, receyving the Barton becke, it proceedeth forward till it joyneth with the Brocke rill, that cometh by Claughton hall, where in Broke holes doth lie, and so thorough Mersco forest. After this confluence, the Plime or Plympton water meeteth with the Calder and then with the Wire, which passeth forth to Mighell church and the Raw cliffes, and above Thorneton crosseth the Skipton that goeth by Polton, then into the Wire rode, and finally into the sea, according to his nature.

"Beying past the fall of the Wyre, wee coasted upp by the salt cotes to Cocker mouth, whose shortnesse of course deserveth no description. The next is Cowdar,[h] which coming out of Wiredale, as I take it, is not encreased with anie other waters more than Coker, and therefore I will rydde my hands thereof so much the sooner."

In the reign of Henry VIII., Leland the king's antiquary and topographer, passed through Amounderness, of which hundred he has left the following description :—

"From Preston to Garstone X mile.

"A mile without Preston I rode over Savok, a bigge brooke, the wich rising in the hilles a iii or iv miles of on the right hand, not very far of goeth into Ribel.

"After I rode over Brock water, rising a vi miles of in the hills on the right hand, and goeth at last into Wyre. Calder rising about the same hills, goeth also into Wyre; I rode over it. By the townes end of Garstone I rode over a great stone bridge on Wyver or I cam to hit. Wyre riseth a viii or tenne myles from Garston out of the hilles on the right hande, and cummeth by Grenehaugh, a praty castel of lord Darby's and more than half myle thens to Garston in Anderness. Sum saith that Garstone was a market towne.

"From Garstane to Sainct Mikels, a village ii miles, and a mile lower on the further side be the places of Mr. Kirkeby of Rancliffe and Mr. Boteler of Raucliffe; so a vii mile to Alhalois village, and thens to the sea. Raudcliffe of Wimmerlaw a mile from Garstan, hath hys place at Wimmerlaw.

"Wyre ebbeth and floweth a iii miles beneath Garstane, and at a chapel of Alhalows, at a x miles from Garstane goeth into the main se.

"Or I came to Garstane, by a mile and an halfe, I left Merscow, a great parke partly enclose with hegge, al on the moor side with pale; on the right it is replenished with redde dere. The Erle of Darby hath it in ferme of the kinge.

"Up towards the hill by Grenehaugh be iii forests of redde dere, Wyredale, Bouland, and Bleasdale; that be partly woody, partly hethe. The ground bytwixt Morle and Preston enclosed for pasture and corne, but were the vast mores and mosses be, whereby as in hegge rowes. by side grovettes, ther is reasonable woode for building, and sum for fier, yet al the people ther for the most part burne turfes. Likewise is the soil bytwixt Preston and Garstan; but alway the moste part of enclosures be for pasturage.

"Whete is not very comunely sowed in thes partes aforesaid.

"Al Aundernesse for the moste parte in time paste hath been full of woode, and many of the moores replenished with hy fyrre trees. But now such part of Aundernesse as is toward the se is sore destitute of woodde.

"From Garstane I passed partely by moore ground, partly by pasture and sum corne, and so riding over Goker river that maketh no grete course or he cum to the sandes by Cokerham village, not a mile of upon which sandes I passed Koker river ous or twis again, not without sum feere of quickkesandes. At the ende of the sandes I saw divers salt cootes wher were divers hepes of sandes of salt strondes. out of the wich, by often weting with water, they pike oute the saltnes, and so the water is drived into a pit and after sodde."

h "This Cowdar, so far as I know, is a nonentity; but the word, however mis-spelt, seems to have been meant by Harrison to denote the Conder, which is the next rivulet to Cocker, though within Loynesdale hundred."—Dr. Whitaker's His. Rich. vol. 2, p. 418.

The eastern portion of Amounderness is hilly, the western, bordering upon the sea, is a level champaign country, varied with slight knolls, and interspersed with moss lands. The level division is termed the Fylde, which is interpreted to mean the field or flat cleared land.[i] This tract of country now abounds with fertile arable, as well as meadow and pasture land Considerable improvements have latterly been effected in the drainage and cultivation of many portions of the district, and others are now in progress.

The population of the hundred of Amounderness, which, with the exception of Preston, Kirkham, and a few minor places, is chiefly occupied in agricultural pursuits, was in 1851, 113,243. According to the ordnance survey, the hundred contains 162,643 statute acres. The annual value of the property, according to the assessment made in 1854, for the county rate, was £414,272. In 1841, it was £364,454.[j]

PARISH OF PRESTON.

Preston parish, besides the township of Preston, includes Lea, Ashton, Ingol and Cottam, Broughton, Barton, Haighton, Elston, Grimsargh with Brockholes, Ribbleton, and Fishwick.

Lea, Ashton, Ingol, and Cottam, four hamlets, to the north west of the town of Preston, form one township for parochial purposes. In the reign of John, Arthur de Estone held a carucate of land in Estone, Tulket, and Ingole.[k] Mr Baines says:—

> "Sir Richard de Hocton, son of Adam de Hocton by his wife Avica, widow of Roger de Ashton, married Sybilla, daughter of William de Lea, and heir of Henry de Lea, 2 Edward II., and he occurs in the Duchy Feodary, as holding the manor of Lea by the service of 3s. 4d. per annum, and a moiety of the town of Ashton by the service of 50s. yearly[l] The other moiety was then held by Lawrence Travers and William Lawrence, in right of their wives."

A Marmaduke Tulketh lived at Tulketh hall in 1124. It afterwards reverted to Lawrence Travers, of Nateby, near Garstang[m] John Travers, of Nateby, in the 36th Edward III., held land and meadow at Tulkethe. The estate afterwards passed to the Werdens and the Rawstornes, and eventually to the Hesketh. The estate was lately purchased by John Abel Smith, esq It is at present the property of Edward Pedder, esq, of Ashton park, and Joseph Bray, esq. The hall, though a building of no

i "This last tract is commonly denominated the Filde, by which is commonly understood the field or champagn country, and this is probably right, for Alfred, in his version of Orosius, has *on fildum lændum* in the plural, to denote level countries"—Whitaker's His. Rich. vol. 2, p 415.

j The increased value is, however, much greater than is shown by these figures, as the following deductions were made in 1854 "From the value of all lands, tithes, canals, navigations, docks watercourses, reservoirs, quarries, delphs, and brick-yards, *one-twelfth part.* From the value of all buildings, (except farm buildings), mines, railways, and gasworks, one-sixth part"

k Rot. Chart. 1. John.

l "It was an escheat of the crown from the earl of Ferrers, at the compilation of the Testa de Neville."

m See page 462.

great antiquity or architectural pretensions, forms a striking object from the bank of the river, owing to its light colour and castellated form. Tulketh was occupied by the monks under Evanus, during the erection of their magnificent abbey at Furness.[m] The woods have been partially cut down and the neighbouring land laid out for the erection of villas. A small but neat church was built at Ashton a few years ago, principally through the exertions of the late vicar, the Rev. R. Carus Wilson. Lea, Ashton, Ingol, and Cottam, in 1851, contained 743 inhabitants, and according to the ordnance survey, nearly 3,488 statute acres of land. The property was assessed to the county rate, in 1854, at the annual value of £8,361.

Broughton most probably derived its name from the circumstance that a small Roman outwark originally existed in the neighbourhood. It is situated on the line of the great road from Preston to Lancaster. Theobald Walter was deprived of lands in Brochton, in the reign of King John. He, however, afterwards regained possession of them. In the reign of Edward I., a rent of 8s. was derived from land in Broughton, by Edmund, earl of Lancaster.[n] A messuage, two mills, fifty acres of land, and a close called Farnihalgh, were held by Gilbert de Singleton, in the 19th Edward II.[o] Mr. Baines conjectures the messuage referred to to have been a massive structure of stone, razed about fifty years ago, called Broughton tower. Some remains of a moat are still visible near the farm house erected upon the site. It continued in the family of Singleton until about the 13th James II., when it passed by marriage to Lawrence Rawstorne, esq., of Penwortham. In 1810, part of the estate was conveyed to the trustees of Kirkham school, and another portion to James Rothwell, esq., of Hoole. Broughton is a township comprising five hamlets, viz., the Church, Ingol Head, Lightford Houses, Dorton, and Sharoe Green. It forms in conjunction with Barton and Haighton, a parochial chapelry. The origin of the church is not known. The older portion of the present edifice is evidently of the time of Henry VIII. Laurence Stadaghe bequeathed his lands, in the event of a school not being founded, for the repair of Broughton church and the church bridges, in the 18th year of the reign of that monarch. The body of the church was rebuilt in 1822, when many interesting inscriptions and carvings were destroyed. On the oaken roof of the chancel, the dates 1537 and 1539 were carved. The old building contained two chapels, one on the north, founded by the Bartons, of Preston; and the other on the south side of the chancel, by the Singletons, of Broughton tower. The old church tower is yet preserved. It bears the date of 1533. On the base of the

m See chapter 3, page 117 and part 3, page 508. n Kuerden's manuscript.
o Escaet. 45 Edw. II. n. 67.

stone pedestal which supports a sun dial in the churchyard, is the following inscripton, "J. B. 1550." The initials, together with the arms of Singleton, Langton, Barton, and Redmayne, carved in stone, which formed a portion of the previous structure, are rebuilt in the east wall of the present edifice. Bishop Gastrell records that in the early portion of the last century, the salary of the master of the free grammar school was £13 7s. 6d., arising from messuages and land, bequeathed in the 18th year of the reign of Henry VIII., by Mr. Laurence Stadaugh, "towards the exhibition and finding of an honest person, sad and discreet, to teach grammar and school at Broughton." By deed, dated 3rd November, 1656, one pound per annum was given and secured on lands for a similar purpose, by William Daniel, yeoman. The widow Daniel bequeathed one pound per annum; and, in 1649, Mr. Thomas Houghton devised "one-fourth part of twenty-two acres of land, to the poor. Bishop Gastrell likewise mentions other legacies of similar character; one, the "interest of £41, taken care of by trustees;" the other, "the interest of £21., given long ago by a person unknown" At Fernyhalgh, a chapel existed in the fifteenth century. The site is still marked by a cross. In the immediate neighbourhood, a modern catholic chapel was erected, about sixty years ago. In 1718, Christopher Tootel, the catholic minister, having refused to take the then legal oaths, was twice summoned to appear before the commissioners at Preston. He still refusing to comply, the officials visited him in a somewhat unceremonious manner, as appears by the following memorandum in the possession of the present pastor:—

"On Monday, June the last, 1718, the two chappells at Holywell, were visited by twenty soldiers, sent from Preston by the commissioners, mounted on hired horses, and conducted by Mr Hitchmugh, the value of the booty is variously reported, but much less considerable than at first it was said to be, as not exceeding £100."

Fernyhalgh and Holywell are situated at the head of a secluded and picturesque valley. A singular tradition of a miraculous character, still obtains some credence as to the origin of the chapel. The estimated annual value of property in the township of Broughton, in 1854, was £6,196, the population in 1851, 685; and the area, according to the ordnance survey, 2,367 acres.

Barton.—Barton in the reign of Henry III., was held by Grimbald de Barton About the year 1612, it passed by marriage to the Shuttleworths, of Gawthorpe. In 1833, the manor was purchased by the late George Jacson, esq, of Preston, whose son, Charles Jacson, esq, resides at the modern mansion, Barton lodge. The old hall has been converted into a farm-house. St. Lawrence's chapel existed before the reformation. It is mentioned as early as 1577 In the parliamentary inquiry, in 1650, it is stated to be without minister or maintenance Bishop Gastrell says:—"This chapell

Repaired by yᵉ Family who enjoyed yᵉ Estate, and lived in yᵉ Manour-house, to wᶜʰ this seems to have been a Domestic Chapell; wᶜʰ House and Estate now belong to Mr. Shuttleworth. Certified that nothing belongs to it."[p] St. Lawrence's chapel was enlarged and decorated with a stained glass window, in 1845, by the late George Jacson, esq. An excellent organ, built by Mr. Joseph Roome, of Preston, comprising fourteen stops (including swell and couplars), was presented to the chapel, in 1856, by Mr. Hawkins, of Newsham house. The population of Barton, in 1850, was 370; annual value of property, in 1854, £3,336; area, 2,707 statute acres.

Haighton.—This township, from the inquisitions in the duchy office, appears to have been held at a distant period by several proprietors. Mr. Baines says "an ancient building, called Haighton house, was occupied in the last century by Henry Haighton, gent., who was doubtless the representative of the local family." There are two mansions, one of which was more recently purchased by Mr. Anderton, from the Gerards, of Holt, in Brindle; and the other, Haighton hall, from the heirs of Edward Pedder, esq., late of Lancaster, by Richard Newsham, esq., of Preston. The township of Haighton contains 1,077 statute acres. In 1854, the property was assessed at the annual value of £1,388. The population in 1851, amounted to 193.

Elston.—According to Mr. William Elston, who wrote, at the commencement of the seventeenth century, a curious work, entitled "Mundana Mutabilia, or Ethelestophylax,"[q] the original name of this township was Ethelestone. He alludes to an ancient deed, which specifies that King Athelstan, when "lyinge in camp in this county upon occacon of warrs, gave the land of Etheleston vnto one to whom himself was Belsyre."[r] Mr. Elston likewise quotes another document, of the 45th Edward III., which, he says, had "a faire seale, with an eagle displayed with two heads in a scuchion, and there was engraven about plainely to be read these words, *Sigillum Johis de Etheleston.*" The land passed through various hands, until Sir John Radcliffe, of Ordsal, disposed of it to Sir Thomas Walmsley. It was again several times transferred, until it fell into the hands of a Mr. Roger Charnock, who was contemplating the sale of the property at the time Mr. Elston was occupied in the compilation of his curious work. The principal owner at the present time is Thomas

p There exists a tradition, that Mr. Shuttleworth being threatened with the honour of a visit by King James I., on his temporary sojourn at Myerscourgh-lodge, in 1617, set fire to his kitchen, in order that he might be armed with a sufficient apology for declining the responsibilities of furnishing entertainment for the monarch's princely retinue.

q Harl MS. 1727, fo. 336. r See chapter 2, page 93.

Walmsley, esq., of Winckley-square, Preston. The population of Elston, in 1851, consisted of fifty-four persons. The area, according to the ordnance survey, is 961 acres. The assessment to the county rate is £1,005. annual value.

GRIMSARGH.—In the 23rd Henry III., William de Eton held the "town of Grymesargh." Roger de Etheleston likewise held property in this township at the same period. Each paid in consideration the sum of three shillings per annum. The manorial rights, including those of Alston, etc., were disposed of by the late Sir Henry Hoghton, bart., to William Assheton Cross, esq., of Red Scar. A small picturesque chapel, dedicated to St. Michael, was erected about the year 1716, by subscription. Bishop Gastrell says:—

"New chapel, lately erected, viz. anno 1716, in ye Township of Grimsargh, but not yet Consecrated, anno 1722, Certified that nothing at all belongs to it. £200. was subscribed by Mr. Peplo, Minr of Preston, Sir Henry Houghton and others, towards ye augmentation, anno 1717, £40. of wch was given by a Gentlewoman who desired not to be known."[s]

The following letter, addressed by the Rev. Samuel Peploe, vicar of Preston, (afterwards Bishop of Chester), to his predecessor, Bishop Gastrell, gives some interesting particulars respecting the origin of this chapel:—

"My Lord,—I beg leave to acquaint yr Ldp yt there are three Townships and part of another in this Parish, wch lie three, four, and five miles from the church, and have no other convenient Place of public worship. That by this unhappy Situation they have still been exposed to temptations and Popery, (wch is too prevalent in these Parts of your Lordship's Diocess,) and are thereby an easier Prey to the Priests of that Communion, we having no less than six of these men in ys one Parish. From my first coming to this place I have wished for some hopeful remedy agt ys growing evil; and I hope we are now in a way for it if yr Lp. please to give your approbation.

"Sir Henry Hoghton, the Patron of ys Church, (and who has done several good things for increasing our Congregation, and is the person who do's me the favour to put ys paper into yr hands), has promised Land to build a Chapel where it will be serviceable to the Inhabts above mentd; and wth his assistance, I doubt not to procure a decent place for ye worship of God among 'em.

"When the intended Chappel is opened, I have taken care already yt there shall be ten pounds per ann. at least, annexed to it, besides what some of the Inhabitants will Subscribe, and wt may be got by Teaching School, it being a place where a diligent man may help himself that way. These together, will be a competency for a Curate in ys cheap Country; and I hope if ye work be perfected, it will be of great use to men's souls, as well as of service to our Church. I wait only for yr Ldp's pleasure to p'ceed. If I have yt encouragement I shall im'ediately set about it, and hope to give you a good account of ye affairs in a little time. I am, yr Ldp's unknown, but very dutifull son and obedient Servt.
Signed, SAML. PEPLOE.

"I was at Chester to pay my Duty to yr Ldp, soon after you went for London.

"Preston, in Lancashire, Deanery of Richmond, Apr. 4, 1715."[t]

The chapel was enlarged about 1815. This edifice was almost covered with ivy, and formed a very picturesque rural object. It was partially

s Notitia Cestriensis, vol 2, page 470.

t Gastrell's MSS. Registry, Chester. St. George's chapel, Preston, was likewise erected chiefly through the exertions of the Rev. S. Peploe.

rebuilt, and considerably enlarged in 1844, the chief expense being borne by John Cross, esq., of Red Scar.[u] It now contains some handsome stained glass windows. A portion of the ivy yet creeps around the old tower.

Brockholes.—The lordship of Brockholes, at a very early period was held by the barons of Manchester. Roger de Brochol in the 38th Henry III., held the land. It passed by marriage to the Ethelestons, of Ribbleton, and the Singletons, of Brockholes; and afterwards to the Winckleys, by whom it was conveyed to Sir John Shelley, bart. Two old buildings are called respectively Higher Brockholes hall and Lower Brockholes hall. Grimsargh and Brockholes form one township, the annual rateable value of which, in 1854, was £3,108; the acreage, according to the ordnance survey, 1,937; and the population, in 1851, 360.

Ribbleton.—According to Mr. Elston's manuscript, previously referred to, Ribbleton was held, in the reign of Henry III., by Avica de Ribbleton. Her grandson conveyed all his lands, buildings, and gardens in Ribbleton, to be held of the chief lords, to Roger de Etheleston. The township is sometimes styled, in the old deeds, Ribbleton Scalis. William, son of Roger del Scalis, gave the manor to Roger de Etheleston, in the eleventh year of the reign of Edward II. From the Elstons it passed to Sir Thomas de Hesketh, bart., of Rufford. Ribbleton hall is the seat of Thomas Birchall, esq., of Preston. A large tract of still unenclosed land called Ribbleton-moor, is celebrated as the battle field where Cromwell overcame Sir Marmaduke Langdale, in 1648. Should the cultivation of this waste be determined upon, doubtless many relics of the contest will be discovered.[v] On Ribbleton-moor, some time ago, were the remains of two stone crosses, one of which yet stands near to the boundary which divides the township from Preston. On the road from Broughton, a curious circular perforated stone, believed to be the pedestal of an ancient cross, may still be seen. The area of Ribbleton township is 648 statute acres. The population in 1851, numbered 189; and the annual rateable value of the property in 1854, was £1,675.

Fishwick.—According to the Testa de Nevill', Roger Gernet held Fisewic or Fyswyc by serjeanty as forester. It was valued at twenty shillings per annum. Sir William Dacre, in the reign of Edward I., acquired the manor of Fishwick by marriage with Joane, heiress of Benedict Gernet. Ranulph de Dacre fell at the battle of Towton-field. His estates were by attainder forfeited to the crown. Sir Thomas Assheton, of Ashton-under-Lyne, held Fysshewick, in the 7th year of the reign of Henry VIII. By marriage with his daughter, it passed to the Hoghton family, by whom it was held till the middle of the last century, when it was disposed

u See page 590. v See page 183.

of to the father of the late Townley Rigby Shawe, esq., of Preston Fishwick during the present century has become attached to Preston, and now forms a part of the parliamentary and municipal borough. The population in 1851, numbered 1,065 persons. The annual rateable value of the property in the township, in 1854, was £5,028. According to the ordnance survey it contained 692 statute acres of land. The population of Preston was 68,537; the annual rateable value of the property £168,770.; and the area 2,126 acres. Total: Population, 69,542; value of property, £173,798.; area, 2,818 acres. Until lately a spring existed at "Common bank," which possessed the property of "petrifying" or covering with earthy matter plants and other objects submitted to its action. Mr. Baines mentions a spring of this character in Frenchwood. Near Boilton wood, between Lower Brockholes and Red Scar, is a spring possessing medical properties It has acquired some fame as "Boilton-spa." It is not much frequented at the present time. Dr Southey says:—"There is a spring about three leagues from hence (Preston), the water of which will burn with blue flame like spirits of wine." [w] It is difficult to say what spring is here alluded to. Mr. Whittle assumes the one at Boilton.[x] But this is neither three *leagues* (not miles as he prints it) distant from Preston, nor does it possess the peculiar property referred to. Dr. Leigh describes several springs in Lancashire. He mentions one at Inglewhite, with a "very sulphureous smell, as strong as that near *Harrigate* in *Yorkshire*" Another at "*Aucliff*," near Wigan, he thus describes:—

"The Well is at the Bottom of a Tree, the *Water* Cold, and without any Smell; when any Person comes to see it, a Man clears the Well from all its Water, that done you will immediately hear a hissing Noise in a Corner of it, and by holding a lighted Candle near to it, the Sulphureous *Halitus* immediately takes Fire, and afterwards spreads itself upon what Water has issued in, and tis only then indeed it ought to be call'd the *Burning-Well*." [y]

This, in all probability, is the spring referred to.

Fulwood, although immediately contiguous to the township of Preston, is an isolated portion of the parish of Lancaster. It forms, however, one of the suburbs of Preston, and in the course of time, will doubtless become incorporated with the town. Fulwood is not mentioned in the Domesday survey, unless it is alluded to by the term Watelei,[z] which is not improbable, as the Roman Watling-street traverses the township Fulwood was one of the parks or forests belonging to the duchy of Lancaster. It was latterly held in fee by the earl of Derby. A large portion was moor or common, until 1814 Some relics of Cromwell's victory over Langdale in

w Letters from England, No. XL, by Don Manuel Alvares Espriella, second edition, 1808.

x His Preston, vol 2, p. 97. y Nat His. Lan. Ches. Book 1, p. 41.

z See chap. 3, page 99

Fulwood Barracks, Preston

1648, have been found on a farm bearing the name of Killingsough,[a] near which an immense quantity of human bones were discovered during some draining operations. Various reasons have been assigned for their deposit in this locality, though none are perfectly satisfactory.[b] A portion of the land in Fulwood, between the brook which separates it from Moor-park and the Watling-street, has been purchased by the Freehold Land society, and laid out for building purposes. Several houses have already been erected. This pleasantly situated suburb is called the "Freehold-park." The new barracks are situated a little to the left of Freehold-park, at the distance of about a mile and a half from the centre of Preston. The land occupied by this military station comprises twenty-eight and a half statute acres. It is built upon a part of the site of the old race course, over which the ancient Watling-street passed. The preparatory works were commenced in July, 1842, and the first stone was laid on the 28th of August, 1843. The whole was completed in June, 1848. The establishment includes a large square for infantry, and a second for cavalry exercise, together with an extensive general parade ground in the rear. The whole of the buildings, which are spacious and admirably adapted to secure the health and comfort of the occupants, are of stone, from the lower quarry at Longridge. They are calculated to accommodate one battalion of infantry, one squadron of cavalry, and demi-battery of artillery. In addition to the offices for purely military purposes, there is a neat chapel, erected over the principal inner gateway, which gives some little architectural character to this large mass of substantial building. The following inscription is placed upon the inner side of the wall near the principal entrance:—

"This Barrack, built by order of
The Master General and Board of Ordnance
was
Commenced in August, 1843, and Completed in June, 1848,
Amount of Estimate, £137,615. 15. 4½.
Amount of Cost, £137,921. 2. 10¾.
T. Foster,
Major & Comᴰᴳ Royˡ Engineers."

Extensive additions are at present in progress. On the west side of the parade ground a range of substantial buildings are in course of erection, calculated to afford suitable accommodation for about eighty married soldiers and their families. The situation of the Fulwood barracks is remarkably healthy, being rather high, and freely exposed to the sanitary influence of both the sea and mountain breezes. The population of Ful-

a See chap. 4, page 196. b See chap. 2, page 64.

wood in 1851, numbered 1,748; the area, according to the ordnance survey, is 2,116 acres; and the annual rateable value of the property, in 1854, was £5,971. In 1707, the corporation of Preston, at the request of the Rev. Samuel Peploe, M.A., the vicar, granted a piece of land in the "townships of Cadeley and Fulwood" for the erection of a school. The sum of one hundred pounds was invested in five acres of land called "Norshaw," and conveyed to Mr. Peploe and the Rev. W. Charnley, curate of Broughton, in trust. Four fifths of the rental were to be applied towards the maintenance of the school; one tenth was to be distributed in bread, by the vicar for the time being, and the remaining tenth to be paid to the said Samuel Peploe, his heirs, and assigns for ever. Mr. Peploe received £80. out of the one hundred so invested under the will of John Hatch, of Preston, for the use of the school, and £10. more for the purchase of the bread to be given to the poor at Preston, on Sacrament Sunday. The remaining £10. Mr. Peploe added himself, hence the reversion of his interest to his heirs.

MYERSCOUGH is likewise in the parish of Lancaster. It was formerly a forest or park pertaining to the crown. In the reign of Henry VIII., Leland speaks of the red deer in "Merscow park." The land of the forest until lately has generally been held by the earls of Derby. The manor is held under the duchy by Thomas Fitzherbert Brockholes, esq., of Claaughton. Messrs. William and John Humber, of Preston, now hold Myerscough park in lease from the crown. Myerscough lodge, the residence of the gallant Sir Thomas Tildesley, has been converted into a farm house. Although much modernised, some portions still retain their original character. Amongst these is the broad staircase with its fine oak balustrade. The "chimney piece," in a small room to the left of the staircase is an extremely massive and elaborate specimen of the oak carving of the period. It occupies the entire space between the firep lace and the ceiling. It contains eight panels. The four lower ones are ornamented with carved heads; and two of the upper ones bear the arms of the Tildesleys, and the initials T. T. The Rev. Canon Raines says:—"Edward Tyldesley, esq., had arms allowed in 1644, and was probably the individual who about this time restored this part of the lodge."[c] The Derby crest is carved over one of the medallion heads, and the Manx arms over the other. Above the door of the stable, there is built in the wall, a stone, ornamented with rude carving, which carries the following singular inscription: "OLD DOG LAD 1714." This has been interpreted to read as follows: "Oswald Lord Derby, Demense of Garstang, Lord Archer

c Annotations to the Assheton Journal, published by the Chetham Society.

of the Duchy." In a manuscript diary of Thomas Tildesley, esq., which commences in March, 1712, and concludes in November, 1714, there is an entry dated March 28th, 1712, in which he styles himself, in a list of parties at dinner, as "Old: Dog: Lad:" From this it would appear that the phrase originated with one of the Stanley family, who held the office of "Lord Archer" under the duchy, and that Mr. Tildesley adopted it as a nickname on account of his connection with the forest. Edward Tildesley, in 1617, entertained King James I. at Myerscough lodge, on his return from Scotland. Charles II. likewise rested there one night, on his way to Worcester.[d] The population of the township, in 1851, amounted to 459 persons; the area, according to the ordnance survey, is 2,706 acres; and the rateable value of the property in 1854, was £4,181.

KIRKHAM PARISH.

From the numerous remains discovered, Kirkham was undoubtedly occupied as a station by the Roman people.[e] Coins, pottery, etc., have been frequently found. The pottery is all of the coarser kind, no specimen of the "Samian or red lustrous ware" having been met with. One extremely rare and interesting relic of the Roman people was taken from the brook in the Mill Hey Field, in 1792. It is of brass, and is considered to be the ornamented boss or *umbo* of a shield. Dr. Whitaker has evidently been mis-informed as to the locality where this relic was found. The same article is described by him as having been discovered on the line of the Roman road, near Garstang, in 1800. It was examined, according to Mr. Baines, by Dr. Hunter, of York, and afterwards passed into the hands of Sir William Hamilton. Dr. Whitaker says it "was purchased soon after its discovery by Charles Towneley, esq., and deposited, with the rest of his collection in the British Museum." The entire diameter is about eight inches. In the centre its form is semi-globular. The diameter of this embossment is about five inches. In the surrounding flat portion, there are four holes, evidently intended for the rivets by which it was originally fastened to the wood of the shield. In the centre is represented a dignified figure, seated, with a bird, apparently an eagle, on the left. This is most probably intended to represent either Jupiter or some one of the Roman emperors.[f] On either side of the boss is a naked figure engaged in some athletic exercise. Beneath the feet of the figure is an eagle and some other birds. The remainder of the level portion is decorated with representations of swords, shields, and military trophies. The Roman road

d See pages 151, 202, 219. e See chapter 1, page 36.

f Dr. Whitaker says this bird has "more the character of a goose than might have been expected in so dignified a situation."

from Fulwood-moor, passed by Kirkham on its way to the "Portus" of Ptolemy, at the Wyre. Some remains of it are yet visible, especially part of an embankment of gravel, over the moss betwixt Kirkham and Poulton. Several remains have been picked up on its line.[g] The farmers in the neighbourhood, however, are very industriously destroying the last remains of the agger, the material being handy for the repair of roads. Kirkham at the time of the Domesday survey, possessed a church, as the name implies. Roger de Poictou conferred the church and tithes of Kirkham, upon the abbey of Sees, for the benefit of the priory of Lancaster. It afterwards passed to the convent of Shrewsbury, and again, after some further partial transfers, to the abbey of Vale Royal, in the ninth Edward I. In the following year, the town was incorporated. At the dissolution of the monasteries, both the manor and advowson of the church were transferred to Christ church college, Oxford The college retains the right of presentation to the vicarage, but the manor is held in fee by the Cliftons, of Lytham. Several other charters have been granted to Kirkham, including one of the 9th Elizabeth, which confirms the previous grant of a weekly market on Thursday, and an annual fair of five days. It was declared, in the 1st Edward, a free borough for ever, with power to hold a free guild, with a prison, pillory, and ducking stool; and assize of bread, beer, weights and measures. The borough, however, never sent any members to parliament, probably on account of its relative poverty. The duties of town council, appear to have been discharged by thirty burgesses, who are styled in the records the "Thirty Men." Kirkham possesses several charities, and a free grammar school, which was in existence before the year 1585. In 1291, the living of Kirkham was valued at £160.[h] per annum; but at the dissolution of the monasteries its revenues were estimated at no more than £21. 1s. 0½d.[i] In 1835, it appears from a petition presented to the house of commons, from the inhabitants, that, with a population of 12,000 persons, scattered over seventeen townships, comprising 130 square miles of land, eight of the townships were without any means of religious instruction; and that in one direction, for a distance of twelve miles, not a single place of worship was to be met with Some little improvement has since taken place. The parish church was probably re-built by Cuthbert Clifton, who died in 1586, and whose arms are engraved upon one of the buttresses. The "church was entirely rebuilt, by the aid of a parish rate, in the year 1822," at a cost of £5,000 [j] In 1845, the tower was taken down, and the present one surmounted by a

g See chapter 1, page 5. h Valor of Pope Nicholas. i Liber Regis.

j Over an arch in the chancel is an inscription as above quoted. It is, however, not strictly correct, inasmuch as the tower and a portion of the chancel of the elder building were preserved.

St. Michael's Church, Kirkham

spire 150 feet in height erected. There are several interesting monuments in the church. Amongst others, it is said, there formerly existed a singular epitaph to the memory of the Rev. Cuthbert Harrison, A. B., a celebrated ejected puritan minister, who founded, by royal license, in 1672, a meeting house, at Elswick Lees, in the parish of St. Michael. The Rev. R. Clegg, vicar of Kirkham, a bitter opponent of Harrison, is said to have caused a satirical epitaph to be placed over his grave. This gave displeasure to the friends of the staunch nonconformist, some of whom altered the version to the disparagement of Clegg. The epitaphs read as follows :—

Clegg's version,

"Here lies Cud,
Who never did good,
But always was in strife:
Oh! let the Knave
Lie in his grave,
And ne'er return to life."

As altered by Harrison's friends.

"Here lies Cud,
Who still did good,
And never was in strife,
But with Dick Clegg,
Who furiously opposed
His holy life." [k]

The truth of the story is, however, denied by the Rev. Canon Raines, who says: "The fact appears to be that the doggrel in question was the harmless effusion of an obscure poet, and written in chalk, a few years since, on a gravestone in the Church-yard."[l] Kirkham possesses several other places of worship in connection with various religious denominations. A handsome catholic chapel, at the "Willows," near Kirkham, erected from designs by the elder Pugin, was opened in April, 1845. It was dedicated to St. John; but is commonly designated the "Church of the Holy Cross." It was erected entirely at the expense of the Rev. Thos. Sherbourne. The tower contains a peal of six bells. A chapel previously existed near the site, erected in 1809. The trade of Kirkham appears to have formerly depended chiefly on the manufacture of cordage, sail cloth, and some coarse and fine linens. One or two cotton mills have lately been introduced, and considerable advance made in the linen manufacture. Kirkham appears to be gradually recovering from the state of retrogression, which was very apparent to even a casual visitor a few years ago. The population of the township in 1851, was 2,799; the acreage, according to the ordnance survey, 857; and the rateable value of the property in 1854, £5,737 per annum. The parish of Kirkham comprises the following townships:—Kirkham, Freckleton, Warton, Bryning-with-Kellamargh, Ribby-with-Wray, Westby with Great and Little Plumpton, Weeton, Medlar and Wesham, Greenhalgh-with-Thistleton, Great and Little Singleton, Hambleton, Little Eccleston and Larbrick, Rosacre, Wharles and Treales, Newton and Scales, Clifton and Salwick, Goosnargh-with-Newsham, and Whittingham. The three last named are contiguous to Preston.

k Baines's Lan., vol. 4, page 334. l Notitia Cestriensis, vol. 2, page 420, published 1850.

CLIFTON-WITH-SALWICK.—Clifton manor has been held by the family of Clifton, of Lytham, from a very early period In the 42nd Henry III., a William de Clifton held, in the hundred of Amounderness, ten carucates of land. The site of an ancient hall, formerly existing here, was, a short time ago, occupied as a farm-house, called "Hall-yards," at the eastern end of the village. This has since given place to the modern hall, the erection of which commenced about twenty-three years ago. It is in the Elizabethan style, and was built by the late Thomas Clifton, esq It is at present the residence of Edmund Birley, esq. The village consists chiefly of a long straggling row of houses, with barns and outbuildings on the opposite side of the street, which is rudely paved with large boulders Salwick hall, the property of Mr. Clifton, is situated in the northern portion of the township. About forty years ago, Salwick possessed a catholic chapel. The small episcopal chapel of Lund, situated in a retired portion of the locality, supposed, from the name, to have been originally used by the Danish settlers as a place of pagan sacrifice, was partially rebuilt about 1825.[m] In 1662, the Rev J. Harrison was ejected from the benefice. The parish registers record that in 1688, a churchwarden was "presented" for setting up a "scandalous font" in this chapel. This objectionable article is further described as a "scandalous trough." Canon Raines conjectures it to have been "a veritable Roman altar, and the honest Warden to have had very loose notions on 'the peril of Idolatry.'" Calamy says, that Joseph Harrison, "the minister of Lun Chapel" was "fixed in a dark corner, where he was wonderfully followed and very useful." Lund chapel is very often described as being in a "lonely part" of the township Such may have been the case at some remote period. At present its situation on a rising ground, and its contiguity to the Salwick station of the Preston and Wyre railway, render the term "lonely" extremely inapplicable. Lund is evidently a very ancient settlement, the chapel and village being situated on the line of the Roman Watling-street, or "Danes' pad," as it is termed by the neighbouring inhabitants In 1840, Clifton-cum-Salwick and Newton-cum-Scales were constituted a district parish, under the 1st and 2nd Victoria, cap 106 The living of Lund has since been increased to the annual value of £342., by the addition of the tithes of the latter townships. The nomination of the minister is vested in the dean and canons of Christ church, Oxford. The population of Clifton-with-Salwick, in 1851, was 471; the area, according to the ordnance survey, 3,044 acres; and the annual rateable value of the property, in 1854, £5487.

GOOSNARGH-WITH-NEWSHAM.—Mr. Baines says "the chapelry of Goosnargh, which contains the townships of Goosnargh, Whittingham, and

m Canon Raines. Mr. Baines says in 1830.

Newsham, each maintaining its own poor, though it appears part of the parish of Kirkham, has nearly lost all traces of any connection with the mother parish, and is generally considered as a distinct parochial district." According to a parliamentary inquiry, in 1650, the parochial chapel of Goosnargh, situated ten miles distant from the parish church of Kirkham, depended entirely upon an allowance of £50. per annum from the "Committee of Plundered Ministers," which it is stated was paid to a "diligent minister" there, named Ingham. The township was so remote from the mother church, that the inhabitants desired their chapelry to be made a distinct and separate parish. Robert de Goosnargh is the earliest known proprietor of lands in this district. He lived previously to the reign of John. There have been since several other holders of land in Goosnargh, amongst others, the Cliftons, of Clifton, now of Lytham. The abbey of Cockersands held two carucates in Newsham or Newsome. In the fifteenth century, Middleton hall was a seat of the Singletons. It was afterwards transferred to the Rigbies. Colonel Rigby, the celebrated partisan of the cause of the parliament in the reign of Charles I., was of "Middleton in Goosnargh." [n] The property has descended to the Rigby Shawes, of Fishwick and Preston. The parochial chapel of Goosnargh, was, in the opinion of Dr. Whitaker, restored in the reign of Henry VIII. A chantry was instituted in 1553, and, according to Mr. Baines, a tradition asserts that a second was shortly afterwards added. Bishop Gastrell says, "Anno 1611, there was an agreement made between the inhabitants of Goosnargh and Whittingham, concerning the share each town should pay towards the repairs of ye church and chancel." In 1715, the church was repaired. On the lead of the tower is the following inscription: "Gulielmus Bvshell, Rector Ecclesiæ de Heysham et hujus Minister, 1715." The church was enlarged in 1778, and a parsonage house was afterwards erected. In the early portion of the last century, the bishop records that the "chief of the inhabitants, who are called the 24, pretend sometimes to nominate ye Curate; but the right is in the vicar." [o] At the present time, the dean and canons of Christ church Oxford, nominate the incumbent. In the Middleton choir, in the north aisle, is an arch for the tomb of the founder, and a curiously carved stone, bearing the initials of a Rigby and three chevronels, the arms of Singleton. Another episcopal chapel, in Goosnargh, dedicated to St. James, called the "White chapel," was enlarged in 1617. Its origin is unknown. Bishop Gastrell says: "White chapel within Goosnargh, al's Threlfall chapel. Certified that nothing at all belongs to it, and is served now and then only, out of charity at ye request of ye people." Its value in 1834, was £104. A catholic chapel at Hill was rebuilt about 1802. An independent chapel

n See chapter 4, page 177. o Notitia Cestriensis, vol. 2, page 420.

was erected at Inglewhite in 1826 Inglewhite lodge has been held by the Sidgreaves family since the earlier portion of the seventeenth century. This family is descended from Robert Sidgreaves, who, as appears from escheats of the period, held lands in Lea, in the 22nd Edward I. A hospital for "decayed gentlemen" was founded at Goosnargh, by Dr. William Bushell, of Preston In his will, dated 21st May, 1735, he devised, in case his daughter Elizabeth should die under the age of twenty-one years without issue, "*all his real estate whatsoever, except certain lands in Heysham, to William Atherton and five others, their heirs and assigns, upon trust, to dispose of the clear yearly rents and profits of the said premises, in maintaining, supporting, and providing for decayed gentlemen and gentlewomen, or persons of the better rank of both or either sex, inhabitants of the towns or townships of Preston, Euxton, Goosnargh, Whittingham, Fulwood, and Elston, in the county of Lancaster, being Protestants, in a house or hospital to be provided in Goosnargh, where he then resided; and he empowered his said trustees to employ a competent part of the rents and profits of the said premises in erecting a convenient house or hospital, or making additions to the dwelling house of his late father, at their discretion; and to employ the same for the reception and entertainment of such decayed persons; and to appoint such officers and servants, and make such rules and orders, as to them might seem meet for the good government and encouragement of the said hospital and the persons to be placed the rein, who were to be elected by the said trustees, provided that no person being a papist, or any one who should have received any relief out of the rates of the poor of the said respective towns or townships, should be capable of receiving any benefit from this his intended charity*" An indenture, dated October 31st, 1809, in which Mr. Bushell's will is recited, declares that the said William Bushell died about the 10th of June, 1735. It further states that his daughter Elizabeth died before she attained her majority, in July, 1745, and that the trustees carried out the injunction of the testator, and converted his dwelling house into a hospital or asylum It appears from the eleventh report of the Charity Commissioners, that at the end of the year 1824, the annual rental received from the trust property was £855. 8s. 6d., exclusive of the house at Goosnargh and the adjoining land Part of the premises in Preston were held under leases for ninty-nine years, by the earl of Derby, which were granted in 1790, at an annual rent of £112 The commissioners state that these leases appear to have been granted upon equitable terms, but owing to the gradual improvement in value, by the extension of the town, and the erection of buildings, etc upon some of the sites, this property may be estimated, on the falling in of the leases in 1889, at from £700 to £800. per annum. Should the town continue to

Goosnagh Hospital near Preston

Clifton Hall near Preston

extend at the present ratio till the conclusion of the century, even this calculation will be far beneath the actual increased value. The amount expended under this trust from May, 1822, to May, 1823, was £674. 5s. 2d. The hospital at that period contained thirteen inmates. In 1844-5, a new wing was added to the building, at a cost of about £2,400. At the present time there are thirty inmates. Other property belonging to the trust has since been leased for building purposes, and its value consequently enhanced. The total annual rental already amounts to between £1,500. and £1,600. The founder was buried at Leyland. The hospital at Goosnargh bears not the slightest resemblance to an ordinary charitable foundation. The buildings and grounds are suggestive of a gentleman's mansion rather than a "hospital" or asylum of any kind. The inmates are treated with courtesy and respectful consideration, calculated to render the "decayed gentlemen and gentlewomen" as happy in the decline of life as circumstances will permit. The Rev. Canon Raines justly characterises this establishment as "one of the finest foundations in the county." It is gratifying to know, that in the lapse of a few years, the revenues of the trust will be still further augmented. It is earnestly to be hoped that a corresponding increase of efficiency will be maintained by the trustees, in the true spirit of enlightened philanthrophy evinced by its generous founder. Bishop Gastrell says:—

"In ye lower side of Goosenargh is a School, Founded (about 1673) by one Thomas Threlfall, of Whittingham, who endowed it wth lands valued at about 7l. per annum, taught in a dwelling-house purchased wth money given by Thomas Waring, of London, for a Free School. Augmented since with 25l. per annum, given by Henry Colborn, of London, and paid by the Company of Drapers there, who nominate ye Master, together wth ye 24 of ye Chappelry of Goosnargh, on account of Threlfall's gift." [p]

The bishop likewise records the following charitable bequests:—

"Given to ye Poor by one Knowles, of Sowerby, in 1686, 50 sh. per annum, charged upon Land in Goosnargh; by William Higham, 20*sh*. per annum, to buy books for children taught in White-Chapel; by one John Parkinson, in 1676, Land in Newsham, now worth 4*l*. per annum to bind out apprentices; by Christopher Helme, 4*l*. per annum for poor householders; by Lawrence Parkinson, 2 closes, worth 30s. per annum, and the interest of 70*l*. to be laid out in Corn called Groats, yearly, for poor householders who receive nothing from the Township; and the Interest of 30*l*. to ye like poor householders in Loaves, (viz. six penny loaves every Sunday), who come to Church, and for want of such Poor to ye like Poor of Whittingham; 4*l*. 5s. per annum by Thomas William Waring, (in 1691), upon lands in Whittingham, 4*l*. of wch to be given to poor Householders there, and 5s. for a Dinner for the Minister and Churchwardens who distribute it; by Henry Colborn, 5*l*. per annum to the Poor of Goosenargh-cum-Newsham and Whittingham, pd by the Drapers' Company."

---

p Notitia Cestriensis, vol. 2, page 421. The bishop's annotator, the Rev. Canon Raines, adds that Lawrence Parkinson, in 1719, bequeathed £20. to this school. Another school is mentioned by Bishop Gastrell "in ye Higher side of Goosenargh, taught in ye White Chapel, endowed (in 1705), first by one William Lancaster, of Goosnargh, wth the interest of 40*l*., and since augmented by William Higham, of Goosnargh, with the interest of 60*l*., (by will dated 17th Feb., 1713.) The master is appointed by the Executors of Lancaster and Higham."

The population of Goosnargh-with-Newsham, in 1851, was 1,453; the area, according to the ordnance survey, 16,726 acres; and the annual rateable value of the property, in 1854, £8,865.

WHITTINGHAM.—The lands in Whittingham were held by Warin de Whittingham, in the reign of John. Mr. Baines says a Richard Whittingham, father of two sons and a daughter, was living in the middle of the last century. The estates passed by sale to the Pedders, of Preston. An old hall, called variously Gingle hall, Chingle hall, Shynglehall, and Shingleton hall, has long remained in the possession of the Singletons, an ancient Lancashire family. Lower Gingle hall is the property of R. T. Parker, esq., Cuerden. The population of Whittingham, in 1851, numbered 677, with an area of 3,191 acres, and property assessed to the county rate at £4,058 per annum.

LYTHAM PARISH.

Lytham is supposed to have formed part of the Saxon parish of Kirkham. It consists of only one township, which comprises, according to the ordnance survey, an area of about five thousand three hundred and nine statute acres. Lidun was taxed with only two carucates of land, at the time of the Domesday survey. In the reign of Richard I, Roger Fitz Roger gave all his land at Lythum together with the church and all things appertaining thereto, to the monks of Durham, for the purpose of founding a Benedictine cell, in honour of St. Mary and St Cuthbert. Dr. Whitaker concluded that there existed no church prior to this foundation, "because no appropriation ever took place and no vicarage was ever endowed." [q] In the charter, as given by Dugdale, the fact, however, is distinctly stated; "totam terram meam de Lythum cum ecclesia ejusdem villæ et cum omnibus ad ipsam ecclesiam pertinentibus" [r] It further appears that the land of Lidun was presented by king John, when earl of Moreton, to the aforesaid Roger Fitz Roger, with the view that he might confer the same on the monks of Durham. The Rev Canon Raines is of opinion that a church existed at Lytham in the thirteenth century, "although it is not mentioned in the *Valor* of 1291, probably on the ground of its being conventual and not parochial" There exists at present in the duchy office, a roll endorsed "Lethum: Copies of Evidence of the prior of Lethum." This roll includes two separate records, as well as the foundation charter referred to. The first is a release by William le Botiller, dated 1268, of the lands of Lythum, the pasture of Kelgmoles, and wrecks upon the sea coast The deed reserves a right of road to the tenants of Layton The other document, which bears date 56 Henry III, is a

q His Richmondshire, vol 2, page 440
r Monast Angl vol. 4, p 282.

settlement of the boundary between Lythum and Kelgmoles, and lands in Laton. Mr. Baines, in reference to these documents, says:—"The last is probably Laton Heys, on the northern extremity of the parish, and Kelgmoles, called Kilgrimol in the foundation charter, is Kellamergh on the east." This, however, is an error. Kilgrimol is situated near the coast, to the north of Lytham, and adjoins Layton, as may be inferred, from the document itself. This is the spot supposed to have been originally occupied by the Culdee priesthood, at the time of the first grant of lands on the Ribble, in Hasmunderness, to the monks of Ripon. The place is named "Cross Slack," on the ordnance map. Kellamergh, may perhaps likewise have been originally a Culdee cell or cemetery.[s] Dr. Kuerden has preserved a claim, without date, of the prior of Durham, to have view of frank pledge in his manor of Lethum, with waif, stray, and infangthef; emendations of the assize of bread and beer; wrecks of the sea in Lytham; exemption for himself and tenants in the manor from suit to the county and wapentake, and from fines and amerciaments; to have soc, sac, and theam, and to be quit of toll, passage, and portage throughout England and its seaports; and free warren in all his demesne lands in Lethum, and all the royal fish taken there.[t] During severe litigation in the reign of Edward I. the prior of Durham proved that his predecessors had enjoyed without interruption, the privilege of "taking wreck" from the time of Richard I. It was shown likewise, that, by a charter of William the Conqueror, the liberties claimed by the prior had been granted to his predecessors. It was however ordered that the liberty should be seized unto the king's hands.[u] In the twenty-third year of his reign, Edward I. granted the wreck, waif, and stray in Lytham, to his brother Edmund, earl of Lancaster. In 1443, Pope Eugenius issued a bull conferring the privileges of perpetual priors upon the occupant and his successors. Previously the priors of Lytham were removeable at the will of their superiors of Durham. In 1554, after the dissolution of the monasteries, the possessions of the prior of Lytham were granted to Sir Thomas Holcroft, whose representative, Sir John Holcroft, disposed of the manor, in 1606, to Sir Cuthbert Clifton, of Westby. The latter held the estate in the 11th year of the reign of Charles I.[v] At the present time it forms part of the possessions of John Talbot Clifton, esq. Lytham was returned in 1650, as "Lithcomb, a very small parish having only one Township." "Thomas Clifton, Esq., a Papist delinquent," is stated to be the patron and impropriator of the whole tithes. The church was rebuilt

s See chapter 2, page 63.

t Manuscript quarto. fo. 56, in the Chetham Library.

u Placit. de Quo War. 20. Edward I.

v Duchy Records, vol. 10, Inq. n. 13.

upon the site of the ancient priory in 1770, and dedicated to St. Cuthbert. This church contained four monuments to the memory of members of the Clifton family. The present edifice was erected in consequence of the demand for additional accommodation, resulting from the increased popularity of Lytham, as a fashionable watering place. The first stone was laid in March, 1834. Thomas Clifton, esq., contributed £500. towards the expense. The still greater favour bestowed upon Lytham, by invalids and temporary residents, necessitated further accommodation, and accordingly, a few years ago, a second church, a very handsome edifice, dedicated to St. John, was erected near the eastern entrance to the village. There is likewise a catholic chapel, built in 1839, and some places of worship for dissenting congregations. Lytham hall is an elegant mansion, rebuilt between the years 1757 and 1764. The Cliftons are now a Protestant family. The ancient domestic chapel is at present occupied as the servants' hall. Bishop Gastrell says of Lytham: "no school nor charities." Before the bishop wrote, however, a free school-house, erected by Richard Salthouse, must have been completed, as in 1702, the Rev. Mr. Threlfall, of Lytham, gave £5. for the use of the schoolmaster. Other donations followed, till in 1732, lands were purchased, which at the time of the Charity Commissioners' investigation, produced nearly £105. per annum. A second school was established at Heyhouses, in the parish of Lytham, about the year 1780. It appears that Lytham has been a favourite watering place for upwards of two centuries, although the first large hotel for the accommodation of visitors, was not erected until 1794, it was called the Wheat Sheaf, and was situated opposite to the present Clifton Arms Hotel. It has since been taken down. Lytham contains five good hotels, together with a large quantity of houses erected for the purpose of providing private accommodation for visitors. A neat and commodious market house has likewise recently been erected. Baths and other conveniences for invalids have been provided. The sanitary condition of the locality and the general accommodation of the public has been further enhanced by the labour of the Improvement Commissioners, appointed under act of parliament. The village is lighted with gas. Lytham is one of the principal life boat stations on the coast of Lancashire. The beach forms an extensive and agreeable promenade, nearly two miles in length. Several spacious and elegant private villas have, within the last few years, been erected in the village and its neighbourhood.[w] The population of Lytham, in 1851, was 2,698. The property in the parish was assessed in 1854, at the annual value of £13,359.

---

w See page 502.

Saint Cuthbert's, Lytham, Lancashire.

(THE PARISH CHURCH.)

BISPHAM PARISH.

The parish of Bispham, comprising the townships of Bispham-with-Norbreck and Layton-with-Warbreck, is situated upon the western coast of Lancashire. It is mentioned in the Domesday survey as containing eight carucates of cultivated land. From the name it is believed to have been held in the Saxon period, by the ecclesiastics of York. The church is first mentioned in the reign of Richard I, when the right to the advowson of Poulton, with the church of Biscopham, was "quitclaimed" to the abbot of Sees, by Theobald Walter. The doorway of the church, a narrow Norman arch, is, in the opinion of Dr. Whitaker, an erection of the period of William Rufus or Henry I John Romanus, archdeacon of Richmond, confirmed to St. Martin's, of Sees, and St Mary's, of Lancaster, in 1246, amongst other matters, the "mediety" of the church of Poulton and the chapel of Biscopham, and granted, after the demise of the then possessor, the other "mediety." By this union the entire advowson rested with the abbey of Sees and the priory of Lancaster. William, abbot of Salop, was likewise a benefactor, about the period of the foundation of the convent of Deulacres. The monks of the latter establishment, in the reign of Henry VIII paid annually to the abbot of Salop, £3. 13s. 4d for lands in Biscopham, and Norbroke. William le Boteler held the manors of Laton, Great Merton, Little Merton, Bispham, and Warebreck, according to the ancient duchy feodary. His son granted the manor of Great Laton, Little Laton, and Bispham, to Henry de Bispham, and Richard de Carleton, chaplains, in the fifth year the duchy was held by John of Gaunt After the dissolution of the monasteries, the site of Deulacres was granted in 6th Edward VI., to Sir Ralph Bagnell, by whom it was conveyed to John Fleetwood, esq, ancestor of Sir Peter Hesketh Fleetwood, bart The manors of Little Bispham, Great Bispham, and Laton were, according to the duchy records, in the possession of Thomas Fleetwood, in the 13th Elizabeth. The church was rebuilt in the seventeenth century The value of the living in 1834, was £275. There is a school, founded about 1658, "free to all ye parish."

Blackpool is situated in the township of Layton-with-Warbreck. It has been styled the "Queen of the Lancashire bathing places." Notwithstanding its present extent and importance, a century ago, with the exception of "Fox Holes," a mansion of the Tildesleys, it consisted merely of a few rude huts On relatively modern maps, there is no such name as Blackpool. The name is derived from a now extinct tarn or pool, visible on the old map, about half a mile in diameter, which lay behind Fox Hall, or Vauxhall as it is sometimes written. In a pamphlet printed soon after the year 1788, by Henry Moon, of Kirkham, said to be written by Mr.

Hutton, but published anonymously, the water of this pool is described as "of a chocolate or *liver* colour, as all water must, which passes through a peaty soil, so that the place might, with as much propriety, bear the name of *Liver* pool, as Black pool." Vauxhall is said to have been used as a place of concealment for persecuted priests; and that it was erected with the view to the reception of the Pretender, in 1715, who proposed to land on the coast of Lancashire. The latter is, however, very improbable. The tradition may perhaps have originated from some unfulfilled promise of James II. when in Ireland.[x] Mr. Baines thinks it was originally built by the Tildesleys as a hunting seat, hence its name. Some portions are yet in existence. It is used as a farm house. The author of the pamphlet before quoted says:—

"Though it contained four or five rooms on a floor, it had no pretensions to grandeur, therefore it could not excite suspicion. It was surrounded by a lofty wall, seemingly as a screen against the winds, but really to convert the place into a fortification. The sea was a guard on the west; the pool, from whence the place derived its name, secured the east; the small rivulet of peaty water, which communicates with the sea, then a swamp, guarded the south, and rendered this little retreat only accessible on the north. It also abounded with secret recesses, communications, and hiding places within, to guard it against surprise."

Some of the walls, which are built of boulders and brick, are very massive, and justify the notion that the builders intended the place as a stronghold as well as a domestic mansion. Some of the "secret recesses" existed at the end of the last century, and were familiarly designated "priests' holes." The "domestic chapel," after being used for some time as a cheese room, was converted into cottages. The arms of the Tildesleys formerly ornamented the gateway, the noble arch of which yet remains. Edward, son of Sir Thomas Tildesley, in anticipation of being appointed one of the knights of the projected order of the royal oak,[y] caused the words of the intended motto, "Seris Factura Nepotibus," to be inscribed above the porch. The crest of the family, a pelican feeding its young, carved in stone, is still preserved in the wall of a barn. Some parties attribute the rise of Blackpool to the priests, who, after remaining in concealment at Fox hall, returned to their friends, and spoke of its magnificent beach and other qualifications as a watering place. Mr. Hutton describes Blackpool, in 1788, in the following terms:—

"Although about fifty houses grace the sea bank, it does not merit the name of a village, because they are scattered to the extent of a mile. About six of these make a figure, front the sea, with an aspect exactly west, and are appropriated for the reception of company; the others are the dwellings of the inhabitants, which chiefly form the background. In some of these are lodged the inferior class, whose sole motive for visiting this airy region, is health. * * *

"During the time of which I have been writing, there could not be another building in Blackpool, that would bear the name of a *house*.[z] This royal dormitory, therefore,

---

x See pages 246 and 249. y See page 207.

z Mr. Hutton refers to the Jacobite invasion, in 1745, and to Fox Hall, the mansion of the Tildesleys.

The Terrace, Blackpool, Lancashire.

Blackpool, from the Sea.

[illegible] Royal Hotel & Queens Place, Blackpool &c.

must have stood, the little hall among huts. Nor were the huts numerous, for many are modern, and seem to tell the observer that the place rapidly improves. None of the superior houses, for the reception of company, seem to be more than seven years old. A gentleman, who had regularly visited this abode of pleasure twenty-seven years, assured me, when he first knew the place, the little white cottage at the lane end, now the newshouse, was the only one of public resort; and the spot now the coffee room, was a blacksmith's shop; it appears, the people who then frequented Blackpool, were chiefly of the lower class."

In 1788, Blackpool possessed accommodation for about four hundred visitors. Half a century ago, the Yorkshire house, Banks's, Simpson's, Dixon's, and Forshaw's hotels, were the only establishments of this class. There were but few dwelling-houses between the two latter, and these were of an insignificant character. A gentleman who visited Blackpool at this period, thus further describes it:—

"Adjoining Forshaw's there were two or three houses of a rather genteel appearance, compared with the many small cottages leading thence to the street, formerly, the principal entrance from Preston. There was at this time a promenade with an arbour at the end of it, and beyond it nearer to Dixon's Hotel stood a cottage then used as a warm bath; but now that promenade as well as the bath house, have long since disappeared; the embankment having been wasted away by the incursions of the sea, and now forming part of the ground daily covered with the advancing tide. Beyond Dixon's there was a public road where two four-wheeled vehicles could pass each other. The road has also succumbed to the power of the encroaching waters, as have likewise the banks on the south shore." [a]

The promenade extended originally from Yorkshire house to Dixon's, (now Rossall's) hotel. The cliffs in the earlier period of Blackpool's existence, where they sloped to the beach, were covered with shrubs and grass, in which birds occasionally built their nests. Near the end of the last century, however, the sea committed great damage to the cliffs, and destroyed a considerable portion of the fine straight promenade. So rapid has been the extension of Blackpool, that at the present time, it is calculated to accommodate ten thousand visitors.[b] It contains about twenty excellent hotels, and establishments of every class, built with the view to provide lodgings for visitors; as well as several mansions erected by private gentlemen, as marine residences for their families. There are convenient baths, and an athenæum, news room, covered market, (opened in 1844,) gas works, etc. South Shore, an extensive suburb, to the south, already contains several excellent hotels and private residences. It will shortly be joined to Blackpool. Indeed at the present time they are generally regarded as one town. Great progress has latterly been made in the drainage of the place, especially since the introduction of the Improvement Act, and the establishment of the Local Board of Health. About sixty years ago, a subscription was raised by the Rev. Mr. Breakell, and the proceeds applied to improving the promenades. A portion of this fund was expended in the erection of suitable railing and an ornamental Chinese bridge.

a Correspondent of the Blackpool Herald. b Walsh's Guide to Blackpool, 1855.

These, however, have been since destroyed. During the past year a committee procured subscriptions, and devoted the proceeds to public improvements near the beach. The "bridge of peace" now occupies the site of the Chinese structure. The promenade has likewise been considerably enlarged and rendered both more ornamental and more convenient for the perambulation of visitors. A project is on foot for building a large public hall, for assemblies, concerts, etc., during the bathing season. The episcopal church was erected in 1821. It was enlarged in 1832-3. An Independent chapel was opened in July, 1835. A Wesleyan chapel was erected in 1838, and at the present time a beautiful Catholic church is approaching completion, built at the expense of Miss Tempest, a pious and liberal member of that church. The cliffs of Blackpool rise in some places to nearly sixty feet in height, and consequently command an extensive prospect seaward. The beach has suffered severely at various times from the encroachments of the waves. A tradition says that a little to the north of Blackpool, a large tract of land has been entirely swept away, and a public house, erected thereupon, destroyed. The site is pointed out by a huge boulder, still to be seen at low water, and named "Penny stone." The tradition says, that travellers passing the hostelry, fastened their horses to hooks fixed in this stone, while they regaled themselves in the interior of mine host's domicile, on ale sold at a penny a glass. The beach at Blackpool having a rapid descent from the cliffs to low water mark, the tide seldom ebbs so far from the promenade as to give it the appearance of a sandy desert, common to other parts of the coast. Visitors generally speak of Blackpool, therefore, as possessing a "finer sea" than any other of the Lancashire watering places. The interior of the country is somewhat destitute of variety, and deficient in timber, but the prospect seaward is truly magnificent, when the condition of the atmosphere is such as to bring within the range of vision the hills in the Isle of Man, and the mountains of Cumberland and North Wales. On such an evening it is worth the expense of a journey of one hundred miles, to visit the "Foreland of the Fylde," that "region of glorious sunsets," and witness the orb of day, the "material god, and representative of the Unknown," sink with calm dignity and gorgeous splendour into the heaving bosom of the western main. The coast about Blackpool is likewise famed for the sublime grandeur of its aspect, when the westerly wind chafes the ocean into foam, and throws the salt spray high over the beach and buildings. The enthusiastic lover of Nature, gazing upon the ocean from the rugged cliffs, will feelingly, and with truth, exclaim, in the language of Byron:—

> "Thou glorious mirror, where the Almighty's form,
> Glasses itself in tempests! in all time,
> Calm or convulsed—in breeze or gale, or storm,

Independent Chapel, Blackpool.

Icing the pole, or in the torrid clime
Dark-heaving—boundless, endless and sublime:
The image of Eternity; the throne
Of the Invisible! Even from out thy slime,
The monsters of the deep are made; each zone
Obeys thee; thou goest forth, dread, fathomless, alone!"

PARISH OF POULTON-IN-THE-FYLDE.

This parish occupies the north west corner of Amounderness. The town of Poulton is situated upon a rising ground, about a mile above the confluence of the Skippon with the Wyre. It is supposed to have been originally a Roman military post, for the protection of the "Portus Setantiorum of Ptolemy.[c] Roger de Poictou gave to the priory of Lancaster, which he founded, "Pulton, in Agmundernesia, and whatsoever belonged to it, with one carucate of land, and all other things belonging to it moreover he gave the tithe of venison and of pawnage in all his woods, and the tithe of his fishery." A feud of a somewhat singular character, originating in a disputed claim to a right of road, existed for a lengthened period, between the priors of St. Mary's and the proprietors of the soil in the neighbouring township of Thornton. In the reign of Edward I., Sir Adam Banastre, John Wenne, William de Thorneton, Richard le Demand, Richard le Brockholes, Geoffrey le Procuratoure, (the proctor,) and Adam le Rive, (the reve) and a number of their followers, attacked Ralph de Truno, the prior of St. Mary's, at Pulton. The worthy ecclesiastic, together with several of his tenants and servants, were carried to Thorneton, soundly beaten, and afterwards detained as prisoners. From an indenture dated 1330, (4 Edward III.) it appears that after numerous fracas, the matters in dispute were arranged. It was, in consequence, agreed that the tenants and servants of the prior should be allowed two sufficient roads over Sir Adam's lands; one from the towns of Pulton and Thorneton, beyond Skeppol, and thence to Singleton park, by a way which led to the ford of Aldewath in the water of Wyre; the other from Pulton and Thorneton to the ford of Bulk, across the same river. The church is dedicated to St. Chad. Mr. Baines says:—"The endowment of the vicarage cannot be found, probably owing to its great antiquity, for it appears that Poulton was undoubtedly an endowed vicarage in 1291, being valued in the taxation of Pope Nicholas, at £6. 13s. 4d." The church was rebuilt in 1751. It contains several monuments to the Fleetwoods and others. The patronage of the living belongs to Sir P. Hesketh Fleetwood, bart. Poulton towards the last century, according to Mr. Hutton, was a "small town on the decline, consisting of seven sleepy streets."[d] It has not very materially advanced since, notwithstanding the formation of the

c See Chap. 1, page 14 and 36.

d Description of Blackpool, page 10.

Preston and Wyre railway, and the general prosperity of the neighbourhood. The population of the township in 1821, was 1011, and in 1851, 1120. Some little improvement has latterly taken place. A gas works has been established; but the streets of the town are not yet lighted. The parish of Poulton comprises the townships of Carleton, Hardhorn-with-Newton, Marton, Poulton, and Thornton.

FLEETWOOD AND ROSSALL are situated in the township of Thornton. The manor was held in the 13th Henry VIII., by Thomas earl of Derby. It is considered however, but in the light of a "manor by reputation." The pasture of Rossall was granted by King John to the abbey of Deulacres, in Staffordshire, at the instance of the earl of Chester and Lincoln. After some litigation at the suit of Edward I., the abbot was mulcted in a large sum as "arrearages" due to the crown. The jury stated that the manor had been held in bailiwick of King John, for seven years, that it was then worth £24. per annum. From the circumstance that a road, through the neighbouring rabbit warren, (on the site of which the new town of Fleetwood has been erected), bears the name Abbot's walk, Mr. Baines conjectures that the grange of Rossall must have been occasionally visited by the abbot of Deulacres. Singleton Thorpe, a village near Rossall, was entirely destroyed, in the year 1555, by an extraordinary irruption of the sea. Mr. Baines suggests that Singleton Thorpe may have been the residence of Thomas Singleton, who resisted the claim of King Edward I., previously referred to. Of late years a considerable quantity of land has been washed away near Rossall point, and a large bank of sand and gravel thrown up nearer Fleetwood. One of the vessels belonging to the Spanish Armada is said to have been stranded for some time on a sand bank in the neighbourhood.[e] George Allen, previously to the Reformation, held Rossall, by a long lease, from his cousin the abbot. Richard Allen, grandson of George, and brother of the celebrated cardinal, left a widow and three daughters, who were ejected in the year 1583, before the expiration of the lease, and deprived of all their goods, substance, and money. Rossall was given to Edmund Fleetwood, whose father had previously, on the dissolution of the monasteries, purchased from Henry VIII. the reversion of the lease. Mrs. Allen and her children endeavoured to recover the property; but "the original writings having been carried off when Rossall was plundered, they were compelled not only to desist but to quit the kingdom, in fear of further persecution." One Anion, a neighbour, seized upon £500. belonging to the children, under pretence that it was intended to be forwarded to Rheims, for the use of the cardinal their uncle. By the marriage of the heiress of Richard Fleetwood with Roger Hesketh,

e See chapter 3, page 141.

Rossall School & Chapel, Fleetwood, Lancashire.

of North Meols and Tulketh, in the early portion of the last century, the Rossall property passed to the Hesketh family. Rossall hall was until lately the residence of Sir Peter Hesketh Fleetwood, bart. In 1844, the premises were adapted to the requirements of the Northern Church of England School, a new first-class establishment, founded "with the object of giving an education to the sons of clergymen and others, similar to that of the great public schools, but without the great cost of Eton or Harrow, and embracing also a more general course of instruction in modern literature and science." The project succeeded so well, that in 1850, the council determined to make Rossall school "a permanent institution, by the purchase of the estate and an ample outlay in new buildings, so that full accommodation might be provided for 300 boys." The estate cost about £8,000. Since that time a chapel has been erected at an expense of £1,800, raised by voluntary contributions. A spacious school room has been built, (said to be one of the noblest halls of its character in the kingdom,) together with class-rooms, large dining hall, dormitories, and rooms for private study, and other offices, etc. A library has been established, containing nearly a thousand volumes, supported by joint contributions from the council and friends. These and other improvements involved an additional outlay of about £10,000. Several Rossall scholars have already distinguished themselves at the universities. There is an exhibition of £10. per annum, in books, tenable for three years, founded by Tatton Egerton, esq., M.P. A fund is at present being raised by the munificence of the earls of Ellesmere, Derby, and Burlington, and other gentlemen, to found others of £50. per annum. The present head master is the Rev. W. A. Osborne, M.A., of Trinity College, Cambridge. The system of education resembles that followed at Marlborough college, and King's college, London. About twenty years ago, Fleetwood first sprang into existence. Prior to 1836, the locality was simply a well stocked rabbit warren, and a favourite haunt of the small black headed sea gulls which frequent the coast. A lime kiln and a solitary hut alone proclaimed to the casual sportsman who visited the place, that humanity had not quite deserted it. In 1830, Sir Hesketh Fleetwood, bart., granted to a company formed for the purpose of constructing a railway from Preston to the mouth of the Wyre, the privilege of passing through his estates, free from the payment of the usual purchase money for land so required. An act of parliament was not however procured till 1835. In the following year the town of Fleetwood, so named in honour of the enterprising baronet, commenced its existence. A regular plan of the intended streets, public buildings, etc., was drawn by Mr. Decimus Burton, which in the main has been followed in the construction of the town. As in the case of Birkenhead, buildings rose faster than the legitimate demand, and a natural reaction ensued. At the present time, however, Fleetwood may be fairly said to have cast off its leading strings, and to rely upon its own intrinsic merits, rather than upon fortuitous or adventitious circumstances. Fleetwood was made a port in 1839, when Preston was degraded to the position of a creek under its jurisdiction. In January, 1844, Preston was restored to its original position, and Fleetwood made a creek under it. In 1846, the latter was declared to be a "subport" under Preston; and, in January, 1850, it was again invested with the privileges of an independent port. The following figures show the gradual increase of the trade :—

FOREIGN TRADE.	1847.	1848.	1849.
Vessels with cargoes Inwards	6	15	36
Ditto Outwards	1	5	15
COASTING TRADE.			
Vessels with cargoes Inwards	752	873	1247
Ditto Outwards	913	857	1059
DUTY PAID ENTRIES.			
Total number	77	175	218

The following return shows the number and tonnage, by admeasurement, of the vessels belonging to the port of Fleetwood, in 1850 and 1855 :—

	1850.		1855.	
	Vessels.	Tons.	Vessels.	Tons.
Under 50 tons	7	221	11	402
Under 100 tons	1	83	16	1064
Under 200 tons	1	113	7	811
Above 200 tons	0	0	3	2323
	9	417	37	4600

This is exclusive of the fine steamers which daily communicate with Belfast. Nor does it include the fishing smacks, which, in 1850, were five in number, and in 1855, eleven. The following table gives a comparative statement of the exports and imports during the years 1855 and 1856 :—

	1855.		1856.		INCREASE.	
	No. of shipments.	Tons.	No. of shipments.	Tons.	No. of shipments.	Tons.
Steamers	1,326	245,724	1,361	269,901	35	24,177
Coasting	1,934	107,564	1,937	107,843	3	279
Foreign	19	11,327	38	18,714	19	7,387
TOTAL	3,279	364,615	3,336	396,458	57	31,843

The trade of Fleetwood would unquestionably expand to infinitely greater proportions, provided suitable docks were formed for the accommodation of large vessels. The railway company possesses the requisite powers under the act of parliament, but the project, though often mooted, and sometimes apparently in earnest, has not yet been carried out. The harbour is

Pier Head, Fleetwood, Lancashire.

Fleetwood, Lancashire 2.

unquestionably the easiest of access of any on the Lancashire coast. The channel is well buoyed and otherwise marked. There are two stone lighthouses on shore at Fleetwood, a beacon at Rossall point, and a "screw-pile" lighthouse at the "foot of Wyre," where the channel unites with that of the Lune. The anchorage ground outside is excellent, and when vessels have once entered they are well protected against every wind. All that is required to develope the capabilities of the port to an almost incalculable extent, is capital and intelligent enterprise, to provide the necessary dock accommodation. Perhaps the present agitation respecting the Liverpool town dues, may direct the attention of the Lancashire merchants and capitalists to the facilities afforded for legitimate competition by the harbour of the Wyre. The imports at the present time consist chiefly of general Irish produce, iron ore, pig iron, and timber. Some manufacturers have found it to their advantage to import cotton into Fleetwood, notwithstanding the drawback resulting from the absence of good dock accommodation. The first importation of cotton, into Fleetwood took place on the 18th January, 1846, by the *Diogenes*, from New Orleans, a vessel of 497 tons registered burthen. In July, 1850, the *Isabella* landed a cargo of 609 bales. The *Isabella* brought a second cargo of 400 bales in January, 1851. The fourth arrival was the *Cleopatra*, with 1,327 bales, on the 10th of April, 1857. On the 21st of the same month, the *Favourite* entered Fleetwood, with cotton direct from America.[f] Fleetwood though small is a well built and pretty little town. A church dedicated to St. Peter, was erected by subscription, in 1841. It contains about 450 sittings, of which 150 are free. The living is endowed with the great tithes of Thornton, which amount to about £66. per annum. The incumbent's salary is augmented by the proceeds of the pew rents, which amount to nearly £200. per annum, when the whole are let. An Independent chapel was opened in May, 1848. The Wesleyan and the Primitive Methodists, as well as the Roman Catholics, likewise possess places of worship. A national school was erected by public subscription, in 1846, as a testimonial to the enterprising lord of the soil, Sir P. Hesketh Fleetwood, bart. It is calculated to afford instruction for about 140 boys and a similar number of girls. A commodious station for the county constabulary has lately been com-

f The Fleetwood correspondent of the Preston Chronicle, referring to the arrival of the Cleopatra in the Wyre, makes the following pertinent observations: "There is now a greater probability of this trade succeeding at Fleetwood than upon the occasion of the first experiment. The gain to the importers of the present cargo upon the item of town dues alone, as charged at Liverpool, is about £23. A similar sum is likewise saved in cartage, as at Fleetwood the cotton is taken direct from the scales alongside of the vessel, and loaded upon the railway trucks. The harbour dues are much less than at Liverpool, and warehousing charges, brokerage, and several other expenses are avoided."

pleted. A spacious cemetery has been laid out, at the distance of about a mile from the town. Fleetwood is lighted with gas, and contains public baths of first-class character, together with four good inns or hotels. The principal hotel, the "North Euston," is a large and handsome edifice, fitted with every accommodation for the highest class of visitors. It is situated near the beach, and commands a magnificent prospect of Morecambe Bay, the mountains of Lancashire, Westmoreland, and Cumberland, and occasionally those of the Isle of Man and North Wales. The "Crown," also a first-class family hotel, is situated very conveniently for travellers, being nearly opposite the railway station. In September, 1847, her Majesty the Queen, honoured Fleetwood with a visit, on her return from Scotland. Great rejoicings took place on the occasion.[g] Fleetwood may be said to be, to some extent, a watering place, as well as a seaport. It is much frequented during the summer months by both pleasure and health seekers. The township of Thornton, which includes Rossall and Fleetwood, contains an area, according to the ordnance survey, of 6,387 acres. The population, in 1851, amounted to 4,134. The property was assessed to the county rate, in 1854, at £13,762. annual value.

There are several schemes for public improvements at the present time occupying the attention of some of the principal landowners in the "Fylde country." One is the construction of reservoirs, and other necessary works, in the higher lands, of such dimensions, as will furnish an ample supply of pure water to the bathing places upon the coast, and the other towns and villages in the district. The laying of the mains along the lines of railway would doubtless considerably lessen the expense of such an undertaking. Mr. Clifton, of Lytham, is understood to be preparing to open a new road from Lytham over the sand hills to Blackpool. The project, mooted some time ago, for a "coast line" of railway from Preston by Lytham to Blackpool, and even to Fleetwood, has been again revived. If such a scheme were carried into effect, the whole shore of Amounderness in a short time would become fringed with watering places and detached marine residences. At the present time, however, these are but projected undertakings, some of which may not be seriously entertained for some years to come.

PARISH OF ST. MICHAEL-LE-WYRE.

A church existed here at the time of the Domesday survey. King John presented the living to a Master Macy.[h] In a process before the officials of Richmond, in 1326, the place is termed Migchalgh. In 1345, the patronage was in the hands of Henry, earl of Lancaster. The advowson was granted in 1403, to the college of Battlefield, nominally by Henry

g See page 309. h Testa de Nevill'.

IV., but really by Roger Yve. Since the reformation, it has passed through various hands, several of whom have been themselves the incumbents. The village and church of St. Michael's are situated in the township of Upper Rawcliffe with Tarnacre. The church which is believed to be a re-erection of the period immediately succeeding the reformation, has a chapel in connection, formerly the burial place of the Butlers, of Kirkland, and therefore called the Butler chapel. On the outside are the arms of the family, the only memorial remaining. This chapel now bears the following inscription :—

"This oratory, known before the Dissolution to have been a Chantry dedicated to St. Catherine, and completely endowed with lands in the neighbouring townships, was repaired by John France, esq., of Rawcliffe Hall, A.D. 1797, being an Appendage to that ancient Manor House."

The Rev. W. Hornby, M.A., cousin to the earl of Derby, is the present incumbent. The living is a discharged vicarage, the advowson belonging to Mr. Hornby's family. A new church was built at Inskip, in 1849. The site and a subscription of £500. were contributed by the earl of Derby. The Rev. W. Hornby, M.A., vicar of St. Michael's, presented the endowment. There are several free schools and other charities in St. Michael's parish, which includes the following townships :—Upper Rawcliffe with Tarnacre, Out Rawcliffe, Great Eccleston, Elswick, Inskip with Sowerby, and Woodplumpton. The latter is contiguous to Preston.

Woodplumpton is a chapelry, including the hamlets of Woodplumpton, Catforth, Eaves and Bartell, which likewise form the manor of Woodplumpton. It was originally held by the barons of Stokeport. It afterwards passed to the De Ardernes, and the Warrens, of Poynton; and again by marriage, in 1,777, to Viscount Bulkeley, whose representatives, the Fleming Leycesters, succeeded to the property. Lord de Tabley is, therefore, the present lord of the manor of Woodplumpton. It appears to have been formerly divided into File Plumpton, Parva, Grauntefelde Plumpton, and Magna Plumpton. Land and cottages, in the two first divisions, were held in the reign of Edward II., by William de Clifton. Gilbert de Clifton held lands in Magna, Parva, and File Plumpton, in the reign of Henry VIII. The last division was held as a manor by Thomas de Lathom, in the reign of Richard II. The duchy records likewise attest to the manor of Woodplumpton being held in the reign of Henry VIII. by John Warren. This family resided at the ancient manor house, called Woodplumpton hall. Woodplumpton chapel, with a low tower, existed in the year 1577. It was rebuilt in 1630, and has undergone many alterations since. A beam of the roof bears the date, 1639. The carved oak of the communion table is inscribed, "W. A. 1635." Several of the pew doors likewise present inscriptions. The oldest is as follows :—" 1649,

James Starkie" An organ was erected in 1849. It was presented by Richard Threlfall, jun, and R. Waterworth, esqrs, of Preston. The handsome stained glass, which now decorates the principal window, is likewise a donation of the latter gentleman. Four other windows have been glazed with coloured glass, and the edifice further ornamented by the old reading desk and pulpit, which were removed from the parish church of Preston, at the time of its last rebuilding These were presented by Mr. Threlfall.[i] The north aisle contains a handsome monument, erected to the memory of Henry Foster, R N, F.R S, son to the late incumbent, who was drowned in February, 1831, in the river Chagres, in the Gulf of Mexico. The monument is of white marble and represents a British seaman, mourning for the loss of the promising young officer. The Roman catholic chapel at Cottam, was destroyed in the election riots of 1768.[k] It was afterwards rebuilt. The one near Hollowforth narrowly escaped a similar fate The date of the erection of the first chapel is not known. Small chapels for the Wesleyan Methodists were erected about 1815 and 1819. A widow named Alice Nicholson, of Bartel, in 1661, by deed, gave the sum of £100. "for the maintenance of a free school within the manor of Woodplumpton." A second donation of £10. by the same lady is likewise recorded In 1676, John Hudson, of Lea, devised to the feoffees of the school, the sum of £20., on condition that the "heirs of the house" in which he resided at the time, should be admitted free of charge, for ever. There are some other charities belonging to Woodplumpton. Previously to 1672, George Nicholson devised £210. to the poor; and Thomas Hoghton left for a similar purpose, the sum of £3 per annum in land The vicar of St. Michael's appoints the curate "The minister of St. Michael's formerly paid to the minister of the Parochial chappel of Woodplumpton, £4. per annum, out of the small tithes of the whole parish"[l] The sum of £50. per annum was allowed by the Committee of Plundered Ministers, but at the time of the inquiry there appears to have been no curate. The ordnance survey gives the area of Woodplumpton at 4,956 acres. The population, in 1851, was 1,574; and the rateable value of the property, in 1854, £8,905.

GARSTANG PARISH.

Garstang parish occupies the northern portion of the hundred of Amounderness. Garstang is a market town, and has doubtless, enjoyed the privilege appertaining thereunto for a lengthened period, Leland, when he passed through it, however, speaks as if he were not quite certain of

i Mr Threlfall likewise purchased the pinnacles of the church, and the whole of the obelisk, which, till a few years ago, stood in the market place. These materials have been used in the construction of a gateway and other fancy erections at his house at Hollowforth.

k See page 331. l Parl Inq. Lamb Libr.

the fact. His words are "Some saith that Garstone was a market towne." Towards the end of the seventeenth century, Blome speaks more positively on the subject. He says "Garstrange, or Garstang, seated upon the river Wire, an indifferent good town, and hath a great market for corn, cattle, yarn, and fish, on Thursdays." [m] A charter of incorporation had been granted in the fourth year of the reign of Edward II., which conferred the privileges of a market, fair, court of pie-poudre, stallage, tollage, lastage, portage, assize of bread, leather, weights and measures. It likewise directed that the town should be governed by seven capital burgesses, who annually elected a bailiff and other officers. A new charter with additional privileges was obtained in the reign of Charles II. The municipal corporation commissioners, in their report, speak of the place as "small, the houses of inferior description; there are no manufactories, nor anything bespeaking prosperity. The trade of the town is said to be on the decrease and its general state declining." A curious relic of the legal formulæ of the Anglo Saxons survived until within a very recent period, in the friburg or constablewick of Garstang, consisting of eleven townships, surrounding the original lordship, to which all except one were subject. Dr. Kuerden says:—

"These handled smaller cases betwixt townsmen and neighbours, and, according to the degree of trespass, awarded satisfaction, made agreements respecting pastures, meadows and corn lands, and reconciled differences among neighbours; but when greater matters fell out, they were referred to the superior justiciaries appointed over them, and whose jurisdiction extended over a hundred of these Freeburgs."

A mound or eminence near the banks of the Wyre, called "Constable hillock," is yet pointed out as the place to which the jury adjourned from the court, in order to proceed with the election of constable, which ceremony was performed in a very peculiar and antiquated fashion.[n] It is not known with certainty when the first parish church was erected. It is mentioned in the reigns of Henry II. and John. St. Helen's, the parish church of Garstang, is singularly enough, situated at a place called Garstang Church Town, in the township of Kirkland, a mile and a half distant from the market town of Garstang. In 1746, it was much injured by an inundation of the Wyre. The walls of both the body and chancel were raised and a new roof constructed in 1811. Besides the tower, nave, side aisles, and chancel, there is a small chapel on the south, and on the south east the family vault of the Butlers, of Kirkland. This contains a beautiful monument in marble with the following inscription:—

"In memory of Alexander Butler, of Kirkland Hall and Beaumont Cote, Esq., who died the 6th day of May, 1819, aged 79; descendant from an ancient and honourable house; he served his country in the important offices of high sheriff, constable of Lan-

m Brit. p. 135. Published in London, 1673. n See chapter 3, page 111.

caster castle, deputy lieutenant and magistrate; he chose an elegant retirement, as most congenial with his literary and philosophical pursuits. This monument was erected by his successor and heir, Thomas Butler Cole, Esq"

The barons of Kendal held the manor of Garstang soon after the conquest It passed successively to the Lindseys, the de Ghisnes, and the dukes of Lancaster. A portion of the manor, however, was granted to the monks of Cockersand, by William de Lancaster, steward of Henry II On the dissolution of the monasteries, the crown rated the manor for John Rydmaden. The Honourable W. Spencer, son of Lord Spencer, leased the manor from the crown in the seventeenth century. His descendant and heiress, Elizabeth, daughter of Digby, Lord Gerard, transferred the estates to the family of the dukes of Hamilton, by her marriage with James, earl of Arran, duke of Hamilton and Brandon. Mr. Spencer's lease expired in 1736, when the manor was sold by act of parliament. The purchaser was Sir Edward Walpole, in whose family it still remains. An action at law, in the 5th year of the reign of John, decided that Garstang had always been a mother and not a filial church. Dr. Whitaker is of opinion, notwithstanding this decision, that it was originally a chapel dependent upon the church of St. Michael. Gilbert Fitz-Reinford granted the advowson to the monastery of Cockersand, which grant was confirmed by King John, in 1215. The living was valued at £26. 13s. 4d., in 1291. At the dissolution, the patronage passed to Christopher Anderton, esq. Previously to the year 1755, it was frequently transferred. Since that time it has remained in the family of the present vicar, the Rev J Pedder, M.A. There is likewise an episcopal chapel at Garstang, rebuilt on an older foundation, in 1666. It was again rebuilt in 1769 An Independent chapel was built in 1777, a Roman Catholic chapel in 1784, and a Methodist chapel in 1814 Two acres of land have been purchased in Barnacre-with-Bonds, on which it is proposed to erect a new Catholic chapel, schools, and a residence for pastors. The remainder of the land will be laid out as a cemetery. The first stone of the chapel was laid in June, in the present year. Although situated in Barnacre, it will not be more than a quarter of a mile distant from the Catholic chapel in Garstang. Garstang possesses a free grammar school, and several charities. Bishop Gastrell says, the "Free Grammar school, was endowed with 100*l*, given by the family of the Butlers. It is an ancient School, built by y[e] Inhabitants, the ground upon w[ch] it stands being given by one of y[e] Butlers of Kirkland, who are lords of y[e] Manour No endowment but the Interest of the above named 100*l*." o A new school, in connection with the establishment, was erected

o By an agreement, dated 9th March, 1602, the administrators of Walter Rigmaden, of Wedacre, bestowed "100 marks, (as a commemoration for theire comodities received of the deceased) too bee the first foundation of a Free schoole to bee erected in the Parishe Church Yard of Garstang."

a few years since. Kirkland hall, the present mansion, is a modern building Garstang, owing to the peculiar taste of the proprietors of the manor, who stedfastly refused to permit any land to be built upon, has acquired the reputation of being "the only finished town in England." This restriction, it is said, has been lately somewhat relaxed. The chartered privileges of the town were unaffected by the Corporation Reform Bill. The parish of Garstang extends over an area of upwards of 24,700 acres, and includes the following townships: Barnacre-with-Bonds, Bilsborough, Cabus, Catterall, Claughton, Cleveley-with-Forton, Garstang, Holleth, Kirkland, Nateby, Pilling, Winmarleigh, and Nether Wyersdale. Greenhough castle, which is in Barnacre-with-Bonds, was erected by royal license, in the 5th year of the reign of Henry VII, by Thomas Stanley, earl of Derby. Camden, in the reign of Elizabeth, describes it as follows.—

"The Wyr, a little river coming from Wier dale, runs with a swift stream by Greenhough Castle, built by Thomas Stanley, the first Earl of Derby of that family, while he was under apprehension of danger from certain of the nobility of this county who had been outlawed, and whose estates had been given him by Henry the Seventh, for they made several attempts upon him, and many inroads into his grounds; till at last these feuds were extinguished by the temper and prudence of that excellent person."

During the civil wars (1643), Robert Plessington was governor, and held the castle for the king. There is no record extant of any siege to which it was ever subjected. Rusheworth, however, says "there remained (1645) of garrisons belonging to the king unreduced, Lathom House and Green Castle, in Lancashire, besieged by the Lancaster Forces." At the conclusion of the war it was dismantled by order of parliament, and little more than twenty years afterwards (1672), Pennant speaks of "the poor remains of Greenhaugh Castle" The original walls formed a rectangle, about fourteen yards by sixteen, with a square tower at each angle. A circular moat defended the whole. But a single tower now remains, and this is in a very dilapidated condition. In the township of Nateby, is "Bower's House," which in 1660, was the seat of Richard Green, gent. In the upper story of this building is a room originally prepared as a place of secret worship by the Roman catholics, when the exercise of their religious formulæ was interdicted The floor has been laid with clay, and every precaution taken to prevent sound issuing beyond the apartment. The staircase winds round a hollow square tube of wood, large enough to permit the ascent and descent of a man. This secret passage it is said was used to convey the officiating priest, and the furniture of the altar, etc., into the cellar beneath the house, when the parties were disturbed at their devotions by the intrusion of unwelcome visitors. Leland speaks of a chapel at "Alhalows at a x miles from Garstang" where the Wyre "goeth into the main se." There is some difficulty in determining what building he alluded to. Mr. Baines says.—

"There is now no village or chapel of All Hallowes, where the Wyre falls into the sea; but a chapel of St. John the Baptist, upon Howarth, is given in the charter of Robert Fitz Bernard to the knights hospitallers in the reign of king John, and the ruins of a chapel called St. John's, in a MS. map of the date 1598,[p] are still existent near that part of the Wyre in the township of Pilling."

This is, however, by no means regarded as a satisfactory solution of the difficulty. Pilling cannot be said to be situated at the mouth of the Wyre, and its distance from Garstang is less than ten miles. Some conjecture that a chapel may have been destroyed near Rossall[q] At Catterall, there formerly existed an extensive calico printing establishment, the property of the Messrs. Feilden. In 1830, the concern was closed, when, according to Mr. Baines, the population of the neighbourhood diminished about one half. The premises were afterwards converted into a cotton mill. The lands in Claughton, (locally pronounced Clighton) were soon after the Conquest, possessed by the Clactons and the Banestres. A portion passed to the duke of Lancaster, in the reign of Richard II. John de Brockholes was in possession in the third year of the reign of Henry IV. The late Joseph Brockholes devised the estates to William Fitzherbert, of Swynnerton Hall, in the county of Stafford, with an injunction to adopt the name and arms of Brockholes His son Thomas Fitzherbert Brockholes, esq, at present resides at Claughton hall, an elegant and spacious modern mansion, situated in the midst of a richly wooded park, and environed by beautiful scenery. The first stone of a reformatory school for North Lancashire, was laid at Bleasdale, on the 23rd of September, 1856, by Mr. Garnett, of Quernmore Park.

p Harl. Coll. No. 6159. q See page 554.

PART III.—THE ENVIRONS.

CHAPTER III. THE HUNDRED OF BLACKBURN.

Blackburn Parish—Townships of Walton, Cuerdale, Samlesbury, Pleasington, Balderstone, Osbaldeston, Salesbury.—Ribchester Parish—Ribchester, Dilworth, Dutton, Alston, and Hothersall.—Chipping Parish—Stonyhurst.

Blackburn hundred is situated to the south and east of Amounderness. At the time of the Domesday survey, a very considerable portion of the land was either waste or covered with wood.[a] An ancient document exists, entitled, "*De Statu Blagborneshire,*" supposed to be the production of an abbot of Whalley, named John Lindeley, who lived in the fourteenth century. It is stated, in this record, that Christianity was introduced into the district as early as the days of Augustine, and that at the end of the sixth century, the churches of Blackburn, Whalley, Ribchester, and Chipping were erected.[b] According to this document, "Blackburnshire," which then included the parish of Rochdale, was but thinly populated; the inhabitants were wild and untractable, and the country infested with foxes and savage beasts. From these causes the bishop of Litchfield appears to have, to some extent, deputed his authority to the resident rectors or deans. The hundred was granted, after the Conquest, by Roger de Poictou, to Roger de Busli and Albert Greslet. After the defection of the first named, the territory reverted to the crown. It was afterwards conferred by William the Conqueror on Ilbert de Lacy, lord of the honour of Pontefract. In the reign of Edward I., Henry de Lacy, earl of Lincoln, obtained a verdict confirmatory of his right to the possession of the "wapentake of Blackburne, and to free chace in all his fees in Blackeburnshire, and to make attachments and distresses by his bailiffs, to try felons, and to have fines and amercements, in all his fees," etc. The possessions of the Lacies were transferred to the house of Lancaster, in 1310, by the marriage of Alicia, daughter and heiress of Henry de Lacy, to Thomas, earl of Lancaster.

---

a See chapter 3, page 99. b See chapter 2, page 62.

The hundred of Blackburn contains the following parishes —Whalley, Chipping, Mitton, Ribchester and Blackburn. The last named adjoins Preston. Blackburn is a large and flourishing manufacturing town, the chief place or capital of an important district. Consequently, any details with reference to it, come not within the province of the historian of Preston. Some of the townships in the parish of Blackburn, however, are contiguous to Preston, and form a portion of its environs.

WALTON-LE-DALE.—It has been previously shown[c] that an ancient British fortress most probably existed at Walton, and that it was afterwards adapted by the Roman conquerors to their taste and requirements. The probability of its being the site of the Roman station Coccium has been discussed elsewhere.[d] The same may be observed with respect to the battle of Brunanburh and several other important events that may have transpired in the township or its vicinity. Waletune is described in the Domesday survey as containing two carucates of land held by the king. The manor was granted to Robert Banastre, about the year 1130, by Henry de Lacy. Walton formed a portion of the dower of Alice Banastre, on her marriage with John Langton. In the 12th year of the reign of Edward III, their son Robert Langton was knighted. The particulars of the feud between the Hoghtons of Hoghton and Lea, and the Langtons of Newton and Walton, in the reign of Elizabeth, through which the last named manor was transferred to the Hoghton family, have been previously related.[e] Walton-le-Dale, in conjunction with Curedale, forms a parochial chapelry. Walton church is believed to have been originally erected in the twelth century. It was endowed with two oxgangs of land, equal to about thirty Lancashire acres. Although situated on an eminence, it is described in the earlier records as Law or Low Chapel. It is not improbable that this term may have been derived from the circumstance of the locality having been previously used as a Saxon burial ground.[f] According to the *Coucher Book* of Whalley, the chapel of Walton, with all the tithe lands and "obventions" belonging to it, was granted, in the year 1229, to the abbot and convent of Stanlow, by Adam de Blackburn, at the request of his lord John de Lascy. The grant, however, was subject to a payment of twenty marks per annum to Richard, son of the dean of Whalley, until he should be promoted to a similar or better benifice. Shortly afterwards (1238), however, the advowson was granted by John de Lascy to the abbey, free from any charges Ralph Langton, of Walton, and baron of Newton, in the 18th year of the reign of Henry VII., bequeathed the sum of twenty marks, "to make and repair the Lawe

c See chapter I.
d See chap 1, and appendix.
e See chapter 3, page 142
f See chapter 2, page 26

Cuerdon Hall, Preston.

(The Seat of R. Townley Parker Esq. M.P.)

St. Leonard's Church & Schools Walton-le-dale.

church, if the parishioners would build the same while his son was under age." The north portion of the chancel belongs to the Asshetons, of Cuerdale; and the south part to the Hoghton family. The arms of both families are carved in stone. Beneath those of the Hoghtons is the following inscription :—"The south part of this chancel belongs to Sir Gilbert Hoghton, knt. and bart. builded ——." The date is erased. Sir Gilbert Hoghton died in the year 1647. In the parliamentary inquiry of 1650, Law is styled a "parochial chapelry, nine miles from the parish church, containing two hundred families." Complaint was made by the inhabitants that £40. a year had been allowed them for a pastor, by the Committee of Plundered Ministers, out of the sequestered tithes of James Anderton, esq., "a delinquent papist"; but that with respect to other charges laid upon these tithes for the maintenance of other ministers, the order had done the inhabitants no good. Another complaint was that the sum of £4 per annum usually paid to the minister at Law Chapel by the vicar of Blackburn, had been illegally detained during the preceding three years. The township was in consequence without both "minister and maintenance." The church is dedicated to St. Leonard. The annual value of the living, in 1834, was returned at £156. The register commences in 1653. The vicar of Blackburn is patron of the living. In 1761, the steeple of Walton church was furnished with a peal of six bells, cast by Messrs. Lester and Pack, of London, at a cost of £322. 19s., including the value of the metal contained in the four old bells, which previously formed the peal. Walton bells are famous for the sweetness of their tone. Whether this is attributable to the skill of the founders, or to the situation of the church, is perhaps difficult to decide; but, from the circumstance that the neighbouring peal at Penwortham enjoys a similar reputation, doubtless much of the proverbial sweetness results from the site. Bishop Gastrell mentions three charities belonging to Walton, one of £10. per annum, bequeathed in 1624, by Peter Burscough, yeoman, to be distributed to the poor on Good Friday; a similar bequest, in 1688, by a Mr. Crook, of Abram, of the tenth part of an estate in Alston and Whittingham, of the value of 22s. and 6d. per annum; and a gift of £20. by Catherine, wife of Richard Park, in 1718, "with her husband's consent." The commissioners' report, (1819,) mentions another charity bequeathed in 1735, "for the poor of Walton and Brindle," by William Gradell. The property is named "Shuttling Field's Estates," and consists of a "farm-house, outbuildings and 24 acres of land, producing annually £50." The bishop records the following facts with reference to the free school :—

"The School here, (wch is free only to the Inhabitants of the Town,) was built by the Inhabitants upon ground Given by Sir Richard Houghton, anno 1672, (the Children being taught in ye Chapel before.) Given to the Master by Peter Burscough, anno

1614, (1624) 100*l*, out of the interest of which was raised 30*l*. more during ye vacancy of ye School in ye time of ye Rebellion. By Mr. Andrew Dandy, Citizen of London, 100*l*., by Thomas Hesketh, of Walton, 20*l*.; by Mr. Crook, of Abram, the tenth part of his Estate in Austin [Alston] and Whittingham, Leased for 11*l*. 10s. 0d. per annum. No Governours being appointed by ye Benefactours, (except ye heirs of Mr. Crook for wt was given by him), the Inhabitants have named six Trustees, but they keep the right of Nominating ye Master."

This school was originally the only one in the township. At the present time instruction is given to from thirty to thirty-five scholars, in the usual branches of a commercial education. The teacher's salary is derived from the interest of the bequests enumerated, lodged in the hands of Sir Henry Bold Hoghton, bart., amounting to £14. 1s. 6d. per annum; £2 yearly from a farm in the parish of Ribchester (Crook's bequest); and pence paid by the scholars. The national schools were erected in 1835, at a cost of £1000., chiefly derived from subscriptions and a grant from the National Society. The upper school is frequented by upwards of 100 boys and fifty girls, the infant school by about seventy boys and sixty girls. About forty girls attend the sewing school. Instruction is imparted in the Sunday schools to about 500 children. There are four teachers, whose salaries are paid from funds derived from subscriptions, interest of money realised by a bazaar, and the pence of the children. It is intended in a short time to erect a catholic chapel in the village of Walton, the premises already in use being merely temporary About thirty years ago, a catholic chapel was erected at Brownedge, in the township of Walton, to which a school is attached. The interior of the chapel is handsomely decorated. There are likewise a methodist and a unitarian chapel, and places of worship for some other denominations. The township of Walton, which includes Moon's mill and Bamber-bridge, now possesses a considerable quantity of cotton mills, as well as a print works, established as early as 1760. There are several old mansions and modern genteel residences in Walton, including Lostock hall, Banister-hall (now a farm house), Walton lodge, the seat of W. Calrow, esq.; Cooper-hill, the residence of Charles Swainson, esq.; and Darwen bank, the seat of Miles Rodgett, esq. It has been stated that the original house at Cooper hill, was designed by General Burgoyne, and that a lightning conductor was put to it by Dr. Franklin. [g] The old hall at Walton, successively the seat of the Banastres, the Langtons, and the Hoghtons, was pulled down about twenty years ago. Some of the offices yet remaining point out the site Sir Henry Bold Hoghton, bart, as lord of the manor, is coroner for Walton-le-dale. Joseph Walker, esq, solicitor, Preston, acts as deputy The township of Walton-le-Dale contains 4,663 statute acres of land. The population, in 1851, amounted to 6,855. The

g Dobson's pamphlet, History of the Parliamentary Representation of Preston, etc., page 29.

Frenchwood, Lancashire

the Seat of Chas Swainson Esqr

property was rated, in 1854, at the annual value of £18,024. Walton has been the scene of many important historical events. These will be found fully described in the preceding chapters.

Cuerdale forms a portion of the chapelry of Walton. Geoffrey de Keuerdale held, of the earl of Lancaster, in the reign of Edward III., three carucates of land, in Keuerdale. It passed by marriage to Thomas le Molynex, who was slain at the battle of Redcote bridge, in the first year of the reign of Richard II. On the birth of Radcliffe Assheton, in 1582, it was transferred to the family of the present proprietor, W. Assheton, esq., of Cuerdale and Downham. Cuerdale hall, formerly a residence of the family, was erected in 1700, but the remains of foundations in the gardens indicate that some more ancient structure preceded the present edifice. Cuerdale has become somewhat celebrated, owing to the discovery of an immense hoard of Saxon, Danish, and other coins, etc., in 1840, by some workmen employed in repairing the bank of the river.[h] The township of Cuerdale contained, in 1851, no more than eighty inhabitants. Its area includes 684 statute acres of land, chiefly situated in the valley of the Ribble. The property was assessed to the county rate, in 1854, at £985. per annum.

Samlesbury is an extensive township lying between the Darwen and the Ribble. From its name, a Roman outwork probably existed here, on a vacinal way from the principal station at Walton to Ribchester and Whalley. The manor was held by Gospatric de Samsbury, towards the end of the reign of Henry II. His grandson, Sir William de Samlesbury, having no male issue, the property became vested in the husbands of his three daughters and co-heiresses. Roger de Haunton espoused Margery, but left no representative. Cecily married Sir John D'Ewyas. In the forty-third year of the reign of Henry III., he held one half of the manor of Samlesbury. The other moiety became vested in Sir Robert de Holland, of Hale, on his marriage with Elizabeth, the youngest daughter of Sir William de Samlesbury. Robert de Holland was knighted in the tenth year of the reign of Edward I. The widow of his grandson, Sir Robert Holland, married the celebrated Edward, the Black Prince, father of Richard II. Sir Robert, son of Elizabeth de Samlesbury, founded the priory of Holland. Being a partizan of Thomas, earl of Lancaster, his estates were confiscated on the attainder of that nobleman. After much litigation, however, they were restored. This property passed by marriage to the Lovel family, and was again confiscated during the wars of the roses, by John Lord Lovel, an adherent of the Lancastrian party. A descendant of Cecily de Samlesbury married Sir Gilbert de Southworth.

h See chapter 2, page 74.

Her moiety of the manor remained in possession of this family till 1677, when it was disposed of by John Southworth, esq., together with the old hall, for little over £2000, to Thomas Braddyll, esq., from whom it descended to the Braddylls, of Conishead priory. An episcopal chapel, dedicated to St. Leonard, was founded by Gospatric de Samlesbury. It was originally a chapel of ease to Law or Walton church, without a cemetery. It appears from the *Coucher Book*, however, that two Irish bishops, on a visit to Gospatric, were prevailed upon to consecrate a cemetery, which act was supposed to render the chapel parochial. This transpired during the absence from England of Hugh de Nonant, then bishop of Litchfield, who held the see from 1185 to 1198. Irritated at this interference with his authority, Hugh, on his return, annulled the consecration. The entreaties of Gospatric, however, mollified the anger of the bishop, who, eventually confirmed the sentence. Dr. Kuerden preserves the following curious letter from the earl of Derby respecting Samlesbury chapel:—

"13 May, 1558. Edw E of Derby to al his louing frends. As I am credibly enformed the church at Sambury is in ruine & indangering people that resort to heare God's worde, I haue thought good to moue my louing frends to help with there charity towards the re-edifying thereof."

According to the Parliamentary Inquisition, in 1650, the parochial chapel of Samlesbury was reported as having had anciently a pension of £4. per annum, paid by former vicars of Blackburn, but at that time detained. The inhabitants, amounting to one hundred families, stated that they were desirous Samlesbury should be constituted into a distinct parish. Richard Smethurst was minister at the time, and received £40 per annum, from the county committee. The value of the living, in 1834, was £110. per annum. The church, although the ancient burial place of the lords of the soil, contains scarcely a single memorial of note, except the knightly ensign of one of the Southworths, and, an alabaster slab, covering the remains of a William, son of Sir William Anderton, who died about the nineteenth year of the reign of Henry VI. The higher hall, commonly called "Samlesbury old hall," situated on the new road from Preston to Blackburn, is a most interesting specimen of the superior kind of domestic architecture of the middle ages. The following observations respecting edifices of this class, by Dr. Whitaker, will be read with interest.—

"The whole structure has been originally a frame work of wood independent of walls, the principals consisting of deep flat beams of massy oak naturally curved, and of which each pair seems to have been sawed out of the same trunk. These spring from the ground and form a bold Gothic arch overhead; the spars rest upon a wall plate, and that is again sustained by horizontal spars, grooved into the principals. It was then of no importance that such erections consumed great quantities of the finest ship timber, and indeed the appearance of one of these rooms is precisely that of the hull of a great ship, inverted and seen from within. Specimens of this ancient style in perfection are, the old manor house at Samlesbury, and the Lawsing Stedes barn, at Whalley. In the reign of Henry IV. we have a deviation from this primitive mode, there the principals have two springers, one from the ground, another from a rude capital about 8 feet from the ground, but the square of the building is considerably raised, and the arch encroaches less upon the apartment within. The style of architecture in wood evidently kept pace with that in stone, and when in the time of Henry VII. the arch became broader and more depressed in the centre, we have a corresponding change in our ancient timber buildings. Wooden posterns still descended to the ground, but they were now become perpendicular and square and fluted. From the top of these, elegant and ornamental springers received horizontal roof beams, while all was still open to the roof above, and the rafters continued to rest on a wall plate. Thus the idea of a complete frame independently of the walls was still preserved; but the low basement story of stone may still be observed in some of our most ancient buildings, advanced to the square, though the cross pikes are generally of wood. This precisely describes the Hall of Little Mitton and another noble specimen of somewhat later date, the west wing of Samlesbury Hall, built by Sir Thomas Southworth, in 1532, of which the outer wall, however, is of brick. The wood employed in the construction of this last mansion must have laid prostrate a forest, and while the principal timbers are carved with great elegance, and the compartments of the roof painted with figures of saints, while the outsides of the building are adorned with profile heads of wood cut in bold relief within huge medallions, it is curious to observe, that the inner doors are without lock or panel, and have always opened like modern cottages with a latch and a string. It was moated round and has contained three sides of a quadrangle, the centre one of which containing the great hall, is a noble specimen of most rude and massy woodwork. Though repaired by Sir Thomas Southworth, in 1532, whose name it bears, it is of high antiquity, probably not later than Edward III."

Mr. Alfred Rimmer is inclined to doubt whether the hall is quite so ancient as conjectured by Dr. Whitaker. He says, "It is somewhat similar in character, and perhaps scarcely so rude, as one formerly standing at Radcliffe hall, and engraved in Whitaker's Whalley, and this was built in the reign of Henry IV."[1] There is some difficulty in deciphering a portion of an inscription in old English characters, owing to its mutilated condition. It has generally been interpreted as "Thomas Southworth, Baronete." Mr. Rimmer, however, says:—

"As the word which was read Baronete occurs before Thomas Southworth's name, and Knight is written very distinctly after, it is not probable that this reading is correct; moreover it is not like Baronet, except in the number of the letters and the initial. As this inscription is later than the room, and as various other parts of the house are of the same age, it might read thus: *Anno Domini Mccccc xxx ii, Bono Statu Thomas Southworth, xx.* The next panel, which contained the remainder, has been destroyed, and when complete the inscription may have stated that Sir Thomas restored the hall, in 1532, to a good condition, which both Baines and Whitaker state to have been the case."

The timber of the screen which separates the gallery for musicians from the body of the hall is elaborately carved. The arched fire place is very large, measuring in height six feet nine inches, and fourteen feet nine inches in breadth. It is lighted by a very fine oriel window, in addition to four others of a plainer character. The entire hall is about thirty-five feet in length, by upwards of twenty-six in breadth. The staircase

1 Lancashire and Cheshire His. Soc. Trans. vol. 4, page 35.

for so noble a mansion is considered narrow and mean. The roof of the entrance hall has an arched fire place in the Tudor style, and a finely carved oak ceiling. It is nearly thirteen feet in height. There is a parlour to the right which still retains its oak ceiling and latticed window Still further to the right is the ancient domestic chapel The window is filled with rich tracery, said to have been brought from Whalley Abbey. It is of the character prevalent during the reign of Henry VII. A room to the left of the entrance hall is in excellent preservation Its fire place is ornamented with six gothic panels and two shields. It bears the following inscription: "Thomas Southworth, Knight, 1555." The front which is 105 feet in length, is ornamented by diamond shaped figures in blue brick, and is surmounted by a coved cornice of lath and plaster, common to buildings erected during the reign of Henry VIII. The moat referred to by Dr. Whitaker has since been filled up. The figures of saints on the ceiling of the hall have likewise disappeared, and modern locks have superseded the primitive latches. Mr. Baines complained in 1836, that the ancient hall was in "a state of dilapidation and converted into two beer shops." In 1852, Mr. Rimmer, however, says:—

"Samlesbury Hall is in a state of high preservation, and the timber even in the most ancient part, is as sound as it ever was. The walls are perfectly true and the glass in most of the windows is entire. The doors do not even need re-hanging, nor does the brickwork require to be pointed; and in all probability if the Southworth family existed to the present day, it would still be their family residence; but at present it presents a sad picture of the mutability of human affairs, and is now occupied as a roadside inn of the meanest description, and a great part of it lies useless.[k] The entrance hall with its lofty ceiling and mullioned windows, is a bar parlour; and the ancient dining hall which has so often rung with the revelry of the first gentlemen of the county, is quite deserted; modern partitions divide some of its finest rooms, so as to render it difficult, in many instances, to discover the original plan of the mansion."

Samlesbury hall was purchased by John Cooper, esq., of the Oaks, Penwortham, in 1851. The evil complained of by Mr. Baines and Mr. Rimmer was some time ago remedied, and the hall of the Southworths converted into a boarding school for young ladies. The "Lower hall" was sold by Thomas Southworth, esq, to Sir Thomas Walmsley, of Dunkenhalgh, in the reign of James I. It has descended to one of the representatives of the family, H. Petre, esq. Samlesbury has gained some notoriety as the *locale* of a band of "Lancashire witches." The superstition was not confined to the humbler classes of the locality. From the evidence of John Singleton, on the trial of the gang, as recorded by Potts, a writer on witchcraft, it appears that Sir John Southworth was in the habit of observing that a relative named Jane Southworth, was

k This is scarcely correct. Samlesbury Hall was certainly a road-side inn, but it was in no way inferior to the general average of such places Indeed, in some respects it was, at one time, rather superior than otherwise.

Stonyhurst College, Lancashire.

"a cruel woman and a witch, and he, Sir John, in going between his own house and Preston, did for the most part forbear to pass the house where Jane the said witch did dwell, doubting that she would bewitch him."[l] The commissioners report, made in 1819, mentions the following charities in connection with this township:—

"Samlesbury School.—The master teaches 6 poor children, and occupies rent free a dwelling house and land of £8. yearly value, and has £8. from the overseers.

"1715. Langdale's Charity.—Dorothy Langdale left £200 for the support of the poor and aged, or for binding out poor apprentices. This legacy, increased by accumulation of interest to £214. 13s. was laid out in a house, cottage, gardens, and land, producing £25. per annum in rent, which for many years has been applied in aid of the poor's rates, instead of being disposed of to charitable purposes.

"1613. Richard Hoghton's Charity.—The rent of 5 acres of land to be divided among 3 townships for their poor, viz: to Preston, £2. 10s.; to Alston, £5.; and to Samlesbury, £2. 10s."

Samlesbury formerly possessed extensive alum works.[m] The area of this township, according to the ordnance survey, is 4,379 statute acres. The population, in 1851, was 1,435; and the annual rateable value of the property in 1854, £5,822.

Pleasington was formerly the property of a family of that name. A deed without date, but supposed from the names of the witnesses to be about the time of Henry III. or Edward I. exists, by which Henry de Plessyngton gave to John de Stodleigh, and Margery his wife, daughter of Henry de Plessyngton, a piece of land in Plessyngton, called Tincfield, together with another piece called Adam's Assart, to be held at an annual rent of 3s. to the end of Margery's life. The property became transferred by marriage to the Winkeley family. Kuerden preserves a document by which John de Wynkerdelegh grants to his eldest son John, his manor and demesne in Plessington, to be held "by the yearly service of one rose, and fealty to the chief lord." In the 4th year of the reign of Richard II. a Robert de Plessington was chief baron of the exchequer. In 1715, a younger branch of the family of Plessington, lost his estate for supporting the Stuarts. His portion of the property was sold by the commissioners for £770., to a Mr. Wickers. The manor passed to the Cunliffes, and afterwards to the Ainsworth family. A descendant, Edward Ainsworth, who, "by vulgar debauchery, wasted the patrimony of a long line of respectable ancestors," conveyed it to the father of the late J. F. Butler, esq., in 1777.[n] The present handsome Roman catholic church, called Pleasington priory, was erected by J. F. Butler, esq., at a cost of £20,000. He died in 1822, leaving the estate to a niece, Miss Julia Butler, who bequeathed it to J. Bowden, esq., of the county of Derby, now J. Butler Bowden, esq.,

---

l See chapter 4, page 147. m See chap. 1, p. 41, and chap. 4, p. 152.

n Letter of Michael Jones, esq., barrister, to J. F. Butler, esq., of Pleasington hall, dated Jan. 1814. Mr. Jones says Lawrence Ainsworth was in possession of the property in 1453.

its present possessor, who resides at Pleasington Hall. About fifty years ago, the last of the family of the Aynesworths sold Fenniscowles to the late W. Feilden, esq. Woodfold was formerly a residence of the Sudells, and afterwards of Paul Fleetwood, esq., of Preston. Pleasington contains an area of 1701 statute acres. The annual rateable value of the property, in 1854, amounted to £2,930. The population, in 1851, numbered 428.

Balderstone.—This manor passed from the family of that name to the Harringtons and the Pilkingtons, by marriage. Dame Margery Pilkington, in the 12th year of the reign of Henry VII., bequeathed her portion to Sir Thomas Talbot, and his wife Jane, her niece. In the nineteenth year of the reign of Henry VII., Sir James Harrington presented a petition to the king and council, praying that he might be restored to the possession of the estate which had been forfeited in the first year of the reign of that monarch. He describes himself as being "sorofull and repentant as any creature may be of all that the same your Besecher have done to the displeasure of your Hignesse, contrarie to his duty of Allegiance." The prayer of the petition was granted. A portion passed to the Dudley family, and afterwards escheated to the crown, in the first year of the reign of Henry VIII. The manor was sold about the year 1821, by Mr. Cross, to Joseph Feilding, esq., of Witton. Balderstone chapel is probably an erection anterior to the Reformation. It is mentioned in the year 1559. It was without endowment or minister, in 1650, although the township contained eighty families. It was in decay during the reign of James I., but was afterwards restored. The building was enlarged in 1755, and 1818. Balderstone contains 1807 statute acres, and a population of 660 persons. The property was rated at £2,301. per annum, in 1854.

Osbaldeston.—Dr. Leigh supposes the name to have been derived from Osalveden, signifying Oswald's Town, a Roman villa in the neighbourhood, in the time of Tacitus. This, however, is ridiculed by the more erudite Dr. Whitaker. Osbaldeston Hall is believed to have been the property and residence of one of the oldest families located in Lancashire. Mr. Baines says it was the property of "Elfi of Osbaldeston, a Saxon, whose son Hugh was living in the 30 Henry III., from whom descended the family of Osbaldeston; while from his brother William, who assumed the name of Balderstone, descended a family, which terminated in two coheiresses, in the reign of Henry VI." The estate remained in the same family till the middle of the eighteenth century, when it passed by sale to the Warrens, by whose representative, the Lord de Tabley, it is at present held. Osbaldeston and Balderstone are pleasantly situated on the south bank of the Ribble, and include some beautiful rural scenery.[o] The

o See page 522.

township of Osbaldeston was rated, in 1854, at the annual value of £1,126. The population, in 1851, numbered 250. The area, according to the ordnance survey, is 1,084 acres.

SALESBURY or Salisbury, is likewise situated on the southern bank of the Ribble, opposite to Ribchester. The manor was held by Award de Salebury, who granted lands therein to the monks of Stanlow about the time of Edward I. The manor was transferred to the Talbots, by the marriage of Isabella, daughter and co-heiress of Richard Mauliverer, by Sybil, daughter and heiress of Sir Robert de Cliderhow, of Salebury. By the marriage of the daughter of John Talbot with Edward Warren, of Poynton, the manor passed to Lord de Tabley. Salesbury hall is now a farm house. It possesses some historical associations; [p] but is chiefly remarkable on account of a magnificent Roman altar, supposed to have been procured from Ribchester, having been built into one of its walls. This stone has been deposited in St. John's college, Cambridge, by the late Dr. Whitaker.[q] Another hall at Salesbury, called Lovely hall, was formerly a jointure of the Talbots. Salesbury green, was, according to Mr. Baines, "a station for the rebels during the last century." The chapel was built in 1808. The patronage for the first sixty years is vested in Lord de Tabley. Salesbury contains 1,215 statute acres, and was assessed in 1854, at the annual value of £1,217. The population, in 1851, amounted to 388.

RIBCHESTER PARISH.

The parish of Ribchester is situated to the east of that of Preston, and includes the townships of Ribchester, Dilworth, Dutton, and Alston-with-Hothersall.

RIBCHESTER, as the name implies, was a Roman castrum on the Ribble. It has been identified with the Rigodunum, of Ptolemy, the Rerigonium, of Richard of Cirencester, the Coccium, of Antoninus, the Bremetum racum, of the Notitia, and the Bremetonacis, of Antoninus. This matter will be found fully discussed in other portions of this work.[r] From the numerous remains which have been discovered, Ribchester, has evidently been a populous and important place, during the period of the Roman occupation. Leland, in his day, found Ribchester "a poore thing." He records, however, that "it hath beene an Auncient Town. Great Squarid Stones, Voultes, and antique coynes be found ther; and ther is a place wher the People fable that the *Jues* had a Temple." He further adds that the "tide floweth and ebbith in *Ribyl* most communely more than half way up betwixt Prestun & Ribcestre, and at Ragis of Spring Tydes farther." Leland has evidently been misinformed on this matter. The backing of

p See pages 130, 170, and 524. q See Appendix.
r See chapter 1, and Appendix.

the fresh water by the tide at the present day, seldom produces any impression above Cuerdale, except in the case of floods; and there is no reason to believe any change has taken place, in this respect, for some centuries.[s] Camden paid more attention to the Roman remains. He discovered the pedestal of a pillar, built into the fabric of Salesbury hall, on the opposite side of the river, which bore the following inscription :—

"DEO MARTI ET VICTORIÆ DD AVGG ET CC NN."

Another altar, dedicated to Apollo, Camden noticed in a neighbouring wall. It was, in 1814, by permission of Lord Bulkeley detached, and presented by Dr. Whitaker to King's College, Cambridge. This relic is considered one of the most interesting Roman altars found in this kingdom. Though much injured, it yet exhibits the remains of a well executed figure of Apollo, with his lyre, and two priests holding the head of a horned animal, intended for sacrifice.[t] The inscription on this altar, being considerably defaced, has given rise to much learned controversy.[u] Camden on his second visit, in 1603, discovered another altar, which he describes as the largest and finest he had ever seen. It is dedicated to the "mother goddesses." It is nearly unique, only one of a similar character having been discovered. It has been placed in the museum at Stonyhurst college. Camden mentions likewise a large stone, bearing the representation of a man on horseback, brandishing a spear over a prostrate enemy. This stone bore the following inscription :—

"HIS. TERRIS. TEGITVR. AEL. MATRONA. QV.VIX. AN. XXVIII. M.II.D. VIII. ET. M. IVLIVIS. MAXIMVS. FIL. VIX. AN. VI. M. III. D. XX. ET. CAM. PANIA. DUBBA. MATER. VIX. AN. L. IVLIVS. MAXIMVS. . . . . AL. SAR. CONIVX. CONIVGI. INCOMPARABILI. ET FILIO. PATRI. PIENTIS. SIMO. ET. SOCERAE. TENACISSIMAE. MEMORIAE. P."

Another relic, called "a poor man's altar," bears the following inscription :—

"PACIFE RO MARTI ELEGAVR BA POSVIT. EX. VOTO."

Dr. Stukeley visited Ribchester in 1725. He thus describes it :—

"The Ribble is very broad in this place, rapid and sonorous, and what is much to be lamented, runs over innumerable Roman antiquities; for in this long tract of time it has eaten away a third part of the city. I traced out the old ground plot, and where the wall and ditch went round it; it lay in length east and west along the north side of the river, upon its brink, 800 feet long and 500 feet broad. Originally, I apprehend two streets ran along its breadth. * * By symmetry I find the whole channel of the river lies, at present, within the precinct of the old city, the original channel on the other side being filled up with city walls and rubbish, for it bends with a great elbow towards the city."

The river has certainly encroached much upon the site of the castrum, though it is doubtful whether to the extent conjectured by Stukeley. Horsley, Leigh, and others, made some additional discoveries. One is a square stone with the figure of a boar sculptured on one side. It bears the

---

s See chapter 1, page 52. t Camden thought the figure a Cupid. u See appendix.

following inscription: "LEG XX VV FECIT" The most important relics of the ancient city have, however, been brought to light within the last sixty years. In 1796, a slip of earth disclosed a bronze helmet of very superior workmanship It is ornamented with figures of armed warriors in conflict. In addition to the head piece, there is a beautiful mask attached, representing a finely proportioned human face. Dr. Whitaker says "the crest, which was unfortunately lost, was a sphinx." From the thinness of the metal and other circumstances, it is believed to have formed part of a statue, and not to have been used as a piece of defensive armour. It is at present deposited along with the remainder of the Townley collection, in the British museum. A few other smaller articles were found at the same time as the helmet. In July, 1811, some workmen, while repairing the river's bank, discovered several fragments of an inscribed stone. When these were adjusted, Dr. Whitaker endeavoured to interpret its meaning. From the imperfect condition of the relic, this is by no means so satisfactory as might be desired. However, the learned antiquary, after much ingenious dissertation, gives it as follows:—

"DEAE MINERVAE
PRO SALVTE IMP M AVREL ANTONINI AVG ET
IVLI PIAE MATRIS DN ET CASTR SVOR ET
VAL CRESCENTIS FVLVIANI LEG EIVS PP PR PR
T FLORIDVS NATALIS LEG PRAEP N ET REGIANE
TEMPLVM A SOLO EX RESPONSV RE—
STITIVIT ET DEDICAVIT"

This Dr. Whitaker extends in the following manner:—

"Deæ Minervæ—Pro salute Imperatoris Marci Aurelii Antonini Augusti et Juliæ Piæ matris domini nostri et castrorum suorum, et Valerii Crescentis Fulviani Legati, provinciæ præsidis, propraetor, Titus Floridus Natalis legatus præpotenti numini et reginaæ templum a solo ex responsu restituit et dedicavit." v

This led to still more important discoveries, which are thus described by Dr. Whitaker:—

"This" (the stone last referred to) "sufficiently proved the existence of a temple, of which this inscription must have formed the tympanum. Accordingly, in the summer of 1813, leave having been obtained to dig in the adjoining gardens, between the river and the church yard, the first appearances, at the depth of about three feet, were a stratum of charcoal, evidently formed by the conflagration of the roof, and nearly in the centre a cavity in the earth had been made, by uniting the ends of the beams at their fall, large enough to contain a man sitting. Beneath this was a confused mass of large amphoræ, some almost entire at first, and many beautiful remnants of pateræ in the red Samian ware, mingled with which lay several human skeletons, all of the largest size, in every direction. Every appearance about the place indicated that it had been taken by storm, and that the defenders had been buried in the ruins of the roof, but the absence of tiles or slates seemed to prove that the outer covering of the building had been previously stripped by the assailants Here, too, was found a very curious Roman statera, or steel-yard, very exactly graduated, and a singular bodkin of polished stone.

v "To the goddess Minerva,—for the safety of the Emperor Marcus Aurelius Antoninus Augustus, and of Julia Pia, the mother of our lord, and of his camp, and of Valerius Crescens Fulvianus, his lieutenant, governor of the province,—the proprietor Titus Floridus Natalis the lieutenant, restored this temple, and dedicated it to the most powerful goddess and queen."

"The progress of discovery was now once more suspended, till the sexton, digging a grave where no interment had taken place before, on the left hand of the entrance of the church-yard, found the base of a column and an anta, or square moulded corner of the naos itself, upright, and in their original situations. Measurements were now accurately made from the place where the inscription was found, which must have been the front of the building, to the base of the column. This gave the entire length, excepting one intercolumniation, for the whole had evidently had a peristyle. The distance of the anta from the column, by the rules of architecture, gave the distance also between column and column; by which data, with the help of a very conspicuous line of mortar, about forty-five feet westward in the churchyard, the site of the west wall was ascertained, a ground plan of the building was laid down, after which, by known proportions of Doric architecture, a complete elevation was obtained. From remains not originally more promising than these, Palladio has restored, in the most satisfactory and convincing manner, several ancient temples But every appearance about this work (far unlike those beautiful specimens of ancient art which that great architect had the happiness to retrieve), indicated, at once, provincial barbarism, and a declining age in art. For the column was ill wrought, and the different diameters so varied from each other, as to show that it had never been struck from a centre.[w]

"Let all these circumstances be laid together, and it will scarcely be doubted that this was a temple of Minerva, restored by command of Caracalla; that the helmeted head of brass was that of the goddess, that the temple had been stormed and burnt in some irruption of the Caledonians,[x] during the last period of the Roman power in Britain, and that the precious object of worship itself had been carefully deposited in the earth, on the approach of the threatened danger, in a situation from which the depositor never lived to disinter it."[y]

Dr. Whitaker likewise mentions the statue of a lion, found within a few yards of the east wall of the temple, apparently an architectural ornament, together with a fragment of an altar, to the west of the peristyle. In Feb., 1833, the upper portion of an altar, the sides of which were decorated with vine leaves, was dug up in the church yard It bears an inscription in rude but distinct letters, which has been rendered as follows:—"Pro Salute et Victoria invicti imperatoris Marci Aurelii Severi Antonini Pii et Juliæ Augustæ Matris Domini et Castrorum suorum—Sep Re—."[z] The Rev. Mr. Allen, of Salesbury, who discovered the altar, observed indications of an ancient conflagration, similar in character to those mentioned by Dr. Whitaker Near the altar, a fibula, a bulla, a ring of brass, and several coins were found. The Rev T B Hazlewood, incumbent of Ribchester, has preserved the last mentioned altar, as well as a large number of coins, pottery, and other interesting remains. Ribchester has been visited by members of various archæological associations; and many other interesting relics have, from time to time, been discovered Amongst others, a small but beautiful gold cup, with handles, was dug up behind the White Bull

w See chapter 1, page 51. x See chapter 2, page 56.

y The helmet was discovered in an excavation filled with fine sand. Doubtless the tradition respecting the temple of the Jews, had reference to the structure discovered by Dr Whitaker. In the middle period of Christianity in England, the only old, or, indeed, different religion to their own, known to the mass of the people, would be the Jewish

z "For the safety and victory of the unvanquished emperor, Marcus Aurelius, Severus Antoninus Pius" (Caracalla) "the happy Augustus, and of his mother Julia Augusta, and for the safety of his camp"

Inn. A "tunnel" is said to have formerly existed under the Red Lion Inn, but this has been destroyed Three rude pillars, now forming part of the porch of an inn, are reported to have been taken from the river. Gold coins are not common at Ribchester. One, however, was found in Jan., 1837. It was of the reign of Nero, and about the size of a modern sixpence. In the following month, another discovery of some importance took place. Some labourers were employed by Mr. Patchett to form a hot-bed in his garden, when they came upon what has been pronounced to be the remains of a Roman bath. It is described as thirty feet in length and fifteen feet in breadth. The walls, which were three feet in thickness, remained to the height of four feet. Mr. Whittle says, "the bottom was regularly paved after the manner of their watling or guethelin streets, and over this was a fine cement, three feet in thickness, a strong coating verily, and upon this was laid tiles or flags, jointed in a masterly style." From the general description of this relic, it was more probably the flooring of a Roman house, of some pretensions. It was formerly the practice to name this class of remains indiscriminately Roman baths. Mr. Patchett has yet in his possession several of the rude stone pillars, nearly a foot in height, which were taken from the foundation These, doubtless, supported the tesselated pavement, and formed the hypocaust or flues by which the apartment was warmed.[a] These interesting remains, with a few exceptions, have been used in the construction of ordinary buildings. Some of the flags, which formed the pavement of the Roman hall, have been degraded to a not very dissimilar service, in connection with a neighbouring pigsty Some fragments of glass, and a few imperfect coins were found during the excavations Coins are still often found. A silver denarius of Titus Vespasian, in capital preservation, was picked up about two years ago. A portion of the fosse and vallum which defended the castrum on the west, is still visible. The latter is termed "Anchor-hill." Roman Ribchester was doubtless destroyed soon after the departure of the legions, by an irruption of the northern barbarians, or by the resident native inhabitants, who resisted the authority of the Britanni, or Romano-British people, by whom they had previously been held in subjection. Tradition says it was destroyed by an earthquake, and again that it was burnt by the Scots.[b] At the time of the Domesday survey, Ribchester was included in Amounderness, and was one of the villages which belonged to Preston Edmund de Lacye held the manor in the forty second year of the reign of Henry III. As early as the 27th Edward III., the Motons are styled "lords of Ribchester." It passed from them to the Hoghtons, of

a See Celt, Roman, and Saxon, by Thomas Wright, page 190, etc.

b See Chapter 1, page 50

Hoghton Tower. According to the duchy records, Rybchester was vested in Sir Alexander Hoghton, in the fourteenth Henry VII On the same authority it appears that in the 36th Elizabeth, Sir Richard Sherburne died seized of the manor. It passed from the Sherburnes to the Welds, and was disposed of by the celebrated cardinal of that name, about twenty-five years ago, to Joseph Fenton, esq., of Bamford hall, near Rochdale, together with the neighbouring manors of Dutton and Bailey. A church is believed to have existed at Ribchester soon after the Conquest. The Domesday book makes no mention of such an edifice. It is certain one was erected previously to the reign of Henry II. In 1291, the living was valued at £22 The present church has been built at various periods. An elaborately ornamented screen, in the Dutton choir, on the south side of the edifice, is supposed to belong to the age of John or Henry III. In the 7th year of the reign of Henry IV., a chantry was founded on the north side of the choir, by Sir Richard Hoghton, M.P. There is a tomb in this choir formed from a solid block of stone, bearing three heraldic devices of the Hoghton family. A moiety of the Dutton choir belonged to the Hoghtons, in right of some possessions in Alston. It was sold by the late baronet to Mr. Rothwell, of Lancaster. A portion of the other moiety, formerly the property of the Townleys, was sold in 1729, to John Riley. It is described as the "middle part of Dutton choir, being a seat therein, five feet square, reserving power to pass and repass to other parts of the said choir, not thereby granted." [c] The further end of Dutton choir, together with an estate in Bailey, was leased in 1740, by Richard Townley, esq., of Belfield. It was lately claimed by Mrs. Alston, of Ribchester, in right of William Pye, gent., deceased, a descendant of the Townleys, of Dutton. The ruins of a chapel in Bailey, which is in Mitton parish, were removed in 1830, by the late Joseph Fenton, esq The chapel of St. John the Baptist, in Bailey, was a chantry, founded by Roger de Cliderhow, rector of Wigan. Roger was a partisan of Thomas, earl of Lancaster. In 1323, he was indicted for high treason, but acquitted He was charged with having preached, in Wigan church, against the king; with having contended that his congregation were liege subjects of the earl; and with having furnished two horses and four foot soldiers on behalf of his patron. The advowson of Ribchester appears to have been possessed from an early period by the dukes of Lancaster On the foundation of the see of Chester, in the reign of Henry VIII, the living was conferred upon the bishopric. The bishop is rector of Ribchester, and possesses all the great tithes in the parish, except those of the township of Dutton. According to the Parliamentary Inquisition, in 1650, the vicar of Ribchester formerly received twenty marks

c Lanc MSS., vol. 31, page 519.

per annum from the bishop of Chester, together with £6. 13s. 4d., a year from the parish of Stede. It was complained that no allowance had latterly been made, and that the minister, Mr. Christopher Hindley, had been suspended by an order from the provincial Assembly of Divines, but for what cause the presentors were not informed. The commissioners for the sale of bishops' lands, in 1647, state that there was no minister at Ribchester, that the people "only heare so often as they can, and pay the minister chiefly out of their own purses. There was one Mr. Harley" [Hindley] "minister, but was put out by the Committee of Divines in Lancashire, for his insufficiency, and being *scandalory* in his life and conversation." At this period the rectory was held by Richard Sherburne, esq., of Stonyhurst, the lord of the manor, by lease from the bishop of Chester A free school was established in 1771. There are likewise some charities which produced, according to the commissioners' report, in 1819, £53. 16s. per annum. There are remains of several stone crosses, some of them believed to be of the earlier Christian period, in the parish of Ribchester and its neighbourhood. A small cross, with a ball in front, found in Ribchester church yard, some years ago, and transferred to Lovely hall, Salesbury, closely resembles those in Whalley church-yard; on which account it has been conjectured that it may have been erected to commemorate the preaching of Paulinus. Remains of crosses are found near the White Lion, Hothersall; at Dutton Lee; at Ward Green, near the Pinfold, below Written Stone in Dilworth; at the north-east extremity of the parish; in Stonygate-lane, upon Alston hill; and opposite the White Bull, in Ribchester. One in Gallows lane, Dutton, is said to be near the spot where the hangman for the early feudal lords plyed his vocation. The Written Stone, in Dilworth, is a square block, inscribed "Rafe Ratcliffe laid this stone here to lie for ever, A.D. 1607." Rafe Ratcliffe owned the estate at the period. Amongst the older edifices in Ribchester, are the Court house, in which the manor courts were formerly held, a hall at Knoll Green, formerly the residence of the Cottams, and Buckley hall, erected by the Sherburnes, in 1666. Ward hall has been modernized The principal trade of Ribchester is weaving and wood turning. The area of the township is 2,211 statute acres; its population in 1851, was 1,650; and the annual rateable value of the property in 1854, was £3,087.

DUTTON has passed through various hands Originally it gave the name to the family of Dutton. In the time of John of Gaunt, William de Dutton granted lands in the township to William Moton and others. In the reign of Edward III., Ralph de Clayton, and Hugh de Cliderhow, and Richard de Caldcotes, held lands in Dutton. The last named is afterwards described as Richard de Townley. The manor remained in this family till 1799. It has since passed from the Welds, by purchase, to the Fentons, of Bamford Hall. The abbey of Whalley held Horrobanks, in this township. After the dissolution of the monasteries, it was rated to Richard Sherborne. Dutton hall is a spacious mansion, built at the latter part of the seventeenth century, it is the joint property of the Rev. Richard Rainshaw Rothwell, rector of Sefton, and his nephew, Richard Rainshaw Rothwell, esq., of Sharples hall, near Bolton. Lower Dutton hall and Huntington hall are objects of interest. The latter is converted into a farm house. A hospital was founded in the reign of John. It is described as a "Hospitale subtus Langrig," and was dedicated to St. Saviour. It was a preceptory of the Knights Hospitallers, dependent upon the house of Newland, near Wakefield, after the order of St. John of Jerusalem was dissolved. Alan de Singleton granted four acres of land in Dilewrhe, to the hospital. In the reign of Henry III., William, son of Walter de Moton, confirmed a grant of lands previously made by his father. Nicholas Talbot, of the family of Bashall, in 1501, by will, appointed a priest to sing for twelve months "at Stead, where Fader and Moder are buried." The manor of Stede, with all its "rights, members, and appurtenances," together with other manors, rents, messuages, and lands, belonging to the knights of St. John and the abbeys of Whalley and Cockersand, were granted to Thomas, afterwards Sir Thomas Holt, of Grizzlehurst, for the sum of £1,727. 15s, on the dissolution of the monastic institutions, in the reign of Henry VIII. The lands were held subject to a chief rent of £9.11s. per year, and an annual stipend of forty shillings to the minister of Stede. The ancient chapel, though in a very dilapidated condition, yet remains. It is believed to be one of the oldest entire buildings in the county. The porch exhibits a fine specimen of the Anglo-Norman arch, with slender clustered columns and floriated capitals. Two of the original small lancet windows yet remain. The font is of grit stone, octagonal in form, and bears the arms of the knights of St. John and others, in rude carving. Two slabs, one richly ornamented, are supposed to cover the remains of priests, formerly attached to the church. There is a monumental stone to Sir Adam de Cliderhow and his wife, who held the manor of Salesbury, in the reign of Edward III. An ancient stone coffin, with a double cross, supposed to have originally contained the body of one of the masters of the hospital, was formerly to be seen on the north side of the altar. The remains of the Roman Catholic bishop of Armorium (Petre), who resided at Showley, and died in 1775, are interred immediately in front of the altar. Externally Stydd chapel appears like a ruin. It is clothed with ivy, and stands in a deserted grave-yard, overgrown with weeds. Some remains of the foundations of the hospital have been discovered in the neighbourhood of the chapel. The living of Stydd has been attached to the vicarage of Ribchester. It is endowed with the tithes of eleven farms within the township of Dutton. Service was formerly performed twice a year, in order to secure the emoluments of the living. The present vicar, Mr. Hazlewood, however, having caused considerable repairs to be made, celebrates divine service in the ancient edifice once per month. In 1650, Stede was returned as a parish church, being a donative from the abbot of Cockersand, then belonging to Mr. Holte, of Grizzlehurst. It was stated to be "worth £6. 13s. 4d., and hitherto paid to the Minister of Ribchester, he being accounted Parson of Stede." At that time there were only seventeen families within the parish [d] A catholic chapel, built in 1795, and alms-houses, together with a residence for the priest, adjoin the Stydd chapel. Dutton possesses a number of charities, amounting to £273. 19s. 9d., the interest of which is annually expended in cloth distributed to poor housekeepers. In 1819, the principal was invested in government securities. Dutton contained 446 inhabitants, in 1851. Its area is 1,898 statute acres. The property was assessed to the county rate, in 1854, at the annual value of £1,597.

Alston and Hothersall.—For a lengthened period, the Hothersalls remained lords of the manor. It afterwards passed to the Lettenbys, and from them to the Martins. Hothersall hall was in existence in 1617-18. The present manor house is a later erection. The thriving village of Longridge is situated partly in Alston and partly in Dilworth. The principal proprietors are the earl of Derby, Sir Henry Bold Hoghton, bart, Mr. Nelson, and Mr. Cross. The latter gentleman is lord of the manor The episcopal chapel at Longridge existed before the Reformation. It is marked upon Saxton's map, in 1577 According to the Parliamentary Inquisition, in 1650, Longridge had "neither minister nor maintenance," although the district contained one hundred and forty families, who humbly desired the government to appoint a minister, furnish a competent endowment, and constitute the district a separate parish. The advowson was purchased by the trustees of the Hulme charity, from Sir H. P Hoghton, bart. The chapel was re-built about 170 years ago, and again about 1783 The present edifice was erected by subscription in 1822-3 The square tower was added in 1841. A parsonage house has likewise been erected, and the living further augmented. A small catholic chapel was erected in Alston, in 1765. A new small, but very beautiful, edifice is at present nearly completed. It is intended to convert the old chapel into a school. There are a few charitable bequests to the poor of these townships. Hothersall-with-Alston is included in

d Par Inq Lamb. Libr.

Amounderness hundred in the county rate assessment of 1854. The property is taxed at the annual value of £886. The population, in 1851, amounted to one hundred and fifty-two persons. The area of the two townships is 1,038 acres.

DILWORTH.—The Cottams long resided in this township. A claim without date is preserved by Kuerden, from the men of Ribchester, Dilworth, and Dutton, to be free from fines, amercements, and tolls in all markets and fairs, and from suit and service in the county and wapentake.[e] In the 20th Edward III., the abbot of Cockersand assumed that, by a charter of King John, he was exempted from the payment of rates and taxes in several specified places. Dylleword is mentioned amongst the number. The township of Dilworth lies upon Longridge fell, and includes a portion of the village. There are two charitable bequests to the poor of Dilworth, of the annual value of £13. 19s. At Tootal height, immediately above Longridge village, there are now several quarries of excellent freestone. The cotton manufacture has been latterly introduced, and Longridge has begun to exhibit signs of rapid progress. The Preston water supply is principally drawn from the neighbourhood. The scenery is very beautiful, and the air pure and bracing; consequently Longridge, since the opening of the railway, is much visited by health and pleasure seekers. The population of Dilworth in 1851, was 833. The area is 1247 statute acres. The property was rated in 1854, at the annual value of £2664.

CHIPPING PARISH.

Chipping, as well as Ribchester, although at the present time in the hundred of Blackburn, is included in the deanery of Amounderness. Chipping was originally written Chepin, a common Danish term referring to a market. Chipping contains only two townships, Chipping, and Thornley-cum-Wheatley. The Status de Blagborneshire mentions Chepyn as one of the three parishes separated from Whalley, previously to the reign of Edward the Confessor. Richard de Chepyn was lord of the manor soon after the conquest. It passed to the Knolles, and afterwards to the Sherburnes, and the Welds. The earl of Derby is now lord of the manor of Chipping and Thornley. The church of Chyppyng is mentioned in the 25th year of the reign of Henry III. The present edifice dedicated to St. Bartholemew, was partly re-built in 1520, and re-seated in 1706. On the font there is an ancient inscription, which has never yet been satisfactorily interpreted. It is supposed by some to partake of the Runic character. Mr. Baines mentions "a brown earthenware coffin, half an inch thick, marked with lozenges, and containing bones perfectly white," found in a lane near the church, about the year 1770. It remained for

e A similar claim was preferred by the inhabitants of Chipping.

some time, but was afterwards destroyed. On the east side of the south aisle is a chapel, called Wolf-house Quyre, the property of the earl of Derby. It was originally a place of sepulture belonging to the Sherburne family. Wolf-house, formerly the residence of the proprietors of the manor, was re-built by the Sherburnes in 1601. It has since been taken down and a farm-house erected on the site. Leagrim hall, the seat of the Weld family, is pleasantly situated on a wooded slope, about half a mile from the village. The living of Chipping is a discharged vicarage, in the patronage of the bishop of Chester. It is valued in the Liber Regis at £36. 13s. 4d. In 1650, the parish was returned as an appropriation of the bishop of Chester, the tithes, then worth £85. 5s. per annum, were under sequestration. Mr. John Kinge, an able divine, had £10. a year paid formerly out of the reserved rent of the bishop, and £50. per annum from the committee of plundered ministers.[f] Chipping and Thornley possess several charities. Chipping free school was built by Mr. John Brabine, and endowed by him, in his will, dated 9th April, 1683. There is a catholic chapel at Chipping, erected in 1827, and two independent chapels, one built in 1807, and the other in 1816. An old residence of the Ashton family, called Hesketh end, built about 1501, has several curious inscriptions carved on the exterior, commemorating the landing of the Romans, Saxons, and Danes, the Norman conquest, and the protestant reformation. These inscriptions Mr. Whittle fancied were Roman, and that the house had been built of inscribed stones from Ribchester. Higher Core and Wood Yate are two old residences of the Parkinsons. Mr. Baines says, "most of the families resident in this parish, even amongst the labouring classes, have occupied their houses for centuries, content in their obscurity and undisturbed by competition." Patten hall, in Thornley, received its name from being the residence of the Misses Patten, who sold the house to the earl of Derby. Bradley hall was originally the residence of the Bradleys. They are mentioned as early as Edward I. The estate was purchased in 1666, by Charles, eighth earl of Derby. There are remains of several old crosses in Chipping parish. One may be seen at Wheatley Brook, another at the Town End, and a third in the churchyard. There is some cotton manufacture, as well as a little iron founding and machine making in the parish. A large quantity of excellent limestone is likewise yearly burned. The neighbourhood of Chipping, owing to its being situated at the foot of Parlick pike and the neighbouring fells, is occasionally liable to sudden inundations, from the overflowing of a mountain streamlet, called Chipping brook, which empties itself into the Loude, a tributary of the Hodder. About six years ago, the entire valley through

f Parl. Inq. Lamb. Libr. vol. 2.

which the brook wends its picturesque course, was swept by a torrent of such a magnitude, that damage to the amount of about £4000. resulted. The advent of the flood was not marked by heavy or continued rain A water spout, after passing over the Fylde district, struck against the side of the pike, and suddenly discharged an immense volume of water, which rushed from the hill side to the plain with frightful velocity; devastating the grounds, reservoirs, and buildings of two cotton spinning establishments, in the upper portion of the valley, and flooding a part of Chipping, and much of the land below. Many sheep and some cattle were drowned on the hill side, as well as in the plain. The growing crops were much injured, and several buildings and some bridges were either wholly or partly destroyed. Chipping, in 1851, contained 1,134 inhabitants, and Thornley-cum-Wheatley 491. The area of Chipping is 5,634 statute acres, that of Thornley-cum-Wheatley 3,220. The former township was rated, in 1854, at the annual value of £4,907., and the latter at £2,441.

STONYHURST COLLEGE.

The relaxation of the penal laws against the Roman catholics in England, together with the proscriptions of the French revolution, induced the principals of the English college at Liege, to found a seminary for the instruction of priests, etc., in their native country. The manorial residence, of the Sherburnes, in the parish of Mitton, was selected as the location, and in 1794, a long lease, on favourable terms, was obtained from Thomas Weld, esq., father of the distinguished cardinal of that name The present mansion at Stonyhurst, erected on the site of a still more ancient manorial residence, was commenced by Sir Richard Sherburne. The edifice was unfinished at the time of his death, in 1628. The handsome west front, a large portion of the quadrangular court, and one wing were, however, completed. Sir Nicholas Sherburne added the cupolas of the towers, and directed the laying out of the gardens and grounds. From the contract deed, preserved at Stonyhurst, it appears the expense of building the cupolas amounted to no more than £40. The loss of his only son, Richard Francis, who died at the age of nine years, in 1702, caused Sir Nicholas to abandon his design of completing the princely structure. His only daughter, married to Thomas, duke of Norfolk, died without issue. Elizabeth, sister to Sir Nicholas Sherburne, married William, son and heir of Sir John Weld, of Lulworth castle, in the county of Dorset. The mansion at Stonyhurst was in a very delapidated condition, when leased for educational purposes by the Jesuits It was not only substantially repaired, but considerably enlarged. In 1832, the first stone of the present handsome church was laid. It is in the Tudor style, or latter period of English architecture, and was built from designs by Mr. J. J. Scholes. It is dedicated to St. Peter. Shortly after the completion of the church, the observatory was erected. The north side of the quadrangle, which was previously only a temporary construction, has been taken down, and re-built, so as to accord with the architectural character of the rest of the edifice. These improvements, which have been effected at a cost of from £8,000. to £10,000., are now rapidly approaching completion. About two years ago, a neighbouring mansion, named Hodder Place, was converted into a kind of preparatory school, for the education of the junior pupils, previously to their entering the college. It is calculated to provide accommodation for about forty scholars. The number of students in the college itself averages about 160. The establishment is well calculated to promote its objects, being delightfully situated in a healthy neighbourhood, and furnished with every accommodation for study. There is a good library, an interesting museum, and a small but valuable collection of pictures. The library contains, amongst other choice and rare works, some beautifully illuminated manuscripts, the prayer book which formerly belonged to Elizabeth of York, queen of Henry VII., the office in honour of the blessed Virgin, used by the unfortunate Mary, of Scotland, mother of James I., together with several ancient missals on vellum, and a manuscript copy of St. John's gospel, of the seventh century, which was found in the tomb of St. Cuthbert, at Durham. Amongst the works of art are two sculptures in ivory, and a small picture of the Crucifixion, said to be the work of Michael Angelo; a fine picture of "Christ taken down from the cross," by one of the Caracci, and an altar piece, the "Immaculate Conception," by Murillo. The buildings, play ground, gardens, etc., occupy an area of about ten acres. The principal edifice is three hundred feet in length. The noble hall of the Sherburnes, sixty feet by thirty, is used as the refectory. Its architectural embellishments are of a very superior character. A magnificent gallery, used as a recreation hall by the preceptors, ninety feet by twenty, is a part of the older building. The hall of study is a large apartment, seventy-eight feet by twenty feet, fitted up with benches, etc., for upwards of two hundred scholars. The philosophical apparatus room, forty-eight feet by thirty-three feet, is embellished with an elaborate frieze. The dormitory, offices, etc., are upon a corresponding scale. Several of the pupils at Stonyhurst, finish their education at the London university. As the college is not an endowed foundation, the pupils' fees, furnish the chief if not the entire revenue of this extensive establishment.

PART III.—THE ENVIRONS.

CHAPTER IV. THE HUNDRED OF LEYLAND.

Penwortham Parish—Howick, Hutton, Farington, and Longton—Brindle Parish—Leyland Parish—Euxton, Cuerden, Whittle-le-woods, Clayton-le-woods, Heapy, Wheelton, Hoghton, Withnell—Rufford Parish—Much Hoole Parish—Little Hoole—Tarleton Parish—Croston Parish—Southport.

LEYLAND hundred is situated to the south of Amounderness, the river Ribble forming the boundary line between them. With the exception of Chorley, it contains no manufacturing town of importance. Although a large portion of its surface is composed of moss, or bog, the remainder is generally of a fertile character. A considerable quantity of the best land in the hundred, indeed, has been formed by the drainage of Martin mere, and the neighbouring swamps.

Originally Leyland hundred consisted of six parishes, viz. :—Leyland, Penwortham, Brindle, Croston, Eccleston, and Standish. Hoole, Tarleton, Rufford, Hesketh, and Chorley, which formerly belonged to Croston, have been formed into independent parishes. A similar sub-division of Leyland has taken place during the present year

According to the Domesday survey, king Edward the Confessor held Leyland. It was granted by the Conqueror to Roger de Poictou, but reverted again to the crown on the defection of that nobleman. In the reign of Richard I., the wapentake was held by the earl of Morton, afterwards king John. In the 13th Henry III , the king confirmed a grant of all lands between the Mersey and the Ribble, to William Ferrers, in right of his wife, daughter of Hu Keuelioc, earl of Chester. Dr. Kuerden describes these lands as "what William Peuerel formerly had, and forfeited in poysoning Randle, the grandfather to this earl, to whom K. Stephen as well as Henry the first's Empress had bestowed what was Roger Pictauensis or Will Peuerels, but never fully confirmed to the Earls of Chester, until this said 13 Hen. III." Kuerden further observes, the wapentake of Leyland "was parted as I conceiue between Agnes the wife of W. Ferars, and Hauis her sister, the wife of Robert Quincy, earl of Lincon, whose daughter Marg't. was maryed to John Lacy, Constable of Chester, and so he became half lord of the afforesaid Wapentak, which he shortly after granted to one Robt. de Heppawel and Margy his wife, who afterwards held the same in soccage by the service of one sparrow hawk." The moiety held by the Ferrers, passed by marriage to the Sherburnes, of Stonyhurst, in the 32nd year of the reign of Edward I. The other moiety returned to the Ferrers family on the marriage of William, son of William Ferrars, with the daughter of Robert Quincy. His elder brother Robert, last earl of Derby, being attainted, his lands were granted to Edmund, earl of Lancaster. W. Ferrars, however, "held the free wapentake of Leyland, of Lord Edm. brother to the king."[g] After this period the lands became more divided, W. Aghton, knt., W. Fleming, esq., the Grays of Groby, the Stanleys, earls of Derby, and the Rigbies, of Burgh and Layton, appear as holders. Kuerden says:—"I likewise find in the 9 Edward II., Rob. Holand acquired to himself & heirs of his body, from Thomas E., of Lancaster, the manor of Derby, with the wap. of Derby, Salford, *Leyland-shire*, & Black. to be held of our lord the king by homage & service of 40*sh.* & 1 Asturc. pro omnibus."

PENWORTHAM PARISH.

PENWORTHAM lies contiguous to Preston. The parish contains about 7,451 acres of land. Penwortham is mentioned in the Domesday survey as having "two carucates of land, which produced ten-pence." This document further states:—"There is now a castle there; and there are two carucates in the demesne, six burgesses, three radmans, eight villains, and four neatherds, between all they have four carucates; there is half a fishery, a wood, and aeries of hawks. As in the time of *king Edward*, it is valued at three pounds." Much controversy has arisen respecting the precise import of the phrase, "there is now a castle there." Some contend that it refers to a structure erected anterior to the Conquest, others to a defensive work constructed by Roger de Poictou. Whatever may have been the meaning of the compilers of the Domesday book, recent discoveries in the "Castle Hill," Penwortham, appear to indicate that the locality was originally used by the Romans as a *specula* or outlook, in connection with the station at Walton, and that it was afterwards fortified by their Anglo Saxon successors. This question will be found fully discussed and illustrated in a previous chapter of this work.[h] Warin Bussel, the first recorded lord of Penwortham, is supposed to have been a son of Roger de Busli, to whom Roger de Poictou had granted a moiety of Blackburn. Warin de Bussel married a lady from Evesham, in Worcestershire, and hence his benefactions to the abbey of that place. The following donations

g Kuerden. h See chap. 3, page 103.

by the Bussel family to the church at Evesham, are recorded in a memorandum entered in the chartulary of the convent, which is believed to be as old as the reign of Henry III :—

"Warin Bussel gave to the church of Evesham, the church of Penwortham, and the church of Leiland, the chapel of Meols, with their appendancies. The same Warin gave the town of Farington with its appurtenances, and Richard Bussel" (his son) "gave to the church of Evesham, six bovates of land in Longeton ;—the entire church of Leiland which returns two marks, and the chapel of Meols, which returns 3s. Albert" (brother of Richard) "gave two bovates in Leiland, and the assart of Blakesawe. Also the aforesaid Richard gave the fourth part of his fishery."

Six daughters of Warin Bussel, on their marriages, were portioned out of the lands of their father, which grants were confirmed by his son Richard.[i] Hugh Bussel, grandson of Warin, was dispossessed by John, earl of Morton. By a suit at law, Hugh was reinstated. On the accession of John to the throne, Hugh was constrained to pay a fee of twenty marks, for a confirmation of his title, and to acknowledge that he held it to the king by the service of three knights' fees.[k] The claim of Hugh Bussel was, however, eventually annulled on the non-payment of a fine, and the barony was transferred to Roger de Lascy, on the payment of the fine.[l] Hugh had agreed to pay four hundred marks for its renewal.[m] Robert Bussell released to Roger de Lascy the barony of Penwortham, in consideration of the payment of a fine of three hundred and ten marks.[n] He, however, still retained two bovates and two carucates of land in Longeton and Leyland, and two carucates in Eukeston.[o] Mr. W. A. Hulton, says, "He still, however, retained some interest in Penwortham, notwithstanding his cession to Roger de Lascy, for he subsequently conferred on the monastery of Evesham, a rent of twelve pence out of his fishery in the Ribble, at Penwortham He also granted to the priory of Penwortham, a small plot of land in Longton, to build a grange." Mr. Hulton is of opinion that there can be no doubt that the lands referred to, descended to the Faringtons, of Werden. He quotes the *Tenant duc. Lanc*, taken anno 1311, where the grant is referred to.[p] Roger de Lacy, constable of Chester, granted to the Penwortham priory, nine bovates of land, situated

i "A daughter (possibly Sibil) married Hamo Pincerna and had two carucates of land in Hocton and Echilston. The present possessors of Hoghton Tower descend lineally from this marriage." —W. Adam Hulton. "Documents relating to the Priory of Penwortham," etc., published by the Chetham Society

k Dugdale's Baronage, vol. 1, page 593.

l Mag Rot 4, John Rot 12 a Lanc

m Rot. Claus 7, John m 6.

n Coucher Book in the Duchy office.

o "Rogerus de Lascy dedit Roberto Bussell ij bovat. et ij caruc terre in Longeton et in Leyland, et servic ij. caruc. in Eukeston faciendo servic decime partis unius militis."—Testa de Nevill.'

p "Rogerus Lacy dedit Roberto Bushell ij. bovat. terre in Longton in Leylond et servic. ij caruc. terre in Ewkeston fac' decime partis unius feodi militis. Henricus dux Lanc. Willus ffarington et Wills de Holand de dicto duce decem partes unius feodi militis in Leylonde et Ewkeston qu. Robertus Bushell guondam tenuit de feodo " in the township of Leyland. The *Coucher Book,* in the Duchy office, records that Ranulph de Blundeville, earl of Chester, and baron of Lancaster, after his claim to the lands between the Ribble and the Mersey had been confirmed by Henry III., held his court at Penwortham castle.[q] The barony passed by marriage to Thomas, earl of Lancaster, and merged into the duchy possessions. The preceding grants to the abbey were confirmed by Thomas, surnamed the "good duke of Lancaster." He likewise granted to the monks of the priory, part of the waste land between Martynns, Bothomy, and Brandelegh, called Whadycthegreues, to be enclosed for their own use.[r] But little information has been preserved respecting the priory of Penwortham. Warrin Bussel's grant to Evesham stipulated that three monks and a chaplain should be provided from the monastery at Evesham, for the performance of divine offices at Penwortham. The chaplain eventually became titular prior. The priory at Penwortham appears to have been dependent upon, or "obedientary" to, the parent establishment at Evesham. The priors were removable at the will of the abbot. They held no property of their own. They were not instituted by the bishop of the diocese; but were regarded as temporal holders on behalf of the abbot of Evesham. They had no seal especially their own, but used that of the superior convent, as agents or factors. Penwortham appears to have been regarded with peculiar dislike by the monks, probably on account of its poverty and dependence. To be removed from Evesham to the Lancashire cell, was looked upon in the light of a punishment. Roger Norreis, formerly a monk at Canterbury, was imprisoned for criminal acts, but contrived to escape by a sewer. He for some time lived a private life. He was afterwards made abbot of Evesham by royal authority, without election by any college, and contrary to the wish of the convent of that church. He is described as pompous, apparently of great literary attainments, eloquent, and possessing great powers of speech. But he was a drunkard, a glutton, and criminal in many other matters. He cruelly oppressed the monks, and so diminished their food and clothing, that for some days they lived on bread and water, and on others on "hard bread, and on beer, differing little from water, without any pittance." Many of the monks, too, "for want of frocks, hoods, and breeches," could neither attend the choir, nor chapter, nor perform divine service.[s] Roger Norreis appeared determined to prevent any one enjoying the benefice after his

q See chapter 2, page 111. This circumstance demonstrates either that the castle remained in existence a little longer than the author had previously supposed, or that some building, on or near the site, retained the title after the defences were destroyed.

r Cotton MSS. Nero D. fo. 246.

s Evesham Ch. fo. 167. See Documents relating to priory of Penwortham, edited by William Adam Hulton, esq., and published by the Chetham society.

demise. It is said that during seven years, he pulled down fixtures, burthened the church with debt to the amount of a thousand marks, and so delapidated the convent, that some of the inmates were not properly sheltered from the rain, and were entirely worn out with hunger. Many complaints were made against him, but he for a long period, contrived to baffle the efforts of the monks to get rid of him. At length, on the visit of Nicholas, bishop of Tusculum, a legate of the Roman see, Norreis was accused, and, by his own confession and the testimony of his brethren, convicted of seven or eight crimes. "And so," says the Evesham record, "to the joy of all the convent, in the year of our Lord M° CC° XIIJ, Abbot Roger was deposed and made ex-abbot, whom may God for ever destroy!" The legate, however, five days afterwards, gave Norreis the priory of Penwortham, in order that he might subsist. His continued excesses caused him, in five months, to be deprived of this humble benefice. He afterwards rambled abroad for some time. About five years after his exclusion from Evesham, Pandulphus, the then legate, "out of pity, and to prevent him from being a wanderer all the days of his life, restored him to the priory of Penwortham." He remained six years, plundered the monastery of some rents, and "never expressed a wish to be reconciled to the abbot and convent." He died, "oppressed with wretchedness, and was buried at Penwortham."[t] The following memorandum reveals something of the nature of the tribute demanded by the parent establishment from its dependent:—

"The convent of Evesham shall have from the Priorship of Penwortham yearly at the feast of St. Egwin, sixty salmon, namely samlets, or twenty-four larger fish which make up that weight. Besides these, the said Prior shall present two larger salmon to the Abbot, and one to the Prior" [of Evesham]. "The Prior shall, nevertheless, be allotted one out of that quantity. But Ralph Wylicote, the Prior of Penwortham, in his time assigned a whole salmon to each of the monks. But lately that custom was commuted into a certain sum of money, which the convent received towards the expences of blood letting." [u]

Another memorandum records how some portion of the revenue was disposed of. The fondness of the worthy fraternity for *good* salmon doubtless resulted from the numerous fast-days, necessitating the consumption of a large quantity of fish:—

"To the celebration of the anniversary of Walter de Walecote, Prior, are assigned all the rents which he acquired at Evesham and Penwortham, that the almoner for the time being may find for the convent, at that anniversary, the best pittance of salmon or some other fish of the best kind that can be procured, together with an allowance of the best wine; and the residue shall, at the almoner's discretion, be faithfully distributed amongst the poor." [v]

t Mr. W A Hulton observes, "It is curious how nearly the transmission of Roger Norreis to Penwortham synchronizes with the appearance in Lancashire of Hugo Norreis, the founder of the ancient family at Speke. Roger was an exile at Penworthan, A.D. 1213, and on the 16th October, 1199, King John confirmed to Hugh Norreis a carucate of land in Blackrod. And both were recipients of royal favour"—Doc. Pri. Pen. page xxxiv.

u Evesh. Ch. fol. 167. v Ibid.

The travelling expences allowed to the prior, when duty required his presence at Evesham, are recorded with great minuteness:—

"Memorandum, that the hostiler for the time being is bound to find the Prior of Penwortham, on his departure from the Abbey to Penwortham, and on his return from Penwortham to the Abbey, hay and provender for his horse, and for the horse which carries his bed, if he travel with a bed, and for the horse of his companion and his squire, if he travel with a companion or squire; and if he travel with more horses or squires, yet the hostiler ought not to find provender except for the horse of one squire and for the horses above mentioned. And then he must furnish hay and provender for two nights on their journey to Penwortham. On their return he must supply provender for three nights if required. So if his companion should come alone, or with a single attendant, the hostiler must furnish provender for three nights on his arrival, and for two at his departure. Nor ought he to find more hay, provender, or beds, except by special favour. Neither ought he to find in any wise provender for the Prior's horses which bring the salmon, nor hay nor beds for the servants, except by especial favour."[w]

At the dissolution of the monasteries, the priory, which was dedicated to the Virgin Mary,[x] was rated (26th Henry VIII.), according to Dugdale, in one place, at £29. 18s. 7d., and in another, at £99. 5s. 3d. Speed gives the amount at £114. 16s. 9d.[y] The abbot and convent of Evesham, by indenture, dated February 20th, 30 Henry VIII., leased to John Fleetwood, of Little Plumpton, their estates in Penwortham and Leyland. The property and conditions are specified as follows:—

"All that ther manor and Lordship of Penwortham within the Countye of Lancastre with ther appurtenaunce and all lands, tenements, howses, barnes, stables, buyldings, meadows, mores, courtletes, and the profitts of the same, waiffs, fyshynges, comon of turbarie, with all the appurtenaunce, in the countie of Lancastre. And all other lands and heredytaments possessions of the said convente, *as well spirituall as temporall* what soever they bee to the said monastre in any wyse belonging. * * All that ther parsonage of Penwortham aforesaid, and also the parsonage of Leylonde in the Countie of Lancastre aforesaid, and all manner of tithes, porcons, and pensions, and all Glebelonds, houses and barns, with all ther appurtenaunces. * * Except and always reserved to the said Abbott and Convente, and all ther successuors, the advowson of the vicarage of the said church of Laylond; and also the advowson of the parsonage of Meles, * * for the term of four score and nineteen yeres. * * Yelding and paying therfor yerly and euery yere * * foure score nynetene pounds fyue shillings and threpence."[z]

By letters patent, dated 24th Jan., 34 Henry VIII., the king granted the priory and lands in Penwortham to John Fleetwood, "he Renderinge to the said kinge the yearly rent of ix^{s} ix^{d}." Lands in Staffordshire were likewise granted to John Fleetwood. The grant was confirmed by letters patent, dated 6th July, 6th Elizabeth. This document states that the "temporalities of the said priory are holden of the Queen in capite by the seruice of the xith p'te of a knight's fee." The following document gives some additional details respecting the Penwortham property:—

---

w Evesh. Ch.

x Beneath the brow, to the left of the present highway from Preston to Liverpool, nearly opposite to the lodge gates, is a spring, called St. Mary's well, believed by many yet to possess great healing properties.

y Notitia Monastica.

z Penwortham Documents.

"Parcel of the Poss. of the late Monastry, in Evesham, in com. Worcester.

"Cell of Penwortham } The tythes .... ix^{s} ix^{d}
rated 13 August, for John Fleetwood, at 20 years purchase, viij August .... xxi^{s} iij^{d}

"The clere yerely value of the landes aforesaid, xi^{s} vi^{d} wch rated at xxviij yeres purchase amounteth to xvj^{l} ij^{s} the clere yerely value of the tenthe aforesaid ix^{s} ix^{d} wch rated at xx^{tie} yeres purchase amountythe to ix^{l} xv^{s} And so Thole amountythe to . .. . } xxv^{l} xvij^{s}

"The money to be p^{d} in hand before the xxvijth Auguste next."[a]

The priory became the residence of the Fleetwood family.[b] It was sold to John Aspinall, esq , of Standon hall, near Clitheroe, who again disposed of it to James Barton, esq., of Ormskirk. The advowson of the church and other property was purchased from the latter gentleman, about the year 1783, by Lawrence Rawstorne, esq , of Hutton and Preston, in which family it still remains. The late Lawrence Rawstorne, esq., son of the purchaser, re-built the mansion, on the site of the priory, in 1832. This family is descended from Captain Edward Rosthorne, one of the defenders of Latham house, in the time of Charles I. The son of Lawrence Rawstorne, esq , the heir to the estate, is a minor. The mansion is at present leased by Mr. Hollins, of Preston. The old building, which was a wooden structure, remained almost entire until the middle of the last century, when the chapel, which formed one side of the square, was taken down and re-built The three other sides still remained. Mr. Baines gives the following description of the edifice:—

"The transformation of a monastery into a mansion, necessarily gave rise to much alteration, but a gallery cloister of fine oak work, with narrow wooden windows, and carved principals and springers of oak, on the south side of the building, served as well to display the little ornament that belonged to these cells, as to convey an idea of their gloomy recesses. A number of portraits of the Fleetwoods and the Rawstornes ornamented the interior of this monastic mansion, the whole appearance of which, with its moated enclosure, carried the mind back to other times, and presented abundant materials for conjecture and contemplation. Within living memory there were many arches and fallen ruins remaining, the bridge over the old moat, at Penwortham old hall, led to the priory, which in 1783 is described as an old brown edifice with dark slates upon it."

A tradition still lingers in the neighbourhood that a subterranean passage beneath the Ribble formerly existed, by means of which the monks of Penwortham held uninterrupted communication with their brethren at Tulketh! The remains of an arched vault in the garden, to the north of the present building, for some time appeared to countenance the absurdity.[c]

---

a Harl. MSS Cod. 607, fol 101b.

b "After the Dissolution, this Cell, and its Chapel, within a Moat, and the Tithes and Lands belonging to it and to Leyland, were sold by Queen Elizabeth to John Fleetwood, of Little Plumpton, Esq, for £3,088, and the Monastery was converted into a dwelling-house by the purchaser."—*MS pen Rev* John Piccope, quoted by the Rev. Canon Raines, in Not. Ces., p. 387. —The letters patent are dated 14th December, 42nd Elizabeth. The estates by this document were not, however, conveyed to John Fleetwood, but to his second son, Richard.

c See page 508.

John Fleetwood, in 1627, married Ann, daughter of W. Farington, esq., of Worden. William Farington, of Leyland, who died about the year 1672, married a daughter of Edward Fleetwood. His representative, the late J. Nowell Farington, was lord of the manor. A court is annually held at Penwortham, at Michaelmas. It is not known with certainty when the original church was erected. It is first mentioned in 1291. It appears to have been claimed and allowed as early as 1343, that the abbot and convent of Evesham, had, from time immemorial, held it, with all its rights and property, by canonical title; that all episcopal dues and other burthens, which would have been charged on perpetual vicars, were paid by them. The monks of the monastery, or other merely temporal vicars, who were appointed and removed at the will of the abbot, without institution or presentation to the bishop, had the cure of the church as well in spirituals as temporals. On the transfer of the property to the Fleetwoods, the living became a free gift of the patron, the institution of whose nominee by the bishop was unnecessary.[d] In the year 1650, Penwortham was described as a parish, the tithes of which, valued at £174. were claimed as the inheritance of "Mr. John Fleetwood of Penwortham Esq." His demesne land, if titheable, would have produced £3. a year; but no tithes had been paid within the "memory of man." The pastor, a Mr. William Seddon, had been "put in by the said Mr. Fleetwood, together with the consent of the rest of the Parish of Penwortham, and his stipend-wages is £60. a year which he receives from Mr. Fleetwood."[e] John Fleetwood, in his will, dated 20th March, 1651, enjoins his heir to see that the parish church should at all times be provided with a "good, able and sufficient preacher," who should be "endowed with lerninge and understandinge, and of a good life and conversacon fittinge for his place and callinge." He was further instructed to allow the said preacher, the sum of "forty pounds by the yeare att least in ready money."[f] The stipend was augmented by a grant from the dispensers of "Queen Anne's Bounty," in the early part of the present century. It is now freed from the "burthen of lay authority," and is subjected to jurisdiction similar to other episcopal establishments. The church is dedicated to St. Mary. The registers commence in 1586. They have been for some time, however,

d Evesh. Ch. fo. 178, published by Chetham society. e Parl. Inq. Lamb. Libr. vol. 2.

f "The terms of this legacy show clearly how miserably dependant the then curate of Penwortham was upon the patron of the living. Mr. Fleetwood, indeed, appears to have had high notions of his power as patron. He interfered to prevent a Mr. Richardson from preaching at Penwortham. In return, Mr. Richardson, who describes himself as going about from church to church to spread the Word of God, revenged himself by penning a rabid attack against Mr. Fleetwood and patrons in general. His verses are curious and afford a strong confirmation of Mr. Macaulay's statement of the manner in which the country clergy were treated." W. Adam Hulton: "Documents relating to the priory of Penwortham," etc. Mr. Hulton prints this curious Latin poem.

very imperfect in several places. A few months ago, they were further injured by an accidental fire. The value of the living in 1834, was £106. The oldest portion of the present church is believed to have been built in the fifteenth century. A new gallery was erected, and the upper portion of the body of the church was refronted in 1812. About two years ago, the nave, which was in a very dilapidated condition, was taken down and re-built, and an organ added. The chancel, with its fine old roof, long covered with plaster, was restored. The arch in the old tower was opened, and the west window exposed to view from the interior of the church. The work was executed from designs by Mr. Paley, of Lancaster. The church-yard was likewise considerably enlarged, on the south side. There are a few tablets to the memory chiefly of members of the Fleetwood family. A window still retains a piece of ancient stained glass, on which is depicted the armorial bearings of the Fleetwoods and the Leighs, with the following inscription: "Richard Fleetwood and Margery his wife, 1595." Margery was the daughter of Thomas Leigh, esq., of Egginton, in Derbyshire. John Horrocks, esq., the enterprising cotton spinner, who represented Preston in parliament, for about two years previously to his death, lies buried beneath an altar tomb, on the east side of the church-yard. In the parish of Penwortham there yet exist fragments of ancient crosses. One is near Penwortham hall, and another in Howick. A third, on the road leading to the church, was removed to its present site from a lane in the neighbourhood. About forty years ago, a piece of boulder pavement was discovered near Penwortham hall.[f] It was four feet in breadth, and was traced about one hundred yards. Mr. Baines says:—"The road surveyor, feeling no sympathy with the antiquary, destroyed the road, and used the materials to repair the public highways! conceiving that, probably, to be the *shortest* way of solving the disputes which had arisen, whether this was a Roman, a Saxon, or a Norman causeway." There can be little doubt, however, that the road was a Roman vicinal way, communicating from the station at Walton with the *specula* at Penwortham. In June, 1836, a very valuable gold coin of Ferdinand and Isabella, was found at the site of the old priory. It is upwards of two inches in diameter, and weighs two ounces and five drachms. On the obverse is the following inscription:— "Fernandus et Elizabet. D. G. Reg. et." The reverse presents armorial bearings and the motto: "Sub. umbra, alarum, tuarum, pro."[g] It was coined towards the close of the fifteenth century. The only ancient residence of note besides the time-honored seat of the Fleetwoods and the Rawstornes, in the township of Penwortham, was at Middleford or

f Mr. Marshall's residence was formerly named Penwortham lodge. The priory is described by several writers as Penwortham hall.

g Whittle's His. Preston, vol. 2, page 167.

Penwortham Church, near Preston.
Rev.d R. A. Rawstorne, Incumbent.

Penwortham Priory, near Preston.

Middleforth, an edifice belonging to the Norris family, which was built in the reign of Henry VIII. A modern mansion, erected on the site, was lately purchased from the executors of the late J Holland, esq, by Mr. Thomas Pearson, of Preston Penwortham possesses several modern mansions, of some pretensions, including Hurst grange,—W. A Hulton, esq.; the Oaks,—Jno. Cooper, esq; Penwortham hall,—W. Marshall, esq.; Penwortham house,—Joseph Pyke, esq; Woodfield,—Joseph Walker, esq., etc. The land to the south of the valley of the Ribble, at Penwortham, has been mapped out, with the view to the erection of villa residences. A free grammar school was founded in the sixth year of the reign of Edward VII., by Christopher Walton, of Little Hoole, who executed an indenture of feoffment, by which he endowed it with lands, then of the yearly value of £2. 13s. 6d. It was further endowed by his son and heir, John Walton, who granted to the trustees, lands and tenements in Kirkham, Killarmergh, and Preston, and in Longton and Hutton, then of the yearly value of forty shillings, for the foundation and maintenance of a school, where young children should be taught the "Absay" (A.B.C.) "catechism, primer, accidence, pervely," and others in grammar, without school hire, except cockpence, to be paid twice a year. The scholars were taught for many years at Longton, first in the chapel, and afterwards in a small cottage. In 1746, the present school at Hutton was erected. In 1825, another school was opened in Cop-lane, Penwortham, and in 1830, a new school house was erected. The trustees have likewise endowed the free-schools in Farington, Longton, and Howick, and by this means have thrown them open to the whole parish. They purpose, also, to immediately open as a school, a small building at the westerly extremity of the village of Longton, formerly used as a residence by one of the teachers The whole of the schools furnish employment for six masters and three mistresses. In consequence of the increased value of some of the property, the annual rental, in 1819, was £635. 15s. 1d.[h] The rental of the trust estates for the year ending December, 1854, was £935. 7s. 7d. There are some charities, by the Fleetwoods and others, producing about £18. per annum, for the poor of Penwortham, Middleforth, and Howick, and for the apprenticeing of Penwortham children The only dissenting chapel in Penwortham township is a small building near Middleforth green, belonging to the Wesleyans. It was enlarged in 1833. The property in the township was rated, in 1854, at the annual value of £7,528. Its population in 1851, amounted to 1,487. Its area, according to the ordnance survey, is 2,230 acres. The white building, now disused, though locally

h Charity Commis Report, XV. p 194.

known as "Penwortham factory," is, nevertheless, in the township of Walton.

HOWICK.—This township was one of the original grants to the abbey of Evesham. Simon Hoghwike, in the 16th Edward II., held messuages and land in Hoghwike, Farington, and Pedwortham, in trust for the abbey of Evesham. Thomas Hesketh, of Rufford, appears to have held the manor in the 15th Henry VIII., and John Flettwood, in the 33rd Elizabeth. In the 21st James I., Robert Hesketh appears as lord of the manor.[1] Much of the land is now freehold. A large portion belongs to the Rawstorne family. The old hall has been converted into a farm-house. Howick House was built by the late W. Rawstorne, esq., and afterwards transferred to the late Thomas Norris, esq., of Redvales, near Bury. It is at present the property and the residence of his nephew, Thomas Norris, esq. Howick is only a small township, its area being 574 acres. The property was rated, in 1854, at the annual value of £1,034. The population, in 1851, was 116.

HUTTON.—Helias, the son of Roger de Hotun, at a very early period, granted to the abbey at Cockersand three carucates of land in Hotton, in Leylandshire. A large portion of the abbey lands was sold to John Ketching, esq., by Henry VIII. Hutton Hall, the residence of the Rev. R. A. Rawstorne, was erected in the seventeenth century. Hutton contains 2124 statute acres. The population, in 1851, numbered 500. The annual rateable value of the property in 1854, was £3,473.

FARINGTON.—William de Farington held in trust, for the abbot and convent of Evesham, one messuage, eight acres of land, and 14s. rent, in Farington and Leyland, in the 10th Edward III. The town of Farington had been granted to Evesham by the charter of Warin Bussel. The manor was held by John Fleetwood, in the 33rd Elizabeth. A considerable portion of the township now belongs to the Faringtons of Leyland. Farington Hall is mentioned in the year 1500. An episcopal church was erected in 1839. It is dedicated to St. Paul. It is calculated to accommodate about 500 persons. The living is worth about £130. per annum. There is a small endowment by Mr. Peter Dawson, of London, but the income is derived chiefly from the rents of the pews, and a grant of £80. per annum by the ecclesiastical commissioners. Cotton spinning was introduced a few years ago by Messrs. Bashall and Boardman, in consequence of which an entirely new village, of considerable extent, has sprung up, a little to the north of the Leyland railway station. Public schools have likewise been erected. The average attendance of scholars exceeds 230. Farington, in conjunction with Leyland, promises to become, in a

1 Duchy Records, vol. v., Inquis. m 16.

few years, a very populous locality. Two large and substantial modern mansions have been erected, by the proprietors of the cotton mill. The township contains 1,860 statute acres. Its population, in 1851, amounted to 1,932. Its property was rated, in 1854, at the annual value of £7,923.

LONGTON.—Roger de Lacy granted the manor of Longton to Robert, brother to Hugh Bussel, the last baron of that name. Richard, the second baron, had previously granted two bovates of land in Longton, to the abbey of Evesham. Robert, son of Richard, son of Sibilla de Longton, granted lands in Longton, to the church of Penwortham, a portion of which were afterwards given by an achronal charter to Richard, Bambel.[k] Geoffery Bussel, of Leyland, quit claimed, by a similar deed, to John de Farington, son of William de Mel, the homages and services of certain of his free tenants in the town of Longeton, with the reliefs, wardships, and other honours belonging to the demesne, viz, the homage and service of Alice, wife of Robert Bussel, and the homage and service of Roger, son of Thomas Bussel, which consisted in the presentation, in each case, of a pair of white gloves.[l] By a deed without date, Thomas Bushell granted to Henry de Longton, a portion of his land, to be held by fealty and one penny yearly rent. There is a charter in the Duchy office, of the 17th Edward II., confirming a previous grant of three acres of land in the field of Turmireacres, and the field of Reskelde, in the town of Longton, by Robert Bussel, to the priory of Burscough A family of the name of Howick, held lands in Longton, at an early period A quarter of the manor was held by Sir William del Lee, in the 46th Edward III. It passed to the Flemings, of Leyland. The whole lordship of Longton was granted to Henry, son of Ralph de Brethirton, by Sir Thomas Fleminge, in the 9th Henry IV. In the 6th Edward IV., a fourth part of the manor was transferred to Willo Fleminge, to hold the same of the chief lord or lords of the fee. Elizabeth Fleming married Thurstan Hall. "The five Lords of the Manor" were, in 1833, represented by Robert Moss, esq. On the 13th of April, in the present year, "at the Court Baron of Sir Thomas Hesketh, Baronet, Joseph Weld, Esquire, John Randolphus de Trafford, Esquire, and Robert Moss, Esquire, Lords of the said Manor," orders were made upon a number of parties, to cleanse and otherwise improve divers watercourses, under various specified penalties. The privileges of the lords are, however, relatively very limited. Canon Raines, indeed, says,—"The Manor appears to have been factitious, and no Manerial privileges are now exercised."[m] The episcopal chapel was in existence in 1517. By a will, dated January 7th, 1527-8, William Walton, priest, bequeathed "to the chapell of Longeton, a Masse boke, a

k Harl. MSS. Cod. 1242, fo. 310. l Ibid. fo. 309 b. m Notes to Notitia Cestriensis, page 338.

chalyce, and all other ornaments belongyng and p'tenyng to the celebracon of masse." Walton further adds :—

"Also, I geve in my life, and bequethe in this my last will, to Robert Farington, sone of Rich[d] Farington, ye chauntre which I of late haue purchased, founded, and putt in feoffame't to certen feoffes. * * The which chauntrie is founded for the chapelle of longeton, w[t] all mess. tenements, burgages, landis, and other th' app'ten'nce y[r] unto belongyng, * * p'o'ided alwayes that whyles the said Rob't doith want lafull age to be p'st (that is to wete vj years,) then I will y[t] Sir John Walton,[n] occupye and solempnize dyvine s'vice at the forsaid chapelle of longeton. But I will y[t] he receyve his wages yerely duryng the said vj years, of, and by the hands off Rich[d] Farington aforesaid."[o]

The testator further directed that the said chantry should be presented to one of his own "blode and kin," and of his "name, (if ther be any,) ov' so descendyng lynally, fro' tyme to tyme." In 1650, although without incumbent or endowment, the chapelry was considered to be eligible to be made parochial. The tithes were valued at £80. per year; but they were claimed by the Fleetwoods, of Penwortham. The chapel was re-built in 1770, and a cemetery added in 1816. The patron saint is unknown. The living was valued in 1834, at £148. The advowson belongs to the Rawstorne family. A methodist chapel was erected in 1807, and enlarged in 1833. The primitive methodist chapel was built in 1837. The population of Longton, in 1851, amounted to 1,687. The area of the township, according to the ordnance survey, is 3,153 acres. It was assessed to the county rate, in 1854, at the yearly value of £5,418.

PARISH OF BRINDLE.

Brindle lies to the south of Walton. On every other side it is bounded by the parish of Leyland. It appears from the Valor of Pope Nicholas, (1291) that no church existed at that period. Dr. Kuerden conjectured that Brindle had originally been a township under Leyland. It was formed into an independent parish anterior to the Reformation. In Henry VIII.'s reign it is entered in the king's books as "Brindle Rectory—£12. 8s. 4d.—£1. 4s. 10d." Possibly it may have previously formed a part of the parish of Blackburn. It is not improbable that the terms Burnhul, Bamberg and Brownedge may have had a common origin. Brindle is variously written Burnhul, or Burnel, in early documents. In the reign of Edward II., its designation is Burnehill. It has become gradually further changed from Brinhill, Brandhill, and Brandle, to Brindle. In the Testa de Nevill', Thomas de Burnul is described as holding three carucates and a

n The term "Sir" is often applied to the clergy in old documents. Shakspere calls the curate "Sir Topas," in the "Twelfth Night." Sir Hugh Evans, the Welch curate, in the "Merry Wives of Windsor," is one of the most characteristic portraits of the great dramatist. In the Iter Lancastrense is the following couplet :

"To cherish learned curates though Sir Jhon
Doe preach for foure pounds vnto Haselingdon."

See page 148, of the present volume.

o Lanc. MSS.

half of land, of "our lord the king in thanage for 35s. and the service of finding one judger." The superior lord was Grelly, baron of Manchester. In the 22nd Edward I., owing to the death of Peter de Burnhulle, the manor was held in wardship, out of which some litigation arose. In the 26th Edward III., it was transferred to William Gerard, esq., by marriage with Joan, daughter and heiress of Peter de Bryn, of Brynhill. Sir Thomas Gerard was created a baronet in the 9th James I. The manor passed, by exchange, in the middle of the eighteenth century, to the Cavendish family. The earl of Burlington is the present lord of the manor: Dr. Kuerden says:—

"Brindle hath a parish church in the midst of the lordship, and adjacent to it a parsonage house, part whereof lately re-edified with a fayr stone building, erected by the worthy and learned parson, Mr. Henry Pygot, likewise Chappelain to the Right Honourable E. of Derby, and Vicar of Ratchdale, [p] a doubly qualified Peter both for souls and fishes, and a complacent associate to the gentry and all learned persons."

The parish church, a small structure, dedicated to St. James, has an elevated site. The date of the original edifice is not known. It is thought that the tower is a part of the ancient building. In 1815, the body of the church was entirely re-built in the "gothic style," at an expense of £1650. The old church had indented semi-circular windows. The chancel had been re-built at some previous period. On the oaken free seats, in the choir, are the dates 1582, and 1634. A large stone coffin lies beneath the eastern gable of the chancel. Nothing further is known of it. In the wall above, however, is a small figure, resembling, somewhat, the impression of a human foot, concerning which, the local antiquaries affect no such ignorance. It is said, by tradition, to have been produced by the heel of a papist's shoe, who, waxing warm in controversy, declared that if some asseverations advanced by him were not true, he wished his foot might sink into the stone; upon which "the reforming stone instantly softened and buried the papistical foot!" The Rev. Canon Raines thinks it not improbable that there were two chantries to the church; as, in the year 1535, sir John Hampton and sir Owen Gerard were priests, and sir Thomas Buckley was rector of Bryndhull. [q] In the inquisition of 1650, the parish of Brindle is described as having a parsonage house, and some other buildings; four acres of glebe, and five cottages, of the yearly rent of 6s. 8d. The tithes were valued at £75. per annum. The value of the living, in 1834, was £515. The duke of Devonshire still retains the patronage. The grammar school, according to bishop Gastrell, was "built by ye towne upon ye Glebe," and, in his day, was "free to ye children of all legall Inhabitants, who were born in ye Parish." One hundred pounds

p "Henry Pygot, B.D., inducted vicar of Rochdale 1662, died April 10, 1722, aged 94. He was rector of Brindle seventy one years, and vicar of Rochdale fifty nine years and seven months." E. Baines.

q Lanc. MSS., vol. IX., p. 46.

were given as an endowment, in 1623, by Mr. Peter Burscough, of Walton. This was subsequently increased, by several small donations, to the sum of £177. 12s., before the date of Bishop's MS. In 1772, the sum amounted to £247. 12s. 6d. According to the commissioners' report, in 1819, the amount had reached £336. 8s. 7½d.; yet, they say: "Though called a free grammar school, it seems never to have borne that character." There are two or three other charities belonging to the parish. The ordnance map shows the sites of the remains of a large number of stone crosses, in Brindle parish. There is a very commodious and handsome catholic chapel, near to Brindle lodge. It was erected in 1780. A school, in connection, was built in 1831, by the late Mr. James Knight, of Chelsea, "for the benefit of the Brindle congregation, and as a token of respect for his native place." A room for service was opened by the methodists, in 1828. Brindle workhouse is said to have been originally erected for a catholic chapel. It was for some time used as a lunatic asylum. In 1816, however, inmates of this class were transferred to Lancaster. There are in the parish a chemical works, a tannery, and a tile manufactory; together with some hand-loom weaving, but no cotton manufactories. There are excellent quarries for millstones and ashlars. Many attempts have been made to discover coal; but they have hitherto proved unsuccessful, notwithstanding the statement of Kuerden, who says, it is "beleeued Brindle hath many mines of cole and channel which in some measure appears in the surface of some bancs and at the side of Lostoc water." There are many springs in the parish On the ordnance map several "wells" are marked. Kuerden records the following particulars respecting the famous St. Helen's well, situated about a mile and a half south-west of the village of Brindle :—

"Over against Swansey House, a little towards the hill, standeth an ancient fabrick, once the manor house of Brindle, where hath been a chappel belonging to the same, and a little above it, a spring of very clear water, rushing straight upward into the midst of a fayry fountain, walled square about in stone and flagged in the bottom, very transparent to be seen, and a strong stream issuing out of the same. This fountain is called Saint Ellen's Well, to which place the vulgar neighbouring people of the Red letter do much resort, with pretended devotion, on each year upon St. Ellen's day, where and when out of a foolish ceremony they offer or throw into the well pins which there being left may be seen a long time after by any visitor of that fountain."

Kuerden mentions two other old residences. He says, "In the way from Brindle church to Clayton Green, nere the brook cald Rodburn, standeth a fayr stone building, the inheritance of Mr. Thomas Walmsley." [r] And again, "In the road from Brindle to Chorle standeth a fair new built house with al appurtenances, belonging to my lady Slater, called the Hall of Deanholme, erected not long since by that worthy Knight, sir Henry Slater, deceased." This edifice, now the property of the earl of Burlington,

r A descendant of the Walmsleys, of Shoigher.

has been converted into a farm-house. It is sometimes called the manor house; but this is merely a modern appellation, the ancient manor house being situated near St. Helen's well, as recorded above by Kuerden. The area of the township and parish of Brindle is 3,103 acres; the population, in 1851, was 1,310; and the annual rateable value of the property, in 1854, was £5,503.

PARISH OF LEYLAND.

The Domesday survey states that king Edward the confessor held Leyland. He had "one hide and two carucates of land, a wood two miles long and one broad, and an aerie of hawks." The same document further records certain privileges enjoyed by the inhabitants of this district:—"The men of this manor and of *Salford* did not work as was customary for the king at the hall, nor did they reap in August; they only made one hedge in the wood; they were subject to fines for wounding and rape, and had all the other customs of the other superior manors. The whole manor of *Leyland*, with the hundred, rendered to the king nineteen pounds eighteen shillings and two pence." Other lands belonging to this manor are described as "twelve carucates of land, which twelve freemen held as twelve manors; in these are six hides and eight carucates; there are woods six miles long, and three and a quarenten broad." Other holders are described as follows:—"Of the land in this manor, *Girard* holds one hide and a half, *Robert* three carucates, *Randulph* two carucates, *Roger* two carucates, *Walter* one carucate. There are four radmans, a priest, and fourteen villains, and six bordars, and two neatherds; between them they have eight carucates, wood three miles long and two broad, and four aeries of hawks. The whole is worth forty shillings—part is waste land." Doubtless this refers not to the parish of Leyland alone, but to the whole hundred, with the exception of Penwortham, as no other villages or manors are mentioned. The parish of Leyland is situated nearly in the centre of the hundred, and contains within its boundaries about 17,000 acres of land. The principal stream is the Lostock, which, rising in Withnell, after a tortuous course, joins the Yarrow, in the parish of Croston. The Darwen forms a portion of the north eastern boundary. One of its tributaries, the Roddlesworth, or the Moulden water, a picturesque stream, rises to the south of Withnell and Wheelton, and joins the Darwen below Hoghton tower. The manor remained in the Bussel family till the time of King John, when one moiety became vested in Roger de Lacy. In the 14th Henry III., (1230) John de Farington, son of William de Meles, coroder of Leyland church, and grandson of Hugh de Meolis, who was living at the period of the Conquest, espoused Avica daughter of Robert Bussel, and received the other moiety of the manor. Lacy's moiety descended to John of Gaunt, duke of Lancaster; the Faringtons still retaining possession of their portion. After the accession of Henry IV., the duke of Lancaster's moiety merged into the possessions of the crown. Edmund II. leased it for a short period to Thomas Molyneux, of Sefton, and afterwards to Thomas Walton, esq., attorney-general of the county palatine of Chester. He is recorded to have still held it in the first year of the reign of Henry VII. The Faringtons still retained their moiety, and shortly afterwards appear to have been possessed of the whole manor. It is on record that William Farington, who died in the 17th Henry VII., held the manor of Leyland by knight's service. Mr. Baines says it is extremely probable that the moiety belonging to the crown was granted by the king to the Faringtons, a circumstance which he suggests would "in some measure account for the fact that no court is held for the manor of Leyland, which has led to the supposition that it is only a factitious manor." Abundant documentary evidence, however, demonstrates that the supposition is entirely groundless. The parish of Leyland includes the townships of Leyland, Euxton, Cuerden, Whittle-le-woods, Clayton-le-woods, Heapy, Wheelton, Hoghton, and Withnell. During the present year, it has been subdivided into the following parishes, viz :—Leyland new parish, which includes Euxton and Cuerden, and that portion of the township of Leyland which lies to the east of the Penwortham and Wrightington turnpike road. That portion to the left of the said road will form a separate parish under the church lately built by Mrs. Farington, at Moss-side. Whittle parish is composed of the townships of Whittle-le-woods and Clayton-le-woods. Heapy parish comprises the townships of Heapy and Wheelton. Withnell parish includes Withnell and that portion of Hoghton which lies beyond the Chorley and Finnington turnpike road. Hoghton parish is the remainder of Hoghton township.

LEYLAND parish church may have existed before the Conquest. There is no record of it, however, in the Domesday book, but that document mentions a priest, and it may, therefore, reasonably be inferred, that there existed an edifice for the performance of his functions. It has been conjectured that some portion of the tower of the present church was erected at the close of the eleventh century. In 1291, it is noted in the Valor of pope Nicholas, as follows : "Ecclia de Laylond. £10....£1". The bodyof the church was re-built in 1816, and somewhat enlarged. It is a plain gothic structure. The old edifice, which was dedicated to St. Andrew, was a very interesting specimen of church architecture. Mr. Baines describes it as "formed of one arch of gothic ceiling, the height of which was 27 feet, and the area from 60 to 65 feet by 33 to 38 feet. The supporting principals were all of plain oak, and the present roof of the chancel resembles that of the ancient pile." The arch, which separates the nave from the chancel, is supposed to have been built in the reign of Edward II. The following additional particulars respecting the old church, are from the pen of Miss Farington :—[s]

"The Church had a good waggon roof, painted blue, and dotted over with gilt stars. There was a western gallery, erected for the organ, in the early part of George the Third's reign ; another and older one along the north wall, and one stretching from north to south across the Chancel arch, which, from its being only wide enough for one row of pews, and from its situation, must, I fancy, have been a 'rood loft.' The pulpit and desk were near the middle of the south wall."

Miss Farington's paper was illustrated by numerous drawings. Amongst others were several of the gargoyles, which were "placed in a curious projecting line, at some distance below the roof." These carved stones were sold as old materials, and purchased by Miss Farington's father. One drawing represented what was termed the "Cat Stone." "To this relic appends the usual story of the stone being removed by night, (in this case from Whittle to Leyland), and the Devil, in the form of a cat, 'throttling' a person who was bold enough to watch." Miss Farington further observes :—

"The tower and chancel were not touched, but the width of the body of the Church was increased nine feet on each side. When the old walls were pulled down, they were no further interfered with than the flooring of the new Church required ; but some alterations in ffarington Chapel (which occupies the south-east corner of the Church) a year or two since,[t] and which necessitated the entire removal of the old foundation, brought to light the fact, that they were partly composed of the fragments of a still earlier Church. The incised slabs drawn out, are of very superior workmanship to those in the Church-yard, and a small headstone, apparently more ancient. There were other portions of stone coffins besides the headpiece I have drawn. * * There seems no reason to doubt the undisturbed portion of the foundations would be equally rich in fragments as this south-east corner. * * The ffarington Chapel had a window (and not a door as now) at its east end. * * It is dedicated to St. Nicholas. * * In 1591, William ffarington obtained a confirmation of his previous family claims to it, from Bishop Chaderton, who confirms to him and his heirs for ever, a right 'to sit, stand, and otherwise repose themselves therein' while living, and after death to occupy 'two several vawtes or toumbes, in the upper of the same lying eastward, to bury the deade bodys of the men, and in the lower standing westward, to bury the dead bodys of the women.' There was a division between the two sexes in the family pew itself, till 1816, and at the present time, the men's free sittings run along the south side of the Church, and the women's the north. Prior to the alterations, all that part of the Chapel wall not occupied by monuments was covered with hatchments, helmets, tabards, and other relics of the age of heraldic funerals, but they were destroyed with the old Church. * * There are three sedilia and a double piscina under four semi-circular arches, and in the opposite wall an ambry, with a small pointed arched door of rude oak, as black as ink, till lately painted over. The roll moulding is the simplest characteristic ornament of this part of the Church, and the windows are the simplest form of decorative. There are some fragments of old stained glass in the east one. In the window seat of that westward of the chancel door, four folios are chained, viz. : Foxe's 'Martyrs,' and Jewell's 'Apology,' in black letter, and 'A Preservative against Popery,' of later date. * * In the outer north wall of the chancel, about three feet above the

s Paper read before Lan. and Ches. His. Soc. Vol. 7, page 18*.

t Miss Farington's paper was read in January, 1855.

ground, is a low arch, the purpose of which is not very clear. It is, perhaps, four feet wide, and nearly two high in front, and there are no indications of its ever having contained a recumbent figure.—We had a venerable yew tree in our Church-yard, but it was blown down in the storm of Christmas, 1852"

A chantry was founded in Leyland church, by James Anderton, esq., of Euxton, in the 15th Henry VIII. The walls of the church are adorned with a number of marble tablets. One, surmounted by a bust, is inscribed to the memory of Sir William Farington, who died in 1781. Another handsome monument, with the figures of two boys and profuse ornamental decoration, records the demise, in 1742, of George Farington, of Worden, esq., and of Margaret, daughter and sole heiress of John Bradshaw, of Pennington, in 1771. A carved wooden tablet is inscribed to the memory of William Farington, of Wearden, esq., and of Elizabeth his wife, the former of whom died in 1714, and the latter in 1703. An inscription testifies that the chapel belonged to William Farington, esq., of Werden, and his heirs, in right of confirmation by the bishop of Chester, in 1591. At the east end of the north gallery are several tablets to the memory of members of the families of Banastre and Parker, of Cuerden. One records the death of Banastre Parker, in 1738, son of Robert Parker, of Extwistle, esq, and of Elizabeth, daughter and co-heir of Christopher Banastre, of Bank, esq., by his wife Anne, daughter and one of the co-heirs of William Clayton, of Liverpool, esq. Another is to the memory of Banastre Parker, of Cuerden, who died in 1788, without issue. A third is to the memory of Thomas Townley Parker, of Cuerden, who died in 1794, at the age of 33. He married Susanna, sole heiress of Peter Brooke, of Astley hall, near Chorley He left one son, Robert Townley Parker, esq., the present possessor of the family estates One monumental inscription records the demise, in 1776, of Sam. Crooke, of Leyland, well known for his charities, and another stone is inscribed to the memory of a kindred spirit, Dr. William Bushell, the munificent founder of the hospital for decayed gentlemen and gentlewomen, at Goosnargh Dr. Bushell's grave is situated at the south-east corner of the church-yard, not far from the small gate leading past the vicarage It is covered simply by a slab of the commonest description. A suggestion, however, has been made that some more suitable monument should be placed over the resting place of one of the worthiest of the many generous benefactors of Preston and its neighbourhood, which it is to be hoped will not be lost sight of. There is a stone in the church-yard as old as the fourteenth century. It covers the burial place of the old family of the Weardens, of Golden hill. On the dissolution of the monasteries, the Fleetwoods, of Penwortham, became patrons of the living. The Rawstornes purchased the great tithes, with the exception of the demesne lands of Worden and some others, the property of the

Faringtons. The advowson of the vicarage was purchased, in 1748, by the Rev. Thomas Baldwin, whose family has since retained the patronage and furnished the vicars. In 1650, the vicarage, with other buildings, and twelve acres of glebe land, were valued at £6. per annum, and the small tithes at £5. per annum. The impropriate tithes, however, were worth £272. per year, and were claimed by several parties.[u] Mr. William Rothwell, M.A., had been appointed vicar, but the puritans would not permit him to officiate. He was dragged violently out of the church, and was persecuted with so much rancour, that he would have died of want, but for the generosity of Mr. Daniel, of Daresbury, in Cheshire. He was reinstated in the vicarage after the Restoration, and died at Leyland, in 1677.[v] In 1834, the living was valued at £400. per annum. The registers commence in 1538. A neat episcopal chapel was erected and endowed in 1854, at Moss-side, by the liberality of Mrs. Farington. The site was given by the Misses Farington, the owners of the Worden estates. A parsonage house has since been added, and the district lately constituted a separate parish. A temporary catholic chapel was opened in the village of Leyland, in 1846, and a much larger and very commodious one, dedicated to St. Mary, erected in 1854. The Wesleyans have a chapel at Golden hill, built in 1814. The independent chapel, situated in the village, a very neat structure, was opened in 1844. The grammar school of Leyland was founded by Queen Elizabeth, and endowed with £3. 18s. per annum.[w] Crooke's school, at Moss-side was founded in 1770. The founder left an annuity of £5. for an organist, and another of £20. as salary for a schoolmaster. Crooke's other charities are described as "cottages and lands, of which the income is given to the masters of Euxton, Clayton, and Cuerden schools, the rector of Croston and curate of Leyland, etc., amounting annually to £76. 4s.[x] The commissioners further report as follows:—

"1792. *Beatson's Charities.*—£200. to the grammar school of Leyland, and £100. to each of the schools of Moss Side, Euxton, and Clayton. Also £200. to the trustees of the poor-house of Leyland, called Albiston poor-house, [Osbaldeston's poor-house,] to be invested in the funds, and the dividends to be paid yearly to six poor women, and £100. in trust to be invested in the funds, and the dividends to be applied to the purchase of bread for the poor of Euxton.

---

u Par. Inq. Lamb. Lib. vol. II.

v Walker's Sufferings of the Clergy, p. 344.

w Par. Com. Rep. According to the Notitia Cestriensis, the queen endowed the school with £3. 6s. 8d. per annum, "to wch hath been given since 100*l*. by Mr. Dandy; 50*l* by James Sherdley; by Mr. Walsh, Curate of Liverpool, 10*l*. the Interest of wch to be paid to the Master, who is Nominated by Trustees, appointed according to a Decree in Chancery, who keep ye Writings. 1717. The Rev. Thomas Armetriding, Vicar, by Will dated the 18th of February, 1718, proved at Chorley, in 1719, gave £200. for the Master, and £50. for the Usher; and Margaret, his widow, by Will dated the 15th of November, 1728, gave £50. for the Usher. The Interest of £20. was given lately for an Usher by John Bury, of Lealand."—Page 381.

x Par. Com. Rep.

"1607. *Farington's Alms Houses* for six alms people, who receive 16s 8d. each yearly; Besides 10s from Osbaldeston's Charity, the Alms House is entitled to the interest of Armetriding's bequests, in 1728, of £160., and to Mary Farington's legacy of £100., in 1811. Annual income, exclusive of the interest of £160 ... £12 5s. 2d.

"*Charities in Land and Money to the Poor*, per annum Osbaldeston, in 1665, left per annum, £117. 5s.; Clayton, in 1754, 10s. *For bread*; 1728, Preston left, per annum, £1. 6s, and Oakenshaw, in 1744, 10s.; yielding annually... £119. 11s. 0d."

An infant school was erected at Moss-side, in 1837, by subscription and a grant from the National Society. Worden or Wearden hall, the ancient seat of the Faringtons, is mentioned in 1509. For twenty-five generations this family has continued in Leyland, in uninterrupted succession by male heirs, until the demise of James Nowell Farington, in 1848. Worden hall is now a farm house. About the time of the first James, Sir Thomas Farington removed to Shawe hall, near the village of Leyland. Sir William Farington, in the last century, enlarged the building, and stored it with a fine collection of marbles, frescoes, etc., which he procured in Italy and other places. The mansion was almost entirely re-built by the late J N Farington. The name "Shawe hall" was discontinued, and "Worden," in remembrance of the title of the ancient family seat, transferred to the modern edifice. The park has been much enlarged, and the approaches, and entrance lodges entirely re-constructed. The latter are now much nearer the village. The mansion called the "Old hall," erected in the time of Elizabeth, formerly the seat of the Charnock family, now extinct, is still in existence, but has been converted into a farm-house. There are several modern residences in Leyland of some importance, amongst others, Golden hill house, erected during the last century, the residence of Mrs Eccles; and Wellfield, the residence of John Eccles, esq. A savings bank was established in 1821. In 1834, the deposits amounted to upwards of £20,000. In 1851 they had increased to the sum of £39,654. 17s. 3d. This amount belonged to 924 different individuals. A few years since a large room, called the Union hall, was erected, in which the meetings of the Leyland Agricultural and Horticultural Association, concerts, lectures, etc., are held. A library or mechanics' institute has lately been established In 1850, gas was introduced. About a quarter of a mile from the village, there is an extensive bleaching establishment, locally termed "The Shrugs." Two customary fairs are held annually in October and March. These fairs are proclaimed with some ceremony, by the "mayor," as the gentleman elected to preside on such occasions, is styled, by courtesy. The township of Leyland contains 3,725 statute acres of land. In 1851, its population was 3,617 The annual rateable value of the property in 1854, was £11,797.

EUXTON.—The township and chapelry of Euxton, or, as it is sometimes written, Euxton-burgh, lies to the south of Leyland, on the line of the

Worden Hall, Leyland, near Preston

The Seat of Mrs [illegible]

Penwortham, near Preston

great Roman highway. From its name, some outwork has evidently existed, to protect the ford over the Yarrow. A much corroded Roman coin was picked up about twenty-three years ago, together with a "circular piece of gold, without superscription or any other proof that it had ever passed through the mint." [y] The manor passed by marriage from the Holands to Sir William Molyneux. He died in 1372. It remained in his family until its transfer to James Longworth, esq., of Liverpool. Dr. Kuerden says that Euxton "hath a fayre chappel" built "by Sir William Molyneux, of Sephton." The date (1513) is inscribed upon the south wall. Canon Raines suggests that the builder was probably the Sir William Molineux, who distinguished himself at Flodden. Kuerden further observes:—

"The corn tyth is worth 55ls. per an. and is the inheritance of Mr. Anderton, of Clayton. The small tyth is worth 50 shill. and belongs to the vicar of Leyland. In this township their is a water corn miln, cald Pincoc Miln, standing vpon the Riuer of Yarrow, and adjacent to it a fayr arched stone bridge ouer the said riuer in London post road, parting the parish of Leyland from the parish of Standish, and below the bridge standeth a paper milne, and a little below that another corn milne cald Hermitriding," (Armetriding) "miln. Vpon the banks of this riuer are some quarryes of stone of very hard flags and slate.

"Nere the aforesaid chappel standeth an antient fabric cald Euxton Hall, the present inheritance of W. Anderton, esq., late Justice of Peace, under K. James, but scince at Manchester, amongst other Lancashire Gentlemen." [z]

James Anderton, of Euxton, in the 15th Henry VIII., founded three chantries, "to pray for the souls of him and Agnes his wife." One was at Leyland church, another at the chapel at Euxton, and a third at Eccleston. In 1650, the great tithes, claimed by James Anderton, esq., of Clayton, were estimated at £50. per annum; and the small tithes at £2. 5s. The incumbent was Mr. Seth Bushell, "a godly pious minister, and conformable to the present government." [a] His salary was £40. per year. He was afterwards vicar of Preston. [b] Mr. Anderton does not appear to have been equally "conformable," for the tithes are described as sequestered for the use of the state owing to his "delinquency." Bishop Cartwright has the following entry in his diary: "1687. Mr. Walmsley of Leland came to visit me, and he deliv^d me a Petition for ye restoring of Euxton Chapel to the Inhab^ts, the key whereof was in the hands of — Molineux, who alledges that it is his, and not theirs, that it has no maintenance, nor any prayers said in it for 20 years last past." Bishop Gastrell says that the Rev. Thomas Armetriding, left £200. after the death of his wife, for "Augmenting this Chapel, together wth ye Queens Bounty." Mrs. Armetriding died in 1730. The chapel was re-built in 1724, [c] and

---

y Baines's His. Lan., vol. 3, p. 454.

z See page 215.

a Parl. Inq. Lamb. Lib.

b See pages 463 and 474 of the present work.

c Mr. Baines says "about 1710." Canon Raines corrects this to 1724.

again in 1816. In 1829, it was enlarged by the "Incorporated Society for the Building of Churches." A chancel has since been added. The font, being in the Norman style, is thought to be much older than the chapel built by Sir William Molyneux. An ancient stone cross, formerly placed inside the chapel, now lies neglected outside the gate. Canon Raines says it is still "used by the Roman Catholics at their funerals as a station." The patron saint is unknown. The value of the living, in 1834, was £125. The advowson belongs to the representatives of the Rev. Thomas Armetriding. Adjoining the hall is a catholic chapel, built in the last century, by Mr. Anderton. It was restored in 1817-18. Euxton hall was most probably built in the reign of Henry VIII., by James Anderton, esq. It was re-built by William Anderton, esq., in 1739. His grandson, William Ince Anderton, esq., in 1849-50, erected a modern mansion contiguous to the old hall. The Andertons, of Clayton and Euxton, are descended from a second son of Anderton, of Anderton, who married Anne, daughter of Henry Banastre, of Bank. This lady was afterwards united to William Farington, esq., of Farington. Charles II. slept at Euxton hall, on his way to Worcester. A puritan newspaper, called the "Mercurius Politicus," of the 16th August, 1650, contains the following characteristic notice of this monarch's progress through Lancashire:—

"August 14th, 1650. This day Charles Stuart lodged at Euxton-burgh, six miles on this syde of Preston, being Sir Hugh Anderton's house, who was prisoner at Lancaster, but sett at liberty by the Scotts. This Anderton is a bloody Papist, and one that when Prince Rupert was at Bolton, boasted much of being in blood to the elbows in that cruel massacre. The next night theyr king lodged at Brine, six miles from Warrington, being Sir William Gerard's house, who is a subtile jesuited Papist. This dissembling Scott, trusts none so well in Lancashire for his hostes as the papists."

Another branch of the Andertons resided at Lostock, near Bolton. Francis Anderton was at Preston in 1715. Patten states that he was reported to have said "he had lost a good estate for being with the rebels but one day."[d] The Bushells formerly resided at "Spout," in Euxton. Mr. Baines says "it does not appear," whether the founder of Goosnargh hospital was descended from Warin Bussel, the ancient lord of the domain. It is by no means improbable, however, as a portion of the lands retained by the representative of Warin, after the transfer of the barony to Roger de Lascy, was situated in Eukeston. In 1684, two other residences, Armetriding house and Glear or Glide hill, are mentioned. The only mansion now existing in Euxton, besides the seat of the Andertons, is Runshaw hall, the residence of G. Johnson Wainwright, esq. Euxton possesses a few other charities, besides those previously alluded to, amounting to £14. per annum.[e] The school, founded in 1758, was re-built,

d See page 237. e Charity Commissioners' Report.

Astley Hall Lancashire.

The Seat of Thomas Townley Parker Esqre

in 1837, on a new site. The necessary funds were furnished by subscription, and a grant from the National Society. The catholics have likewise a good school in the township. The population of Euxton, in 1851, was 1,631. The area is 2,934 statute acres, and the annual rateable value of the property is £7,826.

CUERDEN was granted to Vivian Molineux, by Roger de Poictou. His grandson gave the manor of Kardon, as a marriage portion with his sister, who espoused Siward, son of Anti, son of Elsi. His son Henry de Kuerden and grandson, Thomas, granted lands to the knights of Jerusalem and the abbey of Kokersand. The manor afterwards passed, by grant, from Roger de Kuerden to Gilbert Woodcock, the marriage of whose daughter transferred it to Robert Banastre, baron of Newton and lord of Walton. It afterwards passed to the Amilcorns, the Chernocks, the Langtons, and the Fleetwoods, of Caldwick, in the county of Stafford. By marriage it was transferred to the Banastres, of Bank. On the marriage of Elizabeth, daughter and co-heiress of Christopher Banastre, with Captain Robert Parker, of Extwistle, who died in 1718, it passed to the family of the present proprietor, Robert Townley Parker, esq. Cuerden hall is a large and elegant mansion, beautifully situated upon the higher ground overlooking the valley of the Lostock. The extensive and well wooded park presents some delightfully picturesque specimens of English rural scenery. Astley hall, another mansion belonging to Mr. Parker, is situated on the margin of a streamlet named the Chor, in the parish of Chorley. It was re-built in 1600. It is a large edifice of wood, plaster, and brick, and is well stored with fine examples of antique furniture. Amongst others there is a singular oaken table, called a "shuffle table" or a "shove groat table," formerly used for a game now obsolete. Astley hall passed to Richard Brooke, esq., second son of Sir Peter Brooke, of Mere, in the county of Chester, in the latter part of the seventeenth century, on his marriage with Margaret, daughter and heiress of Robert Charnock, esq., of Charnock and Astley. In 1787, Thomas Townley Parker, esq., of Cuerden, married Susannah, daughter and heiress of Peter Brooke, esq., whose son Robert Townley Parker, esq., of Cuerden, Royle, and Extwistle, succeeded to the property. Mrs. Parker afterwards married Sir Henry Philip Hoghton, bart., who died in 1835, and was succeeded by his son, the present Sir Henry Bold Hoghton, bart. Lady Hoghton resided at Astley hall at the time of her demise. It is at present the residence of her grandson, Thomas, eldest son and heir of Robert Townley Parker, esq. Mr. Parker, sen., has on two occasions represented Preston in parliament. Since his retirement from active political life, a committee has been formed for the purpose of procuring a first-class full length portrait of him, with the view to its being deposited in some public building in the town. From the estimation in which Mr. Parker is held, as a private gentleman, by men of all shades of politics, and his constant attention to the interests of the town and neighbourhood, this proposition has met with general approval. Dr. Kuerden says,—"There is another fayr built hous, but not altogether so modish as the last," (Cuerden hall) "upon the lower Kuerden Green, commonly called the Crow-trees, being the antient inheritance of Mr. John Woodcoc and his family, for 4 or 500 years." This building is generally termed Woodcock hall. It is now the property of R. Townley Parker, esq. In 1646, John Woodcock, a Francescan priest, a member of the ancient family referred to, was executed at Lancaster, as a "popish recusant." Dr. Kuerden speaks of his own ancestral residence, situated below Cuerden hall, on the west side of the London road, in the following terms:—

> "Another fayr square fabrick, a brick building, adorned about with tall pyne and fir trees, situated pleasantly upon the edge of Kuerden Green, not long since built in a fayr court, and a spacious orchard and garden on the south side thereof, planted by Ri. Kuerden, Dr. of Physic, being an antient inheritance descended upon him, and hath continued in his precedent ancestors from K. Stephen's Raigne, then given in marriage to the original of that family, Sywardus filius Anti, with a daughter of the son of Vivian Molineux, who held that lordship, 2 car. of land by the service of ¼ of a Kts fee. This inheritance hath continued entirely in the Dr's family to this day,[f] though the lordship itself hath been twice or thrice alienated."

In 1673, Mr. Andrew Dandy founded a school at Cuerden, and endowed it with a rent charge and interest amounting to £6. per annum. This was afterwards increased by £5. per annum, from Crooke's charity.[g] It has been further augmented by R. T. Parker, esq., and others. Including some annual donations, the schoolmaster's salary is upwards of £40. per year. About 60 scholars, on an average, attend the school, which was erected in 1690. Cuerden shares in some other charities with the neighbouring townships. A very pretty episcopal church was erected in 1836, on land given by Robert Townley Parker, esq., who likewise subscribed £200. towards the building fund. The "Church Building Society" granted a further sum of £200., and the remainder was raised by subscription. It is dedicated to St. Saviour, and will seat about 550 persons. In 1850, an organ was erected by Mr. J. Roome, of Preston. A parsonage house was built in 1847, at a cost of £1200., which was defrayed by subscription and a grant of £600. from the ecclesiastical commissioners. The living is in the patronage of the vicar of Blackburn. The church, indeed, though situated within the Cuerden demesne or park land, is in the township of Walton-le-dale. It is intended chiefly to accommodate the inhabitants of Cuerden and Bamber-bridge. A school, in connection, has been since erected by

[f] The latter portion of the seventeenth century. [g] Char. Com. Rept.

Entrance Hall, Astley Hall, Lancashire.

(The seat of Thomas Townley Parker Esq.)

subscription and a grant of £210. from the National Society. There are three cotton mills in the township. Cuerden contains 807 statute acres of land. The property was assessed to the county rate, in 1854, at the annual value of £2,778. In 1851, the population numbered 521.

WHITTLE-LE-WOODS.—In the reign of Henry I., part of the manor was granted to Gilbert de Witul. It passed from this family to Richard le Butler. John Butler de Rawclif, dying without male issue, it passed, by marriage, to the Standish and Anderton families. In the reign of Charles II., the representative of the latter disposed of a portion to Mr. William Crooke. The other original moiety, described as half a carucate in Whythall in the wood, was granted by the son of Warin Bussel to Richard Fiton. It passed to the Lees, and afterwards to Sir Richard Hoghton, on the marriage of Sibil, daughter of Sir Henry de Lee. Dr. Kuerden says:—

"Nere unto the water of Lostock, is a fayr fabrick of stone cald the New Croke, which was erected by Richard Clayton, Dr. of Divinity and Mr. of St. John's College, Cambridge, who purchased the estate in Whittle cald the New and Old Croke, where the family of Claytons were planted for some generations. The New Croke descended to Rich. Clayton, esq., who dying without heirs male, it descended by a sister to the Leicesters, of Toft, in Cheshire, the present owner thereof. And the other house cald the Old Croke, descended in another brother of the family of Clayton, and by Captain Robert Clayton, now of Fulwood, was sold to one Mr. William Croke, who likewise purchased the half lordship of Whittle from James Anderton, of Clayton, esq."

The episcopal chapel is a handsome edifice. It was erected in 1829, the parish contributing £500., and the remaining expence being defrayed by the church commissioners. At South-hill is a neat catholic chapel, dedicated to St. Chad, with a school in connection. The chapel was built in 1791, and enlarged in 1812. The Wesleyan chapel was re-built in 1839. Whittle shares with the neighbouring townships in some charities. In 1769, a school was founded by Sir F. Standish, bart., and Samuel Crooke, esq. The endowment produces £11. per annum. In 1841, six alms houses, for poor persons belonging to Chorley, were erected in this township by Susannah Brooke. Shaw hill or Shawe hall, a large and eligibly situated mansion, passed to Thomas (Ikin) Bright Crosse, esq., on his marriage with Miss Crosse, the heiress to the estate. Whittle contains several extensive millstone quarries, a few cotton factories, and a calico printing establishment. It is intersected by the Leeds and Liverpool canal, and the branch of the Lancaster canal which connects the tram way from Preston with the more important water communications. Whittle has evidently been occupied, and its stone quarries worked, by the Roman people. About twenty years ago, a hoard of coins, said to have amounted to nearly a thousand in number, were found, on the removal of the rock above the Lancaster canal tunnel. Coins have likewise been found at Whittle-springs, one of which, a medal of Philip the elder, would seem to imply that the Roman people, to some extent, were acquainted with these now celebrated waters.[h] The chalybeate spring has been long known, but the famed alkaline fountain was not discovered till 1836, during some boring operations, undertaken with the view of ascertaining whether the Lancashire coal field extended beneath the estate. A breakage in the instruments employed caused some delay in the borings, and it was not until 1841, that the obstacle was removed, when the water rose to the surface in great abundance. In the strata penetrated, blue grey rag and grey rock greatly predominate. The total depth is about 265 feet. The neighbourhood of the springs has been converted into beautiful pleasure grounds, and a commodious hotel erected, with baths and other conveniences. The scenery of the district is varied in its character and extremely picturesque. From some of the neighbouring eminences, a large portion of the Lancashire coast is visible. The place is much frequented by invalids and pleasure parties. The alkaline water is highly spoken of, and has been compared to that at Baden Baden. The township of Whittle-le-woods contains 1,354 statute acres. The population, in 1851, amounted to 2,310. The property was rated in 1854, at the annual value of £4,894.

Clayton-le-woods.—One moiety of this township was given by Richard Bussel, as a marriage portion with his sister, to Robert de Hickeling, in the county of Nottingham. Their son assumed the name of Clayton. His descendants sold their portion of the manor to the Andertons, of Euxton. About the year 1672, it was transferred by sale, to Caryl, third viscount Molyneux, from whose family it passed to the present owner, Lord Skelmersdale. Richard Bussel granted the other moiety of Clayton to Richard Fiton. It passed by marriage to the de Lees, and afterwards formed part of the portion of Sibil de Lee, on her marriage with Sir Richard Hoghton. Clayton hall, the manorial residence of the Claytons, is now a farm-house. It is a spacious edifice of the age of Elizabeth. A small catholic chapel, dedicated to St. Bede, was erected at Clayton-green in 1823. There is likewise a school in connection with the chapel. A methodist chapel was built in 1830. In 1744, a school was founded by Edward Bootle. The endowment is increased by participation in Beatson and Crooke's charities, and annual donations from Lord Skelmersdale and R. Townley Parker, esq. The poor are entitled to the proceeds from two closes of land, belonging to Clayton's charity, and a participation in Frith's bequests. The population of Clayton-le-woods, in 1851, amounted to 747. The annual rateable value of the property, in 1854, was £2,910. The area of the township, according to the ordnance survey, is 1,430 acres.

Heapy.—A district formerly called Gunoldsmores, or Cunnolvesmores,

h See page 50.

included Heapy, Rothelsworth, Stanworth, Ollerton, Whelton, and Withnil It was granted by Richard Bussel, the second baron of Penwortham, as a marriage portion with his sister, to "Alan son of Suen, and sometimes cald Regenaldus, as is memorised in an ancient scrole."[1] In the reign of John, Randulph, brother to Richard de Ollerton, assumed the name of Heapy, his brother having granted him the manor. In 1299, his descendant, Robert de Hepea, sold the lordship to Hugh de Standish. It still remains in the possession of the younger branch of this family, represented by H. S. Carr Standish, of Duxbury, esq. Dr. Kuerden says, "Heapy had an antient Park belonging to it, and a water miln for graine vpon the Bagir brock." The episcopal chapel was erected by voluntary subscriptions in the year 1752, on the site of an edifice which existed in the previous century. Further subscriptions and a grant from the National Society being obtained, the chapel was enlarged and galleries erected, in 1829. The advowson belongs to the vicar of Leyland. The value of the living in 1834, was £111. It is now worth about £150. per annum, arising from the great tithes of Wheelton, land in Coppul, purchased by a grant from Queen Anne's bounty, and £42. a year, granted by the ecclesiastical commissioners, in 1841. The patron saint is unknown. There are three schools in connection with the chapel. One at Heapy, was built in 1826, another at Wheelton, in 1842, and the third at White Coppice, in 1843. A parsonage house was erected in 1846. In 1851, Heapy contained 495 inhabitants. The area of the township is 1,463 statute acres. The annual rateable value of the property, in 1854, was £1,895.

WHEELTON.—A third portion of the ancient lordship of Gunoldsmores, including this township, and its members, Whelcroft, Brinscoles, Stanworth, Monkshal, and Brightfeld, passed to Roger de Stanworth, on his marriage with the second co-heiress of William Alanson, on which occasion, he appears to have assumed the name of Quelton. Whelton-cum-Heapy was afterwards held by the Hoghtons, as a part of their manor of Hoghton. Kuerden states, that in his day there existed "good store of slate and flag quarries in this lordship called Whelton Delph." There is now a cotton factory within the township. Brinscall or Brinscough hall was in existence in 1650. Another mansion, called Simpson's fold, is considered to have been erected about the same period. By Simpson's bequest, poor housekeepers in Wheelton are entitled to the interest of £30. The population of this township, in 1851, amounted to 1,041. Its area is 1,696 statute acres. The property was rated, in 1854, at the annual value of £8,012.

---

1 Kuerden.

Hoghton.—In the time of Henry II., Hoghton was held by Adam de Hocton, son of Richard Fitz Hamo, and grandson of Hamo Pincerna, who married the daughter of Warin Bussel, first baron of Penwortham, shortly after the Norman conquest. The descendants of this family still retain their ancestral possessions at Hoghton and other places. John of Gaunt, in the 9th Richard II., granted to Sir Richard Hoghton, license to add to his park seven score acres of land. Of Hoghton tower, the ancient seat of the family, Dr. Kuerden gives the following particulars:—

"This tower was build in Queen Eliz. raigne by one Tho. Houghton, who translated this manor-house, formerly placed below the hill nere unto the waterside. Betwixt the inward square court and the 2d, was a very tall strong tower or gate house, which in the late and unhappy civil wars was accidentally blown up with powder, with some adjacent buildings, after the surrender thereof, and one Captaine Starky with 200 soldiers were killed in that blast most wofully.[k] The outward is defended with two lesser bastions vpon the south-west and north-west corners, besides another placed in the midst betwixt them, now serving for an outward gate house. This stately fabric is inuironed with a most spacious park, which in former times was so full of tymber that a man passing through it could scarce haue seen the sun shine at middle of day; but of later days most of it has been destroyed. It was much replenished with wild beasts, as with boars and bulls of a white and spangled coulor, and red deer in great plenty, the last as yet preserved for game by the lords thereof."

King James honoured Hoghton with a visit, on his progress from Scotland to London, in 1617, the particulars of which have already been given.[l] Hoghton tower is now fast falling into decay. Portions are occupied by the cultivators of the neighbouring land. This relic of the past, with its many interesting associations, and its magnificent site, naturally attracts, during the summer months, pleasure seekers from the neighbouring towns. The principal entrance is to the west, beneath an embattled tower, flanked on each side by a somewhat similar but smaller turret. The entire structure forms a rectangle, divided into two courts. The banqueting hall is a noble apartment, with mullion and transom windows, minstrel gallery, and capacious fire place. It measures ten yards by seventeen, and is paved with small square stones. Here, occasionally, the merry laughter of cheap trip parties, enjoying an extemporised quadrille or country dance, disturbs the slumbering echoes of the old baronial edifice. The domestic chapel, on the north side of the inner court, which was used, for a lengthened period, after the Hoghtons removed to Walton hall, has had no public service performed in it for about forty years. It is now fast falling into decay. There are some mouldering portraits yet remaining in the "green room," one of which is said to represent the original builder of the fortress-mansion, Sir Thomas Hoghton. One of the apartments is termed the "guinea room," from its having been decorated with representations of that coin. The family arms are likewise represented in the

k See page 173. l See page 150.

Hoghton Tower, Lancashire.

[illegible]

Hoghton Tower, Lancashire (Inner Court)

(the Ancient Seat of Sir Henry Bold Hoghton, Bart.)

compartments of the wainscot, with the motto "Mal Gre le Tort." The "king's bed room," which is twenty feet square, presents some elaborate carving over the chimney piece. The gallery, ten yards long by eight broad, is relatively in tolerable preservation, and contains a few specimens of antique furniture. It is approached by a flight of low oaken steps, up which, it is said, the late baronet rode occasionally on a favourite pony The draw-well is stated to be forty-two yards in depth.. From its position, this would be necessary, especially when the fortress was beleagured. The statue of king William III, which stands in the centre of the inner court, was brought from Walton hall, after the demolition of that mansion, and placed upon its present site Every thing speaks loudly of past splendour and present decay. And yet the desolation is not sufficiently great to prevent a constantly recurring hope that the edifice may be restored and again rendered habitable. The site is, indeed, a most imposing one, and must have presented even more attractions, when the western side of the pyramidical hill, on which the mansion stands, was covered with forest verdure. From this point, the eye traverses an immense fertile plain, stretching to the Irish sea, and dotted with towns and villages. In the rear of the tower, the Darwen rushes through a richly wooded and secluded gorge, and playfully bounds over the rocky terraces which intersect its path. Within a trifling distance are expansive views and deep shadowy dingles. Here, the majestic wide spreading landscape, with the busy hum of humanity borne over it in subdued cadence, by the unimpeded breeze, there, the solitary glen, with its emerald sward, and its rippling fountains and feathered choristers making sweet harmony with the mystic tones of cool stray zephyrs, coying with wild flowers and the leaves and tiner branches of overhanging forest trees. Truly, Hoghton is worthy of its historic name and princely reminiscences! At the foot of the hill there is another residence of some pretensions, named Riley green. In the reign of Charles I., the resident family was styled "Riley of the Green." The episcopal chapel at Hoghton, situated near the village, was erected, in 1823, by the parliamentary commissioners. The living is in the gift of the vicar of Leyland. In 1790, a methodist chapel was erected at "Hoghton Bottoms" The charity commissioners make the following report respecting Hoghton school:—

"1709. School founded by Sir Charles Houghton, of Houghton Tower, bart., for teaching the English, Latin, and Greek tongues, but about twenty years ago, the national system of education was introduced into the school, and sir Henry Hoghton, and Mr. Sudell, voluntarily contribute £25. each annually to its support About 150 boys and girls are taught reading and writing."

The population of Hoghton, in 1851, was 1,373. The area, according to the ordnance survey, is 2,232 acres. The rateable value of the property, in 1854, was £4,750.

WITHNELL includes the hamlets of Ollerton and Brinscall. The views on the Roddlesworth streamlet, in this township, are extremely varied and picturesque. The series of reservoirs for the storage of water, in connection with the Liverpool works, commences at Withnell, and continues to Rivington. These magnificent sheets of water, which give an entirely new feature to the district, have, from their picturesque aspect, acquired the title of the "South Lancashire lakes." Roger de Withnil received the township as part of the dower of the third daughter, and co-heiress of William Alanson.[m] In the 7th Edward I., Henry de Wythenall held his lands of Sir Adam de Houton. In the 11th Edward III., privilege was granted by the king to Sir Richard de Hoghton, of free warren in all his demesne lands in Hoghton and Withinhul, together with five hundred acres of wood and heath to enclose in the said townships, and permission to make a park. Withnell passed, in the eighteenth century, to Henry Sudell, esq, whose trustees re-sold it to the Messrs. Parke, of Preston, who are now the reputed owners of the manor. The episcopal chapel, dedicated to St. Paul, was erected in 1841 The advowson belongs to the vicar of Leyland. The living is worth about £103 per annum. A good parsonage house was built about twelve years ago Bishop Gastrell says, "Here is a school lately erected, and said to be endowed by Sir Charles Houghton, deceased, but how endowed ye vicar cannot yet learn Anno. 1718." Canon Raines adds that the school was endowed by deed, dated the 30th of June, 1789, with the sum of £400. There are two cotton factories and a paper mill in the township, the property of the Messrs. Parke. The latter was established in 1843. Wesleyan chapels and schools are attached to these establishments. A Wesleyan chapel is now in course of re-erection in Brinscall. The population of Withnell, in 1851, was 1,975. The annual rateable value of the property, in 1854, amounted to £5,010. Its area, according to the ordnance survey, is 3,620 statute acres.

RUFFORD PARISH.

RUFFORD was formerly attached to Croston It was formed into a separate parish in 1793. Richard Bussel, the second baron of Penwortham, granted to Richard Fitun, together with other lands, a moiety of this manor. It passed to Sir William Heskaith, in 1275, on his marriage with Matilda, daughter and co-heiress of Richard Fitton. By the marriage of Sir John Heskayte, knight, grandson of Sir William, with Alice, daughter and only heir of Edmund Fytton, lord of half Ruffourd, he became sole lord of the manor and assumed the arms of Fytton. His descendant, Sir Thomas

m See page 615

G. Hesketh, baronet, holds the unbroken manor, with the exception of one estate belonging to the church. Rufford chapel must have been in existence in 1346, as in that year King Edward III., during his sojourn in Normandy, granted to Sir William Hesketh, a licence to found a chantry in the chapel of St. Mary, of Rufford[n] The Testa de Nevill' records that "Richard Bussel gave to the abbey of Chester, one carucate of land, in Ruchford in alms, which the abbot of Chester holds." By virtue of this grant, the dean and chapter of Chester enjoy a pension, issuing out of this manor, of £40. per annum[o] The monastery of St. Werburgh anciently claimed, as a fine out of the manor of Rufford, the yearly payment of eleven shillings.[p] Whether the licence referred to was granted with one or both of these conditions annexed, is not known. The chantry was dissolved in 1548, restored in 1553, and afterwards suppressed by Queen Elizabeth. According to the parliamentary inquisition, in 1650, Rufford was deemed fit to be formed into a parish distinct from Croston, "in respect that the waters lying between the Town of Rufford and the parish of Croston are for the most part all the Winter time not passable." The same document further records that "Mr. Woods, well qualified, and conformable to the State and Government, doth officiate the Cure, but hath no other Sallary save the benevolence of his Auditory and the Inhabitants there" The chapel was re-built in 1734, at a cost of £1,165., by a brief procured by the Hesketh family. When constituted a district parish, in 1793, it was endowed with the great and small tithes of Rufford and the great tithes of Ulnes-Walton. The advowson belongs to Le Gendre Nicholas Starkie, esq., of Huntroyd. The church, which is dedicated to the Virgin Mary, is a plain brick edifice, with a stone cupola. A small gallery and organ were erected in 1829. On the north side of the family pew of the Hesketh, is an ancient slab, bearing a sculptured representation of an armed knight and his lady, with their hands clasped as in prayer. It is in memory of Sir Thomas Hesketh, knight, and his wife. The former died in 1363 In the 13th Edward III, William de Heskayte obtained a charter to hold a market every Friday at his manor of Rugford There is now no market, but a fair for cattle, etc., is annually held. There are several charities belonging to the parish, including the following:—

"*Charities of Baldwin and others*, amounting to £34. 10s, in several small sums, for which an interest of £1. 14s 6d. was paid towards the support of a schoolmaster until the year 1818, in consequence of a school having been built by sir T. D Hesketh, in 1816,[q] which is supported solely at the worthy baronet's expense, for all the poor children of the parish, on the national system, and books are also furnished for the use of the school. A small payment is made by the children of the farmers. The old school

n Harl Bib 2063, p 135 o Lucas's MSS. p Ormerod's Cheshire, vol. 1, p. 227.

q The date inscribed on the present school is 1821.

house, which stood opposite the Hesketh Arms, supported a still more ancient one of Rufford Old Hall." r

About ten years ago, two cottages were converted into a girl's school. A room was first used as a place of worship by the Wesleyans, in 1813. Rufford old hall, the ancient seat of the Hesketbs, is believed to have been erected in the fifteenth century. It is pleasantly situated amidst park-like scenery. Many of the rooms are pannelled, and profusely ornamented with elegantly carved figures and beautiful foliage. The entrance hall is a magnificent apartment, with a hammer-beamed roof. Though much less in magnitude, this room resembles Westminster hall, in many respects. Much of the carving is similar in character, and is considered equal if not superior in execution. Rufford hall likewise possesses an important addition in its magnificent screen. The drawing room has an open carved roof, and a curious door which originally led to the minstrel gallery. It is the property of Sir Thomas George Hesketh, bart., and is occasionally occupied by the dowager Lady Hesketh. Rufford new hall is an elegant mansion, erected in 1798, by Sir Thomas Dalrymple Hesketh, bart. Holmes wood house, an ancient structure, has been converted into a farmer's residence. A handsome modern house, occupied by the rector, is sometimes styled the Parsonage. The surrounding country generally is flat marsh or moss land. Owing to the improvements in the drainage, however, large tracts have been brought into profitable cultivation, and the general health of the district improved. Immense quantities of potatoes are grown upon the reclaimed moss land of this and neighbouring parishes. Rufford, in 1851, contained 861 inhabitants. Its area is 3,120 statute acres. The annual rateable value of the property, in 1854, was £4,734.

MUCH HOOLE PARISH.

HOOLE was separated from Croston, and formed into a distinct parish, in 1642. In the early part of the reign of Henry III., Thomas Banastre held the manor of Great Hoole. It passed to the Hesketbs, on the marriage of Thomas Heskaith, in 1387, with Margaret, daughter and heiress of Thomas Banastre. Sir Thomas G. Hesketh, bart., G. A. Legh Keck, esq., the Messrs. Rothwell, and others are the principal landowners. The church, which is dedicated to St. Michael, was erected in the fifteenth century, and was re-edified in 1628. The steeple was built in 1720, and, in 1812, the ceiling was renewed. The chancel was added in 1824. On the north side of the steeple is the following inscription: "Vt Hora sic Vita." It has been conjectured that this inscription, together with another, "Sine sole sileo," as well as the sun dial and old clock, owe thei existence to the celebrated astronomer, Jeremiah Horrocks, who resided in

r Char. Com. Rept. XV., abstracted by Baines. The word "supported" should, evidently, be "succeeded."

this parish.[a] The tower, which stands upon four pillars, is curiously ornamented with pinnacles, vases, and arched ornaments. The report of the parliamentary inquisition, in 1650, states that about ten years previously, Hoole had been made a separate parish, by act of parliament. The consent of the rector of Croston had been purchased by Messrs. Thomas and Andrew Stones, for £400., in whom was vested the patronage of the living. It has since passed through various hands. The advowson is at present held by the Rev. F H Sewell, vicar of Cockerham, There are two small charities belonging to the parish, besides the school, noticed as follows in the charity commissioners' report .—

"*School*—By indenture, bearing date the 12th of February, 1774, it appears that this school was endowed with two closes in Much Hoole, called Twelve Acres, and Land called the Mutkell, purchased for £116, raised by subscription, with a view to apply the yearly income to the salary of a schoolmaster The closes are let for £16 6s, which is paid to the schoolmaster, who likewise receives a yearly sum of £10. from the rector. For this salary he instructs gratuitously in reading all the poor children of the parish, whose parents choose to send them."

From the parliamentary inquisition, in 1650, it appears that a £10. per annum was given by Mr Stones, the patron of the living, to a school in Much Hoole Perhaps this is the £10 referred to by the commissioners, as paid by the rector. Bishop Gastrell, has the following curious entries with reference to this trust :—

"There is a School here endowed wth 10*l* per annum, to be paid by ye Rector, as appears by his certificate of ye value of his Living recorded in the Exchequer anno 1708, and by several witnesses now living, anno 1722, but how or by whom it was settled, I cannot yet learn.

"Certificate of ye same Rectour [Mr. James Whitaker] anno 1725, yt there is no Free School or any other School wth in ye Parish."

A methodist chapel was erected near the "Mess Houses," in 1824, and a primitive methodist chapel, near the same place, in 1828 Carr house was built in the seventeenth century, by John Stones, esq This residence is situated in Bretherton, but is subject to the taxation of the parish of Hoole. Mr. Baines mentions a farm-house, in the village of Much Hoole, with some remains of a moat; but he adds that it "is without history." The township of Much Hoole contains 1,746 statute acres of land. The annual rateable value of the property, in 1854, was £2,661. The population in 1851, amounted to 775

Little Hoole, a neighbouring township, is included in the parish of Much Hoole Roger de Montebegon granted this manor to the priory of Thetford. The late Rice George Fellowes, esq., of Edmonton, in Midddlesex, was lord of the manor and proprietor of the soil. Since his demise, a portion has been sold. The remainder is vested in his widow. The manor-house, called Marsh house, is the residence of the rector. A primitive methodist chapel was erected in Little Hoole, near the Raikes-

[a] See part 4, of the present volume, for a biographical notice of Horrocks.

brook, in 1854. The population of the township, in 1851, numbered 202 individuals. The area includes 1,201 statute acres of land. The annual rateable value of the property, in 1854, was £1,553.

TARLETON PARISH.

TARLETON was separated from Croston and made a distinct parish in the year 1821. The island near the "more" of Croxton, the land called Tarlton and Littlehole, with the men and all that pertained to them, were granted by Roger de Montebegon, to the Cluniac priory of Thetford, in the county of Norfolk [t] John Malherbe, supposed to be a brother of Roger de Montebegon, about the same time, gave all the holms, or marsh lands, near the "more" of Tarleton, in Lailondeshire, to the abbey of Cockersand.[u] The prior of Thetford quit claimed to the abbot all his right to the said holms, etc. Alexander Banastre, of Bank, held the manor of Tarleton, in the reign of Richard II. He appears to have succeeded a family named from the township. On the marriage of Thomas Hesketh, with Margaret, daughter and co-heiress of Thomas Banastre, a portion of Tarleton passed to the Hesketh, of Rufford. The remainder continued in the Banastre family, till the marriage of Anne, daughter of Christopher Banastre, with Thomas Fleetwood, esq. It again passed by marriage to the Leghs, of Lyme Anthony James Keck, of Straughton grange, in the county of Leicester, was married, in 1765, to Elizabeth, second daughter of Peter Legh, of Lyme. His son Lieut. Colonel George Anthony Legh Keck, and Sir Thomas G Hesketh, bart, are, at the present time, joint owners of the manor Tarleton church is dedicated to St. James. Mr. Baines says, "The Fleetwoods, of Bank hall, joint lords of the manor, erected Tarleton chapel, now church, in 1717, and on the 24th of July, 1719, the edifice was consecrated." The Rev. Canon Raines says.—"Baines is singularly inexact in his account of this church. * * Bishop Gastrell is wrong in the date 1720, and Ecton in giving St. Mary as the patron saint" Mr. Baines makes no mention of any chapel previously to the one consecrated in 1719. From the bishop's MSS, in the Registry, Chester, it appears, that Thomas Hesketh, esq., and Mrs H. M. Legh, the joint owners of the manor, the Rev Henry Leadbetter, rector of Croston, and twenty-three freeholders of Tarleton, in 1718, petitioned Bishop Gastrell for a license to erect a new chapel at Tarleton The petitioners stated that during "the late unhappy Usurpation an edifice was built by the prevailing Faction, in Tarleton, and used for a pretended place of Worship." After the Restoration, service was occasionally performed, according to the ritual of the church of England. Having never been

t Ellis's Monas. vol. 5, nu. 6, p 150 u Ex. Cart. de Ann 7 et 8. Ric. II n 1 consecrated or endowed, it gradually fell into decay. The lord and lady of the manor gave the site of the old ruined chapel, and the principal land owners agreed to build a new edifice without any expense to the rector. The petitioners likewise subscribed £200. towards the endowment, and hoped to obtain a grant of a similar sum from Queen Anne's bounty. They agreed that the minister should be nominated by the rector of Croston, for the time being, on the recommendation of the lords of the manor of Tarleton and the principal inhabitants, who should be members of the established church. A squabble afterwards arose, when the chapel was nearly completed. It was alleged that the edifice was not built on the site originally intended, but about one hundred rods from the locality where the presbyterian chapel had stood. The principal subscribers assigned the following as their reasons for changing the site:—On the spot selected, there had previously stood a chapel of great note and antiquity, dedicated, according to tradition, to St. Helen. From the bones which had been dug up, especially in preparing for the foundations of the new building, it appeared to have been parochial. The baptistry near the chapel was still called St. Helen's well, which had been much resorted to, within then living memory, by the devotees of the period, although the chapel itself had fallen into decay about the beginning of the preceding century. In addition to these considerations, the site was much superior, and more commodious for the inhabitants of Sollom and Bretherton, who would often make use of the chapel, when prevented by water from attending the parish church. In the year 1548, a chantry in Tarleton chapel was dissolved. In 1650, the parliamentary inquisitors recommended the building of a new church at the end of the lane called the "Black Gate Lane End, *where a church is now building* for the inhabitants of Tarlton, Holmes, and Zollom." They likewise recommended that the church should be made parochial. The number of families in the district was eighty-seven, from which they concluded the congregation would amount to four hundred and thirty-one persons. The living is in the patronage of the rector of Croston. Two charities pertain to Tarleton, besides the following:—

"1650. *School.* There is a school-room in this parish which bears upon it the date of 1650, and which is repaired out of the funds of the parish. Part of a field near Tarleton bridge, supposed to have been given by a Mr. Johnson, was sold to the Leeds and Liverpool Canal Company for £320., which produces in interest £12. 16s. per annum; the other part lets for £6. per annum. Besides this field there are four other parcels of land which let for £10., and another source of income is derived from a sum of £50. The whole number of scholars is about 80, of whom 20 are free. Annual income £31. 6s." [v]

A "school of industry and Sunday school," for girls and the younger

v Char. Com. Rep.

boys, was built in 1839, by subscription and a grant from the National Society. The land was given by the Rev. S. Master, rector of Croston. The school is supported by annual donations from Sir T. G. Hesketh, bart., G. A. Legh Keck, esq., and the Rev. S. Master, and the pence of the children. A methodist chapel, in Tarleton, was re-built in 1832. A small chapel was erected in 1851. A charter was granted by William III., in 1700, to Thomas Fleetwood, esq., of Bank hall, authorising the holding of an annual fair, upon the site of Martin Mere. Other charters were likewise granted, but their powers have fallen into disuse. Thomas Fleetwood was the first who attempted, on an extensive scale, the drainage of Martin Mere, or the "Martinensian Marsh," as it is some times styled.[w] His efforts were not very successful, but since his time large tracts of fertile land have been reclaimed.[x] Upon the strength of the charter alluded to, a convivial party assembles annually at the Ram's Head Inn. The members of the "corporation," after electing a "Lord Mayor" for the ensuing year, regale themselves in the most orthodox manner; the worthy host catering with a liberality calculated to win "golden opinions" from even more distinguished civic functionaries than those who devote their attention to the municipal business of the "antient borough of Tarleton." The parish and township includes Tarleton, Sollom, and Holmes. The total area is 5,534 statute acres. The property was rated, in 1854, at the annual value of £6,844. In 1851, the population amounted to 1,945.

CROSTON PARISH.

The parish of Croston formerly included those of Rufford, Tarleton, Hoole, Chorley, and Hesketh-with-Becconsall. It at present comprises the townships of Croston, Bispham, Bretherton, Mawdesley, and Ulnes-Walton. The parish, which is generally of a low and level character, is watered by the rivers Douglas and Yarrow. King John, in exchange for other lands, in 1201, gave Hugh le Porteur twenty marks in Croxton, and ten marks in the town of Croxton Saracene.[y] Three years afterwards, he granted lands which had been Hugh le Porteur's, together with ten marks of land in Crokeston, which had belonged to William de St. Albans, to G. Luttrell.[z] Roger de Montebegon gave ten carucates and six bovates of land, in Croston, to his brother, John Malherbe, to be held in knight service.[a] At the same period, Aumeric Pincerna held three fees in Crocstun, Bulham, and Filingham. Annabella, one of the three daughters and co-heiresses of Richard Fitton, lord of half the manor of Rufford, "married Edmund Leigh, lord of Crostone, 17th Edward I. He and

w So called on Mr. Fleetwood's monument, in Meols church.

x See page 507.

y Rot. Chancell, 3 John, m. 7.

z Rot. Lit. Claus.

a "Testa de Nevill."

his wife gave their inheritance to Sir William Heskayte, knt., confirmed by Sir William Leigh, 22nd Edward III., 1343." [a] The document quoted further states that "Dame Mawde, d. & co-heir of Richard Fytton," who married Sir William Heskayte, "had all the lands of the co-heirs of Richard Fytton by gift." A moiety of the manor was previously vested in Sir John De la Mere. One of his daughters married Sir Thomas Fleming, of Wath, and another, William del Lee. The latter, in the 46th Edward III., held a moiety of the manor of Croston and Maudishlegh. Elizabeth, daughter of John Fleming, married Thomas Heskayte, and Alice, daughter of William Lee, married Thomas Ashton, about the time of Henry VI. Ann, daughter and co-heiress of Richard Ashton, married John Trafford, who died in 1686. His representative, J. Randolphus de Trafford, esq., is now lord of a moiety of the manor of Croston. The other portion descended to the Hesketh family. Monacha, another daughter and co-heiress of Richard Ashton, married Alexander Hesketh, of Aughton. Thomas Norris, esq., of Redvales, Bury, and afterwards of Howick house, purchased the Hesketh moiety from the Rev. Streynsham Master, D.D., rector of Croston, about the year 1825, who had previously acquired it by purchase from Sir Thomas Dalrymple Hesketh, bart. A church at Croston was in existence at the time of the Conquest. It was granted by Roger de Poictou to the monastery of St. Martin, Sees, in Normandy. The patronage was exercised by the priory of St. Mary, at Lancaster. In 1291, it was valued at £33. 19s. 9d. A stipend of £3. 19s. 9d., was, in 1588, payable to the clerk of Croston, out of the revenues of the duchy of Lancaster. [b] The rectory was appropriated to the abbey of St. Saviour, of Sion, by the pope, Martin V. In 1420, it was ordained a vicarage by the bishop of Litchfield. The patronage passed from the crown, after the dissolution of the monasteries, to Anthony Browne, of Southweld, Essex. It was afterwards frequently disposed of. It became vested in 1755, in Legh Master, esq., M.P. His son the Rev. Robert Master, D.D., sold the advowson to Le Gendre Nicholas Starkie, esq. In 1821, it was transferred to George Smith, esq., brother to Lord Carington. In 1650, the net value of the living was returned at £300. 9s. 3d. per annum. The church comprises nave, aisles, chancel, tower, and two chapels. In the Valor of Pope Nicholas, (1291) the chapels are not mentioned. One of these, a chantry, founded by the Hesketh and dedicated to St. John the Baptist, is called the Rufford chapel. The other is termed the Becconsall chapel. It was styled a chantry in 1538. In the seventeenth century, it passed to the Banastres, of Bank. Both chapels were purchased from Sir Thomas D. Hesketh, bart., by the rector. The church

a Hesketh pedigree, of Rufford. b Birch's MSS. British Museum.

was re-built in the sixteenth century. A brief was obtained in 1743, for the re-building of the church. There is a catholic chapel in Croston, and another in Mawdesley. The latter was built in 1830. A new and handsome structure is now in the course of erection at Croston, by the munificence of J. Randolphus de Trafford, esq. A methodist meeting room was opened in 1828. Croston old hall was built in the seventeenth century. It was taken down at the latter part of the last century, and a new edifice erected. The rectory was built about the same period as the old hall. Bamford house, in Mawdesley, now converted into a public house, was built in the seventeenth century. Black Moor house was erected about the same time. Bispham hall was built in the sixteenth century. Bank hall, Bretherton, long the manorial residence of the Banastres, is mentioned previously to the reign of Edward II. The present edifice, which is of timber and brick, with the date 1608, inscribed over the west door, has undergone a complete restoration. Mawdesley hall, a massive stone building, was long the residence of the family of that name. Heskin new hall, in the adjoining township, was built by this family. A branch of the Nelsons, of Fairhurst, held lands in Mawdesley, in the third year of the reign of Richard II. Mr. Baines says:—

"The celebrated naval hero, Lord Nelson, expressed to Mr. Townsend, the herald, during the search for his pedigree, a strong desire to establish himself as a descendant from a Lancashire family; but the name of Nelson is of considerable standing in the county of Norfolk, and to that county we are obliged reluctantly to surrender this most distinguished ornament to the British arms."

Ulnes-Walton is chiefly occupied by yeomen and small landed proprietors. The Faringtons, however, possess a large estate within the township. An old cross is preserved in the garden belonging to a farmer named Gradwell. Tradition says it marks the site of an ancient cell. There are several valuable charities belonging to the parish of Croston. The free school, situated in the church yard, was erected in 1660, by the Rev. James Hyatt, rector, and endowed with rent charges to the amount of £14. This has since been augmented to £21. 9s. per annum.[e] A school was founded in the township of Bispham, by Richard Durning, in 1675. The base of an ancient cross, near the centre of the village, indicates the origin of the name of the place. Leland, in the reign of Henry VIII., speaking of Croston, says that it then possessed "a poore or no Market." The inhabitants are principally occupied in agricultural pursuits. There is, however, a little fancy hand loom weaving done in the parish. A few years ago, a cotton mill was erected not far from the village; but it has not been in operation for some months past. The following table shows

e Char. Com. Rep. XV.

Southport, Lancashire (from the Sea)

Southport, Lancashire

Birkdale Church, Southport, Lancashire.

Victoria Bath & Promenade, Southport, Lancashire.

the area, population, and annual value of the property, in the townships composing the parish of Croston:—

Township.	Acreage, according to the ordnance survey.	Population in 1851.	Annual Rateable Value, in 1854.
Croston	2,361	1,500	£5,087
Mawdesley	2,934	887	£5,068
Bispham	926	270	£1,643
Bretherton	2,428	818	£3,871
Ulnes Walton............	2,105	556	£3,602
Total	10,754	4,031	£19,271

SOUTHPORT.

This fashionable watering place is situated in the parish of North Meols, and in the hundred of West Derby. It, nevertheless, possesses claims of sufficient importance to preclude its being entirely omitted in a history of the environs of Preston. Mr. Baines says: "From the Teutonic word *Melo*, farina, are derived the Saxon terms *Mell, Meol*, and our *meal*, which have each been figuratively employed to designate this parish, in consequence of the number of *sand* hills which it contains." This is very ingenious; but it is infinitely more probable that the name of the district is derived from the Ancient British word *meol*, or *moel*; which, according to Owen's Welsh dictionary, signifies "a heap or pile, a conical hill, its top smooth, or void of rocks and woods." Southport, like Blackpool, is an entirely modern town. In 1792, the first inn or hotel was built by Mr. Sutton. The locality was known at the period as South Hawes. It is said that an indentation or bay, with water to the depth of seventeen fathoms, formerly existed near to the site of the present town. Previously to the erection of the inn, a few visitors resided at Churchtown, about two miles distant, and were driven in rustic vehicles to the South Hawes, for the purpose of bathing. This inn has lately been taken down. It was originally named in derision, "Duke's Folly." It proved, however, the nucleus of one of the most prosperous and fashionable watering places on the western coast of England. It is said to have received its present name from a Mr. Barton, surgeon, who, on the occasion of the opening of Mr. Sutton's hotel, "christened" the place after the fashion adopted at ship launches. Smashing a bottle of wine, and scattering the contents around him, he exclaimed,—"This place shall be called Southport." In 1809, the village comprised no more than thirty houses, inhabited by about one hundred persons. It gradually, however, continued to progress. The Hesketh Arms Hotel, was built in 1821. The chapel of ease, named Christ Church, was erected in 1820. An independent chapel was built in 1823, to which a school was added two years afterwards. A Wesleyan methodist chapel was erected in 1824, and a national school in 1825. A marine fund was established in 1825, for the purpose of rewarding fishermen and seamen, who might expose themselves in rescuing the crews of vessels and other persons, whose lives might be endangered on the coast. The Strangers' Charity was founded in 1806. Its object is to afford assistance to poor sick persons who may be recommended to try the benefit of sea bathing. This institution has met with so much patronage that a large and commodious edifice, for the reception of patients, has lately been erected near the north end of the town. In 1836, Southport contained about 340 houses and nearly 800 inhabitants. This large number of private residences, lodging houses, and hotels, met with ample support. Baths, a ball room, a billiard room, a news room, a temporary theatre, and other attractions, were provided for the entertainment and instruction of visitors. The progress of Southport has since been extremely rapid. In 1851, the population of the township of North Meols had risen to 8,694. In 1854, the property was assessed to the county rate at the annual value of £27,605. On the previous assessment, in 1841, it was valued at £17,426. It is now approachable by railway in every direction. Magnificent private residences have been built, and several first class hotels offer every desirable accommodation. An extensive promenade overlooks the sands, superior baths have been erected, and a covered market provided. A handsome new and additional episcopal church, some other places of worship, and a very elegant and commodious town hall have likewise been erected. Lord-street, the main thoroughfare, is a truly noble avenue, upwards of a mile in length. The gardens which front the houses on each side give to Southport a more rural character than is possessed by either Lytham or Blackpool, or indeed most other watering places. Southport, like Blackpool, has given birth to a suburb on the south. It is situated in the township of Birkdale, and already possesses a considerable population. A new episcopal church, with a handsome spire, is nearly finished. Many beautiful and elegant villas have been erected here, and land is laid out for others of a similar character. The beach on the Southport coast is low, and the tide retires to a considerable distance, but the sands are very level, and so firm and smooth, that not only pedestrians but vehicles of every description traverse them with the same ease as the public highway. Blackpool has been styled the "Brighton of the North," and Southport the "Montpellier of England." The locality is unquestionably healthy. Many of the native population attain an extreme old age. This is attributed to the general dryness and purity of the atmosphere, arising from the sandy nature of the soil and the slight rainfall. The group of desolate sand hills, lying to the north, with their barren summits but partially clothed with hardy star grass, and deep valleys dressed in a garment of rich verdure interwoven with numerous wild flowering plants, is much frequented by the visitors. The comforts and elegancies of civilization are presented in immediate contiguity with a scene almost as wild and uncultivated as though the foot of man had never previously pressed the sod. The lover of solitude and Nature may enjoy himself here to "the top of his bent," with the comfortable reflection that when his appetite for lonely contemplation loses its zest, and that of the corporeal man, stimulated by the health-laden breezes from the sea, begins to rebel, he may, in a few moments, exchange his barren seat on the apex of the desert *moel* for the couch of the well provided dining room; and when the "crowd, the hum, the shock of men," jars upon his sensative nerves and more refined sympathies, he can again return, "to muse o'er flood and fell," and truly feel and exclaim with the poet,

> "This is not solitude; 'tis but to hold
> Converse with Nature's charms, and view her stores unroll'd."

APPENDIX.

THE ROMAN TOPOGRAPHY OF LANCASHIRE.

After the first chapter of this work had passed through the press, the author received a courteous communication from John Hodgson Hinde, esq., of Acton house, Felton, near Newcastle, calling his attention to a new reading of the inscription on the celebrated Ribchester altar, dedicated to Apollo. In his introduction to the history of Northumberland,[d] a proof sheet of which he kindly forwarded, Mr. Hinde expresses his approval of the old route through Manchester and Ribchester, as the tenth iter of Antoninus; but he removes the station Bremetonacis from Overborough to Ribchester. Dr. Bruce, in the Archæological Journal, (1855),[e] has the following observations upon this subject:—

"To one other altar only will we direct attention. Though not from the region of the Wall, it still belongs to the north of England. It is without doubt the most elaborately carved altar which the Roman residents in Britain have left us. It is now preserved in the quadrangle of St. John's College. Camden mentions it and tells us it was found in the Roman station of Ribchester. The inscription, which he informs us 'was copied for him,' he gives as follows:—

SEO ESAM
ROL NASON
OS ALVEDN
AL. Q. Q. SAR
BREVENM
BEDIANIS
ANTON I
VS MEC. VI.
IC DOMV
ELITER.

"Never perhaps, was so unmeaning a concatenation of letters submitted to the gaze of a bewildered antiquary. Camden could make nothing of the inscription, but suggests somewhat waggishly that it contained little more than the *British* names of places adjoining. Horsely grappled with Camden's corrupted copy, and elicited one portion of the truth. He says, 'I believe the fourth line may be Alæ equitum Sarma [tarum].'

"The altar seems soon after its discovery to have been used as a common building stone in the erection of Salisbury Hall. In 1815, it was disentombed and fell into the hands of Dr. Whitaker, who bequeathed it to St. John's College. Dr. Whitaker (History of Richmondshire, vol. 2, p. 461) thus expands the inscription: *Deo sancto Apollini*

d The Antiquarian society of Newcastle have undertaken the completion of the History of Northumberland, left imperfect by the death of the late Rev. John Hodgson. At the request of the society, J. H. Hinde, esq., has undertaken to prepare the introduction.

e Vol. 12, p. 225. Paper by the Rev. J. C. Bruce, L.L.D., F. S. A.

Apono ob salutem Domini nostri ala equitum Sarmatarum Breneten. sub Dianio Antonino centurione legionis sextæ victricis. The correctness of this reading, in the main, cannot be disputed, but one or two emendations may be suggested. Instead of Apono, which Dr. Whitaker conceives to be an epithet of Apollo, Mapono is probably the true reading. We nowhere else meet with Aponus (indolent) as an epithet of this deity. At Plumpton, in Cumberland, an altar has been found which is inscribed[f]

DEO
MAPONO
ET N. AVG

"To Mr. Roach Smith I am indebted for the reading now suggested, as well as for the idea that Maponus may be the British name for Apollo as Belatucader is of Mars. It is nothing uncommon to address a god both by his classical and local name. The first letter in the fourth line appears to be N (numerus) rather than A (ala); both designations as applied to a troop of cavalry are common. The last letter in the ninth line is worthy of notice. The sculptor seems in the first instance to have made the word *domu* and then to have altered it to the usual form of *domo*.

"The chief value of the inscription depends upon the fifth line. Mr. Hodgson Hinde, in a paper read before the Society of Antiquaries at Newcastle-upon-tyne, and published in their Transactions,[g] conjectured (without having seen the altar) that Dr. Whitaker's reading of Brenceten, should be Bremeten. Such, as is shown in the wood cut, appears to be the fact. He further argues that the station at which the Sarmatian cavalry (Ribchester) were located, was the Bremeten racum of the Notitia. He does so on the same principle that High Rochester is conceded to be Bremenium and Risingham Habitancum."

This was written previously to the discovery of the Roman station at Walton-le-dale, near Preston. After reading the paper, by the author of the present work, published in the Transactions of the Lancashire and Cheshire Historic Society,[h] Mr. Hodgson Hinde maintains his previous position in the following terms:—[i]

"On the 10th Iter of Antoninus. The consideration bestowed upon the 10th Iter by Mr. Hodgson was confined to the northern portion of its route, nor indeed up to the period when he wrote his last volume, had any difference of opinion been expressed as to its course from the southern boundary of ancient Northumberland, by Manchester and Ribchester, to Overborough, near Kirkby Lonsdale. The difficulties were assumed to be confined to the stations north of Overborough.

"Manchester occurs in another Iter (the 2nd) as well as in the 10th, and is there designated Mamucium or Manucium, and described as 18 miles distant from Condate, the next station to the south. In the 10th Iter also Condate occurs, and the next station, at the same distance of 18 miles north, is Mancunium.

"It is not wonderful, therefore, that Mancunium has been identified by all our elder antiquaries with Mamucium, and the site of each fixed at Manchester. Again, the next station but one to the north of Mancunium is Bremetonacum, a name so nearly resembling Bremetenracum, in the Notitia, that it is difficult to divest oneself of the idea that the two names are substantially identical and both belong to the same place. Now Bremetenracum of the Notitia is proved by an inscription to be at Ribchester, and a strong presumption is raised that Bremetonacum, of the Itinerary, is also there; especially as the actual distance from Manchester to Ribchester corresponds, with sufficient accuracy, with the Itinerary distance from Mancunium to Bremetonacum.

"The recent investigations of two gentlemen resident at Warrington, Mr. Robson and Mr. Beamont, have fixed the site of Condate at a place called Stockton Heath, on the Cheshire side of the Mersey,

f "Lyson's Cumberland, p. crv." g "Archæologia Æliana, vol 4, p. 109."

h Vol 8, p 127. In this paper the author entered no further into the discussion of the route than to show that Dr. Robson's theory was supported by the discovery of a station near Preston, as he had predicted. Dr. Robson professed not to trace the iter beyond Lancaster. The substance of the paper referred to is embodied in the first chapter of this volume.

i History of Northumberland, p. 22.

at no great distance from the town in which they reside. Further than this, traces of a Roman road have been discovered at intervals nearly in the line of the modern highway which passes through Warrington, by Wigan and Preston, to Lancaster, and the claims of this road to be considered the true original of the 10th Iter have been enforced with great ability by Mr. Robson and others.

"This theory involves the abandonment of the assumption that Mancunium of the 10th Iter is identical with Mamucium of the 2nd, and that Bremetonacum of the Itinerary is the same place as Bremetenracum of the Notitia It implies also the existence on two nearly parallel lines of road, of two places whose names so nearly resemble each other as Mamucium and Mancunium, and again of two others so similar as Bremetenracum and Bremetonacum.

"These may not be sufficient reasons for rejecting Mr Robson's views, but they are strong grounds for not admitting them without most careful scrutiny.

"It is not enough to show a fair and well-defined Roman road, in order to claim for it a place in the Itinerary of Antoninus. On the contrary, some of the most magnificent specimens of the imperial highways are unnoticed in that document, and were undoubtedly of later construction. Of this we have a striking instance in the Roman road from Lincoln northwards to the Humber.

"The oldest roads indeed were probably those which were least distinguished for their magnificence; they generally passed through an upland country, where the rivers were crossed with facility, near their sources, and costly bridges were thus avoided. In the long period of Roman domination, subsequent to the reign of Antoninus Pius, there was abundant time to substitute or to add level lines of coast road, where hilly tracts alone previously existed, and during that period it is probable the road by Warrington to Lancaster was laid out, after the resources of the country were developed, and the construction of bridges and other heavy engineering works no longer presented an insurmountable obstacle

"This opinion is further confirmed by the account furnished by Mr. Robson, of the formation of the road-way, which he represents as constructed of loose stones and gravel, whereas the majority at least of the older roads, wherever they are met with intact, present a paved surface

"On the whole, the balance of probability seems to be in favour of the views of the older antiquarians, who placed Manchester and Ribchester on the 10th Iter, but the balance of evidence may yet be reversed, if a line from Lancaster should hereafter be traced northward, agreeing with that Iter in its details, and it should be found impossible to connect Overborough with any corresponding northern route. Under any circumstances, the discoveries of Mr. Robson and other active members of the Historical Society of Lancashire and Cheshire are of great value, and will probably lead to the ultimate solution of this most difficult problem, by directing to it an amount of attention which has hitherto been dormant.

"In endeavouring to render intelligible the merits of this controversy, it has been found convenient to reverse the order of the stations as they occur in the Itinerary, commencing at the south end instead of from the north, and thus securing an ascertained starting point. With regard to the inscription by which Ribchester is identified with Bremetenracum, the editor may be permitted to refer to a paper of his own in the Archæologia Æliana, vol. iv. page 109, and to Dr Bruce's remarks on the same inscription in the Journal of the Archæological Institute, vol xii p 225-7

"As regards the Roman road from Warrington to Lancaster, the reader is referred for further information to a series of most interesting papers in the Transactions of the Historical Society of Lancashire and Cheshire, vol. ii. p 27, vol ii. p 34, vol. viii p 127"

This view of the situation of Bremetonacis brings the argument exactly back to its original position, as propounded by Camden Dr. Whitaker, however, was extremely horrified at what he termed "this delusion" on the part of "the father of antiquities," and rejoiced exceedingly at his renunciation of the obnoxious doctrine. After noticing Leland's uncertainty as to the probable origin of Overborough, he says —

"Even Camden, who had better helps than Leland, was long in uncertainty on the subject; for in his third edition of 1590, we find a continuation of the error with which he set out, that Ribchester was the Bremetonacæ of Antonine; and from the imaginary resemblance of Lac, which runs by Overborough, that this was the Roman Galacum. * * Hitherto we see that the father of antiquities was in total darkness, which led him to fix the site of Coccium far too near Mancunium, and in a place where there were no vestiges of Roman antiquity; while he violently transferred Bremetonacæ to Ribchester, and, from a mere resemblance of name, which seems to have been the parent of all these errors, Galacum to Overborough. In this delusion, however, Camden did not die; for in the folio of the Britannia (A.D. 1670), this passage is altered for the better." k

The alteration for the better, in Dr. Whitaker's opinion, consisted in the placing of Bremetonacæ at Overborough. Soon after the receipt of Mr. Hodgson Hinde's courteous communication, the author visited Cambridge, and carefully sketched the letters forming the word which has introduced a new and certainly important item in the list of facts and conjectures relative to the Roman topography of Lancashire. There can be no doubt that the letters as nearly resemble BREMETNN as any others. The B, R, and E, seem pretty certain. As the last perpendicular stroke of the next letter is likewise used for the upright line of the E, and the latter is *reversed* in its form, of course some difficulty exists in saying positively whether Dr. Whitaker's or Mr. Hinde's interpretation is correct. The author would certainly have read it as M, and not as N, had he known nothing of the controversy. The letter has been imperfectly formed by the sculptor, and the surface of the stone has suffered considerable injury. The next letter, given as T, is much injured, and is therefore very doubtful. The two last letters are either N. N., or N. M. On the whole there can be little doubt that BREMETNN is the more probable reading.

It is of the utmost importance that the precise amount of value due to this inscription, as evidence of the name of the station near which it was found, should be determined, inasmuch as the interpretation suggested by Mr. Hodgson Hinde doubtless points to the hilly route as the line of the 10th iter of Antoninus. This, at the same time, not only repudiates the theory of Dr. Robson and others, but clashes, to a considerable extent, with the views of both Dr. Whitaker and the historian of Manchester. It is certainly somewhat singular, that Dr. Whitaker, who had possession of this altar for some time, and who was the first to give anything approximating to a correct interpretation of the inscription, should have felt no sympathy with Camden's original opinion. The difference in the readings of Mr. Hodgson Hinde and the historian of Richmondshire amounts to no more than the change of a single letter. If Dr. Whitaker could for a moment have imagined, from its position in the sentence, or otherwise, that the term applied to the *locality where the altar was erected*, he would neither have written the sentences above quoted nor the following:—

"The word Breneten is to me wholly unintelligible, unless it refer to some subordinate tribe of the Sarmatians, the Sarmatæ Brenetenni. As to the peculiarity of placing an Ala of Sarmatian horse under a Roman centurion, it may easily be solved by supposing

k His. Rich., vol 2, p. 265.

them to be a new levy of raw soldiers placed under an experienced Roman officer, for the purpose of being disciplined. The Sarmatian horse were the Cossacks of the Roman armies."[l]

Mr. Hodgson Hinde contends the inscription intimates that the altar was erected by the centurion commanding a wing or troop of the Sarmatian cavalry, *stationed at* Bremeten; which he, viewing the term, like Sar, for Sarmatarum, to be a contraction, expands to Brementenracum, which he considers sufficiently near to Bremetonacis, or Bremetonacæ, as it is sometimes written, to identify the station in the Notitia with that of Antoninus. This is extremely plausible, and, if supported by other confirmatory evidence, would weigh heavily in the argument. But it is equally probable that the word may, as Dr. Whitaker suggests, have reference to a people or tribe, from amongst whom a portion of the soldiers may have been enlisted. This tribe may either have been foreign or native. Indeed, the term Bremetonacis has been considered as a Latin form of a British word, Bremetonax or Bremetonac, having reference to a tribe of people; the capital or chief location, as is common, being named after the tribe. Ribchester may have been in this district, and therefore a *troop* of horse belonging to this force might be stationed there, without at all invalidating the probability that the remaining portion of the soldiery might be located at the capital or elsewhere. There is no reason why Lancaster should not equally with Ribchester put forth its claims to the distinction of having been the chief Roman city in the county, or even a more extended territory. Lancaster has been comparatively neglected, while Ribchester has been written into notoriety by several distinguished authors. Yet there is nothing either in the size of the camp or the *extent* of the remains at Ribchester to demonstrate that it was a superior post to Lancaster. The latter place appears *never to have lost* its position, but to have remained the chief place under both the Saxon and Norman rulers; consequently its site has been continually subjected to the action of the builder and renovator. Hence the destruction of much of the remains of the Roman city. And yet a careful examination of what has been found on the spot and in the neighbourhood would indicate a much stronger fort and a larger population. There is good reason to believe that Lancaster possessed a stone rampart, a part of which, called the "Wery wall," remained till the time of Camden. Ribchester, on the contrary, appears, like Walton, to have been defended only by an earthen vallum. The vaunted temple of Minerva has evidently been, to borrow a phrase of Leland's, "a poore thing."[m] The ground at Ribchester, over which the remains extend, is very limited. No villas or other indications of a wealthy

l His. Rich., vol. 2, p. 462.

m See page 51.

Roman population have been found in the neighbourhood. At Lancaster, on the contrary, the environs have proved very prolific in remains, including vessels, altars, milliaria, and statues. In the town, Mr. Baines records the finding of altars, tombs, earthenware, coins, a potter's kiln, tiles, sacrificial cups, etc., together with a "large hewn stone, six feet under the surface, about three tons weight, supposed to have been the corner stone of a Roman temple." A number of coins of Vespasian and Domitian were found beneath this immense stone. From the depth, situation, character, and quantity of the remains discovered, it is evident that the many partial destructions of the place must, as stated by Mr. Baines, have had the effect of burying beneath the present town, "in one indiscriminate and impenetrable heap, *magazines of antiquities!*" If Lancaster had been so fortunate as to have possessed a local historian, with the learning and zeal of either of the Whitakers, it would, unquestionably, long since have challenged and received more consideration at the hands of those who have endeavoured to expound the topography of Roman Britain.

Of course, the explanation of the doubtful term now offered is merely conjectural; but it must not be forgotten that the one which identifies in it the ancient name of Ribchester, is conjectural also. The term may really apply to neither. It is by no means certain that Dr. Whitaker is not substantially correct, and that the true reading is NUMERUS EQUITUM SARMATARUM BREMETENSIUM, or a troop of the Bremetensian Sarmatian cavalry. But the Romans were not in the habit of naming their stations from the people composing the auxiliary troops. Still the suggestion of Mr. Hodgson Hinde is most valuable, and if other important facts and inferences could have been reconciled to it, the identity of Ribchester with the Bremetenracum of the Notitia would perhaps never have been disputed.

If it be conceded, likewise, that Bremetenracum and Bremetonacis are identical, then the tenth iter must have passed through Ribchester. In this case Camden's forsaken theory must be again revived and Coccium placed at Bury. Against this, and the confounding of Mamutium with Mancocunium, there are, however, many objections. Dr. Whitaker considered Bremetonacis at the required distance from Manchester, when he placed it at Overborough. Mr. Hodgson Hinde considers it to correspond with sufficient accuracy, when he brings it upwards of thirty miles nearer the latter town. The itinerary distance is only thirty-eight Roman, or about thirty-five English, miles; so that Mr. Hodgson Hinde is much nearer than his predecessor. But if the itinerary distances are referred to at all, they must be stated less vaguely. The distance between Manchester and Ribchester, by the Roman way, is less than thirty miles, so that no favourable evidence can be extracted from this source. The intermediate station, Coccium, if placed at Bury, will agree with the twenty Roman miles of the iter from Ribchester, as Bremetonacis; but no remains have been found near the place; and, again, it is little more than half the distance from Manchester marked in the itinerary as intervening between Coccium and Mancocunium. Antonine gives eighteen Roman miles as the distance of Condate from Mancocunium; while John Whitaker's station at Kinderton demands twenty-three. The next station to the north of Bremetonacis is Galacum, at twenty-seven Roman, or less than twenty-five English miles. Overborough, by the Roman route, is, as before stated, upwards of thirty miles. Beyond Overborough, all indications of the Roman road cease; still there remain three other stations in the iter to be placed! All attempts to find a Roman highway have hitherto failed; and yet, from the nature of the country, the chance of its preservation was immeasurably greater than that of the lower route, which has been the great thoroughfare from the earliest known period to the present time.

The whole of the old theory is based upon an assumption by the elder Whitaker, that the tenth iter met the second at Manchester, ran along its line to Condate, and then proceeded in its original direction. And it is made to perform this eccentric freak merely because the station in the second iter, to the east of Condate, is called Mamucium, and in some copies Manutium; while in the tenth iter appears a station north of Condate, written Mancocunium, but sometimes contracted to Mancunium. Independently of the facts that the distances are unfavourable to the old theory and the direct route is whimsically violated, as has been shown at page 31 of the present work, so far from being a difficulty, it is, in itself, infinitely more probable that Mancocunium and Mamutium were two distinct places, than that they were, as assumed, merely variations of the same name. Many of the different Roman stations in the country are *identitcal* in name, as many towns and villages are in modern times. Witness Alaunum, Venta, Durobrivæ, Mediolanum, etc. Many present but slight variation, as Durobrivis, Durolevum, Durovernum; all neighbouring stations in Kent. Nay, in one of the very itinera under consideration, there is a station Durobrivis, and another DuroCObrivis! Why therefore is ManCOcunium to be necessarily either Mamutium or Manutium?[n] And yet on this slender dogma the old doctrine rested! Truly, it needed some such important aid as that afforded by the reasonable conjecture of Mr. Hodgson Hinde, to delay its consignment to the cabinet devoted to the preservation of exploded theories.

n Manchester was written *Mame*cester till the end of the fifteenth century.

Instead of the itinerary distances supporting the claim of the route through the hills, the very reverse is the fact. The old theory, imperfect as it is, might have been accepted as the most probable interpretation, and the descrepancies attributed to corruptions in the text, previously to the discovery of stations near Warrington and Preston, and of the direct road which entered Lancashire from Cheshire, at the former place. These new facts, however, demand grave consideration. The premises upon which the old structure is erected must be again tested, and their true value assigned in the more complete chain of evidence now existing.

In favour of the line of the tenth iter passing through Warrington, Preston, Lancaster, Dalton, Muncaster, and Egremont, to Maryport, many facts and inferences may be adduced. In the first place, there is a continuous line of road from one end of the iter to the other, and the distances accord with the written figures, not only infinitely nearer than by the old fragmentary route, but much more so than is usually the case with the most approved of the recognised itinera. In the next place, Maryport, a well known flourishing station, abounding with remains, is situated at the mouth of the Solway, and at the end of the direct line of forts by the wall from the Tyne. It was thus the extreme north-west post of the Romans in Britain, and therefore a locality highly probable as the commencement of an iter. By this direction, in conjunction with the Watling-street, a complete line of communication is obtained diagonally across the island, from Maryport to Pevensey. It is the natural route, and most practicable for carriages. Its highway was wider than the hill road. Indeed, the latter, as some of the remains attest, was but about five yards broad; two vehicles could therefore scarcely pass on the crown of the agger with safety. Dr. Whitaker himself describes the road from Ribchester to Overborough, as "one of the most rugged and difficult stages in Britain; and for that reason," he further observes, "as I have elsewhere shown, was probably abandoned under the lower empire for the longer but more practicable line through the low country and by Lancaster." [o] The road through Warrington, Preston, Lancaster, etc., is not only "more practicable" but shorter than either the doctor's old or new route. It has been shown, on the authority of John Whitaker himself as well as others, that it is most probably the ancient British track. [p] The coins and other remains at Walton point to the station having been founded by Agricola on the site of a British fortress. This line of highway crossed the rivers by the nearest practicable fords at the head of the tidal water, and no bridges were either required or constructed. Supposing, for the sake of the argument, it be granted the track was not Romanised, (and then but imperfectly finished,)

o His. Rich., vol. 2, p. 266. p See pages 27 and 35.

till the reign of Julius Philippus. Even this is rather in favour than against its being the tenth iter of Antonine. Some necessity must have caused the repairs or re-construction of the road at this period, which, it is assumed, the milliaria inscribed to that emperor indicate. As the itinerary was not compiled or completed till the commencement of the following century, there is every reason to expect such a route recorded.[q] The very existence of *mile stones* on this highway is, in itself, strong presumptive evidence that it was not only a much frequented but a recorded route. By the new theory the western portion of the second iter likewise accords perfectly with the document. On the old one it does not. A single glance at the map will show that the direct route from York to Chester passes through Warrington. Nay, this line is continued to Segontium, on the coast of Wales, as directly as the nature of the country would permit. Such is the case at the eastern end. The direct course is still preserved from York to Prætorium, on the east coast. Thus, there are two great lines which intersect the country and cross each other, at Condate, nearly at right angles; the one running from the coast opposite France, to the north western extremity of England, and the then Roman Britain; the other from the coast of Wales opposite Ireland, in a north-easterly direction through Chester and York, to near Flamborough Head.

For these reasons, the author feels no inclination to amend that which he has given in the first chapter of this volume as the *most probable* Roman topography of the district; although he cheerfully acknowledges that the suggestion of Mr. Hodgson Hinde is most valuable and should not be lost sight of, as future discoveries may, and no doubt will, throw further light upon the subject. No permanent settlement of so difficult a question ought to be insisted upon, until every means of investigation and all the resources of logical inference have been fairly exhausted.

KILLINGSOUGH.

This name, as suspected (page 64), is of much older date than the tradition records. It is written Kylaneshalghe, in the "Inquisition Post Mortem" of the first duke of Lancaster, in the records of the Tower. The inquisition was taken in the thirty-sixth Edward III. This strengthens the probability that a Culdee cell or Cemetery formerly existed there.

BATTLE OF THE VINWED OR WINWEYDE.—(A.D. 655.)

Mr. Thomas Baines suggests the neighbourhood of Winwick as the probable site of this battle. Others say Winwidfield, near Leeds.[r] As

q Julius Philippus reigned between the years 244 and 249, and the date of the itinerary is given by Mr. Wright at "about the year 320."—Celt, Roman, and Saxon, page 457.

r See page 65.

Bede distinctly states that "King Osway concluded the aforesaid war in the country of Loidis," (Leeds), Winwidfield must certainly be preferred to the Lancashire site.

THE BATTLE OF BILLANGAHOH, NEAR WHALLEY. (A.D. 798.)

(SEE PAGE 66)

Since Dr. Whitaker's death, a relic of the battle of Billangahoh, has been discovered. Canon Raines says.—[s]

"In the year 1836, as Thomas Hubbersty, the farmer at Brock-hall, was removing a large mound of earth in Brock-hall Eases, about five hundred yards from the bank of the Ribble, on the left of the road leading from the house, he discovered a Kist-vaen, formed of rude stones, containing some large human bones and the rusty remains of some spear heads of iron. The whole crumbled to dust on exposure to air. Tradition has uniformly recorded that a battle was fought about Langho, Elker, and Buckfoot, near the Ribble; and this tumulus was opened within two hundred yards of a ford of the Ribble, (now called Bullasey-ford,) one of the very few points, for miles, by which that river could be crossed. The late Dr. Whitaker repeatedly, but in vain searched for remains of this battle, as he appears to have erroneously concluded that the scene of it was higher up the river, near Hacking Hall, at the junction of the Calder and Ribble"

The tumulus at Brockhall is evidently the one described by Dr. Whitaker. His words are:—"Of this great battle there are no remains, unless a large tumulus near Hacking Hall and in the immediate vicinity of Langho, be supposed to cover the remains of Alric or some other chieftain among the slain."[t] The site of the tumulus is marked on the ordnance map. It is scarcely three quarters of a mile from Hacking hall, and rather more than a mile from Langho chapel. No other tumulus is noticed by the ordnance surveyors, on the south side of the Ribble. Doubtless, similar remains would be disclosed, if the "lowes" mentioned at page 68 of this work were removed. Although on the opposite bank of the river, the nearest tumulus is scarcely half a mile from the one at Brockhall.

THE BATTLE OF BRUNANBURH.—(A.D. 934-7.)

(SEE PAGE 74.)

The author made known, at the dinner on the visit of the Lancashire and Cheshire Historic Society to Preston, in June, 1856, that he had devoted considerable time and labour in the collection of evidence, which he considered would demonstrate that the burying of the immense Anglo-Danish treasure at Cuerdale, had some connection with the great fight at Brunanburh; and that he intended to advance the claim of a neighbouring locality as the long lost site of this celebrated engagement. The bulk of what now appears in the second chapter of the present work, on this subject, was at the time written. This announcement created some interest in the question, and caused further investigation. A paper, by Mr. T. T.

s Notitia Cestriensis, vol. 2, page 286 t His. Whalley, page 34.

Wilkinson, of Burnley, was shortly afterwards read before the Lancashire and Cheshire Historic Society, in which that gentleman supported the author's general view, and claimed Burnley as the locality. A lecture, which he delivered on the same subject, being reported in the newspapers, gave birth to some discussion. Mr. C. A. Weddle, of Wargrove, near Warrington, in two communications to the "Preston Chronicle," objects to a Lancashire site, and prefers Brunton, in Northumberland.[u] It is necessary not only that the author should notice some of the objections raised, but that additional evidence, procured since the time of the printing of the matter in chapter second, should be added here. Mr. Weddle's objection to Burnley on the plea that Roman roads do not lead to that locality, is valueless; simply because the reverse is the fact. The great road from Flamborough Head, by York and the Penine Alps, to the Ribble and Wyre, passes over Whalley moor. This line is crossed by two roads from the north to the south; one near Ribchester, and the other near Preston.[v] Mr. Weddle's map may not have these marked. The great road from the Wyre through the Penine chain, however, is laid down on the "six-inch" ordnance map. It was surveyed by the late Mr. Just, of Bury. There are several other connecting causeways likewise given in Dr. Whitaker's "History of Whalley." Mr. Weddle objects to the Welsh allies of Anlaf coming from Wales. They certainly may have been only the Cymri of Strathclyde and Cumberland. The probability is, however, as there was a general confederation against the growing power of Athelstan, that both branches of the Celtic population joined in the confederacy. They were included in the vanquished in 926.[w] It will be seen that the author does not prefer Burnley as the site of the great battle.[x]

u Preston Chronicle, March 2nd, 1857.

v See ante, page 638.

w The Saxon Chronicle says,—"This year fiery lights appeared in the north part of the heavens. And Sihtric perished; and King Athelstan obtained the kingdom of the North-humbrians. And he ruled all the kings who were in this island; first, Howell, king of the West-Welsh, and Constantine, king of the Scots; and Owen, king of the Monmouth people; and Aldred, son of Ealdulf, of Bamborough; and they confirmed the peace by pledge, and by oaths, at the place which is called Eamot, on the 4th before the Ides of July; and they renounced all idolatry, and after that submitted to him in peace." Mr. Wilkinson identifies Eamot with Emmet, near Burnley.

x See page 82. It is there stated as not improbable that the battle in which Athelstan's governor, or deputy, Gudrekir, fell, may have been fought in the neighbourhood of Burnley. Gudrekir may have attempted to prevent the junction of the pirates from the Humber with their allies from Ireland and the north. The tradition records that a *distinguished chieftain* was slain during the heptarchy. At Brunanburh, the poem says there were *five kings and seven earls* "on the battle stead, by swords in slumber laid." Popular tradition does not generally *diminish*, but rather exaggerates, circumstances of this character. The number of battles which have taken place in the neighbourhood of Walton have naturally caused great confusion in the traditions. Every event of this character is associated with the Scotch,—as in the Fylde, the Danes are held responsible for all warlike ravages. Indeed, at Brunanburh, a great number of Scots, with their king and prince were engaged. Bruce advanced to the pass of the Ribble and burnt Preston, in the reign of Edward II. Cromwell defeated the Scotch under the duke of Hamilton, in the same neighbourhood, 1648. Charles II. with a Scotch army passed through in the following year. After the battle

It is too far distant from the sea. The same remark applies to Mr. Weddle's locality. It is a long march from Brunton to the Solway, especially after such a struggle as that at Brunanburh! It will require some very strong facts to shake the authority of the old poem in this respect. Even Mr. Weddle must grant the Roman roads are convenient enough for the pass of the Ribble. The Irish from Dublin, and the rovers from the Humber, have a direct line of road between them. The Cumbrian and the Scots are likewise amply accommodated. The western Welsh, if they formed a part of the confederation, are equally so, by the way of Warrington. This road would exactly meet the requirements of Athelstan. These Roman highways all meet not far from the great "pass of the Ribble," one of the most important military positions in the district. The treasure is found buried in the neighbourhood of the ford, and to the south is Bamber, Brownedge and some other places to be mentioned hereafter. Additional evidence will yet be given to show that Bamber is most probably a corruption of Brunburh. Mr. Weddle says: "Lancashire must have belonged to the Saxons, then, at least," (?) "and not to the Danes; nor do we ever hear of their losing it. And where are the footprints the Danes have left in their pad?" A reference to pages 82 and 85 of this volume, will sufficiently answer the question. Mr. Weddle's last sentence is a singularly unfortunate one. He will find "Danes' pad" enough, in all conscience, and that, too, in connection with the ancient "portus" of the Setantian people, which lies in a provokingly tempting situation, directly opposite to Dublin. The site chosen by Mr. Weddle is open to one serious objection, which he appears to have overlooked. For what earthly reason did the warriors from Norway and the Baltic sail past the Tyne, the Wear, and the Tees, in order to land in the Humber, if their friends and Anlaf's hereditary kingdom were near the Scottish border? Or, if after conquering the south portion of this section of the heptarchy, why did he and all his allies run away to the northern extremity? Anlaf does not appear to have lacked either skill, courage, or ambition, as his after life proves, as well as his conduct during the campaign under consideration. But place him and his victorious friends at the pass of the Ribble, and he stands prepared to retain his conquest, with every facility for safe retreat for himself and allies, in case of misfortune.[y] Mr. Weddle appears to feel that he has a weak point in the fact

of Worcester the Scotch fugitives were pursued through Preston. The Scotch occupied Preston in 1715, when the town was taken by general Wills. In 1745, part of the army of Prince Charles Edward Stuart was encamped at Walton, on their march to Derby; and Preston was a temporary resting place on their retreat. Hence the peasantry associate every thing of a warlike character with the Scotch. Even the Roman station was the burial ground of the "Scotch warriors," till the recent discovery by the author demonstrated the incorrectness of this very popular belief.

y "Fordun relates, that in the year after the battle of Bruningfield or Brunford, in which

that the place to which the name Brunton has been given, "is only a farm, with its accompanying buildings, erected in what *in former ages was called the Chollerford field of Wall*, since the cessation of border raids." It unfortunately happens that the district south of the Ribble severely suffered in the devastations committed by the Norman soldiery at the period of the Conquest. Large portions of the country were laid waste; others were covered with forest. Consequently the Domesday book gives no record, with three or four exceptions, of the townships in the hundred of Blackburn; otherwise the difficulty of showing the Saxon names of the locality now advanced as the scene of the battle of Brunanburh, would be materially lessened. The same observation certainly applies with equal truth to Mr. Weddle's locality. There is no difficulty in determining the meaning of the term Brunanburh. It is simply a fort, or dune, or hill, or defended homestead, situated in a neighbourhood characterised by springs. Bamberg, written in the maps of last century Bamber green, and now Bamber bridge, is not named as either a township or hamlet in the Norman record. The village is situated in the present township of Walton-le-dale; but it adjoins Brindle, which is both a parish and a township in itself. Here abundant documentary evidence is available to trace the corruption of the name. It is variously written in early deeds, Burnhul, Brinhill, Brand-hill; and, after becoming Brandle and Bryndhull, ends in its present Brindle.[z] It is by no means improbable that the land to the south-west of the Darwen, including Brownedge and Bamber Bridge, originally appertained to the Saxon parish of Brindle. The Darwen is evidently the natural boundary not only between the parish of Blackburn and Brindle, but of the hundreds of Leyland and Blackburn.[a] The district abounds in springs. Many are marked on the ordnance map as "Wells." The ordinary directory now records "two fine springs of exceedingly clear water called St. Ellen's Wells," about half a mile south-west of the village. Dr. Kuerden, who was born in the neighbourhood, about the year 1620, says:—

"Over against Swansey House, a little towards the hill, standeth an antient fabrick, once the manor house of Brindle, where hath been a chappel belonging to the same, and a little above it, a spring of very clear water, rushing straight upward into the midst of a fayr fountain, walled square about in stone and flagged in the bottom, very transparent to be seen, and a strong stream issuing out of the same. The fountain is called St. Ellen's Well, to which place the vulgar neighbouring people of the Red letter do much resort, with pretended devotion, on each year upon St. Ellen's day, where and when out of a foolish ceremony, they offer or throw into the well pins, which there being left may be seen a long time after by any visitor of that fountain."

From this the antiquity of the springs cannot be doubtful. Indeed a

---

Constantine and Malcolm (then his heir apparent and Prince of Cumberland), with their ally Anal-phus, son of Sitric, King of Northumberland, were defeated by King Athelstan, that monarch possessed himself of Cumberland and Westmoreland." Lyson's Cumberland, p. 5.

z See ante, page 600. a See ante, page 138.

district could scarcely be found to which the term would better apply. Immediately south of Brindle is Whittle, famous at this day for its alkaline and chalybeate waters. Some springs in the neighbourhood were known to the Romans, as is testified by the inscription on a medal found a few years ago.[b] Mr. Sibson says Bamberg means "war town," a *very significant* corruption of Brunburh, if a battle were fought there, especially with Burnhull or Brinhill in its immediate neighbourhood. Mr. Weddle himself has added another, and a most important link in the chain of evidence in favour of the Lancashire locality. After summing up the various names mentioned and their evident corruption and variations, he says :—

> "Two of them in particular, Weardune and Wendune, I have never seen noticed by any modern writer, yet *Weardune appears to me the most important name, if Brunanburg be excepted,* AND EVEN THIS IS NOT MORE SO. As to Wendune it is evidently a mistake in the transcribing for Werdune, the Anglo-Saxon r being nearly n, with a long bottom stroke on the left."

Mr. Weddle finds a Warden Hill, about two miles from the farm house in "Chollerford field." This he considers as very conclusive in favour of the latter place being the true Brunanburh. If such be the case, the existence of Wearden, at about a similar distance from Burnhull or Brinhill,[c] is equally if not more conclusive. The term Weardune, is sometimes written Weondune, which, after the correction of the n, as indicated by Mr. Weddle, is Weordune. The ancient seat of the Faringtons, of Leyland and Farington, is variously written Werden, Worden, and Wearden. It is pronounced by the inhabitants, Wearden at the present day. It was a place of some importance in the time of the Romans. Coins, and a heavy gold signet ring, bearing the letters S P Q R, have been found there.[d] It is situated near the line of the Roman highway; and if Anlaf's troops covered the pass of the Ribble near Brunhill or Bamberg, Wearden is precisely the spot were Athelstan's forces would encamp in front of them.

These reasons, in conjunction with those advanced in the second chapter of this work, induce the author to prefer the locality, in the present state of the evidence, as the *most probable* site of the "battle of the Brun." Mr. Weddle pertinently remarks, that the very "uncertainty of the whereabouts of the battle field" is, to his mind, a reason why it should be looked for "in some place half forgotten." The *cause* of the temporary oblivion, in the case of Bamberg and Burnhull has been explained.

---

b See ante, page 50.

c Mr. Weddle himself says :—"The variety of names, in my opinion, is caused by the number of meanings that burgh had. It meant a hill, heap, mountain, fortification, castle, tower, city, house, and tomb." Hull is well known as Saxon for hill, or mound.

d See ante, page 40.

THE MIN SPIT WELL.

(See page 210 and page 445.)

In July, in the present year, the workmen employed in laying the sewerage pipes at the bottom of Mainsprit-weind, came upon the ancient well described by Dr. Kuerden. It appears to have been enlarged from time to time. The line of cutting passed over three distinct chambers or reservoirs. The most northerly one was little over a yard, and the next scarcely two yards in breadth. The southern chamber was nearly three yards across, measured internally. It was subdivided by pillars, apparently two rows, which supported the roof. The pillars were of a slightly pyramidical form, and somewhat octagonal, the corners of the square blocks being cut away. There are some other more elaborately wrought stones, which doubtless formed the front of the structure, or opening through which the water was drawn from the last reservoir. The whole was covered with heavy flags. The stones, some of which are very large, have been carefully squared and finished in the inside of the structure. No mortar or any cement had been used. The stone is Whittle grit. The roof was about four feet below the present pavement. The whole of the lower land over the Syke brook, now the main sewer, has been considerably raised. The excavators only passed over the western extremity of the well. Its breadth was not ascertained. The foundation of an old wall, which formerly enclosed the neighbouring "skin yard" passed over it. The part within this enclosure appeared to have been covered over with stout timber. It is known that the well was used many years ago by the skinners. Most probably the making of the large "Folly reservoir," about forty yards distant, in 1729, reduced the supply from the spring, and the smaller well outside the wall, in Syke lane, opposite the bottom of the weind, was erected as a compensation to the public. The ancient well appears to have been closed about this time, with the exception of the portion used by the skinning and tanning establishments previously referred to. The gas company have destroyed the public well in connection with Messrs. Abbott and Kellett's waterworks, but the present improved water supply had rendered it almost useless. During the excavation, the water flowed in abundance from the ancient spring. In one block of stone a cavity was filled with lead. Probably this originally held the chain which secured an iron ladle or other vessel used in drawing the water by the numerous women who patronised the spring in Dr. Kuerden's time, and from which circumstance and the frequent passage of the "milkmaids bringing their daily milk and butter to the town this way from beyond the river Ribble," the "Minspit-lane" was often called "Pettycoat-alley." The public of the present day would scarcely relish the daily gossip of the milkmaids and the drawers of water in Pettycoat-alley. The character of the lactary fluid would be irretrievably ruined from such communion.

CORPORATION SEALS.

(See page 306.)

It has been suggested that the old seal bearing the effigy of King Edward I. and the inscription "S. EDW. REG. ANGL. AD. RECOGN. DEBITOR.," may have been made pursuant to the statute 13th Edward I., "*De mercatoribus*," and used by the mayor as the seal to the ancient securities described as "Statutes Merchant." This is probably correct. A "Statute Merchant" was a kind of bond or recognizance of record, acknowledged before the clerk of "Statute Merchant" and sealed with the seals of the debtor and the king, upon condition that if the former did not discharge the debt upon the day specified, an execution could be granted against his body, lands, and goods; which the creditor could hold until the liquidation of his claim.

ELECTION EXPENSES.

The auditor of the Preston election accounts, Mr. Alderman Thomas Monk, published the official statement in the Preston newspapers, on the 11th of June, 1857. From this document it appears that Mr. Grenfell's election cost £598. 11s. 4d., and that of Mr. Cross £763. 19s. 10d. Sir George Strickland's expenses amounted to £675. 15s. 11d. Total £2,038. 7s. 1d.

MISCELLANEOUS.

Chaplain of the Prison.—Mr. Clay resigned the office in June, 1857. See page 441.

Young Men's Club. (Omitted at page 453).—This institution was established in the early part of the year 1855. The premises in Fishergate were taken in April in that year, and altered to meet the requirements of the members. The following passage from the prospectus, dated August, 1855, will best explain the objects of the society.

"The club is designed for the especial benefit of all employed in shops, warehouses, and offices, being a place for their resort, where they may find innocent recreation and relaxation, with every facility for moral and intellectual improvement. The means provided for these purposes are: A news and reading-room supplied with seven daily, one semi-weekly, and seven weekly newspapers, and a selection of periodicals and magazines; an evening school with competent master, where book-keeping, arithmetic, grammar, etc., components of a commercial education, may be learned; a corresponding room with pens and ink provided, where members can retire free from interruption to write; an amusement room supplied with chess, draughts, and bagatelle; a room for conversation; a music room furnished with a piano—thus affording every facility for a singing class; a gymnasium, being the only one in the town; and a lavatory and dressing room furnished with all requisites. Facilities are also afforded for lectures; and arrangements are being made for French, Singing, Drawing, and other classes, and refreshments."

This club has scarcely yet received the amount of patronage anticipated by its projectors and friends, or which its praiseworthy objects ought to command.

BANKS. (Page 457.)—Mr. Lawe died suddenly in May last, (1857). The bank will shortly be closed.

GRAMMAR SCHOOL. (Page 489.)—In June, 1857, Mr. J. E. Addison was elected a scholar of the University of Dublin.

WALTON-LE-DALE.—A unitarian chapel formerly existed here. It was converted into cottages many years ago. The catholic chapel at Brownedge was erected in 1826, in the place of a smaller edifice, built in 1782. A catholic place of worship previously existed at Killingbourne, near Moon's mill. Killingbourne, is indicative of an ancient Culdee, cell, or cemetery. Mr. Kemble and others regard the term *ing* as refering to a family, clan, or tribe. They make Killinghall, the hall of the Cylingas; Birmingham, the *ham* or residence of the Beormingas, the descendants or clan of Beorm; and so on, with numerous others. See ante, pages 63 and 639.

OSBALDESTON.—An episcopal chapel was erected a few years ago, and a catholic chapel also. The latter is dedicated to St. Marie.

RIBCHESTER.—At page 579, it is stated that the relic, described as a "Roman bath," found at Ribchester, was most probably the flooring of a house. On further inquiry, it appears that both a bath and a house have been discovered near the same spot. In connection with the former there were leaden pipes for the conveyance of the water. Mr. Patchett's house is erected partially from the stone found on or near its site, and which formed the foundation of the Roman residence referred to.

BIOGRAPHY.

Ainsworth, Henry—Allen, Cardinal—Ambrose, Rev. Isaac—Arkwright, Sir Richard—Baines, Edward—Barton, Dr. William—Barrow, Thomas—Baxter, Rev. Roger—Clayton, Dr. Robert—Clayton, Sir Richard—Dunn, Rev. J.—Fisher, Henry—Foster, Captain—Gilbertson, William—Gradwell, Bishop—Haydock, Rev. Geo. Leo—Helme, William—Horrocks, Rev. Jeremiah—Horrocks, John—Kuerden, Dr. Richard—Preston, John—Preston, Rev. Thomas—Rushton, Rev. Edward—Shepherd, Dr.—Sharrock, Dr.—Southworth, Rev. Richard—Tootel, Rev. Hugh—Weever, Dr. John.

Ainsworth, Henry.—This eminent Hebrew scholar, and biblical commentator, was born about the year 1560. He was the second son of Lawrence Ainsworth, of Pleasington. Although a man of extraordinary talent and a voluminous writer, little is known of his life. He finished his education at Cambridge. In the reign of Elizabeth, he left England, and went to Holland. He had adopted the tenets of a puritan sect, named the Brownists, and published a work on the subject of their faith, in 1602. He is highly spoken of as a man of learning and ability; but appears to have been somewhat irritable in temper, and fond of controversy. According to Dr. Heylin, Ainsworth once maintained a dispute on the foolish question, "whether the colour of Aaron's linen ephod was blue or green." It appears that his works are better known abroad than in England. Mr. W. R. Whatton says: "It is difficult to select a writer more highly spoken of, or oftener cited by the learned of all countries, than Mr. Ainsworth." Dr. Worthington, Master of Jesus college, Cambridge, in a letter dated the 11th January, 1660, deeply regrets the loss of some of Ainsworth's MSS. He made some fruitless efforts to recover them. Ainsworth died in 1629. A curious and characteristic story respecting his death is told, on the authority of Neale, who asserts that it was the subject of popular discourse at the time, at Amsterdam. A wealthy Jew merchant had lost a diamond of great value. Ainsworth found it and returned it to the owner, who offered to liberally recompense the poor scholar's honesty. Ainsworth would accept of nothing in the shape of reward; but he induced the Jew to promise him an opportunity of conferring with some learned rabbis, on the prophecies in the Bible relating to the Messiah. The story says the Jew was unable to fulfil this promise, and from a feeling of vexation or shame, he rid himself of the difficulty by causing poison to be administered to the man to whom he owed a debt of gratitude, but whose singular temper refused any recompense except in a form which proved to be impracticable.

Allen, Cardinal.—Dr. William Allen, son of John Allen, of Rossall grange, was born in 1532. In his fifteenth year he entered Oriel College, Oxford, where he studied logic and philosophy under the celebrated Morgan Phillips. His great talents were soon recognised. In his twenty-fourth year, he was made principal of Mary Hall, and in the year following, he officiated as proctor. He was made canon of York in 1558. He refused to take the oath and forfeited his fellowship, on the accession of Elizabeth. He entered the Catholic college of Louvaine in 1560. His first work was written there, and excited great attention. It is entitled "A defence of the Doctrine of Catholics concerning

Purgatory and Prayers for the dead." He was made soon afterwards tutor to Sir Christopher Blount Allen was zealous in the cause of the Roman Catholic religion. With the view of furthering its restoration in England, he visited his native country, at considerable personal risk. He spent three years in England. He fled to Flanders, in 1568; and from thence to Mechlin and Douay. He took his degree of doctor at the last named place, and established an academy for English pupils. The pope granted him a pension. After some further mutation of fortune, he was made canon of Rheims, and under the patronage of the cardinal of Lorraine, opened a seminary in that city. He now became greatly distinguished abroad, and equally detested by the protestant party at home. He published very extreme opinions respecting the obligation of Englishmen to the queen. He denounced her government as impious and unjust, herself a bastard and a usurper, obstinate and impenitent, and recommended her deposition. He is said to have advised Phillip II. of Spain, to invade England. A portion of the armada attempted to effect a landing in the neighbourhood of Rossall. [a] The fate of the invasion is well known. The king of Spain, notwithstanding, made Allen archbishop of Mechlin. He passed, however, the remainder of his life at Rome. He died in 1594, and was buried with great pomp. It is stated that in the evening of his life he regretted the part he had taken in the invasion of his native country, and this is countenanced by a letter of his, found amongst the Burleigh papers, dated Rome, August 14th, 1593, and addressed to Richard Hopkins, in England. He lived at Rome in great splendour, enjoyed the favour of the pope, and had an extensive reputation for learning and eloquence.

Ambrose, Isaac.—This celebrated nonconformist minister was born at Ambrose hall, near Garstang, in 1602. He was curate of the parish church of Preston during the commonwealth. He afterwards removed to Garstang, of which place he was for some time minister. Having adopted the principles of the nonconformists, he published several works, chiefly to enforce their views. The literary productions by which he is now principally known are the "Primo, media, and ultimo," "Looking unto Jesus," and the "Communion of Angels," the two latter works were afterwards edited by the Rev. John Wesley. During his residence in Garstang, Ambrose erected a kind of hermitage or retreat in Woodacre wood, at which he spent one month in the year, and subjected himself to rigorous religious discipline. He appears to have been a truly pious and amiable man, and enjoyed the esteem of numerous friends. He died at his house in the Church weind, (now St. John-street,) Preston, in 1663-4. He had previously resided for some time in Bolton. During his last sickness, many friends from that town and Garstang visited him. Mr. Whittle says: "He was holy in his life, happy in his death, and honoured by God and all good men." Dr. Cole of Preston, who was suspended by the bishop, and afterwards appointed minister of Dedham, in Essex, was a warm friend and admirer of Ambrose.

Arkwright, Sir Richard.—Richard Arkwright was born at Preston, on the 23rd September, 1732. [b] He was not only the son of poor parents, but the youngest of thirteen children. His uncle Richard taught him to read, and he gathered some little further instruction at a school during the winter evenings. He was apprenticed to a barber, which business he followed till 1760, when he began to trade in hair. For some time previously he had resided at Bolton. Arkwright travelled about the country for the purpose of purchasing hair, which he prepared and afterwards sold to wig makers. He is said to have invented a successful process for the dyeing of hair; but this statement rests

---

a See chapter 3, page 140.

b Mr. Baines says, "There are reasons for believing that he was born either in the house now occupied by Mr. Clare, hosier, or that adjoining, in Lord-street." This property has since been taken down and re-built. The south end of the Stanley buildings, Lancaster road, occupies the site of Mr. Clare's shop.

upon very slender authority. Arkwright's first experiments in mechanics were instituted with the hope of discovering a perpetual motion. This study prepared him, to some extent, for the more practical business of his after life. From about the year 1766, Arkwright appears to have devoted the whole of his energies to the discovery and improvement of machinery for the spinning of cotton. His various efforts in this direction, his difficulties, and his ultimate success, have already been traced in detail. His claims, as an inventor, have likewise been fully canvassed in a preceding chapter of the present work.[c] Mr. Whittle relates an amusing anecdote respecting Arkwright and his assistant, Kay, during the time they were employed in fitting up the first spinning machine, in Mr. Smalley's house, in Stonygate.[d] He says :—"The room was very secluded, and behind it was a garden, filled with gooseberry trees. Two aged women, who lived in a thatched cottage hard by, used to say,—'That they heard strange noises, of such a humming nature, that the devil was tuning his bag-pipes, and that Arkwright and Kay were dancing a reel.' This caused a great consternation in the small town of Preston at that time, and many were inclined to break open the place, in order to examine if any traces could be found of the devil, who it was supposed carried on his orgies there, with his two favourites, Arkwright and Kay." Arkwright's first mill was erected at Nottingham, in 1771. The treatment which Hargreaves, of Church, near Blackburn, had received from his neighbours, in consequence of his invention, induced Arkwright and his earliest partners to try their fortune amongst strangers, and thus Preston lost the distinction of first introducing to the world the nucleus of that vast system of mechanical production which has, in so short a space of time, effected peaceably the most important social revolution on record. A second mill was established at Cromford, near Wirksworth, in Derbyshire. He continued to improve his machinery, and notwithstanding the success of a most formidable opposition, which deprived him of his patents, he continued to the last at the head of the manufacturing interest, and died the possessor of a fortune little short of half a million sterling.[e] In 1786, Mr. Arkwright was appointed high sheriff of the county of Derby. He was knighted by George III., after presenting an address of congratulation to the king on the failure of the attempt made on his life by Margaret Nicholson. In the year 1789, Sir Richard Arkwright purchased the manor of Cromford. He had previously, in 1782 bought the estate upon which he erected the mansion called "Willersley Castle." Sir Richard, notwithstanding the suffering to which he was subjected from a severe asthmatic affection, continued to labour unremittingly at his business till the close of his life. He died at his house in Cromford, "of a complication of disorders," on the third of August, 1792, in the sixtieth year of his age. The prejudice against him and his inventions had partially passed away. Thousands of persons crowded the rocks and roads in the neighbourhood of the picturesque village, in order to witness the consignment to their last resting place of the remains of one of the acknowledged extraordinary men of the age. He was buried at Cromford church, where a monument, by Chantrey, is erected to his memory. It is somewhat singular, that every effort which has yet been made, with the view to the erection of a suitable memorial in his native town, has met with little sympathy. Preston owes much, both in reputation and prosperity, to the genius of Arkwright. If it be commendable to erect statues in memory of those whose intellectual labour has been the means of conferring benefit upon society at large, surely Sir Richard Arkwright ought not to be forgotten, either in his native town or in the metropolis of the cotton manufacture.

---

c See page 361.

d This building has been converted into a public-house, and named the "Arkwright's Arms."

e Pen. Cyclop. Some say a million. In the picture gallery of a noble earl, in this county, is a portrait of Arkwright, with the following inscription: "Shaved for a penny; died worth a million; hurrah for the constitution of England!"

BAINES, EDWARD.—The historian of Lancashire was born on the 5th of February, 1774, at the village of Walton-le-dale. His father, Mr. Richard Baines, was the last person prosecuted by the corporation of Preston, for the then heinous offence of trading within the borough without being in possession of the freedom thereof.[f] Mr. Richard Baines was at that period a grocer. He subsequently became steward to the earl of Derby, and likewise a partner in a cotton-spinning concern at Brindle. His son Edward, when two years of age, went to reside with a maternal uncle, at Hawkshead. He attended the free grammar school, then taught by Edward Christian, afterwards chief justice of Ely, and Downing professor of law, in the university of Cambridge. Baines was a sprightly and clever lad. He was a favourite with the master, who is reported to have prophesied that "he would either be a great man or be hanged." The poet Wordsworth was his school-fellow. He returned to Lancashire when eight years of age, and finished his education at the Preston grammar school. At the age of sixteen, he was apprenticed to Mr. Thomas Walker, printer and stationer, Church-street. At twenty-one, he removed, with the consent of his parents and his master, to Leeds. He was from the first employed at the office of the "Mercury." In 1801, by the assistance of a few friends, he purchased the good-will, together with the printing materials, etc., of the "Leeds Mercury," for £1,552. Under his able management it became one of the first provincial papers in the kingdom. Notwithstanding his multifarious duties and the active part he took in local and general politics, Mr. Baines found leisure for literary labour. He published, soon after the close of the war with France, in 1815, a work entitled a "History of the Wars of the French Revolution," in two quarto volumes. The addition of two other volumes afterwards expanded the work into a "History of the Reign of George III." In the years 1822 and 1823, he wrote "The History, Directory and Gazetteer of the County of York." During 1824 and 1825, he published a similar work, in two volumes, octavo, of which his native county formed the subject. This proved the foundation of the largest and most important of his literary labours, the "History of the County Palatine of Lancaster." The latter work further occupied his attention for six years, notwithstanding the assistance retained for various departments. Like his other works, it was originally published in parts. It was completed in 1836, and met with an extensive sale. The biographical department was contributed by W. R. Whatton, esq., F.S.A., and the chapter on the "History of the Cotton Manufacture," by his son, Mr. Edward Baines, jun. The work will ever be regarded as a most valuable contribution to local history. In 1834, Mr. Baines was elected a representative in parliament for the borough of Leeds. In 1835, he was returned a second time, and again in 1837. In 1841, in consequence of his impaired health, he declined to re-enter parliament. Mr. Baines died at Leeds on the 3rd of August, 1848, aged seventy-four years and six months. His remains were honoured by a public funeral. A monument was erected to his memory, bearing the following inscription:—"To commemorate the Public Services and Private Virtues of EDWARD BAINES, who faithfully, ably, and zealously represented the borough of Leeds in three successive parliaments. As a man, a citizen, and a patriot, he was distinguished by his integrity and perseverance, his benevolence and public spirit, his independence and consistency. This monument is erected by voluntary subscription, that posterity may know and emulate a character loved and honoured by his contemporaries." Mr. Baines's sons have done great credit to the training of their parent. The eldest, the Right Hon. Matthew Talbot Baines, who represents Hull in parliament, was for a considerable period president of the Poor Law Board. He is now chancellor of the duchy of Lancaster, and chairman of the Annual Sessions of the Peace for Lancashire. Mr. Edward Baines, of the Leeds Mercury, is the author of the "History of the Cotton Manufacture." Mr. Thomas Baines, long connected with the Liverpool press, has

f See page 287.

contributed much to local historical literature. His "Commercial History of Liverpool" is a most valuable work, the result of long and diligent labour.

BARTON, WILLIAM.—This clever theological scholar was born in Fenkell-street (now Church-street), Preston. He was descended from a respectable family at Barton. He became successively bishop of Rochester and Lincoln, and died in May, 1613.

BARROW, THOMAS.—An artist of no mean pretensions. He was born at Great Eccleston, in the Fylde, on the 15th January, 1737. Barrow painted landscapes, animals, and even history; but he was chiefly employed upon portraits. When about forty years of age, he placed himself under Romney, and remained his pupil for about twelve months. Mr Whittle says, that "during this time he entered himself as a Royal Academician," and, in virtue of this impression, he describes him as "Thomas Barrow, R.A." This, however, is an error. Parties do not enter themselves as Royal Academicians, but a few fortunate artists are elected to that distinction, on account of their real or supposed superiority over their compeers. The number, too, is limited to forty. Indeed, there were but thirty-six at the period referred to. The first perfect list of forty was completed in 1780, by the addition of the names of Edward Birch, Richard Cosway, Joseph Nollekins, and James Barry. Thomas Barrow would doubtless enter himself as a *student* at the Royal Academy, and hence, probably, the error referred to. Mr. Whittle, who visited Barrow some four years before his death, and found him in possession of a "fund of literary anecdote," and "sentiments refined in the highest sense of the word," gives the following anecdote of his first professional success.—"A gentleman invited him to come down to Yorkshire, in order to clean some paintings he had. Barrow accordingly borrowed £15. of Romney, to prosecute his journey thither. When arrived, and having beautified many elegant pictures, the gentleman intimated to him that he could only afford to give him washing, lodgings, and provisions, for the service he had rendered him. This species of conduct was highly improper on the part of the gentleman. A lady, in the vicinity of York, having heard of this business, and wishing to encourage rising merit, invited him to take a full length portrait of her little son. He took it. The lady invited a party on this occasion; they saw and admired; they nearly one and all gave him orders for their portraits to be taken. He took apartments in the city of York; fame blew his trumpet; Barrow amassed £300 in course of twelve months, a part of which he sent to his aged parents at Great Eccleston, and he worked on for more." He died in the year 1822, aged eighty-four years. He was buried at the parish church of St. Michael-le-Wyre. Mr. Barrow possessed an excellent library of books relating to art, the contents of which were dispersed at his death. There is an easy dignity and careful finish in some of his portraits, but the colour is often rather grey and somewhat opaque.

BAXTER, ROGER.—A polemical writer, of considerable ability, was born at Walton-le dale, in 1793. He received a portion of his education at Preston, and afterwards, in 1806, entered the Catholic college at Stonyhurst. He departed for America in 1817, where he became professor of rhetoric and *belles lettres*. He was afterwards appointed pastor to a Roman Catholic cathedral church at Philadelphia. Previously to his departure from England, he had written several controversial works. He published, at Washington, in 1819, a work entitled "The most important Tenets of the Roman Catholic fairly explained." He returned to England in 1826, visited Paris, and afterwards became pastor at Enfield, near Blackburn. He preached several controversial sermons about this time, which attracted considerable attention. He returned to Philadelphia, and assisted the Catholic bishop of that place. He again appeared as a champion of Catholicity, and entered into a controversy with an episcopal clergyman. The whole discussion was printed at George Town, under the title of the "Alexandrian Controversy." He died at Philadelphia, on the 24th May, 1827, at the early age of thirty-four years. His funeral was attended by the bishop and clergy of the Catholic church, and a numerous train of his admirers. A memorial stone was placed by his brother in the burial ground attached to St. Wilfrid's, Preston.

CLAYTON, ROBERT, D. D.—A Roman Catholic prelate, born at Fulwood. He was connected with the Claytons, of Adlington; indeed, according to Mr. Whittle, he was the "24th in descent from William de Clayton, who lost his life in 1441, when Ranulph, earl of Chester, took possession of London." In 1729, he was made bishop of Killala, and translated to Cork in 1735. In 1745, he was promoted to the see of Clogher. He died in February, 1758. He published a large number of works on divinity, was a member of the Royal and Antiquarian societies, and a contributor to the Philosophical Transactions. He was much respected for probity and learning, and corresponded with Bradley, the Astronomer Royal, and other distinguished persons. He presented the copyright of his voluminous writings to Mr. Bowyer.

CLAYTON, SIR RICHARD, BART., F. S. A.—A member of the family of Clayton, of Fulwood. His uncle, Richard Clayton, lord chief justice of the common pleas in Ireland, by will dated March, 1770, left to him his manor of Worthington and Adlington. He was a magistrate in 1772, and was created a baronet in 1774. He was also constable of Lancaster and recorder of Wigan. He was likewise distinguished as an author. The following are the principal productions of his pen:—"A Critical Inquiry into the Life of Alexander the Great, by the Ancient Historians," translated from the French of St. Croix;" "Memoirs of the house of Medici, from the French of Tenhove;" and "The Science of Legislation," from the Italian of Filangieri." He died at Nantes, in France, of which place he was consul, in April, 1828.

DUNN, REV. JOSEPH.—Mr. Dunn was a native of Catterick-bridge, near Richmond. He was educated at St. Omer's, and afterwards at Liege. He came to Preston in 1775. He was actively employed as Catholic pastor for a period of fifty-one years. He was a man of considerable learning, and true practical piety, and commanded the general respect of the inhabitants of every denomination. Although he occasionally wrote on controversial subjects, his tone was always mild and charitable. He enjoyed an extensive correspondence with many learned and virtuous men, both in England and on the continent, and received the special commendation of the pope. Mr. Dunn was not only chiefly instrumental in founding the Catholic chapel of St. Wilfrid, the Fox-street schools, etc., but he was one of the principal originators of the Preston gas company. It is said that he had some interesting correspondence with Sir Walter Scott on this subject. His real name was not Dunn, but Hart. He died on the 19th of November, 1827, in the eighty-second year of his age. A monument was erected to his memory in St. Wilfrid's chapel.

FISHER, HENRY.—The late well-known publisher, Henry Fisher, of Newgate-street, London, was born in Preston, about the year 1775. He served his apprenticeship with Mr. Sergent, in the shop lately occupied as the Chronicle office, in the Market-place. He was in business in Liverpool, where his printing-office was destroyed by fire, in 1821. He afterwards visited Paris, and improved his knowledge of the printing business. His success as a publisher in London is well known. He was elected a member of the common council of the city of London, for Faringdon ward, in 1829. Amongst other important works, Mr. Fisher published Baines's History of Lancashire, in four volumes, quarto, with numerous illustrations. He died in June, 1837.

FOSTER, CAPTAIN HENRY, R.N., F.R.S.—This distinguished young officer was born at Great Eccleston, in the Fylde, on the 20th August, 1794. He was the son of the Rev. Hugh Foster, of Woodplumpton. He was appointed astronomer, or surveyor, to the north-west expedition, in 1824. On this occasion, he received a marked compliment from Captain Basil Hall. He says, in his journal: "I take this opportunity of bearing the strongest testimony to the merits of this young officer, to whose assistance and companionship, in every pursuit connected with nautical science, I stand essentially indebted;

and it is with real satisfaction, on public as well as on private grounds, that I observe his promotion to the rank of lieutenant, his admission as a member of the Royal Society, in November, 1827, and his appointment as surveyor to the north-west expedition now about to sail." He received the Copley medal of the Royal Society, in November, 1827, and was immediately promoted to the rank of commander. In the following year, he was appointed to conduct a voyage of discovery to the south Atlantic ocean. The principal objects of the expedition were experiments with the pendulum, and the determination of the longitude of various localities visited, by means of the chronometer, observations on magnetic and meteorological phenomena, ocean currents, etc. After fulfilling the whole or the greater portion of the proposed duties, Captain Foster was accidentally drowned, whilst descending the river Chagres to his ship, which lay at its *embouchure* in the Gulph of Mexico. His body, wrapped in the flag of his native country, was interred on the bank of the river. A monument was erected in Woodplumpton church, "by several of his companions and friends, as a memorial of the high esteem they entertained for his character, and of the deep regret they felt for his untimely death." The fatal accident occurred on the 8th of February, 1831. Captain Foster was in the thirty-fourth year of his age at the time of his demise. A most valuable work, in two volumes, octavo, was afterwards published, under the sanction of the admiralty, entitled, "A Voyage of Discovery to the South Atlantic Ocean, performed in his Majesty's ship 'Chanticleer,' in 1829, 1830, and 1831, under the command of Captain Henry Foster, R.N., F.R.S."

Gilbertson, William.—Mr. Gilbertson was born in 1788, at Market Weighton, Yorkshire. His family removed to Skipton, and afterwards to Burnley. Mr. Gilberston settled in Preston early in life and commenced business as a druggist. For several years he devoted his attention to the study of the geology of the neighbourhood. He discovered an immense number of new species of fossils in the rich limestone beds of the forest of Bolland, and amassed a collection so large and valuable, that the trustees of the British Museum gladly purchased the greater portion for the sum of £350. Mr. Gilbertson was a life member of the British Association for the Advancement of Science; a member of the *Societe Geologique* de France; an honorary member of the Yorkshire Philosophical Society; and corresponding member of the Manchester Natural History Society. Mr. Gilbertson corresponded with some of the most eminent scientific men in various parts of Europe. His name was well known in London, in France and Italy, long before his fellow townsmen suspected that he had contributed anything of importance to geological science. Professor Phillips, in his "Illustrations of the Geology of Yorkshire," g several times refers to Mr. Gilbertson in a manner honourable to himself for his generous candour, and highly complimentary to the Preston geologist. He says:—"But my greatest obligation is to Mr. Gilbertson, of Preston, a naturalist of high acquirements, who has for many years explored with exceeding diligence and acumen, a region of mountain limestone remarkably rich in organic remains. The collection which he has amassed from the small district of Bolland, is at this moment unrivalled, and he has done for me without solicitation, what is seldom granted to the most urgent entreaty; he has sent me for deliberate examination, at convenient intervals, the whole of his magnificent collection, accompanied by remarks, dictated by long experience and a sound judgment. He had proposed to publish an account of his discoveries, and especially of the Crinoidea, for which no man in Europe had equal materials, and he had made a great number of careful drawings for the purpose; but all these, as well as the specimens, he placed at my disposal—a striking proof of liberal and genuine devotion to science. h * * Mr. Gilbertson's rich collection is the source from which almost all my drawings and examinations" (of Crinoidea) "have been taken. * * Besides the species noticed in

g Published in 1836.

h Introduction, page xvii.

the following classification, Mr. Gilbertson possesses others, and is likely to discover more; his collection is also very rich in varieties and malformations; and I hope that he may hereafter be induced to give to the world the result of his very diligent study of these beautiful fossils.[i] * * *Gilbertsochrinus.* New genus. * * I dedicate the genus to Mr. Gilbertson, whose name will ever be honourably associated with the crinoidea."[k] Mr. Gilbertson did publish at Preston, a small "Catalogue of Fossils, from the mountain limestone of Great Britain, extracted from the works of Messrs. Phillips and Sowerby," in 1837, but although he continued his researches, no work corresponding to Professor Phillips's suggestion ever appeared. He died at Preston, on the 10th of February, 1845. His brother, Mr. John Gilbertson, surgeon, a gentleman of cultivated mind, was one of the founders of the Institution for the Diffusion of Knowledge.

GRADWELL, ROBERT, D.D.—This Roman Catholic divine and polemical writer was born at Clifton, in the Fylde, on the 26th of January, 1777. In 1791, he entered Douay college, and was amongst the parties seized by the leaders of the French revolution, in 1793. Gradwell returned to Clifton, in the following year, much reduced in health, owing to the privations to which he, in conjunction with his associates, had been subjected to at the castle of Doulens. Gradwell joined his former companions at Crook-hall, near Durham, in 1795. He remained there until the new college of Ushaw was built. He was ordained a priest in 1802. In 1809, he was appointed pastor of Claughton. At this period he held a professorship at the college. In 1817, on the re-opening of the English college at Rome, he was appointed the rector. His talents were of such a character as to secure for him not only distinguished academic honours in Rome, but the favour and respect of the popes Pius VIII. and Leo XII., Cardinal Gonsalvi, and other distinguished personages. On the death of Dr. Poynter, he was appointed to succeed him as coadjutor to Dr. Bramston, Roman Catholic bishop of the London district. He was consecrated bishop of Lydda, and died in London on the 15th of March, 1833, a few months after his arrival. His principal literary works are, "A Dissertation on the Fable of Papal Anti-Christs," and a series of papers in the "Catholicon," entitled, "A Winter Evening Dialogue between John Hardman and John Cardwell; or, Thoughts on the Rule of Faith."

HAYDOCK, GEORGE LEO.—This distinguished biblical annotator was born 1774, at Tag-house, near Woodplumpton. His father, George Haydock, was a member of the Society of Friends, but his mother, Ann Cottam, was a Roman Catholic, in which religion young Haydock was educated. He received the additional name of Leo at the time of his confirmation at Mowbray, by Matthew Gibson, Vicar Apostolic of the northern district. He had previously been for three or four years the pupil of the Rev. R. Banister, of Mowbraw. In 1788, he entered Douay college. He was one of the companions in affliction of Dr. Gradwell, in 1793, when the establishment was suppressed by the leaders of the French revolution. After his return to England, he studied nearly a year under the Rev. W. Coombes, of Old Hall Green, in Herefordshire. In 1796, he rejoined his companions at Crook Hall, Durham, then superintended by the Rev. Thomas Eyre, afterwards first president of Ushaw college. He was made priest in 1798. His first mission was at Ugthorpe, near Whitby, Yorkshire. He was afterwards transferred to Whitby, and again, in 1830, to Westby, in the Fylde district. Archdeacon Cotton, in a recent work, says:—"It appears that about this time he had some difference with his bishop, Dr. Thomas Penswick, on account of money due to him on some charitable trust. The bishop refused to pay, and replied to his repeated applications for a settlement, by the summary process of placing him under an interdict. He then appealed to the bishop's successor, Dr. Briggs, but without success: and afterwards to the College of Propaganda

i Page 203. k Page 207.

and the Pope; but he found fresh difficulties thrown in his way, and has complained that his communications to Rome were betrayed to his opponent. After seven years of vexatious proceedings, arising out of that business, he was offered the small and scanty mission of Penrith in Cumberland, which he judged it prudent to accept, and there he passed the remainder of his days. His death took place in 1848. His library was sold by public auction, at Preston, in July, 1851."[1] Haydock did not close his career at Penrith. Mr. Whittle, who was personally acquainted with him, says, in 1837, that, "in 1831, he retired from the pastoral life, and now resides as a private gentleman at the Tag-house, although in holy orders." Haydock is chiefly known in consequence of his elaborately annotated Bible. The project was first conceived by his brother Thomas, a schoolmaster and printer of Manchester, in 1806. The Rev. Benjamin Rayment, who afterwards supplied the principal notes for the New Testament, having declined undertaking the annotation of the Bible, George Haydock, then residing at Ugthorpe, accepted the laborious office. Owing to Mr. Thomas Haydock's leaving Manchester for Ireland, it was supposed that he had relinquished the task, and a Mr. Oswald Syers was induced to announce an edition. The printing of this work commenced in March, 1811. Thomas Haydock, however, returned to Manchester, and, on the 11th of July, 1811, put the first sheet of his brother's Bible to press. Only fifteen hundred copies were at first printed; but as the work, which was issued in fortnightly and afterwards in weekly parts, at a shilling each, progressed, subscribers multiplied, and a second edition was issued at Dublin, where Thomas Haydock had a printing establishment. The last sheet was printed in September, 1814. A third edition was issued at Dublin, in 1813, and a fourth, at Manchester, 1814. There had been no Catholic Bible printed in England for thirty years, at the time Thomas Haydock projected his work. The text, published by Dr. Challoner, was chiefly followed by Haydock: all the notes were supplied by himself. When the New Testament was added, the notes were furnished by Mr. Rayment, Mr. Robinson, and others. Haydock's laborious diligence proved unproductive in a pecuniary sense. He is said, indeed, to have lost upwards of one hundred pounds by the speculation. Haydock likewise composed a "Paraphrase on the Psalms;" a "Treatise on the various points of difference between the Roman and the Anglo-Catholic Churches," etc. "Haydock's Bible," says Archdeacon Cotton, "has attained considerable reputation, and is executed on a different plan from all which preceded it, forming what we may call a 'Variorum' edition of the Scriptures. * * I have the original MS. from which the work was printed, in his own handwriting, in five small but closely printed volumes. His diligence was unwearied; yet he found the greatest difficulty in keeping the press from standing still; so that perhaps he did not always select his notes as judiciously as he would have done if more leisure had been allowed him. In a few instances he introduces allusions to topics and persons of ancient or modern times, not always pertinent to the subject, nor strictly justifiable. For these he was occasionally taken to task by some of his brethren, who seemed more disposed to find fault with his labours than to share and lighten them. * * He does not appear to have possessed high scholarship; but was a pious and warm-hearted man, a most industrious reader, and biblical annotator. It is said that the fly-leaves and margins of almost all his books were covered with notes by his own pen. Certainly this is the case with those few of them which have come into my hands." Several of Haydock's works, and especially his own copy of the Bible, are elaborately annotated in the manner referred to. Some are now in the possession of Mr. Alderman Brown, who likewise possesses two volumes of

---

1 "Rhemes and Doway. An attempt to show what has been done by Roman Catholics for the Diffusion of the Holy Scriptures in English, by the Rev. Henry Cotton, D.C.L., Archdeacon of Cashel, &c."

miscellaneous extracts, and original pieces, written in Hebrew, Greek, Latin, French, and English. During a cursory inspection, the author noticed some poetical pieces, signed with Haydock's name; one of which, on "Death," exhibits no mean power.

HELME, WILLIAM.—Mr. Helme was one of the many poor, but gifted individuals, who, by pure force of character, triumph over apparently insurmountable obstacles. He was born at Warrington, on the 27th of March, 1785, but being brought to Preston while yet an infant, all his self-education and practical knowledge are associated with the latter locality. Although merely a humble warper in Mr. German's mill, he found leisure for study and self culture. He was in the habit of attending a kind of natural history society held at the Green Man Inn, Lord-street, where he both acquired and communicated much useful information. His taste lay chiefly in botanical and entomological studies, and especially the latter. He was much patronised by a Mr. Tomlinson, surgeon, who resided at Albin-bank, and was frequently the companion of his rambles. He held regular correspondence with some of the first naturalists in the kingdom, and amassed a large and valuable collection of insects, which was purchased by subscription, after his demise, and deposited in the Preston Institution for the Diffusion of Knowledge. He died at his residence, in Pleasant-street, on the 11th of April, 1834.

HORROCKS, JEREMIAH.—This celebrated astronomer was born at Toxteth Park, near Liverpool, about the year 1619. He was placed at Emanuel College, Cambridge, previously to 1633. He early devoted his attention to the study of astronomy, and but for his early death, would in all probability have rivalled Newton. He died on the 3rd January, 1641, (old style)[m] and can not therefore be said to have perished in the civil wars, as has been supposed. The first blood was not shed until July, in the following year.[n] A considerable portion of his books and papers, however, appears to have been lost or destroyed in the tumultuous scenes which followed. Others are reported to have perished in the great fire of London, in 1666, after having been used by Sherburne, in the composition of the "Tabulæ Britannicæ." There is some confusion in the records respecting the fate of Horrocks and his manuscripts. He appears to have been introduced by Christopher Townley, of Carr, in Lancashire, to three or four other astronomers, two of whom, Crabtree and Gascoygne, like Horrocks, died very young. After referring to the destruction of a portion of his papers, in the fire of London, the writer previously quoted, says, "The rest of Horrocks's papers were rescued by Dr. John Worthington, afterwards rector of Hackney, from Crabtree's representatives. A lately published work informs us that 'Crabtree the friend of Horrocks, is supposed to have perished in the civil wars; the papers of Horrocks himself were burned, after his death, by a marauding party of soldiers.' We imagine the death of Crabtree is here confounded with that of Gascoygne, and the papers of Horrocks with those of Milbourn." Gascoygne was slain at Marston Moor, and the papers of Milbourn, who was curate at Brancepeth, near Durham, were destroyed by the Scots, in 1639. Although but 22 years of age at the time of his death, Horrocks produced more valuable and original matter on the science of astronomy, than many long-lived celebrities. He was the first observer of the transit of Venus over the body of the sun. He first suggested the true theory of lunar motion, by supposing an elliptic orbit, with a variation in the eccentricity of the ellipse and an oscillatory motion of the line of apsides. A modern authority says: "Newton afterwards showed that both suppositions were consequences of the theory of gravitation, and (book iii., prop. 35. scholium), attributes to Halley a part of what is really due to Horrocks, as explained by Flamsteed. But Horrocks has been more than avenged by the foolish statement of Martin, in his 'Biographia Philosophica,' that Newton made Horrocks's theory the 'groundwork of all his astronomy.' This palpable misconception was copied by Dr.

m Pen. Cyclop. Art. Horrocks, Jeremiah. n See page 165.

Hutton into his Mathematical Dictionary."[o] Horrocks's account of his observation of the planet Venus, on the 24th November, 1639, entitled 'Venus in Sole visa,' was printed at Danzig, in 1662, in conjunction with the 'Mercurius in Sole visus,' by Hevelius. The Rev. Robert Brickel sums up the further claims of Horrocks to the applause of his countrymen, in the following terms :—"He was the first to reduce the sun's parallax nearly to what it has since been determined; the first to remark a phenomenon proving the extreme smallness of the apparent diameters of the stars; the first who began a course of tidal observations, etc., and the first who devised the beautiful experiment of the circular pendulum for illustrating the action of a central force. Besides these things, he effected a great improvement in different astronomical tables, detected the long inequalities of Jupiter and Saturn, made his remarks about the fixed stars, and had his conjectures about the nature and movement of the comets." Horrocks's works were published in 1672, by Dr. Wallis. Some copies are entitled "Opera Posthuma," and others "Opuscula Astronomica." An enlarged biographical notice has lately been announced as in preparation. Costard speaks of Horrocks as a young clergyman, but a doubt has been expressed whether he ever took orders. Horrocks resided at Hoole, near Preston. A great portion of his observations was made there and he is understood to have officiated as minister to the Parish church.[p] The present rector, the Rev. R. Brickel, in a communication to the Preston papers, in June, 1857, respecting the propriety of erecting a suitable memorial to so extraordinary a genius, in the parish of Hoole, says :—"I am proud of my parish, as the place where Horrocks ministered, and am gratified in supposing that he occupied the same old pulpit in the performance of '*his higher duties.*'" There is every probability that a suitable memorial will shortly be raised in honour of one of the most remarkable men of genius to which England has given birth. A townsman, Mr. Moses Holden, astronomer, so highly esteemed Horrocks, that some years ago he devoted the proceeds of one of his lectures to the erection of a marble monument in Toxteth Park, to perpetuate his name. It bears the following inscription, surmounted by a representation of Venus on the sun's disc :—

VENUS IN SOLE VISA, NOV. 24, 1639.
In Memory of
JEREMIAH HORROX, one of the greatest
Astronomers this kingdom ever produced.
Born in Toxteth Park, in 1619.
Died in 1641. Aged 22.
His observations were made at Hoole,
eight miles from Preston, where he
predicted, and was the first person
who saw, the transit of Venus
over the sun.
This memorial was erected by
M. Holden, Astronomer.
1826.

Horrocks's name is sometimes written Horrox. In his copy of Lansberg's "Tabulæ Perpetuæ," preserved by his friend Townley, his name, in his own hand writing, is spelled Horrocks.

Horrocks, John.—The founder of the commercial prosperity of the town of Preston, was born in the year 1768, at Edgeworth, near Bolton. His father, a member of the Society of Friends, originally resided at Bradshaw hall, in the neighbourhood of Bolton. He leased a stone quarry at Edgeworth, and commenced the manufacture of mill stones. John, and his brother Samuel, both worked in their father's quarry. The rapid progress

o Pen. Cyclop.

p See page 620.

of the cotton manufacture, which had already given a new direction to the enterprise and industry of the country, attracted the attention of young Horrocks. He fitted up two or three spinning frames, in a corner of the millstone manufactory, and contrived, by his own labour, to produce saleable yarn. His chief customer at this period was Mr. John Watson, of Preston, then the only manufacturer in the town. Mr. Horrocks soon afterwards transferred his energies and enterprise more directly to Preston. A story is related that on one occasion, Mr. Watson and he differed respecting the value or quality of some yarn; when Horrocks declared that his patron should have no more of his goods; for he would come to Preston and "put out" his yarn to the weavers himself. He had gradually increased his establishment at Edgeworth, and had accumulated some little capital at this period. He rented a small building at the bottom of Turk's-head-court, in Jan., 1791. His business, under his judicious management, gradually increased. He afterwards entered into partnership with Mr. George Bolton, of the firm of Shuttleworth, Bolton, Claytons, and Moore, bankers. Horrocks's sanquine temperament, however, alarmed his colleague, and caused him to withdraw. The late Mr. Richard Newsham, banker, had more confidence, and took Mr. Bolton's place in the firm. So great was his success on the completion of his first factory, that Horrocks set about immediately erecting another, which proved the commencement of the present extensive establishment called the "Yard works." It is named the "Yellow factory," and is yet standing. The building of this mill was commenced in 1791, the first year of Horrocks's residence in Preston. Mr. Watson, Mr. Horrocks's rival, at this time worked the original mill in Moor-lane, and the one called "Penwortham factory," in Walton-le-dale. His residence and warehouses were situated at the north end of the present Avenham-street. Other structures were erected by Horrocks in rapid succession, viz., the "Yard factory," in 1792, which was destroyed by fire, and re-erected in 1796; the old "Moss factory," in 1796; Frenchwood mill, and the new establishment on the "Moss," in 1797; the one near the canal, in 1799, and another at the "top of the yard," in the Dale-street establishment, in 1802. He influenced the establishment of the Heatley-street mill and machine works, and held an interest therein, in conjunction with Messrs. Riley, Paley, and Leighton. The works at Edgeworth were discontinued, so far as the millstone manufacture was concerned, and the premises converted into a cotton mill. There are several different versions of the details of the early career of Horrocks, of a somewhat doubtful character, but the above facts may be relied upon.[q] Mr. Whittle says,—"A small present or rather reward for some personal service to a stranger, enabled the young adventurer to begin business as a cotton manufacturer; and by indefatigable application he soon increased his stock." Another writer says,—"I have heard that the fortune of the first Mr. Horrocks thus began: He was a journeyman muslin weaver in 1791; and was with thousands thrown out of work, at the commencement of the French war; but he had saved ten pounds from the produce of his previous labour. With this he purchased cotton, and manufactured coloured-bordered handkerchiefs. Not being able to sell the first parcel he manufactured, in the country, he came up to London and had them sold by auction. They left him a handsome profit; so, after making an agreement with the auctioneer to sell as fast as the goods arrived, and to be permitted to draw bills for the amount as fast as they were sold, he returned to the country; and in the course of two other years, manufactured it is supposed, above one hundred thousand dozens of them."[r] When Mr. Horrocks became established at Preston, his brother and other relatives joined him. His brother Samuel Horrocks eventually became a partner. He transferred his interest in the Turk's Head-court works to Mr. Isaac Horrocks. When Mr. Newsham

q See Mr. Dobson's pamphlet on the Parliamentary Representation of Preston.

r Pamphlet by Hamilton in Defence of the co-operating system of trading.

retired, Mr. George Horrocks took his place. Mr. John Horrocks, another relative, was afterwards a partner. This firm was then known as that of Horrocks, Jacson, and Co. Mr. Horrocks's energy and business habits soon caused him to be selected for public labour. He was induced, in opposition to the Derby interest, to contest the representation of the borough, in 1796. He was unsuccessful, but in 1802, he was elected in conjunction with Lord Stanley, without a contest. s He did not live long to enjoy the senatorial office. He died in London in 1804, at the early age of 36. He was buried at Penwortham. His estate in money and property, accumulated in about fifteen years, was worth £150,000. Mr. Horrocks resided originally in Turk's Head-court. He successively removed to Fishergate, Dale-street, and Golden-square. In 1801, he built his mansion named Penwortham Lodge; which has since been changed to Penwortham hall, by its present proprietor, W. Marshall, esq. t Mr. Horrocks was buried in the church yard at Penwortham. Mr. Dobson gives the following characteristic anecdote of this eminently practical man:—"On one occasion while M.P., he visited Woolwich, and saw the workmen boring cannon by hand. 'You are a bonny set,' said Mr. Horrocks to one of the heads of a department, 'to do your work in this way. You should have a machine.' 'Oh! it is impossible to use machinery,' said the desciple of red tape. 'Well, I know whether you can or not, but I'll see Pitt to-morrow.' And no doubt he did, for it has been stated that a boring machine was not long after introduced into the government works at Woolwich." Many other stories are told of his promptness, decision, and generosity. When solicited for a subscription towards the erection of an organ in the parish church, he demanded the probable price of a good instrument. On being told that a sum of £500. would be required, he declared he would pay the amount himself, but stipulated that he should have the packing case. No doubt he had some good use for it, and a man of his character, even when cheerfully giving £500. for a public purpose, would not wish to foolishly throw a pound away. He was a great friend to the late Mr. Palmer, town clerk, and was mainly instrumental in securing his appointment as coroner. Mr. Palmer attributed his own habitual punctuality in after life to a practical lesson given him by Mr. Horrocks. Palmer was clerk to the Penwortham bridge trustees. A meeting was called at which Mr. Palmer arrived late. "Have you got a watch, Palmer," said Mr. Horrocks. The clerk answered in the affirmative, upon which his patron demanded the time of the day. "Half-past ten," was the prompt reply. "The meeting was called for ten, and servants should be ready at the time fixed, whether masters are or not," said Mr. Horrocks with firmness, but without severity. He added, "Young man, miss your meals, if you will, miss your rest, and miss your pleasure, but never miss fulfilling an engagement." It appears Mr. Palmer profited much from this advice. It has been stated that during the fifty-three years he held the office of coroner, he never kept a jury waiting a quarter of an hour, except under special circumstances over which he possessed no control. Mr. Palmer died in December, 1852, in the eightieth year of his age. For the lengthened period of sixty-four years, he never missed attending the assizes at Lancaster. His last was his 127th visit. The late Mr. Alderman Miller, who was previously a small manufacturer at Bolton, entered Mr. Horrocks's Preston establishment in 1802, and shortly afterwards became a partner. His eldest son is now the sole proprietor of the extensive manufactories pertaining to the nominal firm of "Horrockses, Miller, and Co.," and which at the present time employ upwards of 3,000 hands. u The erection of a statue, to the memory of John Horrocks, was contemplated a few years ago. The site fixed upon was about the centre of the land proposed to be devoted to the erection of villa residences at Penwortham. Nothing, however, has yet resulted.

Kuerden, Richard, M.D.—A physician, and scholar born about the year 1620, at Cuerden, near Preston. He was a lineal descendant of "an antient Family of H. I. or

s See page 333. t See page 590. u See page 425.

King Stephen date." He received his early education under Mr. Sherburn, at Leyland. In 1638, he was admitted a commoner of St. Mary Hall, Oxford. On the breaking out of the civil war, he removed to Cambridge. He commenced, in 1642, bachelor of arts, in Emanuel College. He remained till the surrender of Oxford to the King, in 1646, when he returned to St. Mary Hall, Oxford. He was incorporated and shortly afterwards elected vice-principal of his college. He remained for seven years, tutor to the principal scholars. He had generally about thirty pupils. Kuerden remained a staunch royalist, and had, in common with many others of the halls of Oxford, to support himself by his own means. He was nominated to the office of proctor of the university, but not feeling disposed to submit to the then government, he declined it, and commenced the study of physic. In 1652, he was appointed replicant in the act of that year, to all inceptors of physic. This office qualified him for the degree of doctor of physic. He paid the fees and was duly registered, but something in the oaths displeased him, and he preferred the loss of seniority in the university, to compliance. On the appearance of Charles II. in England, Kuerden took the, to him, more agreeable oath. This occurred on the 9th September, 1661. He was created doctor of physic on the 26th March, and received his testimonial under the public seal. The defeat of Charles at Worcester, however, completely changed the state of affairs. He left Oxford, and settled at Preston, where he devoted himself to literary pursuits, and the practice of medicine. Kuerden, in conjunction with Mr. Christopher Townley, of Carr hall, contemplated the publication of a complete history of Lancashire. They stipulated that "if either party dyed before impressure, the survyvor should have the other's Manuscripts to himself." These manuscripts were very numerous. Mr. Townley had been engaged about forty years amongst the records in the possession of the nobility and gentry of the county, and had transcribed in twenty folio volumes more than three hundred thousand abstracts. Kuerden carefully perused and abstracted the necessary portions from the Domesday book in the Tally Office, the records in the Tower of London, at Westminster, in the Rolls chapel, the Duchy office, the Pells, etc., as well as those in the Chancery court and Common Pleas, and other minor repositories in the county. Mr. Townley died in August, 1674, when the whole MSS. became the property of Kuerden. He issued proposals for publication, in 1688. The work was to be entitled Brigantia Lancastriensis Restaurata: or a History of the Honorable Dukedom or County Palatine of Lancaster." It was to be published in five volumes. Kuerden intimated that it was "composed and laid ready for the press." It remained, however, unpublished at the doctor's death. Mr. Baines gives the following particulars respecting the manuscripts:—"The magnificent structure announced in the prospectus was never raised: the architects seem to have been overwhelmed by the vast mass of material which they had collected; and this circumstance operated as powerfully as Sir William Dugdale's Warwickshire, to prevent the execution of their plans. [v] All that was done towards the History of Lancashire by Dr. Kuerden and his coadjutor, beyond the collection of abstracts, was an outline of the preface, an unfinished history of Roman Britain, and a small portion of the history of the parish of Leyland, which is also incomplete. * * Of Dr. Kuerden's MS. collections, eight volumes are preserved in the Heralds' College in London, two are in the Chetham library at Manchester, and one is among the Harleian MSS. in the British Museum, the bulk of each relating to the county of Lancaster, but mostly interspersed with extraneous matter. Dr. Kuerden was addicted to the study of judicial astrology, and, besides the calculations which appear in his various MSS., he had prepared for the press a translation from a Latin treatise on

v It has been stated that the excellence of Sir William Dugdale's History of Warwickshire, caused Kuerden to delay the publication of his own work, from a consciousness of its great inferiority as a county history.

that subject. To the title page of this work, formally arranged, he has appended his initials,[w] and the whole is found in the Harleian MSS., which contain the attempted history of Leyland, and in several parts of which he has written his name at length." [x] Kuerden received the patronage of Sir William Dugdale, who, during one of his visits, examined the Roman roads over Preston and Fulwood moors, and pronounced his opinion upon the remains.[y] Kuerden acted as deputy and marshall to Sir William during a visitation for the purpose of disclaiming, at Lancaster, the pretentions of all persons to coats of arms, who were unable to satisfactorily support their title to the armorial bearings assumed.

PRESTON, JOHN.—This celebrated divine was born in Bishopgate, near the old vicarage, in Preston. He received his early education at the grammar school in his native town. He was chaplain to King James I., a preacher at Lincoln's Inn, and afterwards prebendary of Lincoln. A work on the "Divine Attributes" gained him many friends amongst the nonconformists. He was chaplain to Charles I., and, in 1625, he was master of Emanuel college, Cambridge. He published another work, which was re-printed in 1836, entitled "The Golden Sceptre held forth to the Humble."

PRESTON, THOMAS.—Thomas Preston was born at Preston, on the 13th August, 1530. He was a fellow of King's college, Cambridge. He wrote a dramatic piece entitled "Cambyses, King of Persia," [z] ridiculed by Shakspere in act second, scene fourth, of the first part of the historical play, King Henry the Fourth. Falstaff prepares to enact the king, and so train the prince to meet his father. He says:—"Give me a cup of sack to make mine eyes look red, that it may be thought I have wept; for I must speak in passion, and I will do it in King Cambyses' vein." When Queen Elizabeth visited Cambridge, in 1564, she was so captivated with a "pretty young man of the name of Preston, from a town in Lancashire, whose graceful performance in a public disputation, and in the Latin play of Dido, had particularly caught her fancy," that she conferred upon him the title of "her scholar," and granted him an annuity of £20. Preston had likewise the degree of Doctor of Laws conferred upon him. His epitaph, at Oxford, describes him as "Tho: de Prestona, de Prestoniensis, Lanc."

RUSHTON, EDWARD.—A jesuit priest and a member of an old family resident at Great Eccleston, in the Fylde. He was born at Preston, in 1625. Some polemical tracts and a work entitled "De Schismate Anglicano," written by him, and published at Liege, created considerable sensation during the reign of Charles 1.

SHEPHERD, RICHARD, M.D.—Little is known respecting this public benefactor. He was born at Kendal. He practised as a physician in Preston, and died on the 28th Nov., 1761. He bequeathed his valuable library, and funds for its support and extension, to the mayor and aldermen of Preston, for the time being, for the use of the town.[a] He resided in Friargate, near the present King's Head Inn. He is said to have been of a charitable and kind disposition. He cultivated a herb named "Angelica," from which he prepared a kind of candy, which he distributed to the poor. The only memorial of him is a portrait in the library bearing his name.[b]

SHARROCK, DR. GREGORY W., was born at Preston, on the 30th of March, 1742. He received the rudiments of his education at the grammar school, and afterwards "dedicated

w "Ouronomachia, or the Astrologer's Game, first contrived for the refreshment of such as study those arts and Especially of Astrology, now set forth and brought to light p. Gulielm. Falconem of Cambridg. Printed at London, Thomas Æstam and Hen. Midlton at the charg of Will. Jones. 1571. And now translated into English by R. K. M.D."

x His. Lanc. vol. 3, page 465. y See page 48.

z It is styled a "Lamentable Tragedy" by Thomas Preston. It was published in 1570.

a See page 448. b See page 255.

himself to religion," at the age of 16, in St. Gregory's convent, Douay. The Catholic bishop Walmsley thought so highly of his qualities that he petitioned the pope to appoint him his coadjutor. He was consecrated at Wardour, as bishop of Telmessus, in 1781. On the death of Bishop Walmsley, he was appointed his successor. He died at Bath, on the 17th October, 1809. He wrote several tracts, which were published in eight parts.

SOUTHWORTH, REV. RICHARD.—A member of the old Samlesbury family. He was born in 1743, and was removed to Preston when young. He entered Douay, in 1756. He was appointed successively vice president of the college, professor of poetry, rhetoric, philosophy, and divinity. He occupied the chair of divinity from 1792, to the time he left the college, in 1786. He was shortly afterwards made pastor of the Catholic congregation at Brockhamton. He died in November, 1817. Mr. Whittle says,—"He should have succeeded the Rev. and honourable Dr. James Talbot, in the Episcopacy; but this was overruled by some means best known to those who had to do with it, in the year 1790." Another member of this family, the Rev. T. Southworth, was educated at Preston and Douay. He was for a long period president of the Catholic seminary at Sedgley-park.

TOOTEL, REV. HUGH.—A Catholic divine, and theological writer, who assumed the name of Charles Dodd, was born at Durton, near Preston, in 1672. He studied first under his uncle at Fernyhalgh, and in 1688, was sent to Douay. After passing through a course of philosophy and divinity, at the seminary of St. Gregory, at Paris, he returned to Douay, and continued his studies till 1698, about which time he was appointed priest at Fernyhalgh. In 1718, he was again at Douay, busily employed in the collection of materials for his great work on Church History. It was published in three separate volumes, in 1737, 1739, and 1742. He had been appointed priest at Harvington, in Worcester, in 1726, having for about four years been the assistant to his predecessor. Several gentlemen contributed towards the expense of the publication of his Church History, including the duke of Norfolk, and Sir Robert Throckmorton, bart. Tootel or Dodd was a voluminous theological writer. It is said he wrote no less than sixty-four works of this character. He died at Harvington, in 1742.

WEEVER, JOHN.—Mr. Whittle says that the learned author of "Ancient Funerall Monuments," was born at Preston, and not at Lancaster, as some writers have asserted. His parents were poor, but his uncle gave him a good early education, and afterwards sent him to Cambridge. When he left college, he fixed his residence at Clerkenwell. He died in 1632, aged 56. His great work, which was dedicated to King Charles II., was the result of much research and personal investigation. Weever complains in his preface, of the impediments thrown in his way by illiterate officiousness. He says: "I have been taken up in divers churches, by the churchwardens of the parish, and not suffered to write the epitaphs, or take views of the monuments, as I much desired; for I wanted a commission, which would have greatly encouraged me, for Henry VIII. did grant license to John Leland, in order that he might effectually prosecute his antiquarian researches." A monument, with a long poetical inscription, was erected to his memory, in St. James's church, Clerkenwell, London, by John Skillicorne, of Preston, his executor. The Skillicornes were an old and influential family in Preston. Richard Skillicorne was mayor in the time of Richard II.

CHRONOLOGICAL TABLE.

B. C.
55 Cæsar's first invasion of Britain. A. M. 3049. [a]
54 Cæsar's second invasion of Britain.

A. D.
43 The Romans under Plautius invaded Britain.
50 Do. under Ostorius Scapula do.
59 Do. under Suetonius Paulinus do.
79 Do. under Agricola do.
The Roman station at Walton founded on the site of the ancient British fortress.
85 Agricola's fleet first sails round Britain.
410 Britain ceases to acknowledge the Roman dominion.
448 Total extinction of the Roman power in Britain.
449-50 Hengist and Horsa landed in Britain.
547 Ida and a body of Angles conquer the present Northumberland and part of Scotland. He founded the kingdom of Bernicia.
559 Ælla, son of Ida, conquered Yorkshire, and perhaps part of Lancashire. He founded the kingdom of Deira, which when joined to Bernicia, became the kingdom of Northumbria.
596 Augustine arrived in Britain.
627 Paulinus made bishop of Northumbria. King Edwin baptized.
633 Edwin slain.
642 Battle of Maserfeld. (Winwick) Death of Oswald. Victory of Penda, the pagan Mercian king.
655 Battle of Winweyde (Winwidfield, near Leeds) Death of Penda.
705 Grant of lands on the Ribble to the monastery at Ripon.
787 First invasion of the Danes.
798 Battle of Billangahoh (Langho, near Whalley).
871 King Alfred began to reign.
876 Northumbria divided amongst the Danes by Halfdene.
878 Alfred retired to Athelingay. The Danes masters of England.
Alfred defeated the Danish king Godrun, at Eddington, and divided with him the kingdom.
901 Death of Alfred the Great.
910-11 Battle of Wodensfield.
921 Edward the elder subdued the Cumbrian Britons.
923 Manchester fortified by Edward the elder.
926 Death of Sigtryg, Danish king of Northumbria. Expulsion of Anlaf his son.
930 Athelstan grants Amounderness to the church of York.
934-7 Battle of Brunanburh.
940 Death of Athelstan.

a Aspin's Universal Chronology.

941 The Northumbrians chose Anlaf for king.
942 Death of Anlaf.
944 Edmund conquered Northumbria.
948 The Northumbrians again revolted, and chose Eric for king.
954 Edward ravaged the country, and re-subjected it to the Saxon authority.
991 Danegelt first imposed.
993 Sweyn, king of Denmark, conquered Northumbria.
1002 Massacre of the Danes.
1004 Sweyn pillaged various parts of England.
1014 Death of Sweyn.
1017 Canute king of all England.
1041 Edmund the Confessor began to reign.
1066 The Norman Conquest.
1080 } 1086 } Domesday survey made.
1087 William Rufus ascended the throne.
1100 Henry I. succeeded to the crown. The Preston Custumale probably granted in his reign.
1124 Evanus and his monks arrived in England. They were located at Tulketh during the erection of Furness abbey.
1135 Stephen began to reign.
1140 (About) First recorded mention of Lancashire by its present name.
1154 Henry II. ascended the throne.
1164 (About) Preston granted a Municipal charter.
1189 Richard I. ascended the throne. He conferred the earldom of Lancaster on his brother John.
1199 King John's reign commenced. Municipal charter granted.
1216 Henry III. began to reign.
1220 Walter de Preston slain in a feud.
1221 The Friary at Preston founded.
1227 Municipal charter granted.
1252 Second ditto.
1264 Preston probably first represented in Parliament.
1266 Edmund Crouchback created earl of Lancaster.
1272 Edward I. ascended the throne.
1291 Hospital at Maudlands, first recorded notice of.
1295 First recorded parliamentary election.
1306 King Edward I. at Preston.
1307 Edward II. began to reign. Adam de Banistre was slain by the followers of the earl of Lancaster, in a fight in the valley of the Ribble, during this reign.
1322 Thomas, earl of Lancaster, beheaded.
1323 Preston burnt by Bruce.
1327 Edward III. ascended the throne.
1328 Municipal charter granted.
1329 First recorded celebration of the Guild Merchant at Preston.
1333 Battle of Halidown Hill. Edward recruited at Preston.
1343 Preston the wealthiest of the Lancashire boroughs.
1377 Richard II. succeeded to the throne.
1379 Municipal charter granted, and Guild Merchant held.
1399 Henry IV. proclaimed king. In his reign, Walton bridge was re-built.
1401 Municipal charter granted.
1413 Henry V. began to reign.
1414 Municipal charter granted.
1415 Guild Merchant held.
1422 Henry VI. ascended the throne.
1425 Municipal charter granted.
1455 Commencement of the "Wars of the Roses."
1459 Guild Merchant.

1461 Edward IV. proclaimed King.
1465 Henry VI. captured at Clitheroe.
1474 Introduction of the art of Printing into England.
1482 Edward V. began to reign.
1483 Richard III. ascended the throne.
1485 Henry VII. proclaimed King.
1485 Great plague called sweating sickness.
1487 Lambert Simnel landed at the "Pile of Foudray."
1495 Sir William Stanley executed. Henry VII. visited Lathom and Knowsley.
1501 Guild Merchant.
1509 Henry VIII. began to reign.
1513 Battle of Flodden. Euxton chapel re-built.
1520 Chipping parish church re-built.
1532 Samlesbury old hall repaired by Thomas Southworth.
1536 Act for the suppression of the lesser monasteries.
1537 The "Pilgrimage ot Grace." The abbot of Whalley hanged.
1543 Guild Merchant.
1544 Decay of Preston and other Lancashire towns.
1547 Edward VI. ascended the throne.
1548 Rufford chantry dissolved.
1553 Penwortham parish free grammar school founded. It is commonly called Hutton school.
1553 Mary began to reign. A chantry founded at Goosnargh church. Rufford chantry restored.
1555 Village near Rossall destroyed by the sea.
1557 Municipal charter granted.
1558 Elizabeth ascended the throne. Elizabeth founded Leyland grammar school.
1562 Great plague. Guild Merchant.
1566 Municipal charter granted.
1569 General apprehension of all the beggars in the kingdom.
1581 (Abont) Preston parish church re-built.
1582 Guild Merchant.
1586 Kirkham parish church probably re-built.
1588 Meeting at Preston respecting the threatened invasion by the Spanish armada. Expected landing in Morecambe bay. Samlesbury church in a delapidated condition.
1589 Feud. Hoghton, of Lea, killed. The manor of Walton-le-dale granted to the family as compensation.
1602 Guild Merchant. Garstang free school founded.
1603 James I. succeeded to the English crown. Shortly afterwards, a great plague desolated the country. Camden visited Ribchester a second time.
1605 Gunpowder plot. Small Catholic chapel opened in Friargate,—the first since the Reformation.
1611 Institution of the honor and title of baronet.
1612 Lancashire witches hanged.
1615 First discovery of steam power by De Caus.
1617 King James visited Preston and Hoghton Tower. White-chapel, Goosnargh, enlarged.
1618 "Book of Sports" published.
1622 Guild Merchant.
1625 Charles I. ascends the throne.
1628 Hoole church re-edified.
1630 Woodplumpton church re-built.
1631 Calicoes first imported into England.
1633 Second batch of Lancashire witches tried.
1642 Guild Merchant. Commencement of the civil war. Great meeting on Preston moor. Fracas at Manchester. Threatened attack upon Preston. Siege of Manchester. Defeat of the royalists at Chowbent and Hinfield moor. Parlia-

mentary reverse at Hindley, near Wigan. Meeting of royalists at Preston. Hoole parish separated from Croston.

1643 Ruse at Salesbury. First siege of Preston, Feb. 9. The Mayor killed, and the town captured by Major General Seaton for the parliament. Siege of Lancaster. Lancaster taken. Hoghton Tower blown up. Lord Derby failed to take Bolton. He threatened Manchester. Failed before Bolton a second time. Second siege of Lancaster. Preston surprised by the earl of Derby, and the defences destroyed, on the 21st March. Surrender of Blackburn to the earl of Derby. Colonel Ashton surprised Wigan, but afterwards abandoned it. Defeat of the earl of Derby between Whalley and Ribchester. Ashton re-took Wigan, demolished the defences, and drove the earl of Derby out of the county. Ashton captured Liverpool. Warrington surrendered to the parliamentary forces. The royalists defeated in Furness by Col. Alex. Rigby. The castles of Hornby and Thurland surrendered to the parliament. Fairfax defeated on Adwalton moor. Lord Byron succeeded in Cheshire. Siege of Nantwich. Defeat of Byron, and triumph of the parliamentary generals.

1644 First siege of Lathom House. Bolton captured by Prince Rupert and the earl of Derby. Liverpool captured by Rupert. Battle of Marston moor. Prince Rupert at Preston. Imprisonment of the mayor and bailiffs. Shuttleworth defeated the royalists at Whalley. Sir John Meldrum re-took Liverpool, after defeating the king's partisans at Ormskirk. Great suffering.

1645 Battles of Naseby and of Rowton Heath, near Chester. Capture of Lathom House.

1646 General surrender of the royalists.

1647 Charles I. a prisoner.

1648 Threatened invasion of the Scotch to restore the king. Meetings at Preston, etc. Col. Lilburne defeated Sir Richard Tempest. Great battle at Ribbleton moor, Preston, and Walton: Cromwell defeated Langdale and the duke of Hamilton.

1649 Charles I. beheaded. Charles II. proclaimed at Preston. Battle of Dunbar. Charles and the Scotch entered England, and passed through Preston. Lord Derby landed at the Wyre, from the Isle of Man. Meeting at Preston. Lilburne pursued the royalists to near Ribble bridge. Battle of Wigan-lane, and death of Sir Thomas Tildesley. Charles II. defeated at Worcester. The earl of Derby beheaded at Bolton. Greenough and Clitheroe castles dismantled.

1650 The Corporation purchased the "fee farm rent" from the crown. Tarleton school built.

1653 Cromwell made Lord Protector.

1658 Oliver Cromwell died.

1660 Charles II. proclaimed King.

1661 Right of voting in the parliamentary elections at Preston declared to be in the "Inhabitants at large." "In burgesses," nevertheless, only voted. Test and Corporation Act passed. Woodplumpton school endowed.

1662 Act of Uniformity passed. Guild Merchant.

1666 Garstang episcopal chapel re-built.

1672 Feudal tenures abolished.

1673 Municipal charter granted. Goosnargh school founded. Cuerden school founded.

1675 A school founded at Bispham, in the parish of Croston.

1678 A weaving machine invented by M. De Gennes. Failed in practice.

1682 Guild Merchant.

1683 Chipping school endowed.

1684 Judge Jeffreys at Preston. Municipal charter granted.

1685 James II. succeeded to the throne.

1688 The Revolution. William III. proclaimed king.

1690 Preston first lighted with oil lamps. Cuerden school built.

1694 The Lancashire plot disclosed. Trial of Jacobites at Manchester.

1698 Captain Savary patented a steam engine for pumping.

1701 Queen Anne ascended the throne.

1702 Guild Merchant. Blue coat school established.

1705 Savary and Newcombe patented a pumping engine.
1707 Cadley school built.
1709 Hoghton school founded.
1714 George I. proclaimed king.
1715 Jacobite rebellion. Siege of Preston. Capture of the rebels by Wills and Carpenter. Battle of Sherriff moor.
1716 Grimsargh chapel built.
1717 Beighton improves Savary and Newcombe's engine.
1718 Unitarian chapel, Church-street, built. Euxton Catholic chapel restored.
1719 Tarleton chapel built on the site of an ancient edifice.
1720 Douglas navigation act obtained. Hoole church steeple built.
1722 Guild Merchant.
1723 St. George's chapel built.
1724 First fire engine introduced to Preston. Euxton chapel re-built.
1725 Dr. Stukeley visited Ribchester.
1727 George II. began to reign.
1729 "Folly" waterworks commenced.
1734 Rufford chapel re-built.
1737 Scroop, duke of Bridgewater's first act obtained for navigation purposes. Not carried into effect.
1738 Fly shuttle invented. Wyatt's first patent for spinning with rollers.
1742 Guild merchant.
1743 Croston church re-built.
1744 Clayton-le-woods school founded.
1745 Jacobite rebellion. Prince Charles Edward Stuart marched through Preston to Derby, November 27th. Returned December 12th. First Preston newspaper published. Bushell's hospital, at Goosnargh, founded.
1746 Battle of Culloden. Garstang church flooded. The Penwortham free school at Hutton first erected.
1748 Wyatt's second patent for spinning with rollers. Friends' meeting house built; re-erected in 1847-8.
1751 Poulton church re-built.
1752 Heapy chapel built on the site of a previous edifice.
1753 No stage coach left Liverpool.
1755 Penwortham bridge opened. Balderston chapel enlarged.
1756 Packhorses travel from Liverpool to Preston and Lancaster. No coaches on this road. The "Flying coach" from Warrington to London commenced running. Penwortham bridge fell.
1757 Penwortham bridge re-erected.
1758 Francis, duke of Bridgewater's first canal act obtained. Euxton school founded.
1760 George III. ascended the throne.
1761 Dr. Shepherd's library bequeathed to the town. St. Mary's Catholic chapel, on Friargate brow, erected.
1762 Guild Merchant.
1765 Alston Catholic chapel built.
1767 Hargreaves's spinning jenny invented. Highs, of Leigh, said to have invented a spinning machine.
1768 The "great election." Cottam chapel destroyed. Universal suffrage first introduced. Edgworth received the gold medal of the Society of arts, for models of a railway.
1769 Arkwright's first patent for spinning machinery. Watt's first patent "for lessening the consumption of steam and fuel." Garstang episcopal chapel re-built.
1770 Body of Parish church re-built. Lytham Parish church built on the site of the priory. Longton chapel re-built. Crooke's school, Moss-side, Leyland, founded.
1771 Arkwright's second mill built at Cromford. Ribchester Free school established.
1774 A stage coach commenced running between Manchester and Liverpool, and between Liverpool and Preston.
1775 Arkwright's second patent. Watt's second patent.

1776 Bridgewater canal from Manchester to Liverpool opened. Old bank opened.
1777 First cotton mill built at Preston. Garstang Independent chapel built.
1778 A Methodist chapel built in Back lane. Goosnargh church enlarged.
1779 Riots at Blackburn, etc., owing to the introduction of machinery. Crompton's mule jenny completed.
1780 Town Hall fell. Brindle Catholic chapel built.
1781 Arkwright's first trial; infringement of his patent; nonsuited. Watt's third patent.
1782 Guild Merchant. Watt's fourth patent. Douglas navigation opened. Small Catholic chapel at Brownedge built. Since superseded by a larger edifice.
1783 Leeming-street Baptist chapel erected. Longridge chapel re-built a second time.
1784 Watt's fifth patent. First mail-coach despatched from London to Liverpool. Garstang Catholic chapel built.
1785 Arkwright's second trial. His patent invalidated. Power-looms first patented by Dr. Cartwright. Cylinder-printing established at Mosney, near Preston. Bolton and Watt's engine first employed in a cotton-mill.
1788 Workhouse built on the moor. Blackpool contained only about fifty houses.
1789 Withnell school endowed. The first steam-engine erected for a cotton-mill in Lancashire. French Revolution commenced. House of Correction, Church-street, opened.
1790 Arkwright first introduced the steam-engine in his mill, at Nottingham.
1791 South-hill Catholic chapel, Whittle, built.
1792 Kelly's self-acting mule introduced. First inn built at Southport.
1793 Kinlock's first power-loom set up. King of France beheaded. St. Wilfrid's Catholic chapel opened. Rufford parish separated from Croston.
1794 First hotel erected at Lytham. Stonyhurst College founded.
1796 Royal Preston volunteers embodied. Roman bronze helmet found at Ribchester.
1798 Lancaster canal opened. Irish rebellion broke out. Subscriptions raised for government to carry on war with France. Preston volunteer corps formed.
1800 Grand Junction canal opened, with the exception of the Blisworth tunnel, finished in 1805.
1801 Peace of Amiens.
1802 Guild Merchant. Tram-road bridge over the Ribble erected. Trevethick's first patent for a locomotive engine. Theatre Royal built. Catholic chapel at Hill, Goosnargh, re-built.
1803 Prince William Frederick of Gloucester visited Preston, and reviewed the volunteer corps. Revisited Preston in the following year. Horrocks's power-loom first patented.
1805 Battle of Trafalgar.
1806 Ribble Navigation Act obtained. The "Strangers' Charity," Southport, founded.
1807 Bonaparte's Berlin decree. Chipping Independent chapel built. Longton Methodist chapel erected.
1808 Preston volunteers join the militia. Independent chapel, Grimshaw-street, built. Salesbury chapel built.
1809 Dispensary established. Old chapel at Willows, near Kirkham, built. Southport contained only about thirty houses.
1811 Severe distress,—subscriptions for the poor. Blenkensop introduced a locomotive on a colliery railway, near Leeds. Garstang church partially re-built. Remains of a Roman temple at Ribchester first discovered. Penwortham church partially restored.
1812 Bell's first steam-boat on the Clyde. Catholic chapel at South-hill, Whittle, enlarged.
1813 Riots at Middleton, West Hoghton, etc., on introduction of machinery. Proclamation of peace.
1814 George Stephenson introduced a locomotive at Killingworth colliery. Tower of Parish church re-built. Trinity church erected. Vauxhall-road chapel built. National school, Avenham-lane, erected. St. Wilfrid's (Roman Catholic) school, Fox-street, built. Fulwood moor enclosed. Garstang Methodist chapel built. Wesleyan chapel, Golden-hill, Leyland, built.

1815 Battle of Waterloo. Improvement Commissioners Act for Preston obtained. Body of Brindle church re-built.
1816 Preston first lighted with gas. Deficient harvest,—great distress. Chipping second Independent chapel built. Body of Leyland church re-built. Euxton chapel again re-built.
1817 Chancel of Parish church re-built.
1818 Strike of hand-loom weavers at Preston. Balderstone chapel again enlarged.
1820 George IV. ascended the throne. Duke of Bridgewater's canal from Leigh to Wigan opened. Christ church, Southport, built.
1821 Spinners' strike at Preston. Blackpool Episcopal church built. Leyland Savings bank established. Tarleton parish separated from Croston.
1822 Guild Merchant. St. Peter's church erected. Kirkham Parish church re-built.
1823 Seventy-two coaches ran in and out of Preston every Wednesday. St. Paul's church erected. Clayton-green Catholic chapel built. Southport Independent chapel built.
1824 Corn Exchange erected. Brockholes bridge built. Rufford new school built. Chancel added to Hoole church. Hoole Methodist chapel built.
1825 Sharp, Roberts, and Co's. first patent for self-acting mule. Application to parliament for act to make Liverpool and Manchester railway. Countess of Huntingdon's chapel, Pole-street, erected. Lund chapel re-built. Free school opened at Cop-lane, Penwortham. Southport National school built.
1826 Serious riots in Lancashire; some looms destroyed. Ribble and Wyre made ports under Lancaster. Independent chapel, Inglewhite, built. Catholic chapel, Brownedge, re-built. Heapy school built.
1827 Catholic chapel built at Chipping.
1828 Municipal charter granted. Mechanics' Institution opened. St. John's girls' school, Vauxhall-road, built. Trinity school, Trinity-place, built about this time. Hoole Primitive Methodist chapel built. Croston Methodist meeting room opened.
1829 Great distress; soup kitchen established. First steamer on the Ribble. Court house erected. St. Peter's school, Fylde-road, built. St. Paul's school, Pole-street, built. Euxton chapel enlarged. Whittle chapel erected. Heapy chapel enlarged.
1830 William IV. ascended the throne. Sharp, Roberts, and Co's. second patent. Liverpool and Manchester railway opened. Eighty-one coaches, in one day, ran in and out of Preston. New school built at Cop-lane, Penwortham. Mawdesley Catholic chapel built. Blue-coat school re-built. Methodist chapel, Clayton-le-woods, built.
1831 Protestant Wesleyan Methodist chapel, Chadwick's Orchard, erected. Brindle Catholic school built.
1832 Reform Bill passed. Lock-up built in Avenham-street. Preston Water company established. St. Paul's school, Carlisle-street, built. Stonyhurst church built. Tarleton Methodist chapel built.
1833 House of Recovery built. First stone of St. Ignatius Catholic chapel laid. Christ church school, Bow-lane, built. Methodist chapel, Penwortham, enlarged.
1834 Moor Park enclosed.
1835 Corporation Reform Bill passed. Blackpool Independent chapel opened. Walton National school built.
1836 Spinners' strike. The first stones of Christ church and St. Mary's church laid. The town of Fleetwood commenced. Bamber-bridge church built. Whittle alkaline spring discovered.
1837 Queen Victoria ascended the throne. Grand junction railway opened. Poor-law Amendment Act introduced. New Ribble company formed. First stone of St. Thomas's church laid. St. James's church built as a Dissenters' chapel. Primitive Episcopalian chapel built. St. Mary's first school built. Longton Primitive Methodist chapel built. Infant school, Moss-side, Leyland, built. Euxton school re-built on a new site.

1838 A steam vessel first crossed the Atlantic. Manchester and Bolton railway opened. North Union railway opened. First stone of St. Austin's Catholic chapel laid. Wesley chapel, North-road, built. Blackpool Wesleyan chapel opened.

1839 Preston made a port under Wyre. St. Peter's school, Brook-street, built. Fleetwood made an independent port. Farington church built. Whittle Wesleyan chapel re-built. Tarleton "School of Industry" built.

1840 Lancaster, Longridge, and the Wyre railways opened. St. Thomas's school, Lancaster-road, built. St. Ignatius's school for girls, St. Ignatius-square (Roman Catholic), built. Wesleyan school, Croft-street, built.

1841 Railway completed to Manchester from Preston. Lytham dock constructed. Withnell chapel built. New Grammar school, Cross-street, erected. St. Austin's school (Roman Catholic) built. Fleetwood church erected. Longridge chapel tower built.

1842 Serious disturbances. Rioters shot in Lune-street. Guild Merchant. Savings bank, Lune-street, erected. Wheelton school built.

1843 Preston again made an independent port, with Fleetwood under it. White Coppice school built.

1844 First stone of Literary and Philosophical Institution, and Winckley Club, laid. St. George's chapel restored. New Jerusalem chapel, Avenham-road, opened. Commercial schools, Knowsley-street, erected. St. Ignatius's school, Upper Walker-street (Roman Catholic), built. Blackpool covered market opened. Rossall college founded. Independent chapel, Leyland, built.

1845 Bonded warehouses erected at Preston. Scotch Baptist chapel, Meadow-street, built. Kirkham Parish church spire erected. Catholic church of the Holy Cross, Kirkham, opened.

1846 Blackburn railway opened. Ribble branch opened. Lytham and Blackpool branch railways opened. Avenham-walk extended, 1845-6. Trade depressed. Failure of potatoe crop. Foundation stone of Institution, Avenham, laid. All Saints' church erected. St. Mary's second school built. Trinity school, Snow-hill, built about this time. First importation of cotton into Fleetwood. Fleetwood testimonial schools erected.

1847 The Queen visited Fleetwood and Preston. Friends' school built.

1848 Overseers' offices, erected. German's schools, Elizabeth-street, erected. St. James's school, Knowsley-street, built. Ragged schools built. Fulwood barracks completed. Fleetwood Independent chapel opened. Talbot schools, Maudlands, built.

1849 Railway from Preston to Liverpool opened,—(East Lancashire.)

1850 Public Health Act introduced into Preston. First stone of St. Walburge's Catholic church laid. Fleetwood again made an independent port.

1851 Baths and Wash-houses opened. A small Methodist chapel at Tarleton built.

1852 Queen Victoria lunched at Preston,—and again in 1853. Statue to Sir Robert Peel erected. Fire-brigade buildings erected.

1853 The great strike of factory hands commenced. Obelisk removed from Market-place. Zoar chapel (Baptist), Regent-street, built. All Saints' school built.

1854 Militia stores building erected. Moss-side Episcopal chapel Leyland, built. New Catholic chapel, Leyland, built. Little Hoole Primitive Methodist chapel built.

1855 Southport junction with East Lancashire railway opened. Cemetery, Ribbleton, opened. Nave of Penwortham church re-built. Old buildings, Market-place, pulled down. Roman station discovered at Walton.

1856 Temperance Hall built. Preston Banking Company's new offices erected. First stone of a Reformatory school laid at Bleasdale.

1857 Magistrates' Court and Lock-up built. Lancaster Banking Company's new offices erected. Baptist chapel, Fishergate, erected. Christ church school, Wellfield-road, built. Blackpool Catholic church opened. Birkdale church built. First stone laid of a Catholic chapel at Barnacre, near Garstang. Alston new Catholic chapel built. Leyland parish sub-divided. Brinscall Wesleyan chapel built. Croston new Catholic chapel built.

INDEX.

D.

E.

M.

N.

O.

P.

Q.

R.

LIST OF SUBSCRIBERS.

Ashworth, Henry, The Oaks, Bolton.
Ascroft, Robert, Preston.
Armstrong, Councillor Francis, Preston.
Atkinson, James, „
Armstrong, Councillor Henry, „
Ashfield, Charles Joseph, „
Armstead, James, „
Abraham, John, „
Ambler, W. R., „
Adamson, J., „
Anderton, David, „
Anderton, Peter, Coppul, near Standish.
Alexander, John, Preston.
Ascroft, William, „
Ainsworth, William „
Arrowsmith, Robert „
Allen, Anthony, Ashton.
Ashworth, R., Walton-le-dale.
Anderton, Robert, Lostock.
Aitken, W., Ashton-under-Lyne.
Armstrong, Rev. A. T., Ashton-upon-Ribble.
Ainsworth, William, Fleetwood.

Blackburne, J. Ireland, Hale, Warrington.
Brown, Alderman, F.R.C.S., Preston.
Bushell, Joseph, Myerscough.
Boardman, William, Farington house.
Bowdon, John Butler, Pleasington hall, Blackburn.
Banks, William, Preston.
Burnett, Thomas, Hutton.
Blackburn, R. H., Preston.
Billington, Councillor Leonard, Preston.
Burlington, the Right Hon. the Earl of, Holker hall, Milnthorpe.
Bashall, William, Farington lodge.
Brandreth, John Moss, Preston.
Backhouse, Mrs., Preston.
Baldwin, Mrs., Ockbrook, Derby.
Bamber, S. I., Douglas, Isle of Man.
Bairstow, John, Preston.
Brown, Luke, Kirkham.
Barrett, John, Blackpool.
Barker, Thomas, Preston.
Booth, William, Manchester.
Booth, John, Green Bank Morton, Manchester.
Bolton, James, Preston.
Bonny, John, „
Bramwell, John, „
Banks, Thomas, „
Booth & Co's., H., Book Society, Preston.
Birdsworth, William, Lytham.
Bickersteth, Robert, Liverpool.
Bevan, R., Freckleton house, Wigan.
Broughton, H.H., M.D., etc., Preston.
Birkett, Charles, Clayton villa, Fulwood.
Booth, Councillor, J. B., Preston.
Bibby, Walter, „
Bilsborough, Robert, „
Blackhurst, William, „
Burnet, Robert, „
Birley, Thomas Langton, Kirkham.
Blackhurst, James, Liverpool.
Bannerman, Charles, Preston.
Burrow, James, jun., „
Breakell, Councillor Thomas, Preston.
Brooks, F., „
Bannister, Duke, „
Bell, Jas. Alexander, „
Brown, Matthew, „
Bamber, John, „
Begg, William, „
Brown, R., „
Birley, Edmund, Clifton hall.
Blackhurst, John, Preston.
Birchall, Thomas, Ribbleton hall.
Briggs, J., Preston.
Bickersteth, Edmund, Liverpool.

Crosse, Thomas Bright, Shaw hill, Chorley.
Cook, Miss Eliza, London.
Carr, Councillor James, Preston.
Clark, Thos. Rev., M.A., „
Clark, Thomas, „
Cope, J. G., B.A., „
Catterall, William, „

Crookall, Charles, Canada.
Clarkson, Joseph, Ribchester.
Coward, W., Preston.
Coward, R., „
Croft, John, „
Clegg, John, London.
Clough, Councillor Thomas, Blackburn.
Cowell, John, Preston.
Capstick, John, „
Coulthart, John Ross, F.S.A., Mayor of the Manor of Ashton-under-Lyne.
Clarke, Thomas, Preston.
Crook, James, „
Clemmey, Arthur „
Croft, Edward „
Clayton, Edward, Treales.
Clare, Charles St., Preston.
Cross, Richard Assheton, M.P., London.
Cartwright, Samuel, Preston.
Croft, William, Burnley.

Dobson, W., Preston.
Dewhurst, John „
Dixon, Thomas, „
Dodd, Thomas, „
Daynes, Samuel, Norwich.
Durham, W., Blackburn.
Duckett, Thomas, Preston.
Dixon, Robert, „
Dewhurst, John, „
Dawson, Pudsey, Hornby Castle, Lancaster.
Dixon, B., Preston.
Douglas, William, Preston.
Drennan, W., „
Duxbury, John, „
Davies, B. G., Merther Tydvil, Wales.
Dodd, Henry, Fleetwood.

Eastham, Councillor Thomas, Walton-le-dale.
Eastham, Councillor George, Preston.
Eckersley, Peter, „
Eccleston, John, „
Embley, Robert, „
Eglin, Richard, Penwortham.
Eastham, George, Preston.
Eccles, John, Wellfield, Leyland.
Eddleston, Thomas, Preston.

Farington, Mrs., Worden Hall, Leyland.
Farnworth, Henry, Preston.
Fishwick, Crane, Scorton, near Garstang.
Fare, Daniel, Poulton-le-Fylde.
Fort, William, Preston.
Farrington, Isaac, „
France, Robert, „
Feilden, John, Mollington Hall, Chester.
Fisher, William, Preston.
Foster, Edward, „
Feilden, Joseph, Witton Park, Blackburn.
Fair, James, Warton Lodge, Lytham.
Foster, George, Fleetwood.
Fox, William, Lancaster.
Friends' Book Society, Preston.

Grenfell, Charles Pascoe, M.P., Taplow Court, Windsor. (Two copies.)
Green, Joseph, Preston.
Garth, John, „
Grundy, Thomas, „
Grindrod, John, Blackpool.
Greenwood, Joseph, Rochdale.
Goodwin, ———, Bolton.
Greaves, J. J., Preston
Grayston, H., „
Grime, R, „
Grosvenor, W. H., London.
Grenside, Rev. W. B., Melling vicarage, Lancaster.
Gillet, John, Manor house, Fulwood.
Glover, Isaac, Preston.
Gilbertson, J. B., „
Gardner, Robert, „
Gillett, Thomas, „
Guthrie, John, Bradford.
Graham, John, Goosnargh Hospital.
Gardner, Richard Cardwell, Newsham house, Liverpool.

Hornby, Edmund, Dalton Hall, Westmoreland.
Heywood, James, London.
Hoghton, Sir H. Bold, Bart., Torquay. Devonshire.
Hornby, Rev. James J., Winwick Hall, Warrington.
Hull, Rev. John, Vicarage, Poulton.
Hebdon, Rev. Geoffrey, Preston Patrick, Westmoreland.
Hansbrow, Capt., Lancaster Castle.
Horrocks, John, Preston.
Hornby, Mrs., Lytham.
Harrison, Mrs., Old Hall, Samlesbury.
Hunt, Councillor Robert, Longton.
Hollins, Edward, Penwortham Priory.
Howarth, Thomas, Preston.
Horrocks, Mrs. S., Preston.
Holland, W., „
Hobson, John, „
Heathcoate, H. „
Heathcoate, Miss A., „
Hankinson, John, „
Harrison, William, Blackburn.
Hesketh, Sir Thomas George, Bart., Rufford hall, Ormskirk.
Hunter, J. L., Wigan.
Hinde, John Hodgson, Acton house, Northumberland.

Hargreaves, John, Blackburn.
Howarth, John, Preston.
Hogg, John „
Halsall, John, „
Hayhurst, John, „
Harrison, John, Fulwood.
Hulton, W. A., Hurst Grange, Penwortham.
Hayes, Thomas, Liverpool.
Hammerton, Thomas, Preston.
Harrison, Miss., „
Harrison, John, „
Hale, G. C., Knowsley, Prescot.
Harrison, Edward, Preston.
Hornby, Richard, „
Heywood, Sir Benjamin, Bart., Claremont, Manchester.
Harrison, James, Valentine House, Cottam.

Inman, R., Preston.
Institution for the Diffusion of Knowledge.
Ivers, James, Preston.
Isherwood, Councillor Joseph, Preston.
Institution, Literary and Philosophical, Preston.

Jacson, Charles Roger, Barton Lodge, Preston. (Two copies.)
Jacson, John, Oakhurst, Hindley, Wigan.
Jackson, Mr., Preston.
Jesper, Joseph, „
Johnson, John, „
Jones, T. L., „
Jones, J. E., „

Kershaw, Rev. J. C., Walton-le-Dale.
Kirby, William, Preston.
Kitton, Rev. J., Hutton.
Knowles, John, Lytham.

Lyon, John, Preston.
Lambert, Mr., Catterall, near Garstang.
Lowndes, E. C., Preston. (Two copies.)
Lund, James, Chipping.
Leigh, Ralph, Preston. (Two copies.)
Luff, Thomas, Liverpool,
Lee, Henry, Preston.
Lyon, Thomas, Appleton Hall, Warrington.
Langton, William, Manchester.
Livesey, Joseph, Preston.
Livesey, R. N., Lytham.
Livesey, Robert, Preston.
Liddell, William, „
Longworth, John „
Lawe, Robert, the Larches, Ashton.
Ladyman, Thomas, Preston.
Lancashire and Cheshire Historic Society.
Lawson, R., Preston.
Lancaster, W., Preston.

Manchester, the Right Rev. the Lord Bishop of
Myres, Councillor J. J., Preston.
Monk, Alderman Thomas, Preston.
Marginson, James, Fleetwood.
Morrell, John, Beach Villa, Leyland.
Marshall, William, Penwortham Hall.
Marshall, George, Preston.
Mould, George, London. (Two copies.)
Melling, E. G., Ashton.
Milburn, Thomas, Preston.
Moss, Thomas, „
Martang, F., „
Mulby, Thomas, „
Myres, Councillor Miles, Preston.
Mason, W., London.
Meek, Brothers, Preston.

Noble, M., London.
Newsham, Richard, Preston.
Naylor, P., „
Norris, Dr., „
Newsham, Mrs. James, Preston.

Oldfield, R. A., Sierra Leone.
Ord, Thomas, Preston.
Oddie, Thomas, „
Omerod, George, D.C.L., F.R.S., Sedbury Park, Chepstow.
Osborne, Rev. G. Y., Fleetwood.
Oliverson, Richard, Preston.
Oxendale, Thomas, „
Osborne, Rev. W. A., Rossall, Fleetwood.

Pedder, Alderman Edward, Ashton Park.
Patten, Col. J. Wilson, M. P., Bank Hall, Warrington.
Pedder, Mrs., Leamington.
Pedder, Rev. John, Churchtown, Garstang.
Parker, Robert Townley, Cuerden Hall. (Three copies.)
Parker, Thomas Townley, Astley hall, Chorley.
Pedder, Councillor H. N., Whinfield, Ashton.
Peet, Henry, Carlisle.
Paley, Councillor William, Preston.
Pye, George, Preston.
Parker, James, Liverpool.
Pollard, Mrs., Chorley,
Phillips, Thomas, Preston.
Park, J. H., „
Pertoke, F., „
Plant, W. H., „
Pickup, L. P., Broad Green, Liverpool.
Pedder, Alderman Richard, Preston.

Procter, William, Preston
Preston, Rev George, Whalley.
Parr, Rev. Henry, Vicarage, Taunton.
Park, Thomas, Preston
Parker, Councillor James, Preston.
Preston, William, Liverpool.
Parry, William, Preston.
Parker, George, „
Priest, William, „
Pilkington, W. O, the Willows, Ashton.
Park, Philip, Preston.
Powell, Thomas, „
Pedder, Capt. Thomas, 7th Hussars
Pedder, Capt. Charles Denison, 39th Regt.
Price, Rev. T., Aberdare, South Wales.

Roberts, R. W., London.
Rossall, John, Blackpool.
Richards, R. E, Kirkham.
Riley, Richard, Preston.
Rodgett, R. B, Walton-le-dale.
Roscoe, Miss, Preston.
Richson, R., „
Roebank, Jonathan, Preston
Reay, James, Liverpool.
Rawstorne, Rev. R. A., Hutton Hall
Rawcliffe, John, Broughton.
Raw, Councillor John, Preston.
Rigby, John, Preston.
Robinson, Richard, „
Rodgett, William, Woodplumpton
Robinson, Mrs., Preston
Roberts, W. J., Cross Mount, Aughton, Ormskirk.
Rawes, S, Preston.
Rogerson, John, Preston
Rishton, J G. M., London.
Richardson, John, Kendal
Rock, Brothers, and Payne, London.
Roe, James, London.
Roylance, Councillor Oliver, Blackburn.
Richmond, Frederick, Manchester

Spencer, Lawrence, Mayor of Preston
Swainson, W. B, Cooper hill, Walton-le-dale.
Smith, Councillor George, Beech Grove, Moor Park, Preston.
Swainson, Charles, Cooper hill, Walton-le-dale
Shilleto, Rev. Wm., Bleasdale Parsonage.
Smith, Rev. H. R., Preston
Salts, Robert, „
Summersgill, Robert, „
Stanley, Henry, „
Sharrock, J. „
Shorage, George, „
Schofield, John, Bradford
Street, Benjamin, Worksworth
Sudell, John, Finland, Russia
Simpson, Rev. Samuel, Isle of Man
Singleton, Thomas, Preston.
Swarbrick, George, „
Sparrow, Councillor John, Blackburn.
Sykes, James, Breck House, Poulton-le-Fylde
Shawe, Alderman William, Preston.
Smith, William, „
Southworth. John, „
Smith, Councillor Samuel, Charnley house, Fulwood
Smith, Thomas, Ashton.
Sharples, George, Preston
Stout, George, „
Stanley, Daniel, „
Settle, S I, Whittle Springs.
Seward, Charles, Preston
Swarbrick, Thomas
Stanley, the Right Hon. Lord, M P, London.
Strickland, Sir George, Bart., Newton House, near Malton.
Simpson, Isaac, Preston.
Swarbrick, Rev. Edward, Preston.
Sergenson, Thomas, Longridge.
Syms, William, Chorley.
Smith Robert, Longridge.

Tabley, the Right Hon. Lord de, Tabley House, Cheshire
Threlfall, W., Preston
Threlfall, Councillor Richard, Preston (Two copies)
Threlfall, Thomas, jun., Preston.
Turner, John, Preston.
Taylor, E.
Toulmin, George, Bolton.
Tait, Miss, Lytham.
Troughton, T. M., Walton Hall
Teale, Councillor George, Preston.
Tipping, Thomas, Preston.
Taylor, John, Preston.
Taylor, W., „
Thompson, Mrs., Kirkham.
Tuson, Miss, Preston.
Thornley, Jeremiah, Preston
Thompson, R. T, Preston.

Valliant, Thomas, Preston
Vernon, Rev. William, Cambridge

Walton, Miss, Leyland Lodge, Leyland
Wilcockson, Isaac, Preston. (Two copies.)
Watson, Councillor William, Preston.
Warbreck, Miss, Fleetwood.
Wilson, Miss, Lytham.
Wilson, Edward, Broughton.
Walmsley, John, Hoghton.

Watson, Councillor John, Durham.
Walmsley, Alderman Thomas, Preston.
Wardle, W., „
Waddington, J., „
Whitehead, John, „
Winstanley, S. A., „
Worthington, John, „
Wilkinson, J. T., F.R.A S., Burnley.
Whittaker, Robert, Walton-le-dale.
Wallacy, R., Penwortham Priory.
Wilkins, W., Longton.
Winstanley, John, Preston.
Walker, John, „
Woods, Councillor Joseph, Preston.
Walker, Thomas, „
White, Thomas, „
Whitehead, John, „
Williamson, J. B., „
Watson, Richard, Preston.
Walker, H., „
Winder, James, „
Wilding, George, „
Watson, R, G., „
Whittaker, John. „
Wood, Richard, „
Woodhead, Thomas, Bradford.
Wilding, George, Ribbleton.
Worthington, Richard, London.
Worthington, William, Blackpool.
Waugh, Edwin, Manchester.

Young, Murdo, London.
Yates, Councillor R., Preston.
Yates, James, „
Yates, Thomas, „

FINIS.

WORTHINGTON AND CO., PRINTERS, TOWN HALL CORNER, PRESTON.

Lightning Source UK Ltd.
Milton Keynes UK
UKHW020808160620
364898UK00003B/32

9 781344 050999